ROYAL BOROUGH OF GREENWICH

Follow us on twitter @greenwichlibs

Please return by the last date shown

28/4/17

Thank you! To renew, please c~ ~ ~
Royal Greenwich library or ren
www.better.org.uk/greenwic

D1355172

< *Lift flap for map of public transport*   s >

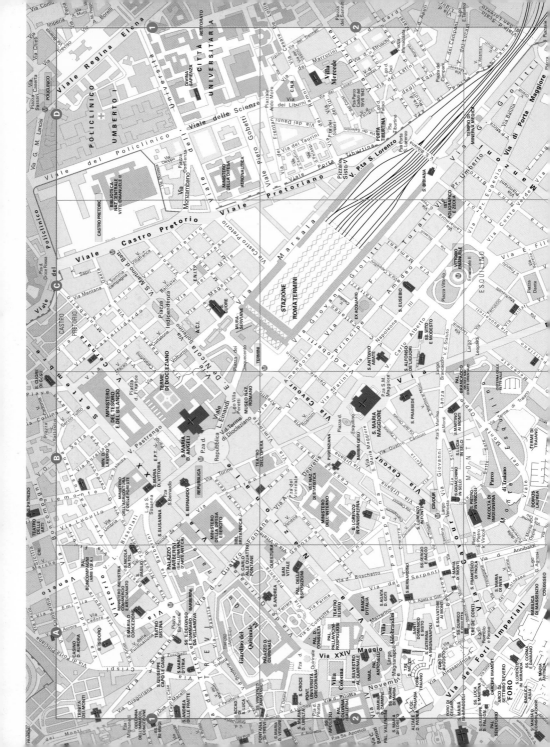

Mauro Lucentini
Paola Lucentini Eric Lucentini Jack Lucentini

Rome

A practical guide to the history and culture of the Eternal City

PALLAS GUIDES

Contents

Statue of Marcus Aurelius, formerly on the Campidoglio Square

of Hadrian – Pantheon – Basilica of Neptune, Baths of Agrippa – 'Sacred Area' of the Argentina – Theatre of Balbus – Portico of Octavia – Theatre of Marcellus – Temples of the Food Markets and the Velabrum – S. Maria in Cosmedin – Circus Maximus – (The Aventine Hill, from S. Sabina to S. Saba) – Baths of Caracalla

Opposite: Castel Sant'Angelo and the Ponte Sant'Angelo

Overleaf: the centre of Rome in about AD 400: detail of the model from EUR

Opposite: courtyard of S. Cecilia

This book is dedicated
to the memory of
Paola Lucentini

Acknowledgements

We would like to thank the librarians, editors, curators, archæologists and others who helped make this book possible. Priceless technical assistance came from Diana Abrashkin, AIA, of Boston, and archæologist Marina Piranomonte of Rome's Sovrintendenza alle Belle Arti. For their advice and help we are indebted to Robert Bernstein, former chairman of Random House; Professor Jane Ginsburg of Columbia University; Mario Gori-Sassoli of Rome's Istituto Nazionale per la Grafica; Hans Heinrich Coudenhove-Kalergi of London; Cheryl Hurley of the Library of America; Inge Heckel of the New York Academy of Interior Design; and Mark Piel of the New York Society Library.

We owe a special debt to the late historian and archæologist Cesare D'Onofrio of Rome for sharing his profound love and scholarly knowledge of his city with us, and to the Biblioteca Hertziana for generously making available to us the wonderful photographs of Rome that Mr. D'Onofrio took over the years, and which appear (many of them for the first time) throughout this book.

Finally we wish to thank friends and family who patiently listened to our endless prattle about Rome and cheered us on, among them Carlo Fruttero, the late Franco Lucentini, Baroness Olga von Kollar, John and Mary Gibbons, Robert and Dina McCabe, Paul and Chantal Cannon, David Olan, Dotty Attie, Sarah Schulte and so many others it would take another book to list them all.

We are grateful to readers who alert us of errors in the book, or provide other useful information or suggestions to help improve and update it. Write us c/o the publisher or by e-mail to mauro.lucentini@hotmail.com. We will do our best to reply to everyone.

How this book works

*I bought some maps and books on Rome and would read them in the
evening, putting the information I thus acquired to use the next day
when I toured the city; this way I soon made myself so thoroughly
a master of the matter, I could have guided my guide.*
— Montaigne, *Voyage en Italie*, 1581

This book is both for people who have not visited Rome and for those whose efforts to understand it have been frustrated by the city's sheer complexity. Although good for visits of any
length, it is especially helpful for people with only a few days to spend in Rome. Also, this
book is for everybody, from the ignoramus to the connoisseur. A short visit does not mean a
short guidebook! On the contrary, a guide rich in easily digestible information can make a
short stay much more meaningful.

This book differs from standard guidebooks in three major ways:

A book to read in advance

Each section describing sights is preceded by several pages that you may wish to read before
you start walking, to add context and enjoyment to your visit. These pages are marked 'Before
Going' and are set in a single column. The site-by-site descriptions which come next are entitled 'On the Spot', and are in two columns. As a whole, the 'Before Going' sections form a
thorough book on Rome. Read them at your leisure – before departure, on the plane or in your
hotel room. Of course, you can also refer to them during the actual visit.

Thoughtfully organized Walks

This book consists of ten Walks covering the essentials of Rome. Within each Walk, sections
that aren't essential are marked 'Detour' and you can skip them without compromising your
aim of mastering 'basic' Rome. The Walks and Detours are designed to provide you with in-
depth knowledge of the basics in the least possible time: they are compact, with no wasted
steps, and have been checked for time length. Particular stress is placed on directions, orientation and transportation, as time wasted on these matters is the main problem for most tourists
in this labyrinthine city.

The Walks take from half to a full day each, depending on their length; your speed; the number of open churches and monuments; and whether you take the Detours.

If you omit the Detours, the Walks total roughly 60 hours, or about seven days of intensive
sightseeing. If you have less time, take only the first – usually more important – Walk in each
section.

If you have more than a week, take one or more of the Detours. Or consider the additional
walks described on pp. 278-295 and 601-639. These provide, respectively, a second, more

Opposite and previous page: the Trevi Fountain

detailed examination of the Forum and the Palatine, and visits to the outlying, 'Beyond the Walls' areas of Rome.

Then there are the museums. The Walks in this book include only the Vatican Museums, those unsurpassed displays of art and civilization. But if your stay is long enough, you should certainly spend time in some of Rome's other important and exciting museums. These are listed and briefly described on pp. 681-688.

Theme-based Walks

Rome is one of the most difficult cities to understand, even for Romans. Paradoxically, the very quality that can take you to the heights of excitement – the city's extraordinarily rich tangle of 27 centuries of history and architecture – can confuse you to the point of utter frustration. The many layers of visual information can be hard to tease apart. Venerable ruins hide within ordinary modern buildings. Pagan temples live on as Christian churches. Baroque façades conceal ancient Roman columns. Styles, shapes, originals and imitations, old and new, blend so closely as to make some objects hard to see, let alone interpret.

But with a bit of determination and the guidance provided in this book you can overcome these difficulties.

We've discovered that a good way to untangle Rome is to follow its different layers one by one, focusing separately on each neighbourhood where the evidence of a particular style or time period predominates. Each walk, therefore, concentrates on a single historical or artistic aspect of the city. This will help you put the various elements together to form a coherent picture, not only culturally and historically, but surprisingly, also from the practical standpoint of finding your way around. (There are some unavoidable exceptions to this organization, however. For instance, the Renaissance Rome walks include descriptions of some Ancient Roman sights.)

The ten Walks – two Walks per theme – are:

§ 'Roma Romantica'. These walks cover the latter part of Roman history: the baroque, the 18th century, the neoclassical period, the Romantic period and the 'belle époque' style.

§ 'Ancient Rome'. These cover Rome before the fall of the Empire in the late 400s.

§ 'Rome of the Popes'. These cover primarily the Holy See and directly associated sites within and without the Vatican, such as St. Peter's, the Vatican Museums, the Popes' 'Castle of the Holy Angel', and St. John Lateran.

§ 'Renaissance Rome'.

§ 'Trastevere' ('Across the Tiber').

The midpoint of each walk is clearly marked in order to help you measure your progress, decide when to take breaks, or plan an abbreviated sightseeing programme if time is limited.

Finally

Practical details about staying and eating in Rome and about the transport system are in the section on yellow paper at the end of the book, together with a comprehensive list of the museums of Rome. There is also a glossary for technical terms (though we have avoided using them where possible) and a biographical index of artists and their works in Rome.

Opposite: Hurrying back to Vatican City

*S. Domenico e Sisto and its conventual buildings.
On the left the gardens of the Villa Aldbrandini*

Some historical background

Preparatory studies are needed for the voyage to Rome.
– Stendhal, *Promenades dans Rome*, 1829.

An outline of the history of Rome will make the arrangement of this book easier to understand and will enrich your visit. Rome's development took place in four basic phases, to which the different sections of this book correspond: origins and the Republic; the Empire; Medieval and Renaissance Rome; and Baroque, Romantic and Modern Rome.

Origins and Republic (8th to 1st Centuries BC)

Rome began as a small settlement on the Palatine Hill – domain of King Romulus, its semi-legendary founder – near the Tiber River, which was essential for transportation, trade and water supply.

Eventually, the neighbouring hills – the fabled 'Seven Hills' and others – were conquered. The hills, located south and east of the present-day city centre, provided excellent defence against invaders and malaria, which infested the marshy nearby land, especially during the frequent floods. The Romans eventually solved one major problem – a scarcity of water on the hills – with aqueducts.

Kings ruled Rome in its murky early period, for some 240 years, projecting its power across central Italy. Afterward, during the half-millennium of the Republic, the dominion grew to blanket the Italian peninsula, most of Europe and parts of Africa and the Middle East (then called Asia Minor).

This period is covered in the first 'Ancient Rome' Walk.

Empire (1st Century BC to 5th Century AD)

The Republic expired in about 49 BC, giving way to the Empire. By this time, Rome commanded such power that a direct attack on the city was unthinkable. Due to the new-found safety and overcrowding on the hills, people began moving to lower-lying areas.

Rome's first emperor, Augustus, and his successors built up the so-called Campus Martius, or Field of Mars, the plain near the Tiber, with drainage projects partially solving the long-standing malaria problem. (The area had previously been used for farming, religious rituals and

Opposite: The Forum

military training.) Even so, under the Empire, the Campus Martius was not as densely populated as the older areas, as it was largely devoted to public buildings, monuments, parks, baths and sports facilities.

Both 'Ancient Rome' Walks cover the sights of this period.

Medieval and Renaissance Rome (5th to 17th Centuries)

Chaos and mass internal migrations followed the barbarian invasions of Rome and the fall of the Empire in the late 400s (more precisely, the fall of the Western Empire, since its Eastern arm held out for another millennium).

The city proper also saw a transformation. With the aqueducts destroyed, life on the hills became impossible and people fled to the low-lying northern quarters. Wars, epidemics, starvation and migration reduced Rome's population to fewer than 20,000 from its estimated peak of about one million.

The population was now concentrated in the western part of the Campus Martius, in the great bend of the Tiber (water being a key consideration), and across the river in the Trastevere area. After several centuries of darkness and misery, Rome slowly began to bloom under papal rule. The popes acquired great international prestige and wealth, and began to beautify the area at the river bend – a trend that reached its first peak during the Renaissance in the 1400s and 1500s.

Around this time Romans began distinguishing between the 'abitato', or inhabited part of the city, and the uninhabited 'disabitato', the previously urban area which had reverted to a rural state.

The sights of this period are covered in the 'Renaissance Rome', 'Rome of the Popes' and 'Trastevere' Walks – six in all.

Baroque, 'Romantic' and modern Rome (17th Century to the present)

By the end of the Renaissance, the population within the Tiber's bend had exploded, and the engineers of the so-called 'builder popes' began to rebuild the aqueducts. The first aqueduct served the zone adjacent to the Tiber bend area, that is, towards the 'disabitato' hills to the southeast, and people soon began moving there. Papal architects developed the zone with straight new thoroughfares which attracted mainly upper-class families and foreigners who could afford the pricey real estate. Artists and craftsmen followed.

This development left many important artistic landmarks from the Baroque (17th century) to the Romantic period (18th to early 19th centuries), leading to the area's general, cumulative name of 'Roma Romantica'.

Modern Rome, from the second half of the 19th century to the present, covers and overlays the whole city, expanding miles beyond all previous boundaries, tunnelling through the hills, and largely (though not entirely) obliterating the distinction between the 'abitato' and the 'disabitato'.

Although modern Rome has squalor to spare, it does boast a few noteworthy features, especially from the so-called 'Belle Epoque' (turn of the 19th-to-20th century) and the first few

Piazza Farnese

decades of the 20th century.

Italy became a unified nation only comparatively recently. For centuries until 1870, Rome was the capital of a small theocracy, covering about a quarter of present-day Italy, under the iron-fisted rule of the popes. (The rest of Italy too was divided into various states, some of them under foreign domination.) This helps explain a Roman peculiarity that often surprises visitors. Rome is speckled with time-worn marble signs threatening heavy fines and corporal punishment to litter-bugs, courtesy of 'Monsignor of the Roadways.' These were hung in the 17th to 19th centuries by the monsignors, the pope's priest-bureaucrats who lorded over every aspect of Roman life.

The sights of this period are covered in the two 'Roma Romantica' Walks.

29

Where to begin? Orientating yourself in Rome

Fortunately, there is one spot in Rome from which you can rapidly acquire a direct feel for both Rome's physical layout and its evolution: a gate in the north section of the old walls of Rome, opening onto a large square called Piazza del Popolo. We suggest you begin by orientating yourself here. The effort will pay for itself many times over during your visit.

Three streets fork off from the side of the square opposite the gate. The one in the middle (Via del Corso) leads to the area that best represents Ancient Rome. The street to the left (Via del Babuino) leads to what we call 'Roma Romantica'; the one on the right (Via Ripetta) points to Renaissance Rome and what we refer to as 'Rome of the Popes'.

In the middle: Via del Corso
Or, more simply, 'the Corso'. The name originally meant racetrack. The Corso can be viewed as the thoroughfare to Ancient Rome. It crosses the Campus Martius, into which Rome expanded during the Empire. Several imperial monuments stood here – some still do – especially west of the street. A mile long, the Corso ends at the edge of the oldest part of Rome – the Rome of its origins and of the Republic – at the Palatine Hill and the Forum. Beyond are the other hills originally inhabited in the south and south-east of the city.

To the right: Via Ripetta
The name means Shore Street and references the bank of the nearby Tiber. The street crosses the Campus Martius in a more westerly direction towards the core of the area within the Tiber's bend. Laid out by the popes in the early Renaissance to serve an area that became thickly populated after the fall of the Empire, it was beautified during the Renaissance. An offshoot of Via Ripetta leads to St. Peter's and the Vatican, which are adjacent to the Tiber's bend on the opposite bank.

Via Ripetta, and the streets that continue and branch off it, are associated with Medieval-Renaissance Rome and 'Rome of the Popes'.

To the left: Via del Babuino
'Babuino' means baboon. This street leads to the area developed after the Renaissance and thus characterized by architecture, history and traditions of the Baroque, pre-Romantic and Romantic periods. From that area it continues in the same general direction by means of

View down the trident over the Piazza del Popolo

straight streets laid out by the great 'builder Popes.' Further east are more modern areas of some interest, developed after Rome was reunited with Italy in 1870. Generally speaking, Via Babuino can be associated with 'Roma Romantica.'

The 'Seven Hills'

Eager for topographic orientation, visitors to Rome often ask: which are the fabled 'Seven Hills' of Rome? This is a surprisingly difficult question to answer because, over the millennia, different elevated areas have been included in the traditional number. The ancient Romans adopted their term for the seven hills, 'Septimontium', in the very early Republic in reference to an area roughly coterminous with that of the 'pomerium'—the official territory within Rome's administrative borders. Sometimes, multiple peaks on a single hill were treated as separate hills (thus, for instance, the original 'Septimontium' included only four actual hills totalling seven peaks). On the other hand, the Pincian elevation, although within the pomerium, has never been regarded as a 'hill', while the important Janiculum and other real-and-proper hills never made the list as they lay outside the pomerium. Nowadays, when people speak of the 'Seven Hills' they informally mean the following: Palatine, Capitol, Esquiline, Viminal, Quirinal, Cælian and Aventine.

Overleaf: the Spanish Steps

31

ROME

Roma
Romantica

View from the Pincian in the early 19th century

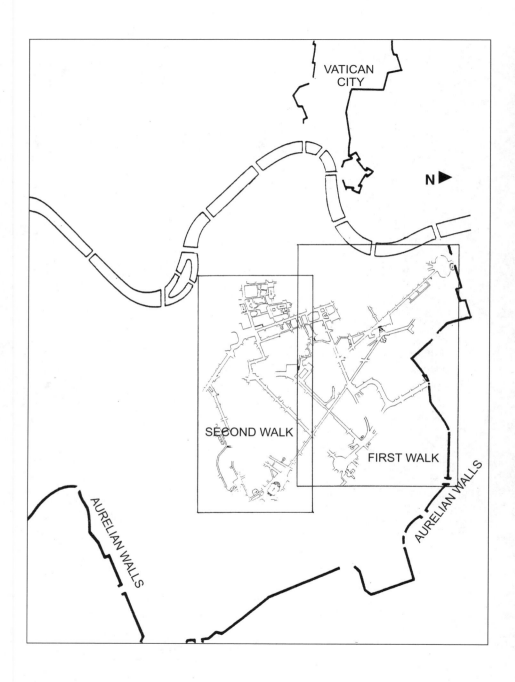

ROMA ROMANTICA

INTRODUCTION

To lovers of Rome the term 'Roma Romantica' indicates those areas of the city that in the late 16th century were the starting point of a slow resettlement, replacing with people and stone the vineyards and wastelands that had invaded much of the city's high ground after the fall of the Roman Empire. The new settlement was intended to spread the population more generously, after the centuries of crowding inside the Tiber bend, where the Romans had confined themselves since the fall (p. 28). Our two Walks will cover this area as well as an adjacent one sharing many of its characteristics.

It is worth stressing that Roma Romantica is merely a rough-and-ready designation that stems mainly from the fact that so many figures of the Romantic movement chose to reside in this 'new' and fashionable area. Yet far from coinciding chronologically with Romanticism (late 18th to mid-19th century), Roma Romantica extends either side, to a total of four hundred years or so – from the 17th to the 20th centuries. Moreover, those who use the term as a topographic definition tend to associate it with contemporary notions of sentimentality and romance ('la dolce vita'), which have little if anything to do with Romanticism as an artistic and literary movement. Yet these modern notions do contribute to the spirit of at least some of the area, and so many (ourselves included) see some value in the Roma Romantica label as a crude but practical aid to conveying general ideas about a place and time.

Among the earliest of these notions is the close historical association of the area with the Counter-Reformation (16th-17th centuries), that sharp reaction to the threat of Protestantism, and its roots in the worldliness and paganism of the renaissance. The idealism and moral uplift of the Counter-Reformation found artistic expression in the Roman baroque, which, though present throughout the city, positively dominates the architecture in this area.

The Triton Fountain

Later, the area took on the elegance of the 18th century, though in a city steeped in religion it never acquired the frivolous tones it had elsewhere. Here, at the heart of Christianity, the experience of Rome powerfully affected two key figures in the history of Romanticism and neo-classicism: Goethe, the polymath and matchless interpreter of the Zeitgeist, whose stay in Rome had a major impact on his thought, and another German, Winckelmann, the archæologist-æsthete whose ideas form the basis of neoclassicism in art. Both lived in the Romantica quarter.

Rome had been an international centre of the arts since the renaissance and a magnet for

English Grand Tourists in Rome, mid-18th century

foreigners seeking artistic and spiritual fulfilment. The flow increased in the 18th century, the quintessential era of the Grand Tour, and came to a climax in the early decades of the 19th century, as the area acquired its most specifically Romantic character. These visitors came above all to see the classical ruins, and spent their time there; but most of them were lodged in the recently redeveloped quarters, where their quest for cultural self-improvement was able to encounter that peculiar blend of religiosity and voluptuousness which was, and in part still is, the Roman way.

After power shifted from the papacy to the Italian state in the late 19th century, Rome underwent a radical and unfortunate transformation intended to make it a 'modern' capital. Many parts of Roma Romantica, however, have escaped major changes. Indeed, some of their elegance and emotional appeal spilled over into new districts nearby built in the *belle époque* period at the end of the century. Other areas have deteriorated badly. Ironically, the districts of Rome which are today most in need of rehabilitation are those built after Rome became the capital of Italy in 1871. In this book they will be included mainly as optional Detours, though even here the visitor will find many sights of interest and much to admire.

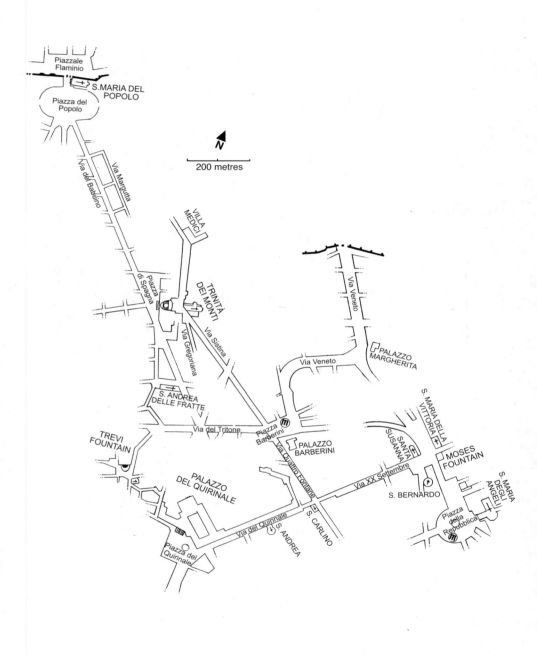

ROMA ROMANTICA
FIRST WALK

Starting point: Piazzale Flaminio
End point: Trinità dei Monti
Duration: 7 hours (without the Detours, indicated above between parentheses).
Strategy: all major sites are open both morning and afternoon. An exception is
the Palazzo del Quirinale, which is only open on Sunday mornings (you will
need to show your passport or similar ID to enter).

BEFORE GOING

1. Porta del Popolo and the Walls

We begin at the foot of the city walls by a massive stone portal now called Porta del Popolo, but known to ancient Romans as Porta Flaminia. This gate is essential to the history of Rome. For centuries it was the main access from the north – from most of the world, that is, given the position of Rome on the Italian peninsula and of the peninsula on the continent.

Generation upon generation of merchants, sightseers, artists and foreign potentates, as well as hostile armies and streams of pilgrims have entered Rome through this gate. They included Martin Luther who, on passing through it in 1510, fell to his knees and exclaimed: 'Hail sacred Rome, land of martyrs, sanctified by the blood they shed here!'

If this isn't reason enough to begin our visit to Rome here, then there is another one. There is no better place to get an initial feel for Rome (as noted in the Foreword, p. 25). The site provides an excellent spatial orientation and speaks volumes about Rome's political, artistic and spiritual past.

Even the walls tell a story. For centuries, the stability of the Empire – the Pax Romana or 'Roman Peace' – and its vastness had forestalled any need for walls: no invader could have got close to the great city without being destroyed. In the late 3rd century AD, when decline had set in, the walls were built by the Emperor Aurelian (not to be confused with the earlier and more famous Marcus Aurelius), and they held firm for two centuries, before finally giving way to the barbarians.

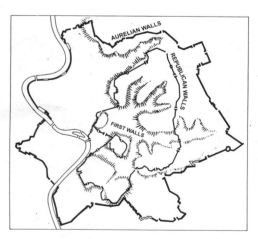

The walls of Rome

Twice before, however, Romans had felt the need for walls: when Rome was founded as a clump of huts on a hill, and during the fledgling years of the Republic, about six centuries before the Aurelian walls, when mortal struggles, such as the Punic Wars, lay ahead. We'll find remnants of these older walls closer to the city centre, since Rome was much smaller then. Visualising the concentric rings of walls will help give you a feel for the city's growth.

The Porta del Popolo was originally named after the Via Flaminia, an age-old artery linking Rome to the north. Today it ends here but originally it continued through the gate into the city. In the middle ages the roadway widened on the inside of the gate, where it became a square. Both the gate and the square received the Latin name Populus (today they are Porta del Popolo and Piazza del Popolo), which means both 'people' and 'poplar': either translation could apply here. 'People' is the more accepted version, though a medieval legend told of a poplar, or walnut tree, behind the gate which supposedly sheltered the ghost of the Emperor Nero. What is true is that his family tomb was actually there.

The gate was rebuilt at the end of the Renaissance. Stylistically interesting, the new gate documents a momentous episode in the Counter-Reformation drama sparked off by Luther on his arrival 150 years earlier: the conversion of Queen Christina of Sweden from Lutheranism to Catholicism and her subsequent arrival in Rome through the Porta del Popolo. This was a sensational diplomatic coup for the pope, all the more so since Christina was the daughter of the king who had led Protestants to victory in the Thirty

The Porta del Popolo

Years' War. After her conversion, she abdicated, and settled in Rome under papal auspices. Little did the pope suspect the embarrassment which this very independent woman would cause him with her free lifestyle, as we shall see later.

ON THE SPOT

1. Porta del Popolo and the Walls
Stand near the news kiosk in the middle of Piazzale Flaminio. The gate is the three-arched marble structure in front of you. Directly opposite is the present end of the Via Flaminia, a great access artery from the north for over two thousand years, until it was replaced by motorways and flight paths.

On both sides of the gate are the walls, largely disguised by more recent constructions (in other walks you'll see them in a more original state). To the right of the gate you can make out three crenelated towers (with notched parapets through which marksmen shot their weapons). With the third tower the walls end abruptly (they were demolished at the end of the 19th century).

On the same side note a large coat-of-arms. It belongs to an 18th-century pope and marks a restoration made during his pontificate. Rome is dotted with similar displays, reminders that before the city became part of the Italian state in 1870, the popes personally directed its upkeep and development. Some of the pontiffs left an especially powerful imprint on the cityscape, thereby gaining

fame as the great 'builder popes'.

The walls, which here double as retaining walls for the verdant Pincio Hill, ascend to the left of the gate. Only part of the masonry is original.

Iron bars that still jut out (at the time of writing) near the top of the wall used to support a safety net installed here during the economic depression of the 1930's, when this had become a favourite jumping spot for suicides.

From the 15th to the 17th centuries a section of the wall a bit further up was known as the Muro Malo, the 'Bad Wall', because the ground was reserved for the burial of prostitutes, 'unless,' said a papal regulation, 'they marry or become nuns.'

The two early 19th-century temple-like structures on the same side mark one entrance to the Villa Borghese, former residence of a still-extant princely Roman family. The grounds of the villa are one of Rome's few public parks (pp. 602-603).

Porta del Popolo. Now observe the outer façade of the gate, keeping in mind that the two side openings are a 19th-century addition. The original central part is an example of the simple yet linear style of the mature renaissance. It is believed to have been designed in the mid-16th century by Michelangelo's bitter enemy, Nanni di

Baccio Bigio, though some attribute it to Michelangelo himself.

Cross at the lights to see the inner façade on Piazza del Popolo. It was built almost a century later, when renaissance simplicity was going out of fashion in favour of the baroque style. The design is by Gian Lorenzo Bernini, one of two supreme masters of the baroque in Rome, the other being Francesco Borromini. These two did more than anyone else to give the city its present appearance. We will shortly have more to say about them, and their lifelong rivalry.

The gate, with its blend of liveliness and solemnity, is a good example of Bernini's style.

The star-over-mountains relief surmounting the gate is a schematic rendering of the coat-of-arms of Alexander VII, a 17th-century 'builder pope' so absorbed in urban planning that he kept a complete model of Rome, in moveable wooden pieces, in his bedroom. He shuffled the pieces around for ideas and to show his architects what he wanted. He commissioned Bernini to redesign the gate for the arrival of Queen Christina of Sweden, and personally composed the welcoming Latin phrase on the façade, *Felici faustoque ingressui* ('To her happy and propitious arrival').

BEFORE GOING

2. Piazza del Popolo and the Church of S. Maria del Popolo

Urban development. Across the square from the Porta del Popolo are two nearly identical domed churches. Three streets radiate from them – Via del Babuino, the Corso and Via Ripetta – mentioned on pp. 30-31 for their handiness as a means of orientation and as a reminder of the historical diversity of the various areas. Together, the three streets are nicknamed the 'Trident'.

On the left, Via del Babuino is the first stretch of our two Roma Romantica Walks, so we'll focus on it now. As noted earlier, Via del Babuino leads to an area developed after the renaissance to ease crowding in the Tiber bend. The development went on for more than three centuries, with the aim of reclaiming the *disabitato*, the area abandoned by Romans after the fall of the Empire (see 'Some Historical Background', Medieval and Renaissance Rome, p. 28). The network of new thoroughfares underpinning the expansion was mostly in place by the late 16th century.

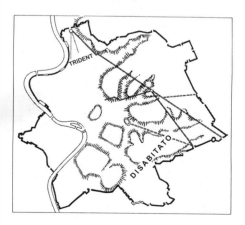

Sixtus V's road building programme

Behind the project was Sixtus V, arguably the greatest of the 'builder popes'. It must be noted, though, that the historian Cesare D'Onofrio, a great myth-slayer, has recently proved that this pope was also moved by a less noble motive than just improving Rome's townscape: to facilitate the enlargement of his private property, Villa Montalto. The villa and its gardens in fact rapidly became Rome's largest (though famous for its beauty, the villa was destroyed in the mid 19th century to give place to the present railway station, p. 80).

The new streets formed a fairly geometrical pattern. At each of the major junctions was a handsome square centering on a huge Egyptian obelisk or Roman column. Piazza del Popolo, with its imposing needle, and Via del Babuino are the stems of Sixtus V's street system.

Slowly the *disabitato* area was repopulated, though for many years – in some places for centuries – people only settled in the new streets, leaving the surrounding area empty. Until the late 19th century vineyards, pastures and even wastelands continued to occupy large patches of Rome, and traces of the *disabitato* are still visible today.

Rome has 48 obelisks, more than any other city, even in Egypt. They tell a strange tale. The emperors brought them back from conquered Egypt to adorn their great stadiums and racetracks. They were found in pieces, half-buried, during the Renaissance, apparently toppled as heathen objects by zealous Early Christians. The builder popes then set them up at major junctions, but not only for decoration.

Recent research has revealed that the needles, topped by crosses and consecrated to the Christian God, were intended as weapons of exorcism, like supernatural lightning rods protecting the city from Satan. Their inscriptions attest to this function, most explicitly the one on the Vatican obelisk (see p. 376). Satan was thought to have a particular grip on Rome because of its many ancient pagan monuments.

Stylistic development. No Roman square better displays the Roman genius for harmoniously blending different styles than Piazza del Popolo. So logical and well-balanced that it seems a single project, its layout actually developed over 300 years. The 'trident' end of the square, though not the twin churches, was built, and the needle set up, in the 16th century. In the next century, Bernini rebuilt the gate, while the twin churches rose in an ornate, later baroque style than that of the gate.

In the neo-classical early 19th century the Roman architect Valadier, together with French designers who had arrived with Napoleon's forces, at that time occupying Rome, added the finishing touches: a fountain, statues around the obelisk, and low buildings and ramps to enhance the symmetry and connect the busy urban scene with the green backdrop of the hill.

If Piazza del Popolo is a real-life textbook on Roman architectural trends from the earliest baroque to the neo-classical, it also contains a splendid example of an earlier style – the unassuming renaissance church of S. Maria del Popolo, tucked in a corner opposite the twin churches.

The real jewel of the square, it is one of Rome's 'Caravaggio churches', containing works by this 17th-century painter, one of the most influential in the history of western art (for a special note on the artist see p. 494). Yet the church's glory had begun more than a century before Caravaggio, when it was a centre of activity for renaissance artists such as Pinturicchio, Bramante and Raphael.

Religious development and the spirit of the times. One of the first popes to bring renaissance artists to Rome was Alexander VI, who has been called one of the most sordid characters in papal history (not to be confused with Alexander VII, the builder pope, who lived 150 years later). He placed S. Maria del Popolo under his special patronage and commissioned many of the artists who were active at that time to work there.

This pope, Rodrigo Borja, was the descendant of minor Spanish nobility and nephew of a previous Spanish pope. As both cardinal and pope, he had several semi-official lovers. One, the savvy businesswoman Vannozza Catanei, bore him children who gained even greater notoriety: Cesare Borgia (the surname was Italianised), a ruthless politician and the model for Machiavelli's cynical treatise *The Prince*; Lucrezia Borgia, accused of poisonings and of an incestuous relation with her father; and Giovanni, Duke of Gandía, assassinated in mysterious circumstances, possibly by his brother Cesare. Vannozza and her murdered son are both buried in S. Maria del Popolo. Alexander's next lover was the Roman duchess Giulia Farnese, called Giulia Bella for her beauty.

The Borgia lifestyle helped precipitate the Protestant Reformation, an upheaval with particular links to Piazza del Popolo. Luther not only entered Rome through the Porta del Popolo, but also spent much of his time in the square, for as an Augustinian monk he was expected to lodge in the Augustinian monastery adjacent to S. Maria del Popolo. (The monastery, which manages the church, is still there but in a newer building.)

We saw how Luther rejoiced when he first arrived in the Holy City. He left feeling quite differently. The simple friar from the north was stunned by the neo-pagan materialism, blatant venality, luxury and corruption around him. He didn't need to go far to get these impressions: the mere association of Alexander VI with S. Maria del Popolo, where Luther prayed daily, would have sufficed. The works of art he saw there, such as the chapel designed by Raphael in which pagan astrological symbols surround God, must have repelled him. When Luther left Rome to begin the fateful Reformation, it is said he cried: 'Farewell, Rome, city that anyone seeking a pious life must flee!'

The popes were slow to see the storm roused by Luther's indignation gathering over their heads. When they finally realised the full scope of the disaster, they acted quickly, but times had changed. Twenty years earlier, when the Dominican preacher Savonarola had railed passionately against clerical excesses, his revolt was snuffed out relatively simply: he was burnt at the stake. But now half of Europe was following the reformers, and the Catholic Church was fighting for its life. The popes' impressive, multi-pronged philosophical, diplomatic, organisational and political counter-offensive is known as the Counter-Reformation, and it has left a deep imprint on the city, which we will trace in both our Roma Romantica Walks.

ON THE SPOT

2. Piazza del Popolo and the church of S. Maria del Popolo

Stand with your back to the gate. At the far end of the square are the twin churches (S. Maria di Montesanto, left, and S. Maria dei Miracoli, right) built in the 17th century by Carlo Rainaldi, a talented contemporary of Bernini, in collaboration with the much younger Carlo Fontana. The three main streets radiate from them to the central areas of present-day Rome.

Immediately to your left by the gate, is the third and most important church of the square, S. Maria del Popolo, to which we'll return in a moment.

In the centre is an Egyptian obelisk measuring 73 ft (24 m) without the base. It is the third tallest but second oldest in Rome (3,300 years old), and was brought to Rome by Augustus after he had annexed Egypt following his victory over Mark Antony and Cleopatra. Originally erected in the Circus Maximus (see p. 267), it lay there in pieces until the 16th century, when Pope Sixtus V had it reconstructed here. (Another obelisk, Rome's tallest and oldest, was also found near the Circus, and re-erected by the same pope in Piazza San Giovanni in Laterano.)

Besides the hieroglyphics dedicating the needle to the Pharaohs Ramses II and Seti I, the base bears inscriptions from the time of Augustus dedicating it to the Sun, and inscriptions, also in Latin, from the time of Sixtus V's time dedicating it to the Holy Cross. One of the latter inscriptions, engraved on the side facing S. Maria del Popolo,

Piazza del Popolo, in a view by the young Piranesi, mid-18th century

1.Madonna di Monte Santo   Piazza del Popolo   2.Madonna de Miracoli

has the 'Christianised' obelisk dedicate itself to the church and say: 'I stand much happier here, before a temple devoted to One whose virginal womb bore, in Augustus' reign, the Sun of Justice'.

The fountains and statuary are part of the early 19th century remodelling of the square by Valadier.

S. Maria del Popolo is on or near the former site of the tomb of the reviled Emperor Nero. It is said that the very purpose of the church – built in 1099, rebuilt in 1227 and again in 1472 – was to exorcise the old tyrant's ghost. If so, the exorcism failed. This corner of the square witnessed ghastly public executions for many centuries. As recently as 1853 a band of brigands was clubbed to death in front of the church.

The façade dates from the second reconstruction of the church in 1472. Note the graceful *Madonna and Child* over the main doorway.

The church is open 07:00-12:00 and 16:00-19:00; Sundays 08:00-13:30 and 16:00-19:00.Inside, medieval tombstones in the floor remind us that the church is much older than the present 15th-century structure.

On the walls all around are tombs and memorials, mostly from the 15th-16th century. Start your tour at the first chapel on the left, which contains some of these wall monuments, as well as two beautiful renaissance reliefs around the fonts.

Go to the next chapel in the left aisle, Cappella Chigi, patronised by a famous renaissance banker (of whom more later, p. 575), and designed by Raphael. Its harmonious lines and splendid decoration reflect the superb sense of proportion and balance typical of this great artist of the early 16th century. His follower, Francesco Salviati, executed the paintings between the windows. Raphael also provided drawings for the mosaics in the chapel dome and for a statue, a merry Jonah escaping from the jaws of a semi-concealed whale, in a niche to the left of the altar. The mosaics represent God creating the Heavens, surrounded by the astrological symbols of the sun and planets. The chapel was completed more than a century after Raphael by Bernini, who added two lively statues, the delightful *Prophet Habakuk Drawn by the Hair by an Angel* to the right of the altar, and *Daniel in the Lion's Den* diagonally opposite.

47

Over the altar is the moving *Birth of the Virgin* by Sebastiano del Piombo, an artist closely linked to Raphael and Michelangelo.

At the end of the left ailse are two small chapels The one to the right contains two masterpieces by Caravaggio: on the right is *The Conversion of St. Paul*: Saul, a Jew, falls from his horse as he hears Christ's call on the road to Damascus. On the left is *The Crucifixion of St. Peter*. Tradition holds that St. Peter asked to be crucified upside-down as a sign of deference to Christ. The prominent Italian art historian Roberto Longhi has called these works 'perhaps the most revolutionary in the whole history of sacred art', thanks to their extreme naturalism coupled with an uncanny sense of abstract form. Over the chapel altar is an *Assumption of the Virgin* by Annibale Carracci, a leading contemporary of Caravaggio and one of the greatest draftsmen and colourists of his time.

If there is no service in progress, you may now go discreetly into the presbytery, the area behind the high altar. Enter through the opening in the middle of the altar rail. Near the left door, on the wall, is a light switch. The ceiling frescoes are by Pinturicchio, a fellow student of Raphael. They represent the *Coronation of the Virgin*, surrounded by amazingly life-like figures of *Apostles* and *Sybils*. One of the most admired painters of his time and famous for his sweetly coloured, airy style, Pinturicchio was amongst the first artists to be called to Rome, and to this particular church, by Pope Alexander VI Borgia at the end of the 15th century. These are some of his best works.

On the presbytery walls, right and left, are two tombs of cardinals by Andrea Sansovino, another important artist in the Borgia circle; the two reclining statues are amongst his masterpieces. The apse itself was designed by Bramante, the most influential architect of the late 15th century, adviser to popes and a pivotal figure of the Renaissance. He was one of the first to study and draw inspiration from the architecture of ancient Rome. This is evident in the solemn apse with its coffered ceiling. The beautiful stained glass windows by the French artist Guillaume de Marcillat are in a style typical of French cathedrals but very rare in Rome.

As you leave the high altar area, note a charming little panel of the *Virgin and Child* over the altar, a Byzantine-style work of the 13th century. Continue along the end wall of the church, where there is another pair of chapels. Vannozza Catanei, mistress of the Borgia pope, and at least one of the children she bore him were buried in the chapel at the far right, but there are no traces of this. A memorial plaque was detached and defaced at an unknown date and inexplicably turned up in the distant church of S. Marco. The bones may still be in a wall or under the floor. Also unknown is the burial place of a related figure who was enterred in the church, the German Johann Burchard, the pope's master of ceremonies, who will be much discussed later. Cross the transept, sumptuously decorated by Bernini (his pupils executed the elegant angels on both sides). Continue down the aisle on this side. Most of the chapels here were decorated, at least in part, by Pinturicchio and his pupils. The most interesting are the third from the last and the last. The former is frescoed, mainly by Pinturicchio's pupils, with *Scenes from the Life of the Virgin*. The last chapel has the delightful *Adoration of the Child*, entirely by Pinturicchio. To the left the tomb of a cardinal by Andrea Bregno, another contemporary of Pinturicchio, is also noteworthy. The exquisite *Madonna* adorning the tomb is by Mino da Fiesole, one of the finest Florentine sculptors of the generation before Michelangelo.

Roman churches abound in macabre symbols of death, but none more gruesome than the marble skeleton grimacing to the right of the exit. A 17th-century gentleman erected this as a monument to himself; his contented face adorns the medallion above.

Outside the church, note the turretted 15th-century bell tower, partly enclosed in the adjoining Augustinian monastery where Luther stayed (rebuilt in the 19th century).

*The Cappella Chigi in the 19th century, by the French architectural artist
and educationalist Paul Letarouilly*

BEFORE GOING

3. From Piazza del Popolo to Piazza di Spagna: Via del Babuino and Via Margutta

As we enter Via del Babuino, the gateway to Roma Romantica, we skirt the Pincio Hill to the left. As noted in the Foreword ('Some Historical Background', p. 28), the high ground was abandoned when the Roman Empire fell, mainly because barbarians had cut the aqueducts.

The popes' campaign to resettle the *disabitato*, begun in the late 16th century, faced two problems: bringing the water back and persuading people to move there.

The first problem was partially solved by repairing the least damaged aqueduct, which ran a relatively short 16 miles (26 km), mostly underground, thus making for an easier reconstruction. The name of the water it carried, Acqua Vergine ('of the Virgin'), dated back to ancient Roman times, when according to tradition a young virgin led some thirsty Roman soldiers to its source.

The Acqua Vergine will accompany us throughout the area. Flowing under the Pincio Hill, the main conduits descend into the area of our next highlight, Piazza di Spagna. From here, several offshoots serve a wide area. One branch runs under Via del Babuino and ends at Piazza del Popolo, where it feeds the fountains under the obelisk. Almost none of the famous fountains that so enhance Rome's beauty existed before the aqueducts were repaired in the late 16th century (two more aqueducts were restored within thirty years of the first).

The second problem – attracting people to the reclaimed area, which the popes wanted to make a showpiece of urban planning and social integration – was handled with fiscal incentives, one of which had an indelible influence on the district. In an early instance of brain drain, foreign painters could settle here free of craft or trade taxes. Scores of them seized the offer. Although rents in the Piazza di Spagna itself were too high for most artists, the vicinity was affordable. Many opened shops in Via del Babuino and the parallel Via Margutta. The artists were also attracted by the market for their work among the wealthy inhabitants of the Piazza di Spagna, and the painters were soon joined by craftsmen in related fields such as framing, colour mixing, and dealing in art and antiques.

The list of Flemish, Dutch and French painters who settled in Via del Babuino and Via Margutta in the 1600's reads like the index of an art history book. The Flemish and Dutch schools were represented, among others, by Rubens, Bril, Van Laer, Van Somer, Van Swanevelt, Van Wittel, De Bruyn, Breenbergh, Poelenburg and Sweerts; the French by Claude Lorrain, Poussin, Valentin de Boulogne and many others. Roman museums overflow with the legacy of those foreign painters, whose works were also exported all over Europe.

A general increase in house prices and rent reduced the artists' numbers in the 18th century, but they returned *en masse* in the next, at which time artists from all over Italy and Europe lived here, including Richard Wagner and his mentor, Franz Liszt, both on Via del Babuino.

The two streets still show traces of this artistic, bohemian character, but ongoing gentrification has diluted it. Most of the studios on the two streets are now luxury apartments, and most of the colourful art-related shops are gone. But several artists still live on Via Margutta, and many antique stores, once famous throughout Europe, remain on Via del Babuino.

ON THE SPOT

3. From Piazza del Popolo to Piazza di Spagna: Via del Babuino and Via Margutta

From the square go down Via del Babuino, left of the twin churches. The street is composed mainly of 17th-, 18th- and early 19th -century buildings, a mixture typical of this part of Rome.

The first palace on your left (No. 9), built around 1800 in the neo-classical style, is the illustrious and romantic **Hôtel de Russie**, famous for housing tzars, kings and princes (it was dubbed the 'hotel of kings'), as well as for its beautiful gardens on the slopes of the Pincio. One famous guest there in the 1930's and 1940's was King Gustav VI of Sweden, a distinguished archæologist.

The Russie is one of several grand hotels that sprang up in the district in the 18th century, when most of the elegant foreign clientele had abandoned the old area of the Tiber bend, and Rome was becoming the meeting point of Romantic Europe. These hotels thrived until the early 20th century, when they were eclipsed by newer establishments on Via Veneto (see p. 85-86).

German forces occupying Rome requisitioned the hotel in 1943. After the war it was rented out as offices for several decades, but in 2000 it was bought by a British hotel chain and reopened, partly as a result of the waning of the Via Veneto as a fashionable area, which has led to the revival of many luxury hotels in older parts of Rome.

Continue along Via del Babuino and at the first intersection turn left into Via Margutta.

(To see the house where Wolfgang Goethe – the great 18th-19th century German poet and one of the founding fathers of the Romantic movement – spent several months (a building of no special interest otherwise), or the minor **Goethe Museum** in the same place (p. 687), turn right instead of left out of Via del Babuino and into Via della Fontanella and go one block. The building is at the intersection of Via del Corso (No. 18). It is possible that the apartment occupied by the museum is the very one in which Goethe spent

Goethe at the window

one of his Roman sojourns in the company of his countryman, the painter Johann Tischbein, who has left us a famous drawing of Goethe at the window there. Return to Via del Babuino and into Via Margutta.)

Via Margutta makes a right angle and then runs parallel to Via del Babuino, skirting the foot of the Pincio Hill. The very name reflects the bohemian character of the street. The artists and artisans who first settled here named it after Margutte, the braggart hero of a 15th-century comic poem (Byron tried to translate it into English, then gave up). Painters and other artists, you will remember, have lived here for centuries.

Discreetly enter one of the typical verdant courtyards, such as Nos 33 or 51A, asking doormen as needed. Through the latter you can reach the slopes of the Pincio – via stairs that start halfway down the courtyard to the left under a stucco eagle – discovering an unsuspectedly rural, idyllic enclave.

At No. 53B the great 18th-19th century English painter Sir Thomas Lawrence founded the British Academy of the Arts, which later gave way to the painters' and sculptors' studios mentioned on the sides of the gate.

Opposite, on the wall at No. 81, is what looks like one of the typical 17th- or 18th-century anti-litter signs of the old papal regime (see p. 29). This one is unique, however, in that it is a fake, recently made and placed here by an antiques dealer as a prank. Its text, threatening 'by order of the most illustrious and reverend Monsignor President of the Roadways ... a fine of 10 scudi plus corporal punishments' to litterers is fairly similar to the ancient warning signs you'll see on many a wall and corner of Rome.

At No. 54 was Rome's glorious Circolo degli Artisti ('Artists' Club'), closed in 1960 for lack of support after about a century of life. Its heyday was between the late 19th and early 20th century, when membership included (besides the greatest names in the visual arts) musicians such as Wagner, Liszt and Puccini, writers such as D'Annunzio and Zola, and actresses such as Sarah Bernhardt and Eleonora Duse. Another member, who lived in Via Margutta, was the Catalan painter Mariano Fortuny, who also created fabulous fabrics and dresses.

Just past No. 54 is a nice fountain dated 1927 and spouting Acqua Vergine.

Backtrack a few steps. Go left at Vicolo dell'Orto di Napoli to return to Via del Babuino. Cross there and go right. At the end of the block is the Anglican **Church of All Saints**, one of the first (1882) of a number of Protestant churches that sprang up in Rome after 1870 and the end of papal rule (for others, see p. 81 and p. 131). A pure example of the English 'Gothic Revival' style, its appearance on an old Roman street was said alternately to clash with it or artfully blend in with a pleasant touch of exoticism. The church was built to provide a spiritual haven to the substantial British population in Rome and is a testimonial to

artistic currents sweeping through Victorian England at the time.

The architect, George Edmund Street, was a follower of the famous mid 19th-century English painter and art scholar John Ruskin. Street and other followers of Ruskin declared themselves foes of the culture of mass-production that was the consequence of the Industrial Revolution and, to oppose it, they emphasised refined craftsmanship and simple but colourful materials. Street, who in 1879 had completed another church in Rome (p. 81), returned to the city with two other prominent advocates of these ideas: the decorator, poet and socialist author William Morris and his friend, the painter Sir Edward Burne-Jones. All went to work on the church. The unusual choice of materials is obvious both on the façade – in the red bricks from Siena, contrasting with the white travertine marble of the windows and portal – and inside, in the pink stone from Arles on the brick structures. Both materials were specially imported. The church is usually open in the mornings, except on Saturdays; and on Sundays it is open at 18:00 for evensong.

The striking mosaics in the apse are by Burne-Jones, while Morris contributed ornamental details, such as the ceramic panels at the base of the walls.

On the left wall as you face the altar is an interesting plaque 'to the English colonel Baron J. W. Keen and his English Legion' who fought with Garibaldi in the 1860 campaign to liberate and unite Italy (see pp. 565).

Continue along Via del Babuino away from Piazza del Popolo. On the next block is **S. Atanasio dei Greci** ('of the Greeks'), built in the late 16th century by the renowned architect and sculptor Giacomo Della Porta for the Greek Catholic priests (as distinct from Greek Orthodox) who fled the Byzantine Empire after it fell to the Turks in 1453. Mass is still celebrated here in Greek in accordance with the rare Greek Catholic ritual. (A little-known fact is that there are thousands of non-Orthodox eastern Christian communities who acknowledge the authority of

'Oriental bishops with long beards' – an image from a 19th-century guidebook to Rome

the Roman papacy but keep many of their own customs, such as married priests; together they can boast millions of adherents, mostly in Eastern Europe but also in the United States.)

The church is our first example of the work of Della Porta, one of the last exponents of the High Renaissance before the advent of Mannerism and another of the prolific artists to whom Rome owes its present appearance. His churches, palaces and fountains grace many Roman squares.

It is only open on Saturday evening and Sunday morning for Mass.

The inside is unusual, with architectural details such as a clover-leaf triple apse (*trikonochos*) and high wooden screen before the main altar (*iconostasis*) typical of eastern churches. Both side apses have early 17th-century frescoes by Cavalier d'Arpino, once the Roman employer and later a heated enemy of Caravaggio.

To the left of the church, large windows indicate the presence of an artists' studio (four generations of a family of sculptors, the Tadolini, worked here in the 19th century). Against the wall is a low fountain surmounted by an old, badly worn statue of a satyr. Popularly supposed to be a baboon, it gave the street its name ('del Babuino' or 'of the Baboon') four centuries ago.

Continuing away from Piazza del Popolo, the next block begins with a late 16th-century palace, the College of the Greeks, built together with the Greek church and now housing a Benedictine seminary.

Further along to the left, No. 79 was the Hotel of America in the 19th century. Wagner stayed here in 1876. At No. 89 is the 18th-century building where Valadier, the architect who completed Piazza del Popolo, lived.

Via del Babuino opens into Piazza di Spagna.

BEFORE GOING

4. Piazza di Spagna

If we had to describe Piazza di Spagna in one word, it would be 'elegance'. The square was born elegant when the popes set out to make it the showpiece of their new district east of the over-crowded Tiber bend. Entrepreneurs offered the modern, airy houses in the uncongested neighborhood at stiff rates that limited prospective takers to the affluent, such as senior clergymen, nobles, diplomats and wealthy foreign travellers.

The cosmopolitan exclusiveness and sophistication of the area grew in later centuries, as we shall see. Today it survives, despite the efforts of populist city authorities, fast food restaurants and tourist agencies to destroy it. Cars are banned, though the crowds that invade the square by day and even more so by night, along with the street vendors, more than compensate in noise and dirt.

Yet there are still moments when, by detaching yourself from the chaos, you can recapture the old magic. Renowned luxury stores such as Gucci, Bulgari and Valentino have their world head-quarters here or nearby. Old-world establishments, such as Babington's Tea Rooms and Caffè Greco also help. Yet the timeless grace of the square lies in its serene physical layout and in the many reminders of a cultural and social life that was among the most intense in Europe.

When the square was built, Spain and France, the most powerful countries in Europe at the time, bought major properties: Spain in the square itself, where it opened its embassy to the pope (it gave the square its name and is still there); and France on the Pincio overlooking the square. The French built a church and convent for their clergy and acquired a splendid villa for an academy of the arts, both of which survive. The two countries so monopolised the square that for a century, half was called Piazza di Spagna ('of Spain') and the other half Piazza di Francia ('of France').

In the 18th century it was the turn of wealthy Britons to dominate the square. They lodged for long periods either in rented apartments or in the many luxury hotels that sprang up in the area (one of the few surviving hotels of that calibre, the Hassler, at the top of the Spanish Steps, is arguably Rome's best). England was then the world superpower, and its upper classes had the cus-tom of taking a Grand Tour of Europe, of which Rome was the uncontested high point. Until the late 19th century, the swarms of *milordi* (as the Romans called rich Englishmen, whether lords or not) on the square earned it the slang nickname 'er ghetto dell'Ingresi', or 'the English ghetto'.

From the square, wealthy visitors went hunting for paintings and antiques to take home. This habit helped sustain the artists and dealers who had settled in the area. A related phenomenon was that the square became a job market for models who were hired by painters, both professional and amateur (the English tourists were avid watercolourists). Many models wore the folk costumes of the surrounding countryside – 'all varnished eyes and daggered hair and swathed legs and peaked hats,' as Henry James wrote. Charles Dickens found the models, who gathered in the square until the late 19th century, 'mightily amusing'.

At the height of the Romantic era, Piazza di Spagna was the cultural rendezvous point of the world, thronging with foreigners, both resident and in transit, all ostensibly engaged in artistic or intellectual pursuits – the point of their visit being, of course, to explore Rome's great classical her-itage. 'Nothing similar exists elsewhere,' noted Stendhal in the early 19th century.

The physical beauty of the square was another draw. While it was divided between Spain and France, each country sought to enhance its own image (in a time of hot political competition) by embellishing its half. The famous 17th-century Italian-born French statesman, Cardinal Mazarin, outdid the Spanish by conceiving a monumental staircase ascending the hill from the square up to the French church and other French institutions. Actual construction had to wait a century, until both French and Italian money backed a design by the Roman architect Francesco De Sanctis.

The Spanish Steps, as they are called in English (Mazarin, who began the project in the name of France, must be spinning in his grave), are the most famous and distinctive feature of the square. Architects particularly appreciate the way in which the steps are viewable from all angles. The designer's 18th-century report, however, reveals that Signor De Sanctis had other than æsthetic considerations in mind: 'I will make the steps visible from everywhere

The Barcaccia in the Piazza di Spagna, looking towards the Column of the Immaculate Conception

because the reverend fathers [of the French church atop the hill] have alerted me to the gross indecencies committed on that shrubby slope by couples who often hide there,' he wrote.

Overlooking the steps is the apartment where John Keats died four months after his 25th birthday (it is now the Keats-Shelley Museum). Keats had arrived in Rome in September 1821, ill with tuberculosis, accompanied by his young painter friend Joseph Severn (Rome's climate was reputedly good for 'consumptives'). Like most of their countrymen, they lodged in Piazza di Spagna. Keats' little bedroom overlooked the steps. There, England's greatest Romantic poet spent his final month gaping at the ceiling which Severn had painted with flowers for him, tortured by thoughts of the woman he loved, Fanny, and writing letters that can make even a strong reader cry:

> The thought of leaving [her] is beyond everything horrible – the sense of darkness coming over me – I eternally see her figure eternally vanishing... Shall I awake and find all this a dream? We cannot be created for this sort of suffering...

> There is only one thought killing me – I have been well, healthy, alert etc., walking
> with her, and now...
> I should have had her when I was in health, and I should have remained well. I can
> bear to die – I cannot bear to leave her. Oh, God! God! God! God! everything... that
> reminds me of her goes through me like a spear.

Nor could he find consolation in religion. Writing home, Severn reported what his friend told him:

> A malignant being must have power over us – over whom the Almighty has little or
> no influence – yet you know Severn I cannot believe in your book – the Bible – but I
> feel the horrible want of some faith – some hope – something to rest on now – there
> must be such a book...

Keats died one dark February evening in Severn's arms. A few hours later, Severn wrote down
his final words:

> Did you ever see any one die – no – well then I pity you poor Severn – what trouble
> and danger you have got into for me – now you must be firm for it will not last long –
> I shall soon be laid in the quiet grave – thank God for the quiet grave – O! I can feel
> the cold earth upon me – the daisies growing over me – O for this quiet – it will be
> my first.

He was buried in the Protestant Cemetery in Rome (p. 624), a fragrant green shaded by pine

Keats

trees and dotted with the daisies he had dreamt of. In accordance
with his wishes, his unmarked tombstone, recognisable only as that
of 'a young English poet', carries the inscription 'Here lies one
whose name was writ in water'. Nearby are the remains of the poet
Shelley, another Piazza di Spagna regular. He also died tragically
young, at the age of 30, perhaps by suicide, when his boat capsized in
a storm off the coast of Liguria; a volume of Keats' poems was in his
pocket (on Shelley's death see also pp. 56, 624). Severn settled in
Rome and lived to 85 in an apartment near the square.

Keats and Shelley were amongst the scores of Romantic era
English and American poets, writers and painters who lived in the
area. Others were Lord Byron, Sir Walter Scott, Sir Thomas Lawrence, Sir Joshua Reynolds, Leigh
Hunt, Rembrandt Peale, Thomas Cole and John Singleton Copley. In nearby Piazza Mignanelli
was the studio of J. M. W. Turner, the great English painter – 'a good tempered, funny little gentleman, continuously sketching at his window,' as one countryman wrote in his diary.

On the Pincio, between the 16th and 19th century, countless French painters, musicians and
writers – from Poussin, Fragonard and Ingres to Chateaubriand, Berlioz, Gounod, Debussy and
Balthus – lived in or near the French Academy.

ON THE SPOT

4. Piazza di Spagna

The square is framed by 17th- to 19th-century ochre buildings; the tall palm trees have grown here for over a century.

The square consists of two triangles, like a bow-tie. We'll first explore the larger one, which we enter from Via Babuino; the other we'll visit in the next section, before leaving it along Via dei Condotti.

Proceed along the right side of the square, which is dominated by the **Spanish Steps** to the left.

Completed by the architect Francesco De Sanctis in 1726 to replace rustic, tree-lined paths that went up the grassy slope, the steps are one of the most scenic city views anywhere. The gently sloping stairway, of typical Roman travertine marble, is grand, sweeping and graceful, something one would expect in a palace or opera house rather than outdoors. It makes the space feel at once theatrical and intimate, sumptuous and comfortable. In springtime, potted azaleas are placed all down the steps for an even more spectacular effect.

Especially at the bottom, the steps once served as a gathering place for artists' models. Today it is hordes of tourists and young people.

At the top of the steps, the church with two distinctive bell towers is **Ss. Trinità dei Monti** ('Most Holy Trinity of the Hills'), a French-run church, to which we'll return at the end of the walk.

The oldest monument in the square is in the middle: the delightful Barcaccia ('Old Boat') Fountain, designed in the early 17th century by Pietro Bernini, father of the famous sculptor-architect Gian Lorenzo Bernini. Some scholars believe it is by the son.

Instead of spouting upwards like all self-respecting fountains, this one leaks water from all sides, like the water-logged shipwrecks that squatted at the nearby river. This adds a fantastic prop to the stage-set of the square, while solving the problem of low water pressure due to the levelling off of the aqueduct as it arrives from the hill. Tourists gather about the Barcaccia for fresh spring water and to bathe their tired feet, though this is naturally forbidden.

If we now face the steps, the building farthest from the steps on the left was renowned for centuries as the Hôtel de Londres; it closed in 1931.

Two elegant 18th-century buildings flank the steps, like the wings of a stage, and were indeed designed by De Sanctis as part of the whole scheme. The building on the left houses Babington's Tea Rooms, founded by a genteel English lady in the early 18th century and still serving authentic, somewhat overpriced British-style breakfast and tea.

The building on the right is where John Keats died. It now houses a small museum devoted to him and Shelley. The apartment, with its charming, typical early 19th-century decor, is worth a peek (for opening times see p. 687).

Further to the right, at No. 31, is a house built in the 17th century by a family of French painters from Burgundy, the Courtois. Its best known members, Jacques and Guillaume, both called *il Borgognone* ('the Burgundian') were soldier-

The area around the Piazza di Spagna

The Barcaccia and the Spanish Steps in the 19th century

painters who specialised in battle scenes. Their dilapidated crest over the portal bears their motto – now barely legible – a pun on their name: 'Though armed with sword, I am courteous' ('courtois' in French, 'cortese' in Italian). After the Courtois, countless artists lived in the building, most recently the famous Italian painter and sculptor Giorgio De Chirico, who died here in 1978. (There is one of his sculptures in the lobby.) Further to the right, on the corner of Piazza Mignanelli, is a building housing American Express. Until the early 20th century it was another grand hotel, the Albergo dell'Europa.

We now visit Via dei Condotti, the street opposite the Spanish Steps, before completing our Piazza di Spagna tour.

BEFORE GOING

5. Via Condotti

Not even most Romans know that Via Condotti, one of the world's most fashionable streets, is named after the humble water-line that, as we learned, permitted development of the area 400 years ago. 'Condotti' refers to the main pipe that still carries water under the whole length of the street. The English equivalent 'conduit' gave its name to a smart street in London.

Via Condotti resembles Piazza di Spagna both in origin and character. Chic stores attest to its sophistication; its cosmopolitanism shows in the illustrious Caffè Greco, one of Europe's oldest coffee houses, which has been open since the 18th century. Its name refers to the Greek-style coffee it served before the *espresso* machine was invented in the late 19th century. From the start, the street was a haunt of international celebrities, including the Venetian adventurer and womaniser Giacomo Casanova.

Indeed, Casanova is one of the personalities who most contributed to the romantic aura of both Via Condotti and Piazza di Spagna, where he lived during an absence from his native Venice. His memoirs describe the 18th-century atmosphere of the coffeehouses here, typified by the Caffè Greco:

> I was walking down the Strada Condotta [an older name for Via Condotti] when I heard someone call me from the coffee house. It was my friend the Abbé Gama ... 'Sit here beside me,' he says. From the next table, I hear a young abbé loudly ridiculing the pope, though without bitterness. Everyone laughs. Another, asked why he had left Cardinal B.'s service, answers that it was because His Eminence did not think himself obliged to pay for certain extra services he demanded in his nightshirt. The laughter is general. Another comes over and tells the Abbé Gama that if he cares to spend a pleasant evening at the Pincio gardens, he would meet him there with two little Roman girls who are satisfied with just a quarter of a gold piece ... amid all that comes in a very pretty gentleman. His hips remind me of a girl in men's clothes; I say so to Gama, who tells me this is the celebrated castrato, Beppino Ricciarelli. The abbé calls him to us and tells him with a laugh that I have taken him for a girl. He looks me full in the face and says that if I will spend a night with him, he will show me that I was both right and wrong.

Also on Via Condotti is the world's smallest sovereign power – the Vatican is gigantic by comparison – the Sovereign and Military Order of the Knights of Malta, a.k.a. Knights of Rhodes, a.k.a. Knights of Jerusalem. This chivalric group, dating back to the middle ages, is recognised as an independent state by the Italian government today, just as it was under papal rule. It issues passports, registers merchant ships and issues stamps which are accepted in a few countries.

The Knights of Jerusalem were Italian philanthropists who obtained Muslim permission in 1048 to build a hospital for Christian pilgrims to the Holy Land. In 1099, after a victorious Crusade, they began to help the new Christian rulers. The Muslims returned a century later and threw out the Knights, who then conquered and settled a series of Mediterranean islands: first Cyprus and then, in 1310, Rhodes. Two centuries later they were again dislodged by the Arabs and settled in Malta. (Each time they moved, they changed their name.) When the British occupied Malta in 1814 the Knights retired to Rome, where they owned the Via Condotti palace and two others. The order runs 200 hospitals worldwide and a leper colony. Some Knights take vows of poverty and chastity. Until about 1960 only the nobility could join, but now anyone can who contributes generously enough. More than half the 5,000 members are Italians; some 2,000 are Americans.

Many Catholic countries accord its Grand Master – currently an Englishman – the honours due to a head of state.

Retracing our steps along Via Condotti, we return briefly to Piazza di Spagna, in a section marked by an antique column re-erected in 1856 to celebrate the Immaculate Conception of the Virgin, which the Church had recently recognised as an infallible truth. The new dogma asserted that Mary was conceived free of the 'original sin' weighing on humanity since Adams' expulsion from the Garden of Eden. Contrary to popular belief, it has nothing to do with the virgin birth of Jesus Christ.

Column of the Immacolata

Because it implicitly elevated Mary to semi-divine status, the belief had met widespread opposition from clerics who deemed it incompatible with the 'one God' axiom of Christianity. It was approved, however, thanks to the fervid support of Pope Pius IX, who wanted to repay the Virgin for having saved him, as he believed, from a frightful accident (see p. 609). Curiously, the story seems to have repeated itself in the last century. Pope John Paul II, who claimed the Madonna helped him survive an assassination attempt early in his reign, pushed to have her recognised as possessing divine powers of redemption on a par with her Son.

This part of the square will also introduce you to the work of Bernini's great competitor, Francesco Borromini.

The two rivals seemed condemned to work constantly at close quarters, sometimes on the same building even. Here, they designed different parts of the Collegio di Propaganda Fide, an organisation founded by the Church after the Reformation to reaffirm and spread the Catholic faith.

Bernini is the more famous of the two, partly because he was also a great sculptor; but Borromini was the greater architect. The dynamic interplay of his surfaces has been likened to Bach chorales in stone. A simple stonemason in his youth, Borromini acquired tremendous craftsmanship and culture through tireless effort. His career was slow and bitter. Bernini, a year younger and the son of an established artist, had it much easier. Once, when working on the same project as Borromini, he was paid ten times more.

The differences in circumstances and personality led to constant friction, with the introverted, neurotic Borromini ('the difficult genius' as he was called) the inevitable loser against the well-connected, self-assured Bernini. Borromini's frustrations drove him to suicide, which he tried to commit by falling on his sword. He changed his mind and called for a doctor, but it was too late and he died after recounting his own desperate attempt to end his life. He was 67. Bernini lived on to the ripe old age of 82, wealthy and honoured. We'll discuss him further when we see his work in the Vatican (pp. 374-6).

ON THE SPOT

5. Via Condotti

The Caffè Greco is about 30 yards down the street on the right. For almost three centuries it was the rendezvous of foreign and native intellectuals and artists. Inside fixtures, paintings and faded photos evoke the characters, landscapes and intimacy of a long-gone world. Amongst the hundreds of famous people who frequented it were Goethe, Gogol, Schopenhauer, Stendhal, Mark Twain, Mendelssohn, Baudelaire, Wagner, Liszt, Henry James and Giacomo Leopardi.

Leopardi, the greatest modern Italian poet, lived in the next building (No. 81) for several months at the height of the Romantic era. Across the street lived the painter Severn after the death of his friend Keats, as well as the poet Tennyson and the novelist Thackeray.

The flagships of world-famous stores – Gucci, Bulgari, Ferragamo, Valentino and others – dot the length of Via Condotti. The side streets sport other elegant shops. Down the right side of the street, at No. 68, a 17th-century palace houses the world headquarters of the Sovereign and Military Order of the Knights of Malta.

In the courtyard one can often see cars with the 'SMOM' license plates of the Order. One of their clinics is around the corner, at No. 68 Via Bocca di Leone. The stamps issued by the Order are sold in the lobby.

Return to Piazza di Spagna and turn right into the smaller triangle of the square dominated by the Column of the Immaculate Conception of the Virgin erected in 1856.

The ancient Roman column is topped by a statue of the Virgin and the base is adorned with statues and reliefs of Moses and other biblical figures and episodes, all in a Michelangelesque style by minor 19th-century sculptors. The best is the statue of *David* – one of the four on the base – by Adamo Tadolini, whose studio we passed on Via del Babuino (p. 53).

On the right side of the square, at No. 57, is the 17th-century palace of the Spanish Embassy to the Holy See, which gives the square its name. Diego Velázquez, the greatest painter of 17th-century Spain (the Siglo de Oro or 'Golden Century'), lived here during his long stay in Rome. In the next century, Casanova lived and worked in the embassy for a few months as a secretary, until he got into trouble over a girl who lived across the square and had to flee Rome.

The end of the square is formed by the 17th-century **Collegio di Propaganda Fide** (Latin for 'propagation of the faith'), created during the Counter-Reformation as a headquarters for missionary work. The bulk of the building, including the simple and well-proportioned façade, is by Bernini. Borromini designed the extraordinary side elevation.

The right side, facing Via Propaganda, with its intriguing and animated succession of concave and convex surfaces, is typical of Borromini's style and a perfect solution for a large surface area that must be neither too showy nor monotonous, and that can only be seen close to.

Inside the building is a very elegant little chapel by Borromini, the Cappella dei Re Magi ('of the Magi'), which is occasionally open to visitors (ask at the Via Propaganda entrance to the building).

Via Condotti in the late 19th century

6. From Piazza di Spagna to the Trevi Fountain

Before leaving Piazza di Spagna, let's discuss the rest of our walk and its continuing relation to the expansion line followed by the builder popes in resettling the district.

An obelisk stands at the top of the Spanish Steps before the church of Trinità dei Monti. As we learned (p. 45), the needle marks a major junction in the expansion scheme. Yet why is the needle so far uphill with respect to our present route? In other words, why doesn't the expansion line continue in the same direction, along the axis of Via del Babuino-Piazza di Spagna? It can't, because if it did, it would hit the steep side of Rome's tallest hill, the Quirinal. Indeed, the street that follows the Babuino-Piazza di Spagna axis ends in a modern tunnel.

Since the expansion line has climbed to the obelisk area, following it would mean climbing the 138 Spanish Steps. Our less taxing route will take us first slightly to the right of it, to the Trevi

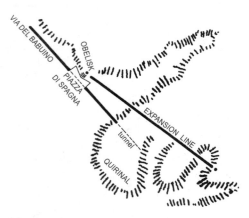

The line of expansion favoured by the builder popes

Fountain, a monument to the genie of the district, the Acqua Vergine. Then we'll climb a gentler slope to the Quirinal Hill and rejoin the expansion line. Finally, we'll go sideways, returning to the top of the Spanish Steps and its lovely, romantic neighbourhood.

On the way we'll see more works by Borromini and Bernini, including the beautiful church of S. Andrea delle Fratte ('in the Thickets'), whose name recalls the rural character of the area before its resettlement by the popes. Before reaching the Trevi Fountain we'll see the dark ruin of the ancient Roman aqueduct that carried the Acqua Vergine. Though now several feet below street level, this segment of the channel once ran above ground (see p. 140).

Approaching the Trevi Fountain we'll see the first signs of another major aspect of urban development in Rome: the post-1870 demolition of huge swathes of the city in the name of modernisation. 'It was the time,' wrote the famous 'decadent' poet, Gabriele d'Annunzio, a few years later, 'when the industry of the constructors and of the destructors of Rome raged at its sleaziest.' We'll cross Via del Tritone, one of the thoroughfares created by the fledgling Italian state to mimic Paris and London, usually with unimpressive results. 'Squalor, misery, ruin and vile stucco ... these are the elements of the modern picture; that is what the great development of modern Rome has brought forth,' the American novelist and resident Francis Marion Crawford wrote in 1880, perhaps with some exaggeration.

One minor consequence of the craze for rebuilding was the destruction at this intersection of the home of Giuseppe Gioacchino Belli, the 'Poet of Rome'. His sonnets in Roman dialect, amongst the highest expressions of 19th-century poetry, are occasionally quoted in this book.

ON THE SPOT

6. From Piazza di Spagna to the Trevi Fountain

Follow Via Propaganda to a four-way intersection. Across the street to the left is **S. Andrea delle Fratte** ('St. Andrew in the Thickets') by Francesco Borromini (the undistinguished façade is a later addition). Worth observing from the outside is the upper part of the church at the rear, with its lively interplay of surfaces typical of this great architect, and the strange, imaginative bell tower. Left unfinished at Borromini's death (by suicide), the church was completed by Giovan Antonio de' Rossi. (Open: 08:00-12:00 and 16:00-18:00.)

The majestic and serene interior was created by Borromini in a relatively small space. As usual, his rival Bernini's work is not far away: two marvellous angels on either side of the high altar. The statues were meant for a bridge (p. 395), but the pope deemed them too precious to be outdoors and moved them here. Copies were made for the bridge.

A bit of historico-religious folklore is in the third chapel to the left of the main entrance, which houses an especially venerated 'Madonna of the Miracle'. This artistically indifferent 19th-century painting is said to be responsible for the sudden, miraculous conversion of a wealthy Jewish visitor from Strasbourg, one Mr. Ratisbonne (described as 'an obstinate Jew' in a French tablet on the wall above a modern bust of the convert). Interviewed in 1842, Ratisbonne described his experience with the painting: 'The Lady was there, sweet, majestic, surrounded by a radiating light, beckoning me to come forth ... I fell to my knees and was struck by the truth as by a thunderbolt.' Ratisbonne became a Catholic priest and died a missionary in a distant land.

The altar is also the one where Maximilian Kolbe, a Polish priest who died in the Nazi concentration camp of Auschwitz in 1943 by sacrificing himself in place of another prisoner, celebrated his first Mass. He was beatified in 1982. On the same side as the chapel, near a side exit, is buried one of the few women painters accorded adequate recognition in the past – the Swiss Angelica Kauffmann, who died in 1807. Her epitaph is on the wall. Exit by the main door.

Diagonally across the street (but don't cross) is Palazzo Bernini, formed by two 17th-century buildings (12 and 11A), both partly remodelled in the 19th century, which the well-heeled architect-sculptor bought and joined. He lived in only part of No. 11A and rented out the rest. His bust and memorial tablet were placed on the wall of No. 12 by mistake.

Take a left at Via S. Andrea delle Fratte and another left into Via del Nazareno. Passing a 16th-century building on the left, at No. 2 is a tiny door topped by papal arms. Across the street are the partly buried ruins of the ancient Roman aqueduct of the Acqua Vergine, the late 16th-century reconstruction of which spurred the resettlement of the whole area. The tiny door opposite gave service access to the aqueduct.

Via del Nazareno runs into the modern Via del Tritone. Cross it and take Via della Stamperia, one of the two streets in front of you. Where the street widens, at No. 77, is the entrance to the historic Accademia di San Luca, the painters' guild and

Route from
the Palazzo
Bernini to
the Trevi
Fountain

academy. (It contains a gallery, see p. 684.) Borromini renovated the 16th-century building a century later and decorated the entrance hall.

The twin columns with the stucco garlands which you see from the entrance were designed by Borromini. They hide the beginning of a spiral ramp that served as a staircase but was also used to send supplies to the upper storeys by mule.

In Via della Stamperia ('of the Printing Press'), No. 6 is the Calcografia Nazionale, a national printmaking centre, founded in 1738 and moved to this building, which was designed for it by Giuseppe Valadier, a century later.

Its collection of over 20,000 engraving plates from all periods is the world's most largest. Italian artists such as Piranesi, famous for his views of Rome, and non-Italians, such as Ingres, are represented, but the old copper plates are not used, nor are modern prints produced here. The collection is open to scholars only and public exhibitions are rare.

Via della Stamperia leads to the Trevi Fountain.

BEFORE GOING

7. The Trevi Fountain and on to the Quirinal

The spectacular Trevi Fountain is not only a work of art: it is the dazzling commemoration of the return to Rome of the Acqua Vergine, which had allowed the redevelopment of the whole area. It marks the end point of the renovated aqueduct.

More modest monuments had served the purpose for almost 200 years, during which time legends sprang up associating the water with nostalgia for Rome. The earliest version simply said that the water was so good that whoever tasted it would return to Rome. Eventually it was said that whoever drank the water on the spot under the midnight moon would have to return. The coin-tossing ritual, mimicked worldwide, replaced the moon tradition after the present fountain became a major tourist attraction. It probably originated in the clever idea of someone who came along later with a rake. Today the coins go to charity.

A bustling scene has always surrounded the fountain. The American novelist Nathaniel Hawthorne described it in 1858:

> In the daytime there is hardly a livelier scene in Rome than the neighbourhood of the Fountain of Trevi; for the piazza is then filled with stalls of vegetables and fruit dealers, chestnut-roasters, cigar-vendors, and other people whose petty and wandering traffic is transacted in the open air. It is likewise thronged with idlers, lounging over the iron railing, and with *forestieri* [tourists] who come hither to see the famous fountain. Here, also, are men with buckets, urchins with cans, and maidens (a picture as old as patriarchal times) bearing their pitchers upon their heads. For the water of Trevi is in request, far and wide, as the most refreshing draught for feverish lips, the pleasantest to mingle with wine, and the wholesomest to drink, in its native purity, that can anywhere be found.

Today, though the scene is quite different – no pitcher-bearing maidens, but chestnut-roasters may be there – the general atmosphere hasn't much changed; indeed, *forestieri* from five continents arrive in hordes. This teeming neighbourhood also has a 350-year-old bakery and a 500-year-old pharmacy, both active, and a small church with strange treasures.

The name 'trevi' is of uncertain origin. It could refer to a site near the source of the aqueduct, or to a 'three-way' crossroads near the fountain.

Leaving the neighbourhood, a short trek will take us up the nearby Quirinal Hill, the tallest of Rome's fabled Seven Hills (see p. 31).

ON THE SPOT

7. The Trevi Fountain and on to the Quirinal

The grandeur of the Trevi Fountain – the splashiest and most monumental in Rome – is enhanced by the small size and intimacy of the square, which acts as a sounding board to its roar. The conceit animating this world-famous mid-18th-century extravaganza is the Court of the King of the Ocean. There is certainly a royal air about the pageant of marble figures and an oceanic feel to the onrushing water.

The overall design is the masterpiece of a relatively minor Roman architect, Niccolò Salvi. The central statuary group is by Pietro Bracci, an 18th-century follower of Bernini. The remaining sculpture is by minor contemporaries.

The colossal centre statue is the Ocean, pulled through waves and reefs in a shell-shaped coach drawn by two sea-horses and led by Tritons, demi-gods that are half-human in form, half-fish . Rarely have architecture and sculpture so well availed themselves of the natural elements, water and rock. A relief over a niche on the right represents a maiden pointing out the water source to Roman soldiers, in the story that gives the aqueduct its name. Film buffs will remember the famous scene in *La Dolce Vita* where Anita Ekberg wades through the pool like a kind of sexual she-wolf challenging Marcello Mastroianni.

Stand with your back to the fountain. On the right, at the corner of Via del Forno ('Oven Street') is an ordinary and very busy bakery, now also a mini-market, which has been open since the 17th century. The sign 'Forno' ('Oven') over the door is early 19th-century. (Other similar signs nearby are imitations.)

Across the street from the fountain, framing the

The Trevi Fountain, in an 18th-century engraving by Giuseppe Vasi

store windows at No. 93, are the relics of a medieval portico with ancient Roman marble columns. To the left is the theatrical façade of the baroque church of **SS. Vincenzo e Anastasio** (Sts. Vincent and Anastasius), the work of Martino Longhi the Younger.

It was founded by Cardinal Mazarin (see p. 55), whose escutcheon, framed by angels, is at the top. For centuries it was the parish church of the district that includes the Quirinal Palace, one of the former papal residences. Thus the church preserves the hearts and other organs of some 30 popes who reigned between 1590 and 1903, removed at their embalming. Ordinary folk saw something almost diabolical in the display. This led to the corruption of the name of the second titular saint, who instead of Anastasio was called Satanasio (Satanas).

To the left of the church is an 18th-century street shrine on the corner of the building. There are hundreds of these in Rome, affectionately called 'Madonnelle' ('Little Madonnas'), regardless of whom they actually represent. Besides their devotional and ornamental use, they offered nocturnal passers-by the dim light of their lamps when street illumination was still to come.

At No. 89 is the Farmacia Pesci, founded in 1522. The interior, including some of the furniture, is 16th-century. The pharmacy preserves a wooden unicorn head which an unconfirmed tradition ascribes to the great 16th-century sculptor and goldsmith Benvenuto Cellini, who supposedly traded it for medicine.

Go around the right flank of SS. Vincenzo and Anastasio and take Vicolo dei Modelli, which skirts the church to begin a slight ascent of the Quirinal Hill. The vicolo is named after the many artists' models who lived here and exhibited themselves in the Piazza di Spagna (see p. 54).

The vicolo leads to the small Piazza Scanderbeg. Scanderbeg was a 15th-century

Madonnella

Alb-anian guerrilla leader who won his country's freedom from the Turks with the encouragement of the popes. During a Roman sojourn he lived at No. 117 in the square, though the present building is 18th-century.

Continue toward the right into Vicolo Scanderbeg. On your left is a solitary street stairway leading to a secondary entrance of the Quirinal Palace, today the residence of the Italian President. Pass under the arch and take the wider Via della Dataria uphill. After about 100 yards take a short staircase to the hilltop, or avoid the steps by following Via della Dataria to its end.

BEFORE GOING

8. The Quirinal

There were human settlements on the Quirinal Hill (probably named after an ancient temple to the god Quirinus) long before Rome itself was founded. At the dawn of history it was the stronghold of the Sabines, whose women, according to a tale that hovers somewhere between legend and fact, were carried off one fine day by the newly arrived Romans from the south, in one of the most celebrated international incidents in history.

For centuries the Quirinal was a literary centre. The ancient Roman poet Martial lived here in a draughty third-floor room with broken windows. Pomponius Atticus, to whom Cicero's famous letters were addressed, lived and ran a flourishing publishing company here. The poet Virgil, a man of peasant stock who had come down from the north, lived nearby. During the Renaissance, sophisticated literary circles gathered here (one such group, which included cardinals, went into such pagan raptures during its poetry readings that the pope jailed the whole bunch in Castel Sant' Angelo). Michelangelo took part in one of these groups, presided over by his great Platonic love, the poetess and princess Vittoria Colonna.

The hill is crowned by the vast Piazza del Quirinale, one of the city's most ancient and beautiful squares. It has been celebrated since the middle ages for a huge Græco-Roman statuary group of two muscular horse tamers of uncertain identity who lead rearing stallions. The sculptures have given the hill an alternative name, 'Monte Cavallo' (or 'Horse Hill').

Impressive buildings frame the square. Foremost is the Palazzo del Quirinale, home to the President of Italy. It was built between the 16th and 18th centuries as a papal summer residence, and was occupied after 1870 by Italian kings.

The palace is the cooperative effort of some of the best architects over three centuries. Yet despite its beautiful façade and solemn air, it is somewhat monotonous. The inside is more interesting, but public viewing is severely restricted under the present democratic regime. (Curiously, when the kings lived here, until the mid-20th century, it was open twice a week.) You'll probably have to content yourself with a look from afar at the courtyard, where sometimes the tall presidential guard, the horse-maned Cuirassiers appear.

The building has witnessed several dramatic moments. Napoleon's soldiers abducted Pope Pius VI from here in 1799 (see p. 572), and his successor Pius VII in 1809. The former died in captivity. When they came for the latter in the dead of night, he had a temperature, couldn't find his glasses and wasn't even given time to take a change of clothes. He was dispatched into exile; but six years later he was back in the palace, and his captor was in exile on St. Helena.

Thirty-three years later, in 1848, it was Pope Pius IX's turn to flee the Quirinal, when revolution shook all of Europe and swept through Rome. He returned to the city in 1850, but not to the Quirinal; both he and his successors preferred to stay all year round in the Vatican. When the king's soldiers of a newly unified Italy entered Rome two decades later, they had to call a locksmith to enter the palace. The kings settled here and the popes retired to voluntary seclusion in the Vatican. A period of bitter church-state relations followed, ending only in 1929 with an agreement under the Mussolini Fascist regime, called the Conciliazione ('Reconciliation').

ON THE SPOT

8. The Quirinal

The Quirinal Palace, now the presidential palace, dominates the square on the left. It is the work of a sequence of architects: in the late 16th century, Martino Longhi the Elder, Ottaviano Mascherino and then Domenico Fontana, right arm of Pope Sixtus V and executor of his great programme of urban renewal; in the 17th century, Flaminio Ponzio and Carlo Maderno, another of the highly prolific baroque architects to whom Rome owes much of its cityscape; and in the 18th century Ferdinando Fuga. The best part of the exterior is the portal by Maderno, surmounted by a window and balcony by Bernini, once used for papal blessings of the crowd, and flanked by a powerful round bastion by Mascherino.

At the time of writing, guided tours take place on some Sunday mornings starting at 09:00, but the queue of would-be visitors begins to form at dawn. A passport or similar ID is required.

Starting from the vast courtyard by Fontana we go up a grand staircase frescoed with a *Christ in Glory among the Angels* by Melozzo da Forlì, the great late 15th-century master. We then pass a series of chapels and galleries, some sumptuously decorated by famous 16th-century painters, such as Pietro da Cortona, Giovanni Lanfranco and Guido Reni. Furniture from four centuries, ancient Roman mosaics, ceramic vases, bronzes and paintings are scattered everywhere. The large gardens are marvellous. (Entrance to the gardens is sometimes allowed on the afternoon of June 2, the anniversary of the foundation of the present Italian Republic.)

The grand statuary group in the centre of the square has been one of Rome's most famous monuments since the early middle ages. According to tradition they represent the **'Horse Tamers'**, the twins Castor and Pollux (also called 'Dioscuri', 'Sons of Zeus'), Greek mythological heroes worshipped by the Romans from early times as Rome's protectors (see p. 282). Recently revived early medieval interpretations, however, see them as two versions of a single subject: Alexander the

The Quirinal Palace with the Horse Tamers, from an early 20th-century postcard

OPVS FIDIAE

OPVS·PRAXITELIS

The Horse Tamers as they were in the 16th century, engraving by Lafreri

Great training his famous horse Bucephalus.

The statues, originally in different positions, belonged to the Baths of Constantine or to a Temple of Serapis, both nearby, or to both. They are Greek or Roman copies of a 5th-century BC Greek original (see p. 311 for the concept of 'copy' in this context). They are not by the famous Greek sculptors Phidias and Praxiteles, as the late renaissance pedestal proudly asserts. In the middle ages the statues served as military emplacements and were so badly damaged that the horse attributed to Phidias was reduced to little more than its head.

The obelisk, an ancient Roman imitation of an Egyptian needle, and a later addition, is the twin of another we'll see later (p. 97). Both originally stood at the entrance to the Tomb of Augustus, which we visit in the Second Ancient Rome Walk. The fountain, installed in the early 19th century, has a great granite basin from the Roman Forum, where it was used as a horses' drinking trough in the middle ages.

The white building to the right of the presidential palace is the noble-looking **Palazzo della Consulta** ('of the Council'), which rests partly on the foundations of the vanished Baths of Constantine. It was built by one of the finest architects of the 18th century, Ferdinando Fuga, with proceeds from the official lottery. It houses the Italian Constitutional Court, and was formerly the Papal Tribunal.

On one side of the square is a balcony that offers a fine view of Rome sadly marred by TV antennæ. Directly before you, left of the balcony, is a low-lying building with a papal coat-of-arms (entrance at No. 13). This imposing 18th-century structure, by Fuga and others, looks grand enough to be another royal palace; it is the former papal stables. There are often interesting shows here: tel (06) 6966270 or visit www.scuderiequirinale.it.

69

BEFORE GOING

9. From the Quirinal to Quattro Fontane

Here begins a spacious, straight avenue flanked on the left by the huge Quirinal Palace. It ends in the distance at a brick building and a gate where, on a fateful September day in 1870, Italian government troops invaded Rome to wrest it from papal rule.

About a third of the way down the avenue, you'll reach a famous crossing where you'll be back on the northwest-southeast expansion line (see pp. 62) of the builder popes. The four corners are called 'le Quattro Fontane' ('the Four Fountains') and are right on the crest of the hill. From this vantage point you can see the whole stretch of a long thoroughfare built through this part of the former *disabitato*. In the distance to the left is the obelisk of Trinità dei Monti overlooking Piazza di Spagna. Closer and to the right is another needle by the great church of S. Maria Maggiore, to be visited later. Both obelisks mark major junctions of this part of the expansion line. The street system, you may recall, was laid out in the 16th century by Sixtus V, perhaps the greatest of the 'builder popes'. He enlisted the services of Domenico Fontana, first of a family of great northern Italian architects who moved to Rome and worked here for two centuries, greatly contributing to the present appearance of the city. As well as the various Fontanas themselves, the family included Domenico's nephew Carlo Maderno; and Borromini was a distant relative.

The axis of streets linking Trinità dei Monti with S. Maria Maggiore, once known as the Strada Felice after the baptismal name of Pope Sixtus V, Felice Peretti

What made the project possible in this area was the restoration of an ancient aqueduct – the second after the Acqua Vergine. Sixtus, whose first name was Felice ('Happy'), celebrated the event by naming the new water supply Acqua Felice ('Happy Water'). He also named the new, long thoroughfare Strada Felice, but various parts were later renamed. The first segment, from Trinità dei Monti down to a valley between the Pincio and Quirinal hills, received Sixtus' papal name, becoming Via Sistina. The second part, from the valley up to the Four Fountains Crossroads, is Via Quattro Fontane. The part leading to the great church of S. Maria Maggiore is Via Depretis, after a late 19th-century politician.

ON THE SPOT

9. From the Quirinal to Quattro Fontane

Take Via del Quirinale, skirting the presidential palace. On your right are public gardens. Past them, on the left, a side door to the palace allows a peek at the presidential gardens. Almost opposite is the beautiful entrance to Bernini's church of **S. Andrea al Quirinale** ('St. Andrew by the Quirinal').(Open: 08:00-12:00 and 16:00-19:00. Closed August afternoons. Ring the bell at No. 29.)

The elliptical interior, sumptuous and grand despite its small size, is a jewel of baroque architectural, decorative and pictorial harmony. The shallow depth of the church confronts the visitor with the main altar, and this sense of movement is further exploited by the vivid portrayal of St. Andrew's ascent into heaven, rising from the altar painting via a carved figure that is welcomed by angels above. Of all Bernini's works, this was his favourite, and his son reports that he often came here to sit in his later years.

Statues and paintings are by minor masters of the 17th and 18th century. Most noteworthy are the paintings in the first chapel on the right by the 17th-century Genoese painter G. B. Gaulli, better known by his nickname of Il Baciccia, amongst them the *Death of St. Francis Xavier* over the altar. The imposing sacristy is nearby. In the adjoining convent are the beautiful rooms of a 17th-century Polish saint, Stanislas Kotska, sometimes open (ask in the sacristy).

DETOUR
30 MIN

Past S. Andrea, enter the other public gardens and go through them to the other side. Continue straight into Via Genova and on to the important modern artery Via Nazionale (further discussed on p. 81) and turn right. Nearby, at the bottom of the steps, is **S. Vitale**, officially first consecrated in the 5th century but in fact even older. It is so far below street level as a result of both its age and the construction of the modern avenue. Remodelled several times in the middle ages, it was made narrower in 1475 by eliminating the aisles. The columns separating the aisles from the nave were

S. Andrea al Quirinale in the 17th century, shortly after it was built; engraving by Falda

incorporated in the new walls; you can see traces of them on the right. Recently, the removal of baroque embellishments brought to light the original, simple façade. It is of a rare type called 'open' because above the arches of the portico there were others on the façade (later walled up).

The magnificent wooden doors of the 15th-century entrance were designed and carved two centuries later by the Jesuit priests who ran the church in the period of the early Counter Reformation. The church evokes the missionary fervour of the era through gruesome paintings of martyrdom, meant to prepare young priests for the perils of their vocation. Moreover, only plants and insects symbolising martyrdom in Christian iconography were allowed to grow in the vast gardens of the church, which were destroyed to build Via Nazionale. The fine portico, with its ancient columns and 5th-century capitals, was once frescoed with devices of torture. (Open: 07:30-11:00 and 17:00-19:00.)

Inside, 17th-century frescoes and paintings mostly depict atrocious scenes of torture, such as a soldier covered with honey and exposed to the insects (on the entrance wall to the left of the doors). Some of the works are by Jesuits priests themselves; for instance, over the first altar on the right is the *Martyred Virgins* by Giambattista Fiammeri. Others are of uncertain attribution. The most notable frescoes are those in the transept by the Florentine painter Agostino Ciampelli. Return to Via del Quirinale.

END OF DETOUR

Go 300 yards further on. At a four-way intersection is the diminutive church of **S. Carlino** ('Little St. Charles') officially called S. Carlo alle Quattro Fontane (from the crossroads mentioned below), by Borromini. Cross the intersection carefully to appreciate the spirited façade (the last work of the great architect, completed in the year of his suicide, 1667), the bell tower and the lantern of the dome from different angles – all in the master's seemingly whimsical but in fact rigorous style. The statues and central medallion are not by Borromini. (Open: Mon-Fri 09:00-12:00 and 16:00-18:00; Sat 09:00-12:00; Sun 11:00-12:00.)

The church is so small that its friars delight in telling visitors how it could fit inside one pier of St. Peter's. Yet the inside feels spacious, partly due to the subtle geometric interplay and to the way in which the paintings and sculptures (by minor 17th-century artists) are integrated with the architecture. Equally remarkable is the tiny, yet

S. Carlino at the crossroads shortly after it was built; from the same suite of engravings by Falda as the image on p. 71

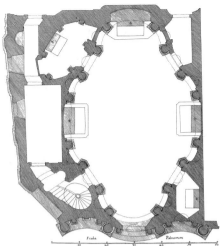

S. Carlino: plan showing the subtle wavy curves of Borromini's design, all of which are resolved in the regular oval cupola

majestic cloister. Its architectural elements can be read in different ways: a good example of Borromini's sense of flux and movement, that was to prove very influential in the later development of the baroque.

In comparing these two small, oval churches by Bernini and Borromini, most architects tend to give the palm to Borromini, since he has achieved his aims with simplicity. None of Bernini's rich materials, colours and theatrics here, just brick, stucco and white surfaces. 'One looks at Bernini's buildings with the eyes; one feels Borromini's with the whole body,' wrote Anthony Blunt, the great Borromini scholar.

S. Carlino is at the crossroads of the Quattro Fontane. The four fountains after which the intersection is named are late renaissance works representing two deified rivers, the Roman Tiber and the Tuscan Arno, and two goddesses, Juno and Diana.

This is the only spot in Rome from which three obelisks are visible: two mark the nodal points of Trinità dei Monti and S. Maria Maggiore; the third is atop the statuary group of the Horse Tamers in Piazza del Quirinale. The fourth terminus of the intersection is a monumental gateway in the Aurelian Walls, built by Michelangelo, through which Italian troops entered on 20 September 1870. (This gate, the Porta Pia, is described in one of our excursions 'Outside the Walls', see p. 607.)

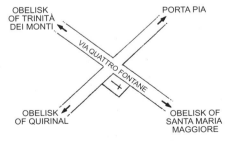

see p. 607.

◈ MIDPOINT OF WALK ◈

73

BEFORE GOING

10. The area of the Baths of Diocletian: from S. Maria della Vittoria to S. Maria degli Angeli

This part of our walk unfortunately starts with almost 500 yards of drab government buildings, and there are no buses. You'll soon be rewarded, however, with the sight of a most singular Roman phenomenon: an entire neighbourhood that sprouted from the remains of just one ancient ruin, the colossal Baths of Diocletian, one of those lavish public establishments built by the emperors to keep the masses happy and their minds distracted from politics.

The ghost of this great monument has influenced the layout of the neighbourhood in fascinating ways. We'll see more examples elsewhere in which urban topography reflects the outlines of vanished monuments, such as the Stadium of Domitian – transformed into Rome's largest square – and the Theatre of Pompey, which bequeathed its contours to later buildings and streets. The striking difference here is that major chunks of the Baths survive, both as themselves and as new buildings, enough to give a clear and palpable impression of their original appearance and staggering size.

Two of several churches in the area are exceptional: S. Maria degli Angeli, created by Michelangelo within the main hall of the Baths, and S. Maria della Vittoria. The latter's fame is tied to one of Bernini's most celebrated and controversial works, a statue of the great Spanish mystic St. Theresa of Avila in the ecstasy of a transcendental union with Christ. The work was inspired by a passage in the saint's autobiography.

The powerful, unprecedented rendering of an emotional climax has evoked a sense of awe

The Baths of Diocletian, as seen by Piranesi in the mid-18th century

throughout the centuries, as well as shock over what could seem like steamy eroticism. 'Si c'est ça l'amour divin, je le connais,' ('If this is divine love, then I know what it is,') wrote the French *magistrat* Charles de Brosses, a famous 18th-century traveller, while Jakob Burckhardt, the 19th-century Swiss art historian, expostulated: 'Let's forget the fine points of style here, as we look at the shameful degradation caused by this exaggerated realism.'

A page in the saint's autobiography, the famous *Book of my Life*, inspired Bernini here. Reading it, one can indeed wonder what were the true feelings of this woman, to whom the noted American psychologist Robert Richardson Sears has attributed 'a distinctive combination of great ardour and utter candour':

St. Teresa

> On my left I saw a very beautiful angel standing (…) carrying a long dart of gold, tipped by a little fire. This he planted in my bosom and pushed it right into my heart, and then he pulled it back so that it seemed that the heart was being extirpated; and he repeated that over and over. And every time that left me full of a great, ardent love of God. It gave me a piercing pain, such that I had to utter small cries; yet at the same time, this pain was a sensation so sweet, that one would wish that it would never end…

The erotic overtones of this part of our walk do not end here, however, but in the fine, circular Piazza della Repubblica, also called Piazza dell'Esedra. It is a large square, yet it is contained entirely within a single apsed terrace, or exedra, of the ancient baths. Today the space is graced by a turn-of-the-century (19th to 20th) fountain so spicy as to have caused almost an urban riot in its time. The bronze naiads, or water nymphs, frolicking naked on the rim are the work of a fiery Sicilian sculptor, Mario Rutelli, whose amorous exploits with his models were the talk of the town. The fountain so shocked city authorities that they repeatedly postponed the unveiling until someone knocked down the fence around the fountain, triggering a hasty inauguration.

The fountain found reluctant official acceptance. 'It is not the nude in the art that offends us, but the poses and the expressions,' fumed a city councillor. With time, Rutelli's naughty nymphs have come to be judged as one of the very few modern improvements to Rome's landscape. Unfortunately, air pollution and water corrosion are damaging the bronze, which is not, apparently, of the highest quality. So despite repeated restorations – the latest, incidentally, under a Rome mayor who is a direct descendant of the sculptor – sometimes the shapes of the group are hard to discern, let alone the coquettish mien that caused such a scandal.

ON THE SPOT

10. The area of the Baths of Diocletian: from S. Maria della Vittoria to S. Maria degli Angeli

Take the continuation of Via del Quirinale, Via XX Settembre (the date of the conquest of Rome in 1870; before this and other name changes imposed with anti-clerical animus by the new government, both streets shared the graceful name of 'Via Pia', the Pious Way, after a Pope Pius). Staying on the right-hand side, pass the late 19th-century Ministry of Defence buildings on both sides, all the way to an open space, Piazza S. Bernardo. Continue on the same side, then cross to a round church, **S. Bernardo alle Terme** ('St. Bernard at the Baths'). The fine façade is early baroque, but what makes the church unusual is that it was built at the end of the 16th century out of one of the cylindrical halls at the corners of the immense Baths of Diocletian. Later, our walk will lead to the centre of the baths; the distance from here will give you an idea of their size.

Occasionally open, S. Bernardo is softly lit by an oculus in the beautiful domed ceiling, like that of the Pantheon. The rich decoration, including paintings and statues, is mostly by minor early 17th-century artists. A chapel to the right of the main altar contains the tomb of the painter Friedrich Overbeck (left wall), one of several important German artists who lived in Rome in the 19th century. It is by his countryman Karl Hoffman.

Across the square from S. Bernardo is **S. Susanna**, a very ancient church (9th-century, perhaps much earlier) totally rebuilt in the Renaissance and completed in 1603 with a baroque façade by Carlo Maderno. It is currently the national church of the United States Catholic community in Rome. The original church was built over the ruins of ancient Roman houses, vestiges of which have been uncovered. They include the ruins of a house which according to legend was that of Susanna, the niece of a 3rd century pope, who was beheaded here for refusing to marry a son of the Emperor Diocletian. (Rejection

of exalted suitors to preserve virginity is a leitmotif of early Christian martyrology.) The overpowering remains of the Baths in the area may have coloured the story too. (Open: 08:00-12:00 and 16:00-19:00.)

The interior decoration is by minor late 16th or early 17th-century artists. Especially noteworthy are four large tapestry-like frescoes by Baldassarre Croce, a painter from Bologna, with scenes from the life of Susanna the Martyr, and from that of another Susanna, the biblical one. Under a 17th-century crypt are the remains of the ancient Roman houses (ask at the sacristy for admission).

Leaving the church, go left and cross at the lights. At the corner is **S. Maria della Vittoria** ('of the Victory'), also by Maderno (the façade is by Giovan Battista Soria). The name, another reminder of post-Reformation convulsions, comes from an image of a 'Victorious Madonna' donated by Catholic Austria to the church in 1620 after defeating Protestant Bohemia in the Battle of Prague early on in the disastrous Thirty Years' War. The tiny image, found in the wreck of a castle, was credited with rallying the Austrian troops in the battle. (Open: 07:00-12:00 and 16:30-19:30.)

Inside, the mid-17th to 18th-century decoration is Roman baroque at its most exuberant. On the entrance wall note the warlike ornaments of the choir and organ. In the second chapel to the right, the painting over the altar of the *Madonna and Child with St. Francis* is a late work by Domenichino, the great 17th-century master whose tragic vicissitudes we'll deal with in a later walk (see pp. 508, 513).

In the next chapel are the remains of St. Victora, a saint whose name is unrelated to that of the church but which, in one of the literal analogies that curiously influenced the clerical mind, may have motivated the deposition of her body here, together with the fact that, like Susanna nearby, she was said to have been martyred under Emperor Diocletian. The remains are encased in wax, but real teeth show through the parted lips.

Over the main altar of the church is a copy of the venerated image of the 'Victorious Madonna'.

The original was lost in a fire which devastated the apse in the 19th century. The redone apse decoration shows the image being carried aloft by triumphant troops.

The main attraction is the last chapel on the left, designed in 1648 by Bernini and decorated by him with the statuary group of St. *Theresa Pierced by the Love of God*. Bernini, a dramatist and stage-set designer as well as a sculptor, emphasised the event by the subtle use of different light sources and the setting as a whole. A golden shaft of light rains down from the lacunar ceiling, leaving the alabaster walls and the columns of African marble in a suggestive penumbra. The light strikes the group in the centre: the famous angel with his dart and 'ambiguous smile' and the prostrate saint with her mouth half-open and eyelids drooping. On the walls on both sides, groups of statues watch the scene as though from theatre boxes. They are members of the noble Venetian Cornaro family who sponsored the chapel. Bernini may have designed some of the busts, but they were all sculpted by assistants.

In the next chapel down the aisle, the painting of the *Holy Trinity* over the altar is by Guercino, another major 17th-century master. The tomb on the wall (upper right) is of Cardinal Gessi, one of Galileo's judges; his painted portrait is by Guido Reni, a great fellow-student of Guercino and Domenichino.

In the sacristy are relics of the 17th-century Austrian wars, including a Turkish flag said to come from the epoch-making Battle of Vienna of 1683, which halted Turkish expansion in Europe. On the walls, four large panels depicting the Battle of Prague are by an anonymous German painter who appears to have participated in it. On the short wall to the right of the entrance another painting, by the noted 18th-century artist Sebastiano Conca, is related to the story of the victorious image.

Across from the church and around the corner to the right is the great Fountain of Moses, created by the architect Domenico Fontana in the late 16th century as the grand terminus to the aqueduct brought by Pope Sixtus V to repopulate the district (p. 70). In other words, the monument does for the Acqua Felice what the Trevi Fountain does for the Acqua Vergine.

The late 16th-century statuary depicts water-related biblical scenes. The relief on the left, with the story of *Aaron Leading the Jews to a Spring in the Desert*, is by Giovan Battista Della Porta (no relative of Giacomo Della Porta). The other, showing *Joshua on the Banks of the River Jordan*, strangely dressed as a Roman officer, is by the Roman sculptor of Spanish origin, Flaminio Vacca. If the reliefs are unimpressive, the statue in the middle is decidedly clumsy, a corpulent *Moses Ordering the Red Sea to Part*. From the outset it was an object of ridicule which, magnified by the inevitable comparisons with Michelangelo's *Moses* (pp. 104-105), is said to have caused the artist responsible (a minor sculptor) to die of a broken heart. The beautiful Egyptian lions are copies.

Past the fountain, continue into Via V.E. Orlando. Here the block is taken up by the turn-of-the-century (19th-20th) Grand Hôtel, once Rome's classiest and still one of the best, awkwardly renamed St. Regis Grand in 2000 upon its acquisition by an American chain. Turn round the corner with the hotel. Across Via Parigi the remains of the Baths of Diocletian begin again. Cross Via Parigi and continue straight. A first chunk of the ruins at the corner (one of the great halls) was taken up until recently by a planetarium supplied by Germany as reparation after the First World War (note the pretty art déco door-frame); it is presently an annex of the Roman archæological museum (see p. 682).

At the end of the block step into Via Cernaia, where the ruins continue to the right and left; note the floor mosaics on the right. Return to Via V.E. Orlando and continue left. Now largely masked by brickwork of various periods, the ruins continue until they form a niche occupied by a church (officially a basilica) facing Piazza della Repubblica.

Now try to visualise the size of the Baths of Diocletian, the grandest in Rome, built at the end

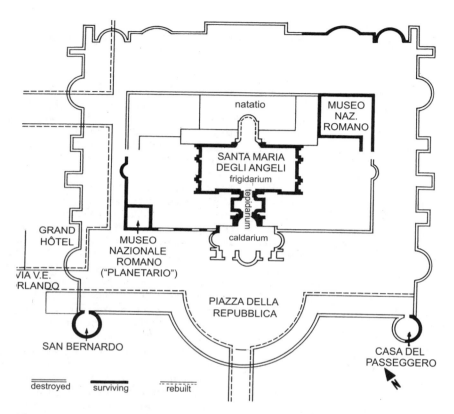

natatio

MUSEO
NAZ.
ROMANO

SANTA MARIA
DEGLI ANGELI
frigidarium

tepidarium

caldarium

GRAND
HÔTEL

MUSEO
NAZIONALE
ROMANO
("PLANETARIO")

VIA V.E.
'RLANDO

PIAZZA DELLA
REPUBBLICA

SAN BERNARDO

CASA DEL
PASSEGGERO

N

destroyed   surviving   rebuilt

The Baths of Diocletian, with the church of S. Maria degli Angeli, laid out by Michelangelo within the ruins of the baths

of the 3rd century AD. They covered 34 acres (14 hectares) and held more than 3,000 bathers, twice as many as any previous Roman bath. (For general information about ancient baths, see pp. 275–276).

The baths were located within a huge rectangular perimeter wall, with a great apse on one side. The entrance to the present basilica marks the centre of the rectangle. In other words, the distance you walked from the church of S. Bernardo (p. 76) to this church is the distance from one corner of the baths to the centre.

The large circular Piazza della Repubblica was originally an open space within the perimeter wall

devoted to physical exercise. The curved modern buildings correspond exactly to the great apse of the perimeter. An avenue (Via Nazionale) presently cuts the semicircle in half, but it was originally unbroken. It was probably built with steps where people could sit to watch the activities.

The basilica of **S. Maria degli Angeli** ('of the Angels') is entirely comprised of the ruins of the baths, though it occupies less than a quarter of their vaulted space (the rest of the original establishment within the perimeter walls was open-air). Michelangelo transformed the ruins into a church in 1561, three years before his death, but his plans were altered by Luigi Vanvitelli in 1749. Like the Pantheon (p. 238), the church is owned by the Italian state and used for official functions (funerals, etc.) involving political and military figures.

The niche forming the church façade in front of you is now outdoors, but it used to be one curved wall of a hall in the covered part of the baths. If you are facing the church, the hall extended behind you (another piece of its wall survives on your left); this was the Calidarium (or Caldarium), the 'Hot Area' where bathing started with a kind of sauna. (Open: 07:00-12:30 and 16:00 19:00.)

Enter to a sense of vastness unparalleled by any other Roman church, even St. Peter's. The present vestibule was an intermediate hall of the former baths, the Tepidarium or 'Lukewarm Area', where people began adjusting to the cool main area. Today the main elements of interest here are the tombs of two painters. To the right of the entrance is the tomb of Carlo Maratta (17th-18th century), who designed it himself; his brother Francesco executed the bust. To the left is that of Salvator Rosa (17th century); the bust is by a minor contemporary. In the passage linking the vestibule to the great hall is the large, expressive statue of *St. Bruno of Cologne* (right) by the renowned 18th-century French sculptor Jean-Antoine Houdon. Immediately past it, a chapel on the left contains *St. Peter Receiving the Keys* by the distinguished northern Italian painter Girolamo Muziano (late 16th century), noted for his subtle use of colour and light.

Proceed to a huge rectangular transverse hall, which Michelangelo adapted from the central hall of the baths, respectfully leaving its outlines intact. The central hall was the main meeting place, used for cold water dips in the Frigidarium, massaging, strolling and socialising. This may be the best place to get an idea of the grandiosity of an Imperial Roman public interior. Though Michelangelo had to raise the floor by about 6 ft (2 m), the ceiling is still 90 ft (28 m) high. Its immense original vaults rest on eight enormous monolithic columns of red granite from the original structure. Another eight columns flanking the two passages to the hall were added during its conversion to a church; they are painted brick.

Huge, dramatic pictures decorate the hall, mostly by minor 18th-century artists. Italian painting in this period, except for the wonderful art of Venice, had begun sliding into a cold academicism, from which it would recover only a couple of centuries later.

On the right side of the hall the finest picture is Muziano's *Sermon of St. Jerome* on the left wall nearest to the centre of the hall. On the right the hall also contains the tombs of three Italian First World War leaders: the army commander Diaz, the Navy commander Thaon di Revel, and the prime minister Orlando. On the ground a ray of sunlight traces the arrival of noon on a sundial, or meridian line, of 1701. Research published in 1999 by the American historian of science J. L. Heilbron shows that these devices, which are found in a few Italian churches and the church of St. Sulpice in Paris, were important aids in astronomical computations. For instance, they helped determine the exact length of the lunar month and the solar year.

On the left side of the hall, a painting on the left wall (second from the centre of the hall) depicts the *Fall of Simon Magus* ('the magician') by Pompeo Batoni, a masterpiece of 18th-century Central Italian art (for the biblical episode, see p. 196).

In Michelangelo's design, the great hall represented the nave, or main body, of the church. This was changed drastically about two centuries later, when Vanvitelli altered the orientation of the church and opened a new nave perpendicular to Michelangelo's, which consequently became the transept. In order to do so, Vanvitelli broke through the wall of the Frigidarium – something Michelangelo, out of respect for the great ruin, would never have done – and invaded another part of the ancient complex, the giant outdoor swimming pool (*natatio*) where the Romans finished their bathing in summer.

In Vanvitelli's part of the church, on the right wall (second panel) is a powerful *Martyrdom of*

St. Sebastian by Domenichino (17th century). Opposite is the *Baptism of Christ* by Carlo Maratta, one of the finest works by this 18th-century painter, whose tomb we saw near the entrance.

From the left of Michelangelo's nave one arrives at the sacristy, passing other giant rooms of the baths. The sacristy and an adjacent choir room are covered with vivid frescoes of debated 18th-century authorship.

The other rooms of the baths extended all around the church: dressing rooms, locker rooms and even libraries. More ruins are to the right of the church, towards the main railway station in the vast Piazza dei Cinquecento.

DETOUR
20 MIN

The backdrop to Piazza dei Cinquecento is the **Termini Railway Station.** It is not so called because it is the terminus of all tracks to Rome (though it has been since the mid-19th century). The name refers instead to the presence of the Thermæ, or Baths, of Diocletian nearby. The station, renovated in 1999, is considered a masterpiece of modern Roman architecture. Unfortunately, the deterioration of its early 20th-century neighbourhood, the crowds, the shady dealings, partly connected to illegal immigration, and the petty crime for which the station is notorious, cast a shadow over its undoubted æsthetic merits.

In 1938 Angelo Mazzoni del Grande began to refurbish the 19th-century station and he built the two sides in one of the more ponderous keys of the 'Rationalist' (i.e. Fascist) style. The war put a stop to the project, until it was picked up again in 1947, when the front was built in a much lighter vein by a team of architects headed by Eugenio Montuori and Leo Calini.

The new part is a marble façade over 400 yards long, with ribbon windows, from which hangs a most daring corrugated eave following a pure horizontal line. The result is an exemplary meshing of two substantially different styles. The completion of the project in 1954 was celebrated in the Italian-American film *Terminal Station* by the great director Vittorio De Sica, starring Montgomery Cliff and Jennifer Jones.

At the left end of the façade is an important section of the Republican Walls, built 600 years before the Aurelian Walls (p. 42). In the section here they were powerfully fortified and further protected by a moat. The two walls – Republican and Aurelian – ran very close in this part of Rome.

(If you wish, you may extend the detour further by going 'outside the walls' and seeing the Tiburtina and Maggiore Gates of the Aurelian Walls – a longish walk starting along the left side of the station. The two gates are described on p. 636 and p. 632.)

On the way back to Piazza della Repubblica from the right end of the station, we pass Palazzo Massimiliano Massimo (the last building on the left in Piazza dei Cinquecento). This late 19th-century palace is the main part of the National Roman Museum of Archæology (p. 682). The other major sections of the museum are: across the square within the ruins of the Baths of Diocletian, in the former planetarium nearby (pp. 77-80, 682), and at some distance from here in Palazzo Altemps (p. 451). Via delle Terme di Diocleziano starts in front of the entrance to the palace. Near the beginning of the street are two less obvious sights.

On the right, amidst trees, in a pathetic state of neglect, is the Monument to the Fallen of Dogali – these being the Five Hundred to whom the square is dedicated. Even if there were anyone alive today to realise the connection between the name of the square and the unhappy Fallen, at this point the square is their only remaining claim on public memory, since the battle in which they fought and died at Dogali (in Eritrea) in 1887 has long been forgotten. It was the starting point of Italy's misguided colonial adventures in Africa.

For fifty years the monument stood proudly right in front of the 19th-century train station. When the station was redone, it was quietly removed. It is topped by an Egyptian obelisk from a temple, the Iseo Campense, which will be mentioned later. The inscription refers to the deeds of the great Pharaoh Ramses II.

The monument knew another moment of glory in 1936 when, having conquered Ethiopia, Mussolini added to the base a bronze 'Lion of Judah' – the Ethiopian national symbol – that he had looted. It was returned in 1944. (For a similar experience with the stele of Aksum, see p. 274.)

On the other side of the street, where Via del Viminale starts, you can see what is left of the second cylindrical hall that formed one of the two front corners of the immense square-shaped Baths of Diocletian. The 'cylinder' matches the one that is now the church of S. Bernardo (p. 76). Today it contains modest dwellings. Next to the ruin was a day hotel (called the 'Casa del Passeggero' or 'Traveller's Home') created in 1929 and connected to the station. In its day it was highly publicised as one of the most modern and efficient establishments of its type in Europe.

After the Second World War it was reopened and reclosed several times. At present it is not in use and severely dilapidated. If accessible, it's worth a peek to see what remains of the art deco style decoration.

Via delle Terme di Diocleziano leads back to Piazza della Repubblica.

END OF DETOUR

Turn your attention to the square in front of the church, Piazza della Repubblica. Named after the present Italian Republic, it was originally called Piazza dell'Esedra, after the great apsed terrace of the baths which the square now occupies (many still call it that). In the middle is the Fountain of the Naiads (1901), with Rutelli's gambolling nymphs which seem drawn from a naughty *belle époque* magazine.

Another pleasant expression of post-1870 architecture is the square itself, with the elegant curved buildings, designed by Gaetano Koch, faithfully following the curve of the ancient exedra. The architect, who was responsible for many of the better features of turn-of-the-century Rome, was the grandson of the Austrian painter J. A. Koch, also active in Rome. The semi-circle is bisected by Via Nazionale, an artery built along with the square to link the nearby railway station to downtown Rome, thus slicing through the ancient urban fabric.

Originally a chic, tree-lined avenue like Via Veneto and also frequented by society figures such as D'Annunzio, the great *belle époque* poet and hedonist, Via Nazionale has deteriorated badly in recent decades and is now garishly commercial.

Three blocks down on the left is **S. Paolo dentro le Mura** (St. Paul within the Walls), another church of the American community – this one Episcopalian – and currently open only on Sundays for a 10:30 service. It was built in 1879 in a neo-romanesque style by the British architect G. E. Street, following the æsthetic principles he would apply three years later to another, neo-gothic Protestant church in Rome (see p. 52).

St. Paul within the Walls was the first American Protestant (though not the first Protestant) church allowed in Rome after the end of papal rule in 1870 (for the very first one, see p. 131). This accounts for its name, an ironic commentary on the papal defeat and a pun on the much more famous basilica of S. Paolo fuori le Mura ('St. Paul outside the Walls'). The church's sponsors, including the American banker J. P. Morgan, also gave it a tall bell tower to spite the pope, 'so that he can see it from the Vatican as he gets up every morning,' as it was said. (Open: 09:00-16:00.)

The church has some of the few really beautiful modern mosaics in Rome, by the British artist Sir Edward Burne-Jones (late 19th-century).

The itinerary picks up again at Piazza Barberini, about half a mile (800 m) from here. You can easily get there by metro (look for the 'M' sign in Piazza della Repubblica. Piazza Barberini is one stop in the 'Battistini' direction. If you are walking, retrace your steps on Via V. E. Orlando, then take Via Barberini on the left downhill past Largo S. Susanna.

BEFORE GOING

11. Piazza Barberini and Via Veneto

Unlike Piazza di Spagna, Piazza Barberini kept the semi-rural, suburban flavour of the *disabitato* even after it was included in the popes' development plans. Sheep and cows wandered here as recently as the first decade of the 20th century. These qualities appealed to the many artists who lived here in the Romantic era. For about a century after the mid-18th century it was the haunt of Germans, Austrians, Scandinavians and Russians in particular. Amongst the Germans were the famous archæologist and art historian J. J. Winckelmann, the great historian of medieval Rome Ferdinand Gregorovius, and the painters J. F. Overbeck – founder of the Nazarene School – and J. C. Reinhart. The Austrian painter Joseph Anton Koch, founder of a school of Romantic landscape, and two famous Danes, the sculptor Bertel Thorvaldsen (his Piazza Barberini studio is now a movie theatre) and the fairytale writer Hans Christian Andersen, also lived here. So did the eminent Russian novelist Nikolai Gogol, who wrote his masterwork *Dead Souls* here. He wrote to a friend in 1838: 'Goats and sculptors, my dear lady, roam under my windows ...'

Just off the square, in Via S. Nicola da Tolentino, was the studio of the renowned American sculptor Augustus St. Gaudens, in the late 19th century. The centre of the square is dominated by another fabulous Bernini creation, the Triton Fountain. (It gives its name to the wide street off the square, which you crossed further down after leaving Piazza di Spagna, pp. 62, 63). The water

Piazza Barberini with the Triton Fountain by Bernini; engraving (18th century) by P. Schenck

spouting from the mythological creature, half-man, half-fish, is Pope Sixtus' Acqua Felice.

On the side of the square bounded by the lower slope of the Quirinal is the imposing Palazzo Barberini, the home of a still extant princely family that has given Rome one pope and several cardinals, high prelates and government officers. Sir Walter Scott, a key figure of the Romantic movement and the first great exponent of the historical novel, was a guest there in the early 19th century. Some decades later, the American sculptor, poet and jurist William Wetmore Story rented a wing.

On the opposite side of Piazza Barberini the Via Veneto begins. It is a meandering modern avenue and international rendezvous point of what used to be called 'café society'. The avenue and the district it crosses were built at the turn of the last century in a final burst of the building craze that swept through Rome for four decades after the city became part of the Italian state in 1870. Luckily, toward the end of the period the style outgrew its initial dullness (p. 62). Yet the construction here wiped out Rome's most beautiful park, the historic Villa Ludovisi. The outrage, attended by blatant speculative abuse, raised an outcry amongst lovers of Rome worldwide.

Near the foot of the rising avenue is the Church of the Capuchins, one of two Roman churches famous for their 'believe-it-or-not' collections of human skeletons and mummified bodies. (The other church, S. Maria dell'Orazione e Morte, is part of the first Renaissance Walk.) The macabre exhibits were meant as *memento mori*, reminders of our mortality. Ironically, the church now finds itself on Via Veneto, epitome of the 'sweet life' celebrated in Federico Fellini's famous film *La Dolce Vita*, shot here in 1955.

ON THE SPOT

11. Piazza Barberini and Via Veneto

Piazza Barberini, on a slight gradient, is dominated by Bernini's festive yet imposing Triton Fountain (1643) spouting water through a Triton's conch-horn. The dolphins at the base hold up the Barberini family escutcheon with their tails.

On the side of the square skirting the Quirinal is the massive flank of the Palazzo Barberini, behind a cinema. This is the main wing built by Carlo Maderno in 1625. The 1875 destruction of its monumental entrance, however, which opened onto the square, has greatly impaired its powerful æsthetic effect.

DETOUR
10 MIN

To better appreciate the building go to what was originally a side entrance but has now become the main entrance. Climb up Via Quattro Fontane, which starts at the bottom of the square (this street you saw from above at the 'Four Fountains' crossroads, pp. 70, 73). About halfway up the hill, on the left, is the entrance to the palace. This wing was completed in a mature baroque style, partly by Bernini and partly by Borromini in 1633, circumstances having as usual forced the two to work together.

The palace was commissioned in 1623 by Maffeo Barberini, who had been elected pope as Urban VIII. Like Innocent X and Alexander VII (p. 44) after him, he was a 'builder pope' and an admirer and patron of Bernini. For his palace he chose Carlo Maderno as architect, who decided to use an open renaissance villa model rather than the closed block more characteristic of urban palaces. Maderno died in 1628 and his work was finished by his kinsman and assistant, Borromini.

The iron gates resting on marble statuary are a 19th-century addition. Bernini designed the magnificent façade, with columns in the three orders

Palazzo Barberini in the 18th century; etching by Piranesi

of classic architecture (Doric, Ionic and Corinthian, progressing from the bottom floor up), and the grand stairway; Borromini, the rich and entirely original windows where the façade connects with the wings, and under the portico to the right, an elegant spiral staircase. The palace

Borromini's windows at the Palazzo Barberini: the first to dramatize Michelangelo's central shell motif by making the two side elements splay out

houses a national museum of Old Master paintings. The splendid ceiling frescoes designed and executed by Pietro da Cortona for the Barberini may also be viewed (see p. 683).

Ongoing excavations of the palace grounds have found remains of Imperial era houses, including a room transformed in the 3rd century AD into a mithræum, with interesting frescoes of the Persian cult of Mithras (see Glossary); it is not open to the public.

Return to Piazza Barberini.

END OF DETOUR

At the upper part of the square the turn-of-the-century, tree-lined avenue of Via Veneto begins; it was the heart of the *dolce vita* celebrated in the 1950's Fellini film of that name. At the very beginning of the avenue, on the right side, is the Fountain of the Bees (bees are the Barberini's heraldic symbol) by Bernini, much altered by restoration.

A few yards up the avenue, on the right, a double staircase leads to the plain 17th-century façade of S. Maria dell'Immacolata Concezione ('of the

Immaculate Conception'), a Franciscan church familiarly known as the **Chiesa dei Cappuccini** ('Church of the Capuchins'). The Cappuccini (or 'Hooded Ones') are Franciscan friars. Cappuccino coffee, incidentally, gets its name from the colour of their habit. (Open: 09:00-12:00 and 15:30-17:30. In the afternoons the famous crypts open half an hour earlier and close half an hour later.)

The gloomy main floor has several noteworthy 17th-century paintings; there are light switches on the left wall of each chapel. First chapel to the right: on the altar is the original *Archangel Michael Smiting the Devil* by Guido Reni, one of the most copied paintings in history. Imitations are in hundreds if not thousands of churches all over the world. The devil is supposedly a portrait of Pope Innocent X (see p. 456) whom Reni hated. On the left wall is the *Mocking of Christ* by an important Dutch follower of Caravaggio, Gerhard Honthorst. Second chapel to the right: *Nativity* by Giovanni Lanfranco over the altar (together with Reni and Domenichino, a pupil of Annibale Carracci, see p. 508). Third chapel to the right: over the altar, *Ecstasy of St. Francis*, and on the left wall, *Death of St. Francis,* both by Domenichino. Sacristy: on the right wall, *St. Francis with a Skull,* a minor but wonderful work by Caravaggio (p. 494), though some scholars think it is a copy.

The underground crypts are the special tourist attraction. No fewer than 4,000 Capuchin monks' skulls and bones adorn their walls, intended as a weird reminder of man's common fate. In the same spirit, until the end of the 19th century the monks slept in their own coffins. The soil on the floor comes from the Holy Land. In the first crypt, a skeleton hanging from the ceiling is said to be that of a princess from the nearby Barberini palace who had requested that her remains be used in the same way as those of the friars.

Continuing up Via Veneto, you can take in the *belle époque* luxury hotels and cafés that inspired Fellini. The blend of opulence and vulgarity, sensuousness and neurosis depicted in *La Dolce Vita* is less evident today, and the avenue is neither as glittering nor as lively as it used to be.

For several decades the post-1870 urban modernisation mania drove upper and upper-middle class Romans out of the time-worn historic centre toward the gleaming new *quartieri alti*, or high-ground neighbourhoods, such as the Via Veneto. The trend reversed about 1960, and the flow of people back to the centre has accelerated the decline of the Via Veneto.

Since the first half of the avenue is of no special interest, consider catching a bus in front of the Chiesa dei Cappuccini – any line, one stop – or walk up to the second wide curve. The curve is dominated, on the right, by the American Embassy, an 1888 building by Gaetano Koch. It is also known as Palazzo Margherita since until the 1920's it was home to the dowager Queen of Italy, Margherita, who moved here from the Quirinal Palace after an Italian-American anarchist from Paterson in New Jersey murdered her husband in 1900 (p. 239).

The tasteful, well-proportioned building, the best of its type and time in Rome, is somewhat spoiled by the U.S. mission's addition of a penthouse and showy eagles under the cornice.

Proceed uphill. On the left, at the corner of the intersection with Via Ludovisi, is the elegant Grand Hôtel Palace, once famous as the Albergo Ambasciatori, by Marcello Piacentini and Giuseppe Vaccaro (the hotel of this name has now moved to a lower section of the avenue).

The bar near the lobby has great frescoes by Guido Cadorin, a painter protegé of the famous 'decadent' poet, Gabriele D'Annunzio, representing the foyer of the hotel at the time of its inauguration in 1926, and which capture the sophisticated atmosphere of these luxurious hotels in their prime. The frescoes portray well-known personalities of Roman high society of the time.

Further up, at a wide intersection, the four-star Hôtel Excelsior is on the right (founded 1905). It is popular with jet-setters, including movie stars and middle eastern potentates, and guests have included two exiled monarchs, Farouk of Egypt and the last Shah of Iran, as well as Richard Burton and Elizabeth Taylor.

Other luxury hotels and many grand open-air cafés line the avenue.

Via Veneto ends at Porta Pinciana, the first gateway through the Aurelian Walls after the one we saw down the hill at the start of the Walk (pp. 43-44).

The gate proper is the marble one, to the left of a marble cenotaph commemorating local men who fell in the First World War. All other openings in the wall here are recent. The best view of the interesting gate is from the outside. Go to the other side.

The gate is called Pinciana because the high grounds here are the slopes of the same Pincio Hill we saw earlier from Piazza del Popolo (p. 43). An ancient Roman family, the Pinci, owned part of the hilltop.

The gate saw some of the furious battles during which Belisarius, a 6th-century general and military genius, reconquered Rome for the surviving eastern part of the Empire, Byzantium, after nearly a century of barbarian rule. Byzantium eventually lost Rome again, together with the other huge swathes of the former Roman Empire it had wrested from the barbarians. Meanwhile, Belisarius was accused of aspiring to the throne of the Byzantine Emperor Justinian and was demoted. A medieval legend, popular with artists well into the 19th century, says that his eyes were gouged out and he was reduced to beggary, but this has recently been disproved.

The two cylindrical towers were added by Belisarius, who was quartered nearby. A Greek (Byzantine) cross carved at the time on the outer keystone of the archway, between the towers, is a reminder of his feats. A completely eroded medieval Latin inscription, still legible in the 19th century, said *Date obulum Belisario* ('Give alms to Belisarius,'), in reference to the legend of his sad end.

From here look at the march of the walls on both sides of the gate. On the right (if you face the gate) they descend, punctuated by Rome's beautiful pines, toward the Porta del Popolo. In the background are the two turrets of the Villa Medici, a highlight of the end of the Walk.

Behind you is Villa Borghese, whose lower entrance you saw from outside the Porta del Popolo (p. 43). Behind you, to the left, lies a post-1930's middle and upper-class residential district, Parioli.

Note: there is a complete description of Villa Borghese on pp. 602-603.

To return to the main itinerary, go back to Piazza Barberini and take Via Sistina, which begins there. By bus: just inside Villa Borghese take the bus uphill. It goes to Piazza Barberini and, just past it, stops at the beginning of Via del Tritone. Alight there and walk back a few yards to Piazza Barberini and the beginning of Via Sistina.

Rome from the Pincian in the 1950's

12. Via Sistina and Trinità dei Monti

We resume our walk along Sixtus' Via Felice on a segment now called, as you may remember, Via Sistina. This elegant, romantic street will take us back full circle to Piazza di Spagna, this time to the top of the Spanish Steps.

The terrace here is called Trinità dei Monti ('Trinity of the Hills') after the church that crowns it. Terrace, steps and a section of the square below have had links with the French ever since a French king bought part of it in the 15th century.

Three major French institutions still operate here: the 16th-century church of Ss. Trinità dei Monti ('Most Holy Trinity of the Hills'), owned by France and served by French clergy; an adjacent 17th-century convent of French nuns; and the Roman seat of the renowned French Académie des Beaux-Arts, founded in the 17th century.

The convent, originally controlled by the French priests who ran the church, was turned over in 1828 to an aristocratic French order of nuns that needed a base for an exclusive girls' school they had founded. The nuns, called Dames du Sacré Cœur ('of the Sacred Heart of Jesus'), devoted their lives to education and were initially semi-cloistered. When they took the veil, they had to cede all their property to their family, except a 'dowry' for the convent and, optionally, their books for its library.

These great ladies were very popular with the Roman public. Until a few decades ago, on special days the convent opened its doors to visitors seeking advice on education and family matters (or, it was said, just curious to see the secluded nuns). Their admirers included the German composer Felix Mendelssohn-Bartholdy. In the 1830's, he would go and listen to them sing in the church adjoining the convent. 'The music', he wrote, 'is bad, and the organ playing absurd. But it is twilight, and the singing nuns are the sweetest voices in the world ... Pity that no one is allowed to see the fair singers.'

The nuns are no longer cloistered and don't relinquish their property. Most wear ordinary clothes, and they don't sing, at least not in a choir. The convent is internationally famous as an exclusive girls' school, with branches in many countries, including the USA.

Public gardens today cover a large part of the Pincio Hill on which Trinità dei Monti stands. In classical times the hill was famous for its opulent villas. The most splendid belonged to the fabulously wealthy Lucullus, whose name has entered our vocabulary as 'luxury', the epitome of the good life. After changing hands a few times, the villa became the property of the Emperor Claudius' third wife, Messalina, who obtained it by forcing its owner to commit suicide, and used it for her prodigious orgies. Claudius found out and sent a detail of guards to slay her. They found her crouching in the garden. One soldier gave her his dagger. She pressed it timidly to her breast, but lacked resolve. It fell to the commanding officer to dispatch her with a lance. No one knows exactly where this took place. But ruins of Messalina's gardens have turned up, of all places, in the back yard of the Sacred Heart convent.

ON THE SPOT

12. Via Sistina and Trinità dei Monti

The appearance of Via Sistina owes much to a drastic post-1880 remodelling of most of its buildings. Yet it lacks the pompous, cheerless look of many Roman arteries built in the same period, such as the nearby Via del Tritone. Indeed, there is a feeling of an aristocratic, cosmopolitan and intellectual past, that makes Via Sistina one of the most alluring streets in this part of Rome.

On your right, at No. 104, is the house, untouched by late 19th-century renovations, where the Danish fairytale writer Hans Christian Andersen, lived in the early 19th century. Across the street further on, at No. 48, lived his friend and compatriot, the sculptor Thorvaldsen, whose house (now remodelled) was for decades a gathering place for Scandinavian and German artists and intellectuals, including King Ludwig I of Bavaria, who was often a guest there. A century earlier, the famous Italian engraver, Giambattista Piranesi, whose prints of ancient Roman monuments (p. 64) are amongst the supreme achievements of the medium, lived and had his press here.

Further on, the building at No. 59 is an 1890's reconstruction done for Count Stroganoff, a Russian grand seigneur of the family who gave us 'Beef Stroganoff'. His splendid home, with its famous art collection, was chosen by Gabriele D'Annunzio as the setting for his 'decadent' masterpiece of 1905 *Il Piacere* ('Pleasure'). A century earlier the French author Stendhal and the painter Ingres lived in the original building. And 200 years before that, it was home to the renowned Italian painter Salvator Rosa, whose heirs sold it to Stroganoff three centuries later.

Passing the distinguished early 20th-century Hôtel de la Ville on the right, we reach Piazza Trinità dei Monti. On the right is another hotel, the Hassler, also 20th-century, one of Rome's most exclusive and expensive. Over the garage is a pretty 18th-19th-century street shrine.

Overlooking the Spanish Steps is the church of **Trinità dei Monti** ('Trinity of the Hills'). You've already seen the late 16th-century façade from Piazza di Spagna below. The sight it composes together with the Spanish Steps is one of most familiar to tourists in Rome.

Probably owing to the wishes of the French who commissioned it, the church is vaguely gothic, a style alien to Rome. This appears in the twin bell towers, a faint echo of the great French cathedrals, while inside are a pointed dividing arch and cross-vaulted ceilings. The design, long thought to be by Carlo Maderno, has recently been attributed to Giacomo Della Porta. You may notice its similarity to his S. Atanasio dei Greci, of a few years later, which we saw on Via del Babuino. (Open: 09:30-12:30 and 16:00-19:00; on Tuesdays between 16:00 and 17:00 there is a guided tour that includes a section usually closed to the public.)

The third chapel on the right is frescoed by the late 16th-century artist, Daniele da Volterra, with the *Assumption of the Virgin*, an unusual, powerful composition with dramatic colours. The first figure on the right is a portrait of Michelangelo, Daniele's greatest influence.

Over the altar in the second chapel on the opposite side is the *Descent from the Cross*, also by Daniele. The great French painter, Nicolas Poussin, who lived next door to the church in the following century, called it the third most beautiful painting in the world.

Other chapels are frescoed by major artists, including Raphael's assistant, Giulio Romano, and two late renaissance painters, the brothers Federico and Taddeo Zuccari, who lived nearby. But these are only visible on Tuesdays (see above), because the chapels are past a closed choir screen that divides the church.

Attached to the church, to the left of the portal, is the Convent of the Sacred Heart. Occupied by nuns, and by monks before them, the building was once owned by the painter Poussin, who moved here from Via del Babuino. The convent has exquisite 18th-century frescoes, but admission is rarely allowed.

Like the one you saw on the Quirinal, the

obelisk before the church is not Egyptian, but an ancient Roman imitation. Note the casual, un-Egyptian stance of the figures at the bottom.

On the right facing the church is a small palace with a four-columned porch, separating Via Sistina from Via Gregoriana. It is Palazzetto Zuccari, built in the late 16th century by the Zuccari brothers, whose frescoes in Trinità dei Monti we've just mentioned. (They went bankrupt building it.) Their frescoes also grace some of the rooms here.

Other important painters, as well as the illustrious mid-18th-century archæologist Winckelmann, who had his first Roman lodgings here, lived in the palazzetto. They included Claude Lorrain in the 17th century, who moved here from Via Margutta – he spent most of his life in Rome – and the 18th-century Englishman, Sir Joshua Reynolds. Jacques-Louis David, the painter of the French Revolution and of Napoleon's day, also lived here in the late 18th century, where he painted his masterpiece, the *Oath of the Horatii*.

Another famous tenant in the early 18th century was a former Polish queen, Maria Casimira, widow of the Polish national hero Jan Sobieski, later King John III. The distinctive round porch attributed to the Sicilian architect Filippo Juvarra was added then.

Around the corner from the palazzetto is Via Gregoriana, a quiet street that preserves its baroque and 'romantic' aura wonderfully. No. 30, formerly the garden entrance to Palazzetto Zuccari, has a fanciful portal and windows shaped like monsters' mouths. Designed by the Zuccari brothers, these exemplify a typical current in Mannerist art. The lovely garden was destroyed when one of the last and richest members of the German community here, the art student Enrichetta Hertz, bought the building and made this part into a library. She later bequeathed the library to the German government (which still owns it) and it became very important in documenting the artistic development of the city. It includes a huge photographic archive of Rome.

Return to Trinità dei Monti. Enjoy the view from the top of the steps. Down the tree-lined avenue on the right, you can get a good view of the 16th century **Villa Medici,** seat of the Académie de France, and is normally closed.

In the 17th century France's 'Sun King', Louis XIV, established the academy, which was originally in a different building. Napoleon moved it to the Villa Medici when he occupied Rome, after buying the villa from Florence's famous Medici family. The coveted 'Prix de Rome', bestowed by France on outstanding French artists, has always involved a paid three-year sojourn at the academy here. Most famous French artists living in the area were Rome prize winners. Some were also appointed directors of the academy, including Horace Vernet in the early 19th century, and after him Ingres. Among the most important directors of the academy in recent years was the painter Balthus.

If you wish, go and see whether this is one of the days on which the Villa Medici is open to the public. It is a charming spot, in any case, and is graced by a pretty, quiet late 16th-century fountain in front, familiar in countless Romantic-era paintings.

Built in 1564 by Annibale Lippi, the son of Nanni di Baccio Bigio, the villa was modified shortly afterwards, especially the garden façade, by a more famous Florentine, Bartolomeo Ammannati. Galileo was held under house arrest here for his 'heretical' views (see p. 106).

The most interesting part of the building is the rear façade, which is sumptuous and extremely lively, in a pure Florentine style, and in striking contrast to the very simple front. It is adorned with dozens of ancient statues, reliefs and marble fragments dug up in the Renaissance, including garland reliefs from Augustus' famous Ara Pacis (see p. 222). Fountains and statues decorate the lush park, amongst them a colossal ancient Roman seated goddess, later restored as the 'Goddess Rome'. The 17-acre park extends to the Aurelian Walls and offers impressive panoramas. It is open on Saturday and Sunday mornings, 10:00 to 12:30.

Note: here the Pincio Gardens border on the Villa Borghese (see note on pp. 602-603).

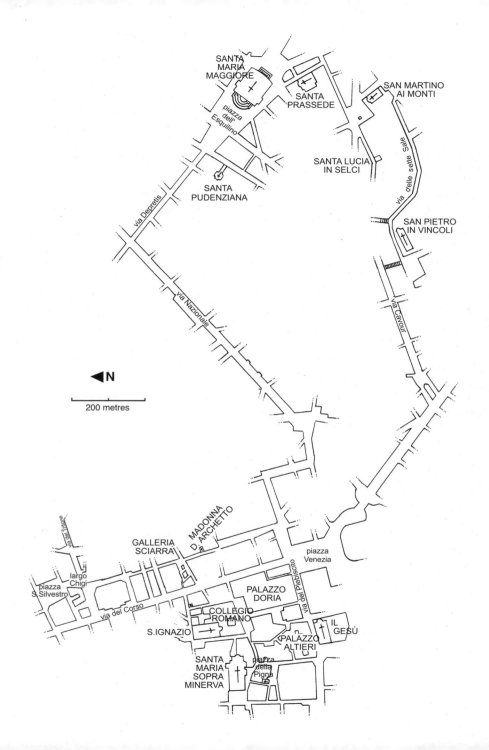

ROMA ROMANTICA
SECOND WALK

Starting point: Via Urbana (Piazza Esquilino)
End point: Largo Chigi
Duration: 6 hours (without the Detours, indicated above between parentheses).

Notes: 1) Whether you go in the morning or afternoon, try to start early in order to find
as many churches as possible open. S. Maria Maggiore, however, is open almost all day.
2) Short shorts (for both men and women), miniskirts, bare shoulders and so forth are
not allowed in S. Maria Maggiore.
3) The excavations under S. Pudenziana are rarely accessible, but you have a better
chance of seeing them in the morning. You may also try calling the church the day
before (tel. (06) 4814622) for an appointment.

BEFORE GOING

1. The Viminal and Esquiline churches: S. Pudenziana

The Second Walk resumes the trip along the 'Via Felice' of Sixtus V and the expansion line of the resettlement plan for the *disabitato*, climbing three of the Seven Hills, the Quirinal, Viminal and Esquiline.

We now encounter three venerable churches harking back to ancient Roman times, all very dear to Christian tradition. One, the great basilica of S. Maria Maggiore, has special importance as part of the pilgrimage route of the 'Seven Churches', followed annually by streams of the faithful in search of 'indulgences' (years off Purgatory, in this case 300 years if you visit all seven churches).

For centuries, people had to forge their way through semi-abandoned wastelands to reach these churches, as they were isolated in the *disabitato* after the fall of the Empire. This caused the Church authorities constant concern, and one of the main purposes of their resettlement plan was to reclaim the churches. Thus the expansion line leads straight to them. The grid went even further – to another isolated yet supremely important church: S. Giovanni in Laterano, which we'll visit in the second walk in the Rome of the Popes. This branch of the grid ended there at the Aurelian Walls after having crossed the whole city from Piazza del Popolo.

The other two churches in this area, S. Pudenziana and S. Prassede, are witnesses to a centuries-old story. Tradition holds that when the Apostle Peter came to Rome amid an increasingly bloodthirsty pagan backlash against his religion, a Roman senator, Pudens, converted to Christianity and sheltered Peter in his home. After Peter's death the senator's daughters, Pudentiana and Praxedes, devoted their lives to helping perse-cuted Christians and recovering the blood of martyrs as sacred relics. The home of Pudens and his daughters also became a refuge for the perse-cuted and a centre of worship, one of the many so-called 'home churches' (*ecclesiæ domesticæ*) characteristic of Christianity before its legalisation in the 4th century. (In these walks we'll see many examples of these Early Christian meeting places, which later became regular churches. They were also called *tituli*, since they were usually assigned as 'titles' to the dignitaries of the Early Church and entrusted to their care. The practice has con-tinued in modern times, when newly created cardinals are assigned their own 'titular' churches.)

The factual basis of the story of Pudens is unknown, but it is typical of many tales which were presented as fact for centuries in Rome, and

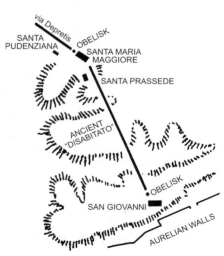

The expansion line over the Esquiline: from S. Maria Maggiore to S. Giovanni in Laterano

have since been found to be mostly or wholly figments of the popular imagination. Such stories, especially frequent in the middle ages, were sometimes encouraged by the Church for their edifying value. There was even a name for them: *pia fraus* ('pious fraud').

S. Pudenziana, the first of the two churches dedicated to Senator Pudens' supposed daughters, rises on the ruins of a private house of the 1st century AD, that is, one contemporary with St Peter's supposed stay in Rome. The house was located on an ancient Roman street mainly inhabited by senatorial and patrician families, the *Vicus Patricius*. But other than this supporting evidence for the story, our earliest records of it are from the middle ages, centuries later.

A Senator Pudens may have existed, and he may or may not have had any connection with Peter. (Incidentally, we don't even know for certain whether Peter ever set foot in Rome.) His house could have become a Christian refuge and then a church. His daughters, however, appear to be completely fictitious. Their legend, as we shall see, probably began with a misinterpretation of a word and two figures in the ancient mosaic of the apse. The sisters' blood-collecting activities, too, seem to be a creative elaboration on certain physical features of the church.

The church contains yet another example of this medieval myth-making ability. In some periods it was dedicated not only to St. Pudentiana, but also to a supposed friend or relative of Pudens, St Pastor. His name and effigies appear in various parts of the church. Recent archæological work, however, suggests that his legend developed from another of the mosaics in the church, now lost, showing St Peter as a shepherd (pastor).

ON THE SPOT

1. The Viminal and Esquiline churches: S. Pudenziana

The entrance to **S. Pudenziana** is on Via Urbana, the ancient *Vicus Patricius*.

Little is known about the true origins of the church, one of the oldest in Rome. Excavations have shown that it was built around the 4th century by adapting an existing 2nd century public bath, which in turn had been built on top of a two-storey private house from the 1st century.

The church was remodelled at least five times between the 8th and 19th centuries. Due to the phenomenon of progressive burial, which we'll explain later (p. 140), it is 12 ft (4 m) below the present street level – and remember that beneath it are the remains of a two-storey house. The exterior, entirely redone in the 19th century, is not much to look at, except for the door, which is flanked by precious ancient Roman columns and surmounted by a lovely frieze (11th-century or older). With its plant motifs and figures, it is one of the most refined examples of medieval sculpture in Rome. The medallions show the two saintly sisters Pudentiana and Praxedes, their father Pudens and 'St Pastor' with the Lamb of God in the middle. (Open: June-October, weekdays 07:30-12:00 and 15:30-18:30, closing half an hour earlier from November to May. Sunday 09:00-12:00.)

The main attraction inside is the splendid 4th-century mosaic in the apse (the last five figures on the right are 19th-century), showing an enthroned *Christ among the Apostles*. Behind these are two women, probably representing the Jewish and Christian faiths, though for centuries they were mistaken for the sister saints (and are often even now). In the background are the Cross and the holy city of Jerusalem; in heaven, the symbols of the Evangelists. This is the oldest known mosaic representation of these symbols, and also the earliest realistic representation of life-size human figures surviving in a Roman church.

The grave, classical and monumental style is strictly in keeping with ancient Roman tradition. The eminent scholar Richard Krautheimer has interpreted this as an attempt to play down the eastern origins of Christianity, and give it local credentials, which would have been more acceptable to the pagan part of the populace. The powerful figures appear very 'Roman' and official: Christ could be a consul or emperor, the apostles senators, the building a Roman portico.

Christ holds an open book, which says the Lord (*Dominus*) is the keeper (*conservator*) of the church of Pudens (*Ecclesiæ Pudentianæ*). The last word means 'of Pudens' not 'of Pudentiana', suggesting that the church was originally named after Pudens, the former senator. The word, however, was mistaken for 'of Pudentiana' in the middle ages, and since it was displayed so prominently and repeated so often, it caused a change in the name of the church. Together with the misidentification of the two women in the mosaic, this fact almost certainly spawned the whole story of the two saintly daughters.

The columns of the ancient church are visible on both sides, embedded in later masonry. The original plain mosaic floor shows through here and there. In the left aisle, a square water-chute, probably from the public baths that preceded the church, was interpreted throughout the centuries as a pit, which led to an elaboration of the sister saints' story. It was said that they poured and kept the martyrs' blood there. The girls are matter-of-factly engaged in the operation in a 17th-century oil painting of uncertain attribution on the left wall near the entrance. Near the 'pit' is the entrance to a very richly decorated chapel, one of several added to the church by Francesco da Volterra during a total renovation in the late 17th century, completed after his death by Carlo Maderno. Monuments, multi-coloured marbles and mosaics are by minor contemporaries.

At the very end of the left aisle, a chapel

dedicated to St Peter contains a statuary group by Giovan Battista Della Porta, a minor late 16th-century sculptor (no relation to Giacomo Della Porta).

The beautiful dome, the first oval one in Italy, is visible from inside the presbytery. It was designed by Francesco da Volterra and painted by his contemporary and fellow Tuscan, Niccolò Pomarancio.

In the sacristy, entered from the right side of the church, a fresco in the vault attributed to Domenichino represents the *Conversion of St William of Aquitaine*.

Scattered throughout are inscriptions and other remains from the buildings that preceded this church.

Ask in the sacristy to be shown the excavations of the putative Senator Pudens' house under the church. Past a layer of construction belonging to the ancient public baths are floors from different periods in a two-storey house. The different pavements represent the best collection of their sort in Rome. Some date to the 1st century BC, though the final walls are two centuries later. An even later ancient Roman road crosses the rooms in one place, an intersection of the *Vicus Patricius*. Most of the site remains unexplored.

Also ask the guide to show you the oratory, a medieval annex to the church covered with naive 11th-century frescoes of episodes from the lives of the two sisters.

Leaving the church, note the 12th- or 13th-century (some scholars say 11th-century) bell tower on the left. It is one of the most striking of many medieval bell towers flanking Roman churches, almost all of them romanesque – a linear and serene style far more common in Latin countries than the pointed and ornate gothic style that became the norm in Northern Europe.

Reach your next stop by reclimbing Via Urbana to Piazza Esquilino, in view of the rear of the great basilica of S. Maria Maggiore.

BEFORE GOING

2. S. Maria Maggiore and S. Prassede

The grand 5th-century church dedicated to Mary was called Maggiore ('the Great') because its builders wanted to make it the greatest of all churches dedicated to the Virgin. The gesture was deemed necessary to erase an insult recently aimed at Her. A group of heretics (the Nestorians) had maintained that She was not really the Mother of God, because Jesus had lived as a man – not as a god – and merged with the Godhead only after death. A papally convened council of bishops at Ephesus in 431 declared the notion blasphemy. The following year work began on the church – actually a basilica, the form that imitates the public halls of pagan Rome. (The word 'basilica' would later be applied as a liturgical distinction to designate certain important churches, whatever their form.)

The builders kept the promise of the name. To this day no other Marian church – and few others for that matter – are comparable to it for grandeur and beauty. Its historical and liturgical importance is such that it is part of the Vatican state territory.

It also offers a remarkable selection of works of art, though as an anthology it differs from that of Rome's other treasure-chest churches. For instance, in S. Maria del Popolo, we saw renaissance and baroque works; in S. Maria Maggiore they span an incredible 1,300 years. The church has the most beautiful surviving set of late imperial (5th-century) wall mosaics, as well as rich 12th-century marble floors and another wonderful set of 13th-century mosaics. The 14th-century romanesque bell tower is the tallest and most impressive in Rome. The splendid late 15th-century ceiling displays the first gold brought back to Europe after Columbus' voyage to America, donated by the Spanish monarchs Ferdinand and Isabella to the Spanish Pope Alexander VI Borgia. The originally simple exterior was rebuilt several times, the best results coming from the most recent remodellings. The back, or apsidal part, visible as we approach from Via Felice, is a Roman baroque masterpiece; and the 18th-century façade is one of the most spirited scenic creations of the period. It is particularly elegant in the way it shows the 13th-century mosaic-covered façade through imposing arcades, as though it were in a jewel case. At the time, everyone applauded Ferdinando Fuga's renovation, except Pope Benedict XIV, who had commissioned it. 'Fuga must have thought we were theatrical impresarios,' he said. 'This looks like a dance hall.'

The building materials used for the church are even more ancient than the edifice itself, enhancing the impression of a time-capsule. As in many other Roman churches, including very early ones, the nave columns, which give the interior the serene and strikingly authentic look of an ancient Roman basilica, are spolia from pagan temples. Recent roof repairs have revealed tiles imprinted with trademarks from Nero's day in the 1st century AD.

The church contains the remains of many characters by now familiar to us. One is Gian Lorenzo Bernini, buried with his father Pietro, also a sculptor and architect. Another is Sixtus V, the great builder pope of peasant birth, of whom the German historian Ferdinand Gregorovius wrote: '... this astounding man, who as a child herded swine, and as an old man commanded peoples and kings... filled Rome with so many works, that from every side his name, like an echo, rings in the traveller's ear.'

S. Maria Maggiore, mosaic of the Coronation of the Virgin

The mosaics are the greatest treasure of S. Maria Maggiore. Together with those of our next stop, S. Prassede, they form an unequalled compendium of mosaic art through the centuries.

The 5th-century mosaics of S. Maria Maggiore are in the ancient Roman style, but much looser and more dramatic, stylistically and emotionally, than those in S. Pudenziana (pp. 93-94). Colour, composition and gestures display classical mosaic art at its most expressive.

The 9th-century mosaics of S. Prassede are totally different. They are a poignant memento of the 200 years when Rome, after its fall, was reconquered by Justinian, ruler of the surviving eastern branch of the Empire, Byzantium (formerly Constantinople, now Istanbul; see p. 83). The trance-like, other-worldly look of Byzantine figures deeply influenced Roman art. The mosaics of S. Prassede are the most important Byzantine monument in Rome. The splendour of their profoundly mystical figures and golden background has earned them a nickname the 'Garden of Paradise'.

Another sweeping change is evident in the 13th-century mosaics of S. Maria Maggiore with their much more human, realistic representation. This is a reaction against the hypnotic rigidity of Byzantine art and foreshadows the great renewal of the visual arts begun soon afterwards in Rome by Pietro Cavallini and in Florence by Cimabue and Giotto. The change extends to the materials themselves: the more recent wall mosaics use marble chips, as opposed to the gem-like glass chips of Byzantine workmanship.

The original builders of S. Maria Maggiore are not known. Nor is it known whether the 5th-century basilica is a remodelling of a 4th-century one attributed to Pope Liberius – called the Basilica Liberiana – and connected to the poetic 'legend of the fall of snow', which we'll see represented in a bas relief inside, and which gives a different explanation of the origins of the church. The earlier basilica may have left traces now entombed in the foundations of the present building, or else may have stood on a separate site nearby and been demolished. Again, nobody knows.

ON THE SPOT

2. S. Maria Maggiore and S. Prassede

Approaching **S. Maria Maggiore** the first thing we see is the apse end, so beautiful and architecturally complex that it can be mistaken for the main façade. The work of various major architects of the late 16th and 17th centuries (including Carlo Rainaldi), it is one of the highest expressions of the Roman baroque.

The obelisk that completes the square is the twin of the one we saw on the Quirinal, both spolia from Augustus' mausoleum and both ancient Roman imitations of the Egyptian form.

Go round the church to the right, up Via Liberiana. At No. 24 is the house which Pietro Bernini built for himself and where his son Gian Lorenzo lived and worked until his early forties, when he moved into his own palace (p. 63). In the courtyard of No. 17 are remnants of a 12th-century palace, the Patriarchìo di S. Maria Maggiore, which served occasionally as a papal residence.

You are now in front of the basilica, an elegant, yet solemn 18th-century creation by Ferdinando Fuga, whose work we admired on Piazza del Quirinale.

The architect preserved and exploited some of the existing elements of the older church. For instance, of the two five-storey buildings that flank Fuga's façade, the one on the left was already there, having been joined a century earlier to the original 13th-century façade. Fuga just added its twin to the right. The original 13th-century mosaics – representing Jesus, Mary and Saints, and signed by an otherwise unknown mosaicist, Filippo Rusuti – were left visible, framed by the great loggia on the upper floor. The overall stage-set effect is enhanced by the many decorative sculptures and by the 14th-century bell tower, the tallest in Rome, at 240 ft (75 m). (Open 08:00-20:00; in winter 08:00-19:00.)

The church interior has remained structurally intact since its construction in the 5th century. Its great size (282 ft/86 m in length), harmonious proportions and powerful rows of monolithic marble columns (40 in all) offer a rare example of how ancient basilicas, both Christian and pagan, looked.

The 12th-century floor is a fine specimen of the Cosmatesque technique employed by generations of medieval masons, architects, sculptors and decorators, many of them belonging to a family of artists called Cosma, from whom the whole group takes its name. The warmly coloured geometric designs of the marble – used for floors and furniture, such as candelabra and pulpits, and often inlaid with coloured pieces of marble or glass – is typical of many Roman churches.

The imposing gilded ceiling bearing Alexander VI Borgia's coat-of-arms in the middle is probably by Giuliano da Sangallo, a younger contemporary of Michelangelo.

Along both walls of the central nave, above the colonnades, runs a cycle of superb mosaics from the 5th century, of great rarity due to their antiquity, complexity and excellent state of preservation. The biblical scenes, in 36 rectangles, bear the imprint of ancient Roman art both in their solemnity and in their vividness. The scenes on the left wall illustrate the lives of Abraham, Isaac and Jacob, and those on the right the lives of Moses and Joshua.

Connected with these mosaics theologically, and from the same period, are the equally vivid **mosaics** in the triumphal arch framing the apse. They represent scenes from Christ's nativity and childhood.

In the apse itself is the monumental mosaic by Iacopo Torriti, signed and dated 1295, representing the *Triumph of Mary*, to whom the basilica is dedicated. Note the refined ornamentation in the upper part, with doves, peacocks and other Christian symbols. (See p. 96 for the nature and style of all these mosaics, where they are discussed within the general context of mosaic art in Rome).

In the lowest section of the apse wall are four 15th-century marble reliefs of disputed authorship referring to the history of the church. One of them shows the *Miracle of the Snow*. The legend holds that Mary herself indicated in a dream to Pope

S. Maria Maggiore, interior

Liberius, the supposed founder, where her great church was to be built. She confirmed this by having snow fall on the site even though it was August. Thus the basilica is also called S. Maria della Neve, or 'St Mary of the Snow'. Of course, the legend, referring to a 4th-century basilica, would only apply to the 5th-century basilica if the former were indeed the predecessor of the latter on the same site, and this is not known.

Return to the main entrance and go counter-clockwise. In the right aisle, the first door leads to the 17th-century baptistery. On the left wall is the tomb and black marble bust of an ambassador sent from the Congo to the Vatican in the early 17th century. The emissary Europeanised his name, Ne Vunda, to Antonio Emanuele, Marquis of Funta, but everybody called him 'Negrita', as the Latin inscription says. Bernini sketched his portrait, and for this reason the bust was long attributed to Bernini, though it is in fact by another, lesser sculptor. It is also said that Bernini used the ambassador's features for his Fountain of the Moor in Piazza Navona (p. 461)

On one side, the baptistery leads to the beautiful sacristy, with its massive 17th-century furniture; on the other, to a 15th-century former chapel, whose very dilapidated frescoes are sometimes attributed to the great renaissance painter Piero della Francesca, who worked for a time in Rome. Note the beautiful Cosmatesque pavement. From this side you can leave the church for a moment to see a small column commemorating the conversion to Catholicism of Henry IV, the first Bourbon king of France (see p. 370).

Return to the aisle. The last chapel on the right (actually, the right terminal of the transept) is the stunning Sistine Chapel, not to be confused with Michelangelo's Sistine Chapel in the Vatican. The latter takes its name from a different pope, Sixtus IV, while this one was commissioned by Sixtus V, the builder pope. The late 16th-century chapel contains the monumental tombs of two popes: on the left, St Pius V (d. 1572), and on the right Sixtus V himself (d. 1590). Chapel and monuments were designed by Domenico Fontana, artistic adviser to Sixtus V. Note the contrast between the coloured marbles of the structure and the papal figures in white.

Leaving the chapel, on the floor almost in front of it, near the next-to-last column in the nave, you will see a simple tombstone over the remains of the two Berninis, Pietro and his more famous son Gian Lorenzo.

Continuing down the right aisle, at the very end on your right is the sepulchral monument to a late 13th-century prelate, Cardinal Rodriguez, by Giovanni Cosma of the Cosma family (see glossary), a gothic work of great pathos.

Cross the transept in front of the altar (below is a kneeling statue of Pope Pius IX, who had to flee Rome during the 1848 revolution, p. 565) to the left aisle. The first great chapel here is the Pauline Chapel, built for Pope Paul V Borghese by Flaminio Ponzio. Designed two decades after the Sistine Chapel, but clearly following the same scheme, it too contains the great tombs of two popes, Paul V to the left and Clement VIII to the right. In the middle is a sumptuous altar surmounted by a Byzantine painting of the *Madonna* (9th-century or perhaps later). Striking 17th-century frescoes adorn the ceiling. Especially noteworthy are those by the great Guido Reni above and around the two monuments. In the chapel dome a *Madonna* by the 16th-17th-century Florentine painter Ludovico Cigoli, rests her feet on the moon, a standard motif, though here the moon is a scientific first: it was based on Galileo's description to Cigoli of what he could see through his telescope. The chapel has a crypt (not open) containing the remains of members of the Borghese family, including those of the ravishing Paolina, Napoleon's sister, who married a Borghese prince (see p. 602).

Next down the aisle, the simple and solemn Sforza chapel, long attributed to Michelangelo's follower Giacomo Della Porta, is now thought almost certainly to be by the master himself.

The space has undoubtedly a Michelangelesque imprint, obvious also in some individual features, such as the graves with their ornate lids. On the other hand Della Porta was usually very

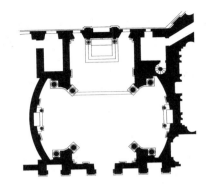

The Sforza Chapel in S. Maria Maggiore: the novel arrangement of the columns prefigures baroque inventiveness

mindful of the great master's motifs. A further complication is that some figures in the frieze recall the hand not of Giacomo, but of Guglielmo Della Porta (no relation). Recently discovered documents show, however, that Michelangelo's involvement can no longer be doubted.

Excavations under S. Maria Maggiore, unfortunately closed to the public, have uncovered the remains of a large ancient Roman building and a frescoed portico.

As you leave the church, note the tall marble column erected in the square by a pope. It was the only one left in the great ancient Basilica of Maxentius, which we'll see later.

If you wish to continue the main itinerary, cross the square to take the narrow Via S. Prassede to the far right (see sketch map on p. 102).

If you take the following side trip, cross the square to the column and go from there straight into Via Carlo Alberto.

DETOUR
1 HR 30 MIN

On this side of S. Maria Maggiore, Via Carlo Alberto and its direct continuations are part of the original arrow-straight Via Felice planned by

Sixtus V to connect the newly settled district to the *disabitato* by crossing the whole city from north to south (pp. 44, 70). Just on the left (No. 2) is a church dedicated to **S. Antonio Abate** (St Anthony Abbot), an ancient desert hermit, sufferer from and protector against erysipelas, or 'St Anthony's fire', so called after him (Queen Christina of Sweden died of it, p. 366). The church originated as part of an early 13th-century hospital for this and other skin diseases, a scourge in the middle ages. Rebuilt many times, it now has a 19th-century appearance, excepting the original portal by Vassallectus, a principal exponent of the Cosmatesque style. The double staircase is recent, added because of the lowering of the street level. (Open: Saturday at 07:00 and Sunday at 10:00, and occasionally at other times.)

The interior is 18th-century. Much of the liturgical furniture is linked to eastern, or Slavic, rites, since in modern times the church was annexed to the adjacent Vatican seminary of the Russian Catholic (as opposed to Orthodox) clergy (Collegium Russicum).

Proceeding down Via Carlo Alberto, on the right, near No. 45, are remains of the Republican walls (p. 42). Just past them is **SS. Vito e Modesto**, a church founded in the early middle ages to honour these two martyrs, then rebuilt in 1477 and restored many times since. On the façade elements of the 15th-century structure survive: the central oculus ('eye'), the mullioned windows and the simple portal. (Open: 07:00-10:00 and 18:00-20:00.)

Behind a grate is a stone, a fragment of an ancient Roman cenotaph, called the *Pietra Scellerata* ('Evil Stone') in the middle ages because the cenotaph was believed to have been near the spot where the two saints honoured by the church, together with many other Christians, were martyred. The stone was supposed miraculously to cure rabies. A renaissance altar follows, with a 15th-century fresco of the *Virgin with Sts Modestus, Sebastian, Margaret and Vitus* attributed to Antoniazzo Romano. On the opposite wall a votive plaque of 1620 recalls how the stone healed a prince of the Colonna family (pp. 128-130) after he had been bitten by a rabid dog. Under the church are vestiges of the Republican walls and an aqueduct (ask the sacristan for admission).

Near the church is the **Arch of Gallienus**, actually the Esquiline Gate of the Republican walls, built by Augustus in the 1st century AD and restored by an ordinary citizen in 262. The inscription says the donor, M. Aurelius Victor, dedicated the gate to the *Clementissimo Principi*, the Emperor Licinius Gallienus, and his wife Salonina. Originally the gate included two minor arches on either side.

From the arch take Via S. Vito to Via Merulana. The popes built the street, named after an ancient Roman road nearby, as part of Sixtus V's urban project connecting S. Maria Maggiore to S. Giovanni in Laterano. Take it, to the left, to Largo Brancaccio (the 19th-century Palazzo Brancaccio here is now the Museum of Oriental Art, p. 685). Go on for another block to Largo Leopardi. In the middle is the so-called **Auditorium of Mæcenas** (Open: 09:00-13:30; from April 1-September 30 also 16:00-19:00 on Tuesday, Thursday and Saturday; closed Monday.)

This is a great hall, now partly underground, with faint remains of frescoes. Of unknown purpose, it belonged to a villa which one of the richest men in ancient Rome, Mæcenas, a friend and supporter of Augustus, had built for himself (see p. 223). Before Augustus the whole area, including the streets and squares ahead of us in the detour, was the grim Campus Esquilinus, a pauper's cemetery where animals were buried too. Mæcenas decided to beautify the site as part of Augustus' programme of urban renewal (p. 216) and so he covered the land with a thick blanket of soil and built a villa.

From Largo Leopardi take Via Leopardi to **Piazza Vittorio Emanuele II**. The huge square was made in the late 19th century by widening the Via Felice, that is, Via Carlo Alberto – which we find again on this side of the square if we advance a few yards, and will use as a reference point. A vast new development centred on the square was meant to accommodate a surge in the lower and middle classes after Rome became the capital of Italy in 1870 (see p. 28). The newcomers included many who came from the northern region of Piedmont to join the new bureaucracy, which is why the square, dedicated to the king who unified Italy (p. 238), resembles the famous porticoed squares of the king's former capital of Turin.

Alas, the neighbourhood has come down badly. Shoddy materials were used when it was built, and later the construction of the metro so weakened the foundations that some buildings collapsed. Petty crime and shady dealings connected to the nearby mainline station (pp. 80-81) have not helped. In the last few years, a Chinatown has sprung up in the area – the first in Rome's history – but this has not improved matters. Efforts to regenerate the area have given scant results.

Just inside the square, on the Via Carlo Alberto side, is a large ancient Roman ruin. This was the terminus, showcase fountain and water distribution point of an aqueduct,.

The structure is traditionally, though erroneously, called the **Trophies of Marius**, since it was believed for centuries that two grand marble 'trophy' sculptures depicting war symbols, which once adorned it, were from the Republican era and celebrated the wars of the famous general Marius (p. 256). Actually they, and indeed the whole fountain, were from the time of the Emperor Domitian in the 1st century AD. Now they decorate the balustrade of the Capitol (p. 145).

Behind the ruin is the so-called **Magic Door**, with monstrous statues of the Egyptian god Bes on the sides. It is the curious relic of an 18th-century villa on the Via Felice that belonged to an enthusiastic alchemist. With its pseudo-Egyptian sculpture, cabalistic signs and mysterious inscriptions, it reflects the mystical, supernatural manias prevailing in the century that gave us Mozart's *The Magic Flute* and figures such as Cagliostro (p. 387) and Casanova (p. 59).

Nearby, in an indentation of the corner of the square, is the very ancient church of **S. Eusebio**. It is built over ruins of a 4th-century Roman house, said to be the *ecclesia domestica* of a priest called Eusebius, a staunch Christian at a time (4th century) when the Emperor Constantius II had embraced the Arian heresy (which denied the divinity of Christ.) Eusebius is supposed to have been imprisoned and starved to death by the emperor in this house. In the middle ages it became an official church and was later remodelled several times. Its present appearance dates from the 18th century. (Open: 07:00-11:00 and 18:00-20:00.)

Inside are 17th- and 18th-century paintings by minor artists. There are very impressive carved walnut seats (late 16th-century) in the choir. In the basement (inaccessible due to cave-ins that have weakened the church) are vestiges of ancient Roman buildings.

Every year on January 17 horses and other animals are blessed in front of the church.

Leave the church and walk to the other end of the long side of the square. Take Via Lamarmora (left) and continue into Via G. Pepe, dominated by several grandiose arches of the 3rd century aqueduct that fed the Trophies of Marius reservoir-fountain. On the right is an attractive and once important theatre of the turn of the 20th century, the Ambra Jovinelli, in the *art nouveau* style; it is currently under restoration.

Cross Via Giolitti. The desolate railroad neighbourhood is the setting of the exquisite little church of **S. Bibiana**, the architectural debut in Rome of the 25-year-old Gian Lorenzo Bernini (who still lived in the neighbourhood at the time, see p. 97). Its early 17th-century appearance, still echoing renaissance models, belies its much greater antiquity, Bernini's work being the last of several reconstructions. Tradition holds that the church was founded in the 4th century over the home of a wealthy Christian family, including the young Bibiana, all murdered by order of Julian the Apostate (p. 427), though no persecution in Rome by this emperor is in fact recorded. Nevertheless 4th-century structures were found underground during Bernini's restoration. These included a priceless alabaster tub, obviously from a rich household. Bernini turned it into the funerary urn of bones said to belong to the martyred family, which had been in the church's possession since remote antiquity. (Open: 06:00-10:30 and 16:30-19:30.)

The evocative columns of the nave are spolia from ancient Roman monuments and the brick walls are medieval. The 17th-century nave frescoes tell Bibiana's story; those on the left are by the famous Pietro da Cortona, those on the right by the minor but vigorous Florentine painter Agostino Ciampelli. The aisles contain medieval tombstones. At the end of the right aisle is Bibiana's mother, *St Dafrosa*, by Pietro da Cortona; at the end of the left aisle, Bibiana's sister, *St Demetria*, by Ciampelli. The main altar and the statue of *St Bibiana* are by Bernini. Under the altar is the alabaster tub, an exceptional archæological find, with the relics of the martyrs.

Near the exit, to the right, is a small column to which according to tradition Bibiana was tied during her martyrdom. A plaque under the portico commemorates thousands of bodies found here in the course of various works, no doubt originally burials in the ancient Campus Esquilinus Cemetery.

Continue along Via Giolitti. Walk by the underpass after the church; 200 yards past it you will see a great ruin erroneously called the **Temple of Minerva Medica**, probably a nymphæum from a 3rd century AD villa owned by the Emperor Gallienus (p. 100).

Originally marble-covered and adorned with a statue in each of the great niches, it has an unusual decagonal ground plan. Much admired in the past, the monument now stands forgotten in the squalid neighbourhood.

Go back to the underpass and cross it. On the other side you can see the Aurelian Walls (p. 42). Cross them at Porta San Lorenzo in front of you and go left for 300 ft along the walls to reach the ancient **Porta Tiburtina** (Tiburtine Gate).

The picturesque gate, in an equally picturesque

stretch of turreted walls, was originally a passageway cut by Augustus through an aqueduct in 5 BC (the lower arch). It was incorporated 270 years later in the Aurelian Walls and remodelled in the early 5th century by the co-emperors Arcadius and Honorius. Adorned with *bucrania* (carved ox skulls), the Augustan passage bears inscriptions commemorating Augustus and Titus, who restored the aqueduct in 70 AD. Arcadius and Honorius' remodelling, more evident on the other side of the gate, is recorded in an inscription celebrating these 'triumphant victors, who have restored gates, walls and towers of the Eternal City and removed many ruins.' Three aqueduct conduits crossed the attic.

Bus No. 71 stops (at least at the time of writing) at Piazzale Tiburtino before the nearby Porta San Lorenzo. You can board it to go back to S. Maria Maggiore where you may pick up the main itinerary with the church of S. Prassede.

END OF DETOUR

Via S. Prassede takes us to a side entrance of the church of that name. This is the everyday entrance.

From S. Maria Maggiore to S. Prassede

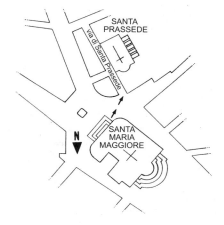

S. Prassede (St Praxedes) was erected in the 9th century – when the tradition of the sister saints Pudentiana and Praxedes (see pp. 92-93) was already centuries old – by the 'builder pope' St Paschal I, near the ruins of a pre-existing Christian basilica in an area where Praxedes was supposed to have assisted her first martyrs. (Open: 07:00-12:00 and 16:00-18:30.)

The entrance leads directly into the right aisle. Halfway down the aisle is the **Chapel of St Zeno**, Rome's most important Byzantine monument, called the 'Garden of Paradise' in the middle ages. It is covered with exquisite 9th-century, Byzantine-style mosaics representing Christ, angels and saints, including the sister saints, on a golden background with symbolic animals and foliage. (For the nature and style of these mosaics, see p. 96 where they are discussed in the general context of mosaic art in Rome.) Above the left door, the woman with a square halo – indicating that she was still alive at the time – is Theodora, mother of Pope Paschal, who is buried here. The chapel has the circular form of a small mausoleum (pp. 216, 385), as Paschal intended it for his mother's resting place. She had also been given the title *episcopa*, or 'female bishop'.

The mosaics in a niche over the altar, representing the *Virgin and Child with Sts Praxedes and Pudentiana*, are a later, possibly 13th-century, work.

The floor is a very rare, wonderful example of pre-Cosmatesque patterned marble work. (The Cosmatesque floor in the rest of the church is a modern reproduction.) A small oriental jasper column is displayed in an adjacent space. It was brought from Jerusalem by a crusader in the 13th century and is said to be the one to which Jesus was tied when he was scourged. Indeed, some paintings of later periods show Jesus attached loosely with ropes to the small column rather than tied tightly to a full-size column, as more commonly depicted. (The retrieval of putative relics from Jerusalem and the East was a typical phenomenon of Early Christianity, often with political overtones; see also pp. 107, 417, 631)

The chapel is delicately ornamented on the outside wall, too, where a window is surrounded by 9th-century mosaics of *Christ, the Virgin and Saints* (much restored), including the two sisters again. The window also encloses a beautiful ancient Roman urn. Two columns of black granite flanking the door, together with a rich marble frieze surmounting it, are spolia from pagan buildings. Outside the chapel, on the pillar just in front, note a marble bust of a bishop called Santoni. This is the first work by Bernini in Rome, made when he was just 16 and lived in the area (p. 97).

Other impressive 9th-century mosaics decorate the triumphal arch and the apse. On the arch they depict the Heavenly Jerusalem, with jewelled walls, inhabited by Christ, the Virgin, the Apostles, angels and saints, including the two sister saints. A procession of martyrs and the 'elect' head towards the gates. On the apse, Christ blesses the sisters, who wear gala Byzantine dresses and are presented to Him by Sts Peter and Paul. St Zeno and Pope Paschal I are present, the latter with the square halo of the living. Other figures and symbolic animals and palms, in a flowered landscape by the River Jordan, complete the scene. Pope Paschal's monogram is on the arch and at the top of the apse.

At the end of the right aisle is a chapel with a modern altar and a beautiful 16th-century wooden crucifix. Opposite the altar is the 13th-century Cosmatesque tomb of a cardinal, Pantaleon Archier de Troyes, titular head of S. Prassede, who was killed here during a riot.

The main entrance to the church, opposite the apse, is sometimes open, giving a view of the quiet courtyard (formerly with a colonnade) in front of the church and the simple 9th-century façade (with its renaissance doorway). A stepped hallway leads to a small entrance porch that we'll see later from the outside.

3. On the Esquiline Hill: S. Martino ai Monti and S. Pietro in Vincoli

The Walk continues at the top of the Esquiline Hill, along a ridge that in ancient times was the fringe of Rome's most populous and boisterous district, the Suburra (p. 154). After the Empire fell the area and all high-lying residential districts were abandoned, because of the destruction of the aqueducts. Today it remains strangely silent, one corner of the city that still gives the impression of solitude and dereliction that for centuries characterised the *disabitato* (p. 28).

Along with abundant vestiges of pagan antiquity, the area offers a mixture of remains from Early Christianity, the middle ages, and the baroque and romantic eras. Several churches survive of the many that sprang up here when Christianity was legalised in the late Empire, for the inhabitants of the proletarian district were the first and most numerous converts to a religion that offered compassion to the downtrodden.

One of these churches has become a temple of renaissance art thanks to the great Michelangelo: S. Pietro in Vincoli, the site of Michelangelo's tomb of Pope Julius II with the famous statue of Moses. It also evokes the unfortunate career setback suffered by Michelangelo. (Not a financial setback, apparently. The art historian Rab Hatfield, who has recently published a study of the bank accounts of the time, maintains that contrary to general belief, Michelangelo was very well paid and had become extremely rich. He was also very tight with his money.) The monument,

S. Pietro in Vincoli as it was in the 18th century, still surrounded by other buildings; engraving by Giuseppe Vasi

104

including the statue, was originally meant for St Peter's; Michelangelo designed it to be four times larger and to include forty statues. He wanted it to be his artistic testament. But first the delays of Julius II, who had commissioned it, and then the opposition of Julius' successor and enemy, Leo X, forced Michelangelo to drop the project, which had absorbed some of his most productive years. Julius II's heirs had Michelangelo resume the work in his old age, but on a much smaller scale. He agreed to finish only the statuary which he had begun as a hopeful young man, and a bit more, assigning the rest to other artists, with unhappy results. 'I have wasted my youth chained to this tomb,' wrote Michelangelo bitterly.

Yet the monument's central statue, Moses, would alone be enough to ensure any artist eternal fame. The biographer Giorgio Vasari, a younger contemporary of Michelangelo and himself an artist, wrote: 'There was no

Moses, by Michelangelo

other work to be seen, ancient or modern, to rival it.' He also reports that Rome's Jews would go every Sabbath, 'like flocks of starlings, to visit and adore the statue ... And it well may be, for they are adoringa thing not human but divine.' In the 19th century the French novelist Stendhal wrote: 'Those who have not seen the statue cannot realise the full power of sculpture.' And the young Sigmund Freud devoted an entire book to analysing the feelings animating Moses as represented in Michelangelo's statue.

We leave the hill down a dark, narrow lane that recalls a bloody episode of Rome's most remote, semi-legendary past. The ancients called it *Vicus Sceleratus*, or 'Street of Crime'. When Rome was still a monarchy, Tullia, daughter of the wise King Servius Tullius, conspired to replace him with her husband, the Etruscan Tarquin. Hired assassins attacked Servius and left him dead in the street. When Tullia rode home in her carriage, the driver stopped at the sight of the body, but the ferocious daughter ordered him to ride over it, and was spattered with her own father's blood. The usurper Tarquin, nicknamed 'the Proud', and his wife were expelled some years later when his regime proved to be too oppressive. He was Rome's last king; the Republic was established in the 6th century BC.

105

ON THE SPOT

3. On the Esquiline Hill: S. Martino ai Monti and S. Pietro in Vincoli

Leaving the church of S. Prassede, take Via S. Prassede to the right, then take another right at Via S. Martino ai Monti. On your right, at No. 28, is the austére medieval vestibule entrance to the front courtyard of S. Prassede, with two ancient Roman columns (also note the fine frieze). The whole is not unpleasantly sandwiched between more recent buildings. Further down, No. 20A incorporates the first two floors of the **House of Domenichino** (17th-century).

The life and work of Domenichino, one of the great painters of the 17th century, are discussed on pp. 510-513. Here an inscription reads in part: 'He, who gave glory to painting, took refuge in this house from the implacable hostility of the envious.' This alludes to the misfortunes that befell Dominichino, though he seems to have sinned as much as been sinned against, especially in his relations with his rival, the painter Lanfranco, as we'll see later.

In the basement of No. 8, a fascinating relic from Augustus' time (early 1st century AD) was found in 1885. If you see anyone going in or out, ask permission to see the ruin, of which the tenants are justifiably proud.

Grateful for his good rule, the Roman people gave Augustus a gift of money every New Year. Augustus, however, did not use the money personally, but spent it on part of his plans for urban embellishment; more specifically, on putting marble statues of the gods near all the main crossroads. (There is more on Augustus' plan in the second Ancient Rome Walk, p. 216.) The ruin is the base of one of these monuments, to the god Mercury, with an inscription recalling all this. The statue is gone. The base rests on tufa blocks, once covered with marble, which in turn rest on the ancient street.

Via S. Martino ai Monti ends in the square of the same name, a place of ancient pathos, marred by the modern Via G. Lanza, which slashed through it in the drastic late 19th-century renovations. Dominating the square are the two medieval **Capocci Towers**, one of which you can see better as you advance along the right side of the square. They are named after one of the baronial families who last owned them in the 15th century. The free-standing one is 98 ft (30 m) tall; both are heavily restored.

The towers, of uncertain date, were probably built with materials from the nearby Baths of Trajan, then attached to the now vanished castles of feudal families whose internecine battles bloodied medieval Rome (see p. 144). Today they are divided into apartments and offices.

At the bottom of the square take Via in Selci. Its name is old: *selci*, the typically Roman flint paving stones now so common, were something to boast about in olden days, when most roads were dirt. On a steep slope such as this, they were needed to keep the surface from sliding off.

In even remoter times the street had a different name. It was the age-old Clivus Suburranus, a main peripheral street of the ancient Roman Suburra district (see p. 154). The grim building on the left, with walled-up archways and windows, is from that time (5th century AD), with many medieval additions.

Some believe the building contained the older, original church of S. Martino. (We'll visit the present church shortly.)

At No. 82 is the portal of a 17th-century convent of Augustinian nuns, built over another convent several centuries older. It includes the small church of **S. Lucia in Selci**, to which the nuns admit visitors when they are not too busy. Go in. The nuns are cloistered, so you must ring the bell near the drum on the wall, the device through which they communicate with the outside. Leave an offering.

First documented in the 5th century when it served as a *diaconia*, or food distribution centre (p. 254), the church was rebuilt several times, most recently at the beginning of the 17th century by Maderno, who designed the portal and impressive wooden doors. Inside it bears the imprint of

Borromini, who restored it a few decades later. The beautiful stuccoes are 17th-century, as are most of the paintings, amongst which the most notable are the *Annunciation* over the main altar, by Anastasio Fontebuoni, and the *Martyrdom of St Lucy* by Lanfranco over the first altar on the right. Roughly opposite is a niche, or chapel, designed down to its minutest details by Borromini, one of his first works. He also designed the choir balcony over the entrance.

Return uphill to the square and keep to the right there. Past a pretty neo-baroque 19th-century building is the massive, ancient apse (9th-century) of **S. Martino ai Monti**, our next stop. To the left of the apse take Via Equizia, noting on the right the blocks of lava stone (tufa) from pre-2nd century BC structures used for the foundations of the church.

The façade of S. Martino ai Monti ('St Martin on the Hill'), and most of the present church, are from the 17th century, when the 9th-century structure was partly rebuilt. The church is even older, however. The current building replaced an early 6th-century building, which in turn replaced a semi-clandestine *ecclesia domestica* (see p. 227) established three centuries earlier by the priest Equitius, after whom the street beside the church is named. (Open: Monday-Saturday 07:00-12:00 and 16:00-19:00; Sunday 07:00-12:00.)

The beautiful columns are ancient Roman, probably from the 6th-century church. The interior is decorated by minor 17th-century painters. Most notable are frescoes by Gaspare Dughet, a pupil and brother-in-law of Poussin and, like him, a Roman by adoption. They run in rectangular and square panels on the aisle walls and depict events from the *Life of the Prophet Elias*. The airy, romantic rural views are amongst the best of their genre.

Admission is sometimes granted to the cellar (ask the sacristan). Below a 17th-century crypt are 3rd-century ruins, with fragments of the marble furnishings of the 9th-century church and faded frescoes with saints from the same period. The original function of these structures is unclear.

They were once a rather important building or buildings, originally two-storeys at least (there are remains of stairs), that opened onto the Clivus Suburranus. Are they from the original church (which some scholars place near the Augustinian convent, see p. 106)? Or from the house of the priest Equitius, as was long believed? The style suggests public rather than private architecture, so these may even be later annexes to the nearby 2nd century AD Baths of Trajan (p. 213).

Leave the church and go right, keeping right past the fork in the road. A five-minute walk along the street, Via delle Sette Sale, takes you through one of the most evocative areas of Rome's old *disabitato* (p. 28). A military base was built on the right in the late 19th century. (Several of these mysterious bases, mostly reserved for the armed services, a few for state intelligence, and marked *limite invalicabile* ('limit of prohibited area'), are to be found at various points throughout the city, some strategically located on hills.)

Immediately after it, as you pass No. 22A, note up on your left the medieval belfry and then the apse of the great church of **S. Pietro in Vincoli** ('St Peter in Chains'), our next stop.

The street ends at Piazza S. Pietro in Vincoli. On your left is the church façade, a harmonious late 15th-century porch topped by a bland super-structure of a century later.

The renaissance look of the church belies its much greater antiquity. Its history is similar to that of S. Martino ai Monti. It was built in the early 5th century to house the chains from St Peter's Palestinian imprisonment, which the dowager Empress Eudoxia claimed to have found in Jerusalem (on this kind of retrieval, see pp. 103, 358, 368, 417, 631). It replaced a lower-level church from a century earlier, which in turn had arisen over a 3rd-century *ecclesia domestica*. Possible traces of these earlier buildings were found in 1957 and can sometimes be visited.

The church structure is basically 5th century, despite changes and additions in the middle ages, renaissance, and 18th and 19th centuries. The door has a great 15th-century frame; bases of columns from an earlier porch peek out at the sides. (Open 07:00-12:30 and 15:30-18:00, or 19:00 in summer.)

Some of the 5th-century brickwork of the entrance wall is visible from the inside.

The splendid columns of the wide nave and triumphal arch before the apse are spolia from ancient Roman buildings. Together with an elegant 18th-century frescoed ceiling, they lend a certain grandeur to the interior. The subject of the ceiling fresco is the *Miracle of the Chains*. When St Peter's chains from Palestine were made to touch those that fettered the saint during his (undocumented) stay in Rome, the two sets joined together miraculously.

Openings recently pierced in the ceiling offer a view of huge ancient beams. Other beams, inscribed with the date 1465, can be seen to the right.

Going counter-clockwise, over the first altar is a *St Augustine* by the 17th-century master Guercino. Next is the tomb of a cardinal whose portrait is by Guercino's great contemporary Domenichino; then an altar with a copy of the *Liberation of St Peter* by Domenichino (the original is in the sacristy, see below); and next, another cardinal's tomb designed by Domenichino, who also made the portrait.

The church's treasure is in the transept: the *Tomb of Pope Julius II* with the statue of *Moses* by Michelangelo. Moses, on his return from Mount Sinai, grasps the Tablets of the Law and gazes balefully upon the Hebrew worshippers of the golden calf – a figure of inexpressible monumentality and power. (The horns are a traditional attribute of the image of Moses, derived from a mistranslation of the Hebrew word 'rays' – of wisdom – as 'horns' in the first Greek version of the Bible.) The two gentle figures beside Moses are the biblical *Rachel* and *Leah*, symbolising respectively the contemplative and the active life. The figures were carved by Michelangelo 36 years after the *Moses*, and were considered until recently – apart from the general design – the only other part of the monument by the master. They were completed and polished by assistants.

The remaining statuary was done by subcontractors, and Michelangelo was understandably unhappy with the results. The able sculptor Raffaele da Montelupo (better works by whom we'll see later) made the three standing figures on the upper level, which are all mediocre apart for the *Madonna* in the middle. It was said that the sculptor was ill at the time. Over the *Moses*, the reclining statue of *Julius II*, attributed to the even lesser sculptor Maso del Bosco, was labelled 'unforgivable' by the great Swiss critic Burckhardt. Yet one theory advanced in 1999 maintains that it is by Michelangelo himself. If this is so, then he must have been at his wits' end at this point in the long saga of the tomb.

In the 16th-century sacristy behind the monument are paintings by various 17th-century artists, including Domenichino and Pier Francesco Mola, and a delightful 15th-century altar built with medieval Cosmatesque pieces. The marble floor of the sacristy is said to come from the nearby Baths of Trajan.

Return to the transept. The apse, frescoed in the late 16th-century, has a 19th-century structure containing the legendary chains of St Peter in a shrine. Its bronze doors, with scenes from the *Life of St Peter* in relief, are a delicate 15th-century work. The chains are occasionally exhibited over the shrine. In a crypt under the altar is a 4th-century Christian sarcophagus, said in legend to contain relics of the biblical Maccabee brothers.

On the way out, in the aisle on your right are three altars. Note a 7th-century Byzantine-style mosaic of *St Sebastian* on the second one. At that time the martyr was depicted as a bearded old man, not as the winsome youth of later art. The third altar is surmounted by a *Deposition* by Cristoforo Pomarancio, a 16th-17th-century Tuscan painter, no relation of Niccolò (p. 94). Past it is a relief by the renowned 15th-century sculptor, Andrea Bregno, of *St Peter Holding His Chains*, alongside a cardinal whose tombstone is on the right. On the other side of the last pier is the simple, late 15th-century tomb of the Pollaiuolo brothers, famous Florentine sculptors and painters. Their remains were discovered inside during recent restorations. Over the tomb a very worn 15th-century fresco depicts a *Procession to Exorcise the Plague of 1476*. The mosaic of *St Sebastian* (see above), carried in the procession, was said to have ended the plague.

In the nearby Via Eudossiana is the slightly run-down cloister of the church, designed at the end of the 15th century by Giuliano da Sangallo, and currently part of the Rome University engineering department. If you wish to see it, take Via Eudossiana to the left, enter the university building and go through the glass doors on the left.

Return to Piazza S. Pietro in Vincoli. The whole area, of military importance because of its commanding height, was once heavily fortified. Across the square is another medieval tower.

Except for the 15th-century balcony, the tower dates from the 12th century and belonged to the feudal Margani family. (We'll see another Margani tower later, p. 532.)

Pass under the very low archway near No. 39 and start down the stairs. Note the gothic door to the left in the covered passage. The spooky alley is traditionally identified with the last part of the *Vicus Sceleratus*, scene of Tullia's heinous crime (p. 105). Past the passage, turn to the **Palazzo dei Margani** behind you.

Commonly but mistakenly called **Palazzo dei Borgia**, the complex, which today houses a world-renowned Art Restoration Institute, dates from different periods. On the left is a truncated medieval tower. The bulk of the palace is also medieval; note the black-and-white stonework characteristic of medieval fortifications. The upper middle part is 16th-century, with an elegant balconied window in the style of the northern

Michelangelo and assistants: The Julius tomb

architect Serlio. The top is a later addition.

Halfway down the stairs, on the left, is a square. At the far side are the monastery and church of **S. Francesco da Paola**, a Counter Reformation saint (16th-century) from the southern city of Paola.

The church, incorporating the tower which we saw on the upper square, is sometimes open. It is notable for its airy 17th- and 18th-century decorations, and for a fresco on the sacristy ceiling of the *Virgin Appearing to S. Francesco da Paola* by the distinguished 17th-century painter Sassoferrato.

Return to *Vicus Sceleratus* and go down to Via Cavour.

❧ MIDPOINT OF WALK ❧

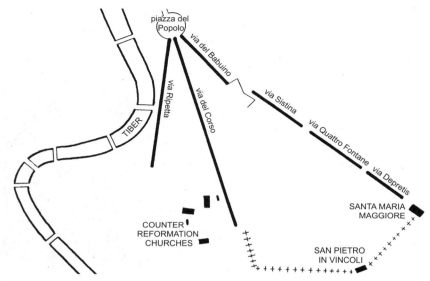

The route from S. Maria Maggiore to the Gesù

We now leave the neighbourhood for the Counter-Reformation churches to the west of the Corso, a 10 minute walk, or easily reached by public transport.

Cross Via Cavour, go down the hill to Via dei Fori Imperiali, where you turn right to Piazza Venezia. At the far end of the square take Via del Plebiscito left for two blocks to Piazza del Gesù on your left.

By bus, catch No. 84 near the end of Via Cavour, and it will take you to Piazza Venezia. From there, continue as above. Alternatively, go right on Via dei Fori Imperiali and take No. 87 at a stop on the right. It will take you to a traffic island in the middle of Via del Plebiscito. Cross to the kerb by whichever side looks less murderous, and walk in the same direction as the bus was going. Pass a four-way intersection, and walk one more block to Piazza del Gesù on your left.

BEFORE GOING

4. The Counter-Reformation churches: Il Gesù

The Walk leaves the hilly former *disabitato* area of the Esquiline Hill to descend directly to a low-lying area near the Corso on the fringes of the Tiber Bend. It lies between the medieval-renaissance district near the river (p. 28), and the post-renaissance settlements we have explored so far. This was the home base of two religious orders, the Jesuits and the Dominicans, which competed ferociously to be the standard-bearers of the Counter-Reformation. There has never been any love lost between them, and the situation is not so different today. Furthermore the Jesuits, a fiercely independent order, were often suspected of conspiratorial schemes and dictatorial ambitions by all their brethren of a different cassock.

First we'll visit the original Jesuit headquarters. The order was founded by a young Spanish nobleman, Iñigo de Loyola (later St Ignatius) soon after the Protestant revolution and had a quasi-military character. Drilled into perfect discipline and obedience, it was called a 'company' and its head a 'general'. Its goal was to combat the new heresy, Protestantism, with the weapons of intellect, politics and diplomacy, in a war that could be open or covert as needed. Once papally approved, the order flourished, in part thanks to the support of the many noble families with whom its founder had connections. It gave the church no fewer than six saints in rapid succession: its founder St Ignatius, his companion St Francis Xavier, his young disciple St Aloysius Gonzaga and his followers St Francis Borgia, St Robert Bellarmine and St John Berchmans. The suspicion of celestial favoritism did not endear the Jesuits to the other orders. They attracted criticism for other reasons, too. Initially the order adhered to traditional precepts of priestly austerity, but later, as it slipped more and more out of its founder's control it veered toward worldliness and ostentation, reflected artistically in the flamboyant decoration of their churches. But it was their meddling in political and diplomatic affairs that most compromised them, so much so that during the Enlightenment the order was suppressed in several countries,

St. Ignatius

and finally abolished by the Pope. With the post-Napoleonic reaction spreading all over Europe after 1815, however, those who remembered the Jesuits for their good educational work and for their devotion to dangerous missionary work in many parts of the world got the order reinstated.

The historic Jesuit headquarters consist of Il Gesù (the Church of Jesus) and an adjoining administrative building. Today, the order also has much larger offices elsewhere. The church exterior is solemn; the interior was originally intended to be as sober, but as the 17th century progressed, a style of architectural, colouristic and ornamental grandiloquence emerged that was meant to smother any possible doubt about the superiority of Roman Catholicism with an onslaught of devotional and æsthetic emotionalism. In this way, art served St Ignatius' multifaceted offensive. The Gesù is famous for its spectacular frescoed ceilings and fantastically ornate chapels. One, containing the body of St Ignatius, is covered in gold, silver and lapis lazuli, including a lapis lazuli globe alleged to be the world's biggest piece of this semi-precious stone. 'A marvellous work, unique and without parallel in its kind,' enthused the French lawyer Charles de Brosses, one of the most astute 18th-century visitors to Rome (p. 74).

The administrative building, of the same period as the church, contains the rooms where St Ignatius lived and where he died in 1556.

In bygone times, the area in front of the Jesuit headquarters was said to be Rome's windiest. One of the less malicious jokes spread by the Jesuits' enemies in the 18th and 19th centuries is that the Devil and the Wind were taking a walk together. When they came in front of the Gesù, the Devil said to the Wind: 'Wait here a minute, please. I have something to do in there.' He went in, but never came out, and to this day the Wind waits outside for the Devil to leave the Jesuit sanctuary.

ON THE SPOT

4. The Counter-Reformation churches: Il Gesù

Piazza del Gesù is dominated by **Il Gesù**, or Church of Jesus, the late l6th-century mother church of St Ignatius and his Jesuit order, whose offices were initially housed in the building next door. The façade, by Giacomo Della Porta in collaboration with Vignola, was to be the prototype for hundreds of Jesuit churches all over the world. (Open 06:00-12:30 and 16:00-19:15.)

The grandiose, theatrical style of the high baroque appears in full force in the interior, where the most famous decoration is the frescoed nave ceiling. This is the masterpiece of the 17th-century painter Baciccia, a close friend and pupil of Bernini. It is of exuberant, almost explosive power, showing the *Triumph of the Name of Jesus* (represented inside the halo by the monogram I.H.S., the first three letters of Jesus' name in Greek, and also the Jesuits' emblem). A tour de force of modelling and perspective, with its mixed torrents of human and heavenly figures rising toward infinite bliss or plummeting to damnation, it is one of the happiest results of the Jesuit effort to make mystic truths immediate and tangible.

Most of the chapels too are meant as an exercise in pomp and magnificence, with multi-coloured marble, semi-precious stonework, and conspicuous paintings and sculptures. A few highlights are described here.

The third chapel on the left has a 16th-century *Holy Trinity* over the altar by the Venetian painter Francesco Bassano. The chapel opposite (third from the right) is entirely decorated by Federico Zuccaro (also 16th-century).

Note in particular the glorious chapels at both ends of the transept. The one on the right is dedicated to St Francis Xavier, St Ignatius' companion. It is by Pietro da Cortona, one of the greatest architects and painters of the 17th century.

In the left transept is the celebrated chapel of St Ignatius, designed by the Jesuit lay brother Andrea Pozzo (late 17th-century), whose fantastic frescoes in other Jesuit buildings we'll see shortly. The columns are covered with lapis lazuli; the head of the statue of St Ignatius is silver (originally the whole statue was silver, but a pope had to melt it down to pay war reparations imposed on the papal armies by Napoleon). The assorted statuary groups by various minor sculptors are battle cries of the Counter-Reformation crusade. At the lower left of the altar is *Faith Confronting Idolatry*; at the lower right, *Religion Striking down Heresy*, in which hideous figures represent Protestantism.

Before leaving the church, on the wall to the left of the main altar note Bernini's marble bust of the cardinal-saint Robert Bellarmine, the Jesuit theologian who started heresy proceedings against Galileo (see p. 116).

Next to the church, in the original **Jesuit Headquarters**, are the rooms where St Ignatius lived and died. (Open 09:30-12:30.)

The modest apartment upstairs consists of a waiting room, a bedroom-study, a private chapel (where St Ignatius died) and a service room. Mementos include a piece of his vest, his cloak and a pair of his shoes. Outside the rooms is a corridor decorated more than a century after his death by the same artist, Andrea Pozzo, who designed the St Ignatius chapel in the adjoining church. Pozzo, a supreme master of perspective, was known throughout Europe for his technical virtuosity, which he elaborated in a famous treatise. The frescoes here, a tribute to the saint, use every trick of perspective to give the little hallway a feeling of immensity, filled with complex architectural and human forms. Walls and ceiling must be seen from a marble rose inlaid in the centre of the floor. If you move from there, you see that seemingly straight lines are curved, and vice versa, as lines and figures collapse into optical distortion.

Back in the square, No. 46 is an 18th-century palace by Ferdinando Fuga, famous as the seat of the main Italian party for decades after the Second World War, the Christian Democrats. Now a

Contemporary architectural print showing the façade and internal structure of the Gesù

FACIES EXTERNA CVM PROSPECTV INTERIORIS TEMPLI AB ALEXANDRO
CARDINALI FARNESIO SOC. IESV ÆDIFICATI

PARS EXTERIOR Iacobo de la Porta Architecto . PARS INTERIOR Iacobo Baroño à Viniola Architecto .

Scala palmorum.

20

small minority, they are called the Popular Party.

Across Via del Plebiscito, Piazza del Gesù is flanked by the rich façade of the 17th-century Palazzo Altieri (No. 49), built by the Roman brother architects, Giovan Antonio and Mattia de' Rossi. The palace, once owned by a princely family that died out in 1955, is rented out to commercial firms that sometimes allow visits to the interesting frescoes.

Cross the square and go round the left-hand corner of the palace into Via del Gesù. At No. 85 on your right is a beautiful renaissance doorway. On your left take the wide Via della Pigna ('of the Pine Cone'), which opens into a small square of the same name.

The pine-cone emblem of the Rione

The name 'pine cone' designates the entire neighbourhood. It comes from a giant pine cone sculpture, which probably decorated an ancient Roman temple to the Egyptian goddess Isis near here, part of one of the oriental cults popular in imperial Rome. You'll find several traces of the temple in your walks, and the cone itself in the Vatican (p. 317), where it has been for the last twelve centuries.

In the square is **S. Giovanni della Pigna** ('St John of the Pine Cone'), a church that existed in the 10th century but was rebuilt in the 17th. It is occasionally open.

Inside, note three tombstones of the baronial Porcari family that sponsored the church. The oldest dates from 1282. They are on the walls by

the entrance, two on the left and one on the right.

It was once common for a church to enjoy a close link with a noble family that would support it and in exchange have its own chapels and bury its dead there. These 'family chapels' existed until 1850 (see p. 406).

Outside, on the left wall of the church, is an 18th-century street shrine (see p. 66) with a lovely fresco. Continue into the adjacent Vicolo delle Ceste.

At No. 25, behind the first door (and its renaissance frame) to the left, are the remains of the Porcari House, birthplace of Stefano Porcari, a baron who in 1453 plotted to kill the pope and establish a republic. He was caught and hanged together with nine conspirators (see p. 386).

The name Porcari ('Swineherds') probably alludes to very humble origins in an obscure past. The Porcari, however, like many aristocratic renaissance families (pp. 517, 527), claimed a fictitious ancient Roman lineage – in this case from the statesman Cato the Censor, whose family name, Porcius, also came from the Latin for 'pig'. The Porcari coat-of-arms, showing a pig, is over the doorway. Under it, Stefano's failed plot is sympathetically described in a tablet from 1871 – right after the overthrow of papal rule, a period of great anti-clerical feeling. A street near the Vatican was renamed 'Stefano Porcari' around this time.

Continue along Vicolo delle Ceste ('of the Baskets') and turn right into Via dei Cestari ('of the Basketmakers'), named long ago after the many basket-weavers who once had their workshops here. Today the many shops in this and nearby streets specialise, instead, in clerical attire and religious articles. Many have been here a century or more, sometimes managed by the same family.

At the end of the block, the shop in front of you, at No. 34 Via S. Chiara, belongs to the Gammarelli family, tailors to the pope since 1792. The last time we entered they were busy on a chasuble and pyjamas for John Paul II.

A few more steps in the same direction take you to Piazza della Minerva.

BEFORE GOING

5. S. Maria sopra Minerva

A short way from the Jesuit headquarters is the main church of the rival Dominican order, S. Maria sopra Minerva –'Over [the Temple of] Minerva' – with its adjoining monastery.

The Dominicans, a much older order than the Jesuits, are famous for their preachers and learning, and boast such figures as St Thomas Aquinas. They clung to a stern and simple way of life even throughout the neo-pagan excesses of the renaissance. No less an ascetic than Savonarola (p. 46) was amongst their preachers. In Spain, the pitiless Inquisition, zealous defender of the true faith, was always headed by a Dominican. They could, and did, take an 'I-told-you-so' stance when the upheaval of the Reformation arrived, and quickly placed themselves at the forefront of the ensuing struggle. They did so by managing to have the Inquisition re-established in Rome, though the Vatican had disavowed it after the Spanish atrocities committed under Cardinal Torquemada, which included the expulsion and massacre of Jews. The Dominicans once again led the Inquisition offensive, their mandate confirmed by the Council of Trent (1563) where key anti-Protestant strategies were planned.

Rivalry soon flared up between the two Counter-Reformation orders, the newly-arrived Jesuits and the long-established Dominicans. The Jesuits fought subtly, through connections and propaganda; the Dominicans employed fiery preaching and stubborn dogma. Some Dominicans considered the Jesuits as diabolical as their common enemy, the Protestants, for the Jesuits, with their accent on pragmatism, did not always observe their founder's rules of chastity and poverty. The Dominicans probably abetted the movement that led to the 18th century disbanding of the Jesuit order, which was then revived in the 19th. (The Jesuits returned the hostility of their

S. Maria sopra Minerva in the 17th century; engraving by Falda

colleagues by stressing their excessive dogmatism and ferocious intransigeance, creating for them the punning sobriquet *Domini Canes*, 'Bloodhounds of the Lord.')

The Dominican headquarters comprise the monastery and church, whose name comes from its location near the former ruins of the ancient Temple of Minerva.

The church is much older than that of the Jesuits, and its treasures, of a more varied kind, span a longer period. Much like its owners, it is sombre both inside and out. Moreover, it is Rome's only genuine example of gothic architecture. Its links to the Inquisition appear in various ways. It contains the tomb of another Cardinal Torquemada – uncle of the notorious cleric – and that of Pope Paul IV Carafa, a zealot and antisemite of whom Stendhal wrote: 'This old Neapolitan seriously believed he would be eternally damned if he did not yield to the dark urges that commanded him to persecute.'

A major backer of the Inquisition, this 16th-century pontiff ordered the Jews of Rome into a ghetto for the first time. (We visit the neighbourhood in the second Renaissance Rome Walk.) He was so hated that at his death the people beheaded his statue and threw it in the river, where it was retrieved much later (p. 393). They also tried to storm S. Maria sopra Minerva and its monastery, seat of the Inquisition. The Italian government confiscated the Dominican monastery, along with many others, after annexing the city in 1870, but the friars still occupy some rooms.

The Inquisition held its trials and imprisoned some of its most famous victims in the building. Here, in 1600, it sentenced Giordano Bruno, the great philosopher (himself a defrocked Dominican) who was the first to realise that the stars were other suns, to burn at the stake (we visit the execution place in the first Renaissance Rome Walk). It condemned the Spanish mystic Miguel Molinos to life imprisonment for his gentle spiritual doctrine of Quietism. And most famously, it tried Galileo Galilei and forced him to recant his view that the earth moved around the sun. Galileo is said to have mumbled 'e pur si muove' ('and yet it moves') after his recantation, but this seems to be mere legend.

ON THE SPOT

5. S. Maria sopra Minerva

In the middle of Piazza della Minerva is the delightful Elephant of the Minerva, which Romans affectionately call *il pulcino della Minerva*, the 'chick of the Minerva'. Bernini designed it in the 17th century to bear an Egyptian obelisk found nearby, where a temple to Isis once rose (see pp. 114, 121); the carving, however, is by assistants. Elaborating on the concept that Minerva is the goddess of wisdom, a Latin inscription on the base says that 'the strongest of beasts' can 'support in its robust mind a solid wisdom'; it was dedicated to the god of wisdom by Pope Alexander VII (the last of Bernini's great papal patrons and one who loved writing dedica-tions, see p. 44). Piazza della Minerva itself was named after another old temple nearby, dedicated to the Roman goddess. In the 8th century a church built over the ruins of the temple was called **S. Maria sopra Minerva** ('over Minerva'). Five centuries later it collapsed and was rebuilt a short distance from the original site, while still keeping its name.

Dominating the square, the 13th-century rendered façade, redone in the 15th century, has a mystically bare, almost gaunt look, enlivened only by three marble doors.

On the right side of the façade are touching mementos of the Tiber floods that for many centuries were the scourge of Roman life, especially in low-lying districts such as this one (p. 140, 236). Marble tablets placed on the wall for over four centuries indicate the level reached by each flood from 1422 to 1870, after which the Tiber was embanked. Photographs from the last flood show people boating in the area. The record flood height was in 1598, as the uppermost tablet says, despite the 'cursing of the whirlpools by the pontiff'. The flood killed hundreds and forced a postponement of the famous trial of Beatrice Cenci (pp. 517-525).

A renaissance restoration wiped out the gothic style of the church on the outside, but inside it is visible in the ogival arches and cross-vaulted ceilings, though it is not readily apparent because of a drastic mid-19th century restoration. The church was probably designed by Dominican friars from Florence and resembles the Dominican church of S. Maria Novella there. The key feature is the width of the nave, essential for preaching.

The church is open: 07:00-12:00 and 16:00-19:00. Start from the right. The fifth chapel, midway up the aisle, has a pleasant early 16th-century painting by Antoniazzo Romano. It shows Cardinal Giovanni Torquemada – uncle of the dreaded chief of the Spanish Inquisition – introducing to the Virgin a group of girls who had received a dowry from the church.

Two chapels further along, a cenotaph to a Dominican bishop (right wall) by Andrea Bregno features a fresco by the great 15th-century master, Melozzo da Forlì, whose marvellous music-making angels grace the Vatican museum (p. 314). Two musical angels appear in this fresco too, albeit less impressive.

The next wide opening in the aisle – the right arm of the transept – is the famous **Carafa Chapel**, decorated by Filippino Lippi, another Florentine painter invited to Rome at the end of the 15th century. Lippi – the son of another famous painter and ex-priest, Filippo Lippi, and a nun he had abducted from a convent – has left us works of great elegance and tender feeling. His painting of the *Annunciation* over the altar and his frescoes – the *Assumption* (centre wall), episodes in the *Life of St Thomas* and *St Thomas Confounding the Heretics* (lower right wall) – are

amongst his masterpieces. In the latter fresco, the two boys on the right are two cousins of the great Florentine Medici family, who became popes in the next century, Leo X and Clement VII. Both are entombed in the church, as you'll see shortly (Lippi must have had prophetic gifts).

On the left wall is the tomb of Pope Paul IV (of the Carafa family, patron of the chapel), a man so redoubtable, it was said, that even the great Spanish general, the Duke of Alba, who feared no one, quaked before him. Some of the awesomeness is clear from the statue by the 16th-century sculptor Giacomo Cassignola. Before leaving the chapel note the marvellous renaissance archway and Cosmatesque floor.

The 'chick of the Minerva'

117

On the upper left wall of the chapel is the late 13th-century tomb of a bishop, a signed work by Giovanni Cosma.

Overhead on the left, note the spectacular baroque organ (with a matching section on the other side of the transept). Move along the transept to the main altar. The coffin under the altar contains the body of St Catherine of Siena, patron saint of Italy, a great 14th-century mystic who was instrumental in bringing the popes back to Rome from their voluntary exile in Avignon (see p. 300). She spent the last part of her life in a convent nearby (p. 241). The walls and floor of the room where she died were later brought to the church and rebuilt near the sacristy.

Behind the altar, on the walls of the presbytery, are the tombs of the two Medici popes portrayed as teenagers in the Carafa Chapel. On the right rests the unfortunate Clement VII, whose reign was embittered by the Sack of Rome (p. 381) and by England's withdrawal from the Roman Church under Henry VIII. The statue is by Nanni di Baccio Bigio. On the left is Leo X, son of the 'magnificent' Lorenzo de' Medici, destined to the papacy from the cradle (he was a cardinal at 17). He devoted his reign to pleasure and the patronage of artists, first among them Raphael. His statue is by a minor 16th-century sculptor.

Outside the presbytery, standing against the pier to the left of the main altar, is the *Redeemer* by Michelangelo. Finished, retouched and polished by minor sculptors, there is something awkward about it, not to mention the ludicrous bronze loincloth added by scandal-fearing friars. Yet it retains much of the physical power and psychological depth that only Michelangelo knew how to instill in the human figure.

Near the left wall of the next chapel to the left, a 15th-century tombstone on the floor covers the remains of the beatified Fra Angelico, the famous painter and Dominican friar of whom the painter-biographer Vasari wrote that 'he never painted a crucifix without tears in his eyes.' (For the chapel frescoed by him in the Vatican palace, see p. 335.)

Cross the transept on this side. The transept ends in a large chapel rebuilt in the 18th century by the Neapolitan architect Filippo Raguzzini. It contains the tomb and funerary monument to Benedict XIII, a pope who tried unsuccessfully to curb the luxurious life-style of the cardinals and the worldliness of the priests, which had become widespread. More successfully, he also initiated campaigns to restore Rome's ancient churches. The sensitive statue is by Pietro Bracci. Leave the chapel. On the right is the tomb of Andrea Bregno, the 15th-century sculptor, many of whose works we have already seen.

Now walk down the aisle, stopping by the second pier on the left to see another of the famous sculptural portraits of women saints by Bernini, the relief of the Venerable Maria Raggi. At the very end of the aisle, on the right-hand wall, are two 15th-century tombs, one above the other. The lower one is a masterpiece by Mino da Fiesole, a delicate Tuscan sculptor of the early renaissance.

Before you leave, gaze at the 19th-century ceiling. The cavernous attics above were used by the Dominican friars to hide Jews, escaped Allied prisoners of war and Italian dissidents during the Nazi occupation of Rome. Supplies were sent up by rope and basket at night.

Outside the church, at No. 42 immediately to the right, is the late l6th-century cloister, covered with worn frescoes painted in 1602 by minor artists.

Noteworthy here, at the end of the side in front of you, are the tombs of two cardinals, the one on the left attributed to Mino da Fiesole. All around are the walls of the Dominican convent where Galileo and others were tried and asked to recant their views.

BEFORE GOING

6. S. Ignazio, the Collegio Romano and the Caravita Oratory

Across the street from the Dominican headquarters is another Jesuit stronghold, the church of S. Ignazio (St Ignatius), which is within a great Jesuit academy, the Collegio Romano (Roman College).

Edification and Education. The church was built about half a century after the Gesù (pp. 110-112), but in the same style; the interior is also somewhat similar, as it was responding to the same pressures of anti-Reformation propaganda. Its fame comes from the tremendous ceiling frescoes by the Jesuit lay brother Andrea Pozzo (p. 112), especially one that simulates the interior of the dome on a flat surface. The ingenious artist achieved the illusionistic feat after plans to build a real dome were scrapped for lack of funds. Like the Gesù, S. Ignazio has a wealth of sumptuous chapels. One contains the remains of the order's youngest saint, St Aloysius Gonzaga, in a precious lapis lazuli urn.

A nobleman like S. Ignazio, indeed the scion of one of Italy's oldest and most illustrious families, Aloysius renounced his property and title of marquis at the age of 17 to be a simple soldier in the Company of Jesus. He lived in two rooms of the building that encloses the church, and died at 24 while helping plague victims. He was so handsome, it is said that every girl in Rome was secretly in love with him and wept at his demise. His rooms may be reached through the church. (There is a full-length, life-size portrait of him by his contemporary, the great Guercino, in New York's Metropolitan Museum.)

The solemn façade of the Collegio Roman, now Liceo Visconti, in the 19th century; engraving by Paul Letarouilly

The large building that encloses the church, its solemn façade facing the opposite side, also originally belonged to the Jesuits. It was built in the late 16th century – four decades before the church – as a school, the Collegio Romano, intended to mould the young élite to fill the upper echelons and cadres of the multifaceted Counter-Reformation campaign. The Jesuits have always set great store by education and the school was the first of a chain that would include hundreds of schools and universities worldwide, some of them famous, such as Fordham University in New York and Georgetown University in Washington. The Collegio Romano has produced important scientists, scholars, and political and religious leaders, including eight popes. When the Italian state annexed Rome in 1870, it took over the school. For a few decades it continued to maintain the highest standards, boasting famous teachers, such as the great poet Carducci, and famous alumni. It then declined, and is now an ordinary high school.

Piety and Pain. One way in which the Dominicans and Jesuits competed for primacy was by outdoing each other in pious zeal. A remarkable token of this is to be found in Via del Caravita, a street running from S. Ignazio to the Corso. It is a little Jesuit church, technically an oratory, founded in the 17th century as a base for charitable activities, but also used for a renewed, and indeed extraordinary, ritual of penance: self-flagellation. In keeping with their astute and pragmatic spirit, however, the Jesuits did not so much practice this edifying ritual as exhort others to do so. The oratory is not much to see, so you won't miss much if you find it closed, as it usually is. Yet it is worth remembering for the bizarre ceremony that unfolded there every Friday at Vespers, until about 1870. A 19th-century traveller, Lord Broughton, described it thus:

> The pious whipping is preceded by a short exhortation, during which a bell rings, and strings of knotted whipcord are distributed quietly among the audience. On a second bell the candles are extinguished – a loud voice issues from the altar, which pours forth an exhortation to think of unconfessed, or unrepented, or unforgiven crimes … while the audience strip off their garments, the tone of the preacher is raised more loudly at each word, and he vehemently concludes: 'Show, then, your penitence – show your sense of Christ's sacrifice – show it with the whip.' The scourging begins in the darkness, the tumultuous sound of blows reaches you from every direction while the words 'Blessed Virgin Mary, pray for us' burst out at intervals. The flagellation continues fifteen minutes.

Rome's great 19th-century poet, Gioacchino Belli, made fun of these fanatics in his poetry. In one marvellous sonnet, two young lovers, who have just met on the Corso, look for a place to relieve their sudden amorous urges.

Je curze incontro a braccia uperte: "Oh Ghita!	'I ran to her with open arms: "Oh, Ghita!
Proprio me n'annerebbe fantasia!" Dice: Ma indove?"	Wouldn't it be great!" "But where?" she said…

They sneak into the oratory and end up making love in a confessional as soon as the candles are put out for the ritual.

ON THE SPOT

6. S. Ignazio, the Collegio Romano and the Caravita Oratory

Return to the front of S. Maria sopra Minerva, turn left along the side of the church (Via S. Caterina da Siena) and continue into Via Pie' di Marmo ('of the Marble Foot'), named after a colossal foot found in the ruins of the Temple of Isis (see p. 114). The ruin of the temple was razed in the 16th century, but in a shop at No. 24A you can still see vestiges of an arch (called Arco di Camilliano in the middle ages) which was the temple entrance.

At the end of the street, on the right, you'll see the marble foot on a pedestal. We are here at the corner of Via S. Stefano del Cacco ('St Stephen of the Macaque'), so called after a little church of the same name which is up the street. The church name is another age-old reminder of the vanished temple, since 'macaque' must be a reference to the statue of a monkey, a sacred animal in ancient Egypt, that belonged to the temple. The statue no longer exists.

If you wish to visit the little church – unexceptional on the outside and only open on Sundays at 11:00 – it's a bit further along Via S. Stefano del Cacco on the right. It dates from the 11th century

Plan of the Piazza S. Ignazio, showing Raguzzini's unique layout

but was redone in the 17th.

The church has beautiful columns and minor paintings showily arranged in the apse. Connected to it is a Benedictine monastery, sometimes open to visitors.

The intersection of Via Pie' di Marmo and Via Stefano del Cacco is near the edge of Piazza del Collegio Romano, dominated on the left by the powerful late 16th-century façade of the former Jesuit school, now a public high school. We'll see more of this building shortly.

Without entering the square, turn left into Via S. Ignazio, flanked on the right by the great bulk of the Jesuit buildings and to the left by the former Dominican headquarters (curiously, a bridge joins the seats of the rival orders). The street ends in **Piazza S. Ignazio**. In front of you are graceful 18th-century buildings, so evocative of rococo chests of drawers that they were nicknamed the *bureaux*; hence the name of an adjoining street, Via dei Burrò. (Another theory, however, is that the street name comes from the *bureaux*, or offices, of the French occupiers of Napoleon's time.) These buildings and the layout of the square are the work of the Neapolitan architect Filippo Raguzzini. To your immediate right is the façade of the second of the historic Jesuit churches, **S. Ignazio**.

The façade, in the 'Jesuit style' established half a century earlier with the Gesù, was designed in 1626 by the illustrious Jesuit mathematician, Father Orazio Grassi, who also planned the interior with Carlo Maderno.

A peculiar aspect of this beautiful church is its subtle connection with the world of science, culture and education, where the Jesuits have always excelled. Besides Grassi, the other great figure associated with the church is Andrea Pozzo, the painter who in the late 17th century was responsible for the fantastic *trompe-l'oeil* ceiling perspectives. He was the tenured professor of geometry and perspective in the adjoining Collegio Romano, and used his frescoes in the church as a permanent workshop for his pupils. His students may actually have painted much of the famed ceiling under his direction. (Open 08:00-12:30 and 16:00-19:15.)

The great vault fresco of the *Entry of St Ignatius into Paradise* and the clever false dome are best seen by standing on a yellow disc in the middle of the nave. As with the Gesù, it could be said that the beauty of S. Ignazio is even more in the general effect of its spectacular decorations than in any specific work of art. Note particularly, however, the two altars designed by Pozzo at either end of the transept, topped with splendid high-reliefs by other artists. The relief on the right depicts *St Aloysius Gonzaga*, and was carved in the late 17th century by the French artist Pierre Legros. Under the altar is a lapis lazuli urn with the saint's remains. The left altar, crowned by an 18th-century *Annunciation*, contains an urn with the remains of another Jesuit saint, the Flemish St John Berchmans, who died at the age of 22 in the service of the order and is the patron saint of altar boys.

The link between the church and the Jesuit world of science is clearly felt when you visit the adjoining college, where St Aloysius Gonzaga lived and died. The sacristan can lead you to it through a passage from inside the church and there, besides the saint's rooms and memorabilia, you'll see the

Andrea Pozzo's false dome, from his textbook

students' old recreation rooms, the rooms of other Jesuit saints and grandees and the great courtyard.

The courtyard has an old solar clock (to the left of the regular clock). The priests say Galileo installed it during one of his frequent visits to his friends and rivals, the Jesuit professors. Across the courtyard rises the dome of an observatory where one of the college's 19th-century professors, the world-renowned astronomer Father Angelo Secchi, studied Mars and the light spectra of the stars.

Leave the church and turn right into Via del Caravita, where you'll pass the Caravita Oratory on the right after an intersection. It is so called after the corrupted name of a Jesuit father, Pietro Gravita, who founded it in the 17th century.

The inside, occasionally open, is mainly notable for a *Holy Trinity with St Francis Xavier* over the altar by the distinguished 18th-century painter Sebastiano Conca. Above it is a fresco of *Our Lady of Compassion* attributed to the great 15th-century artist, Baldassarre Peruzzi. Commissioned for a different church, detached in fragments and reconstructed here, it has been heavily restored. Via del Caravita leads to the Corso.

BEFORE GOING

7. The Corso in modern times

The straight, mile-long road now called Via del Corso, starting from Piazza del Popolo, is the main link between Rome's ancient core and the north. Its role and importance in early antiquity will be discussed below in the section on Ancient Rome (pp. 226-227).

In the middle ages it reverted to a mainly rural state, but around the 15th century it was renewed for several reasons. One was the new importance of a commercial river harbour near its Piazza del Popolo end (p. 541). Another was a papal decree allowing those who promised to build large palaces on the street to expropriate land and small houses. A third was the gradual transfer, ordered by the pope in 1466, of all carnival festivities from other neighbourhoods to the street – including the hugely popular races, which give the street its present name, Il Corso ('the Race Course').

The racing tradition dates back to the famous chariot competitions of classical times. They were abandoned in the depth of the middle ages, but later modestly revived as foot races and races between animals, such as horses, asses, cows and water buffaloes.

Detailed chronicles of these events from the renaissance show that the foot races were organised much as they are today: people ran in separate age groups and the winners received prizes, usually in the form of pieces of cloth.

Here are excerpts from the 1487 diary of Johann Burchard, the pope's master of ceremonies (see p. 48):

> *Sunday, Feb.18.* After dinner, around the 20th hour [i.e. mid-afternoon] Jews aged 20 and under raced for a prize of red cloth... The winner was a Spanish Jew who, though he was first to touch the prize, was actually preceded by another contestant who tripped over a horse right at the finish line and fell. Thus the race had to be repeated. Later today men 50 and over ran for a similar prize. A German won.
>
> *Monday, Feb. 19.* The very reverend Cardinal Colonna [see p. 130 and p. 190] racing with three other cardinals, all of them masked, had a bad fall along with his horse.
>
> *Tuesday, Feb. 20.* Twenty- to thirty-year-old young men raced for a prize of baby blue satin. A certain Vignaro, formerly groom to Signor Virginio Orsini, won. On the same day boys under 15 ran, but owing to a false start the race had to be run again. The 4-yard length of baby blue satin was awarded to Federico de Larica [a member of the large Spanish community], but only after much squabbling, because the son of the watchman of the Castle of the Holy Angel tied for first ... Many were injured.
>
> *Wednesday, Feb. 21.* Today there was a donkey race ... The prize was a 4-yard length of blue cloth ... The donkey of a grocer from Via del Paradiso won.
>
> *Sunday, Feb. 25.* The race of riderless horses took place. The prize, decorated with gold brocade, was won by a horse of the personal chamberlain of His Holiness the Pope ... A race whose prize was a length of purple velvet was won by the mare of Lodovico Mattei, a Roman. At the end of the day the killing of the bulls took place, during which several persons were wounded and a few died.

The Corso races in the 19th century; engraving after H. Regnault

With the rise of anti-semitism after the Counter-Reformation, male Jews, both young and old, were forced to run at carnivals as objects of ridicule, often wearing only loincloths. This custom was abolished in the late 17th century, but until the mid-19th century only on condition that the Jews pay for one of the most popular animal races, that of the riderless horses.

In this race, horses were prodded with goads and firecrackers all along the Corso, starting at Piazza del Popolo. As the only Corso race to survive until modern times, it was the climax of the world-famous Roman Carnival, Europe's greatest festival in the 18th and 19th centuries. Countless paintings, books and even musical pieces, such as Berlioz's *Roman Carnival Overture*, describe the carnival. Goethe lived on the Corso (p. 51) in the late 18th century and spent much time at his window, as a famous drawing by his painter friend Tischbein shows. In his diary, Goethe observed the unique spirit of the carnival and its resemblance to the ancient Roman Saturnalia feast (p. 161):

> On a foreigner who sees it for the first time, the Roman Carnival cannot make an altogether agreeable impression: it will neither please his eye nor appeal to his emotions ... There are no fireworks, no great lights, no brilliant parades. All that happens is that, at a signal, everyone has leave to act as mad and foolish as he likes, and almost everything, except fisticuffs and stabbing, is allowed. The difference between the social orders seems abolished; everyone accosts everyone else, all good-naturedly accept

whatever happens to them, and the insolence and licence of the feast is balanced only by the universal good mood ... It is not really a festival given for the people but one the people give themselves ... The state contributes next to nothing. The merry-go-round revolves automatically and the police regulate it very leniently.

The festive spirit of the Corso conditioned its very architecture: balconies sprang up all around for confetti-tossing and race-watching. Balconies were often rented like theatre boxes, outright or by the seat ('luoghi, luoghi' – 'places' – cried scalpers in the streets). 'If year after year, and season after season, it had rained balconies, hailed balconies, snowed balconies, blown balconies, they could scarcely have come into existence in a more disorderly manner,' wrote Charles Dickens. Today they have mostly vanished, and the festivities ended in 1896 because of frequent accidents. Yet the Corso remains the first street of Rome thanks to its key role in communication across the city, its many shops and the panache of its palaces. Moreover, it is the first choice for the sunset promenade, an ancient Italian custom from big cities to tiny villages. Sadly, the street, which Stendhal called 'the most beautiful in the universe' has declined sharply recently, especially towards the Piazza del Popolo end, where cheap stores have replaced elegant shops.

ON THE SPOT

7. The Corso in modern times

At the crossing you are about 300 yards from the end of the Corso. Off to the left is Piazza del Popolo, with its familiar obelisk. On the right the Corso ends in the area covered by the next Walk, the most ancient core of Rome. The giant colonnaded monument you see there, however, has nothing to do with ancient Rome; it is a much-criticised early 20th-century patriotic memorial (p. 535). The antiquities lie behind it.

Of the many palaces along the Corso, mostly 16th to 18th century, one is just across the street, **Palazzo Sciarra**, built in the 16th and 17th century for the Sciarra branch of the Colonna family (see below, pp. 189, 190). It is by Flaminio Ponzio, a renaissance architect whose work foreshadows the baroque; note the imposing doorway. The palace is now owned by a bank.

Cross the Corso and turn around. Opposite, on the right (corner of Via del Caravita) is another palace owned by the same bank; it is ancient, but was rebuilt in the mid-19th century in a renaissance style.

Go a few steps along the last stretch of the Corso to a widening called Piazza S. Marcello. In front of you is another palace, this one by Alessandro Specchi (18th-century), also currently a bank – they all have headquarters on the Corso. The palace was once famed as the centre of French diplomatic, cultural and social life in Rome.

It was the residence of Cardinal de Bernis – ambassador of both Louis XV and Louis XVI to the Holy See, a key figure in 18th-century politics, and the hero of many amorous exploits shared with his friend Casanova (p. 46). During the French Revolution, the palace was refuge to several members of the French royal family. Later it was the residence of the great French writer Chateaubriand, ambassador to Rome (p. 56).

Here the Corso is dominated by the concave,

The Corso, and the Palazzo Sciarra

EXTERIOR FACIES ECCLESIÆ S.ⁱMARCELLI PP. SERVITARVM, AD VIAM CVRSVS, AB ILL.ᵐᵒ.ᵉᵗ
R̃E.D.MARCO ANTONIO BONCOMPAGNIO DE CATALLIS VTRIVSQVE SIGNATVRÆ REFERENDARIO ᴇxᴛʀᴠᴇᴛᴀ Àᴺⁿ

Façade of S. Marcello in an early 18th-century engraving designed for use by architects

tion he pursued throughout his career, and the results were easily imitated and consequently very influential.

The statues on the façade are by Fontana's assistants; the great square frame overhead was supposed to contain a *bas relief* but was never completed.

A church had been built on the spot in the 4th century to honour the Roman Pope Marcellus I, who was said to have been condemned to forced labour here by the Emperor Maxentius (this was the site of the ancient Roman post office, the *catabulum*, and Marcellus was presumably working as a slave here). The original church was destroyed by a fire in 1519 and work on the present building was begun shortly afterwards. (Open 07:15-12:00 and 16:00-19:00.)

The elaborate ceiling is 16th-century. The most important monument in the church is the early renaissance tomb of Cardinal Michiel to the left of the entrance. The cardinal was one of the many victims of Pope Alexander VI Borgia (pp. 46, 329), who had him poisoned in the prison of the Castel Sant' Angelo in 1503. The tomb is a double one, as it also holds the remains of the cardinal's nephew. The sculptors were Andrea Sansovino and his pupil Jacopo Sansovino; the latter also designed the church interior. The cardinal, who lived nearby, bequeathed his property to the church, including his library, a donation symbolised here by the books supporting the coffin. No hint of his tragic demise is evident from the monument.

late 17th-century façade of **S. Marcello** by the architect Carlo Fontana, a distant relative of the famous Domenico (p. 70), but a generation younger. The church is one of his masterpieces. Fontana, an important theorist and student of classical architecture, was among the first to abandon the flourishes of the mature baroque, in favour of balance and clarity of design. This direc-

In the third chapel to the right is a damaged 15th-century fresco over the altar of the *Madonna and Child* set in a beautiful marble frame. On the side walls are frescoes by Francesco Salviati, a mid-16th century follower of Raphael. The next chapel contains a 15th-century wooden crucifix, called 'miraculous' because it survived the fire that destroyed the original church in 1519 and is said to have stopped the plague (see p. 246) when it was carried in a procession in 1522. In the vault are frescoes by Perino del Vaga, a close follower of Raphael; under the altar, a 3rd century AD block of marble with military symbols on the sides. The multi-coloured marble chips were added when the block was made into a reliquary in the 12th century. The chapel opposite contains paintings by the Zuccari brothers (late 16th-century) on the side walls, as well as marble busts of the noble Frangipane family; the three on the right are by the important 17th-century sculptor, Alessandro Algardi.

Access to the crypt is through the sacristy. There are remains of a 5th-7th century brick basin used for baptismal immersion in the old church. The excavation can also be seen, in part, from inside the bank next door.

Leave the church and go left. At No. 5 is the 15th-century doorway of the (demolished) home of Cardinal Michiel. Continue along the Corso in the same direction for just a few yards. Across the street is **S. Maria in Via Lata**, founded in the 7th century as a *diaconia*, or welfare centre (see p. 254). At the time this part of the Corso was called Via Lata ('Broadway') because it was wider than the rest of the street. In ancient Rome it was part of the Via Flaminia; there used to be an important imperial arch in front of the church (see p. 226). In the renaissance, both church and arch were demolished and the church was entirely rebuilt. The bell tower survives from the late 15th century.

The facade was added in the 17th century by Pietro da Cortona, one of the great architects of the high baroque. The main problem was that the Corso, though wide, was not wide enough here for the façade to be seen fully, except sharply foreshortened. In the nearby S. Marcello the problem had been solved by setting the church back in a small square and curving the facade, but here there was no further space. Cortona solved the problem in a novel and effective way with a high, deep loggia surmounting a portico of the same size and design, both open and both articulated with freestanding columns. This creates an extraordinary effect of plasticity and depth, which passers-by can appreciate, even from the side, without having to stand at a distance.

The church is open 17:00-22:30, closed August 15 to September 10. The interior exhibits a rich interplay of multi-coloured marble, stucco and gilding. The columns, spolia from ancient Roman monuments, were later covered with jasper scalework. Frescoes and paintings, mostly by minor 17th-century artists, decorate the walls and chapels. The main altar is notable, and together with the surrounding decorative arrangement (including alabaster columns and a 13th-century image of the *Virgin* by an otherwise unknown Petrus Pictor – 'Peter the Painter') is attributed to Bernini. The wooden choir dates from 1628. In the chapels at the far ends of the aisles are remains of the Cosmatesque pavement. The chapel on the right contains the tombs of some members of Napoleon's family (Palazzo Bonaparte was nearby, p. 535).

Beneath the church, though rarely accessible (ask in the sacristy), are ruins from the 2nd century AD and rooms belonging to the original church, with a few marble fragments and vestigial frescoes.

Note: the church abuts the grand Palazzo Doria-Pamphili, which in turn faces the Corso on one side and Piazza Venezia on another. The palace is described in the context of Piazza Venezia, where the Corso terminates (p. 535).

Leave the church and continue left to the corner of Via Lata – not the original Via Lata, which was the same as the present Corso, but an intersection that has inherited the name. At the very beginning of the street note the picturesque Fontana del Facchino ('Fountain of the Porter'), probably late 16th-century, representing one of the water-carriers with his little barrel who sold water door to door.

This used to be one of the 'talking statues' where pranksters and dissidents would affix their posters (see p. 461).

BEFORE GOING

8. From the foot of the Quirinal to S. Silvestro

The Walk continues with a detour to the level-ground to the west of the Corso along the foot of the Quirinal Hill. The area was quite lively and densely populated even before the restoration of the aqueducts, since it was the main route up the hills from this side. Even when it was *disabitato* (see p. 28) the hills did have villas, vineyards and farms. This communication role has since passed to Via Nazionale nearby, built in the late 19th century with the further aim of linking the down-

Vineyards on the Quirinal in the 17th century, from a contemporary map

town area to the railway station. The neighbourhood is consequently quieter than it used to be.

Until recently, some of Rome's most influential families lived here, together with the multitude of servants and artisans they employed. Amongst the noblest were the Colonna, who throughout the middle ages were as powerful as the popes or the secular authorities occasionally established by the citizenry. With their vast country estates, private militia and entourage of allied minor nobility, the Colonna were a redoubtable financial and military power, as well as a political force to be reckoned with. There were also the Riario, the della Rovere and the Odescalchi – families that gave the church scores of high prelates and popes, including Sixtus IV and Julius II. As patrons of illustrious artists, these popes left an indelible imprint on Rome. Michelangelo, protegé and victim of Julius II, also lived nearby.

In keeping with this lively past, several neighbourhood churches were the scene of bloody events in the middle ages and the renaissance. Just as in S. Marcello we saw the tomb of Cardinal Michiel, poisoned by the Borgia pope, so in SS. Apostoli we find the tombs of Riario family cardinals who were involved in bloody conspiracies. And it was in front of the church of S. Silvestro in Capite that Pope Leo III was attacked and gravely wounded during a procession in 799.

Resuming our main itinerary and returning towards the most crowded part of downtown Rome today, we find additional signs of demolitions and alterations connected with the post-1870 'modernisation': the widening of Via del Tritone, two mall-like *gallerie* and 'La Rinascente', Rome's first department store (and still one of the very few). The Walk ends in view of yet another planning monstrosity, the transformation of the ancient monastery of S. Silvestro into the main post office, with a depressing 19th-century façade. Few people today pay much notice to the old monastery, where loud postal transactions take place around the once serene cloister, or to the adjacent church, over a thousand years old. And to think that the latter boasts the possession of the head of St John the Baptist, the very one presented to King Herod's daughter Salome, on a plate after she had him killed for rejecting her advances!

ON THE SPOT

8. From the foot of the Quirinal to S. Silvestro

If you choose to skip the following detour, return to Palazzo Sciarra (see p. 125) and take Vicolo Sciarra, skirting the right flank of the palace to Piazza dell'Oratorio.

DETOUR

30 MIN

Cross the Corso once more. Take Via SS. Apostoli, in front of you, to Piazza SS. Apostoli on the right. Dominating the square is the church of **SS. Apostoli** ('Holy Apostles') so called for the putative bodies of Sts Philip and James in the crypt.

The basilica was founded in the 6th century and restored or rebuilt several times. The porch is 15th-century, while the loggia above it and the statues are 17th-century. The bulk of the present church is 18th-century, while the spare neo-classical façade behind the porch and loggia was built in the early 19th century to a design by Giuseppe Valadier.

The assorted marble monuments and fragments under the porch are either ancient Roman or medieval. On the right wall is a beautiful 3rd century AD imperial eagle and below it, a 13th-century, much-eroded 'gatekeeper' lion signed by Vassalletto of the famous Cosma clan. Near the door are more medieval lions and, at the sides, late 15th-century tombstones. On the left wall is a funerary stele by Antonio Canova (19th-century).

The vast interior (open: 07:00-12:00 and 16:00-19:00.) exudes an air of solemn magnificence, enhanced by the luminous early 18th-century fresco in the vault of the *Triumph of the Franciscan Order* by Baciccia (more sedate than his earlier and more famous *Triumph of the Name of Jesus* in the Gesù, p. 112) and by the roomy chapels, each with its own dome. In the third chapel on the right are 15th-century frescoes. The other chapels contain 17th- and 18th-century paintings. The chapel at the very end of the right aisle has eight 4th-century spiral columns used in the original church.

In the middle of the church, before the apse, a 19th-century double staircase descends to a crypt with the putative remains of the two apostles. There is also an unfinished cenotaph, perhaps by Andrea Bregno, to the man who was brother to Pope Sixtus IV and father to Pope Julius II, Raffaele della Rovere, who died in 1477.

In the apse is the *Martyrdom of the Two Apostles* by the minor early 18th-century painter, Domenico Muratori; it is the largest altarpiece in Rome. Overhead there was once Melozzo da Forlì's marvellous fresco of music-making angels, fragments of which we'll see in the Vatican picture gallery (p. 314). Also in the apse are the early 16th-century tombs of other relatives of Sixtus IV: on the left wall, the tomb of Cardinal Pietro Riario by Bregno (though the *bas relief* is attributed to Mino da Fiesole); on the right wall, the Michelangel-esque tomb of Cardinal Raffaele Riario (more on him later).

At the very end of the left aisle is Antonio Canova's first Roman work: a monument to Pope Clement XIV (late 18th century). There is also the tomb of the great baroque composer Gerolamo Frescobaldi (see the tablet on the floor).

To the left of the church stands the imposing late 15th-century **Palazzo SS. Apostoli**, perhaps by Giuliano da Sangallo, built as a residence for the titular bishop of the church, who was then Giuliano della Rovere, the future Pope Julius II and patron of Michelangelo and Raphael. The windows of the palace and a tower on the corner are adorned with the della Rovere escutcheon. The portal leads to two communicating cloisters, the first late 15th-century, the second early 16th-century, with assorted funerary monuments from both centuries. One commemorates the fact that Michelangelo's body was temporarily deposited here before being taken to Florence. The attractive fountain is by Domenico Fontana.

To the right of the church is **Palazzo Colonna**, not actually visible from here because a low building with shops, an unusual 18th-century structure, stands before it. The palace may be entered only as part of a visit to the important picture gallery within (p. 684); the entrance is at the far right.

The vast, elegant palace, built in the 15th century and entirely restructured in the 18th, is still the seat of the historic Colonna family. It incorporates another small 16th-century palace. Bridges at the back, visible if you go around to Via della Pilotta (you'll see them later, p. 190), link the palace to a large villa, also belonging to the Colonna, that reaches the foot of the Quirinal. In this villa Michelangelo took part in the literary gatherings organised by his friend, the princess and poetess Vittoria Colonna (p. 67).

Across the square from the church is the long façade of the 17th-18th century **Palazzo Odescalchi**. The left part of the main building – the eight pilasters on the left – follows a harmonious design by Bernini. The wings, added later, alter the delicate proportions. The palace inaugurated a building type with a giant order of columns that gave a vertical emphasis and contrasted with the horizontality of Palazzo Farnese; this new type (which took its cue from Michelangelo's designs on the Capitol) remained popular in Europe for centuries. The back of the palace faces the Corso and was redone in the 19th century. The courtyard, with its arches and statues, is by Carlo Maderno (early 16th-century).

The short side of the square displays the 17th-century **Palazzo Balestra** with a narrow baroque façade. The last of the Stuarts, Prince Cardinal Henry of York, lived here when he took refuge in Rome together with his brother, the pretender to the thrones of England and Scotland (p. 371).

On the left side of the palace take Via S. Marcello. At No. 41B on your right a passage leads to the minuscule **Chapel of the Madonna dell'Archetto** ('of the Little Arch'). (Open evenings only, 18:30-20:30.)

The delightful mid-19th century oratory, which a private group uses for prayer meetings, is noteworthy for its jewel-like decoration and especially for its small frescoes by Costantino Brumidi. The artist, who used the rare encaustic technique, where the pigment is diluted in melted beeswax, felt that his art was not sufficiently appreciated in Italy – where indeed he is still little known – and moved to the United States. There he used his method to fresco the dome of the Capitol in Washington (where his paintings are now a highly popular draw since their careful restoration).

Continuing along Via S. Marcello, note on your left, at No. 24, the rear façade of a grandiose *art nouveau* palace (the main façade is on the Corso, but this one is better). Via S. Marcello ends in Piazza dell'Oratorio. Note on the upper right-hand corner of the street a charming 1860 Madonnella (street shrine).

END OF DETOUR

Piazza dell'Oratorio takes its name from the **Oratorio del Crocifisso** (to the left of the gallery), a 16th-century prayer hall, named after and dedicated to the crucifix in the nearby church of S. Marcello, said to have ended the plague after being carried in a procession (see p. 127). The finely proportioned façade is by Giacomo Della Porta. (Open 07:00-12:00 and 16:00-19:00; in August, 09:00-12:00.)

Late 16th-century frescoes by minor artists cover the interior, forming a resplendent ensemble. On the sides are episodes from *The Invention of the True Cross* (see p. 368). On the entrance wall to the right is *The Procession of 1522 to End the Plague*, in which the crucifix was carried; to the left is *The Crucifix Remains Intact in the Fire of St Marcellus* by Cristoforo Pomarancio. A 16th-century copy of the miraculous crucifix is over the main altar.

On the left side of the square, if you are facing the oratory, there used to be a good restaurant where Ernest Hemingway was wont to eat in the years after the Second World War. Near the oratory is the *belle époque* Galleria Sciarra, wistfully evocative of a bygone world, with its naive frescoes by the Roman artist Giuseppe Cellini (1888) celebrating domestic life and its dusty, once smart shops. It seems to have been a not quite successful attempt to make a shopping mall for Rome in the manner of London's Burlington Arcade.

Cross the gallery (if closed, go around to the right) and continue straight into Via S. Maria in Via. (You're in the neighbourhood of the Trevi Fountain now, covered in the first Walk.) The left side of the second block was also transformed into a covered mall at the turn of the century, the Galleria di Piazza Colonna, bigger and more pompous than the Galleria Sciarra (restored 2004, when it was incongruously renamed in memory of a cinema actor, Alberto Sordi).

Via S. Maria in Via opens into the end of Via del Tritone (which we have seen from various viewpoints, pp. 63, 83). Here Via del Tritone widens on the left, taking the name Largo Chigi, one of Rome's busiest spots. The Rinascente department store, opened in 1877, is here.

On the corner of Via del Tritone is the church of **S. Maria in Via**, founded over a thousand years ago and last remodelled in the late 16th century to a design by Giacomo Della Porta and Carlo Rainaldi. (Open 09:00-12:30 and 16:00-19:00.)

The first chapel on the right contains a sweet 'miraculous' fragment of a 13th-century fresco known as the *Madonna of the Pit,* which was said to have popped out of a well in the chapel. The golden crown was, as usual, added later to indicate the miraculous nature of the image.

Largo Chigi on the left ends in the Corso. The rest of the Corso, from Piazza Colonna to Piazza del Popolo, especially notable for its ancient Roman antiquities, is described in the second Ancient Rome Walk (pp. 216-233).

Cross Via del Tritone into the busy double square of Piazza S. Claudio-Piazza S. Silvestro. Until 1940 the squares were separated by a row of buildings (demolished to improve traffic flow), one of which was the Anglican Trinity Church (1872), the first Protestant church built in Rome after the collapse of the papal regime in 1870 (see pp. 52 and 81).

Facing you is the central post office, a former convent, very ancient and once very rich. Its possessions included the nearby Column of Marcus Aurelius (p. 232)! Along with many other convents (p. 116), this one was expropriated by the new Italian state after the annexation of Rome in 1870 and turned into offices. It is now marred by the new façade added at the time. Inside, at the far left end, is the church of the former convent, **S. Silvestro in Capite** ('St Sylvester of the Head'), so-called because of the astonishing relic within: a head alleged to be that of St John the Baptist.

An 8th-century pope built both church and convent in his own home, at a time when the papacy was flourishing thanks to the protection offered by the Franks. It was rebuilt in the early 13th century, when the fine romanesque bell tower was added, topped by a bronze cockerel, the only such weathervane remaining in place in Rome. The complex was again remodelled in the late 17th century.

Before the church, currently served by Pallottine priests (p. 475) of various nationalities, is a courtyard with a modern collection of old inscriptions. In front of the low baroque façade is a porch (part of one built in the 13th century) which also contains tablets and inscriptions. On the wall near the right-hand corner, one inscription curses and threatens to excommunicate any future abbot or abbess who might sell the Column of Marcus Aurelius.

Inside (open: 07:00-19:15; Sunday 07:00-12:45 and 15:30-19:15), the church has a wonderful 17th-century organ and many paintings of the same period. Among them, *St Francis* by the Pisan artist Orazio Gentileschi in the second chapel to the right; in the dome of the same chapel are frescoes by his fellow countryman Cristoforo Pomarancio. Remains of the 13th-century Cosmatesque floor of the church are in the last chapel on the left. The precious 14th-century reliquary with the putative head of St John the Baptist – the upper part of a skull embedded in a ball of wax – is in the first chapel on the left.

In the crypt, partly visible from the transept and sometimes open, there are ancient Roman tufa blocks and other remains of the primitive church.

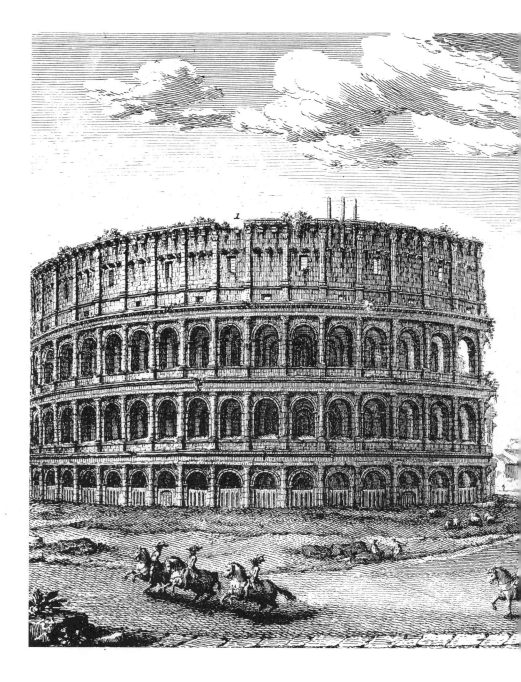

Ancient Rome

The Colosseum in the mid 18th century, by P. Schenk

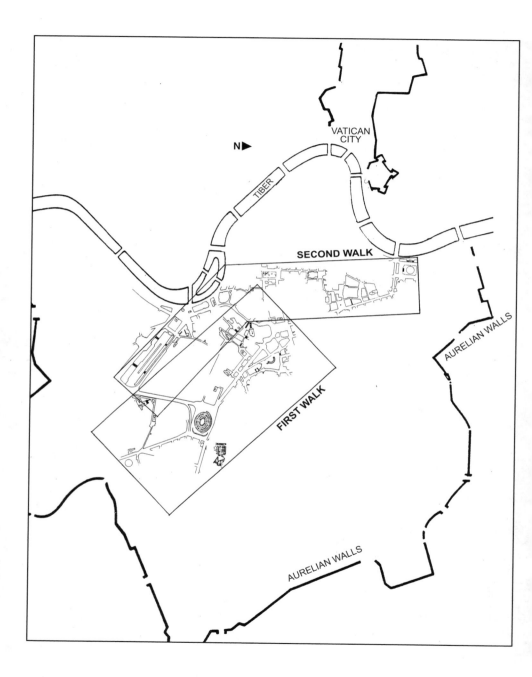

ANCIENT ROME

ANCIENT ROME

INTRODUCTION

From Livy on, historians have attributed the strength and greatness of ancient Rome to certain well-defined traits of the Roman character: a habit of pious observance, respect for tradition and authority, and a simple lifestyle that included traditional pastimes with civic and religious overtones. These two Walks show evidence of these Roman qualities. Rome's Sacred Hills, the Capitol and the Palatine, as well as the Roman Forum and Imperial Fora, exude the sense of tradition, religion and destiny that informed Roman life. Here and in the Campus Martius area, developed later by Augustus and his successors, we'll see how the Roman state and its institutions evolved. The Colosseum, the Theatre of Marcellus and the Circus Maximus all evoke the world of Roman entertainment and daily life.

The Gladiator: one of the most famous ancient statues yet unearthed in Rome

Public monuments make up most of what remains of ancient Rome; after all, they were built to last. You can, however, still get fascinating glimpses of private dwellings inside the city. You'll see more of these if you later explore the ancient harbour town of Ostia outside Rome, or Pompeii and Herculaneum further south – places that vividly evoke daily life because, ironically, they were abandoned. Rome, on the other hand, never froze in time, and continued human habitation has taken a higher toll than the natural elements in terms of wear and tear.

Our Ancient Rome Walks begin at the end of the Corso, exactly one mile (1.6 km) south of the Porta del Popolo where we began our first exploration of the city. Since this gate was, as we saw, part of the Aurelian Walls that marked the perimeter of the antique city, you may ask why we go south one mile to visit ancient Rome. The reason is that, in order to see ancient Rome in chronological order, we must start at its very core. The mile between the end of the Corso and the Porta del Popolo traces later phases of urban growth, so we won't visit it until the second Ancient Rome Walk.

How the Romans lived: model of a typical multi-storey apartment house
(based on one at Rome's port, Ostia Antica)

We must also recall the shift of Rome's centre of gravity from south to north, essential to understanding the city. This shift occurred in two distinct phases. One was at the outset of the Empire – at a time when the Roman state was seven centuries old and still had five more to go – and is due to Augustus (see pp. 27-28) and his successors. The shift was planned to ease crowding; immigration had surged with the growing global importance of Rome, and the population was probably about a million.

The first phase of the shift from south to north at the time of Augustus

The second shift occurred after the Empire fell, and was due mainly to the destruction of the aqueducts (p. 28). In this case, however, the move was not related to overcrowding, but rather to the depletion of the city, now reduced to a few thousand souls. Strictly speaking, only the first shift interests us in the Ancient Rome Walks. The results of the second are discussed in the Renaissance Rome Walks, and we have already noted its final developments in the first Roma Romantica Walk.

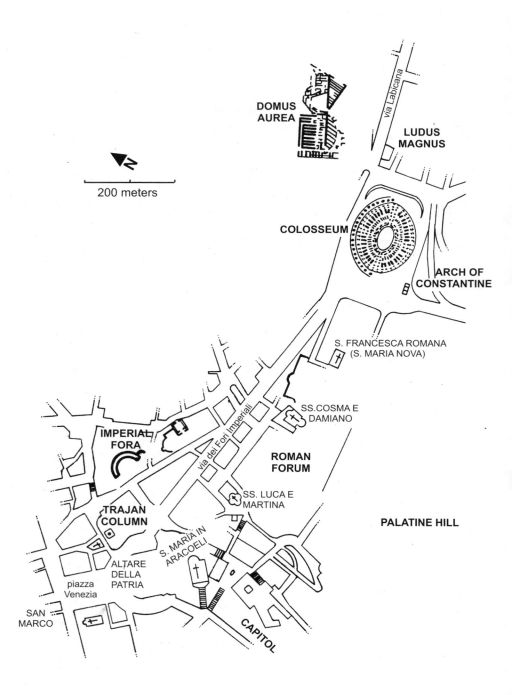

200 meters

DOMUS
AUREA

via Labicana

LUDUS
MAGNUS

COLOSSEUM

ARCH OF
CONSTANTINE

S. FRANCESCA ROMANA
(S. MARIA NOVA)

SS.COSMA E
DAMIANO

IMPERIAL
FORA

via dei Fori Imperiali

ROMAN
FORUM

SS. LUCA E
MARTINA

TRAJAN
COLUMN

PALATINE HILL

S. MARIA IN
ARACOELI

ALTARE
DELLA
PATRIA

piazza
Venezia

SAN
MARCO

CAPITOL

ANCIENT ROME: FIRST WALK

Starting point: Piazza Venezia   End point: Via Labicana
Duration: 8 hours (without the Detours, indicated above between parentheses).

Notes: 1) All major sites are open morning and afternoon. 2) If you wish to stick to the tight schedule of these walks, you must limit yourself to seeing both the Palatine and Roman Forum from the terrace of the Capitol. This should suffice to introduce you to these very complex sites, especially now that some essential features, such as the House of Vestals, are closed and can only be seen from above (see p. 285 and pp. 288-289). (If you have time, however, you should return for an in-depth visit, which will take almost half a day; see the detailed guide of the Palatine and Forum on pp. 279-294) For the visit to the Domus Aurea, at the end of this Walk, a sweater is suggested even in summer. Guided tours only: reserve a place by calling (06) 3974 9907 (not always necessary).

BEFORE GOING

1. Piazza Venezia and the approach to the Capitol

We approach the oldest core of Rome from Piazza Venezia, the large square at the end of the Corso. As we prepare to climb our first site, the Capitoline Hill, historic seat of the Roman government, we see a jumble of mouldering bricks, which vanish into a hole in the ground, topped by a funny-looking belltower. Most people don't even notice it, yet these are fairly well preserved remains of an ancient Roman five-storey apartment house, one of the few remaining examples of a private dwelling in the city, as mentioned above (p. 136). This gives striking proof of the ability of some Roman landmarks to escape the untrained eye.

The bell-tower was added in the middle ages, when what remained of the upper floors was turned into a small church, later demolished. The building itself is hidden in a hole. Go near and peer down, and you'll see an 1,800-year old shop on the ground floor and a stretch of original roadway. It would not have been unlike the model shown on p. 137.

The vertical shift. This is another of the countless instances of ancient ruins at considerable depth underground (we saw this in the first Walk, pp. 52, 71). Why has the surface level changed so much? Even more puzzling, many of the ruins are not underground. Why is there a difference?

The reason why some are not underground is either because a whole area has been excavated, and so you are on the same level as the ruins, or because the ruins themselves have escaped burial thanks to their position. There are several reasons why many of Rome's monuments were buried: fire, particularly frequent in early antiquity; the habit of rebuilding on top of old ruins without clearing them (in many Roman buildings, the foundations are based on ancient buildings, which in turn are based on structures older still); landscaping by the ancients; and, last but not least, silting caused by river floods. For 2,500 years, a basic fact of Roman life was that the Tiber flooded frequently; and two or three times in a century these floods would be catastrophic (pp. 116-117).

In ancient Rome the floods were less frequent and disastrous, because the river-bed and banks were cleaned and smoothed out regularly. Nonetheless, low-lying areas were vulnerable, which is one reason why people preferred the hills and why, after Augustus and his successors expanded the city into the low-lying Campus Martius, it remained sparsely inhabited and was mainly used for monuments and entertainment. In the middle ages, when the aqueducts supplying water to the hills collapsed (p. 28), the people were forced to settle in the Campus Martius, even though the floods there worsened. The authorities had largely forgotten how to manage the river-bed, and, to make things worse, they had to install watermills that obstructed the current, in order to process flour, which in antiquity had arrived ready-milled from distant lands.

Nor were the damage and the casualties of these terrible floods limited to what the waters achieved on their own; the floods were sometimes followed by outbreaks of cholera, or invasions of plague-bearing rats. Popes and cardinals on occasion toured the city in boats, bringing comfort to the people. In the 1880's the newly established Italian state took the more practical step of embanking the river with high walls, and the Tiber was finally tamed.

The heights reached by the flood waters are recorded throughout Rome on wall tablets dated between 1276 and 1870; photographs of the 1870 flood show people boating in the Pantheon.

The Capitol, overshadowed by the Altar of the Fatherland: from a 1930's postcard

ON THE SPOT

1. Piazza Venezia and the approach to the Capitol

Piazza Venezia, used by the Fascist dictator Mussolini for what he called 'oceanic' meetings of the populace, is dominated by a vast, dazzling white monument, the largest to be built anywhere in modern times. This 'Altar of the Fatherland', built at the dawn of the 20th century to commemorate the unification of Italy, is tragically out of place here in the context of ancient Rome, and indeed belongs to another of our walks. (See p. 535 for a description, and also for a discussion of Palazzo Venezia, the oldest of Rome's great renaissance palaces, which is on the right side of the square as you face the memorial.)

Go to the right flank of the monument – pedestrian crosswalks will help you brave the traffic – and walk along it to the bus stop, where you'll find the ruins of a 2nd century AD **Apartment House** are here.

The 1800-year-old building, one of the few and best preserved of its kind in Rome, is 27 ft (about 8

m) below street level. It has five storeys and a staircase. Its ground floor were *tabernæ* (shops). Most apartment houses had these *tabernæ*, which the owner would rent out. They typically included one large room at mezzanine level, with a window over the door of the shop, for the shopkeeper and his family. Ancient authors say that when shopkeepers were late with their rent, landlords threatened to trap them upstairs by removing the portable ladder to the store below. Many of the stores sold take-away food, because apartments, unlike houses, lacked kitchens and running water. They had no bathrooms either and so most people used public lavatories (*foricæ*), which were quite luxurious and not unpopular for socialising.

The top storey now consists only of bits of masonry. In the middle ages the top was the only part above ground; it was turned into a tiny church, later torn down (see p. 531), leaving just the diminutive belfry and altar wall, with a 14th-century fresco. The small roof is only for protection. The house, excavated only in part, extends underground on both sides. On the far left it faces a section of original pavement.

2. The Capitol

The Capitol was the most sacred area of ancient Rome, the hub of its political and religious life. Other seats of power around the world are named after it, including Capitol Hill in Washington DC. But why was it so important?

The answers are confusing even to most present-day Romans. Misleading notions and false analogies abound concerning the Capitol. First, unlike its successors worldwide, the Capitol is not a building, it is a hill – the Capitoline Hill – crowned by buildings. Second, the present buildings do not look as if they have anything to do with ancient Rome; they are majestic structures enclosing a magnificent square, but they all date from the middle ages or renaissance. In contrast to the Roman Forum on the other side of the hill, no ancient Roman buildings, not even ruins, are visible. But the great antiquity of the site will gradually become apparent as we explore it.

The hill has two low peaks, each of which played a key role in Roman history; the medieval and renaissance constructions are situated in the flat area between them (the *Intermontium*).

The peak to the left as you ascend was the main fortress of early Rome, the so-called Arx, similar in purpose to the Acropolis of Athens. Here, when Rome was still little more than a village of shepherds, the first Romans fought their first desperate battles. Here, sometime at the beginning of the 4th century BC, the sacred geese of Juno gave the alarm that the Gauls (or Celts), who for a long time had threatened Rome from the north, were approaching; a warning that did not, however, prevent the Gauls from inflicting a miserable defeat on Rome. Here, then, was a place that inspired reverential reflection on the past in subsequent generations. Here, too, the Augurs, priests of the Auguraculum, studied the flight of birds to predict Rome's future.

On the right peak, the holiness of the hill was more tangibly embodied. There for centuries stood the most splendid, ancient and holy of all the hundreds of temples in Rome, the Temple of Jupiter, the supreme god. Precious marbles covered the structure, its doors and roof were gilded. As a result, the whole hill was dubbed *Capitolium Fulgens*, 'Resplendent Capitol'. The temple was used for most major state ceremonies, both religious (like a pagan St. Peter's) and political. The Senate, Rome's governing body throughout its history (though in name only, after the Emperors had stripped it of all its power), met here for its solemn inaugural sessions. Subsequent meetings were held at its ordinary seat, the palace of the Curia, or Secretariat, in the Roman Forum, which was down the hill on the other side. Incidentally, Shakespeare erred in locating on the Capitol the meeting of the Senate during which Julius Cæsar was killed. Nor did it happen in the Curia, which was then under restoration. Cæsar met his fate far from here, in the annex of a theatre being used temporarily by the Senate. We go there in the second of these two Walks (p. 244).

Alas, of the famous Temple of Jupiter only traces remain. We do know, however, what it looked liked, because the Capitoline Museums have a marble bas-relief of the temple from imperial times.

The historian Livy tells us that early Romans would drag their vanquished enemies to the heights of the Capitol to celebrate their victories. This ritual gradually evolved into a highly

The Campidoglio in the 18th century, by Piranesi

formal ceremony, the *triumphus*, a spectacular parade granted by the Senate to generals after their greatest victories, which wound up on the Capitol near the golden Temple of Jupiter. The word (from which, of course, 'triumph' derives) originally referred only to the parade itself, the highest honour Roman society could bestow. Led by the victor – draped in royal purple, his face painted red to display his affinity to the gods – the march ascended the hill from the Forum side of the hill, starting along a traditional path, the Via Sacra ('Sacred Way'), whose ancient stones we'll see. Amidst the clamour of victorious troops and cheering crowds, and the piercing blasts of long trumpets (some of which have been found), soldiers marched with the enslaved enemy – men, women and children in chains, hauling their own captured regalia and heavy war spoils. Sometimes, during the march, the enemy king and generals would be slaughtered in the dark Mamertine Prison, which we'll visit later, at the foot of the Forum side of the hill. Traitors were hurled to their deaths from the Tarpeian Rock, a cliff on the right peak, the location of which, perhaps surprisingly, has only been tentatively identified.

Other features illustrate the civic role of the Capitol. There were two major buildings along with the Temple of Jupiter and several others. One, on the left peak (Arx), was the Mint, next to the Temple of Juno Moneta ('Juno the Monitor' or Prophetess). The coins struck there were called *moneta*, the origin of our word 'money'. The other building, in the gentle dip between the peaks, was an imposing State Archives, the Tabularium, after the *tabulæ* ('tablets') on which all laws were inscribed. This building, or paradoxically what was left of it, was destined for a long and glorious future.

The transformation. The opulent buildings on the Capitol were mostly destroyed after the fall of the Empire. The hill was a wasteland in the dark ages, a good place to graze goats; hence it was called Monte Caprino ('Goat Hill') for centuries, while for similar reasons the plain of the Forum at its foot was called Campo Vaccino ('Ox Meadow') until the 19th century. Yet the importance of the hill was never quite forgotten. In 1143, when the Romans revolted against the pope and dreamt of restoring Rome to its former glory, albeit only in the city and its surroundings, they chose the imposing ruins of the Tabularium as the site for a rebuilt Senate.

The medieval republic didn't stand much chance against the popes, the warring noble families in their towers, who divided the city amongst themselves, and foreign intruders, usually German emperors, who claimed to have inherited the Roman Empire. The medieval history of Rome is virtually that of the unending conflict of these forces. Yet a semblance of the revived institution tottered on for centuries, sometimes in opposition to, usually in cooperation with, if not abject subservience to, the other powers. Progressively reduced from a score of senators to two, then one, the office survived to the 19th century, when the 'Senator of Rome' was actually a papal bureaucrat.

Another revolt occurred in 1348, when Cola di Rienzi, a charismatic leader with a talent for rousing the people by conjuring the ghosts of past grandeur, actually took control of the city. (Opera-goers may remember the story from one of Wagner's early works, *Rienzi.*) But Cola's triumph was short-lived. Undermined by the feudal families, whose power he had broken, and accused of corruption, he was lynched by a mob as he tried to flee the Capitol during a demonstration. His statue is on the hill at the spot where he fell (a description of his death is on p. 219).

In the renaissance, when artistic and philosophical currents fed by memories of classical times swept across papal Rome, one pope decided to carry out a drastic renovation of the Tabularium-Senate area that so potently symbolised Rome's past. The artist and architect called to this grand task in 1536 was no less than Michelangelo. So it is to Michelangelo's genius that we owe the sight that greets us as we reach the hilltop. And it is a wonderful sight indeed. But it is a creation of the renaissance and therefore somewhat confusing to a visitor who arrives expecting the remains of ancient glory.

The building that had risen on the old Tabularium was remodelled by Michelangelo and renamed Palazzo Senatorio ('Senator's Palace'). It was still standing when papal rule finally ended in 1870. It then became, and still is, the seat of the Mayor of Rome. So, in a limited sense, the Capitol continues to be a symbol of ruling power in Rome.

The horizontal shift. The approach to the Capitol gives a dramatic visual confirmation of the shift from south to north of Rome's historic centre, discussed on p. 137. This in turn helps us better understand what we see. The present buildings and monumental staircases of the Capitoline Hill, all medieval and renaissance, face northward, i.e. toward us as we arrive, as if stretching their arms out to greet the 'new' part of the city, settled in the plain and within the river bend after the fall of the Empire. Yet the ruins of the old Roman structures they replaced show that the original buildings and stairs all opened to the south, thus saluting the Forum, the hills and the original and most venerable part of Rome.

ON THE SPOT

2. The Capitol

A few steps further on you reach the foot of two grand staircases to the Capitol (Campidoglio). The steep one on the left leads to the peak once called *Arx* ('Citadel'), former site of the Temple of Juno Moneta and its adjoining Mint, now that of the church of S. Maria in Ara Coeli, with its stern 13th-century façade. The other peak, with only vestigial ruins, will be discussed later (p. 163). The steps were built in 1348. (The church entrance on this side is often closed. For a visit, see p. 148.)

Not so steep and more ornate is the stepped ramp to the right leading to the depression between the two peaks. This is the famous Cordonata, or stepped ramp, designed in the 1500's by Michelangelo as part of his renovation of the legendary area. Its base is adorned with two Egyptian Lions from a sanctuary of Isis that once stood in the Field of Mars nearby (p. 114).

Climb the ramp. In a small garden on the left is a small modern monument to Cola di Rienzi, ancient marble fragments decorating its base.

Note the statues on the balustrade above, best seen from three-quarters of the way up the ramp. These are ancient Roman pieces that were placed here in the renaissance when the site was rearranged. The giant twin statues depict the mythical Horse Tamers, Castor and Pollux (p. 68); they are ancient Roman copies of 5th-century BC Greek originals. To right and left are two interesting marble trophies, sculptures representing captured arms, shields and armour hanging from crossed tree-trunks that were used by the Romans to symbolise their military victories. The one on the right also shows a chained female figure, symbolising Germany. Both are from the reign of the Emperor Domitian in the 1st century AD. On either side are, respectively, statues of the great Emperor Constantine who adopted Christianity (left) and his son and successor Constantine II (right), both 4th century AD. Note the awkward style characteristic of the declining arts in the twilight of the empire. At either end of the balustrade are two 1st century AD milestones from the ancient Appian Way.

We reach **Piazza Campidoglio**, one of the first examples, and surely the most splendid, of a modern square built entirely to a single design.

Mid-19th century view up the Cordonata to the Campidoglio

H. Cock, The Capitoline Hill c. 1544, before Michelangelo's renovations

Michelangelo's project was executed in part by him and finished over the next hundred years, with modifications, by his followers.

The square is not big, yet it gives an unexpected impression of grandeur, thanks to a subtle trapezoidal design – it seems rectangular, but the sides are actually oblique – and the fact that the buildings define it without actually enclosing it.

At the centre, where all the perspectival lines converge on a star, part of an intricate pattern in the convex pavement, stood the world's most famous equestrian monument, the 2nd century AD **Statue of the Emperor Marcus Aurelius**. Until recently: today it is replaced by a frankly unsatisfactory copy.

After a long restoration, the gilt-bronze original was moved to the nearby Capitoline Museums to protect it from air pollution. Unbelievably, the authorities won't let you see the original statue – a paramount symbol of Rome, for centuries freely and proudly shown to streams of visitors from every latitude – without buying a museum ticket.

The statue is the only one of its kind to have survived. It escaped destruction in early Christendom because it was mistakenly thought to portray Constantine, the first Christian emperor (see p. 401). In fact it shows the emperor-philosopher, Marcus Aurelius, famous for his wisdom and devotion to the welfare of the state, riding on a heavy Hungarian horse and addres-sing the people. Its extraordinary majesty and grace have drawn admiration through the ages, and it is the prototype of all modern equestrian statues.

It was transferred to the Capitol from its original site near S. Giovanni in Laterano, against the advice of Michelangelo, who opposed this violation of the intentions of the ancients. The pedestal by Michelangelo is in itself a thing of beauty.

Michelangelo's project for the Campidoglio

The twin palaces on either side of the square are the Capitoline Museums (Palazzo dei Conservatori on the right, Palazzo Nuovo on the left; to visit these famous museums, the oldest open to the public anywhere in the world, see p. 682).These palaces exhibit all the strength and individuality of Michelangelo's genius, and their main innovation, the giant order of Corinthian pilasters supporting an entablature across the whole building, was copied everywhere. Stately and rich as these structures are, all covered with the luminous travertine stone of Rome (see Glossary), they yield in historic importance to the simply stuccoed middle building, the venerable **Palazzo Senatorio**. This is the renaissance renovation of a medieval structure, which in turn had risen over the ruins of the ancient Roman **Tabularium** (p. 144). The palace now houses the offices of the Mayor of Rome.

The building, surmounted by a powerful bell-tower, is by Michelangelo's followers, but the central double staircase, the most impressive part, is by the artist himself. Preceded by a fountain, the staircase includes a niche with an ancient Roman statue of the goddess Minerva, changed in the renaissance to the goddess Rome. It has been criticised as too small; Michelangelo wanted a larger statue or a group. Flanking her are imposing 2nd century AD river gods, the Nile left, the Tiber right.

Some of the emblems on the façade are emblazoned SPQR, *Senatus Populusque Romanus* ('the Senate and People of Rome'). Created well over 2,000 years ago to symbolise Rome's glorious rule, this acronym is used everywhere on city property from buses to manhole covers, unselfconsciously thanks to its uninterrupted use through the centuries.

DETOUR
20 MIN

Take the wide steps to the left of the Senator's Palace halfway up, then go up to the left to the side door of **S. Maria in Ara Coeli** (open 6:30-12:00 and 15:30-18:00, to sunset in summer.) This fascinating church rises atop the Arx peak of the Capitol (p. 142) where the Temple of Juno Moneta once stood. Another major ancient Roman institution was probably there, too, which left an important mark on the church and its history: the Auguraculum, or 'Office of the Augurs', priests who predicted the future from the flight of birds. The high ridge of this most sacred Roman hill was clearly suitable for ritual bird-watching.

We don't know when the first Christian buildings replaced the pagan ones here. Records from the 8th century are the earliest to mention a

The Santo Bambino

church on the site dedicated to Mary. In the late 1200's the church and its adjacent monastery were assigned to the newly founded Franciscan Order (p. 411), which rebuilt them both. The new church, completed in the early 14th century, was much larger than the earlier one and perpendicular to it; its transept covered the whole area of the old church.

Some time before its reconstruction the church acquired the supplementary name of *Ara Coeli* ('Altar of Heaven' in Latin) appended to the old name of St. Mary. The addition derived from a legend, already centuries old, linking this site with the Emperor Augustus. It said that Augustus was once 'in his room on the Capitol' (actually he never lived there), when he had a vision of a beautiful Virgin over an altar holding a Child in her arms, while a voice from above proclaimed: 'This is the altar to the Son of God.' Augustus fell on his knees, and prayed to the Saviour Who was to come; then he had an altar built on the spot of the apparition.

What are the origins of this legend? A visit to the church uncovers the poignant answer and reveals another fascinating instance of medieval myth-making (compare the legend of Sts. Pudentiana and Praxedes, p. 94, or that of Sts. Rufina and Secunda, pp. 400-401, amongst others).

Over this (side) door of the church is a 13th-century mosaic of the school of the great Roman artist Pietro Cavallini.

Entering here brings you to the right aisle. Go left down this aisle to the main entrance and start your visit from there. If the main entrance is open, first go out to see the façade close up, and the captivating view. The late 13th-century romanesque façade is enlivened by three delicately ornamented portals, the minor ones surmounted by striking 16th-century reliefs of the Evangelists. The long flight of marble steps was inaugurated in 1348 by Cola di Rienzo (p. 144), as witnessed by an inscription left of the main portal. Now re-enter the church.

The 13th-14th century cosmatesque floor, strewn with tombstones, is everywhere colourful, especially so in the apse, which we'll reach shortly. Symbols of naval warfare adorn the splendid wooden ceiling installed to celebrate the victory of the Venetians over the Turks at Lepanto in 1571, which ended Turkish expansion in the Mediterranean. The columns articulating the church all come from ancient Roman buildings and are all different.

It is best to tour the church clockwise. Move to the left-hand row of columns. High up the third column bears a mysterious ancient Roman inscription, *A cubiculo Augustorum* ('From the room of the consecrated ones'). Recent research by the archæologist Cesare d'Onofrio has linked the inscription to the office of the Augurs, the Auguraculum. Indeed, according to the ancient historian Suetonius, the adjective 'augustus' was etymologically connected with the study of bird flight. All this indicates that 'Augustorum' meant none other than 'of the Augurs' and that the column comes from the grounds of the church itself where, as we mentioned, the Auguraculum was once located. A curious hole pierced in the marble at eye level was probably used for ritual sky-gazing. It is very probable that the words 'Augustorum' and 'cubiculo' (room) echoing through the centuries in the medieval subconscious and associated with the ancient dedication of the church to Mary, fuelled the legend of Augustus' vision of Mary 'in his room'. A fourth element of the legend, the *ara* ('altar') erected by Augustus, will be explained shortly.

The chapel behind the column has a 15th-century fresco by Benozzo Gozzoli over the altar of *St. Anthony and Two Faithful*; on the right wall is a tomb dated 1509. In the chapel to the left of this one, a famous *presepe* (nativity scene) is shown at Christmas. On a pillar between the two chapels is a fine statue of Paul III attributed to Guglielmo Della Porta (not to be confused with Giacomo).

Return to the row of columns. On the fourth column, converted into an altar, is an early 15th-century fresco of the *Madonna*, by a painter of the Sienese school. The fifth column is decorated with a fresco of *St. Luke* (15th-century); in front of it

lies the effaced tombstone of the *magister murator* ('master builder') of the new church completed in the early 1300's.

Continue up the left aisle. Outside the last chapel are two interesting epitaphs. On the left is the tomb of Prince Francesco Ruspoli (we'll see his palace on the Corso, p. 227). He was killed by a raging elephant in 1893, aged 27, while exploring East Africa. On the right is the tomb of Felice de Fredis, who discovered the famous statue of the Laocoön (p. 212) in the 1500's.

Climb the steps to the transept (the area covered by the earlier church perpendicular to the present one). Before you is a 17th-century canopy (actually a 19th-century copy) over an opulent 13th-century porphyry marble tomb. Go to the right of it, where you'll see a light switch. The tomb was pried open in 1963, revealing a marvellously carved 13th-century sandalwood box containing the relics of St. Helena, mother of the Emperor Constantine. Below (use the light switch) is a fascinating 13th-century altar with cosmatesque decorations and a relief of *Augustus' Vision of the Virgin* (upper corners). In 1963 probes under the altar showed that it rests on an ancient Roman wall – 2nd century AD or earlier – probably belonging to the old office of the Augurs (see above). The wall goes down many feet and was probably partly above ground in the early middle ages. In all likelihood the top of the wall sticking out of the floor of the older church suggested the idea of an *ara* or altar built there by Augustus – the fourth and last element of the legend.

On the end wall of the transept is the grand early 14th-century tomb of a cardinal, in the cosmatesque style and with a fresco by Cavallini. To the left is the early 16th-century monument to the portly Pope Leo X, the pleasure-loving patron of the arts (p. 117), by a minor sculptor. A door opposite the monument leads to a chapel with the Santo Bambino ('Holy Child'), a modern copy of a famous wooden doll in swaddling clothes. The 15th-century original, one of Rome's most venerated images, was stolen in 1993, presumably for

Savelli tomb in S. Maria Aracoeli, perhaps by Arnolfo di Cambio

the jewels pinned on it. Despite the national uproar, it has never been recovered. Said to possess miraculous healing powers, for centuries the doll used to be carried out of the church to comfort the sick and the dying. Moreover, children from all over the world used to write to the Bambino of their sorrows, and some still do. The letters are not opened, but placed around the doll for a time and then burned.

Return to the church and the transept. In the apse is a grand baroque altar surmounted by a 10th-century image of the *Madonna* from the earlier church. Diagonally opposite the altar are two late 12th-century pulpits signed by Lorenzo Cosma and his son (founders of the famous Cosma family), originally from the older church,

where they formed a single unit. When they were separated their shape was unfortunately changed.

Move to the other end of the transept. A chapel to the right of the main altar has its own side chapel, on the wall of which is a beautiful late 13th-century mosaic of the *Virgin and Child with Saints and a Donor* (it is visible from the gate). The donor, kneeling under the left saint, wears a medieval Roman senator's costume (p. 144) and has been identified as a member of the Capocci family (p. 106). In the remaining chapel at this end of the transept are two 13th-century tombs of one of the great baronial families of the time, the Savelli. On the right-hand tomb is the statue of Pope Honorius IV, a member of the family. The tomb on the left, the lower part of which is a 3rd century AD sarcophagus, is attributed to Arnolfo di Cambio. In the wall to the left of the monument are buried the remains of Brother Ginepro ('Juniper'), a lifelong companion of St. Francis of Assisi.

Go down the steps. In the first chapel restorations begun in late 2000 have uncovered extensive medieval frescoes, probably by Cavallini, contributing to our growing appreciation of this Roman artist, who now seems to have been comparable in importance to the Florentine masters in the development of painting on the eve of the renaissance.

Continue down the aisle. In the passage to the side door are two 16th-century tombs: the one on the left (1504) by Andrea Sansovino, the one on the right (1544) designed by Michelangelo, though not carved by him.

The next chapels in this aisle are frescoed by minor 16th- and 17th-century artists, except for the last one. The 15th-century paintings here are the work of Pinturicchio, and are amongst his masterpieces. They show the *Life of St. Bernardine of Siena*, a famous preacher and Franciscan friar who often visited the church. One of the paintings shows him with St. Francis and other saints; another shows St. Francis receiving the stigmata, the supernatural wounds of Christ. St. Bernardine died a few years before the birth of

Pinturicchio, who was christened Bernardino after him.

Left of the main entrance is the 15th-century monument to a cardinal by Andrea Bregno, one of his best works. On the wall next to it (left) is the tombstone of another prelate of the same era. It is signed in the upper left-hand border by the greatest Florentine sculptor before Michelangelo, Donatello, but is almost completely worn down, since it used to be on the floor.

END OF DETOUR

Underneath the Senator's Palace, a corridor was created in modern times to connect the different buildings. At the time some very interesting ruins came to light; they are accessible to the public through the Capitoline Museums.

Among the ruins are vestiges of private buildings from the imperial era, a stretch of an ancient street and the remnants of a 2nd or 1st century BC Temple of Veiovis, or Vediovis, an obscure, very ancient divinity of Etruscan origins, perhaps a 'young' Jupiter. There is also a colossal, headless statue of Veiovis. Near the temple are Republican era stairs that came up the hill from the Forum side but were later interrupted for the construction of a temple in the Forum. From the corridor one can pass to the front porch of the ancient Tabularium and its basement (which we'll discuss in a moment), with vestiges of mosaics and private buildings older than the Tabularium itself.

Walk to the right around the Senator's Palace. Before leaving the square, notice in the distance on your left the 13th-century **Torre delle Milizie** ('Soldiers' Tower') silhouetted against the sky. This is amongst the most impressive extant towers

View of Torre delle Milizie

of the feuding medieval barons, though an earthquake has knocked off at least one storey. It also leans a bit because of a sinking phenomenon similar to that of the leaning tower of Pisa. The tower will be in view for much of this Walk.

The right side wall of the Senator's Palace clearly shows how the structure combines various eras. Most of the left-hand and upper parts of the wall are from the medieval building preceding the renaissance remodelling. The right-hand and lower part are ruins of the ancient Tabularium, the monumental ancient State Archives. The powerful 1st century BC stone blocks of its walls are visible here, together with the ancient main doorway, which was here on the flank of the building, as the original front facing the Forum looked out over a cliff (p. 160). Left of the doorway is some of the original pavement.

BEFORE GOING

3. The Palatine and the Forum

The Palatine, cradle of Rome. Opposite the Capitol are another hill, the Palatine, and a valley, the Roman Forum. Of these three historic sites, the oldest is the Palatine. Here, a hardy band of shepherds, traders and farmers from the countryside to the south settled in remote antiquity. It was an ideal site for these future Romans. The proximity of the river ensured water and good transportation, while the hilly ground promised healthy air and a good defence. According to tradition, the momentous arrival took place on 21 April 753 BC, a date annually celebrated in Rome. Recent discoveries have shown that there is more to the story than sceptics had thought: traces of an 8th-century BC village have come to light just where the Romans believed the first walled city ('Roma Quadrata' or 'Square Rome') stood. Remains of what could have been the walls themselves were found in 1988.

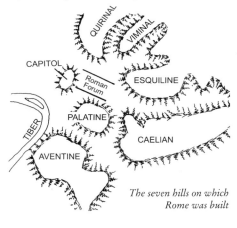

The seven hills on which Rome was built

All Rome's fabled beginnings have been tied to the Palatine. Tradition placed the den of the she-wolf that raised Romulus (Rome's supposed founder) and his twin brother Remus at the foot of the hill near the river. They had been abandoned by their mother Rea Silvia, who according to legend, was a princess of a nearby kingdom and a Vestal Virgin. As such, she would have betrayed her vows of chastity, though she claimed the god Mars had raped her. Did Romulus really exist? Until the time of the Emperor Nero (1st century AD) a thatched hut within Roma Quadrata, said to have been his house, was reverently maintained and re-thatched every year.

The first settlers dedicated the hill to their god of flocks and shepherds, Pales, hence the name Palatine.

The Forum, the original town square. This phase of the earliest beginnings also includes the birth of the Forum in the nearby valley, an area discussed in more detail later, but which we must mention now since its history is intertwined with that of the Palatine.

The valley, overlooked by the Palatine and the Capitol, as well as other, more distant hills, was a natural meeting place for all the people of the area. Here they began to gather to trade and to socialise, just as villagers everywhere still do today. In addition, before the Romans had conquered the neighbouring hills, this was the scene of their earliest conflicts, such as the battle against the Sabines of the Quirinal Hill, following the famous rape of the Sabine women (see p. 67).

Palatine chic. With the takeover of the surrounding hills – the first act in Rome's conquest of the world – and as the city burst out of the limits of Roma Quadrata, its nerve centres shifted from

The Forum and the Colosseum in Maggi's map of 1625

Julius Cæsar, Augustus and Tiberius, as shown on coins

the Palatine to the Capitol and the Forum. The Capitol became the civic centre and defensive citadel. The Forum became the place where votes were cast, soldiers enlisted, justice was rendered and transactions were sealed.

The Palatine became a sort of holy ground, where the richest and most eminent lived. The rest of the population spread out over the various hills, while the lowest classes huddled in the Suburra, a slum across the other side of the Forum and 'under' the city on the hills, as the name (meaning 'sub urbe') indicates. Beautiful patrician homes crowded the crest and slopes of the Palatine, hence the word *palatium* or 'palace'. Quite a journey for a word that originally came from the farming god Pales! Amongst the most famous politicians who lived on the Palatine in the first flowering of Roman life were Caius Gracchus, champion of the downtrodden and of democracy, who gave up his sumptuous home to live in the Suburra, and Julius Cæsar's friend and later enemy Mark Antony (Cæsar himself, though very rich, preferred the Suburra). The great orator and lawyer Cicero also lived here, along with his perhaps even greater lawyer colleague, Hortensius (we cannot judge, since Hortensius' speeches have not survived). On the slopes of the Palatine lived a rich family of the lesser nobility, the Octavii, which later spawned a fateful man, Caius Octavius, who was to become Octavianus Augustus.

The Palatine again the centre of power. At the twilight of the Republic, the roles of each area changed again. The death of Cæsar, the dictator assassinated in a desperate attempt to save Republican liberties, and the short struggle that followed, sounded the death knell of the Republic. When the young Octavius, who had been adopted as son and heir by his great-uncle Cæsar, emerged victorious, the basis was laid for the greatest and most powerful monarchy the world has ever known. Octavius, also known as Octavianus and later as Augustus ('the Consecrated One'), was first in a long line of monarchs to whom fell the task of holding together western civilization for the next five centuries.

Augustus was born on the Palatine. He lived there for the 40 years of his long, wise reign, first in his parents' villa, then in that of the lawyer Hortensius, bought and given to him by the people. Because of his charisma and his enormous impact on the Roman world, his successors also chose to live on the Palatine, though in far more lavish homes. Thus the Palatine once more became the centre of Roman power and the Forum lost its primacy, though it acquired an almost sacred character as a great symbol of the past, as we shall see. Both in the Forum and on the Capitol the once all-powerful Senate continue to convene, but after Augustus it was little more than a rubber-stamp.

Caligula, Claudius and Nero, as shown on coins

The emperors' presence on the Palatine and their fabled palaces inspired the poet Claudian to write the following verses (in Addison's translation):

The Palatine, proud Rome's imperial seat,	Ecce Palatino crevit reverentia monti
(An awful pile) stands venerably great:	Exultatque habitante deo potioraque Delphis
Thither the kingdoms and the nations come	Supplicibus late populis oracula pandit
In supplicating crowds to learn their doom.	Atque suas ad signa iubet revirescere laurus

Augustus' successors outdid each other with ever more splendid palaces; the poet Statius mused they were such 'as to make Jupiter himself envious of such a court'. Yet, after Augustus, an emperor's life was not easy, for assassins lurked around every corner. Such terrible stress may help explain some of the rulers' unbalanced personalities.

Looking at the Palatine from the terrace of the Capitol, one sees impressive foundations belonging to the oldest of the palaces, built by Augustus' immediate successor, Tiberius, and completed by Tiberius' successor, Caligula. There Tiberius saw his only son die, poisoned, it was said, by his son's own wife and her lover, Tiberius' right-hand man. Fearing for his own life, he left Rome to reside permanently on the inaccessible heights of the island of Capri, whence he kept in occasional touch with Rome through a primitive telegraph system. Caligula was insane; he walked around the palace in the most fantastic attire, male or female as he chose, and had a bridge built from there to the Capitol so that he could 'go chat with my friend Jupiter' in his golden temple (p. 142). He was brave enough to stay in Rome but was murdered near the palace.

In a new wing of the same palace, Caligula's successor, Claudius, was at dinner when news came of the execution of the wife he had once idolised, Messalina (p. 87). He listened silently and then told a servant to pour him some more wine. A few years later he ate deadly mushrooms which his fourth wife Agrippina had prepared in order to gain the throne for her son, Nero.

Nero built a complex of palaces, offices, pavilions and pleasure grounds so vast that the Palatine could not contain it; its thousands of rooms sprawled to the foot of the hill and onward to other hills. Only a small fraction of this Domus Aurea ('Golden House'), as it came to be called for its riches and marvellous art, survived Nero, whose suicide brought the Augustan dynasty to an end. The founders of the new Flavian dynasty, Vespasian and Titus, razed the immense compound and returned the land to the public, a populist gesture meant to earn them political capital (but see

View of the Forum in the 16th century by Martin Heemskerk

pp. 210 -211). They spared Nero's private residence, however, which still exists.

The third and last Flavian emperor, Domitian, built a new palace atop the Palatine. This great persecutor of Christians lived in hourly terror of assassination (though not by Christians), seeing a dagger around every corner. In the end he was stabbed by one of his most trusted aides, who faked a broken arm and hid a knife under his sling. The emperor ran around the room screaming, then vainly tried to fend off the killer bare-handed, but co-plotters entered and finished him off.

Rise and fall of the Forum. The origins. The word 'forum' almost certainly comes from *foras* ('outside') and initially referred only to the communal area outside the primitive town on the Palatine. As noted earlier, it was a meeting place and trading point for the people from the various hills, both before and after they were absorbed into the city-state that was born on the Palatine.

The site was then just a marshy plain, a backwater of the Tiber with little streams and ponds, where shepherds, farmers and traders bartered their goods. The valley was also used for burials, under the very ancient taboo on allowing these within the city limits. The remains of a necropolis contemporary with the traditional date of the foundation of Rome have been found there.

Shortly afterwards, the valley was reclaimed by channelling a single waterway underground to serve as a sewer for the now densely populated hills. This is the first recorded architectural feat of these ancient peoples, and it is a major one. The Cloaca Maxima, as it was called, is still partly in use (the original marble outlet in the Tiber is seen in the next Walk). Branches built later in other areas were so wide that they were inspected by chariot. The Romans learned how to build from their northern neighbours and sometime masters, the mysterious Etruscans (pp. 682-683), who probably directed the sewer construction.

Already in this initial phase the Forum was used for assemblies: Romans met there to vote, to be counted, to be drafted and to worship. The Comitium, a small area originally designed for these aims, is still identifiable. It contains remains of a primitive religious shrine. Others existed nearby, including the first Temple of the Vestal Virgins, a circular wood and straw hut. The Vestals were a religious sisterhood dating back to the original tribe. Their sacred duty was to keep a flame eternally burning, an important task in early times, when starting a fire was not easy. As we know, Rea Silvia, mother of Romulus and Remus, was a Vestal.

A humming centre of life. In the first centuries, these commercial, civic and religious functions quickly expanded and were housed in a growing collection of buildings. The village market became a permanent commercial mall. We know exactly where the stalls and *tabernæ* (stores) of different merchants were – spice-sellers, butchers, booksellers, jewellers and so on. A building went up just outside the Comitium area for Senate meetings; it is still there, albeit several reconstructions later.

The Forum became a throbbing centre of community life, reaching its heyday in the last centuries of the Republic, when the throngs and bustling activity became a literary leitmotif. People of all races and nations, rich and poor, citizens and slaves, poured in, preyed upon by pickpockets from the neighbouring Suburra. Public announcements were made, transactions, both public and private, took place, either in the open air or in the halls of the vast basilicas*. The latter were also used as courts, and, though virtually razed, are still an imposing sight.

The Via Sacra, the main artery of the Forum, and the other streets that still wind around the basilicas, temples and commercial areas, were jammed with pedestrians during rush hour (vehicles were barred). Idlers – who were legion once a welfare system was set up, paid for by conquered lands – loitered on the steps to play board games, which remain carved in the stones. Special events also attracted the public. On some days people were admitted to the Temple of the Vestals (now an elegant marble edifice, though still circular like the original hut) to see the ancient flame. Part of the temple still stands. Elsewhere they could see spears dedicated to Mars (*Martis hastæ*) hanging from a rope. These supposedly trembled at the approach of war. Priests also watched them for signs of earthquakes, like primitive seismographs. Then there were the ceremonies of the Salii priests (the name originally meant 'leapers'). The higher they could jump, the higher the next wheat harvest would be, another prehistoric ritual. Some temples, endowed with priceless works of art, also served as museums.

* 'Basilica' is a Greek word but a Roman architectural invention: a vast covered hall articulated by rows of columns and lit by a central window high up in the nave. This successful model was later adopted by Christians for their places of worship. Amongst the differences between a pagan and a Christian basilica are: pagan basilicas were surrounded by giant, usually two-storeyed, porticos, while the main entrance was on the long instead of the short side. Pagan basilicas had a civic not a religious function, which was fulfilled by temples. Pagan temples were reserved for priests, while worshippers assembled outside. Christians, on the other hand, all worshipped together, and so the basilica model was adopted as eminently suitable for large gatherings. Later the basilica model was taken over by the Muslims, who added a large courtyard to the long side to accomodate the large communal prayer meetings.

The hubbub often increased at events such as a politician's speech, a triumph (pp. 142-143) or macabre displays, as when the dictator Sulla, during the great civil clashes preceding the fall of the Republic, had his enemies' heads impaled around a fountain. The Forum was where Cæsar's body was taken after his assassination, and where Mark Antony made his famous funeral speech, immortalised by Shakespeare. The people built a pyre for the body, while veterans of Cæsar's wars came to throw their weapons on it and Jews – to whom Cæsar had been a strong protector – came to mourn. (Cæsar had defended the Jews' religious freedom and exempted them from public duties that conflicted with their pious obligations.)

From business centre to civic showcase. We have seen how, with the advent of the Empire, the Palatine replaced the Forum as the centre of political power. At the same time, however, the Forum acquired enormous symbolic importance. The amazing expansion of Roman power and civilization conferred an almost divine aura on the place where so many memories and legends of conquerors were born. For this reason Cæsar, and even more emphatically Augustus, the first emperor, began to transform the Forum into a monumental showcase. Commercial enterprises were pushed to new public areas developed nearby, the Imperial Fora (our next stop). Moneychangers were perhaps an exception: we believe this because coins have been found melted into the marble, where they may have fallen in the great panic and fire following the first barbarian invasion.

Meanwhile, ever more lavish temples, basilicas and monuments proliferated in the Forum. For the first time, statues and other monuments commemorating individuals people – such as triumphal arches and honorary columns – began to spring up. Augustus started the fashion by building a memorial column and temple to the 'God Cæsar' on the site of his cremation. This was also the first time that a defunct leader was deified, a custom which later became common and which some emperors even extended to themselves without waiting for death. Like the transformation from Republic to centralised monarchy, the practice of deification was an attempt to unify the domain by a transcendental bond between the far-flung masses and their ruler. One emperor even poked fun at the custom on his deathbed: 'I feel myself becoming a god,' smiled a waning Vespasian. Some emperors placed huge equestrian statues of themselves in the Forum, where the bases of the statues of Domitian and Constantine remain.

Twilight. Another turning point for the Forum was in the closing decades of the empire, when Christian rulers shut down the temples, a cruel blow to traditions that were still dear to many. The writer Zosimus describes a brooding old woman, the last of the Vestals, wandering through the deserted halls of the House of the Vestal Virgins, the flame that had burnt for over a thousand years gone out forever. In the Senate, the statue of the winged Victory, an age-old symbol of Rome as conquerer, was considered idolatrous and removed, precipitating one of the final crises in the relations between the Christian and pagan communities.

With the soul of the Forum extinguished, physical deterioration was quick to follow. No new monuments rose, except a gigantic column in honour of the Byzantine Emperor Phocas in 608, long after the western Empire had fallen. A wave of destruction and depredation accompanied the barbarian invasions. Yet the wealth of monuments in the Forum was such that it kept its appearance more or less intact throughout the 10th and 11th centuries. Meanwhile, the ground and

Cattle were still grazing in the Campo Vaccino ('Ox Meadow') at the end of the 19th century, when this photograph was taken

accumulating debris had begun to rise, covering the bases of the monuments.

Ironically, the wholesale destruction of the Forum really began in the renaissance, a time fanatically devoted to antiquity and classical ideals. Whole temples were demolished for use as raw material in buildings for the aristocracy and papacy. Columns were removed by the hundreds. An entire triumphal arch, Augustus' Triple Arch, was dismantled in 1540 for use in the new St. Peter's. Kilns worked round the clock converting marble into lime. The ground level of the Forum meanwhile rose inexorably. Soil and grass covered the area, which became ideal for grazing. Medieval buildings, including several churches, appeared over the ruins.

Already in the renaissance Raphael had started some archæological work, but it was only in the 18th century that people began to examine what lay beneath the greenery. The excavations intensified in the following century. At this time the area was still called *Campo Vaccino* ('Ox Meadow'), a name that persisted well into the 20th century. Romantic artists painted scenes of cattle grazing amongst the solitary marble chunks that jutted from the ground. Phocas' Column, the only monument never buried, presided mournfully over the landscape, eliciting wonder from painters and poets, though nobody knew what it was. 'Thou nameless column with a buried base,' Lord Byron called it.

In the last 150 years, the removal of 27 ft (8m) of accumulated soil, the demolition of medieval superstructures – with notable exceptions – and the restoration of some of the monuments have uncovered the scattered, broken remains. Yet this venerable clutter still echoes with the ideas, peoples and institutions that helped spawn western civilization.

Clivus Capitolinus

Temple of Vespasian

Temple of Saturn

ON THE SPOT

3. The Palatine and the Forum

Your view of these sites from above – which, as explained on p. 139, can be a substitute for actually walking through them – is best effected from more than one perspective. So the Walk will lead you to various viewing points: the terrace to the right of the Tabularium, then to its left, and then downhill. The sketches above should help identify what you are looking at.

Past the Tabularium, you are on the other side of the hill on a terrace overlooking the Palatine and the Forum.

On the terrace, stand near one of the middle pillars of the railing, preferably the largest one. To your left the wall of the main Capitoline building plunges down, the upper half formed by the renaissance rear façade of Palazzo Senatorio, the lower half by the front façade of the Roman Tabularium. A fuller description of this comes later.

To your right, at eye level, is the green **Palatine Hill**; the massive walls rising against it are foundations and service buildings of the Palace of

Tiberius and Caligula which rose on the hilltop. The palace, the first great imperial residence, is gone. Parts of it remain buried. Ruins of a bigger palace of a later dynasty are on another part of the hilltop. In another Walk we'll see, from the other side of the Palatine, many of these remains (p. 267, unless you decide to do the complete Forum-Palatine tour now, which is described separately on pp. 288-295).

At your feet is the **Roman Forum**. It covers the whole area from here to the heights marked by a white church and a very tall bell-tower, beyond which looms the Colosseum, one of our next highlights. Let's look at the Forum methodically.

Right under the terrace, a colonnade forming an obtuse angle was the **Portico of the Harmonious Gods (Dei Consenti)**. Between the columns it once held statues of the twelve major gods of Olympus, peacefully deliberating in mixed couples (Jupiter and Juno, Neptune and Minerva, Mars and Venus, Apollo and Diana, Volcanus and Vesta, Mercury and Ceres). It is a forlorn memento of paganism on the wane. The cult dated from the time of the Republic, and the portico probably dates from the time of Hadrian; it was

BASILICA JULIA

extensively repaired under the emperor Julian the Apostate, the 4th-century emperor who vainly tried to restore paganism after the triumph of Christianity under Constantine. This reconstruction is the last pagan monument in the Forum.

In front of the middle of the Tabularium are three beautiful columns, all that remains (one corner) of the 1st century AD **Temple of Vespasian**, built by the Emperor Domitian for his deified father (the one who joked as he died about becoming a god).

To the right of the three columns is a road made of big paving blocks called the *Clivus Capitolinus* ('Capitoline Climb'), the uphill stretch of the triumphal route (pp. 142-143) that ended on the summit of the Capitol at the Temple of Jupiter, now gone.

On the other side of the Clivus are eight columns in a double row, which formed the entrance façade of the very ancient **Temple of Saturn**. Attached to the columns is the brick core of the platform that supported the big rectangular temple. The structure, built in the 5th century BC and remodelled in the 1st century BC, was dedicated to a god who was hugely popular due to his

association with a mythical golden age in which all men were equal, an age fleetingly revived during the raucous *saturnalia* festivals. These precursors of the famous Roman carnival of later centuries, (pp. 123-125) began in mid December in front of these columns and consisted of two weeks of license in which slaves could take liberties, such as eating at their masters' tables. The temple also housed the city treasury and was looted by Julius Caesar during the civil wars. The Clivus Capitolinus started in front of the temple, where it joined the famous **Via Sacra**, the oldest street in the Forum, and the route traditionally taken by generals in triumphal procession. If you let your eyes follow the double row of columns, almost in line with them, but slightly to the right, you will see the paving stones of the Via Sacra.

To the right of the Via Sacra, the vast expanse of marble slabs with stumps of pillars and columns was the **Basilica Julia**, a magnificent three-storeyed, multi-naved hall donated by Cæsar for use as a courthouse. This is our first encounter with a prototype of that very successful Roman invention, the basilica (see footnote on p. 157).

To the left of the Via Sacra is a row of pedestals,

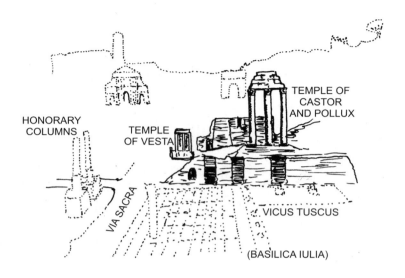

HONORARY COLUMNS

TEMPLE OF VESTA

TEMPLE OF CASTOR AND POLLUX

VIA SACRA

VICUS TUSCUS

(BASILICA IULIA)

two of which still bear columns. These were all columns erected to honour imperial dignitaries. Where the pedestals end on the left and the Basilica Julia ends on the right the Via Sacra turns sharply left, though you can't clearly see this from here. At the same point, the Via meets another ancient street, not visible from here, that turns sharply to the right. This was an elegant shopping street, the Vicus Tuscus ('Etruscan Street'), whose continuation, now a modern street outside the Forum, is in the Second Walk (p. 262).

Across the Vicus Tuscus rises a confused bulk of masonry and concrete together with three gigantic columns, perhaps the single most familiar feature of the Forum. These all belong to the **Temple of Castor and Pollux**, the mythical twin horsemen whom Romans believed would appear to help them in battle. We have already seen their statues elsewhere (pp. 68 , 145).

Left of the tall, free-standing columns are three much smaller ones, part of the circular **Temple of Vesta**, where the sacred fire burned. Behind it to the right was the **House of the Vestals**, where the virgin priestesses lived (now a low ruin). Like

nuns, they spent much of their days in the cloister-like courtyard, partly visible from here, which was decorated with statues of former Chief Vestals. With some effort, you can distinguish two of these. The Vestals were revered and enjoyed extraordinary privileges. Yet if they broke their vow of chastity, they faced death. Since on no account could their sacred blood be spilled, they would be buried alive. The man involved would be publicly flogged to death near the Temple.

In 1988 part of a wall was excavated behind the House of the Vestals which could be the one protecting the original group of huts on the Palatine. This wall of Romulus' Roma Quadrata seems to have been reinforced by a moat like the much later Republican Walls (p. 80). Behind the House of the Vestals rises a ridge, crowned by the Arch of Titus, that represents the limit of the Forum. It is more visible from other observation points and will be discussed later (pp. 209, 287-288).

Now observe some features in the far left-hand part of the Forum. Go to the far right of the iron railing and continue 10 to 20 yards along the low brick wall. Stop here, taking as a reference point

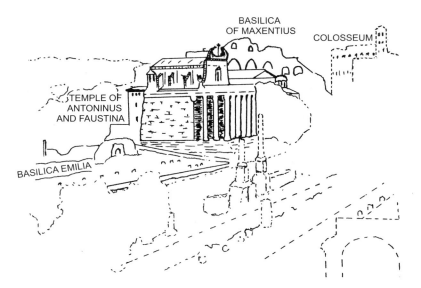

the top of the Colosseum beyond the ridge that marked the boundary of the Forum.

Starting from the Colosseum end, scan the Forum from right to left. First comes the top of the massive brick **Basilica of Maxentius**, with arched openings, an immense construction of the early 4th century AD, which we'll see again from further down the hill (p. 180). The next prominent building, with marble columns, is the sumptuous **Temple of Antoninus and Faustina**, both deified in the 2nd century AD. The temple was later turned into a church. (We'll approach it from a different direction shortly, the better to see its magnificent columns and frieze.)

Left of the temple are the low ruins of the other great meeting hall in the Forum, the **Basilica Æmilia**, built over a century before the Basilica Julia, but then rebuilt fifty years after it. It was somewhat smaller than the Basilica Julia but also had a two-storeyed portico. Part of the entrance wall facing the Forum still stands; one doorway has been rebuilt.

Before you leave: at your feet is the impressive continuation of the Clivus Capitolinus ascending

to the Capitol. Behind your back and to your right is the second of the two low peaks of the Capitol (see p. 142), the one where the resplendent Temple of Jupiter once rose. Only traces remain.

DETOUR:
10 MIN

Leaving the terrace, take Via Monte Tarpeo (behind you) away from the Tabularium, then take the first right into Via del Tempio di Giove up to the second peak of the hill, where you reach a wall with an arched window open to the sky. At the foot of the wall a low rectangular enclosure marks a deep excavation revealing a few blocks of stone. This is a corner of the foundation of the **Temple of Jupiter Capitolinus**, the greatest sanctuary in Rome.

The ruin was unearthed in 1919. Some pieces of a wall also survive, embedded in the basement of the nearby Capitoline Museums (p. 164), where further excavations of the temple sub-structures are presently underway.

A few steps to the left is a garden overlooking the cliff. Some scholars identify this site as the Tarpeian Rock, whence traitors were hurled to their deaths. As one of the 'improvements' introduced in the Jubilee Year 2000, this area has been closed to the public.

Return to the terrace overlooking the Forum.

END OF DETOUR

Go back to Capitol Square in order to reach another fine view of the Forum. Pass in front of Palazzo Senatorio and turn right at its end. Immediately past the corner, mounted on a column to your right is a small-scale reproduction of the famous Capitoline She-Wolf.

The original, housed in the Capitoline Museums, is a bronze masterpiece of great antiquity (6th or early 5th century BC), and is probably Etruscan. The She-Wolf has always been the symbol of Rome, linked to the legendary brothers, Romulus and Remus (p. 153). The suckling twins on the statue were added in the 15th century by the Florentine master Antonio Pollaiuolo.

On the left flank behind the She-Wolf is a 15th-century tower. Across the street in a little garden are remains of the walls of the Arx, dating back almost to prehistory.

Go down the left flank of Palazzo Senatorio; like the right, it is a mixture of ancient Roman and medieval parts, the latter prevailing. The most recent are from the 1400's, including another massive crenellated tower.

As you again reach the panorama of the Forum, you'll be at the top of steps descending the hill. Go down these steps all the way to the level of the modern street, where you'll find yourself facing a marble arch. This is one of the greatest triumphal arches ever erected by the Romans, the **Arch of Septimius Severus**, built by the Senate in the early 3rd century AD to honour this valiant emperor,

The Roman Forum as it appeared in the 18th century, with the Arch of Septimius Severus still partly underground, by Giuseppe Vasi

The Capitoline Wolf (5th-6th century BC); Romulus and Remus are a renaissance addition

who was born in the African colonies and was once just a simple soldier, and his two sons and later co-emperors, Antoninus and Geta.

After Septimius' death his eldest son Antoninus (nicknamed Caracalla, from a fancy Gallic gown he wore and wanted all Romans to wear) waited a year, then dispatched his co-emperor brother Geta by having him killed before their mother's eyes. He then had Geta's name removed from the inscriptions on either side of the top of the arch, according to a traditional procedure called *damnatio memoriæ* ('condemnation of the memory') inflicted on public figures fallen in disgrace. The erasures on the fourth line of the inscriptions are still obvious, even though they were covered with the words 'optimis fortissimisque principibus', 'best and strongest princes' in praise of the two imperial survivors. (This is more visible on the other side, but do not go there just yet.)

Of harmonious, majestic proportions, the arch

is architecturally splendid, even though the reliefs, representing Septimius' victories and his barbarian captives (the latter on the bases of the four columns), reveal the incipient coarseness of late-imperial workmanship, partly overcome by the expressive force and variety of the figures.

Immediately to the right of the arch is a round brick structure, the remains of the Umbilicus Urbis ('Navel of the City'), marking the very centre of Rome.

This is also the best spot to complete our viewing of Palazzo Senatorio: the impressive medieval tower on the corner and the Tabularium comprising the whole lower half of the structure. Try to visualise the ancient Roman part of the building as it was when it formed the monumental backdrop to the northern end of the Forum: a huge two-storeyed portico running the entire length of the façade. You can still see three arches of the lower storey; the rest have been walled up. The ancient

165

TEMPLE OF SATURN

TEMPLE OF VESPASIAN

PORTICO OF THE HARMONIOUS GOD

Tabularium was as tall as the present building; it had marble revetment and each arch framed a statue. Picturing it will also help you visualise the appearance of the ancient Roman basilicas, which were similar.

At this point it is worth trying to recognise the monuments we saw from the other terrace, especially the nearest ones: the Temples of Vespasian (three columns) and Saturn (eight columns), the Portico of the Harmonious Gods, and the Via Sacra winding round the Temple of Saturn, becoming the Clivus Capitolinus and ascending to the crest of the Capitol. (After the Arch of Septimius Severus was built, the triumphal processions occasionally passed beneath it.)

Now move along the brick parapet to the other side of the Arch, where the parapet forms a balcony over the Forum.

On your right, an esplanade at the centre of the Forum paved in travertine is the Piazza del Foro ('Forum Square') proper. It is dominated by the **Column of Phocas**, rising in solitary magnificence. This was the last monument to be erected in the Forum, in honour of the Byzantine Emperor Phocas. (This usurper, once described as 'the most perverse and ferocious tyrant that ever donned the imperial diadem', was one of the few to make the visit to Rome, in 608, long after the collapse of the Western Empire. He gave the Pantheon to the pope, but was beheaded, dismembered, disembowelled and burnt, on his return to Constantinople.) The art of making a column of such splendour had long been forgotten by the time Phocas visited, and this column was simply taken from a much earlier temple, of the 3rd century AD.

Behind the column and along the Via Sacra runs a line of seven pedestals for more honorary columns (of the columns themselves only one and a half survive). Where the pedestals end, the Forum Square ends too. You may remember that here the Via Sacra curved inwards, marking the shorter side of the square. Just beyond the shorter side are the few remains of the **Temple of the Deified Cæsar**, built by Augustus on the site of Cæsar's cremation. On the Ides of March, the

166

anniversary of Cæsar's death (March 15), people still bring flowers and light candles here.

Now let's consider the area nearest to our vantage point. Immediately to the left is a tall, unprepossessing brick building, the original seat of the ancient **Roman Senate** (called the Curia in its day). This is the third reconstruction of the building, following a fire in 283 AD. It was found more or less in its present state when a medieval church, built as a shell around it, was dismantled in the early 20th century. The brick façade was once covered with stucco, some of which is still visible under the cornice. The bronze door is a copy; the original was transferred by Borromini to the church of S. Giovanni in Laterano, where we'll see it in another walk.

The space before the Curia is the oldest official part of the Forum, the Comitium. Here, surrounded by a rectangular steel railing, is a small underground room with a primitive sanctuary of very great antiquity. Its nature is unclear. Historically, it was venerated as the Tomb of Romulus, though initially it must have had a dif-

ferent cult meaning, possibily a sanctuary to the god Vulcan (see p. 202). In the room is a stone with the oldest known Latin inscription (6th century BC or earlier); it has never been satisfactorily interpreted. An adjacent railing surrounds a black marble slab, the *Lapis Niger* ('Black Stone'), placed there in Cæsar's time to mark the holiness of the site. Access to the underground room is now barred. Immediately to the right is the pedestal of a column commemmorating wars against the barbarians (303 AD) and showing winged victories and sacrificial rites.

If at this point you feel inspired to embark on the full on-site visit of the Forum and the Palatine, turn to p. 279. The entrance is slightly further on in this walk.

Turning around, on your right you see the baroque church of **SS. Luca e Martina** (Saints Luke and Martina), a mid-17th century masterpiece by the painter and architect Pietro da Cortona. Observe the elegant façade and lively dome. It was built over the ruins of a 6th-century church, which had gradually been buried and

S. Luca e Martina and the Arch of Septimius Severus in 1775, by the French artist Barbault

which had occupied, in its turn, part of an office annexe of the adjoining Roman Senate.

The façade has a sculptural, monumental quality which, as the baroque scholar Anthony Blunt observed, is emphasized by the simplicity of the material, the rough travertine that Cortona favoured. In the middle section, coupled columns are set into the wall, following a formula devised by Michelangelo; but here the columns are spaced out and separated by projecting planes, carved with reliefs. This arrangement, and the presence of two rectangular blocks that frame the façade on both sides, produce an effect of overcompactness. Apparently Cortona meant to build two further bays outside these blocks, alleviating the pressure, but he died before the completion of the church and his plan was never fully realized.

DETOUR
10 MIN

The visit to the church is another short detour, only possible, however, if the promise to re-open the church has been kept. (It was closed eight years ago for restoration and excavations and was still closed at the time of writing.)

Besides building the church, Cortona, whose body lies under the nave, bequeathed it his entire fortune, which was sufficient to fund the splendid decoration of the interior.

Two notable paintings are: a contemporary copy of Raphael's *St. Luke Painting the Virgin* over the main altar and the *Assumption of the Virgin* by Sebastiano Conca (18th century).

Through a door to the left of the main altar you

descend into the 6th-century church, now serving as a crypt, with several marble columns and other architectural elements probably from the office annex of the Senate building. A corridor in the crypt leads to an octagonal room – over an altar is a terracotta relief of the *Dead Christ* by Cortona's contemporary, Alessandro Algardi – and to a chapel devoted to S. Martina, with a beautiful bronze altar by Cortona. Another terracotta relief by Algardi, depicting a group of saints, is in a nearby chapel.

END OF DETOUR

Detail of travertine stone used in S. Luca e Martina

Just past SS. Luca e Martina is a marble porch inscribed MAMERTINUM surmounted by the church of S. Giuseppe dei Falegnami ('St. Joseph of the Carpenters'), built in the early 17th century by the Guild of Carpenters and dedicated to their patron saint. The church stands over the oldest, most terrible Roman prison, the **Mamertine**. Indeed, it bestrides the path that originally led to the prison, on which were stairs (now only traces remain) called the *Scalæ Gemoniæ* ('Stairs of Moans') in ancient Rome, because of their destination (not so different from the 'Bridge of Sighs' in Venice).

The church is occasionally open, and has a charming interior decorated by minor 17th- and 18th-century artists.

The porch inscribed MAMERTINUM is not the entrance to the ancient prison, but was built at the same time as the church above it as a kind of advertisement. The real entrance to the Mamertine Prison is one floor down. (Open: 9:00-12:30 and 14:00-18:30.)

Go down the steps. The stern façade belongs to a 42 AD restoration by the Consuls Rufinus and Nerva, as the original inscription says. The dungeon itself is extremely ancient. Initially Rome's only prison, it was later used only for the detention and execution of political prisoners.

The prison consists of two chambers, one above the other. The lower one is now reached by a modern staircase, but originally it could only be entered – and, of course, not easily left – through a hole in the floor. The lower, more ancient chamber (around 6th century BC) was originally called *Tullianum,* the place of the *tulla* (or 'spring'), because it must initially have been a cistern. In this 'so silent, so close and tomb-like' space (Dickens' description) many famous adversaries of Rome perished, including Jugurtha, the African king who was starved to death in 104 BC; Vercingetorix, the Gallic hero who vainly tried to stop Cæsar's advance in 45 BC; and Simon Bar Giora, the valiant defender of Jerusalem against Emperor Titus in 70 AD. The last two died as the victors celebrated their triumphs on the Capitol above. Others who fell here were the alleged co-plotters of Catiline, a politician accused by Cicero in a famous oration, for unclear motives, of hatching a revolution (Cicero reported their execution to the people with the single word *vixerunt* – 'they have lived') and Sejanus, the Governor of Rome accused of having murdered the son of the Emperor Tiberius (p. 155).

A medieval tradition, now considered a legend, has it that Saints Peter and Paul were imprisoned in the lower chamber to await their execution, tied to a column which is still visible. A 19th-century altar in the upper chamber commemorates them.

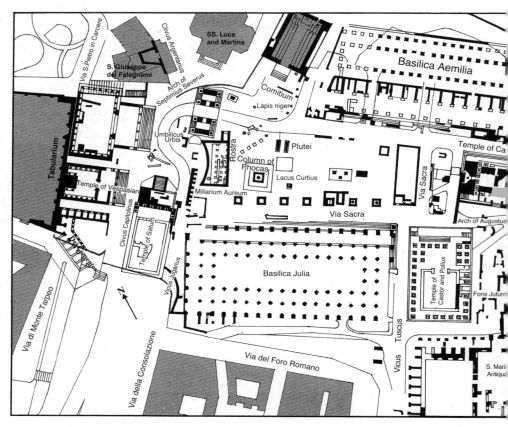

Plan of the Roman Forum

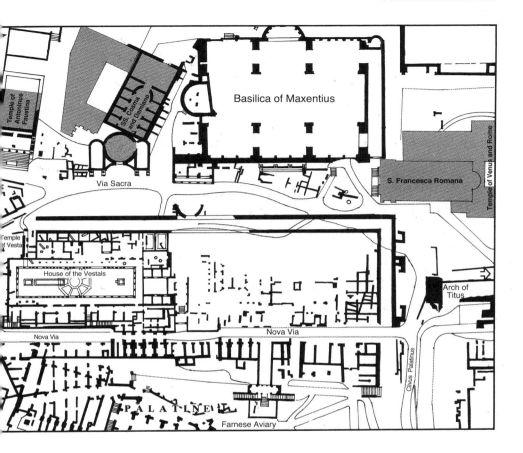

Temple of Antoninus Faustina

SS. Cosma and Damian

Basilica of Maxentius

Via Sacra

S. Francesca Romana

Temple of Venus and Rome

Temple of Vesta

House of the Vestals

Nova Via

Nova Via

Arch of Titus

Clivus Palatinus

P A L A T I N E

Farnese Aviary

BEFORE GOING

4. The Imperial Fora

You may recall that the decommercialisation and transformation of the Forum into a patriotic showcase involved the creation by the first emperors (or more precisely, the autocrats who ruled at the end of the Republic and who were later called emperors) of new public business centres suitable for the public activities of the growing State.

These *Imperial Fora* border on the old Roman Forum and together they form one monumental area, the largest and most famous of any city in the ancient western world. All this is very difficult to visualise today, however. All you initially see is a wide modern avenue, peppered with excavations whose meaning, interrelation and connection to the general picture are far from obvious. It takes some mental acrobatics and some understanding of the complex evolution of the area to reconstruct the ancient appearance of this key aspect of classical Rome.

Mussolini's legacy. We can divide the post-imperial history of the Fora into four phases: the middle ages to the early 1900's; the Fascist era to the end of the Second World War; the post-war period; and the time since the Jubilee Year 2000.

The area remained more or less unchanged in appearance for some six centuries after the Empire collapsed, before many of its monumental features were pillaged or gradually fell. Their collapse raised the ground level, and houses and churches were built on various levels going up, with the modern street level being about 27 ft (8 m) above that of ancient Rome. Far from being an open air museum, it was a living part of the city, much like any other part of Rome. It was not until the end of the 19th century that archæological research begun some decades earlier in the Roman Forum expanded into the Imperial Fora and parts of the quaint, mostly still medieval district were razed in order to dig out patches of the old Fora.

In the early 1930's Benito Mussolini, eager to show off the splendours of classical Rome (with which his Fascist movement had always identified) ordered the construction of the avenue you now see between the Capitol, the Fora and the Colosseum. He called it 'Via dell'Impero' ('Empire Street') in reference not only to antiquity but, more pointedly, to Italy's colonial expansion in Africa, to which he himself had contributed with the annexation of Ethiopia. The new road had perforce to run through the Imperial Fora. Building it required not only flattening new sections of the old medieval district, but re-filling some sections of the Fora unearthed earlier. (Even more insanely, a major relic near the Colosseum – the Meta Sudans fountain, discussed below – was destroyed to ease traffic.) To enhance the drama of the new avenue, Mussolini's men lined it with bronze reproductions of statues of the ancient emperors (as if Rome hadn't enough originals) and hung one wall along the street with five large marble maps: four showed the evolution of the Roman Empire, the fifth Mussolini's budding colonial empire. All this gave the area a new-fangled, theatrical sort of monumentality that awed visitors, including Adolf Hitler on his visit to Rome in 1938.

Romans were less impressed. They used the reproduction statue of Augustus for an anti-fascist pasquinade: protesting against the inedible bread supplied as part of war-time rations, they hung a loaf on the statue with the verses: 'With your iron stomach, eat the bread of the [Mussolinian] empire' ('Co' sto stomaco de fero, magna er pane de l'Impero.')

The present scene. After the defeat of Fascism at the end of the Second World War the avenue was politically cleansed by a change of name – becoming 'Via dei Fori Imperiali', its present name, without any reference to modern imperialism – and by the removal of Mussolini's fifth marble map. Otherwise, it remained unchanged, even down to the bronze reproduction statues. The small unearthed sections of the Fora were visible, and though they formed a disjointed patchwork quite unlike the ancient, majestic ensemble, at least most of the basic elements of each forum were there, isolated but clearly recognisable.

Then came the Jubilee Year 2000. An archæological frenzy took hold, fuelled by the 'political-antiquarian complex' (see pp. 678-679). Here it was a campaign to unearth all of the Fora and turn them into a promenade, despite the obvious obstacle of the avenue. The result is confusion and frustration. A string of excavations have revealed large new patches of the Fora, but centuries of destruction have ensured that they include practically nothing of note, and most of what is visible is an indecipherable jumble of remains from the middle ages to the 19th century. This has complicated the already difficult task of mentally reconstructing the ancient Fora, and also made it harder to approach some of the older, more significant excavations. A plan to make the whole area directly accessible inside the excavations was not carried out (except sporadically) owing to a lack of personnel, and even if it did happen, it would do little to increase the comprehension and enjoyment of the average visitor.

The present scene is thus one of dazed masses of tourists wandering about the avenue, anxious to see the ancient glories but repelled by the incomprehensible clutter of the new excavations and barely aware of the old ones, which in some places are smaller and further off. Many people are reduced to observing, photographing or filming the fake statues, which they mistake for the main ancient feature, and the Fascist-era maps. Their remaining attention is taken up by costumed Roman soldiers, who are now permitted to circulate amongst the tourists, Disneyland-style, and be photographed with them for a price. Even the authorities seem disoriented by the mess: a pamphlet issued by the city's Department of Culture calls the present avenue, built in 1932, 'one of the most beautiful roads of the Imperial Age'!

An effort of mental reclamation. To counteract, at least mentally, these pernicious developments and get a rough picture of the ancient Fora area, we suggest you: (1) try to understand the spatial layout of the archæological site and its components by patiently reading the indications in our On the Spot section; (2) be on the alert in distinguishing the ancient features from the Fascist fakes; (3) ignore as much as possible the results of the archæological fervour that has taken a heavy toll in the area in recent years.

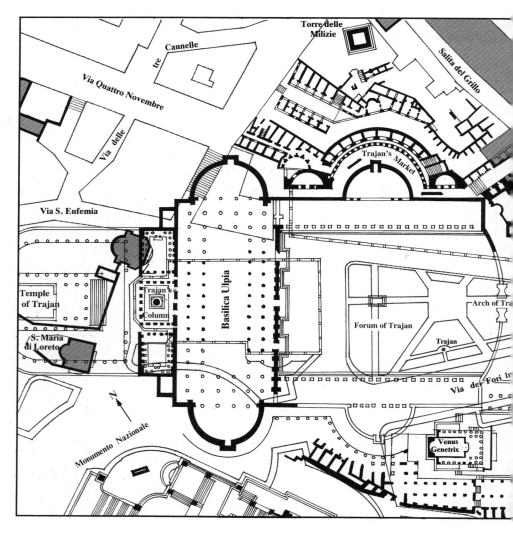

Plan of the Imperial Fora

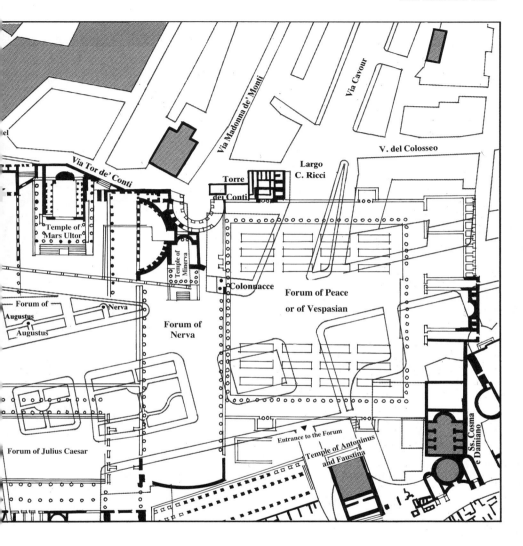

ON THE SPOT

4. The Imperial Fora

Leave the prison and walk down the left-hand side of the church of SS. Luca e Martina in front of you (Via del Tulliano), stopping at the end.

Here we can get a picture of the great extent of the Imperial Fora. The area is a very irregular rectangle extending from the two church domes on the left to the group of traffic lights on the right on the modern avenue. The depth of the rectangle is marked by the leaning Torre delle Milizie, visible amongst the trees in front of you. Remember that behind you the rectangle joined the Roman Forum in a single vast, monumental complex. Let's investigate the main features of this rectangle, trying also to follow its development in time.

Go back toward the Mamertine Prison and start (right) up the Clivo Argentario; the name, now Italianised, of this ancient Roman street means 'Financial Hill'. It recalls the commercial-cum-financial nature of these newer fora, which were added to the Roman Forum for mainly practical reasons. Along this street were offices, the stark brick ruins visible on the right. The street pavement is *basolato*; though originally flat, it is now worn and bumpy, and in part rebuilt.

At the top of the Clivo, across the street at the foot of the huge Altar of the Fatherland (see p. 545 – the entrance to the Museo del Risorgimento is here too, see p. 686) are some blocks of volcanic *tufa* rock, vestiges of a very ancient wall, though it is not known whether they are from Rome's pre-imperial walls, which circled this hill (p. 188).

The imperial fora in the 4th century AD, from the model at EUR. Trajan's Column can be seen standing between the Temple of Trajan and the Basilica Ulpia; beyond are the Fora of Trajan (with the markets to the left), of Augustus (with the Temple of Mars Ultor) and of Julius Cæsar. The narrow sliver of the Forum Transitorium, or of Nerva, is clearly seen filling in the space between the Forum of Augustus and the Forum of Vespasian. The much smaller spaces of the Roman Forum, dominated by the Palatine, are clear on the right

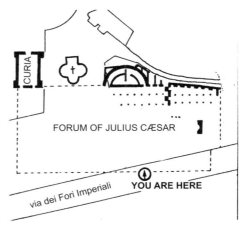

FORUM OF JULIUS CÆSAR

YOU ARE HERE

via dei Fori Imperiali

The Forum of Cæsar, the first of the new complexes added to the Roman Forum at the end of the Republic

Go downhill and around to the modern avenue. Before continuing to your right along the avenue, at the corner there is a small column marking its inauguration in 1932 under Mussolini, whose name is conspicuously listed. It is our first hint of the Mussolinian face of the avenue, originally called Via dell'Impero and rebaptised Via dei Fori Imperiali after the fall of Fascism.

Walk along the excavation a short distance to a large bronze statue of Julius Cæsar on the pavement near the parapet, just before the end of the first part of the excavation. The statue is one of several statuary reproductions of Roman rulers placed along the Fora in the Fascist era, the originals of which belong nowhere near here.

The parapet behind the statue is the best spot to view the excavated **Forum of Julius Cæsar**, built in the late 1st century BC. Cæsar, who monopolised power briefly toward the end of the Republic, was the first of the dictators who would rule the Roman commonwealth, now a full-grown empire; and this forum was the first of the new communal Fora built at the dawn of the imperial

177

era. It already shows all the features of these great plazas: a porticoed square, commercial buildings, a basilica for meetings and one or more temples.

Cæsar's Forum is a rectangle lying more or less parallel to the modern avenue, which covers more than half of it. On one long side the forum bordered the Roman Forum: on the left it extended to the foot of the present church of SS. Luca e Martina; on the right it went all the way to the corner of the modern Altar of the Fatherland. In Cæsar's day that corner was blocked by a high earthen spur linking the Capitoline and Quirinal hills, which as we'll see later was later levelled by Emperor Trajan, at the same time as he was renovating most of Cæsar's Forum.

In front of you the double row of columns was part of a portico framing the entire square. The large, arched brick structure behind the columns was the Basilica of the Argentarii ('of the Money-changers', equivalent to today's bankers), a primitive bank and stock exchange built in the Forum after Cæsar's death. As you may recall, behind the basilica is the ancient Clivus Argentarius ('Financial Hill'). Nearby are some ruins of a three-storey residential building. In the area were found the largest ruins of ancient Rome's *foricæ*, or public latrines (p. 141), not visible from the outside.

Three tall columns dominate to the right. They belong to the left side of the Temple of Venus Genitrix ('Venus the Ancestress'), dedicated by Cæsar to the goddess from whom his family claimed descent to thank her for his decisive victory at Pharsalus with which he gained power. The temple stood against the spur mentioned above. It was one of the temples that was turned into a museum. Cæsar began his collection with several priceless works of art, including a gilt statue of Queen Cleopatra of Egypt, his mistress and later Mark Antony's. In front of the temple he erected a statue (since vanished) of his famous horse, which he had nursed when he was a child and which he rode into all his battles.

Excavations under Caesar's Forum started in 2006 have found remains of prehistoric tombs dating back to 1000 BC, three centuries before the traditional date of Rome's foundation. These are the oldest indication of human settlement ever found in this general valley area (see also pp. 153, 156, 263 and 286).

Continue along Via dei Fori Imperiali in the same direction (towards the Colosseum) as far as the traffic lights. On the way, ignore the digs on the right, the result of an unsuccessful archæological campaign in 2000-01. Cross at the lights. Then come back on the other side, along the low railing with street lamps overlooking the dig, and stop when you get to another of the bronze reproduction statues. Inside the excavated area is a broad white marble staircase; take up a position directly in front of it. This is the **Forum of Augustus**. As Augustus succeeded Cæsar, his forum borders on Cæsar's (at a point now lying under the modern avenue). Remember that Cæsar's Forum, in turn, adjoined the Roman Forum, and all the Fora formed a continuous complex.(See map opposite.)

The wide marble staircase belongs to the most noteworthy feature of the Forum, the Temple of Mars the Avenger (Mars Ultor), erected by Augustus to celebrate having avenged Cæsar's assassination by his victory at Philippi, where Cæsar's murderers met their deaths. You can see the platform, columns, part of the inner sanctum, or *cella,* and a stepped base at the back that originally supported statues of Mars, Venus and Cæsar.

Notice the mark left by the structure on the monumental wall at the far end of the Forum, which separated it from the Suburra, the ancient slums. As you may remember (p. 154), the Suburra ('Suburb') is where the poor had moved in the initial expansion from the Palatine settlement. Augustus' purpose in erecting such a massive wall was probably to contain the frequent fires in the crowded slums, which consisted mainly of wooden hovels. Beyond the wall the Suburra extended at the foot of the hills, which begin to rise gradually here.

The Temple of Mars the Avenger, too, doubled

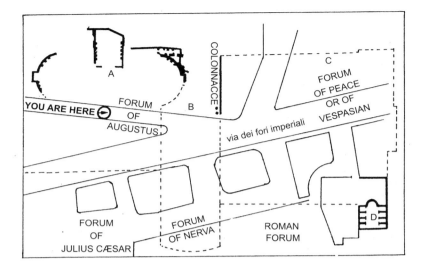

The complex of the Fora of Cæsar, Augustus, Nerva and Vespasian (partly covered by the avenue built in the 1930's to link Piazza Venezia with the Colosseum)

as a museum, containing amongst other memorabilia Cæsar's sword. A statue of Augustus on horseback stood before it. Parts of the temple are still faced with marble, though much of this revetment was used in the 1600's for a great fountain on the Janiculum (p. 564). Some of the multi-coloured marble paving also remains.

Vestiges of other buildings survive in the Forum. To the right and left are marble staircases that led to the Suburra.

The Forum is bounded on all sides by curved walls, once decorated with colonnades and statues. Amongst the latter was a colossal statue of the 'Genius of Augustus', of which a footprint remains on the left side. At the curve on the left is the House of the Knights of Rhodes, built over the ruins in the 1100's and remodelled in the 1300's, which we'll discuss shortly (p. 191).

For 73 years the complex formed by the Roman Forum and the Fora of Cæsar and Augustus sufficed as the civic and commercial centre of Rome. None of the immediate successors of Augustus, from Tiberius to Nero, felt the need to enlarge it. But as the metropolis began to expand again, so did this public area.

It is worth glancing at the map to follow the expansion visually. The Forum of Augustus, where we are standing, is at (A). To the far right are two ornate columns (B). For now just use them as a reference point. Beyond them was the first addition to the complex, a gigantic Forum of Peace (C) built by the Emperor Vespasian (pp. 192-194) on his return from the war in which he had crushed the Jews of Palestine in 70 AD, with the help of his son and successor, Titus. Of the entire Forum of Peace, only one hall (a library) survives, transformed into a church that stands across the avenue (D). We visit the church later.

The successor of Vespasian and Titus, Domitian, was a great builder (his Stadium is the modern Piazza Navona, p. 452). He continued the expansion by developing the sliver of land left between the Fora of Augustus and Vespasian. After his assassination (p. 155) his successor,

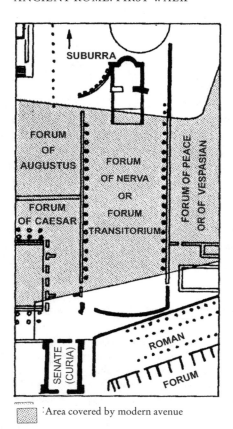

: Area covered by modern avenue

*The Forum of Nerva, also called
the Forum Transitorium*

Nerva, finished the project in 93 AD. It is called the **Forum of Nerva** or Forum Transitorium. Its most obvious features are the two grand columns we used earlier as a reference point. Go to them.

Known since the middle ages as the 'Colonnacce', which translates roughly as 'those old columns', they now look like part of a temple, a mistaken impression accentuated by the (over-restored) gate between them. Actually, together with the lavish frieze, they belonged to a dazzling double array of 38 columns bordering both sides of the Forum, and extending behind you across the modern avenue. This was a false portico – there was no space between columns and perimeter walls – and a superb solution to the problem of conferring grandeur on a narrow strip. Nerva's Forum linked the Roman Forum to the Suburra and to the other nearby Fora; hence its many gates (past the one between the columns, there is another wide portal, now walled up, which led to Vespasian's Forum) and its other name, 'transitorium'. Nerva's Forum was dedicated to Minerva, goddess of wisdom and crafts. What remains of her temple is the grassy mound and a base of large blocks. Here the emperor had his chamberlain Vetronius Turinus asphyxiated by smoke for influence peddling: 'He who sells smoke must perish by smoke,' was Nerva's verdict. Above 'those old columns' are a relief and a frieze, traditionally said to represent Minerva and the feminine crafts she protected, but recently interpreted as part of a much longer frieze symbolising the provinces of the Roman Empire. In front of the columns, a stretch of the old street leading to the Suburra is visible, heavily marked by cart tracks.

Nerva's successor, Trajan, was the first emperor chosen not by birth or by his predecessor's designation, but because he was judged the best by the Army and Senate. A Spaniard, he was also the first non-Italian emperor. Under him the Empire reached its maximum expansion across three continents. In 107 AD he decided to celebrate his conquests by further enlarging the Forum complex. What he did is the subject of the next section.

5. The Imperial Fora continued

As there was no more space in the valley when he decided to expand the Fora, Trajan and his great architect, Apollodorus of Damascus, razed the spur of the Quirinal hill to the left of the Forum of Augustus which, as you may recall, bordered on the Forum of Cæsar (pp. 177-178). This operation created a broad new space at the foot of the Quirinal. (It also connected the Fora with the other monumental area which Augustus had built in the Campus Martius, the object of the second Ancient Rome Walk). The earth-moving feat took just a few months. The resulting space was the largest and most majestic of the monumental areas that the emperors had added to the Roman Forum. Trajan's architectural feat inspired awe in the ancients themselves, not only when it was performed, but even more so later, when well before the great Empire fell the Romans were already reminiscing about the golden age of their forefathers.

An episode in the history of Trajan's Forum illustrates this nostalgia. In the late 3rd century AD the Empire still had two centuries of life, but the emperors had begun to abandon Rome as their administrative capital. The imperial courts and government increasingly moved to cities in the outer reaches of the empire in order to bolster defence against mounting barbarian pressure. Some emperors had never even been to Rome, including Constantine II and Constantius II, sons and successors of Constantine. They ruled the Empire from Constantinople, the city Constantine had founded on the Bosphorus, astride Europe and Asia. In 356 Constantius visited Rome with an escort of European and Asian dignitaries and was overwhelmed by the monuments. The soldier-historian Ammianus Marcellinus, who may have been present at the occasion, wrote:

> But when he [Constantius] came to Trajan's Forum, a creation that in my judgment has no peers under the heavens and the gods themselves must envy, he was awestruck. He stood there transfixed, surveying with an astonished eye the gigantic fabric, of such grandeur that it defies description and can never be replicated by mortals. He said he would never attempt to imitate such a work, and that he would be content just to have a reproduction made of Trajan's horse, whose statue stands in the square with the emperor on its back. Hormisdas, the Persian prince who was part of the retinue, remarked with Oriental finesse: 'Yes, sire, but first you must have a similar stable built, if you can. The horse wants the same space to range.'

After the fall of the Empire, in the darkest periods of Roman history, Trajan's complex continued to cast its spell. Venantius Fortunatus, a 6th-century poet and Bishop of Poitiers, tells of listening to recitals there of the works of Virgil, the bard of Rome's golden age and by then a heart-rending memory from an irretrievable past. With its quiet promenades, schools and libraries, its Hall of Liberty, arts and aura of mystery, Trajan's Forum still fills us with a sense of timeless civilization.

Almost a movie and 1,900 years old. This book will attempt to do something as yet unachieved by any guidebook to Rome that we know of: to make one of the most famous and dramatic monuments of the Imperial Fora, Trajan's Column, fully legible. The huge marble shaft is covered from top to bottom with reliefs chronicling in extraordinary, vivid detail two major campaigns against the barbarians. In antiquity the column was flanked by buildings from which one could see the reliefs close up. These buildings fell in the middle ages, so it is hard to see the reliefs from the foot of the 132 ft (40 m) monument, not to mention follow their story, especially if you don't know it. We attempt to overcome such problems by selecting some of the narrative highlights, explaining the story they tell and where best to view them from. This requires your patient co-operation, but the reward is great. We willingly spend money and time to watch a fanciful re-enactment of a Roman battle in a Hollywood movie, whereas here you can see these struggles unfold on a marble scroll created in authentic, fascinating detail by the very people who fought them.

ON THE SPOT
5. The Imperial Fora continued
Continue in the same direction (though a 'temporary' obstruction created here during the archæological frenzy mentioned on p. 173 was still here a few years later and may force you to go right around). Just beyond the Forum of Augustus you'll be on the edge of the area reclaimed by Trajan when he had the spur flattened. Stand at the railing at a point facing the

Trajan's Market, part of Trajan's Forum

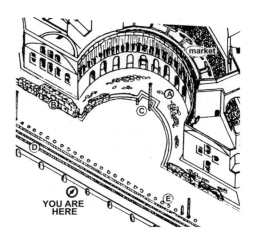

middle of the excavation, or as close as possible to it. (In the more recent excavations behind you, the base of the famous equestrian monument to Trajan was found – see p. 181 – but otherwise there is nothing much of interest to see.) The **Forum of Trajan**, last of the Imperial Fora, is as large as all the others combined and of a majesty that quickly made it one of the marvels of the classical world.

First let's look in front of us. The backdrop is a great semicircular structure (labelled 'Market' in the diagram). Take it as a reference point. A street (A) runs around the semicircle, continuing straight on either side of it. Our side of the street was once bordered by a wall of the same shape (straight, apsed, then straight again); of this wall only a few inches at the bottom remain, though note a substantial portion still standing on the extreme left (B). The centre of the curved wall formed a niche articulated by two columns (C), the one on the right re-erected. Directly before you, at the top of the three steps (D), ran a row of columns (E), of which you can now see one to the left, one and a half to the right and the outlines of the bases of the rest. All this grandly ornamented ensemble – apsed wall, niche, columns – formed one end of an immense central square (P in the next diagram). It was surrounded by magnificent arcades, entered behind you and to your right through Trajan's Arch, long since destroyed.

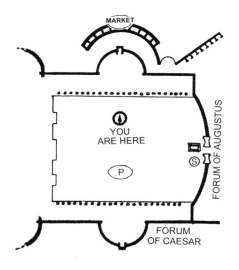

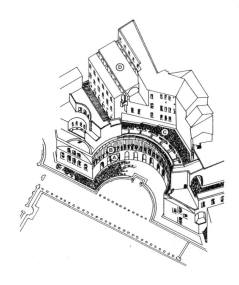

Plan of the central piazza of Trajan's forum, now partly covered by the road

The grandiose structures of Trajan's Market, one of the main commercial and administrative centres of the ancient city

Near the entrance was the equestrian statue of Trajan, now gone except for the outline of the base. In antiquity it was the most celebrated of its kind. Considering the breathtaking equestrian statue of Marcus Aurelius, p. 146, we can only imagine what this one must have been like. The opposite end of the central square adjoined Cæsar's Forum. The whole square was paved with multi-coloured marble slabs, some of which are still visible, especially in front of the niche.

The square was just one of the five giant elements of the Forum. The second was the great semicircular structure itself ('Market') and what lies behind it. The building served to buttress the cut-off hillside. It was a fabulous, unprecedented construction commonly called **Trajan's Market**. This modern name is based on the theory, recently called in doubt, that it was a shopping mall. At some time there must have been a series of stores (*tabernæ*), but the building must have had more than commercial functions. Some schol-

ars think that it was a civic and administrative centre used, amongst other things, for the distribution of welfare food and educational activities.

On the ground floor rooms (A) open onto the square. On the second floor (B) is a row of arched windows; behind them is a long corridor and behind that a row of rooms (shops or offices perhaps?). The façade of the third floor was destroyed in the middle ages when the structure was turned into a castle. Behind the missing upper façade was a third row of rooms, the outlines of which are still clearly marked. They opened onto a marvellously preserved upper street, which we'll see later (C).

To the left the structure is topped by further floors, partly occupied by stores and rooms, partly by a giant atrium (D) – the entrance to the market from the hillside, which we'll also see later. Finally note (top right) a medieval superstructure with two Gothic windows and in the background

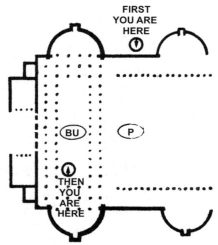

Plan of the central piazza of Trajan's Forum and, left, of the Basilica Ulpia

the Torre delle Milizie (p. 151). Before moving on, notice on the far right an original flight of steps that led to the Suburra. The large structure with the arcaded loggias to the right of the steps is the medieval House of the Knights of Rhodes, which you saw from the Forum of Augustus (to be discussed shortly).

Ignoring the new and unproductive excavations behind you (if you are still looking at the market) go left a few steps, then turn and look at the older excavations on the same side.

The slightly lower area to your left (P) is part of the main square of Trajan's Forum. As we said, it was the first element of the great complex, the second one being the so-called market. In the area in front of you with many standing columns are the remains of the third element, the **Basilica Ulpia** (BU), named after Trajan's family. A gigantic edifice, it was almost twice as big as the older basilicas in the Roman Forum. It ran parallel to the main square and had one nave and four aisles.

The two rows of columns mark the nave (on either side are some of the bases of the columns forming the four aisles). Like the other basilicas, it had two storeys and so the rows of columns we see were surmounted by another set of smaller columns. We see only part of its length; the rest, including two great apses at both ends, is buried. Of the two apses, the one farthest from you housed the *Atrium Libertatis* ('Hall of Liberty'), a hall used for ceremonies of manumission, marking the enfranchisement of slaves.

In the centre of the great nave, the section farthest from you still shows the original pavement design; make your way round to it for a better view.

Next to the basilica is the fourth of the five elements of the complex, an architectural group centred on the marvellous **Trajan's Column**, depicting as on a scroll the two wars in which Trajan conquered Dacia (Romania). Little more than the column itself remains of the architectural group which it dominated, but originally there were two tall buildings next to it, aligned with the basilica: a Latin library and a Greek library (in Rome's heyday, the upper classes were bilingual). Remains of the ground floor of one of the libraries, with recessed walls holding shelves for scrolls, are accessible from the Basilica Ulpia, but are rarely open. From the upper floors of the libraries the public could see the spiralling relief on the column at close range.

Walk up to the column. Including the base it is 132 ft (40 m) high, the exact height of the spur of the Quirinal before it was swept away by Trajan's engineers. Indeed the formal purpose of the column was to commemorate this great technical feat, which it does in the last two lines of the wonderful inscription on the base, which read: 'to indicate how high was the hill cut down in such a great enterprise'. The script here is considered a marvel in itself, the most beautiful of its kind in existence. (We have used it for the word Rome on p. 33.)

Trajan's column in the 1930's

A small door in the base leads to a sepulchral cell, now empty, where a golden urn once held Trajan's ashes. Those who, like Trajan, had received a 'triumph' were exempt from the ban on burials within the city. A winding staircase carved inside the marble drums of the column leads to the top, which was originally crowned by a statue of Trajan. The present statue of St. Peter was placed there in the renaissance.

One of the most memorable of Roman works of art, as well as a major source of information on Roman military strategy, the frieze is 610 ft (200 m) long and includes 2500 finely carved figures. It was originally polychrome.

With the disappearance of the two adjacent libraries, the reliefs cannot be easily seen today. Yet much of the action can be made out if you follow these directions:

With your back to the staircase and street some distance away, stand facing the small window-slits in the column; on this side most of the especially interesting scenes centre on these slits.

First (lowest) band. Some isolated buildings and depots of a Roman encampment on the Danube. All is quiet, but a torch from a window on the right is flashing signals.

Second slit (fourth band). Hostilities have begun. Roman scouts bring back severed heads of Dacians.

Band above second slit. Left: Dacian cavalry drown in the Danube. Upper right: Sarmatian horsemen, from a nomadic people allied with the Dacians, enter the fray. Scaled armour protects them head to toe, as well as their mounts. (The scales were made from horse's hooves, patiently sliced.)

Third slit. The Sarmatians are pursued and defeated. One of them tries a Sarmatian specialty: shooting arrows while turning around in the saddle.

Fourth slit. A Dacian leader submits to Emperor Trajan (in officer's uniform with a pleated skirt). To the right of the Dacian are a long-trumpet major (see p. 143) and bearers of the Roman Eagles and other standards.

Fifth slit. Left: Roman heavy infantry try to conquer a Dacian fort by forming a 'tortoise' with their shields against the wall. Right: the heads of the Dacian leaders are presented to Trajan.

Band above fifth slit. Far left (move left as needed): Dacians surrender (note their dragon-head standard). Centre: women, children and old people are forced to leave their home towns (depicted behind them) to be replaced by Romans and their cattle.

Different details of the same part of the war can now be seen by moving around to the right, with your back to the house at No. 83, and again using the slits as reference points.

First slit. Left: a sacrificial procession around a Roman fort. Bottom centre: a failed infiltration attempt by a Dacian guerrilla, who falls from his horse. Far right: Trajan addresses his troops from a platform.

Band above first slit. Left: a Roman camp is attacked with battering rams. Roman relief troops arrive by boat from the right.

Second band above second slit. Top left: supply carts, one with the Dacian dragon standard, are abandoned amid a mound of Dacian bodies. Bottom centre: a Dacian stabs himself rather than be captured. Right: Dacian dependents pass to the Romans.

Third slit. Left: prisoners within a Roman fort. Centre: a soldier kisses Trajan's hand. Right: furious Dacian women torch naked Roman prisoners.

Band above third slit. Left: inside the encampment Trajan, wearing a toga and with his head covered, makes sacrifices to the gods. A bull, a ram and a pig (the classic *suovetaurilia* sacrifice) are led to immolation. Opposite Trajan note the flute player and eagle and standard bearers, the latter with their regulation headdress, a bear's head.

Skip fourth slit. *Fifth slit.* Dacians attack; note their curved daggers. Top left: their king, Decebalus, directs the battle with extended arm.

Band above fifth slit. Winged Victory inscribes the word *Pax* ('Peace') at the end of the First War. On both sides are trophies of Dacian armour and weaponry, like those we saw on the Capitol (p. 145).

Skip sixth slit. *Second band above sixth slit* (hard to see). Two years have passed and Decebalus has renewed hostilities. Trajan has arrived from Italy and is sacrificing (left) in view of the immense bridge (top of band) which his architect, Apollodorus (p. 181), has constructed over the Danube in the intervening years. A few of the pylons supporting the bridge, which replaced a temporary one of barges and thus enabled the assimilation of the conquered land, still survive at the Iron Gates, the border between Romania and Serbia.

Move around to the right, to a third set of slits.

Bottom band. Here we are again at the start of the First War. The Romans leave their border fortifications and cross the Danube on a temporary bridge of barges. Each soldier wears his helmet on his shoulders over his regulation sword (*gladius*) and carries the regulation knapsack on a pole. The God of the Danube emerges to watch.

Skip first slit. *Second band above first slit.* Far left (move as needed): tiny Roman heads are impaled on the wall of a Dacian fort. The Dacian dragon standard flies overhead. Right: Trajan addresses his troops.

Skip second slit. *Band above second slit.* Left: Dacian leaders are beheaded. Centre: medical officers attend two wounded Romans (note the different uniforms). The doctor on the right disinfects a leg with vinegar.

Skip third slit. *Band above third slit.* Romans cut a tree for construction. Dacian heads are impaled on poles (far right).

Fourth slit. Trajan orders allied Moroccan horsemen, who use no bridles, saddles or stirrups, into battle. They rout the Dacians. Their leader would later be made a Roman citizen, senator and consul.

Skip fifth slit. *Band above fifth slit.* The Second War has begun. Romans embark from the harbour at Ravenna.

Sixth slit. Dacians prepare for action. By now they are partly Romanised; one wears a Roman sword at his belt (next to slit).

Band above sixth slit. Trajan, dressed in a civilian toga (right), receives leaders of different allied forces, in their exotic outfits and headdresses. In the background is a Romanised Dacian town with an amphitheatre (upper left) and portico. (The Romanization of the area was rapid and long-lasting; hence the modern name Romania, and the modern language, which is closely based on Latin.)

The upper part of the shaft depicts objectively and respectfully the Dacians' heroic struggle. After a traitor delivers the keys of the main fort to the Romans, the routed Dacians set fire to their capital. Many poison themselves. King Decebalus escapes, but then stabs himself-to avoid capture.

As in an immense trophy, the column illustrates in detail, all around the base, the weapons, uniforms, dragons standards and other insignia of the vanquished.

Note: if you have time one day to see the Museum of Roman Civilization (p. 686), you can see a full-size cast of the entire frieze at eye-level.

The fifth and final element of Trajan's Forum was the sumptuous **Temple of Trajan** in a piazza facing Trajan's Column. Except for a colossal capital and a fragment of an equally huge granite column, which have been moved and can now be seen near the foot of Column, the temple and its piazza are gone. On the site they once occupied, beyond the two churches opposite the Column, now stands Palazzo Valentini (p. 190), where some ruins are visible. Of the two churches themselves, the one on the left, S. Maria di Loreto, is a renaissance work, possibly by Bramante. Its dome was added by the Sicilian architect Giacomo del Duca. The lantern has been nicknamed the 'cricket cage' for its unusual shape. The church on the right, Ss. Nome di Maria ('Most Holy Name of Mary'), was built in the 1700's.

6. The Imperial Fora concluded. The medieval towers and the church of SS. Cosma e Damiano

The next stretch of our Walk starts with the ancient marble tomb of a certain Caius Bibulus, rising incongruously amid intense traffic. (This gentleman is also remembered because his name – 'bibulous' – is quoted amusingly by the poet Horace.) The tomb is here because before Augustus expanded the city into the Campus Martius ('Field of Mars') Rome ended at this point (p. 42) and, as you may recall, ancient custom forbade burial within the city walls.

Just as the presence of a 2,800-year-old necropolis in the Forum confirms the site of the earliest city, Roma Quadrata, next to it (pp. 156, 286), so the Tomb of Caius Bibulus tells us that these were the Republican city limits. And just as what are thought to be vestiges of Roma Quadrata walls were found in 1988 not far from the necropolis (p. 288), so blocks of more recent walls – the Republican or Servian walls – have been found on the slope of the Capitol near this tomb.

Add to this what you already know about the (third and final) late-imperial set of walls seen at the very beginning of your visit (pp. 42-44) and you will have a very graphic idea of Rome's development.

The Walk continues behind the Imperial Fora through the once teeming Suburra district, now a sleepy, appealing neighbourhood where medieval and modern buildings rub shoulders. Few traces of the ancient buildings in the area and none of its original character survive. Instead we find no fewer than four original towers erected by the feuding factions of medieval Rome; actually six if we count simple vestiges and even nine if we include the three we saw in a contiguous area on a previous Walk (pp. 106, 109). Amongst these are the famous Torre delle Milizie (pp. 151, 184) and Torre

View from the Vittoriano over the Torre delle Milizie and Trajan's Markets during the Mussolinian renovations

Colonna, the latter bearing the name of one of the most powerful families in medieval and renaissance Rome. This princely family, still extant, gave its name to the area (Rione Colonna), while the name itself comes from the nearby Trajan's Column (Colonna Traiana), which they use as a heraldic device. In the struggle to dominate Rome that raged throughout the middle ages, the family was in fierce competition with other noble families, the Roman populace, the pope and foreign rulers. In some periods they had a private army and a powerful faction, called the Colonnesi, to support them.

Before leaving the area we'll complete our exploration of the Fora by visiting the site of the largest forum, Vespasian's, now almost completely vanished. Only then, having traversed the whole area (over 200 acres or 100 hectares) of a monumental ensemble unequalled in size and opulence, can you try

The Emperor Vespasian

to reconstruct the full picture. A look at the three-dimensional model of Imperial Rome (see p. 176) will help too.

Completing the section is a visit to SS. Cosma and Damiano, the only church that occupies the site of not one but two ancient Roman monuments, built almost three centuries apart. It is decorated with early medieval mosaics.

After the church, we skirt the massive ruins of the Basilica of Maxentius, which are closed on this side and so can only be visited in an 'on site' tour of the Roman Forum (see 'A Closer Look at the Forum and the Palatine', pp. 286-287). The Emperor Maxentius began this immense construction as if to prove that under him Rome, then in an advanced state of decline, could still produce architectural feats like those of the past. Yet it was Maxentius' co-emperor, Constantine, who completed it, after installing himself in Rome in 312 AD as sole ruler. The site is a reminder of the mortal struggle between the two co-emperors, in which Constantine, who controlled Gaul (France) and Spain, defeated Maxentius, who controlled Rome, by allying himself with the Christian party and killing Maxentius at the Battle of the Milvian Bridge (pp. 605-606). We'll soon see another reminder of these epoch-making events, the Arch of Constantine.

ON THE SPOT

6. The Imperial Fora concluded. The medieval towers and the church of SS. Cosma and Damiano

Before leaving the vicinity of Trajan's Column, walk along the marble paving towards the Altar of the Fatherland. Without crossing, from the corner look over the wide avenue. On the grassy patch bordering the Altar is a small white marble ruin, an isolated doorframe. This is the **Tomb of Caius Bibulus**, who lived in the final years of the Republic (1st century BC), one of the most ancient remains of its kind to be found in Rome.

Now walk back past the two churches that stand across from Trajan's Column. Go around the flank of the second church (Via S. Eufemia) to the first crossing (Via Tre Cannelle). At this point Via S. Eufemia skirts the imposing **Palazzo Valentini** (from the name of one of its more recent owners), built by a cardinal in the late 16th century and modified in the 19th. In 1707 the Anglo-German composer George Frederick Handel was a guest in the palace, and it was here that he wrote his great Resurrection oratorio. In the basement, sometimes open, are the remains of an ancient Roman bath, probably connected to the Temple of Trajan (p. 187). If you go into the courtyard, where there is sometimes a sign saying 'Mostra' advertising an exhibition in the basement, you may have a chance of seeing the vestiges of the bath. From Via S. Eufemia go up Via Tre Cannelle to a modern avenue (Via Quattro Novembre).

We are here on the fringes of the Suburra. Right at the crossing is the first of the many towers that sprang up in the area in the middle ages, the 11th-century **Torre Colonna**. It bears the Colonna shield with the device of a column. Under it are fragments of Roman reliefs. The family still lives in the neighbourhood. If you face the tower, on the far right you'll see the bridges that connect the present Colonna palaces with their villa on the slopes of the Quirinal (see p. 130).

Go uphill from the Torre Colonna. At the end of the block, on the left, is the best close-up view of another, more famous tower, the Torre delle Milizie, which we first saw from the Capitol (p. 151) and will discuss in a moment.

Going up the next block you will see first, beyond a low wall on your right, the remarkable Via Biberatica, a shopping mall in Trajan's Market.

The street dates from around 110 AD; it has original paving, sidewalks, houses and stores, which are those of the third floor of the market. You may recall (p. 183) that this floor opens onto a well-preserved street (this stretch continues around the top of the structure which we saw from below). Some of the stores must have sold spices or wine, as the name of the street derives either from *biber* (a late corruption of *piper*, pepper) or *bibere*, 'to drink'. The street is a fine early example of urban planning. Note especially the balconies along the first and second storeys, which doubled as fire escapes, a new feature in Roman architecture, which was introduced after the catastrophic fire of forty years earlier, the one during which Nero supposedly fiddled (see below and p. 210).

Today the rooms on the right are classrooms used by the state school next door, in one of those cases of symbiosis between past and present not unusual in Rome. You can even try to see the classrooms by entering at Nos 94–95 of the avenue and being very discreet (ask janitors or teachers if you see any).

A few steps further along the avenue brings you to the upper entrance of Trajan's Market.

From the pavement you can see the grandiose entrance hall with its cross-vaulted ceiling, whose architectural details were inspired by oriental models known to its Syrian architect, Apollodorus of Damascus (pp. 181, 187). Similar structures exist in the Middle East.

Having seen the Market from below, the entrance and Via Biberatica, a visit to the site is not essential.

The **Torre delle Milizie** ('Soldiers' Tower') is accessible from the entrance to the Market, but at the time of writing is only open once a week for guided tours (Wednesdays at 19:00; reservations required, call +39-06-6781883).

Built in the early 1200's, it was the tallest of the 600 or so towers that dotted Rome in the middle ages. Originally 164 ft (50 m) tall, an earthquake reduced it to 138 ft (42 m) a century after its construction. Looming over the heart of the former Suburra, its position helps explain the medieval myth that Nero played his lyre atop the tower (which obviously didn't exist in his time), while below in the Suburra the fire raged. (Suetonius does record that Nero watched the great fire from a tower, but that was part of Mæcenas' famous villa and was so tall that the poet Horace wrote 'it brushes the clouds'.) The foundations of two other towers have turned up close by.

At the end of the block on your right is a 17th-century church, **S. Caterina a Magnanapoli**, while before you at the top of an elaborate staircase is the 16th-century church of **SS. Domenico e Sisto**. In the distance on your left you will recognise Piazza del Quirinale, from your first Roma Romantica Walk.

Turn sharply right. The street narrows and descends into the quiet, picturesque Salita del Grillo ('Grillo Hill'). Halfway down the steeper part of the slope on the right are the barely decipherable remains of ancient Roman houses built back-to-back with Trajan's Forum, one of the few remaining traces of the Suburra. Near the foot of the hill is the 12th- or 13th-century **Torre del Grillo**, another baronial tower stronghold.

The ornate roof-terrace was added at the end of the 17th century, when the tower was bought by a certain Marquis del Grillo, as an inscription around the top says. He also built the adjacent palace, connected by an overpass, one of the few examples in Rome of the rococo style. The best view of the palace is from the other side of the arch in Piazza del Grillo.

Past the arch the street is intersected by Via Campocarleo, which retraces the route of an ancient street between Trajan's Forum and the Suburra. The far end on the right, with steps which you already saw from the Forum side, is still in part the original street, and includes the walled-up entrances to five *tabernæ* in the Forum (see p. 141).

At No. 1 Piazza del Grillo is the entrance to the **House of the Knights of Rhodes,** also known as the Knights of Malta (pp. 59-60). The house bears the order's older name because it was bought while the group was still based in Rhodes, before fleeing to Malta. You have seen the front of this beautiful medieval palace (built in the 12th century and remodelled in the 15th) from the Forum of Augustus (p. 179).

The palace is usually closed, which is unfortunate since it is interesting for several reasons. First,

The salita del Grillo behind Trajan's Forum

it is partly embedded in some structures of the Forum of Augustus, visible only from inside. Second, it has a small museum of remains from the Forum, located in the adjacent *tabernæ* of Trajan's Market, whose entrance you just saw on Via Campocarleo. The museum also contains memorabilia of the long medieval history of the Knights of Jerusalem-Rhodes-Malta and the balcony has a marvellous view onto the Fora. A ground-floor chapel is open Sunday mornings after 11:00, notable for its intact ancient Roman structure and for a renaissance altar.

Further downhill to the right is the tremendous 98 ft (32 m) stone wall of the Forum of Augustus. The wall served both as a backdrop to the Forum and as a firebreak against the frequent fires in the Suburra.

Note the alterations in the wall effected across the centuries, including a 16th-century fresco from a demolished church and convent, a renaissance portal and medieval gothic windows.

Just before the wall ends, a monumental arched gate, part of the original structure, opens into the Forum of Augustus. (From the middle ages until about 100 years ago, when the street was much lower and the gate still crossable, it was called Arco dei Pantani, 'Arch of the Puddles', because of the conditions of the ground.) Have a closer look from here at the powerful flank of the Temple of Mars the Avenger. Continuing straight, you see a small and very simple medieval house, which looks like a farmhouse, almost free-standing in the middle of the street. Found here some decades ago embedded in newer buildings, it has been isolated and heavily restored. It is presently a club for senior citizens.

Behind the house is the last medieval tower of this short stretch, the early 13th-century **Tor de' Conti** ('Tower of the Counts'), reduced to a stump by the same earthquake that damaged the Torre delle Milizie (p. 191). Go around it from the left and stop for a moment opposite No. 38a.

Area of the Forum of Peace, or of Vespasian, now almost completely built over

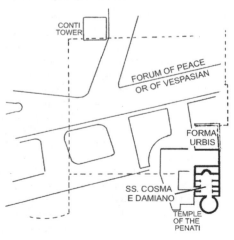

Famous in the middle ages for its size, this was the largest of the medieval towers in Rome; the poet Petrarch called it 'unique in the world'. It was built by Pope Innocent III of another historic clan, the Counts of Segni (hence its name) to protect the city and papacy from the ambitions of the competing feudal families. Though only the base remains, disfigured by windows inserted later at different times, the squat structure, with its massive spurs and rough wainscot of black and white rocks, exudes brute force. It was maintained at public expense as essential to law and order. A marble inscription in Latin on the base to your right was added in the 13th century by one of its commanders, who describes himself as 'a valiant, loyal and powerful soldier' (*miles*) before adding, 'nobody can overstate the internal strength and external solidity of this edifice'.

Proceed to the front of the tower (No. 44) for a further look, then continue along the pavement for 30m. Stop near a marble capital on a pink column rising from the pavement. Excavations in the 1930's showed that the Tor de' Conti had incorporated an apse of the wall encircling **Vespasian's Forum of Peace** (pp. 179-180). The ruins in the tower are closed off, but other traces of the great forum are visible, such as the column before you, one of 98 that stood around its central square. Other parts of the complex will be seen shortly.

Cross Via dei Fori Imperiali at the lights. You again face the new excavations, which continue in different segments to the left, all of them part of Vespasian's Forum. The excavations of 2000-01 found very little of note, but they do give some idea of the extent and position of the forum. What you see here is part of the great piazza at its centre.

The Forum of Peace was a great walled and columned square surrounded by halls and flanked by a Temple of Peace. The latter was meant to celebrate the victory that Vespasian and his son Titus had won in the Jewish War, and to display treasure pillaged from the Temple of Jerusalem, such as the Tables of the Law, the Silver Trumpets and the Seven-branched Candlestick (*menorah*). (These objects were also reproduced and their

The temple of Antoninus and Faustina, converted to a church, S. Lorenzo in Miranda,
as seen from the Roman Forum in the 18th century, by Piranesi

capture celebrated in the reliefs on the triumphal Arch of Titus, p. 287) The digs have revealed that the square included a garden, a patch of green amidst so much marble.

Continue straight on, between the excavated segments, all the way to the entrance to the Roman Forum in Largo Romolo e Remo. (For an 'on site' visit to the Forum, see note p. 139.)

Climb the steps at the far left-hand corner of Largo Romolo e Remo. Once in the street above, Via in Miranda (Miranda is the name of an old convent here), take a closer look at the flank of the Temple of Antoninus and Faustina (p. 163), converted into the church of **S. Lorenzo in Miranda** between the 7th and 10th centuries. The columns are magnificent, as is the frieze with griffins and candelabra, one of the finer examples of ancient Roman decorative art.

In the 15th century control of the church was given to the adjacent Collegio Chimico

Farmaceutico (Guild of Pharmacists), which is still here and through which one can enter. (Open Thursdays only, 10:00-12:00.)

The interior was remodelled in the 17th century and contains some important works of the same period. In the first chapel to the left is a *Madonna with Child and Saints* by Domenichino, in poor condition despite or perhaps because of its restoration in 1985. Over the main altar, designed by Pietro da Cortona, is a beautiful *St. Lawrence Led to Martyrdom* by the same artist.

Go back (not down the steps) and around the corner (marked by a ludicrous modern statue) to the entrance of another church, **SS. Cosma e Damiano**. The church was built in the 6th century as a *diaconia*, a centre of assistance for the poor, in a peripheral hall of Vespasian's Forum originally used as a library. The conversion and a 17th century modernisation conceal the pagan origins of the building. But if you look into the old excavations just to the left of the church entrance, you can see the fragmentary remains of another hall of Vespasian's Forum. It marked the end of the great square of Vespasian's Forum of Peace where it bordered on the Roman Forum.

The brick wall over the excavations divided this hall from the library, and is very interesting in itself because it was used under the Emperor Septimius Severus (p. 165) to exhibit an enormous map of Rome engraved in marble. The holes left on the wall by the iron hooks are still visible. Many fragments of the map (the *Forma Urbis*)

Fragment of the ancient map of Rome known as the Forma Urbis

were found at the foot of the wall, in one of the luckiest archæological strikes ever. They are the most important document we have for reconstructing the topography of ancient Rome. Unfortunately, they are in storage and inaccessible to the public.

This is the only church in Rome to occupy two adjacent ancient Roman buildings. The first, which constitutes the main body of the church, is the library of Vespasian's Forum. The second is a circular temple that was part of the Roman Forum proper and was only connected to the library when the latter was converted into a church in the 6th century. It was used as a vestibule, since the church entrance was then from the Forum. In its present, 17th-century, form the entrance is through a long hall (note its rough left wall, the original wall of the library), a cloister with indifferent 17th-century frescoes and a side door. (Open: 07:00-12:45 and 16:00-18:45.)

Inside the main attractions are two mosaics, the one in the apse contemporary with the church (6th century), the other added a century later on the triumphal arch.

The apse mosaic shows the *Second Coming of Christ* against a background of multi-coloured clouds. He meets the white-robed Apostles Peter (right) and Paul (left). They present to Him, respectively, the martyrs Cosmas and Damian – Arab Christians, brothers and physicians, said to have been beheaded in the 3rd century in the Middle East, and the patron saints of doctors. On the far right is another eastern saint, Theodore, in a dazzling gown, and on the far left is Pope Felix IV, who founded the church in the 6th century, though his image is a 17th-century restoration. Under the main scene, a flock of lambs represents the faithful. In the later mosaic on the triumphal arch, angels adoring the Lamb of God, and various Christian symbols.

These mosaics are the best examples in Rome of Christian art in transition. The ancient Roman, classical style still dominates, in the monumentality and psychological characterisation of the human figures as well as in the realism of the details and the free sense of space. But Byzantine influences from the East – the Byzantines had reconquered Rome in the 6th century – have begun to come through, in the fixed gaze and total frontality of the figures. The transitional character of the mosaics shows in their very materials, a mixture of marble and glass (p. 96), the latter prevailing in the flesh tones.

Other highlights of the church are the beautiful wooden ceiling and rich altar, both 17th-century (the centrepiece of the altar is a 13th-century icon), a 13th-century cosmatesque candlestick near the altar and, in the first chapel to the right of the original entrance, a curious 8th-century Byzantine fresco of *Christ on the Cross* fully clothed and crowned.

If the original entrance is open, it leads to the vestibule in the ancient round temple of the Roman Forum (Temple of the Penates). At Christmas an 18th-century Neapolitan *presepe* (nativity scene) is exhibited here.

When the church was rebuilt in the 17th century, the floor was raised considerably; however, the old floor, in the earliest cosmatesque style, is accessible several feet below, through a metal gate (often closed) halfway along the cloister. This early part of the church also contains the original altar.

Leaving the church, the huge ruin on your right is the 4th-century AD Basilica of Maxentius, which you already saw from a distance. It is closed on this side, but you can visit it later from the Forum side, see pp. 286-287. It has gigantic coffered vaults, which were a major inspiration to renaissance artists and architects. A glimpse of them may be had from here. The basilica was finished after Maxentius' death by Constantine, who set up the colossal statue of himself, of which fragments survive in the Capitoline museums.

Mosaic of St. Peter in SS. Cosma e Damiano

Go on toward the Colosseum, walking past the powerful masses of the Basilica of Maxentius. On a wall are four black-and-white marble maps, a Fascist creation showing the growth of the Roman Empire. A fifth map on the far right showing Mussolini's 'empire', including Ethiopia, was quietly removed after the fall of Fascism and was retrieved only recently from a mound of rubble. Its present whereabouts, however, are uncertain.

If buses still run on Via dei Fori Imperiali and you are not taking the Detour below, you can go back to the bus stop near SS. Cosma e Damiano and take any bus one stop to the Colosseum.

The hilly ground on your right as you approach the Colosseum square is the ridge that closed the Roman Forum to the southeast, on which are the ruins of the Temple of Venus and Rome and the Arch of Titus (see below, pp. 208-209).

The main itinerary resumes on p. 197. The Detour site is reached by climbing a staircase just past the four Fascist maps or by taking, a few steps further on, a steep street on the right of Via dei Fori Imperiali.

❧ MIDPOINT OF WALK ❧

DETOUR
15 MIN

BEFORE GOING

S. Maria Nova (S. Francesca Romana)

One of the most remarkable cases of metamorphosis and multiple reincarnations of Roman monuments is the object of this detour to the ridge overlooking the Roman Forum.

Here one of the minor ruins of the Temple of Venus and Rome (discussed in the next section) was turned into a small church dedicated to St. Peter at the dawn of the Dark Ages, possibly the 5th or 6th century. It commemorated a legendary episode of the Apostle's (perhaps equally legendary) stay in Rome, which would have occurred here on the ridge of the Forum. A famous magician, Simon Magus, who could levitate, challenged Peter to demonstrate his own supernatural powers. As Simon soared over the ridge, with the Roman authorities (including Emperor Nero) watching, St. Peter – who knew the performance was the Devil's work – knelt on the stones of the Via Sacra and prayed for the fall of Simon, who promptly crashed to his death. Tradition says that Simon's murder was later a principal charge against St. Peter at his trial, and led to his death sentence (see p. 560). In the church the faithful were shown stones, called *Silices Apostolici* ('Flintstones of the Apostle'), said to be the ones on which Peter had knelt and which bore the miraculous imprint of his knees. (They are still exhibited today.)

In the same period another church was built in a different part of the Forum within another ancient ruin, but with a very different aim. It was part of a network of welfare centres (*diaconiæ*) created to give out food and help in the period of desperate need that followed the fall of the Empire. The *diaconiæ* were set up by Pope Gregory the Great, a major figure in Christian history, who was also responsible for the mission to England and possibly for the introduction of what is now called Gregorian chant – unless this is due to one of his early successors by the same name.

The *diaconia* in the Forum was dedicated to the Virgin Mary. By the 10th century both it and the little church of St. Peter were so decrepit that the authorities decided to merge them as one fully rebuilt church. They chose the site of the church of St. Peter on the ridge, which was renamed Sancta Maria Nova ('New St. Mary's'). The other church was then dubbed Sancta Maria Antiqua ('Old St. Mary's') and soon abandoned. You will see its ruins if you take the Forum Walk described in 'A Closer Look', p. 284, and if a decades-long restoration is completed by then.

In its second lease of life, S. Maria Nova enjoyed great popularity and artistic renown, especially after it was decorated in the early 15th century with frescoes by the great central Italian painter, Gentile da Fabriano, which Michelangelo admired and often studied. Unfortunately, nothing of this period survives, the church having been again rebuilt in the 17th century (Gentile was buried in it, though exactly where is unknown).

Before the reconstruction, however, another major event took place in the church. In the early 15th century a woman destined to become one of Rome's most popular figures began to frequent it: Francesca Ponziani, a rich lady who devoted her life to helping the poor and the sick, especially during a devastating bout of the plague. She and a group of companions, who had joined her in an order of nuns she founded with papal approval, took their vows in S. Maria Nova, and Francesca was buried there. (In the Second Renaissance Walk we'll see the convent she founded.)

When S. Maria Nova began its third lease of life after its second reconstruction in the 17th century, it was soon being called the 'Church of S. Francesca Romana', as Francesca had by then been canonised. The name has stuck, alternating with the official one.

St. Frances is now the patron saint of car drivers. Every year on her saint's day, March 9th, car owners from all over Rome gather near the church to have their vehicles blessed.

ON THE SPOT

The church of S. Maria Nova, also known as S. Francesca Romana, and the adjoining monastery, the property of Benedictine friars since 1352, are on the crest of the ridge enclosing the Forum in the former area of the Temple of Venus and Rome (discussed below). The church façade has a conventional 17th-century design. The romanesque bell tower, one of Rome's tallest and visible before you reach the façade, is 12th-century. (Open: 9:30-12:00 and 15:30-17:30.)

The interior is basically early 17th century but parts of the recently restored floor are original cosmatesque work: a square in the middle and part of the paving in the transept. Proceed counterclockwise. In the vestibule of a side entrance to the right are two medieval tombs: right, that of a cardinal who died in 1394, by an unidentified, but possibly Roman sculptor; left, that of a commander of the papal guard who died in 1475, possibly by the Neapolitan Mino del Reame. At the end of the right wall a marble tablet commemorates a recent abbott of the monastery, who was mugged and strangled with a church vestment here shortly after the Second World War. The robbers had approached him on the pretext of discussing a Mass for the recently executed dictator Mussolini.

In the apse are two beautiful remains from the older church. At the top is a mid-12th century mosaic of the *Madonna and Saints* in the Byzantine style (there is a push-button light to the left behind the statue of an angel). Over the altar is an image of the *Madonna* on wood from the same period. In 1949 it was discovered that the image covered another much older one, variously dated between the 5th and 8th century. This very rare early Roman-Byzantine icon, which probably comes from the church of S. Maria Antiqua, was separated from its overpainting by skilled restorers and is sometimes exhibited in the sacristy. We'll see it shortly.

Take the steps on the right to the transept. Against the wall in front of you is a late-16th century monument to the 14th century Pope Gregory XI, who brought the papacy back from Avignon to Rome (p. 300). The beautiful reliefs of *St. Gregory* and *St. Catherine of Siena* (p. 118) are signed by Pier Paolo Olivieri, a Roman sculptor. On the right wall, behind two iron grilles, are the *Silices Apostolici*, the paving stones shown for centuries as proof of the story of Simon Magus.

From the transept descend to the crypt, restored in the 19th century, where the skeleton of S. Francesca Romana is on display. Go right to return to the church.

At the left end of the transept, near the entrance to the sacristy, are a beautiful 15th century marble shrine guarding the Holy Oil and paintings by minor 16th and 17th century artists. Enter the sacristy for a moment to see the ancient icon mentioned above.

Leaving the church, return to the avenue and proceed toward the Colosseum.

END OF DETOUR

The Piazza del Colosseo is dominated by the huge mass of the amphitheatre. It would be better, however, to visit another monument on the square first, unless the closing time of the Colosseum dictates otherwise, as seeing it afterwards would make the Walk somewhat longer.

BEFORE GOING

7. The Arch of Constantine

Recent archæological research has revealed that the plain southeast of the Forum, delimited by a ridge and three hills – the Palatine, Celian and Oppian – was densely populated throughout the early Empire. It was then swallowed up by Emperor Nero's palace compound, which sprawled from the Palatine to the slopes of the Oppian, and the area became a park landscaped around an artificial lake. Nero's successors, Vespasian and Titus, razed most of the palace and restored the area to the public. The drained lake served conveniently as a foundation for the Colosseum.

Next to the Colosseum is one of Rome's most imposing late-imperial monuments, fascinating both for its historical importance and its visual impact. It is the arch honouring the Emperor Constantine, who in 312 AD had become sole ruler by defeating his co-emperor, Maxentius, in battle. By so doing he not only freed Rome from an unpopular ruler, but changed the course of history by allying himself with the growing Christian community and for the first time sanctioning its religion.

An inscription over the arch eloquently reminds us of the 'divine intuition' that guided

Constantine. His motives for accepting Christianity have long been debated. Some have called it an astute bid to tap into a new source of support; others have seen it as a statesman's wise strategy to reinvigorate the declining Empire with a shot of religious fervour. Both may be true. Yet the most important reason, which comes across clearly from Constantine's letters and religious edicts, was that after 312 he sincerely believed himself destined to serve what he called 'the highest divinity', identified with the Christian God who had given him military victory and raised him to supreme power. He was convinced that proper Christian devotion would nourish his and the empire's fortunes and that neglecting this duty would call down the vengeance of a powerful and offended God.

More superstition than idealism, perhaps, but it accorded perfectly with the religious tenor of the times. Constantine converted to Christianity years later, apparently shortly before he died. At the time he told his biographer, Eusebius of Cæsarea, that when he had been debating whether to attack Maxentius, he had lifted his eyes toward the sun and

Constantine the Great: colossal head in the Palazzo dei Conservatori

seen amidst the blinding rays the shape of the Cross – a vision that turned him decisively toward Christianity and encouraged him to grant ever increasing favours to the Christians.

It was long thought that the Arch of Constantine was built in 315, the tenth anniversary of his reign and third anniversary of his triumph over Maxentius. But in 1994 the archæologist

The Arch of Constantine in the 18th century, with the Colosseum in the background, by P. Schenk

Anna Maria Ferroni of Rome's Central Restoration Institute concluded from fresh archæological evidence that the arch was in fact two centuries older, and dated from the reign of Hadrian, with new reliefs being added later in honour of Constantine. Indeed, the arch is a compendium of artistic styles. It was decorated with pieces from older monuments – a practice that became commonplace at the time – and reflected an artistic decline that had been underway for a century, amid growing social, economic and political unease. The arch is the first major example of a practice that continued throughout the late Empire and early middle ages. In this particular case, however, it may have been due not so much to the plunder of older monuments as to the reuse of admired pieces that had escaped a fire. At any rate, the statuary on the arch, ranging from the early 2nd to the early 4th centuries, allows us to ponder the deterioration of sculpture from the supreme standards of Trajan's and Hadrian's time to the 'rudest and most unskilful' level, as the English historian Gibbon wrote of the later decoration.

ON THE SPOT

7. The Arch of Constantine

Turn right into the square. Go along the edge of the square, with its original flagstones (the central part next to the Colosseum is paved with marble), for about 100 yards, where you pass on the right the entrance to the Via Sacra towards the Forum. We saw the other end of this famous road from the Capitol (pp. 161-162).

Note: if you go about 165 yards (150 m) further along the Via Sacra you reach the Arch of Titus in the Forum, which we also saw from the Capitol (p. 162). We'll get a closer view of it from the top of the Colosseum, but without seeing its internal reliefs depicting the plunder of the Temple of Jerusalem, which can be seen in the 'on site' visit to the Forum and Palatine. If you wish to visit the Arch of Titus now, however, the description starts on p. 287.

In front of the entrance to the Via Sacra, a round platform indicates the former site of the Meta Sudans ('Sweating Cone') fountain, so called because of the way in which water oozed from it. It was said to be a resting and refreshment place for victorious gladiators. Its substantial remains were absurdly torn down in 1937 by the Fascist authorities to ease traffic around the monumental area (p. 172).

Immediately behind it is the **Arch of Constantine,** generally dated to 315 AD, unless one accepts the recent theory (pp. 198-199) that it was much older, and only refurbished later with new sculptural elements dedicated to Constantine.

Constantine's reign was highly controversial at a time when pagans still controlled many centres of power. The political and religious circumstances are ambiguously suggested by an inscription on the arch (third line) which mentions an *instinctu divinitatis* ('intuition of the divine') along with greatness of mind and military prowess as the reasons for Constantine's success. Obviously, his alliance with the Christians could not yet be stated too bluntly.

In size and design, the arch resembles that of Septimius Severus (pp. 164-165), built a century earlier, or rather later, if the new theory mentioned above is true.

The sculpture comes from various periods and makes up what the Italian scholar Filippo Coarelli has called 'a real museum of official Roman sculpture, perhaps the richest and most important'. The statues at the top of the arch, representing Dacian prisoners, are from the reign of Trajan, *c.* 105 AD. Still at the top, the beautiful reliefs front and back (but not on the sides) are from the reign of Marcus Aurelius' reign, *c.* 180 AD. They depict this emperor's wars. Note that the heads of the statues and those of the emperor in the reliefs are an 18th-century recreation. The big roundels over the minor archways at the front and back (but not on the sides) are from Hadrian's reign, *c.* 130 AD, and depict vivid scenes of hunting and sacrifice,

The Meta Sudans before its destruction in the 1930's

Arch of Constantine: details of earlier and later carving (above and below respectively)

which include Hadrian's youthful lover, Antinoüs. Four rectangular panels with dazzlingly beautiful reliefs, two within the main archway (right and left) and two on the sides of the arch at the top, are from Trajan's reign (one frieze may come from the Basilica Ulpia, p. 184, detached when the building was damaged by fire). They show scenes of Trajan's Dacian Wars. All the other sculpture is in the tell-tale crude style of Constantine's reign, which Raphael called 'very stupid' (remember the clumsy statues of Constantine and his son on the Capitol, p. 146).

A band of six long rectangular reliefs girding the arch is of particular interest. From the side facing the Forum-Palatine complex and moving right, they depict: Constantine's army leaving Milan; the Siege of Verona; the Battle of the Milvian Bridge against Maxentius; Constantine's entry into Rome; his speech in the Roman Forum; and the distribution of money to the people in Cæsar's Forum.

Continue walking counterclockwise toward the present Colosseum entrance (to the south, in the center of the side lacking an outer wall).

201

8. The Colosseum

We all think that we know what went on in the Colosseum: bloodthirsty crowds goading the unfortunate, brutish gladiators to fight to the death, or watching innocent Christians, including old men, women and children, being hacked to pieces by executioners or devoured by wild beasts.

Yet such a cliché, which inevitably colours our feelings as we approach this most immense and majestic of Roman monuments, should be qualified. For instance, no historical or archæological record proves that a Christian was ever killed here. Several historians, including the famous Jesuit scholar Hippolyte Delehaye, have shown that such executions took place elsewhere. At any rate, they were not routine, but rather exceptions, occurring in given historical moments, in a polity normally marked by great religious tolerance.

The gladiators themselves were seldom forced to fight against their will. True, criminals were often forced to kill or be killed as a form of capital punishment. But many gladiators were prisoners of war, who were given the choice between enslavement (the enemy would have reserved the same treatment for Romans) or a career in the arena, if their physical constitution suggested it. Their career had a contractual time limit, too, after which survivors would be freed and allowed to keep the considerable sums of money they had accumulated. One such captured barbarian was Spartacus, who later led a famous slave rebellion. Other gladiators were debtors in dire straits or ordinary people attracted by a career offering financial rewards and popularity, especially with women (*suspirium puellarum* – 'the sigh of girls' – the champions were called). Some participated occasionally as amateurs, just for thrills. Often these were members of the aristocracy. The historian Tacitus writes that many Roman knights became so passionate about proving themselves in the amphitheatre that the emperor, who considered such behaviour indecorous for the upper classes, forbade it. Of course, these facts do not diminish the atrocity of the massacres of humans and animals which occurred in the arena, but they do show that the phenomenon was more complex than we may think.

Gladiator, from late Imperial mosaic

Another major factor, which is often overlooked, is religion. In ancient Rome, sports and games had a religious connotation. As in other ancient civilizations, they were often rooted in strange and sometimes bloody prehistoric rituals. For instance, every June 8th a fishing contest took place on the Tiber, which ended in a great fish bake traditionally held near the sanctuary of the god Vulcanus. Everybody took part and had a good time. Yet ancient historians knew that this innocent custom had begun with human sacrifices offered to Vulcanus to avert volcanic eruptions: *pisciculi pro animis humanis* ('little fish instead of human souls'), as the grammarian Festus put it. After all, the Romans came from the countryside to the south, a highly volcanic area.

Originally, gladiatorial combats were organised by private citizens before the tomb of a beloved relative, to pacify his soul and prevent new deaths in the family: *falcigerum placant sanguine* ('they placate the scythe-bearer with blood'), observed another Latin writer, Ausonius. Only in the 1st century BC did public contests replace these private combats.

Another neglected aspect of the games was their role as a test of character, a benchmark of the virtues of courage and endurance so critical first to Rome's survival, then to its greatness. 'Nothing better exists to prove contempt of suffering and death,' wrote Cicero. This explains why so few Roman writers and philosophers, including some of very high moral standards, had much to say against the games. The first rule of a gladiator, whether Roman or barbarian, drafted or volunteer, was to behave with manly dignity. If he did so, he had a good chance of getting out alive, even if he lost. It is well known that the crowd, led by the emperor who was often present, could stop a fight and spare the loser's life by a waving of handkerchiefs or gesturing with their thumbs (the nature of this gesture, though, is not known; that of the opposite gesture is also unknown, because *pollice verso* only means 'turned thumb'). The criterion was always the combatant's valour and contempt of death. All these practical, religious and moral overtones are rarely appreciated today. Think of the grotesque portrayal of the atrocities of the arena in the Oscar-winning film *Gladiator*, accepted as fact by today's public.

Gladiator, from late Imperial mosaic

The regular attendance of the emperor takes us to a fourth, often forgotten aspect of the games: their civic and political import. They were a manifestation of the bond between citizen and leader, through the sharing of a public event. For this reason, spectators had to wear proper attire – in the lower tiers, the official toga for men was obligatory – and eating or drinking during the games was forbidden.

The gladiators presented their arms to the emperor at the start of the contest with the famous words reported by Suetonius, *Morituri te salutant* ('Hail, Cæsar, we who are about to die salute you'), although this may not have happened on every occasion. The emperor also gave the signal for another introductory ceremony related to the religious and civic nature of the games: the parade of statues of dead emperors around the arena.

Last but not least, the games were meant to entertain the people, and sometimes even to distract them from other problems. The same was true of the circus, hence the contemptuous phrase, *panem et circenses* ('bread and circuses'), referring to the political laziness of the masses. The theatre, too, had this function. When Augustus reproached a famous mime, Pylades, for creating an aura of scandal and gossip around him, the actor boldly retorted: 'You know, Cæsar, it is in your interest that people should concentrate on us.'

For greater excitement, gladiators expert in different weapons were often pitted against one other. Some fought with the short army sword (*gladius*) and shield, some with daggers, others with long tridents and nets to enmesh opponents. In certain periods, the fights were limited to mock encounters with no bloodshed. In any case, Christian emperors abolished the games at the beginning of the 5th century AD, possibly because of an incident in which a monk, Telemachus, leapt into the arena to stop the violence and was stoned to death by the crowd.

There were *naumachiæ* ('sea battles') for which the arena was temporarily flooded and fights with wild beasts in which sometimes thousands of animals were massacred. These, too, are often mentioned as evidence of savagery; on the other hand, lions and other dangerous animals still roamed highly populated areas of the empire, such as the Middle East, and it was necessary to control their numbers. Sometimes people were exposed defenceless to the wild beasts (thrown *ad bestias*) as a form of capital punishment. Trained animals performed: there is a record of feats, such as an elephant writing Latin words with its trunk. Some games closely resembled today's bullfights. In others, men protected themselves only by escaping at the last moment behind comb-like turnstiles, such as those used in some underground stations today, or by donning spiked overalls called 'hedgehogs'. There were four gladiator training schools, the biggest of which, complete with a small arena, was near the Colosseum. We'll see its ruins.

The Colosseum was built between 70 and 80 AD by Nero's two successors, Vespasian and Titus, on the site of an artificial lake (*stagnum*) in Nero's palace complex, the Domus Aurea ('Golden House'), which had been razed to immense public enthusiasm (see p. 155). The planners, however, saved from the entrance a colossal gilt bronze statue of Nero, crowned by a halo of the sun's rays, and put it in front of the new arena. It was as tall as Trajan's Column, over 100 ft (35 m), and was the biggest bronze monument ever built. With its ray-girt head periodically replaced by

19th-century reconstruction of Colosseum area, showing the 100-foot high Colossus, the Arch of Constantine and the Meta Sudans

that of the current ruler, the statue remained there for several centuries as an important symbol of Rome, until it was torn down in the dark ages. (The statue was so important that Christians seeking pardon were obliged to swear their loyalty to the state in front of it.) This famous Colossus, and not the size of the arena, gave the Colosseum its name, though it was not so called until much later. The name first appears in a manuscript of the 7th-century English monk, the Venerable Bede, in which he attributes the following prophecy to Anglo-Saxon pilgrims: 'While the Colosseum stands Rome shall stand; when the Colosseum falls, Rome shall fall; and when Rome falls, the world shall fall.'

The Romans called the arena the Amphitheatre. The word, meaning 'double theatre', was coined a few decades earlier in reference a smaller wooden prototype, a new invention in which two semicircular theatres were joined on a pivot and could be used either individually or combined as one round theatre. Previously, only semicircular theatres had existed.

The ancestor of all modern super-stadiums, the Colosseum is bigger than most of them. It normally seated 50,000, but with standing room and special adaptations it could hold over 70,000. Formed as a slightly elliptical circle 573 ft (188 m) across at its widest, it had a feature which no other open-air arena of its size can boast: it could be protected from sun or rain by a system of sailcloth curtains, extended by means of moveable masts and railings. The rigging is still visible. Sailors from the imperial fleet were specially trained to operate the ingenious system.

The Colosseum was, and is, an example of immense architectural prowess and assurance. The architect is not known, but the workforce included thousands of Jews captured by Titus in the Palestinian Wars (pp. 179, 192).

Plundered for material from the middle ages to modern times, the Colosseum was reinforced under Pope Pius VII in the early 19th century, and the sections in danger of collapse were rebuilt. Pius and his successors also removed a tangle of greenery and flowers that had eroded the ruin, but enhanced its singular beauty, celebrated by artists for centuries. A loss to botany, too, since it turned out that the flora in the Colosseum were unique, since they included exotic plants which had found their way there as seeds brought with the wild beasts used in the games.

Since the middle ages the Colosseum has been one of Rome's supreme wonders, attracting streams of visitors day and night, when the full moon gives the gigantic mass a ghostly look ('an exquisite moment,' wrote Goethe). Dickens, who visited it both by day and by night, called it 'the most impressive, the most stately, the most solemn, grand, majestic, mournful sight conceivable,' and mused, 'To see it … is to see the ghost of old Rome, wicked, wonderful old city, haunting the very ground on which its people trod.'

ON THE SPOT

8. The Colosseum

Over the ridge of the Forum is the **Colosseum**, Rome's largest and most famous monument, completed in 80 AD, symbol throughout the centuries of the majesty and indestructibility of the *caput mundi*, the head or capital of the world. Part of the square around it is still paved with the original travertine marble slabs. (Open: 09:00-19:30; no entry after 18:30.)

Note: one innovation introduced in the Jubilee Year of 2000, charging admission to the Colosseum for the first time in history, has created huge bottlenecks at the only ticket office. Perhaps in compensation, men in centurion garb are allowed outside the arena to be photographed with tourists for a price. If when you get there the queue reaches the steps, it will take an hour to get in; and you may prefer to put off your visit to the interior to a less crowded day. In that case, a visit to the Arch of Titus mentioned in the note on p.200 can make a pleasant alternative.

The southern side of the amphitheatre is the worst preserved. The great arcaded exterior wall has disappeared, either through natural decay or looting for stone, and only the dilapidated internal ring remains. Shattered by several earthquakes and used for centuries as a quarry, the Colosseum is less than half its original mass, though its grandeur is undiminished. It is built mainly of travertine and tufa with a concrete foundation and concrete vaulting.

We'll inspect the exterior later from a better preserved side. For now, suffice it to say that the ground floor arcade of the oval arena, whose two axes measure 617 ft (188 m) and 512 ft (156 m), has 80 entrance arches, 76 of which were used at any one time by a public of up to 70,000 (entrance was free but the seats were assigned). The four entrances at the cardinal points of the oval were for official use, such as the entrance of the religious processions that always preceded the games.

Enter at the southernmost of the four entrances. Walking in, you see before you the arena, or rather its bowels, the floor having been removed to show the complex underground workings. Various plans are presently being discussed to cover up the underground tier, while at the same time making it accessible. All around is the skeleton of the *cavea*, the huge circle where the audience sat.

The best overall view is from the second floor. It is reached via stairs situated to your left, a few steps past the next (western) entrance. Having reached the top of the stairs, turn left to the railing and left again to look down into the arena. You'll see the other three official entrances on the ground floor; the one to your left (north entrance), flanked by pillars and today marked by a cross that dates back to the time when it was erroneously thought that thousands of Christians had been executed here, was for the emperor and his retinue. They sat over this entrance in the imperial box, while near them, in a balustraded section, sat other authorities, including the Vestal Virgins.

Everyone else sat on the steps covering the *cavea*, divided by rank. Two main circles, up to the penultimate ring of square windows, were for male Roman citizens, in order of eminence. These distinctions were marked on the marble steps, some of which are restored to the left of the east entrance. A third circle above these two, now gone, had wooden bleachers, and was for women and non-citizens. Slaves stood on a colonnaded terrace above the bleachers, also missing. The crowds entered in an orderly way through a network of corridors and staircases, some of which still have the original steps. Then the people were figuratively 'vomited' into the *cavea* through 160 doors called *vomitoria* (some remain).

The wooden floor of the arena was thickly covered with sand (*arena* in Latin, hence the name given to all similar sites ever since). During animal fights, tall wire netting topped with elephant tusks pointing inwards protected the public, while archers stood in bunkers ready to stop escaping animals. Originally, there was underground plumbing to flood the arena for mock sea battles, but when animal fights gained in popularity, the

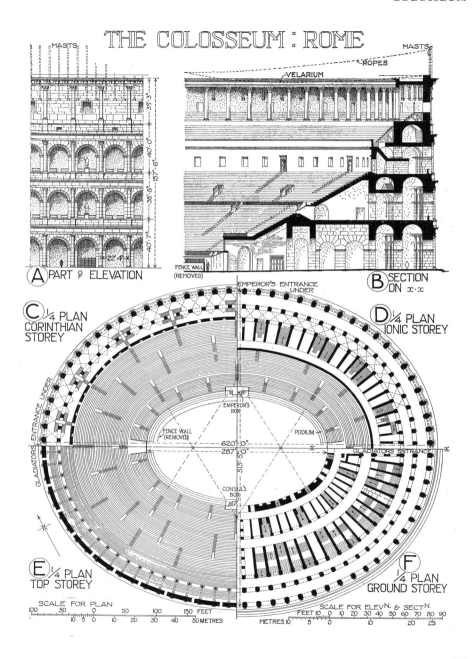

THE COLOSSEUM : ROME

MASTS

MASTS

ROPES

VELARIUM

35'-3"

40'-0"

157'-6"

38'-8"

40'-7"

22'-4"

Ⓐ PART ᵒᶠ ELEVATION

FENCE WALL
(REMOVED)

Ⓑ SECTION
ON x·x

Ⓒ ¼ PLAN
CORINTHIAN
STOREY

Ⓓ ¼ PLAN
IONIC STOREY

EMPEROR'S ENTRANCE
UNDER

GLADIATORS ENTRANCE UNDER

EMPEROR'S
BOX

FENCE WALL
(REMOVED)

PODIUM

620'-0"

287'-0"

513'-5"

x

x

GLADIATORS ENTRANCE

CONSUL'S
BOX

Ⓔ ¼ PLAN
TOP STOREY

Ⓕ ¼ PLAN
GROUND STOREY

SCALE FOR PLAN
100 50 0 50 100 150 FEET
10 5 0 10 20 30 40 50 METRES

SCALE FOR ELEVᴺ ᵉ SECTᴺ
FEET 10 0 10 20 30 40 50 60 70 80 90
METRES 10 5 0 10 20 25

naval games were moved elsewhere so the arena could have more elaborate stage mechanisms and backstage facilities underground.

The underground maze we now see contained cubicles for attendants, animal cages, storage rooms, first aid stations and a complex system of chutes, trap doors and counterweight-driven elevators to bring up the animals and hoist the scenery.

A tunnel under the eastern entrance (the one opposite you) linked the arena to the gladiatorial school, which we'll see outside the Colosseum. Another led to a hospital, another to a morgue (*spoliarium*). The latter tunnel probably passed through the underground gate visible under the eastern entrance, called the *Porta Libitinaria* (Libitina was the goddess of corpses). When the games became a form of assembly-line execution, human corpses were hauled, sometimes along with animal carcasses, toward *carnaria*, common graves that perhaps remain under the nearby Via San Gregorio.

After each combat, attendants wearing masks of the God Mercury – the guide to the netherworld – checked whether the fallen were really dead by tapping them on the forehead with a mallet, and sometimes gave them the *coup de grâce*. During large scale fights and hunts, the smell of blood, burnt flesh and wild animals was overpowering, despite attempts to cover it with perfume and incense.

Now let's look at the exterior. Go back out to a marble balustrade. Before you is the ridge we passed earlier (p. 195), a spur of the Palatine closing in the Forum. It is covered by the ruins of the double **Temple of Venus and Rome** (the city deified), Rome's largest temple, built in the 2nd century AD by Trajan's successor, Hadrian, and rebuilt a century later after a fire. We see a giant coffered apse and rows of columns on either side. The other half of the double temple stood where a church now stands (S. Maria Nova, p. 196, whose medieval bell tower we can see).

Hadrian was himself an architect of considerable creativity (see p. 385) and his idea of a double temple was new. Each of the two apses, placed back to back, contained a giant seated statue of one of the two goddesses. Hadrian had proudly shown his creation to Apollodorus, the famous architect of his predecessor Trajan (pp. 181, 187) and now his own adviser. Apollodorus dryly noted that if the goddesses stood up, their heads would go through the roof. According to one historian, Hadrian never forgave him, and some time later he first exiled Apollodorus, then put him to death on trumped-up charges. Perhaps at the time the emperor was already showing signs of the senile dementia that was to lead to his death.

The temple stands on the site of the vestibule of the Domus Aurea, built by Nero seventy years earlier, and the 107 ft (35 m) statue of himself, the Colossus. The statue was moved to the front of the Colosseum (12 pairs of elephants were needed) after the destruction of Nero's compound, whose immensity you can now estimate by considering that it descended the ridge to a park and artificial

The ruins of the double temple of Venus and Rome, the largest in the ancient city

lake in the present Colosseum area and continued on the other side for a total of 250 acres. (The exact spot to which the Colossus was moved is now marked by a small modern platform.)

Along the ridge to the left is the **Arch of Titus** (not to be confused with the larger Arch of Constantine, which is nearer to you on the left). Built to celebrate Titus' victory over the Jews (p. 179), the elegantly proportioned arch has reliefs showing Titus' triumphal procession, in which the seven-branched candlestick and other spoils from the Temple of Jerusalem are carried. Until the 19th century Roman Jews avoided passing near the arch.

Go back inside and around to the left, to the better preserved northern side of the amphitheatre. Remains of the original internal stairs are visible in places. On the right, the imperial entrance below can be identified by the Christian symbol of the cross raised in front of it in later times. Thirteen or fourteen arches past this point (three or four arches beyond the one with a stone coffin, near which you will note a bit of the original floor), the arches frame the area where the Domus Aurea continued along a green slope and behind palm trees. Part of the main palace remains; we'll go there in the next section of the walk.

Brick ruins on the lower part of the slope, near the street, are remains of the Baths of Titus, perhaps a simple conversion to public use of the private baths of the Golden House. Continue around, then descend to the exit (western gate). Before leaving, in the hall to the left note marble blocks commemorating restorations in ancient times. Two of these blocks, engraved in the rough lettering of advanced decline (5th century AD) thank various notables for restorations after 'abominable' earthquakes. On the pilasters of the arcades are tablets that visitors can kiss to acquire indulgences; they date from the 18th century, when the Colosseum was considered a holy site (see p. 202).

Leave the Colosseum and go right in order to see its better preserved northern side from the outside.

Here the solemn travertine exterior is almost intact. Each of the three arcaded storeys is decorated with columns of a different order: Doric for the base, Ionic for the middle and Corinthian for the top, with Corinthian pilasters for the blind storey at the very top. Over most of the arched gates on the ground floor are Roman numerals corresponding to those on the spectators' tickets, so that everyone could find their seat. A series of marble brackets runs around the building on the blind top storey, slightly below the cornice. These supported the 240 pine masts that went through holes in the cornice to hold up the sailcloth cover of the *velarium*.

Between the arched gates numbered 38 and 39 (XXXVIII and XXXVIIII) is the imperial entrance, which is larger than the others and unnumbered. It was lavishly decorated in stucco; there are remains of a geometric pattern over the second inside archway and on the vaulted ceilings.

The curve ends with a huge brick buttress, one of two added in the 19th-century restoration by pope Pius VII (whom Romans suspected of graft, see p. 461) to support the plundered wall, whose tremendous slabs seem to crumble even now – an awesome sight. Here, on the spot where the marble pavement ended and the flint paving stones began, are five of the low pillars, once connected by an iron railing, which originally surrounded the theatre and may have anchored the ropes of the *velarium*.

Past the brick buttress, in an area with the original marble floor, you can get a close-up view of some of the innards of the arena, including the underground corridor leading to a gladiator school, our next stop.

Leave the Colosseum from this side by the modern steps nearby on the right. Carefully cross at the treacherous traffic lights on your right and go left two blocks to the parapet of an excavation. These are the ruins of the **Ludus Magnus**, the largest of Rome's four gladiator schools, with an underground connection to the Colosseum.

The excavation has uncovered little more than a third of the school grounds. The curved ruins

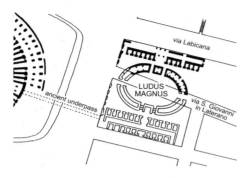

The ruins of the Ludus Magnus, the city's main gladiatorial school

continue under the present Via San Giovanni in Laterano to form an oval. This was a mini-arena where gladiators practised, surrounded by a *cavea* or circle of steps for trainers and colleagues to sit on. At each end of this part of the oval are remains of triangular fountains; two more decorated the

buried site opposite. Flanking the arena are the remains of a row of fourteen cells, the dormitory of the trainee gladiators. There was another row of cells on the unexcavated side.

Nearby were the three lesser gladiator schools: the Ludus Dacicus for fighters in the Dacian (eastern European) style; the Ludus Gallicus for the French style; and the Ludus Matutinus for wild beast fights. Only traces of the first survive.

Go to Via Labicana, which borders the excavation, and is flanked by a hilly park. Cross Via Labicana at the lights and enter the marble park gate there. A few yards from the gate, the first lane to the left leads to the site of the Domus Aurea.

What would appear to be a new wing of the Domus, with frescoes depicting an unidentified city, was discovered during excavations in 1999 at the corner of Viale Monte Oppio and Via delle Terme di Tito. The site is still closed to the public at the time of writing, but you can check the present situation by calling the Soprintendenza Archeologica di Roma (see p. 659).

BEFORE GOING

9. The Domus Aurea (Golden House of Nero)

Not the least attraction of this Walk is the chance to pursue the traces of the vanished residence Nero built for himself after the terrible fire of 64 AD, which he was accused of having started, though without proof (he contributed generously to the rebuilding out of his own pocket).

More than a palace, it was an enormous complex of several palaces with thousands of rooms, guesthouses, casinos, baths, gymnasia and theatres, interspersed with pools, a mile-long portico, rows of exquisite Greek statuary, and gardens and artificial woods stocked with wild and domestic animals. New aqueducts brought in extra water, including sea-water from the coast and sulphur-water from the mountains for special bathing pools. The main palace was Nero's residence, where he dined with guests, while perfumes and flowers were dropped from ivory ceilings, and where his mistress, and later wife, Poppæa, bathed in tubs of asses' milk. It was gilt on the outside (hence the name) and decorated inside with frescoes by Fabullus, the best painter of his time. It is said that he was practically imprisoned in the house, being forbidden to leave before he had finished the decoration. Some walls (according to Suetonius, writing several decades later) were inlaid with mother-of-pearl and semi-precious stones.

The whole complex covered sizeable areas of four hills (the Palatine, Esquiline, Oppian and Cælian) and the valleys in between, all on expropriated land. Such extravagance was a major cause of Nero's unpopularity. Yet modern historians detect some political bias in such criticism.

Emperors' residences had always included administrative and public buildings, and Nero's expansion could well have been necessary in order to handle the swelling bureaucracy of the greatest empire on earth. (Modern historians still wonder at how this bureaucracy worked so smoothly and effectively throughout the empire.) Thus, a famous phrase attributed to Nero during the palace house-warming party, 'Well, here I can finally start living as a human being,' always quoted derisively, might not have been so preposterous after all. (Indeed, contrary to widespread belief, Nero was not universally detested by his subjects. Tacitus, a most reliable annalist, writes that many regretted his passing, especially the poor, and that he left a valuable political legacy, which some of his would-be successors attempted to exploit in the troubled months after his demise. A false Nero even appeared on the scene and gathered a substantial following, until he was unmasked and executed.)

As we know (pp. 155-156), Nero's successors found it politic to tear down the Domus Aurea. Yet its most private area, Nero's own residence, was left standing for a few years and used as an extra imperial palace. Then it was sealed into the foundations of another massive public building, the Baths of Trajan, where it lay forgotten.

Baths of Trajan: considered the finest surviving Roman wall

In the middle ages the memory of 'Nero's folly' was never lost, but nobody remembered exactly where the palace was. So the accidental discovery in the renaissance of a set of underground rooms with exceptional frescoes and stuccos, though it caused a sensation, was not connected to the fabled Golden House of Nero. (Some years later, another clamour of enthusiasm greeted the fortuitous discovery in the same area of the *Laocoön*, the sublime statuary group now in the Vatican.)

The transformation of the rooms into the substructures of a later building deformed and darkened them, so that the renaissance artists who flocked to them compared them to natural caverns. They called them 'grottoes', and their frescoes – the work of Fabullus – 'grotesque'. Later the term 'grotesque' took on a different meaning, but technically it still denotes a style of mural decoration. Day after day, Raphael and his friends lowered themselves into the rooms from a hole in the ceiling to study and copy the paintings. Graffiti signatures, such as that of Raphael's assistant, Giulio Romano, remained there until recently, but have since been erased by humidity. Fabullus' work influenced Raphael's own style.

Only in the 19th century did scholars realise that this had been Nero's residence. Meanwhile the flow of artists and other lovers of antiquity had continued unabated. At a time when people thought nothing of firing a musket into a painted ceiling in order to collect a few fallen fragments, one can imagine the fate of the frescoes. We are lucky to have the renaissance copies.

Today it requires a feat of imagination to recognise in these dim underground chambers Nero's marvellous home, and in the gloom of walled-up windows to believe that sunlight once drenched the palace and vistas of gardens and colonnades once lightened the spirit. Yet some frescoes remain, some of the silent rooms still impress us with their noble design and a fabulous past still hovers over Nero's bedroom, dining hall and other as yet identified features.

ON THE SPOT

9. The Domus Aurea (Golden House of Nero)

Open: 09:00-19:00. Accompanied tours only. To be sure of a place, book by calling 06-39749907. A sweater is recommended for the visit even in summertime.

See p. 210 about a separate wing of the Domus Aurea discovered in 1998-1999, access to which is restricted at the time of writing.

Access to the **Domus Aurea** is through the substructures of baths built over the domus by the Emperor Trajan. These foundations invade, distort and shut out daylight from all the rooms of Nero's palace that have been excavated (others remain unexplored).

A revolutionary masterpiece, the Domus Aurea marked the first use of concrete as the building material of choice for fine architecture, and the break with Greek design based on a support system of walls and columns. Using vaulted architecture in concrete, Nero's architects arranged a harmony of simple shapes in empty space – rectangular and triangular prisms, cubes, octagons and hemi-cylinders.

The excavated part is divided into two main wings separated by a great trapezoidal courtyard (1). The left wing was once preceded by a long portico (2). This wing contains a frescoed corridor (3), a *nymphæum* (4) with seashells and other decorations near the ceiling, including a fragment of glass mosaic depicting *Ulysses and Polyphemus*, and twin rooms (5 & 6), possibly bedrooms, flanking what may have been a *triclinium*, or breakfast room (7).

These private apartments, if that's what they

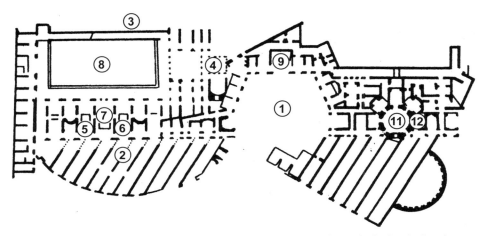

The Domus Aurea, part of the grandiose residence of Nero, built after the fire of 64 AD

were, were lit from two sides: the entrance portico (now missing) on one side, with a view of the future Colosseum valley, at the time an artificial lake; and a great peristyle, or columned courtyard (8), on the opposite side. The windows are now walled up and parallel foundation walls of the Baths of Trajan invade the courtyard, in the centre of which traces of a fountain are visible.

Around the trapezoidal courtyard (1) between the two wings are several rooms with frescoes, which have deteriorated severely in recent years. The rooms include the famous hall with the gilt vault (9), originally lit from the courtyard, with highly refined stuccos and traces of Fabullus' work. Most of the paintings are imaginary architectural and mythological vignettes and naturalistic friezes. The technique and style resemble those of the celebrated red frescoes of Pompeii, but here white backgrounds predominate.

In the right wing are another decorated corridor (10), in which renaissance artists left graffiti with their names, and a great octagonal hall (11), probably the dining hall which the historian Suetonius said could rotate to follow the sun. The latest excavations have found what seems to be a round platform, or the imprint of one, in the middle of the hall, and a sort of water chute in a wall, which could have powered a rotating device. Light comes from a great oculus in the domed ceiling, like that of the Pantheon (p. 236). The room (12) next to the hall had stuccos and a frescoed vault depicting *Hector and Andromache*, and is probably where the *Laocoön* group was found.

Above the Domus Aurea, the **Baths of Trajan**, designed by the great Apollodorus (pp. 181, 187), occupied most of the present park. Vestigial ruins lie about, amongst which a powerful minor apse with coffered ceiling. To see it, walk around the Domus Aurea to the right, to the upper end of the park, where it is bordered by Via delle Terme di Traiano.

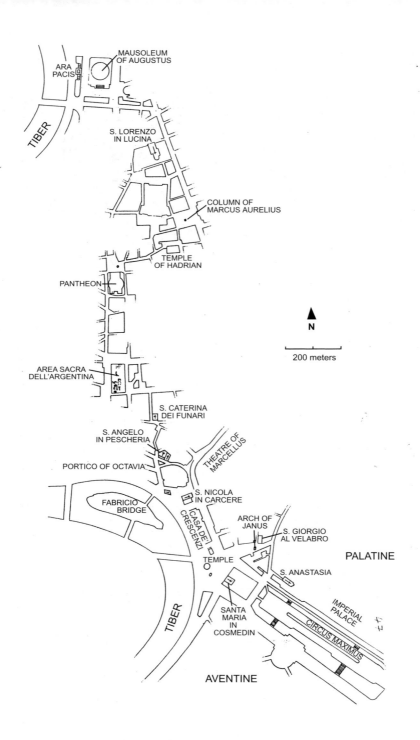

MAUSOLEUM
OF AUGUSTUS

ARA
PACIS

TIBER

S. LORENZO
IN LUCINA

COLUMN OF
MARCUS AURELIUS

TEMPLE
OF HADRIAN

PANTHEON

N

200 meters

AREA SACRA
DELL'ARGENTINA

S. CATERINA
DEI FUNARI

S. ANGELO
IN PESCHERIA

THEATRE OF
MARCELLUS

PORTICO OF OCTAVIA

S. NICOLA
IN CARCERE

FABRICIO
BRIDGE

CASA DEI
CRESCENZI

ARCH OF
JANUS

S. GIORGIO
AL VELABRO

PALATINE

TEMPLE

S. ANASTASIA

IMPERIAL
PALACE

TIBER

SANTA
MARIA
IN
COSMEDIN

CIRCUS MAXIMUS

AVENTINE

ANCIENT ROME: SECOND WALK

Starting point: Piazza Augusto Imperatore
End point: Viale delle Terme di Caracalla
Duration: 6 hours and 30 min (without the Detours indicated between parentheses)

BEFORE GOING

1. In the footsteps of Augustus through the Campus Martius: the Mausoleum of Augustus

In 14 AD, on the 19th day of the eighth month, then called the Sextile, Augustus, the first emperor, died. A grieving world renamed the month after him in the justified view that Augustus had contributed something fundamental to civilization and that after him times would be different for Rome and for the world.

The second Ancient Rome Walk unfolds under Augustus' great shadow. It takes us to the Campus Martius, which owes its initial development to him, and along a string of monuments connected with him. Most of the Walk will follow the Corso, which you may recall (p. 25) is associated with ancient Rome, since it crosses an area of imperial monuments towards the oldest core of the city. So we now visit what we bypassed in the first Ancient Rome Walk (see pp. 136 -137).

From Rome's very beginnings, this area was dedicated to Mars, the god of agriculture, later transformed into the god of war. The zone was outside the Republican Walls and was for centuries reserved for farming, ceremonial and military uses. But as republic mutated into empire, a development characterised by a period of explosive growth and internationalisation, Augustus found it essential to expand the city in this direction.

The expansion was part of a general plan of urban renewal, which Augustus later summed up in the statement, 'I found Rome a city of bricks, I left it a city of marble.' This proud observation crowned and symbolised feats of political and constitutional reform which made this man the rebuilder and, many would say, the saviour of the land. Augustus ended the civil wars that had bloodied and weakened the polity for over a century, subdued the proud patrician families who had come to consider the Republic their own fiefdom, thwarted revolts in the provinces and united the increasingly anarchic, far-flung commonwealth under a central imperial government.

As we begin our Walk from the edge of the Campus Martius toward the core of ancient Rome, we immediately reach the ruin of one of Augustus' most poignant monuments: his own grave, the Mausoleum. Of a size and splendour unprecedented in Rome, it was patterned after the fabled mausolea of eastern kings and named after the first to be built, in honour of King Mausolus of Halicarnassus. Augustus inaugurated it in 28 BC, when he was 34, a year after taking office as undisputed master of Rome. It was meant as a tomb for himself and his successors, whom he expected to continue his wise and benevolent rule. Though the system he established allowed for emperors to designate anyone as their successors by adoption, he fervently hoped to give the people someone of his own blood, as the first of a carefully selected set of rulers. His dream never came true.

All the young relatives whom Augustus deemed worthy to continue his work preceded him to the Mausoleum. What followed was a dynasty of distant relatives and strangers, mostly corrupt or incompetent, sometimes murderers and madmen. Indeed, the greatest tribute to the solidity of the government created by Augustus is that, despite such rulers, Rome enjoyed peace, prosperity and good administration until the death of Nero, the last and most notorious member of Augustus' Julio-Claudian dynasty. Only then did internal strife erupt again.

Augustus had no male heir. Sickly and rumoured to be homosexual (the rumour originated

Augustus

with his enemies, who had said the same of his great-uncle Julius Cæsar: it was unfounded in both cases), he had only one daughter, Julia, from his wife Livia. He concentrated his dynastic hopes on his nephew, Marcellus, son of his beloved sister Octavia. Marcellus was married to Julia at 15 and was carefully groomed for the throne. He showed great promise but died of malaria at 19. His ashes were the first to enter the new Mausoleum, with a grand funeral recorded by Virgil in Book VI of the *Æneid*:

Quantos ille virum magnam Mavortis ad urbem	What a moan will rise in the great city
Campus aget gemitus! Vel quæ, Tiberine, videbis	from the Campus Martius! What rites will
Funera, cum tumulum præterlabere recentem! ...	you see, O Tiber, when lapping the shore
Heu, miserande puer, ...	in front of a recently opened sepulchre! ...
Tu Marcellus eris.	For you, alas, unhappy boy, Marcellus.

217

The Mausoleum of Augustus: 18th-century reconstruction by Mariano Vasi

The emperor then married off the widowed Julia to his ablest general, the young, strong and wise Agrippa, whom he now considered his heir. Nine years later Agrippa died and his ashes too entered the Mausoleum. Augustus next designated his grandchildren, Caius and Lucius, as possible heirs, only to see them predecease him. Lucius succumbed to disease in Marseilles at 19; Caius died of wounds at 24 during a campaign in Armenia.

The 67-year-old Augustus' dynastic ambitions were shattered. He settled for his stepson, Tiberius, his wife Livia's child by a previous marriage, a valiant general but a sullen, vicious and narrow-minded aristocrat given to drink (his soldiers called him Biberius, rather than Tiberius) whom the puritanical Augustus had never liked. Augustus' bitterness in adopting Tiberius as heir is clear from the famous preamble to his will: 'Since an atrocious fate has torn away my sons ... let Tiberius Cæsar be my heir.'

His sister Octavia, along with the Empress Livia, had always been closest to Augustus. Octavia was an unhappy figure. As a young woman Augustus had forced her to marry Mark Antony, who promptly betrayed her with the Egyptian queen Cleopatra and whom Augustus himself later destroyed. Octavia too entered the Mausoleum before the ageing emperor; her ashes were placed near those of her son Marcellus, under a common epitaph. Augustus followed his relatives there at the age of 76, with the most solemn state funeral Rome had ever seen. His body was cremated at the Mausoleum on a pyre so huge that it burned for five days, during which the Empress Livia, dishevelled, barefoot and attended by a group of senators, waited to collect the ashes in her bare hands. (At that time, witnesses affirmed having seen Augustus' soul being taken to Olympus by an eagle: his *apotheosis*.) Livia herself entered the Mausoleum fifteen years later, at the age of 86. In Robert Graves' bestseller *I, Claudius* the characterisation of Livia as a serial killer, who murdered all Augustus' heirs and then Augustus himself, is entirely fictional.

Most members of Augustus' dynasty were buried in the Mausoleum: Tiberius, his son Drusus (poisoned), Caligula, Claudius and his son Britannicus (all three assassinated), together with a multitude of relatives (many of them murdered too). The most notable exception was Nero, too damned in senatorial circles for his body to be moved to the Mausoleum from the family tomb near Piazza del Popolo (p. 42), where it had been deposited after his suicide. Another person to whom Augustus himself denied the honour of burial in the Mausoleum was his daughter Julia. In her later years she had been exiled to an island for scandalous conduct, which included making love to five nobles at a time (probably a euphemism for a political conspiracy). The same fate befell her own daughter for similar reasons.

A few emperors after the Augustan dynasty were buried there, the last being Nerva. By then the Mausoleum was full. Trajan was buried at the base of his column (p. 186). Hadrian built a new imperial sepulchre, which we'll see in a later Walk in its medieval reincarnation as the Castel Sant' Angelo.

The last cremation at the Mausoleum occurred long after it had fallen into ruin, when the body of the revolutionary Cola di Rienzi (p. 144), after having been hung from the balcony of a nearby church, was burned there in the 14th century, in mockery of the man who had professed to be a new Augustus. Here in the words of the 'Anonymous Roman' (a chronicler who probably was present) is what happened to Rienzi's corpse after the mob killed him as he fled the Capitol:

> Someone brought a rope and tied the feet. They threw it on the ground, dragged it around, bruised it and shattered it … They dragged it to S. Marcello, where they hung it from a balcony. It had no head; the skull was lost along the way … It was horribly fat and as white as bloodied milk. It was so fat that it resembled a large buffalo or a cow from the slaughterhouse. There it hung for two days and one night. Boys threw stones at it. On the third day they dragged it to the field of Austa [Mausoleum of Augustus]. There they made a fire of thistles. They put it on … Because of the great fat it burned eagerly. This way the corpse was consumed and reduced to ashes … not even a stitch was left.

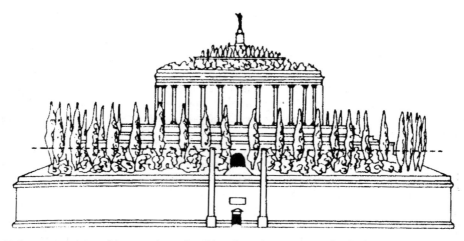

Modern reconstruction of the Mausoleum; dotted line shows the present street level. Alternative reconstructions have been proposed

ON THE SPOT

1. In the footsteps of Augustus through the Campus Martius: the Mausoleum of Augustus

The entrance to the massive ruins of the Mausoleum usually being closed, we'll have to settle for a survey of the exterior. The original appearance of the tomb is uncertain, but there was probably a high enclosure around the base crowned by two or more receding cylinders laid one on top of the other and encircled by colonnades. The whole was faced with travertine and topped by a statue of Augustus. The entrance was eventually flanked by two obelisks. Many centuries later, one of these was taken to the Quirinal, the other to S. Maria Maggiore (pp. 69, 97). A great bronze plate over the entrance carried Augustus' autobiographical statement, which he dictated shortly before dying. The plate has disappeared, but its text has been found reproduced in Roman temples worldwide (the best preserved is in Ankara, Turkey).

The tomb was inspired by oriental and Etruscan models, which were topped with earth and evergreens. Cypresses have been planted in a recent attempt at restoration, but the ruin is basically unrecognisable, having undergone more transformations over almost two millennia than any other Roman monument. It has served as a fortress, a marble quarry, a vineyard, a bull ring, a theatre and in the 19th century as a refuge for needy old women. As recently as 1936 it was a concert hall.

The internal structures are mostly gone, but a small square room in the centre has been identified as the cell containing the ashes of Augustus and Livia. A circular corridor around it has three niches. The one on the left probably contained Octavia's urn, which has been recovered, and that of her son Marcellus; the other two contained those of Augustus' grandchildren, Lucius and Caius.

BEFORE GOING

2. The Ara Pacis (Altar of Peace)

A few steps from Augustus' tomb is an extraordinary marble tribute to his rule, the Altar of Peace, or more precisely, of the Augustan Peace: *Ara Pacis Augustæ* is its full Latin name. Tomb and altar together form a sort of compendium of Augustus' life and times, though originally the altar wasn't very near the tomb, as we'll see. At the time of writing, the monument is closed for remodelling of the protective structure.

'When I returned to Rome from Spain and Gaul after my successes in those provinces, the Senate decreed that an altar of Augustan Peace should be consecrated in the Campus Martius in honour of my return.' So said Augustus in the autobiographical statement that hung outside his tomb. Yet the Ara Pacis Augustæ is more than an honorary altar. Unlike the tomb, which evokes the demise of Augustus' dynastic ambitions, the altar symbolises the greatness of his achievements and high hopes for the future. Its most striking feature is the great processional frieze, depicting Augustus and his entourage at the height of success. The historian D. R. Dudley has observed, 'This is the high noon of the Principate and Augustus is shown with his family, his friends and his grandchildren. The death of Marcellus is, so far, his only personal loss; death has not touched his friends, nor scandal his daughter Julia. The succession seemed amply provided for; who could guess that it would eventually fall on the uncongenial Tiberius?'

In the frieze serious men appear deeply conscious of their awesome responsibilities, serene

Panel of the processional frieze on the Ara Pacis enclosure

221

women chat, while children, some more intimidated than others by the state function they attend, grab their elders' cloaks. A less pretentious or more human and expressive state monument is hard to imagine. The art is the best that the golden age of Roman sculpture had to offer. Equally fascinating are the allusions to peace, prosperity and Rome's great traditions in the other panels.

The archæological history of the monument is unprecedented. It was founda third of a mile away, shattered, awash in water infiltrations and over 20 feet underground. The first fragments emerged in 1568 near the foundations of a palace on the Corso. Everyone admired them but no one suspected a link with the fabled altar of Augustus, even though Augustus had said in his autobiography that the altar celebrated his return from the North, which implied that it was on the northern approach to Rome, the present Corso. Collectors, including the Florentine Medici family, bought many pieces. They were eventually scattered amongst various Italian museums, the Vatican Museums, Vienna and the Louvre.

In the 19th century more ruins were found in the foundations of the old palace. In the latter half of the century German archæologists definitively identified them as belonging to the Ara Pacis. An initial, essentially correct, theoretical reconstruction of the monument was drawn. Systematic excavations were attempted, but a heavy water influx hampered work. In 1903 renewed efforts involved tunnelling under several buildings. More pieces were found, but water stopped work again. In 1937 Italian engineers devised a clever system to stop the water. They froze the basement using refrigerating pipes, permitting the remaining fragments to be extracted. It was decided to rebuild the altar on its present site, as it could not be placed under the old palace. All the pieces in Italian hands, including those in museums, were reassembled. Pope Pius XII donated what was in the Vatican and the Vienna museum sold its pieces to Italy. Only the fragments in French hands, which are either in the Louvre or embedded in a wall of the French Villa Medici (p. 89) are missing. They were replaced by casts, in the hope that one day France will follow the example of the other nations and allow a full reconstruction.

The fecundity of Mother Earth,
from the Ara Pacis

ON THE SPOT

2. The Ara Pacis (Altar of Peace)

The project for a new protective structure, entrusted by the city to the prominent American architect Richard Meier, has unleashed a huge controversy because of the unnecessary destruction of the Rationalist-style 1930's pavilion that stood here, and because of the style and disproportionate size of the new design, publicly called a 'horror' by a member of the national government. Work is still in progress at the time of writing but should be completed shortly. There is also a very dubious plan to redesign the whole square as a modern promenade.

Walk to the modern pavilion by the river, a few steps west of the Mausoleum. This shelters the rebuilt **Altar of Augustan Peace**, which was originally in the open. The monument consists of a square enclosure of richly sculpted marble, which contains the actual altar.

The main interest is not the altar but the enclosure, where the reliefs show the head of the imperial court procession that was held to consecrate the altar during its construction. The first three panels are almost obliterated, but in the third we can see the lictors, or *fasces*-bearers (A), preceding the authorities. Where the third panel joins the fourth is the veiled, wreathed figure of Augustus (B), unfortunately almost erased, flanked by two other wreathed notables, the consuls, one of whom (right) is probably the future emperor Tiberius (C).

Four priests, or *flamines*, follow the group, recognisable by their strange spiked hats (D). Next comes a religious attendant bearing an axe (E). The solemn, veiled figure that follows is probably Agrippa (F), Augustus' right-hand man and son-in-law. Clinging to his toga is his older son, Caius (G), caressed on the head by a lady in the background. Next to him is his mother, Augustus' daughter, the 'erring Julia' (H), see p. 219. The youth beside Julia is probably Iulus (I), Octavia's son by the unfortunate Mark Antony, see p. 219. Next to him is his half-sister Antonia (J), holding her child by the hand. In the next group are one more small child in a miniature toga (K) – Domitius Ahenobarbus, Nero's future father – and a young girl with her hair in a bun. The old man behind her is probably Mæcenas (L), the fabulously rich philanthropist (whose name has become synonymous with patronage of the arts) and Augustus' fervent backer, see p. 100.

The opposite side of the enclosure shows senators, magistrates, widows of Augustus' family and others bringing up the rear of the procession. The erased panel probably depicted the emperor's wife, Livia, see p. 218. Many of the heads of the figures on this side were reworked or added in the 16th century, as they were amongst the first fragments to be found. The toddler raising his arms to be carried is Agrippa's other son, Lucius, see p. 219.

The front and back of the enclosure depict allegories of tradition and prosperity: (front right) the Trojan Æneas – legendary forefather of Augustus

The third and fourth panels of the frieze of the Ara Pacis enclosure

A B C D D D D E F G H I J K L

and of Romulus, founder of Rome – sacrificing to the Penates, or ancestor-gods, his head veiled; (back left) the fecundity of Mother Earth.

On all sides of the enclosure, acanthus leaves of amazing delicacy adorn the lower parts of the panels, enlivened by swans and other fauna. All the leaves originate from central stalks of marvellous design. There are tiny animals near the bases of the stalks; a small snake approaching nests of frightened birds (one fleeing) and lizards. On or near other stalks are a frog, a cricket and a scorpion.

Now enter the enclosure. Its interior surface is garlanded with leaves and fruit, while the lower part represents a fence, a reminder of the wooden fence that enclosed the shrine at the time of its consecration by the imperial procession – a moment of history captured in stone.

The altar itself displays scenes of animal sacrifice by Vestal Virgins (inside) and priests with

Vegetal decoration from the Ara Pacis

sacrificial victims (outside). Indeed, the altar was created to thank the gods annually through such sacrifices for Augustus' successful return.

As you leave the pavilion, notice a modern inscription on its base that repeats Augustus' autobiographical statement, *Res Gestæ*, 'The things I have done' (p. 224).

Cross the street and turn right. Pass the 19th-century Palladian façade (by Valadier) of the much older church of **S. Rocco**, dedicated to the protector of the plague-stricken. Turn the corner. On the side wall of the church, a tall marble strip inserted in 1821 records the levels of the worst river floods in the past few centuries (see pp. 116-117, 140).

A modern double arch separates S. Rocco from another church, **S. Girolamo degli Schiavoni** (St. Jerome of the Slavs). It was built in the renaissance as the national church of the Slavic community of refugees, mainly Croats, Serbs and Bosnians, who fled when Turks invaded their homelands around 1400. It is still used by people from the Balkans, including refugees from the wars in the 1990's.

On the support of the double arch is a small drinking fountain of Acqua Vergine (p. 50), a charming, though damaged, mid-18th century work. A wine barrel is surmounted by a smiling face, either an *oste* (innkeeper) or a stevedore from the river harbour nearby (p. 123), where wine was brought from the north. The harbour was demolished in the late 19th century when the river was embanked. This ancient, smaller harbour – called Porto di Ripetta ('of the Little Jetty') in order to distinguish it from the main Porto di Ripa Grande downriver – was famous for its curved steps, built by Alessandro Specchi in the early 18th century, which inspired those of Piazza di Spagna.

Pass the arch. At some distance before you, rising above a well-designed apse, is a church dome, one of the most beautiful in Rome. It is the work of Pietro da Cortona, who created it in 1668 to surmount the church of S. Carlo al Corso, which had been designed a few decades earlier.

Leave the modern square, going between the pillars on the right into the equally modern Via Tomacelli .

Piranesi's view of Alessandro Specchi's Porto di Ripetta, mid 18th-century

DETOUR
10 MIN

On the Corso, go left to the church of SS. Ambrogio e Carlo, better known as **S. Carlo al Corso** ('St. Charles on the Corso'). It is the national church in Rome of the Lombards (immigrants from the northern region, centred on Milan) and was built in honour of the famous Milanese cardinal, St. Charles Borromeo, after he was canonised in 1610. It replaced an earlier church nearby dedicated to St. Ambrose, patron saint of the Lombards, which had served the Lombard community in Rome since the 1200's, and was then torn down.

S. Carlo was designed and begun by a Lombard architect, Onorio Longhi, and completed within a few decades by his son Martino. The unusual, flashy façade was designed by Cardinal Luigi Omodei, an amateur architect and patron of the arts.

The church is open: 09:00-12:00 and 16:00-19:00. The interior is very grand. An ambulatory encircles the deep apse: this is unique in Rome but follows Gothic examples, notably the cathedral of Milan, to which it probably refers. Elaborate baroque stuccos and frescoes adorn the vaults and walls. Those of the main vault and transept follow designs by Pietro da Cortona. The main altar has a sumptuous altarpiece by Carlo Maratta (1690) of *Sts. Ambrose and Charles in Glory*. A niche behind the altar holds a reliquary with the heart of St. Charles Borromeo. On the pier to the left of the altar, the 15th-century shrine for holy oil comes from the original church of St. Ambrose. In the vestibule of the sacristy is a dramatic 17th-century *Crucifixion* by Borgognone.

The doorway next to the church (No. 437) leads to a connected building, which includes the beautifully decorated Chapel of St. Ambrose on the site of the original church. Ask the custodian for access. Leave the church and go right a few yards.

END OF DETOUR

BEFORE GOING

3. The Corso in Antiquity

You are again on the Corso, Rome's high street since the middle ages (pp. 123-127). Already in antiquity it was a very important route, as part of the Via Flaminia (pp. 42-43), the highway linking Rome to the North. In the 3rd century, with the building of the Aurelian walls, this segment of the Via Flaminia was enclosed within the city, and its name changed to Via Lata ('the Broadway'), and much later still to Corso ('Racecourse'). Originally, the street did not end at Piazza Venezia, as it does today, but continued to the spur of the Quirinal, before this natural barrier was flattened by Trajan's engineers (p. 181), where it joined the Clivus Argentarius, which we saw near the Forum of Julius Cæsar.

Characterised today by a parade of palaces, the street was conceived as monumental from the very start. Before it was part of the city, it served as a burial ground for notables (custom forbade interment within the city walls. From the tomb of Nero and his family (p. 42) to that of Caius Bibulus (p. 188), funerary monuments lined the whole street, as did imposing crematory ovens (*ustrina*). Augustus was following Roman custom when he built his Mausoleum next to it.

Temples and other public buildings gradually rose along the Corso, beginning with Augustus' plan to expand the city, especially the public areas in the Campus Martius. Amongst the first was the Ara Pacis, which, as already mentioned, was not on its present site but further along the Corso. Much later, several emperors built celebratory columns and triumphal arches along the Corso: at least five arches spanned it in classical times.

The Corso in 1625, detail from the bird's eye view map by Giovanni Maggi

None of the columns or arches remains, except Marcus Aurelius' great column, which we'll see later. These and other monuments were torn down in the middle ages and renaissance. Raphael, in charge of modernising the street near Piazza del Popolo in the early 16th century, pleaded in vain with the pope to halt the destruction. The last arch was razed in the next century by Alexander VII, the great builder pope (p. 44), to ease traffic and make the street more uniform.

Marble fragments come to light periodically all along the Corso. Amongst the greatest and most mysterious of the vanished temples was the Temple of the Sun, built by Emperor Aurelian in the 3rd century after a trip to the Orient. It did not long survive the fall of the Western Empire. Eight of its columns have turned up half a continent away in the Church of St. Sophia in Constantinople, where they were taken in the 6th century by Justinian, ruler of the Eastern Empire.

One of Augustus' first public works along what was then the Via Flaminia was the aqueduct bringing the Acqua Vergine from the countryside, a tremendous engineering feat organised by his son-in-law Agrippa. The aqueduct was destroyed after the fall of the Empire; only its reconstruction a millennium later allowed the area to be redeveloped (p. 50).

ON THE SPOT

3. The Corso in Antiquity

The Corso now crosses a busy five-way intersection, Largo Carlo Goldoni, named after a famous 18th-century Venetian playwright who stayed in the building on the right-hand corner with Via Condotti, with its theatrical backdrop of the Spanish Steps, which we visited in the first Roma Romantica Walk. Near the intersection, at No. 126 of the Corso, is the Hotel Plaza where the opera composer Pietro Mascagni (who wrote *Cavalleria Rusticana*) lived and where he died in 1945. Cross the intersection all the way to the right. You are about one-third of the way up the Corso here. Looking down the street, on the left is the obelisk of Piazza del Popolo, while on the right is the pompous pseudo-classical marble Altar of Piazza Venezia (p. 535), which hides the Capitoline Hill from view.

Excavations have revealed ancient ruins all along the Corso, from 9 ft to 15 ft (3 m to 5 m) underground. From a point across the street slightly to the right, and continuing right for a few blocks, five separate digs between 1893 and 1960 yielded many fragments of red oriental granite columns, probably from Aurelian's Temple of the Sun. Surface remains still existed in the renaissance and we have a complete floor plan of the temple by the great 16th-century architect Andrea Palladio.

On our right the string of great Corso palaces begins. The one nearest to you in Largo Goldoni is **Palazzo Ruspoli Memmo**, a fine example of late 16th-century architecture, by Bartolomeo Ammannati. Its original owner was the princely Caetani family (p. 248), whose heir was murdered by another nobleman in the early 17th century in front of its main entrance on the Corso. The door was sealed in mourning, until very recently, when an art gallery was installed on the ground floor.

In the 18th century the palace passed to the Ruspoli, a banking family, in partial payment of a gambling debt. After Napoleon's fall, some of his relatives lodged here, including the future Napoleon III as a child.

At the time of writing some members of the Ruspoli family still live here. The present owner is an Italian financier, Roberto Memmo, who has set up an art foundation in the palace (the art gallery is linked to it) and sometimes opens its frescoed salons to visitors.

BEFORE GOING

4. From S. Lorenzo in Lucina and the Solar Clock of Augustus, past the Column of Marcus Aurelius and on to the Pantheon

Many of the earliest Christian churches were not churches at all, but the homes of well-to-do believers, placed at the disposal of the faithful so that they could perform their rites sheltered from official persecution. After the legalisation of Christianity, many of the homes became regular churches. One of these home churches (*ecclesiæ domesticæ*, also called *tituli*, because the early prelates were each entitled to one) was just off the present Corso, and is probably still there in its reincarnation as the ancient church of S. Lorenzo in Lucina.

In the middle ages the church was dedicated to St. Lawrence, when relics found there were thought to be those of the legendary martyr, notably the gridiron on which he was roasted to death. ('I'm cooked on this side,' he is supposed to have said during his torture, 'now turn me over.') For many centuries before, the church was named after a certain Lucina. Who was she? According to tradition, she was a rich Christian matron, owner of the ancient home church. But Lucina was also a cult name for Juno, mother of the gods, in her capacity as protector of sick or pregnant women. Could the name of the church have actually come from a sanctuary of Juno Lucina on the site? This idea has been reinforced by the discovery of traces of what might have been an ancient sanctuary under the structure tentatively identified as the original home church.

Furthermore, amongst the vestiges of the presumed sanctuary, a pit was found under the centre of the church during digs in 1987. It may have been a well where women drank health-giving waters, a typical feature in sanctuaries of healing gods, which often doubled as medical centres (see p. 599). Curiously, S. Lorenzo has always been, and still is, preferred by pregnant and sick women, who pray before an old mosaic of the *Madonna of Good Health* over the main altar. Coincidence? Or proof that customs and beliefs survive through religious upheavals and through the ages?

The 1987 digs proved that S. Lorenzo is one of the oldest churches in Christendom; its basic structure has been in continuous use as a church from the start. The church uses wall for wall the structure of an ancient Roman house found beneath, quite probably, the original home church. The supporting posts of the house continue directly into the chapel piers one floor above, the ground having risen that much between the two constructions. Such continuity also appears from the north-south orientation of S. Lorenzo, which follows that of the house, instead of the ritual east-west layout of other early churches.

Lucina's home church was one of Rome's most important Christian community centres (at times, the most important) well before the 4th century, when the emperor Constantine allowed Christians to have official places of worship. It seems to have served occasionally for meetings of church prelates as early as the 2nd or 3rd century. At least one pope was elected in it, the Spaniard, Pope Damasus, in 366 AD. The church proper dates from the 5th century.

Where does all this leave us concerning Augustus' footsteps, the theme of our Walk? We find them here once again, hidden beneath S. Lorenzo in Lucina. The digs mentioned above, which confirmed tentative reports from the renaissance and later, have shown that under the church and the neighbouring streets and squares is a huge marble sundial. It is the Solar Clock of Augustus,

S. Lorenzo in Lucina in the 18th century, engraving by Giuseppe Vasi

built in the emperor's honour by his supporter and intimate friend Mæcenas (see pp. 100, 223), and one of the architectural and technological wonders of ancient Rome.

The clock had three components. First, a travertine pavement on which people could walk, which was actually a sundial inlaid in bronze with markings of the months and the hours of the day. Second, a great Egyptian obelisk, the pin, or gnomon, of the sundial. And third, of all things, the Ara Pacis, which originally stood a stone's throw away from S. Lorenzo (the old palace under which its fragments were found is next to the church).

The clock not only told time and date: the width of its shadows gave the length of days and nights in the different seasons. It also fulfilled an honorific function: every year on September 23, Augustus' birthday, the shadow of the obelisk fell in a line ending at the Ara Pacis. Thus, the Egyptian astronomers and mathematicians who planned the monument to Mæcenas' commission paid obeisance to the greatness of Augustus, prince of peace.

At the time of writing the public cannot visit the underground structures of the church or the solar clock excavations, which continue intermittently under S. Lorenzo in Lucina and in the nearby area. There is talk of a general exhibition when the work is finished and funds permit.

The Walk continues from the point where the Ara Pacis was discovered to where the obelisk-gnomon of the Solar Clock was found in pieces, then on to a piazza where the obelisk was set up three centuries ago. Continuing through an area once crowded with imperial monuments, past two that still stand (the Column of Marcus Aurelius and the Temple of Hadrian), we reach the greatest monument of all, pride of the Augustan era, the Pantheon, built by Agrippa, Augustus' right-hand-man, general and son-in-law.

ON THE SPOT

4. From S. Lorenzo in Lucina and the Solar Clock of Augustus, past the Column of Marcus Aurelius and on to the Pantheon

Taking the Corso to the right, walk in front of Palazzo Ruspoli and turn right into Piazza S. Lorenzo in Lucina. Across the piazza, at Nos 2-4, is another palace, the mediocre Palazzo Fiano-Almagià (built in the 14th century and remodelled in the 17th) under which the Ara Pacis was found.

Next to the palace is the medieval narthex (porch) of the church of **S. Lorenzo in Lucina**. (Open: 07:00-12:30 and 16:00-19:30 in winter, 17:00-19:30 in summer.)

As a church the building dates to the 5th century; as a house (now underground) to two or three centuries earlier. Yet the visitor sees no trace of its great antiquity. Rebuilt and remodelled several times (notably in the 12th century and finally in the 17th), S. Lorenzo looks like a mixture of the two later periods.

To the 12th century belong the fine romanesque bell tower and the porch with two marble lions. They are mentioned in one of Robert Browning's poems, in which the heroine, who has been baptised and later married in S. Lorenzo, says: 'I used to wonder, when I stood scarce high / As the bed here, what the marble lion meant.' Actually the lions symbolise the Christian Church: (left) a ferocious one, the Church militant; (right) a tame one, the benevolent Church.

The interior is 17th century. On the right, a coffer under the altar in the first chapel contains the gridiron venerated since the middle ages as the one on which St. Lawrence was burned to death in the 3rd century. On the pillar to the left of the second chapel is a memorial to Poussin. It was erected to the great 17th-century French painter, who lived and died in Rome (p. 88), by his countryman Chateaubriand, the early 19th-century novelist and ambassador to Rome, who wrote the Latin epitaph. The fourth chapel was designed by Bernini, who also carved the angels in and around the pretty little dome and the bust of a bearded gentle-

Putti over the Fonseca tomb, by Bernini

man (the papal medical doctor, Gabriele Fonseca) on the left. His pupils executed the two impressive busts on the right. The *Annunciation* over the chapel altar, attributed to Guido Reni, is in fact a period copy. The greatest ornament in the church is above the solemn main altar: the *Crucifixion*, a Guido Reni masterpiece, with its stormy and tragic sky. Over the altar, in an oval frame, is a mosaic of the *Madonna of Good Health* (p. 228) of uncertain date.

Behind the altar, in the massive wooden choir stalls (ask in the sacristy in the right transept for permission to see them) a small door opens to reveal a marble bishop's throne dated 1112. Its inscription records the transfer of St. Lawrence's relics to the church. A chapel in the right transept has a fine 16th-century wooden crucifix and a private memorial to Italy's last king, Umberto II, who died in exile in 1983.

Ask in the sacristy whether the underground level of the church, which includes remains of the 5th-century structure and of the Roman house which could be the original *ecclesia domestica*, is now open to the public.

230

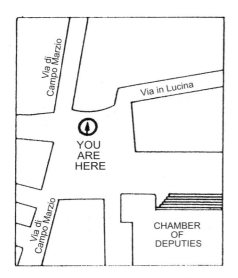

Piazza del Parlamento, with the Chamber of Deputies

brick and travertine rear façade of the Italian **Chamber of Deputies**, a conspicuous example of the early 20th-century 'floreated' style (*floreale*, an Italian off-shoot of *art nouveau*). The building is an extension of a much older one which we'll see shortly.

Stand with your back to the tablet commemorating the obelisk.

DETOUR
10 MIN

Skirt the piazza going left and enter the narrow Via in Lucina. No. 33 is the fine early 16th-century **Palazzo Vacca** (partly rebuilt).

It was originally home to the noble Spanish family De Vaca ('of the Cow' – note the emblem over the portal), one of the many that followed Pope Alexander VI Borgia (p. 45) to Rome. The family later Italianised its name to Vacca. A late 16th-century descendant, Flaminio, became a well-known sculptor (pp. 77, 239). A Latin inscription over the portal reads: 'My bones and my laboriously earned wealth I leave to thee, O Rome.' Another over a window reads, 'Nothing is certain in this miserable life'.

Further along on your left is the rear and more attractive façade of Palazzo Fiano-Almagià, whose main entrance you saw flanking the church of S. Lorenzo. Further still, street and palace form an angle. This is where the Ara Pacis was found under the palace (p. 222).

Continue in the same direction until you reach the Corso again. A Latin inscription of 1665, recalling the demolition of the last Roman triumphal arch on the Corso – the Arch of Domitian, rebaptised the Arch of Portugal in the middle ages after the name of a cardinal who lived nearby – is on a wall near here, where the Corso crosses Via della Vite (look up to your left).

Return to Piazza del Parlamento.

END OF DETOUR

Leaving the church, go left and left again into Via di Campo Marzio. At No. 48 archæologists are sometimes at work excavating the marble slabs of Augustus' sundial. The dig is in the courtyard behind a small door. On the front of No. 47 a bar displays a marble illustration of the excavated part of the clock.

Via di Campo Marzio leads to Piazza del Parlamento, where on your left above the door at No. 3 is an 18th-century marble tablet. A pope had it placed over the spot where the needle, or gnomon, from Augustus' sundial was found, in pieces. The obelisk was then re-erected in a square nearby, where we'll soon see it.

The Latin inscription speaks of 'the obelisk elegantly carved with hieroglyphs brought to Rome by Emperor Augustus after the conquest of Egypt, erected in the Campus Martius to project the sun's shade and the length of days and nights on a paved esplanade marked with copper lines.'

Piazza del Parlamento is dominated by the

Cross Piazza del Parlamento and pick up Via Campo Marzio again, which continues on the other side. It leads to Via Uffici del Vicario (at the corner look up to see a fine 18th-century street shrine). Turn left along Via Uffici del Vicario. On your right is Giolitti's, Rome's most famous ice-cream parlour. Pass it – if you can resist stepping in – and go on to Piazza Montecitorio, dominated by **Palazzo Montecitorio**.

Begun by Bernini in 1650 and completed by others, the very simple lines of the palace belie its grandeur. It was a courthouse under papal rule. Lottery numbers were drawn on its central balcony on Sundays before uproarious crowds. ('Damn the guy who invented lotto,' cries a player in a sonnet by Gioacchino Belli, Rome's great poet of the 19th century.) In 1871 the first Chamber of Deputies of a unified Italy adopted the palace as its seat, and it was doubled in size at the turn of the century by the addition which you saw from the back (p. 231). Remains of the crematorium where Marcus Aurelius was cremated have been found in a basement.

In front of the building is the 6th-century BC Egyptian obelisk from Heliopolis, formerly the needle of Augustus' sundial (p. 231). Papal engineers crowned the obelisk with a bronze ball, designed with a hole through which the rays of the sun shine on marks on the piazza, telling the time like the ancient sundial. The markings are gone, however, and the spot of light is hard to see.

Behind the obelisk, where the square narrows, veer left to Via Colonna Antonina (look out for the store sign 'Camiceria Caleffi'). It leads to another square, Piazza Colonna, dominated by the 2nd century AD **Column of Marcus Aurelius**, also called Colonna Antonina after the emperor's dynastic name.

Erected here soon after the death of the emperor-philosopher (p. 146) Marcus Aurelius, it celebrates his arduous campaigns to secure the Danube frontier (during which he also wrote his classic *Meditations*). The column obviously mimics Trajan's Column (p. 184) of a century earlier both in its size and 'unfurled scroll' design. The reliefs are cruder, however, though remarkably expressive. In the first episode Romans cross the river on a bridge of barges. The following scenes mostly depict battles and the subjugation of the barbarians. The human element dominates; the natural setting is less prominent than in Trajan's Column. A statue of Marcus on top of the shaft was missing by the 16th century, when a statue of St. Paul was placed there.

The column has been a major Roman landmark since the dark ages. It was once even taller than its present 120 ft (42 m). Rising street levels have buried two thirds of the pedestal, as well as a large platform beneath.

Nearby in the 18th century archæologists found another, shorter shaft which an earlier generation had dedicated to Marcus' father, the Emperor Antoninus Pius. Soon afterwards it was damaged by fire and cut up to repair other monuments. Its marvellous sculpted base can be seen in the Vatican museum (p. 312).

To view the square, stand near No. 355 (on the side that continues Via Colonna Antonina).

In antiquity major public buildings covered the square, including a temple dedicated to Marcus behind his column, porticoes and two crematoria (*ustrina*). Traces of these have appeared all around. Homes occupied the area beyond the Corso to your right. Even after Augustus' settlement the Campus Martius was never as densely populated as 'older' Rome, but some areas were exceptions. One residential building near here was a sort of skyscraper called 'Felicula's block' (*insula*) and was famous in antiquity. Its height is unknown, but people called it 'the monster'.

To your right in the square is an attractive late 16th-century fountain of the Acqua Vergine (p. 50). Across the Corso is a Galleria from about 1900, which faces a wider section of the Corso, called Largo Chigi, on the left, one of the busiest spots in the city and a nodal point of its modern traffic grid (see p. 131).

Continuing counterclockwise: the palace in front of you is the early 17th-century Palazzo

Chigi, which houses the Prime Minister's office. On the left side of it, at No. 366, is a large early 19th-century building, **Palazzo Wedekind**, now the headquarters of a newspaper. It is distinguished by ancient Roman columns from a villa near the lost Etruscan city of Veii not far from Rome, which articulate its portico. The columns were dug up a few years before the building was erected. A temple to the deified Marcus Aurelius probably once stood on the spot.

Retrace your steps toward Via Colonna Antonina. You'll pass the 18th-century façade of the church of S. Bartolomeo, once the chapel of Rome's first mental hospital (then called 'Ospedale de' Pazzarelli', now relocated). Past the church, turn left into Via dei Bergamaschi, which leads to Piazza di Pietra ('of Stone'), so called because of the massive **Temple of the Deified Hadrian**, built by Antoninus Pius in memory of his adoptive father in 145AD. This is part of the right flank, with 11 of the original 13 columns.

The temple, which was eight columns wide, opened to the left, towards the Corso (then Via Lata), behind a wide staircase and a triumphal arch. Although columns and parts of the cornice had been visible throughout the centuries (while the building served first as a hospital, then a customs house, before becoming, in 1882, Rome's Stock Exchange, which it remains), the identity of the remains was only confirmed in the 1920's. The temple was then restored and part of the base excavated. Look down into the trench to see how much deeper the ancient street level was. Behind the columns is the outside wall of the cella, or inner sanctum, which once contained the emperor's statue and altar. Other remains of the cella are in the Stock Exchange.

In antiquity this area, from the ancient Via Lata to our next destination, was a series of porticoes (see p. 245) and temples, of which fragments of isolated columns sometimes turn up here and there.

Bear right beside the columns and into Via dei Pastini. At the second crossing on the right, Vicolo della Spada d'Orlando ('Lane of Roland's Sword'), is an attractive late renaissance Acqua Vergine drinking fountain on the wall (p. 50). Opposite, a bit further on, is a shapeless marble lump, the stump of a column. In the middle ages this was said to owe its condition to the mythical Roland, Charlemagne's greatest knight, who sharpened his sword on it. The stump, and some bricks opposite, were from a temple which was an unprecedented kind of tribute: Hadrian built it in honour of his mother-in-law, Matidia. In the distance we can see the façade of the mid-15th century Palazzo Capranica, much reworked, though the beautiful windows and doorway are original.

Proceed along Via dei Pastini. At the next crossing, Via degli Orfani, immediately to your right is a wall tablet marking the height of one of the worst river floods, in 1870 (pp. 116-117). The coffee house on the corner serves some of Rome's best espresso. You have reached Piazza della Rotonda with its famous Augustan temple.

Temple of Hadrian in the 1830's

BEFORE GOING

5. The Pantheon

Agrippa (p. 218) conceived of a magnificent, unusual temple that would give a unique character to the newly settled area of the Campus Martius, which Augustus wanted rich in public and religious buildings, as well as in recreational spots such as theatres, baths and gardens. The site was chosen because of a great tradition: it was said that here, eight centuries earlier, Rome's founder Romulus had been carried up by an eagle to Heaven to join the gods (his *apotheosis*).

Yet, though Agrippa's name figures conspicuously on the temple front, what you see is not what Agrippa built. The original was restored by Domitian after a fire in AD 80, only to be struck by lightning in AD 110 and again burnt down. (According to another theory, the foundations collapsed.) The Pantheon was rebuilt in its current form by the Emperor Hadrian, to whom we owe other huge buildings, including the Temple of Venus and Rome (p. 208) and his own Mausoleum (p. 388). An accomplished architect, he probably designed the present Pantheon too. The fact that Agrippa's, and not Hadrian's, name is on the front is explained by the latter's customary modesty and by the fact that Augustus' famous son-in-law was still venerated at the time. Until recently the great bronze inscription with Agrippa's name caused much confusion. Only the discovery of bricks and clearly marked tiles from Hadrian's time convinced scholars of the real authorship.

How Hadrian's building differs from Agrippa's is unknown. The size was probably the same, but the innovations under Hadrian must have been drastic. Construction techniques had greatly improved, and the inventive emperor would not have slavishly followed the older design.

The temple is ancient Rome's grandest and most august building to have survived virtually intact. Originally dedicated to all pagan deities ('Pantheon' in Greek means 'of all the gods') and later to all Christian martyrs, since the darkest ages it has been considered one of Rome's most majestic and venerable architectural wonders. In the early 19th century Byron wrote of it:

> Simple, erect, austere, sublime ...
> .... spared and blessed by time
> Looking tranquillity, while falls or nods
> Arch, empire, each thing round thee, and man plods
> His way through thorns to ashes – glorious dome!
> .... Sanctuary and home
> Of art and piety – Pantheon! pride of Rome!

As an engineering feat, the temple is extraordinary. The exquisitely proportioned dome is the largest built in concrete until the 20th century. (St. Peter's, which is slightly narrower, is the largest in brick.) The crushing weight is dispersed by an intricate system of relieving arches that reveal a profound knowledge of construction techniques. The concrete is also formed by layers of materials whose density decreases as the height increases.

Dome and oculus of the Pantheon

Architecturally, the building is a provocative mixture of two styles: a powerful cylindrical main structure, characteristically Roman, and a Greek-inspired oblong portico. The combination is typical of Hadrian, who was known for his fanciful, eclectic tastes, as witnessed by his unprecedented 'double' Temple of Venus and Rome (p. 208) and by his exotic villa at Tivoli near Rome. The most impressive feature of the interior is the oculus (or 'eye'), a circular opening in the centre of the dome. As the only light source, it suffuses the vast hall with a serene radiance.

To Mme de Staël, the famous 18th-century French writer, the great oculus, with its cascade of sunbeams alternating with the procession of clouds in the intense blue Roman sky, symbolised a celebration of life: 'Pagans felt the divinity in life in the same way as Christians, after them, felt the divinity of death, and that is the essential difference between the two,' she reflected.

Not even the river floods, particularly bad in this low-lying area (photographs of the 1870 flood show boats in the Pantheon), have seriously damaged it. Incidentally, it seems to be one of the few ancient temples conceived not only as a sanctum for priests, but as a meeting place for the faithful (see p. 157).

If the elements have been easy on the Pantheon, the same cannot be said of people. A few decades after Constantine legalised Christianity, the Pantheon, then 200 years old, was closed like other temples of pagan worship. It lay unused for centuries, while thieves and barbarians, both before and after the fall of the Western Empire, plundered altars, statues and anything that wasn't nailed down. Like so many other temples, it would have gone to ruin had not an early pope converted it into a church, when it was about 500 years old.

Yet there were further mishaps. The Eastern Roman Emperor, who still nominally ruled Rome,

Pantheon: section

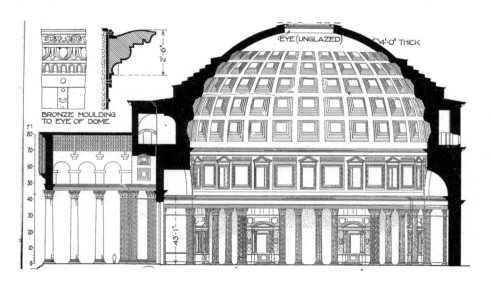

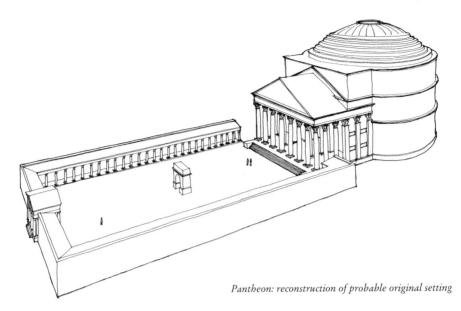

Pantheon: reconstruction of probable original setting

took all the gilt bronze roof tiles while visiting the city. During the war-torn middle ages, the potent structure often served as a fortress – once, in the 11th century, as the redoubt of a papal pretender, or 'anti-pope', in his sallies against the legitimate pope.

In the 17th century, a pope of the princely Barberini family, Urban VIII, appropriated the gilt bronze cladding of the portico ceiling, weighing some 200 tons. Part of it was forged into 80 cannons for the papal Castel S. Angelo (p. 381). The pope's architect, Bernini, used the rest in St. Peter's, where you'll see how it was transformed (p. 368). For this reason, history has branded the Barberini pope with the quip: *Quod non fecerunt barbari, fecerunt Barberini* ('What the barbarians didn't do, the Barberini did').

During the renaissance, admiring foreigners and especially artists used to climb the dome to look inside the oculus. The Emperor Charles V did so when he visited Rome to patch things up with the pope nine years after his troops had so viciously sacked it (discussed later, p. 381). A Roman youth of the noble Crescenzi family was sent to escort him. The youth later told his father that he had felt a strong urge to push the emperor down the hole: 'In my time, we did things, we didn't just talk about them,' the father is supposed to have replied.

The Pantheon is the resting place of several great renaissance artists, including Raphael. Near his tomb is a memorial to a cardinal's niece to whom Raphael was betrothed, though it is said that he kept postponing the marriage because he was in love with a 'baker's little daughter' (p. 574). When he died at 37, unmarried, Rome wept. Before he was laid to rest, the pope appeared in the temple, knelt beside the sublime artist's body and kissed his hand – drenching it with tears, the chroniclers assure us.

237

ON THE SPOT

5. The Pantheon

You are before one of the most important monuments of Roman, indeed, all architecture – designed, wrote Michelangelo, 'by angels and not by men.' It was originally preceded by a flight of steps, now buried, and flanked on both sides by statues and long porticoes. Various bronze ornaments are gone, including an imposing frieze on the triangular pediment of the porch that included the eagle that recalled the apotheoses of both Romulus (p. 234) and of Augustus (p. 219). Otherwise, despite having been converted into a Christian church, the **Pantheon** looks much as it did when Hadrian rebuilt it over the ruins of temples of Agrippa and Domitian in the 2nd century AD.

The colossal grey and Aswan rose-pink granite columns of the portico are a sight in themselves, as is the massive bronze portal, which may be original or a later, possibly renaissance, reproduction. The three columns in the left row are slightly different. One comes from Domitian's villa at Castelgandolfo and another from the nearby Baths of Nero; they were erected here in the 17th century to replace missing ones. The portico exterior is better preserved on the right side (Via della Rotonda). Step around to look at it and at the massive cylindrical body of the temple, with powerful relieving arches embedded in it. (It is always open in the mornings and often in the afternoons, but the schedule changes constantly.)

Stepping inside, you get much the same impression as an ancient Roman would have had, since the interior, like the exterior, is basically intact. The floor, restored several times, has its original appearance (you may recognise the patterns from Trajan's Forum). The prodigious coffered dome with its oculus, the columned chapels punctuated by a majestic apse opposite the entrance and the tabernacles between the chapels, with alternating triangular and curved pediments, are just as they were. Imagine pagan statues in place of the Christian ones and you are in a Roman imperial temple. The only major change is under the dome, where a band of rectangular panels and blind windows was added in the 18th century. To the right over the apse, a section of the band was rebuilt in 1930 to imitate its original appearance, with two grilled windows and multicoloured marble pillars.

The rhythm and grandeur of the interior are due not only to the symmetry of the decoration, but also to the geometric harmony of the structure. The diameter of the dome at its widest for instance (143ft or 43.3m) is equal to the height of the whole building.

Go around counterclockwise. The first chapel has a 15th-century fresco of the *Annunciation*, perhaps by Melozzo da Forlì or Antoniazzo Romano. The second chapel has the tomb of Italy's first king, Victor Emmanuel II, whose memorial we saw in Piazza Venezia; the tomb here would seem to make that colossal monument even more redundant. (Though it is a church, dedicated to 'S. Maria ad Martires', the Pantheon is Italian state property, like S. Maria degli Angeli (p. 79). Both have been used for the burial of national figures.) The third chapel has a 15th-century painting and medieval tombs on the floor. A small door, usually locked, leads to rooms in the ancient structure. Past the apse with the main altar, the fourth chapel contains a 16th-century crucifix and the tomb of Cardinal Consalvi, Pope Pius VII's) right-hand man, by the prominent 19th-century Danish sculptor, Bertel Thorvaldsen.

The tabernacle which follows contains the **Tomb of Raphael** (died 1520; see p. 333), the first of several artists to be buried here. His body lies in an ancient Roman sarcophagus with a famous Latin epitaph by Cardinal Bembo, one of his major literary contemporaries. It can be translated: 'Here is Raphael, by whom Nature, the great mother of all things, feared to be outdone when he lived; but when he died, she feared to die.' Over the coffin is a statue of the *Virgin* by Raphael's friend Lorenzetto, which Raphael himself commissioned for his grave. To the left is a bronze bust of Raphael dated 1883.

On the sides of the tabernacle are inscriptions

The Pantheon in the early 20th century

commemorating Raphael (left) and his fiancée, the niece of a cardinal (right). On the lower right are the epitaph and tomb of the great 17th-century painter Annibale Carracci .

In the fifth chapel are the tombs of two more members of the House of Savoy: Umberto I, second king of Italy, assassinated in 1900 by an Italian anarchist emigrant who had returned from New Jersey for the purpose; and of his wife Queen Margherita (see p. 85). The next tabernacle contains the tomb of Baldassarre Peruzzi, a prominent architect and painter, and friend of Raphael. The sixth chapel has the tombs of other 16th-century artists, including Taddeo Zuccaro, Raphael's pupil Perino del Vaga, the sculptor Flaminio Vacca (p. 231) and the 17th-century composer Arcangelo Corelli.

BEFORE GOING

6. From the Pantheon to the Argentina

Before the middle ages, as you may recall, the Campus Martius was lightly settled, especially in the area nearest the river. In their abundant leisure time the Romans flocked to this tranquil plain, a pleasant respite from the congestion of the residential hills. 'The ground covered with grass throughout the year and the crown of hills above the river offer a spectacle from which you can hardly tear your eyes,' noted the famous Greek geographer and travel writer Strabo, when visiting the Campus Martius in the time of Augustus. This idyllic character is still faintly echoed in the names of some streets and buildings: 'the valley' (*valle*), 'the little valley' (*vallicella*) and 'river sands' (*arenula*).

Strabo speaks of 'all sort of equestrian exercise ... ball-playing, hoop-trundling and wrestling' in the Campus Martius. Bathing and swimming, for which the area near the river was ideal, were also popular. Swimming contests took place in the Tiber. Shakespeare described one of these, between Julius Cæsar and his future assassin Cassius:

> Once upon a raw and gusty day,
> The troubled Tiber chafing with her shores,
> Cæsar said to me, 'Dars't thou, Cassius, now
> Leap in with me into this angry flood,
> And swim to yonder point?' Upon the word,
> Accoutred as I was, I plunged in,
> And bade him follow – so, indeed, he did.
> The torrent roared, and we did buffet it
> With lusty sinews, throwing it aside,
> And stemming it with hearts of controversy.

Augustus' plan to settle the Campus Martius (p. 137) and make Rome a 'city of marble' gave Roman water sports a more formal setting. The Campus Martius offered the perfect locale and social ambiance; so here were built the first public baths *(thermæ)*, which in imperial times would become a key feature of Roman daily life.

Like many of Augustus' monuments, the first baths were built and funded by his friend and son-in-law Agrippa (p. 218), who also brought to Rome the very first aqueduct. The ruins of the baths are just steps away from Agrippa's other great project, the Pantheon. Though much smaller than Rome's future imperial baths, the Baths of Agrippa had all the conveniences that would later become standard in such establishments: large hot and cold communal tubs, sauna-like rooms, gyms and swimming pools. The basic plan for *thermæ* remained substantially the same for centuries.

The large Baths of Nero, the first to follow Agrippa's, were also built in this area, adjacent to the Pantheon square. Only a few gigantic columns remain here and there. Two were used to replace lost originals in the portico of the Pantheon (see p. 238) and we'll see more in this section of the Walk. Just how much these establishments pleased the people is echoed in a verse by the poet Martial: 'What was worse than Nero? But what is better than Nero's Baths?' Less happy was Nero's tutor, the philosopher Seneca, a sophisticated millionaire who lived in front of the baths and could not stand the noise (for his lament in a letter to a friend see pp. 275-276).

Another water project by Agrippa, his *stagnum* or 'sailing pond', was also near the Pantheon. The historian Tacitus has left us a vignette of Nero banqueting on the pond in a golden barge, surrounded by highborn ladies and naked courtesans.

Besides sports, the Campus Martius was a good spot for popular gatherings, once these became too large for the Forum. We'll see traces of the *Sæpta* (or 'Courts'), a huge structure used for voting, abutting the Pantheon.

ON THE SPOT

6. From the Pantheon to the Argentina

Before leaving the picturesque Piazza della Rotonda (so called after the medieval name 'rotunda' for the Pantheon) let's look at its other main features. The 1578 fountain by Giacomo Della Porta is topped by a small Egyptian obelisk, the twin of the one over Bernini's Elephant of the Minerva (p. 116). The monster and animal figures, are 19th-century copies of Della Porta's originals.

The **Albergo del Sole** ('Sun Hotel'), the oldest Roman hotel in continuous operation, documented since 1467, is at No. 63. Only the right half is original.

One of the greatest Italian poets, Lodovico Ariosto, stayed here in 1513, when it was called the Albergo dell'Ariete ('Hotel of the Ram'); the name changed to the current one a century later. An inscription records a letter he wrote to a cousin in rhyme: 'In high spirits, but dirty and drenched to the bones, I went to dinner at night at the Ram.' Another tablet records the (then unknown) opera composer Pietro Mascagni's stay on the eve of his triumphant 1890 première of *Cavalleria Rusticana*. The famous European adventurer Count Cagliostro also lodged here for a few days in the 18th century, before being arrested for hitting a waiter (for Cagliostro, see p. 387). The German writer Thomas Mann often stayed in the building to the left of the Albergo del Sole.

Unlicensed vendors have plagued the square throughout history and still do so today, despite sporadic attempts to remove them. A house facing the Pantheon bears a large tablet extolling the early 19th century Pope Pius VII's success in getting rid of these 'ignoble businesses' (*ignobilibus tabernis*), which of course were back under the next pope.

In antiquity the Baths of Nero began on the square. Some of the columns survive. Two have been re-erected nearby; you can see them, one at a time, by walking from the fountain to the Pantheon and looking down to the end of the street on your right. Another two were inserted,

together with their splendid capitals, at the left end of the Pantheon portico to replace missing ones (see p. 238).

Return to that side of the portico, and then carry on around the building, following the Via della Minerva. Along the curved part of the Pantheon runs a long low brick wall. Originally covered with marble, it was part of the long side of a vast (10 acre) porticoed rectangle with buildings, called the *Sæpta* (or 'Courts'), where people gathered to vote in Republican times. After Augustus came to power there was no longer talk of elections, so it became an art exhibition area and later an art and antiques market.

Across the street, at No. 7 Via della Minerva, is an authentic 15th-century tenement block.

Turn right into Via della Palombella. Attached to the powerful curve of the Pantheon are the remains of another imposing building originally erected by Agrippa adjacent to the Pantheon: a **basilica** dedicated to Neptune, god of the sea, thanking him for Agrippa's naval victories on behalf of Augustus.

This is part of the long far side of the oblong basilica – all the rest rose behind you – with a wide apse which still contains ruins of the pedestal of Neptune's statue. (Entrances to pagan basilicas were on the long side and so the apses were placed opposite, p. 157.) There remain two columns, walls with niches and a very elegant frieze with marine motifs – dolphins, seashells and tridents – from a restoration under Hadrian.

Continue along Via della Palombella, turning left at Via della Rotonda. At the first crossing on the left is the 19th-century façade of the 16th-century church of **S. Chiara** (St. Clare), served by French clergy. Opposite, at No. 14, is the convent where St. Catherine of Siena died in 1380 (p. 118). Continue straight on, as the Via della Rotonda becomes Via Torre Argentina. At the first crossing on the right (Via de' Nari) is the area where once was the *Stagnum Agrippæ*, the sailing pond created by Agrippa with the Acqua Vergine he had brought to Rome (p. 227).

From the second intersection you can see at the

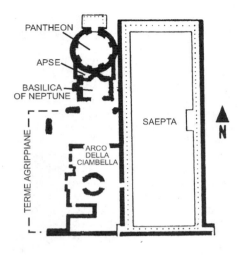

The complex of the Pantheon area

end of the street on the right one of the medieval underpasses which were once so common that you could cross entire neighbourhoods in them. A house nearby, long since gone, was the birthplace in 1791 of Rome's great poet, Gioacchino Belli.

At the second intersection, Via Arco della Ciambella ('Arch of the Doughnut'), turn left. Overhead, between Nos 9 and 15, are the remains of the **Baths of Agrippa**. The building was aligned with the Pantheon and Basilica of Neptune.

Stand across from No. 13 and look up to see the remains of a large semicircular wall, the 'doughnut arch' which gave the street its medieval name. The wall belonged to a vast central hall, over 80ft (25m) in diameter, from which the various rooms of the baths radiated.

At the bottom of the brick wall on the left is an elaborate renaissance Madonnella reworked in the 19th century.

Return to Via Torre Argentina. Before you is the church of SS. Benedetto e Scolastica, patron saints of the Umbrian town of Norcia, north of Rome. This is the small community church of immigrants from Norcia to Rome, the *norcini*. Since Norcia is famous for its pork products, being a *norcino* has always been synonymous in Rome with being a pork butcher. Until the last century *norcino* stores were concentrated in the area, as recalled in a vituperative sonnet by Belli: 'I'd sooner get myself castrated by a norcino at the Rotonda [the Pantheon]...' ('...prima me vojjo/fa castrà da un norcino a la Ritonna...'). One pork butcher's, which is still across the street from the church, has been here for the last 150 years. The church itself is 15th-century, but was remodelled in 1619.

Continue on Via Torre Argentina and after a few yards you reach a broad square.

BEFORE GOING

7. The Sacred Area of the Argentina

Crossing the Campus Martius (Field of Mars), we have covered more than two thirds of the mile (see p. 137) separating the last ring of Roman walls from the oldest core of the city: the Palatine, Capitol and Forum. We now begin to see an older, pre-Augustan construction layer, when the Campus Martius was on the outskirts of the city. At this time the area was already used, as later under the empire, for religious and political ceremonies, as well as for recreation, but the religious aspect was dominant, stemming as it did from the original agricultural character of the flat, well-watered terrain.

Mars, god of the field, was an agricultural deity who later took on a war-like character. Originally a god of the Sabines (called Mamers in Oscan dialect), he was probably identified with the field from pre-Roman times, when the Sabines of the Quirinal Hill (p. 67) farmed the area.

One of the earliest episodes in Roman history is linked to the agricultural nature of the Campus Martius. Tradition claims that the early Romans' first action after expelling their last king, the Etruscan Tarquin (p. 105), and founding the Republic, was to toss the corn he had planted in part of the field into the Tiber (according to the story, the corn then formed the foundations of the Isola Tiberina).

The most ancient surviving religious monuments in the Campus Martius are in a square called Largo Argentina (which has nothing to do with the country). This fascinating group of temples was excavated in the 1930's, when archæologists called them the 'Sacred Area'. It is unclear to whom they are dedicated, but they seem to form a set, like another group further on in our Walk (p. 240). Both groups face east.

Near the Sacred Area rose the first Roman stone theatre (previous ones were wooden). It was given to Rome by the general Pompey the Great, Julius Cæsar's adversary in the years of conflict before the Augustan Peace. The only faint trace of the theatre is in the outline of a square nearby, part of the second Renaissance Rome Walk (p. 514). Here, adjacent to the Sacred Area, we'll see the low wall of a building related to the theatre, witness to a crucial moment in history. Pompey had been murdered four years earlier in Egypt, where he had tried to escape Cæsar's cold resolve. On the morning of 15 March 44 BC, the Senate met in an annexe of the

Denarius minted by Brutus to commemorate the Ides of March, showing two daggers flanking a cap of liberty

huge portico attached to the Theatre of Pompey (its own building in the Forum was being restored, see p. 167). Cæsar, the dictator, went to preside over the session. There he was attacked and stabbed 23 times by conspirators led by his adopted son, Brutus, and by Cassius (p. 240). It is said that Cæsar, uttering his famous last words, 'You, too, my son' (but in Greek and so not 'Et tu, Brute') died before the statue of his dead rival Pompey, staining it with his blood.

ON THE SPOT

7. The Sacred Area of the Argentina

An excavation in the centre of the square marks the Sacred Area, the oldest Republican ruins in the Campus Martius. Cross to the nearest corner. On the right, before viewing the ruins, note the façade of the 18th-century **Teatro Argentina**, where Rossini's *Barber of Seville* was given its triumphant première.

View the excavation from the street, since it is usually closed. Along the wall parallel to the theatre are remains of a marble *forica* (p. 140), an ancient Roman public latrine (the seats are missing).

Walk left along the dig and stop a few yards

past the next corner of the site on Via S. Nicola de' Cesarini.

The area contains four temples, all very old, though their ages vary enough for the floors to be on different levels. The temple (A) in front of this end of the street (right) is the second oldest, dating from the 3rd century BC. It has two rows of columns articulating the sides, and front steps rebuilt in brick. Except for two added in a restoration after the fire of AD 80, the columns are not travertine or marble, which were sparingly used at the time, but a brown volcanic rock called tufa (which was however covered by white stucco to look like marble). In the middle ages the temple was converted into a church. The altar, two apses,

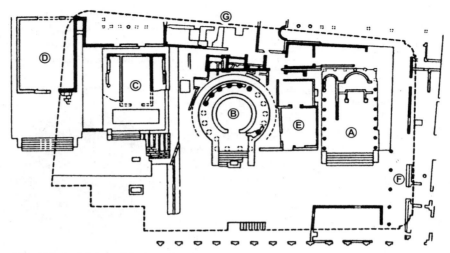

Plan of the Sacred Area of the Argentina

and traces of frescoes under the small protective roofs remain.

The marble pavement in front is from imperial times, and so is much later than the temple itself. The ruins of the walls (E) to the left of the temple, as well as a set of columns (F) to the far right of the site, of which four are still standing, are from later secular buildings. The columns formed part of a Portico of a Hundred Columns, now gone.

Move on to the left. In the centre of the site is a circular temple (B), of which six columns still stand. This is the most recent of the four temples (early 2nd century BC), as the higher floor indicates. It was probably dedicated to the Goddess of Good Fortune on This Day. The columns, the original platform and steps are in tufa. The temple was restored under the Empire.

Move far enough to the left to see some of the area behind the temple. Some brick and tufa ruins there (G) belong to the wall of an annexe of Pompey's theatre complex (pp. 243, 511) where Julius Cæsar was killed.

Left of the temple (B) are the powerful tufa platform and some of the walls of the oldest of the temples (C), dating from the 4th or early 3rd century BC, as the squat, archaic design suggests. At your feet note sections of the earlier, lower tufa paving.

Along the whole left side of the excavation, as far as the end, runs one side of the platform of the largest of the four temples (D), covered in travertine marble. It dates from the 2nd century BC. There are remains of the wall above it. The rest is under the street. (At the far corner, a private benevolent association has created a flourishing refuge for the ubiquitous Roman cats.)

At the left end of Via S. Nicola de' Cesarini is an over-restored 12th-century tower, which was found inside a building razed during excavation of the area. Medieval documents call it the Torre del Papetto ('Tower of the little Pope'), probably in reference to a famous anti-pope (or papal pretender) of the time, Anaclete II (pp. 594, 597), a descendant of converted Jews. The tower has a medieval porch, rebuilt rather freely in 1932 from pieces found in the area.

MIDPOINT OF WALK

BEFORE GOING

8. From the Argentina to the Velabrum: the Portico of Octavia and Theatre of Marcellus

The theatre district of Augustus. We mentioned that the Theatre of Pompey (1st century BC) was the first to be built in stone. The reason it was so late – the Greeks had been building marvellous stone theatres for centuries – is that austere Republican Rome frowned on such frivolous pursuits as theatrical performances. Thus anything more lasting than a makeshift wooden theatre was discouraged. When Pompey built his stone theatre he erected a temple dedicated to Venus over the orchestra in order to avoid problems with the censors by showing that the building had a religious aim.

Augustus was powerful and open-minded enough to bypass such scruples. When he added theatres to his new monument-filled recreation area in the Campus Martius, he insisted that they be permanent. Either directly, or indirectly through his generals and officials, who were expected to prove their devotion to the common good by funding large construction projects, Augustus built two theatres and an amphitheatre. The location of the amphitheatre is uncertain (see p. 467). The theatres are in the present segment of our Walk – one still standing, the other in the guise of underground ruins and salvaged pieces of decoration. The extant theatre is the Theatre of Marcellus, a major monument begun by Cæsar (in reply to Pompey) and completed by Augustus, who dedicated it to his deceased young nephew and heir, Marcellus (p. 218).

In the golden age of Augustus and for some time after, the theatre was used for classical plays, but it soon declined as cultural entertainment along with Latin drama in general. Rome's drama never attained the excellence of the Greek, nor did it occupy the same eminent place in Roman society as in the more refined Greek culture. Taste soon became so corrupted that serious works were rarely performed. Most were a pretext for pornographic or sadistic displays. Actresses appeared nude with an abandon that made even the broadminded poet Martial wince. From the reign of Domitian onwards, criminals were sometimes put to death by substituting them for actors in the goriest scenes.

The porticos of the Campus Martius. In classical Roman architecture, a portico was not just a porch, but could also be a large and complex structure: a roofed rectangle with long double rows of columns enclosing other buildings, such as temples and libraries, ornamented with sculptural groups and other works of art. It was a typical Roman form of architecture, common in the showcase area of the Campus Martius, and one which could be rich and imposing.

Such was certainly the portico which Augustus dedicated to his beloved sister, Octavia (p. 217). Actually, he rebuilt an older and smaller portico a few yards from the theatre honouring her son Marcellus. The new portico had over 100 columns and covered an area of 4 acres (almost 2 hectares). It contained several buildings, including two great temples, surrounded by marvellous works of art, the finest of the age.

Apart from a few scattered columns, all that is left to see is the entrance – a gate-like, temple-like structure known technically as a propylæum. People usually mistake the entrance for the whole and conclude disappointedly that the celebrated Portico of Octavia was just a modest marble structure, now blackened and corroded. It is like mistaking the gatehouse for the castle. What you do see is, nevertheless, very important: it is the only surviving entrance to one of these characteristic complexes in Rome, and one of very few left in the Roman world. It survives because in the middle ages a small church nestled in it, using the entrance as its own to conform with current prototypes, early Christian churches often having an arcaded entrance.

The church itself is interesting, since it borders on what was to be the Jewish Ghetto in the Counter Reformation. At that time it became a centre for indoctrinating the neighbourhood. Jews were required to attend a weekly sermon on the errors of their ways and how to repent. Before entering they were checked to make sure they had not stuffed their ears with cotton or wax, as they were wont to do.

Such proselytising must have pained the Jews even more, since the portico had been the site of another historic humiliation for them fifteen centuries earlier. It was from here that the Emperors Vespasian and Titus began their triumphal parades after conquering Jerusalem and destroying the Temple (pp. 179, 192-193). The Jewish historian Josephus records the event, which he witnessed after coming to Rome in the victors' entourage; 'we owe to this base courtier the description of the splendid and festive pomp of this triumph,' the German historian Gregorovius later wrote.

The Tiber Island. Near the Portico of Octavia is the river and in it is a tiny island, the only one in Rome, whose legendary origins we mentioned on p. 243. Its history is connected to that of ancient Rome's oldest hospital.

An outbreak of plague occurred *c.* 300 BC, when Rome was still a young Republic. After consulting the oracles, the Senate sent emissaries to Greece to seek advice from the priests of the Temple of Æsculapius (the Greek god of medicine) at Epidaurus, who quite sensibly suggested that the Romans build a hospital in an isolated spot. Religion required that it be put under the protection of Æsculapius, so a temple dedicated to the god was to be joined to it. The double building was quickly built on the Tiber Island, which was then only accessible by ferry and thus an obvious choice for quarantine purposes.

Three centuries later, in the 1st century AD, with the hospital and temple attracting increasing traffic, bridges were built to the island from both banks. The authorities also decided to embellish and aggrandise the island. To recall the original sea mission to Greece, they made the island into a ship by encasing its banks with marble slabs. A snake carved near the prow of the 'ship' alludes to the legend that the envoys had returned with a sacred snake from Epidaurus, a gift from the Greek priests to the Roman people. (A snake coiled around a staff was Æsculapius' emblem and remains to this day the symbol of medicine.) When the returning ship sighted the Tiber Island, the snake slithered overboard and swam to it, indicating that this was the place for the temple and hospital.

The original hospital is gone, but medical centres have continued to occupy the Isola Tiberina, as the island is now called. Today a monastic order runs a large hospital there, which was built in the renaissance. During a severe outbreak of the plague in the 17th century, the island was used to quarantine the victims. The bodies of those who died were shipped directly down the river for burial at sea in order to reduce the risk of contagion.

When the Nazis occupied Rome, the monks hid many Jews from the nearby Ghetto in the hospital, passing them off as patients.

Theatre of Marcellus and columns of the Temple of Apollo

ON THE SPOT

8. From the Argentina to the Velabrum: the Portico of Octavia and Theatre of Marcellus

From this corner of the square take the continuation of Via Florida to your left. (The name has as little to do with the North American state, as the Largo Argentina with South America, but derives from the nearby 'Field of Flowers', p. 482). Walk along the right-hand side of this street, the Via delle Botteghe Oscure. The medieval name ('of the dark shops') comes from the rope-maker and dyer workshops that were then nestled in an annexe of the ruined **Theatre of Balbus**, built in the 1st century AD by Augustus' general of the same name.

This was the smallest of the three theatres, but had the finest decoration. All that remains are the foundations and ruins of the cavea (seating area) in the cellars of the first block in Via delle Botteghe Oscure, remains of the annexe (Crypta Balbi) in the second block and many salvaged marble fragments decorating courtyards and buildings nearby.

The first block comprises several palaces, each of which was originally occupied by a different branch of the same family, the ducal house of Mattei. The first, at No. 32, was built for the Mattei in the mid-16th century by Nanni di Baccio Bigio, or his son Annibale Lippi, but is called **Palazzo Caetani** after its later owners.

If the door of this solemn building is open, you may ask permission to look inside. The palace is run by the Caetani family foundation and is mostly rented as office space, like many palaces in Rome which belong to nobility.

Both courtyards are in the sober Tuscan renaissance style and both, particularly the second, are decorated with fragments of marble from the Theatre of Balbus complex. Some of the rooms are covered with renaissance frescoes, but they are not usually open to the public.

Continue along the block. At the crossing with Via Caetani is the entrance to the Crypta Balbi, an oblong, porticoed and apsed underground annexe to the Theatre of Balbus. Its use is uncertain but it is similar in shape to the annexe behind the Theatre

of Pompey (p. 244).

The ruins include very fine marble fragments, a marvellous capital and powerful walls. Excavations of the crypt were completed in the year 2000. Amongst the exhibits on the site are remains of the ancient artisan activity in the area.

Turn into Via Caetani. A third of the way down the street to your left, an interesting bell tower belongs to S. Caterina dei Funari, which we'll visit shortly. Further down the block, on the left between Nos 8 and 9, a tablet indicates where the body of the former Italian premier Aldo Moro was found in a car boot after he was abducted and murdered by terrorists in 1978.

On the right at No. 32 is another Mattei palace. Built by Carlo Maderno at the beginning of the 17th century, it was highly influential in its layout. Now state property, it houses offices (among them a centre for American studies) and is open during office hours. The impressive double hall and two courtyards, all richly decorated with statuary and ancient reliefs, mostly from the Theatre of Balbus complex, are usually accessible, though the frescoed salons are not. One of the greatest Italian poets, Giacomo Leopardi (p. 61), who was related to this branch of the Mattei family, stayed here in 1822-1823.

Via Caetani ends in Via dei Funari ('of the Rope-makers'). In the second Renaissance Rome Walk, we'll explore the area to the right, where the street continues around the block of palaces once belonging to the Mattei (there are two more). Now we turn left and admire the rich design of the façade of **S. Caterina dei Funari** (many rope-makers worked in this neighbourhood), built in the 16th century by Michelangelo's pupil, Guidetto Guidetti.

This is one of the best examples of a renaissance 'ædicular' façade designed in two superimposed storeys. The interior, rarely open, contains works by Federico Zuccaro and other late 16th-century painters.

The church used to be the motherhouse of the Sisterhood of Wretched Virgins in Peril (Compagnia delle Vergini Miserabili Pericolanti)

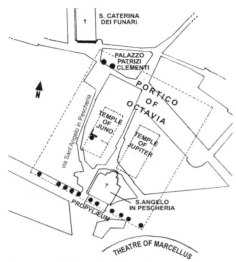

The area of the Portico of Octavia

founded by Ignatius Loyola (pp. 110 -111) to save women from prostitution.

To the right of the church on the wall is an *art nouveau* tablet commemorating the poet Gigi Zanazzo, who wrote in Roman dialect (d. 1929).

Also to your right (facing the church) is the late 16th-century **Palazzo Patrizi-Clementi**, not especially noteworthy except for two column stumps embedded in the wall on the right. Walk over. The columns belong to the far left-hand corner of the oblong Portico of Octavia. Seeing them here will give you a better sense of the vast layout of the Portico, when we visit its entrance shortly.

The small square you are in now, Piazza Lovatelli, consists almost entirely of late 16th- and early 17th-century buildings. At No. 1 is Palazzo Lovatelli, remembered for the highly intellectual and cosmopolitan salon held there in the *belle époque* years (at the turn of the last century) by Countess Ersilia Lovatelli, a noted *savante* and beauty. She died in 1925.

The composer-pianist Franz Liszt, poets and writers such as Gabriele D'Annunzio, Giosuè Carducci, Emile Zola and Anatole France, the

historians Ernest Renan, Theodor Mommsen and Ferdinand Gregorovius all frequented the salon. The Lovatelli family survive but do not live here. When we were last here, there was still a dusty box for calling cards hanging at the end of the hall, which is occasionally open. It is a reminder of a bygone, pre-telephone era, when leaving one's card was an essential part of the mechanics of social life.

Past the palace, enter Via S. Angelo in Pescheria ('of the Holy Angel in the Fish Market'), a name whose meaning will shortly become clear. At No. 30 note a small 15th-century portal.

You are probably not aware of it, but walking down this picturesque old street you have actually been within the rectangular enclosure of the Portico of Octavia. Is there anything left to see of this majestic double array of columns, enclosing two famous temples? The basements of several houses on the left (especially No. 12) and a garage (No. 11) contain ruins, but they are not easily accessible. Go to No. 28 on your right; if you are lucky and find it open, go up two flights of stairs. Through the window on the first landing, look into the courtyard across the street: there is a fluted column with a splendid capital from the Temple of Juno, one of the two temples in the Portico of Octavia. The base of the column is in the garage at No. 11.

Nothing remains of the other temple, dedicated to Juno's spouse, Jupiter. Pliny relates that the twin temples contained the wrong statues, since porters had mistakenly put Juno's statue in Jupiter's temple and vice-versa. The priests, who believed that nothing ever happened by chance, thought the error divinely inspired, and never dared rectify it.

The street ends in view of a small group of picturesque tenement houses (right), which are medieval in origin but have undergone countless alterations. Continue under an archway. This is part of the main entrance to the **Portico of Octavia**, which we now see from the other side.

Desultory and mostly fruitless digging in front of the Portico by the archeological-political complex has been angering the locals and hindering visitors for years.

The brick arches on the sides are an early medieval addition. The front inscription mentions a restoration under Emperors Septimius Severus ('Imp. Cæsar L. Septimius') and his son Caracalla ('Imp. Cæsar M.') after a fire, when the Portico was nearly 200 years old.

The entrance gateway, or propylæum, was on the short (south) side of the rectangular Portico. After examining the structure itself (note that its base is several feet below street level), look for what's left of the columns on the short side. There are more than you think. To the right of the propylæum, in an excavation also surrounding the Theatre of Marcellus, which we now begin to see on our right, are several columns from this side of the Portico, going all the way up to the near right-hand corner (see map on p. 249).

In Piazza Lovatelli we saw stumps of columns belonging to the far left-hand corner (see p. 249), so we can now begin to visualise the location and enormous size of the structure.

To the left of the propylæum, on the pavement in front of a restaurant, are five more columns from this side, one just a stump. All these granite and marble columns are smooth, as befits a simple enclosing structure, while the columns from the propylæum and inner temple, which you may have seen from a window (p. 249), are fluted, as befits more noble edifices.

Apart from two temples, the Portico enclosed two libraries, one Greek, one Latin (pp. 184, 277) It also contained statues, either originals or copies, by three supreme Greek artists, Phidias, Praxiteles and Lysippus. The last of these was represented by a row of equestrian statues of Alexander the Great and his generals. The celebrated Medici Venus, now in the Uffizi in Florence, was found here.

The propylæum area has added a lively note throughout the centuries to this colourful corner of old Rome. From the early middle ages to 1880 it was the main fish market in Rome. Stone counters, belonging to noble families and rented to fishmongers at great profit, lined the structure both inside

and out. Fish from the nearby Tiber were hauled in, making this the only part of Rome lit during the hours of darkness. By day noise from the market mingled with that of the Ghetto to the left of the propylæum, and with that of the shacks and hovels encrusting the Theatre of Marcellus to the right.

An ancient marble fish-cutting block can be seen at the front end of the propylæum (lower right) under a 16th- or 17th-century tablet in Latin saying that the heads of all fish longer than the tablet must be given as tax to the market managers. Another tablet on the left forbids gambling and games in the market.

Within the ruined propylæum is the small 7th-century church of **S. Angelo in Pescheria** ('Holy Angel in the Fish Market'), originally built as a *diaconia*, or food distribution centre. It has been remodelled several times, most recently in the 19th century. Traces of medieval frescoes are on the propylæum itself.

A secondary entrance to the left is sometimes open. The church is the only one in Rome, as far as we know, to hold folk religious services, with jazz and pop songs, usually on Saturday evenings.

The interior is early renaissance. Over a side altar at the entrance end of the left aisle is a 16th-century *Crucifixion*. In another altar area at the end of the left aisle is a fresco of the *Virgin and Child* attributed to the 15th-century painter Benozzo Gozzoli. It would be one of the few works of this great Florentine master in Rome. In a corresponding area in the right aisle are late 16th-century frescoes with tales from the *Life of St. Andrew*, protector of fishermen and fishmongers.

To the right of the propylæum (No. 33) is a small deconsecrated church, the **Oratory of the Fishmongers**. Over the door of the charming late 17th-century stuccoed façade is another image of St. Andrew. The oratory is now a wedding gift shop. (The Ghetto, to the left of the propylæum, is visited in a later walk, p. 522-528.)

Also to the right of the propylæum, at No. 28 Via Portico d'Ottavia, is the **Casa Vallati**, named after the family who owned it in the middle ages and renaissance. No. 28 is a 16th-century addition to a much older house built by the family, which adjoins it on the right and turns the corner into the archæological site. The older part, dating from the 14th century, was restored in 1930 and now houses municipal offices. Return now to No. 28.

Over the archway is a renaissance inscription in Latin: 'Wish only for what you can have'. A plaque on the wall recalls that here, on 16 October 1943, Nazi troops occupying Rome began their 'pitiless hunt for the Jews'; 2,091 were deported to death camps.

Walk past the house and the archæological area to the left, which we'll visit later. Proceed along Via Portico d'Ottavia toward the tree-lined river drive. Just before it on the left is **S. Gregorio della Divina Pietà** (St. Gregory of Divine Compassion), built in the middle ages in the place where it was said, probably wrongly, that St. Gregory the Great grew up (for the more likely candidate see p. 425). The church was rebuilt in the early 18th century. When the Ghetto was walled in, the church faced one of its gates and was sometimes used, like S. Angelo, for the forcible indoctrination of Jews.

An extraordinary inscription in Hebrew and Latin on the façade rebukes the Jews in the words of God as recorded by the Prophet Isaiah: 'I have spread out my hands all the day unto a rebellious people, who walketh in a way that is not good, after their own thoughts; and a people that provoketh me to anger continually to my face.'

The church was also the headquarters of a lay brotherhood devoted to helping upper-class families in need. On the right flank is an 18th-century slot for giving 'alms to poor but honourable and embarrassed families'.

At the lights, cross the river drive (which in Italian is called Lungotevere, 'along the Tiber') to the pavement along the parapet.

Here is **Ponte Fabrizio**, also called Ponte Quattro Capi ('of the Four Heads') for the two four-headed posts (ancient Roman originals) adorning this side of the entrance. This bridge to the Tiber Island is one of the oldest in Rome, built in the 1st century AD, and in continuous use since then. Another bridge reaching the further bank is almost as old, but was rebuilt in the 19th century using a little of the original structure. (The island is

The Tiber island in the 18th century: by Piranesi

The Theatre of Marcellus, before and after, by Piranesi. Above, as it appeared in the 18th century; opposite, as Piranesi imagined the ruins would look once the medieval and renaissance additions had been removed. He has added plants like the ones that grew on the Colosseum in his time, and remembered to allow for the rise in ground level

described as part of the Trastevere Walk, p. 597-600.). Over the arches of the bridge on both sides, an inscription (better preserved on the right) records that the builder, Fabricius Curator Viarum ('Master of Roads') personally tested the bridge (*idemque probavit*). The bridge was originally faced with marble; the masonry we now see is a 17th-century restoration.

The view of the island with its old buildings, some medieval, is Rome at its most alluring. Practically nothing remains of the Temple of Æsculapius and its associated hospital, which were to the left of the bridge. In their place is a church whose medieval belfry is visible from here. To the right of the bridge is the latest of many hospitals which have occupied the island throughout the centuries. The present one was built in the renaissance and is run by priests, as was Æsculapius'.

To see traces of the 'hull' shaped by the Romans

on the banks of the island in order to make it resemble a ship, go a hundred yards to the left of the bridge. Where the buildings on the island end, there is a large white patch of travertine stone revetment installed by the Romans (look for it under a scalloped balcony). On the travertine slabs are some damaged and worn reliefs: a bust of Æsculapius, with his symbolic snake coiled around a staff, and a bull's head. From this distance you need binoculars to see them (under the third scallop from the left). You can get a close-up view by going down to the banks of the island via steps near the hospital (see also pp. 597-598).

From Ponte Fabrizio cross the river drive again at the lights and go right into the square opposite, Piazza Monte Savello ('of the Savelli Hill', from the name of the baronial family we'll discuss shortly), first walking along the pavement and then crossing towards a parapet overlooking some

ruins. As you go, you'll see a private driveway on your left marked by two pillars with bears; this is the entrance to Palazzo Orsini. Orsini is the name of the princely family who once owned it and means 'little bears'. The family still exists but resides elsewhere. The palace was built during the renaissance in the ruins of the Theatre of Marcellus; you'll see it from the other side. Continue along the parapet to Via del Foro Olitorio, descend it and then go left for about 100 yards.

You are now in front of the massive **Theatre of Marcellus**, which will possibly remind you of the Colosseum. It was begun by Julius Cæsar to emulate his adversary Pompey, who had built the first stone theatre in Rome (p. 243), but was completed in 11 BC by Augustus, who dedicated it to his deceased nephew Marcellus. It is thought to have inspired the Colosseum, built 83 years later, though it is much smaller and a half-circle, not an amphitheatre. Moreover, while the Colosseum has three superimposed arcades topped by a fourth non-arcaded storey, the Theatre of Marcellus had only two arcaded storeys (the right columns of the present ground floor have been rebuilt), with a non-arcaded storey above. The top storey was replaced, first by a medieval fortress, then by the renaissance Palazzo Orsini, the entrance to which you saw on Piazza Monte Savello.

The palace originally belonged to the Savelli family, one of Rome's oldest and most famous (p. 269), who dominated the area for centuries but died out in the 18th century. The Orsini then bought the palace, which more recently has been subdivided into luxury apartments.

The interior of the theatre is inaccessible, but virtually nothing remains of it anyway. It originally held 15,000 people, half as many as the Theatre of Pompey but 2½ times the capacity of New York's Radio City Music Hall. Today the garden of the palace occupies part of the stage and seating area.

253

9. The vegetable and cattle markets and the Velabrum

With the Theatre of Marcellus we have reached the immediate vicinity of the ancestral city. The Capitol, with the Palatine behind it, is across the avenue. The history of the area is older than Rome itself. A trading post supplied by the nearby river was here even before the Latin settlement on the Palatine; at least part of the settlement probably grew out of the post. So, if the Palatine is the cradle of Rome, this is its nursery. Legend hints as much by placing the discovery of Romulus and Remus (p. 153) at the foot of the Palatine in a marshy area called the Velabrum.

Originally the area was a border between the city proper and the undeveloped Campus Martius (pp. 27-28). After Augustus it was a junction between the densely populated old city and the district of monuments and public amenities he created in the Campus Martius (p. 234). In the middle ages, when the 'old' city had become the *disabitato* and the Campus Martius the 'core' city (p. 28), and later, the district retained its role as a link between these two main urban areas.

The markets. Being a natural junction, this area had some key service roles. First and foremost it was an age-old trading centre, a purpose to which it was well suited, since it was between the Tiber and the Fora and their shops. The main vegetable market of ancient Rome (the Forum Holitorium) began in front of the Theatre of Marcellus. Further down the present road, it joined the cattle and meat market (the Forum Boarium), where it ran with the Roman Forum. Throughout the centuries the area was used for markets, fairs and storage, and saw colourful shopping activity until the 1930's, when major excavations and ill-advised Fascist-era 'cleanups' chilled the atmosphere. Adding a boisterous, if sad note, poor immigrants from the countryside were hired here for the construction gangs that built post-1870 Rome.

On this Walk we find many relics of the original commercial nature of the district, especially in the lower section by the Roman Forum, where it is called the Velabrum, a very ancient name still in use, which probably means 'marshes'. We might remember that the Forum too was marshy at the beginning (p. 156).

Two extremely old churches there, S. Maria in Cosmedin and S. Giorgio in Velabro, are fully in tune with its commercial character. They originally doubled as food distribution centres, part of a group of churches, called *diaconiæ*, conceived by the remarkable 6th century Pope Gregory the Great (p. 425) to distribute the produce from Church-owned farms, a project that was vital in relieving the desperate poverty following the fall of the Empire (p. 28).

Diplomacy and war. Another very different role of this border zone in antiquity was for activities that, whether by law or tradition, could not take place within city limits. Thus there was a civic centre, Villa Publica (now gone), for assemblies and census-taking, which sometimes served as a place to greet arriving foreign ambassadors and other dignitaries, since they were barred from entering the city until their credentials had been presented and accepted. In the nearby Temple of Apollo the Senate met for business or rituals traditionally performed outside the walls. A third building of this sort was the famous Temple of Bellona, goddess of war, where victorious generals returning to Rome had to wait for a decision if they had requested a 'triumph'. No soldier in active service, unless he belonged to Rome's military guard, could enter the city.

Before the temple was the equally famous *Columna Bellica* ('War Column') in front of which every new war was declared. Protocol required that this be done by a sacred herald, the *fetial*, who hurled a blood-smeared spear in the direction of the enemy land; this was legally equivalent to a declaration of war. Julius Cæsar himself once performed the task, throwing the spear toward Egypt and its queen, Cleopatra, who later became his lover.

The Temple of Bellona, to the north of the early city, had its counterpart to the south in a temple dedicated to Mars, god of war, on the old Appian Way (p. 616). Whoever

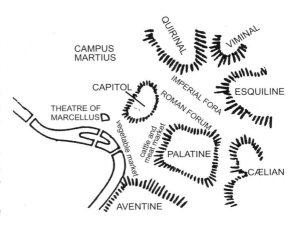

The food markets, midway between the Tiber and the Fora

approached Rome from either direction was thus forewarned of the warlike character of its inhabitants.

Ghosts from the past. You'll find a few more temples in the area, all extremely ancient and some of uncertain identity. No trace can be found, however, of another use to which the area was supposedly put in remote antiquity. Confirming the practice of human sacrifice in ancestral Rome (p. 142), the historians Livy and Plutarch record two occasions on which people were buried alive in the Forum Boarium. This was done to circumvent a prophecy in the Sybilline books, age-old oracles attributed to the Sybils, that 'Gauls and Greeks will one day possess Roman soil'. The idea was that the victims would 'possess' Roman soil instead, thereby fulfilling the prophecy. During the First Gallic War, a Gaul and his wife were interred there. The same fate befell a Greek couple during the Second Punic War.

Another remarkable sacrificial rite took place nearby. It was connected with the oldest bridge in Rome, the Ponte Sublicio. This was a wooden bridge that stood downstream and is long gone; it was replaced by a stone one of the same name, that stands somewhat closer to the markets. 'Sublicio' comes from *sublicæ*, a proto-Latin Oscan word meaning 'wooden pylons'. These pylons were in fact quite special, as they could be pulled out and the bridge dismantled as soon as enemies were detected on the horizon. Every 15 May a sacrifice called *sexagenarii de ponte* ('sexagenarians from the bridge') took place here. Twenty-four 60-year-olds were thrown off the bridge – if they couldn't swim, too bad for them – to appease the ghost of the river god, Tiberinus, who according to myth had drowned in the river. In later times, straw puppets replaced the unfortunate elders.

ON THE SPOT

9. The vegetable and cattle markets and the Velabrum

Before leaving the Theatre of Marcellus, let's see some other features close by. The three tall columns just to the right of the theatre are the corner of the **Temple of Apollo**, founded in the 5th century BC and dedicated after an outbreak of plague (earlier than the one mentioned on p. 246) to Apollus Medicus. It was rebuilt 400 years later under Augustus.

The marvellous columns, which date from the Augustan reconstruction, bear some of the richest and most perfectly sculpted capitals anywhere, and an equally superlative frieze of laurel branches (symbol of Apollo), ox skulls and candelabra. The temple doubled as a museum containing famous Greek statuary (see p. 157).

Behind the columns is a pretty medieval house with a small iron balcony: the 13th-century hotel, Albergo della Catena ('Inn of the Chain'), Rome's oldest extant hotel building. Its name derives from a moveable chain in the river that regulated access to the fish market. No longer an inn, it houses offices of the city government, which isolated and over-restored the building in the 1930's.

Some 20 yards to the right of the three columns, a half-buried platform is the remnant of the early 3rd century BC **Temple of Bellona**. The War Column that rose in front of it and the Villa Publica nearby are gone.

During the fierce civil wars leading to the end of the Republic, the conservative Sulla (p. 158), having defeated the populist Marius, imprisoned 3,000 of Marius' followers in the Villa Publica. He promised to spare their lives, then massacred them as the senators, meeting in the Temple of Bellona, heard the screams in helpless silence.

Return downhill and stop in front of the steps to the excavation. On a platform to the left are two isolated columns and the 7th-century church of **S. Nicola in Carcere** ('St. Nicholas by the Jail'), a reference to a prison once located here. The church incorporates the remains of three very old

temples all next to each other, like those in the Sacred Area of the Argentina (p. 243), and like them facing east. They have been tentatively identified. Disentangling what is the church from what are the temples is not easy, but it's easier once you realise that the church engulfs the whole middle temple. Columns from the other two temples are embedded in the side walls of the church. Those in the right flank are the left side of the right temple (whose central structures are gone), matching the two free-standing columns near you, from the right side of the same temple. The columns you'll soon see on the left side of the church are from the right side of the left temple, whose other sections are also gone.

The three temples are called the Temples of the Forum Holitorium, for we are now in the area of the ancient vegetable market of the same name. The two side temples date from the 3rd century BC, while the middle one is from the 2nd century BC. All three were rebuilt in later classical times. The columns on the right flank of the church are of middling size, since the (right) temple to which they belonged was similarly modest. The rim of its platform is also embedded in this side of the church. The gothic side door is 14th-century.

Go next to the front of the church. Three columns on the façade are from the middle temple. Near you is a flight of steps that once led up to the temple; and there are more remains of the temple inside.

Go around to the left-hand side of the church. Here we can see the columns and cornices of the left temple, the smallest of the three, thought to be the Temple of Hope – a touching dedication, since it was built during the desperate First Punic War.

The church is dedicated to the Byzantine St. Nicholas and stands where the Byzantines built a jail during their occupation of Rome in the 7th century (p. 83). The district was densely populated by them. The church façade was totally rebuilt in the late 16th century by Giacomo Della Porta; 13th-century bells peek out from the belfry to the right, originally a medieval fortified tower.

The church is open sporadically. Its interior

was rebuilt in the 12th century, as indicated by a dedicatory tablet at the entrance end of the right aisle, and was restored in the 19th. Near the tablet is a 17th-century painting of the *Holy Trinity* by Guercino and, just past it, a 15th-century fresco by Antoniazzo Romano.

The church contains traces of all three temples. There are fragments of the middle one to the left of the entrance and elsewhere. A column from the right-hand temple is near the right wall, while there are columns from the left-hand temple in the sacristy.

Complicating matters, the columns of the nave, with beautiful and varied capitals, are spolia from other unrelated temples. A 9th-century inscription in Latin on the second column to the right records a generous gift to the church by a *majordomus* ('chamberlain') called Anastasius (a Byzantine name): a vineyard, livestock and money.

Leaving the church, note an over-restored medieval house across the street. To the right are the ruins of the ancient porticoes of the Forum Holitorium. Proceed down the avenue past a long Fascist-era building housing Rome's registry office. The commercial harbour of ancient Rome was here, serving the food markets, and beyond them to your distant left, the Fora (in imperial times the harbour and most of the commercial businesses were moved to more spacious quarters downstream, see p. 624).

The far corner of the modern block has a remarkable monument, the small late 10th-century **Casa dei Crescenzi** ('House of the Crescenzi'), partly built and almost entirely decorated with spolia from ancient Roman buildings. The practice was fairly common (p. 95), but while countless examples survive in churches, they are less frequent in houses. This one is the oldest and most elaborate.

It was owned by Rome's most feared family of the time, the ancient and powerful Crescenzi. They were still extant 450 years later, as we saw in connection with an attempted regicide in the Pantheon (p. 237), but later died out. The house

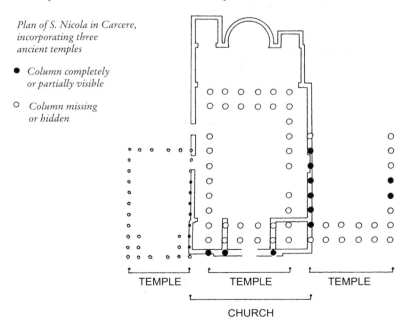

Plan of S. Nicola in Carcere, incorporating three ancient temples

● *Column completely or partially visible*

○ *Column missing or hidden*

TEMPLE   TEMPLE   TEMPLE

CHURCH

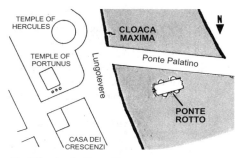

The Tiber by the Ponte Rotto

was originally crowned by a tower that served as a watch for the nearby river at a point where the island made it easy to cross.

A Latin inscription engraved over the portal identifies the builder as Nicola Crescenzi. It exudes great pride, suggesting that these buildings embellished with Roman spoils were more costly than one would think. Indeed, even in the darkest ages, the plunder of pagan monuments was officially restricted.

'I am well aware that the glory of the world is unimportant, and if I have built a house like this one, it was not out of vanity but to pay homage to my city,' says Nicola, in a rhyme typical of medieval Latin poetry. 'But when you live in a beautiful house, never forget that you are not going to be there long. So think of the grave … Death arrives on wings … You can barricade yourself in a castle sky-high, lock a hundred doors, command a thousand armies or flee like the wind, and you will still not escape.'

The arches over the portal and window on the right are from Roman temples. The window sill is a deeply carved piece of coffering from the ceiling of some basilica. Over the portal and window runs a cornice framed by late-imperial friezes with winged cupids. It continues along the side of the house, which has brick columns and pilasters with rustic terracotta capitals, other friezes and various decorations. Part of the second floor wall survives. A curved piece of marble on the lower right bears the Latin inscription: 'Now that you have seen this

magnificent house, come in and meet Nicola in person'.

The old meat and cattle market, the Forum Boarium, was across the intersection. It closed many centuries ago. Until the mid-19th century, however, cattle continued to be brought here and to the nearby Roman Forum to graze and be branded.

Nearby are two more very ancient temples, famous for their excellent condition. In the middle ages both were turned into churches, now rarely if ever used, which contain worn, moderately important frescoes.

The first of the two temples is opposite the side of the Casa dei Crescenzi (do not cross), the 2nd century BC **Temple of Portunus**, god of harbours. Remember the commercial harbour was nearby. It is also called the Temple of Fortuna Virilis, since it has been misidentified as such for several centuries.

This highly original temple combines Greek and Roman republican styles. Some columns are travertine, others volcanic stone (tufa), and the two materials are combined in other parts of the structure too.

We'll describe the second temple shortly. Skirt the side of the Casa dei Crescenzi and go towards the river. Cross the Lungotevere to the bridge. About halfway along the right side of the bridge, you can see the **Ponte Rotto** ('Broken Bridge') on your right. This was originally the Pons Æmilius, Rome's oldest stone bridge, built in the early 2nd century BC by the man who gave Rome the Basilica Æmilia in the Forum (p. 163). Since the current is particularly strong here, the bridge has twice collapsed and been rebuilt, the last time in 1568. It fell again 30 years later, during the most catastrophic flood of the Tiber on record (p. 117), and was abandoned. Beatrice Cenci, who was in jail at the time for the murder of her father (p. 518) and whose trial had been postponed due to the flood, offered in vain to rebuild it at her own expense if her life were spared.

An ancient rumour claimed that the Menorah from the Temple of Jerusalem looted by Titus' armies (pp. 192-193, 287) had been thrown into the water near this bridge and was still at the bottom; but it has never been proved or disproved.

The view of the broken bridge, with the Tiber Island in the background, is famous. The surviving arch consists of an elegant early baroque upper structure (note the papal arms) over the original Roman piers.

From here you can also see the other ancient bridge linking the island to the bank over the left branch of the river, the **Ponte Cestio**. This was rebuilt in the 19th century reusing materials from the original Roman structure, but with major changes in the design. It is faced with marble, as the Ponte Fabrizio on the other side once was (p. 251).

The mouth of the ancient sewer, the Cloaca Maxima, is visible from the other side of the bridge on which you are standing. To see it, we must cross appalling traffic without any lights or make wide detours, and we'll have the same problem returning. It is not essential to see it, however. If you do not, return to the Temple of Portunus, skirt it to the avenue and continue right until you see the round Temple of Hercules on your right (see below).

If you elect to see the Cloaca, go to the other side of the bridge. The **Cloaca Maxima**, early Rome's greatest technological feat, is under the left bank of the river. The first branch of this huge sewer, which is still in use today, was built to drain the Forum (pp. 156, 282), probably around the 5th century BC. It was later extended to elsewhere in the city, with tunnels so wide that they could be inspected by chariot.

The sewer outlet is the smaller hole within the modern marble arch in the embankment. It was probably built when the sewer was enlarged and improved in the 2nd century BC. This particular outlet is not used today, since modern outlets were opened downriver.

The Romans learnt construction from their northern neighbours, the mysterious Etruscans, who may have ruled the city for a time during the period of kings (p. 27) and probably directed the sewer construction.

Return to the embankment and again brave the traffic to a grassy slope with a circular temple. This is the second of the temples in the Forum Boarium, now known as the **Temple of Hercules** after centuries of fame under the name of the Temple of Vesta, owing to a mistaken analogy with the circular Temple of Vesta in the Forum. Go down across the garden to the avenue in front of the temple.

Built in the 2nd century BC, it is not only the earliest known marble temple in Rome (all earlier ones were in tufa, see p. 244) but was built in the fabulously expensive Pentelic marble from Athens, probably by a Greek architect. It is also one of the very few round temples in Rome. Hercules, the legendary hero to whom it was presumably dedicated, was considered the protector of butchers and cattle dealers (from a famous episode in his life when he killed the cattle thief Cacus). Indeed, the temple was probably donated by one of the rich meat dealers of the Forum Boarium. It originally had twenty columns (one is missing). The roof is modern. A marble frieze over the columns is missing, which distorts the proportions.

Nearby is the Fountain of the Tritons by a minor 18th-century artist, inspired by Bernini's fountain of the previous century in Piazza Barberini (p. 83). From the fountain, walk to the nearest traffic lights and cross to the medieval church of **S. Maria in Cosmedin**.

This is another of Rome's very ancient churches, but the first on our visits that actually looks ancient both inside and out, since it was restored to a medieval-looking state in the late 19th century, when new ideas of archæological integrity began to prevail.

The church opened in the 6th century as a *diaconia* (see p. 254) on the site of two abandoned buildings often identified as the central food distribution agency (or Statio Annonæ, whose role the *diaconia* partly inherited) and a large memorial to Hercules (Ara Maxima Herculis). (By a twist of fate, during the Second World War Rome's central food rationing office, also called 'Annona', was across the street from St. Maria in Cosmedin to the right.) The church was rebuilt in the 8th century and elements continued to be added from the 11th to the 13th centuries. Stylistic overlays added in the 18th century were removed in the late 19th-century restoration, leaving the present 8th- to 13th- century appearance, the serene and mystical romanesque style.

The church served the Byzantine community, which settled in the area at the time of Justinian (p. 83) and swelled in the 8th century thanks to mass immigration from the East triggered by the schism with Rome that followed the advent of iconoclasm in the Byzantine empire. The name 'in Cosmedin' is a corrupted Greek word of uncertain meaning (perhaps from the Greek *kosmidion* or 'ornament') and dates from this time.

The 12th-century porch has a central canopy

S. Maria in Cosmedin, interior

over four red granite pillars. The seven-storey romanesque belltower, one of the most beautiful of its kind, is 13th century. The main portal is 11th century.

On the left wall of the narthex (or porch) is the legendary **Bocca della Verità** ('Mouth of Truth'), a round marble face. For centuries it was said that the mouth would bite anyone who put their hand in its mouth and lied. It was even used as a lie detector in medieval trials, especially of adulterous wives. It has been variously identified as an ancient foutainhead, or a manhole from the nearby Cloaca Maxima (p. 259). (The *bocca* is famous world-wide thanks to the 1953 film *Roman Holiday* in which Audrey Hepburn puts her hand in the hole. It now sees a constant flow of tourists. Japanese agencies organise 'Roman Holiday' tours to Rome, in which the visit is limited to the sites of Hepburn's adventure.) Opening times are irregular.

The interior of the church is 8th century, except for the 11th- to 13th-century liturgical furnishings. These include a marble choir enclosure (*schola cantorum*) with pulpits and a tall candelabrum (right) held up by a lion, a gothic canopy over the main altar and a bishop's chair (*cathedra*) behind it. All these marble pieces have rich cosmatesque inlays. The canopy was signed by Deodatus, third son of Cosma the Younger. The beautiful floor is cosmatesque too, though much of it was redone in the 19th century. All the columns in the nave are ancient Roman spolia, as are their beautiful capitals, except some with simple stylised leaves, which were added in the 12th century.

Many of the columns are from the Statio Annonæ, the original ancient Roman structure: three in the left aisle (one of the short sides of the Statio); seven near the portal, in the bell tower, in a chapel and in the sacristy gift shop (the long side of the Statio); and one in a recess of the sacristy gift-shop (the other short side of the Statio). In this room there is also an important mosaic fragment from 706 depicting the Christ Child receiving a gift from one of the Three Kings, one of the few ornaments rescued from the destruction of old St. Peter's (p. 373). In a choir room next to the sac-

The Arch of Janus and S. Giorgio in Velabro in the 18th century, by Giuseppe Vasi

risty gift-shop is a beautiful 15th-century Roman painting of the *Virgin and Child* above the altar.

A crypt is accessible from the *schola cantorum* (ask the sacristan). It was built in the 8th century, but is all modern except for the columns and a mosaic. The crypt is carved out of the tufa blocks that originally formed the platform of the Ara Maxima Herculis, though this is hardly apparent. A 6th-century marble altar in a small apse contains many early Christian relics brought here from the catacombs, including a skull, supposedly that of St. Valentine, which was traditionally exhibited on the saint's feast day crowned with roses.

Leaving the church, go around the block to the right. Cross Via de' Cerchi and aim for an open space, Via del Velabro, with a peculiar marble arch-like structure. Here was the centre of the Velabrum area, which linked the great wholesale markets to the Roman Forum. So busy and noisy in antiquity, so sleepy and remote now! The massive travertine cube is the **Arch of Janus**. It is not a regular arch, nor was it dedicated to the god Janus. In Rome a 'janus' was a four-way covered passage,

which is what the structure was, a shelter and meeting point for merchants at one of the city's busiest crossroads. It was built under Constantine in the 4th century AD, possibly in his honour.

The cornice and decorative superstructures were removed in the middle ages, when the arch was turned into a fortress, thereby distorting its proportions and appearance. The niches all around, especially the deeper ones, probably held statues. Small mutilated sculptures on the keystones of the four archways are the goddesses Rome and Juno (seated) and Minerva and Ceres (standing).

To the right of the monument, in a private garden at No. 3, is a stretch of the Cloaca Maxima near the surface, but the gate is usually locked.

In 1993 a terrorist bomb devastated the area, especially the front of S. Giorgio in Velabro, which had been beautifully restored. Since then, acccess to the area has been restricted, but you can still visit it by using the elevated walkway on the left leading to the church.

Just opposite No. 3 is a small marble structure

leaning against the church wall, the intriguing Arch of the Moneychangers, built by their trade association and the cattle merchants – *argentari et negotiantes boari*, as the last line of the inscription reads – to honour the Emperor Septimius Severus and his family. It is contemporary with the early 3rd century AD Arch of Septimius Severus which we saw in the Forum, but displays even cruder sculpture, since as a private monument it was made by less skilled craftsmen than those in the imperial workshop, who were maintained under exclusive contract.

The arch was probably an ornamental entrance to the Forum Boarium from a now vanished side street. A poignant touch is the removal of the name and figure of Prince Geta in several places. The erasures were ordered by Geta's brother, Caracalla, after he had killed him (p. 165). Caracalla also murdered his wife, Plautilla, and her father, Plautianus, whose figures were removed from the arch. Geta's name is probably replaced at the end of the third line of the inscription by *fortissimo felicissimoque principi* ('strongest and best of princes'), referring to Caracalla, whose name on the arch is the official one, Bassianus Marcus Aurelius Antoninus.

On the left pilaster a worn-away figure in the middle is thought to be Caracalla himself. The inside panel shows him sacrificing on a portable altar; the empty space contained erased figures. The third panel shows Roman soldiers with a barbarian captive.

On the right pilaster are Septimius Severus and his wife sacrificing. The empty space near her probably contained another erased figure.

Other reliefs represent Hercules, protector of cattle merchants and butchers, bulls led to sacrifice, sacrificial and butchering tools, and musical instruments.

The holes that appear here and there were thought to have been made in the middle ages by treasure hunters looking for the elusive gold of the moneychangers; in fact the treasure here, as elsewhere, was more likely to have been the iron dowels that the Romans used to hold the stone blocks together.

Flanking the monument is **S. Giorgio in Velabro**, a church similar to S. Maria in Cosmedin in age, style and history. Like S. Maria, it was founded in the 6th or 7th century as a *diaconia* and used originally by the Byzantine community. St. George, the legendary Roman soldier and martyr, slayer of the mythical dragon, was a saint much venerated in the East and patron of the Byzantine army. After repeated remodellings in medieval, baroque and later times, the church was restored to its romanesque simplicity in 1926. (Open: 08:00-13:00 and 16:00-18:30; closes at sunset in summer.)

The façade, narthex (porch) and bell tower are 12th-century; the Latin inscription around the narthex refers to a 13th-century restoration.

Typical of early basilicas, the interior is articulated by columns plundered from ancient Roman buildings, though the capitals are 7th-century. The main altar is in the cosmatesque style. The apse contains much-reworked late 13th-century frescoes of the *Madonna and Saints*. At the entrance end of the aisles are pieces of the 9th-century marble choir. A small 11th-century marble altar can be seen at the far end of the right aisle.

Relics said to be the skull of St. George, his sword and part of his banner are venerated in the church, though the Vatican has recently decided that he (like others in a long list of saints) never existed.

From the church, proceed uphill along Via del Velabro to Via San Teodoro. No. 1 on the right is an interesting tall house of uncertain age. Via San Teodoro was the ancient Vicus Tuscus, or 'Etruscan Street', linking the Velabrum and the market area to the Fora on the far left. You may recall seeing the other end of the Vicus as we looked over the Roman Forum from above (p. 162). The high wall in the distance used to be the firebreak of the Forum of Augustus (pp. 191-192). The ancient Vicus was a very busy street with all sorts of shops, some very elegant, including fashionable tailors and sellers of Chinese silks and rare perfumes.

Turn left. Past the Via dei Fienili crossing is **S. Teodoro**, one of Rome's few round churches (see p. 428). Its origins are murky, but harmonise with the neighbourhood character. It was built over the foundations of one of the great granaries connected to the Forum, and later dedicated to one of the saints favoured by the Byzantine community in the area. It began as a *diaconia*, or welfare centre, but little else is known about it. The plain brick façade, round dome and escutcheon of Pope Nicholas V record a major reconstruction of the church in the mid 15th-century; the cupola is attributed by Vasari to Bernardo Rossellino. The semicircular outer court and double ramp were added in the 18th century.

The church is occasionally open. Inside the apse contains a mosaic of *Christ with Saints*, imitating the 6th-century one in SS. Cosma e Damiano, which suggests that S. Teodoro was already in existence then. The mosaic is very damaged and was restored in the 17th century. The rest of the decorations are mainly 19th-century and include a few minor paintings.

Retrace your steps to the crossing with Via dei Fienili and take it to the end. On the right is **S. Maria della Consolazione** ('St. Mary of Consolation'), which began life as the chapel of a large 15th-century hospital behind it, where St. Aloysius Gonzaga (p. 119, 122) caught the plague while attending the sick. The hospital closed in 1936 and the building is now a police station. The church was rebuilt in the late 16th century to a design by Martino Longhi the Elder. The upper storey of the façade was completed in the same style in the 19th century. The front steps are modern. (06:30-12:00 and, in summer, 15:00-18:00.)

The decoration inside is mainly by minor late 16th- and 17th-century artists. There are notable frescoes by Taddeo Zuccaro in the first chapel to the right. On the side walls are an *Assumption* and a *Nativity* by Cristoforo Pomarancio. The sacristy has a marble relief of the *Crucifixion* by Luigi

Capponi (late 15th-century) and fragmentary frescoes by Antoniazzo Romano from the same period. The chapel nearest the exit in the left aisle has a relief by Raffaello da Montelupo (1530) of the *Mystical Marriage of St. Catherine*. Over the beautiful main altar, designed by Longhi, is a delicate fresco by Antoniazzo Romano of the *Madonna of Consolation*. Antoniazzo painted this when the church was built, in the late 15th century, but he was reworking an earlier, anonymous picture in the street outside the church which had been placed there in fulfilment of the last wish of an executed criminal. It was said that another man under sentence of death had prayed before this image and had then been miraculously saved when the hangman's rope got tangled up; this man later turned out to be innocent. The church was built specifically to hold the miraculous image.

Opposite the church is Vico Jugario, the street where the great Roman poet Ovid lived. 'Jugum' is Latin for yoke and in ancient times the street was named after oxen yoke makers who worked here. Halfway down it, on an elevated platform to the left, is the little church of **S. Omobono** (late 16th-century). Rarely open, it contains an apse fresco of uncertain authorship from the same period. The church is on the edge of a vast archæological zone, excavated at various times in the mid-20th century, the Sacred Area of S. Omobono. The zone is highly interesting because the deeper layers have revealed 9th- to 6th-century BC objects, for both domestic and cult uses, of Etruscan, Greek and Roman manufacture. These suggest an inhabited spot, similar to the huts on the Palatine (p. 290), which served as a meeting place for some of the ancient peoples who lived here before Rome was founded, and of whom our knowledge hovers between legend and history. The very ancient name, Vicus Tuscus, given to a nearby street (pp. 162, 282), could refer to an Etruscan settlement.

Return along Vico Jugario and take Via S. Giovanni Decollato on the right. This neighbourhood was spared the Fascist-era demolition frenzy, which nevertheless left it isolated and semi-deserted. On the right is **S. Eligio dei Ferrari** ('St.

Eligius of the Ironsmiths'), built in the 16th century by the Guild of Ironsmiths, which still owns and runs it. St. Eligius is also patron saints of goldsmiths, whose guild built another church dedicated to him a few years earlier (see p. 473). The church is open for Mass at 07:30 every day and on Sundays at 11:00, when the choirs of the guild members precede Mass.

The sumptuous interior contains works by minor 16th- to 18th-century artists. A *Madonna Enthroned* by Sermoneta (*c.* 1500) on the main altar is noteworthy. There is a small museum with memorabilia of the guild.

Further along, on an elevated pavement to the right, is **S. Giovanni Decollato** ('St. John Beheaded'), a church once famous as the seat of the Brotherhood of Compassion. These hooded monks followed criminals to their execution, pressing a holy picture to their lips (see p. 491). In the final centuries of papal rule, and until 1870, most executions took place in the nearby Piazza de' Cerchi near the Circus Maximus. The confraternity was founded in the 16th century in Florence, and in Rome one of its volunteers was Michelangelo. The Roman chapter had the privilege of saving one condemned Roman a year, who was then led through the city in a solemn procession. The populace took a morbid interest in these survivors' actitivities, drawing inspiration from them for numbers to play in the state lottery. The brotherhood still exists and is now dedicated to helping prisoners. The church, with its sober brick façade, was completed in the mid-16th century. Sadly it is rarely open.

The decoration inside, and that of an adjacent oratory, includes works by Vasari (the main altarpiece), Salviati and minor Florentine mannerist painters of the 16th century. Amongst the latter is Jacopino del Conte, whose *Deposition* here is his masterpiece. A door to the left of the main altar leads to a cloister which served as a cemetery for the executed. From the portico one passes into a room with mementoes of executions, such as some of the religious images that the condemned had to kiss, the basket that caught Beatrice Cenci's head

(p. 518) and Giordano Bruno's hood (p. 484).

Further along on the left, at No. 22, the Oratorio per Misericordiam is also run by the Brotherhood of Compassion. It is marked by a 17th-century alms box for the families of the executed, engraved with a decapitated man's head.

Return to the crossing of Via S. Teodoro and Via S. Giorgio in Velabro.

END OF DETOUR

On your right take Via S. Teodoro, which runs along the foot of the Palatine. Halfway down the block, behind a gate to the Palatine, is the area where according to legend the she-wolf nursed Romulus and Remus (p. 153). At the time of writing, the gate is planned as a new entrance, or exit, to the Palatine. Where the street ends, at No. 90 on the right, is a beautiful renaissance doorway.

Opposite is **S. Anastasia**, another early home church (p. 228), founded in the 4th century by a woman called Anastasia and later dedicated to a Byzantine martyr of the same name. Its ancient origins are hidden since it was rebuilt several times, the exterior remodelled in the 17th century and the interior in the 18th. Of key interest are the underground rooms with remains of the Circus Maximus complex, unfortunately closed to the public for over twenty years. The church is occasionally open.

The richly appointed, spacious interior has a typically 18th-century elegance. Twelve ancient Roman columns from the early church, which were plundered from a temple, are adapted here to a purely ornamental use. The chapels are furnished with paintings by minor 17th-century artists. Under the main altar is a 17th-century statue of *St. Anastasia Dying* in the style of Bernini. A medieval canopied altar is in the chapel to the left of the main altar.

Ruins under the church were shops or annexes from the Circus Maximus, separated by an ancient road from an unidentified building and 1st-century AD portico.

BEFORE GOING

10. The Circus Maximus

In ancient Rome, circuses were arenas for shows and athletic events. As the name implies, the Circus Maximus was the biggest, but also the oldest and most famous. Today only a wide grassy esplanade used for jogging remains. One consolation, however, is that what you see is what the first Romans saw when they began to use this little valley between two hills for games. It was conveniently shaped: the villagers who came from the Palatine could sit on the slopes of the hills to watch.

At first there were no benches and only the crudest of sporting equipment. This changed when Rome became a large and wealthy town. Races, especially chariot races, became all the rage. Stadium structures, elaborate props, furnishings and service buildings, of which only the faintest traces remain, sprang up in and around the arena, which is still shaped as it was when chariots dashed past roaring crowds.

The extremely old Circus Maximus is the greatest structure ever built for entertainment: it had a capacity of 250,000, or 300,000 including standing room. It was soon exclusively used for chariot races, while less popular sporting events took place on other tracks and stadiums, such as the Stadium of Domitian, which we'll see in its modern incarnation as Piazza Navona (p. 452).

No other permanent sports complex has matched the Circus Maximus for capacity. Most of Rome's population attended it for major events. Admission was free. In the Late Empire, chariot racing became a national mania; whole fortunes were made or lost in betting. Teams and their fans also acquired political clout, a development that was even more extreme in the Eastern Empire and the second capital established there, Constantinople.

Lew Wallace's novel *Ben Hur* faithfully portrays the tremendous excitement and risk of the races. Immense skill was required from the drivers (*aurigæ*), but the prizes were colossal. There were four traditional teams: Whites, Greens, Reds and Blues, which hired and traded stars for sums comparable to those paid today for professional sports players. The chronicles are replete with names of young chariot champions who perished in the frequent crashes, a mortality rate well above that of Formula One racers. Other dangers included mad emperors placing bets. Vitellius had the whole Blue team executed when it was thought to be about to beat his favorites. Caracalla did the same to the Greens, who had disappointed him.

Races often went on from dawn to dusk, up to 100 daily. Each had seven laps and each lap was counted by mechanical counters on the central track divider: great wooden 'eggs' rising and falling, or bronze dolphins flipping. The classic races involved chariots drawn by four horses (*quadrigæ*), but contests amongst other chariot-horse combinations, from two-in-hand to ten-in-hand, were common. For more variety, there were acrobatic performances on horseback and fights between exotic animals.

The audience faced risks too. Once 24 elephants knocked down the iron railings around the track, injuring many. Another time, just before the wooden bleachers were replaced by marble seating, the old planks were heard to creak. Only the level-headedness and courage of Augustus, who rushed from the imperial box to the threatened section and calmed the people, averted panic

The remains of the Circus Maximus as they appeared in the 17th century, with the imperial palaces of the Palatine in the background; engraving by P. Schenk

and allowed a smooth evacuation.

As in the Colosseum, events in the Circus Maximus were often accompanied by ceremonies and the music of high-pitched wind instruments and a hydraulic organ. Clever diversions, sometimes invented or sponsored by the emperors, included showering the audience with colourful packets (*missilia*) containing candy, money or gift coupons. The gifts could be huge, reminiscent of modern television game shows. Suetonius tells us that they included houses, farms and even ships.

The Circus was also an important social meeting place. In his famous manual, *Ars amatoria*, Ovid, prince of erotic poets, recommended attending the races as the best way for boys to meet girls. The general fever, he said, and the elegant naughtiness of the girls' attire (people in the best sections dressed somewhat as they do today at Ascot or Longchamps) were favourable to amorous encounters. As in many other arenas (p. 452), the fun-loving Romans added plenty of pleasure and entertainment facilities to the Circus, such as inns, eateries and brothels. Traces of these are under the nearby church of St. Anastasia and on the edge of the Stadium of Domitian in Piazza Navona (see p. 460).

ON THE SPOT

10. The Circus Maximus

Via S. Teodoro ends in view of the vast open space of the Circus Maximus, which covers the valley between the slopes of the Palatine and Aventine hills. Cross to the edge of the grassy area and go to the middle of this short side of its perimeter. The Palatine is to your left, the Aventine to your right.

The arena was about 2,000 ft by 660 ft (600 m by 200 m) and its tiers for public seating were enclosed in a huge three-storey structure, of which a few ruins remain. The arena was several feet lower and substantially wider than it is now, since the present slopes didn't exist, but the shape was about the same. Under the large modern building behind you were the chariot starting pens (*carceres*). Along the central axis of the arena was the 'spine', a long low structure, suggested by the present earth mound, with ornamental architecture and lap-counting devices. Two Egyptian obelisks stood on the spine. The first, erected by Augustus, is now in the Piazza del Popolo (see p. 46), and we'll see the second, erected 300 years later by Constantius II, in another Roman square (p. 410). Racing close to the spine shortened the distance, but one risked disaster if a wheel caught on the wall. The last competitions were held in the 6th century, long after the fall of the Empire.

The only extant ruins of the Circus are visible from here by looking at the far short side of the oblong, where the tiered structure curved. There are remains of sub-structures, a segment of bleachers and stairs to an upper floor. Over the ruins is a small 12th-century medieval tower.

A 3rd century AD Mithræum, including a large relief of the god Mithras killing the bull, was found under the modern building behind you, which covers the chariot *carceres*. It is only accessible with the permission of the the city authorities.

Originally the emperors and their courts watched the races from a multi-storeyed marble box on the long Palatine side of the tiers. Later they could watch directly from their new imperial palace on the Palatine, overlooking the long left side of the Circus. The ruins of the palace are a stunning sight today, especially at sunset. (There is a detailed guide to the Palatine in 'A Closer Look', pp. 275-295).

A curious 17th-century façade with the top curved downwards is nearer to you on the left. It is the entrance to a late renaissance villa on the Palatine (p. 288).

On the right is the Aventine Hill, an aristocratic residential district during the Empire, which was devastated by barbarians and remained virtually deserted until recently. In the 17th century a Jewish cemetery was created on its slope. It was in use until 1895, when the remains were moved to a new general cemetery (p. 633). Only tombstones with inscriptions were moved, however, and these were very few, since a papal decree in force until 1846 forbade inscriptions on Jewish tombstones, except for those of rabbis. All that is left of the cemetery are a few beautiful cypress trees on the avenue.

If you are not taking the following Detour, move to the opposite end of the Circus. The main itinerary resumes on p. 274.

Mithras as a sun-god

DETOUR

2 HR

BEFORE GOING

The Aventine

In Rome's earliest days, the Aventine was used to settle prisoners from wars with nearby tribes. The word 'plebeian' originated in reference to these people, as opposed to Roman citizens, who were 'patricians'. The Aventine was home to these lower classes throughout the late Republic. By then, two other underprivileged groups had joined them: foreigners and people from Italian cities allied to Rome but who were not Roman citizens, such as people from surrounding Latium, who gained political equality only in 90 BC.

Friction between plebeians and patricians arose early and lasted for centuries. In the 5th century BC the plebeian leader, Menenius Agrippa, threatened the nobility with secession. He thereby wrested concessions, such as the right of the poor to elect magistrates (*tribuni plebis*) to represent them. The Aventine remained relatively cut off from the rest of Rome for centuries, both because it was a stronghold of proletarian opposition and because it was hard to climb. Until the reign of Claudius (1st century AD) the Aventine wasn't even within the *pomerium*, the sacred confines of Rome. As a by-product of the social struggles, a number of untraditional temples appeared on the hill, which have left many traces. These were also refuges and fortresses for political groups. The most important of the temples, the Temple of Diana on the summit, was founded in the remote era of kings (p. 27) and was the Roman seat of a league of Italian cities that initially resisted Roman power in Italy. Similarly, the Temple of Minerva housed an often rebellious union of craftsmen, writers and actors. Temples to 'foreign' deities existed thanks to the Roman custom of giving 'homes' to images of gods captured from enemy cities.

The historian Plutarch poignantly relates the end in 121 BC of Caius Gracchus, an elected magistrate and great advocate of the poor. Hunted by nobles, he fled from one to another of the temples amid the myrtle tree thickets covering the Aventine (which, incidentally, is also called Myrtle Hill). He hid with his men first in the Temple of Diana, then in the Temple of Minerva. Losing ground, some of his friends gave their lives to buy him time. He went to the Temple of the Moon at the western end of the hill, near the church of St. Anselmo today. Again forced to run, he leapt off the temple platform and sprained his ankle. A slave helped him hobble to the valley, cross the river and hide on the Janiculum. Reaching a small sacred woodland dedicated to the Furies, he felt faint and asked the slave to kill him. The slave obeyed, then committed suicide; their enemies found both bodies. They desecrated Caius' remains, ripping out his heart, and announced that the Furies (avenging deities) had rid Rome of his presence (pp. 154, 560).

With the end of the Republic, Rome's commercial centres (see pp. 254-262) moved from just north of the Aventine to a larger site, a plain south of the hill, the Emporium (p. 624). Thus the nature of the Aventine changed. Most of its residents, who worked mainly in the food markets, moved to the plain or to Trastevere. The fall in population was accelerated by several fires, including Nero's notorious fire of 64 AD. Then rich Roman families discovered the Aventine. The ruins

S. Maria del Priorato, the chapel of the Knights of Malta on the Aventine: the only building actually designed and built by Piranesi

of villas, including those of Trajan and Hadrian before they became emperors, have emerged, together with their private baths. Gentrification, however, led to ruin: in 410 AD the Vandals, led by Alaric, sacked the Aventine. Deserted and reduced to farmland, it was well suited for the construction of churches and convents. Many still survive, including S. Sabina, S. Prisca and S. Balbina, which was built over the ruins of a former villa.

History revisited the hill about 1000 AD, when the 20-year-old Germanic Emperor Otto III, heir to the Holy Roman Empire (p. 303), came to visit his friend Adalbert, former bishop of Prague, who had retired to a monastery on the hill. The cultivated, likeable and visionary Otto came to propose the creation of a 'universal Christian empire' with Rome as capital. It would be no less than the Roman Empire reconstituted in a broader form, based on an alliance between Otto, the pope and the peoples of Europe. Otto's dream found some support from the pope, the Germanic peoples and eastern Europeans, but the Romans themselves did not appreciate the idea of having a Germanic ruler. Ejected from Rome by an uprising, Otto died at 22, while trying to recapture the city (p. 597).

Soon afterward Otto's palace became a fortress, and later home to one of Rome's warlike baronial families, the Savelli (p. 253). The ruins of the Rocca Savella are the first thing to strike the eye when you climb the hill from the Circus Maximus. Yet, overall, the Aventine spent the next millennium peacefully, dominated by its solitary churches and farmland. In the 1930's gentrification recommenced and the present calm residential neighbourhood developed.

ON THE SPOT

The Aventine

Climb the hill. (If at any time this detour seems too long, it is worth remembering that it follows the bus no. 175 route coming from the centre.) Take Clivo dei Publicii on the right (*clivus* meant 'climb' in Latin). This is the same street, with the same name, laid down by two magistrate brothers of the plebeian Publicii family in 289 BC. It was the first street in ancient Rome to be paved for traffic and have a walkway for pedestrians.

The street soon turns right and becomes Via S. Sabina. (The ancient road continued straight and over the hill.) Pass the poetic Clivo di Rocca Savella ('Ascent of the Savelli Fortress') on the right. Just beyond is a garden bordered on the right by the crenelated ruins of the fortress. Initially, it was an imperial palace, built by Otto III in 1000 AD. The warlike barons Savelli turned it into a 'rocca' or fortress in the 12th century. The garden has a lovely view over Rome. Go on to Piazza Pietro d'Illiria, named after the 5th century priest who founded the church of **S. Sabina**, the side of which borders the square.

The church was founded *circa* 425 AD as an *ecclesia domestica* or 'home church' (p. 228), according to tradition in the house of Sabina, a Roman matron. Ample remains of a Roman house are indeed below, but are not presently accessible. Later the church was dedicated to a 1st or 2nd century Christian martyr also called Sabina. It was renovated in the 9th, 13th and 17th centuries, but restored to its original appearance in the early 20th. So it is probably the best example in Rome of an Early Christian basilica. The major event in the history of the church was in the 13th century, when the pope entrusted it to the future St. Dominic, after approving the monastic order of Dominicans (p. 115), who still officiate here. The romanesque belfry dates from this time. (Open: 06:30–12:45 and 15:30–19:00.)

The most precious item in the church is the 5th-century wooden double door of the central entrance. To see it, first go down the right aisle (note the elegant 15th-century portico), then cross the 13th-century hall with assorted memorial tablets, ancient Roman sarcophagi, beautiful sarcophagi fragments reused in the middle ages as tombstones, and other pieces of marble from the early church. The door itself, which is made of cypress, is surrounded by splendid marble carving from imperial times; it survived because it was long embedded in the Savelli fortifications. The 18 extant panels (of the original 28) show biblical scenes beautifully framed by vines and little animals. The first panel at the top is one of the earliest depictions of the Crucifixion. A few panels betray 19th-century restorations.

The interior of the church was restored to a primitive plainness when the baroque ornamentation was removed. The columns are original and were made especially for the church. The bands at the top depict Roman military insignia (identified through comparison with an imperial army almanac). These are in turn surmounted by crosses to symbolise the triumph of Christianity over paganism – the whole composing an exquisite multi-coloured 5th-century marble frieze, whose motif is echoed in the apse. Over the main entrance are remains of the vast mosaic decoration from the original church: a band with an inscription in blue mentioning the founder, the priest Peter of Illiria, and Pope Celestine (who was pope at the time). Two female figures at the ends symbolise the two glorious faiths, Christianity (right) and Judaism (left), as in S. Pudenziana (p. 93).

The large windows have been rebuilt according to the original medieval design. In the middle of the central aisle is the tombstone of a 14th-century Master General of the Dominicans, the Spaniard Muñoz de Zamora, the only such mosaic in Rome. Many of the marble furnishings, such as the beautiful *schola cantorum* in the centre of the nave, were reconstructed from original 5th- to 9th-century fragments found during the restoration.

Halfway up the right aisle, a half-buried column belongs to the Roman ruins below. Just past it is the Chapel of St. Hyacinth, with frescoes by Federico Zuccaro (late 16th-century). His brother

Taddeo frescoed the apse of the church, following the design of the primitive mosaic, but these frescoes were ruined by 19th-century restorations.

Cross to the other aisle. Halfway down is the beautiful, vividly frescoed baroque chapel of St. Catherine of Siena (p. 118). Over the altar is a notable oil painting by Sassoferrato of the *Madonna with St. Dominic and St. Catherine*, typical of this 17th-century master's pure and luminous work.

Next to the church is a 13th-century convent and cloister accessible from the outside hall of the church (ask in the sacristy). St. Thomas Aquinas taught here and St. Dominic's own cell can be seen, transformed into a chapel in the 17th century.

In Piazza Pietro d'Illiria, note a fountain with a mask and basin from ancient Roman baths.

Continue along Via S. Sabina. In an 18th-century enclosure, at No. 23, is the very ancient porticoed church of **S. Alessio** (St. Alexis) within a courtyard. It was founded at an unknown date and rebuilt in the 13th century, when the romanesque bell tower was added. Its present appearance dates from 18th- to 19th-century restorations. Originally dedicated to another saint, it was re-dedicated in the middle ages to the young son of a senator who was supposed to have lived next door in imperial Rome. The traditional story is that Alexis, vowing to remain chaste and not consummate a marriage that his parents had forced upon him, fled and wandered for 17 years in the East. When he returned to Rome, he worked, unrecognised, as a servant in his parents' house. For years he lived under a stair, until he felt death approaching. He then revealed himself to the pope, who in turn informed his father and wife. We'll see his story in a famous fresco in another church (p. 422). (Open: 8:00-12:30 and 15:30 to dusk.)

The doorway and floor inside are 13th-century cosmatesque work. In the right transept a 13th-century Madonna is said (anachronistically) to be a picture venerated by Alexis during his oriental wanderings. In the apse two exquisite little columns survive of the 19 originally here. Napoleon's troops carted off the rest. The columns

Detail of the door of Santa Sabina

are by the heads of the Cosma family, Jacopo and Lorenzo; the right-hand one is signed. In the romanesque crypt – the only such one in Rome –

are an interesting altar and 11th- to 12th-century frescoes (ask in the sacristy for access). The rear wall has an 18th-century glass shrine glorifying the space under the stair where Alexis used to sleep.

Next to the church is a 16th-century cloister with ancient capitals (on one side only) plundered from Roman ruins. The courtyard was damaged in a 19th-century explosion and restored. On the wall is a funeral tablet to Stefano Massimo dated 1012, one of the oldest that mentions this ancient and illustrious Roman family (see p. 504).

A little further along, Via S. Sabina opens into the picturesque Piazza dei Cavalieri di Malta ('of the Knights of Malta'). Two great memories fill this space: that of the Knights themselves (see pp. 59-60), who owned property here, and that of the 18th-century artist and engraver Giovan Battista Piranesi, whose designs are the most passionate evocation of classical Rome ever captured on paper. The marble enclosure of part of the square was built to his design; its obelisks, steles and panels, depicting the military and naval symbols of the Order, recall the fantastic architecture of his prints.

On the right is the monumental entrance to the **Villa of the Priorate of Malta** (of the 'Prior' or 'Grand Master' of the order) designed by Piranesi. Look through the keyhole for a famous view of the dome of St. Peter's. To enter, permission is required, obtainable at the headquarters of the Order in Via Condotti. The complex includes a medieval convent and the small 16th-century church of **S. Maria del Priorato**, both restored and decorated by Piranesi.

In the square the cypress trees behind the enclosure belong to the modern Benedictine International College (a seminary), which also houses the abbot of this old monastic order. It is accessible from an avenue of cypress trees leading to **S. Anselmo**, a serene late 19th-century church, interesting partly because beneath it are 2nd and 3rd century AD ruins, including a magnificent floor mosaic, now in the college (ask to see it).

Back on the square, retrace your steps along Via S. Sabina to the entrance of the Savelli Fortress, then turn right into Via S. Alberto Magno. Go to the end and take Via S. Eufemiano (the senator father of Alexis) to Piazza del Tempio di Diana ('of Diana's Temple', now gone).

The square, which is named after the most important of the many temples that once rose on the hill when it was the stronghold of the Roman plebeians, is at the centre of an area rich in archæological sites, all unfortunately inaccessible to the public. The rustic farmhouse on one side of the square, for instance, is over the remains of the 3rd century Baths of Decius (with mosaics and frescoes) and other ancient and medieval buildings.

Continue across the square and take Via del Tempio di Diana down to Piazza S. Prisca. Take the steps at the higher end of the square to the church of **S. Prisca**. Note the ancient Roman ruins in the basement under the steps to the right.

The church is first documented in the 5th century, but is actually older and was built over houses of which you have just seen traces (the ruins are closed to the public). Tradition says that these houses belonged to a Jewish couple called Aquila and Priscilla who, with their young friend Prisca, had invited Peter and Paul to stay with them. Prisca was thrown to the lions for this. Almost three centuries later, a pope claimed a body he had unearthed on the Aventine belonged to the martyred saint. The names of the Jewish couple are mentioned in the New Testament in reference to St. Paul's life, but their connection with St. Prisca and this church is probably legendary (note the similarities with the legend of Sts. Pudenziana and Praxedes, pp. 92-93).

At some point the houses under the church may have served as an *ecclesia domestica* or 'home church' (p. 228), which later became the church proper. The ruins also include rooms that were used as a Mithræum. The primitive church was rebuilt several times and shortened in the 15th century after a fire. The present façade is 17th-century. (Open: 06:00-12:00 and 16:00-20:00.)

Two ancient Roman columns adorn the doorway. Inside other ancient columns embedded in 17th-century pilasters articulate the nave. Over the capitals and in the presbytery are early 17th-century frescoes by Anastasio Fontebuoni. At the beginning of the right aisle is a baptismal font made out of a 2nd-century AD capital on a 13th-century base. These ancient pieces come from the crypt (currently closed), where according to a tradition obviously at odds with their real age St. Peter used them to baptise the two Jews and Prisca. Over the main altar is the 17th-century *St. Prisca Baptised by St. Peter,* the masterpiece of the Florentine painter Domenico Passignano. The presbytery has frescoes by Fontebuoni. At the beginning of the left aisle are fragments of a heavily restored 15th-century Roman *Annunciation.*

In the sacristy are various arches from the front of the church before it was shortened in the 15th century; they are now reduced to windows.

From Piazza S. Prisca take Via S. Prisca down to Piazza Albania at the foot of the hill, where a modern equestrian statue commemorates the hero of the Albanian struggle for independence, Scanderbeg (p. 66). Near the corner of the square symmetrical? to the one from which we came and in the adjacent Via S. Anselmo are long stretches of Republican walls (p. 42).

This stretch was rebuilt in the 1st century BC. An arch is visible that opened onto a 'ballistic chamber', a room containing the ancient missile-hurling machine called a *ballista.*

Return to the corner of Piazza Albania and Via S. Prisca. Cross the avenue, Viale Aventino, at the intersection with Via S. Saba and climb another smaller hill.

In front of you are steps topped by a small 13th-century romanesque portico that lead to the courtyard of **S. Saba**, founded in the 7th century by Greek monks, who were refugees from Palestine. In the 5th century a Christian hermit called Saba had built for himself and a number of companions a monastery, the Great Lavra of Mar Saba, between Jerusalem and the Dead Sea (which still exists). Two centuries later the Arabs conquered the region. Some of its eastern community fled to Rome and founded another monastery here. Its oratory is this church, which was later taken over by western Benedictine monks.

The church has been repeatedly remodelled and its romanesque façade is covered by a 15th- century structure topped by an elegant loggia.

The portico was rebuilt in the 18th century, when rough pilasters replaced the original columns. Various important ancient Roman sarcophagi, inscriptions and beautiful marble fragments are inside the portico. Note on the left an 8th-century relief of a falconer on horseback. The early 13th-century cosmatesque doorway is signed Jacopo Cosma. (Open: 06:30-12:00 and 16:00-18:30, Sundays to 19:00.)

The interior is enlivened by columns plundered from ancient Roman ruins. The cosmatesque floor, probably contemporary with the doorway, was restored in modern times. Fragments of the marble choir and the original presbytery enclosure are along the right nave, including spiral columns signed by Magister Bassallectus (Vassalletto). Late 16th-century decorations in the apse probably retrace an earlier mosaic. In the middle is a beautiful but over-restored 14th-century *Crucifixion;* up under the roof is a 15th-century *Annunciation.* Behind the altar is a beautiful cosmatesque bishop's throne. Steps from the presbytery lead down to a 9th-century crypt in the traditional ring shape used to display relics (pp. 367, 431).

On the left is a sort of supplementary aisle, probably a walled-up portico, with late 13th-century frescoes. Fragments of much older frescoes (7th- to 10th centuries) are in the sacristy and in an oratory downstairs (ask in the sacristy).

Leave from a rear door opening onto Piazza Bernini. Walk along Via Salvator Rosa, Via Ercole Rosa and Via S. Balbina for a few minutes to the picturesque and isolated church of **S. Balbina**, dedicated to a martyr traditionally held to have been beheaded in the early 2nd century. The church is first mentioned in the 6th century, but existed in the 5th, when it was a Roman magistrate's 'home church' (p. 228). The latest of several remodellings, in the 1930's, was an effort to restore it to what was presumed to have been its original appearance. A portico in front of the plain brick façade incorporates materials from excavations.

The church entrance is from the convent next door, now a rest home for the elderly, a large medieval building and tower built over a group of 2nd century AD ruins. Some are visible in the right wall as you go in. (Open: 07:00-17:00 October 1-April 30; 07:00-19:00 May 1-September 30.)

The church floor is an invention of the restorers, who reused beautiful 1st century AD Roman mosaics found in the Fora during the construction of Via dell'Impero in the Fascist era (p. 172). The ceiling beams are 15th-century. On the entrance wall to the right is a tomb of an early 14th-century cardinal, signed by Giovanni Cosma himself. In the first chapel on the right are fragments of 14th-century frescoes of the *Madonna and Saints* and a wonderful 15th-century marble *Crucifixion* by Mino da Fiesole and Giovanni Dalmata (fourth niche on the right). The late 16th-century frescoes in the apse, depicting *St. Balbina and other Saints*, are by Fontebuoni. Behind the altar is a beautiful 13th-century cosmatesque bishop's throne.

Coming back down the left aisle, the first chapel contains a brick structure on the floor, which could be a traditional early Christian altar with a well for relics, from the original 'home church'. Three chapels further down is the most important medieval fresco in the church, partly covered by a later fresco: the *Madonna with Sts. Peter and Paul* under a medallion of *Christ Blessing* – all 13th-century and attributed to the school of Cavallini.

Below the square in front of the church is Viale Baccelli. At the time of writing a bus running left goes to Porta Capena (see below) then on to the centre. The Baths of Caracalla are nearby.

END OF DETOUR

Before you is a wide intersection of several major roads, Piazza di Porta Capena ('of the Capua Gate'), named after a gate in the primitive walls that stood here in Republican times (p. 42). The first great consular road, the Appian Way, going south towards the city of Capua and beyond, started here. The road, currently called the Via Appia Antica, now starts a bit further south at the less ancient Aurelian Walls (see p. 42).

Until 2003, a 79 ft (24 m) tall obelisk dominated one side of the square. This very interesting granite monolith or stele was a 4th-century AD pre-Christian funerary monument from Aksum, ancient capital of Ethiopia and spiritual home of the Abyssinian religion and civilization. It was brought here in 1937, when Fascist Italy had made Ethiopia its colonial 'empire'. The Roman authorities have been promising to return it since the end of the Second World War, and it is currently in storage pending its delivery to the legitimate owners, although this is repeatedly postponed, owing to alleged transportation difficulties. (For another mortifying conclusion to Italy's colonial adventure, see p. 81).

The white building on the right by the subway station is the Food and Agriculture Organization, a Rome-based agency of the United Nations.

Viale delle Terme di Caracalla ('of the Baths of Caracalla') begins at the intersection and follows the initial stretch of the Appian Way. Go down it for about 500 yards, or take a bus if possible. On the right is the evocative little church of **SS. Nereo e Achilleo**, sometimes open. It was founded around the 4th century on the spot where, according to legend, after escaping from the Mamertine Prison, St. Peter lost the bandage on his chain-damaged foot (p. 169). Indeed, it used to be called *titulus fasciolæ*, 'the church of the bandage'. It was rebuilt in 800 AD and again in the 15th century, when it acquired its present simple appearance. A handsome Roman column stands before it.

The stark interior contains beautiful 15th-century pilasters and 16th-century frescoes of *Stories of the Martyrs* by Niccolò Pomarancio, who specialised in these gruesome, 'edifying' scenes (see pp. 428-429). Also by him is the oil painting of *St. Domitilla* over the left altar. On the outside of the triumphal arch, the vivid Byzantine-style mosaic dates from the 800 AD reconstruction; in the middle is the *Transfiguration*. In the presbytery area are notable 11th- to 15th-century marble furnishings: candelabra, a pulpit and a bishop's throne with lions, some of them cosmatesque.

BEFORE GOING

11. The Baths of Caracalla

The concept of sumptuous baths, whether public or private, goes back to ancient Egyptian and Ægean civilizations. Yet it was the Romans, with their technical bent, love of luxury and dedication to the more popular aspects of social life, who raised the baths to their peak, both as architectural creations and as public institutions. The oldest public baths in Italy have been found in Pompeii. Rome itself had none until Augustus. Custom had precluded such amenities: heated water, like the theatre (p. 245), was considered too frivolous for the stern Roman nature. Augustus, however, wanted Rome to look rich and monumental and ordered his son-in-law, Agrippa, to provide the first public baths, which were relatively small and located behind the Pantheon (p. 242).

Under later rulers, it became the policy to keep the people distracted and happy. Emperors competed in building the most impressive baths. Admission was very cheap and the baths became essential community centres. True to a certain Roman egalitarian spirit, though they were intended mainly for the populace, nobles and even emperors, such as Hadrian, often attended. Traces of smaller, more refined and exclusive baths have however been found in especially elegant districts, such as the Aventine. We've already seen how huge the Baths of Diocletian were in their reincarnation as a renaissance church; now we'll visit the best preserved, most decoratively splendid and technically innovative of the baths: the Baths of Caracalla. All baths followed the same basic layout. Service areas, shops, gyms, a stadium, even libraries with giant reading rooms surrounded a vast courtyard and garden used for exercise. The baths proper included dressing rooms, oiling rooms and saunas for sweating and resting, where the oils, dust and sweat were scraped off with curved metal or bone implements called strygils. You'll see a strygil on the famous statue of Apoxyomenos in the Vatican (p. 320). Bathers could choose between hot, warm and cold pools. On one side was a great swimming pool, used only in summer. Men and women had separate hours, though mixed bathing was not unusual, though deplored by moralists such as Quintilian, and occasionally prohibited by emperors, including Hadrian and Marcus Aurelius.

It must be added that historians don't agree on the precise rules and customs of the baths. The function of some spaces remains unknown. What is certain is that the baths were of paramount importance to the Romans, as many ancient writers have emphasised. Seneca, tutor and future victim of the emperor Nero, describes a day at the baths in a letter to his friend Lucilius:

I can't stand the noise any more – I live right over the public baths. The racket makes me regret having ears. When I hear that heavy breathing, those throaty rasps, the moans real or for show, I can just imagine those athletes twisting and turning and lifting their leaden weights. Actually most of them take it easy and go for the massage and the greasing, but then I get slapping noises, which differ depending on whether the masseur's hand is hitting flat or hollow.

Let's not talk of the ball players when they start keeping score! That's the pits! Add to this the din of the brawlers and the screams of the thief when he's caught. Not to mention the guy's voice who likes to listen to himself while he bathes. And all the diving with great splashing. But at least all these people have normal voices. My nightmare is the depilator with his thin reedy voice, now loud, now soft, with which he tries to make himself noticed over the crowd. He never shuts up, but when he pulls out underarm hairs, then it's the other guy who yells. And all the while the concessionaires are walking around calling for attention, each with his own special intonation – the drink vendor, the sausage seller, the pastry chef ...

The Baths of Caracalla were planned and begun by Emperor Septimius Severus, but built mainly by his son Caracalla (p. 165), officially called Marcus Aurelius Antoninus Bassianus (hence their official name, the Antonine Baths). One of the largest and best preserved of the ancient thermal complexes, the baths served up to 8,000 people daily in two or three shifts. They were renowned even in their own day for their technical perfection, the abundance and purity of the water – Caracalla built a new aqueduct for them – and the quantity and quality of the artwork. The baths were in perfect condition three centuries later, when they were named one of the wonders of Rome, but were abandoned shortly afterwards when Gothic invaders cut the aqueducts.

In the early middle ages the baths of Caracella became a source of building material, like other Roman monuments. Much of their contents was dispersed through Rome and elsewhere. Capitals from the libraries have turned up on the columns of S. Maria in Trastevere. Capitals from a gym, with eagles and lightning bolts symbolising Jove, are in the Cathedral of Pisa. Yet even during the renaissance the amount of art turning up in the excavations caused wonder. It included famous sculptural groups, such as the Farnese Bull and the Farnese Hercules, now in the National Archæological Museum in Naples, the two granite basins in Piazza Farnese (p. 480) and the mosaic of the Athletes now in the Vatican Museum (p. 680). The variety of marble floors and mosaics, a few still in place, was one of the largest decorative schemes of its kind in Rome.

ON THE SPOT

11. The Baths of Caracalla

On a ridge behind SS. Nereo e Achilleo stand the Baths of Caracalla, hidden by a brick wall erected 20 years after the inauguration of the baths in 216 AD. A portico (now gone) preceded the baths and a specially built street ran in front of the portico. This is one of Rome's most evocative and impressive monuments, only slightly smaller than the Baths of Diocletian (pp. 77-80) built 90 years later. Today the entrance is through the right end of the brick wall. (Open: 09:00- one hour before sunset; Mondays and holidays 09:00-14:00.)

From the entrance turn left and into the main body of the complex. Not all of the rooms have been identified with total certainty. A huge gymnasium (1) and service rooms lead to the *frigidarium* (2), the cold water room and heart of the establishment. On the other (eastern) side of the *frigidarium* is another gymnasium (3), symmetrical with the first. Parallel to this central suite of halls is another suite on the left, including changing rooms (4,5) and a *natatio*, or swimming pool (6). The area along the right side of the central suite was being restored at the time of writing, after half a century of misuse as a summer opera house; it is now closed, and the misuse has already recommenced, after a few years of restraint. It includes sauna-like rooms called *sudatoria* or *laconica* (7,8), a *tepidarium* (9), which had basins for lukewarm water, and the ruins of the *caldar-*

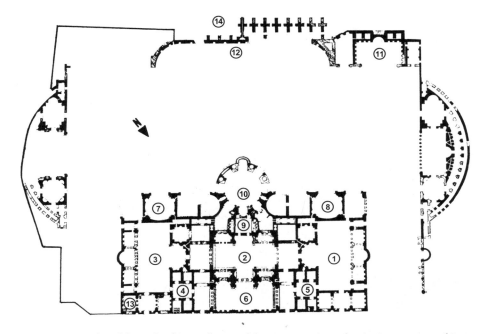

Plan of the Baths of Caracalla, one of the most evocative and majestic monuments of Rome

ium (10), a huge circular hall for hot water baths, once domed. (The imposing ruins of the *caldarium* are used as the opera stage.)

Some of the accessible spaces contain marvellous capitals, carved with images of gods, and pieces of multi-coloured floor mosaics. A walk through the huge exterior courtyard leads to the ruins, near its western corner (11), of one of two libraries – the one on the opposite corner has left no trace – and then to what remains of a stadium (12).

Deep beneath the eastern corner (near the eastern gymnasium), excavations begun in the 19th century have uncovered a 2nd-century AD house, which was destroyed to create the landfill on which the baths were built. Several frescoes detached from the house, depicting oriental and Roman divinities, are exhibited in one of the service rooms of the gymnasium (13), not always open. Some scholars feel they foreshadow the mania for exotic cults that gripped Rome at the time.

Highly interesting, but usually inaccessible (try ringing 06 6987 3017 to book a visit), is the substratum of the baths, a network of tunnels containing a heating system, firewood storage space and a mill probably connected to the eateries serving the baths. One of the tunnels later became a Mithræum (see glossary), of which a few architectural details remain. A dense web of narrower tunnels was for lead pipes and conduits, connected to large water tanks in the south side of the complex (14) and to the special aqueduct that fed them (see pp. 614-615).

From this point, the Walk can be continued in the direction of Porta S. Sebastiano and the Appian Way (see Excursions Outside the Walls, p. 612).

A CLOSER LOOK
AT THE FORUM AND THE PALATINE

Starting Point: the main entrance to the Roman Forum on Via dei Fori Imperiali (Largo Romolo e Remo, halfway between Piazza Venezia and the Colosseum). End point: See options on p. 295. Duration: $3^1/_2$ hrs.

Notes: 1) This description assumes you've viewed the Forum from above, an ideal way to get orientated generally, as suggested on p. 139. If you haven't, you can complete the description here by using all cross-references and reading the 'Before Going' section, pp. 153-159. This description also assumes you'll enter the site from the main entrance (see 'Starting Point' above).

2) The site is open daily until 19:15 in summer and until dusk in winter. Last admission an hour earlier.

3) All the Palatine, except the ruins of the main imperial palace, was closed to the public at the time of writing. On rare occasions restricted sites of the Forum and Palatine are open briefly for guided visits. Enquire at the Soprintendenza Archeologica: (06) 39967799 or (06) 6990110.

4) There are no eating facilities and picnicking is not allowed. There are water fountains at the main entrance, at the end of the Vicus Tuscus and near the Arch of Titus. Restrooms can be found at the main entrance, at the end of the Vicus Tuscus, in the Antiquarium on the Palatine and at the secondary exit on Via S. Gregorio.

Walk down the ramp. Where the first railing ends, to the right, is the razed **Basilica Æmilia** (p. 163), the oldest surviving prototype of the pagan and, later, Christian basilica. It takes its name from the ancient and aristocratic family who built it in the 2nd century AD (and who also built the great consular road, Via Æmilia, in northern Italy).

The nave, with two aisles, is 230ft (70m) long, about half the length of St. Peter's. After being burnt down it was rebuilt by Augustus with a grandiose two-storey portico. To the right are casts of part of the frieze that ran around the top of the first storey of the portico depicting the *Rape of the Sabine Women* and other early Roman episodes. The originals are in storage. Around the corner to the left of these casts are elements from the second storey, a simpler frieze and fragments of columns.

In the nave, to the left, is the partly standing side wall. The tufa blocks belong to the original

2nd century BC building, the marble blocks to its reconstruction under Augustus two centuries later. Note the remains of decorative frames around the entrances (remember that pagan basilicas opened on the long side).

Going around the basilica from the left, try to visualise its portico, of which two and a half pink columns of the ground floor still stand together at the far right. Behind the portico ran a row of shops, including moneychangers (who were also moneylenders and bankers). The ruins of these shops, part original, part rebuilt, are still visible.

Two-thirds of the way down this side of the basilica, near two ornate capitals on the floor, is a round marble base that belonged to the famous statue of *Venus Cloacina* ('of the sewer' – a reference to the Cloaca Maxima, see p. 282). Here, according to tradition, an early Roman stabbed his daughter, the virtuous Virginia, to death to save her from the lust of a powerful politician.

The Arch of Titus in the 1930's

Move on to the corner of the basilica. Behind the corner began a long street, the Argiletum, which climbed the Esquiline Hill (across the modern avenue outside the excavation). The famous Sacellum (small temple) of Janus, whose doors were always closed in peace time but open during war, was on this corner.

Excavations of the older basilica are at this end, under a protective roof. Note that everything in the earlier building was made of tufa, as in the oldest Roman temples (p. 243), including the columns, whose bases remain.

Here, too, you can see scattered green and dark spots on the marble floor – these are coins, perhaps dropped by the moneychangers working here, which melted in the fire that destroyed the building during the barbarian invasions.

After the Argiletum intersection the Comitium area begins; it was once the very centre of Roman political life. On the right is the **Curia**, meeting place of the Senate (p. 167).

Inside, the large steps supporting the 300 seats of the senators are still visible on the long sides,

while on the far short side, between the doors, is the dais of the presidency. A pedestal against the wall in the middle of the dais once supported a statue of the Winged Victory, source of a famous controversy (p. 158). In its place is a statue of an emperor which was found behind the Curia.

The multi-coloured marble floor has been restored by following a few of the original pieces. On both side walls are niches for statues flanked by columns. The remains of early medieval frescoes belong to the church built inside the Curia and dismantled when the Curia was restored in the 1930's.

Two marble reliefs from the time of Trajan (1st to 2nd century AD) are usually exhibited in this room. Originally the parapets of a vanished building in the Forum, they depict two glorious events in the emperor's reign: Trajan instituting a system of free food distribution for poor children and orphans, and Trajan ordering the records of tax arrears to be destroyed. The buildings in the reliefs are those of the Forum at the time of Trajan. The sacred fig tree (p. 281) appears in both reliefs.

The eastern end of the Forum

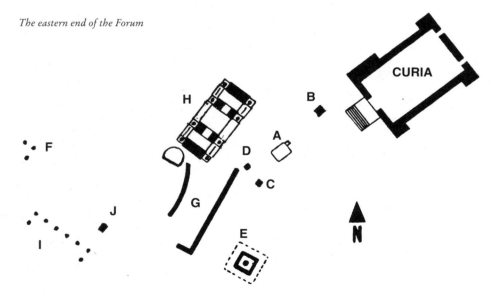

On the ground opposite the Curia is the **Lapis Niger** with the so-called Tomb of Romulus (A), which was possibly a Sanctuary of Vulcan (p. 167). It contains a mysterious archaic inscription and despite its great interest is usually inaccessible, ostensibly for lack of security personnel.

Several interesting monumental pedestals are in this area. Between the Lapis Niger and the Curia is a pedestal (B) dedicated to Mars and the founders of Rome by Emperor Maxentius, whose name was chiselled off in *damnatio memoriæ* when he was ousted and killed by Constantine in 312 AD (p. 198). (This 'obliteration of the record', literally 'condemnation of the memory' was a not infrequent formal procedure.) The name is still faintly visible over the line 'Invictus Aug'.

Beyond the Lapis Niger on the left is a pedestal (C) dedicated to three co-emperors whose general, the great Flavius Stilicho, defeated the barbarian Goths in 403 AD. Stilicho's name was also chiselled off (over the 'S.P.Q.R.') when jealousies and intrigues led to his execution. On the right (D) is the elaborately sculpted base (303 AD) of a column commemorating victories over the barbarians, which we have already seen from above (p. 167). One relief shows a procession of senators; another, the emperor drinking ceremonially to the god Mars. In his retinue is a *flamen martialis*, a priest of Mars, with the strange spiked helmet which we saw in another relief three centuries older (p. 223).

Face the pedestals with the Lapis Niger behind you: beyond them, in front of you, is the tall **Column of Phocas** (E); see p. 166.

Phocas was a 7th-century emperor of Byzantium, the Eastern Empire, which then ruled over the city of Rome from its capital, Constantinople (modern Istanbul). The Roman authorities honoured him with this column, after he donated the Pantheon to the Church on a visit to Rome. Phocas had taken power by murdering his predecessor and his five children, and was himself murdered upon returning to Constantinople.

Between the Column of Phocas and the three columns from the **Temple of Vespasian** (F) on the right (p. 161) is a modern wall (G). It incorporates fragments of the famous **Rostra**, the dais from which politicians addressed the crowd.

The dais was decorated with bronze rams from the ships captured in a crucial 4th-century BC naval battle. The word *rostrum* originally meant 'ram'; it has since acquired the additional meaning of 'dais' because of the association of the two in this particular monument.

Julius Cæsar moved the Rostra here from its site near the Curia when he renovated the whole Comitium area of the Forum. Vestiges of the original Rostra have been found under the present pavement, and the earlier tufa block pavement of the Comitium has been identified under the marble one that Cæsar built.

Near the Rostra, on the right, is the grand **Arch of Septimius Severus** (H); see pp. 164-165. Walk through it, admiring its beautiful ceiling. Keeping to the left, proceed to the base of the **Temple of Saturn** (I) with its eight columns; see p. 161. A few yards away from the base, on the right, is a rounded fragment with a frieze; this is the base of the *Milliarium Aureum* (J), or Gilded Milestone, erected by Augustus to indicate an ideal convergence point of all the roads of the Roman Empire. The distance of all other cities was measured from this stone.

If you now go around the Temple of Saturn to the right and up, you can approach the podium of the **Portico of the Harmonious Gods**; see p. 160. (Then return to the base of the Temple of Saturn.)

Here you are standing on the last level stretch of the Via Sacra, before it becomes the Clivus Capitolinus and starts climbing the Capitol. With your back to the Temple of Saturn, concentrate on this last stretch.

To the left, a short distance from the Column of Phocas, a fig tree, an olive tree and a grapevine grow on an unpaved square area. These plants were sacred to Rome, and were planted here symbolically (we saw the sacred fig engraved on one of Trajan's parapets, p. 280). They are on the edge of an esplanade, a rectangular area paved in travertine (the Forum square proper) in the centre of the

Forum. On the long side (your side) the square is marked by a row of huge brick pedestals which were once marble-covered and surmounted by large honorary columns. These are all gone, except for two, which have been re-erected at the end of the row. Proceed until you are between the second and third pedestal.

On the ground in front of you, there is a wheel with spokes crudely sketched on the marble; it is one of the many board games (*tabulæ lusoriæ*) that the idle scratched on the pavement or monuments of the Forum. They are round or square and include checkerboards and boards for tic-tac-toe-like games.

To the left of the sacred plants the pavement is inscribed with the name Lucius Nevius Sordinus, the magistrate who last restored the esplanade in the time of Augustus (the bronze letters have recently been redone).

Go to the next space between the pedestals that makes an indentation. Before you a tufa and marble enclosure marks the site of the last puddle of the Forum marsh, *Lake Curtius* (see p. 156).

According to tradition, the warrior Curtius jumped into the lake with his horse and vanished in the 5th-century BC, after an oracle demanded such a sacrifice in order to avert disaster for the city. The relief is a cast of one that was here in Republican times.

Slightly to the left is a square pit, one of several in the area that formed a system of underground galleries and elevators like the one in the Colosseum. It was created by Julius Cæsar when gladiatorial games were held here, before the great amphitheatre was built.

Further ahead, in an excavation on the Forum square, is the base of a colossal statue of Emperor Domitian on horseback, which no longer exists. It stood almost 40ft (13m) high.

The underground supports which anchored three of the horse's hoofs – the fourth was raised – are still visible. The statue was destroyed in *damnatio memoriæ* after the emperor's gruesome murder (p. 156).

Beyond the dig is the raised base of a much

smaller equestrian monument to Emperor Constantine, which has also gone.

An additional bit of history: this is the very spot on the Via Sacra where, in the year-long commotion following the death of Nero (68-69 AD), the first of three short-reigning emperors, Galba, was tossed from his litter and killed by rebel soldiers.

Let's now examine the other side of the Via Sacra. In front of us, on a raised platform of long marble steps, is the **Basilica Julia** (p. 161), which we'll now approach.

The grandest building at this end of the Forum, it stood within a double-colonnaded, two-storey portico. The interior was 270ft (90m) long, with a nave, two sets of aisles and three floors One of the piers on the porch is a 19th-century reconstruction. Next to it, flanking what was the main entrance in the middle of the long side, are two plinths labelled with the names of two great Greek sculptors, Trimarchos and Polyclitus (p. 319), statues by whom were placed here in the 4th century.

Here and there on the upper steps more board games can be seen (on the left note grooves in the marble for minature billiards and, further on, a circle with the carved word *oraculo*).

In order to build his basilica, Cæsar destroyed a much older, smaller basilica which had in turn been built over the house of the great general Scipio Africanus, nemesis of Hannibal in the second war against Carthage. Recent digs have found remains of both these buildings.

Continue along the Via Sacra. Where the Basilica Julia ends, the Vicus Tuscus, the famous commercial street, begins on the right. On this short side the basilica borders the massive base of the **Temple of Castor and Pollux** (p. 162). Across the Vicus, under the platform of the Basilica Julia, is one of the original entrances to the **Cloaca Maxima**, the ancient sewer that allowed reclamation of the Forum valley and was later extended under most of the city (pp. 156, 259). Proceed along the Vicus in order to see the ruins of huge buildings of uncertain nature on your left, perhaps the service buildings of the first imperial palace on the Palatine, which we saw earlier from above

(p. 160). A tablet here saying 'Tempio di Augusto' does not indicate an actual ruin, but only the general area in which a temple to Augustus once stood. Where the excavation ends are the ruins (generally closed) of great grain storehouses, *horrea*, that flanked the commercial street where it met the food markets of the Velabrum (p. 256) outside the Forum.

Return to the Via Sacra where it turns sharply. Don't turn with it but pause and look for large white marble slabs lining the pavement before you. They indicate the approach to the former **Arch of Augustus**, 30 yards away beyond a couple of steps, now reduced to a few sad marble blocks. (The arch was torn down in the 1540's to provide material for the new St. Peter's, see p. 357.) Go as far as the steps in order to see the remains, which belong to the central opening (the arch was the first to be built with three openings). Then, without taking the steps, go sharply left. At mid-block, as the climax of an area full of memories of Cæsar and Augustus, is the ruined **Temple of the Deified Cæsar**, built by Augustus on the spot where Cæsar's body was placed after his assassination (p. 166).

The temple proper rose over and beyond the semicircle of tufa blocks. The semicircle encloses older blocks, beyond which is a mound, the site of Cæsar's funeral pyre. This is where Mark Antony read Cæsar's testament to the people. In antiquity, the temple had a front balcony adorned with other Rostra (see p. 281), those of the Egyptian fleet that the future Augustus captured from Mark Antony and Cleopatra.

Continue to the crossing. You are back at the Basilica Æmilia. Turn right, picking up the Via Sacra in its main stretch. At the first corner on the left a large inscription exalts Lucius, grandson of Augustus and heir apparent (p. 218), as *princeps juventutis* or 'prince of youth' ('L. Cæsar ... principi,' etc.).

Along with a similar inscription to Lucius' brother, Caius, the slab was part of the Arch of Lucius and Caius that spanned the Via here, concluding the Augustan section of the Forum.

Directly across the modern entrance ramp, take a dirt path leading you back to the vestiges of the Arch of Augustus (A).

If the decades of inconclusive restorations are over and the area is reopened, proceed through it in the same general direction, keeping the three columns of the Temple of Castor and Pollux (C) on your right. Otherwise the itinerary picks up on page 284, at the Temple of Vesta.

From the Via Sacra to the Oratory of the Forty Martyrs

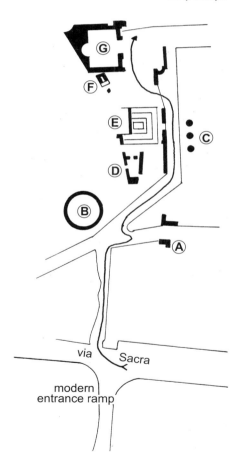

The building immediately to the left (D) housed the Office of Waters that managed the aqueducts. Past it is a rectangular basin (E), an ancient fountain marking the spot where the early Romans, long before the first aqueducts were built, found one of their major sources of drinking water. They identified it with a divine spirit, and called it the 'Spring of the Nymph Juturna'.

Legend had it that after Castor and Pollux helped the Roman army win a crucial early battle, the twin demi-gods came to Rome to bring the good news and were seen watering their horses at the fountain. Reliefs on an altar nearby (a cast) depict Juturna and the twins.

Past the fountain and slightly to the left (F) are a marble shrine, rebuilt in modern times using original fragments, a basin and an altar, all part of late imperial renovations of the cult area of Juturna.

Beyond the Spring of Juturna, set back on the left, is an ancient Roman building (G), which was turned into an oratory or reliquary in the early middle ages; it is the first Christian monument we see in the Forum. Later abandoned, it was excavated in 1901. It is called the **Oratory of the Forty Martyrs** from the subject of its apse frescoes, which are almost gone.

The martyrs were imperial soldiers in Armenia, who were executed for having converted to Christianity. (More on this on p. 582.) The frescoes are from the 8th century; the one on the left wall, better preserved, depicts saints.

Abutting the Palatine here are more service buildings of the imperial palace (the first one, built by Tiberius and Caligula). The building before you, perhaps the barracks of the emperor's guard originally, was partly turned into a church and *diaconia* (p. 254) in the 6th century; it is still called by its Latin name, **S. Maria Antiqua** ('the Old').

The history of the name is as complex as that of the church. Damaged in a 9th-century earthquake, the church was abandoned and the cult moved to a new church nearby, S. Maria Nova (now also called S. Francesca Romana, see p. 196). Later, another church was built over this one, which was forgotten. When the superimposed church was torn down during excavations in 1902 the ruins of the old church were found.

The church is artistically and historically important for its cycles of 7th- to 9th-century frescoes, sometimes overlaid in as many as three layers. As the great scholar of Roman medieval art, Richard Krautheimer, observed, 'Continually redecorated and repainted for three centuries, the church reflects the successive currents of painting in Rome during that period... All [the paintings] testify to an invasion of Rome by Byzantine contemporary art, to its taking root, being absorbed and quickly transposed into a local dialect.'

At the entrance a corridor to the left leads to a covered ramp rising to the Palatine. Past an open forecourt (or atrium) with traces of frescoes, and an inner narthex or porch, the central nave of the church is full of marble remains from the choir. In the left aisle is the base of a pulpit with an 8th-century inscription in which Pope John VII proclaims himself 'Servant of the Mother of God'.

In the left aisle are pagan and Christian sarcophagi, one with the biblical story of Jonah and the whale, and three bands of frescoes, the two upper ones with episodes from the Old Testament, the lower one with Christ and saints of the Latin and Greek Church.

In the right aisle are fragments of frescoes and one detached from the atrium, the *Madonna Enthroned between Saints and Angels*, with a portrait of the late 8th-century Pope Adrian I, who was alive then, as the square halo shows.

Around the presbytery are frescoes of biblical episodes. In the apse are mid-8th century frescoes of *Christ Blessing the Faithful* and the *Virgin introducing Pope Paul I to Christ*. This pope too has a square halo.

To the right of the apse are three layers of 6th- to 8th-century frescoes.

In a chapel to the left of the apse is a Crucifixion in a niche. To the left is Pope Zacharias (mid-8th century, see p. 404) with a square halo; to the right is a fresco of his contemporary, Theodotus, a high prelate, and his wife, presenting two children to the Virgin. Near the entrance, to the left, Theodotus asks the protection of St Quiricus and St Julitta. To the right is the *Unknown Martyrs* (a Latin inscription reads: 'Their name is known to God').

Retrace your steps to the remnants of the Arch of Augustus. Observe the round **Temple of Vesta** (B) nearby; see p. 162. Most of the structure has been rebuilt, but some marble fragments date from imperial times (originally it was just a straw hut). The roof was open to let out smoke from the sacred fire.

In the temple was an inner sanctum, which only the priestesses could enter, containing objects thought to influence the future of Rome, including the *palladium*, an archaic image of Minerva.

Behind the temple is the (destroyed) **House of the Vestals** (p. 162), preceded by a rectangular shrine-like structure with the base for the missing statue of the goddess Vesta.

As part of a 'Jubilee Year 2000' programme to make the Forum more accessible to the crowds, the House of the Vestals, one of the most interesting features of the Forum, was put off-limits and at the time of writing it is still closed. If it has not been re-opened, you'll have to pick up the itinerary five paragraphs down.

Rebuilt after Nero's fire and again later, the house is entered by a footbridge, which is over tufa traces of the earlier, Republican building. It comprises a central cloister-like atrium, with three enclosures of uncertain use in the middle, amid statues of the dowager vestals (Vestales Maximæ). The statues are all from the last two centuries of paganism. Found in a heap and unidentifiable, they were put back on pedestals haphazardly. The pedestal inscriptions exalt the holiness and piety of these elder priestesses, except for one in a corner across from the footbridge, whose name was erased in *damnatio memoriæ* (p. 165). The base could belong to the statue of one of the last Vestales Maximæ, Claudia, who converted to Christianity in the dying days of paganism, thereby incurring the wrath of the other priestesses.

The building had three floors. On the short side

near the footbridge there was probably a communal dining room. At the other end there is a large hall with a high ceiling which was probably used for rituals. It is surrounded by six rooms, one for each Vestal (there were always six). They did not live in these rooms, but in much more comfortable quarters on the second floor of the long side, opposite the footbridge, where traces of several heated bathrooms have been found. On the third floor lived their many servants. Kitchens and other service rooms were on the ground floor.

The six priestesses varied greatly in age, as they were chosen from patrician families at the age of six to ten and had to serve at least 30 years: ten as novices, ten in active duty and ten as teachers. (See p. 162 for a discussion of the restrictions and privileges of their lives.)

Take the footbridge back. Leave the site and go straight. Before reaching the Via Sacra, behind a platform on the left are the foundations of the Regia, the ancestral office of the Pontifex Maximus, high priest of the Roman state. In the remote period of the monarchy (8th to 6th centuries BC) the kings themselves performed this role, and excavations in 2005 suggested that they too had their residence on this spot.

The Regia is a confused complex of buildings, some so ancient that they were little more than primitive huts, as their foundations show. Other structures included a Sanctuary of Mars, which also served as an archive for important documents and which contained the hanging 'Spears of Mars' and a temple to an ancient agricultural goddess served by the 'jumping priests', the *salii* (p. 157).

Reaching the Via Sacra, before you (slightly to the left) is the superb **Temple of Antoninus and Faustina** (p. 163), occupied by the church of S. Lorenzo in Miranda, which is why the temple was not destroyed like the others. Not for lack of trying, however. High up on the columns you can see deep indentations left by the ropes of medieval marble pillagers when they tried to pull the building down. Evidently it was too sturdy for them.

The mid-2nd century AD temple was dedicated by the emperor Antoninus, father of Marcus

Aurelius (p. 146), to his wife, Faustina senior, whom he deified when she died, and to Antoninus himself, similarly deified by the Senate. The top line of the inscription was added then.

The brick steps in the front are modern, but the brick ruins of an altar in the middle are original. The statue, which is higher up, was found inside. The church, which occupies the inner cell of the temple, is entered from the other side, p. 193.

On the right flank of the temple the remains of an early Iron Age cemetery, originally covering much of the Forum valley, were found in 1902. The cemetery, contemporary with the traditional date of the founding of Rome (753 BC), dramatically confirmed that there were indeed human settlements at that date on the nearby Palatine (p. 156).

About 40 tombs from the 9th to 7th centuries BC have been excavated. Their fascinating contents are in a small museum in the Forum, which we'll reach shortly, but which is (at the time of writing) closed most of the time.

Proceed uphill along the Via Sacra. Past the cemetery are the ruins of a Republican era building at a level lower than the street. Its layout suggests a small hotel or perhaps a prison.

Next is another temple which also owes its survival to having been turned into a church (SS. Cosma e Damiano, whose entrance is on the other side, see p. 193). Confused with a similar temple depicted on an ancient coin, until recently it was wrongly thought to be dedicated to the deified son of Emperor Maxentius, Romulus, who died in childhood. (The wrong identification tablet was still hanging there at the time of writing, even though the error was discovered ten years ago.) The temple was indeed built by Maxentius (p. 198) in the early 4th century AD, but as a **Temple of the Penates**, twin deities who protected families.

An earlier Temple of the Penates had stood further uphill, but when Maxentius built the enormous basilica we shall shortly see there, he rebuilt the temple here. The central structure is flanked by two halls, now in ruins, each of which must have contained the statues of the twin gods.

The right hall still has two columns in front. The temple has beautiful bronze doors whose lock still works perfectly. The frieze over the entrance is too fine and classical to be from the age of Maxentius and Constantine, when decadence had set in (p. 201). It must have come from the earlier temple, or some other earlier building. The roof and the tiny dome are part of its transformation into a church.

Notice that most of the foundations of the temple are laid bare; two sewers are visible. This is because the early 19th-century archæologists who first unearthed the rising section of the Via Sacra destroyed the street at the entrance level of the building, mistaking it for a medieval construction, though it was in fact contemporary with the ancient buildings. The present level is at least three centuries older.

A few steps further uphill, on the left, is a five-arched medieval porch, whose position indicates the level of the street at that time.

Continuing, on the right are the confused, unidentifiable remains of ancient shopping malls called *Piperataria* ('of the pepper', meaning spices from the Orient in general) and *Margaritaria* ('of the pearls', meaning jewellery in general). On the left we come to the **Basilica of Maxentius** (or of Constantine, who finished it), which we passed on Via dei Fori Imperiali (p. 195).

Maxentius began this immense construction – which served as a meeting hall, a tribunal and occasionally a trade centre – as if to prove that under him, Rome, then well into its decline, was still capable of its great architectural feats of the past. This is indeed the last building to bear the full imprint of Roman genius.

But it was Maxentius' co-emperor, Constantine, who completed it, altering it substantially, after installing himself in Rome in 312 AD as sole ruler.

The basilica was entered from this side and consisted of a central nave and two side aisles. Advancing to where it is fenced off, we can see the whole colossal display of ruins. And this is just one of the aisles; the other one and the nave, which are gone, we crossed as we entered. The nave was

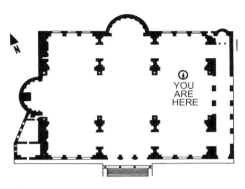

Basilica of Maxentius

wider than the aisles and much higher, reaching 115ft (35m)! The piers that divided the nave from the aisles were flanked by eight huge columns, all missing except for one that was moved to the square of S. Maria Maggiore in the 17th century (p. 99).

The stumps in the centre are the piers of the nave. The immense pillars and the vaults of the ceiling, the largest ever built, with their magnificent octagonal coffers, exude an unforgettable grandeur, and were a major inspiration to Renaissance architects and artists.

An apse at the end of the nave held a colossal statue of Constantine, fragments of which are in the Capitoline Museum. One of its feet alone measures 6 ft (1 m 80) long. On the floor is a giant chunk of the ceiling, which collapsed during an earthquake in 1349.

This is the only ancient basilica with vaulted concrete ceilings; these were normally used for the giant baths, so the early archæologists mistook it for a bath.

Next to the basilica are the convent, bell tower and façade of **S. Maria Nova/S. Francesca Romana**, entered from outside the Forum (p. 196). Here in the Forum, at the rear end of the right side of the church, is the unmarked entrance (at the time of writing) to a small **Museum of the Forum**, containing full reconstructions of the Iron

Age tombs mentioned on p. 286.

It displays artefacts from the necropolis – human remains, including coffins of children dug out of tree trunks – and statues, architectural elements, inscriptions, etc. from the Forum. According to the Soprintendenza Archeologica (based in the same building), custodian of Italy's archæological assets, the museum is officially open. In reality, it is almost always closed and the sign on the wall advertising its existence was stealthily removed some time ago.

Approach the nearby Arch of Titus. You are now on the Velia, the ridge that enclosed the Forum valley on this side. The Via Sacra passed under the Arch, then ended in the Colosseum area (p. 200).

The **Arch of Titus** (p. 209) was erected after the death of Emperor Titus to honour him and his father, Emperor Vespasian, for their victory in the Palestinian War of 70 AD (pp. 192-193).

The arch is thought to have been built by the brother and successor of Titus, Domitian (p.156). But this is disputed, mainly because of the dash and vigour of the reliefs, which are more characteristic of the stylistic perfection of sculpture reached a few years later under Trajan. For many centuries the arch was embedded in a medieval fortress, which helped preserve it. It was isolated and extensively restored by Valadier in the early 19th century. You can easily recognise the parts that were rebuilt, especially on the outside and the top. Because of the grievous error made when the road was excavated (p. 286), the arch appears to be suspended in mid-air, with its foundations exposed. The Colosseum side is better preserved.

The famous reliefs in the arch are unfortunately badly eroded, even more so after a recent cleaning. They depict the triumph celebrated by the two emperors in the Forum. One shows the start of the parade, with soldiers carrying treasures from the destroyed Temple of Jerusalem: the seven-branched candlestick and the silver trumpets. The other depicts Titus on his triumphal chariot being crowned by Victory. The horses are led by the deified Rome; the Senate and the people of Rome

Arch of Titus before the Valadier restoration, from an 18th-century print

are symbolised by two men, one in a toga, the other bare-chested. In the centre of the vault is Titus lifted to the heavens by an eagle.

Pass in front of the arch on the Forum side and go just a couple of steps up the ancient street, called in modern times the Clivus Palatinus or 'Palatine Climb'. On the right turn up the Via Nova ('New Street'), which is unpaved at this end. The street was another main artery of the Forum; to the right it overlooks excavations begun in the early 1990's, which unearthed remains of walls thought to be those of Rome when it was still a village on the Palatine (pp. 42, 188).

After a few steps, turn left to reach the hilltop, up a double staircase that forms the entrance to an early baroque building. In the late 16th century the slope and hilltop were bought by the princely Farnese family (pp. 46, 478) and turned into a botanical garden by the architect Girolamo Rainaldi. There were probably already steps leading from the Forum to the hilltop in ancient

Roman times. Those you are now climbing form two landings, enlivened by artificial grottoes, a typical baroque creation. The lower one frames a fountain, the Nymphæum of Rain. The space was once decorated and frescoed (traces remain).

On the hilltop you reach a building consisting of two wings, which formed an aviary, the main ornament of the botanical garden. Just in front of it, behind a parapet, is the ancient tunnel (*Cryptoporticus)* connecting the two imperial palaces.

If the part of the Palatine closed to the public has not yet been reopened, proceed directly to the 'expanse of ruins' of the newer palace on p. 292.

Since the Jubilee Year 2000, the year in which the Roman authorities promised to introduce the world to the splendours of Rome, much of its most revered site, the Palatine Hill, has been closed to the public. The fascinating features described on the following pages, down to paragraph four of page 292, are at present inaccessible for the first time in modern history. You'll probably have to follow a sharply curtailed itinerary, heading directly for the newer imperial palace. Even if areas are still closed, it is still worth reading the next few pages for the sake of orientation, for the bits and pieces that can still be seen in the distance and to ponder what you are missing.

The magnificent botanical garden, the oldest in the world conceived as a systematic exposition of plant species, covered part of the hilltop. Past the aviary we find the first ruins of the imperial palaces. Proceed to the middle of a brick parapet overlooking a two-level baroque fountain. From the parapet look down to the right at the start of a long gallery. This is the *Cryptoporticus* ('secret' or 'hidden underground' portico) linking the two main palaces. Do not go down yet, as you'll reach the tunnel later from the opposite end.

Viewed from the parapet, the whole area to the right was the grounds of the oldest imperial palace, that of Tiberius as enlarged by Caligula (Domus Tiberiana; see p. 155). Practically nothing of it remains above ground. Archæological probes in

the 1880's revealed a grand central courtyard, but the probes were not pursued and the building is still basically unexplored. For an idea of where it stood, take the path leading off to the right, roughly in line with the parapet, and you'll be walking over the buried palace. Continue straight to the rim of the hill, then look down into the Forum. On the slope are impressive ruins of the service buildings and substructures of the palace. We saw these ruins earlier from below (p. 282), as well as those of other service buildings, including the one turned into the church of S. Maria Antiqua on the slope around the corner (p. 284).

From the rim of the hill, as you may recall (p. 155), Caligula built a bridge joining the palace (at the point where you are now standing) to the Temple of Jupiter on the Capitol.

Nearby look for a solitary headless statue. Directly in front of it, take the path that crosses the botanical garden (the buried palace is still beneath you) and leads to an octagonal maze of hedges that reproduces an ancient brick labyrinth, which we'll see later. Past it, continue over the buried palace

Plan of the Farnese Gardens

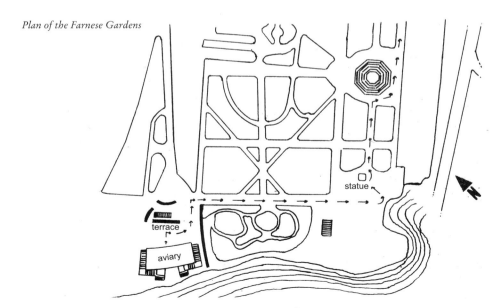

until you come to a metal railing. Go down the steps at the end of the railing to the left and stop. On your left is the little that has been excavated of the **Palace of Tiberius**, a row of store rooms. Recently more probes have been made in preparation for further digs.

Let's forget the imperial palaces for a while and explore an extremely ancient area. On the right, a large shapeless mound of gravel and bricks is the base of the **Temple of Cybele**, a mysterious mother figure and goddess of the forces of nature, whose cult the Romans borrowed from the Middle East in very ancient times.

During the Second Punic War (218-201 BC; p. 256), part of the desperate struggle against Carthage, the Romans, facing defeat, feared they had lost favour with their gods; so they thought of importing new ones such as this. The cult was based on a black stone, possibly a meteorite, whose owners lent it to the Romans for some years, during which time it was kept in this temple. A majestic statue of the *Great Mother*, which was found headless near the ruin, has been placed in the Palatine Antiquarium (p. 294).

Beyond the Temple of Cybele is an area tied to the very origins of Rome. Here the ancient Romans piously maintained in perfect condition a thatched hut which they claimed was the original house of Romulus, Rome's mythical founder (not to be confused with the son of Maxentius by the same name, see p. 286). They replaced its straw roof regularly.

The hut is gone, but traces of others from a similarly remote time are nearby. Leave the area between the store rooms of the Palace of Tiberius and the base of the Temple of Cybele. Keeping the temple base to your right, proceed to a roof covering a tufa platform with a pattern of holes in the ground. These holes are the foundations (excavated in 1948) of three early **Iron Age huts**. Whether one of these was Romulus' matters little. The fact is that these are the earliest traces of human settlement on the Palatine and belong precisely to the period to which tradition assigns the foundation of Rome (pp. 27, 286).

The largest hut had a rounded rectangular base 12 ft x 16 ft (3.65 m x 4.8 m). Six holes on the perimeter held poles that supported walls of straw and mud. Another hole in the centre held a taller pole to support the roof. Two smaller holes on the short side mark the location of the door; another two in front of these, perhaps a small canopy. The model corresponds exactly to cinerary urns shaped like miniature huts found in the tombs of the ancestral cemetery in the Forum (p. 286).

On one side of the excavation are rough steps cut in the tufa; they are thought to be the remains of a theatre built by a Roman magistrate on the Palatine in the 2nd century BC. It was promptly torn down by conservative authorities still opposed to any permanent theatre. (p. 245).

With your back to the excavation, take a short detour to the right to see an archaic cistern and other extremely ancient remains. Return to the Temple of Cybele and continue along the row of rooms belonging to the Palace of Tiberius. To the right are more archaic cisterns. At the end of the path descend the three steps to the left of the ramp. In the first structure on the right is the present entrance to the House of Livia, a wing of a larger compound of houses belonging to Augustus, and to Livia herself.

What is traditionally called the **House of Livia** was found in the mid-19th century by archæologists looking for the residence of Augustus, which they knew was in the area, a relatively modest villa formerly belonging to the lawyer Hortensius (see p. 154). It may well be this house, but was identified more excitingly as the House of Livia after the dramatic discovery of lead water-pipes marked 'Juliæ Aug.', a name applicable to the wife of Augustus as member of his adoptive Julia family. Roman regulations required those few citizens with private water supplies to put their names. It is indeed possible that this part of the compound was at some point reserved to Livia, although this Julia could be one of a number of Imperial ladies.

In any case there is no reason to doubt that this building was part of the compound of Augustus, who had added several buildings to Hortensius'

Paintings in the House of Livia, late 1st century BC; as seen at the end of the 19th century

villa. He didn't seek luxury but did need space, as rulers were expected to conduct public business in their homes (see p. 211).

The remains of the House of Livia consist of a courtyard with a mosaic floor surrounded by four rooms, all with late 1st century BC frescoes (i.e. from the time of Augustus), the style of which recalls the frescoes of the destroyed city of Pompeii (the 'Second Pompeian' style). Three of the rooms face the long side of the courtyard. The middle one (perhaps a reception and living room, or *tablinum*) has a fresco reproducing a famous Greek painting of the myth of Io. The princess Io, turned into a cow by a jealous goddess, is imprisoned by the many-eyed giant Argos; the god Hermes arrives to free her. The famous lead pipes with Livia's name on them are usually shown here. The two other rooms, as well as the fourth on the short side of the courtyard (tentatively identified

as the *triclinium* or dining room) have splendid ornamental frescoes.

Service rooms and another courtyard are at the back of the house. The other buildings of the compound abut the house on this side. Though partly obliterated by the construction of the imperial palace (see below), they have been fairly certainly identified by archæologists. A two-storey building is likely to have been the **House of Augustus** proper, which has been excavated and identified only in recent years, and is presently being reinforced. The house can be divided on the basis of the richness of its decoration into a private part (with simple mosaic floors) and a public part (with multi-coloured marble floors); the latter faces a colonnaded courtyard. Three rooms with frescoes in the Second Pompeian style are of special interest here: a 'room of the masks', a 'room of perspectives' and a delightful, exquisitely coloured 'small study of Augustus' (the identification is uncertain). Two libraries, Greek and Latin, frequent components of public complexes (p. 184), have also been identified in the compound.

Resume your walk in the same direction. At the end of the path on the left the *Cryptoporticus* begins, which we saw from the opposite end near the aviary (p. 288). It marks the edge of the Palace of Tiberius on the left, to which it was connected by several entrances (now walled-up). Walk down the tunnel for a few yards to see its most interesting features, the refined ceiling stucco (a copy; the original and fragments of faded frescoes from the walls of the corridor are in the Palatine Antiquarium, see below p. 294) and the floor in herringbone brickwork and mosaic. You may recall that the tunnel linked the imperial palace of Tiberius and Caligula to that of their successors, which we'll reach next.

Walk back and take the steps around to the right. Past an oval ruin in the ground (a fish-pond), continue up, then to the right and down again. As you arrive at the foot of the steps, an expanse of ruins comes into view.

The part of the Palatine at present off-limits ends here. From here you can get a glimpse of the end of the *Cryptoporticus*, the beginning of which we saw near the aviary (p. 288).

This expanse of ruins belongs to the final, magnificent imperial palace. We'll just use them as a reference point for now. Approach them along the dirt path leading to the right. Stop several yards before the entrance to the site, marked by steps.

Note a dark, shapeless mound to your far right (but don't go to it). This was the base of the Temple of Apollo built by Augustus next to his compound and famous for its splendid coloured marble columns and statues by the greatest Greek masters. The Sybilline books (p. 255) were kept here under a statue of Apollo.

Turn your attention again to the ruins of the **Imperial Palace**. Before entering, read the basic information in the next seven paragraphs.

By the mid-1st century AD the palace built only a few years earlier by Tiberius and enlarged by Caligula on the Forum side had already become inadequate for the needs of the emperors. Caligula began a new building, which Claudius and Nero continued after him, on this side of the Palatine overlooking the Circus Maximus (see p. 267). It encroached on splendid private homes (including the 'House of the Griffins' and others discussed on p. 154). The *Cryptoporticus* was built last, on the orders of Nero.

In 64 AD the 'Fire of Nero' (p. 155) ravaged two-thirds of the city, devastating the buildings on the Palatine too. So Nero built for himself the huge Domus Aurea, which began elsewhere on the Palatine and spread to other hills (p. 210). His successors Vespasian and Titus tore down most of the complex and returned the land to the people (p. 211), but spared the main house, in which they took up residence themselves. It survives at the foot of the Oppian Hill (pp. 212 -213).

Domitian, brother and successor of Titus, and a great builder (pp. 156, 161, 180, 235, 287, 452), rebuilt the imperial palace on this side of the Palatine at the end of the 1st century AD, entrusting the project to his famous architect, Rabirius. Before us is this last, glorious edifice. It served as a dynastic seat for rulers, not only in the remaining four centuries of the empire, but into the middle ages, when barbarian kings, Byzantine emissaries, Germanic emperors and even popes lived there.

The fact that this is a single palace is often blurred by the assortment of names used to designate it or parts of it, such as the Palace of Domitian, Domus Flavia or Domus Augustana (the latter meaning 'of the Augusti', as all emperors were called in honour of the first, not 'of Augustus' the individual).

Before us, the section of ruins strewn along the remains of once towering walls defines one side of the palace. On another side (to the right if you face the present entrance) the palace overlooks the Circus Maximus. The opposite side, extending to your left at the top of the Palatine, was the original front with its main entrances. It opened onto a flat area, the Area Palatina, which is now gone, the soil having slid down.

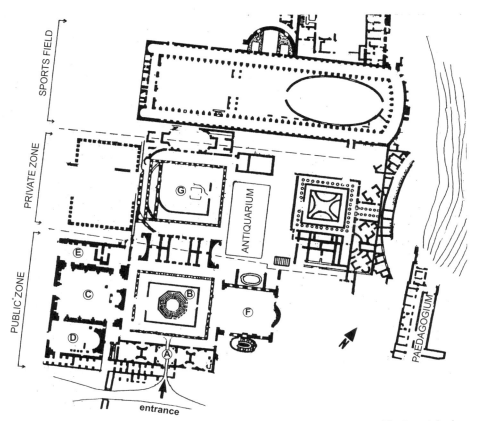

The Imperial palace

On this esplanade, the wise Emperor Pertinax, predecessor of Septimius Severus, was murdered by his own soldiers in 193 AD, the chaotic 'Year of the Five Emperors'. He had reigned for only a few months.

Under the palace ruins are others related to Nero's construction and to two sumptuous private Republican-era homes. The best preserved is the 'House of the Griffins', so-called for its frescoes. Public access, however, is normally restricted. Frescoes from the two houses, along with other objects found in the Palatine excavations, have been moved to the Antiquarium (see below).

The palace complex has two general zones, one for the public activities of the emperors, the other for their private use. Enter the site: you now are in the public zone.

The Public Zone. Past the remains of a porch (A) is a huge, columned courtyard, called a peristyle (B), centred on a ruined octagonal fountain shaped like a labyrinth – the one which inspired the maze in the Renaissance botanical garden (p. 289). The columns, now stumps, are of rare marbles.

Towards the Area Palatina side, to the left, the peristyle meets three large rooms (now fenced off). The middle one (C), the largest, is the *Throne Room*, where the emperor gave audience sitting in state in the apse. At the opposite end a colonnade articulated the façade of the building, which opened onto the Area Palatina. The majestic Throne Room had niches all around, with colossal coloured marble statues (two have been found). The ceiling is estimated to have been at least 100ft (33m) high. The room (D) to the left (with your back to the apse) resembled a basilica, with a nave and two aisles. Here the emperor, again sitting in an apse, presided over meetings of his tribunal (some judgments were reserved for him), or cabinet. The use of the third room (E) is unknown.

Return to the peristyle. On the Circus Maximus side, it meets the Banquet Room complex, called *Coenatio Jovis* ('Jupiter's Dining Hall'). The splendid main room (F) has a floor of coloured marbles, double-bottomed for a hot-air heating system (some badly buckled edges remain), and an apse for the emperor, with part of the original floor restored. Through side windows, the diners, lounging on their day beds, enjoyed a view of two oval fountains. The right one, as you face the apse, survives.

Descend the modern steps into the crumbling dining room. Other steps there (inaccessible to the public) lead to the older structures mentioned earlier (p. 293). Return to the peristyle (B) and enter the second main area of the compound from the right-hand side.

The Private Zone. You enter a second peristyle (G), shaped like the first one, with the brick ruins of a large pool. Across the pool a footbridge leads to the base of a small temple. The temple isn't there any longer; its place has been taken by a grand pine tree.

Unidentified ruins are next to the courtyard on the Area Palatina side. (Some scholars think these belonged to the public zone.) The whole area next to the courtyard on the Circus Maximus side was the private residence of the emperors. Its layout is not obvious, since part of it now houses the

Palatine Antiquarium (see p. 685), a converted 19th-century convent.

The private residence had several floors above and below the one on which we're standing. Go to the first large arched passage to your right. On this floor most of the room partitions are gone and not much is discernible. Partly because the slope of the hill was cut and excavated to provide another flat surface, the lower storeys have a clearer layout, but the uses of their rooms are unknown.

The private residence, with its monumental elliptical façade, whose ruins make such a stunning sight from the foot of the hill, overlooked the Circus Maximus (p. 267). You can see the façade from here too, from a railing facing the valley, by going around the palace ruins to the right.

From here a row of modern pillars supporting the ruins of the *Pædagogium*, a school for imperial pages and servants, is visible midway down the slope to the right. Many examples of graffiti have turned up in its rooms. A famous one mocks a Christian servant by showing him praying before a donkey-headed man on a cross, with the words 'Alexamenos worships his God'. The building is usually closed to the public and the famous graffito is now in the Antiquarium.

On the hilltop nearby is the Loggia de' Mattei, a Renaissance building containing 'grotesques' and other frescoes attributed to Baldassarre Peruzzi or his school.

The Palace Sporting Grounds. As you face the Circus Maximus, go completely around to the left of the private zone. You will see an enormous arena from above. Its precise function is unknown, but some of the most luxurious private residences had tracks for horse riding, chariot races and other athletic activities. This arena was in a two-storey portico. A monumental viewing stand is on one of the long sides. At one end is an oval enclosure, a sort of corral, thought to have been built by the barbarian king Theodoric, who lived in the palace after the Empire fell.

Beyond the racetrack you can see other powerful brick constructions on this corner of the hill; these are the substructures of a lost platform that supported an extension of the palace which was level with the rest. It was added a century later by Septimius Severus, the emperor from North Africa (p. 164-165). At the foot of the hill on this side Septimius also built a famous decorative colonnade on four floors, a sort of glorified theatre backdrop called the Septizodium (a play on the emperor's name and the seven planets of the zodiac – themselves symbolic of his name – which decorated all the floors; the name was latter corrupted to Septizonium). It was said that the purpose of the building was to impress Septimius' fellow Africans who came to Rome. (They would arrive from the Appian Way, the main link between Rome and the south, which is just opposite this corner.) The building still stood in the 16th century and was greatly admired by Renaissance artists, who have left many drawings of it. It was destroyed by Pope Sixtus V in order to obtain materials for his huge building projects.

You now have several options.

1) You can go all the way back to the main entrance of the Roman Forum.

2) You can start back, but break away near the Arch of Titus, where there is a secondary exit to the Colosseum area (occasionally at closing time the guards direct everyone to this exit).

If you take this option, upon exiting you'll see the ruins of the Temple of Venus and Rome (p. 208) close-up. Just past the exit on your right Via S. Bonaventura begins, which goes uphill outside the Palatine enclosure. Midway, behind a portal to your left, is the small church of **S. Sebastiano al Palatino** (ring the bell), founded in the 10th century near the spot where S. Sebastiano was traditionally said to have been martyred (p. 618). He was supposedly shot by arrows on the steps of the Temple of the Sun founded by the Emperor Heliogabalus in the early 3rd century AD. Its foundations, resting on a giant terrace, and other traces, are nearby and under the church. (A later Temple of the Sun is discussed elsewhere, see p. 227) The church was rebuilt in the 17th century,

but still has naive 10th- and 11th-century frescoes in the apse.

At the end of the road is another small church, **S. Bonaventura**, from the late 17th century. It has a quiet garden with a view of the Colosseum.

3) You can descend by going around the arena and taking a path and steps on the other side down to a third exit on Via S. Gregorio.

If you take this route, first you will see more massive foundations of the palace extension built by Septimius Severus on the right. At the foot of the hill you can see whether the path to the right has reopened; it is inaccessible at the time of writing. It would lead you the *Pædagogium* (p. 294) – itself possibly reopened – and on to the ruins of the ancient Republican walls that enclosed the city on this side before the expansion ordered by Augustus (pp. 42, 80). You would then have to retrace your steps around the foot of the hill to the Via S. Gregorio exit. If the path is still closed that way, take it on the left to the exit, passing the arches of the Aqueduct of Nero (see pp. 404, 431). The exit is adorned on the outside with the great mannerist portal of the botanical garden, by Vignola and Girolamo Rainaldi (p. 288).

Until around 1900, the doorway was on the Forum side of the garden, where it looked much grander, since it had additional arches at the base and was included in a massive wall. It was dismantled during the excavations and recently rebuilt here.

4) A new exit path is being prepared. From the Houses of Augustus, it will go down to Via S. Teodoro (see p. 264) and the church of S. Anastasia. This way should allow visitors to see the remains of the Republican Walls, the extremely ancient Cacus Stairs on the Palatine slope (named after the cattle-thief, a monstrous giant, who was slain here by the legendary Hercules) and the *Pædagogium*.

If you want to reach the bus routes to the centre of town on Via S. Gregorio, cross the street to the bus-stop roughly opposite Vignola's doorway (the stop is usually hidden by tourist buses).

Rome of the Popes

Boniface VIII, in the crypts of the Vatican. Boniface invented the Jubilee, or Holy Year, which created a tourist industry, with hundreds of thousands of pilgrims flocking to Rome. He also stretched the papal tiara to the Biblical length of the ell for greater effect

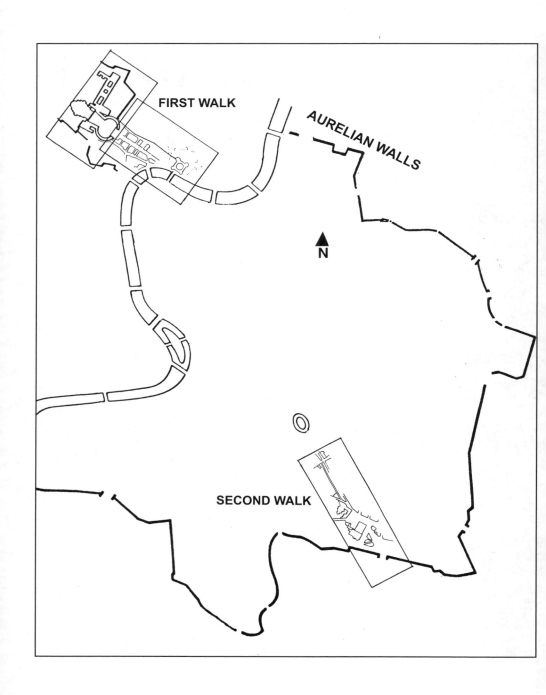

ROME OF THE POPES

Planning your walk: this is the section of the sightseeing plan of this book that requires the greatest organisational effort for those pressed for time, owing to the conflicting, erratic and altogether inadequate opening hours of the various landmarks. (Those who can allow several days for their visit to the Vatican could hardly spend them better.)

Both Walks could in theory be done (without the Detours) in a single day – the Vatican and S. Pietro (St Peter's) starting early in the morning, Castel Sant'Angelo and S. Giovanni in Laterano (St John Lateran) in the afternoon. But the problem is that the queues at the Vatican Museums are at their worst in the first part of the morning – from about 11.30 they dwindle or disappear.

The alternative is then to visit the castle in the morning, as close as possible to opening time, and not to tarry there. Then go on to the Vatican museums and palaces, and then proceed to S. Peter's and S. John Lateran, both open until evening (but try to be at the Lateran before 18:00, when the cloister closes).

The situation is somewhat eased by the fact that all three main sites are not far from Metro stations, and on the same A line. The Vatican is reached from the CIPRO or the OTTAVIANO stations; from the Castle, the line is reached by a relatively short walk to the G. CESARE station; S. Giovanni in Laterano (S. GIOVANNI station) is several stops away in the direction of the ANAGNINA terminus.

INTRODUCTION

All Rome is 'of the popes' in a sense: they ruled it for centuries, took a direct interest in its development and left their mark everywhere. In this section, however, we speak of 'Rome of the popes' in a limited sense, including mainly the parts that were the administrative seat of the Church's world-wide spiritual dominion for 1700 years – the 'Holy See'.

In 312 Emperor Constantine, thanks to his alliance with the Christian faction in a civil struggle, overthrew his rival and co-emperor Maxentius. The next year he legalised Christianity and donated land and materials for a papal headquarters and for several imposing cult buildings – the first official churches (as opposed to private or semi-clandestine ones, see p. 228).

Lateran and Vatican. We habitually think of the papacy as based in the Vatican, but the original, Constantinian headquarters were elsewhere: the Lateran complex, which comprised a palace joined to one of the newly created cult buildings, a church modelled on a classical Roman basilica. (Indeed, all Constantinian churches were basilicas, the typical Roman form for a public meeting place.)

The church was initially dedicated to the Redeemer, later to St John. The name Lateran came from the location – the former site of the patrician Laterani family mansion of imperial Rome. It was situated on the fringe of the city. The outlying location was chosen for political reasons: to avoid unduly provoking the pagan party, which still held great power.

The popes were based in the Lateran for a thousand years. But their rule was repeatedly challenged by Roman warlords, the Roman populace or European rulers ; and in 1309, at the climax of one such struggle, the pope was forced to flee Rome and to take refuge in some papal property in France, at Avignon. There the popes stayed for 68 years. The eventual return to Rome was partly in response to the entreaties of the Romans, who had seen their city decline in power and prosperity in the interim. Further strife followed, however, which at one point threatened the very survival of the papacy. By the 1420's the popes again had the upper hand, and were determined to assert much stricter control and set up an unassailable defensive position. The Lateran, on the edge of Rome and indefensible, was unsuited to either goal.

The Vatican area, however, very close to what had by then become the centre of the city in the river bend, indeed just across the river, fitted these requirements. From it, popes could monitor events in Rome. Assuring an easy defence were the river in front of it, hilly and easily fortifiable land behind it, and a gigantic fortress, Castel S. Angelo, next to it that could be connected to the papal palaces.

The transition was smooth, since the Church already owned buildings in the Vatican equivalent to those in the Lateran: a palace and, nearby, a Constantinian basilica as beautiful as St John's. It was dedicated to St Peter.

Christianity and the Vatican. The ties of the Vatican area with Christianity began centuries before the papal Curia moved there. Christian and Jewish cemeteries had long been there. In ancient Rome, the left bank was inhabited by middle easterners, mostly slaves and the poor, who included many followers of the two 'foreign' eastern cults, Judaism and Christianity. The area also witnessed the massacre of Christians. Emperor Caligula built a circus (race-course) there, which

The Courtyard of the Pine Cone in the 18th century; engraving by Giuseppe Vasi.
In the niche the bronze pine cone mentioned by Dante

was completed by Emperor Nero, who found it handy to blame the Christians for a fire that had ravaged Rome (pp. 190-191) and so decided to enhance the thrill of the races by killing Christians there. They were torn apart by animals, crucified, or tarred and burnt as torches to light the festivities. Tradition holds that the martyrs included St Peter, who was crucified upside down at his request, in deference to Christ, who had died facing the sky. (The Caravaggio painting which we saw on the first Roma Romantica Walk depicts this scene, see p. 48.)

Three centuries later, Emperor Constantine built one of his Christian basilicas on the same spot (with the major exception of the Lateran, most of the Constantinian churches mentioned at the outset of this chapter were built over Christian cemeteries, or where martyrs' blood had been spilled). In the early middle ages, St Peter's acquired special prestige since, as Christ's vicar, St Peter was considered the predecessor of the popes, who were increasingly powerful. Moreover, since St. Peter had come to be seen as the greatest martyr, his church and the Vatican attracted the largest crowds in the steady stream of pilgrims who came to imbibe the miraculous, supposedly healing aura of the martyrs' bones.

Many centuries before the popes moved to the Vatican, the area had become a key attraction to foreign visitors, especially Germanic ones (who then included the French and English). Kings and queens visited: Ceadwalla, King of the West Saxons, came to be baptised and died there immediately after; Carloman of France (uncle of Charlemagne) came to be absolved of his sins and stayed on as a monk. Others came to be crowned there, such as Charlemagne, who stayed in the Vatican palace and received his imperial crown in St Peter's on Christmas Eve 800 AD.

The Vatican and Rome. The Vatican area was thriving by the time the papal Curia moved there. Its big tourist industry had spurred a large public works programme that spread throughout the city. We have already seen that Via Ripetta was built to lead pilgrims to the Vatican from their major entry point, Piazza del Popolo (p. 42). In the Renaissance Rome Walks we'll also see how the whole area in the Tiber bend – across the river from the Vatican – was renewed and beautified because of its close ties with the Vatican, and spawned a hotel industry dependent on it, as well as crafts and shops specialising in religious objects. This area was also home to many artists in the Curia's employ.

The Vatican today. The year 1870 saw the end of papal rule in Rome and Central Italy. Rome became the capital of a new, unified Italy, and the popes secluded themselves in the Vatican palaces in protest. Sixty years of extreme church-state tension and clashes followed. In 1929, under Mussolini's Fascist regime, there was a grand compromise called 'la Conciliazione' ('the Reconciliation'), which included the creation of the tiny State of the City of the Vatican, enjoying extra-territoriality and subject only to papal authority. This is the present situation.

The Vatican city-state covers one sixth of a square mile (0.44 km²) and has about 500 citizens. It includes not only part of the Vatican area (the complex of the papal palaces housing the pope, his court and the world-famous museums, several administrative buildings and St Peter's Basilica with its square), but several other historic Church possessions around Rome, including the Lateran complex and the basilica of S. Maria Maggiore. The streets between the river and St Peter, known as the Borgo (or Borough), are not included.

Most of the city-state is surrounded by ancient walls, different from those of Rome, built by the popes over the centuries. A long, elevated passage links the Vatican palaces to the huge, independently fortified Castel Sant' Angelo ('Castle of the Holy Angel'), which on several dramatic occasions served as a refuge to the popes. The castle is no longer Church property or part of the city-state.

These two Walks cover most of these areas, whether part of the city-state or not: the Vatican palaces and museums, St Peter's (not the Constantinian basilica, which no longer exists, but a newer one, which replaced it) and its square, the Borgo, Castel Sant'Angelo and, in another district, the St John's Lateran complex. We'll also visit some venerable churches strung along the way between the two complexes.

Constantine, Charlemagne and papal authority. Both the Vatican and the Lateran are inextricably tied to the figures of Constantine and Charlemagne, a fact of which you'll find many visual reminders in your visits. Not only did Constantine, donor of the Lateran, the Vatican and other Early Christian basilicas, legalise Christianity in the 4th century (p. 198), but his name was used for centuries thereafter as the theoretical foundation of papal authority. Five centuries after him, a very different kind of emperor, Charlemagne, turned that theoretical foundation into reality.

A constant in the history of the papacy has been the contrast between its global ambitions and its puny material power ('how many divisions has the pope?' Stalin jeered). In the centuries of chaos following the fall of the Western Empire, these ambitions were embodied in the popes' claim to have inherited the imperial mantle, which they defended against competitors, such as the eastern (Byzantine) emperors and the successors of the barbarian rulers who had conquered the West.

In the 8th century, the popes formalised their claim by forging a document, the 'Donation of Constantine,' in which the Roman emperor had supposedly handed the Church title of ownership to Rome and the Western Empire. The document went unquestioned until it was proved a fake in the 15th century, but by then papal power was entrenched.

A few decades after the forgery, the popes found an ingenious way to enforce its contents. They took it upon themselves, as recipients of the supposed donation, to bestow the crown of the Western Empire on an outsider – a great, ruthless leader of ex-barbarians, Charles, called 'the Great' or Charlemagne, King of the Franks. But the compact between the papacy and Charles implied various conditions. The Emperor would act on behalf of the Roman church, source of his legitimacy, and this was reflected in his title, Holy Roman Emperor. The papacy expected that not only Charles, but all future emperors and kings in Europe would have their authority confirmed in Rome by the Pope, through the rites of unction and coronation.

On a practical level, this symbolic relationship committed the leaders of the 'Holy Empire' to use force against anyone who might contest the papacy's secular rights. Charlemagne, who had already destroyed and absorbed the kingdom created in Italy by other German ex-barbarians, the Longobards (from whom the name Lombardy is derived), which had posed the most immediate danger to papal authority, had also engaged himself to bring under papal control the lands still occupied in the Peninsula by the Byzantine Emperor (Ravenna, Venetia and Spoleto in the north, Benevento in the south). This last part of the compact, despite some false starts, was never honoured, because Charlemagne was more interested in gaining Byzantine recognition of his new title than in fighting. When Charles died of pneumonia at Aachen 14 years after his coronation, his empire was divided up amongst his sons. The German rulers, who kept the imperial title, immediately began trying to impose their will on the popes and Rome, ignoring the original pact.

By the 11th century, tension between the two powers had already caused many clashes. Things came to a head when the uncompromising Pope Gregory VII took office and tried to restore the absolute primacy of the Church over Rome and the Western Empire. The German emperor replied by disowning him and having an 'anti-pope' elected. Then he invaded Rome, as Gregory took refuge in Castel Sant'Angelo.

Gregory escaped the predicament with an agreement not unlike that between an earlier pope and Charlemagne: an alliance with a new, potent force on the European scene, an adventurer from Normandy in France, Robert 'Guiscard' ('the Astute'). Robert rescued Gregory; he chased off the emperor, and meanwhile eradicated the remnants of Byzantine power in Southern Italy.

There were complications, however. In Rome Robert's troops went on a spree of looting and plundering that deeply scarred the history of the city. You'll see some of its effects at the end of these two papal Walks, at the churches of the Quattro Coronati and S. Clemente. And Gregory's victory did not end the conflict with the Germanic emperors: it continued for centuries, often involving, as a third and fourth party, the great families and the people of Rome. The bloodiest episode was the 1527 Sack of Rome, which crushed the great flowering of the Renaissance there, and traces of which we'll also follow in one of these Walks.

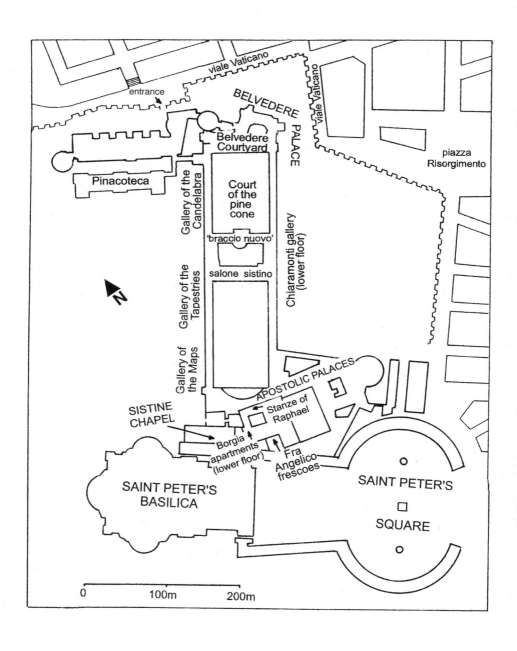

ROME OF THE POPES
FIRST WALK

1. The Vatican Palaces and Museums 307   Pinacoteca 312; Court of the Pine Cone 317; Chiaramonti Sculpture Gallery 317; Scala del Bramante 320; Cortile del Belvedere 320; Room of the Animals 322; Gallery of the Statues 322; Room of the Masks 323; Room of the Busts 324; Room of the Muses 325; Round Room 325; Greek Cross Room 326; Room of the Chariot 326; Room of the Candelabra 327

2. The Papal Apartments of Raphael 329   Gallery of Maps 334; Raphael's Loggia 335; Room of Heliodorus 335; Stanza della Segnatura 338; Room of the Fire 339; Apartments of Pope Alexander VI Borgia; Room of the Saints 341; Room of the Mysteries of the Faith 341

3. The Sistine Chapel and Michelangelo's Masterpieces 343   Sistine Chapel ceiling 347; Last Judgement 348 ; Aldobrandini Wedding 353; Museo Gregoriano Profano 355; Museo Pio Cristiano di Antichità Cristiane 355

Midpoint of walk

4. S. Pietro (St. Peter's Cathedral) 357 S. Pietro 360; Museum of the Basilica, 369; Sacred Grottoes 370

5. St. Peter's Square 374   Colonnade 376; Obelisk 376

Starting point: Viale Vaticano   End point: Piazza S. Pietro
Duration: 7 hrs (without the Sacred Grottoes detour).

Planning: 1) Dress code. Scores of tourists are turned away daily from St. Peter's for lack of proper attire. Short shorts on men or women, mini-skirts, bare backs, bare arms and ultra-low necklines are not allowed.

2) Umbrellas, walking sticks and large bags (but not cameras) must be left in the cloakroom of the Vatican Museums and Palaces. Unfortunately this precludes taking the short-cut exit suggested on p. 352. Check whether you really need to bring these items.

3) Visits to the excavations under St. Peter's (guided tours only, about 90 minutes) – including the ancient cemetery and St. Peter's (putative) grave– require reservations at least three weeks in advance. Children under 14 are not admitted. (Contact the Excavation Office (Ufficio Scavi), to the left of the basilica (open 9 am-5 pm), by fax ((06) 698 73017) or email (scavi@fsp.va) in a major language addressed to: Rev. Fabbrica di San Pietro, Ufficio Scavi, 00120 Città del Vaticano. Requests must include a list of applicants by name; language group (Italian, French, German, English or Spanish); an address and, where possible, phone number in Rome where the Vatican can confirm the reservation.)

4) Visits to the Vatican gardens (guided only) take place on Tues, Thurs and Sat at 10:00 from 8 March to 29 October. Places must be reserved at least one week in advance: call (06) 698 84676 between 1 & 2 pm.

5) General papal audiences are held most Wednesdays at 11 am (for confirmation, call (06) 6982 in Rome). Invitations must be requested at least one or two days in advance, either in person at the Bronze Gate (p. 377) to the right of the basilica or by letter to the Prefettura della Casa Pontificia, 00120 Città del Vaticano. You can get a ticket on the same day, but probably not a good seat. Dress must be very conservative, preferably black or dark; white is allowed for ladies; ladies must cover their heads.

6) Wheelchairs are available at the Vatican Museums and Palaces, but it is advisable to reserve them by calling (06) 6982.

7) There are lavatories in the Vatican Museums and Palaces, and near both colonnades in St. Peter's Square.

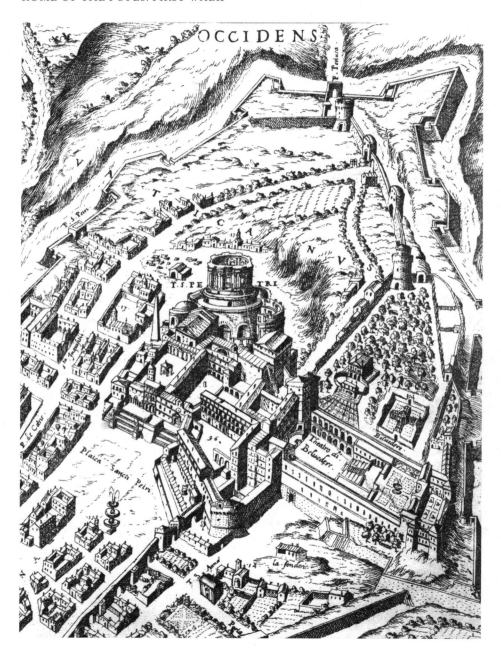

BEFORE GOING

1. The Vatican Palaces and Museums

> *On we went from chamber to chamber through galleries of statues*
> *and vases and sarcophagi and bas-reliefs and busts and candelabra –*
> *through all forms of beauty and richest materials –*
> *till the eye was dazzled and glutted with this triumph of the arts.*
> *Go and see it, whoever you are. It is the wealth of the civilized world.*
> Ralph Waldo Emerson

> *In Rome, the history of art and the history of mankind confront us simultaneously.*
> Johann Wolfgang von Goethe

The Palaces. When the papal court moved from the Lateran to the Vatican in the early 15th century, the building it took over, adjacent to St. Peter's Basilica, was about 200 years old. Actually parts of it dated to the 6th century – we saw that Charlemagne stayed there in 800 – but the palace had been mostly rebuilt in the early 13th century.

The first adviser to the popes in their new residence, the great renaissance humanist and architect, Leon Battista Alberti, said on his deathbed: 'If the authority of the Church is visibly displayed in majestic buildings, the whole world will accept it.' This advice was immediately followed. A great construction programme, starting about 1450, gave the palace a new wing and subsequent additions, including the Sistine Chapel, destined for artistic glory. All this forms the original palace compound, which we'll see at the end of our visit (not earlier, for reasons we'll soon see).

There was another great expansion around 1490, when a pope decided that the compound, which lay on low ground near the river, was unhealthy. He had a new residence built 600 yards further uphill, where there was fresher air and an open countryside view. He called it *Il Belvedere* ('the Beautiful View').

This project had two great consequences. First, the pope's successors found the hillside building ideal for housing their budding art collections. In the glorious days of the Renaissance, wonderful ancient statues were being unearthed every day throughout Rome and Italy, eliciting universal awe. The courtyard of the Belvedere, and eventually almost the whole building, was devoted to this purpose. Thus the first great museums of the modern world were born. Today the public can visit the whole palace and museum complex, entering from the side of the museum, which is why your visit starts at a distance from the original compound near St. Peter's.

The second major consequence of the Belvedere construction was that it gave new direction to the papal building fervour by supplying the next logical objective: to join the old and new palaces. In the early 16th century the new artistic director, the great Bramante, presented a plan

Rome in 1577, from the map by Du Pérac and Lafreri. St. Peter's is still only half built,
but the Vatican is beginning to spread out

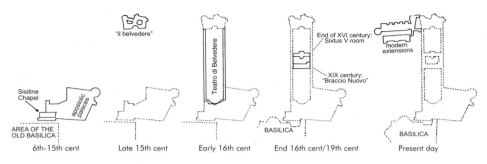

The expansion of the Vatican Palaces

to bridge the expanse between the two. The final project involved two huge parallel corridors, three stories high each, following the gradient separating the two complexes and joining them at either end, and thereby producing an oversized rectangular courtyard.

Visualising this rectangle is essential to orientate yourself in the labyrinthine Vatican palaces and museums.

In the great courtyard Bramante and his papal employers saw potential for outdoor, grand-scale entertainment. Terraced, with gardens and fountains, and with great niches at both ends, one of them with steps as in a theatre, the upward-sloping courtyard was in fact called 'Teatro di Belvedere' and was the scene of tournaments, plays, banquets and fireworks for a whole century. The hedonistic renaissance popes loved it so much that for a time the space was nicknamed the *Atrio del Piacere* ('Court of Pleasure'). Then in blew the cold wind of the Counter Reformation: in the late 16th century Sixtus V decided that the *Atrio del Piacere* was too worldly and destroyed it by halving it with a transversal wing. (This builder pope, who was celebrated for his urban planning (pp. 44-45), was apparently less proficient at individual projects. John Varriano, an American scholar of the baroque, has called him 'insensitive' and subject to lapses 'in creative imagination ... and good taste'.) Sixtus' immediate successors considered demolishing the addition, but didn't. About two centuries later, the divided courtyards were further fragmented by the insertion of another wing parallel to Sixtus', the *Braccio Nuovo*, ('New Arm'), used for a separate, major sculpture collection, which we'll visit in this Walk.

To complete this sketchy presentation of the palaces, we must mention the lavish landscaped gardens around them within the Vatican walls. We'll further discuss the original compound (called the Apostolic Palaces) in the next section on the papal apartments and Sistine Chapel.

The museums. Historians have long debated the social, economic and psychological causes of the cultural upheaval of the Renaissance, or 'Rebirth'. But there is no doubt that the dramatic reappraisal of pagan antiquity which it involved was prompted largely by the actual discovery of Greco-Roman relics in the earliest excavations, and of long-forgotten manuscripts in old monasteries. These objects stirred a wave of awe and inspired renaissance generations to emulate the great achievements of the past. An immense, double patrimony of art and culture, old and new, thus burst forth.

The Vatican museums – comprising several vast exhibition areas, mostly within the Belvedere palace and the great corridors linking it to the Apostolic Palaces near St. Peter's – differ from other museums in that they were repositories of this double patrimony from the start. Many of the unearthed works that shook the human mind from its medieval slumber, and some of the greatest works created then, are in the museums, rooms and chapels of the Apostolic Palaces, where they were amassed at the height of the Renaissance.

Most museums get their art from the commercial market or through bequests and donations. The Vatican museums are a first-hand, direct showcase of the ideals that produced, amongst other things, the Vatican museums themselves. Visiting them is like visiting the sources of our spirit; they are to Western civilization what the house or studio of a great artist is to the artist's lifework. Another comparison could be the Air and Space Museum in Washington D.C., where spaceships and lunar rocks illustrate a new age at the very moment of its birth.

The museums and Michelangelo. No renaissance artist admired the newly recovered ancient works in the Belvedere more than Michelangelo, whose Sistine Chapel would come to be seen as the culminating glory of the Vatican. Two works in particular stunned him, both of which we'll see. One was a powerful torso from a broken statue of Hercules or Marsyas – the Belvedere Torso – which the young Florentine master visited time and again; indeed it seems to anticipate by some 2,000 years Michelangelo's own formidable visions. The other is the famous Laocoön statuary group, found just a few years after Michelangelo moved to Rome (p. 196).

Proof of Michelangelo's prodigious sense of balance and design relates to the restoration of the *Laocoön*. After the sculpture was found, a good sculptor, Montorsoli, was asked to replace the missing right arm of the main figure, which he did, using a fully extended arm. Michelangelo must have thought it wrong, because he started, unrequested, sculpting his own version of the arm, folded back toward the head. Then, pressed by other projects, he dropped the task. The *Laocoön* kept Montorsoli's outstretched arm for four centuries, during which none of its millions of admirers – artists, critics, and experts included – found anything wrong with it. In 1905 a fragmentary arm was found that was later positively identified as the missing original, and in 1960 it was added in place of Montorsoli's arm. It was folded back toward the head, just as Michelangelo had designed it. (There could be an entirely different explanation for Michelangelo's apparent prescience, though, if a startling theory put forth in 2005 by the American scholar Lynn Catterson of Columbia University is true. She maintains that the *Laocoön* was a forgery by Michelangelo, who followed the description of the lost Greek masterwork given by Pliny the Elder to create a statuary group that he then plotted with others to 'antique' by burying, have it dug up again and finally sold as ancient. Derided by many of Catterson's colleagues, this theory cannot be totally rejected as it is known that in his youth the sculptor did precisely this sort of fraud with at least one other sculpture, and possibly more.)

Planning your visit. Visiting the Vatican museums is a great experience. The drawback is battle fatigue. The museums are by far the world's largest collection of ancient art and, together with the Apostolic Palaces, cover about 500,000 sq ft (50,000 m²). In a straight line, the exhibits would stretch five miles (8 km). Often the harried visitor is spent before seeing the essentials.

To avoid this, it is very important to head straight for the highlights, bypassing the mass of

exhibits that only regular visitors have the luxury of enjoying. We present quite a selective visit on the assumption that given the choice between visiting the place exhaustively and not getting exhausted yourself, you'll pick the second option.

We call the Vatican collections 'museums' rather than 'museum' since they vary widely in nature and origin. Our Walk includes only the major art collections. Others, including those unrelated to the unique renaissance character of the place (the Egyptian and Etruscan museums, for instance), are briefly described on pp. 680-681. Minor and very specialised collections are skipped entirely. Do read the 'planning notes' on p. 305 concerning the dress code for St. Peter's, bags and umbrellas; they can save you a lot of time, but not unless you read them before going!

A note on the sculpture. Most of the exhibits in the museums proper – that is, in the Belvedere area, not in the old Apostolic Palaces – are statues, all excavated in Rome or Italy. Most are labelled 'Roman copy of a Greek original'. This doesn't mean they are minor reproductions. Virtually all the ancient statues we know (with the main exception of temple friezes, such as of the Parthenon) are copies. In Greece and Rome, successful original sculpture served as models, to be copied repeatedly over the centuries. There were some variants, but the replicas were not considered less worthy than the originals, which in any case are lost. In short, these 'copies', the main source of our knowledge, and of æsthetic pleasure both for the ancients and for us, are amongst the great treasures of civilization.

You may have noted the emphasis on Greek, rather than Roman sculpture. Sculpture was more widespread in Greece; the Romans focused on a more practical art form, architecture. The Roman sculptures we have are mainly portraits, often strikingly beautiful, sarcophagi and the above-mentioned copies. But this requires further qualification. Often these 'Roman' works were made by Greeks in Rome, many of whom were slaves or ex-slaves brought to Rome for the purpose. So 'Roman' in sculpture often simply means 'made in Rome' or even 'found in Rome'.

Another important point is the distinction between 'classical' Greek and 'hellenistic' sculpture. The latter is late Greek art, produced not only in Greece, but in the sprawling realms born of the breakup of Alexander the Great's empire in the 4th century BC, areas that Rome later conquered. In Rome, hellenistic sculpture was widely produced and imitated. This Greek-inspired art is characterised by greater realism and less abstraction than classical (pre-4th century BC) Greek sculpture and, though often of high technical virtuosity, is æsthetically less impressive.

Charlemagne, by Agostino Cornacchini: an early rococo variant on Bernini's statue of Constantine, to which this was a pair

311

Chimneypiece in the Borgia Apartments

ON THE SPOT

1. The Vatican Palaces and Museums

It is worth bearing in mind that after seeing the Sistine Chapel you may well prefer to use the secondary exit onto St. Peter's Square. The 'regular' route involves walking back a fifth of a mile (over 300 m) to exit near the main entrance in a part of the city which is out of the way of subsequent destinations. You can't use the secondary exit, however, if after the visit you want to return to the cloak room or go to the museum restaurant, which is also near the entrance. In summer a snack bar is sometimes open near the Sistine Chapel.

Open: July 1 to September 30 and at Easter, Monday-Friday 08:45-16:45, Saturday 08:45-13:45. Other times, 08:45-13:45; no admittance in the last hour. Closed on Sunday, except the last Sunday of every month, when admission is free. Also closed on holidays: January 1 and 6, February 11, March 19, Easter and Easter Monday, May 1, Ascension Day, Corpus Christi Day, June 29, August 14-15, November 1 and December 8, 25 and 26.

In summer the Pinacoteca inside the complex closes at 13:30; the Belvedere courtyard area closes between 13:45 and 14:45. For more information and/or confirmation, call (06) 6982.

The entrance and exit to the museums are modern doors in the 17th-century brick walls around the Vatican (the earlier walls are inside the compound). Plain, except for papal emblems and two stone angels near Piazza Risorgimento, the walls zig-zag, forming large spurs characteristic of state-of-the-art fortifications in the 17th century.

The ultra-modern, glass-and-concrete entrance pavilion was inaugurated in the Jubilee Year 2000. Past the ticket booths, go right to see the Pinacoteca ('Picture Gallery') first. If you start your visit by going left, you'll probably end up missing the picture gallery, because you'll be too tired to return all the way here, or in any case to enjoy the paintings. Of course, if you are really pressed for time and decide to skip the picture gallery entirely, go left.

The **Pinacoteca** is an early 20th-century structure. Before entering, go into the courtyard in front of it to see, on a terrace, the base of the Column of Emperor Antoninus Pius, found in the 18th century near the column of Antoninus Pius' successor Marcus Aurelius (see p. 232).

Parts of the shaft were also found, but were later destroyed or scattered. The column was set up in 161 AD to honour the deified emperor by his sons Marcus Aurelius and Lucius Verus. One side of the wonderful base depicts the apotheosis of Antoninus and his wife Faustina Senior (we saw their temple in the Forum, pp. 163, 193); they rise up to the heavens, led by a winged spirit and two eagles. The goddess Rome and the personified Campus Martius look on. Another two sides show the ritual joust, at the funeral, of the imperial horseguard (*equites singulares*, see pp. 396-397) and of foot soldiers.

The following overview covers the foremost works of the Pinacoteca. Those with limited time will find the diagrams help locate the main pictures quickly.

FIRST HALF OF THE PINACOTECA, ROOMS I TO VIII

These galleries trace Italian painting from the middle ages to the renaissance. Most of the artists are from Central Italian cities – Florence, Siena and Perugia – whose 'schools' (characteristic styles) deeply affected artistic development in Rome.

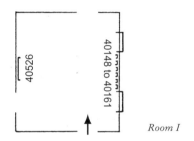

Room I

Room I (12th century- early 14th century)

All the works here are by the 'primitives', painters still tied to the stiff, intensely mystical early medieval style, which in turn draws on the Byzantine tradition exemplified by some of the mosaics that we saw earlier (pp. 95-96). Highlights:

No. 40526: Giovanni and Nicolò, *Last Judgment*.

Nos 40148 to 40161: Bernardo Daddi, episodes from the *Life of St. Stephen*.

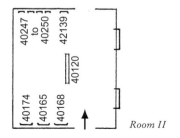

Room II

Room II (late 13th-14th century)

This room is devoted to Giotto and his direct followers. Giotto, the founding father of modern painting, broke with rigid Byzantine schemes to discover a new world of naturalism and human drama. Among his followers, Lorenzetti is closest to him in vision; Martini and Gentile da Fabriano stress the decorative, fable-like aspects of their narrative in a style sometimes called 'Late Gothic'.

No. 40120 (in the middle): Giotto, triptych with *Christ and the Virgin Enthroned* and *the Martyrdoms of St. Peter and St. Paul*; on the back, *St. Peter Enthroned and other Saints*.

No. 40168: Pietro Lorenzetti, *Christ before Pilate*.

No. 40165: Simone Martini, *The Redeemer Giving His Blessing*.

No. 40174: Bernardo Daddi, *Madonna of the Magnificat*.

Nos 40247-40250: Gentile da Fabriano, *Episodes from the Life of St. Nicholas*.

No. 42139: Sassetta, *Madonna and Child*.

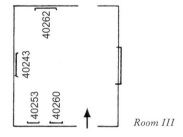

Room III

Room III (early 15th century)

Technical research, a special concern of the 'Late Gothic' painters, was advanced by masters such as Masolino, who combined psychological insight and a new sense of perspective, and Fra Angelico, famous for his gem-like colours and his deep spirituality (p. 118). Angelico's pupil, Benozzo Gozzoli, added a festive mood and great ornamental richness. Another of Angelico's direct followers, Filippo Lippi (father of Filippino, p. 117), showed the feel for line and volume that became the hallmark of the dawning Renaissance.

No. 40260: Masolino, *Crucifixion.*

No. 40253: Fra Angelico, *Madonna and Child with Saints.*

No. 40243: Filippo Lippi, *Coronation of the Virgin.*

No. 40262: Benozzo Gozzoli, *Madonna of the Girdle.*

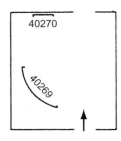

Room IV

Room IV (mid- to late-15th century)

Abstract geometrical beauty and the first daring experiments in foreshortening characterise the splendid images of Melozzo da Forlì.

No. 40269: Melozzo, *Music-making Angels* and *Apostles* (fragments of a destroyed fresco from the church of the SS. Apostoli, p. 129). These are the quintessential angels, perhaps the most famous ever painted. We've seen others by Melozzo elsewhere (p. 117).

No. 40270: Melozzo da Forlì, *Sixtus IV at the Inauguration of the Vatican Library.* In this famous painting the celebrated scholar, Bartolomeo Sacchi, called Il Platina, kneels to be appointed head of the library. The pope is surrounded by four of his nephews, his assistants. A cardinal in red, Giuliano della Rovere, is the future Pope Julius II. In grey, to the right, is the future cardinal, Raffaele Riario, who would later be involved in a plot to unseat or kill another pope (p. 483). To the left, in blue, is Girolamo Riario, Pope Sixtus' military henchman, who arranged the killing of prominent members of the rival Florentine family, the Medici. He was then murdered himself.

Go directly from Room IV to Room VI.

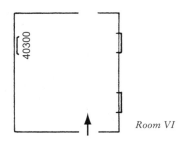

Room VI

Room VI (late 15th century)

No. 40300: Carlo Crivelli, *Pietà.* This important master from the Veneto region combined renaissance advances in perspective and modelling with bold experiments with the human figure, including distorting it for expressive purposes.

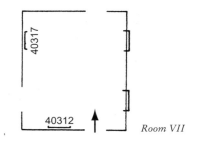

Room VII

Room VII (late 15th-early 16th century)

We approach the high noon of the Renaissance, entering the circle of artists that spawned Raphael. Perugino, a great innovator, famous for his sober clarity and the delicacy and strength of his characters, was Raphael's teacher. Pinturicchio, many of whose works we saw elsewhere, was Raphael's fellow pupil in Perugino's studio.

No. 40312: Pinturicchio, *Coronation of the Virgin.*

No. 40317: Perugino, *Virgin and Child with Saints.*

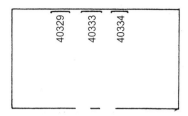

Room VIII

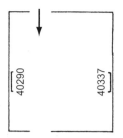

Room IX

Room VIII - Raphael (1483-1520)

No. 40334: *Coronation of the Virgin.*
No. 40329: *Madonna di Foligno.*
No. 40333: *Transfiguration.*

The first of these three great paintings, dating from 1502, still shows Perugino's influence, though the pupil has come into his own, with a style full of spirituality like his master's, but less posed, less formal, and livelier. The second work, dated 1512, and the third, painted just before his death (p. 333), show Raphael at his most mature and renaissance art at its peak. The perfectly matched colours, clarity of line and impeccable feeling for atmosphere and volume produce an almost magical balance. Balance, indeed, characterises Raphael more than anything else. Only the upper section of the *Transfiguration*, where Christ levitates in view of the Apostles blinded by His light, is all by Raphael; the lower, depicting the related evangelical episode of the possessed child, is partly by his pupils (but following his drawings). The small showcases contain minor works by the master. Around the room are eight of ten tapestries made in Brussels based on his cartoons (preliminary designs), which are now in the V&A Museum in London.

SECOND HALF OF THE PINACOTECA, ROOMS IX-XV.

This contains paintings of other renaissance giants, Florentine and Venetian, plus baroque and later works, Italian and foreign.

Room IX (early 16th century)

No. 40337: Leonardo da Vinci, *St. Jerome.* Monochrome (one-colour) sketch for a painting on wood, admirable for its anatomical knowledge and for insight into the mystic's anguish and ecstasy. The work, which had been cut in two, was found by accident, one part in a cobbler shop, where it was part of a stool, another in an antiques shop, where it was a coffer lid.

No. 40290: Giovanni Bellini, *Pietà.* The foremost master of the Early Renaissance in Venice, creator of timeless figures immersed in heavenly luminosity and religious silence.

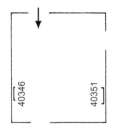

Room X

Room X (16th century, Venetian school and others)

No. 40351: Titian, *St. Nicholas and the Virgin.*
No. 40346: Veronese, *Allegory.*

Both masters represent renaissance painting at its apex in Venice, where it attained a total command of colour, sumptuous in Veronese's elegant compositions, passionately warm in Titian.

315

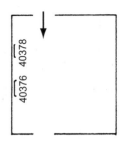

Room XI

Room XI (late 16th century)

No. 40378: Barocci, *The Blessed Michelina*. A masterpiece by a Central Italian artist who advanced beyond the Raphaelesque tradition with a warmth and pathos foreshadowing the baroque.

No. 40376: Barocci, *Annunciation*. Another delicate, lively work by this master.

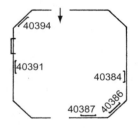

Room XII

Room XII (late l6th-17th century: the Baroque)

The paintings here exemplify the baroque reaction to the all-too-perfect, idealistic solutions of the Renaissance. Caravaggio, Guercino and Reni express ground-breaking realism and drama through vivid, even clashing colour juxtapositions. Domenichino and Poussin, whose largest painting is here, take on similar experiments by more sober means: delicate matching of hues and studied symmetry of shapes attaining an abstract, at times almost surreal atmosphere. The room is dominated by a stunning Caravaggio, so inspiring that Rubens and Cézanne made copies.

No. 40384: Domenichino, *Communion of St. Jerome*.

No. 40386: Caravaggio, *Deposition*.

No. 40387: Reni, *Crucifixion of St. Peter*.

No. 40391: Guercino, *St. Mary Magdalen*.

No. 40394: Poussin, *Martyrdom of St. Erasmus*.

Note: from a window of this room, enjoy a view of the Vatican gardens.

Go directly from Room XII to Room XIV.

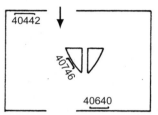

Room XIV

Room XIV

No. 40442: Jacques Courtois, *Battle Scene*. The 17th-century soldier-painter called 'Il Borgognone', whose house we saw in Piazza di Spagna (p. 57).

No. 40746: Murillo, *Martyrdom of St. Peter Arbuens*. A graceful work by the great 17th-century Spanish master.

No. 40460: C. Maratta, *Pope Clement IX*, (late 17th century).

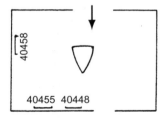

Room XV

Room XV (Portraits)

No. 40448: Sir Thomas Lawrence, *George IV of England*. Dated 1816 and typical of the 'grand manner' of English portraitists.

No. 40455: Pompeo Batoni (18th century), *Pius VI*. A vivid portrait of the pope who died a prisoner of Napoleon (pp. 67, 355).

No. 40458: G. M. Crespi (1665-1747), *Pope Benedict XIV*. A powerful, subtle portrait; the brushwork creates an almost tactile effect.

A side room (Room XVII) contains clay models of beautiful *Angels* and other sculptures by Bernini.

Leaving the Pinacoteca turn left and then right around a courtyard. Past a four-gate hall, the 'official' path turns, at times, left up a flight of steps, leading to the Egyptian Museum (see p. 681).

Note: this Walk doesn't include a visit to the Egyptian Museum, whose entrance is from the first landing of the steps. If you visit it, pick up the Walk again as follows. At its exit, you'll be on another landing. Go down, then enter the Chiaramonti Sculpture Gallery before you, the description of which starts below. If you visit the Egyptian Museum, don't miss the Pine Cone, the highlight described in the next few paragraphs, also accessible from this museum.

Don't climb the steps. Proceed straight through a door into another courtyard (if closed, ask to have it opened), the **Court of the Pine Cone**. The Cone is by the niche on your left.

The courtyard was originally almost three times longer – the so-called 'Atrio del Piacere'. Bramante made it in the early 16th century when he built two multi-storey parallel corridors to link the late 15th-century Belvedere Palace (left) to the even older Apostolic Palaces near St. Peter's. These can't be seen because the courtyard was later halved by transverse wings between the two corridors (the present short side of the courtyard opposite the Pine Cone). At the time of writing, the courtyard centres on a modern sculpture completely inappropriate to the place, further spoiling its atmosphere.

The *Pine Cone*, a colossal ancient Roman bronze, was originally a fountain. It stands at the top of a double staircase attributed to Michelangelo, which resembles his staircase on the Capitol (p. 147). The Cone was found in the middle ages in a district to which it gave its name (p. 114). Once it adorned a courtyard of old St. Peter's Basilica, where Dante saw it ('his face seemed to me as long and huge as St. Peter's Pine Cone,' he wrote of a giant in the Divine Comedy).

The Cone now stands on a marvellous 3rd century capital with a victorious athlete in relief, between copies of two 2nd century AD bronze peacocks, the originals of which we'll see shortly (p 318).

Continue on this side of the courtyard, cross the door in front of you and turn right. We are now in the long **Chiaramonti Sculpture Gallery**, contained within the first section of one of Bramante's parallel corridors (later we'll walk along the whole other corridor on an upper floor).

Planning: the gallery has nearly 1,000 ancient sculptures of all kinds, none of outstanding interest. We'll have to walk to the end, to another more

From the Atrio dei Quattri Cancelli to the Galleria Chiaramonti

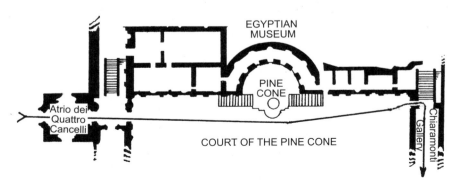

important side gallery, then come all the way back. We advise looking at the right-hand exhibits of this gallery on the way there, and at the other side when returning. We'll point out the highlights.

The walls are divided into panels, identified by Roman numerals: even numbers on the right, odd on the left. On the right:

Panel X: (No. 26) on the floor: funerary monument to *P. Nonius Zetus*, miller and flour merchant, 1st century AD. The marble has holes for the cinerary urns, one of which survives. Two reliefs depict a mill turned by a donkey and flour-processing equipment.

Panel XII: (No. 4) sarcophagus fragment with horses turning a millstone, 3rd century AD.

Panel XVI: (No. 3) colossal head of *Athena*, Roman copy of a Greek sculpture, possibly by the great Phidias (5th century BC).

Near the end of this gallery, on the right, a magnificent gallery opens.

It is housed in the building known as the *Braccio Nuovo* ('New Wing'), one of the two transverse buildings dividing Bramante's original *Teatro di Belvedere*.

The gallery is divided into niches. Start from the right: The third niche has a very fine statue (No. 11) of *Silenus Holding Dionysus in his Arms* (Dionysus was the god of wine and Silenus was his tutor), Roman copy of a work by the school of Lysippus. Later (p. 320) we'll see a masterwork by Lysippus himself, a 4th century BC sculptor who was one of the giants of classical Greece.

In the fourth niche (No. 14) is the famous *Augustus of Prima Porta*, the best depiction we have of the first Roman emperor. It is named after a place near Rome where it was found in 1863 during the excavation of a villa of Augustus' widow, Livia. It is a copy, probably commissioned by Livia after his death, of an honorary statue made when the emperor was about 40. He addresses his soldiers, armoured and barefoot as customary in these heroic portrayals. The wonderfully modelled face exudes intelligence and vigour. Note the extremely fine relief of the armour: encircled by gods and personified natural forces, Augustus'

general, the future emperor Tiberius, recovers from a Barbarian king the Roman military insignia lost in an earlier battle. At the foot of Augustus is Cupid astride a dolphin, symbolising the goddess Venus, who was said to be an ancestor of Augustus through his adoptive father, Cæsar.

In front of the statue is the most interesting of various 2nd century AD Roman floor mosaics, depicting the adventure of Ulysses and the Sirens.

Continue on the right side. Past the column is a statue of *Emperor Titus* (late 1st century AD) in his civilian garb, the toga (No. 26).

In front of the great square niche that follows is a bust of *Julius Cæsar*, so heavily reworked that little of the original remains (No. 30). It is flanked by two wonderful bronze peacocks, the originals of those we saw near the Pine Cone (p. 317). These symbols of immortality came from the tomb of the Emperor Hadrian (p. 389).

Past another column, the third bust is *Emperor Trajan*, early 2nd century AD (No. 41).

Go to the end of the gallery and pass to the opposite side.

In the first niche is *Demosthenes* (No. 64), an admirable portrayal of the great Greek orator, a Roman copy of a 3rd century BC Greek statue.

In the second niche, the *Wounded Amazon* (No. 67), Roman copy of a work by another major Greek sculptor of the 5th century BC, Kresilas. Arms and feet are a modern restoration. The original was entered in a famous competition on this theme; we'll see another entry further on (p. 325).

Past the third niche, No. 71 is a bust of *Julia*, Emperor Titus' daughter (1st century AD). The following bust, No. 74, is *Emperor Hadrian* (2nd century AD).

Proceed to the great round central niche.

It contains a colossal statue of the personified *River Nile* (No. 106), a 1st century AD Roman work, possibly based on a hellenistic original. It was found in 1513 near S. Maria sopra Minerva, where, as you may recall (pp. 114, 116), there was a temple to the Egyptian goddess Isis to which the statue probably belonged.

Sixteen children play with animals and scramble

The Belvedere statue of the River Nile, as drawn in the 16th century by Francisco de Holanda

over the great river god, who lies near a sphinx and carries a horn of plenty, symbol of the Nile's fertilising power. Around the base, on the sides and on the back, are whimsical fights between pygmies, between crocodiles and hippos, and between ibises and crocodiles, evoking life on the banks of the Nile.

Go past the great round niche. Before the column is another statue of *Julia* (No. 108), daughter of Emperor Titus, found along with that of her father now opposite it. The hairstyle is typical of the Flavian era (1st century).

First niche: (No. 111) *Athena*, goddess of wisdom, the best known, Roman copy of a 4th-century BC Greek original.

Past the niche, (No. 112) bust of *Domitius Ahenobarbus,* Nero's Father, whom we saw portrayed as a child in the Ara Pacis (p. 223).

Second niche: (No. 114) the head is that of *Emperor Claudius*, 1st century AD; the body, with toga, does not belong to it.

Before the fifth niche: (No. 121) bust of *Emperor Philippus the Arab*, a striking portrait of a ruler in the declining empire (3rd century AD).

Fifth niche: (No. 123) the *Doryphoros* ('the Spear-bearer'), Roman copy of a lost original by Polyclitus, a seminal work of classical Greek art. The 5th century BC sculptor was the first to study the proportions of the human body and the dynamics of its balance, producing sublime, vastly influential works (note the many other statues with similar postures, including that of Augustus across the hall). Polyclitus is known to have created a statue that summarised his æsthetic principles, and it is probably this one.

Sixth niche: statue of *Emperor Domitian* (late 1st century AD).

Exit again to the long gallery, and backtrack to

its beginning, this time observing, rapidly, the works on your right. Note in particular:

Panel XLVII (Nos. 14, 15, 16): portrait of a *Lady of the Imperial Family* (first half of the 1st century AD), followed by two typical portraits of *Citizens* of the same period.

Panel XXXI (halfway down): (No. 2) relief of the *Three Graces*, Roman copy of a 5th-century BC Greek original.

Panel XXIX: (No. 2) head of *Augustus*. (No. 4) Statue of *Tiberius*. (No. 5) Head of *Tiberius*.

Panel XIX: (No. 13) portrait of a *Roman of the End of the Republic* (1st century BC). (No. 5) Head of *Agrippina* (early 1st century AD), mother and victim of Nero.

Panel XI: (No. 12) head of *Cicero* (1st century BC).

Panel VII: (No. 2) fragments of a relief representing the *Dance of the Aglaurid Sisters* (the mythical dispensers of nocturnal dew) and the *Dance of the Hours*. Roman copy of a 4th-century BC Greek model.

Panel V: (No. 3) statue of *Emperor Antoninus Pius* (2nd century AD) in armour (he is the one being taken to heaven on the first sculpture we saw in the museum, p. 312).

Panel III (last): (No. 16) the last bust to the right on the lower shelf represents *Emperor Geta*, co-emperor with his brother, Caracalla, and murdered by him in the early 3rd century AD (see pp. 165, 262).

The gallery ends with stairs (lavatories on the left) leading to the late 15th-century Palazzo del Belvedere, where the original museum was founded. Go upstairs and straight through a square room and a round hall to a smaller room. There, in solitary splendour, is the *Apoxyomenos* ('the Scraper') by Lysippus, the only existing Roman copy of a lost Greek masterpiece.

It represents another basic stage in the development of sculpture after Polyclitus' *Doryphorus* (p. 319). Working a century later, in the 4th century BC, Lysippus adds to his predecessor's canons a new spontaneity and emotional commitment, and a deeper feel for three-dimensionality. Through

the movement of the extended arms, torso and legs, the statue more fully commands its space and can be admired equally from all sides, not mainly from the front as in earlier sculpture.

The statue is of an athlete scraping off sweat, dust and the olive oil used in wrestling. The bronze Greek original adorned the Baths of Agrippa in Rome (p. 242).

Proceed straight to a final vestibule. On the wall are mosaics depicting circus and arena scenes.

This room opens onto the spiral **Scala del Bramante**, built by the great early 16th-century architect to allow access to the palace on horse- or mule-back.

Inspired by the ramp we'll see in Hadrian's Tomb (Castel Sant' Angelo), the stairway is the prototype of many others, including Borromini's (p. 64) and the modern double ramp near the exit of the museums.

From the vestibule return past the *Apoxyomenos* and go toward the round hall. In the archway between these two rooms, on the right, a tablet states in Latin that Leonardo da Vinci often lodged and worked in these rooms between 1513 and 1516. The door on the right leads to the **Cortile del Belvedere**, housing the first masterpieces collected and exhibited in the Renaissance. (This is the original name of the space; it was later changed to Octagonal Court to avoid confusion with a newly created subdivision of the central courtyard – p. 308 – which was then called by the same name, Belvedere Court. The mixing up of these names in Vatican and other publications is a perpetual source of confusion.)

Go to the left corner. In an enclosure is the *Apollo Belvedere*, one of the most famous works in art history. This is a Roman copy; the original is dubiously attributed to Leochares, a 4th-century BC Greek sculptor. Winckelmann (p. 39) thought it the 'highest ideal' of art. Goethe was 'swept off his feet'. It has enjoyed almost unparalleled renown from the moment it was unearthed at the end of the 15th century. Critics today, however, are a bit more reserved. The lithe proportions, sensuous, powerful body, stately posture and

The young Taddeo Zuccaro drawing the Apollo Belvedere and the Laocoön

dominating gaze are truly godlike, perhaps even too declaredly so. There is a tinge of affectation that seems to presage the end of serene classicism and the advent of the more rhetorical, less spontaneous Hellenistic era.

Continue clockwise to the next corner. An enclosure there contains the *Laocoön* group. One of the few sculptures comparable to the *Apollo Belvedere* in renown, it is and was even more famous, in antiquity as well as today. The 1st century AD Roman historian, Pliny the Elder, called it the greatest sculpture then known. His detailed description allowed the identification of the statue when it was excavated in Rome 1,500 years later (p. 212), shortly after the *Apollo*. The statue immensely influenced Michelangelo and other renaissance artists, and has enthralled every generation since.

Laocoön was a Trojan priest in post-Homeric myth, who tried vainly to warn his countrymen of the threat posed by the wooden horse donated by the Greeks. This incensed Athena, the protectress of the Greeks, who sent two snakes to strangle him and his two sons.

The work is thought to have been made in Rome in the 1st century AD by three otherwise unknown Greek masters, reproducing a Greek original, probably in bronze, of the 2nd century BC. Its extraordinary virtuosity may make it the masterwork of Hellenistic sculpture. To today's eyes, however, not even the Laocoön escapes the common shortcoming of that age of sculpture, an overly self-conscious desire to impress. Note, though, the wonderful modelling, the extremely dynamic, yet cohesive composition and the great pathos. (For a theory that the statue is in fact a forgery by Michelangelo, see p. 309.)

Leave by the right-hand door. In the next passage two *Molossian Dogs*, Roman copies of 3rd century BC Hellenistic works, guard a door. Proceed to the third corner of the courtyard.

Here stands the *Hermes*, Roman copy of a late classical, 4th-century BC Greek bronze original, serenely portraying the messenger of the gods. Poussin called it 'the most perfect example of the male human body'.

Behind you, in the right niche of the arch, (No. 6) is an ancient Roman Priapic (phallic) statue of the *Wealth of Nature*, of uncertain date.

Continue clockwise. Noteworthy in the following passage are:

Between the columns on the right (No. PN 45)

a large tub-shaped (two ends juxtaposed) sarcophagus with *Fighting Animals*, a powerful 3rd century AD work.

Opposite, on the wall above is a typical sarcophagus depicting the half-closed door of the Netherworld (3rd century AD).

In the niche at the centre, *Venus*, a late 2nd century Roman work. The body is a replica of a famous statue by Praxiteles, which we'll see and discuss shortly (p. 323). The head is that of a Roman lady, possibly Emperor Marcus Aurelius' wife Faustina Junior (noted for her misbehaviour).

Continue straight to the last corner. In the enclosure are three statues by Antonio Canova (late 18th–early 19th century), a great Italian artist, so famous in his time that he almost personified the neo-classical period of European sculpture.

Before Napoleon exiled him, Pope Pius VII (p. 67) commissioned these works to try to replace the many ancient statues taken from the Vatican to Paris on the orders of Napoleon (most were returned after the fall of the emperor). Pius' choice was appropriate, since no other sculptor alive knew better than Canova how to revive the ideals of classical art in the spirit of those principles of 'noble simplicity, calm grandeur' that Winckelmann (p. 39) had recently declared to be central to the classical vision. Canova added a touch of late 18th-century gracefulness.

In the centre is *Perseus*, son of Zeus and slayer of the serpent-haired Medusa. On the sides are *Kreugas* and *Damoxenos*, Greek boxers, who, according to a 2nd century AD report, were involved in what must be the worst episode of bad sportsmanship in history. When he saw that he was losing, Damoxenos stabbed Kreugas in the belly and ripped out his intestines. The referee disqualified Damoxenos and declared his dead victim the winner; it was the most he could do.

Cross the court back to the passage flanked by the *Molossian Dogs*. From here enter another set of rooms in the Palazzo del Belvedere, all devoted to statuary. Here you are about one third of the way into your visit.

These statuary halls are not usually all open at once. The first is the **Room of the Animals**, divided into a left and a right section (sometimes only one is open).

Most of the animal statuettes are by an 18th-century sculptor-restorer, Antonio Franzoni, either heavy reworkings of ancient fragments, or entirely his own. In the left section, most noteworthy is the boar-hunting *Meleager* with his dog in the central niche of the short side (No. 40). It is a Roman copy of a Greek work, possibly by Skopas, one of the most dynamic and dramatic classical sculptors (4th century BC).

To the right, under the window, is a colossal *Camel Head*, Roman copy of a 2nd century BC hellenistic work, once part of a fountain.

In the right section, in the middle of the right wall, are two small mosaics from Hadrian's Villa (2nd century AD), made with tiny chips and representing bulls attacked by lions and goats grazing (Nos 138, 152). They are the finest of several mosaics of various periods on the walls and floors of this group of rooms.

Standing between the two small mosaics is a Mithras group (No. 150), a Roman religious work of the 2nd century, when the Persian cult of Mithras was popular in Rome alongside Christianity and other eastern religions. The sun-god is usually represented, as here, killing the primeval bull, symbol of the procreative force. Since Creation starts with the flowing of the bull's blood, the evil spirits, symbolised by a scorpion, a snake and a dog try to prevent the sacrifice.

Now take the arched passage toward the great window.

If this section and/or passage are closed, leave the Room of the Animals from opposite the courtyard door and enter the Room of the Muses, picking up the description on p. 315

Turn left into the short end of the long **Gallery of the Statues**.

First statue on the left: (No. 1) head of *Lucius Verus*, co-emperor and brother of Marcus Aurelius (2nd century AD), superimposed in an old restoration on an earlier body of *Emperor Augustus*.

Gallery of the Statues, engraving by the early 19th-century architectural historian and educator Letarouilly

Third on the left: (No. 5) a striking *Hermes*, the messenger god, Roman elaboration on a 5th-century BC Greek model.

At this end of the long gallery are two candelabra from Hadrian's Villa (2nd century), a Roman work, the richest and possibly the most beautiful objects of their kind we have from antiquity.

They flank a *Sleeping Ariadne*, a high quality Roman copy of a 2nd century BC hellenistic original (No. 11). The statue has been placed over a late 2nd century AD sarcophagus carved with a *Struggle between Giants*.

Continue clockwise and walk up to the large window. Enter a square room to the right, the **Room of the Masks**, so called after the beautiful mosaics on the floor (2nd century AD) from Hadrian's Villa.

At the far left (visible even if the room is closed) is an ancient Roman toilet or bidet in red marble (No. 26), the *Sedia Stercoraria*, whose strange role in papal history is related on pp. 413-414.

In the niche opposite the entrance is the *Venus of Cnidos* (No. 37), a Roman copy of a famous statue by the Greek Praxiteles (4th century BC), the artist who introduced grace and sensuousness into classical Greek sculpture, which previously had stressed force, dynamism and balance. The movements of his figures are just hinted at. The expression is dreamy and veiled, yet there is great vitality and warmth. Praxiteles was as influential in the development of art as his great predecessors. This work was especially famous, as it was the first time the goddess was represented nude.

To the left of the statue are the *Three Graces*, a

323

The Belvedere Torso, engraving by Letarouilly

charming copy of a late hellenistic work (No. 35).

Leave the Room of the Masks the way you came in.

Back in the long Gallery of the Statues go left all the way up to the columned passage flanked to the left by a seated statue of the Greek dramatist *Posidippus*, Roman copy of a 250 BC Greek original (No. 50), and to the right by an unidentified seated portrait (No. 51) found with it. Both heads are much reworked.

Past the columns enter the **Room of the Busts**, divided into three sections. Proceed clockwise.

Between the windows are marble 'anatomical' votive offerings of the sick from pagan sanctuaries: a rib cage (No. 13) and an open abdomen (No. 15), analogous to those placed later in Christian churches.

Keeping to your left, pass to the second section.

On the lower right shelf are the busts of two children: the first (No. 63) is the future emperor *Caracalla* (2nd century AD); the second (No. 65), dressed as chief of the army, is probably the imperial heir, *Diadumenianus*, assassinated in 218 AD at the age of 11.

Continue to the third section.

In the niche at the end is *Jupiter Enthroned*, Roman replica of the cult statue in the Capitol Temple (pp. 142-143, 163), originally by the 1st century BC Greek sculptor Apollonius (No. 77).

In front of the statue, a celestial globe with zodiac and stars (No. 91).

Continuing clockwise, return to the first of the three bust sections. The wall opposite the windows exhibits on shelves a parade of original Roman busts of emperors. On the lower shelf (left to right):

No. 122: *Julius Cæsar* (d. 44 BC).

No. 123: *Augustus as a Youth*.

No. 124: *Augustus as a Priest* (reigned 27 BC-14 AD). The wreath of wheat ears is the symbol of a religious brotherhood.

No. 127: *Nero as Apollo the Lyre-player*(?), reigned 54-68 AD.

No. 130: *Titus* (reigned 79-81 AD).

No. 131: *Nerva* (reigned 96-98 AD).

No. 132: *Trajan* (reigned 98-117 AD).

No. 133: *Hadrian* (reigned 117-138 AD).

Upper shelf (left to right):

No. 112: *Antoninus Pius* (reigned 138-161 AD).

No. 113: his son, the 'philosopher emperor' *Marcus Aurelius* (reigned 161-180 AD).

No. 114: *Lucius Verus*, Marcus Aurelius' adoptive brother and co-ruler.

No. 115: *Commodus*, Marcus Aurelius' son, a deranged tyrant (reigned 176-192 AD).

No. 120: *Caracalla*, also mentally unbalanced (reigned 211-217 AD).

Return to the long gallery. Toward the middle of the left side is the *Wounded Amazon* (No. 59), a badly restored Roman copy of a 5th-century BC work (the head does not belong to it) which was another entry in the competition mentioned on p. 318. The original is attributed to Phidias, another supreme Greek master, coordinator and possibly creator of the famous sculptures of the Parthenon.

Next, No. 62, is a famous masterwork by Praxiteles, *Apollo Sauroctonos* ('he who kills the lizard'), Roman copy of a 4th-century BC original). The playful attitude, flexibility and naturalness show how far sculpture had progressed technically from the time of Polyclitus (p. 319). Yet one also feels that some pure, almost transcendental sense of beauty has been lost and that the hellenistic decline is not far away.

Approach the exit. Near it is (No. 85) a delicate adolescent *Eros*, Roman copy of a Greek 4th-century BC work.

Return to the Room of the Animals. From there, at the passage opposite the courtyard, turn right to enter the **Room of the Muses**.

Here begins an 18th-century addition to the 15th-century Belvedere Palace by the architect Simonetti. Originally an entrance to the museum within the Vatican walls, the addition connects the Belvedere to the structures built in 1932 and 2000 to form the present entrance and exit.

The main attraction of the Room of the Muses is in the middle: the *Belvedere Torso* by the Greek Apollonius (see p. 324), who worked in Rome in the 1st century BC. It is famous for the boundless admiration it drew from renaissance artists, especially Michelangelo.

Found in the early 15th century, it represents Hercules or another mythological character. The influence of this powerful, muscular figure on Michelangelo's art, as we'll see shortly in the Sistine Chapel, is easily seen. Three and a half centuries later, the piece also inspired the French sculptor Rodin for his famous *Thinker*.

Around the room is a set of statues representing the *Muses*, found in the 18th century in the ruins of a Roman villa. They include portraits of famous Greeks. Most are Roman copies of 3rd-4th century BC Greek originals. The most striking are on the right wall (if you face the *Belvedere Torso*):

No. 23: *Erato* (muse of lyric poetry, and often love songs).

No. 21: *Homer* (from a 5th-century BC original).

No. 20: *Socrates* (philosopher).

No. 18: *Calliope* (the muse of epic poetry).

No. 16: *Apollo as lyre-player* (the master of the Muses).

As you leave the room, the last portrait on the right is *Pericles* (No. 44), from a 5th-century BC original by the famous Kresilas (see p. 318).

Represented here with his helmet of supreme commander, Pericles was the Greek democratic ruler whose name is forever tied to the golden age in Greece. This statue is the source of all images of him in history books.

Enter the great **Round Room** (built by Simonetti, who was inspired by the Pantheon).

On the floor is a great 3rd century AD Roman mosaic; in the centre, a vast porphyry basin carved from a piece found in front of the Curia (p. 167) in the Roman Forum.

Then, going counter-clockwise: No. 3, bust of *Jupiter*, Roman copy of a famous 4th-century BC Greek statue of the king of the gods.

In the niche is (No. 4) *Antinous*, Emperor Hadrian's lover (pp. 200-201), though the identification is not quite certain; with the attributes of the cult of Dionysus, the god of wine, probably a 2nd century AD Roman work. Famous for his beauty, the youthful Antinous drowned in the Nile in 130 AD and was deified by Hadrian.

No. 5, bust of *Empress Faustina Senior* (p. 312), mother of Faustina Junior (p. 322) and mother-in-law of Marcus Aurelius (2nd century AD).

In the niche (No. 6) is a *Goddess*, Roman copy of a 5th-century BC Greek work (school of Phidias, p. 325).

No. 7, head of *Emperor Hadrian* from his tomb in Castel Sant'Angelo (2nd century AD).

In the niche is (No. 8) a gilt bronze *Hercules*, unearthed in 1864 from the ruins of Pompey's Theatre (p. 514), a 2nd century AD Roman work.

No. 9, bust of *Antinous* from Hadrian's Villa, a 2nd century AD Roman work.

In the niche is (No. 10) a *Goddess*, Roman version of a late 5th-century Greek prototype (school of Phidias). Skip the next bust, niche and bust.

In the niche is (No. 16) *Emperor Claudius* (Messalina's husband, pp. 84, 155) dressed as Jupiter, 1st century AD.

In the niche is (No. 19) *Juno*, from a temple of the goddess, a 2nd century AD Roman work.

Pass into the **Greek Cross Room**, so-called from its shape. In the middle of the floor is a 3rd century AD Roman mosaic with a bust of *Athena* and the *Phases of the Moon*.

On the right is the magnificent *Sarcophagus of Constantina*, daughter of Constantine, the emperor who legalised Christianity in the 4th century (p. 198). The sumptuous porphyry marble coffin, from her mausoleum (p. 610) depicts symbolic figures common in the Early Christian cult (cupids harvesting grapes, peacocks, etc.) drawn from a traditional pagan repertory.

On the other side is the *Sarcophagus of St. Helena* (p. 399), mother of Constantine, carved a few decades before that of her grand-daughter and equally magnificent (p. 368). The subject of the reliefs is war, which may mean that the sarcophagus, which was found in Helena's tomb outside Rome, was originally meant not for her, but for her emperor husband (Constantius Chlorus, the father of Constantine), or for Constantine himself.

Take the stairs to an upper landing. (The entrance to the Etruscan Museum, which is not part of the Walk, is another floor up, see p. 681).

On the right is the **Room of the Chariot**, often closed (something can be glimpsed through a gate). In the middle is the impressive *Chariot (Biga)*, though only the box of the marble cart and part of the body of the left horse (if you are facing the group) are ancient, and moreover these 'original'. They were put together and completed for exhibition here by the same 18th century sculptor, Franzoni, who created most of the animals in the Room of the Animals (p. 322).

The exquisitely sculpted chariot body, whose wheels are by Franzoni, is a Roman work, perhaps 1st century AD. It may have been a votive offering to a god. During the middle ages it was used as a bishop's throne in the church of S. Marco.

Along the walls, going right from the entrance:

First niche: (No. 608) *Bearded Dionysus*, Roman copy of a Greek original from the school of Praxiteles.

Around the room are sarcophagi of children (2nd-3rd century AD), showing cupids competing in circus races, a symbol of the human condition.

Before the third niche on the left side: (No. 615) *Discobolus Pacing to Measure the Distance*, Roman copy of a 5th-century BC Greek original, probably by Naukydes, son of Polyclitus.

Past the third niche: (No. 618) *Discobolus Throwing the Discus* (the head is a modern addition), Roman copy of a famous 5th-century BC work from Hadrian's Villa. It is the masterwork of Myron, another founder of classical Greek sculpture, greatly influential especially with regard to problems of human movement in art.

Leaving the room we start toward the Apostolic Palaces, the oldest Vatican complex. Here you're

Room of the Chariot, engraving by Letarouilly

at the beginning of one of Bramante's parallel corridors, across from the one you walked through in the Chiaramonti Sculpture Gallery (p. 317), but you are one floor higher.

There are no really major works here. Your attention is best spent on the few indicated here.

The gallery is called the '**Room of the Candelabra**' after several great candelabra, all impressive 2nd century AD Roman works, in the openings around the arches.

Go past the first section. In the second section (in the middle on the right) is (No. 22) a statue of the *Diana of Ephesus*, 2nd century AD copy of a cult statue of this middle-eastern fertility goddess, from Hadrian's Villa.

Section 4: first niche left: (No. 94) *Young Prince*

of the 1st century AD, with the amulet-pendant worn only by patrician children around his neck; second niche right: (No 38) *Old Fisherman*, Roman copy of a 3rd century BC hellenistic work, extraordinarily realistic. Under the third window left: (No. 66) *Child Strangling a Goose*, Roman copy of another famous hellenistic work of the 4th century BC.

Section 5, immediately right: (No. 5) *Female Runner*, with a palm branch on the base symbolising victory, 1st century BC copy.

In the last section over a sarcophagus on the left is a *Persian Soldier*, copy of a 2nd century BC hellenistic original (No. 32).

This is now the end of the visit to the Vatican Museums proper.

BEFORE GOING

2. The Papal Apartments and frescoes in the Apostolic Palaces; the Stanze, or Rooms, of Raphael

The decoration. Along with their monumental construction programme, the popes launched an intense decoration programme after moving to the Vatican, focusing on the early complex of buildings, the Apostolic Palaces adjoining St. Peter's.

From 1450 the Vatican called in over a dozen masters from Florence and other Central Italian cities that were the cradle of renaissance art. The first were Fra Angelico, Perugino and his pupil Pinturicchio, Piero della Francesca, Andrea del Castagno, Botticelli and Signorelli. Some worked in the papal apartments, others in the adjacent Sistine Chapel, of which we'll say more in the next section.

Unless you are admitted to a private audience (as distinct from the collective ones mentioned on p. 305) you cannot enter the section of the buildings occupied by the present pope and his court and offices; in any case, apart from its ceremonial splendour, it is not the most important part artistically. But you can tour the older apartments with their priceless frescoes and get a feeling of their fabulous past, though almost no furniture or fixtures remain to remind us that these rooms were once actually lived in.

We'll see rooms dating back to the 13th century, adjacent to the present papal court. Near them – in the structure added to the original one two centuries later (p. 307) – we'll pause in the private chapel of an austere mid-15th century pontiff decorated by the sweetest and chastest of the old masters, Fra Angelico. Later we'll step, one floor down, into an entirely different atmosphere.

The Borgia Apartments. At the end of the 15th century Cardinal Rodrigo Borgia (p. 45) became pope, taking the name Alexander VI. To house himself and some of his many illegitimate offspring, he chose a suite beneath the rooms frescoed by Angelico and others. A few years later, a political opponent described life in Alexander's home in a letter:

> Who would dare describe in full the monstrous acts of libido that take place within those walls? The rapes, the incests, the violence on children of both sexes? The number of whores and pimps permitted to roam freely in St. Peter's See is infinite. In comparison, Rome's brothels are the purest abodes.

We might consider these partisan exaggerations, were they not confirmed in some detail by the Vatican's icy, punctilious master of ceremonies, the German Johann Burchard (p. 48), whose diaries are considered reliable. Famous is his concise report of a party attended by the pope and his children, Cesare and Lucrezia, to which fifty high-class courtesans were invited and danced 'first dressed, then nude,' and also performed 'carnal acts' with the guests in public. On 31 October 1501 Burchard reported, as unruffled as when he was talking about the running competitions (p. 123):

Raphael: The School of Athens (detail)

Silk coats, sandals, caps and other gifts were exhibited, to be given those who could copulate the most times ... Everybody did everything with them under everybody else's eyes; then the prizes were awarded.

Burchard passes no judgement on how the popes led their lives. He only grumbles when protocol is violated in a procession, the pope is wearing the wrong clothes, or a cardinal's tonsure is unshaved. At one point in his diary he states, without comment: 'Now, for the first time, people are starting to go around with masks on their faces.' Assassination and theft were becoming the order of the day and people were being stabbed in churches. The Borgias made a way of life out of murder and torture, for political or personal motives. In one room of the apartments Lucrezia's first husband, young Prince Alfonso of Aragón, of whom her family wasn't fond, spent his last hours. He had been brought there that morning after 'unknown assailants' had wounded him just outside the papal palace the night before. Burchard reports:

> The prince was kept under close guard, but since he had no intention of dying of his wounds, he was strangled in his bed around three in the afternoon. His doctors and a hunchback male nurse were arrested and interrogated, but could prove that they were innocent, as those who had arrested them knew perfectly well.

The apartments retain no trace of these dramas except for Pinturicchio's frescoed walls. Along with edifying allegories, they give a fabulous record of Alexander's times, including the pope's portrait and perhaps – the identification is uncertain – those of his children.

Also portrayed is the Turkish sultan's brother and rival to his throne, Prince Djem, who had been arrested in Italy and held at the papal court. The Sultan paid the popes amply for this service. He also tried repeatedly, by offering large sums, to have his brother murdered, but failed at first, possibly because the prisoner was more valuable alive than dead. Alexander VI was later forced to give him up to the King of France who had invaded Italy. Djem died in the hands of the latter, 'having ingested some food or drink unsuited to him, and to which he was unaccustomed,' Burchard diplomatically noted.

Among the rewards the sultan gave the popes for Djem's detention was a supposedly precious relic, which the sultan claimed had been found in Palestine: nothing less than the spearhead used to kill Christ on the Cross.

Burchard relates that several cardinals and other papal advisers contested the authenticity of the relic and urged the pope to reject it. But accepted it was, and it has been treasured ever since. It is one of four major relics in the Vatican, kept in St. Peter's to be displayed on special occasions.

Alexander VI died abruptly in 1503 (according to one story, he drank by mistake a cup of poisoned wine he had reserved for one of his cardinals at dinner). Here is what happened that day in his apartments, as related by Burchard:

> The duke [the pope's son Cesare Borgia] sent his aide Micheletto, with many men, to shut all exits from the apartment. There, one of them pulled his dagger out and threat-

ened to cut Cardinal Casanova's throat and throw him out the window, unless he delivered the keys to the pope's coffers. Terrified, the cardinal handed them over. Then these men, entering the room behind the pope's bedroom, opened two strong-boxes full of gold pieces which they took away, together with all the silver objects they could find ... Later, the pope's servants got in and took what was left: they did not leave anything, except the pontifical seats, some pillows and the cloth on the walls.

Julius II's Apartments and the Stanze of Raphael. During the reign of Alexander, his son Cesare Borgia – the model for Machiavelli's hero in *The Prince* – had managed with his father's help to slice off and appropriate pieces of the papal domains and neighbouring lands.

Alexander VI's successor reigned less than a month. Then a brutally energetic man, an able politician and fierce warrior rose to the throne, assuming the name of Julius II. He promptly began to repair the damage the Borgias had done to the Church's interests. He had Cesare arrested and briefly detained in the papal apartments, before letting him flee to Spain, where he later died in battle. Papal forces quickly recovered the lands he had seized.

Julius lived briefly in the Borgia apartments. He then moved to a suite one floor up because, as Paris de Grasses, the master of ceremonies who replaced Burchard after the latter retired, wrote in Latin in his diary, 'non volebat videre omni hora figuram Alexandri praedecessoris sui' ('he could not stand seeing the portrait of his predecessor all the time').

The new pope vigorously resumed the building and decorating programmes of his predecessors, aided by his artistic adviser Bramante, whom he engaged to construct the great courtyard (pp. 307-308) and rebuild St. Peter's Basilica (p. 357).

Bramante suggested hiring several new artists, including Perugino and his pupil Pinturicchio. He advised Pope Julius to invite to Rome another promising pupil of Perugino, Raffaello Sanzio, from the city of Urbino. The pope agreed, and decided to test the young man on one of the walls of the new suite. Most of the walls had already been frescoed by some of the most prestigious painters working in the Vatican: Perugino, Piero della Francesca and Andrea del Castagno.

Raphael started to paint. Pope Julius, another 'universal man' of the Renaissance, was as sensitive in artistic matters as he was decisive in political ones. When he saw Raphael's work, he told him to keep painting, not only the blank walls, but the whole apartment, erasing what had been done by much more famous colleagues. He also put a team of assistants under Raphael's command.

Some of the paintings destroyed (against Raphael's will, it is said) represent a tremendous loss, especially those by the great Piero della Francesca. But thus the sublime *Stanze di Raffaello* ('Raphael's Rooms') were born. The *Stanze* are an extraordinary document of the development of an artist who possessed an enormous ability to profit from external influences without ever altering his basic style.

The fervid cultural milieu then flourishing in Rome, especially at the papal court, provided Raphael continuous inspiration from varied sources, including the works he had been forced to destroy. We can follow room by room the fascinating evolution of his style that took place in a few short years.

As we know, Raphael had begun as a pupil of Perugino. His early works show traces of the easy, airy lyricism of Perugino's school. But under the impact of classical Rome, Raphael's vision became more solemn and sedate without losing its grace and harmony. His encounter with Michelangelo led to greater plasticity and monumentality in some works. Then, in the latter part of his brief career, a rush of colour was added to his palette, evidence of his contact with the colour-drenched Venetian school, whose works were just then gaining exposure in Rome. But Raphael's style throughout remained faithful to the same inner motives, as if he were expressing the same quiet, serene melodies in different keys.

Three years before Raphael's arrival Julius II had summoned to Rome another young man, the Florentine sculptor Michelangelo Buonarroti. The artist, in his early twenties, had proved his vast talent in a previous visit to the city, when on the commission of a French cardinal he had created a stupendous group of the Virgin Mary holding her dead Son (later called the *Pietà* or 'Compassion'). Pope Julius offered Michelangelo a contract for a spectacular series of sculptures, but then changed his mind and engaged him in an odd task for a sculptor: the completion of the frescoes in the great official chapel not far from the wing where Raphael was working. This will be the subject of our next section. The point here is that for four years, two of the three greatest geniuses of the Renaissance were at work in the Apostolic Palaces, only yards away from each other. The third, Leonardo, worked also intermittently at the Vatican, but in a different part (p. 320) and on smaller jobs.

This created another extraordinary artistic synergy, though the influence was almost exclusively Michelangelo's on Raphael's art, for reasons connected with the former's temperament, which we'll discuss later.

The two would meet in the corridors, Raphael serene, self-assured, followed by a train of assistants, Michelangelo alone, gloomy and introverted. There was usually a sardonic exchange of wisecracks, in which Michelangelo was most often the loser. There was no love lost between them. Yet they understood and deeply respected each other's genius. When the German notable Johann Goritz, who had commissioned a small fresco from Raphael of a prophet for the church of S. Agostino, complained that he had been overcharged, Michelangelo dryly noted: 'The knee alone is worth what you paid.'

Raphael kept trying to see what the secretive, suspicious Michelangelo was up to, despite the fact that the latter had barred visitors from his workplace and kept the chapel locked. One night Raphael persuaded Bramante, who as artistic adviser to the pope had the key, to sneak him into the chapel. The sight shook him to the bones. From that day his style was enriched, as the decoration of the *Stanze* clearly shows. Raphael paid tribute to his rival by putting his brooding figure in a fresco representing great historical contributors to the discovery of Truth.

A note on Raphael and Michelangelo. The Raphael-Michelangelo duet synthesises the flowering of renaissance art in Rome in the 16th century, much as the Bernini-Borromini duet encapsulates the blooming of baroque art in Rome a century later.

Raphael's essence was grace, harmony, limpidity of design and colour. He succeeded in being miraculously ethereal and robust at the same time. The uniqueness of Michelangelo resided, on the contrary, in the almost superhuman strength, dramatic power and wonderful sculptural quality of his conceptions.

Raphael and Michelangelo, from an early edition of Vasari's Lives

The two artists' lives had very different courses. Michelangelo, though famous and apparently very rich (see p. 104), was unhappy. Morose, physically uncomely (he was short and his nose had been flattened in childhood by an envious fellow-student), a perfectionist and terribly stingy, he was always at odds with his fellow men. His covert homosexuality did not aid his peace of mind. A further source of his gloom was that, though he loved sculpture passionately, circumstances and the will of popes forced him to be most often a painter and an architect. 'Universal men' of the Renaissance, both he and Raphael had an enormous range of interests; both have left us major architectural works.

Raphael, of sunny disposition, very handsome, loving everybody and loved, even idolised, by everyone in Rome, had an easy, satisfying life. But this bright existence was cut short at the age of 37 by an illness which his contemporaries discreetly gloss over; Michelangelo carried on his labours to the age of 89.

The great renaissance biographer, Vasari, tells us that Raphael died of a sudden illness contracted 'because of his excessive amorous exertions' and because his doctors weakened him by draining his blood with leeches. The agony lasted only a few days. His adoring assistants said he had died by decree of destiny, because he had given everything human art could give. They hung his last monumental painting, the *Transfiguration* (which we saw in the Vatican Pinacoteca, p. 315), over his deathbed. As we saw when the Ancient Rome Walks led us to his tomb (p. 237), all Rome, including the pope, wept at his demise.

2. The Papal Apartments and frescoes in the Apostolic Palaces; the Stanze of Raphael

If you want to keep to your tight schedule, you will have to hurry through the flow of visitors, which is intense here. In the first galleries, where the exhibits are not of paramount importance, you should stop rarely, if at all.

The first gallery we cross is called 'of the Tapestries', from the beautiful, mostly 16th-century tapestries hanging all along it. The first ten to the left were made in Brussels after cartoons by Raphael's pupils. The rest come from Flemish and Italian workshops.

Next is the **Gallery of the Maps**. Between 1578 and 1580 the walls were frescoed with 40 maps of the regions and cities of Italy. They are incredibly accurate for their time, and represent a crucial record of renaissance cartography and geography.

The gallery affords, on the right, views of the Vatican gardens and dome of St. Peter's. The latter view is especially precious, since it is difficult to see the dome close-up from the street.

As you leave the second gallery you come to the end of Bramante's corridor on this side, and enter the compound of the Apostolic Palaces. The buildings here vary in age from the late 16th century of the first rooms you enter (the most recent additions to the original core) to the early 13th century.

The most interesting exhibits here are (first room, on the left) two very rare and beautiful 15th-century Flemish tapestries representing the *Last Supper* and other episodes from the Passion.

Turn left into a large room dominated by a gigantic late 19th-century painting. None of the works here is particularly memorable. But note, here and in the following rooms, the ancient Roman mosaic floors.

The main interest of the next room is that it is within the Borgia Tower built by Pope Alexander VI on the corner of the original Apostolic Palaces. The door at the other end of the room leads to the Apostolic Palaces and to the suite of Raphael's *Stanze* ('Rooms').

Now your itinerary will depend on which route is in use at the time of your visit. Usually the one-way route has you enter the suite, but then leave it immediately, shunting you to a long outer catwalk leading to the suite from the opposite end (on the way the catwalk gives a view of the lower half of the original '*Teatro di Belvedere*', p. 308).

When there are no large crowds (which is rare), the one-way route goes straight through the suite. To use this book at such times, once in the suite proceed through the door in front of you, pass two more rooms and start your visit from the large hall beyond.

You are now in one of the original Apostolic Palaces. It served for a long time as the private residence of the popes, including Alexander VI Borgia, whose apartments you'll visit on a lower floor. From the catwalk you enter a large hall which is considered part of the Stanze, though it was actually frescoed by Raphael's assistants after his death in 1520. These frescoes are nonetheless beautiful and intriguing. The most notable (opposite the windows) is the *Battle of the Milvian Bridge* by Giulio Romano, possibly based on sketches by Raphael.

Constantine won the battle against his co-emperor Maxentius after adopting the Christian Cross as his insignia (see p. 198).

The other frescoes are: to the left, *Constantine's Vision of the Cross before the Battle* by Giulio Romano. Opposite it: the *Baptism of Constantine by Pope Sylvester*; on the window wall, *Constantine Donates Rome and the West to Pope Sylvester*, both by Gianfrancesco Penni.

Pope Sylvester, recipient of the legendary 'Donation of Constantine' (p. 303) is depicted here with the features of the pope reigning at the time the fresco was painted, Clement VII. The papacy long based the legitimacy of its political rule on this supposed donation, which never actually happened. The baptism of Constantine by Sylvester is also legendary, since Sylvester died before Constantine was baptised at the end of his life.

Briefly postponing your entry into Raphael's *Stanze* proper, you now visit two adjacent rooms to which you could not easily return later.

Take the passage opposite the catwalk door to a sumptuous room, the *Sala dei Chiaroscuri*, richly decorated in the 16th century and once devoted to consistories (assemblies of cardinals) and ceremonial papal functions. It is divided by pillars, which mark the connection between the 15th-century wing of the palaces and the oldest, early 13th-century core.

This is the farthest you'll go in the old compound of the Apostolic Palaces, and the closest you can get from this side to the wings housing the present pope's residence and court, which face onto St. Peter's Square.

At the time of writing, an impressive group of late 14th-century wooden sculptures representing the *Flagellation of Christ*, is exhibited here. It does not have any historic connection with the palaces.

Behind the wall with the large windows is **Raphael's Loggia**, the middle balcony in a stack of three whose construction Bramante had begun. Raphael completed it after the death of Bramante, and also designed its decoration, though his assistants executed it. Sadly, the works have long been deteriorating and the loggia is generally closed.

If a planned restoration is finished, the loggia deserves a visit mainly for the extremely fine frescoes in the 'grotesque' style by Giovanni da Udine and the stuccoes, also by him. The small figurative frescoes in 13 sections are by Raphael's other assistants, Giulio Romano, Gianfrancesco Penni, Perino del Vaga and others. The first twelve sections are Old Testament scenes, the last, episodes from the Gospels (the cycle has been called 'Raphael's Bible' as opposed to 'Michelangelo's Bible' in the Sistine Chapel). The more strictly decorative and imaginative elements of the loggia were inspired by the discovery of the frescoes in Nero's *Domus Aurea*, which Raphael, who had succeeded Bramante as Superintendent of Antiquities, used to visit with his friends (p. 212).

From the room with pillars, a passage diagonally opposite the entrance leads to a small chapel, which is inside a tower in the 13th-century structure and was decorated in the mid-15th century by Fra Angelico.

In excellent condition, the frescoes depict episodes from the lives of two early martyrs, St. Stephen (above) and St. Lawrence (below), in the simple, noble manner proper to this deeply religious artist. The characters possess great human dignity and the colours a quiet radiance in this masterwork of Fra Angelico's full maturity. On the blue starry vault are portrayed the four evangelists and their symbols. The floor is from the time of Angelico.

From the chapel, backtrack through the adjacent room, skirting the left wall, cross two vestibules and enter the suite of Raphael's *Stanze*.

The first one is called, after one of its frescoes, the **Room of Heliodorus** and contains some of Raphael's greatest creations. There are four principal frescoes, and all the subjects, chosen specifically by Pope Julius II, concern miraculous interventions by God to protect the Faith and the Church.

Chronologically the room is the second painted by Raphael. When he arrived, it was already decorated with frescoes by the great Piero della Francesca, but he was forced to paint over them.

Please note that the two greatest works in the room are not, curiously enough, those on the two main walls, but those on the window walls, as if the cramped space and predetermined framework had stirred the master's imagination and compositional ability to the utmost.

The most stunning of these two masterpieces is in front of you, the *Liberation of St. Peter* (1514).

This monumental night scene is famous for the fantastic effects created by three distinct sources of light: the moon, the torch held by a guard and the angel's halo. One of the most stupendous pictorial blendings of the real and the supernatural, it achieves an almost hallucinatory power through the play of light – especially the back lighting – vivid colour and stark outlines against the shadow. Raphael may have been inspired by works which he himself had obliterated in the room by Piero della Francesca, who was known for such hypnotic effects. Raphael advanced them to a degree that would only be attempted again a century later by Rembrandt.

Turn to the second masterpiece on the opposite window wall, dated 1512 and entitled the *Miracle of Bolsena*.

This event occurred in the 13th century, when a priest who had doubted the Blessed Sacrament (that the sacred wafer, or Host, was really the body of Christ) saw blood gush from the Host while saying Mass. In a symbolic time warp, Raphael shows, opposite the stunned priest, not the medieval pope but his own patron, Pope Julius II, kneeling in prayer. A political allusion to the fact that before starting his expeditions against Cesare Borgia, Julius had placed his enterprise under the patronage of the Blessed Sacrament.

Behind the pope are two of his cardinals. The first is the pope's cousin, Raffaele Riario, whose portrait by Melozzo, together with that of the future pope himself, you saw in the painting of Sixtus IV's family in the Pinacoteca (p. 314). In the painting by Melozzo, the cousins were 37 years younger. All the portraits here are amongst

Raphael's most powerful.

In the lower space to the right are officers of the Swiss Guard, a group portrait famous for its life-like immediacy and vividness.

Perfect mastery of a difficult composition, the grace and expressivity of each figure and deep brilliance of the colouring unite to make an unforgettable scene. This is one of the first instances in which Raphael appears to have exploited the colouristic advances of the Venetian school (p. 315), of which he had just learned.

The third fresco, on your left, *Heliodorus Driven from the Temple*, is only partly by the hand of Raphael.

It refers to the biblical episode of Heliodorus, a Syrian potentate who tried to rob the treasury of the Temple of Jerusalem. A celestial horseman sent by God and two other celestial soldiers smote him and his accomplices as they left, and the gold was recovered. Symbolically the scene stands for the victory of Julius II over Cesare Borgia, who had tried to steal Church lands. To drive the message home, Pope Julius himself appears, sternly and incongruously, on the left.

Some scholars believe that the long-robed youth in the foreground is Raphael. The other two figures, supporting the pope's chair, are Raphael's painter friends, Marcantonio Raimondi and Baldassarre Peruzzi. The left side of the painting, with its splendid colour contrasts, is probably all by Raphael.

Note the originality of the composition, which leaves the middle space – between the calm scene on the left and the convulsed one on the right – empty, emphasising a mystical background and a powerful architectural and perspectival design.

On the remaining wall is the fresco of *Attila Repulsed from Rome*. Raphael began it with much help from his assistants in 1513, the year the great Julius II died, which is why one of the two main characters is not portrayed as Julius, but as his successor, the portly Leo X (whose portrait as a child you saw in S. Maria sopra Minerva).

Raphael: The Stanza of Heliodorus, general view and detail of window shutter, engraving by Letarouilly

Leo also chose to emphasize episodes involving some of the predecessors who carried his name.

The barbarian leader, Attila the Hun, who invaded Italy with a murderous army shortly before the Roman Empire fell (5th century), was stopped by Pope Leo I. Here, astride a black horse, Attila appears terrified by the miraculous appearance of Saints Peter and Paul in the sky, threatening him with swords. The meeting is depicted in view of the gates of Rome, though it actually took place in Northern Italy. Moreover, it is probable that rather than being terrified, Attila withdrew after being paid a ransom.

Pass into the **Stanza della Segnatura** (Julius II's study), where the newly arrived Raphael was tested in 1509 at the pope's request. All the major works here are by the young artist's hand. The decorations evince the theme of the human spirit in its highest manifestations: religion, science, art, philosophy and ethics.

As you enter, opposite is the *Glorification of the Blessed Sacrament*, symbolic of theological Truth.

Here again the focus of the composition is the sacred Host (the Blessed Sacrament of the Eucharist, transubstantiation of the flesh of Christ) as the quintessence of Catholic doctrine. The sacred wafer is displayed on an altar, and the scene of its glorification is divided into two zones: above are the forces of Paradise, including saints and prophets, while below, on Earth, are the defenders of the Faith, amongst them great theologians, popes and visionaries.

As usual, many of the figures portray real people. Amongst those certainly identified is the first on the left, an ecstatic monk in a Dominican cassock, the painter Fra Angelico. To the right of the altar are, amongst others, St. Augustine (an imaginary portrait) dictating to his secretary, and two popes, of which the second is Sixtus IV (builder of the Sistine Chapel and uncle of Julius II, see p. 314). Behind Sixtus, crowned with laurel, is Dante, the greatest Italian poet. The second figure after Dante, hooded and partly hidden, is thought to be Savonarola, the great rebel mystic, a still controversial figure at the time, who had been burnt at the stake by Julius II's predecessor, Pope Alexander VI Borgia (p. 46). Curiously, Julius II himself is not portrayed, unless he is to be identified with God Omnipotent, Who resembles him!

The very complex symbolic scene was certainly conceived with the help of papal theologians. Raphael's style is still reminiscent of his teacher Perugino in the compositional scheme, design and palette, but the artist already shows abundant individuality. The portraits are incisive, the conception monumental, some of the figures breathtaking, such as the virile angels careering through the sky against a background of golden rays and floating cherubs.

Proceeding counter-clockwise, on the next wall over the window are *Allegories of the Christian Virtues*, personified by women and cupids. The fresco to the right of the window is by Raphael's workshop. It depicts the 13th-century Pope Gregory IX, who founded ecclesiastical law, represented as Julius II. The cardinals near him are Raphael's contemporaries: left, Giovanni de' Medici, the future Leo X (pp. 117, 337), and right, Alessandro Farnese, brother of Giulia 'Bella' and the future Paul III (p. 46). The minor fresco to the left of the window is not attributed to Raphael's circle.

On the next wall is the *School of Athens*, symbolising scientific Truth, a composition of absolute formal perfection.

In contrast with the infinite sky of theological Truth, characterising the fresco opposite, the scene here is contained within a limited, though majestic man-made structure, as if to emphasise the triumph of human reason. Ancient thinkers and scientists – some with the features of Raphael's contemporaries – converse as they stroll in an imposing basilica (on a design supplied by Bramante, inspired in turn by the Basilica of Maxentius, p. 287).

Advancing from the depths of the hall towards the steps are the two princes of philosophy, Plato (to the left, probably with Leonardo da Vinci's features) and Aristotle. To their left, grouped around the philosopher Socrates (counting on his fingers) are dialecticians, logicians, grammarians, mathematicians and musicians. Reclining on the steps in contemptuous isolation is the cynic philosopher Diogenes, who despised worldly pleasures.

In the foreground, near the far left, is the wreathed hedonist philosopher Epicurus. In the next group, the philosopher-mathematician Pythagoras writing. Near the centre, the pensive, lonely figure writing on a small sheet is the philosopher Heraclitus, with Michelangelo's features. The cartoon for the fresco, which is preserved, reveals that this space was originally empty. Raphael added the portait in homage to his rival after seeing his work in the Sistine Chapel, the profound impact of which is reflected in the marked stylistic affinity of the portrait with the Sistine Chapel figures.

The group to the right centres on a man bending to draw with a compass on a blackboard. He is Euclid, father of geometry, with the features of Bramante. On his shirt collar (hard to see) is Raphael's signature, R.V.S.M. ('Raphael from Urbino, by his Hand'). To his right, holding a globe in his left hand, is Ptolemy, founder of the Ptolemaic system of astronomy. Here Raphael made a mistake common in the renaissance, confusing him with the Ptolemies who were Pharaohs of Egypt and giving him a crown. The very last figure on the right is the painter Sodoma, while next to him is Raphael himself.

The fresco on the last wall, the *Parnassus*, is a tribute to music and poetry – artistic Truth. The perfect, almost musical rhythm of the design and ineffable beauty of the figures in themselves express the subject matter.

The Muses surround the god Apollo in his mythical abode, Mount Parnassus. To the left are the three supreme poets, the blind Homer with Dante on his right and Virgil on his left. The lower left-hand group includes the 14th-century poet Petrarch (just left of the tree) and the Greek poetess Sappho (seated). In the right section, just next to the Muses, are probably the 16th-century poet Ariosto and the 14th-century novelist Boccaccio. Famous Greek and Latin poets follow.

On the vaulted ceiling are large medallions with allegorical female figures thematically connected to the frescoes below: over the *Glorification of the Blessed Sacrament* is the personification of *Theology*, followed, counter-clockwise, by *Justice*, *Philosophy* and *Poetry*. In the vault corners are four rectangles containing episodes symbolically linked to the medallions (following the *Theology* medallion counter-clockwise are: *Adam and Eve*, the *Judgment of Solomon*, *Astronomy*, and *Apollo and Marsyas*). All are by Raphael.

Note the beautiful Cosmatesque floor.

The last room is also the last chronologically (1514-1517) of the three decorated by Raphael or under his direction, though most of the work is by his assistants. It was the living room of the pope, and takes its name of **Room of the Fire** from the most important of its frescoes, the *Fire in the Borgo* on the wall opposite the window.

The Borgo district (between St. Peter's and the river, and one of our next highlights) was devastated by fire in the 9th century. Tradition has it that Pope Leo IV put it out with a simple sign of the cross. Depicted here with the features of Leo X, who was reigning at the time of the painting, the medieval pope appears in the background on a balcony connected with old St. Peter's Basilica, whose façade is partly visible. The old basilica still existed in Raphael's day; it was being demolished under the direction of Bramante in order to be rebuilt much more lavishly. This fresco is one of the few documents of its appearance.

Raphael designed the scene, though Giulio Romano and other assistants handled most of the brushwork. The most famous detail, the family of four fleeing the fire at the extreme left, is by the master's own hand. Here the painter certainly had in mind an episode from the Trojan War as related by Virgil: Æneas escaping the burning city with his father on his back. The figures are magnificent. In the rest of the fresco one feels the influence of Michelangelo's Sistine Chapel (for instance, the muscular amphora-bearer on the extreme right).

The frescoes on the other walls are all by assistants and are of minor importance. The vault

Raphael and assistants: The Fire in the Borgo

decorations by Perugino, depicting allegories of the Trinity, are very beautiful.

Rest rooms are available here (the door in the wall of the 'Fire' fresco).

Through the door opposite the fireplace enter a chapel entirely decorated and frescoed in the 17th century by Pietro da Cortona. From here take steps (straight ahead and right) leading down to the **Apartments of Pope Alexander VI Borgia** decorated by Pinturicchio and assistants.

The private apartments consist of the first few rooms in a suite of 52 devoted to a gallery of modern religious art. In the context of our Walk you should visit only these first few rooms.

Note: here you'll start seeing signs directing you to the Sistine Chapel. If at all possible (the guards might want to enforce the indicated route here) ignore these signs and follow the directions in this guide. Keep in mind that after the few rooms of the Borgia Apartments, you'll want to reach the Sistine Chapel without passing through the 52 rooms of the modern religious art gallery, a huge detour that contains nothing that could be thought artistically indispensable.

You are now on the lower floor. The first room is part of a defence tower built by Alexander VI (see p. 334) and abutting the corner of the apartments. It is soberly frescoed by Pinturicchio's assistants. The floor is original, as in most of the following rooms. The room, occasionally used as a prison, is where Prince Alfonso of Aragón was strangled (p. 330). Three years later Cesare Borgia was imprisoned here by his father's successor, Julius II (p. 331).

(You may enjoy the second room, on the left, exhibiting some works by modern artists, including Matisse and Rodin, and also some by Goya.

The third room, on the right, is also frescoed by Pinturicchio's assistants.

The fourth room, the pope's study and occasional dining room, is frescoed with *Allegories of the Arts and Sciences* personified by enthroned women. All were designed by Pinturicchio, who also painted some of them (all the other frescoes in the room are by later, minor artists).

Over the fireplace, on the right, before the personification of Geometry, kneels the father of geometry, Euclid. Again, as in Raphael's *School of Athens* (p. 338), he has Bramante's features. The marvellous 16th-century fireplace is by Jacopo Sansovino.

The pope was laid out in this room after he died

in the adjacent bedroom. If you wish to see the latter, identifiable today only by a marble fireplace bearing the pope's name, it is past the door opposite the window. Past the bedroom is a cubicle, possibly the bathroom. Beyond that is the room where the pope's treasure was found by Cesare Borgia's emissaries (p. 331).

If you've made this brief detour, return to the frescoed fourth room.

Proceed to the fifth room through the door to the right of the window. It is called the **Room of the Saints** after the subject of the wonderful frescoes, mostly by Pinturicchio. Over the door through which you entered is the *Visitation*. Continuing left, the *Meeting between St. Anthony and St. Paul the Hermit*.

The next fresco is the famous *Speech of St. Catherine of Alexandria before the Roman emperor*, which depicts most of the Borgia family (except the pope, whom we'll see in the next room), Borgia court notables and Pinturicchio himself.

The identifications are tentative and controversial: most of the characters are here, but deciding who's who is not easy. The ravishingly beautiful St. Catherine – discussing Christian doctrine against the background of the Arch of Constantine – is traditionally thought to be a portrait of Lucrezia Borgia, the pope's daughter by his lover, Vannozza Catanei (pp. 45-46). We have scant clues, however, such as the fact that St. Catherine was the patron saint of bastards, a possible allusion by Pinturicchio to the pope's children.

The emperor is thought by some to portray Cesare Borgia, Lucrezia's brother. On the far left, the figure in red holding a square is the architect Antonio Sangallo the Elder; to his right is Pinturicchio. In the area to the right, the two teenagers in front of a group of sages are thought to be Goffredo, the youngest of the pope's children, and his child wife Sancia of Aragon, sister of the unfortunate Alfonso, (p. 340). She later became the lover of her brother's murderer, Cesare. The fourth child of the pope and Vannozza, Giovanni

Borgia, Duke of Gandía, is thought to be in the crowd, but there is no reliable identification. He was murdered under mysterious circumstances, possibly by Cesare (pp. 46, 355).

The Turkish knight on horseback on the right is the tragic Prince Djem, poisoned to please his brother (p. 330).

On the next wall, to the left, is the *Legend of St. Barbara*, then *Susannah and the Elders*.

Over the door is a *Madonna* thought to bear the features of Giulia Bella Farnese (p. 46), who succeeded Vannozza as the pope's lover.

Alexander VI had three more children by her. During this period another baby also appeared in his household. Alexander had it recognised as his son Cesare's illegitimate son, but it was almost certainly his own. It has repeatedly been suggested that the child, who passed into history as the mysterious *Infans Romanus*, was born of an incestuous tie between the pope and Lucrezia.

Over the window is the *Martyrdom of St. Sebastian*. Note in the background the Colosseum and, further right, the Palatine.

The fantastic decoration of the room is completed with Egyptian motifs by Pinturicchio's assistants (the sacred bull Apis is an allusion to the bull in the Borgia coat-of-arms).

The next room, known as the **Room of the Mysteries of the Faith** from the subject of the frescoes, is the last decorated by Pinturicchio, though he left much of the brushwork to his assistants. Most notable is the *Resurrection* over the door which you passed through, including a marvellous portrait of *Alexander VI Borgia*.

If you are now forced to proceed along the one-way route (see note on p. 340), you have no choice but to trek through the extremely long Gallery of Modern Religious Art, from where signs will direct you to the Sistine Chapel. Otherwise, your best option would be to return to the first room of the apartments and from there take the stairs back up, where you should follow the signs to the *Cappella Sistina* that lead back downstairs by a different route.

Michelangelo: The Prophet Joel, from the Sistine ceiling

BEFORE GOING

3. The Sistine Chapel and Michelangelo's Masterpieces

In order to defend the western side of the papal palaces Sixtus IV (not to be confused with Sixtus V, the great urban planner, who reigned over a century later) decided in about 1450 to erect a massive blockhouse next to the Vatican compound. As built it included an external gallery and battlements on the side of the compound facing St. Peter's.

In normal times the building served peaceful uses. The cavernous interior was an ideal space to gather the cardinals in conclave, as they could thus be isolated and easily watched – in those days papal elections were an occasion for frauds, blackmail, bribery and other shenanigans. The space also served as a giant chapel for the pontiff, where he could perform the most solemn religious rites and ceremonial state functions. It was from these uses and after the name of its builder, that this essentially military installation came to be called the Sistine Chapel.

To embellish the ungainly interior of the rectangular block was amongst the first aims of the great decoration programme launched by Sixtus and his successors. Perugino, Botticelli, Signorelli and others covered the lower part of the walls with large frescoes symbolising the recovered strength of the papacy, the legitimacy of its power and the discomfiture of its enemies. A simple blue fresco of a starry sky covered the ceiling. A strip comprising the upper part of the walls and the edge of the ceiling remained blank at first.

It is not known why Pope Julius II decided to impose on Michelangelo, a sculptor, the task of completing the frescoes in the chapel. The idea was all the more unlikely, since the pope and Michelangelo had already had a falling out when the pope postponed indefinitely the gigantic architectural-sculptural project of his own tomb, which he had commissioned from Michelangelo (see p. 332).

When this happened, Julius tried instead to involve Michelangelo in rebuilding St. Peter's, but the artist, who had spent months selecting the marbles for the forty statues he envisioned for the tomb, left Rome in protest when the job was shelved.

He was virtually forced to return, however. After a commission the pope had given him as a consolation (casting a bronze statue of the pope for a church in Bologna; the sculpture was later destroyed in a military operation), he was again faced with a request which had little to do with his chosen profession as a sculptor: frescoing the blank spaces of the Sistine Chapel.

Michelangelo, multi-talented like many renaissance artists, was not without painterly qualifications. He had actually begun his career as a child apprentice in the studio of the great Florentine painter Ghirlandaio, and had produced some remarkable pictures in Florence. But he considered himself a sculptor, loved sculpture passionately and wished to devote his life to it. Furthermore, he did not feel especially competent as a painter of fresco, a difficult, unforgiving medium.

It is conceivable that the pope, with his unerring taste, understood Michelangelo's potential better than Michelangelo did himself. Another theory is that it was all a scheme engineered by Bramante, the official artistic adviser to the pope, who had good reason to fear Michelangelo's competition in his own field of architecture, and who wanted to see him discredited and ridiculed by pushing him into a great job for which he was unsuited.

Be that as it may, Michelangelo, embittered and challenged, yet with boundless faith in his own genius, responded with bravado. He would do the chapel, and he would paint not only the large blank strips, but also the vast ceiling, then adorned with a simple starry sky. He would accept no advice regarding subject or style, no supervision and no help. None but the pope could see the results before completion.

The pact was struck. Michelangelo went straight to work. He asked Bramante, the architect and engineer, to build the scaffolding needed to reach the ceiling, but Bramante's structure proved unusable because its beams contacted areas of the walls that had to be painted. Michelangelo had it replaced with a free-standing structure of his own design.

He then hired seven assistants, but only in order to learn fresco technique from them. After the first sections were done he released them and continued alone. He worked on the ceiling for four long years, mostly standing, his head tilted back, dust and paint raining into his eyes, with a doggedness and a singlemindedness that bordered on the insane, bringing his food and a chamber pot up with him on the scaffold each morning to save time. (Julius II often visited him, always urging him to hurry, once threatening to throw him off the scaffold if he didn't.) Vasari writes that for some time afterwards, Michelangelo could not read or look at a painting except with his head tilted back.

Michelangelo's sketch of himself at work

The result fully vindicated Julius' choice. It did indeed require the unlimited powers of an architect, sculptor and painter to produce such a grand compositional scheme, populate it with figures of such individual power and maintain in the whole such a wonderful balance of lines and tones. Even in terms of sheer quantity the achievement is amazing: the ceiling measures 45 ft x 128 ft (14 m x 39 m), there are 343 figures, which means Michelangelo completed one every four days.

The paintings were unveiled on 14 August 1511 and on 31 October the first Mass was celebrated in the newly decorated chapel.

Its impression on Michelangelo's contemporaries was enormous, and has not abated. Many consider the frescoes the highest expression of the human mind through the visual arts. Michelangelo's style 'is the language of the gods,' wrote Reynolds, the late 18th-century English painter. Apart from a handful of dissenters in the Romantic era, when Michelangelo's monumentality offended some sensibilities, few have disagreed. Goethe, who visited the Sistine Chapel countless times and once fell asleep there on the papal throne, wrote:

> Whoever has not seen the Sistine Chapel can have no idea of what man is capable of accomplishing. One hears and reads of so many great and worthy people, but here, above one's head and before one's eyes, is living evidence of what one man has done … The master's inner security and strength, the grandeur of his conception are beyond all description … I am so engrossed by Michelangelo these days that even Nature makes no appeal to me, since I cannot see her with the eye of genius as he did. If only there were means to fix such pictures in one's soul!

The Erythræan Sibyl, from the ceiling of the Sistine Chapel; 19th-century engraving

Goethe's accent on Michelangelo's 'inner security and strength' is especially apt. Michelangelo had embraced art since childhood with a passionate love for the human form as a synthesis of all the feelings and forces of the universe. He interpreted this form in a powerful, dramatic and highly personal way, and translated it into stone and colour with an almost infallible assurance.

He seldom revised, rarely had those second thoughts that in Italian art are called *pentimenti*, regrets. In sculpture, he sometimes attacked the stone and extracted his muscular figures without studying them first in clay or in drawings. In painting, he could never have executed such gigantic works alone had it not been for his formidable confidence.

Another facet of Michelangelo's unique character, which differentiates him even more from his fellow artists – Raphael, for instance – was his imperviousness to the influence of the styles of other

345

artists, with the crucial exception of the great examples of the past. He did not care what his contemporaries were doing. He was true to himself throughout his long career. We must add that if he never imitated anybody, the many who mimicked him in the following ages never really succeeded; his monumental style seems to be an end of the line in art history.

The best example of Michelangelo's constancy is to be found in the Sistine Chapel. He returned there when he was 60 to start the fresco on the altar wall of the Last Judgment, another prodigious work. The painting, the largest single composition ever frescoed – 48 ft x 44 ft (14.6 m x 13.4 m) and with over 200 figures – took five years. Despite the 25 years separating the two creations, they are recognisably imbued with the same vision.

Evenness of style does not imply uniformity of atmosphere. Indeed, very different emotions permeate the two masterworks. The ceiling celebrates man's relations with God; the

Altar wall of Sistine Chapel: Michelangelo gave St. Bartholomew the features of his friend the poet Aretino (later a severe critic of the painting), and made the saint's flayed skin into a self-portrait

wall is a terrifying portrayal of His wrath. Contemporaries related with awe that when Pope Paul III unveiled the fresco he broke into prayer: 'Lord, charge me not with all my sins when the Day of Judgment comes.' Historically and psychologically these two modes of Michelangelo's art may reflect the horrors of the Sack of Rome, which occurred in the years between the two frescoes (see p. 381). In any case, together they prove the tremendous range of Michelangelo's expression.

The Sistine frescoes have suffered during the almost half-millennium of their existence, especially from the smoke of candles and incense used in the chapel on ceremonial occasions until recently. In 1547 they were already reported to be obscured by dirt. Restorations were carried out in 1565-68, 1712, 1797 (after an explosion in the nearby Castel Sant'Angelo dislodged a piece of the ceiling), 1903-05, 1935-38 and 1980-1994.

This last cleaning – carried out by Italian specialists with Japanese funding – was the most extensive and was, of course, very advanced technologically. It wiped off layers of grime and the lacquers of previous restorations, giving the colours a brilliance they had not had for centuries or which – some critics say – they never had. A controversial point, since according to a minority of scholars the restoration removed a patina that Michelangelo himself had applied to subdue the colour and give more sculptural relief to the figures. Others maintain that the grime had accidentally acquired a protective function and that the fragile colours are now more vulnerable to the increased pollution in modern Rome.

ON THE SPOT

3. The Sistine Chapel and Michelangelo's Masterpieces

We begin with the ceiling.

The pope wanted it illustrated with stories of the twelve Apostles, but Michelangelo, realising the immense scope of his task, decided that only a subject equally vast would do. Thus he set out to depict the Creation and the human family at the dawn of history, as described in the Bible. The idea was highly unusual, the execution unconventional.

Michelangelo obviously needed to impose some structure on such an immense surface. So he divided it into zones by painting an extremely elegant, fictive architectural framework that followed the strip-like fashion traditionally used for large frescoes. But he added a new element: figures of all sizes breaking out of the painted frames. The result is a fantastic population of figures, each an individual, yet united by an almost magical feat of balance and narrative. As we'll see, Michelangelo abandoned the surviving traces of formal organisation in the second giant fresco – the *Last Judgment* – painted a quarter of a century later on the altar wall.

The depiction of *Genesis* and of the biblical *Flood*, the crux of the ceiling decoration, is a strip running the length of the middle of the vault. This strip is in turn split into nine panels, every other one surrounded by four marvellous *Nudes*. A possible symbolic meaning has long been discussed for these nudes; but the artist's love of beauty and proportion is explanation enough.

Planning: it would be confusing to see all the decoration – the central strip and margins of the ceiling, the upper and lower walls – by circling the chapel just once. The best way to get a reasonably complete viewing with minimal effort is to make three tours, each starting from the altar wall, as we'll explain.

First Tour: proceeding from the altar wall to the opposite wall, look at the nine central panels of the ceiling – the order in which the Genesis story progresses. Michelangelo actually painted them the other way around. Perhaps he felt that the last scenes were easier to handle from the standpoint of fresco technique, with which he was not yet very familiar.

Glance at the four *Nudes* around each panel, but don't concentrate on them individually as you go; do so on your way back to the altar wall.

Here are the subjects of the nine panels:

1) *God Dividing Light from Darkness* (this and the other odd panels also include monochromatic roundels with related stories).

2) *Creation of the Sun and Moon, and of the Plants on the Earth.*

3) *God Dividing the Waters from the Firmament.*

4) *Creation of Man*, one of the greatest works in the history of painting, its spiritual force only equalled by its tremendous formal power. One indeed feels the spark of creation between the two fingertips.

5) *Creation of Eve.*

6) *Temptation and Expulsion from Paradise.*

7) *Noah Sacrificing to God after the Flood* (this episode and the next are chronologically reversed, perhaps because the first required less space).

8) *The Flood*, with famous scenes such as a husband carrying his wife, a sinking boat which a woman tries to stop others from boarding, an old man trying to save a younger one, etc. Part of this panel and of the next fell off when a powder keg exploded in Castel Sant' Angelo in 1797.

9) *Drunkenness of Noah.*

God dividing the waters from the earth, from the Sistine ceiling

The Last Judgment

Back at the altar, look at the fresco of the **Last Judgment** on the altar wall, keeping in mind that Michelangelo painted it 25 years after the ceiling.

Michelangelo's style is similar, but his compositional technique and his mood are not. To accommodate an even more awesome vision, he left out the structure – the division into zones – that he had used in the ceiling (possibly because his now perfect fresco technique allowed him to do so).

The mood has changed from serene to tragic, as required by the subject. The Last Judgment had extra resonance for a city recently traumatised by the great Sack of Rome in 1527 (see p. 381), which was considered divine punishment for the loose, semi-pagan ways that had prevailed in Rome. The subject – unheard of over a main altar – was probably conceived as a reminder of divine wrath.

The composition is a tremendous whirlwind set in motion by Christ's gesture of condemnation and propelled, in the lower part of the fresco, by the blasting trumpets that announce the day of reckoning. Christ is unconventionally depicted as a titanic figure (the face resembles the Apollo Belvedere, which probably inspired it, p. 320-321). Near him is the Virgin, averting her eyes in pity. At their feet are two patron saints of Rome: left, St. Lawrence carrying the gridiron of his martyrdom, and right, St. Bartholomew holding his own skin (he was flayed alive). The features of St. Bartholomew are claimed to be those of Aretino, a renaissance satirist sometimes said to have blackmailed Michelangelo over his homosexuality. The skin itself is a caricaturised self-portrait of the sorrowful Michelangelo.

The fresco is roughly divided into four large bands. The two upper ones are Heaven: above are angels carrying the symbols of Christ's sacrifice; below is Christ surrounded by saints, patriarchs and martyrs, all dismayed by the wrath of God as He judges the world, together with a host of more ordinary people. The most prominent figures in the crowd are St. Peter with his keys (right) and St. John the Baptist symmetrically opposite.

In the lower band, around the celestial trumpeters, are the Elect rising to Heaven (left) and the Damned hurled to Hell by demons (right). The Elect are helped by angels; two of them are hoisted by a rosary, an interesting anti-Protestant note (Lutherans denounced rosaries as superstitious trinkets).

The lowest band on the left represents the *Resurrection of the Dead* – their bodies are being recomposed – and on the right, *Hell*, dominated by two Dantesque figures. To the left is Charon, boatman of the dead, beating the Damned as he ferries them from above. On the far right is Minos, the archdevil. He is donkey-eared and resembles the pope's master of ceremonies, Biagio da Cesena, who had criticised the fresco (when Biagio complained to the pope, he got the answer,

'Sorry, not even the pope can save people from hell.')

Biagio's attack was based on the nudity of the original figures. The accusation of obscenity, promptly taken up by, of all people, the pornographic writer Aretino, who compared the fresco to a brothel, gained strength in subsequent decades. In the prudish climate of the Counter-Reformation, the fresco risked being destroyed. In a compromise, one of Michelangelo's followers, Daniele da Volterra, was commissioned to paint over the private parts, for which he gained the nickname *il Braghettone* ('Mr. Pants'). (For technical and historical reasons, these early overpaintings weren't removed in the last restoration, though other more recently added drapes were.)

Second Tour: starting again from the altar, go around the chapel counter-clockwise to see the rest of the ceiling decoration by Michelangelo (down to the arches over the windows, but excluding the sides of the windows).

The long strip with the Genesis panels is surrounded by three sets of paintings: 1) Four triangular frescoes at the corners of the vault, representing instances of the *Miraculous Salvation of Israel*; 2) all around the Genesis strip, twelve individual figures of *Prophets and Sibyls*; 3) below these, in triangles and arches down to the windows, are figures and scenes representing the *Ancestors of Christ* according to the Gospels.

(The names of the figures in sets 2 and 3 are indicated on the frescoes).

As you go, you can look at all three sets in the area above you at the same time, starting with the first Prophet over the altar (the powerfully foreshortened figure of Jonah) and with the triangular fresco in the right corner representing the *Bronze Serpent*.

Sibyls and prophets fit into the general scheme of man and his redemption, as they are characters from the pagan and Old Testament worlds who, according to Christian tradition, foresaw or prefigured the coming of Christ.

The enthroned figures have an inexpressible monumentality; they are surely the marvellous statues Michelangelo dreamed of sculpting for the pope (see p. 105). It is hard to say which figures are the most beautiful; we'll point out two that hold a

The ceiling of the Sistine Chapel

349

Two ignudi from the Sistine Ceiling

special interest beyond their æsthetic value.

The last prophet on the first long wall, *Joel*, is a portrait of Bramante.

The next triangular fresco (right-hand corner of the wall opposite the altar) represents *David and Goliath*; the third (left-hand corner of the same wall), *Judith and Holofernes*.

Swinging back to the altar, the last prophet, *Jeremiah*, a tragic symbol of the anguish of knowledge, is a pensive self-portrait of Michelangelo.

The last triangular fresco (left-hand corner of the altar wall) represents the *Punishment of Haman*, another biblical scene.

Third Tour: start again from the altar wall (counter-clockwise). As you walk to the opposite wall and return, look at the frescoes under the windows and at the individual figures on the sides of the windows. These paintings represent the pre-Michelangelesque decoration of the chapel commissioned by its builder, Sixtus IV, from the best Florentine painters of the late 15th century.

The frescoes on the first side wall comprise the series of episodes from the life of Moses; those on the opposite wall, episodes from the life of Christ. Beside the windows are imaginary portraits of the first thirty popes (up to the 4th century). All the imagery had a political aim: it symbolised the legitimacy of the papacy not only as a spiritual, but also as a temporal power. All the subjects are related in some subtle way, theological or historical, to this theme, as are many details. One example is the frequent appearance of the Arch of Constantine, an allusion to the spurious claim by the Church that Constantine had given the popes the sovereignty of Rome and the West (p. 303).

The double series of frescoes (including imaginary portraits of the popes beside the windows, some of which we'll mention) is listed here:

(1) *Moses' Journey in Egypt* by Perugino with Pinturicchio, his assistant at the time. The portrait of the *Pope* overhead on the right is by Domenico Ghirlandaio (see the note on him below in connec-

The prophets Jonah (with his whale) and Ezekiel from the Sistine Ceiling

tion with fresco No. 10), the one on the left is by Sandro Botticelli (see the note in the next paragraph);

(2) *Seven Episodes from the Life of Moses* by Botticelli. In this multiple-scene painting, Moses is the man in yellow. Botticelli, a pupil of Filippo Lippi, was one of the star artists in the highly intellectual circles of renaissance Florence. His refined elegance, fluid design and sweet colour are coupled with great solidity of form and touching pathos. Later in life he passed from the poised, classical ideals characteristic of his time to a deep, tormented mysticism. This fresco, from his transitional period, is amongst his masterpieces. The *Pope* overhead on the left is by Ghirlandaio.

(3) *Crossing of the Red Sea* by Cosimo Rosselli, a relatively minor painter.

(4) *Moses Receiving the Tablets of the Law* by Rosselli.

(5) *Punishment of the Rebels against Moses* by Botticelli. Another multiple-scene painting. Moses wears green. Behind Moses on the far right is Botticelli (in black). The *Pope* overhead on the left is by Botticelli.

(6) *Testament of Moses* by Luca Signorelli, an early renaissance artist who is considered the only real precursor to Michelangelo, in his celebration of the dynamism and flexibility of the human body. His works in the chapel are amongst his earliest. The third figure from the left is Signorelli. The *Pope* overhead on the right is by Botticelli.

On the wall opposite the altar wall are minor, heavily restored late 16th-century frescoes.

The great door here is the official entrance. Behind it are halls used in major ceremonies, closed to the public.

The hall visible from here, by the architect Antonio da Sangallo the Younger, is fantastically decorated by late 16th-century artists, including the painter-biographer Giorgio Vasari, Francesco Salviati and the Zuccari brothers. The room is called the 'Royal Hall' because it has been used to receive kings and ambassadors.

Next to it is the Loggia of Benediction, a balcony from whose central window, facing St. Peter's Square, the pope gives his blessing *Urbi et Orbi* ('to the City and the World').

The most important of the last halls situated behind these – inaccessible except by special permission – is the Pauline Chapel, with the last two frescoes painted by Michelangelo before his death (the *Conversion of St. Paul* and *Crucifixion of St. Peter*).

The tour continues with the other side wall.

(7) *Last Supper* by Rosselli. The *Popes* overhead are by Botticelli (right) and Ghirlandaio (left).

(8) *Handing over of the Keys* by Perugino, one of his masterpieces. The fourth and fifth figures from the right are said to be Pinturicchio and Perugino.

(9) *Sermon on the Mount* by Rosselli.

(10) *Calling of Sts. Peter and Andrew* by Ghirlandaio. This excellent painter, known for his clear outlines and bright colours, taught the young Michelangelo for a time in Florence. Both *Popes* overhead are by Ghirlandaio.

(11) *Temptation of Christ* (in the background – the façade is that of the Hospital of the Holy Spirit, which we'll see in the Borgo, pp. 382-383) and the *Purification of the Lepers* (in the foreground) by Botticelli. The far right-hand figure, with a baton, is Girolamo Riario, Sixtus IV's nephew and henchman, whose portrait by Melozzo we saw earlier (p. 314). The *Pope* overhead on the left is by Botticelli.

(12) *Baptism of Christ* by Perugino, inscribed with his name in small letters on the marble cornice just over the medallion figure of God. Perugino probably directed the team of artists in this first phase of the decoration; his is the only signature found in the chapel. The *Pope* overhead on the left is by Ghirlandaio.

Another fresco by Perugino was on the altar wall, but Michelangelo had to erase it in order to create his *Last Judgment* (along with figures he himself had painted over two windows 25 years earlier). The windows were walled up at that time.

Going toward the exit, near the great door, we'll get a chance to see further interesting elements of the chapel.

The beautiful Cosmatesque-style floor is 15th century. Beneath it, incidentally, were once the offices of the masters of ceremonies, including Burchard (p. 329), De Grasses (p. 331) and Biagio da Cesena (p. 348).

The false curtains painted on the side walls, just under the frescoes, were covered on ceremonial occasions with the tapestries designed by Raphael and his assistants, that we saw earlier, pp. 315 and 334.

There are two wonderful marble relief works in the chapel: one is a balcony midway on the left wall, used by the famous Sistine Chapel Choir; the other is the partition dividing the Chapel. Both are the work of one of the greatest 15th-century Florentine sculptors, Mino da Fiesole, possibly in collaboration with Andrea Bregno and Giovanni Dalmata.

You are now back at the great ceremonial door. Here we'll see two much smaller doors, one in the right-hand corner and the other on the left near the marble partition. The right-hand one leads directly to Piazza S. Pietro (St. Peter's Square), and is generally open, except on special occasions. The one on the left leads to the adjacent building and the main exit (near the original general entrance), a very long walk.

Planning your visit: you may want to take the shortest way out to Piazza S. Pietro; if the door is closed, you could try to have it opened for you). If so, you should first see a key highlight on the floor above, which is very near here, then return to the chapel and the exit to the basilica. The highlight is a room containing an important ancient Roman fresco, the so-called *Aldobrandini Wedding*. Before you go, however, ask the guards whether the room is open.

Rest rooms and, in summer, a snack bar are located at the bottom of the stairs that you took to enter the chapel.

To see the *Aldobrandini Wedding* and, if you so decide, go toward the main exit, take the door to the left. A few steps lead to the end of one of Bramante's corridors, which you left to enter the Sistine Chapel, but one floor down. You must now walk the whole corridor again to return to the general exit. The corridor consists of a series of rooms, generically called the Vatican Library, though only the central ones actually house the library. Many of the rooms contain relatively minor objects which you can skim over.

The first three rooms contain religious objects of various ages.

Room I: Church vestments from the 14th to the 18th centuries.

Room II: (frescoed by a minor 16th-century artist) a showcase contains objects found in 1903 under the altar of the Lateran *Sanctum Sanctorum* (p. 403); amongst which, in the centre, is a unique 8th-century enamelled gold cross with episodes from the life of Christ (another gold cross of comparable importance was stolen from the case).

Room III: especially notable are Roman and Early Christian glassware (the case immediately to the left), amongst which, in the lower centre, is a cup with sea animals in relief made in Germany in the 4th century; ivories (2nd and 3rd case to the right) and enamels (6th and 7th cases to the right).

Off the end of the room, to the left, is a room with the most important exhibits in this wing: ancient Roman frescoes, including the famous *Aldobrandini Wedding*. Note: the room is being rearranged at the time of writing.

The fresco, named after the cardinal who first owned it after it was found in 1605, is on the wall opposite the entrance. It is one of the most beautiful and best preserved of ancient Roman frescoes, possibly after a series of Greek paintings from the time of Alexander the Great (4th century BC) depicting the wedding of Alexander and Roxane. It represents the preparations for a wedding. The bridegroom waits near the bed, while a maid encourages the bashful bride. Other women prepare washbasins and garlands.

Continue around the room. In the upper part of the two longer walls are frescoes with landscapes and episodes from the *Odyssey*.

Found in a 1st century BC villa, they represent the hero, Ulysses, amongst a mythical, man-eating tribe of giants called the Lestrygons, his visit to Hell and his stay in the palace of the sorceress Circe. The prevalence of landscape is typical of hellenistic painting of the period.

On the entrance wall, to the left of the entrance, is a fragment from Ostia (the port town near Rome) showing *A Merchant Ship Being Loaded with Grain* (3rd century AD) and, to the right, the god *Mars*.

On both longer walls of this section of the room (before the windows), under the *Odyssey* landscapes, are six fragments representing *Heroines of Greek Tragedies* from a 2nd or 3rd century AD Roman villa.

Far section of the room: on the right wall under the landscapes are two very fine 2nd century AD mosaics; the one with garlands and fruits is from Hadrian's Villa near Tivoli. On the left wall under the landscapes are two fascinating fragments showing a *Religious Procession of Children from Ostia* of the 3rd century AD. They flank a *Chariot Race* of the 2nd century AD.

On the floor is a 3rd century AD mosaic of *Achilles Dragging Hector's Body*. On the ceiling are frescoes by Guido Reni of the story of *Samson*.

Return to the corridor. The final section of the museum is presently being reorganised, so the following paragraphs may have been outdated.

In the next room are copies of ancient papyri and clay models of statues by Bernini, as well as gilt glass medallions of the 3rd-4th century AD from the catacombs. Next is a room with Early Christian and Byzantine artefacts; in the cases are lamps and other objects from the catacombs.

In the next gallery, where the library proper begins, are two early 16th-century navigational maps to the right and left.

The one on the right is by Girolamo da Verrazzano, brother and partner of the sailor who discovered, amongst other places, the Hudson River and Manhattan Island. Globes and planispheres of the same period are also exhibited, the latter based on the theory of geocentricity, with

Michelangelo's projected design for St. Peter's, from a fresco in the Vatican

the Earth as the centre of the solar system.

An interesting exhibit here – at the right end of the room, but often moved around – is an early 15th-century engraved German brass disc representing the world as it was known or imagined before the great explorations.

Eurasia and Africa are shown upside-down (south up) surrounded only by ocean. Interesting historical and geographic references are mingled with imaginary ones, such as black people with dogs' heads in South Africa. The museum shop nearby sells costly reproductions of this precious document.

The next two rooms and a long hall that branches off after the second room are the creation of Pope Sixtus V, the great 16th-century builder and urban planner, who reigned a century after Sixtus IV of the Sistine Chapel fame; thus these rooms are also called 'Sistine'. They are all notable

for their fresco decoration from the time of Sixtus V, mostly by minor artists, showing the changes made in Rome by this pope.

First Sistine Room: over the entrance is a fresco of *St. Peter's Basilica*, then under construction, as it would have been if Michelangelo's plan had been used (see pp. 359-360). Over the opposite door is the *Transfer of the Vatican Obelisk to St. Peter's Square*, a legendary feat in its time (pp. 376-377). A 16th-century stamping device invented and built by Bramante to print the pope's great Lead Seals is often displayed in this room.

Second Sistine Room: past the entrance, near the first window on the left wall is a 16th-century view of the area between the Mausoleum of Augustus and the Tiber, including the churches of S. Rocco and S. Girolamo, which we saw in a previous Walk (p. 224). It was then a desolate area where, as Burchard tells us, human and animal waste was thrown into the river. In the same spot, some decades before the fresco was painted, the corpse of Alexander VI Borgia's son, the Duke of Gandía, was fished out (p. 46). A local boatman said that the night before he had seen five men throw a body into the river. Asked why he hadn't reported it, he said he had seen so many corpses floating there, he considered it normal. Pope Alexander shut himself up in his room, weeping and refusing food for almost a week.

Sistine Hall: this is the transverse wing built by Sixtus V to halve Bramante's enormous *Teatro di Belvedere* (p. 308); it is now often used for special exhibitions.

Of the many frescoes, mostly views of Rome, the most interesting is behind and over the second arch of the hall to the right; it shows Sixtus V's entire urban plan, with its long, straight arteries, as described in the Walks (pp. 44-45, 92).

The last rooms along the corridor are traditionally named after the popes who had them decorated.

Pauline Rooms (of which there are two): on the end wall of the first room is the *Canonisation of St. Charles Borromeo* (pp. 225, 516, 604).

Alexandrine Room: early 19th-century frescoes with episodes from the *Life of Pope Pius VI*, who was imprisoned by Napoleon (see p. 67). The last four scenes on the left wall depict in reverse order his exile in 1798 and death in captivity in 1799.

Two cases on the left contain an 11th-century Italian embroidered white linen altar-cloth and a 10 ft (3 m) wide, very finely embroidered 13th-century English red silk cope.

Clementine Rooms (of which there are five): early 19th-century frescoes with episodes from the *Life of Pius VII*, who succeeded Pius VI and, like him, was arrested and exiled by Napoleon (p. 67). In the second room, the second fresco on the right shows the Colosseum as Pius VII repaired it in 1807 (the restoration was pointed out when visiting the site, p. 209).

Third room: the last fresco on the right depicts *The Pope Arrested in 1809 at the Quirinal* (the French officer holds Napoleon's order).

Fourth room: the first fresco on the right shows the *Arrival of the Pope at Fontainebleau Castle* (near Paris), where he was exiled for five years; the second fresco on the right, his temporary *Deportation to Savona* (near Genoa) in 1814.

A showcase on the right contains ancient Roman bronzes, including an especially fine *Head of a Girl* (upper shelf, far left).

Fifth room: the first fresco on the right shows *Napoleon Exiled from France in 1814*, with Pius VII returning triumphantly to Rome from Piazza del Popolo; the church of S. Maria del Popolo is hidden by a temporary structure built for the celebration. The second fresco on the right depicts *The Pope Leaves Rome for Safety after Napoleon's Escape and Return to Power in 1815*. The last fresco on the left depicts a scene which took place two months later: *After the Final Defeat of Napoleon at Waterloo, the Pope Returns to Rome. He Enters St. Peter's Square.*

The door of the last room is flanked by two porphyry columns with reliefs of the *Tetrarchs*, the four co-emperors who ruled the empire between the 3rd and 4th centuries AD.

Leaving the galleries, descend a staircase leading to the courtyard of the Pinacoteca. You pass the joint entrance to the **Museo Gregoriano Profano**, a collection of Roman and Greek statuary, and the **Museo Pio Cristiano di Antichità Cristiane**. Also nearby is the entrance to the Missionary-Ethnological Museum (For all of these, see the brief descriptions on p. 681).

To reach the main exit, pass a two-storey 1932 building, by Giuseppe Momo, with a sumptuous double spiral ramp (one side goes up, the other down) inspired by Bramante's near the Belvedere court (see p. 320)

Before leaving admire the wonderful modern mosaic (1940) by the Florentine painter Massimo Campigli.

❧ MIDPOINT OF WALK ☙

BEFORE GOING

4. S. Pietro (St. Peter's Cathedral)

The first basilica. You may recall that Caligula ordered a circus (race track) to be built in the Vatican area. It was almost a third of a mile long, running the length of the space presently covered by St. Peter's Basilica and St. Peter's Square. Tradition has it that St. Peter was crucified here in 67 AD, the last year of Nero's reign, and buried nearby in a public cemetery just outside the northern wall of the circus. (For a different tradition, see pp. 560-562) Whether or not this is true will probably never be known; it is debatable whether Peter was in Rome at all. Yet Early Christians venerated his grave there, and there an oratory (chapel) rose by the 2nd century. It is also believed that during a period of severe persecution of Christians in the next century his remains were moved to catacombs near Rome for hiding.

When the Emperor Constantine came to power in the 4th century and promoted Christianity, he replaced the oratory with one of his great basilican churches (p. 397). Its foundations were set near the north wall of Caligula's circus, which was being demolished. Constantine's basilica stood for over 1,000 years, its simple grandeur the wonder of Europe. Then part of the foundation began to crumble, threatening the whole basilica. The popes razed it to build a new one under the direction of Bramante, their artistic adviser. Construction began at the outset of the 16th century and lasted 120 years. Parts of the old basilica, called the Sacred Grottoes, survive below.

The new basilica. Controversy surrounded the building of the new basilica, which was far more extravagant than the old one. The first architects said they aimed to build 'a Pantheon on top of a Basilica of Maxentius', that is, the sum of the largest pagan temple and the largest pagan civic building. The first price was demolition on a tremendous scale. Not only was the old basilica destroyed, but so were its priceless treasures, which Bramante laid waste with such abandon that he was nicknamed *Maestro ruinante*, the 'Master of Ruin'. Countless ancient Roman monuments were also torn down in order to provide materials. A great early 20th-century Italian archæologist, Rodolfo Lanciani, wrote:

> Building the new St. Peter's did more harm to ancient classical remains than ten centuries of so-called barbarism … Of the huge and almost incredible mass of marbles of every type, colour, value and description used in the building, there is not an inch, not an atom that was not removed from classical buildings, many of which were levelled for the sake of one or two pieces only.

The heavy cost of building and maintaining the structure forced the popes into desperate fundraising measures, including a tax on prostitutes and the sale of indulgences (the forgiveness of sins for a fee). The latter triggered Martin Luther's outrage (p. 46) and it has been argued that if it had not been for the rebuilding of St. Peter's, the Roman Church would not have stumbled into the disaster of the Reformation.

St. Peter's and Bernini's colonnade

St. Peter's bones. Let's return to Constantine's time. While the first basilica was being built, the emperor announced he had discovered St. Peter's bones hidden one century earlier in the catacombs (for this sort of recovery, see pp. 107, 368, 417, 589, 630), and had them interred in the original grave. He then had a monument built over them in the centre of the church, over the primitive oratory. The faithful could not see the bones, since the only access was through a hole in the monument from which the inside, several feet down, was invisible.

For centuries the monument over the grave was fanatically worshipped. The 6th-century deacon of the basilica, Agilulf, records that the faithful would lower cloths (weighted, and tied to strings) through the hole to touch the apostle's coffin and thereby acquire healing powers. It was also said that if the fabric weighed more when retrieved than before, Heaven had granted the wish accompanying it.

In the 9th century the basilica was looted, probably by Arab pirates, who devastated Rome in 846. The monument over the grave was damaged and fell out of use. When the basilica was demolished in the 15th century, the monument, by then topped with medieval structures, was preserved as its most precious possession and inner sanctum. In the new basilica, as in the old, the monument was in the most prominent location, a crypt below the main altar beneath the centre of the dome.

By then the exact meaning and history of the multi-layered monument had been forgotten. So it came as a sensational discovery when the architect Giacomo Della Porta (p. 53), levelling the floor over the crypt in 1594, saw through a hole a recess that looked like a grave. Here is what followed, according to contemporary accounts, as reported by the archæologist Lanciani:

> On hearing of the discovery, the pope descended into the crypt with three cardinals and, with the help of a torch which Della Porta had lowered in the hollow space, saw what no one had seen for over 1,000 years: the grave of St. Peter ... The impression this wonderful sight produced on the pope was so great that he caused the opening to be sealed at once.

Today it is believed that what the pope saw was not St. Peter's tomb, but one of the primitive graves near it, which we'll discuss in a moment.

In 1940, after another accidental sighting of ancient structures under the crypt, Pope Pius XII ordered thorough excavations, which lasted until 1949. The report published caused a new sensation. Not just one grave, but a whole ancient Roman cemetery had been found (guided visits are possible upon application, see the note on p. 305). The tombs were from the 1st (some scholars believe 2nd) to 4th centuries AD, mostly pagan, some Christian. (More tombs of the same period were discovered accidentally in 2003 during the construction of a parking garage under the Vatican. The site was still being excavated at the time of writing.) These remains did not by themselves prove that the burial place of Peter was here, but they did show that since early times, Christians wanted to be buried in a spot revered as the Apostle's resting place. Graffiti on the wall of a 3rd century tomb says 'Peter prays for the holy Christians buried near his body'.

There were remains of Peter's traditional tomb, or more exactly, of the original oratory and the base of the multi-layered monument: the foundations, parts of a related 'red wall' and niches with two small columns. The desecration by medieval Arab pirates was evident in the damaged base, where there was an empty niche large enough to have once contained a casket. Ancient graffiti nearby read 'Petrus' (Peter) in Greek letters. Human bones were found in a crevice near the wall. Initially mistaken for animal bones, they were stored for a time in a shoebox. In 1965 it was announced that they were human, possibly of St. Peter's time. And there the tormented question of St. Peter's bones stands.

The exterior of St. Peter's. Today we tend to forget the controversy around the building of the new St. Peter's, in view of the artistic merit of the achievement. Yet criticism abounds on that score too.

Some fifteen major architects working in Rome during the 120 years of its construction had a hand in it, including Bramante, Raphael, Baldassare Peruzzi, various members of the Sangallo family, Michelangelo, Giacomo Della Porta and Carlo Maderno. Each altered the others' plans. The floor plan was changed five times, between a Greek Cross (with arms of equal length, the preference of both Bramante and Michelangelo) and a Latin Cross (a short segment crossing a longer one, Raphael's project, later modified by Maderno and others). The Greek Cross was associated with the idea of a martyrium, a church dedicated to the martyr Peter; but the Latin Cross, closer to the basilica form and traditional for episcopal churches, was more suitable for the processions and ceremonies that became increasingly important to the Roman Church. Papal ambition also naturally preferred the more extensive and awe-inspiring option. The early 17th-century pope who set the final shape, Pope Paul V Borghese, changed Michelangelo's plan – which would have made St. Peter's somewhat similar to St. Sophia in Constantinople and, along with it, one of the most beautiful buildings in the world – because the pope said that he wanted the new church to cover the whole space occupied by the original church, which had also had a Latin Cross plan. More likely he did it because the Latin Cross was bigger than the Greek, hence presumably more imposing. The pope topped the façade with the gigantic bronze inscription *Paulus V Burghesius Romanus*, prompting the popular quip : 'The front is Paul's, let's hope the back at least is Peter's'.

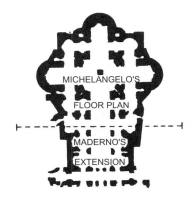

From Greek to Latin cross

The result of all these vagaries is a hybrid of two churches. One is by Michelangelo, who provided a simple, imposing structure on a Greek Cross plan, under a breathtaking, innovative and majestic dome. The other is by Maderno, who, after Michelangelo's death, added a row of three chapels on either side in front of Michelangelo's structure, turning it into a Latin Cross, and sealed the whole thing behind a monumental screen façade.

Of the two contributions, Michelangelo's is the greater, quantitatively and qualitatively. Yet,

359

ironically, this is extremely hard to perceive. Inside the church, grasping Michelangelo's vision requires a determined mental effort, since Maderno's part is what first meets the eye, and thus imposes its character on the whole. Outside, Maderno's wide façade conceals Michelangelo's structure. Only glimpses of the latter are visible by going around the church, a task hindered by access restrictions to the surrounding Vatican City.

The main victim of this split personality is Michelangelo's dome. It was meant to crown the building dramatically, but Maderno's Latin Cross lengthened the church, setting the dome far back and blocking the view of it from the front. To admire it as Michelangelo intended, you must see it from afar – it is the supreme landmark of the Roman cityscape – or, again, go around the church. Only by such efforts can you fully realise the majesty and power of Michelangelo's conception.

Maderno's façade has also been criticised as too wide. We need not agree with two 19th-century novelists – Thackeray, who found the façade 'ugly and obtrusive', and Stendhal, who called it 'a sad veneering' – but it does go on and on. This is not all Maderno's fault. The pope wanted an added bay at each end, an over-extension meant to be balanced by two end towers, which, as we'll see, were never built. As we'll also see, it was only Bernini's later idea of a colonnade embracing square and church in one, titanic design, that substantially corrected the general disproportion.

The interior. The architectural shortcomings are less disruptive inside the church. The huge size overwhelms us with a sense of boundless monumentality. Especially on sunny days, when golden rays pour in from the giant inverted funnel of the dome onto Bernini's fantastic monuments in and around the centre of the Latin Cross, one feels as though one had stepped into God's antechamber, or at least into its nearest earthly equivalent. Yet some regret that St. Peter's fails to inspire the intimate, warm spirituality conveyed by many other beautiful churches, though Michelangelo's famous statue of the *Pietà* (the Virgin Mary and Her dead Son) goes a long way towards conveying those tender, fervent human feelings which are in rather short supply in the architecture.

In the end everyone can decide for themselves what sense of the divine St. Peter's inspires. It certainly bespeaks the power of the church, which was probably the main aim of the Renaissance popes. The great ceremonies held here enhance the aura of Christianity Triumphant, such as the papal coronations, when all the princes and high prelates of the Church, the pope's civil and military staff, together with representatives of all the great religious orders gather by the thousands in colourful robes to perform the rituals amid torrents of sacred music. These grand events are rare, and invitations hard to get, though minor ceremonies are more frequent, do not require special admission and can be just as interesting.

Bernini's role. Not too pleased with the appearance of the new basilica, the first pope to reign after its completion, Urban VIII, ordered a series of improvements from the young prodigy of baroque Rome, Gian Lorenzo Bernini.

Appointed architect of St. Peter's at the age of 25, already at the peak of his fame as a sculptor and architect, Bernini first worked on the interior, producing his famed *Baldacchino*, a spectacular bronze canopy under the great dome. He then addressed the exterior, though his first attempt was a disaster. He built one of two end towers originally meant to balance the overly wide façade, but the tower was quickly dismantled when the façade beneath cracked, almost costing Bernini his career.

He returned to the façade thirty years later. At the age of 58, an inspiration led him not only to correct the problem of its width (he never solved that of the hidden dome), but simultaneously to create one of the world's most dramatic architectural ensembles, the *piazza*, discussed in the next section.

Profane footnotes. Amongst the many enthralling objects you'll see in the church, some are decidedly unchurchlike. One statue, originally shown in the nude, had such allure that the popes had to have it covered with metal drapery. This is one of the female figures on the tomb of Pope Paul III Farnese. Arguably the finest tomb in the church, this is the masterpiece of Michelangelo's contemporary, Guglielmo Della Porta (no kin of Giacomo Della Porta, who built the dome designed by Michelangelo and much else in Rome).

The statue prompted embarrassing incidents. Belli, the early 19th-century poet of Rome, relates in one of his more unrestrained sonnets:

She was so beautiful, that an English lord	E ttanta bella, ch'un zignore ingrese
Was once surprised by a guard while committing	'Na vorta un zampietrino sce lo prese
An obscene act and with his bird in hand	In atto sconcio e cco l'uscello in mano
In front of her...	

In another version of the story, Belli adds, the hapless protagonist was an altar boy.

Although there are some who say	Cuantuncue sce so' ccerti ch'hanno detto
that it wasn't a milord jerking off	che nun fussi un milordo su sta scicia
on this stone doll, but an altar boy..	De pietra a smanicà, mma un chirichetto

Of course, both versions could be true.

The model for the statue may have been the sister of the pope whose tomb this is. She was known as Giulia Bella ('Giulia the Beautiful'), and was the lover of her brother's notorious predecessor, Alexander VI Borgia (pp. 45-46); Paul III was rumoured to owe much of his career to his sister and her prestigious connections.

Also struck by the statue's beauty 350 years later was the great Italian poet and sensualist, Gabriele D'Annunzio (pp. 83, 88), who recalls in one poem: ' ...as once upon a time in Borgia's bed, in rose-coloured marble lives the naked Giulia'.

Another cause of wonder in the church are the marble pedestals of Bernini's canopied Baldacchino, which have an odd decoration: the face and belly of a woman in labour. This was Bernini's way of satisfying Pope Urban VIII, who had vowed to introduce some special artistic feature in the church to thank God for a niece's happy delivery.

ON THE SPOT

4. S. Pietro (St. Peter's Cathedral)

A wide platform and shallow steps, designed by Bernini as part of his remodelling of the square, introduce Carlo Maderno's grand façade of **S. Pietro**, finished in 1614.

The corners of the platform are flanked by huge early 19th-century statues of St. Peter (left) and St. Paul (the latter by Adamo Tadolini, p. 53).

The slow rhythm of the façade, with a long row of embedded columns and pilasters, is discreetly enlivened by the slight projection of the central part and equally slight recession of both ends. Across the top are thirteen 19 ft (5.8 m) statues of the Apostles (minus St. Peter and plus St. John the Baptist) and the Saviour. At both ends are clocks added in the early 19th century by Valadier.

Over the central portal is the balcony from which the election of a new pope is announced with the Latin phrase *habemus papam* ('we have a pope') and from which the new pope gives his solemn blessing *urbi et orbi* ('to the city and the world'). To see the dome even partially you must go back to the entrance to the square. The superb apse and sides of the church, designed and built by Michelangelo (for a fresco of his project, see p. 354), are even more hidden from view. You can see all these parts from the windows of the Vatican Palaces (p. 334) or from the Vatican Gardens, which are, however, only accessible upon special request.

The immense dome (*cupola* in Italian, and *er cupolone* in the Roman dialect) is the largest ever built in brick, at 448 ft (over 13 6m) high, including the drum at the base and the lantern at the top. It was designed by Michelangelo, but slightly modified and built by Giacomo Della Porta. Michelangelo designed it at the age of 71, but only lived long enough to see only the drum completed.

The design is based on the famous *Duomo* (cathedral) in Florence, but endowed with the special force and élan that only Michelangelo could muster. Here the effect comes from the upward thrust of a powerful ribbing which forms seg-ments, each enlivened by three superimposed windows (called *oculi* or 'eyes') of decreasing size. The dome rests on a base, or drum, with paired columns, framing magnificent windows.

Enter the large vestibule behind the façade from the first entrance to the right. At the far right a closed glass door faces a hall at the foot of a ceremonial staircase, the *Scala Regia* ('Royal Staircase'), the official entrance to the Vatican palaces. Only the landing is visible here, and the staircase will be discussed in the context of the square (p. 377). On the landing is one of the finest, liveliest equestrian statues in history, *The Emperor Constantine* by Bernini, the prototype of all such monuments in Europe for 150 years.

The church has five entrances. As you come back from the right end of the vestibule, the first is the *Porta Santa* ('Holy Door'). This is not only usually closed, but bricked up; it can only be opened by the pope, who first knocks on it with a silver hammer. This happens every 25 years, during the Church's Jubilee year. In the year 2000 it was the frail John Paul II who opened it.

The second entrance is the one regularly used. The third, central entrance, has fabulous bronze doors from the old basilica, commissioned by Pope Eugene IV in the mid-15th century from the Florentine sculptor Antonio Averulino, called 'Il Filarete'. Bronze bands, recognisable by their rougher craftsmanship, were added top and bottom to make them fit the new entrance.

The central panels depict *Sts. Peter and Paul*. Peter hands the kneeling pope the keys to Paradise. Note the enamelled clasps on the gowns. Above are *Christ* and the *Virgin Mary*. The lower panels show *Peter's Crucifixion* and *Paul's Beheading* (as a Roman citizen Paul was spared a shameful death) with interesting views of ancient Rome.

Small horizontal panels between the large ones portray the main event in the reign of Pope Eugene IV, a Council of Bishops he convened to try to reunite the sects within the Church in order to deal with the Turkish threat. The arrival of the Byzantine Emperor Palaeologus with

Looking down to St. Peter's Square from the façade of the basilica

a delegation of eastern prelates caused a stir, especially since in the group were Ethiopian monks, whose existence was barely suspected. In the upper reliefs the emperor, wearing an odd pointed hat, arrives by boat. In the lower reliefs his sovereign power is confirmed by a new coronation by the pope himself. The Ethiopians are recognisable by their turbans. All around are countless little animals and mythological figures.

The fourth and fifth entrances have modern bronze doors. Those of the fifth, with reliefs of the *Descent from the Cross* and others, were made in 1963 by the most prominent Italian sculptor of the time, Giacomo Manzù.

On the far left is an 18th-century equestrian statue of Charlemagne. The French king was crowned Holy Roman Emperor by the pope in old St. Peter's in 800 AD, an historic event that revived the ideals of the Roman Empire and European unity (p. 303).

Return to the central door. Just opposite, up under the vestibule ceiling (hard to see due to the back lighting) is a famous 14th-century mosaic by Giotto, the *Navicella* ('Little Ship'), from the old basilica. It is badly damaged by restorations. It shows Jesus walking on the water and inviting a hesitant Peter to leave the ship where the Apostles are cowering, and to follow Him. Peter, the fisherman on the left and the saints in the clouds are 17th-century reworkings or additions.

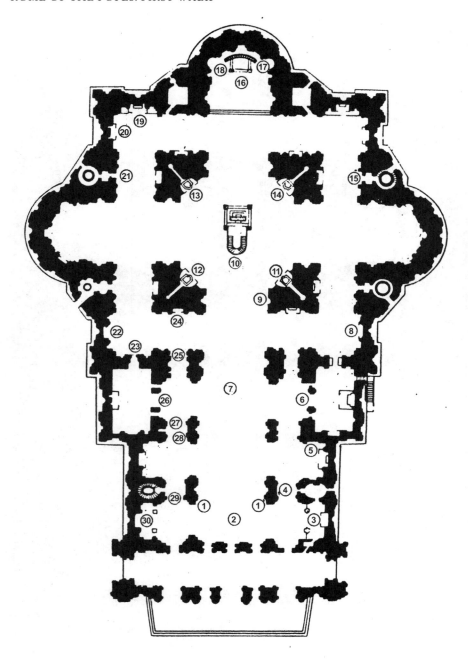

Enter the church. (Open: April to September 07:00-19:00 and October to March 07:00-17:30. The dome and the Sacred Grottoes close an hour earlier.)

Stand with your back to the central doorway. A first impression belies the immensity of the church. This effect is due to the exactness of the proportions and the lack of scale comparisons. To appreciate the real dimensions, consider that the marble cherubs supporting the holy water fonts at the bottom of the nearest nave pillars (1) are almost as tall as a man. The church is over an eighth of a mile (211 m) long. The arches between the nave pillars are as tall as a six-storey building.

The first third of the church, up to and including the third bay on both sides, is what Maderno added to Michelangelo's basic plan, changing its shape from a Greek to a Latin Cross. Keep in mind the distinction between the two parts in order to appreciate the visions of both architects. An effort to isolate mentally the last two thirds of the church will help you visualise the interior as Michelangelo planned it.

Before starting the tour, note within the central doorway, at the very bottom right, a curious little relief (quite hard to distinguish), a sort of signature of the 15th-century sculptor Filarete, whose wonderful panels we saw on the other side of the door. The seven figures on foot are said to be Filarete (to the right) and his assistants, waving their tools. Two unexplained figures flank them, one on a mule and the other on a camel, playing the pipes. The obscure Latin inscription seems to say that the work did not bring its authors much money, but great pleasure.

On the floor a few steps in front of you is a great red marble disk (2); it is the porphyry slab on which Charlemagne knelt to be crowned Holy Roman Emperor on Christmas Eve in the year 800 AD (see p. 303). The disk was moved here from the old basilica, where it lay before the high altar.

Bernini designed the great allegorical stucco figures over the nave arches and the multicoloured marble inlay on the inside of the piers, with medallions of the early popes supported by cherubs.

On the pillars of the arches, to the right and left, upper and lower niches hold statues of the founders of all the religious orders of the Church, by minor 18th-century and later sculptors.

In the upper niche of the first pier on the right, for instance, is Madeleine Sophie Barat, the early 19th-century French saint who founded the order of the Sacred Heart of Jesus (whose nuns so fascinated Mendelssohn, p. 87).

Tour the church counter-clockwise. In the first chapel to the right is the celebrated *Pietà* (Mary and her dead Son) by Michelangelo (3). Bulletproof glass was installed after a lunatic defaced the statue in 1972. It has been carefully restored.

Mary appears as a young girl. 'Purity enjoys eternal youth,' said Michelangelo, himself 24 at the time, when questioned about her age. She cradles the Saviour – a magnificent, manly, yet infinitely sweet figure – across her knees, gazing at him with an unforgettable look of tender sorrow. This is not one of the power-packed, tormented, awe-

Detail of Michelangelo's Pietà

inspiring works of the artist's maturity, such as you saw in the Sistine Chapel. It attains nevertheless an astonishing formal perfection, a forceful blend of psychological insight, beauty and religious passion almost unprecedented in the history of art. Created in the last year of the 15th century, it has been called a synthesis of all the artistic experiences of that first great century of the Renaissance, and a premonition of the second. It is the only work ever signed by Michelangelo (on the band across the Virgin's breast).

In the passage to the second chapel, on the left, is the *Memorial to Queen Christina of Sweden* (4), who abjured Protestantism in 1655 (pp. 43, 478). The relief (dated 1702) is by a minor French sculptor and represents her recantation.

The queen is actually buried in the Sacred Grottoes below (p. 372). She died of a combination of illnesses, including the disfiguring *erysipelas* ('St. Anthony's Fire'). In her coffin a silver mask covered her face.

In the second chapel (5) is the monument to *Pope Pius XII* (left), who reigned during the Second World War, by the Italian sculptor Francesco Messina. The pope, who has been criticised, unjustly in our view, for his allegedly weak reaction to the wartime plight of the Jews, but whose beatification is nevertheless being considered by the Vatican, is entombed in the Sacred Grottoes below the church (p. 371).

(There are, at the time of writing, the remains of 139 other popes within the basilica and grottoes (basement rooms, some of them remaining from the earlier church). We'll only be describing the most noteworthy monuments.)

Over the altar of this chapel is a mosaic copy of a fresco by Domenichino. During the 18th century many of the frescoes and oil paintings in the basilica were replaced by these mosaic copies because of the humidity. Most of them will not be discussed, since you have seen, or will see, many of the originals.

The third chapel (6) has a fine 17th-century iron gate designed by Borromini. In this richly adorned chapel is a gorgeous gilt-bronze and lapis lazuli

tabernacle by Bernini (1674), who loosely followed Bramante's famous *Tempietto* design (p. 561). Above it hangs the *Trinity* by the major 17th-century painter and architect Pietro da Cortona. Spiral columns from the old basilica flank a side altar.

Walk across to the middle of the central nave (7). This is where the main entrance to the basilica would have been in Michelangelo's Greek Cross plan.

On either side of you is the third bay of the nave. Pass by the right bay and turn right into an area which, like a great corridor, goes all around the Michelangelesque section of the church. Beneath the altar to your left is the embalmed body of Pope John XXIII (d. 1963), who was beatified in 2001. On most days the faithful line up to pay homage to this popular pope. At the end of the corridor is an altar (8) framed by a sumptuous chapel of coloured marbles and mosaics, built by Giacomo Della Porta to Michelangelo's design. Over the altar is a small but greatly venerated 12th-century Madonna (much repainted) from the old basilica.

Return to the middle of the nave. Here you have a fine view of the basic structural elements of Michelangelo's church: four huge polygonal piers supporting the colossal dome.

On the nave side of the pier to your right (9) is the bronze, seated statue of *St. Peter* in the act of blessing. A centuries-old tradition invites the faithful to kiss the toes, now almost worn away. The statue comes from the destroyed basilica, where it was already one of the most famous cult objects. Until recently it was attributed to the foundation period of the basilica, the 4th century. In the Renaissance it was thought to be a pagan image adapted to Christian use, possibly the *Jupiter* from the ancient Capitoline temple (p. 163). Now the head at least is thought to be a 13th-century work, probably by the Tuscan sculptor Arnolfo di Cambio, who was active in Rome at the time. It bears his hallmark of quiet dignity and high expressiveness. The sculptor may have simply replaced the head and hands of an older statue,

The interior of St. Peter's, early 20th century, by the Anglo-Russian artist William Walcot

which is what happened to another statue of St. Peter in the Sacred Grottoes (p. 373). None of these attributions is conclusive, however.

The statue has the facial features that have always been attributed to Peter, according to a tradition that has prompted a close resemblance amongst all images of him throughout the centuries (compare Caravaggio's, p. 48).

You now reach the focal point of the church, the high altar over St. Peter's grave, where only the pope or his designee can say Mass. It has a great bronze canopy under the awe-inspiring, light-drenched sweep of the dome.

The 19th-century French author, Mme de Staël, wrote: 'Even when looking at it from beneath, this dome inspires a sort of terror; one has the impression of abysses suspended over one's head.'

A few details will give you a sense of its dimensions. The pens held by the Evangelists in the mosaic roundels at the base of the dome (all the mosaics are by minor late 16th- or early 17th- century artists) are almost 5 ft (1.5 m) long. The angels flanking the roundels are 12 ft (3.5 m) tall. The lantern at the top of the dome is 52 ft (16 m) deep. Around the base of the dome, the words of Christ to St. Peter as quoted in the Gospels are inscribed in Latin: 'Thou art Peter (*Petrus*) and upon this rock (*Petram*) I will build my Church, and I will give thee the keys to the Kingdom of Heaven.'

Before the high altar is the curved balustrade of the stairs (10) leading down to St. Peter's crypt. The landing, on the level of the old basilica, faces a niche of the multi-layered monument over St. Peter's presumed grave (p. 358).

Around the balustrade are 95 perpetually lit oil lamps. Carlo Maderno designed the crypt and rich marble decoration. Two tiny columns of transparent alabaster at the foot of the banister are said to come from Nero's Golden House. Pius VI, who died a prisoner of Napoleon (pp. 67, 355), is

Angel from the Cupola

buried in the Sacred Grottoes below here.

The canopy over the high altar is the famous *Baldacchino* by Bernini (Borromini contributed to the architecture and ornaments), an incredible feat of bronze casting and one of the grandest flights of fancy of baroque Rome.

Commissioned by Pope Urban VIII Barberini, it used bronze stripped from the Pantheon, prompting the popular quip, 'What the barbarians didn't do, the Barberini did' (see p. 237).

The imposing, airy structure, as tall as a six-storey building, has spiral columns inspired by much smaller marble ones from a similar tabernacle in the old basilica. These are now in the elaborate balconies (also by Bernini) on the four piers supporting the dome. The vines on the columns swarm with the heraldic bees of the Barberini. Four of Bernini's most magnificent angels top the canopy. The structure is meant to create a festive atmosphere; it resembles ceremonial canopies carried in church processions.

Inside the Barberini escutcheon on the pedestals is the face of a woman in labour (p. 361). Follow the reliefs around clockwise. Note how the escutcheons decrease their swell, to represent, it is said, the woman's belly. The last face is that of a smiling newborn.

On the side facing the Baldacchino, the four colossal piers (remember the small church of S. Carlino could fit into one of them, p. 72) are divided horizontally into two sections. Above are the balconies designed by Bernini, where four major Christian relics are exhibited during Easter Holy Week. Below are great niches with statues relating to the relics.

The most interesting of the four statues is *St. Longinus with his Lance* by Bernini (11). Longinus, a Roman soldier, thrust his lance into Christ's chest to end His agony on the Cross. What is said to be the lance (kept behind the balcony overhead) was given to the pope in the 15th century by a Turkish sultan who ruled the Holy Land. Its dubious authenticity, the fact that it was a veiled compensation for unsavoury services, and the Muslim faith of the donor were all noted at the time by Burchard in his diary (p. 330).

The other statues, by lesser 17th-century sculptors, are: *St. Andrew* (12) with the X-shaped cross of his martyrdom (the corresponding relic is the presumed head of the saint, encased in silver) by the Fleming François Duquesnoy, called Fran-cesco Fiammingo in Italy; *St. Veronica* (13), who gave Christ a veil to wipe His brow while on the road to Calvary (the relic is the veil on which Christ's face is said to be miraculously imprinted) by Francesco Mochi, a Tuscan sculptor; and *St. Helena* (14), mother of the Emperor Constantine (pp. 399, 415, 630), who found what she said was the True Cross in Palestine and brought it to Rome (the relic is the largest fragment of the Cross), by Andrea Bolgi from Carrara, one of Bernini's assistants.

(There are entrances to the Sacred Grottoes, the substructures that partly occupy the space of the earlier church, at the base of the piers; only one at any given time is in use. If you want to visit the Grottoes, a 30 minute Detour (pp. 371-373), we recommend you first finish seeing the church.)

Pass between the two piers to the right of the main altar and swing round to the left. On the wall to the right is the late 18th-century monument to *Pope Clement XIII* by Canova (15), an early work by this great neo-classical Italian sculptor, and one of his best.

Move on to the front of the apse, to another dazzling creation by Bernini, the *Cathedra*, or Chair, of St. Peter (16). It is a monumental decorative ensemble, ablaze with light and gold, encircling an oval stained glass window with the Dove of the Holy Spirit. (The dove has been damaged and restored several times. The present version is a 1929 work by the Roman artist Renzo Marzi.) Below the oval window is a gilt bronze chair. Bernini designed it to encase and preserve an ancient wood-and-ivory throne traditionally thought to be St. Peter's pontifical chair, but actually a 9th-century work donated by the Frankish King Charles the Bald to the popes.

The chair is borne aloft by Bernini's colossal statues of the four Doctors of the Church, the great teachers of Christian doctrine: in front, St. Ambrose and St. Augustine (representing the Latin Church), and behind St. Athanasius and St. John Chrysostom (representing the Greek Church). Angels and cherubs with the papal symbols of the keys and tiara surround the chair.

From this part of the bronze decoration an enormous 'glory' of gilt stucco radiates amidst clouds and a mass of angelic creatures. The 'glory' is the grandest example of this typically baroque type of decoration, and one of the most beautiful.

Two of the finest papal monuments in the church flank the *Cathedra* ensemble.

On the right (17) is Bernini's *Tomb of Urban VIII* (d. 1642), the Barberini pope who commissioned the Baldacchino. Urban was the first and most ardent champion of Bernini, who sculpted this last homage to his patron. The details are hard to see from a distance. On the casket, a crouching Death writes the name of the deceased. Barberini heraldic bees rest here and there, as if pausing before a final flight.

On the left (18) is the *Tomb of Paul III* (d. 1549), the masterpiece of the mid-16th century sculptor Guglielmo Della Porta.

The two female figures left and right symbolise *Justice* and *Wisdom* respectively. The younger figure is the one which had to be clothed with metal drapery (see p. 361). It is said to have been modelled on the pope's sister, Giulia Bella Farnese. The older figure is said to be her mother.

Continue counter-clockwise past the apse. Just before the corner note on the wall (19) the *Altar of St. Leo the Great*, with the relics of this 5th-century pope, who blocked Attila the Hun's advance on Rome. A huge marble relief by Alessandro Algardi, a contemporary of Bernini, depicts the famous episode, which we also saw illustrated in Raphael's *Stanze* (pp. 366-368). This dramatic relief is one of the largest extant and amongst the best of its kind from the baroque period.

How Leo in fact persuaded the fierce barbarian king, Attila, to turn back from Rome is unknown. Like the Raphaelesque fresco, the relief invokes the legend of the miraculous intervention of Sts. Peter and Paul.

Under the next altar (20) are the relics of three more popes called Leo, including Leo IV, who miraculously stopped a fire in the Borgo in the 9th century (he too is portrayed in Raphael's *Stanze*, p. 339). Leo XII lies under the floor before the altar. Before dying in 1829 he modestly asked to be buried here with a Latin epitaph calling him 'least (*minimus*) amongst the heirs to such a great name'.

In the next passage to the right (21) is the *Tomb of Alexander VII* (d. 1667), created by Bernini for another of his great patrons, one of the builder popes. You may recognise, high up, the star-over-mountains emblem of the pope's family (the Chigi), which we first saw over the Porta del Popolo. In the papal palaces and St. Peter's Square, Bernini also created for Alexander VII the *Scala Regia* (p. 373) and grand Colonnade (p. 376).

This dramatic tomb is one of Bernini's last works. He left it to his pupils to make several of the figures. A grisly *Death* wielding an hourglass beckons the kneeling pope to rest under the blanket of the Netherworld (a huge slab of jasper, a type of quartz). Of the four allegorical female figures, the one in the foreground on the right, representing *Truth*, was originally naked, as truth is supposed to be (the drape is painted metal).

Pass the transept. In the next passage, on the right, is the door to the **Museum of the Basilica,** or Treasury of St. Peter's. (This is not part of the Walk; for information see p. 681.)

The next altar (22) is dedicated to St. Gregory the Great, an early 6th-century pope and key figure in Church history (pp. 425-433).

St. Peter's: The Memorial to the Last Stuarts

The mosaic is a copy of a 17th-century painting; it shows Pope Gregory with one of the pieces of cloth with which the faithful used to touch the relics of St. Peter or other martyrs (see p. 358). He pierces the cloth which, having gained miraculous powers, gushes blood.

Next (23) is the *Tomb of Pius VII*, the second pope exiled by Napoleon (p. 67), by Bertel Thorvaldsen, an eminent Swedish neo-classical sculptor and long-time resident of Rome in the early 19th century (pp. 82, 238). The sober, surprisingly modern stone portrait stirred controversy at the time because it was by a Protestant artist, the only such work in St. Peter's.

The great mosaic facing the passage (24) is a copy of Raphael's *Transfiguration* (p. 315)

Continue into the next passage. On the right (25) is the *Tomb of Leo XI* (d. 1605), another work by Algardi, who created the general design and the figure of the pope. The rest is by minor 17th-century sculptors.

As a cardinal, Leo XI accepted the conversion to Catholicism of the Protestant king of France, Henry IV, who is supposed to have said 'Paris is well worth a Mass' (see p. 88). The relief records the event. The flowers adorning the base of the tomb, with the Latin motto 'thus it bloomed', allude to the mere 27-day reign of the pope.

We are now back in Maderno's part of the church. The very rich chapel that follows (26) is by Giacomo Della Porta. In the next passage, on the right (27), is the *Monument to Pope St. Pius X*, in which the pope is shown invoking peace on the eve of the First World War (when he died).

Opposite (28) is the *Tomb of Innocent VIII* by the great 15th-century Florentine sculptor Antonio Pollaiuolo. It is the only funerary monument transferred from the old basilica to the new.

This pope, who was the first to employ the Swiss master of ceremonies Burchard (p. 329), accepted the dubious gift of the Sacred Lance (p. 330), seen here in his left hand. His tomb is the first to depict a pope enthroned, though he is also shown lying in eternal rest. All the figures are intensely expressive, including the small allegories.

Go to the next passage. On the left is the *Memorial to the Last Stuarts*, a late work (1819) by Canova, on the spot where these unhappy princes are buried in the grottoes below.

Refugees first in Paris, then in Rome, these last heirs in a direct line to Mary Stuart, Queen of Scots were, each in turn, pretenders to the English throne: James III, Charles Edward ('Bonnie Prince Charlie', who unsuccessfully invaded Britain) and his brother Cardinal Henry, Bishop of Frascati near Rome. The memorial was gallantly commissioned and paid for by the British King George IV, a fact upon which Stendhal remarked: 'In homage to his reputation as the most perfect gentleman of his kingdom, King George has honoured the ashes of these princes, whom he would have sent to the scaffold had they fallen into his hands.' Stendhal found the monument 'of a beauty impossible to describe'. In the 19th century the two curvaceous guardian angels received metal trousers, later removed.

The last chapel is the Baptistry. The red porphyry basin of the font was originally a sarcophagus lid, probably from Hadrian's tomb (p. 392) and possibly the emperor's own. The font's bronze lid is from the late 17th century.

DETOUR
40 MIN

The **Sacred Grottoes** are on the foundation level of the new basilica and the floor level of the old.

They are usually reached from under the St. Longinus pier (No. 11 in the figure on p. 364), where the visit and our description begin counter-clockwise. Occasionally entrance is from other piers, and the initial part of the visit goes in the other direction, and our description will have to be adapted.

Steps and a frescoed corridor lead from the pier to the grottoes. The grottoes form a semicircle joined to a long nave. Some of the space is the same as that which the old basilica once covered, but the grottoes are the result of a complete replanning and rebuilding carried out over centuries after the old basilica was torn down.

Leaving the corridor, go right. The first three chapels are modern, with some medieval furnishings, and not of great interest. Past the third chapel, on the opposite wall is a relief of the *Head of St. Andrew Held by Two Angels* by the 15th-century Tuscan sculptor Isaia da Pisa. It comes from the old basilica, the first of many fragments spared from Bramante's demolition (p. 357) and which were either left or returned here. In a wall niche opposite the relief is the first of a series of statues from the old basilica of the *Twelve Apostles* by 15th-century artists, including Mino da Fiesole and Giovanni Dalmata.

Past the first niche is the frescoed corridor to the next pier overhead, that of St. Helena. Past more niches, the first chapel contains the remains of Pope Pius XII (p. 366). Opposite is St. Peter's Chapel, richly decorated between the late 16th and 18th centuries. Until the mid-20th century it was the closest a visitor could get to St. Peter's presumed grave, which is just behind, under the precious malachite altar containing another simple early medieval altar (not visible).

Past the corridor leading to the next pier (St. Veronica) an opening in the wall on the left offers a glimpse of the masonry that surrounds the upper part of the shrine built by Emperor Constantine over the supposed burial place of St. Peter (p. 358).

On the wall nearby is the cross that once topped the old basilica. Opposite are two chapels dedicated to the Virgin Mary. Over the altar of the first is a fresco of the *Virgin and Child* attributed to the great 14th-century Roman painter Pietro Cavallini. The second has a fresco of the same subject attributed to Melozzo da Forlì (15th century) and flanked by reliefs of angels, also 15th century. Past these chapels on the right wall is an 8th-century mosaic, badly altered by restorations, with 15th-century reliefs of saints on either side.

The nave now comes into view, beneath the nave of the present St. Peter's. Just to the left is a chapel with two ancient Roman sarcophagi, one of them re-used as a pope's tomb. Over an altar is a fine 15th-century relief. The wall just past this chapel was torn down after the 1940's excavations in order to give a frontal view of St. Peter's crypt (which you saw from above, see p. 367). This is the part of the grottoes nearest to St. Peter's traditional burial place. It is on the other side of the malachite altar of St. Peter's Chapel, which we saw a few minutes ago. The upper part of the multi-layered monument is visible, with a medieval mosaic of Christ of uncertain date. St. Peter's possible burial place is at the foot of the monument, several feet below. In a renaissance box before the mosaic are the 'holy lambswool' scarves (*pallia*) the pope gives to newly appointed bishops as a symbol of the authority they wield on his behalf. (They derive their sanctity from having been so close to the Apostle's grave – a vestige of the liturgy of the cloths made miraculous by touching St. Peter's body; see pp. 358, 370).

The right side of the nave (with your back to the crypt) is usually closed; if not, we can see it now. The first tomb is that of Pius XI, who was pope when Mussolini gained power. Past the steps is the sepulchre of the last of the Stuarts, underneath the memorial in the basilica overhead (p. 371). On the right is the entrance to the archæological sites below, which may be seen only by appointment (see p. 305) and include the ancient cemetery and putative tomb of St. Peter. Past the entrance, the most interesting tombs are:

1) An Early Christian sarcophagus, reused for Urban VI, who died in 1389 after a controversial reign that prefaced the great schism, or separation, between western and eastern Christianity. The front of the sarcophagus was reworked to include the *traditio clavium,* or delivery to the pope of the keys to heaven, meant to re-emphasize Urban's disputed legitimacy.

2) Last on this side is the sarcophagus of Gregory V (d. 999). The epitaph is a rare example of contemporary vernacular Italian. At the end of the nave is an altar with small cosmatesque columns and a much-restored 10th-century mosaic depicting *Christ between Sts. Peter and Paul.* To

the left is the Early Christian sarcophagus of the Emperor Otto II (d. 983).

Go back to St. Peter's crypt and continue past it to the chapel at the end of the aisle, which contains, on the left, the tomb of Pope Pius VI, who died in exile under Napoleon (pp. 67, 355). It is a simple ancient Roman sarcophagus topped by a 4th-century relief which has, on the left, the oldest known depiction of the biblical story of the *Joseph sold into slavery*, and on the right, behind the throne of the Virgin, the oldest known depiction of a *Latin Cross* (p. 352). Over the chapel altar is a 15th-century sculpture of the *Virgin and Child between Sts. Peter and Paul and Pope Eugene IV* (p. 362), perhaps by Isaia da Pisa.

Down the aisle and immediately on the left is a chapel where the *Tomb of John XXIII* (d. 1963) lay until 2001, when he was beatified. The body was then moved to the church above (p. 366). Four years later, his place was taken by the remains of the Polish pope John Paul II, who had specifically requested in his will to be buried in the grotto. Past the chapel and before the steps, on the left, is the *Tomb of Queen Christina of Sweden*, whose memorial is directly above in the church (p. 366).

Past the steps, the first two tombs on the left and the second on the right belong, coincidentally, to popes who only ruled for a few weeks. The first on the left is Innocent IX (late 16th century), who spent his short reign (less than two months) bedridden and was nicknamed *Pontifex clinicus*, the 'clinical Pontiff'. Next is Marcellus II, in a fine 4th-century sarcophagus with reliefs of *Christ and Saints* in the middle and of the two original occupants, a husband and wife, on the sides. This pope reigned less than a month in the mid-16th century (though he had the time to inspire the famous Mass, *Missa Papæ Marcelli*, by his choirmaster Palestrina). Across from him is John Paul I, who died in 1978 after 138 days on the throne (unverifiable rumours claimed that he had been poisoned).

Past the arcade, a corridor from the left crosses the nave on the right to lead to the excavations under the basilica. These include the ancient cemetery and the site venerated as St. Peter's burial place (see p. 305). On the left the corridor leads to the **Hall of Inscriptions** (generally closed) with important epigraphs, sarcophagi and fragments of early 8th-century mosaics from the ancient basilica. Some of these – depicting Pope John VII, Christ, St. Peter, the baby Jesus washed by his Mother – are visible from the entrance. We saw another of the same series in S. Maria in Cosmedin (p. 260).

Picking up again along the aisle past the corridor, on the left is the *Tomb of Innocent VII* (early 15th century) simply engraved with the figure of the pope. Beside it a crude 15th-century statue and even cruder ancient Roman sarcophagus form the *Tomb of Nicholas V*, one of the first great builder popes. In the 1450's, he began the expansion of the Vatican palaces (pp. 307, 329) and called great renaissance artists, including Fra Angelico, to work there. He was also the last pope to crown a Holy Roman Emperor in St. Peter's (p. 303), the Austrian Frederick III. Here you can see close up, at the end of the central nave, the kneeling statue of *Pius VI* (whose grave is at the other end of the aisle, p. 372). For almost two centuries the statue of this victim of Napoleon had a place of honour in St. Peter's crypt in front of the shrine. (It was moved here in the 1980's.) The head and hands are by Canova, the rest by Tadolini.

The last tombs in the aisle are of two 14th-century popes, Nicholas III (right) and Boniface VIII (left), contemporaries of Dante. In his *Divine Comedy*, Dante calls them corrupt and consigns them to Hell, stuck together to a rock in the same infernal pit. Strangely enough, their bodies, which were moved here at different times from the old basilica, wound up beside each other in their marble tombs. We should add that both are remembered as great pontiffs and that, at least in the case of Boniface, Dante's indictment appears unjustified. Nicholas rests in a superb 4th-century sarcophagus, with a figure of *Christ* in the middle (at Christ's feet are the couple who originally occupied the tomb) flanked by episodes from the life of St. Peter. Opposite are the early 14th-century tomb and statue of Boniface by the great Arnolfo di Cambio. Note the humanity of the portrait and the fine drapery.

Go down a corridor at the end of the aisle. Just on the right is a late 15th-century tabernacle framing a lovely mid-14th century *Madonna* (at the time of writing replaced by a photograph); on the sides are the four *Doctors of the Church* (p. 369).

Moving on, note the bases of the columns of the old basilica on the left. On the right are remains of the once sumptuous *Tomb and Monument to Callixtus III*, a 15th-century Borgia pope, uncle of the notorious Alexander VI, who ascended the papal throne 34 years after him. The nephew erected this large monument to his uncle in the old basilica. Only a statue of the pope reclining on the lid of the coffin, surrounded by a few statuary fragments, remain. The coffin is empty. In a bizarre string of events, the bones of Callixtus were mixed with those of his nephew, and all wound up in an obscure chapel of the Spanish national church in Rome (see p. 472). Among the contemporary reliefs over Callixtus' tomb one on the right depicts *St. Osmond of Salisbury*, who was sanctified under Callixtus.

Near the exit, on the left, is another statue of St. Peter, recently moved here from the place now occupied by that of Pius VI. The head is from the middle ages, perhaps by Arnolfo di Cambio, who grafted it onto an ancient Roman statue, probably of a philosopher. The hands were added even later (compare it with the statue of St. Peter in the upper basilica, p. 366).

The exit is near the lift to the dome. A trip there adds at least 30 minutes to this Detour, if there is no queue. The lift only goes part of the way and the remaining climb is taxing. But the glimpse of the structure of the great dome and the views from on high – of the church interior, St. Peter's Square and Rome – make it well worthwhile.

END OF DETOUR

As you leave, note on the base of the column to the left of the outer central entrance signatures carved by visitors centuries ago – one dated 1617, before the new basilica had even been dedicated.

BEFORE GOING

5. St. Peter's Square

Bernini was assigned the task of completing the new St. Peter's by designing the surrounding square, which he did with mastery and innovation, creating a monumental complex that straddles two eras, the Renaissance and the Baroque.

As mentioned in the last section, in so doing he also solved the problem of the too-wide façade of the church. His solution was a spectacular semi-elliptical colonnade enclosing the square in front of the church, and thereby giving the façade a new proportion within the overall design. Together, the squat basilica and the two curving sections of the colonnade acquire a monumental horizontality, conveying the impression of arms wide open: outwards, perhaps to proclaim God's dominion; or inwards, to gather in God's flock.

The emotions this invention evoked were summed up in 1840 by the novelist George Eliot: 'The piazza, with Bernini's colonnade, gave me always a sense of having entered some millennial new Jerusalem, where all small and shabby things were unknown.' Sadly, the effect was marred in the 20th century by the destruction, in the name of modernity and convenience, of an entire side of the square, in conjunction with the demolition of the old Borgo (discussed in the next walk).

The spirit of the square. Like all great Roman squares, St. Peter's has its own aura, shaped obviously by the centuries-old traditions and spiritual influences of the Roman Catholic Church. These are best appreciated during the frequent ceremonies and holy days, when huge throngs, animated by the colourful garments of the many religious orders, gather in the square in a noisy, but orderly and joyous scene. Such events include the announcement from the central balcony of the church of the election of a new pope, and various ceremonial blessings given by the pope periodically, either from the balcony or from his apartment window.

Until the late 19th century these papal appearances were customarily greeted by a festive shooting of cannons from Castel Sant' Angelo (p. 385). This inspired a sonnet by Gioacchino Belli, which perfectly evokes the peculiarly Roman blend of sensuality and spirituality. The scene is a garret in Rome where a couple are making love. She says:

Oh, this is good ... push ... Shhh,
    did you hear that?
Enough, enough now. Take your bird out.
It was the Castle cannon. It means the Pope
Has come out to the balcony.
Let's both get out of bed, let's kneel together;
Brother, we've had enough today;
Some for the body, some for the soul. Come on.
Now let us take his blessing.
	Fa'... che gusto!...spi...Zzitto!
	    Ecco er cannone!
	abbasta, abbasta, sù, caccia l'uscello.
	Nu lo senti ch'edè? Spara castello:
	Seggno ch'er Papa sta sopra ar loggione.
	Mettèmece un'e ll'antro in ginocchione:
	Per oggi contentàmesce, fratello.
	Un po' ar corpo e un po'all'anima; berbello;
	Pijiamo adesso la bbonidizzione.

A note on Bernini. Born in Naples of a Florentine father and Neapolitan mother, Bernini inherited a Tuscan precision and a Neapolitan temper. He was 'harsh by nature, single-minded in his

St. Peter's Square, with Bernini's colonnade

work, passionate in his wrath,' his son Domenico recalled. From early childhood he was steeped in the artistic life of his father, a well known sculptor. He was mesmerised by the masterworks of ancient, especially hellenistic, sculpture (p. 311), and studied them assiduously. Coupled with a complete self-confidence, his talent assured him an extremely successful career from the start. He made his first important work at the age of 14.

Amongst his countless works, St. Peter's colonnade won him the widest acclaim. This may seem odd, given that he was more famous as a sculptor than as an architect, yet his greatness ultimately consisted in his extreme sensitivity to space and unique ability to fuse architecture and sculpture.

What intrigued him most in sculpture was the expressive potential not so much of the rock, but of the surrounding void. He did not understand the one without the other. He often quoted Michelangelo's precept that it isn't hard to sculpt, since all it requires is to remove from the stone, not add anything.

He reinforced the psychological impact of his creations with multiple effects, often drawing from more than one artistic field, in the renaissance tradition of the 'universal genius'. The famous 17th-century English diarist John Evelyn reported after a visit to Rome: 'Bernini ... gave a public opera wherein he painted the scenes, cut the statues, invented the engines, composed the music, writ the comedy, and built the theatre.'

Thus most of Bernini's works should be read not just as the products of a sculptor, but as those of an architect and set designer too. Another work which, together with the colonnade, exemplifies his dramatic, almost theatrical, instincts is the row of angels crowning the bridge to Castel Sant' Angelo (see next Walk, p. 395).

Characteristic of Bernini as a sculptor was his passionate striving to depict movement, transformation and transition, not only in his rendering of human figures, but in the most elusive of subjects and with the most solid of materials. No one has ever more daringly translated into stone the flickering of flames, the quivering of shadows, or the fluttering of drapery.

Another characteristic of Bernini's art was (like Michelangelo's) its incredible consistency. In 56 years he produced more than 100 large works of statuary and architecture in and around St. Peter's, not to mention innumerable others in Rome. As the late Rudolf Wittkower, the most eminent Bernini scholar of the 20th century, observed of his work for St. Peter's, in spite of the great variety in content and scale, 'he never lost sight of the whole, and dove-tailed early and late undertakings even after an interval of half a century.'

ON THE SPOT

5. St. Peter's Square

The best view is from just outside the square, standing with your back to the faceless modern buildings and the pretentious Via della Conciliazione. In the background of the square is the basilica with its dome, which is not fully visible even from here. The description of the facade and a discussion of the dome and rear of the church are on p. 362.)

Enclosing the giant ellipse, almost one and a half times the area of the Colosseum, are the two arms of the imposing **Colonnade** by Bernini. There are 284 columns, in rows of four, and 88 piers. The skyline is dotted with a parade of more than 150 statues of saints, sketched by Bernini and sculpted by his assistants.

Over the right colonnade rise the Apostolic Palaces of the popes. The papal apartment is in the great square building to the right. The window from which the pope blesses the crowd (except after his election, when he appears at the central balcony of the basilica) is the second from the right on the top floor. The blessing, often followed by a speech, occurs on Sundays at noon when the pope is in Rome.

In the square are two marvellous granite fountains, adding a festive note to the solemn picture. The one on the right was designed by Carlo Maderno (1613) and the other by Carlo Fontana (1677). Head to the ancient Egyptian **Obelisk,** which is between them. It once stood in the centre of Emperor Caligula's circus, and is where St. Peter was supposedly martyred (p. 357). Caligula had the needle brought to Rome in the 1st century AD on a specially built 400-ton barge.

The circus (race track) and obelisk were alongside the old basilica. By the middle ages the obelisk was the only one left standing in Rome. It was a great attraction, partly because a bronze globe on top (now in the Capitoline Museums) was believed to contain the ashes of Julius Caesar.

During the construction of the new basilica in the late 16th century, Pope Sixtus V (pp. 44-45) had the needle put here. The obelisk was the first raised in Rome since antiquity. Moving it from 300 yards away and hoisting it was an engineering feat that even Michelangelo had deemed impossible. A fresco in the Vatican Library (see p. 354) shows how this was done, and the machine invented by the architect Domenico Fontana for the job, which took 900 men and hundreds of horses more than four months (see the contemporary illustration opposite).

A famous incident occurred during the hoisting. Since it was so difficult, the pope ordered it done in strict silence; violators would be hanged, no less. All went well until the giant needle was within inches of standing upright. Then the ropes began to creak as if they were tearing! A Genoese sailor in the crowd defied the order and shouted: 'Water on the ropes!' Water was poured on them, they strengthened and the day was saved. Instead of being hanged, the sailor received, along with his descendants, the exclusive and lucrative right to supply the palms on Palm Sunday for St. Peter's.

The obelisk, the second tallest in Rome (p. 410), measures 77 ft (25.50 m). It is 125 ft (38 m) high, including the pedestal, the base with baroque lions and eagles, and the emblem on the top. The emblem, which contains a relic of the True Cross (p. 368), is the star-and-mounts of Pope Alexander VII Chigi (pp. 44, 369), who completed the square. It also appears on the colonnade. On the base Latin inscriptions proclaim God's triumph over evil, and announce the exorcising power of the obelisk (see p. 45): *Ecce Crux Domini, Fugite, Partes Adversæ* ('Here is the Cross of God, begone, fiendish Host'). Further up, near the eagles, are ancient dedications to Caligula, whose real name was Caius (Caligula was a nickname meaning 'little boot', after the military-style shoes he wore as a child, which won him the affection of soldiers). The other two sides recall the role of Sixtus V.

From the obelisk, look at a crowded jumble of papal buildings just to the right of the basilica. The one with a triangular front and one walled-up window is the Sistine Chapel. From the chimney come the famous smoke signals during papal elections. Black smoke signals an inconclusive vote, white smoke, a decision. On April 29, 2005, the ringing of church bells all over Rome was added for the first time, to celebrate the election of the German cardinal Joseph Ratzinger as Pope Benedict XVI.

Halfway between each fountain and the obelisk are two doughnut-shaped paving stones (do not confuse them with the circular or oval discs with astrological and meteorological symbols). If you stand on either of these doughnuts and view the colonnade, it seems formed by a single row of columns, not four.

Go to the right-hand side of the colonnade and

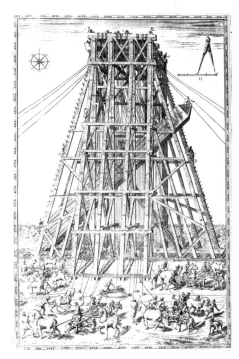

Lifting the obelisk into place: a contemporary engraving

turn left under it to the end. Here, watched by Swiss Guards in renaissance uniforms, is the ceremonial entry designed by Bernini for the Apostolic Palaces. You may climb the steps to the first landing. Without entering, from the *Portone di Bronzo* ('Bronze Gate') you can see the long, silent corridor. At the end, not visible from here (see p. 362), is the equestrian statue of *Constantine* by Bernini, followed by another of his dramatic inventions, the *Scala Regia*.

A perspective effect, created by the decreasing size of the side columns, makes the steps look much deeper, larger and more regular than they are, evoking a sense of grandeur in a relatively small space. Bernini may have been inspired by Borromini's Perspectival Gallery which we'll see in Palazzo Spada (p. 474).

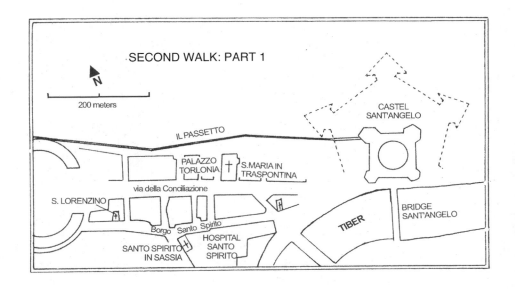

SECOND WALK: PART 1

N

200 meters

IL PASSETTO

CASTEL
SANT'ANGELO

PALAZZO
TORLONIA

S.MARIA IN
TRASPONTINA

via della Conciliazione

S. LORENZINO

Borgo Santo Spirito

HOSPITAL
SANTO
SPIRITO

SANTO SPIRITO
IN SASSIA

TIBER

BRIDGE
SANT'ANGELO

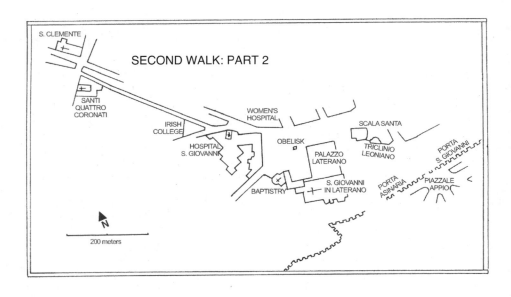

S. CLEMENTE

SECOND WALK: PART 2

SANTI
QUATTRO
CORONATI

IRISH
COLLEGE

WOMEN'S
HOSPITAL

SCALA SANTA

HOSPITAL
S. GIOVANNI

OBELISK

PALAZZO
LATERANO

TRICLINIO
LEONIANO

PORTA
S. GIOVANNI

BAPTISTRY

S. GIOVANNI
IN LATERANO

PORTA
ASINARIA

PIAZZALE
APPIO

N

200 meters

ROME OF THE POPES
SECOND WALK

Part 1
1. The Borgo 380
S. Lorenzo in Piscibus 382; S. Spirito in Sassia 382; Palace of the
Commendatore 382; Ospedale di Santo Spirito 382; Annunziatina 383;
S. Maria in Traspontina 384
2. Castel Sant' Angelo 385
3. Ponte Sant' Angelo 395

Midpoint

Part 2
4. S. Giovanni in Laterano 396
Triclinium Leonianum 402; Sanctum Sanctorum 403;
S. Giovanni in Laterano 404; Cloister 408; obelisk 410; Baptistery 410;
Ospedale di S. Giovanni 411; Women's Hospital 411;
SS. Andrea e Bartolomeo 411
5. The Papal Way to St. Peter's and the church of the
Quattro Coronati 412
SS. Quattro Coronati 414
6. S. Clemente 416
S. Clemente 419; Mithræum 422
(The Cælian Hill and its churches: S. Maria in Domnica,
S. Stefano Rotondo, SS. Giovanni e Paolo and S. Gregorio
Magno 424
S. Maria in Domnica 427; S. Stefano Rotondo 428; SS. Giovanni
e Paolo 429; S. Gregorio Magno 432; S. Barbara, S. Andrea and
S. Silvia 432)

Planning your visit: the Metro links the Vatican (OTTAVIANO station)
and Lateran (SAN GIOVANNI station) in ten stops. When you get off,
go past the turnstile and follow the right wall around to the right exit.
Alternatively, from the vicinity of Castel Sant' Angelo (Piazza Cavour),
take a No. 87 bus directly to the Lateran.

BEFORE GOING

1. The Borgo

Facing St. Peter's Square is the Borgo ('Borough'). Once one of the most intimate, picturesque neighbourhoods in Rome, it is now a cold, sterile space except for a few crannies. The change occurred between 1936 and 1950, one of a series of follies committed by the authorities to ease traffic – abetted, in this case, by the Church, which owned much of the real estate.

A long row of ancient buildings ending in front of the square, known for centuries as the 'Spine of the Borgo' due to its central position in the district, was demolished and replaced by a noisy avenue with faceless modern buildings.

The Spine, containing quaint little houses and narrow alleys, home to many generations of artisans and shopkeepers, was a poetic place, a unique preface to the splendours of St. Peter's. Stepping from it into the square was a revelation, somewhat like suddenly hearing heavenly choirs with the whispers of the human family still echoing in one's ears. The Englishman, Augustus Hare, writing on Rome in the 1870's, noted, 'the whole external effect of St. Peter's depends upon a sudden entrance in the sunlit piazza from the gloomy street.'

What replaced it is a wide avenue (with grotesque modern obelisk-like street lamps) called Via della Conciliazione ('Reconciliation Street') in memory of the 1929 pact between Church and State (pp. 67, 302). It reveals and trivialises St. Peter's from half a mile away. With a kind of back-handed poetic justice, the demolition, meant to ease traffic, brought in streams of cars and pollution both chemical and visual. Huge tour buses replaced the ochre-coloured houses and bustling shops. Incidentally, the real estate so casually destroyed would now be of astronomical value.

What remains of the Borgo is interesting nevertheless. Since Early Christianity, that is, since the first basilica dedicated to St. Peter was built, the area had been favoured by Germanic settlers. Gothic invaders occupied and fortified it in the 6th century, giving rise to the Germanic name Borgo. In the early middle ages the neighbourhood was called the 'Borough of the Saxons'; there were also Longobards, Franks and other Germanic immigrants. Many came as pilgrims and stayed, including wealthy people and kings and queens. Ceadwalla, King of the West Saxons (or Wessex, one of the kingdoms of southern England), came to be baptised and died here shortly after. His successor, King Ine, arrived in the early 8th century and donated money to build a church, S. Spirito in Sassia, the 'Holy Spirit of Saxony'. The church, rebuilt several times, is near Via della Conciliazione. Two other foreign potentates, King Kenred of Mercia (another kingdom in southern England) and Carloman of the Franks, stayed on as monks, abdicating their thrones. The list goes on.

Catastrophe struck the Borgo in 847, a terrible fire depicted in the fresco by Raphael in the Vatican (p. 339). The district was rebuilt, however, and prospered once again, aided by the proximity of St. Peter's. During the Renaissance, it was home to prelates, wealthy merchants, nobles, diplomats and famous artists. Raphael lived here too; he died in a building dismantled in the demolition of the 'Spine' and rebuilt on Via della Conciliazione. Nearby is the palace that housed King Henry VIII's embassy to the papal see until the Anglican schism and Reformation.

Calamity revisited the Borgo in 1527, during one of the periodic conflicts between the popes and Holy Roman emperors (p. 303). A German army under a Frenchman, the Constable of Bourbon, stormed and ravaged Rome to an extent rarely seen in history, in the infamous Sack of Rome. The Borgo in particular suffered. The pope fled to Castel Sant' Angelo (our next highlight) through a raised passage that still survives. From the windows in the passage he could see invaders spearing women and children with their long halberds. A cannonball from the castle took out the Constable, but the atrocities continued for weeks: witnesses described wholesale hangings, gang rapes of nuns and hideous tortures to force people to give up their money. Finally, an outbreak of the plague forced the invaders to leave. Almost 500 years later, memories of the terror and the dreaded Constable echo in a popular lullaby of working-class Rome: 'Sleep my love and go away Barbone' (a corruption of Bourbon, also meaning 'bearded man' or ogre).

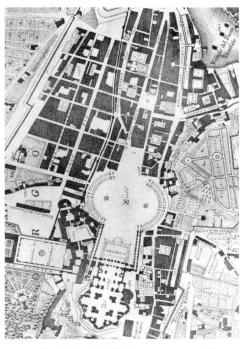

Detail from Nolli's 18th century map of Rome, showing the original approach to St. Peter's, not altered until the demolition of the Spine of the Borgo

The Sack was an epoch-making event. It brought such misery that artists who had flocked to the city during the Renaissance, especially from Florence (p. 444), left in droves for good. Urban development and cultural life lay dormant for decades. The better-off left the Borgo, which was in an especially pitiable state, for the nearby districts beyond the river. Thus the Borgo acquired a lower-class, yet charming and placid character, until the 20th-century demolition and 'urban renewal' dealt the final blow.

Another memento of hard times in the Borgo is the 'ruota degli esposti' ('wheel of the exposed', or foundlings), a contraption that can still be seen, built into the doors of an ancient hospital. The newborn were brought to this wheel from all over Rome and left to public charity. In the 19th century an average of 3,000 infants appeared there yearly. Their descendants are recognisable by the last names given to the orphans by Church authorities, including Proietti, a very common Roman surname, meaning 'the ejected'; Esposito, also very common, 'the exposed'; and Diotallevi, 'May God raise you'.

ON THE SPOT

1. The Borgo

Our description starts from St. Peter's Square and goes towards the river. If you have planned your walk (p. 299) so that you arrive from the castle and the river, take Via della Conciliazione from there and start with the description of S. Maria in Traspontina on p. 384. Continue to the piazza, reading that page to the end, then pick up the description here.

The main modern access to St. Peter's Square is the Via della Conciliazione, which replaced the 'Spine of the Borgo', a row of old buildings and narrow streets. Some of its key buildings were spared and face Via della Conciliazione, as described in the last part of this section. A few buildings of the demolished 'Spine' were rebuilt nearby.

A possible source of confusion is that while the name Borgo refers to the whole district, some streets here are also individually called Borgo, such as 'Borgo S. Spirito' ('Street of the Holy Spirit').

From the edge of Piazza S. Pietro and with your back to it, take Largo degli Alicorni on the right and cross the street called Borgo S. Spirito at the crosswalk. Continue along this street. As you reach No. 9A, look across the street at the apse and bell tower of a church we'll reach shortly. Continue straight on. At Nos. 7-8 is an interesting 16th-century palace.

Cross the street, then go down the steps nearby on your left. At the bottom, there is a passage between buildings at the start of the street you are now in (Via P. Pfeiffer). This is currently the only access to the church we just passed. Called **S. Lorenzo in Piscibus** ('St. Lawrence in the Fish Market' – a long-gone feature), or more familiarly S. Lorenzino ('Little St. Lawrence'), this ancient jewel of a church was isolated amid modern buildings when the area was modernised. It is run today by an International Youth Centre, open every day 11:00-19:00.

This Romanesque church is first mentioned in the 12th century, though the foundation date is unknown. After many changes and a long period of abandonment, the church has been recently restored to its 12th-century appearance. Grace and spirituality radiate from both the interior, with its simple sloping ceiling and noble columns from Roman temples, and the rough brick façade.

Return to Borgo S. Spirito by the steps and continue left. At the corner of the next crossing is the church of **S. Spirito in Sassia** ('the Holy Spirit in Saxony') with its svelte 15th-century belfry. ('Sassia' is an archaic version of the Italian word for 'Saxony' and refers to the 'Saxon Borough'.) King Ine of Wessex donated the church in the 8th century for use by the pilgrims of his nation. It was rebuilt several times, most recently in the 16th century. The façade is by Antonio da Sangallo the Younger. (Open: 07:00-12:00 and 15:00-20:00.)

The interior is delightfully proportioned and richly adorned, mostly by minor 16th-century painters. The grand wooden ceiling is also 16th-century. As you leave, enjoy a view from the top of the steps of St. Peter's dome on the left.

Continue along Borgo S. Spirito. Next to the church, at No. 3, is the solemn mid 16th-century **Palace of the Commendatore**. It was designed by Nanni di Baccio Bigio, a contemporary and rival of Michelangelo, originally as the home of the president of the nearby hospital, hence its name.

It houses a medical library founded in the 18th century. Visit the airy, frescoed renaissance courtyard, graced by a 17th-century fountain. The whimsical six-hour clock is early 19th century; note the single lizard-shaped hand. Reach the upper floor by a door to the left of the fountain (or take the elevator; press 1). On the left wall is the tombstone of an early 15th-century notable.

Across the street, at No. 78 is another 16th-century palace, reconstructed here after it was torn down with the rest of the Borgo 'Spine'.

Immediately past the Palace of the Commendatore begins the very long wall of the **Ospedale di Santo Spirito** ('Hospital of the Holy Spirit'), founded in 1198 and rebuilt in 1471, the

The church of S. Spirito in Sassia and the surrounding buildings: the Palace of the Commendatore is at 1; the hospital entrance at 2, and an old entrance gate to the Borgo S. Spirito at 3. Engraving by Falda, mid 17th-century.

oldest continuously used hospital in the world. Its most striking exterior feature is the octagonal room in the middle, with gothic windows, ceramic disks and emblems. Beneath it is the baroque entrance to this part of the hospital, now a drug rehabilitation centre. It is open to visitors 09:00-12:45 and 15:30-18:30.

Go in. Behind the baroque entrance is a marvellous 15th-century marble portal attributed to Andrea Bregno. Go through it and you'll be under the octagonal structure, impressively decorated with early renaissance frescoes and later statuary by minor artists. From the octagon radiate two hospital wards (not accessible), where the frescoes continue, covering over 10,000 sq ft (1000 sq m).

The hospital houses a museum of the history of medicine (p. 687).

Back on the street, on the right wall as you exit and behind a grill, note the Wheel of the Foundlings, which no longer turns. Note, too, the inscription, 'alms for the poor infants thrown into ['proietti'] the hospital'.

Continue to the end of the block. Around the

corner is the old hospital front. Much decayed, it was rebuilt in 1928 by copying the original 15th-century structure from a Botticelli fresco which we saw in the Sistine Chapel (p. 344). It has since deteriorated again. The more modern part of the hospital continues along the riverside. When the water is low, to the right of the modern hospital you can see what remains of the piers of a large oblique bridge built by Nero as a direct continuation of the Via Recta (see p. 447). Its purpose was to connect the Via Recta to the stadium begun by Caligula and completed by Nero near the present St. Peter's.

More or less opposite the hospital façade, across Via S. Pio X, is the lively, theatrical façade of the 18th-century **Annunziatina** ('Little Church of the Annunciation'). Originally on the other side of the street, it was dismantled and moved here in 1950 during the reconstruction of the area.

It is open sporadically. Inside is a late 16th-century fresco and a *Madonna and Child* of the circle of Antoniazzo Romano (late 15th-century).

Take Via S. Pio X one block to Via della

Conciliazione, built under the direction of the Roman architect Marcello Piacentini.

From here, past the buildings in front of you, you can see the arches of the Passetto, an elevated corridor built over medieval walls by Pope Alexander VI Borgia (p. 329) as a sheltered link from the Vatican Palaces (to the left) to Castel Sant' Angelo (visible to the right). The pope used it to visit his prisoners in the castle; his successors used it to flee to the castle on many a dramatic occasion, beginning with the 1527 Sack of Rome.

Cross Via della Conciliazione. A few steps to the left is the late 16th-century **S. Maria in Traspontina** ('St. Mary beyond the Bridge'), by Cavalier d'Arpino, which was once well known as the parish church of the nearby castle artillerymen. (Open: 06:30-11:30 and 16:00-19:00.)

The first chapel to the right is dedicated to St. Barbara, patron saint of artillerymen, and both sides of the archway have stucco designs of guns and ammunition. The decoration of the chapel, including the altar painting, is by minor early 17th-century artists. Advancing to the transept, note the very low dome: the castle guard wanted it that way, so it wouldn't block their firing line.

Over the main altar, a sumptuous marble and bronze tabernacle and statues, all from the 17th century, surround an ancient Byzantine icon of the Virgin, the date of which is unknown. Before leaving, in the last chapel before the exit note a wonderful 15th-century terracotta *Pietà*, of unknown authorship.

Leave the church and turn into the narrow street on the right, Vicolo del Campanile. At No. 4 is a renaissance house with an 'illustrated' façade (for this type of decoration, see p. 449). Note, too, the early 17th-century bell tower of the church and the continuation of the Passetto.

Return to Via della Conciliazione. The next blocks are lined in part with important palaces, now sadly out of place in the banal context of the modern street.

At No. 130 is the late 15th-century Palazzo Torlonia, which housed the English embassy until King Henry VIII broke with the Roman Catholic Church in the early 16th century, because it would not consent to his divorce, and severed diplomatic ties. Bought in the 19th century by the princely Torlonia family, it still houses the offices that run the family's assets. There is a project to convert the palace into a public museum of the family art collection.

The elegant marble palace is contemporary with the Palazzo della Cancelleria, which we'll see in the next Walk, and resembles it, too, though it is less impressive. It may be by the same unidentified architect.

Cross the street to visit the beautiful Palazzo dei Penitenzieri (Church judiciary officials) directly opposite; it is now a hotel. This was built in the mid-15th century in an early renaissance style similar to the better-known Palazzo Venezia (p. 535).

Enter the courtyard, which gives a view of S. Spirito in Sassia (p. 382); the ancient marble well and the walls with original architectural frescoes are worth a glance.

Further along on this side, Nos 43 and 51 are mid- and late-16th century palaces. No. 43, by Martino Longhi the Elder, was once the embassy of Florence to Rome. Opposite are two more renaissance palaces, moved here from elsewhere in the Borgo 'Spine'. No. 44, on the left, is late 16th-century; No. 34 is where Raphael died in 1520 (p. 237). It dates from the end of the 15th century and is perhaps by Bramante.

Take the street to the left of No. 44 (Via Rusticucci) to the end. From here you can see almost the entire Passetto. To get to Castel Sant' Angelo from here, skirt the Passetto all the way to the right, or take one of the buses going in that direction for one or two stops. The castle entrance faces the river.

BEFORE GOING

2. Castel Sant' Angelo

Always a famous Roman landmark, and a key stronghold of papal defence, the Castel Sant' Angelo (Castle of the Holy Angel) played a crucial military role as late as the 19th century. Its history, however, long predates both its use as a fortress and the papal dominion.

Hadrian's mausoleum. The massive structure was first a tomb built by Emperor Hadrian for himself and his successors in the early 2nd century AD. By then, the Mausoleum of Augustus, p. 220, had been filled and Hadrian's predecessor, Trajan, had been buried under his own memorial column (p. 186). Hadrian may have designed his own mausoleum. As noted (p. 208), he was an able and creative architect. The tomb followed traditional Etruscan models, a squat cylinder on a rectangular base, but it is so much bigger that it is tempting to compare it with Egyptian pyramids. Like them, it has a central sepulchral chamber, which contained golden urns holding the ashes of the imperial family (except Hadrian's own, which were buried near the top, according to a recent theory) and those of Hadrian's successors, at least until Caracalla in the early 3rd century.

The tomb becomes a fortress. The use of the mausoleum as a fortress dates to imperial times. Its position on the river bank provided convenient defence. Aurelian, the 3rd century emperor who provided Rome with a new set of encircling walls (p. 42), incorporated the awesome mass into his new defence complex. The monument was crenellated, the first change in its outer appearance. Many more additions and changes followed.

In the 6th century the mausoleum was used to hold back a siege of Goths (p. 380). The defenders showered the invaders with all the statues on the mausoleum and most of the marble revetment, thus accelerating the change in its external appearance. On a different occasion, however, the Goths won; they took the castle and nearby district, giving the whole the gothic name 'burg', which then became 'borgo'.

The Angel's sword. The edifice received its present name and dedication to the Archangel Michael, leader of the forces of God, in the middle ages when the popes began using it for defence. Just what prompted the change in name, first documented in the 9th century, is unknown. An old tradition, recently shown to be legendary, holds that in the 5th century, during a bout of plague, Pope Gregory the Great (p. 425) led a procession of citizens to St. Peter's to beseech divine aid. Reaching the great tomb-fortress, Gregory had a vision: the Angel of God atop it, replacing a bloody sword in a sheath, showing that the divine fury had abated. The plague then ended and a grateful Gregory gave the edifice its new name.

Throughout the ages, statues of the angel and his sword were placed on the top of the monument, where the statue of Hadrian once stood. The first ones symbolised the military might of the Church. We'll see an older version with a sword-brandishing angel. The present version simply recalls the legend of merciful intervention during the plague, as the angel sheathes the blade.

In the late middle ages, rooms were added over the building for the popes, who often sought refuge there. In the renaissance the rooms became a full-blown palace.

A mirror of the history of Rome. The long history of the monument as a fortress has mirrored the history of Rome, especially in the middle ages, when the city was in the grip of a constant

The Castel Sant'Angelo and the Castello Gate in the 18th century, by Giuseppe Vasi

struggle between four powers: the pope, the Roman people, the great feudal lords, and the rulers of the essentially Germanic empire created by Charlemagne (see pp. 144, 300, 303). Whoever held the castle controlled the city. Even much later, during Napoleon's occupations and the fight for Italian independence and unity, the castle was a major strategic-political consideration.

Besides its role in battle, it was a dungeon for prisoners of rank, not unlike the Tower of London. In the 10th century Marozia, a lady of the most powerful family in Rome, managed to have Pope John X imprisoned and strangled in the castle. A couple of years later her son, still in his early twenties, became Pope John XI. Cola di Rienzi (p. 144) fled to the castle in an episode early in his tumultuous career. In the 15th century the last attempt by a Roman faction to wrest the city from the popes before such efforts were revived four centuries later ended with the hanging of its leader, Baron Stefano Porcari (p. 114), from a castle bastion. After this the popes bolstered the fortress even more, transforming its interior and closing its original entrance to create a new, totally controlled access.

Alexander VI Borgia had several victims, including at least one cardinal (p. 126), strangled, poisoned or starved to death in the castle. Here are some entries from the diary of his master of ceremonies, the unflappable Burchard (pp. 329-330):

Oct. 28, 1497. Bartolomeo Flores, formerly the Archbishop of Cosenza and private secretary to His Holiness, having been deprived of every honour, rank and benefice and imprisoned in the Castle, was today stripped of all but his shirt ... and given a wooden crucifix. He was then transferred from his cell to another called Sammalò ... where a bed of wooden planks with a straw mattress, two blankets and a headrest to protect him from the damp coming from the wall had been prepared for him. He received a prayer book, a Bible and a copy of the letters of St. Peter; also, a barrel of water, three round loaves and an oil lamp. The Keeper has been instructed to bring him new provisions two or three times a week. He is to stay there until he dies...

July 23, 1498. The former Archbishop of Cosenza died today in the Castle. It is said he departed with great composure and piety ... His body was brought to S. Maria in Traspontina [p. 384] where it was buried with no ceremony. May he rest in peace.

Benvenuto Cellini, a famous Florentine renaissance sculptor and the greatest goldsmith who ever lived, went to the castle with the fleeing pope during the Sack of Rome in 1527, and manned a cannon. He claimed to have fired the shot that killed the Constable of Bourbon (p. 381); this did not end the siege, however. A rambunctious character, he returned to the castle a few years later as a prisoner, accused of robbing the papal treasury. He escaped by tying strips of bedsheets together, but was recaptured and put in one of the most dismal cells within the castle, which he describes in his wonderfully vivid memoirs. He was eventually pardoned.

Other famous inmates included, 60 years after Cellini, Beatrice Cenci, heroine of one of baroque Rome's most lurid tales (of whom more later, p. 517), and in the 18th century the self-styled Count Cagliostro, adventurer, occultist, alchemist and freemason (p. 241). Arrested in Rome by the Inquisition and held in an apartment of the castle, still known today as 'La Cagliostra', he was later moved to an ordinary prison, where he died miserably. Until recently an object of simple curiosity, he is now being belatedly rehabilitated for what now appear to have been, in part at least, genuine contributions to the natural and social sciences.

In the 19th century the castle prisons held Roman patriots of the movement to reunite Italy, often destined to execution in the yard below. The most famous of these, though, is fictional: the painter Mario Cavaradossi in the opera *Tosca* by Puccini. In the last act Cavaradossi is imprisoned and executed in the castle; his lover Tosca follows him to death by leaping off the battlements.

The rediscovery of the castle's past. While the origin of the castle as Hadrian's tomb was never forgotten, until not long ago the interior structure of the tomb was hidden by many alterations and the walling up of several sections after the late middle ages. In 1823 a papal guard officer lowered himself through a trap door and discovered a long spiral ramp, the original main access. Since then, exploration and restoration have gone on by fits and starts, especially after the union of Rome with the rest of Italy in 1870. Some late 19th century identifications of parts and details of the building have been disproved by recent research, but are still retailed by many books. Thus a vent in the ramp ceiling has been misidentified as the Sammalò, the worst prison cell in the castle. The famous elevator, built in 1734 by a castle keeper, is incorrectly said to have been installed by the portly Pope Leo X (p. 117) more than 200 years earlier. Later the elevator was removed and the shaft walled up for defence, because the opening led to the inner core of the castle.

ON THE SPOT

2. Castel Sant' Angelo

The best view of **Castel Sant' Angelo** is to be had from halfway along the bridge opposite it. The Castle of the Holy Angel, looks like a huge drum emerging from a box formed by walls, with a polygonal bastion at each corner. The walls and bastions are medieval. The drum is the original Mausoleum of Emperor Hadrian, at least to a certain height. The ancient Roman structure is revealed by rougher, massive stonework (once marble-covered) up to the level marked with the papal coat-of-arms of Pope Alexander VI Borgia, one of the main rebuilders of the castle (pp. 45, 329). At this level, in Hadrian's day the drum was topped by another, much smaller cylinder resembling a round temple, ringed by columns. The round building is still there, without the columns, but it is hidden. It is embedded in brick structures of the middle ages and later, including a renaissance papal palace (note its balconied windows). Also in Hadrian's day a cypress garden topped the drum (as in the Mausoleum of Augustus, p. 220), surrounding the temple-like building.

A statue of Hadrian on a triumphal chariot with four horses topped the whole; today there is a statue of the Angel sheathing a sword, which however is only visible from a certain distance. Originally the drum rested on a square base, whose sides approximately matched the medieval walls (the box you see). The castle is also enclosed on all sides except the river in a pentagonal fortification, built by the popes, which included two concentric moats. These features, not visible from the front, are some distance from the castle walls. They are presently used as public gardens and occasionally for street fairs. The remains of this base are partly above ground and partly below, the street level having risen irregularly all around.

The castle is open 09:00-19:00, with last admission one hour before closing time, but is closed on Monday. Pass the gateway on the riverside. The original oblong entrance hall of the mausoleum is before you, but several feet lower; modern steps descend to it. Before entering, though, you must buy a ticket. (The access in use at the time of writing winds circuitously around the base of the monument, which we will therefore describe first. But the route often changes. You may have to adapt the description of this area around the base to what is in use. Sometimes it will be easier to see this part at the end of your visit rather than at the beginning.)

Go right a few steps around the base of the monument to the ticket office. Just before the office, on the right, are old models of the castle as it changed through the ages.

The ticket office is inside a charming 16th-century building, the 'Oliara', or olive oil reservoir of the castle (we'll discuss the defensive function of the oil during sieges on p. 392). There is a gate, generally closed, on the right. On the outside – which you can see from a distance later, or reach from the filled-in moat – the gate is decorated with a majestic mid-16th century doorway, which was moved there from the front of the monument during the late 19th-century embankment of the river. Near it is a large fragment of sculpture, one of those flung from the top of the castle during the 6th-century siege.

The level we are on here is the original 2nd century street level of the Mausoleum of Hadrian, but modern steps on the right lead to a more recent level, the Courtyard of Executions. Here the sentences were carried out differently through the ages; in the mid-19th century by a firing squad, when the victims were many and mainly patriots of the Italian unification movement (pp. 565-567). On one side of the courtyard a brand new American-style souvenir shop disfigures the old building in which it has been installed. This building is still noteworthy, however: it is the Chapel of the Condemned, built in the late 16th century for castle prisoners to use before their executions nearby. Note its façade.

Continue, under a strident and perfectly useless metal and plastic canopy. After a few yards, where the canopy ends, on your right is a large 16th-century building with papal emblems. Inside is the

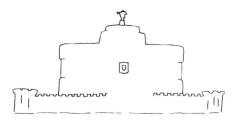 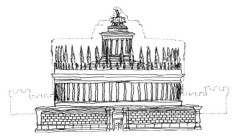

Left: The cylindrical structure of the Castle today, after the rise in the street level. Right: Reconstruction of Hadrian's mausoleum, now encased in the later castle

entrance to the Passetto, an elevated passage linking the castle to the Vatican Palaces, (you saw it from the outside, p. 384) usually closed to the public (but you can check). You are now back on the bottom level of the original structure. Near the end of the tour (with public lavatories on the right) you'll see on your right colossal fragments of statuary and of the original cornice, flung from the top of the mausoleum during the siege (p. 385). Also on the left, embedded in the wall, is the top of the final pilaster of the left parapet of the original Roman bridge, built by Hadrian.

You have now ended the tour of the base and are back where you first entered. Through a modern entrance and new steps, descend to the original entrance hall in the ancient rectangular base of the mausoleum. The floor level here is level with the bridge on the Tiber. The original gateway opened this way, beneath the present one, forming a continuous structure with the bridge. The oblong hall ends in a square space.

The marvellous bronze peacocks in the Vatican Museums (p. 318) were found here. The walls were originally lined with yellow marble. The great niche held the colossal statue of Hadrian, whose head is also in the Vatican Museums (p. 326).

Up on the left is the entrance to an elevator conceived and built in 1734, a 'suspended chair' used daily by the keeper and sometimes by the popes. The entrance was later walled up to ensure the impregnability of the interior.

On the right a spiral (or more exactly helical) ramp begins, the ancient Roman access to the sepulchral chamber. Very well preserved, it rises gradually to 38 ft (12 m), completing three-quarters of a circle.

Processions with the imperial ashes moved up the dark ramp by torchlight, shadows dancing on the yellow marble-lined walls and the mosaic-covered floor. Ventilation and drainage were provided by huge shafts through the barrel-vaulted ceiling. The first of four shafts is about 40 steps from the start. Note the gutter, which also drained the ancient cypress garden.

The ramp has inspired similar structures in other historic Roman buildings (pp. 64, 320). It ends at a doorway. Just before this, on the right, are the wooden guides and the pulley of the 1734 elevator overhead. This was the first of its two stops. Past the doorway (pause here a moment) the ramp used to continue more steeply just in front of you (part of its opening is visible on the wall) for maintainance of the cypress garden and in order to reach the temple-like structure that probably contained Hadrian's ashes. On the left a corridor, which was level with the doorway and not sloping as now, led to the last room, the tomb chamber of the imperial family.

The popes changed everything when they turned the mausoleum into an impregnable fortress. They walled up the spiral ramp in front of and behind you. So you could not have come up the way you did; remember the ramp was only rediscovered in 1823 (p. 387). They now needed a new way to enter the building, so they broke through the stone wall on the right.

They also needed to create obstacles against enemy incursion. The first inner obstacle was the wooden trap door you see in the floor near the new entrance. The present sloped, stepped ramp replaced the level corridor. It still leads to the sepulchre, but now opens on to the room in mid-air through the top of the original Roman archway. Papal engineers narrowed what remained of the archway, the top half, changing it from arched to square. Square holes were added on either side; from these, cannon would greet whoever managed to pass the trap door.

Go up to the sepulchral chamber and enter on the mid-air bridge.

The room where the imperial ashes were kept is empty. Its golden urns were stolen in antiquity and the decoration is gone. Hadrian's own ashes were probably kept in the temple-like cylinder above, but a modern inscription in this room quotes the famous lines he wrote on his deathbed: 'Little soul, gentle and wandering, guest and companion of my body, you are going to dwell in pallid places, stark and bare; will you cease your play of yore?'

The wall opposite the entrance originally had no opening, since the interior of the mausoleum, as we mentioned, ended at this room. The popes had the present door opened in order to make the upper levels accessible from here.

Until 1822 part of the bridge before the door was a drawbridge. Any intruder getting this far had to drop to the floor and scale the wall. On the way, he had to deal with boiling oil poured from above (6,000 gallons – 22,000 litres – of olive oil were always kept in the upper level reservoirs or in the Oliara, p. 388).

In the renaissance and later, the most infamous prison cell in the castle, the Sammalò, was probably here, in the arched recess to your right.

Leave the sepulchral chamber and take the 'new' ascending corridor. On the way, note within the wall the top of one of the vents (the second) we saw from the spiral ramp. The corridor leads all the way out, to the first upper level and the Papal Palace.

Once outside, sit on the marble bench facing the statue of an angel. In antiquity the cypress garden was here. It encircled the cylindrical temple-like structure which is still there, hidden inside the palace before you.

First look at this side of the former garden, which is now a courtyard. It has had several names: 'of the Bell', after a large bell which topped the palace (we'll see it later) and was rung during executions with a chain that hangs down the front of the building here; 'of the Balls', after cannon and mortar rounds which were piled up against signs stating their calibre (the 17th-century signs are on the wall); finally, 'of the Angel', after the mid-16th century marble angel by Raffaello da Montelupo, a follower of Michelangelo. The statue was moved here from the top of the castle in the 18th century, when it was replaced by the present bronze angel.

Behind you, if you are still sitting on the bench, are medieval structures. Near the entrance from which you came, they contained the old guard-room; it was also used by prison guards to prepare special meals for prominent inmates. Today part of the building houses the armoury, a major collection of weapons and militaria.

Assuming you are still on the bench, the courtyard is bounded on the right by a 16th-century wall designed by Michelangelo as the façade of a chapel. To the left is a somewhat matching wall by Raffaello da Montelupo, built a few years later. To the right, by the steps, is an ancient Roman well, attesting to the original garden-like character of the area.

Now look at the palace, built gradually in the 15th and 16th centuries.

Many popes lived in these apartments. Those who have left the most marks are from the first half of the 16th century: Julius II, the first great patron of both Michelangelo and Raphael (p. 331); the pleasure-loving Leo X and the unhappy

Clement VII, whose tombs we saw in S. Maria sopra Minerva (p. 117); and Paul III, Giulia Bella's brother (p. 363).

The palace consists of two wings, which are connected internally, and can be entered from the left or right. Go to the left entrance; on this floor the wing was used as offices.

The first room has a splendid fireplace and terracotta and stone reliefs over the doors, all 18th-century. Go right into a room in the middle of the palace, that is, the centre of the castle. This is part of the ancient Roman mausoleum, the base of the cylindrical, temple-like structure at the top of the main drum (p. 388).

During the papal dominion this was called the Justice Room, because from here awful sentences were handed down to the involuntary guests of the castle. It is frescoed with an Angel of Justice by Perino del Vaga, one of Raphael's assistants (early 16th century). Pieces of ancient artillery are sometimes displayed here.

Return to the courtyard. Enter the papal apartments proper through the door at the other end.

The first is the Apollo Room, with mythical subjects illustrated in 16th-century frescoes in the 'grotesque' style (the Domus Aurea had just been discovered, see p. 210) by Perino del Vaga and others. To the right of a majestic fireplace, bearing the arms of Paul III, is the entrance to the chapel commissioned by Leo X, the façade of which, by Michelangelo, we saw outside. On the floor by the entrance is the opening of the second and last stop of the 1734 elevator. At floor level in the same wall is another opening, 27 ft (8 m) deep, perhaps for emptying chamber pots; the apartment has no traces of a lavatory.

The chapel is now used to display works of art unrelated to the history of the castle. Two more rooms to the left of the Apollo Room fireplace have a similar use. They were private rooms with magnificent friezes by minor 16th- and 17th-century painters.

Past these rooms go through an exit on the right into the other side of the former cypress garden, now subdivided into two courtyards.

In the first, the Courtyard of Alexander VI or 'of the Well', is a wonderful late 15th-century well bearing the arms of Alexander VI Borgia. (The courtyard often displays a catapult or other ancient war machinery. All such machines here and elsewhere in the castle are reproductions, as are the cannons, except those exhibited in the collections.) To your left (if you are facing the palace wall) is the passage to the second, smaller courtyard. Note here the beautiful renaissance design of the windows and doors. This is the Courtyard of Leo X, or 'of the Oven', with a wood-burning oven, whose opening is visible in the shorter wall with the door. It was used to heat water, the purpose of which we'll see shortly.

Back in the passage between the two courtyards, steps lead to the famous palace bath, built in the early 16th century for Pope Julius II, possibly by Bramante. The water heated in the oven which you just saw was for this bath. Note, too, for future reference, that the bath can also be reached from the floor above.

The bathroom is unique due to its age and fine condition. The highly refined decoration (note the real shells) is of disputed authorship. The diary of Johann Fichard, a German visitor in 1536, notes: 'Here in an arched recess His Holiness wallows in hot water poured from the statuette of a naked girl. More of these naked statuettes are around, which certainly inspire His Holiness with great spiritual feelings.' The statuettes are gone.

Return to the Courtyard of the Well. There are several manholes in the floor. Some fed river water brought up by mules into a reservoir. The stored water, tapped through the wells here and in the Courtyard of the Angel, was used for the old cypress garden and for plants which also adorned the area in papal times. The popes installed filters in the reservoir for drinking water.

Other manholes fed olive oil storerooms, which we will visit shortly.

Opposite the papal palace is a semi-circular building, probably ancient though modernised in the renaissance and adorned with graffiti (p. 449) of nude pagan deities typical of the time.

Sometimes some of the rooms served as the least grim of the prison cells, such as the one in which Cellini was held before his famous escape (an unsubstantiated tradition asserts that he was in the room farthest to the right). After he was recaptured, he was put in one of a set of dungeons under the building; you can see its barred window at ground level near the small drinking fountain.

These underground dungeons, which we're about to visit, follow a curve like that of the building overhead, for an interesting reason. They were formed by partitioning the last section of the second ramp, the steep ramp which originally led to the cypress garden so that it could be watered and maintained and which was walled up in papal times (as we saw before entering the sepulchral chamber, p. 389).

Let's now descend to the dungeons.

Note: the regular entrance is a small arched doorway to the right of the small drinking fountain and past the two barred windows, but this is often closed. If so, you must go in through a doorway to the left of the drinking fountain; unfortunately, you then miss Cellini's cell and the section described in the next two paragraphs.

After crossing a large room (once used for visitors to the prisoners) enter a corridor with three gloomy cells with low doors. Two more follow. In the last one Cellini spent almost a year, tormented by the dark, the damp from the adjacent water reservoir and 'spiders and poisonous worms'. Traces of a charcoal drawing, behind glass, are said to be the Christ and God the Father he sketched to console himself, as he mentions in his memoirs.

Climb a few steps to a small room from which you can see, just to the right, an outer latrine. Tradition has it that from here Cellini escaped in 1539, lowering himself with sheets. This is unlikely, partly because of the great height (80 ft / 25 m) and because Cellini, as noted above, was on another floor during his first detention.

Descend into two cavernous olive oil storerooms, containing 83 jars. Nearby are five pit-like giant silos, with a capacity of 400 tons of grain, and more prison cells.

Return to the courtyard and climb the steps to the left of the drinking fountain. You are now on the battlements. Turn left. After a few steps, a staircase under a low arch leads to the upper floor of the sumptuous Apartments of Pope Paul III.

You first come to the Library, once the secret Church archives (now in the Vatican). Its lavish decoration is by minor 16th-century artists, the fireplace by Raffaelo da Montelupo. Through a door to the right of the one through which you came, go and see two more rooms adorned with ancient Roman and mythological subjects. The rooms are often used to exhibit paintings unrelated to the history of the castle. (From here, a few steps lead to the Cagliostra, the wing where the 18th-century adventurer was imprisoned; it was named after him shortly after his death. The wing, however, is usually closed to the public.)

Return to the Library. Go to the wall where the plaster is missing near the floor, exposing rough stonework. (Unless it has been restored recently, the plaster is missing because archæologists wanted to show that this is a medieval construction predating the papal palace. It was built in the 14th century in order to square up the cylindrical structure behind the wall.) Pass through the door in the middle of the wall. This door dates from the time of Hadrian. It opens into the temple-like structure which once topped the mausoleum – an isolated, round, once columned building – and was later embedded in the medieval and renaissance masonry.

You will note that the room is circular. In Hadrian's day it was majestic (36 ft/11 m high). In the middle ages the present ceiling was added, splitting the space into two rooms, upper and lower. The original tall room, just under Hadrian's triumphal chariot, was probably the tomb of the Emperor, as noted above. (Hadrian's enormous red marble coffin must have been here; only the lid survives, now used as the font of St. Peter's.) In papal times, this lower section, which was the highest, most defensible recess of the castle, was the Treasury; it is still so called. Note the two big coffers and heavy walnut cabinets, all 16th century.

We'll now leave the Apartments of Paul III, but we'll return to them from another side after a trip upstairs.

Climb the narrow ancient Roman staircase, which today, as in the time of Hadrian, goes around the temple-like structure.

A modern door midway opens onto what was once the upper part of Hadrian's tomb. This section is not always open, but if so pass from this room into other rooms of the papal palace used for an interesting medieval sculpture exhibition. This includes a wonderful *Bust of the Redeemer* (with the large inscription 'Salvator'), which once adorned the castle entrance, by the 15th century Tuscan sculptor Isaia da Pisa; and a huge, defaced marble *Head of Pope Paul IV*, the late 16th century founder of the Ghetto and a stern inquisitor, found in the Tiber where an enraged mob had thrown it (p. 116). The ceilings of the rooms have late-1920's stuccoes by Duilio Cambellotti celebrating Italy's victory in the First World War.

Return to the winding staircase and continue on up.

You now come to the uppermost terrace of the castle. Here, on the spot where the statue of Hadrian on his triumphal chariot once stood, is the bronze Angel by the minor 18th-century Flemish sculptor Peter Anton van Verschaffelt.

It replaces the stone statue we saw in the Courtyard of the Angel (p. 390), which in turn replaced earlier ones, going back to the early middle ages. It is rightly admired for its graceful spiritedness. To the French writer Stendhal it was 'a naive teenage girl, struggling with the sword she is trying to put away'. The two, vandalised, escutcheons below are of Paul III Farnese (above) and Alexander VI Borgia.

To the left of the Angel is the Campana della Misericordia ('Bell of Mercy'), which tolled during executions (p. 390).

Enjoy the famous panorama from the terrace. It is just the right height and distance to embrace the most venerable features of the city, composed in a timeless picture by the twisting river.

Of special interest is the general view of the great Vatican buildings to the right: St. Peter's, with a fine view of Michelangelo's dome; the papal palaces to its right, up to the Belvedere Palace (p. 307); and the Passetto (pp. 384, 389) connecting the castle to the papal palaces. Today the two-thirds of the structure adjoining the castle belong to Italy, the rest to the Vatican.

Leaving the terrace, do not take the winding staircase up which you came, but the other one.

On a landing halfway down is the entrance to the Apartments of the Castle Keeper (18th century), seven rooms notable mainly for the view, and presently used as offices (closed to the public).

At the foot of the steps go back into the Apartments of Paul III. Here is the magnificent Pauline Hall, or Council Hall, frescoed in the early 16th century by Perino del Vaga and his assistants.

The main subjects are episodes from the *Life of Alexander the Great* (a reference to the real name of Pope Paul III, Alessandro Farnese) on the ceiling and most of the walls, and from the *Life of St. Paul* (the chosen name of the pope) on the monochrome wall roundels.

Hadrian is portrayed on the entrance wall; opposite is the Archangel Michael, by Perino del Vaga's distinguished assisant, Pellegrino Tibaldi.

The room has two interesting false doors painted by Tibaldi. The one on the right of the entrance depicts a courtier of the pope entering; the other, on the Archangel wall, two handymen leaving. (These are portraits of the castle staff at the time; one of them has been tentatively identified.)

From a door to the right of the Archangel wall enter two private papal rooms decorated by Perino del Vaga. In the first room note, on the left, a small door. Pope Paul had it put there to give access to the bath below (p. 391) via steps excavated in the ancient Roman temple-like structure. The wonderful frieze depicts the story of Perseus and Andromeda. The second room, the papal bedroom, has pagan ceiling decorations with the story of Eros and Psyche. The antique furniture is not original to the castle, with the possible exception of the bed.

393

Return to the Pauline Hall. To the left of the Archangel fresco, take a corridor adorned with 16th-century grotesques. This corridor coincides at least partly with one which, in the time of Hadrian, started from the cypress garden and spiralled around the temple-like structure to its entrance (that is, to the door you took when leaving the Library, p. 392). The corridor leads to the Library, which we've already seen.

Return once more to the Pauline Hall and this time go out onto the battlements. Here we are on the front balcony of the castle loggia. It was designed in the early 16th century by Bramante (or, perhaps, Antonio da Sangallo the Younger) for Julius II. Don't miss the beautiful marble columns and grotesque decoration.

(Just below is Bernini's Bridge of the Holy Angel described in the next section. You might like to read that part now (p. 395), especially since Bernini designed the bridge as part of an ensemble including the castle and St. Peter's.)

On the battlements, turn to your right. A few steps further and the Courtyard of the Angel can be seen on the right. From this angle we can see both the old marble angel in the courtyard and the new bronze one at the top of the castle. (We also have another view of the 'Bell of Mercy'.)

A door to the left of the archway opens onto another interesting armoury. Lavatories and a snack bar follow. Past these, we come to an arcaded loggia built by Pope Paul III at the back of the castle. It was designed by Raffaello da Montelupo and frescoed with grotesques, now badly decayed.

Go back to the Courtyard of the Angel and from there turn immediately to the right and descend again to the base of the drum via the stepped corridor. Go straight all the way down, that is, do not turn into the spiral ramp.

Near the exit (which, as you may remember, was the only access to the fortress from the Renaissance to the late 19th century, p. 390) is the old guard room. Nearby is the mechanism of an old drawbridge which no longer exists.

A bridge leads to the top of the medieval walls. Turn right at the top in order to tour the bastions.

Pass the first bastion. From the second bastion, steps (usually closed) lead down to the beginning of the Passetto to the Vatican (pp. 384, 389). Between the second and third bastions the façade of the 'Chapel of the Condemned' is visible. Pass the third bastion; on the castle wall, near the escutcheon of the Borgia pope, is the outside latrine from which Cellini is said to have lowered himself. The fourth, and last, bastion is topped by an extra turret (recently rebuilt) armed with reproduction cannons.

Near this bastion, look out and down to an area where a moat used to be. Farther away among the trees, note the pentagonal ring of walls (mentioned on p. 388) encircling a second moat.

Past the last bastion, you are again at the front of the castle. Descend the steps to the ground floor. On the way down, note the reconstructed workshop of a 16th-century gunsmith. Further along are two ancient Roman busts, one of a bearded Hadrian.

Soldiers, by Stefano Della Bella (17th c)

BEFORE GOING

3. Ponte Sant' Angelo

Emperor Hadrian built Ponte Sant' Angelo (the Bridge of the Holy Angel) as the passage to his great mausoleum. Its original name was Pons Aelius, after his family name. If we observe the lower part, its Roman origin is obvious. The upper part is quite different: it is another magnificent example of the Roman baroque and genius of Bernini.

For well over a millennium before Bernini, even in the centuries when it was still called Pons Ælius, this was the bridge that streams of pilgrims had to cross in order to reach the centre of Christianity: St. Peter's. The throng was at times so thick that a two-way traffic system was set up (p. 442). With the stupendous castle as a backdrop, the bridge was a sort of prelude to the pilgrims' mystical fulfilment at the end of a long and arduous journey.

With his theatrical flair (see pp. 375-376) Bernini quickly grasped this connection and capitalised on it. He put a double row of marvellous angels on the parapet, some to his own design or even by his own hand, others by assistants. 'An avenue of the heavenly host assembled to welcome the faithful to the shrine of the great Apostle,' proclaimed Bernini's patron, Pope Alexander VII. This is the monument that fully fuses Bernini's qualities as sculptor, architect and stage director. The angels are beautiful as individuals, each with a distinctive personality and grace. Yet it is the procession and the design their gestures carve into the sky that convey the unique meaning of the whole. It is as though Bernini – true to his minimalist principle of achieving maximum effect by subtracting from, rather than adding to space – appropriated through the gestures of the angels the whole sky and vista, making them into a hymn to the marvels waiting beyond.

ON THE SPOT

3. Ponte Sant' Angelo

Of the original Pons Ælius, inaugurated in 134 AD and considered in antiquity to be the most beautiful bridge in Rome, only the three great central arches remain. They were once preceded by smaller arches supporting ramps, destroyed in 1892 when the embankment was built. Two new arches were then built at the ends.

The parapets were rebuilt in 1668 to a design by Bernini. Each of the ten angels upon them carries a symbol of the Passion of Christ: the column, the whip, the cross, the nails, the spear, and so on.

Bernini carved two of the angels himself. He gave his talented pupils and followers sketches of the others and supervised their work, but left them some freedom of execution, as is apparent in the individual style of each statue.

Once finished, the two angels by Bernini, one with the Scroll of the Cross and the other with the Crown of Thorns, were deemed too precious to leave outdoors and promptly replaced with copies by his pupils (the second and fourth on the right from the castle end). We saw the original statues in S. Andrea delle Fratte (p. 63).

At the end farthest from the castle, the bridge is adorned with two early 16th-century statues which predate Bernini's renovation, and which were originally housed in two small chapels: St. Peter by Lorenzetto (a friend of Raphael) is on the left as you face the castle, and St. Paul by Paolo Taccone. (The word 'Borgo' on the pedestal indicates the border of the district beyond the river.)

MIDPOINT OF WALK

We now leave the Vatican area and move to that of the original 'mother church' of Christianity, S. Giovanni in Laterano ('St. John Lateran'); see 'Planning your visit' on p. 379.

BEFORE GOING

4. S. Giovanni in Laterano

Your exploration of Rome has taken you from one end of the walled city to the other. Having started at the traditional northern entrance, Porta del Popolo, you are now at one of several southern gates.

You will not find this formerly *disabitato* area (p. 28), rebuilt in modern times and resettled in the 20th century mainly by low-to-middle income people, particularly attractive; it's rather shabby and noisy, and choked with traffic fumes. But fragmentary ruins found all around and still under the present buildings tell a different story, recalling a time when the district was one of the wealthiest, greenest and most tranquil in Rome. Foundations of large villas have been tentatively identified as the homes of two related noble families, the Pisoni and the Laterani. Co-plotters in a mid-1st century AD attempt on Nero's life, the chiefs of the two families were caught and executed, along with the philosopher Seneca, Nero's detested tutor. He was accused of helping them, possibly falsely. Yet the Laterani name lived on, and the area has been called the Lateran ever since ancient times.

A century after Nero's death, the mother of Marcus Aurelius (p. 146) lived here, and here the future emperor grew up.

In the early 4th century, probably where the Pisoni-Laterani villas once stood, rose the princely home of Fausta, sister of the Emperor Maxentius and wife of his co-emperor and rival, Constantine. As we know (p. 198), the political marriage of Fausta to Constantine – she was 10 at the time – failed to preserve peace in the Empire.

Nearby were the barracks of an elite cavalry corps, the *Equites Singulares* ('Excellent Horsemen'), the bodyguards of the emperors. You saw their parade at the funeral of Marcus Aurelius' father on a bas relief in the Vatican Museums (p. 312). Ruins of the barracks have been found.

Mother and head of all churches. The defeat of Maxentius by Constantine marked a turning point in the history of the Lateran. As soon as Constantine took over as ruler of Rome in 312, he began to pay off his debt to the Christian party which had supported him and to the God who – he was sure – had helped him prevail.

From Porta del Popolo to Porta San Giovanni

He first legalized Christianity, then began a programme of aid, which included building the first public – as opposed to private or clandestine – Christian church. Soon afterwards, he provided the pope with a residence and an administrative centre. Then he built more churches, all on sites already venerated as burial places of famous Roman martyrs.

Constantine contributed land and materials himself. As noted earlier (p. 300), the first church – a Roman basilica design, the most appropriate for big public meetings – was built in an outlying area to avoid offending the still powerful pagan party. Most senatorial families were pagan, and Constantine was a prudent man; recall his cautious inscription on his triumphal arch, p. 198. He chose as his site the Lateran district near the southern walls, as far as possible from the city centre, a district where he had personal and public lands of which he could dispose. These estates were the home of his wife Fausta – probably the ancient Pisoni-Laterani complex – and the barracks of the *Equites Singulares*.

These 'Excellent Horsemen' had done their duty, lining up to defend the ruler Maxentius, but his ruin meant their disgrace. The 200-year-old corps was dissolved and its barracks were razed. In Fausta's home, the church hierarchies had already been gathering for some time: one of the first episcopal synods had been held there by Pope Melchiades, and there may have been an *ecclesia domestica* (p. 228) on the site too. Fausta's villa was now levelled, along with the barracks, to make room for the basilica.

Perhaps the destruction of her home was meant to punish the empress, who may have only half-heartedly backed the struggle of her husband against her brother, Maxentius. One thing is clear: relations between the royal couple now began to corrode. A few years later, the emperor had Fausta suffocated in the hot vapours of her own bath.

In contrast to the righteous, wise aura which the Church has created and maintained for 17 centuries around the monarch who assured its salvation and triumph, Constantine does not seem to have been a particularly benevolent person. Some time before putting his wife to death, he had his extremely popular eldest son and heir apparent, Crispus, convicted of plotting against him and executed. Most contemporaries thought him jealous. Some, fearing for their lives, anonymously denounced him as a new Nero. Some ancient authors explain the deaths of Fausta and Crispus with a single story: Fausta, working to put on the throne one of the children she had borne Constantine, accused Crispus, son of Constantine from a previous marriage, of having tried to rape her, and urged the emperor to execute him. St. Helena, Constantine's mother, exposed the ruse, so Fausta was executed too. But it so happened that all of her children – Constantine II, Constantius II and Constans – did indeed ascend the throne.

The first Christian church, which Constantine personally helped build by carrying the first buckets of earth, was originally dedicated to Christ the Redeemer – a dedication appropriate to the first great, formal recognition of the cult of Jesus Christ – and only centuries later acquired the present dedication to St. John or rather to both Saints John, the Baptist and the Evangelist. Its primacy among churches was and is absolute: 'Mother and Head of all Churches', as an inscription on its façade proudly proclaims. (The title, however, was based more on resentment than dispassionate recognition: the church rectors had requested it when they realised that St. John's was losing status to St. Peter's; the pope found it expedient to grant their wish.)

The Patriarchy. St. John's importance was enhanced by the construction nearby of a palace for the pope and his officials. The palace underwent many transformations and additions through the ages until it became a compound not unlike the present Vatican palaces. It occupied most of two great squares now next to St. John's. Since the pope, first bishop of the western empire, was called 'patriarch' in the early days of Christianity – like the Bishop of Constantinople, who still carries the title – the complex was called *il Patriarchìo*, the Patriarchate. (The name 'pope', from the Latin *papa* or 'father', used to be given to any bishop and even to simple priests as a sign of affectionate respect. Only in the 9th century was the name reserved in the West for the Bishop of Rome.) One palace contained a whole row of *triclinia*, dining rooms, where the faithful received meals on special days. Another palace, used for banquets honouring the kings who came to Rome to be crowned by the popes, was added at the end of the 8th century, just in time for the arrival of Charlemagne and his coronation as head of the Holy Roman Empire. The last famous construction was a most ornate loggia, or arcaded gallery, from which the pope announced the first Holy Jubilee in 1300.

Throughout this time, the Lateran area saw intense activity and traffic. Yet for centuries after the fall of the Empire it was isolated from the populous areas, since the people of Rome left the hills for the district within the Tiber bend. The Lateran was thus cut off from the *abitato* by the wild expanse of the *disabitato* (p. 28).

When the popes left Rome and the Lateran for their long self-imposed exile in France in the early 14th century (p. 300), the Patriarchate compound lost its *raison d'être* and began to decay. A great fire devastated it a few years later and no one repaired the buildings. When the popes finally returned later in the century, for practical and political reasons discussed elsewhere (pp. 300, 329) they renounced the Patriarchate in favour of the Vatican.

The urban plan of Sixtus V. Despite this relocation, St. John's Basilica remained an object of great veneration and frequent pilgrimage. In the late 16th century, the basilica, the greatest landmark at the southern end of the city, became the natural terminus of the urban renewal project set in motion from the northern end by Pope Sixtus V (pp. 44, 92). This project was mainly aimed at creating a street grid to serve the resettlement of the *disabitato,* which, incidentally, was not really completed until the 20th century. In previous Walks we followed the expansion plan of Sixtus V from Piazza del Popolo to S. Maria Maggiore near the geographical centre of the city. From S. Maria Maggiore, one main branch of the line was extended to St. John's, partly retracing vanished ancient Roman streets through the hills. There, to mark the furthest and final node of the great road plan, another obelisk was erected – the largest in Rome, or for that matter in Egypt, whence it came.

Locally, the plan involved restoring the basilica area. A monumental renaissance gate was inserted in the walls, just as one had been created in Piazza del Popolo. A new papal palace abutting the basilica replaced the crumbled Patriarchate complex.

Though badly damaged, many of the buildings of the Patriarchate were still standing. Unfortunately, Sixtus V had them torn down, starting with the famous Jubilee Loggia; an act which later contributed to criticism of this great, but somewhat insensitive, builder pope (p. 308). Three fragments of the old Patriarchate were spared: the apse of a dining room (*triclinium*) where

*Piazza San Giovanni in the 18th century, by Giuseppe Vasi. In the foreground
stands the obelisk raised by Sixtus V as the climax of his town planning project*

Charlemagne had dined following his historic coronation; the popes' private chapel in the original
papal palace; and the grand staircase of the palace. The last two were joined into one, by moving
the staircase to make it serve the isolated chapel. Two strange leftovers – the apse minus the dining
room and the chapel plus the staircase – survive at another end of the square facing the Basilica.

The leftovers were spared because of their great political and religious significance. The *triclinium* apse, which was adorned by a mosaic, was kept due to its link with Charlemagne, a figure
whom the Church would invoke for centuries to exemplify the proper relation between papacy
and empire – the former conferring legitimacy on the latter, the latter conferring power on the former. The papal chapel was spared because popes had performed the highest rites of the Church
there – it was the predecessor of the Sistine Chapel (p. 343) – and because it once contained so
many holy relics as to be dubbed *Sanctum Sanctorum* (like the 'Holy of Holies' in Jerusalem). The
staircase was salvaged because a medieval tradition held that it was the staircase of the Jerusalem
residence of the Roman governor Pontius Pilatus, which Jesus climbed before being led to death
(the story probably stemmed from the fact that the steps originally led to a part of the Patriarchate
used as a court of law). The steps were said to have been brought to Rome by Constantine's
mother, St. Helena, that great mover of relics also credited with bringing the True Cross to Rome
(p. 368). The Church certified the legend as true in the 16th century and it has not been disclaimed

since. Thus the staircase is officially holy (it is called the Scala Santa) and must be climbed on one's knees. Pope Pius IX, at the age of 78, climbed the steps on his knees the day before Italian troops entered Rome in 1870 (p. 70), in a vain last-minute bid for divine help. Incidentally, mystical knee-climbing is common to different ages and cultures; Julius Cæsar once ascended to the Temple of Jupiter on the Capitol (p. 142) on his knees.

St. John's Basilica, the rebuilt palace and the Sanctum Sanctorum/Scala Santa were made part of the Vatican State in 1929 (p. 67).

A mystical aura. The mystical, legendary aura of St. John Lateran dates back to before Christianity, indeed before history, when the area was used for a festival to celebrate the arrival of summer. Incredibly, this festival continues. It is the Feast of St. John, beloved by Romans and celebrated on the night of June 23 in the two connecting squares. In the middle ages the feast was also meant to ward off devils and witches by means of bonfires – including one to burn the ropes used in hangings the previous year – and the eating of garlic and snails, considered demon-repellent. In more recent centuries the feast became rowdy and somewhat orgiastic, to the point that the popes imposed restrictions. It is still a colourful evening, devoted to songs, wine, flirting and feasting. Snails are still sold and garlic reigns supreme as seasoning, for *porchetta*, too, a spiced roast suckling-pig. Fireworks have replaced the bonfires.

The Scala Santa in a 17th century guidebook

Another extraordinary document linking distant antiquity with a relatively recent past, which adds to our wonder at the myth-making power of the medieval mind (p. 93), is in the cloister of St. John's Basilica. It is a small marble tablet once erected in a cemetery by two male slaves in memory of a departed young female co-worker. The Latin inscription, difficult to decipher due to its many abbreviations, brings a strong whiff of life in bygone times: 'To the sacred spirits of the dead and to the well-deserving Secunda, hairdresser to our (lady) Rufina and at (the court of) Emperor Titus, dead at 19; dedicated by the two Zosimi, her co-slaves'.

We do not know who this girl was, who departed at so tender an age and was so movingly honoured by her humble friends. Nor do we know how this 1st century AD tablet ended up in a church built three centuries later. The tablet was probably brought here from the catacombs in the early middle ages. At that time churches avidly collected and treasured bones, inscriptions and relics of any type found in cemeteries of the poor, often incorrectly assuming that these belonged to Early Christians, usually identified arbitrarily as martyrs (p. 597).

The story is not over. In the Baptistery of St. John's a whole chapel and altar are dedicated to 'Saints Secunda and Rufina' – the two names mentioned on the tablet in the cloister. Searching the records for these two saints, we find only the testimonial of a 12th-century deacon, Joannes, who relates that his contemporary, Pope Anastasius IV, had placed in St. John's Baptistery 'an altar to the two holy virgins Rufina and Secunda, whose precious bodies were found before he became pope'. A medieval tradition held that these two saints were beheaded during the 3rd century persecutions under co-emperors Valerian and Gallienus for refusing to give up their Christianity or their virginity. Two more churches (one still extant, p. 552) had been built in their honour. With no proof of the existence of the virgins, it seems likely that the story goes back to that humble 1st century memorial to a 19-year-old hairdresser and the names carved on it, misinterpreted and elaborated upon in an age in which a correct reading of Latin had become rare even in the clergy.

Marcus Aurelius mistaken for Constantine. Another historical misunderstanding, a lucky one, originated in the Lateran area. As noted, Marcus Aurelius grew up here. This fact was celebrated late in his life, or after his death, with a marvellous statue of the emperor on horseback placed near his childhood home. After the Empire fell, the area was engulfed in the *disabitato*, and the statue was neglected and became overgrown with weeds. It was not destroyed, like other reminders of the pagan past, only because medieval Romans, who remembered the Constantinian connotation of the Lateran area, mistook the statue for one of Constantine, the great ally of the Church.

In the early Renaissance the artistically sensitive popes carefully restored the work, still thought to depict Constantine, and moved it to the side of St. John's Basilica, where it became one of the most admired monuments in Rome. When Michelangelo restored the Capitoline square the statue was moved there (p. 146), to an appropriate place of honour. By then it had been correctly identified, but the renaissance had no qualms about celebrating a great pagan figure. In 1963 the original pedestal of the statue was found near the underground ruins of Marcus' childhood home and placed in storage, Michelangelo having already given the statue a base of great beauty.

ON THE SPOT

4. S. Giovanni in Laterano

This description starts outside Porta S. Giovanni at the S. Giovanni metro station (the square there is called Piazzale Appio). If you arrive by metro, once through the turnstile follow the right wall round to the right exit.

We are just outside the late 3rd century AD walls built by Emperor Aurelian. It is a more impressive stretch here than the one we saw from the opposite end of the city (pp. 43, 83).

Inside the walls are the two vast squares surrounding St. John's Basilica. Before going there, examine a large marble gate in front of you and, to the left, a castle-like brick structure.

The marble gate is the renaissance Porta S. Giovanni ('St. John's Gate') built in 1574 and a few years later made part of the urban plan of Sixtus V.

The structure to the left is the ancient Roman Porta Asinaria ('Gate of the Ass-drivers'), a southern entrance to the city. Crossing Via Sannio at the pedestrian crossing, go straight until you see it in full on your left. Its recently excavated base is a few yards below street level owing to the usual 'ground rising' phenomenon (see p. 140) The cylindrical towers and battlements were added during a general bolstering of defences in the early 5th century AD.

(From this point, the Walk can also be continued in the direction of S. Croce in Gerusalemme, Porta Maggiore and S. Lorenzo Fuori le Mura; see 'Excursions outside the Walls', pp. 630-636.)

Cross the walls through the square passage and walk around to the left to see Porta Asinaria from the inside.

You are now in the lower of the two squares surrounding St. John's Basilica (Piazza di Porta S. Giovanni). Stand with your back to Porta Asinaria. To your left is the basilica façade; the upper square (Piazza S. Giovanni in Laterano), which faces the other end of the basilica, is not visible from here. In front of you, at some distance, are two remnants of the demolished papal palaces: the mosaic-decorated *triclinium* apse and next to it the Sanctum Sanctorum/Scala Santa.

From Piazzale Appio to Piazza San Giovanni

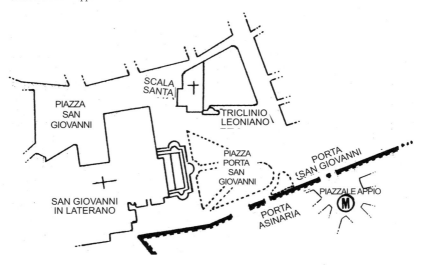

It's best to see these two landmarks first, then visit the basilica, since from the interior of the basilica you can exit directly onto the upper square and go on to your next destination.

Without yet crossing the part of the square with traffic, go toward the huge mosaic-decorated apse, which belonged to the papal dining room, called the **Triclinium Leonianum** after Pope Leo III, who built it shortly before he crowned Charlemagne in Rome in 800 (pp. 303, 365). You can comfortably view the apse from a marble bench here.

Unfortunately, this mutilated relic is not very authentic. In the 18th century, when the apse had already stood for two centuries, the sole remnant of a demolished palace, it was dismantled and rebuilt several yards back in order to enlarge the square. Its mosaic crumbled, and the 'restoration' amounted to replacing most of it with a copy, and not a very accurate one at that. The figures on the upper corners are still of interest, however; those to the right, which are known to follow the original design, are St. Peter with Pope Leo and Charlemagne kneeling at his feet (with the square haloes of the living). Those to the left, which seem entirely designed or redesigned by the restorers, are Christ with Pope Sylvester and Emperor Constantine. The legend of the donation of Rome and the West by Constantine to Pope Sylvester (see p. 303) was invented just around the time of the pact between the popes and the Frankish kings, and was considered a precedent for the coronation of the Frankish king Charlemagne – an emperor committed to the defence of the Church, whence the title of Holy Roman Emperor.

The 18th-century structure framing the apse is by Ferdinando Fuga.

Joined to the apse on the left is the **Sanctum Sanctorum/ Scala Santa**, created at the end of the 16th century to enclose the original papal chapel and the added 'Steps of Pilate'. (06:00-12.30 and 15:00-19:00 in winter / 15:30-19:00 in summer.).

Cross at the pedestrian crossing and go to the entrance. In the vestibule is 19th-century statuary of unusual sweetness.

The central staircase, with 28 marble steps, wood-covered to prevent wear, is the holy one to be climbed on one's knees. Tradition holds that the blood of Christ stained the 2nd, 11th and 28th steps (note the peepholes in the wood). Four flights of ordinary steps flank the Scala Santa to allow visitors a normal climb. It is also surrounded by frescoes of Old and New Testament subjects, painted around 1589 by minor artists.

On the upper floor, behind gratings is the Sanctum Sanctorum, or 'Holy of Holies', the former papal chapel. A Latin inscription over the altar reaffirms the concept, implicit in the name of the chapel, that 'no place in the whole world is holier'. The chapel is permanently closed, but the interior is visible through the gratings. Structurally, it belongs to one of the palaces of the Patriarchate, possibly the oldest, from the time of Constantine (4th century), but rebuilt and redecorated in the late 13th century.

The room is a very rare example of an early medieval Roman sanctuary. Unfortunately, its most striking decorations – a 13th-century ceiling fresco and mosaic at the back – cannot be seen. What is visible includes the graceful twisted Cosmatesque columns of a 13th-century false balcony that runs all around (the figures between them are late 15th-century) and the splendid Cosmatesque pavement, also 13th century.

Over the central altar, an often closed tabernacle has an image of Christ which, tradition holds, was painted by angels. It is an icon of indeterminate age, possibly 5th or 6th century, heavily restored and covered by a later, medieval copy in silk. Throughout the middle ages and later, the image, one of the most famous in Christian history, was carried by the popes in processions to implore divine help against calamities.

Relics and precious objects found under the altar in 1903 are in the Vatican Museums (though one has been stolen, p. 353).

To the right of the Sanctum Sanctorum is a large oratory belonging to the late 16th-century edifice and richly frescoed by the same artists who decorated the staircase.

Enter it to see, in the left wall, the 4th-century door to the Sanctum Sanctorum, originally from the primitive Patriarchate compound, dramatically locked with two huge bolts; the upper one medieval, the other added later, possibly in 1521, when the chapel was last officially open to the public. The bolts were obviously meant to foster the aura of mystery and inaccessibility of the monument. (Doors and their opening and closing have always had a sacred symbolism; think of the Sacellum of Janus – a god whose name itself means passageway – of the gateway to the netherworld on tomb monuments, and more recently, the Porta Santa of St. Peter's and other major churches.)

Go to the altar end of the oratory. Take the door on the left to a room where for the past few years a remarkable 15th-century Crucifix recently restored, though unrelated to the sanctuary, has been displayed.

As you leave, note before you, adjacent to the basilica, the austere Lateran Palace, built by Pope Sixtus V to replace the ruined palaces of the Patriarchate.

Designed by Domenico Fontana in 1586, it is obviously inspired by Michelangelo's Palazzo Farnese, which we'll see in a later Walk, and though it cannot compare with it in beauty, it does inspire a sense of majesty and power. Particularly opulent coats-of-arms surmount the entrances.

The space between the Scala Santa and the Lateran Palace was once almost totally occupied by the papal compound.

With your back at the Scala Santa, on your far right are some surviving arches of a 1st century aqueduct built by Emperor Nero to serve his immense palace (pp. 208-209) and the nearby area.

Between the Scala Santa and the arches of the aqueduct stood a lofty tower, erected by the 8th-century Pope Zacharias to guard the compound. A piece of the base of the tower is on the ground floor of the Convent of the Passionist Order, custodians of the Scala Santa, at No. 14 near the Sanctum Sanctorum.

Normally the convent is not open to the public, but you can try asking the doorman to see the ruin, which is at the end of the corridor to the right. Pope Zacharias erected the tower not only for security but also for prestige, because it closely imitated one that guarded the Byzantine emperor's compound in Constantinople (p. 73). Its addition conferred a somewhat similar status on the Lateran and, indirectly, on Rome itself.

Cross the square again and head for the basilica façade.

Constructed in the early 4th century, **S. Giovanni in Laterano** ('St. John Lateran') was rebuilt five times over the next twelve centuries due to an earthquake, fire and pillage. In the 17th century Borromini drastically renovated the interior. In the early 18th century a new façade was added, the masterpiece of the architect Alessandro Galilei, most notable for its definitive dismissal of a highly decorative baroque in favour of a more severe classical style.

The church is crowned by a procession of oversized statues by minor 18th-century sculptors. In the centre is *Christ the Redeemer*, to whom the basilica was originally dedicated, flanked by the two *St. Johns* – the Baptist and the Evangelist – and *Twelve Doctors of the Church* (p. 369)

On the lower sides of the central entrance is a Latin inscription, repeated twice, proclaiming 'the sacrosanct Lateran church ... mother and head of all churches in the city and the world'. A 12th-century marble strip over the entrances, originating from a previous façade, specifies (starting left) that such attributes are due 'to papal and imperial dogmas... confirmed in the name of the Saviour'.

In the great vestibule are two important ancient Roman remains: to the far left is a 4th-century *Statue of Constantine* found in the Baths built by the emperor on the Quirinal Hill (p. 69); and in the central doorway are the 3rd century AD *Bronze Doors of the Roman Senate*, brought here from the Roman Forum by Borromini (see p. 167). The star-studded bronze bands (a reference to the stars on Pope Alexander VII's coat-of-arms, p. 44), were added to make the doors fit the new entrance.

On the upper section of the walls, at either end,

The Basilica of St. John Lateran, with Alessandro Galilei's solemn 18th-century façade; by Giuseppe Vasi

are reliefs depicting episodes in the *Life of St. John the Baptist* by minor 18th-century sculptors.

The smaller, 'holy' door at the right end is opened only for Jubilee Years, like the one in St. Peter's.

The interior is open: 07:00-18:00 in winter / 19:00 in summer. The cloister closes one hour earlier, so if it's late start with that (p. 408).

Borromini was entrusted with a major renovation of the basilica in the mid-17th century. He could not impose a general design of his own on the interior, since he had to respect certain pre-existing features, especially the splendid 16th century ceiling. Yet the originality of his solutions shows in every detail, another testimonial to his great inventiveness.

The most important of his careful innovations is the nave (look at it as soon as you enter). Its rows of giant niches between archways, with oversize statues of the Apostles under marble reliefs and frescoed medallions, is a novel conception. Decried by conservative critics in the past, it is in fact grand

without being theatrical. The actual statues, reliefs and paintings, by capable minor artists, weren't added until the early 18th century. They form an interesting display of the art of that time; if you wish to look at these works individually, do so, then return here. The cosmatesque style floor is 15th century.

Move on to the double aisle on the right in order to begin a counter-clockwise tour (as we go, we'll often move from one of these parallel aisles to the other). The aisles and most of the chapels, down to the last ornamental detail, were designed by Borromini. His countless new patterns – friezes, moldings, cherubs and so on – form an extraordinary repertory which has had considerable influence on the decorative arts and architecture. Another novelty was that Borromini occasionally used the medieval monuments in the church as the basis for his own creations by inserting them in frames that he designed, sometimes even dismantling and rearranging them.

One of the heroic statues carved for the restored St. John Lateran: St. Bartholomew, by Pierre Legros

In the wall at the very beginning of the far right aisle is a 1527 tomb to which Borromini added a charming fresco of a *Madonna and Child* from the previous century – now much damaged – by an unknown follower of Melozzo da Forlì.

Past the first chapel is the wall tomb (1574) of a young duke appointed cardinal as a teenager, who died at 28. To the tomb Borromini added two 15th century statuettes by Isaia da Pisa taken from another monument, which we'll see shortly. Opposite, on the pier of the parallel aisle, is the central part of a fresco by Giotto, the only surviving piece of a work from the demolished Jubilee Loggia of the Lateran from which Pope Boniface VIII proclaimed the first Holy Year in 1300 (p. 398). The fresco depicts this event. The next chapel is the last private chapel built by a noble family in a Roman church (p. 114), dated 1850, belonging to the princely Torlonia family (p. 384)

Return to the parallel aisle. On the pier is a medieval inscription commemorating Pope Sylvester II, who died in 1003. He was reputed to be a magician, and for centuries after his death it was said that the inscription sweated and crackled when the death of any pope was imminent. In 1909 the slab was inserted in a monument donated by a Hungarian to thank the pope for having crowned the first Hungarian king, St. Stephen Árpád.

On the next two piers are the tombs of Pope Alexander III (who died in the 12th century, though the monument was erected to him by Alexander VII in the 17th century); and Pope Sergius IV, who died in the 11th century (the inscription and bust are from that date; the rest is by Borromini).

On the wall opposite is the 13th century cosmatesque tomb of Cardinal Casati (again, Borromini has rearranged and framed the various parts); next, on the wall by the steps, is Borromini's rearrangement of the 15th century tomb of Cardinal De Chaves, with sculptures by Isaia da Pisa, some of which Borromini used for the tomb of the young cardinal-duke, which we saw earlier (p. 406).

In the right arm of the transept – belonging entirely to the most ancient, 4th century part of the church – especially noteworthy is the chapel in the far corner containing a relief portrait of Pope Boniface IX (late 14th century) in a Cosmatesque setting, near its far right-hand corner. A recent epigraph on the left wall of the chapel commemorates Lorenzo Valla, the 15th century scholar who showed that the so-called 'Donation of Constantine', which had served to legitimise the claims by the popes on the former western Empire (p. 303), was an 8th century forgery. He was buried in the church, but only after recanting his revelation. The exact burial place is unknown, but a fragment of his tombstone with his portrait is in the cloister (see below). The epigraph was put here in the mistaken belief that the sarcophagus of a medieval gentleman below was Valla's.

At the right end of the transept, the whole wall is devoted to a remarkably rich baroque organ (late 16th century).

Borromini's hand is absent from the colourful and grandiose transept decoration, because a complete redecoration by Giacomo Della Porta had already begun a few decades earlier. The reliefs and statuary, by minor sculptors, are excellent. The frescoes are by minor late 16th and early 17th century artists, heavily reworked in the 19th century. The vigorous compositions are also interesting for their subject: on the wall to the right of the organ are legendary episodes from the life of Constantine, including his baptism in the Lateran Baptistery (in fact it took place in what is now Turkey, just before his death). Opposite are episodes from the *Foundation of the Basilica* with Constantine present.

Below is the entrance to the Treasury, a small museum with magnificent 17th and 18th century vestments and important sacred objects. Most notable is a 12th century reliquary box 'of St. John's habit' (third case, No. 8); a late 13th century gilt silver cross (fifth case) and a 15th century gilt silver procession cross (seventh case). On the left wall is the tomb of Alessandro Galilei, architect of the façade.

Return to the transept. In the middle is an exuberant gothic canopy of 1367; twelve frescoed panels are by early 15th century artists, including Antoniazzo Romano and possibly Melozzo da Forlì. Eight 14th century statuettes adorn the corners. The upper part of the canopy contains the purported heads of St. Peter and St. John the Evangelist in two silver reliquaries, which are late 19th century copies. The 14th century originals were melted down a century earlier to meet payments imposed by Napoleon on the popes (see p. 112).

Under the canopy is the modern papal altar, enclosing an ancient wooden table on which, according to tradition, St. Peter and the first popes celebrated Mass. Under the altar is a crypt built in the 19th century similar to that of St. Peter's. Go around and look down into it. It contains a very fine 15th century tombstone of Pope Martin V in the floor, the only work in Rome by the Florentine Simone Ghini, and a splendid 15th century wooden statue of St. John the Baptist.

The rear of the church – everything behind the canopy – was rebuilt in the late 19th century. The presbytery was much enlarged and its decorations were destroyed, to be replaced by mediocre paintings. The late 13th century mosaic of the apse was replaced by a copy. This mosaic is now mainly interesting for its subject, all the more so because the 13th century design was probably based on that of an older mosaic in the original, 4th century church. The figure of Christ in the clouds was thought in the middle ages to have been the first ever exhibited 'officially', which is not implausible, since the church was the first to have been built after the legalization of Christianity. This, in turn, gave rise to a legend – celebrated for many centuries with special processions – that the face of Christ had appeared to the crowd during the inauguration of the basilica. (Connected to this legend is the one of the 'face painted by angels' in the Sanctum Sanctorum, see p. 403.) In the lower section, the jewelled cross symbolises the Faith, from which flow four rivers (the Gospels) quenching the thirsty deer (souls). On the left are the Virgin Mary, Saints and Pope Nicholas IV, who commissioned the 13th century work. Below are nine Apostles; amongst them, to the right and left, are the minuscule figures of the two 13th-century mosaicists, Jacopo Torriti and Jacopo da Camerino.

Proceed to the left arm of the transept. Amongst the stories illustrated by the frescoes are, on the right wall, the legend of the miraculous apparition of the face of God; and, on the left, the equally legendary *Dream of Emperor Constantine* in which St. Paul persuades him to embrace Christianity in order to defeat Maxentius (p. 198); and the *Triumph of Constantine* with the Colosseum in the background.

At the end of the transept is a magnificent baroque altar with early 17th century statues of biblical characters by minor artists. The four great columns are bronze; they were moved here from the presbytery. According to tradition, they are spolia from the Temple of Jerusalem or that of Jupiter on the Capitol (p. 142).

Turn toward the double aisle on this side of the church; from the top of the steps note, on the left pier, the beautiful 16th century tomb of a noblewoman.

A door on the right leads to the early 13th century **Cloister**, a masterwork of cosmatesque art. The paired and twisted columns of the small arches, some inlaid with exquisite golden or multicoloured mosaics, discreetly twinkle in the sunshine. Sculpted human and animal figures of different sizes lend the serene atmosphere a touch of the fabulous (note the little men in the capitals of the colonnettes opposite the entrance slightly to the right; others we'll find later). In the centre of the cloister is a 9th century wellhead.

Around the cloister are many reminders of the ancient Roman and medieval past of the basilica, the latter including many cosmatesque works.

Tour counter-clockwise. On the wall right of the entrance (north corridor) are renaissance statuettes from tombs dismantled by Borromini. On the floor (No. 229) is a very rare 5th century cylindrical altar used by oblates, lay persons who devoted their life to Christ without taking ecclesiastical vows. The names of the oblates are inscribed on the altar. Based on one of these names, Italica, a name mentioned in one of St. Augustine's works, some scholars have identified them with upper-class friends of this great Doctor of the Church and author of the *Confessions* (p. 438).

At the start of the second (west) corridor of the cloister are bronze doors of 1196, signed by the artisans. These were once no less than the doors to the Scala Santa in its original place (p. 399); they now lead to lavatories! In the anteroom to the lavatories are an ancient door (left) and ancient columns; the latter continue into some of the stalls, possibly the only ones in the world with such decor.

In the same corridor (No. 188) is the only remaining fragment of the tomb of the humanist Lorenzo Valla (see above, p. 407). Two more interesting tombs are further on. No. 174 covered the remains of an English knight who died in 1384, depicted with his dog at his feet. No. 158 is from the grave of a Spanish gentleman, probably come to Rome with one of the Borgia popes (p. 373), who died in 1506 and whose relief and inscriptions were defaced for unknown reasons.

At the start of the third (south) corridor is an early 15th century fresco of the Madonna and Child, fragmentary and very damaged. Further on, No. 126 is the fully uniformed effigy of an ancient Roman officer, from his tombstone.

From this corridor you can see across the courtyard the original, medieval wall of the transept of the basilica.

Just before the middle of the corridor, on the wall (No. 97), is the small 1st century AD funerary tablet to Secunda, hairdresser (*ornatrici*) to Rufina and the court of Emperor Titus (*T. Aug.*), which probably prompted the story of the martyrs Secunda and Rufina (p. 400).

On the left two sphinxes guard the garden entrance. Opposite is the stump of a column with Hebrew lettering. Past it are pieces of one of the most beautiful monuments dismantled by Borromini, the tomb of a 13th century cardinal with a statue of the deceased surmounted by figures of priests engaged in a ceremony that was called the 'absolution of the body'. It is a marvellous work by Arnolfo di Cambio, probably one of his first in Rome.

At the start of the fourth (east) corridor, on the wall above, is the damaged fragment of a fresco, one of the many depictions of the Face of Christ in the Lateran area (see pp. 403, 407, 411). It was identified in 2001 as an early work by Bramante, possibly among the first in Rome by this famous architect and adviser to the popes (see p. 462).

Next along the corridor is the entrance to a room where, amongst several exhibits, you should note a 13th century embroidered priest's cope in a display case on the right wall; a beautiful *Madonna and Child*, a drawing questionably attributed to Raphael, on the end wall, to the far right; a 15th century painted tablet of thanksgiving, on the left wall, donated by a famous man of letters, Inghirami, after surviving an accident.

Back in the corridor, look into the garden. On the left side, on a dividing pillar under a mosaic inscription and the word 'claustri', is the signature of the builders of the cloister, two of the ablest members of the Cosma clan. It says that 'Vassallectus ... instructed in this noble art, began this with his father, and finished it alone'. On the cornice are heads of women and lions.

Halfway down the fourth corridor are remains of a showy cosmatesque arrangement for the episcopal chair of the 14th century Pope Nicholas IV (portrayed in a mosaic of the basilica, p. 408). Almost at the end of the corridor, note the little devils and monsters on the capitals of the cloister colonnettes.

Return to the church and complete the visit of the double aisle. In the first chapel is a fresco by Guillaume Courtois, of the 17th century Borgognone family, whose house we saw in Piazza di Spagna (pp. 57-58). In the second chapel, note the elegant upper half, the dome and 18th century stucco decorations. The third chapel has a memorial to papal soldiers who died defending church domains in the 19th century. The beautiful crucifix on the altar is attributed to Stefano Maderno (17th century); below it is a 16th century fresco. Note the oval dome. Before the last chapel, above the confessionals, is the tomb of an early 14th century prelate. The beautiful last chapel is by Alessandro Galilei, the 17th century architect of the church façade. Inside, on the left, is the tomb of Pope Clement XII (18th century), with a sarcophagus and columns of porphyry from the Pantheon.

Cross the church diagonally to the right end of the transept and exit from a side door.

You are now in the upper square, Piazza S. Giovanni in Laterano. Cross to the obelisk and turn around to see the other, wonderful prospect of the church. Its two-storey arcaded portico was added by the architects of Sixtus V when they transformed the area in the late 16th century (p. 398). The extension of the portico to the right is late 19th-century. Behind the portico is the façade of the transept (opposite the one we saw from the cloister); two romanesque belfries stand out against the sky. Remodelled in the 14th century, they are at least two centuries older – the only remaining outer feature of the medieval church, besides the baptistery.

The **Egyptian obelisk**, erected in the square by Sixtus V to mark the terminus of his urban plan (p. 44), is the tallest anywhere – 94 ft (31 m) not including the base – the oldest (15th century BC) and perhaps the most beautiful in Rome.

Pharaohs Thutmose III and IV placed it in front of the Temple of Ammon in Thebes. Constantius II, a son of Constantine, brought it to Rome on a specially built ship and erected it in the Circus Maximus (p. 267). Papal engineers retrieved it there, where it lay in three pieces.

An inscription from the time of Sixtus V on the base repeats the misleading claim that Constantine was baptised here.

On the side of the square opposite the basilica are more surviving arches of Nero's aqueduct (p. 404), picturesquely embedded in old buildings to the left. An ancient hospital is at the left end of the square, which we'll see later.

Across the street from the left end of the hospital, the octagonal brick structure in the square is the historic **Lateran Baptistery**, probably built in the area of the baths of the ancient villa of the Pisoni and Laterani (p. 396). It is the prototype of nearly all baptisteries since. (Open: 08:00-12:00 and 15:00-18:00 in summer /15:00-17:00 in winter.)

Erected by Constantine together with the basilica, it was entirely rebuilt a century later (5th century), then restored or renovated several times, most recently in 1637. Most of what we see dates from the 5th century, and some from the 17th.

Entering through the 16th century door, you see a ring of eight porphyry columns beneath smaller white ones. Everything is from the 5th century, including the Latin inscription exalting baptism : 'Be reborn from this divine seed ... Dip, O sinner, in this sacred river ... Re-emerge purified, whether thou sinned, or thy fathers did ... Those who are not reborn here will not enjoy the afterlife of the blessed...' In the middle, encircled by a 16th century rail, is an ancient green basalt font used for baptism by immersion at a time when many converts were adults. The walls are frescoed by minor 17th-century artists with episodes from the life of Constantine, in commemoration of his claimed baptism here.

Ancient chapels and rooms are all around. The first on the right has 5th-century bronze doors. Over the door of the second is a late 15th-century crucifix.

This second chapel is the one dedicated to Sts. Rufina and Secunda (see p. 400), who are depicted in a 17th century painting in the small apse to the right (ancient documents state that Pope Anastasius IV had put the supposed bodies of the saints under the altar, but they are gone).

Another small apse opposite contains an extremely refined 5th century mosaic with plant motifs. The chapel was the original entrance hall of the baptistery; as you exit, you can see what remains of the 5th century façade and entrance, with its wonderful porphyry columns. Note, on a marble slab to the right, the centuries-old graffiti of visitors.

Re-enter and continue counter-clockwise. The next chapel, built in the 7th century (note the ancient columns), has a wall mosaic from that time. It depicts, just under the ceiling, the symbols of the Evangelists and the holy cities of Jerusalem and Bethlehem. In the apse, Christ with angels; and, below, the Virgin and saints with the popes who had the chapel built, John IV and his successor Theodore. (All this is hard to see, so use the coin-operated light.) On the sides are eight martyrs. The style is Byzantine, though influenced by the more down-to-earth manner of Roman craftsmen. The wooden ceiling is 16th century.

The next chapel has bronze doors of 1196. In the barrel-vaulted ceiling are 5th century mosaics of birds and flowers.

Leave the baptistery. Behind the steel railing to the left is the main Roman Catholic seminary (Seminario Romano Maggiore). The railing ends next to the ruin of the central hall of 3rd century AD baths, which were probably part of the Laterani-Pisoni Villa and later of the home of

Empress Fausta. Is it here that she was suffocated (pp. 410-411)?

Across the street from these ruins is a garden, visible through a railing, with two luxurious fluted spiral columns and a frieze, remnants of a sumptuous Roman villa. (Crossing is difficult here; you may prefer to go around to the traffic lights downhill.) Other ruins have been found nearby, all probably from the residence of Marcus Aurelius' mother (p. 396).

Walk uphill, then around to the left, the short side of the square. It is occupied by the **Ospedale di S. Giovanni** (St. John's Hospital), founded in 1348, modified throughout the ages and still active. The façade was designed by Giacomo Mola and Carlo Rainaldi in the 17th century. Don't miss the elaborate doors, large windows and the little belfry, which lightens the long construction.

The core of the hospital dates to the 1348 structure, a small infirmary (it replaced another even older one down the hill, where St. Francis of Assisi first slept when he came to Rome about 1200 to seek papal approval of his new Franciscan Order). Several additions were made over the next centuries and more followed in modern times.

Passing the façade, on the corner of the hospital and on a building opposite, see the marble reliefs depicting the *Holy Face of Christ* flanked by candelabra. These reliefs and similar ones here and there on the walls of the square date from the 15th to the 17th century and refer to the miraculous apparition of the face of Christ in St. John's (p. 408) and to the famous image 'painted by angels' in the Lateran Sanctum Sanctorum (p. 403).

The church-like building opposite is the 17th century **Women's Hospital** (A), which incorporates a 13th century hospice, still in use.

Going around the corner of St. John's Hospital, 50 yards down the street is the very old little church (B) of **SS. Andrea e Bartolomeo** (Sts. Andrew and Bartholomew), possibly 6th century, with an 18th century façade. The doorway – with another Holy Face, see above – dates from the 15th century.

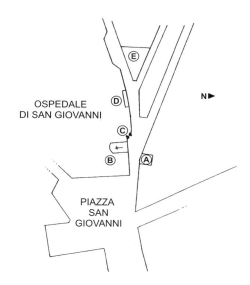

Piazza San Giovanni and the Ospedale di S. Giovanni

The church is rarely open. Inside, the 15th century floor and a fresco of the *Madonna and Child* in the Byzantine style (possibly 15th century) are worth seeing.

Just past the church is a 15th century entrance (C) to St. John's Hospital. It is framed by reliefs of the Holy Face and Lamb of God, and a Latin inscription of a century earlier, when the hospital was founded. Surmounting this in turn is a later inscription offering 'refuge to the poor and the sick'.

Past the entrance is a 14th century porch (D), part of the original hospital; inside are ancient Roman fragments found nearby.

You are now at a fork in the road. The two streets enclose the modern seat of the Irish College (E). Founded in the 17th century, it houses an urn with the heart of Daniel O'Connell. This early 19th century Irish patriot, who died in Italy, left in his will 'my soul to Heaven, my body to Ireland and my heart to Rome'.

5. The Papal Way to St. Peter's and the church of the Quattro Coronati

We will now go, in the return direction, along the most famous of Rome's papal processional routes.

After the popes left their Lateran residence in the 14th century (p. 300) to set up the Holy See in the Vatican, they felt a need to reaffirm periodically their rights over the Lateran with a procession called *il possesso*, 'the possession'. Each newly elected pope led this procession, the richest and most colourful of many that took place in the city. The pope usually rode a white horse or mule, under a special umbrella, with all his cardinals, high prelates and other civil and military officials. As he passed, a bursar distributed coins to the kneeling crowd.

The ceremony kept alive the memory of the original sources of the legitimacy and power of the Church: of the first official church, the Lateran, of the Emperor Constantine, who founded it, and of his supposed 'donation' (p. 303). Especially during war among factions and nations, in which the popes were often involved, this had the important aim of stressing the rights of the popes not only over the Lateran and Rome, but over all of the former western Empire. It also indirectly reaffirmed the popes' purported supremacy over the eastern branch of the Church.

In the Renaissance Rome Walks we'll often follow the Via Papalis, or Papal Way – as the route of the procession was called – in its first stretch from St. Peter's. In the stretch here, the itinerary follows a hilly ridge between the Lateran and the Colosseum and has an interesting military aspect. It is protected by the only 'fortress-monastery' left in Rome, the age-old church of the Quattro Coronati ('Four Crowned Saints') with an adjoining monastery. This was evidently to protect the approach to the Lateran for the papacy.

By a telling coincidence, the compound of the Quattro Coronati contains a fresco depicting the story of Constantine, one of the oldest representations of the subject. It includes some legendary flourishes added in the middle ages. According to these elaborations, Constantine, after legalizing Christianity, changed his mind and the persecutions started again. The famous pope of the time, St. Sylvester (p. 335), had to hide in a mountain cave. A wrathful God struck the emperor with leprosy. His doctors told him only the blood of infants would cure him. The night before the children were to be sacrificed, Constantine dreamed of two wise men advising him to call off the killings and seek the help of the pope instead. This he did that very morning. When Sylvester arrived, carrying the insignia of St. Peter and St. Paul, the emperor recognised in the images the faces that had appeared to him. (These two patron saints of Rome have frequently intervened at critical moments in Roman history; see p. 369). Constantine agreed to be baptised and was promptly cured. This supposedly led to his gratitude and the famous 'donation' (an 8th-century forgery, as we know).

Our route here is the setting of an even more bizarre medieval story. It apparently stemmed from the name of a side street, called Vicus Papissae after the noble medieval family of the De Papa or Papareschi. The word 'Papissæ' led to the legend of a popess, a woman disguised as a man who was elected pope in the 8th century under the name John VIII. The most common of the many versions of the legend describes her as an English maid, enamoured of theology, who disguised herself as a man to be admitted to a seminary. A lightning ecclesiastical career was crowned by election to the papal throne. As she approached the Lateran during the 'possession' parade, she went into labour and bore a girl. A mob of parade-watchers stoned her and the baby to death.

Pope crossing the 'disabitato' in the Possesso procession to the Lateran, 17th century

The story was taken so seriously that for centuries afterwards papal processions detoured around that part of the road. The legend of 'Popess Joan', as she came to be called after her official name, was accepted as fact throughout the Renaissance. Famous authors, such as Petrarch and Boccaccio, based major writings on it, and its doctrinal implications were debated at a Church Council in the 15th century. Carved and painted portraits of the popess were among the collections of the early papacy. It was not until the the 17th century that the story was proved to be a fiction.

Related to this legend and to another even stranger misinterpretation of a word was a medieval ritual performed after papal elections. Before their 'possession' parade, newly elected popes had to sit on a marble chair with a hole, a luxurious ancient toilet seat or bidet found in Roman baths, apparently originally mistaken for a throne. From this chair they distributed money to the people, while choirs sang verses from the first Book of Samuel (2.viii) stating that the Lord 'raiseth the poor from the dust, and lifteth the beggar from the dunghill' (*stercora* in Latin). The chair came to be associated with the word 'stercora' and became known as the *sedia stercoraria*, or 'dunghill chair'; an apt definition considering its design, but puzzling in liturgical terms. Then the disaster of the popess supplied an explanation for the perforated throne: the hole, it was said, was for cardinals to discreetly check the gender of the pope-elect, to prevent a repetition.

Use of the chair was discontinued in 1503 by Julius II (p. 331), a no-nonsense pope. It lived on, however, in popular memory three centuries later, when the great Roman vernacular poet, Gioacchino Belli, wrote:

413

A chair has been in use for them to grope
From underneath and check that lusty zone
To see they have not a popess but a pope.

Da allora st'antra ssedia ce fu messa
Pe ttastà sotto ar sito de le vojje
Si er Pontecife sii Papa o Papessa

The chair is in the Vatican museums, where you saw it (p. 323).

The high ground you'll walk on here is the Cælian Hill, one of the original Seven Hills of Rome (p. 31). This means we are again entering the former *disabitato*, the hilly area abandoned after the fall of the empire, which for many centuries was used only for vineyards and fields.

ON THE SPOT

5. The Papal Way to St. Peter's and the church of the Quattro Coronati

Take the street to the right of the Irish College, Via dei SS. Quattro Coronati ('of the Four Crowned Saints'). This was for some decades the route of the papal 'possession' parade from St. Peter's to St. John's, instead of a wider parallel road going downhill to the right, the more traditional link between the two basilicas. The detour was used to avoid the stretch where Popess Joan had supposedly given birth (p. 419).

From the end of the street you begin to see a squat medieval compound, the church and convent of **SS. Quattro Coronati**.

Pass under a massive bell tower, the oldest in Rome (early 9th century) and originally a defence tower. Inside is a gothic archway and the emblem of a 15th-century Spanish cardinal. Such a gate-tower is still a familiar feature north of the Alps, but unique in Rome today. You are now in the first of two courtyards. Straddling the two courtyards, high up, are the walls of the sprawling 12th- to 13th-century convent. It originally doubled as a fortress, a fact more easily appreciated from another viewpoint later on your route.

Restorations on an upper floor of the convent have revealed, under the wall plaster, very large 13th-century frescoes of religious and agricultural subjects. When and how they will be open to the public has not yet been decided. You might like to enquire at the church during your visit.

To understand the layout of these courtyards and of the complex, keep in mind that this church, built in the 4th or the 5th century and rebuilt a few times on the same plan, was destroyed, probably when Norman hordes pillaged Rome in 1084 (p. 295). It was then rebuilt, but much smaller, in the early 12th century. The smaller church, comprising parts of the earlier building, has been renovated several times.

The first courtyard corresponds to the porch of the original church (the passageway has late 16th-century frescoes). The second courtyard was the front part of the original church; you can see the columns of one of its aisles embedded in the right wall. Over the entrance, preceded by a narrow porch, is a naïve late 16th-century fresco of *Nuns and Orphans Praying to the Four Saints*. (Open: 09:30-12:00 and in summer 15:30-19:00/winter weekends 15:30-17:30. If closed, go straight to the St. Sylvester Oratory, which is usually open, off this courtyard.)

The church is dedicated to four saints who, according to one tradition, were Roman imperial policemen; according to another, four (or five) marble-cutters from the East. Either way, all were martyred. Sometimes the stories merge: the cutters refused to make a pagan statue and the officers refused to arrest them.

The church interior corresponds to the nave of the older church. Again you will see columns embedded in the walls, here in the two side aisles . Later the smaller church was itself divided into a nave and two aisles. The aisles support an upper level for women (called a *matroneum*) common in medieval churches.

The cosmatesque floor is 12th-century; the wooden ceiling, 16th-century.

Inside, on the entrance wall and the adjacent walls are remains of 13th- and 14th-century frescoes of saints and priests in painted frames, followed by later frescoes and oil paintings.

Continue counter-clockwise. At the end of the right colonnade is an altar with a 16th-century fresco of the *Crucifixion*. Symmetrically opposite is an exquisite late 15th-century tabernacle.

The huge presbytery (behind the main altar) is actually the apse of the older, larger church; the contrast with the smaller church produces a grandiose effect. The fine frescoes are by a minor early 17th-century painter, Giovanni da San Giovanni. The lower register shows grisly episodes involving the martyred officers and marble-cutters; above is a depiction of paradise with all the saints.

Steps on the left (permission needed) lead down to a semi-circular 9th-century crypt, renovated in modern times, with 13th-century marble tubs containing bones brought here from the catacombs. The crypt is a typical feature of medieval churches, designed to present treasured relics for the faithful to venerate. Here, as in many other churches, the crypt contains a list of the names of the presumed martyrs (see p. 400) to whom the bones belonged.

From the left aisle we pass to the 13th-century cloister, one of the most evocative in Rome. The part of the cloister next to the church was originally a section of the left aisle of the old church. The 12th-century well was recently moved here from one of the courtyards. On the left is what remains of the 9th-century Cappella di S. Barbara (a nun will open it for you; leave an offering). Originally entered directly from the left aisle of the old church, the chapel looks like that of S. Zeno in S. Prassede (p. 103) of the same period; it has traces of 9th- to 12th-century frescoes and striking ancient Roman vault capitals.

Leaving the church, enter the vestibule of the 13th-century convent on the left, originally home to Benedictine friars, but since the 16th century to Augustinian nuns. Frescoed on three walls are the remains of a rare 13th-century liturgical calendar. (See the note above for recent discoveries.)

Ring the bell. A semi-cloistered nun will appear

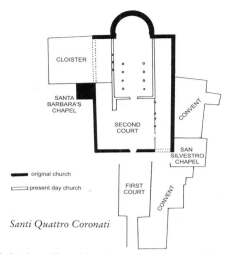

Santi Quattro Coronati

behind a grille and hand you, through a revolving device, the key to the adjacent Cappella di S. Silvestro (leave an offering). It was built in 1246 and since the 17th century has belonged to the association of Italian marble-cutters, whose patrons are the Four Crowned Saints.

The fascinating Byzantine-style frescoes are 13th-century. Those on the entrance wall depict, above, *Christ between the Virgin and Saints on Judgement Day* (one angel awakens the dead with his trumpet; another terminates the starry universe by rolling it up). Below begins a fascinatingly detailed series of episodes from this history of Emperor Constantine and Pope Sylvester, which continues along the left wall (see p. 412). On the right wall are two unrelated episodes: *Sylvester resuscitates the bull killed by the Jewish priest* (the Jews, in amazement, convert); and *St. Helena finds the True Cross* (p. 368). A Jew who knows where the Cross is hidden is forced to tell by being lowered into a pit; a disarming medieval mixture of ignorance, cruelty and naïveté.

The wonderful cosmatesque floor and the ceiling are original. The latter holds a cross of ceramic roundels of Islamic origin, the only one of its kind in Rome. Around the altar are late 16th-century frescoes in stucco frames.

6. S. Clemente

Historical intricacy and structural complexity are intertwined in many Roman monuments, yet none exemplifies this better than the church of S. Clemente, a unique superimposition of four construction levels spanning 22 centuries.

St. Clement: a multiple personality. The intricacies start with the name. Who was St. Clement? The history of this church, based on tradition only, speaks of 'a martyr and pope of the 1st century'. Two Christians with that name living in that century have left their historical mark. One was the consul Titus Flavius Clemens, a cousin of the emperor Domitian, who was killed for his faith – a martyr indeed, but no pope. The other was Pope Clement, third successor to St. Peter, known mainly for an energetic letter with which he ended an episode of ecclesiastic insubordination. He was certainly a pope, but no martyr.

The St. Clement to whom the church is dedicated seems to be a hybrid of the two, perhaps facilitated by a possible relationship between them. Based on the custom that freed slaves usually assumed their master's name, researchers have hypothesised that Clement, the pope, was a former slave of Clement, the consul; that he was a Christian, since most of the consul's household had converted along with him; and (based on certain characteristics of his writings) that he was perhaps a converted Jew.

The two lower levels. Running parallel to the complicated story of St. Clement the man is the equally convoluted tale of St. Clement the building. Of its four layers of construction, the third from the top (the fourth, or lowest, one is still unexcavated and belongs to houses destroyed in Nero's fire, see p. 191) was partly occupied by a large house known as a Christian refuge in the 1st century and later; an example of an *ecclesia domestica* or a *titulus* (discussed above, p. 228). Its existence under the name *Titulus Clementis* is documented. Since such private religious centres were normally named after the wealthy host, not after a saint or martyr, this original home church may have belonged to a benefactor called Clemens, possibly none other than the consul, or a descendant of his.

In the 4th century, after Emperor Constantine had allowed Christians to practise openly, a real church, or rather a basilica (second level from the top), was built over the *ecclesia domestica*. It was called St. Clement. The name then ceased to be interpreted as that of the old benefactor and began to be considered that of the old pope, who had had a major role, as third successor to St. Peter, in establishing Christianity in Rome. But Pope Clement, as titular of a major new church, had one drawback compared to his namesake the consul: he was not a martyr.

Imagination apparently filled the gap. The 4th century gave birth to an elaborate legend conferring the crown of martyrdom on Pope Clement. The real martyr, Consul Clemens, was virtually forgotten. The legend is worth telling not so much for its own sake, as because it led to momentous events in the history of the basilica and because it is the subject of fascinating frescoes there.

The legend recounts that Pope Clement was persecuted in the reign of Trajan. A Roman police chief, Sisinnius, was sent to arrest him, but was miraculously blinded along with his men, so they dragged a column off to prison instead of Clement. Clement was eventually captured, however,

416

and sentenced to work in the dreaded Crimean mines. There he began converting guards and fellow prisoners. Martyrdom was inevitable. He was tied to an anchor and thrown into the Black Sea. Some time later the waters parted, revealing a splendid tomb: Clement's, built by angels. From then on, the waters parted every year, allowing the faithful to pray over the tomb of the martyr. Once a child was drowned by the waters when they flowed back, but his mother found him miraculously alive on the same spot when she returned the following year!

One block, two Gods. Before proceeding, we must return to the original *titulus* in the private home (third level). For about a century, the Christian meeting place was next door to that of another eastern religion, Mithraism. Mithraic priests, called *patres*, like the Christian fathers, must have rubbed shoulders with their Christian colleagues. Mithras worship long predated Christianity; it was widespread under Alexander the Great. The two religions bore some resemblance. Like Christianity, Mithraism urged stern moral precepts, though not so much love and chastity as loyalty and courage (it was especially popular with soldiers). It, too, envisioned the arrival of a Redeemer, the god Mithras, source of all life and goodness (see p. 322). Spread by soldiers returning from the East, the cult took root in Rome about the same time as Christianity.

Ample remains of a Mithraic temple, called a Mithræum, are at the third level of S. Clemente, bordering on those of the original *titulus*. When the second level – the basilica – was built over the filled-in ruins of the *titulus*, the Mithræum continued to function next to it for a few decades, though at a lower level. Mithraism was the last pagan cult to fall; in 395 AD, shortly after the prohibition of other pagan religions, it too was forbidden and soon vanished. The basilica above was then extended by adding an apse, built atop the Mithræum as a gesture of triumph.

The eastern connection: Sts. Cyril and Methodius. Because of Pope Clement's legendary disappearance into the Black Sea, the church was particularly venerated in the middle ages by Christians with Byzantine connections. This in turn spurred a momentous development several centuries after its foundation. In the 9th century the Byzantine emperor asked two distinguished Christian priests, the brothers Cyril and Methodius, to civilise the barbarian hordes north of the Black Sea. The missionaries were exceedingly successful; Cyril, a brilliant linguist, even invented an alphabet for the illiterate tribes, now known as Cyrillic and still in use in Slavic countries.

The conversion and civilization of present-day Russia and other lands by Sts. Cyril and Methodius, as they are known today, was a truly epoch-making event. When later in life the brothers decided to visit Rome, this should have sufficed to grant them an enthusiastic welcome, but they apparently thought they needed more. Before heading for the centre of Christianity, they announced another feat: finding the body of St. Clement on an island in the Black Sea, complete with the attached anchor (see above; and pp. 103, 107, 368 etc. on these miraculous retrievals).

They arrived in Rome in 867 with the supposed body of the supposed martyr (no further mention of the anchor is made) to a triumphant welcome. The relics were taken in a great procession to S. Clemente, as illustrated in the frescoes we'll see shortly, and they still are there. St. Cyril died in Rome soon afterwards and was solemnly buried in the church of S. Clemente. His brother returned to the East. The bones of St Cyril underwent many vicissitudes, though less spectacular than those of the body of St. Clement. Dispersed in 1798, when Rome was briefly under an insurgent republican, anti-clerical regime inspired by the French Revolution, they were considered

*S. Clemente at the end
of the 19th century*

lost, until a box containing part of them was found in 1963 in another city. They were then reburied in the church of S. Clemente.

The first level. You would think that these stories were enough for the saga of S. Clemente, but they are just the beginning. The church discussed so far, the second level of construction, is not the one in use today. Of course, the one being used is the topmost one, though it too is far from recent, having stood for nine hundred years.

Here is what happened. In the 12th century the second-level Constantinian basilica was crumbling, possibly because of the depredations of the Norman king, Robert Guiscard, also accused of having destroyed the church of the Quattro Coronati nearby (p. 303). So it was filled with rubble, as the original *titulus* had been 700 years before, and served as the foundations for a new basilica, which was like the previous one only slightly smaller.

In 1677 the church, until then run by Augustinian friars, was given to Irish Dominican friars who had fled the Protestant persecutions in their country. (They still run the church.) By then, the existence of the lower buildings had been forgotten. As late as the mid-19th century, everyone thought that the extant church was the one of which St. Jerome had spoken in the 4th century, a mistake abetted by the fact that many features of the lower church, such as the precious marble choir, had been moved to the upper one.

Back to the past. In 1857 an erudite, astute Irish Dominican prior, Father Mullooly, had inklings of the remote past of the basilica. He broke through a wall and began a chain of discoveries that continues to this day; it is one of the greatest archæological adventures in the history of the

Church. The excavation of the second level (the original basilica) is complete. That of the third level (the Roman house and *titulus*, and the Mithraic temple) is partly so. There have been glimpses of the fourth level, the Roman houses preceding Nero's fire. The enterprise of the Irish friars has been enormous. Over 130,000 cartloads of rubble have been removed, and an underground canal reaching as far as the Colosseum has been built to drain water from the lower levels.

The ghost of the popess. S. Clemente rises along the ancient Vicus Papissae, near where Popess Joan (p. 419) was supposedly stoned to death in the 8th century. A 1518 guide book to Rome states 'that English woman was buried here without any ceremony, but her death was commemorated by the shrine we still see.' A badly deteriorated street altar, dating from before 1000 and now dedicated to the Virgin Mary, may be the one mentioned in the guide.

ON THE SPOT

6. S. Clemente

Continue downhill on Via SS. Quattro Coronati (take the stairs on your left to save a few steps). As you go, a look back at the massive Four Saints compound will help you better appreciate its defensive, fortress-like character.

The first crossing on your right is Via dei Querceti ('of the Oak Groves'), a name recalling the thick woods covering the slope in antiquity. On this corner, to the right, is a thousand-year-old street altar, possibly the one once dedicated to the legendary Popess Joan.

The much repainted, dilapidated little fresco is from the 14th century. An early 19th-century inscription reads: 'Mary's smile / will gladden this site / if the passer-by / addresses Her: Hail, Mother.'

Continue along Via dei Querceti to Via di S. Giovanni in Laterano. For centuries this street was the 'official' part of the Papal Way from the Vatican to the Lateran. Cross it. The block to your left is occupied, above and below ground, by the double church of **S. Clemente** and its convent, run by Irish Dominicans. The original entrance (not in use, but do and go and see it) is on the continuation of Via dei Querceti.

A marble vestibule (a 'prothyrum') with delicate friezes is against the convent wall. It belongs to the 12th-century church and is a typical Romanesque feature. Behind the wall are a colonnaded forecourt of the same period and the modest façade of

the church, redone in the 18th century. Both are visible only from within the church, if and when the door is open on this side.

Return to Via S. Giovanni and enter the church from the side. (Open: 07:30-12:15 and 15:30-19:00. Lower church: weekdays 09:00-12:15 and 15:30-18:00, Sundays 10:00-12:15 and 15:30-18:00. If you're running late, visit the lower church first.)

An 18th-century restoration makes the interior of the upper church look late-baroque at first. By disregarding the surface stucco work and paintings, you can envisage the original 12th-century lines of the design, practically intact and typical of the time, with a double row of columns from ancient Roman temples and a beautiful cosmatesque floor. Move toward the centre to see another typical feature, the marble *schola cantorum* (choir enclosure) with cosmatesque pulpits and twisted candlesticks. It is 12th-century, but many of the marble pieces were taken from a similar structure in the primitive, 4th-century (lower) church. The enclosure was donated in the 6th century by Pope Johannes II, whose name appears as a beautiful monogram on some of the marble slabs. (Pope John or Johannes had been a parish priest of S. Clemente, at which time he was called Brother Mercurius. He began the custom of changing one's name when elected pope, probably because his own was that of a pagan god.)

Behind the choir is the 12th-century tabernacle, a marble canopy over a crypt containing the reputed relics of St. Clement (note the anchor, symbol of the saint). The relics of St. Cyril, who brought those of St. Clement to Rome and was originally buried in the lower church, are in one of the right aisle chapels. Against the apse wall is the 12th-century marble bishop's throne (the back, which was re-cut from an older, inscribed marble slab, is from the 4th century).

In the apse is a 12th-century *Mosaic*. Some of its glass and marble pieces come from an older, possibly similar mosaic which was in the lower church. It is a masterpiece of the Roman school, with marvellously harmonious colours, and is remarkably intact. A crucifix, unusually adorned with twelve doves symbolising the Apostles, grows out of lush acanthus leaves and scrolls. Over it the hand of God emerges from Heaven offering a crown. Many types of birds, animals, tiny people (including the Doctors of the Church), fruit baskets, lamps and farmyard scenes are among the scrolls: at the bottom left a woman is feeding her chickens, and and at bottom right there is a shepherd with his goats and a slave. Other figures, at the bottom in the centre, are more traditional: the four rivers of Faith (the Gospels) quenching the thirst of deer (the faithful), and the peacocks of the afterlife (p. 318). Below is a frieze of the *Lamb of God among Twelve Sheep* (symbolizing Christ among the Apostles).

The mosaics continue on the arch around the apse in a style indicating the hand of another artist. On the walls of both sides, in four vertical tiers, are the mystic cities of Bethlehem and Jerusalem; the prophets Isaiah and Jeremiah, who foretold the coming of Christ; Sts. Lawrence, Paul and Peter, Rome's great martyrs, and St. Clement; and the symbols of the Evangelists flanking a bust of Christ.

Below the apse mosaic is a much-repainted late 13th-century fresco of *Christ and the Apostles*. To the right, on the false pillar supporting the arch, is an exquisite wall shrine attributed to Arnolfo di Cambio, donated around 1297 by a cardinal, nephew of Pope Boniface VIII (p. 373). Uncle and nephew are shown in the left corner.

To the right of the main apse, in a beautiful 15th- or 16th-century chapel and secondary apse,

is a fine statue of St. John the Baptist, of unknown authorship.

On the wall nearby are two 15th-century funerary monuments. Most noteworthy is the one to Cardinal Roverella, a papal ambassador, by Giovanni Dalmata. Roverella's coat-of-arms includes the head of an African, perhaps an allusion to his work in faraway lands.

Move around to another secondary apse at the end of the opposite aisle. The painting here, the *Madonna of the Rosary*, is one of many in the church by a fine 18th-century Roman artist, Sebastiano Conca. On the wall to the left is the monument to a cardinal which, though erected in the 15th century, uses columns with Byzantine capitals from a 6th-century tabernacle from the lower church.

Set against the wall of this aisle, on both sides of the exit, are the under-drawings (called '*sinopie*') that served as guidelines for the frescoes we are about to see; they were uncovered in 1955 when the frescoes were detached for restoration.

At the beginning of the aisle is a chapel with these famous frescoes by Masolino, a member of the early 15th-century Florentine school, which was soon to abandon the fairy-tale, hyper-decorative International Gothic style and introduced new naturalistic and human elements.

Masolino often collaborated with a younger, more radical and famous member of the group, Masaccio, whom historians believe had a hand in these paintings, though which parts are his has been debated.

On the left wall is the *Legend of St. Catherine of Alexandria*, said to have protested against the persecution of Christians during the reign of Maxentius (p. 198). Upper section, from the left: she is convicted; in prison, she converts the empress; the empress herself is martyred. Lower section: the saint converts the philosophers assembled by Maxentius to refute her arguments; she is tortured; she is beheaded. (It is worth going back to compare the frescoes with the *sinopie*. Often the original intention was ignored in the actual painting – which, because of the nature of fresco, had to be carried out speedily. For instance, in the scene of Catherine's beheading. the *sinopia*, exhibited next to the chapel, shows the saint lying wounded, while in the painting she has not yet been hit. Masolino also omits the moment when Maxentius sentenced fifty of the ineffectual philosophers to be burned alive.)

On the right wall is the *Life of St. Ambrose* and on the centre wall the *Crucifixion*, both very damaged.

Outside the chapel on the left is *St. Christopher*, the legendary giant ferryman who, without knowing it, carried the infant Jesus across a river and felt the weight of the world crushing his shoulders. Nearby there are many examples of graffiti etched by pilgrims, some almost contemporary with the fresco; dates from 1459.

(Reproductions of 19th-century copies of other frescoes, those in the lower church, are usually exhibited near the chapel and are on sale in the souvenir shop; they are worth looking at here, since they will help make sense of the frescoes themselves, which have been badly damaged by humidity.)

Pass the wall of the official entrance. If open, step outdoors to enjoy the medieval forecourt. Then go back inside.

In the first chapel in the right aisle, more paintings by Conca (the one on the right) and pupils (episodes from the *Life of St. Dominic*).

Nearby is the sacristy-souvenir shop, from which a staircase, with fragments from the lower church embedded in its walls, descends to the lower church.

The lower church was built in the 4th century over the already existing structures of a private, late 3rd-century Roman house, probably one of the several *ecclesiæ domesticæ*, or Christian community centres (also called *tituli*) where Christians gathered before their religion was legitimised (p. 198). These structures, in turn, rose over even older Roman buildings, which we'll visit later.

The staircase landing continues into a corridor (a), which is actually the porch of the ancient church (the ceiling is now much lower than it was

originally, because the upper church is partly encased in the lower one). There are several 11th-century frescoes. The best preserved is the *Miracle of the Child in the Black Sea* (see p. 417) on the right wall. Below are St. Clement and the donor, Beno de Rapiza, with his wife, Maria Macellaria, and their children. Nearby is the *Translation of the Relics of St. Clement to the Church*. The Latin inscription reads: 'I, Maria Macellaria, gave this in awe of God and for the salvation of my soul'.

Opposite, on a turning device, is a pagan tombstone, the back of which was reused as a Christian one. The pagan epitaph reads: 'To the spirits of the dead and to Sabinus, nicknamed the Little Wanderer (*vagulus*). A most beloved child, who outshone by far many of his own rank and age'. The Christian epitaph: 'To Surus, may he rest in peace. By his brother Euticianus'.

From about midway along the corridor go to a long wide room, the central nave of the old church (c to f). It is hard to recognise because of several piers (d) supporting the upper church, and even more so due to a reinforcing wall on the right (e),

S. Clemente: plan of the lower church

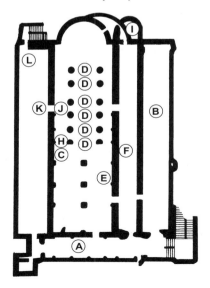

which cuts away the right side of the nave, turning it into a sort of corridor (f). Keep in mind that flanking this nave are two aisles, which you cannot see because they are walled off by the foundations of the upper church; we'll visit them later.

On the entrance wall, just to the left, are 9th-century frescoes (g): the *Ascension of Christ with the Apostles* below, and on the sides, Pope Leo IV (p. 369), with the square halo of the living, and St. Vitus, Bishop of Vienna. In the corner is a *Crucifixion*. Note the columns of the early church emerging from the wall. About halfway down the left side (h) are more frescoes from the 11th century, contemporary with those in the corridor (a) and possibly by the same hand. The first is the strange *Legend of St. Alexis* (see p. 271). After his marriage, this rich young man, wanting to live as a pauper and a virgin, flees home. Later he returns there to work incognito as a servant. Only at his death does he reveal his story to the pope (centre), who tells it to his father and wife (right).

Further on is the *Legend of Sisinnius* (pp. 416-417). In the central band, Sisinnius, the police chief (second from right) comes to arrest St. Clement, who is saying Mass, but he is blinded. On the front row to the left are the donors, while below is the inscription: 'I, Beno de Rapiza, and my wife Maria gave this for the love of God and of Clement'. In the lower band, the servants of Sisinnius, also blinded, take a column into custody thinking it is Clement. Sisinnius goads them in archaic Italian (except for some legal documents, this is the earliest extant record of the Italian language): 'You sons of bitches, pull! Gosmario, Albertello, pull! You, Carvoncello, push from behind with your pole!' St. Clement sneaks away mumbling in Latin – still the upper-class language: 'You hard-hearted people, it serves you right to pull a stone.'

Opposite the fresco and slightly to the right, enter the false corridor (f) – remember that this is really a portion of the nave – and walk down to the left end. There, on the right, is the 9th-century fresco, *Christ Descends to Limbo and Saves a Soul* (on the left is the donor, a priest). Through the passage enter a curved space (i) containing what

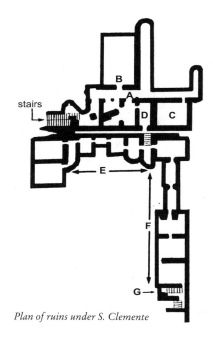

Plan of ruins under S. Clemente

remains of two original apses of the lower church and, further on, the foundation wall of the apse of the upper church. Keep going; you'll now be back in the old central nave. Through a passage on the right (j) a third of the way down, enter the left aisle (k). At the right end (l) under a modern altar are the remains of a tomb, possibly that of St. Cyril.

From here pass a door and descend a staircase (4th century AD) to older Roman ruins, the third level, another 12 ft (4 m) underground.

The first ruins you meet are unrelated to the church. They are the partly excavated remains of a 2nd century AD apartment house, the ordinary Roman *insula*, which rose near the ancient *ecclesia domestica*. Some of the ground floor rooms were turned into a **Mithræum** in the 3rd century AD, a century after the construction of the *insula*. Off the beginning of the corridor to your right (A on the diagram above) through a passage marked by two square pillars is the entrance hall to the Mithraic temple, partly blocked by the apse foundations of the early church overhead; against the walls are benches for the faithful and on the vaulted ceilings, traces of stucco decoration. Go back into the corridor. Opposite is the Mithræum proper (B), the hall for worship. It is actually the converted courtyard of the *insula*. Covering it is a barrel vault with seven holes symbolising the planets, and stucco stars; the vault is worked in rough pumice stone to simulate a cave. Along the walls are benches where the faithful (only men were allowed) reclined for ritual banquets. In the centre is a marble altar with figures pertaining to the cult (see p. 322); an inscription near the top says it was donated by the priest (*pater*) Cn. Arrius Claudianus. In a niche is a cast of a small statue of the god; the original is stored for safety. A bust of the sun god, Apollo, was stolen from this room in 1991. Continue to the end of the corridor; on the right is a room (C) with stucco decorations, benches, a mosaic floor and remains of frescoes (notice the figure of a man between the niches on the right wall). The room was probably for initiation rites, as the presence of seven wall niches, a symbolic number, indicates.

Here you'll start hearing the rumblings of an underground spring behind the walls. This is the (perfectly drinkable) water, perhaps carried by an ancient aqueduct, which flooded the site shortly after its excavation and was channelled with immense effort by the Irish priests through the fourth layer of the ruins (the pre-Neronian buildings) to the Cloaca Maxima (p. 261) near the Colosseum.

Retrace your steps to the first passage on the left (A). Turn immediately into a small room (D). Continuing across a passageway opened in modern times you'll find yourself in a sort of trench. This is a very ancient Roman alley the bottom of which is unexcavated. Drainage work beneath the alley has revealed the fourth layer of buildings, gutted in the Neronian fire of 64 AD (p. 191) and used as the foundations for later buildings. Before you is the oldest ruin, the upper part of a powerful, 90 ft (30 m) wall of tufa blocks (p. 243) from the 2nd century BC.

Cross this wall through another passage opened in modern times. You'll enter the remains of a 1st century AD building totally distinct from the apartment we saw earlier. It is very important in the history of the church of S. Clemente, as it was the earlier home church, or *ecclesia domestica*, which was later filled with rubble and became the foundations of the first basilica.

From its plan, it appears originally to have been a public building, possibly a mint, before being turned into a private residence and home church. Wander (first right, then left) through two suites of rooms perpendicular to each other (E, F); they belong to two of the four sides of the building, which is still mostly unexplored, around an unexcavated courtyard.

You'll reach two sets of stairs (G). The shorter one descends to a dark cubicle, a small catacomb with 16 wall tombs. (The ban on burials within the city lapsed around the 5th century.)

Leave the site via the longer staircase. You'll be in an oblong room (b); this is the right aisle of the old church, which we skipped earlier. Note the columns embedded in the foundation walls of the upper church. In a niche is a 9th-century fresco of the *Madonna and Child*. The Madonna is dressed as a Byzantine Queen, while the female saints who flank her are in Byzantine court attire, typical of much earlier times. This indicates that the fresco is a reworking of an older painting, possibly a 6th-century portrait of the Empress Theodora, wife of Justinian (p. 83). Near the end of the aisle is a 1st century AD pagan sarcophagus.

On your left, before you leave the aisle, note a door with an iron grate. Beyond it, excavations have uncovered the baptistery of the old church, where people were baptised by immersion.

Before taking the stairs to the upper church, peek through an iron grill on the floor into one of the wall tombs we saw earlier.

The walk ends here, near the Colosseum and its many means of public transportation. If you take the following Detour, however, go downhill on Via S. Giovanni in Laterano. At Piazza del Colosseo go left two blocks to Via Claudia.

DETOUR
2 HR

BEFORE GOING

The Cælian Hill and its churches: S. Maria in Domnica, S. Stefano Rotondo, SS. Giovanni e Paolo and S. Gregorio Magno.

An archaic defensive wall is transformed into a city gate, then into an aqueduct, then again into the wall of a hospital enclosing the cell of a holy man. An imperial temple provides the foundations for a monastery, a private house nearby spawns a basilica. Nowhere else are the mutations Rome underwent, especially during its passage from the capital of a worldly empire to that of a spiritual empire, more evident than in this stretch.

From Paganism to Christianity. In an area of the Cælian Hill still immersed in the solitary aura of the *disabitato* (p. 28) is a string of the very earliest Christian churches. One, SS. Giovanni e Paolo, is a most remarkable instance of a pagan building transformed into a Christian one, at a time when Christianity was rapidly spreading, but still very far from general acceptance.

The story of this building begins in the 2nd century AD, when two new houses, comfortable but not lavish, were built on the slopes of the Cælian Hill near a temple dedicated to the emperor Claudius, and provided with tasteful pagan murals. In the 3rd century a third house was built uphill adjacent to the other two, and adorned with one of the earliest Christian paintings. A few years later, the owner of the third house bought the other two and combined all three into one building. A century later, in the late 4th century, as if in a contest between Christian and pagan imagery, the Christian frescoes spread to other parts of the edifice, while the largest pagan mural was plastered over. The purpose of this structure is unclear. Several people are buried in it and the decoration seems closely associated with worship of the dead. What is clear is that soon afterwards the site became an object of intense veneration by Christians. In the early 5th century a large church was built over the graves and dedicated to saints John and Paul.

Several unresolved questions remain. Why a small cemetery in the heart of the city in violation of age-old laws forbidding burials within the walls (p. 156)? What is the link between the church and cemetery? Why the dedication to Sts. John and Paul?

A tradition that would answer all these riddles exists, though it surfaced only in the 5th century, possibly inspired by the questions themselves. It holds the John and Paul of the church are not the apostles, but two Christian military officers who served at the court of Emperor Constantine, the 'legaliser' of Christianity (p. 198). The emperor left the duo a sizeable legacy. They used it to buy a large house on the Cælian slopes, which they then turned into an *ecclesia domestica* (p. 228) for the assemblies of their fellow believers.

Over 20 years later, the throne was occupied by Julian the Apostate who, during his brief and vigorous reign, tried to reverse history by re-criminalising Christianity and restoring paganism. He asked the two officers, now retired, to recant their faith. They refused and were murdered in their own home, along with some supporters. Because of the popularity of the victims, their execution was kept secret and the bodies were buried on the spot.

S. Stefano Rotondo in the 19th century

There are some problems with this story, however. One is that it refers to the 4th century, while the site, with its Christian paintings of almost unprecedented antiquity, already had Christian connotations in the 3rd. There is also an almost identical legend referring to Julian's anti-Christian persecutions in the eastern Empire. Moreover, Julian is not recorded as having executed any Christians in the west.

In 1887 the discovery of the ancient Roman structures under the church set off a spirited debate on the truth of the traditional story, and scholars have been divided into two camps ever since. The sceptics include the famous Jesuit historian and myth-debunker Hippolyte Delehaye (p. 202). They maintain that an age-old *ecclesia domestica* did indeed exist under the church, but that nothing more can be said about it, and that the Paul and John of the dedication were simply the apostles.

Major church excavations and restorations promoted around 1950 by Cardinal Spellman of New York and funded by Joseph Kennedy, bootlegger, former U.S. ambassador to the Court of St. James and father of the U.S. president, have not provided answers. Further excavations are planned.

The dawning of the middle ages. Our brief excursion through the *disabitato* ends, appropriately, in an area tied to a pivotal figure of the time when the *disabitato* came into being: Pope Gregory I 'the Great'. An aristocrat and former high official in the period of ruin and despair after the fall of the Empire (p. 28), he had the sense to reorganise society on new, viable foundations, both psychological and practical, in the name of Christian values, which he adapted to the uncouth mentality of the time. The eminent German-American scholar Richard Krautheimer has called St. Gregory the Great 'the last pope of Christian antiquity [and] the first pope of the middle ages'. On the lower slopes of the Cælian Hill is the ancestral home of St. Gregory, which he turned into a monastery. It included the first of a series of welfare centres to help a populace ravaged by famine and disease (for his programme of charity based on these *diaconiæ*, see p. 254).

Rome's most trying times did not immediately follow the barbarian invasions; in fact, one barbarian ruler, the Goth Theodoric, insured relative tranquillity for some decades. The true blight followed the long struggle for control of Rome between the barbarians and the Byzantine emperors (p. 83). The Byzantines won, but only after immense damage to Rome and Italy, and no efficient government could be set up from the distant eastern capital of Constantinople. St. Gregory restored some government, provided survival assistance and developed a simplified Christian doctrine which, though bordering on superstition, was better suited to the emotional needs of the time and became a hallmark of medieval culture ('Vulgarkatholizismus', the German scholar A. V. Harnack has called it). New, highly effective liturgies, such as processions and chants, were also instituted. Politically, St. Gregory laid the basis for the future commanding role of the papacy in the former Empire. He also set in motion the 'conversion' of Britain, where the Celtic church had been submerged by the Saxon invasions. (Some Christian communities survived, however, including those in Kent, where King Ethelbert had married a Christian.) Gregory entrusted the enterprise to his closest collaborator in the monastery he had founded in his family mansion, the prior Augustine (later St. Augustine of Canterbury, not to be confused with St. Augustine of Hippo, the famous Doctor of the Church). Despite his hesitations, Augustine eventually arrived in Britain in 597 with forty monks, where Ethelbert installed them in a house in Canterbury and allowed them to preach. Over the next sixty years Britain was converted and the native churches brought into line. Augustine himself died in 604, having been installed as the first archbishop of Canterbury. The part that the practical and populist methods of Gregory had in his success can be surmised from Gregory's still extant letters of instruction to Augustine, where he enjoins his missionary to adopt the liturgical usages most congenial to local temperament, not to destroy pagan temples, only the idols, and to adopt pagan rites for Christian feasts.

Places change, their spirit endures. Even more impressive than the physical changes undergone by this section of Rome in its transition from paganism to Christianity is the persistence through the centuries of the new spiritual values. The mission of helping the desperately needy, begun in the 6th century with Pope Gregory's welfare centres, continues today in the original compound, thanks to the efforts of successive religious orders, most recently a Tuscan branch of the Franciscans.

After 1870, when an anticlerical state administration requisitioned most monastic buildings (p. 116), the Franciscans were able to lease back their main one here. Recently, the heroic nun-nurses of Mother Theresa have moved into the compound to care for the sick and aged, astutely invited by the Franciscan prior, Father Anselmo Giabbani. He invited them as the lease expired, when a Communist-led city council announced plans to use the building as a Marxist study centre. The people of Rome sided with Father Anselmo and the nuns, and the lease was renewed.

Equally striking is the story of another monastic order we'll meet in the first part of this stretch, the Trinitarians. Created at the end of the 12th century by a French contemporary of St. Francis of Assisi, St. John de Matha, to help the victims of Arab pirates, it still pursues its basic mission. Today it helps prisoners, slaves where slavery survives, political refugees and victims of human rights violations. The latter have included members of Eastern Europe's 'churches of silence' during the decades of Communist domination, and today include persecuted Christian communities in countries such as China, Pakistan, Indonesia and Sudan.

ON THE SPOT

The Cælian Hill and its churches: S. Maria in Domnica, S. Stefano Rotondo, SS. Giovanni e Paolo and S. Gregorio Magno.

Via Claudia gradually ascends the Cælian Hill. The street, of ancient Roman origin, is dominated on the right by massive walls, the foundations of the Temple of Claudius. It was dedicated to the 1st century emperor by his fourth wife, Agrippina, when he was deified upon his death – a death arranged, it is said, by Agrippina herself (p. 155).

The structures, which supported the base of the temple, and similar ones on the opposite slope of the hill, are all that remain of the temple, one of the largest in Rome.

Cross the street and walk up Via Claudia to the hilltop, or better yet, take any bus at the stop about 80 yards (80 m) uphill, for one stop. Whether you walk or ride, go to the bus stop just past the hilltop, which will be used as a reference point.

Walk a few steps back from the bus stop. At No.12, a massive 17th-century baroque gate adorned with awkward figures is the entrance to a public park, the Villa Celimontana (p. 431).

In the centre of the square is the *Navicella* ('Little Ship'), a monument modelled on an ancient Roman warship, recently adapted as a fountain.

It has given its name to the whole area for centuries. The present sculpture – perhaps by Andrea Sansovino – is early 16th century, but is thought to reproduce an ancient version, a votive gift from Roman soldiers stationed in barracks nearby.

In contrast with its present sleepy, *disabitato* (p. 28) look, in imperial times the *Navicella* neighbourhood was one of the liveliest in Rome. Two troops ('cohorts') with police and fire duties were based here (at stations like the one unearthed in Trastevere, see p. 548) ; ancient sources mention several Lupanaria, or state-regulated brothels. Despite this, the district was aristocratic and residential. Here was the grand villa of Senator Simmachus, one of the last champions of paganism, near a civic basilica donated by a famous jeweller and pearl trader, Hilarus. Traces of both have been found.

Across from the *Navicella* is **S. Maria in Domnica** (the meaning of 'in Domnica' is uncertain, perhaps 'of the Lord') built in the 6th or 7th century, possibly over the barracks of one of the cohorts, as a *diaconia*, or food distribution centre (p. 254). It was rebuilt in the 9th century and

The Navicella outside S. Maria in Domnica

modified in the 16th; its appearance is a mixture of these two periods. The 16th-century façade is by Andrea Sansovino. (Open: 08:00-12:00 and 16:00-18:30 in winter, 16:00-19:00 in summer.)

All the columns come from ancient Roman buildings (pp. 95, 257). The wooden ceiling is 16th-century, with liturgical motifs of the Virgin which also recall the image of the *Navicella*. Under the ceiling runs a fine 16th-century frieze by assistants of Raphael.

In the apse are splendid Byzantine-style mosaics commissioned by Pope Paschal I, the 9th-century restorer of the church. You may remember that he was responsible for the great mosaics in S. Prassede (p. 103). The two sets are indeed stylistically similar. In both, Pope Paschal is shown as the donor, wearing the square halo of the living. Here, he kneels at the foot of the Virgin, who is amidst a crowd of angels. Note the beautiful flowers. The Redeemer, the Twelve Apostles and two angels are on the triumphal arch; below them are two large prophets. An inscription mentioning the restoration of Paschal I is in the beautiful script of the period, the age of Charlemagne, when memories of classical beauty resurfaced briefly. In the mosaics themselves, this reminiscence tempers the stark austerity of the Byzantine style.

Below the mosaics are vivid 17th-century frescoes by a minor painter. Three fine ancient Roman sarcophagi stand in the right aisle; they were unearthed under the church, along with remains of 3rd century AD buildings.

Exit and turn left. A few steps downhill is a giant brick pier from one of the aqueducts that Nero built to serve his palaces (pp. 206, 404) and the adjacent areas. The ruins of the aqueduct are scattered here and there.

At the height of the Empire the Roman aqueduct system provided about 264 gallons (1,000 litres) of water per person daily, more than twice the amount considered adequate nowadays.

To the right of the aqueduct pier, step into Via Santo Stefano Rotondo. A wall on the right is formed by walled-up arches of the aqueduct which continue for a while; go and have a look. An open-

ing in the wall at No. 7 leads to **S. Stefano Rotondo** ('the Round'), the oldest circular church in Rome.

This was built in the 5th century, imitating the Holy Sepulchre in Jerusalem, over a demolished Mithraic temple, whose ruins have been found. (The oriental religion of Mithras – the last in Rome to survive the collapse of paganism – was especially popular among soldiers; remember the barracks were nearby, p. 427.)

In the 12th century the church was restored, and the porch, formed by ancient Roman columns, was added. A complete remodelling took place in the 15th century. The church, which originally contained two concentric rings of free-standing columns, was reduced in size by removing the outer wall and filling in the outer ring of columns. (Opening hours vary; enquire by calling the German-Hungarian College, which owns the church: (06) 4819333.)

Enter the church through the 15th-century portal and a vestibule. Inside, note the outer ring of 34 columns embedded in the wall. Towards the centre of the church, two giant ancient Roman columns and two pilasters, all added in the 12th century restoration, support the ceiling.

To the left of the entrance is an imperial Roman marble chair, later used as a bishop's throne. Past it is a chapel with a small apse in which a 7th-century mosaic in the other-worldly Byzantine style depicts two saints, Primus and Felicianus, whose relics were brought here from the catacombs at the time. They are dressed as dignitaries of the Eastern Empire.

Inside and outside the chapel are more decorations by minor late 16th-century artists. The octagonal marble enclosure and the tabernacle at the centre of the church, as well as the extraordinary frescoes all around the wall are from the same period. Commissioned from late 16th-century artists, including Niccolò Pomarancio, by the Jesuits at the height of the Counter-Reformation (pp. 110-111), to instruct missionaries on the risks of their jobs, they depict in gory, almost sadistic, detail the tortures the martyrs had suffered. (Or had suffered according to Christian tradition. Many scholars, from Gibbon on, deny that such extreme cruelties ever too place.) The French author Stendhal found these images 'too frightful for me to set down'. Once common, today this sort of picture is rare in Roman churches (see pp. 72, 274 for more examples).

The ruins of the Mithræum under the church may be visited on request. For more on the Mithraic cult, see p. 417. Recent excavations have also found traces of military barracks.

Leaving the church, go back toward the isolated giant aqueduct pier on the left. Cross the street here to the wall with the street sign 'Via della Navicella'. The wall is the continuation of the aqueduct, which is walled up. A few steps down-hill from the street sign, two street-level arches of the aqueduct have been turned into portals. The first (No. 4) was outlined in marble in the 13th century and surmounted by a shrine in which a mosaic shows the Redeemer holding by the hand two prisoners, one white and one black, the mean-ing of which we'll see in a moment. The whole is signed (below the mosaic on the arch) by two members of the Cosma family. The next portal (No. 2) is in the pointed gothic style of the same period. Both were entrances to an early 13th-cen-tury hospital-monastery, no longer here. Called S. Tommaso in Formis, or 'in the Arches' (of Nero's aqueduct), it was managed by Trinitarian priests who specialised in ransoming hostages captured by Arabs in the Mediterranean – the captives depicted in the mosaic. The Trinitarians are still there, as we'll see shortly.

Continue along the wall to a marble arch. This is the so-called Arch of Dolabella, actually a gate in Rome's early Republican walls, built long before the final Aurelian walls of the declining Empire (p. 42).

Dolabella and Silanus were consuls, mentioned in a barely visible inscription over the keystone, who rebuilt the gate for the last time under the first emperor, Augustus (early 1st century AD).

A few years later, the gate and a section of the old walls became part of Nero's aqueduct. Pass

under the marble arch and look up, to the right, at the huge arch of the aqueduct. On the left is the present entrance, usually locked, to the Trinitarian compound, now reduced to a small medieval church, reconstructed in modern times.

Turn and look up above the arch of Dolabella. In the masonry of the old aqueduct, a small win-dow, cross and door mark the cell where the founder of the order, St. John de Matha, died in the early 13th century. A simple chapel is now there.

Continue downhill on this street, which follows the ancient Roman layout (note the particularly *disabitato* look of this stretch). You come to a secluded, evocative medieval square dominated by the church and monastery of **SS. Giovanni e Paolo** (Sts. John and Paul).

The whole right side of the square is 12th-cen-tury. It includes the monastery façade and the Romanesque bell tower, one of the most beautiful in Rome, built on a corner of the marble base of the Temple of Claudius (p. 427). More of the tem-ple foundations are visible in the monastery courtyard; if the door at No. 14 is closed, try later, through the church sacristy.

Colourful ceramic discs adorn the bell tower. They are copies inserted in a recent restoration; the precious Mozarabic (Hispano-Moorish) originals are in the monastery. The uppermost part of the church façade, with the four small columns, once free-standing, belongs to the original 5th-century construction. The escutcheon is that of Cardinal Spellman of New York, sponsor of the 1951 restoration.

The street-level portico was added in the 12th century by a Cardinal Johannes, mentioned in the inscription, during restorations following a ram-page of Norman mercenaries (see p. 303). The wall and windows over the portico, as well as a gallery leading to the monastery, are 13th-century.

Inside the portico, embedded in the 12th-century wall, are two ancient Roman columns, the remains of the 5th-century façade colonnade. Together with the uppermost part of the church, also colonnaded, which we saw from outside, this lower colonnade composed a double-tiered set of

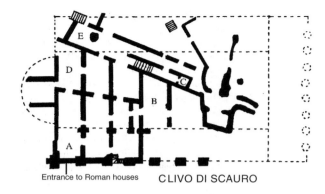

Entrance to Roman houses CLIVO DI SCAURO

Plan of SS. Giovanni e Paolo (dotted line) over the remains of ancient Roman houses underground

free standing arches, unique in old basilicas. Today a beautiful 18th-century iron gate connects the exterior columns of the portico. Symbolic lions (see p. 230) flank the cosmatesque doorway.

(Open: 08:00-12:00 and 15:30-17:30.; but note: after a major restoration completed in 2002, the visit to the underground level (the Roman house) requires a paid ticket and a reservation: tel. and fax (06) 721660; email spazioservizi @libero.it.)

A radical 18th-century restoration inside the church has effaced the ancient appearance and atmosphere. Even some of the original nave columns (taken from ancient Roman buildings, p. 95) were enclosed in new piers. The 12th-century cosmatesque floor is mostly over-restored. A real surprise are the crystal chandeliers hanging in rows from the ceiling: they come from the Waldorf Astoria Hotel in New York and were given to the church when the hotel underwent re-novation! The idea was that of Cardinal Spellman.

Toward the middle of the nave and to the right, a 17th-century rail marks the supposed site beneath the present floor of a shrine to the two titular saints in what was thought to be their house (*in ædibus propriis*, 'in their own house', as the Latin inscription says). Actually, excavations have found a religious shrine slightly beyond the railed area (in 1951 it was made visible through a hole in the floor, now closed).

Go to the apse. The frescoes in the half-dome are by Niccolò Pomarancio (1588). Those in the lower part depicting scenes from the martyrdom of the two titular saints are by minor 18th-century artists. Under the altar, an ancient Roman tub of porphyry contains the supposed relics of the two saints. A door on the left side of the presbytery – tip the sacristan to have it opened – leads to a 1255 fresco of *Christ among the Apostles*, still rigidly Byzantine in style.

The visit to the Roman houses underground begins from the street that descends along the flank of the church (Clivo di Scauro). We enter a row of rooms that were used as supplementary chapels of the church even after the church was built. On the right, one of these rooms (A) has 9th-century frescoes (a *Crucifixion*, with Christ, unusually, in a tunic) and 12th-century frescoes (*Christ and saints*). Bypassing the minor rooms on the left, we next reach a space (B) from the period when the two houses, from the 2nd and 3rd century, were joined by new owners. They were unquestionably Christians, as the decoration, with frescoes of lambs and vines, is typical of Early Christian iconography; on the upper left-hand corner of the side wall it includes a man praying in the Early Christian way, with outstretched arms (*orans*, to use a traditional Latin term). The painting, from the late 3rd century, possibly earlier, is amongst the oldest and best preserved of its kind.

Continuing in the same direction we pass into

the newer (3rd century) house, where a modern stairway leads up to a small room, or shrine (C), with a small window.

Here other graves were found, traditionally considered those of the two martyrs and their companions. On all the walls are frescoes from the 4th century, showing another *orans* figure and some not clearly identified scenes of martyrdom. The shrine is part of the primitive *ecclesia domestica* set up in the houses before the church above existed. Through the small window (*fenestrella confessionis*), a typical feature of these Early Christian shrines (we found one in St. Peter's, p. 368, and elsewhere,) the faithful could peek at the relics of the martyrs. The presence of the shrine was later marked in the church above by the floor inscription which you saw there.

Returning to the lower level and going left you enter a room (D) of the oldest of the two houses (2nd century AD) with frescoes from the 2nd-3rd century representing winged deities and flower friezes, presumably pagan, though there are also birds, vines and other details from traditional Christian imagery. A nearby room (E) of the same house – a courtyard subsequently covered – has remains of a fountain adorned with a beautiful pagan fresco depicting deities and winged children in boats. The fresco was found in 1909 under a plaster layer that partly remains. It was probably added when the houses became Christian property in the 3rd century. In the courtyard is a well shaft. Traces of human burials have been discovered both in the shaft and the base of the fountain. An interesting collection of finds has been installed in an adjoining room.

Leave the church and stop for a moment to examine the side of the square on your right. Uphill is another 17th-century doorway, that of the Villa Celimontana, which we saw near the bus stop (p. 427). To its right are remains of the façade of an early 3rd century AD building, which included shops (*tabernæ*, see p. 140) and was at least two storeys high.

Start downhill on Clivo di Scauro ('Scaurus Climb'), one of the most evocative streets in Rome.

It dates back to the 2nd century BC, with the same name, which is that of the magistrate who built it. Ruins from various periods are on both sides. The first part of the street is bridged by the buttresses of the church of SS. Giovanni e Paolo, necessitated by damages suffered during the 5th century barbarian invasions. Only the furthest, tallest buttress is from that time, however; the others were rebuilt in the late middle ages. Going downhill, on your right, the masonry up to the top of the buttresses belongs to the two three-storey houses over which the church was built (p. 430): first to the 3rd century AD house (note the outlines of the walled-up *tabernæ* and windows), then to the 2nd century AD one (a few ruins).

The entire wall on your left belongs to the monastery-welfare centre founded in the 6th century by Pope Gregory the Great in his family mansion (the main building of the compound has vanished). Past the last buttress, a 1607 portal (No. 3) bears a faded painting of the saint. Continue downhill. Immediately past the baroque doorway are the curved ruins of an early 6th-century building that St. Gregory incorporated into the compound. It was probably a library built by Pope Agapitus, an immediate predecessor of St. Gregory, to help fight illiteracy, which was widespread after the fall of the Empire. In the area are other ancient ruins, notably, a low 2nd century AD house, recognisable by its (later) marble window, nestled between taller structures. (Further remains of the monastery compound are discussed shortly.)

Continue all the way down to where the wall ends on the right, revealing a wonderful new view.

First look back at the poetic Clivo di Scauro (A on map on p. 432), reproduced in pictures of all ages. Observe the original 5th-century apse of SS. Giovanni e Paolo, graced by the small arches of a 13th-century gallery. The part between the gallery and the roof is 12th-century. The dome on the left is a 19th-century aberration.

Turn around and go a few steps forward to see the slope of the Palatine across the avenue. The giant brick arches across the pavement (B) belong

Layout of monastic complex of S. Gregorio Magno

to an extension of Nero's aqueduct up to the imperial palaces on the hill.

Turn around again. Everything centring on a white 2-storey church (C) is linked somehow to St. Gregory. To the left of the church is the area we skirted coming down the Clivo, where Gregory's house and monastic compound stood (D). Soon we'll see better what remains of it. The building (E) on the right of the church belongs partly to a 'new' monastery, partly to a hospice for the sick, the homeless and the aged.

The church itself is **S. Gregorio Magno** ('St. Gregory the Great'). Its exact origins are unknown. Perhaps built over some part of St. Gregory's monastery, its existence is only documented from the later middle ages (traces of medieval constructions survive). The present structure is 17th-century. The austere, harmonious façade is the masterpiece of Giovan Battista Soria, an important early baroque architect. Go towards the church, but before you go in, it is worth visiting the area behind the wall to the left of the steps, where St. Gregory's monastery once stood. The most important elements there today are three little chapels combined into a single structure:

from left to right, **S. Barbara**, **S. Andrea** (St. Andrew) and **S. Silvia**.

Originally there were only the two medieval chapels; S. Silvia was added in the 17th century. At that time the two older chapels, which were originally completely independent, and the new one were combined into one building, which we now see, with the pretty little porch before the central chapel. The chapel of S. Barbara is said to have been a soup kitchen for the poor in the time of St. Gregory. It contains a marble table dating back to the 3rd century AD on which it is said St. Gregory personally used to serve meals to twelve people; one day, tradition adds, an angel sat as a thirteenth guest. Two Latin verses inscribed on the table in the 15th century evoke this legend, and it is shown in an early 17th-century fresco by Antonio Viviani (called Il Sordo, 'The Deaf Man'), a minor painter from Viterbo near Rome. Other frescoes by the same artist illustrate the evangelization of Brtain by St. Gregory and his missionary, St. Augustine of Canterbury: among them, *Gregory inspired by seeing young English slaves for sale in Rome* (a famous episode, in which he declared the blond youths 'were not so much Angles as angels', and that such a race deserved to be saved for Heaven by baptism); *Gregory blesses Augustine and his companions on their departure; Meeting of the missionaries with King Ethelbert.* The chapel stands over the ruins of the lower floor of an early 3rd century AD apartment house, with recently excavated *tabernæ* (accessible from the back).

The chapel of S. Andrea, which once opened on the other side, was perhaps the original small church of St. Gregory's monastery. The ancient Roman columns of the porch may have belonged to the original construction. Inside are frescoes by three 17th-century masters. On the entrance wall is *St. Gregory and his Mother, St. Sylvia* by Lanfranco. On the right wall is the *Scourging of St. Andrew* by Lanfranco's rival, Domenichino (see pp. 508-509). On the left wall is *St. Andrew Led to Martyrdom* by Reni. Remains of 11th-century frescoes, including a *Christ Blessing* in the Byzantine style, have come to light recently.

The chapel of S. Silvia has another wonderful fresco by Reni of *Music-making Angels*.

To the right of this chapel, and linked to it by an ancient Roman wall, is a 15th-century three-storey house with geometrical graffito work (see Glossary), built over ancient Roman remains.

Between the house and the church of St. Gregory the Great, the Missionaries of Charity of Mother Theresa of Calcutta, who was beatified in 2003, are housed in a former chicken coop. The main task of the young nuns, who scurry about in their white habit and veil striped with blue, is to assist the elderly poor lodged in the monastery on the other side of the church. The order accepts even the humblest of donations.

S. Gregorio is open 09:30-12:00 and 16:30-18:00.

Before the church is a solemn, well-proportioned portico by G. B. Soria. It is lined with 16th- and 17th-century tombs, including three of special interest. In the first two on the left rest two English dignitaries, Robert Peckham and Edward Carne. Carne was an emissary of Henry VIII to the pope in a vain attempt by the king to obtain a divorce from his first wife. This was the immediate cause of the separation of the Church of England from Rome. At the far end on the left is a refined 16th-century tomb, highlighted by a relief of the *Madonna*. It presently contains the bones of a 17th-century prelate, but is said to have originally held those of Imperia, a famous renaissance courtesan (see pp. 495-496). Directly opposite is a sensitive, delicate monument to two brothers called Bonsi by the early l6th-century Milanese sculptor Luigi Capponi.

The interior, with ancient Roman columns and patches of cosmatesque floor, is mainly decorated by minor 18th-century artists. A marble altar at the far end of the right aisle is another fine work by Capponi, with three reliefs of scenes from the *Life of St. Gregory*. On the altar is a narrow panel painted by artists of the school of Pinturicchio. To the right of the chapel, in a small room which an unverifiable tradition calls St. Gregory's monastic cell, is an interesting 1st century AD marble chair said to have been Gregory's episcopal throne.

Façade of S. Gregorio Magno, by Giuseppe Vasi

Through a door in the left aisle (ask the sacristan to open it) we reach a large chapel designed by Francesco da Volterra and Carlo Maderno at the end of the 16th century. On the right wall is a venerated 14th-century fresco of the *Madonna and Child*, repainted several times. On the left a large 15th-century relief, perhaps by Bregno, depicts at the top the legend of the angel appearing to St. Gregory at the top of the Mausoleum of Hadrian, now Castel Sant' Angelo (p. 385). The same scene appears on a late 16th-century fresco behind.

From the church you can reach the Colosseum area with its many means of transport, including the metro, by taking the tram that stops just ahead on your right (if you have your back to the church) for one stop. Or you can go down to Via di S. Gregorio, in front of the Palatine Hill, via steps that are somewhat hidden among the bushes on the other side of the tram tracks, and from there take a bus, also for one stop.

Renaissance
Rome

Ceiling from the Villa Madama, decorated in the 1520's
by followers of Raphael

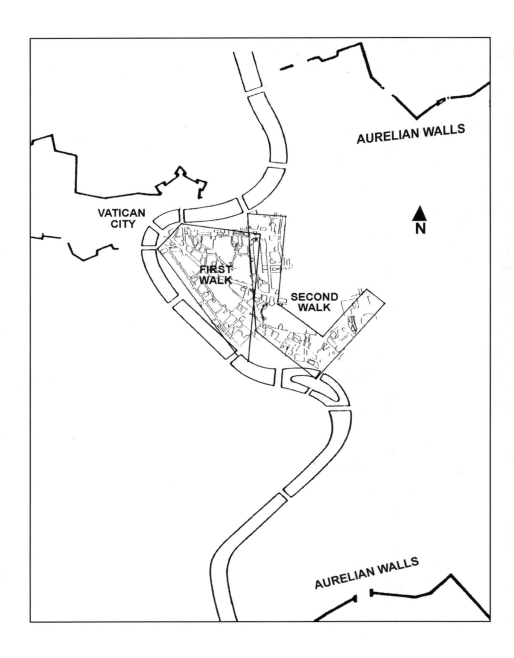

RENAISSANCE ROME

INTRODUCTION

The previous Walks have shown us the great monuments of Rome. The next two will put us in touch with the life of the city, that of today and that of centuries past. No other part of Rome is as vibrant and colourful as the one we'll now visit, nor as rich in art or history. If one had a time machine for a one-day trip back to Rome, this area would be a good choice to visit, since at every point spanning two millennia something fascinating would be going on.

There was one especially glorious era in this neighbourhood, the Renaissance. The word means 'rebirth', not simply an æsthetic awakening. Five to six centuries ago, first in Italy then throughout Europe, people sloughed off the fatalism and mystical introversion that followed the traumatic fall of the empire. They rediscovered the importance of life on earth and the greatness of their pagan past, against which they now ambitiously wanted to measure themselves. This sea change led to an unprecedented artistic flourishing, prosperity and social development which, in Rome, was centered on this district, which is thus traditionally called 'Renaissance Rome'.

The area borders on and slightly overlaps with that we visited in the second Ancient Rome Walk, when we explored the eastern section of the Tiber Bend and saw the monuments of imperial expansion in the Campo Marzio. We'll now visit the western section, close to the river bend, which encloses it on two sides and separates it from the Vatican.

You may remember that under the emperors, the inhabited areas of Rome were mainly limited to the eastern section of the Tiber Bend, away from the river and its marshy and frequently flooded banks, whereas the western section was mainly for gardens, theatres, temples, stadia and so on (pp. 27 -28). The situation changed drastically after the Empire fell. A population decimated by the horrors of invasion abandoned most of Rome and huddled together in the Tiber Bend. People settled near the river banks, both for access to water – the destruction of the aqueducts had forced them to abandon the hills – and for communication with the countryside, crucial for food supply, since all links with distant lands had been severed.

Of those desperate times we know little. A sad, introverted mood set in, foreshadowed by the writings of St Augustine. He urged Christians to give up thoughts of happiness in the City of Man – powerfully symbolised by Rome – and turn all hope toward the City of God. Constant external threats, disease and famine made everyday life a nightmare in the newly settled area, which would later be known as the *abitato* ('inhabited'), as opposed to the rest of Rome, which had been abandoned, called the *disabitato* ('uninhabited'). Chroniclers have handed down scenes of misery and decay to us. Signs of ancient glory gradually faded. Proud monuments fell; the dull grinding noise of demolition by thieves rumbled through the night. Statues and precious marbles were burnt for lime. Muslim corsairs, plundering foreign armies, floods and plagues brought periodic devastation and death.

After several wretched centuries, the lot of the people gradually improved. Two factors helped this: a growing stream of the faithful from all parts of Europe, the first pilgrimages; and the transfer of the Holy See from the Lateran to St Peter's (p. 300), which made the Tiber Bend a sort of ante-room to the centre of power. Moreover, during those times in the middle ages, when civilian authorities temporarily wrested power from the Church (p. 144), the importance of the district was enhanced by its location midway between the two centres, the secular one on the Capitol, and the spiritual one in the Vatican.

The pilgrimages, a much more substantial, organised form of tourism than is often thought, boosted commerce and local crafts. A sophisticated hotel industry bloomed. As the papacy gained worldwide influence in the middle ages, the area began to flourish, especially after the popes returned from their long exile in Avignon in the late 14th century (p. 300). Their vast spiritual authority translated into great political power and wealth.

Soon the popes started to invest massively in beautifying the Vatican and Rome itself. In the late 15th century they began calling great artists to Rome from elsewhere in Italy, mainly Florence, where the artistic renaissance had already yielded splendid results. The artists naturally settled near the source of their commissions, the Tiber Bend area by the bridge to the Vatican.

The Fountain of the Tortoises

Here they built and decorated homes both for themselves and their patrons.

This is the main reason for the renaissance character of the area, from a visual standpoint. Yet the contribution of the Florentines was not just artistic. It expressed itself in a refinement of customs and even of language, as the crude southern dialect of Rome aquired cultivated inflections from Dante's speech. On a more practical level, emissaries from the great banks of Florence, then one of the most thriving commercial centres in Europe, settled near their artist compatriots to aid the papal development programs. The general atmosphere of affluence and opportunity also boosted the size of other foreign communities that had long lived there – merchants, diplomats, seamen, financiers and prelates – usually near their own national churches, of which there are dozens in Rome, particularly in the renaissance area. We'll see most of them in these Walks – the German and the English, the French and the Portuguese, the Flemish and the Spanish, as well as those of the Italian regions that were formerly separate states. Almost all are still served by clergy from their respective countries. Apart from works by artists from these countries, they contain the relics of their national popes and saints, and tombs of prominent members of the foreign communities.

Adding to the bustle and colour of this part of Rome were vast numbers of courtesans, some very stylish and often famous for their learning as well as their beauty, others more humble. They found a ready market among the wealthy, the pilgrims and, it was rumoured, the supposedly celibate clerics. It has been estimated that in the early 1400's, one tenth of a population of about 60,000 were prostitutes and their associates.

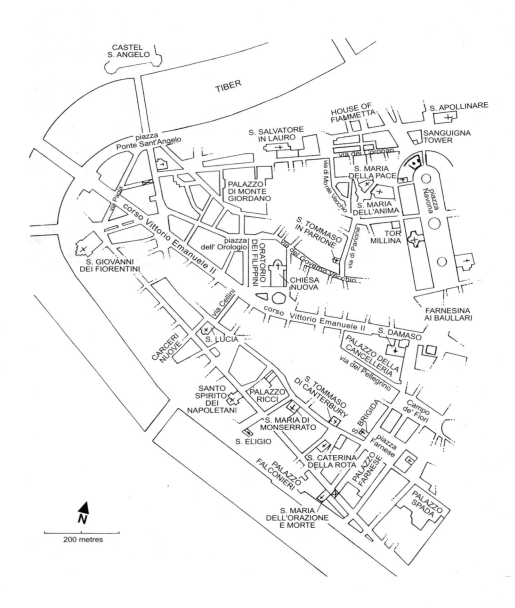

CASTEL
S. ANGELO

TIBER

HOUSE OF
FIAMMETTA

S. APOLLINARE

piazza
Ponte Sant'Angelo

S. SALVATORE
IN LAURO

via dei Coronari

SANGUIGNA
TOWER

S. MARIA
DELLA PACE

PALAZZO
DI MONTE
GIORDANO

S. MARIA
DELL'ANIMA

piazza
Navona

corso Vittorio Emanuele II

via di Monte Vecchio

via Paola

S. TOMMASO
IN PARIONE

TOR
MILLINA

via di Parione

piazza
dell' Orologio

ORATORIO
DEI FILIPPINI

via del Governo Vecchio

S. GIOVANNI
DEI FIORENTINI

CHIESA
NUOVA

FARNESINA
AI BAULLARI

via Cellini

corso Vittorio Emanuele II

S. DAMASO

CARCERI
NUOVE

S. LUCIA

PALAZZO DELLA
CANCELLERIA

via del Pellegrino

SANTO
SPIRITO
DEI
NAPOLETANI

PALAZZO
RICCI

S. TOMMASO
DI CANTERBURY

S. BRIGIDA

Campo
de' Fiori

S. MARIA DI
MONSERRATO

piazza
Farnese

S. ELIGIO

S. CATERINA
DELLA ROTA

PALAZZO
FALCONIERI

PALAZZO
FARNESE

PALAZZO
SPADA

S. MARIA
DELL'ORAZIONE
E MORTE

N

200 metres

RENAISSANCE ROME
FIRST WALK

Starting point: Piazza Ponte S. Angelo
End point: Corso Vittorio
Duration: 6 hours (without the Detours, indicated above between
parentheses).

Planning your walk: you can take this Walk in the morning or afternoon.
Unfortunately, you will find that many of the smaller, non-parish churches
are almost always closed, though there is a higher probability of finding
them open on Sundays.

BEFORE GOING

1. From Ponte S. Angelo to Via dei Coronari

Two famous triplets from Dante's *Divine Comedy* tell us that during the Jubilee Year of 1300 (proclaimed by Pope Boniface VIII from the 'Jubilee Loggia' of S. Giovanni in Laterano, p. 398), the traffic on the bridge from the Vatican to the centre of the *abitato* (pp. 28, 438) – where our first Renaissance Rome Walk begins – was so intense that a system of one-ways for pedestrians was implemented:

> Come i Roman per l'essercito molto,
> L'anno del giubileo, su per lo ponte
> Hanno a passar la gente modo colto,
>
> Che dall'un lato tutti hanno la fronte
> Verso'l castello e vanno a santo Pietro;
> Dall'altra sponda vanno verso il monte.

In Longfellow's groundbreaking translation:

> Even as the Romans, for the mighty host,
> The year of the Jubilee, upon the bridge
> Have chosen a mode to pass the people over:
>
> For all upon one side towards the Castle
> Their faces have, and go until St. Peter's;
> On the other side they go towards the Mountain.

(The castle is, of course, Castel S. Angelo, while the mountain is the hillock of Monte Giordano, which we'll visit shortly.) In a terrible incident in 1450, a cardinal's mule caught in the throng began to kick, triggering panic. People were crushed against the parapets, which collapsed; 176 unfortunates fell into the river and most died.

Other tragic memories haunt the landing area of the bridge inside the Bend. We'll see a marble tablet of 1276, the oldest extant of the many that record the periodic river floodings that brought destruction and death. The first victims were usually the inmates of the Tor di Nona prison, a gloomy old tower that rose at the edge of the water. In the early middle ages the bodies of executed prisoners were strung up for days from the top of the tower. Later, and until the 1800's, executions took place in the piazza in front of the bridge. (Other sites were also used. Guillotine executions took place, for instance, in Via dei Cerchi near the Circus Maximus.) Among those hanged, decapitated, drawn and quartered or otherwise put to death was young Beatrice Cenci, the 16th-century heroine of Rome's most lurid, sensational family drama. Her story will be told later on this Walk, as we approach her palatial home (pp. 517-518).

Ponte Sant'Angelo, Castel Sant'Angelo and St. Peter's in the 19th century.
One of the most popular views of Rome, reproduced countless times

Contemporaries saw nothing strange in the fact that this macabre site before the bridge, Piazza di Ponte ('Bridge Square', now called Piazza Ponte S. Angelo) also served as a festive vestibule to the Vatican area beyond the river, with colourful papal parades, and foreign princes and ambassadors going back and forth.

It was also the anteroom to the financial district, which began right off the piazza in Via Banco di Santo Spirito ('Street of the Bank of the Holy Spirit'). This street still exists, as indeed does the bank after which it is named, 400 years after it was set up as a public service by the Holy Spirit Hospital, which we saw in the second Rome of the Popes Walk, pp. 382-383.

Other streets nearby are also named after particular 'banchi'. There were the offices of the medieval Florentine bankers, as well as those of other nations, such as the Fugger of Augsburg. Even before the renaissance, street stalls called 'banchi' (the original 'banks' – the Italian word simply means 'benches') were set up here by moneychangers to serve pilgrims arriving in Rome.

As noted, the pope was the most important customer of these financiers. But the creditworthiness of the Holy Father was not unlimited; On one occasion, a bank took the jewelled papal tiara as collateral.

ON THE SPOT

1. From Ponte S. Angelo to Via dei Coronari

Piazza Ponte S. Angelo, memorable for its pageantry and processions no less than for its public executions, affords a beautiful view across the river of the Castle that we visited in the second Rome of the Popes Walk.

On this side of the river, the piazza forms the terminal of a trio of streets. Approach the right-hand street, Via Paola, named after Pope Paul III (brother of 'Giulia Bella', p. 361), who built it in the 16th century. From here we can see the noble façade of **S. Giovanni dei Fiorentini** ('St. John of the Florentines') at the far end, built in the heyday of the renaissance as the national church of the Florentine community in Rome. As mentioned above, the Florentines congregated in this district, the cultural and economic mainstay of the city.

The church, in the simple, stately style of the Florentine renaissance, is one of Rome's largest. It was designed by a series of architects spanning

two centuries. Jacopo Sansovino made the basic design and began work in the early 1500's. Work then continued under Antonio da Sangallo the Younger and Giacomo Della Porta; in 1559, five years before his death, Michelangelo tried to have the plan changed from Latin Cross to Greek Cross, but this could not be done for lack of funds. The dome was added in the early 1600's by Carlo Maderno, and the façade a century later by Alessandro Galilei, whose façade of S. Giovanni in Laterano we have already seen, p. 404.

DETOUR
15 MIN

This is essentially a visit to the interior of S. Giovanni dei Fiorentini, which has the same unadorned and typically Florentine look as the outside. (Open 07:00-11:00, to 13:00 on Sun; 17:00-19:00, except in winter, 16:30-18:30).

Counterclockwise: halfway up the right aisle,

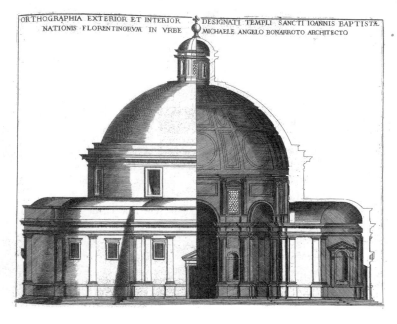

ORTHOGRAPHIA EXTERIOR ET INTERIOR   DESIGNATI TEMPLI SANCTI IOANNIS BAPTISTÆ
NATIONIS FLORENTINORVM IN VRBE   MICHAELE ANGELO BONARROTO ARCHITECTO

Michelangelo's unbuilt but influential design for S. Giovanni dei Fiorentini:

in a vestibule in front of the sacristy, are two 17th-century busts of Florentine benefactors of the church, the one on the left by Pietro Bernini, the other by his more famous son Gian Lorenzo. In a niche over the door is a graceful late 15th-century statue of *St. John the Baptist*, Florentine school, perhaps a youthful work by Michelangelo. At the right end of the transept is the *Martyrdom of Sts. Cosmas and Damian* (see p. 194), the only known altarpiece by Salvator Rosa (p. 88), a 17th-century artist of great originality, who specialised in proto-romantic genre subjects.

At the end of the aisle, an elaborate chapel has a small delicate 15th-century fresco of the *Madonna and Child* over the altar. All around are stuccos and frescoes by minor late 16th-century artists.

On the transept floor, under the dome, is the tomb of Carlo Maderno, one of the most active architects of late renaissance and early baroque Rome, whose countless works include the dome of this church. The tomb also contains the remains of the great Borromini, who also worked in this church in the mid-17th century; his name is not marked, perhaps because he had committed suicide (p. 60). That such a giant should have ended up in a grave bearing the name of another man seems somehow in tune with his tormented, isolated life. Only in 1955 and 1997 did commemorative inscriptions appear in the church (on the third pier of the left aisle and on the floor near the grave).

Borromini designed the impressive main altar (the statuary is by minor artists) and the tombs on the walls to the right and left of it. Both are of the Falconieri family, one of his patrons (we'll see the palazzo he built for them later). The tombs receive natural light from openings designed for the purpose. The presbytery – the space around and behind the altar – is by Pietro da Cortona.

In the Chapel of the Crucifix, to the left of the altar, are paintings by Giovanni Lanfranco, an influential early 17th-century artist (left: *Christ Falling under the Cross*; right: *Christ Praying in the Garden*).

In the church you may hear the sacristan mum-

S. Giovanni dei Fiorentini: pendentive by Lanfranco in the Chapel of the Crucifix

bling about indiscretions by dogs and cats around the pews. It is the only one in Rome that allows visitors to bring pets.

As you leave, on your right is the arrow-straight Via Giulia, an important renaissance thoroughfare we'll visit later in the Walk. Opposite the church is Via del Consolato, from the Florentine consulate that stood here when Florence was a foreign nation.

On the left side of Via del Consolato, at Nos 19 and 20, are three late 15th-century houses of the Florentine community. The two doors are later replacements for three exterior staircases. Opposite (No. 14) is another house in typical Florentine style, a few decades older. Return to Piazza Ponte S. Angelo.

END OF DETOUR

Go to the central street of the three, Via Banco S. Spirito ('Street of the Holy Spirit Bank'); but pause to look at the 15th-century palazzo on the right-hand corner, the Palazzo Bonadies (from the name of the local family who built it), recently rather arbitrarily restored. The ground floor includes remains of a medieval portico, three of whose columns frame a store (Nos 60-61) built in part with wonderful marble pieces from an ancient Roman cornice.

Take Via Banco S. Spirito. Before the first corner, to your left, is the pretty façade of **S. Celso**, one the oldest churches in Rome (5th century), but entirely rebuilt in the 18th century.

Occasionally open, it has an elegant interior. Over the altar is an impressive *Christ in Glory* by a youthful Pompeo Batoni (18th century); in the third chapel on the right is a 15th-century wooden *Crucifix*.

A few steps beyond the church and across the street from it is a low-arched passageway, Arco dei Banchi ('Arch of the Banks'). Such passageways were common in medieval Rome, but almost all have now vanished (p. 242). Step under it for a moment.

On the left-hand wall is the oldest surviving marble tablet marking a river flood, dated 1276 (see p. 140). A passerby carved his name in the marble in 1640. The faded starry ceiling is from the 18th or 19th century.

Back on the street, further ahead, see on the left and right (Nos 12 & 42) two austere 16th-century palaces. At the widening in front of you is the small Palazzo di Santo Spirito (No. 31), marking the beginning of the old financial district.

This elegant early 16th-century structure, with a façade by Antonio da Sangallo the Younger, resembles an ornate piece of furniture. It was initially the papal mint, where Benvenuto Cellini, the great Florentine goldsmith and sculptor, worked for a time, as did his and Michelangelo's friend Sebastiano Luciani. One of the boldest renaissance painters, Sebastiano became curator of the pope's great lead seal, a post Cellini coveted. In order to qualify Sebastiano had to become a priest; he was henceforth called Fra' Sebastiano del Piombo ('of the Lead').

In the early 1600's the mint moved elsewhere and the Hospital of the Holy Spirit (pp. 382-383) took over the building to use it for a new venture – a bank dedicated to helping the poor. The bank (Bank of the Holy Spirit, which gave the street its name) is still there, though recently renamed in a merger.

As you look at the façade, notice on your immediate left (No. 27) another 16th-century building. On its wall a rich tablet from the time of Pope Julius II – patron of Raphael and Michelangelo – extols Julius as restorer of the Church dominions (see p. 331) and builder of magnificent streets in the district (such as the Via Giulia, p. 470, named after him).

At the start of Via dei Banchi Nuovi ('of the New Banks', a street that was part of the Via Papalis, p. 412) No. 1 is a fine house which the architect Carlo Maderno built for himself in 1601. From here we can also see, in the distance, a clock tower by Borromini, which we'll look at more closely later.

Go one block down Via dei Banchi Nuovi. Take the narrow alley on the left, Vicolo della Campanella. A few yards further on, this winding alley turns sharply left, and takes you past picturesque little houses, enlivened by greenery and a charming street shrine. The next few yards are a jumble of houses too modest to have a clear style, though some date from the renaissance or earlier. Over No. 28 (left) is another, 18th-century street shrine. At No. 4 (left) is a renaissance doorway; across from it is a former 17th-century church, now a house. Go on past the church (we're now on Vicolo San Celso) and go left on Via di Panico to the next corner. Stop here to re-orientate yourself.

This is Piazza dei Coronari. In front of you, beyond the buildings in the piazza, is the river, with Piazza Ponte S. Angelo, where you began this Walk, slightly to the left. Take Via dei Coronari, which is on the right.

BEFORE GOING

2. Via dei Coronari and on to Piazza Navona

A few steps from Piazza di Ponte S. Angelo we reach the streets built or improved in the early middle ages to serve the area newly settled after the fall of the empire, then expanded in the renaissance. At the start of these Walks in Piazza del Popolo we saw the approach to this street system from the opposite end. You may remember Via Ripetta (p. 30), the westernmost street of the 'trident'. Some of the thoroughfares in this system, such as Via Ripetta, also served to lead pilgrims arriving from the north through the Porta del Popolo to St. Peter's and the Vatican. Seen from this end, the street system starts with Via dei Coronari, a long, straight street called Via Recta ('Straight Street') in ancient Rome. Once it ended directly, at a right angle, in the continuation of Via Ripetta, Via della Scrofa. Today the link is less direct because of post-1870 alterations.

Via dei Coronari means 'Street of the Rosary-makers', a reminder of the intense artisan and tourist-related activity in the area. We'll find dozens of other streets nearby named after the various artisans whose workshops filled these streets: Trunk-makers' Street, Crossbow-makers' Street, etc. Rosary-makers catered directly to the passing pilgrims, who then took their rosaries to be blessed by the pope during his general audiences, as is still done today. They also supplied the vendors who plied, then as now, the Vatican area.

Many great renaissance artists lived on or around Via dei Coronari. The tormented Michelangelo's first Roman home and studio were here. The carefree Raphael also lived nearby.

From the Porta del Popolo to the via dei Coronari

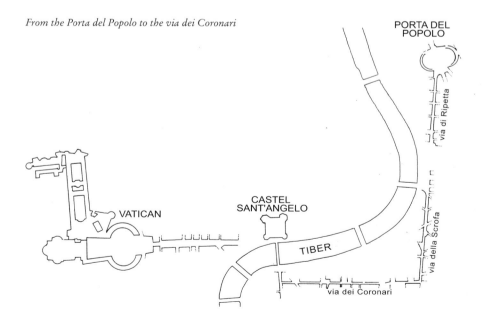

Leonardo da Vinci, the third member of that supreme trio, lodged in the Papal Palace (p. 320) and was often seen strolling, elegant, reserved and somewhat supercilious, through the district's crowded streets. Countless other renaissance figures lived here: Sebastiano del Piombo, Parmigianino, Raphael's great assistants Giulio Romano and Gianfrancesco Penni, as well as the rambunctious sculptor and goldsmith Benvenuto Cellini, when he was not imprisoned in the pope's castle across the river (p. 387).

All the buildings on the narrow streets of the area are old, many dating from the renaissance or earlier. Crumbling tenements, architectural jewels and grand palaces are all mixed together: Rome is one of the few great cities where rich and poor, humble artisans or shopkeepers and aristocrats, have always lived side by side. 'Here it is all palazzi and pigsties,' wrote a famous tourist, the French magistrate Charles de Brosses, in 1739 (pp. 74, 111, 463). This goes back to classical times, when the grandest of patricians, Julius Cæsar, lived in the poorest district, the Suburra, and when hovels and mansions shared the crowded space with splendid temples.

Lately things have begun to change. Rocketing real estate prices have attended the 'rediscovery' of old Rome by locals and foreigners; many who had left the district for more modern neighbour-hoods have returned. But rent control and strict laws against modifying ancient buildings have reined in the gentrification. The age-old picture of different classes rubbing shoulders lives on in the Tiber Bend. Some back streets are downright slummy. Artisans still abound, thanks in part to the restoration business generated by antique stores that have proliferated in the area since the Second World War. Former junk dealers turned antique sellers practically monopolise Via dei Coronari. The liveliness of the tradesmen and artisans carries echoes of the renaissance, when neighbourhood life rolled on in a climate of hard work and artistic enthusiasm.

Cellini's memoirs marvellously describe this area at the height of the renaissance. He had a house and shop in Via dei Banchi and was a regular at the artists' lively parties. He tells us of their dreams and miseries, their jealousies and generosities, their loves and sometimes deadly enmities. He reports the comings and goings of papal officials, and sometimes of the pope, who could not resist dropping by to see how a particular art work he had commissioned was coming along. Cellini describes Pope Paolo III, Giulia Bella's brother (p. 361), as a lover of food and drink, who had a regular vomiting hour to undo his excesses. He was one of those Sybaritic, neo-pagan popes not uncommon before the reformation, who nonetheless evoked the deepest religious awe in the faithful, including the most roguish, such as Cellini, and the most free-thinking. Right behind Via dei Coronari, between the street and the river, Cellini caught his girlfriend, the high-class courtesan Pantasilea, with his friend Luigi, a poet. He wounded both with his sword, while another friend, the painter Bachiacca, was so frightened that he had to relieve himself behind a bush.

Highlights of Via dei Coronari include a small late 15th-century house, the first of two thought to have belonged to Fiammetta Michaelis, known simply as Fiammetta, most famous of the great courtesans and mistress of Cesare Borgia (see p. 331). We'll see her second home in the nearby Piazza Fiammetta, a square so called since the 1600's, and one of the few public spaces in the world dedicated to a representative of the world's oldest profession. This home is far grander than the first and, though almost totally rebuilt, it is a delightful example of early renaissance architecture. The buildings reflect the sensational rise of Fiammetta from a poor young girl, who emigrated from Florence in search of better luck, to official lover of the pope's nephew, one of Italy's most powerful men.

We'll say more about Rome's high-class courtesans, many of whom lived in this area and were major figures of the period, in the second Renaissance Rome Walk when we visit S. Agostino, a nearby church that was a favourite with them.

Our Via dei Coronari neighbourhood visit ends with one of the few remaining *graffito* houses, a peculiar artistic expression of the Roman renaissance.

Starting with Raphael, many artists in the district adorned the outside of their homes and palaces either with fresco, or *graffito*, a technique in which the artist applied two layers of differently coloured plaster and scratched away the outer one to form a picture. Both frescoes and *graffiti* were made to last centuries, and did so, until the post-1870 modernisation frenzy. Then authorities cut the projecting roofs protecting the artwork, which soon disappeared under the double assault of the elements and pollution. The biggest losses are Raphael's own decorations and those of two of his followers famous for this type of art, Polidoro da Caravaggio (not to be confused with the great painter Michelangelo da Caravaggio) and Maturino da Firenze.

These decorations were considered a highly important artistic expression in their time, an integral part of the landscape of renaissance Rome. They conditioned the very architecture of a building, a fact we must remember when, for instance, we see an old building in the area with windows that seem too far apart. The blank space in-between probably contained a fresco or *graffito* work, perhaps depicting a mythological scene or at least a coat-of-arms.

Taddeo Zuccaro frescoing the Palazzo Mattei. Buxom angels bruit his fame,
while Michelangelo and Vasari admire his skill

ON THE SPOT

2. Via dei Coronari and on to Piazza Navona

At the beginning of Via dei Coronari, on the right (No. 123), is the so-called Casa di Raffaello ('House of Raphael'). The attribution is misleading, because Raphael never actually lived here, though he may have shared the ownership. But it is a delightful, authentic private 16th-century house with a charming design and decoration. The two upper floors are a later addition.

At the first corner on the right (Vicolo Domizio) is a street-level 16th-century street shrine, designed by Antonio da Sangallo the Younger. Sadly, the fresco is almost gone. Benvenuto Cellini probably lived in Vicolo Domizio for a while in 1530, in a house on the left. He writes in his memoirs that his house being on a hill, he was able to escape a sudden flood of the river that year. Continuing along Via dei Coronari, on the left (No. 148) is another private house of the 16th century. A few steps further on to the left (No. 157) is the first, and more modest, of the two reputed Case di Fiammetta, a rough mid-15th-century construction.

The street opens into a piazza named after the church dominating it, **San Salvatore in Lauro** ('The Holy Saviour in the Laurel'). The name indicates that a laurel thicket once grew here, possibly the bushes where Cellini surprised his unfaithful Pantasilea with her lover. The church is medieval, but was rebuilt in the late 16th century. The façade dates from 1862. (Open: 08:00-11:00 and 16:00-19:00.)

The bright interior is in the serene style of the great 16th-century Northern Italian architect, Palladio. Note the dramatic 18th-century altar by Antonio Asprucci and, in the third chapel to the right, the *Nativity* by Pietro da Cortona (17th-century). All other paintings are by minor 16th- and 17th-century artists.

In the refectory of the adjoining convent, sometimes accessible, is the *Marriage at Cana* by Francesco Salviati (16th century). On the walls are two monuments of the late 15th century: one to

Pope Eugene IV (see p. 362), from his tomb in old St. Peter's, by Isaia da Pisa, the other, attributed to Giovanni Dalmata, commemorating Maddalena Orsini (for the powerful Orsini family see p. 253).

At No. 15 of the piazza, to the left of the church, is its quiet cloister and a delightful adjoining courtyard with renaissance relief and stucco work.

Left of No. 15 notice the curious Fontana della Tana del Leone ('Fountain of the Lion's Den'), made in the 16th century by re-using an eroded medieval allegorical church lion like the one at S. Lorenzo in Lucina (p. 230).

Proceed along Via dei Coronari. Past an intersection to the right (Via della Vetrina) you reach a deep indentation, also on the right, with two interesting 16th-century palaces (Nos. 44-45).

A few steps further on, the street widens into the intimate Piazzetta San Simeone. On the right, at the corner of the intersecting Vicolo di Montevecchio ('of the Old Pawnbroker's') is a small building (No. 31), Rome's first official pawnbroker, founded by the pope in 1585 to help the poor (rebuilt in the 18th century). We'll see how this institution was later moved to much larger premises (p. 512). Across the street is another 16th-century building (No. 28).

Turn aside for a moment into Vicolo di Montevecchio. Where the vicolo skirts the typical, small Piazza Montevecchio, and just past it, are three charming 16th-century palaces (Nos 3, 4 & 6). Two of them (Nos 3 & 6) are by the architect and painter Baldassarre Peruzzi, a friend of Pinturicchio and Raphael.

Return to Via dei Coronari and Piazzetta San Simeone. The fountain in the piazza is by Rome's great 16th-century architect and fountain-maker Giacomo Della Porta. Dominating the square is the monumental doorway of the most important palace in the area, the late 16th-century **Palazzo Lancellotti** (No. 18) by Carlo Maderno and others.

The doorway was designed by the painter Domenichino, one of the giants of the 1600's. On the corners of the palace are street shrines, charming religious images in stucco added in the 1700's.

Leave Piazzetta San Simeone by Vicolo San Simeone, right of the restaurant. The short street ends in Via della Maschera d'Oro ('Street of the Golden Mask'). Stop at the corner. On the right is a typical renaissance house (No. 9) with *graffito* scenes on two sides drawn from the first panels of Trajan's Column (p. 186); they were restored in 2000. Past No. 9, on the other side of the street is the entrance (No. 21) to a 16th-century palace where Galileo Galilei was often a guest. Opposite (Nos 6, 7 & 8) is what was once one of the most important and best decorated of the neighbourhood's *graffito* houses; the decoration is almost gone now, but a mask in the middle of a garland, which gave the street its name, is still identifiable.

Continue down the street. Just before the first intersection (Vicolo S. Trifone), you'll see the second, much richer, of the two Houses of Fiammetta on the left (though, as with the first, identification is not certain). It is a charming 15th-century palazzetto, but restored to the point of falsification; indeed, not one element seems to have been left in its original state.

Walk around the house and return to Via della Maschera d'Oro.

A short side trip down Vicolo San Trifone will bring you to the medieval Via dei Tre Archi ('of the Three Arches') at the intersection with Rome's narrowest alley.

Return to Via della Maschera d'Oro and turn right into Piazza Fiammetta (more a wide street than a piazza), flanked right and left by renaissance palaces. The piazza leads to the post-1870 Via Zanardelli. In front of you is the Ristorante Passetto, one of the oldest, best and costliest in Rome. To the left is Palazzo Altemps (don't cross

over to it), built in the late 15th century but restyled a century later by the eminent late renaissance architect Martino Longhi the Elder.

This grand specimen of a Roman upper-class family home was originally built for a nephew of Pope Sixtus IV, Cardinal Girolamo Riario (p. 314). After he died a family of German descent, the Hohenems, whose Italian branch translated their name to Altemps, bought it. It is now a branch of the archæological museum (p. 682).

Go right along Via Zanardelli to the end of the block. Without crossing, look again across Via Zanardelli to the opposite corner for a building with a vertical row of single windows, No. 21a, with the Via Zanardelli street sign on it. It is the 14th-century Tor Sanguigna, a tower built by the feudal Sanguigni clan. It is hard to recognise now, embedded as it is in a block of buildings.

The Sanguigni died out in the 1700's. The tower is one of many that dotted medieval Rome, a reminder of a time when the city was divided into many armed camps, each with a warlord and a stronghold (p. 144). Indeed, there were so many towers that 140 were levelled in a single civil conflict. The windows of this tower and some architectural features are later additions, but the bulk is original. Notice near the top on both sides six marble rings that supported canopies – or weapons.

A famous courtesan, Antea, Rome's most beautiful and admired woman (according to Cellini), lived near the tower. (There is a portrait by Parmigianino in Naples' Capodimonte Museum that supports Cellini's opinion, but the identification is alas uncertain.)

Cross over to a modern building with a portico of seven rectangular openings.

3. Piazza Navona (formerly the Stadium of Domitian)

Piazza Navona is properly mentioned in the context of the renaissance: it was a vibrant urban centre then and has several renaissance buildings. But this extraordinary space transcends that or any other era, historically, stylistically and spiritually.

The mood. Considered the most beautiful in Rome, the piazza is, above all, a state of mind. If Piazza di Spagna evokes the word 'elegance', then Piazza Navona brings the word 'joy' to mind. Belli, Rome's great vernacular poet, wrote in the early 1800's:

Piazza Navona! It couldn't care less	Se pò ffregà piazza Navona mia
About Piazza di Spagna or St. Peter's.	E de San Pietro e dde piazza de Spaggna.
It's not a square. It's the great outdoors,	Cuesta nun è una piazza, è una campaggna,
A party, a stage, a hell of a good time.	Un treàto, una fiera, un'allegria.

Piazza Navona must be the only public area in the world that for 1,900 years, through too many regimes and catastrophes to count, has always been devoted to fun, with one exception, as we'll see.

Domitian gave the Roman people this area in 90 AD as a stadium (with a capacity of 30,088) dedicated to athletics. In the middle ages this building collapsed, but the games continued, so that the place was renamed *campus agonis*, the 'competition field'. The shape of the piazza still follows the outline of the original arena. Some of the stadium structures are visible, embedded in a modern building. By a curious word corruption, 'agonis' became 'navona', which means 'big ship' in Italian. The change was probably aided by the fact that the square does resemble a ship.

From the beginning, the masses came to watch sports and enjoy the inns, eateries and brothels that sprouted up around all ancient arenas (see p. 266). The brothels usually occupied the vaults, or *fornices*, supporting the arena structure, and this association is so old that the word ' fornication' derives from it.

A tragic exception to the merrymaking occurred sometime during the empire. According to tradition (though the more sensational details are likely to be embellishments), a young girl was burnt alive here for being a Christian.

To further humiliate her, the execution took place in a brothel, directly facing the arena, and she was stripped naked. But miraculously her long braids came undone, covering her body. An even greater miracle followed, when the flames of the pyre parted around her. Finally a soldier dispatched her with a sword. A devotional book of the romantic era relates that her last words were this prayer:

> It is to Thee that I appeal, to Thee the all-powerful, adorable, perfect, terrible God. I come to Thee, O my Father, to Thee Whom I have loved, to Thee Whom I have sought, and Whom I have always chosen.

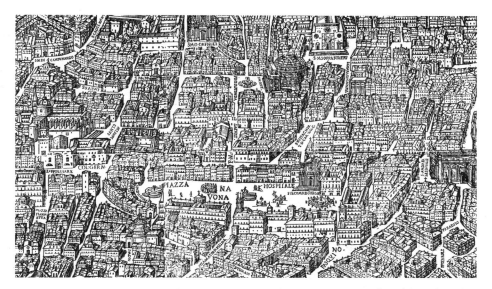

Piazza Navona in 1625, from the map by Maggi

The young martyr's name is unknown, but on account of her sweetness she acquired the name Agnes, from the Latin *agnus* or 'lamb'.

St. Agnes is especially dear to English-speaking peoples because of a belief, widespread amongst English girls for centuries and recalled in a poem by Keats, that if they fasted and drank only spring water on the Eve of St. Agnes, they would see their future husband in a dream that night.

During the dark ages sports and festivities took place in the square alongside the athletic competitions. One such event was the climbing of a tall greased pole, the Albero della Cuccagna ('Cockaigne Tree'), crowned by sausages and other goodies donated by the rich as a prize for the first person to reach the top. A nearby alley is still called Via della Cuccagna. During the age of chivalry, jousts and tournaments took place in the square, which was hung with cloths of gold and silver. The renaissance witnessed other sports, including bullfights, of which Cesare Borgia (p. 330) was occasionally an expert impresario.

The odd thing is that there is no real link between these different, successive forms of entertainment. No specific structure housed them; no fixed city agency planned them. It is as though the square itself, always a favourite with Romans, catalysed the fun.

Over the next centuries the square saw pageants and colourful parades to honour visiting notables. Chroniclers tell us of a 1634 horse show in which Roman princesses awarded diamonds to competing aristocrats. In the mid-17th century there was a new diversion: since the square had developed a concave bottom and had three fountains, someone plugged the drains and let the water overflow to form a lake. The prank was a huge success. For another 200 years, every Saturday and

Overleaf: Flooding of Piazza Navona in the 18th century; engraving by Giuseppe Vasi

Sunday in August the square was flooded and crowds gambolled in the water, a custom which contributed to a misunderstanding about the name of Navona having something to do with ships or naval battles. Everyone joined in, young and old, poor and rich alike. Nobles and high prelates splashed about in fancy carriages. The ordinary people horsed around. Many paintings and prints of the period capture these scenes of jollity

All this ended when papal authorities restored and levelled the paving in the mid-1800's . But the festive mood persisted. No place was deemed more suitable than Piazza Navona for fairs, promenades, serenades and the famous puppet shows. Every January 6, on the feast of the Epiphany (the Greek word for 'apparition', referring to the star that guided the Three Kings to the infant Jesus), the square becomes a children's paradise. Roman lore has corrupted the mysterious word Epiphany into 'Befana', a word that has come to denote a little old lady who, like Santa Claus, brings good children gifts. The night before, stalls sprout in the piazza selling inexpensive toys and candies for parents to buy their little ones, in a bright, poetic atmosphere. Clay figurines used in traditional nativity scenes (old ones are now rare antiques) are also sold in the piazza a few weeks earlier.

Today the square is reserved for pedestrians and remains a scene of tranquil amusement and relaxation. Peddlers peddle, painters paint portraits, musicians perform, and people look on and enjoy the famous ice cream of the neighbourhood – a sublimely rich chocolate concoction called *tartufo* ('truffle') – at the sidewalk cafés or sitting, more economically, on the stone benches of the square.

The backdrop. Of course, the pleasures of watching life in the square would not be the same without the marvellous setting.

The renaissance character of the area is recalled by one of the highlights of the piazza, the graceful church of Nostra Signora del Sacro Cuore ('Our Lady of the Sacred Heart'). But the quintessence of the square is baroque and bears the imprint of the two great masters and bitter rivals, Bernini and Borromini, who were forced in this case, as usual, to work within a stone's throw of each other. The splendid church of S. Agnese, Borromini's creation, a fantastic fountain in front of it by Bernini, as well as other fountains and buildings all around contribute to the baroque character.

The Barberini Pope Urban VIII, one of Bernini's great patrons (see p. 83) died in 1644, leaving a string of major monuments to pay tribute to himself and his princely family, including the *baldacchino* in St. Peter's (p. 368) and the grand Palazzo Barberini (pp. 83-84). The new Pope, Innocent X, from another great Roman family, the Pamphili, wanted to leave no less a mark. He promptly began another series of public works, centred on the square of his birthplace and his family home, Piazza Navona.

Pope Innocent did not share the admiration of his predecessor for the great Bernini, whom in fact he rather disliked. He recruited other architects. His first project, rebuilding his family home on the square, was entrusted to Girolamo Rainaldi, a good but not great architect, who transformed it into a palatial residence. His second undertaking was to rebuild, next door to the palace, an ancient church dedicated to St. Agnes. A floor with remains of Roman mosaics had been dug up there, possibly the brothel where the girl was said to have been martyred, perhaps the very floor where she had knelt down, wearing only her unbraided locks, as the screams of the stadium crowd wafted in through the open doors. The pope assigned the church project to Girolamo Rainaldi and his son Carlo, but soon afterwards switched to Borromini. His usual morose self, the great architect could not finish the job without quarrelling with his employer and quitting the job midway. His genius is evident, however, in the solemn yet spirited façade.

This church in Rome's most popular square became very popular itself during the following centuries, drawing picturesque crowds that further added to the colourfulness of the scene. One 19th-century English traveller, the art historian Anna Jameson, wrote:

> Often have I seen the steps of this church, and the church itself, so crowded with kneeling worshippers that I could not make my way among them; principally the women of the lower orders, with their distaffs and market baskets, who had come thither to pray, through the intercession of the patron saint, for the gifts of meekness and chastity – gifts not abounding in these regions.

As his third project, Pope Innocent gave the space before the church a monumental fountain bearing yet another of the ancient obelisks that had resurfaced. Artists were invited to submit ideas.

Bernini, who had been biding his time, saw his chance. He knew the pope's bias against him, and so he devised a ruse. It was well known that the pope, a weak, tepid character, was dominated by his sister-in-law, Donna Olimpia, for whom he had a morbid passion. An English biographer describes her as so powerful that during her short absences, she locked the pope into his chambers. No papal appointment was made without her consent, and then only 'in consideration of a proportionable sum paid down into her own coffers.'

Bernini addressed himself to this virago, rather than to the official commission in charge of judging the bids made by artists. He sent her a silver cast of his project as a gift. The woman, bribed and flattered by the attention of the great artist, got him the commission. The pope himself was won over, and henceforth Bernini was once again Rome's principal architect. 'It's better not to see Bernini's models,' Innocent said in later years. 'Once you have seen them, you cannot resist having them built.'

The pope did not err on this one: Bernini's Fontana dei Quattro Fiumi ('Fountain of the Four Rivers') is one of the most fantastic baroque creations, and confirms art historian Richard Norton's judgment: 'No one ever understood the artistic value of water as Bernini did.'

A story concerning the rivalry between Bernini and Borromini, apocryphal but too famous not to be told, is associated with the fountain. For centuries the gestures of two of the statues personifying the great rivers of the world have been interpreted as Bernini's way of mocking Borromini's nearby church of S. Agnese. One figure raises his hand as if to shield himself from the imminent collapse of the façade; the other covers his head and turns away in horror. Historians reject this story, pointing out that when Bernini designed the fountain, Borromini had not even started on the church.

ON THE SPOT

3. Piazza Navona (formerly the Stadium of Domitian)

Behind the seven rectangular openings of the portico of the modern building we are now facing, can be seen some ancient ruins; even more striking ones come into view if we move left, to a larger opening. These are all remains of the Stadium of Domitian, which covered the space of the present Piazza Navona, which lies on the other side of this building. The ruins emerged when it was put up, in 1937, and they caused a sensation, since for many centuries the stadium had survived only as a memory and in the outline of the piazza. As usual, the ruins are well below street level (see p. 140).

Before leaving, look back to your far right. Over No. 2 you can see one of the most elaborate of the many Madonnelle, or street shrines, adorning old buildings in Rome.

Left of the ruins, go to the end of the block, to the short Via Agonale, named after the old *campus agonis*, leading to Piazza Navona. Before taking it, from this corner look at the 18th-century façade of the church visible from here, **S. Apollinare**, and at the adjacent brick **Palazzo S. Apollinare**, both elegant works by Ferdinando Fuga. The top floor of the palace is a later addition.

Take Via Agonale to **Piazza Navona**. After absorbing the initial visual impact of the square – its shape follows that of the ancient stadium – go right, to the front entrance of the building we observed from behind (No. 49). If it's open (office hours) go in to see the ancient ruins close up.

At No. 45 of the square, in a courtyard which at the time of writing is part of a café-restaurant (see if they'll open it for you) is a fine and completely unexpected 16th-century palazzetto.

A parade of ochre-coloured buildings surrounds the square – simple houses, noble palaces and two churches – spanning about 250 years, from the late 16th to the early 19th century.

The square has three fountains. The one in the centre has an obelisk. The two smaller ones at either end are twin creations by Giacomo Della Porta (16th century). The nearer one is the Fountain of Neptune, with statues of conventional marine subjects added in the 19th century. We'll describe those on the other Della Porta fountain later. Neither these, nor perhaps any others in the world, could compete with the the central **Fontana dei Quattro Fiumi**, crowning the square with a bold granite needle. This is the masterpiece of Gian Lorenzo Bernini.

People, animals and plants gather around the base of this wonderfully vivid creation. Four human figures, symbolising the great rivers of the four known continents of the period, sit on a jumble of rocks and caves from which exotic animals emerge to drink. Some of the carving is by Bernini, but most is by his pupils based on his designs. Yet the whole group has a superlative coherence and immediacy. Particularly striking is a lion emerging from its den under a wind-swept palm, followed by a freely rendered armadillo, which looks more like a creature from science-fiction.

The two statues thought to be scoffing at Borromini's church in front of the fountain (p. 457) are the Rio de la Plata and the Nile. The first – oddly represented by a black man rather than a native South American – extends his arm toward the church. The second turns his veiled head away. The veil refers to the fact that the source of the Nile was still unknown at the time.

The Egyptian obelisk was found on the Appian Way near the Circus of Maxentius, which it decorated (p. 619). Originally it had been brought to Rome by the emperor Domitian, and had graced the courtyard of the Temple of Isis (p. 114).

Facing the fountain is the façade of **S. Agnese in Agone**, dating from the middle ages but entirely rebuilt in the 1600's. (The name is another reference to the *campus agonis*, and distinguishes the church from a more ancient one dedicated to St. Agnes in another part of the city, p. 607). The church, started by the Rainaldi father and son team, but continued with radical changes (especially on the exterior) by Francesco Borromini,

Bernini's statue for the Fontana del Moro in the Piazza Navona

S. Agnese in Agone

further exemplifies that blend of playfulness and restraint typical of his architecture, and of his 'musicality in stone' achieved through the interplay of concave and convex surfaces. Note also the lone, noble statue of St. Agnes silhouetted against the sky, of uncertain authorship. The church is generally open in the afternoon on weekdays and in the morning on Sundays, but it is usually closed in August.

Mysterious shadows fill the ornate interior. The frescoes in the dome and pendentives are from the late 1600's; especially notable are the *Cardinal Virtues* in the pendentives by Baciccio (you may remember his famous ceiling in the Gesù, p. 112).

Instead of pictures, marble reliefs and statues by minor 17th-century sculptors grace the altars. Over the entrance is a monument to Pope Innocent X (p. 456), who is buried, together with other members of the Pamphili family, in a crypt to the left of the main altar.

Most notable, but rarely open (ask in the sacristy), are underground rooms with remains of an ancient mosaic floor and structures belong-

ing either to the stadium or related buildings – possibly the brothel, but at any rate the place where Agnes is said to have been martyred. A recent tablet in Latin speaks of 'this place of turpitude'. On an altar is the statue of the *Miracle of Agnes' Hair*, the last work by Bernini's talented contemporary, Alessandro Algardi.

Left of the church, as you face it, is the mid-17th century Palazzo Pamphili, Pope Innocent's ancestral home. Its remodelling for the Pope is the dignified but somewhat uninspiring work of Girolamo Rainaldi, father of the better known Carlo Rainaldi, who created the twin churches in Piazza del Popolo and other important works. The palazzo is now the Brazilian Embassy. From here you can observe the other features of the square, especially the second of the two Della Porta fountains, the **Fontana del Moro** ('Fountain of the Moor').

The statues, again, are later additions. The central one, a Moor battling a dolphin, was made in the mid-17th century from a spirited design by Bernini. Tradition claims the face portrays the ambassador of the Kingdom of the Congo, Ne Vunda (p. 98). The other statues are copies of originals by minor late renaissance artists.

On the other side of the fountain from Palazzo Pamphili is the late 15th-century church of **Nostra Signora del Sacro Cuore**, a mid 15th-century church with a simple facade, the entire upper part of which was redesigned in the 19th century. The original, finely worked central doorway is adorned with two angels signed 'Opus Mini' (Mino del Reame; left) and 'Opus Pauli' (possibly Paolo Romano; right).

The church is open 07:00-09:00 and 17:00-19:00. The interior is notable for its unusual hall church design (marred however by 19th-century mutilations) and some late 15th-/early 16th-century features: the multi-coloured marble choir by 'Magister Petrus' of Florence, the elaborate marble backdrop of the main altar and the beautiful Chapel of St. James by Antonio da Sangallo, with a copy of Jacopo Sansovino's statue of the saint. (St. James of Compostela is the patron saint of Spain, and for centuries this building, under the name of S. Giacomo degli Spagnuoli, was the Spanish national church in Rome. After the Spanish revolution of 1868 it was sold to French missionaries, who gave it the name of their order. Most of the statues and paintings in this church were moved to the present Spanish national church of S. Maria di Monserrato.)

Two palaces bound the short side of the square at this end. On the right is the 18th-century Palazzo Braschi, which we'll see better on the other side (p. 506); on the left is the mid 16th-century Palazzo Lancellotti, built for another branch of the family who owned the palace we saw earlier in this walk (p. 450), by the Neapolitan architect Pirro Ligorio.

DETOUR
5 MIN

Turn right around the corner of Palazzo Pamphili into Via di Pasquino. At the end of the block, on the left, is the ruin of a famous statue long nick-named 'Mastro Pasquino', from the name of a local hunchbacked taylor famous for his wit, who was presumably the first to use it as a support for his lampoons, as explained below. Actually, the statue is what remains of a Roman copy of a 3rd century BC Hellenistic sculpture depicting Menelaus supporting the body of Patroclus, a popular subject from Homer's *Iliad*. Artists, especially Michelangelo, much admired it for its powerful modelling (it was less eroded then).

The statue was found in 1500 and bought by a cardinal, who placed it here on the corner of his palace. People immediately adopted it as a sort of poster-board for dissent and it became the custom for locals to stick ferocious satires against the papacy on it. The tradition lasted through to the end of the papal dominion in 1870.

One example of what is called a 'pasquinata' was a famous attack on the Barberini Pope Urban VIII for pillaging the bronze cladding of the Pantheon dome: *Quod non fecerunt Barbari, fecerunt Barberini*; 'What the barbarians didn't do, the Barberini did.' (p. 237). Another pasquinade was directed against Pope Pius VII (see p. 209), restorer of the Colosseum and sometime victim of Napoleon, widely suspected of financial misappropriations: 'Seventh, thou shalt not steal,' intoned the biblical commandment stuck on Pasquino's breast – the addressee being, clearly, the 'Seventh' Pius. It is only fair to add that this strict pope must not have been terribly popular amongst certain groups: remember his ban of the Pantheon vendors, p. 224. Pasquino was the first of many 'statue parlanti' ('talking statues') that soon dotted Rome (pp. 127, 511, 533).

END OF DETOUR

Return to the front of Palazzo Pamphili. Retrace your steps on this side of Piazza Navona to the first intersection, Via S. Agnese in Agone. Across the street is the imposing **Palazzo de Cupis**, built around 1500, named after the original owners. An example of a grand early renaissance Roman residence, the façade was probably originally frescoed.

4. From Piazza Navona to the Chiesa Nuova

In the winding streets behind Piazza Navona we'll visit two fascinating, almost contiguous churches: S. Maria della Pace ('St. Mary of Peace') and S. Maria dell'Anima ('St. Mary of the Soul'). The first, along with the little square where it stands, strikingly exemplifies the careful urban planning of Alexander VII, the builder pope who kept a wooden model of Rome in his bedroom (p. 44). Nowhere is his love for the beauty and order of his city clearer. The church has frescoes by Raphael, which were particularly admired by Goethe, who visited them almost daily. Also famous is its cloister, the first project by Bramante in Rome; after coming to the city from the north he had declined commissions for three years to devote himself to studying Roman ruins.

The second church, S. Maria dell'Anima, is another of the many national churches we see in these Renaissance Walks, built by foreign communities in the area. It was built in the middle ages by the German community – which then included the Dutch and Flemish – along with a hospice for German pilgrims. It contains the remains of and monument to a Flemish pope, Adrian VI Florensz., who tried in vain to prise the Roman Church away from the luxury and neo-paganism of the heyday of the renaissance. He fired the great artists and philosophers of the papal court and stopped work on the sumptuous new religious buildings saying, 'We need more priests for the churches, not more churches for the priests.' His campaign ended when he died after one year's reign. Had he lived longer, history might have been different: art would have suffered, but the Reformation might have been pre-empted. Ironically, the monument built to Adrian in this church by his successor, the patron of Cellini and Michelangelo, Clement VII, has some of the very neo-pagan symbols he detested, such as a river god. At his death the artistic community felt freed of a nightmare. A group of revellers one night hung a garland on the door of the home of the doctor who had treated him with his nostrums, inscribed in Latin: 'To the liberator of the land'. Adrian was the last non-Italian pope until John Paul II Wojtiła in 1978.

Moving away from Piazza Navona, through colourful winding streets, our Walk leads us past several large and small renaissance buildings, including one where Raphael's great romantic love, 'La Fornarina' (p. 237), lived for a time. We'll also pass the little church of S. Tommaso in Parione (St. Thomas in Parione), which became a national church recently under the management of gentle old Ethiopian priests of the Alexandrine rite (similar to the Coptic). It is a religious centre and meeting house for a colony of refugees from Ethiopia and Eritrea who settled in Rome after the Second World War.

Though this part of the Renaissance Walks does not cross any ancestral Jewish neighbourhood – which is at end of the Walks, in the Ghetto and Trastevere – here you'll begin to get impressions of Rome's Jewish life in times gone by. We'll see the luxurious palace built by the last descendant of an important Jewish family, the Corcos, in the late 1500's, who converted to Christianity and thus escaped life in the Ghetto that the fiercely anti-semitic Pope Paul IV had established (p. 116).

We'll then reach a corner where, from the middle ages until the Counter-Reformation, a strange ritual was held, defining the relation between the Jews and the Catholic Church. It took place at the approach to a street called Via del Governo Vecchio ('of the Old Government'). The street lay along the Papal Way, traditional route of the most important papal procession, the one made by every newly elected pope to take possession symbolically of the papacy's old seat in the Lateran (see p. 412). Before entering Via del Governo Vecchio, the cortege passed a famous old fortress-palace on a hillock. This hillock was called Monte Giordano ('Mount Jordan') after Giordano Orsini, the head of a baronial clan in the 14th century, whose stronghold was here. The origin of the name was forgotten in time, and people came to think that the area had a mystical link with the biblical River Jordan. So, starting in the late renaissance, the ritual involving the Jews was held here after the election of each pope.

When the Lateran-bound pope arrived here, the Jewish elders, veiled, would kneel and present him with a gold-bound copy of the Torah. Then the chief rabbi would say in Hebrew: 'Your Holiness, we Jews beseech you, in the name of our Synagogue, to assure us that the Laws of Moses given by the Almighty God on Mount Sinai will be confirmed and approved by the Christian Church.' The pope would reply in Latin: 'We confirm the Laws, yet we condemn your faith, because He Who you say is still to come, the Lord Jesus, has in fact come already, as our Church teaches and preaches.' A papal purser would then present a gift of money to the Jews.

The street also includes a renaissance house where Pope Pius XII, accused by some of not having opposed strongly enough the Nazi persecution of the Jews (see p. 366), was born.

Further on, we'll see the headquarters of St. Philip Neri, an attractive Counter-Reformation character, totally unlike the pugnacious St. Ignatius or the inflexible Dominican friars (p. 115). Romans of the time called him 'Pippo buono' ('good Phil'). In the late 16th century he founded an organisation with the help of young Roman nobles devoted mainly to spreading literacy, education and Catholic doctrine. Many of its affluent young members, the 'Filippini', wore rags, a bit in the vein of the hippie communes of the 1960's, and as in those communes humour and music filled their unconventional lives. They prized group prayer; hence their building was called the 'Oratorio dei Filippini' (the word 'oratorium' – 'prayer hall' – has also come down to us in a different sense, as a musical term, because the music-loving Filippini organised concerts there). 'Get there well in time,' recommended Charles de Brosses, the 18th-century French magistrate (p. 448), to his friends, 'for everything here deserves your atten-

St. Philip Neri

tion: the audience, the voices, the music, the place, the church, the chapel, the paintings, the stuccoes, the statues – all is brilliant, agreeable and in good taste.'

As an educator, St. Philip foreshadowed Dr Spock, the American pædiatrician who fathered the 'permissive' generation. 'Behave if you can, but if you can't, never mind,' Philip is said to have admonished unruly pupils.

The seat of St. Philip's oratory and educational crusade was, and is, a wonderful building by Borromini, attached to a church popularly called the Chiesa Nuova ('New Church'), which Philip also founded. Both buildings contain artistic masterpieces.

ON THE SPOT

4. From Piazza Navona to the Chiesa Nuova

Take Via S. Agnese in Agone to the first crossing. Here is another of Rome's medieval towers (see p. 188), the 15th-century Tor Millina, erected by the feudal Millini (or Mellini) family, whose name is in proud brass letters high up. Continue straight into the street, Via Tor Millina, and notice on the left (No. 25) a small renaissance palazzetto decorated with *graffiti* (p. 449).

Turn right at the end of the block. Before you is **S. Maria della Pace**, built shortly after the end of one of the chronic conflicts between Italian states in 1484 (hence the name). It substantially modified in the mid-1600's on the orders of Alexander VII, when the graceful convex façade and unusual protruding porch were added by the great architect and painter Pietro da Cortona, in a careful plan to make of this church, the streets to either side, and the little square before it an elegant and unified backdrop to the lively street scene.

It is a baroque jewel, best appreciated by viewing it from different points, both while approaching and leaving.

The little square before the church is one of the earliest protected landmarks on record. A marble tablet placed on the wall in 1656 by papal order – at No. 13, left of the church – forbids any alterations, such as new buildings or additions.

The simple, original 15th-century door of the front entrance of the church is locked. To enter, you circle to the left, under the arch, and into a street called Via Arco della Pace. At No. 10 is a small medieval house that still has stone rings on the front which once held wooden poles used to hang out laundry. Opposite (No. 5) is the side entrance to the cloister and church of S. Maria della Pace. (Open erratically, though the posted hours are 10:00-13:00 and 15:00-17:00; Sat, mornings only; Thurs and Sun closed.)

We first enter the late 15th-century cloister, Bramante's classical and serene creation – the result of his long study of ancient Roman architec-

S. Maria della Pace in the 18th century, engraving by Giuseppe Vasi

ture, here reinterpreted through a feeling of quiet religiosity. Pass into the church from a side door.

The interior, as we mentioned, dates to the late 1400's. It is a curious coupling of two halls, one octagonal and domed, the other rectangular. All the major pictorial decoration mentioned here was carried out at the beginning of the 1500's. In the octagon under the cornice are four large paintings. The most notable is the *Presentation in the Temple* (third from left) by Baldassarre Peruzzi, a friend of Raphael. Going down the rectangular hall, the last chapel to the right has a tender *Virgin and Saints* frescoed over the altar by Peruzzi, who also executed the small biblical vignettes on the walls. Outside the chapel, on the right, is a tomb with charming reliefs of two little sisters who fell to the plague in 1505.

Over the opposite chapel are the famous *Four Sibyls* by Raphael beneath the *Four Prophets* also designed by him but probably executed by assistants. Painted after the master had sneaked into Michelangelo's Sistine Chapel (see p. 332), these frescoes, of wonderful plasticity, lighting and composition, show the lessons Raphael drew from the work of his great colleague. Next, on the same side, is an elaborate, unusual 16th-century chapel with a marble arch of striking richness outside.

When you leave, return to the little square before the church and cross over to the left to No. 20. Here enter the hospice and church of **S. Maria dell' Anima** (open 07.30-19:00; Sun 08:00-13:00 and 14:00-19:00).

The complex comprises this building, erected in 1378 as a German and Dutch pilgrims' hospice, and an adjoining church reachable through the building, added in 1510 with the financial help of Johannes Burchard, a German courtier of Alexander VI Borgia (p. 329). German priests still own and manage the church and hospice, currently a study centre.

Cross the charming, secluded hospice courtyard and enter the church from the side. The interior is architecturally interesting. The unknown, possibly German architect used the late gothic hall church design – typical of Germany but rare in Rome – in

S. Maria della Pace: detail of Raphael's frescoes in the Chigi chapel

which nave, aisles and chapels are all the same height.

All the decoration by Italian artists mentioned here dates from the first half of the 1500's. As you enter, the first chapel on the right is frescoed by a distinguished follower of Raphael, the independent-minded, stylish Francesco Salviati. The opposite chapel contains a poignant reinterpretation of Michelangelo's *Pietà* by two of his contemporaries, Lorenzetto and Nanni di Baccio Bigio. Inside the deep presbytery the main altar is surmounted by a beautiful *Holy Family* by Raphael's assistant Giulio Romano. On the right wall is the monument to the unhappy Flemish pope, the would-be reformer Adrian VI, designed by Baldassarre Peruzzi. Most of the other statues and paintings around the church are by minor German and Flemish artists.

Leaving the way you came in, turn right into

Vicolo della Pace, a picturesque alley between the two Marian churches. To the left is the main, late 15th-century part of S. Maria della Pace, which predates Pietro da Cortona's façade by about 170 years. To the right is S. Maria dell'Anima. Circling it all the way to the right you reach the beautiful, austere early 16th-century façade. The front entrance is always closed. A relief by Andrea Sansovino of the *Virgin between Two Praying Souls* – which gave the church its name – adorns the middle door. From the corner, diagonally opposite, see the bell tower, topped by coloured tiles and unique in Rome for its German style.

On the same corner is the small **S. Nicola dei Lorenesi** ('of the Lorrainers'), built in 1636, the national church of Lorraine, now part of France.

Rarely open, the warm interior is rich in stuccos, frescoes, reliefs and paintings by minor 17th-century artists.

Leaving this little church, go left. At No. 65, just past the façade of S. Maria dell'Anima is the **Casa di Giovanni Sander**, with *graffito* work from the renaissance (p. 449) but over-restored in the 1800's. It was the house of Johannes Sander, a 16th-century German lawyer of the papal tribunal, who together with Burchard helped fund the German church.

Retrace your steps to the little square before S. Maria della Pace. Take the wide Via della Pace. On the left (No. 21) and right (No. 8) are imposing 17th-century palaces. At the end of the block proceed straight into Via di Parione. Left, at No. 7, is the so-called Casa di Sisto V ('House of Sixtus V'), built by the 16th-century pontiff, not for himself but for his great-niece (see p. 44). Look for the stuccos and frescoes by minor renaissance artists in the picturesque courtyard and high up on a façade beyond.

Leaving the building, turn around for a last look at the setting of S. Maria della Pace from this angle. Then, directly from No. 7, glance down a street branching off here, Via della Fossa. Without entering it, you will notice, 60 yards down on the left, a building covered with renaissance *graffito* work imitating stonework.

Resume your walk down Via di Parione. Past an assortment of late 16th-century and early 17th-century palaces (No. 12 and 17 on the left, No. 37 on the right – the latter with a 15th-century doorway) is the little 16th-century church of **S. Tommaso in Parione**.

You may be lucky enough to find it open. If so, step inside to see the present-day Coptic-style decorations added by the Ethiopian priests who officiate here. On Thursday and Sunday afternoons and evenings, the priests sing accompanied by drums and the sistrum, an instrument of Egyptian origin belonging to the immemorially old Egyptian ritual. A Gregorian-like chant mixed with echoes of African tribal song rises in an incense-laden atmosphere.

The street ends at Via del Governo Vecchio. Turn left for a few yards to see another group of early buildings. At the far right-hand corner of the first crossing is a simple 15th-century house; just past it (No. 104) is another, though this time largely rebuilt and redecorated in the 18th century, with *graffito* work, frescoes and medallion portraits of famous jurists. Across the street (No. 62) is a 17th-century palace.

Backtrack past the Via di Parione crossing. Go straight on until you see on your right, at No. 48, the 15th-century doorway of a palace remodelled in the 19th century. An inscription in the entrance hall recalls the sojourn here of Raphael's girlfriend 'La Fornarina' (p. 237). Further along on the same side (No. 39) is the partly 15th-century palace where the papal governor of Rome worked, hence the name of the street, 'of the old government'. Opposite (No. 123) is an early 16th-century palazzetto.

Pass two more renaissance buildings on the right, No. 14, 16th- century, and No. 13, 15th-century. On the right before the piazza (No. 3) is the late 16th-century palace built by the member of the Jewish Corcos family who converted to Christianity.

You now reach the colourful Piazza dell' Orologio ('of the Clock'), under the spirited 17th-century clock tower by Borromini, of which we

The façade of the Oratory (left) and the Chiesa Nuova

had a glimpse earlier (p. 446). The mosaic beneath the clock face was designed by Pietro da Cortona. The structure crowns the back of Borromini's Oratorio dei Filippini, which we'll see shortly.

Take the short street next to Palazzo Corcos, Via degli Orsini. Left, at No. 34, is the palace where Pope Pius XII, who came from a wealthy family, grew up. The street ends in view of the entrance to the rambling Palazzo di Monte Giordano complex, in the area where Jewish elders used to await the pope's passage to renew their pact with him (this sometimes happened near the Castel Sant' Angelo instead).

Some archæologists think that the hillock, a landmark since the early middle ages and mentioned by Dante in his *Divine Comedy* (see p. 442), is formed by the ruins of an ancient Roman amphitheatre built by Augustus' general Statilius Taurus on the orders of the princeps (see p. 245).

Now subdivided into homes, the palace is closed to the public, but through the impressive entrance you can see the sprawling courtyard with an unusual 17th-century fountain.

Around the right-hand corner from the entrance, above No. 37 in Via Monte Giordano, is a comparatively rare late renaissance street shrine with a *Madonna and Child*.

Retrace your steps to Piazza dell'Orologio, pass under Borromini's clock and proceed into Via dei Filippini (the Filippini were the followers of St. Philip Neri). The street leads into a piazza, actually part of the modern Corso Vittorio Emanuele. Here, around the corner to the left, are the adjacent façades of the **Oratorio dei Filippini** and **Chiesa Nuova**. When building the *oratorio*, Borromini said he was inspired by imagining 'the human

The Oratory: the façade (above) and opposite, one of the fireplaces designed by Borromini

body, opening its arms to embrace all who enter.' In its façade (left of the church) he has indeed blended warmth, refinement and monumentality to a degree rarely equalled in the history of architecture. Characteristically, he has done so with unpretentious materials, stucco and finely cut brickwork.

The interior, with its marvellous courtyards, fountains and halls, is based on Borromini's drawings; it is generally closed to the public, but one can occasionally gain admission from the doorman at No. 18. The oratorium room is on the ground floor, second door to the left in the lobby.

The adjoining church, traditionally dubbed the Chiesa Nuova ('New Church'), is not by Borromini but by two comparatively minor architects, Martino Longhi the Elder (the plan) and Fausto Rughesi (the façade), and is an example of the transition in the late 16th century from late renaissance to baroque design. The church, as the adjective 'nuova' implies, is the reconstruction of a much older building. Its official, and ancient, name is Santa Maria in Vallicella ('in the Little Valley'), a reminder of the original garden-like character of the area (p. 239). (Open: mornings, 08:00-12:00; evenings, May to Sept 17:00-19:30 and Oct to April, 16:30-19:00.)

The church has an extremely rich interior and one of the world's most beautiful organs (18th century). The ceiling has a luminous, magnificent fresco by Pietro da Cortona, *A Vision of St. Philip during the Building of the Church*. (Unless otherwise noted, all the frescoes and oil paintings mentioned here are from the first half of the 1600's.) More of Cortona's frescoes are in the dome and apse vault. Over and around the main altar are three large paintings on slate by Peter Paul Rubens, very early examples of the intensely colourful style of the great Flemish painter; most famous are the *Three Saints* on the right.

Left of the main altar, in a richly adorned chapel (the paintings are by minor artists; the picture over the altar is a mosaic reproduction) is the tomb of St. Philip Neri, whose remains are exhibited under the altar, a silver mask over the face. Over an altar in the left arm of the transept is the delicate *Presentation of the Virgin* by Federico Barocci (late 16th-century).

A door nearby leads to one of Rome's most beautiful sacristies. On the ceiling is a fresco by Pietro da Cortona; over the altar, the statue of *St. Philip and the Angel* by Alessandro Algardi was donated, as the inscription says, by Pietro Corcos, the converted Jew (pp. 462-466). Over the door is the bronze bust of a pope, also by Algardi. Ask in the sacristy to be let into the rooms where St. Philip Neri lived, now with frescoes and other paintings by Pietro da Cortona and Guido Reni.

Heading back toward the exit, pause at the second chapel on the right to see another beautiful painting by Barocci, *The Visitation*. You may ask to have it lit.

MIDPOINT OF WALK

BEFORE GOING

5. From the Chiesa Nuova to Piazza Farnese: Via Giulia

We now cross Corso Vittorio Emanuele II (Corso Vittorio for short), another bland post-1870 arter ,which divided the renaissance district in two, and enter the southern section.

Here small renaissance homes, solemn palaces, sleepy old piazzas and ancient churches follow each other almost uninterruptedly. You'll find three more ancient national churches, each very different: S. Maria di Montserrato (Spain), stout and austere; the harmonious S. Tommaso di Canterbury (England); and S. Brigida (Sweden), a bit stiff in its northern elegance. Then, after seeing a little church designed by Raphael, S. Eligio degli Orefici ('St. Eligius of the Goldsmiths'), you'll reach an astonishing one, S. Maria dell'Orazione e Morte ('St. Mary of Prayer and Death');. Its mouldy crypt displays skeletons of the dead who in centuries past were often found in the Roman countryside, victims of bandits, malaria or vendettas. Until 1885, this church also organised famous 'religious shows' exhibiting actual corpses. Another Roman church, that of the Capuchins in Via Veneto (p. 85) has similar lugubrious displays, though of different origin. Some social historians believe such exhibits had the healthy effect of familiarising people with death, which in those days struck often, suddenly and early.

All these churches are on or very near Via Giulia, a stately, straight renaissance avenue. Once the widest in Rome and considered the most beautiful, it was created in the early 1500's (probably after a plan by Bramante) by one of the great builder popes, Julius II, patron of Raphael and Michelangelo (p. 331), to add dignity to the teeming area within the river bend and ease its traffic.

S. Maria dell'Orazione e Morte, seen at the end of via dei Farnesi (1950's)

He named it after himself. Via Giulia remained the foremost street in Rome for about two centuries. During this time the half-mile (1 km) long avenue served in place of the Corso (p. 124) for races and parades. A hunchbacks' race in the 1600's at carnival time is documented. The avenue also witnessed famous incidents. Cellini avenged his brother's murder here, ambushing and killing the assassin, a jeweller, with two dagger blows. Then in the mid-1600's a brawl between French soldiers and the pope's Corsican Guard triggered a full-blown diplomatic incident whose repercussions lasted decades.

On the avenue is one of the world's first 'humanitarian' prisons, built in the 1600's on remarkably enlightened principles to re-place the terrible Tor di Nona jails (see p. 442). This prison had spacious, well-lit cells and spiritual counselling rooms called 'conforterie'. It was used until the construction in the the late-1800's of the much larger Regina Cœli prison across the river, which is still in use, together with a more modern one in an outlying district, as the city's main prison.

After 1870, the neighbourhood was devastated during the campaigns of modernisation aimed at making Rome a city worthy of its new role as capital of Italy. A long sliver of colourful old buildings on the river behind Via Giulia was razed to make way for the Tiber embankments (p. 140). A monumental fountain designed as backdrop to the street where it ended at the river was dismantled. Then in 1938 some buildings on and around Via Giulia were torn down as part of a project, luckily abandoned, to create a link road to the northern part of the area within the river bend. Part of the avenue's lustre is gone, but much remains, enhanced by several noble palaces. In its final stretch the street offers a view, through a garden gate, of the imposing back façade of what is considered Italy's greatest 16th-century palace, our next highlight, Palazzo Farnese.

ON THE SPOT

5. From the Chiesa Nuova to Piazza Farnese: Via Giulia

Leaving the church, note a strange fountain shaped like a soup tureen, and indeed called Fontana della Terrina, a late 16th-century work by Giacomo Della Porta and others. An inscription around the top (now almost illegible) – 'Love God and do not sin, do good and let others talk'– might be read as the artists' answer to criticisms directed at the fountain.

Cross Corso Vittorio at the lights (traffic can be dangerous here). On the opposite pavement bear right for a few yards, past Via dei Cartari, and turn into Vicolo Cellini. On the left, at No. 145, is a 1st century AD boundary stone marking the official borders of Rome, the *pomerium*, extended there by order of Emperor Tiberius. (For another of these stones, see p. 592.)

You are now in an area that was the main haunt in the renaissance of low class prostitutes, including many desperate *marranas*, refugees from Spain who had been forced to renounce their Jewish faith. Up to the 1800's Vicolo Cellini was called Via Calabraga, which literally means 'Drop-your-pants Street'. In the prudish post-1870 era, authorities changed the centuries-old name to that of the famous goldsmith Cellini. Ironically, recent research suggests the name Calabraga was simply that of a local medieval family.

At No. 31 is a house that once belonged to a high-class courtesan. It has traces of 16th-century *graffiti*, once mistakenly attributed to Cellini. At one time Cellini did live nearby, attending the church of **S. Lucia del Gonfalone** ('St. Lucy of the Banner'), which is now before you on Via dei Banchi Vecchi ('of the Old Banks') at the end of the alley. Founded in the 13th century, the church was entirely rebuilt in the 18th century, and the interior redecorated in the 19th.

Go right along Via dei Banchi Vecchi. The first block is almost as it was during the renaissance, with mostly 15th- and 16th-century buildings on both sides. Most notable are a 16th-century palace by Antonio da Sangallo the Younger on the corner across from the side of the church, and further on, at Nos 22-24, another palace of the same period, with striking stucco reliefs (the top floor was added later).

Retrace your steps. Past S. Lucia you come to an area left desolate by the unfortunate 1938 demolitions. Before you, at No. 148, is a small 15th-century building with remains of frescoes on the two upper storeys.

Turn right into the demolished area. Take the street to the right of the gutted building, Vicolo del Malpasso ('of the Bad Passage', since in the distant past the road could be swampy due to the nearby river). Follow it one block to where it crosses Via Giulia. There look at this beautiful, straight renaissance thoroughfare (try to ignore the disaster zone to your left). To the right, in front of you (No. 52), are the 17th-century **Carceri Nuove** ('New Prisons').

The building still houses prison-connected activities: the Juvenile Court, the Directorate for the Struggle against the Mafia, an institute for penal studies, a United Nations centre for research on the same subject, and a museum of criminology (see p. 687). A 1655 Latin tablet declares the purpose of the building: 'For justice, clemency and the safer and more humane custody of the guilty'.

Turn left down Via Giulia toward the arch in the distance. In the first block to the left is the pretty 18th-century façade of a church dedicated to St. Philip Neri (p. 463). Pass the razed area. At the end of the next block, on the right, is the national church of Neapolitans in Rome, **Spirito Santo dei Napoletani** ('Holy Spirit of the Neapolitans'). It has medieval origins but was rebuilt in the 17th century; the façade is 19th century.

It is occasionally open. The second chapel on the left has fragments of a *Madonna and Child* fresco attributed to Antoniazzo Romano (15th century); in the last chapel is the *Martyrdom of St. Januarius* by the most prominent artist of 17th-century Naples, Luca Giordano. The presbytery contains the tombs of the last sovereigns of the Kingdom of Naples, Francesco II and Maria Sofia of the Bourbon family, who died in the late 1800's. On the right wall is a typical Neapolitan *presepe* (nativity scene) from the 18th century.

Across the street from the church take Via S. Aurea (on a wall is one of the ubiquitous ancient tablets warning against littering) to a very typical renaissance square. Just to your right, No. 129, is the elegant façade of the early 16th-century **Palazzo Ricci**, with remains of once famous frescoes by Polidoro da Caravaggio (p. 449) depicting ancient Roman legends. (Many were repainted in the 1800's.)

The piazza opens onto Via di Monserrato. Go

right, noticing on the corner the delightful façade of **S. Giovanni in Ayno**, a tiny renaissance church-turned-house. It was once used for macabre shows of the same sort as those held in the better-known S. Maria dell'Orazione e Morte, to which we'll come shortly (p. 473).

Continue along the block. Just before the first intersection (No. 117) is a renaissance house. Then cross the intersection (Via della Barchetta). Just past this is **S. Maria di Monserrato**, the 16th-century Spanish national church which gives the street its name. The façade, by Francesco da Volterra, has a relief (also by Volterra) depicting a *Virgin and Child* intently sawing off the mountain of Montserrat, a famous Catalan shrine after which the church is named ('montserrat' means 'sawed-off mountain', referring to the miraculous origin of the site). The present entrance is at the rear, on Via Giulia, where you now return by taking Via della Barchetta. Admission is not always allowed (ask the doorman).

If you do get in, you will first go past a beautiful courtyard with several funerary monuments to Spanish prelates, mostly late 15th- or early 16th-century and mostly by the Bregno school.

In the first chapel to the right, against the right wall, is a curiously shaped marble box, a unique coffin for two. It contains the bones of the Spaniard Alexander VI Borgia, that most corrupt and powerful of renaissance popes, and his uncle and predecessor, Callixtus III, also a Borgia. How they wound up here in the same coffin is unclear. They were initially buried, as was customary for popes, in St. Peter's (p. 373), in the nephew's case despite his lifelong crimes (he supposedly died drinking poisoned wine which he had intended for one of his cardinals at a banquet). When St. Peter's was rebuilt, both bodies were removed to the Spanish church of S. Giacomo degli Spagnuoli in Piazza Navona (p. 461) and then to this church. During these wanderings the remains were mysteriously mixed up and never properly buried, so that in 1879, three centuries later, they turned up here together in a dusty, unmarked lead box. At this point a wealthy

Spaniard had the monument built. In the same chapel, over the altar, is a painting of *S. Diego* by Annibale Carracci (17th century). On the opposite side of the church, the last chapel before the presbytery contains a statue of *St. James* by Jacopo Sansovino, a major 16th-century sculptor and architect (not to be confused with his master Andrea Sansovino, whose name he took).

Crossing the presbytery on this side, we reach a conference hall. Here, beside a beautiful 15th-century relief of the *Crucifixion*, is a wonderful bust of a Spanish cardinal, a youthful work by Bernini.

Across Via Giulia take the continuation of Via della Barchetta, called Via S. Eligio. The whole street was once called Via della Barchetta, ('of the Little Boat') because of a ferry that used to cross the Tiber here. At the end of the street is the little church designed by Raphael of **S. Eligio degli Orefici**. (Open daily except Sun, ring at No. 9 Via S. Eligio; closed in August.)

This exquisitely proportioned building – climb the steps to the river embankment to see the dome – is flanked by small renaissance houses. Both these and the church have always been owned by a goldsmith's guild, whose offices are here. (St. Eligius, a 9th-century bishop of Noyon in France and founder of an important monastery, was a goldsmith in his youth; he is also patron saint of blacksmiths, whose guild built him another church soon after this one, see pp. 263-264.)

The church interior is as strikingly harmonious as the outside, its simple lines contrasting with the many radiant frescoes by minor 16th-century artists. On the right wall, to the left, is the epitaph of a Roman goldsmith, Bernardino, who fell fighting the invaders in the 1527 Sack of Rome (p. 381).

Try to imagine this solitary little corner of Rome as it was before the embankments existed, when the quiet alley ended directly on the shore. The atmosphere is unfortunately marred by the looming mass of a nearby high school, built in the Fascist era, one of the worst architectural crimes committed in the area.

Return to and walk down Via Giulia again, toward the arch. Pass a building (No. 16) by Carlo Maderno of 1618; look into the courtyard. Next, on the left, is the ancient church of **S. Caterina da Siena**, rebuilt in the 1700's. Following is the imposing **Palazzo Falconieri** at No. 1. The façade, whose corner pilasters end in female torsos with falcon heads in an allusion to the owner's name, is by Borromini.

Adjoining the palace is the macabre late 16th-century church of **S. Maria dell'Orazione e Morte**, or, in its starker original dedication, simply S. Maria della Morte, 'Our Lady of Death'. The façade, added in 1733 by Ferdinando Fuga with his usual elegant touch, is encrusted with symbols of death: winged skulls and, near the side entrances, two marble tablets with grinning skeletons reminding us in an old Latin phrase, *Hodie mihi cras tibi* ('Me today, you tomorrow'). Another inscription on one of the tablets recalls in 18th-century Italian the aim of the brotherhood running the church: to bury 'li poveri morti che si pigliano in campagna' ('the poor dead picked up in the countryside').

The interior, too, sometimes open Sundays for evening Mass (18:00) and closed in August, is elegant, beautifully decorated and proportioned. Both on the right and left between the first and second chapels are 17th-century frescoes by Giovanni Lanfranco representing hermits; they come from a hermit's refuge built for himself by a devout cardinal Farnese. It stood on the left of the church, in front of his family's palatial home (we'll come to it in a few minutes), but was later demolished.

The uniqueness of this church, however, lies in its mouldy underground crypt exhibiting heaps of dusty bones and skeletons. This once led to a much larger covered cemetery, similarly adorned and used for religious shows, but destroyed when the river was embanked. A marble tablet in the crypt depicts a terrifying *Death Raising its Scythe*, which inspired equally terrifying lines by Belli, Rome's great 19th-century poet, about 'the skinny lady of Via Giulia raising her hook' ('la comaraccia / secca de strada Ggiulia arza er rampino').

You are almost under an arch, actually an

arched bridge, built in 1603, possibly to a design by Michelangelo, to link the nearby Palazzo Farnese with other property the Farnese owned on the river bank, including the hermitage mentioned above. The project was never completed. At the bridge, behind a garden gate on the left, is the imposing rear façade and lawn of **Palazzo Farnese**. We'll see the front soon. This part was built in the style of Michelangelo by his followers, Giacomo Della Porta and Jacopo Vignola.

At the next crossing, on your left is the splendid side of Palazzo Farnese, on your right is an inventive renaissance fountain, Il Mascherone ('the Big Mask'), much diminished after its original river backdrop was blocked off.

Walk another block along Via Giulia and turn left into Vicolo del Polverone ('of the Big Dust'). Here Via Giulia ended beautifully with a monumental fountain, which was moved across the river in 1879 to make way for the embankment (p. 140).

Take Vicolo del Polverone. Halfway down on the right is the side of the noble mid-16th century

The Perspectival Gallery, Palazzo Spada: plan and section

Palazzo Spada. Turn the corner to see the fanciful, stuccoed main façade, a highly inventive concept and surprising harbinger of the coming baroque. It is of controversial authorship. The statues in stucco are by Guido Mazzoni from Piacenza.

Step into the courtyard, which Mazzoni decorated even more richly with statues and stucco reliefs of mythological subjects. The great shield belongs to the noble Spada family, original owners of the palace, who later sold it to the Italian government, along with their important art collection (now a major museum, p. 684).

On the left side of the courtyard is a glass door. Through this, past a library and beyond another courtyard, see the **Perspectival Gallery** by Borromini, said to have inspired Bernini's Royal Staircase in the Vatican (p. 377). It is a veritable feat of perspective: when you enter (a doorman can show you there) you see that it is four or five times shorter (24 ft or 8 m) than it looks from afar, while its seemingly tall statue is only 2 ft (65 cm) high. Another courtyard in the building is also worth a look.

In one of the halls of the palace, occupied by an important administrative body of the Italian government (the Council of State), but not publicly exhibited, is a 1st century AD statue once famous because tradition held that it was a statue of Pompey, at whose feet Cæsar died (p. 243). The tradition was found to be baseless over half a century ago.

The main itinerary resumes on p. 478.

DETOUR
45 MIN

Leaving Palazzo Spada go right into Via Capodiferro. The neighbourhood we are about to visit (its name – Regola – is a corruption of 'arenula', meaning 'sandy spot') is bounded by Via dei Pettinari, Lungotevere (the river drive) and Via Arenula. It feels particularly intimate and remote, being outside the bustle of both foot and vehicular traffic.

No. 12 of Via Capodiferro is a 16th-century house with vestiges of a painted façade. No. 7 is the elegant mid-16th century **Palazzetto Spada** (with a late 16th-century portal) attributed to either Baldassarre Peruzzi or Jacopo Vignola. It has shops on the street and, over them, low-ceiling dwelling rooms for the shopkeepers' families (essentially the ancient Roman formula, see p. 140). Paul Letarouilly, a 19th-century French authority on Roman renaissance architecture, considered the palazzetto amongst the jewels of classical inspiration in Rome.

No. 31 is a 19th-century house with a medieval porch; the columns and capitals are 13th-century but the bases are ancient Roman.

At the corner of Via Capodiferro and Via dei Pettinari (Piazza Trinità dei Pellegrini), at Nos 81-84 Via dei Pettinari, is **Palazzo Salomoni-Alberteschi**, dating from the 15th-century but partly remodelled. In it lived two now-extinct medieval families.

Note the renaissance doorways, the original Latin inscription of the names of the owners – *D(omus) Salomonia-Albertiscorum* – and the pattern of heraldic knots and lions under the cornice.

Walk down Via dei Pettinari ('of the Mattress Wool-combers'), a medieval street retracing an ancient Roman one, both created to serve a new bridge built over the river (see below). Near the end, on the right, is the church of **San Salvatore in Onda** ('The Holy Saviour by the Wave'), a name deriving from the frequent and devastating river floods in this area (p. 576). The church is 11th-12th century but has been remodelled several times, especially to raise it above the river level, and it now has a mid-19th century look. In 1844 it was assigned to a teaching order founded by S. Vincenzo Pallotti, called Padri Pallottini ('Pallottine Fathers'), whose schools operate today worldwide. The saint designed and paid for the simple façade and also supplied part of the church furnishings. (Open 07:00-11:00 and 16:30-19:00.)

The evocative interior is articulated by columns of various designs and types of marble, some of whose capitals date back to the foundation of the church or earlier. The bases can't be seen, as the floor was raised. The saint's body is in an urn under the main altar.

In the house to the right of the church are the rarely accessible steps to the old crypt, which contains two ancient Roman columns. Under the crypt are remains of a 2nd century AD house.

Turning the corner, the house facing the river is the world headquarters of the Pallottine Fathers. Besides their educational work, they also founded an internationally known lay apostolate called Catholic Action. S. Vincenzo Pallotti lived here; you may ask to visit his room and chapel.

Via dei Pettinari ends at **Ponte Sisto** ('Sixtus Bridge'), built in the renaissance on the site of the 2nd century AD Pons Aurelius. The old bridge collapsed in the middle ages and was rebuilt for the Jubilee Year 1475 by Pope Sixtus IV, using the ancient pylons (see also p. 572).

The marble-lined bridge is a masterpiece, both for its harmonious design and its technical perfection. The massive piers have withstood the strong current for centuries, while the big *oculus* ('eye') served to reduce stress when the water rose. The bridge did not do so well in the 19th and 20th centuries: during the construction of the embankment the design was altered, and it was further damaged by wheeled traffic. Now restricted to pedestrian use, the bridge has recently been restored.

Retrace your steps along Via dei Pettinari. An intersection on the right, Via delle Zoccolette ('of the Little Clog Wearers') is named after the residents of a nearby 18th-century home for 'poor spinsters', who typically wore clogs, and not (as some think) in honour of prostitutes, who are referred to in the same way, and for the same reason, in Roman dialect. When you reach Piazza Trinità dei Pellegrini, on the right you'll see the church of **Ss. Trinità dei Pellegrini** ('Most Holy Trinity of the Pilgrims'). Of uncertain medieval foundation date, it was restored in the early 17th century and dedicated, together with the hospice next door, to the streams of pilgrims flowing into Rome in the Jubilee years. Church and hospice were famous as places where noblemen, high

475

prelates and even popes ritually washed the feet of arriving pilgrims.

During the 1849 revolution to wrest Rome from the French-supported popes, the hospice became a hospital, where several heroes of the battles on the Janiculum died (p. 566). Amongst these was the poet Goffredo Mameli, one of whose poems, set to music in the 1800's, is the Italian national anthem.

The church is only open in the mornings. It contains two works by Guido Reni (17th century): a fresco in the dome of *God the Father with Saints* and a *Trinity* over the main altar. Next to the altar are beautiful 17th-century candelabra donated to the church by the Roman people when it was consecrated.

Leave the church and take Via San Paolo alla Regola on the right (Regola, you may remember, is the name of the district). It leads to Piazza San Paolo alla Regola, dominated by the 18th-century church of **S. Paolo alla Regola**. The church stands on the spot where tradition holds St. Paul rented a house. This, and two other churches near the end of this side trip, are remarkable mainly for the charming façades gracing the quiet streets and squares. S. Paolo is rarely open.

Under No.16 are remains of an old Roman *insula*, accessible only by special permission from the city (see p. 659).

At the end of the street is a complex of medieval houses (13th century), the largest such complex in Rome. Various medieval elements – a loggia (covered balcony), mullioned windows, pieces of ancient Roman columns and marble fragments – are visible. Two tower-houses frame the complex to the left and right.

Known as the **Case di S. Paolo** ('Houses of St. Paul'), the complex would be bigger if it had not been partly demolished in the early 1900's to make way for the massive Ministry of Justice, which now blocks this part of the district, contributing to its sense of isolation.

Turn into Via S. Maria in Monticelli. Here is the church of the same name, **S. Maria in Monticelli** ('St. Mary on the Mounds'). The 'mounds' are the hillock on which it stands, probably formed by ruins underneath. Perhaps dating from as early as the 4th century, the church has been remodelled several times, lastly in 1715, when it acquired its present appearance (restored 1990). The beautiful brick romanesque bell tower (12th century) stands in picturesque contrast to the 18th-century façade.

Rarely open, it contains a fresco by Antonio Carracci of the *Flagellation of Christ* in the second chapel on the right. In the apse is a fragment of a 13th century mosaic *Head of the Redeemer*. In the second chapel on the left is a 14th-century wooden *Crucifix*. The furnishings in the sacristy are 18th-century.

Turn the corner of Via S. Maria in Monticelli. Opposite the side of the church, at No. 66, is the 18th-century Palazzo Panizza. A few more steps lead to Piazza **S. Salvatore in Campo**, with its early 17th-century church of the same name ('The Holy Saviour in the Field').

From the right side of the church take Via S. Salvatore in Campo. No. 43 is the **House of Alessandro Lancia**, built in the 16th century by this courtier of Pope Paul III (p. 369). The pope's coat of arms is between the second floor windows; on the façade are time-worn decorations. Under the house and many other buildings nearby, almost to the river, are (inaccessible) ruins of ancient Roman buildings.

The street ends in Via degli Specchi, named after an eminent local family, with picturesque homes and courtyards. On the right is one side of Palazzo Santacroce (p. 519). No. 17, left, has a fine renaissance doorway. Continuing, cross Piazza Monte di Pietà, go left and back to Piazza Trinità dei Pellegrini at the corner of Via Capodiferro. From here you may pick up the main itinerary in front of Palazzo Spada on your left.

END OF DETOUR

Map of Rome in c. 1625, showing the Ponte Sisto at the centre

From Palazzo Spada go left a few steps to the picturesque Piazza S. Maria della Quercia ('of the Oak'), named after an 18th-century church with a façade by Filippo Raguzzini, which was in turn named after an oak in the square. Opposite the church is an elegant early 16th-century palazzetto (No. 1), possibly by Peruzzi. As you face the church, the street to your left is Vicolo dei Venti. Take it to the nearby Piazza Farnese.

BEFORE GOING

6. Piazza Farnese to Campo de' Fiori

Built for his own use by Cardinal Alessandro Farnese, Giulia Bella's brother and later Pope Paul III (see pp. 46, 361), this majestic residence, Palazzo Farnese, the focus of Piazza Farnese, bears the stamp of Michelangelo's genius. Indeed, it was Michelangelo who took over the project after the death of Antonio da Sangallo the Younger, the first architect of the palace, and redesigned the upper third of the façade, thus making the whole the foremost example of high renaissance palace architecture in Italy.

More a royal palace than a mere palazzo, this grand structure has housed foreign sovereigns and potentates for centuries. Queen Christina of Sweden stayed here with her court for almost a year after her arrival in Rome (p. 43). An independent-minded woman and a lesbian, her wild lifestyle and language proved an unexpected embarrassment to her host, the pope. (At a party, she said publicly of her lady-in-waiting that she was 'as pleasant in conversation as she was in bed.')

Queen Christina

The Bourbons, the royal family of the Kingdom of Naples, also lived in the palace for a decade after losing their domains in the reunification of Italy. Now the French Embassy occupies the building.

The inside, as beautiful as the exterior, contains the masterpiece by Caravaggio's great 17th-century contemporary, Annibale Carracci, who frescoed the ceiling in the main gallery. For the seven-year project the princely Farnese family paid him wages equivalent to those of a house painter. Much embittered, the already depression-prone artist stopped working and died soon afterwards. If his great work was little appreciated then, it cannot be at all today, at least by the public. The French, who once allowed weekly visits, now require an elaborate application from visitors (to be faxed to the French Cultural Service: +39/06/

Palazzo Farnese in the 1950's

68601508). It is to be hoped that Italy will reclaim the building when the lease comes up for renewal, but that isn't until 2035.

The palace covers a whole side of the lovely square and, with its perfect proportions and decorations, gives it an ideal backdrop. An aristocratic, intimate space, the square is surprisingly quiet despite being near a lively workaday area.

A few steps from Piazza Farnese, the curtain will indeed rise on a boisterous scene, Campo de' Fiori, Rome's ancient produce market square. Not many palaces here, but a cluster of old tenements of all shapes, heights and hues, some dating back to the renaissance. No hushed ambience broken by the gushing of fountains, but the shrill cries of vendors hawking vegetables – another chapter of the perennial study in contrasts that is Rome.

ON THE SPOT

6. Piazza Farnese to Campo de' Fiori

Palazzo Farnese, the grandest and possibly most beautiful of all 16th-century palaces, covers one side of Piazza Farnese. Michelangelo designed the central balcony and the third storey, whose celebrated cornice stands out in all its magnificence thanks to its deep projection and the generous height above the windows. The artist considered it so essential to the general effect that he asked the pope to approve it specifically when he was shown the model.

Palazzo Farnese is the culmination of the long development of renaissance palace architecture, from the simple, sober lines of the early phase, exemplified in Rome by the 15th-century Palazzo Venezia (p. 535), through the livelier designs and more complex statements of later decades (Palazzo della Cancelleria, a coming highlight), to the majesty of the high renaissance. Here, as in the dome of St. Peter's, Michelangelo has mobilised and synthesised the strengths of an entire era.

Sadly, even a peek at the superb courtyard requires special authorisation from the French

Farnese Palace, window by Michelangelo

Embassy. In the interior, the influence of Michelangelo is felt even in the parts designed by Sangallo. The rooms are rich in sculpture and stuccos, and in frescoes by the Carracci school and other accomplished artists, such as the Zuccari brothers. On the main floor, the famous Carracci Gallery is frescoed with stories from Greek mythology by Annibale Carracci, with the help of his brother Agostino and his students Domenichino and Lanfranco. Ancient Roman ruins with intriguing mosaic floors have recently been discovered in the cellars, possibly lodgings for the Circus charioteers (see p. 482).

The square has two three-tiered fountains built in 1626, whose middle basins are large granite tubs from the Baths of Caracalla (p. 276). They prompted the 19th-century American novelist Nathaniel Hawthorne to muse that water, used in Rome by the popes as a 'way of immortalising their memories... has proved a more durable record than brass or marble.'

Opposite the palace to the right is a pleasant 18th-century building, the **Palazzo Roccagiovine**, by Alessandro Specchi. On the square is the Swedish national church, S. Brigida, founded in the late 1300's and rebuilt in the late 1600's. The statues represent the Swedish mystic St. Bridget and her daughter and successor as superior of the Bridgettine nuns, St. Catherine. The bell tower is late 1800's. Next to it is the house (No. 96), rebuilt several times, where the two saints lived in the 1300's. Indeed, the house must have been a haunt of saintly ladies, as Catherine was a friend of the homonymous saint from Siena, Caterina, who lived near the Pantheon (p. 241).

Step into Via Monserrato, left of the Swedish church. Just to the left (No. 61) is a 16th-century palace. At the end of the block is the old church of **S. Girolamo della Carità** ('St. Jerome of Charity'), built and rebuilt several times (last in the baroque period, with a façade by Carlo Rainaldi) on the site where the saint lived around 380 AD. The saint is usually shown in the desert with a lion. Not so well known is that he moved to the desert to flee gossip about his relations

Palazzo Farnese: Hercules and the Sphinx, *fresco by Annibale Carracci in the Camerino, executed as a sample of his work before he embarked on the more famous Gallery*

with a lady who had taken him in as a guest in the house here. The church, which is seldom open, has splendid chapels, including one by Borromini (1660) and another by Juvarra (1708), the only work definitely by him in Rome.

In the next small square to the left is another little church, **S. Caterina della Rota** ('of the Wheel'), founded in the 12th century but rebuilt several times (last in the mid-19th century).

Named after St. Catherine of Alexandria, the martyr who was tortured on a spiked wheel, (see pp. 420, 481), for centuries the church was devoted to helping prisoners ransomed from Saracen pirates. The beautiful ceiling dates from the 18th century.

Opposite is the national church of English Roman Catholics, **S. Tommaso di Canterbury** (dedicated to the archbishop of the 12th century, also known as St. Thomas à Becket, murdered in Canterbury Cathedral). Founded in the 8th century, when it was dedicated to the Holy Trinity its

priests were already then helping English and Scottish pilgrims. It was rebuilt several times, last in the 19th century. It has works by minor 16th-century artists but is not open to the public. Connected to the church is a college for English Roman Catholic seminarians, where the poet John Milton was a guest in 1638.

To the left of the church, at Nos 43-45, there used to stand a jail managed on behalf of the papacy by the powerful baronial family, the Savelli (p. 253), who more often than not used it for their own grudges and vendettas too. Called Corte Savella, this was the building where the heroine of a bloody 17th-century saga – Beatrice Cenci, whom we'll meet later (p. 518) – was held during her trial, and whence she was led to her execution.

At No. 91 on the square is a 17th-century palace with an interesting doorway and rich window detail. Returning to Piazza Farnese, stay on the left in order to turn into Vicolo del Gallo, which leads to Campo de' Fiori.

481

7. Campo de' Fiori and Palazzo della Cancelleria

Campo de' Fiori ('Field of Flowers') is named after the abandoned meadow which this area became in the middle ages. In ancient Rome it was a desolate neighbourhood, where the stables of the *factiones*, the racing teams of the Circus Maximus, were all located. (Their ruins have been found to stretch from Piazza Farnese to Piazza Cancelleria.) In the late 1400's the pope decided to develop the area, the only rustic one that remained along the southern approaches to the Vatican. A new street, Via del Pellegrino ('Pilgrim Street'), was driven through to ease traffic from the south, and sewers and other basic services were added. The square soon flourished. By the 1500's it was considered the most important centre of city life, roughly comparable to the more commercial parts of the forum in ancient Rome: a centre for markets, meetings, public discussions and important announcements. Public tortures and executions also took place here. Energetic activity went on all day, boosted by the passage of popes, kings and ambassadors, for the square was sometimes included in the Via Papalis (p. 412). The major papal 'bulls' (edicts, so named after the large seal – *bulla* – attached to them) against heretics and rebels were hung up here. A 1739 bull raged against 'licentiousness during the festival night of S. John'. The last one, in 1860, attacked the patriots who were unifying Italy.

Until recently, almost every building around the square had an inn, as did many adjacent streets. The most notorious included the Taverna della Vacca ('Inn of the Cow') opened by Vannozza Catanei (pp. 45-46) in 1513 after her lover, Pope Alexander VI Borgia, died. A shrewd businesswoman who had outlived three husbands, in her old age Vannozza invested her considerable capital in real estate, hotels and inns. The 'Vacca' – said to be frequented especially by prostitutes – was amongst her most successful enterprises. She was a greedy old sinner, yet when she died five years later she left everything to religious institutions and charities. Her much eroded coat-of-arms is still on the wall near the corner of the square where her inn once stood.

The piazza was an important arts and crafts centre, too, as witnessed by the names of most of the streets around it (baullari – 'of the trunk-makers'; cappellari – 'of the hat-makers'; giubbonari – 'of the jerkin-makers'; chiodaroli – 'of the nail-makers'; balestrari – 'of the crossbow-makers', and so on).

A very high gibbet loomed over the square until 1798. People were hanged by the arms from it for minor crimes. This 'torment of the rope' caused an excruciating shoulder dislocation. Via della Corda ('of the Rope') off this corner of the square is a reminder of such torture, not, as is often said, of the ropemaker's craft.

Executions here took many forms. People were often hanged from windows. Three monks condemned for having tried to kill the pope with black magic were burnt on a pyre. The following entry from Burchard's meticulous diary (p. 329) reports an execution by garroting in 1498, which also reflects the racial, religious, social and sexual intolerance of the time:

> April 9, Monday. (…) A courtesan, or honest prostitute, known as Corsetta, was arrested a few days ago for living with a Moor, who had been dressing as a woman.

Both were led around the city to show the scandal. She was wearing a black velvet dress ... The Moor had his arms forced together and tied behind his back, while his gowns were hiked up to his navel, so all could see his testicles or genitals, making the deception clear. After the tour, Corsetta was released while the Moor was jailed in Tor di Nona [see p. 442] until Saturday the 7th. Then he was taken from the prison along with two bandits. The three were led to Campo de' Fiori by a constable on a donkey, who was carrying, at the end of a stick, the testicles of a Jew who had had intercourse with a Christian woman. The two brigands were immediately hanged, while the Moor was placed against a wooden plank and strangled against the gibbet by twisting a rope around his neck, with a stick from behind. A fire was made under him but it went out because it rained. His legs though, nearest to the fire, did turn to ashes.

Most memorable is the execution in 1600 of Italy's greatest renaissance philosopher, Giordano Bruno (p. 116), who was burnt at the stake in the centre of the square for his very modern, materialistic conception of God as the universal soul of the world. Four hundred years later, in 2000, the Church issued an apology for this and similar crimes.

What remains today of all these multifarious activities is a very colourful fruit and vegetable market, Rome's largest, which has taken place in the square every morning except Sunday since 1869. The ubiquitous inns have given way to a few very popular restaurants and some food stores.

Right off Campo de' Fiori is Palazzo della Cancelleria, by an unknown architect, Rome's most splendid example of early renaissance palace architecture. It is also a memento of the once inveterate habit of popes enriching their nephews (or in some cases their sons, since there were exceptions, some legitimate and others in defiance of the rule of celibacy amongst the clergy), a custom that gave us the word 'nepotism.' Often these youngsters received the rank of cardinal, too, and there even existed a quasi-official title of 'cardinal nepote'.

The statue of Giordano Bruno in the Campo dei Fiori

One of the few positive results of nepotism is a group of beautiful Roman palaces built by these privileged relatives. The Cancelleria is the most magnificent. It was built in the late 1400's by Cardinal Raffaele Riario, a nephew of Pope Sixtus IV (whose portrait by Melozzo we saw in the Vatican, surrounded by Raffaele and three other nephews, all cardinals or destined to be, p. 314). Young Cardinal Raffaele invested not only his own funds in the palace, but also money he won from the nephew of his uncle's successor, Innocent VIII, in a night at dice. Pope Innocent tried to recover his nephew's money – 14,000 gold ducats, almost a million dollars today – but in vain, the money having already gone to the contractors. Cardinal Riario did not enjoy his palace for long, however. A few years later it was seized by Pope Leo X on account of the cardinal's participation in a plot to unseat him.

When Michelangelo arrived in Rome at the age of 21, he was introduced to Cardinal Riario, who housed him in an annexe of his palace but was not otherwise very helpful. (Around this time, according to his biographer Vasari, and by his own admission, Michelangelo tried unsuccessfully to palm off to the cardinal a 'sleeping cupid' that he had carved and then antiqued in order to sell it for a higher price as a genuinely ancient piece; see p. 309.) It was through the contacts made at Riario's court, however, that Michelangelo received the commission for his *Pietà* (pp. 365-366) from a French cardinal, and it was this work that established hs fame.

The palace interior is magnificent, but unfortunately closed to the public. Its most impressive features are a courtyard attributed to Bramante and a cycle of frescoes by the Florentine painter Vasari, who is also famous as a biographer of renaissance artists. Forced to execute the frescoes in 100 days, Vasari was miserable about the results. An often told but apocryphal story is that he showed them to Michelangelo boasting of how quickly he had done them and Michelangelo replied 'I can tell'.

For more than four centuries the palace has been the administrative offices (or 'chancellery' hence its name) of the papacy and seat of its high court, the Sacra Rota. The court still tries ecclesiastic suits here, though it lost most of its prime business, annulling marriages, when divorce was introduced in Italy in the 1970's. The palace, together with the Vatican (see p. 302), enjoys extraterritorial status.

The Cancelleria encloses in its fabric one of Rome's oldest churches, S. Lorenzo in Damaso, whose great antiquity is obscured by alterations. Excavations begun in 1988 have revealed foundations dating back over 1,600 years. Inscriptions previously found under the church show that in pagan times this area served as barracks and stables for the green faction of the Circus Maximus charioteers, the favourites of the Roman populace.

ON THE SPOT

7. Campo de' Fiori and Palazzo della Cancelleria

Almost at the end of Vicolo del Gallo (whose name comes from the sign of an inn) on the left (No. 13), in a late medieval building, was the notorious Taverna della Vacca owned by Vannozza Catanei, whose escutcheon is still on the wall. It bears the arms of her family, those of her last husband and, proudly inserted, those of her lover, Pope Alexander VI Borgia (a bull and stripes). Just around the corner is a stucco-framed 18th-century wall shrine.

Enter **Campo de' Fiori**. The monument in the middle, one of few first-class late 19th-century statues in Rome, is the brooding, woeful figure of the philosopher Giordano Bruno, burnt at the stake on that spot for heresy in 1600 (p. 116). The statue, by Ettore Ferrari, was erected after Rome was wrenched from the popes in 1870. The pedestal is decorated with medallions showing other famous heretics and bears an inscription by Giovanni Bovio, an Italian naturalist philosopher of the late 19th century who, like Bruno, had been excommunicated for his ideas: 'To Bruno, the century that he foresaw erected this here, where the pyre burnt.' Bruno, who professsed the need for philosophical freedom in a Christian context, and battled the Aristotelian constraints that had shackled Western thought since the early middle ages, remains to this day a powerful symbol of liberty. (His hood, incidentally, still survives, p. 264).

A stroll around the square will show you the warm, down-to-earth atmosphere of this typical plebeian Roman piazza, an endangered species in the historic centre, and in exceptional condition. Next, go to the corner of the Campo, which is at your back to the left if you are facing the front of the Bruno monument.

DETOUR
10 MIN

Leave the Campo from this corner by Via del Pellegrino, part of the main pilgrimage route to the Vatican from the south.

The street existed in ancient Rome, but in the middle ages it was reduced to a fetid alley. Pope Alexander VI, Vannozza's lover, renovated it in the late 1400's, as mentioned by the inscription and coat-of-arms on the first house to the left at the corner of the Campo.

Go down Via del Pellegrino. On the right you'll have the magnificent right side of the Cancelleria, whose façade we'll soon return to see. On the left, at No. 19, an archway leads past ancient column stumps of uncertain origin, embedded in walls, to a spectacularly operatic courtyard formed by centuries-old houses, some with typical medieval external stairs.

Continue down Via del Pellegrino. On the left, at a corner above No. 53, is one of Rome's most beautiful Madonnelle (street shrines), a stucco *Virgin and Child* very delicately sculpted at the beginning of the 18th century. Beneath is a bust of St. Philip Neri (p. 463).

At No. 58 is the house of Vannozza Catanei, where she lived during her long affair with the Borgia pope and where at least one of their sons, the famous Cesare Borgia (p. 331), was born. Further along, still on the left, at Nos 64 and 67, are two renaissance houses with badly faded frescoes.

Those at No. 67, depicting episodes from ancient Roman history, are attributed to Daniele da Volterra (16th century, p. 349). Those at No. 64 – medallions of the Three Kings – are also 16th century but of unknown authorship. They are probably the insignia of a Three Kings Hotel that is known to have been in this neighbourhood.

Retrace your steps and return to the beginning of Via del Pellegrino.

END OF DETOUR

Around the corner is the façade of the **Palazzo della Cancelleria**, designed by an unknown architect at the end of the 15th century. The façade, one of the purest and most noble expressions of renaissance architecture, is of travertine, which gives it an ivory hue. Two slightly bulging corners soften its exceptional length. Balconies accent its rhythm; the one on Via del Pellegrino is especially notable. On this corner is the majestic escutcheon of Pope Julius II, patron of Michelangelo and Raphael.

The solemn inscription 'Corte Imperiale' over the main door was added during the short Napoleonic occupation of Rome, when the building served as the Supreme Court of the French-controlled state. In 1849 it housed the assembly that proclaimed the short-lived Roman Republic of Garibaldi and Mazzini (p. 565).

The building, which currently houses the ecclesiastical High Court, and its second floor great hall frescoed by Giorgio Vasari are closed to the public. During office hours, however, you can go into the splendid courtyard, which some scholars attribute to Bramante. The architect, whoever he was, created the harmonious three-storey structure when he incorporated the church of S. Lorenzo in Damaso next door into the building. He cut off the part of the church that would have intruded into the courtyard and remodelled the rest (it is now to the right of the courtyard). Columns from the church, some marble, some granite, were removed and reused to brilliant effect in the courtyard – a third reincarnation, since they were already spolia from an ancient Roman building.

Excavations begun in 1988 under the courtyard have uncovered the foundations of the early 14th-century church as it was at the time of Bramante, the last of many remodellings, and at lower levels, remains of 4th- and 5th-century church structures, some with traces of fresco. Further excavations

485

Detail of the interior courtyard,
Palazzo della Cancelleria

under the palace proper have uncovered ruins of the chariot depot of the Circus Maximus, the tomb of a 1st century AD Roman general and a *mithræum*. All the excavations are closed to the public, but admission can be applied for at the Vatican (Pontificia Commissione di Archeologia Sacra, see p. 658).

S. Lorenzo in Damaso (open 07:00-12:00 and 16:30-20:00 in winter, 17:00-20:30 in summer), entered from a door to the right of the main portal of the Cancelleria, is one of Rome's oldest churches, having been built by the Spanish pope, Damasus, in the late 4th century (see pp. 228, 554)

on a pre-existing *ecclesia domestica* dedicated to St. Lawrence.

The architect (perhaps Bramante himself) gave the truncated space the simple, linear proportions of the renaissance style, but subsequent remodellings and redecorations have given the interior a heavier appearance. A rather drastic overhaul was necessary in the early 1800's after Napoleon's occupying forces, who were using the nearby palace as a tribunal, used the church as a stable.

Moving counterclockwise, in the first chapel of the right aisle is a 14th-century wooden *Crucifix*, before which St. Bridget of Sweden, who lived nearby (p. 480), used to pray. The great painting over the main altar, *The Coronation of the Virgin and Saints*, is by Federico Zuccaro (late 16th century). At the main altar end of the left aisle is the 1505 tomb of a warlike cardinal, called Trevisan-Scarampi, who as a general defeated the Turks in a famous battle. A chapel further down the aisle has an early 12th century icon of the Virgin over the altar. Continuing down the aisle past tombstones and cenotaphs of different ages in the wall, towards the end you reach the late 16th-century tomb of Annibal Caro, an eminent Italian renaissance humanist. Cross the church and leave through a door at the beginning of the right aisle, framed by an exquisite 15th-century doorway.

You are now back on Corso Vittorio Emanuele. Go right as far as the first crossing after Piazza della Cancelleria, Vicolo dell'Aquila (an 'L' shaped alley). Turn into the vicolo, where on the left side of the first segment of the 'L' is the main façade of the so-called **Farnesina dei Baullari**, one of the most distinguished small renaissance palaces in Rome. It is almost certainly the work of Antonio da Sangallo the Younger, Bramante's pupil and Michelangelo's rival in the early 16th century.

Proper appreciation of this palazzetto is impossible without keeping in mind that it was greatly altered at the end of the 19th century in connection with the creation of Corso Vittorio. The main façade, for instance, is weighed down by the addition (on the left) of a sliver of stonework corresponding to a new front built to face Corso Vittorio (we'll discuss this new front later). Nonetheless, the main façade still strikingly conveys how a relatively small 16th century aristocratic home looked.

Turning into the second segment of the 'L', we see the side of the building that is almost intact, except for an ugly pipe and some walled-up windows, and gives the most authentic impression of the original sobriety and nobility of the design.

The problem is that the next two sides are either heavily altered (the first) or a modern invention (the second). But it gets worse: since these sides are much more visible in the present street layout, in which Corso Vittorio is a major artery, they are routinely mistaken for the originals. (They have even been publicized as such in the only photograph of the palazzetto in an official, government-sponsored guide to Rome.) People don't even look for the 'real' façades, tucked away in the narrow vicolo behind.

The vicolo ends at Via dei Baullari ('of the Trunk-makers'). This side of the Farnesina dei Baullari, with its large airy windows and enclosed balconies (or 'loggias'), was originally the rear and opened onto a garden, now gone. Recreating the garden with your imagination helps complete the picture of the patrician renaissance palazzetto. The effort is complicated, however, by a showy terrace with a ramp that was added to the rear façade in order to connect the original ground level of the building to that of the new Corso Vittorio nearby.

The fourth and final side, on Corso Vittorio, is even more deceptive: it was built from scratch in 1887 with a pretentious neo-renaissance design inspired by the rear or garden side (notice the superimposed 'loggias'). This new front was necessary, since the palazzetto adjoined other buildings here which were demolished when the Corso was created, but of course it could have been built in a much more neutral style.

Even the present name of the palazzetto comes from a misunderstanding: 'Farnesina dei Baullari' implies that this building 'on Via dei Baullari' was once owned by the noble Farnese family (p. 484), but it wasn't. It was built and owned by a French cardinal, called Le Roy. A mix-up between the lilies in the Le Roy family escutcheon (found in the decoration of the palazzetto) and those in the Farnese coat-of-arms, which was better known in Rome, led to the error.

During the 1887 renovation, fragmentary ruins of a 4th-5th century AD ancient Roman building were found under the building. They can be seen, on request, by visitors to an interesting archæological museum, the Museo Barracco, housed in the palazzetto (p. 685).

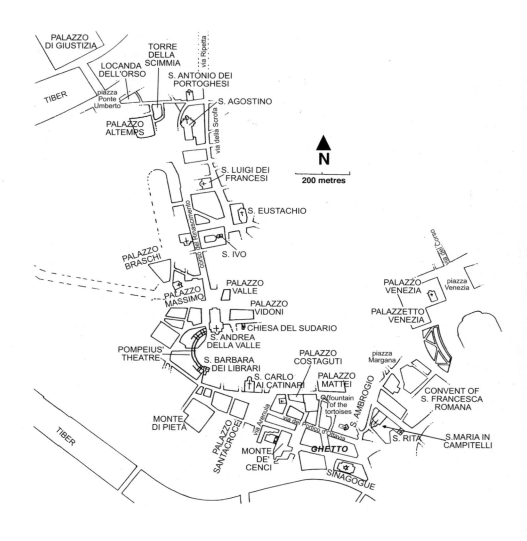

PALAZZO
DI GIUSTIZIA

TORRE
DELLA
SCIMMIA

LOCANDA
DELL'ORSO

S. ANTÓNIO DEI
PORTOGHESI

via Ripetta

TIBER

piazza
Ponte
Umberto

PALAZZO
ALTEMPS

S. AGOSTINO

via della Scrofa

N

200 metres

S. LUIGI DEI
FRANCESI

S. EUSTACHIO

corso del Rinascimento

via del Corso

PALAZZO
BRASCHI

S. IVO

PALAZZO
MASSIMO

PALAZZO
VALLE

PALAZZO
VIDONI

PALAZZO
VENEZIA

piazza
Venezia

PALAZZETTO
VENEZIA

CHIESA DEL SUDARIO

POMPEIUS'
THEATRE

S. ANDREA
DELLA VALLE

S. BARBARA
DEI LIBRARI

PALAZZO
COSTAGUTI

piazza
Margana

S. CARLO
AI CATINARI

PALAZZO
MATTEI

CONVENT OF
S. FRANCESCA
ROMANA

fountain
of the
tortoises

MONTE
DI PIETÀ

PALAZZO
SANTACROCE

via Arenula

via del Portico d'Ottavia

S. AMBROGIO

S. RITA

S.MARIA IN
CAMPITELLI

MONTE
DE'
CENCI

GHETTO

TIBER

SINAGOGUE

RENAISSANCE ROME
SECOND WALK

Starting point: Piazza di Ponte Umberto

End point: Piazza Venezia

Duration: 5 hours (without the Detours, indicated above between parentheses).
Planning your walk: you can take this walk in the morning or afternoon. Unfortunately, you will always find many of the smaller, non-parish churches closed. On Sundays, however, they are more likely to be open.

FACCIATA DELLA CHIESA
DI SANT' ANTONIO
Della Nazione de Portoghesi

Architettura di Martino Longhi il Giouane

BEFORE GOING

1. From the Locanda dell'Orso to the Torre della Scimmia

The second Renaissance Rome Walk unfolds along a sliver of the Tiber Bend area. To its west are the districts first and most densely settled in the middle ages, which we visited on the first Renaissance Rome Walk. To its east is the zone dotted with ancient Roman monuments explored in the second Ancient Rome Walk. Predictably, a mixture of periods is in evidence here, with medieval and renaissance landmarks and traces of Roman antiquity.

The Walk begins in an area not far from Via Coronari, which was on the route of pilgrims to the Vatican and other travellers from the north, and so it was full of tourist accomodation; indeed there were periods when the hoteliers and landlords here enjoyed a kind of monopoly, since taking in foreign boarders was forbidden elsewhere. We know the names and locations of a dozen hotels, hostels and inns active here in the middle ages. Especially in the official Jubilee years, foreigners of all classes crowded them. Dante himself, Italy's greatest poet, presumably lodged in one of these inns – we don't know which – during his stay in Rome for the first Jubilee in 1300 (p. 442). Most of the inns are gone, but one of the most popular, considered during the renaissance to be one of the best , is at the start of our Walk. It is called the Locanda dell'Orso ('Inn of the Bear') and operated as a hotel until nearly the end of the 19th century, though by then it was fourth-rate. Lately it has become a luxury restaurant.

The French philosopher Montaigne left a record of his stay at the inn in 1581. But he soon moved to a more convenient apartment around the corner which he rented 'for just 20 scudi a month, including firewood for heating and the services of a cook,' not to mention walls covered with gilt leather. In his travel diary Montaigne describes how each morning he explored the neighbourhood on horseback. One scene that particularly struck him was a bandit led to execution. You may recall that nearby were both the main prison of the time, the dreadful Tor di Nona, and one of the most common public execution places, Piazza di Ponte (p. 442):

> The prisoner was a dark man of about 30, but we never saw his face ... the two monks who accompanied him on the cart kept pressing a picture of Our Lord against his face, that he was forced to kiss continually. They kept the picture against his face while he went up the gibbet, and until he hung. After he died, he was drawn and quartered ... Right afterwards, three or four Jesuit priests stood above the crowd and lectured the people on the moral value of what they had just witnessed.

Older records describe severed heads and hands hanging for days along the streets around the inn, while pilgrims walked by unconcernedly.

From the inn a short walk leads to another landmark with a zoological name, the Torre della

S. Antonio dei Portoghesi, one of the many churches built to serve foreign communities in Rome

Scimmia ('Tower of the Monkey'), a medieval fortified house. It owes its fame both to a medieval story and to a tale spun around it by the American novelist Nathaniel Hawthorne in the 1800's. In the middle ages it was said – we don't know on what basis – that a pet monkey of the lords of the tower escaped out of the window one day with the family's newborn baby under its arm. The father prayed to the Virgin, promising that if the child were returned unhurt, he would place a lamp, which would burn forever in her honour, at the top of the tower; whereupon the monkey brought the baby back unharmed. Sure enough an oil lamp burned for centuries over the tower (today the lamp is an electric bulb). Hawthorne incorporated the story in his 1860 bestseller *The Marble Faun*, a rambling ghost story set in Rome, whose heroine, a New England girl, lodges on the top floor of the tower, where she is in charge of keeping the lamp lit.

ON THE SPOT

1. From the Locanda dell'Orso to the Torre della Scimmia

The Walk starts at Piazza di Ponte Umberto, named after the modern Umberto Bridge (a reference to the ill-starred second king of post-papal Italy, see p. 239), at the other end of which looms the bulky early 20th-century Palazzo di Giustizia or Law Court. This building, which does not deserve more than a glance from here, is another of those elephantine turn-of-the-century constructions – such as the notorious Vittoriano, see p. 535 – meant to celebrate in Rome the new monarchical order, this one in an awkward imitation of the 'Grand Palais' style from Paris. In the 1970's it collapsed under its own weight and has only been partially re-opened since.On Piazza di Ponte Umberto, opposite the bridge at No. 1, is the Museo Napoleonico (Napoleonic Museum, p. 686), containing memorabilia left by members of Napoleon's family in Rome (see pp. 227, 535). As you face it, a flight of stairs is to your left. Go down them; at the bottom is Via dell'Orso ('of the Bear') on your right.

The difference in street levels here is due to demolition and construction for the river embankment in the 1880's. It shows just how near the pre-embankment river waters were to the houses, and how easily they could be flooded. Safety was achieved, however, by destroying the fascinating natural river bank setting, and truncating and deforming the old street system. Originally the street continued along the river bank toward St. Peter's. It then served – together with Via dei Coronari, which was roughly parallel – to carry the pilgrim traffic, hence the hostelries.

Between the stair landing and Via dell'Orso is the multi-arched **Locanda dell'Orso** ('Inn of the Bear'). It is one of the best preserved examples of an ordinary Roman house of the 15th century. It became a hotel at the start of the 16th century, and for a time it had a high reputation. Its many illustrious guests included the French writers Rabelais

Area around the Locanda del' Orso and the Palazzo Altemps

The Palazzo di Giustizia, nicknamed 'Palazzaccio' (bad , or ugly, Palace) by the locals because both of its preposterousness and of its function

and Montaigne (16th century) and Goethe (in the late 18th). It then declined and became a favourite of stagecoach drivers, coachmen and stable hands, before closing at the end of the 19th century.

The columns and capitals, the refined brickwork and the terracotta decoration of the arches and cornices are all noteworthy.

Go on to Via dell'Orso. Embedded in a corner is a copy of a fragment of an ancient Roman tomb sculpture, showing a lion devouring a boar. The original of this striking piece, here since the middle ages, when the lion was mistaken for a bear and gave its name to the inn, was recently stolen.

On Via dell'Orso, the right flank of the inn has faint geometric frescoes and a beautiful protruding annexe with an intricately decorated terracotta balcony. Further down on your right, at No. 87, is another marble lion – this one original – identical to the other and from the same ancient tomb.

Continue down the street. At the next crossing on the right, Via Gigli d'Oro ('of the Golden Lilies'), step in to see, at No. 25, a house built in the 16th century by Antonio da Sangallo the Younger. Around the corner glance, without stepping in, at the picturesque Via dei Soldati ('of the Soldiers'), with the imposing 16th-century rear façade of Palazzo Altemps (p. 451). Continue down Via Gigli d'Oro and take Vicolo della Palomba ('of the Dove') on the left, which forms

an angle. At Nos 14-15 is a 16th-century palazzetto (notice the mottoes over the windows and the wide expanse between them, once covered with frescoes or *graffito* work).

Continuing along Vicolo della Palomba, you are back on Via dell'Orso. Go down it to the right. Where the street widens, its name changes to Via dei Portoghesi. Here, on your left, is the small, very elaborate baroque façade of the 17th-century **S. Antonio dei Portoghesi** ('of the Portuguese'), another national church (open: 07:00-12:00 and 16:00-18:00).

Rare coloured marbles cover the very rich interior. Note the marble funerary relief of a Portuguese dignitary, by the most famous early 19th-century sculptor, Canova (first chapel to the right), a painting by Antoniazzo Romano (15th-century) of the *Virgin and Child with Saints* (first chapel to the left) and the sumptuous 18th-century gilt organ.

As you leave the church, on your right (No. 18) is the **Torre della Scimmia** ('Tower of the Monkey'). It was built in the 15th century by the Frangipani family, one of the most warlike of the middle ages (p. 127), which has since died out. The perpetual lamp burns on the top of the tower next to a statue of the Virgin. The house around the tower, with an interesting doorway and balcony, dates from the 16th century.

BEFORE GOING

2. S. Agostino, S. Luigi dei Francesi and Palazzo della Sapienza

This short stretch includes no fewer than five churches and five palaces, all major examples of the renaissance or early baroque, within a small area bounded on one side by the long Stadium of Domitian (Piazza Navona, p. 458) and on the other by a string of Augustan monuments headed by the Pantheon (p. 241).

Two great churches are of particular interest. The first is the only one in Rome dedicated to St. Augustine, the foremost Latin Father of the Christian Church, author of the *City of God* (see p. 438). The second, dedicated to the French King Louis IX (St. Louis) is a French national church (of which you saw another on Trinità dei Monti). Both S. Agostino and S. Luigi dei Francesi possess some of Caravaggio's most beautiful works, a privilege they share with S. Maria del Popolo, which we visited at the beginning of the first Roma Romantica Walk. Michelangelo Merisi, called Caravaggio after his native town in northern Italy, came to Rome in 1593 at the age of 20 and stayed for 13 years, producing masterworks that ushered in a new era in painting. A strange and violent man, always the odd one out, he was implicated in a series of incidents that culminated in his killing a man during a tennis match.

Exiled from Rome, he wandered around for four years, spending time in Naples, Sicily and Malta. Everywhere he went he left important works, and indulged in bloody quarrels, one of which left him badly wounded. After partially recovering, he again headed for Rome, hoping for a papal pardon. On the way a minor accident stranded him – alone, ill and penniless – on a desolate beach north of the city. Delirious and tormented by the scorching sun, he died there at the age of thirty-nine.

His art, coming several decades after the measured equilibrium and splendid harmony of the renaissance, starkly brings back the brutality of real life through several pictorial innovations. He used strong contrasts between light and shade (it was even said that he painted at night by torch light). He also paid close, respectful attention to the humblest aspects of everyday life: the people in his paintings are always shown as ordinary and vulnerable, even if they are saints or the Madonna herself; and inanimate objects have the plasticity and weight of real matter. At the same time, his uncompromising realism is founded on a strong sense of the abstract values of drawing and composition. Few other painters have so vividly felt the latent geometry and interplay of shapes in the natural world.

This unprecedented blend of abstract and concrete may have been what particularly appealed to his fellow artists. His vision was widely imitated almost immediately, and its influence spread to most schools of painting all over Europe. To this day it carries a special charge, and admirers include artists such as Manet and Picasso.

S. Agostino, the adjacent Augustinian monastery (of the same order as that of S. Maria del Popolo) and some of the nearby homes were a focus of renaissance intellectual life, when many great artists, such as Raphael and Michelangelo, worshipped there. S. Agostino was also the preferred church of the famous courtesans. Artists and courtesans joined in lively discussions on art and literature at gatherings organised in nearby gardens owned by a high official of the Holy See,

Caravaggio's only print, The Denial of Peter: *technically uncertain but full of the artist's immediacy and psychological realism*

the Apostolic Protonotary, Johann Goritz, from Luxembourg (he was called Coricio in Rome). At their meetings, which ended in banquets, it was customary to read new poetry and to hang poems and garlands on trees. Some of these poems have survived. They typify the renaissance spirit, exuding Christian sentiments dressed in pagan literary garb, with the Virgin extolled as a goddess and the saints as gods.

The high-class courtesans who came to S. Agostino to pray and confess gave generously to the church and were often buried there in chapels donated by them and decorated with their funerary monuments. The most famous of them, Fiammetta Michaelis (p. 448), was interred there. But these tombs, and possibly the remains, have entirely disappeared, no doubt swept away during the counter-reformation.

To pass judgment on these remarkable figures of an extraordinary age is not easy. It is hard to draw a line between these courtesans and their thousands of poorer colleagues who plied their trade in the streets. Yet there was something special about them that redeemed them in the eyes of their contemporaries, who commonly called them 'honest courtesans'. Their beauty and perceived spirituality exempted them from conventions; a comparison with Japan's geishas might be apt. Highly polished, stunningly beautiful – remember that a sharp-eyed man like Cellini considered one of them, Antea, Rome's most beautiful woman (p. 451) – they placed themselves firmly in the renaissance ambiance of high culture and a passion for classical ideals of beauty and knowledge. This attitude could also invite ridicule, however: the scorching 16th-century satirist Aretino – a great writer but a spiteful man (pp. 348, 349) – gives us a devastating portrait of these women as a ludicrous blend of pretentiousness and greed, posing as heiresses to the famous *hetæræ* ('companions') of Greece and Rome. One, nicknamed 'Matrema-non-vuole' ('Mummy-doesn't-want-me-to'), afflicted clients with long recitations of passages from Latin classics (Woody Allen's short story *The Whore of Mensa* comes to mind).

Yet many had true, even great literary talent, such as the poetesses Gaspara Stampa, Veronica Franco and Tullia d'Aragona, as well as Camilla da Pisa, who is remembered for her letters. Their intelligence and learning were often real. They were respected fixtures at the best parties and could hold their own in conversation with the highest minds of that gloriously intellectual era. When they joined a permanent partner, they were expected to be faithful; hence Cellini's murderous fury when he found his Pantasilea, a courtesan, with another man (pp. 448, 450). The Church seems to have accepted them: they could be buried in S. Agostino rather than in unconsecrated ground at the foot of the Muro Malo (p. 43), as was prescribed by law for common prostitutes. These courtesans may even be considered proto-feminists, judging from the sonnet addressed to men by Veronica Franco:

Had we the power and had we the knowledge,	Quando armate ed esperte ancor siam noi
We could be the equal of any man,	Render buon conto a ciascun uom potemo
As we have hands, and feet, and heart	Che mani e piedi e core avem qual
just as you have (...)	voi (...)
Women have not realized it yet,	Di ciò non se ne son le donne accorte
But should they once resolve on doing it,	Che, se si risolvessero di farlo
They could fight with you men until they die.	Con voi pugnar porian fino alla morte.

The aura of high learning around the church of S. Agostino is enhanced by the nearby Palazzo della Sapienza ('Palace of Wisdom'), former seat of the University of Rome. This renaissance building saw lectures by famous scientists such as Galileo and Copernicus; another claim to fame is its chapel, S. Ivo, one of the most exhilarating examples of baroque architecture in Rome, and the masterpiece of Francesco Borromini.

ON THE SPOT

2. S. Agostino, S. Luigi dei Francesi and Palazzo della Sapienza

Across the street from S. Antonio dei Portoghesi, at No. 12 Via dei Portoghesi, is one of the entrances to a renaissance Augustinian monastery, together with the adjoining church of S. Agostino. The monastery was rebuilt in the 1700's by the distinguished architect and painter Luigi Vanvitelli, son of the Dutch painter Gaspard Van Wittel, who had stayed in Rome and Italianised his name. The building is closed to the public but you can see the courtyard from the entrance.

In Vanvitelli's architecture, the elegance of the early 18th century has an unwonted sobriety that uncannily foreshadows the solemn, linear neo-classical style prevalent later in the century. On the left side of the courtyard are four 15th-century funerary monuments by unknown sculptors, moved here from the adjoining church.

The Italian state confiscated the monastery after 1870, along with that of S. Maria sopra Minerva (p. 116) and many others. It is now the office of the Italian Solicitor General.

Via dei Portoghesi ends in Via della Scrofa ('of the Sow'), which is the continuation of Via Ripetta, as you will realise when you see, from the crossing here, the Piazza del Popolo obelisk in the distance to the left. You'll then recall the role of this street axis as a direct line of access into renaissance Rome (see p. 30).

Turn right into Via della Scrofa. In the wall of the Augustinian monastery, at ground level between the second and third windows, is the marble relief of a sow that gave the street its name. The ancient Roman relief was put there in the 16th century as part of a small fountain of the Acqua Vergine, which was later moved to the corner of the building (it is mentioned in the small plaque).

Opposite, at No. 39, is the headquarters of the neo-Fascist party ('Alleanza Nazionale'). Continue down Via della Scrofa; if No. 82 (right) is open, as it rarely is, enter and see the harmonious, theatrical entrance hall of the monastery,

attributed by some scholars not to Vanvitelli but to his Sicilian contemporary Juvarra.

At the end of the block turn right into Via S. Agostino to reach the late 15th-century church of **S. Agostino** (St. Augustine). The façade resembles that of S. Maria del Popolo (p. 47) but is more ornate. Indeed, the two were built a few years apart and are Rome's best examples of orderly and graceful early renaissance church façades. (Open: 07:30-12.30 and 16:30-19:00.)

The simple, geometric interior was partly remodelled by Vanvitelli in the 1700's, to no great advantage.

In order to see the highlights quickly, we'll depart from our usual counter-clockwise order. Next to the central door (usually closed) is a statue of the Virgin and Child by Jacopo Sansovino, an early 16th-century masterpiece whose strength and serenity reveal the influences of both Michelangelo and ancient classical sculpture. It has been called the *Madonna del Parto* ('of Childbirth') ever since the 19th century, when a mechanic left it a votive offering, imploring protection for his wife during delivery. The faithful have always considered the statue particularly responsive to prayers and vows, and have left offerings of all kinds (only a fraction are there now). The foot of the Virgin, now protected by a silver sheath, is worn down by kisses and caresses. Votive pictures and objects extend inside the central door. Until the 1800's the statue also received an unusual category of gifts: the knives of criminals seeking salvation.

With your back to the statue, look at the arches to the left: on the third pillar is a fresco by Raphael of the *Prophet Isaiah* (1512), clearly inspired by Michelangelo's Sistine Chapel frescoes of prophets. Even so, and despite heavy restoration, the intense expression and the force of drawing betray the individuality of a great master. Michelangelo himself, no friend of Raphael, greatly admired the fresco. When the Vatican Protonotary, Johann Coricio (p. 332), who commissioned it, later complained that he had overpaid the artist, Michelangelo supposedly rebuked him, saying 'The knee alone is worth what you paid.' Isaiah carries a scroll in Hebrew with the biblical verse 'Open the door to the believers' under a dedication in Greek 'to St. Anne, Mother of the Virgin, and to the Virgin, Mother of God,' signed 'Io(hann) Cor(icio)'.

Beneath the fresco is a statuary group of *St. Anne with the Virgin and Child*, a moving family portrait by Andrea Sansovino (Jacopo Sansovino's master), commissioned together with the fresco. All the frescoes of prophets on the other pillars are minor 19th-century works.

In the first chapel to the left is the marvellous *Madonna dei Pellegrini* ('of the Pilgrims') by Caravaggio (1605). The Virgin carrying her splendid Child is portrayed as a common Roman woman. She has descended from her tenement apartment and stands in one of the old doorways, of which we've seen many in the renaissance district. Two poor, battered old pilgrims are transported by joy while gazing at these two sweet figures. It is one of the greatest religious representations of all time.

Continue up the left aisle, past the transept, to a small room on the left. Dedicated to St. Augustine, it was frescoed by Giovanni Lanfranco (17th century), of whom there's much more later (p. 508). In a large chapel between this room and the main

S. Luigi dei Francesi, early in the 20th century

altar is the tomb of St. Monica, St. Augustine's mother (4th century AD), herself one of the great figures of early Christianity. On the left wall is a 15th-century tomb chest topped by a statue of *St. Monica* by Isaia da Pisa; her relics have been moved to beneath the chapel altar.

The majestic main altar was designed by Bernini (17th century), who also made the two angels overhead (the little angels over the doors are by minor 18th-century artists). Over the altar is a 14th-century *Madonna* in the Byzantine style.

Continue clockwise. Over an altar at the end of the transept is a painting by Guercino – one of the great painters and draughtsmen of the 17th century – of *St. Augustine and other Saints*. Other paintings on the walls are by Guercino or his pupils. The beautiful sacristy, immediately past the transept, was designed by Luigi Vanvitelli. In the chapel past the sacristy door is an interesting early 15th-century crucifix, before which St. Philip Neri (p. 463) used to pray.

Leaving the church, return (left) to Via della Scrofa and continue in the same direction as before (right) along a block formed by a late 18th-century building. It belongs to the Vatican and contains the Papal Institute of Sacred Music. It is worth looking through the gate of No. 70 to see the courtyard with its colourful fountain.

Continue straight for another block to **S. Luigi dei Francesi** ('St. Louis of the French'), the most important of the French national churches in Rome, owned by the French state and run by French clergy. The stately high renaissance façade was designed at the end of the 16th century by Giacomo Della Porta. The statues are by a minor 18th-century French sculptor; flanking the doors are *Charlemagne* (left) and *St. Louis* (right). The crowned salamanders below these statues were the emblems of the French king Francis I. A French coat-of-arms tops the façade. (Open: May to Sept, 08:00-12:00 and 16:00-19:00; Oct to April, 07:30-12:30 and 15:30-19:00. Closed Thursday afternoons and evenings.)

The warm atmosphere of the interior comes from the play of light on the pink and yellow marbles and the glow of golden stucco. The lavish ceiling centres on a gorgeous fresco by the 18th-century French painter C. J. Natoire of *The Death and Apotheosis of St. Louis.*

In here we'll go clockwise. See the interesting pulpit on the left, with painted panels by an unknown 16th- or 17th-century artist, then go to the left aisle. (Note: most chapels have a light switch just under the altar rail. The Caravaggio chapel has a coin-operated light.) The third chapel was designed and elaborately decorated by Plautilla Bricci, a 17th-century Roman painter and architect. The *St. Louis* over the altar is also by her.

Go to the last chapel on the left, dedicated to St. Matthew, with fascinating paintings by Caravaggio (1600). The most stunning is *The Calling of St. Matthew* to the left. There is magic in the dramatic way Jesus summons the profligate youth, intent on playing dice in a lowly inn. Light, texture, colour, shape, and psychological insight are mobilised together here to an unparalleled degree. To the right is the moving *Martyrdom of St. Matthew*. Over the altar is *St. Matthew and the Angel*, a toned-down version, by the painter himself, of an earlier work whose ferocious realism had offended the priests of this church (not an unusual occurrence in Caravaggio's career). The original ended up in Berlin, where Allied bombing destroyed it in the Second World War.

Just above the chapel altar is a sweet, naive 15th-16th-century statuette of the *Virgin and Child*, of unknown authorship, saved from an old church demolished nearby. A doubtful tradition holds that the lover of the Borgia pope, Vannozza Catanei (pp. 45-46), posed for it.

Over the main altar is a large and impressive painting of the *Assumption* by the Venetian Francesco Bassano (late 16th century).

Continuing clockwise down the right aisle, the second chapel on the left is illustrated with *Episodes from the Life of Clovis*, the first French king to convert to Christianity (in the 5th century), a work by Pellegrino Tibaldi and other, less important, 16th-century painters.

The next to last chapel on the left, dedicated to

St. Cecilia, is frescoed by Domenichino with episodes from her life. It is considered among the masterworks of this great pupil of Annibale Carracci. The painting over the altar is a copy by Domenichino's fellow pupil Guido Reni of a *St. Cecilia* by Raphael.

Opposite the church, at No. 37, is a 16th-century palace by Carlo Maderno.

Unless you're running late and risk finding S. Andrea della Valle closed (see opening times on p. 510) a short side trip is suggested here. The main itinerary resumes on p 501.

DETOUR

10 MIN

After leaving the church, continue right into Via della Dogana Vecchia ('of the Old Customhouse'), named after the papal office which was torn down in 1690 and moved to Hadrian's Temple (p. 233). The austere 17th-century palace on your left, in which Borromini had a hand, now houses the President of the Italian Senate.

Continue down this typical renaissance artery. On your right is the beautiful curved rear elevation of Palazzo Madama, seat of the Italian Senate, whose façade we'll see shortly. At the end turn left into Piazza S. Eustachio, named after the church of **S. Eustachio** on the left. The church was originally a chapel built by the emperor Constantine in the 4th century (p. 357) on the site of the reputed house of Eustace, a general under Hadrian (2nd century) who converted to Christianity. He was said to have been martyred here with his wife and two sons, all burned alive inside a brass bull. The bodies are said to lie under the main altar. (Open: 17:00-19:30; Sun 11:00-12:30.)

Rebuilt several times, the church is presently late baroque (but notice the beautiful medieval bell tower). At the top of the church, a stag's head with a crucifix between its antlers represents a vision Eustace had while hunting, and which spurred his conversion. He is thus the patron saint of hunters. Popularly, St. Eustace is also considered the protector of, and his church a spiritual refuge for, betrayed husbands, because to Italians horns (stag's or otherwise) symbolise marital infidelity.

On the corner across from the church is a charming late 16th-century palazzetto, the exterior decorated with frescoes attributed to the Zuccari brothers. A fresco on the right side, over the arms of the ruling pope, illustrates the legend of St. Eustace.

From the church, go right a few yards. The right end of the piazza is formed by the Palazzo della Sapienza and S. Ivo complex with its beautiful dome and incredible, innovative spiral lantern, all by Borromini. We'll visit the complex later, unless one of the two portals on this side happens to be open, in which case enter now and read the description on p. 502.

The building at Nos 80-83 is the 16th-century Palazzo Stati (also known as Palazzo Maccarani), designed in classical renaissance style by Raphael's chief assistant, Giulio Romano.

The building was originally owned by a feudal clan who had lived in the area since the middle ages and who took their name from it: 'Stati' comes from the Latin 'Eustatii' or 'Eustace's'. Later, it belonged among others to the Cenci family at the time of the bloody saga we'll recount (p. 517). The bar on the ground floor is famous for its *espresso* coffee.

From Piazza S. Eustachio pass into the adjacent Piazza dei Caprettari ('of the Goat-dealers'), with a typical cluster of renaissance and baroque buildings of all shapes; amongst them, at No. 70, is Palazzo Lante, an elegant work by Jacopo Sansovino (early 16th century).

Return to Piazza S. Eustachio and leave it via the street to the right of the S. Ivo complex, Via degli Staderari ('of the Scale-makers'). The fountain in this street is a gigantic ancient Roman granite basin excavated in 1987 during renovation work inside the nearby Senate.

Continue down Via degli Staderari (with, on the left, a nice art deco fountain). To return to the main itinerary, skip the next paragraph.

END OF DETOUR

A loggia at the Palazzo Madama, before its reconstruction, when it included a collection of statues, in an engraving by the 16th-century Northern artist Martin van Heemskerck

After leaving S Luigi dei Francesi, go right and then turn immediately right. On the left of this street, Via del Salvatore, is the side of Palazzo Madama, which houses the Italian Senate.

Follow it to the end, into a broad artery, another misguided modernisation project of the 1930's, when several old alleys were gutted.

This artery has as an imposing backdrop to the far left the church of S. Andrea della Valle with its majestic dome. It is one of our next highlights. Cross over to have a first look at it from here, though if it is getting late it will be better to go directly to the church (for opening times see p. 510) and return here afterwards.

Before you (if the church is on your right) is **Palazzo Madama**, seat of the Italian Senate (those who have taken the Detour will need to walk a block to the left). Built in the 1500's it was re-modelled in 1642 in a somewhat overdone baroque design by the Roman architect Paolo Marucelli. Owned by the ruling family of Florence, the Medici, the palace was called Madama after one of the great Medici ladies who lived in it (as did two future Medici popes and Catherine de' Medici, future queen of France). The Italian Senate took over the building when Rome was annexed in 1871. The foundations of the façade rest on ruins of the walls around the Baths of Nero (p. 241).

501

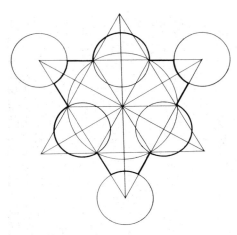

Diagram of the complex floor plan of S. Ivo (in bold) showing how Borromini worked it out from the simplest geometrical elements

To the right of Palazzo Madama, and joined to it by a later two-storey passageway, is another 16th-century palace. It once stood in the area which was demolished to create this artery, but the planners rebuilt it on its present site to serve as offices for the Senate.

The next building (as you go, notice the medieval tower of S. Eustachio in the background) is the **Palazzo della Sapienza**. It was built by Sixtus V (p. 44) at the end of the 16th century for the University of Rome (also called *della Sapienza*, 'of Wisdom'), which was then 200 years old. The campus was moved in 1935, and the building is now contains the State Archives.

Over the centre window of the main façade is the Latin motto: 'The fear of the Lord is the beginning of wisdom'. The palace is by Giacomo Della Porta; its most striking feature is the courtyard, onto which faces the wonderful 17th-century church of **S. Ivo** (St. Ives), the university chapel, by Francesco Borromini. Cross the street to enter the courtyard (if closed, try the two back entrances on Piazza S. Eustachio).

Of all the architecturally planned open spaces of Rome, only Michelangelo's Campidoglio (pp. 145-147) compares in harmony and magnificence with Della Porta's courtyard. Remarkable, too, is the way in which Borromini took off from Della Porta's Michelangelesque manner to create the baroque church of S. Ivo facing the courtyard. There is such continuity between the two styles, that it is still a matter of debate which architect did the lower half of the church facade, which is both part of the courtyard and the church. Yet the individuality of each architect remains marked.

The church dome, a daring multi-lobed design, and the unique snail-shell lantern above it are prime examples of Borromini's genius, which unites unbridled fantasy and geometrical rigour. In the church interior (accessible from the end of the courtyard on the far right; unfortunately only open on Sunday mornings) the master's inventiveness has had free play, through the rhythm of concave and convex surfaces that is his trademark, the momentum of the structural lines and the luminous simplicity of the colour scheme. Borromini's ability in drawing complexity out of basic geometrical elements finds its most complete application in the plan. The superimposition of two equilateral triangles generates a six-pointed star; circles drawn at the points and midpoints of the triangles give alternately concave and convex expression to the points of the star. Borromini then draws this plan upwards with such artistry that the convex areas mutate into concave, and vice versa. The figure has layers of symbolic meaning as well, since the star represents wisdom, the *sapientia* of the university's name.

On the main altar is a dramatic 17th-century painting of *St. Ivo*, of disputed authorship.

Opposite the Sapienza is the rear of the early renaissance church of Nostra Signora del Sacro Cuore. We saw its façade in Piazza Navona on the previous Walk (p. 461). This side is a modern creation in the 15th-century style, though the main doorway is original.

Interior of S. Ivo; the highly regular plan is translated into an undulating wall surface

BEFORE GOING

3. The 'Valley'

We now cross a part of the Campus Martius ('Field of Mars') which in very ancient times, when the Campus Martius was still outside the city proper, was called the 'valley' owing to its slight depression and rural setting; remember, too, that this area was used until the middle ages for outdoor activities (p. 239). We already crossed this area in the first Renaissance Rome Walk, but much closer to the river, where we saw the church of Santa Maria in Vallicella ('in the Little Valley').

In the past, the recreational aspect was evident in several features, some of which we've already mentioned: Agrippa's *stagnum* or pond, where Nero feasted (p. 240); the Euripus, a canal crisscrossed with small bridges that ran along the valley from the pond to the river; the Stadium of Domitian nearby (Piazza Navona, p. 458); and injecting a note of mysterious awe, the Tarentum, a crevice in the ground emitting natural fumes, considered an entrance to Hell and consecrated to the infernal deities.

There were intellectual pursuits, too. Next to his stadium, Domitian built an *odeon*, or musical auditorium, for over 10,000 people, devoted to musical entertainment and poetry competitions. A few steps away was the Theatre of Pompey, the first stone theatre in Rome (p. 519).

After the area had been densely settled in the middle ages, its frolicsome traits faded. But an echo remained in the frequent colourful processions, after the old 'Valley' became part of the Via Papalis, the official path of the papal cortège (p. 412). The district was also famous for special illuminations, known literally as 'fires of joy', organised by the Church authorities. The intellectual aspect continued to dominate, however, accentuated by the establishment of the University of Rome nearby. Scholars and artists, including Antoniazzo Romano, lived in the area. Giuseppe Calasanzio (St. Joseph Calasanctius), a Counter-Reformation saint, who like St. Philip Neri (p. 463) specialised in public education, set up the headquarters of a network of elementary schools here, which were destined to acquire global importance. Ever since the middle ages, publishing companies and bookstores have favoured the area, and some are still here. The first newspaper-like publications also appeared here.

This short stretch has more than its share of noble renaissance palaces, including one possibly designed by Raphael and another by his distinguished contemporary Peruzzi. Peruzzi's palace has the further distinction of having been for several centuries the home of the longest-living aristocratic dynasty in Italy– and possibly the world – the Massimo family, said to go back to Hannibal's foe Fabius Maximus (3rd century BC). When Napoleon asked the great-great-great-grandfather of the present prince whether this was true, he got the answer: 'I can't say for sure, sir. The rumour has been running in my family for only a thousand years.'

ON THE SPOT

3. The 'Valley'

Let's assume you face the doorway of the Nostra Signora del Sacro Cuore across the avenue from the Palazzo della Sapienza (this modern avenue is aptly called Corso Rinascimento or 'Renaissance Boulevard'). Continue left, passing on your right Via dei Canestrari ('of the Basket-weavers'): rattan and wicker furniture has been sold here for centuries; at the time of writing, there was still one such store at the end of the first block). The next crossing is Via S. Giuseppe Calasanzio, named after a saint we'll discuss shortly. Take it to a small square dominated by a column: recently unearthed and re-erected, it belonged to the Odeon of Domitian, which stood here almost back-to-back with the Stadium of Domitian.

The square is called Piazza dei Massimi. On it stands **Palazzo Massimo Istoriato** ('Illustrated'), one of several palaces and houses on a block belonging mainly to the princely Massimo family.

The simple façade was tacked onto older houses by Baldassarre Peruzzi (a major 16th-century architect and painter in the circle of Pinturicchio and Raphael), and then frescoed by his pupils, including Daniele da Volterra. Graffiti and frescoes on Roman renaissance houses usually depicted mythological subjects, but this façade is an exception in showing biblical scenes. The decoration is very faded, but still identifiable on the penultimate floor are *Esther and Ahasuerus* (left), *Judith Slaying Holofernes* (centre) and *Judith with the Head of Holofernes* (right). On the top floor, above a large battle frieze, are the *Marriage of the Virgin* (centre) and some unidentifiable scenes.

The Massimo hosted two famous German printers at the Palazzo Istoriato in the 1400's, Konrad Sweynheym and Arnold Pannartz. Here in 1467 they produced one of the first books ever printed in Rome, a splendid edition of Cicero. It was their innovation to abandon the 'Gothic' typefaces always used hitherto and to print their texts of the ancient writers and the fathers using a typeface designed to imitate the ancient lettering they could see in inscriptions all around them and in the clear forms of the rediscovered manuscripts. This innovation is the ancestor of all modern type, including the one you are reading now. Sweynheim also cast the first Greek typeface. In only eight years, he and Pannartz published almost forty titles and printed 12,000 books, making them one of the forces of the Renaissance. Later, many of the neighbouring streets housed bookstores and printers and publishers.

The walls at an angle to the frescoed façade,

with 16th-century windows, belong to the church of S. Pantaleo (whose own façade is on the other side of the block) and a related monastery. Church and monastery can be entered here, at No. 4, which is the headquarters of a major religious order, the Piarist Fathers (from the 'pious' schools they founded for poor children, which were amongst the first free primary schools). Established in the early 17th century by a counter-reformation saint, Giuseppe Calasanzio, (the Spaniard, José Calasanz) the order runs schools and monasteries on four continents.

DETOUR
15 MIN

Ring the bell at No. 4 to be let in by the friendly and enthusiastic Fathers – mostly Spaniards and Latin Americans – to the saint's rooms, where you can still find his belongings, including his three-cornered hat. You should also be able to see a poetic little cloister and the church of **S. Pantaleo**.

Founded before the 1100's and dedicated to Pantaleo, a martyred 4th-century Christian physician and the patron saint of doctors, the church was extensively remodelled in the 17th century, when Calasanz and his order took it over. In the first chapel to the right of the main entrance is an 18th-century multi-media composition of a sort rare in Rome, by an unknown painter, depicting *Christ on the Cross with Mary Magdalene*. Most other art works, including the vivid ceiling fresco, are by minor 17th- and 18th-century artists. Under the main altar is the porphyry tomb of the saint.

The front door is rarely open; we assume that in any case you will go out the way you came in.

END OF DETOUR

From Piazza dei Massimi take the picturesque alley next to the monastery, Vicolo della Cuccagna (the name refers to the greased pole used for climbing contests, see p. 453). Along the side of the Piarist monastery is a charming 15th-century

The entrance vestibule of the Palazzo Massimo alle Colonne, built on a curve

house (No. 13b). Turn left again – you are still going round the block of Massimo buildings – to Piazza St. Pantaleo, which opens onto the modern Corso Vittorio (p. 470). Here you are on the edge of the 'Valley' and the ancient Euripus canal, both of which are echoed by the layout of the present Corso Vittorio; you are also standing on the former Via Papalis.

On the piazza is the quiet, neo-classical façade of S. Pantaleo, added to the church in the 19th century by Valadier, the architect of Piazza del Popolo. At No. 10 is **Palazzo Braschi**, dating from the renaissance, but totally rebuilt in the late 18th century, when it was purchased by Pope Pius VI (p. 67), for his nephew. It was once the seat of the fascist party. It is the last palace acquired by a papal family in Rome (p. 483). The Braschis died out in the early 1900's.

You have seen the rear of the palace from Piazza Navona (p. 461). The 18th-century interior, by the Bolognese architect Cosimo Morelli, is a solemn, noble design, with a very beautiful staircase. It houses the museum of the history of Rome; the collection is rich and fascinating, but, thanks to Rome's cultural authorities, never fully open (Museo storico di Roma, p. 686).

Continue left around the Massimo block. The three first buildings here belong to the Massimo family, and are connected internally. No. 145 was built in the early 16th century. More important is the adjacent No. 141, **Palazzo Massimo alle Colonne** ('of the Columns'), from the same period. It was built by Peruzzi on the site of the Massimo ancestral home, burnt down during the Sack of Rome (p. 381).

The Massimo still live in this palace. While their origins in the 3rd century BC are probably legendary, the name appears in 4th century AD records. The family is related to many royal dynasties of Europe, such as the Savoy, Bourbon and Saxony.

The word 'columns' in the name of the palace refers to the columns from the Odeon of Domitian that once adorned the original façade and were destroyed in the fire.

In Peruzzi's reconstruction, the beautiful front portico preserves the memory of these columns.

The shape of the façade follows that of the ancient odeon, showing that the previous palace was built over its ruins. The slight curve, together with the effects of light and shadow created by the deep portico, make the palace both monumental and lively.

Past the portico with refined ceiling stuccowork and an entrance hall, also with fine stucco, one enters the first courtyard, wonderfully proportioned and decorated with archæological finds. Another hall leads to the second courtyard – rebuilt in the 1600's – which belongs to the connecting Palazzo Istoriato (p. 505). Two unusual granite columns seem to be spolia from the Temple of Isis nearby (p. 121), and may even come from the destroyed palace 'alle colonne'.

Every year on March 16, morning masses (open to the public) are held every hour on the hour in a second-floor chapel, which was once the sickroom of young Paolo Massimo. On that day in 1584 Philip Neri (p. 463) resuscitated the child, a miracle for which he was canonized.

Continue to the end of the block. The 17th century fountain nearby is attributed to Carlo Maderno, though the upper basin is modern.

Stucco ceiling decoration, Palazzo Massimo alle Colonne

4. S. Andrea della Valle

Before leaving the 'Valley', we'll visit a famous church whose name seems to be an obvious reference to its location: 'St. Andrew of the Valley'. Yet nobody actually knows whether this alludes to the valley, or to the eminent Cardinal Andrea della Valle, of the Spanish La Valle family, whose palace was opposite. Another coincidence further muddles the question. The church was called S. Andrea (St. Andrew) not as a tribute to the cardinal, but because it replaced a smaller, much older church dedicated to the Apostle Andrew.

Let's leave this puzzle (how many of these ambiguities crop up in the history of an ancient city, tormenting historian and tourist alike!) The church is famed not only for its beauty, but as the location of two dramatic stories, one fictional, the other true. The first is from Puccini's opera *Tosca*. Its first act is set in the nave, which the painter Mario is decorating before he sings a beautiful duet with his lover Tosca (p. 387). The second story concerns the real authors of the frescoes, two major artists of the early baroque, Domenichino and Lanfranco. We have seen a few of their paintings elsewhere, but some of their greatest works are here. The story is tied to a long and bitter feud between them which, according to their biographer and contemporary, Bellori, endangered and possibly shortened both their lives.

They were both young pupils of the great Annibale Carracci, in a circle that included other future giants, such as Reni and Guercino. Domenichino was unpopular because of his peculiarly introverted, suspicious nature. He was short, bowlegged and very slow; his fellow students called him 'the ox'. He never showed his drawings to anyone and was so punctilious that he devoted exactly one hour a day to socialising, making a list of seven friends and rotating them each week. He would only make a new friend when there was a vacancy on his list. His teacher Carracci saw his genius, however, and esteemed him more than any other pupil, choosing him as his spiritual heir. He also reserved the best commissions in the studio for him.

Domenichino took full advantage of this, much to the chagrin of his colleagues. The most incensed was Lanfranco, who at first tried unsuccessfully to destroy his rival by accusing him of plagiarism. He printed and passed around engravings of Domenichino's works next to the alleged source material. One day the greatest opportunity of Domenichino's career arose. The friars of S. Andrea della Valle asked him to fresco the dome and part of the apse of their new church. Domenichino gave this commission priority and started making painstaking preparations. He went so far as to act out privately the roles of the characters, 'to enter their souls' as he said. Months passed before he felt ready to put hand to brush. Lanfranco exploited the delay to approach the impatient friars and offer to do the job himself, quickly, while he disparaged his rival's drawings as old-fashioned and imitative.

Domenichino was indeed a conservative follower of the sedate, classical style of the late renaissance, while Lanfranco championed the passionate new manner of the baroque, though this does not imply any superiority on Lanfranco's part.

Lanfranco succeeded in persuading the friars just as Domenichino had finally got down to business and started painting great figures at the base of the dome. Thus one morning Domenichino

S. Andrea della Valle before the creation of the Corso Vittorio, by Giuseppe Vasi

saw his sneering rival enter the church, climb up to the highest level of scaffolding and start painting. Domenichino, realising he was being cashiered, was so shattered that he could barely finish the frescoes left to him, those in the apse. Worsening the blow was the initial public reaction, which favoured Lanfranco's trendier work. Someone even asked that Domenichino's frescoes be painted over by Lanfranco.

This judgment would be reversed within a few years, however, when Domenichino came to be regarded as a genius second only to Raphael. His serene, incisive and at times monumental style found enthusiastic supporters, and has remained influential down to the abstract art of our own day. Lanfranco, on the other hand, is less highly esteemed, but is considered to be the artist who first adopted the baroque style in painting, and a precursor to Bernini.

If the conflict between the two can be (and indeed is) seen as a clash between two schools, then it is no less personal. One morning Lanfranco, climbing to the dome, noticed a thin line in the scaffolding supports. They had been sawn through and would have collapsed had Lanfranco not jumped back. Domenichino was accused of attempted murder, though without proof.

Domenichino is traditionally considered a victim of others' malice; those who have seen his house in the second Roma Romantica Walk may remember a tablet expressing sympathy with him for this reason (p. 106). But if he really tried to kill Lanfranco, he cannot have been a very tender soul himself; and he was second to none in double-crossing his fellow artists. More on this when we visit one of our next highlights, S. Carlo ai Catinari.

ON THE SPOT

4. S. Andrea della Valle

Across Corso Vittorio is the imposing façade of
S. Andrea della Valle, built in the 1600's by Carlo
Rainaldi after drawings by Carlo Maderno, and
notable for its strong plasticity and chiaroscuro
effect. Also by Maderno is the magnificent dome,
the second largest in Rome after St. Peter's.
Halfway up the left side of the façade, an angel
with one wing extended replaces the ornamental
scroll which would normally complete the geometric design. There is no matching angel on the
other side: the story goes that the sculptor, a
minor 17th-century artist, refused to produce the
second one after Pope Alexander VII (p. 44) criticised the first.

Cross Corso Vittorio Emanuele. The church is
open weekdays 07:30-12:00 and 16:30-19:30;
Sundays 07:30-12:45 and 16:30-19:45.

The grandiosity and luminosity of the interior
are due to the vastness of the nave, the barrel-
vaulted shape of the very high ceiling, the
marvellous dome by Maderno and the large apse
resplendent with gold and colour.

The chapels are opulent. Start by looking at
two of these: the first on the right, rich in
coloured marbles, and the second on the right,
which some scholars think is based on a
Michelangelo design (early copies of his statues
and marvellous bronze candelabra decorate it).
Proceeding up the nave, stop just short of the
dome area. Note, over the last (smaller) arches of
the nave, right and left, the tombs of the two
Piccolomini popes. This prominent Sienese family, still extant, has given Italy several important
figures since the middle ages, including these two
renaissance popes, whose tombs were originally
in old St. Peter's, but were moved here when the
old basilica was torn down (p. 357). The late 15th-
century tomb on the left is of Pope Pius II, Æneas
Silvius Piccolomini, poet, historian and humanist;
he was a very influential figure in the early renaissance. The tomb on the right (early 16th century)
is of his nephew, Pius III. The two exquisite sets

of sculptures are of different and unknown
authorship; the second imitates the structural
model of the first. On both, the second panel
from the bottom represents the pope lying in
state. Below are scenes of ceremonial gatherings,
above, scenes of the pope being presented to the
Virgin and Child.

The frescoed further half of the church – from
the dome onward – is one of the most significant
showcases of 17th-century pictorial decoration.

In the dome is the great fresco of *The Glory of
Paradise*, a masterwork by Giovanni Lanfranco, a
painter of deep emotional strength, seminal in the
early development of the baroque. The four powerful figures of the *Evangelists* in the pendentives
(corners) of the dome are by Domenichino,
whose monumental style, lightened by a perfect
sense of balance, renews the ideals of the renaissance.

In the presbytery and apse Domenichino's
frescoes cover the area overhead, that is, the
curved space over the cornice. Depicted over the
central window is the *Calling of St. Andrew*, St.
Peter's humble fisherman brother. To the right of
this, *St. Andrew Led to his Martyrdom*, with the
X-shaped cross on which he was martyred looming in the background. Left is the *Flagellation of
the St. Andrew*, spread-eagled on his cross. These
three panels converge in a smaller one, the
Apotheosis of the Saint, next to which is the scene
of *Behold the Lamb of God*. Symbolic female
figures and ornamental male nudes, all of exceptional clarity and vigour, surround these scenes.
The four male nudes to the left and right of the
Lamb of God scene – carrying garlands from
which putti pick pears – were judged in their time
to be of unsurpassed beauty.

Below the work of Domenichino, five gigantic
frescoes surround the altar; they are by lesser
17th-century painters of a younger generation.
The best are the three central ones by Mattia
Preti, culminating in a powerful rendering of the
Death of St. Andrew.

Before leaving the church, stop at the last
chapel on your right. Against the left wall is a

statue of *St. John the Baptist* by Pietro Bernini; the marble putti over the two side doors are also by him and by his more famous son Gian Lorenzo.

As you leave, across Corso Vittorio to the right (do not actually cross it) is Palazzo della Valle, built in 1517 for Cardinal Andrea della Valle, whose name is over the door, by the sculptor and architect Lorenzetto, a close friend of Raphael.

Walk right and turn right into Piazza Vidoni. Just behind this square began the huge portico of the **Teatro di Pompeo** (Theatre of Pompey), where Julius Cæsar was murdered (we saw the other end when visiting the Argentina , p. 244).

Follow the flank of the church as far as the beautiful old palace at a right angle to it, No. 6, which belongs to a convent. On the lower left-hand side of the wall is some mysterious graffiti, mainly French, in typical 16th-century writing. They are thought to be by French soldiers billeted there, possibly from a unit that accompanied Charles V on his 1536 visit to Rome (p. 237). Until recently the graffiti were shielded by glass panels, but they were shorn of their protection, sandblasted, overpainted and almost obliterated in one of the vaunted 'restorations' of the Jubilee Year 2000.

From the piazza, take Via del Sudario ('of the Shroud'), which starts with No. 10, the minor entrance to a very long building. This is the 16th-century **Palazzo Caffarelli Vidoni**, built by Lorenzetto, possibly on a plan by Raphael. Charles V is believed to have stayed here during the same visit.

In order to appreciate the balance and liveliness of the building, bear in mind that only the central part is authentic; the penthouse, too, is an unfortunate later addition. The side on Corso Vittorio, around the corner, is from the 1800's.

A few steps further on to the right, at No. 44, is the **House of Burchard** ('Casa del Burcardo'), built for his own use in 1503 by the German papal court dignitary whose diaries are a valuable source of information on life in renaissance Rome (pp. 123, 329-31). He was Master of Ceremonies to five popes, including the notorious Alexander VI Borgia. Though privately shocked by the excesses he saw, he never opposed them; indeed, he criticised the reform faction led by Savonarola. His reward was a quiet life and this beautiful home, in the typical style of an early 16th-century German residence. It incorporates a pre-existing tower (now truncated and indistinguishable from the rest of the building), which Burchard called 'Torre Argentina' in honour of his home town Strasbourg, whose Latin name is Argentoratum. This in turn gave its name to the whole neighbourhood (see p. 243).

Visit the pleasant courtyard. The building, presently owned by an association for the protection of copyrights, houses a theatrical library.

To the left and right of the house are two small 17th-century churches embedded in residential buildings. Left is **S. Giuliano Ospedaliero** ('St. Julian Hospitaller'), the Flemish national church in Rome. Right is **Il Sudario** ('The Shroud'), which gives its name to the street, the national church for Savoyards and Piedmontese. The church is dedicated to the Holy Shroud (the 'Turin Shroud'), which is said to bear the imprint of Jesus' body (compare the Veronica Veil, p. 368) and actually to originate from His grave. This famous relic, also called 'Sacra Sindone', was owned for centuries by the royal family of Savoy and Piedmont, who ruled Italy from 1866 to 1946, and who later donated the Shroud to the Italian state. It is still kept in a church in Turin, but radiocarbon tests in 1988 proved that it had been made in the 1300's.

❧ MIDPOINT OF THE WALK ☙

5. The area of the Teatro di Pompeo and S. Carlo ai Catinari

Another striking example of the way in which ancient Roman topography determines the layout of modern Rome appears in this stretch of the Walk. It goes mainly along streets and in view of buildings that were built over the ruins of one of the great monuments of antiquity, the Theatre of Pompey (which has nothing to do with the buried city of Pompeii near Naples). Pompey, or Pompeius, was a great Roman general and would-be dictator, who met his end as a result of his rivalry with Julius Cæsar (p. 243). We've already seen (p. 245) that this was Rome's first stone theatre. It was also one of the biggest ever built, the predecessor of all the important theatres and amphitheatres of the city, including the Colosseum, as well as of the many whose ruins survive throughout the former empire. Its own ruins are virtually gone, but its presence is still apparent, almost tangibly so, in this neighbourhood.

To an even greater extent than in the areas of renaissance Rome we visited before, noble palaces here alternate constantly with plebeian dwellings and downright slums, though this situation is rapidly changing, as even the worst hovels in what is improperly called the *centro storico* have soared in price and renovations are going on everywhere. A scene of industrious age-old poverty is present in the streets bordering the boisterous Campo de' Fiori, for centuries the abode of humble artisans, from which the streets still take their names: Trunk-makers' Street, Cabinet-makers' Street, Key-makers' Street, Nail-makers' Street and so on.

This once underprivileged neighbourhood includes what is probably the grandest pawnshop in history, the 17th-century Monte di Pietà ('Mount of Pity'), founded by the popes (as its statutes declare) 'to protect the people from suffering from the usury of the Jews'. It was moved here from earlier, more modest premises which you saw on the previous Walk (p. 450). Its constitution was written by the Milanese saint, Charles Borromeo. Despite the scepticism of customers, who nicknamed it 'Monte d'Empietà' ('of Impiety'), it has always offered reasonable interest rates. A bank now runs it on behalf of the city. One of Gioacchino Belli's (p. 547) sonnets describes a woman hurrying to the Monte to pawn her bedsheets, one of the last possessions of the desperately poor. The building contains a splendidly adorned prayer chapel, where people in dire straits could seek solace. Another poignant *oratorio* for the same use is on a nearby street.

At the end of this stretch you'll reach another of Rome's beautiful and grand baroque churches, dedicated to the same Milanese counter-reformation saint, S. Carlo Borromeo. Its name is S. Carlo ai Catinari, a reference to the 'catinari' or basin-makers who worked in the neighbourhood.

The church contains some of the last works by Domenichino and Lanfranco, and witnessed the final episodes in the rivalry between these two great artists. Two years after abandoning the frescoes of S. Andrea della Valle to his competitor (p. 509), Domenichino was commissioned to paint the big new church of S. Carlo. The way he got the job belies the claim that this strange man was always an innocent victim in the bloody quarrels and intrigues of the art world at the time of the Carracci and Caravaggio. The frescoes in S. Carlo had already been commissioned from the young assistant of one of Dominichino's co-disciples in the Carracci workshop, a certain Sementi, the protegé of a cardinal. Hearing that the cardinal had died, Domenichino rushed to another cardinal who was indebted to him and succeeded in having the commission reassigned to himself. The young Sementi is said to have died of a broken heart.

Domenichino painted a set of figures under the dome comparable in size to those he had painted at the base of the dome in S. Andrea, but different in that they show for the first time a hint of baroque emotionalism. He may have decided to join the stylistic bandwagon, which had led to such great success for the hated Lanfranco (p. 509), who, incidentally, was just then producing a large oil painting for the same church.

After finishing the frescoes in S. Carlo, Domenichino moved to Naples, but he soon had to flee the city due to threats from local artists who monopolised the market there – a repetition of Caravaggio's experience a generation earlier (p. 499).

Domenichino: Frescoes in S. Carlo

On his return to Rome, he met with new troubles. Someone had mixed ashes into the plaster he had prepared as a base for his frescoes, causing the finished painting to peel off. His own family gave him problems too – his wife's relatives and his daughter. Ever more embittered, he worked less and less and died at 60 of a mysterious illness; rumour had it he had been poisoned. Lanfranco meanwhile got another lucrative commission in S. Carlo, to paint the frescoes in the apse. He had drawn the cartoons and was about to begin painting when his drawings disappeared: stolen, it was said, by unknown persons just at the critical moment when the plaster was drying. Had Domenichino not been dead, he would naturally have been a prime suspect. Lanfranco improvised the fresco, giving it an extraordinary immediacy and making it another admirable piece. But it was his swansong: that year, aged 65, he followed Domenichino to the grave.

ON THE SPOT

5. The area of the Teatro di Pompeo and S. Carlo ai Catinari

Retrace your steps to Piazza Vidoni and S. Andrea della Valle. Past the church façade turn left into Largo dei Chiavari ('of the Key-makers'). Cross lengthways and to the right into Piazza del Paradiso (actually a street connected to a small square). From here the buildings on your left follow an unbroken irregular line bending left. We'll soon see the reason for this curve and the lack of streets interrupting it.

Piazza del Paradiso (move ahead to the square proper) was so called in the middle ages for two now-vanished inns, the Grande Paradiso (Great Paradise) and Piccolo Paradiso (Little Paradise). A third inn, also gone, was called 'dell' Inferno' ('of Hell'), a name perhaps more apt for this place: across the square to the right was a pillory where petty criminals and over-bold prostitutes were exposed to public scorn. At No. 68 is the very old, possibly 16th-century, Albergo della Lunetta ('Little Moon Hotel'), rebuilt in the early 1800's.

Go on to the adjacent Piazza Pollarola ('of the Poultry-sellers'). On the left, at No. 76, is the **Albergo Sole** ('Sun Hotel'), the oldest hotel in Rome (as a business, though not as a building).

It opened in the early 1400's or even before, and so is at least fifty years older than the one of the same name in Piazza della Rotonda (p. 241), though the building that currently houses it dates back only to the early 1800's. More recently, its ancient stables were converted into a garage. It used to be a first-class hotel.

Cross Piazza Pollarola lengthways. At the end of the block to your left (No. 43) is the **Palazzetto di Ceccolo Pichi**, built in the 15th century by a rich shopkeeper. Only the central part is original. Notice the beautiful portal with cherubs and the name of the owner in Latin over the windows.

Left of the palazzetto, on the ground floor, a tablet dated 1755 declares that the pope has exempted the poultry and egg dealers in the neighbourhood from sales tax.

As you face the palazzetto, the street crossing the piazza to your right is Via dei Baullari ('of the Trunk-makers'). At a corner on the left, a store still marked (at the time of writing) by a fictive trunk under the windows is another reminder of the many luggage makers who gave the street its name in the middle ages. Without crossing you can see, diagonally across the street (No. 140), picturesque old residential buildings and, next to them, an unusually designed 16th-century *oratorio*, or prayer chapel, now closed. The backdrop here is the marble-clad Palazzo della Cancelleria that we saw on the previous Walk (p. 485).

Return to the Albergo Sole and take Via del Biscione, on your right, to Piazza del Biscione ('of the Snake'). One side of this square (No. 95) is a large mid-15th century building, **Palazzo Pio**, which once belonged to the noble Orsini family (p. 253).

It no longer bears the Orsini coat-of-arms (bears), but the prominent snake emblem of a later owner probably gave the square its name. Other animal ornaments on the building derive from the coats-of-arms of still other owners.

Until about 1890 a public scribe sat in front of this palace to help the illiterate write letters.

On another side of the square is a pretty little building – originally the stables of the nearby palace – with traces of frescoes and, between the windows, a *Madonna* painted in the 1700's. Between this building and the large palace is a narrow, covered passageway which you will only see if you go right up to it. We'll return there in a moment.

You may have noticed that the square here is the first interruption in the long, continuous curved row of buildings mentioned earlier. The reason for this layout is that these buildings were all built over the ruins of the **Theatre of Pompey** (55 BC) to your right. The houses follow very loosely the line of the *cavea*, or orchestra, of the theatre, the remains of which are embedded in them, mainly in the cellars. Large blocks of brickwork – the *cavea* foundations – are visible downstairs in the Pancrazio restaurant, at No. 94 (ask permission to see them).

The link between the ancient and present layouts is even clearer if you see the curve from the inside. Take the covered passageway mentioned above, Passetto del Biscione. In it is some faded 18th-century decoration; the icon, a reproduction, is a modern addition.

(The passage is sometimes closed. If so, to reach the other side, backtrack to your left, through Piazza Pollarola, Piazza del Paradiso, Via dei Chiavari and Largo del Pallaro.)

On the other side is Via di Grottapinta ('of the painted Grotto'), probably so called in the middle ages after a now-vanished remnant of fresco from the inner theatre. There you'll recognise the curve of the *cavea* traced by houses repeatedly built and rebuilt over the old ruins. Look left and right (Largo del Pallaro). It is a somewhat eerie sight, like facing the ghost of the vanished theatre.

The theatre, built by Pompey after his military victories, when his power still far outstripped that of Julius Cæsar, was one of the most splendid buildings in ancient Rome. It displayed countless statues and other art works and seated 30,000, more than any other theatre ever. One of the statues, the giant bronze Hercules now in the Vatican (p. 326), was unearthed here in 1864.

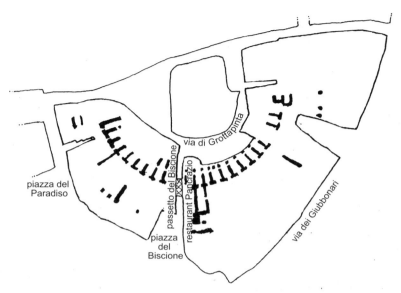

The group of buildings built over the ruins of the Theatre of Pompey;
the curving streets follow the cavea of the ancient structure

At the beginning of Via di Grottapinta is a small renaissance church, S. Maria in Grottapinta, converted to private use. This spot gives another fine view of the dome of S. Andrea della Valle (to the right).

Retrace your steps to Piazza del Biscione; take the opportunity here to look at two small medieval arches on the top floor of No. 4. Proceed straight ahead and you'll be in Campo de' Fiori ('Field of Flowers'), which we visited on the previous Walk (pp. 482-485). At this end of the Campo, on the corner of Via dei Balestrari ('of the Crossbow-makers') is a 1483 inscription celebrating the renovation of this 'floral' neighbourhood under Sixtus IV (p. 483). Keep left and leave the Campo by the lively Via dei Giubbonari ('of the Jerkin-makers').

In the humble tenement house at No. 64, on the left, people still talk about the day in the mid-1800's when Pope Pius IX, seeing a priest giving last rites to a gravely ill old parishioner there, left his carriage to comfort the dying man himself.

Almost opposite, at No. 47, is a small 16th-century house embedded in a 19th-century building. The ground floor and two upper floors are the more modern part. The house has faint traces of fresco – one can make out two figures between the third floor windows – attributed to Peruzzi, the first to introduce the graffito technique to house decoration in Rome (p. 449).

A few steps further on, from No. 42 to the end of the block, is a late 16th-century palace in disrepair, built for the Barberini family (whose newer and grander palace we saw elsewhere, pp. 83-84), by several architects, including Maderno.

Opposite the palace is a small trapezoidal square, Largo dei Librari ('of the Booksellers'), so called in the middle ages after the Guild of booksellers which was located here. Bookstores were once abundant in this area; a last second-hand one in the square closed only a few years ago. On the far side is the doll's house-like old church of

515

S. Barbara dei Librari, founded in the 11th century, long before printing or bookstores existed, and rebuilt in the 18th century. (Occasionally open.)

In the first chapel on the right is a 15th-century painting of the *Madonna and Child with Saints*. The other decorations are by minor 17th- and 18th-century artists.

To the right of the church is a tiny, old and inexpensive restaurant serving almost nothing except delicious deep-fried cod fillets and wine.

Crossing Via dei Giubbonari take Via Arco del Monte in front of you, to Piazza Monte di Pietà, dominated by the monumental **Monte di Pietà** ('Mount of Pity'), or municipal pawnshop.

It was built at the end of the 1500's by the architect Ottaviano Mascarino (or Mascherino), incorporating previous buildings, in one of which Caravaggio spent his first months in Rome, as a guest of a Monsignor Pandolfo Pucci, whom he nicknamed 'Mr. Salad' because the sober meals served in his home consisted mainly of vegetables. In the early 1600's Carlo Maderno enlarged the façade and added the fountain, the great dedicatory tablet with papal escutcheons, the fine relief of the *Entombment of Christ* (commissioned from another, unidentified artist) and the elegant clock-tower.

In the courtyard, at No. 33, are another fountain by Maderno and the entrance to a magnificent chapel. The splendid baroque decorations, and the marbles, statues and reliefs, are 17th- and early 18th-century; they were mistakenly attributed to Maderno, but are actually by the lesser-known architect and sculptor Francesco Peparelli. Permission to visit may be requested at the bank (open 08:00-13:00).

At No. 30 is a renaissance palace, another of the many created by the Roman aristocracy.

Go around the right end of the Monte di Pietà façade into Via dell'Arco del Monte ('of the Arch of the Mount'). The flank of the Mount here was remodelled in the 1700's. On the right, past the archway and sandwiched between two buildings, is a tiny chapel built in 1781 and dedicated both to the Virgin and to the sufferings of those whom poverty has forced to pawn their possessions.

Retrace your steps along Via dell'Arco del Monte back to Via dei Giubbonari and go right. Past another typical street, Via dei Chiavari ('of the Key-makers'), notice two charming baroque doors on the left (Nos 107 and 109). You're now in a piazza dominated by **S. Carlo ai Catinari** ('St. Charles by the Basin-makers') on the left.

The work of two prominent architects, Giovan Battista Soria and Rosato Rosati, the church is another striking example of the 17th-century Roman baroque, notable for its lofty façade (by Soria) and the distinctive, dynamic design of the dome (visible only from a distance; we'll see it shortly). The façade medallion originally framed a portrait by Reni of St. Charles Borromeo, to whom the church is dedicated; it was recently removed for security reasons and is now in the sacristy. (Open: 07:00-12:00 and 16:30-19:15.)

All the art work inside is 17th-century. Much of it illustrates episodes from the *Life of St. Charles Borromeo*, the beloved cardinal of the Milanese, a Counter-Reformation figure famous for his social work and assistance to plague victims.

In the first chapel to the right is Lanfranco's marvellous *Annunciation* and an unusual wooden *Madonna of the Sorrows* of the Neapolitan school (1865). The last chapel to the right, dedicated to St. Cecilia, is a very effective, typically baroque creation by a little-known artist, Antonio Gherardi. Notice the soaring luminosity of the small dome surrounded by music-making angels. The chapel also contains the tomb of Rosa Giovannetti, a young cellist from the neighbourhood, who died in 1929 'in the odour of sanctity'; the process of beatification is underway.

Over the main altar is Pietro da Cortona's *St. Charles Leading a Procession during the Plague*. In the apse is a fresco of *St. Charles Rising to Heaven*, Lanfranco's last work, and the one he had to improvise on plaster, a dramatic representation in a restrained range of colours. The pendentives of the dome are decorated with four powerfully drawn, splendidly coloured *Cardinal Virtues* by Domenichino.

BEFORE GOING

6. The Saga of the Santacroce and the Cenci – on the edge of the Ghetto

God save us! See that house,	Dio sia con noi! Lo vedi, eh? cquer casino
With the windows all broken... There	Co le finestre tutte svetrïate?
In the days of the Cenci woman, a pilgrim	Lì, a ttempi de la Cenci, un pellegrino
In the dead of night did a priest in.	De nottetempo sciammazzò un abbate.
Since then, if you pass there around	D'allor'impoi, a ssett'ora sonate
Midnight, you see a point of light roaming inside,	Ce se vede ggirà sempre un lumino,
Then hear a scream, a very faint, faint one,	Eppoi se sente un strillo fino fino
A noise of dragging chains. . .	E un rumor de catene strascinate. . .

We don't know which house Belli is referring to in his 1832 sonnet *Li spiriti* ('Ghosts'), but surely it was in the neighbourhood we are now entering, site of the most notorious and macabre affair of the late renaissance. The story has left an indelible imprint on the popular mind, because of the youth and beauty of its heroine, Beatrice Cenci, who has inspired painters and poets throughout the centuries, including Shelley, who made her the subject of a tragedy. (The theme was suggested to Shelley by his wife Mary – author of *Frankenstein* – when he joined her in Rome; and it squared with the poet's preoccupation with the tension between individual rights and social convention.) As we shall see, however, the only palace in Rome which was, and is, thought to be haunted does not belong to the Cenci family, but to their close neighbours, the lords of Santacroce.

The histories of the two families, the Cenci and the Santacroce, are closely intertwined. Amongst the most powerful of the baronial clans since the middle ages, they were frequently allied by marriage. In the renaissance, after the rediscovery of classical antiquity, both families claimed descent from the great ancient Roman families. The Santacroce added the surname 'Publicola' to theirs, claiming to be blood heirs of the great Valerius Publicola, one of the founders of the Roman Republic in the 5th century BC. The Cenci asserted lineage from the Cincii, an ancient Roman family. (Neither claim, however, is anywhere as plausible as that of the Massimo, see p. 504.)

Throughout the middle ages and the renaissance the two families shared a *de facto* lordship over the district and reinforced their image by donations to local churches which, as you will see, still contain the remains of many of their members. Yet neither their claim to ancient nobility, nor their help to churches masked their overbearing behaviour, notorious for centuries and the root of many of the scandals and bloody conflicts in the area. In the 1400's the situation reached a point where the pope ordered the Santacroce's houses and towers to be razed. The family moved to another district, but returned a few years later and rebuilt their palaces near those of the Cenci, themselves responsible for a series of bloody brawls, abductions and murders.

In the late 1500's the head of the Cenci family, Francesco, married a Santacroce, who bore him a daughter, Beatrice, and eleven sons, three of whom died in brawls and duels.

Francesco was considered an obnoxious, despotic figure. Notorious for his greed, temper and vices, he was once arrested and fined for sodomy. His main victims were his own family – his sons, whom he hated and planned to disown, his second wife (widowed, he had remarried for money) and his daughter. Apparently in order to avoid giving Beatrice a dowry or the money required to enter an upper-class convent, he forbade the beautiful 20-year old to leave the house or see anyone. She and her stepmother Lucrezia were virtually imprisoned for three years. There were rumours of incest, though they could never be substantiated.

The two women, and two sons who lived at home, gradually hatched the idea of murdering the tyrant. In our Walk we shall see the gloomy city stronghold of the Cenci where the plot took shape. The actual deed was carried out on a country estate in the nearby Apennine mountains. Francesco was killed in his sleep with a shower of hammer blows to the head. The body was thrown from a balcony to mimic an accident. But bloody sheets were found, suspicions aroused and the plotters arrested. Long interrogation and torture led to confessions.

Extenuating circumstances – the foul behaviour of the victim – might have saved the murderers in an era when a noble title was a strong shield against prosecution. Yet a crime that the Cenci's neighbours, the Santacroce, had just committed, and a similar one involving another great family, the Massimo (p. 504), had exasperated the papal authorities. Paolo Santacroce, Beatrice's cousin, suspecting his mother would disinherit him, had killed her and fled the papal states. Days earlier Prince Marcantonio Massimo had killed his elder brother to usurp his inheritance.

So the pope decided to make an example of Beatrice and her co-plotters. After a trial lasting months (interrupted at the end of 1598 by one of the most catastrophic floods of the Tiber ever, which caused 1,500 deaths), the murderers were all condemned to die, except the teenage son Bernardo, who was made to attend the execution of his relatives and then go to the galleys. The family escaped extinction through Bernardo, the only surviving Cenci; his descendants live in a house we'll see. The Santacroce are now extinct.

Giacomo, elder brother of Beatrice, was led to his death in an open cart while, in a savage medieval custom, shreds of his flesh were torn off with red-hot pincers. Beatrice and their step-mother preceded him on foot. In Piazza di Ponte, the site of most executions (p. 442), they were all dispatched by the executioner, while hooded members of a religious brotherhood pressed an image of Christ to their faces (p. 491). First Lucrezia was beheaded, then Beatrice. Giacomo's head was crushed by a sledgehammer, his body drawn and quartered and the pieces left hanging on hooks.

Probably for no reason other than her youth and beauty, an aura of innocent victimisation has always surrounded the figure of Beatrice, though the trial records, which are fully preserved, clearly show her to be the instigator and prime mover of the crime. Even today people take flowers every year to the little church near the Cenci stronghold, where a mass is said on the anniversary of her death.

As you will see, the haunts of the Santacroce and the Cenci are on the edge of the old Ghetto. Actually, if you elect to visit the Synagogue you'll find it most convenient to do so during this part of the Walk. Our visit to the Ghetto proper will be in the next segment of the Walk.

ON THE SPOT

6. The Saga of the Santacroce and the Cenci – on the edge of the Ghetto

Opposite the entrance to S. Carlo ai Catinari is the façade of Palazzo Santacroce, one of several owned by the family in this district. It was said to be haunted, a rumour still not completely dispelled. Built at the end of the 16th century, the exterior is mid-17th century, but partly remodelled in the 19th.

Cross the square, skirt the left side of Palazzo Santacroce (Piazza Cairoli) and step into the garden to see the late 19th-century fountain, which incorporates a large round granite basin from the Roman Forum. This is also a good spot from which to look back at the dome of S. Carlo.

Cross the nearby avenue, Via Arenula, dating from ancient Rome, but widened in the late 1800's. Its name, meaning 'of the little beach' (recalling the nearby river) is also very old. Opposite the fountain take Via S. Maria dei Calderari, a name referring to a demolished church (the craft of the 'calderari', or coppersmiths, akin to the basin-makers, was once typical of the area). Embedded in the wall at No. 23b is the ancient Roman archway of an unidentified building.

A few steps further on, to the right, is Via dell'Arco dei Cenci. The name refers to a medieval archway, finely reworked in the 16th century (now badly deteriorated), linking four buildings, as we'll see in a moment. These buildings were the Cenci family stronghold, birthplace of the famous renaissance heroine Beatrice Cenci.

Pass under the arch into Piazza Cenci. All the buildings on the left and one on the right belong to the Cenci stronghold.

At No. 56 is the so-called **Palazzetto Cenci**, still owned by the family. Erected in the middle ages, it was remodelled in the 16th century by Martino Longhi the Elder. The courtyard, with its ancient arcade, reveals the medieval origins of the building.

Starting on the side of the square which is offi-

cially part of Via Beatrice Cenci, let's now survey the main buildings of the complex – 'a vast and gloomy pile of feudal architecture,' as Shelley put it. The two façades on this side, however, were remodelled in the baroque style. From Via Beatrice Cenci go round the complex by turning left into Monte de' Cenci ('Cenci Hill'); the façades on this uphill stretch maintain their grim medieval appearance.

The hillock is probably formed by the ruins of a short side of the Circus Flaminius, a sports stadium built in the 3rd century AD for the use of the Roman populace by the same magistrate who built Via Flaminia. The rest of the circus probably extended into the nearby area of the old Ghetto.

At the top of the hill is an intimate and picturesque little square, under the solemn façades of the larger building of the Cenci complex (Nos. 17, 20 & 21).

Opposite is the small church of **S. Tommaso a Monte Cenci**, once under the patronage of the Cenci. Built in the 1100's by a Cenci bishop, it was remodelled in the Jubilee Year 1575, as the tablet on the façade commemorates, thanks to 'Franciscus Cincius' – none other than Beatrice's father, tormentor and victim.

The interior, seldom open, contains a beautifully frescoed 16th-century chapel, a fine 13th-century cross and two marvellous ancient

Palazzo Cenci, in a typically gloomy print of the Romantic era

Roman marbles (1st century) supporting a side altar. There are also several Cenci family tombs. One, unmarked, was prepared by Francesco Cenci for himself, but instead covers the quartered limbs of one of his murderers, his son Giacomo. (Francesco was buried in the mountain village where he died.) Beatrice was buried in the distant church of S. Pietro in Montorio; her tomb was under the main altar and, like her brother's, had no mark or inscription. She had asked to be buried there, away from the haunts of her tragic family (later, it seems to have mysteriously disappeared, p. 561). Every September 11, the anniversary of their execution in 1599, a mass is said for their souls in the church of S. Tommaso.

Descend the hill to the left of the church; a part of the Cenci stronghold is still on your left. At the bottom, turn completely around to see another of its façades on the left, renovated in the early 1800's and with 'Cenci-Bolognetti' inscribed over a grand portal (the princely Bolognetti title was inherited in the 1700's by a descendant of Beatrice's only surviving relative, her brother Bernardo).

Stand with your back to the portal. A 16th-century fountain before you is one of many by Giacomo Della Porta (p. 53) and one of the most famous. For centuries it was the centerpiece of the nearby Piazza Giudìa ('of the Jews'), the main gathering place of the Ghetto Jews, though the piazza itself was outside the main gate of the Ghetto. The fountain was moved here when the adjacent Piazza Giudìa was eliminated during the wholesale clearance of the old Ghetto and its replacement by new buildings in the 1880's.

You are now on the fringes of the old Ghetto; later you'll walk through the little that survives. A word of orientation: the space you are in is called Piazza delle Cinque Scole ('of the Five Schools'). (The name, meant to recall the vanished Piazza delle Scole nearby, comes courtesy of a recent brainstorm of the city authorities. It was imposed in 1999 on a space that for over a century after the demolition of the Ghetto had borne the touching name of Via del Progresso, suggested by the Jewish elders to express the general enthusiasm for the area's rehabilitation.)

The Ghetto wall ran along its long open side to your right (if you are still with your back to the Cenci-Bolognetti portal), while just behind it, in a now demolished square to your right, were the five 'schools' or synagogues. The bland, relatively modern buildings to your right, geometrically laid out, cover most of the former Ghetto. All the way around to the right was a large tract of land that disappeared when the river was embanked (see diagram on p. 523). In the distance in front of you are the surviving streets of the Ghetto we'll visit later.

DETOUR
10 MIN

This detour is for those interested in the modern synagogue, and is very short unless you decide to visit the interior. Take Via Catalana, opposite the fountain, for one block, then turn right into Via del Tempio ('of the Temple').

The main front and ceremonial entrance of the synagogue, by architects Armanni and Costa (1904) is here (the ordinary entrance is on the riverside drive). The pavilion-shaped dome is covered with aluminum, then a high-tech metal. The synagogue was built in a fanciful neo-babylonian style, otherwise unknown in Rome, in an effort to strike an independent note, while recalling the middle-eastern origins of the Jewish faith. It has beautiful stained glass windows by Cesare Picchiarini and Duilio Cambellotti.

Across from the synagogue notice the art nouveau decorations on an early 20th-century building belonging to the 'new' Ghetto.

Go round the synagogue to see its riverside façade and marble tablets commemorating the ordeals of the Roman Jews: their dead in Italian wars; 2,091 victims of Nazi deportations; the Nazi massacres in Rome and the sacrifices of Jewish members of the Italian resistance during the Nazi occupation.

A visit to the synagogue and the small Jewish museum attached adds at least 40 minutes to this detour, since only guided group visits are allowed and one has to wait for the next tour (for visiting hours, see p. 687).

Return to the fountain in Piazza delle Cinque Scole.

END OF DETOUR

Across the square from the Cenci-Bolognetti portal is one of the façades of **S. Maria del Pianto** (literally 'of the Wailing'), another church used forcibly to indoctrinate Jews. It is embedded in a medieval apartment house.

The name of this 17th-century church, sometimes misinterpreted as a reference to the 'wail' of persecuted Jews or to the 'wailing wall' in Jerusalem, alludes to the miracle of an icon of the Virgin over the main altar that was seen shedding tears during one of the bloody brawls then typical of the neighbourhood (p. 517).

Near here the Duke of Gandía, son of the Borgia pope and Vannozza Catanei, was seen for the last time before his body was fished out of the Tiber (pp. 46, 355).

Continue around this protruding building to the next intersection on the left, Via S. Maria del Pianto; at the beginning, on the left near the street sign, is another entrance to the church, also embedded in an old building.

Go into Via S. Maria del Pianto. At the end of the block on your right is another **Palazzo Santacroce** (late 1400's), the first that the family rebuilt after their houses were razed on papal orders.

The warlike character of the original tenants is visible in a corner tower, which is not very obvious, since it is engulfed by a third storey added later to the building. This interesting, exceptionally preserved edifice has a base cut into square diamond points, the only example of this style in Rome.

Go round the palace into Via in Publicolis

(from the Latin name that, as you may remember, the proud Santacroce had added to theirs). On the left is **S. Maria in Publicolis**, the Santacroce family church, just as St. Thomas was the Cenci's. It was already here by the 8th century, but was entirely remodelled in the 17th. It is occasionally open.

Inside, rows of Santacroce notables in lace and velvet peer from statues and paintings adorning their graves, almost as if still surveying the situation in their church and neighbourhood – their fiefdom.

Walk across from the church into Piazza Costaguti. On the left side of the square and its continuation are two palaces belonging to other baronial families of the area. The first, Nos. 10-14, is the early 18th-century **Palazzo Boccapaduli** (the marquesses of this name died out in 1809). The second, No. 16-17, is the late 16th-century **Palazzo Costaguti** (this is the rear; we'll see the front later). There are still members of the Costaguti family living here.

The styles of the two palaces, built slightly more than a century apart, are interesting to compare. The passage – right to left – from the mature baroque to the rising rococo is evident especially in the decorative elements of the windows. An added extra floor has spoiled both buildings, especially the older one.

Pass Palazzo Costaguti and leave the piazza. Just around the corner there is a beautiful window with a balcony belonging to the same palace. Under the building next to it, a dark passage, typical of days gone by, leads to a courtyard as shabby as it is picturesque, amid tall old tenement buildings, at least some of which are amongst the few still standing of the old Ghetto, as we'll see later on the other side (p. 527).

Return to the street. Just on the left is a curious protruding chapel built in 1759. This, too, was sometimes used for compulsory Saturday sermonising of the Jews (p. 246) by the papal clergy. Deconsecrated, it is now used for storage.

7. The Ghetto

Four dates must be remembered when visiting the old Ghetto: 1556, when it was founded as a legal institution – a walled enclosure where all unconverted Jews had to live, and stay from sunset to sunrise; 1848, when the walls were torn down, though the Jews were still forced to live in the area; 1870, when the new Italian state abolished all restrictions; and 1885, when authorities razed nine-tenths of the buildings in the old enclosure in the name of progress and hygiene, with the enthusiastic approval of most Jews, replacing them with monotonous new buildings.

All you'll be able to see of the old Ghetto, therefore, is a mere tenth of the buildings once within its walls – one short street and part of another. Besides being tiny, this section is not very representative. It was built only two decades before the walls of the original enclosure were demolished, and so did not share most of its three-century existence. Yet what remains of the old Ghetto, together with the surrounding newer area, gives a vivid impression of Rome's ancient Jewish community, the oldest in Western Europe. Although apparently fully assimilated and never seen in special garb or hairstyle, the Jews of Rome maintains a close-knit and highly independent community, and many observe all the age-old Jewish customs and traditions. One amazing piece of genetic research, published in 2000 in the American *Proceedings of the National Academy of Sciences*, suggests that most of the Eastern European Jews, the Ashkenazim (meaning 'German'), descend from Roman Jews.

But who are the Roman Jews? The first Jewish immigration predates written history. Many more arrived in the 1st century BC, when Pompey the Great (of the theatre, p. 243) conquered Jerusalem and brought many prisoners to Rome. A century later there was also a large influx of Jews as slaves, following the destruction of the Temple in Jerusalem and the victories of Vespasian and Titus over Jewish insurgents in Palestine. Several thousand worked to build the Colosseum. Diaspora Jews trickled in during subsequent centuries; there was a particularly great influx after the massive expulsion of the Sephardic (meaning 'Spanish') Jews from Spain in 1492.

You can sometimes guess the origins of a Roman Jew from his or her last name. Until a few centuries ago, the origins of different groups could still be clearly identified, especially since each group tended to frequent a synagogue or 'school' and observe a liturgy peculiar to it. For example, of the five schools existing when the Ghetto was razed in 1885 ('of the Temple', 'Sicilian', 'Catalan', 'Castilian' and 'New'), one, the 'School of the Temple', served mainly 'Titus Jews', those whose roots went back to ancient Rome. (You can still hear the words 'Titus Jews' used in reference to particular families in the Ghetto.)

As we have seen (p. 520), one large modern synagogue now serves all. In ancient Roman times there were thirteen or fourteen; in the middle ages, ten. Jews originally lived all over the city, though they were concentrated in an area straddling the river formed by the Trastevere district, where most Orientals, Jewish or otherwise, tended to settle, and the opposite river bank (which we are exploring today, in the streets near the Portico of Octavia (for the history of the Jews in Trastevere, see p. 597). Around 1200 AD, for unknown reasons, most or all of the Trastevere Jews crossed the river to join the rest of the community here, where they have remained ever since.

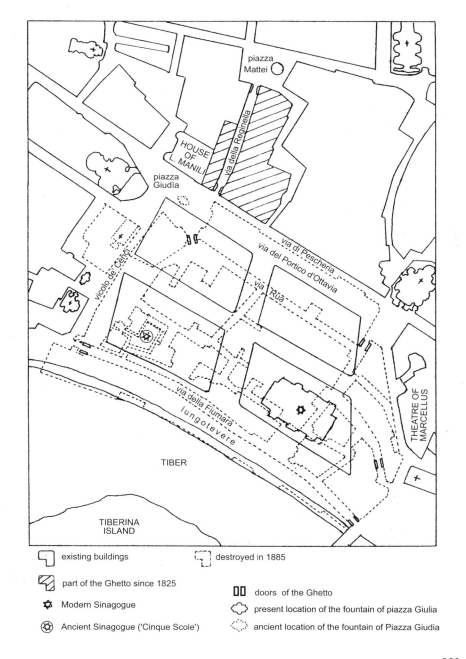

piazza Mattei

via della Reginella

HOUSE OF L. MANILI

piazza Giudia

via di Pescheria

via del Portico d'Ottavia

vicolo de' Cenci

via Rua

via della Fiumara

lungotevere

TIBER

THEATRE OF MARCELLUS

TIBERINA ISLAND

existing buildings

destroyed in 1885

part of the Ghetto since 1825

doors of the Ghetto

Modern Sinagogue

present location of the fountain of piazza Giulia

Ancient Sinagogue ('Cinque Scole')

ancient location of the fountain of Piazza Giudia

Both before and after the era of compulsory confinement to the Ghetto, however, many Jews lived in other neighbourhoods, as they do today. The Jews of the old Ghetto tend to be those of more modest means, mostly small traders and shopkeepers, while professionals and others live elsewhere.

The Roman Ghetto is but one facet of the history of anti-Semitism in Rome. In ancient Rome, Jews suffered some discrimination, especially under Caligula and Domitian, but overall their lot was much better than that of Christians and they escaped real persecution. The authorities, though very tolerant in matters of religion, disliked both Jews and Christians because, unlike all other followers of foreign creeds in Rome, they refused to accept the state religion alongside their own. Christians were the greater nuisance, however, with their aggressive proselytising, so alien to, indeed the opposite of, Jewish behaviour. After Christianity became the official religion of the State, Jews continued to enjoy a relatively quiet life, probably thanks to their excellence in medicine, which made them valuable members of society in a disease-plagued age.

Only in the late middle ages did the sorrows of the Roman Jews begin. The popes made them wear distinctive clothes, exposing them to public hatred for their alleged responsibility in Christ's death and making scapegoats of them. This official attitude allowed the populace to vent its sadistic impulses on the Jews. Though pogroms never took place, Jews were humiliated and abused. We have mentioned (p. 123) the forced participation of Jews, naked but for a loincloth, in the carnival races (the custom was abolished in 1668, when they were allowed to pay for horse races instead). In the 'game of the barrel', Jews overpowered by the populace were sometimes imprisoned in rolling barrels, whence they emerged more dead than alive. Jews consorting with Christian women risked castration (p. 483).

Starting in 1556, in a climate of fanatic orthodoxy spawned by the Counter-Reformation (pp. 115-116) all Jews, who then numbered about 7,000, were forced to live in the area near the Portico of Octavia and the river. This seven-acre zone was initially called Vicus Judæorum but in a few decades it acquired the name of 'ghetto'. The origin of the word is controversial: it is most plausibly an abbreviation of 'borghetto' ('little borough'), while the other theory, identifying it with the Venetian district of the 'getto' ('foundry') now seems less likely.

Walls rose around the Ghetto, and gates – initially two, later as many as eight – opened at dawn and inexorably closed at dusk. Other grievous restrictions were added, such as exclusion from any trade except usury and trade in rags, scrap iron and textiles. The Jews were forced to listen to Christian sermons to which, a chronicle of 1600 reports, they were 'dragged by the head and hair, against their obstinate hearts, to partake of the heavenly graces'. This requirement, exacerbated by being imposed on the Jewish Sabbath, was only lifted in 1847. The reform was one of several promulgated by an initially liberal pope, Pius IX; unfortunately, shocked by the revolutionary events of 1848-49 (see p. 67) Pius soon reverted to an oppressive régime. In 1858 a notorious case of a Jewish child being kidnapped by the Inquisition scandalised Europe and came to symbolise the tyrannical obscurantism of the church that secular Italy had to overcome; it has recently been the subject of a best-seller, *The Kidnapping of Edgardo Mortara* by David Kertzer.

Conditions in the Ghetto were always described as unbearable and cramped, and dangerous to boot, thanks to the nearby river with its frequent floods. The plague of 1656 killed one in five Ghetto inhabitants. Sanitary conditions must have improved later, if it is true that during the great cholera epidemic which beset Rome in the mid-19th century fewer died in the Ghetto than elsewhere. Illiteracy was also lower amongst the Ghetto Jews than in other parts of the city, and cultural and religious life never ebbed despite restrictions and lack of means.

Here is a description by the German historian Ferdinand Gregorovius of life in the Ghetto around 1870, when the perimeter walls had been demolished two decades earlier but the buildings had not yet been razed:

> On entering the Ghetto, we see Israel outside its tents, in full restless labour and activity. The people sit in their doorways, or outside in the streets, which receive hardly more light than the damp and gloomy chambers, and grub amid their old trumpery, or patch and sew diligently ... The whole world seems to lie around in countless rags and scraps ... It is chiefly in the Fiumara, the street lying lowest and nearest to the river [this street disappeared a few years later with the embankment of the Tiber] and on the street corners, one of which is called Via delle Azzimelle, i.e. of the unleavened bread, that the mending of rags is done. With a feeling of pain I have often seen the pale, stooping, starving figures, laboriously plying the needle – men as well as women, girls and children. Misery stares forth from the tangled hair, and complains silently in the yellow brown faces ...'

The abolition of the Ghetto in 1870 by the Italian state after its victory over the papal régime initiated a rapid emancipation of the Jews. A happy period of peace, then prosperity, opened up for Roman and Italian Jews, who were easily integrated with the rest of society, reaching the highest positions, including premiership and high military command. A sort of late love affair blossomed between the Jews and the Italian nation, heart-rendingly witnessed on a wall of Rome's new synagogue by a tablet to Roman Jews fallen in the Italian wars against Germany of 1866 and 1915, which speaks of sacrifice endured 'for the sake of our adored Italian fatherland'.

Little did this unfortunate minority suspect what the 'adored fatherland' had in store for it. Only a few years later, Mussolini, in order to ingratiate himself with his former pupil and now master, Adolf Hitler, enacted the infamous Racial Laws of 1938. Short of reinstituting the Ghetto, these re-established many of the old restrictions on the Jews. Much worse happened when the Germans occupied Rome in 1943-44. Many Jews managed to flee the city, but when the Nazi SS raided the Ghetto area on a tragic October day in 1943, over 2,000 residents were captured and taken to German concentration camps in sealed rail cars. Few returned.

After the war the old Ghetto area and many nearby streets were slowly repopulated. Today they offer a lively scene of everyday activity. Many little Jewish shops conduct flourishing businesses in the traditional fields (textiles, mattresses, trimmings, etc.). On Sundays the streets are crowded at sunset with people who chat and flirt, following old customs. A frequent spectacle is splendid weddings overflowing from the nearby synagogue. With luck, you may catch snatches of conversation in the Jewish-Roman dialect still spoken by some of the older generations, a peculiar mixture of deformed Roman vernacular and Hebrew. (Private courses in this idiom are now held in an attempt to save it from extinction.)

ON THE SPOT

7. The Ghetto

At this point (assuming you are still standing with the protruding chapel to your immediate left), you are not yet in the old Ghetto enclosure but are facing what remains of its famous satellite square, Piazza Giudìa ('of the Jews'), which used to extend past the crossing in front of you and to the left of it. Part of the square is now occupied by the corner of one of the large modern buildings, a public school, built over the main entrance to the razed Ghetto. In this vanished square Della Porta's fountain (p. 520) once stood, around which the Jews used to gather. There was also a long police barracks, with a gibbet for the rope torture next to it, like the one in Campo de' Fiori for everyone else (p. 482). The Jews' open-air court met here.

Most of the features of the piazza are gone; one, however, still stands, and though not Jewish, it is the most ancient and striking. It is the building on the near left corner. Look at both sides: the main one faces Via Portico di Ottavia, the main street of the present Jewish quarter. This is the so-called **Casa dei Manili,** the house built by a certain Lorenzo or Rienzo Manei for his family in the mid-1400's. (Manei, not Manili: research carried out in 2001, the first ever to investigate the matter, has corrected the tradition; it was also discovered that Manei was a simple pharmacist. Also very recently discovered in the cellar of this house are vestiges of a Temple of Neptune.) Its decoration is one of the simplest, yet most telling tributes of the dawning renaissance to the reborn ideals of classical antiquity. Latin and Greek inscriptions encircle it, in an ancient lettering style so beautifully and carefully done that until the late 1800's antiquarians were fooled into thinking they were authentically classical. The main inscription runs across the façade facing the intersection (Via

The 16th-century fountain by Giacomo Della Porta in the ancient Piazza Giudia, by G. B. Falda

Portico d'Ottavia) and reads in Latin: 'While Rome is reborn to its ancient splendour (referring to the beautifications mentioned on p. 439) Laurentius Manlius, as a token of love for his city and in proportion to his modest means, built on this square of the Jews ('ad Forum Judæorum') this house that after his name will be called Manliana, in the year 2221 since Rome's foundation (1468 AD).'

The ambition of Manei, a commoner, to link his name to that of an illustrious Roman family, the Manli, is also apparent in these inscriptions. The search for classical roots evidently was not limited to exalted families such as the Massimo or the Santacroce.

The name of the owner is repeated four times, in Latin and in Greek, over the doors of the longer façade on Via Portico di Ottavia. Over the windows of the shorter façade is an invocation in Latin to the classical spirit: 'Ave Roma' ('Hail Rome'). Also note, on the longer façade, beautiful fragments of classical sculpture – a lion devouring an antelope (similar to those in Via dell'Orso, pp. 492-493) and a dog catching a hare.

Two more buildings were combined with the main Manili house in Via Portico di Ottavia. Four ancient Roman funerary busts are embedded in the last one, at No. 2. Under these is an old alms box for Jewish orphans.

Now we come to the Ghetto proper. As noted, the main entrance was on a corner of the former Piazza Giudìa opposite the Manili house. For most of its life, the Ghetto was contained roughly within the area now covered by the relatively modern buildings, together with a row of buildings facing the river and a few others. In 1825 another section was added, formed by the street behind the Manili house block (Via della Reginella) and part of Via Portico d'Ottavia (which was then much narrower and named Via della Pescheria, after the local fish market). New gates were installed to enclose these houses. The few remaining houses of the Ghetto are on these streets, which were only part of the Ghetto for a few years, since the walls were torn down in 1848.

At the end of the Manili house block take Via della Reginella on the left. This is actually the only part of the Ghetto still intact, as Via Portico d' Ottavia has been widened and one side torn down to make way for modern buildings. An iron gate, the last of the eight gates of the Ghetto to be installed, rose at the end of this street. We saw the rear of some of the buildings on the left a short while ago, when entering an old courtyard (see p. 521).

Via della Reginella ends in Piazza Mattei, where we are again outside the Ghetto. In the piazza is the enchanting **Fontana delle Tartarughe** ('Fountain of the Tortoises') of 1585. It was designed by the great 'fountaineer' of Rome, Giacomo Della Porta, and enriched by the late renaissance Florentine sculptor Taddeo Landini, with four delightful bronze boys playing around it, each with a foot on a bronze dolphin. It is so exquisite that some scholars have attributed the design to Raphael and only the execution to Landini. In 1658 Bernini gave the fountain a final touch by adding the four turtles.

The longest side of the square includes two more palaces of the Mattei block. These are the last two and the oldest of the block which we visited in the second Ancient Rome Walk (p. 248) and which, as you may remember, was entirely occupied by different branches of the Mattei ducal family. Incidentally, the Mattei managed all the Ghetto gates by contract with the papal government.

No. 17 was built in the 1500's by Nanni di Baccio Bigio, Michelangelo's rival. It has a fine courtyard with a portico. No. 19, by an unknown architect, is from the end of the 1400's. Its façade was once entirely frescoed by Taddeo Zuccaro (see illustration on p. 449) ; its courtyard is even more beautiful than the other.

Opposite, at No. 10, is the main entrance to Palazzo Costaguti, which we saw from the other side (p. 521). It was built in the 1500's by a certain Don Ascanio Costaguti ('don' and 'donna' are titles of Spanish origin still used by Italian princely families). A descendant of the same name and sev-

Portico of Octavia in the 19th century

eral relatives still live here in rooms frescoed by Domenichino, Guercino, Lanfranco, Zuccaro and the like.

Leave the square by Via S. Ambrogio, all the way to the left. At No. 3 is the entrance to the monastery and church of **S. Ambrogio**, built over a house where according to tradition St. Ambrose, the 4th century Church Father, bishop and patron saint of Milan, spent part of his life. Admission is usually allowed only on St. Ambrose's Day, December 7.

A few steps further on, at No. 5, you can see what was once the monastery cloister, and is now used by nothing more exalted than the department of sanitation. There are two impressive renaissance doorways (No. 5 itself and another one inside). Over a wall to the left you can see the simple façade of the church, which was already standing in the 9th century but was rebuilt in the 17th.

Continue to the end of Via S. Ambrogio and stand with your back to it. You are now back on Via Portico di Ottavia. The section of the street to your right was part of the Ghetto in the 1800's.

Of the section to your left, the side opposite is formed by the relatively modern buildings that cover the razed Ghetto. The side on which you are standing was never part of the Ghetto and consists of a row of tall medieval and renaissance houses.

Two of these (Nos 8-11 and 12-14) are from the 15th and 16th centuries. They once belonged to another baronial family, the Fabi, now extinct, who claimed descent from the Latin *gens* or noble family of the Fabii. (Fabius Maximus was also a member, so the Massimo family – p. 504 – would have been relations.) Don't miss the original iron hooks under the eaves for hanging out laundry.

Enter No. 13 to see a renaissance courtyard with a typical arcade, belonging to a distinguished building that later became a poor tenement house and has recently been renovated.

Further on, at No. 25, within a truncated 13th-century tower, is a simple store (until 1992 a butcher's shop). Since the middle ages it has been framed by ancient Roman marbles that would have honoured a palace. Where else but in Rome can one find such a juxtaposition of the lowly and the regal? And how long will this exist with gentrification on the march?

Here, in front of the Portico d'Ottavia, which we visited on the second Ancient Roman Walk (p. 251), the old Ghetto ended at a secondary gate. On that Walk we saw two other churches connected with Ghetto life – S. Angelo in Pescheria within the Portico and S. Gregorio della Divina Pietà a few yards away, both used to forcibly indoctrinate Jews – as well as a tablet marking the spot where the Nazi round-up of the Jews began (pp. 251, 525).

To the left of the Portico di Ottavia is the old restaurant Da Giggetto, which neighbourhood people call 'Giggetto er Cattolico' ('Giggetto the Catholic' in Roman dialect) from its founder's name and nickname. Giggetto was one of the few Catholics living here, though the restaurant has always served the most delicious 'carciofi alla giudìa' (artichokes Jewish style).

BEFORE GOING

8. From the Ghetto to Piazza Venezia

Outside the Ghetto proper, other streets in the traditional Jewish quarter border on the Portico of Ottavia. Between the portico and the next highlight of this stretch, Piazza Campitelli, the Jews were intensely active by day, even in periods when, by night, they had to retire to the Ghetto. Several of their little stores and workshops were here, in the shadow of the great Teatro di Marcello ('Theatre of Marcellus'). There were also warehouses and garages for wagons and push-carts, things indispensable to their trades and for which the stifling, cramped Ghetto had little room. Today this border area is still home to a few Jewish-owned shops dealing in mattresses, textiles and haberdashery.

Leaving these streets, the Walk continues through quaint little squares, medieval fortifications and churches of all shapes and sizes. But not for long: the ancient fabric of the city is soon torn again by late 19th-century modernisations, and you find yourself in the presence of the blinding mass of the Altare della Patria ('Altar of the Fatherland') in Piazza Venezia (p. 535). Here, aptly

Palazzo Venezia

concluding your journey through all the phases and sights of the renaissance in Rome, is one of the earliest and greatest monuments of that glorious era, the Palazzo Venezia.

Built in the mid-1400's, this was Rome's first renaissance-style palace, the first example of a movement of architectural renewal whose triumphant conclusion we saw in the 16th-century Palazzo Farnese. Unfortunately, the appearance of Palazzo Venezia is today marred by later transformations around and inside it. Its isolation, a result of modern demolition, is an anomaly: a pope built the palace purposely to be in closer touch with his city and subjects than he was in the Vatican palace. Moreover, parts of the palace complex were later moved and rearranged, to no great advantage. Finally, the overpowering mass of the 'Altar of the Fatherland' nearby has dwarfed the palace and disturbed the subtle, classical balance of its proportions.

The large, noisy Piazza Venezia, originally a modest terminal widening of the Corso, but enlarged in the 17th century and more than tripled in size when the Altar was built, is not much for Rome to be proud of. What's more, the latest alterations involved destroying irreplaceable historic buildings, such as the house where Michelangelo spent his last years.

The history of Palazzo Venezia is long and varied. It was built by a Venetian pope, Paul II, a lover of feasts and fun like all Venetians, who disliked the stuffiness of his court and moved here to be in the midst of city life. He also ordered the carnival and carnival races, which had previously taken place elsewhere in the city, to be moved here, to what was then called Via Lata (p. 226), so that he could watch them and bless them from the comfort of his balcony. It is thus due to Paul II that the Via Lata came to be called Il Corso – the race course – and that the Roman carnival acquired the monumental backdrop which would help make it Europe's most famous for several centuries. The *ripresa* ('catching') – the place where the riderless horses were stopped at the end of their race by a large white sheet drawn across the course – was under the pope's windows. He also endowed the palace with magnificent gardens, which still exist, though in different positions.

Ownership of the palace passed from the Venetian pope to the Maritime Republic of Venice, which made it its outpost and embassy in Rome, while the adjoining ancient church of S. Marco became the national church of the Venetian community. In the early 1800's, when Austria absorbed the collapsed Venetian Republic, the palace too passed to Austria and housed its ambassador until the eve of the First World War, when Italy went to war against Austria. The Italian state then requisitioned it. Another chapter in its history began when, during the Fascist era, Mussolini made it his office. He delivered his famous speeches to the crowds from its balcony. It was in Palazzo Venezia that the Great Council of Fascism held its last, dramatic session on July 24, 1943, when Mussolini was asked to resign. The next day he was arrested and the regime collapsed.

ON THE SPOT

8. From the Ghetto to Piazza Venezia

Pass under the arch and then go left between the columns of the Portico; you are now in Via S. Angelo in Pescheria. We saw this street on a previous walk (p. 249), so leave it here and go right into Via Tribuna di Campitelli. This street splits off to the right (in the distance is the Theatre of Marcellus, p. 253), but keep left. At Nos. 23-23a, embedded in a much remodelled renaissance building, are parts of an ancient Roman colonnade of unknown origin.

Further on to the left, at No. 15a, is a renaissance doorway with a Latin inscription meaning 'God will provide'. Inside is a small garden, a nice example of modern restoration in a renaissance building; it communicates with Palazzo Lovatelli, which we saw from the other side on a previous Walk (p. 249).

The street leads to the long rectangular Piazza Campitelli, which is unspoilt by any modern intrusion – no recent buildings, no bars, no shops – and thus preserves the noble appearance it has had for centuries. The short side nearest to you (Via Cavalletti) and the long side in front of you are occupied by a succession of aristocratic palaces built between the early 16th and early 17th centuries. Most of the original families who resided here have died out (with the exception of the Cavalletti and the Campitelli; the latter gave their name to the whole district).

On the other long side, the square is occupied by the monumental **S. Maria in Campitelli**, built in 1667, and other 17th-century buildings. The church is the masterpiece of Carlo Rainaldi; the strong interplay of the architectural elements and the chiaroscuro effects of the façade make it one of the most dramatic creations of the Roman baroque. (Open April to Oct, 7.30-12 and 17.00-19.30; Nov to March 7.30-12 and 15.30-18.30).

The interior, too, is very lively and follows an unusual winding scheme. Over the altar in the second chapel to the right, designed and decorated by Rainaldi, is a *Virgin and Saints* by Luca Giordano, a prominent 17th-century Neapolitan painter.

Above the main altar is a spectacular decoration, a *Glory of Angels and Sunrays Bursting from Golden Clouds*, conceived by Rainaldi but executed by others (compare it to the one by Bernini in St. Peter's, p. 369). It encloses a tiny medieval (11th-century) icon of the Virgin, the story of which is behind the foundation of the church. When the faithful attributed the end of a terrible plague in 1656 (p. 246) to prayers addressed to this image, Pope Alexander VII (p. 44) had the church built as an expression of popular gratitude.

On the wall under the dome, to the left, is a delightful oil painting by Baciccia (the 16th-cen-

tury painter of the great ceiling fresco in Il Gesù, p. 112) of an unusual subject, the *Birth of the Baptist*.

The church rises where the house of the noble Albertoni family once stood. Their daughter, who died in 1533, is better known as the Blessed Ludovica and as the subject of a marvellous statue by Bernini (p. 585). The family once owned the last chapel on the right as you exit; the 18th-century relief over the chapel altar depicts *Ludovica's Vision of the Holy Family*. The two early 18th-century monuments on the side walls are to members of the Altieri family (p. 114).

At the other end of the square is another of the many beautiful fountains by Della Porta (late 16th-century); beyond it (Via Montanara), on the right, is the elegant little church of **S. Rita**, of medieval origins but rebuilt in 1665.

The church once stood at the foot of the Capitoline Hill (across the modern avenue) on the site of an excavation which we visited on a previous Walk (p. 141). Because of the excavation in 1928, St. Rita was dismantled and rebuilt here. It is now deconsecrated and closed.

Step out onto the modern avenue, Via del Teatro di Marcello (the theatre, which you saw on a previous Walk, p. 253, is to the right). To the left stretches the solemn convent of **S. Francesca Romana**, founded in 1432 by St. Frances of Rome, a noblewoman and mystic who devoted her life to caring for the sick (pp. 196-197). Over No. 40 is an 18th-century fresco of the *Virgin and St. Frances*.

Using the same mortar and pestle that the saint used five centuries ago, the convent nuns still produce an ointment of aromatic herbs which she devised to cure various ailments.

The site of the convent is traditionally called Tor de' Specchi ('Tower of the Mirrors'), probably because an early medieval tower that once stood here had architectural details evoking mirrors. It was also said, in a science-fiction-like medieval fantasy, that the ancient Romans had kept magic mirrors in the tower, with which they could see everything in their vast empire and thus spot incipient insurrections.

Return to Piazza Campitelli and take the first

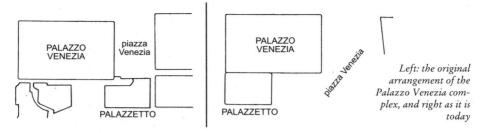

Left: the original arrangement of the Palazzo Venezia complex, and right as it is today

street to the right, Via Capizucchi, skirting the grim rear of the convent. We reach Piazza Capizucchi (mainly formed by the rear of the palaces whose façades we saw in Piazza Campitelli). Cross it and go on straight to Piazza Margana, amongst the most intimate and picturesque of Roman squares. As you cross it lengthways, on your right are an 18th-century palace (No. 21) and a 16th-century one (No. 19). Before you are buildings of medieval origin (Nos 38-41) that once belonged to the Margani, another medieval baronial clan (see p. 109); they died out in the 1600's. No. 40 is the base of a 14th-century tower, Tor Margana, adorned with an ancient Roman column, a medieval eagle relief (near the lamp) and other marble fragments. The 15th-century marble doorway at No. 41 is made of ancient Roman spolia.

Cross the piazza again lengthways. Take Via Tribuna di Tor de' Specchi to the left. Immediately to the right is a charming old house (No. 5), followed by a sliver of a 15th-century house with walled-up windows; the latter is adjacent to the rounded apse of a church inside the convent of S. Francesca. The convent wall continues on the right, ending, as it protrudes slightly into the street, with another truncated medieval tower (15th century or possibly earlier).

On the right the street ends with a palace built in the middle ages and remodelled in the 1500's by Giacomo Della Porta. He lived nearby, though exactly where is unknown.

(If you did not visit S. Maria in Ara Coeli as a Detour on the first Ancient Rome Walk, you can do so now – if, of course, the church is still open at this late point in your walk. It is just across the avenue, at the top of the steep steps to the left. But since the entrance there is often closed, it is better to climb the Capitoline Hill via Michelangelo's ramp to the right, then reach a side door of the church using the stairs to the left of the Senators' Palace. The description is on pp. 149-151. Return here after the visit.)

With your back to Della Porta's palace, notice another of Della Porta's omnipresent fountains a little ahead to the left; go and see this especially delightful one (1589), with smiling children pouring water from little barrels.

Cross to the foot of the raised patch of greenery opposite the fountain. From here, look back across the street at the interesting 17th-century palazzo at No. 23. Now walk along the pavement a few steps downhill to a gravel path in the green; take it and follow it left to the top of the hillock, then continue all the way to the left. You can conveniently sit on one of the marble benches facing Via San Marco (preferably the one on the right).

Across the street, to the far left, is the rear of the early 17th-century headquarters of the Jesuits, which we saw in the second Roma Romantica Walk (p. 112). Next to it – that is, in front of you – is the imposing bulk of **Palazzo Venezia**. Its complicated history needs some elucidation.

From here you can see the three elements of the complex. Left is the so-called Palazzetto, a rectangular structure protruding toward you. Next to it is one flank of Palazzo Venezia; this flank incorporates the church of S. Marco, with white marble arches and a belfry. The oldest part, by far, is the church, which had been here for eleven centuries when Palazzo Venezia was built in the mid-15th century. Later in the century the Palazzetto was added, but in a form entirely different from the present one. It now takes some effort to imagine the complex as its builders intended it, and to ignore the devastations wreaked by later planners.

The Palazzetto did not look at all as it does now; moreover, it was not where it is. Originally, it was an airy, arched structure enclosing a garden which Pope Paul II had added to his palace, Palazzo Venezia. For various reasons, including an earthquake, the arches were later filled in; thus what was meant to be a sort of open cloister became a heavy, rather non-descript building. A garden is still inside – you can see treetops from here – but it is normally inaccessible.

The cloister-cum-palace was originally at the far right end of this flank of Palazzo Venezia. The layout defined and embellished the modest-sized square then in front of the Palazzo's main façade.

After 1900 the square was tripled in size to accommodate the gigantic patriotic memorial on your right. The Palazzetto was dismantled and rebuilt here. Having lost its original appearance and function, it might as well have been demolished, especially since it now alters and conceals the view of Palazzo Venezia from this side. There is not much point in tarrying at the Palazzetto, so we'll proceed to the flank of Palazzo Venezia.

Cross at the crosswalk and walk to No. 49. The marble ruin near the wall is what remains of a big statue of the Egyptian goddess Isis, almost certainly from the Temple of Isis, which was not far from here (see pp. 114, 121). In the 18th century the Romans dubbed it 'Madama Lucrezia' (from the name of an 18-year old Neapolitan girl who lived near here and was said to be a protégée of the pope) and it became another of the so-called 'talking statues' (p. 461) to which dissenting posters were affixed.

No. 49 is one of the side entrances to Palazzo Venezia, the only ones leading to a very interesting courtyard with garden. We start our visit from this courtyard for two reasons: in order not to have to return afterwards, and because its architecture

gives us the occasion to discuss a key question: who built Palazzo Venezia?

(Access to the courtyard is sometimes restricted. But you can still see it from the lobby. Another side entrance, opposite this one – on Via del Plebiscito – is occasionally open and so you can also try later from there.)

The courtyard contains one of the purest, most characteristic expressions of the early renaissance, the arcades of a great unfinished portico. They are so beautiful and typical of the period that experts have even attributed them to one of the inventors of the new, post-medieval style, the Florentine Leon Battista Alberti. This great architect and artistic adviser to the popes (p. 307) was amongst the first to revive the technical and æsthetic principles of ancient classical art. He and one of his Florentine followers, whose name is also mentioned as a possible architect, Giuliano da Maiano, are known to have been in Rome during the construction of Palazzo Venezia.

Other names have also been proposed as the architects of the portico and palace. It is uncertain even whether they are by the same person. There are no convincing records of the authorship of Palazzo Venezia, and the matter is one of the most controversial in Roman renaissance architecture.

The ten arches belong to two sides of a rectangular portico which was never completed and which was planned to have 26. The design is directly inspired by ancient Roman monuments, including the Colosseum.

In the middle of the garden is an 18th-century fountain with a statue representing the marriage of Venice (in the person of a doge) to the Sea.

From here you can enjoy a view of the flank of S. Marco and its belfry, as well as another renaissance tower, built together with the Palazzo.

Leaving the courtyard, pass to the church of **S. Marco**. Its harmonious façade, with a portico, was built at the same time (late 15th century) as the main portico and courtyard of Palazzo Venezia and is probably by the same unknown architect. A visit to the interior follows as a detour.

DETOUR
10 MIN

Confusing homonyms and coincidences mark the history of the church of S. Marco. It was built in 336 AD, adapting a pre-existing *ecclesia domestica*, in honour of St. Mark the Evangelist, by a pope called Mark, who was himself later canonised. At the time, the church dedicated by one Mark to another had nothing to do with Venice – the city didn't exist then – nor with the fact that St. Mark the Evangelist was to become patron saint of Venice. Yet it so happened that eleven centuries after its foundation the church came under the special protection of a Venetian pope, Paul II, and subsequently became the church of the Venetian community in Rome.

The architectural history is just as confusing. The 4th-century church is gone; vestiges have been found under the present church, along with those of ancient Roman structures and two later reincarnations of the church, the last one from the 9th century. These excavations and a crypt can occasionally be visited. Some of the 9th-century structure – part of the walls, the apse and the crypt – survive as parts of the present church, which was built together with the nearby palace in the 15th century and frequently restored and modified thereafter. The present belfry was added in the 12th century.

Under the portico are tombstones and marble fragments from the earlier churches. On the lower right wall is a recently found Latin epitaph to Vannozza Catanei ('Vannotiæ Cathaneæ'), Pope Alexander VI Borgia's lover (p. 45). Nobody knows how it turned up here, since she was buried in S. Maria del Popolo (p. 48). The inscription was defaced, obviously on purpose, but the names of Vannozza and the children she bore the pope – Cesare, Lucrezia, Giovanni and Gioffrè – are still legible. Over the beautiful 15th-century central portal is a relief of *St. Mark the Evangelist* from the same period, attributed to Isaia da Pisa.

The church is open 09:00-12:00 and 16:00-19:00. Inside, the ceiling and gothic windows are 15th century, the columns 18th-century. There are remains of a cosmatesque floor in the nave and apse. At the beginning of the nave is a 9th-century well, used today as a baptismal font. It has a Latin inscription in which a priest called John invites one and all to partake of the water, but curses whoever draws the water to sell it.

Tour the church counter-clockwise. Over the altar of the first chapel in the right aisle is the *Resurrection of Christ* by Palma the Younger, one of the masters of the colour-drenched 16th-century Venetian school. Next to it is the tomb of a cardinal who died in 1570. Over the altar of the third chapel is the *Adoration of the Magi* by the distinguished late 17th-century painter Carlo Maratta from the Marche region.

Continuing down the aisle, as you ascend a flight of steps you'll see on the right the 1796 tomb of a young man by Canova. The aisle ends in a grand chapel designed by Pietro da Cortona in the 17th century. Over the altar is a painting by Melozzo da Forlì portraying Pope (St) Mark.

Under the main altar (18th century) a porphyry sarcophagus, possibly ancient Roman, contains the remains of Pope St. Mark. Access to the 9th-century crypt and the excavations is also from here.

In the apse are 9th-century mosaics: to the right of Christ, the first of three saints is Pope St. Mark; to the left, the second saint is St. Mark the Evangelist, while the third figure is Pope Gregory IV (pope at the time), with the square halo of the living, holding a model of the 9th-century church.

Go to the other aisle. Left of the steps is the late 15th-century tomb of an archbishop; view the reclining figure from the top of the steps. The sacristy contains a depiction of St. Mark the Evangelist by Melozzo (under restoration at the time of writing), as well as the late 15th-century altar and tabernacle of the church, dismantled in the 18th century and arbitrarily rebuilt later. Many parts are missing. It was carved by Mino da Fiesole and Giovanni Dalmata, who did the two angels with open wings and the biblical scene on the left.

END OF DETOUR

Around the corner continue to the front of **Palazzo Venezia**. For a good view of both the palace and the entire square, go to the grassy patch in the middle of the square.

No Roman landmark illustrates better than Palazzo Venezia the transition from the austere, bellicose middle ages to the refined renaissance. Note the contrast between the huge tower, the crenelations, the stark, heavy walls and the splendidly proportioned windows and finely worked central doorway.

The palace contains an important collection of sculptures, paintings and minor arts from the renaissance and middle ages (see p. 684). The entrance is on Via del Plebiscito.

Opposite the entrance, on Via del Plebiscito, is the 17th-century façade of **Palazzo Doria**, one of Rome's grandest palaces, belonging to a princely Genoese family closely related to the Pamphili (see pp. 456, 637), one of whose ancestors is mentioned in Dante's *Divine Comedy*. Members of the family still live there. The palace is larger and richer than many royal residences in Europe; indeed, it covers an area which is two-thirds that of the Colosseum! Yet, for all its grandeur, it has ordinary shops on two sides of the ground floor, a typical Roman feature. The palace houses a major collection of 16th and 17th-century paintings (see p. 684).

Next, at the corner of the Corso, is the 17th-century Palazzo Bonaparte, named after Napoleon's mother, Letizia, who lived there from the fall of the emperor until her death in 1836. The old lady used to watch passers-by from behind the green Venetian blinds on the corner balcony, one of the few remaining balconies of a type once ubiquitous on the Corso (p. 125). 'The mother of that great colossus,' as Belli called her, is portrayed by him as waiting for death in this palace, 'hunched up on a sofa… all shrivelled, no fatter than a ham bone'.

Across the square from the main façade of Palazzo Venezia is a modern building mimicking the shape of the palace, on the right side of which a tablet marks a site once occupied by Michelangelo's house. (Another house where Michelangelo was said to have lived was demolished nearby in 1941, though its façade was moved to the Janiculum hill, p. 637)

On the south side of the piazza, the **monument to King Victor Emmanuel II** (also known as the Altar of the Fatherland, and the Vittoriano or Vittoriale, the victory memorial) is a legacy of the highfalutin' nationalistic rhetoric fashionable at the turn of the last century. It was originally meant to commemorate the unification of Italy (1860-71) and the king who sponsored it (the king's statue is so huge that twenty people once had lunch inside the horse's belly). Later the immense structure was adapted as a memorial to the Italian victory in the First World War, and the Tomb of the Unknown Soldier, with a perpetual flame and guard of honour, was added at the top of the stairway. Inside the monument is a museum partly dedicated to the war (Museo del Risorgimento, p. 686).

Begun in 1885, it is the world's largest civic monument, and represents a mistake both in æsthetics and urban planning, as was realised soon after its completion in 1911. Each passing year has made the error more obvious. The marble, of a variety foreign to the Roman region, is jarring in its blinding whiteness. The overblown style and rows of columns and statuary have earned the structure the sobriquets of 'wedding cake' and 'typewriter'. Worse than the embarrassment has been the devastation of irreplaceable features of this most ancient and sacred part of Rome – either destroyed in the construction or hidden behind the giant monument. As the 1920's Ward-Lock guidebook put it with typical British understatement: 'This colossal building is hardly an ideal substitute for the view of the Capitol formerly existing.' The monument's only saving grace, and justification for survival, is the genuine patriotic fervour that prompted its construction.

The architect was Giuseppe Sacconi. A dozen other architects and sculptors, the best that Italian academic art had to offer, also contributed.

Before leaving the square, visit the small baroque chapel in Palazzo Venezia; the entrance is to the right of the doorway on the main façade.

Trastevere

Galatea, detail of Raphael's frescoes from the Farnesina

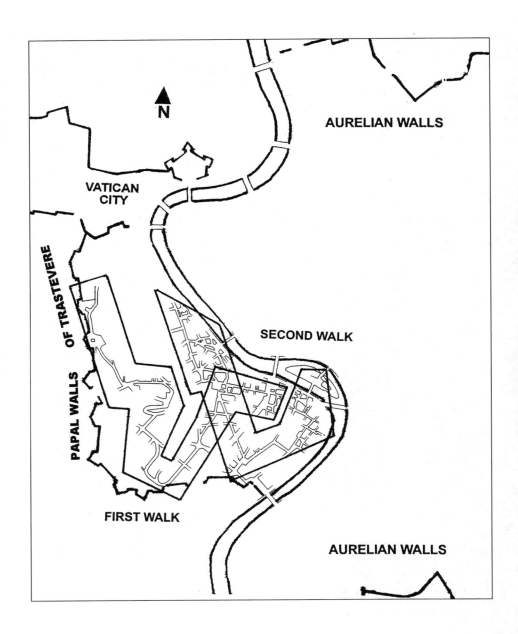

AURELIAN WALLS

N

VATICAN
CITY

PAPAL WALLS OF TRASTEVERE

SECOND WALK

FIRST WALK

AURELIAN WALLS

TRASTEVERE

INTRODUCTION

To Romans and foreigners, the word Trastevere has always suggested a dignified indigence; the neighbourhood has been poor for some two millennia. William Wetmore Story, an American sculptor, jurist and man of letters, who was amongst Rome's famous guests in the mid-19th century (see p. 83), relates his first encounter with the district in his book *Roba di Roma*:

> … and then we plunged into long, damp, narrow, dirty streets… Twilight was deepening into dark as we passed through them. Confused cries and loud Italian voices sounded about me. Children were screaming, men howling their wares for sale. Bells were ringing everywhere. Priests, soldiers, peasants, and beggars thronged along. The Trasteverini were going home, with their jackets hanging over one shoulder. Women, in their rough woollen gowns, stood in their doorways bare-headed, or looked out from windows and balconies, their black hair shining under the lanterns. Lights were twinkling in the little cavernous shops, and under Madonna shrines far within them…

The picture has been cleaned up a good deal, though not entirely, in recent decades, thanks to a steep rise in real estate value and well-to-do immigration from across the river. This includes foreigners, and especially Americans. A special affinity between Americans and Trastevere has existed ever since the foundation of an American Academy on the Janiculum Hill at the end of the 19th century. Academy residents have included many influential American artists, architects and musicians. Also in Trastevere are two churches run by American priests – one Roman Catholic (S. Onofrio), the other Baptist – two American universities and an American Roman Catholic seminary. The poverty, on the other hand, has always been softened by the charm of the neighbourhood, dotted with medieval buildings and touching little churches, and by the industriousness and pride of its inhabitants. These natives boast of being the oldest and most genuine Romans: 'Romani de Roma' (Rome's own Romans), or simply 'noantri' (we others), as they say in their dialect, which is Rome's purest and the closest to that of Gioacchino Belli's immortal sonnets (p. 62).

The 'Festa de Noantri' held in Trastevere is a yearly celebration of their uniqueness. Joined to a sense of independence and even antagonism towards the rest of the city, which may date back to the social struggles of ancient Rome, the Trasteverini, as the local residents are known, have not mixed with the rest of the Roman population for centuries. Until recently, many claimed never to have crossed to the other side of the river. There are perhaps genetic consequences, as it has always been said that pure-bred Trasteverini – those in the past especially, since today there are very few left – are a particularly classical, 'old Roman' and in any case handsome race.

The proud poverty of the district, though not its pretence to any special Romanness, dates back to before the Empire. At that time penniless immigrants from the East settled in the area, which was isolated by the river and outside the city limits. Many were slaves who had come as prisoners of war and were later freed (and if not them, their descendants). Most lacked Roman citizenship and so, in imperial times, weren't even entitled to state welfare. The majority were Syrians and

Playing the morra

Jews, encouraged to settle here by special concessions which Emperor Augustus had granted as part of his policy of urban development. The Jews were also attracted by the fact that outside the city they could openly practise their faith, whereas only official or assimilated cults were allowed within the city limits. Most Jews, though, left for the opposite bank many centuries later, for reasons that remain unclear (p. 522).

These humble and hard-working settlers found their main resource in the great river docks, an essential feature of this side of the river until the late 19th century. (There were other, secondary docks upstream, p. 123.) Most of the city supplies arrived here, in part reshipped from vessels anchored downstream at the port of Ostia. Foodstuffs were stored here for further distribution or, in antiquity, forwarded straight to the markets across the river. Thus Trastevere's population specialised in small businesses, just as in the renaissance areas on the opposite bank the humbler classes were mainly craftsmen. Until the mid-20th century a majority of traders here dealt in foodstuffs, such as preserved meats, poultry, milk products and vegetables. Though the official emblem of the district (the '*rione*') is a lion's head, its true symbol could well be the magnificent statue of a turkey gracing one of its churches (p. 587), a gift from the Università dei Pollaroli (Poultry-sellers' Guild) in the 18th century.

As in all big city dock areas, crime abounded, and the police were sorely tested. Augustus was the first to create an efficient police corps; they even doubled as firefighters. The remains of its station in Trastevere are a district landmark. In ancient times, slaves guilty of killing their owners or

Garibaldi

other murderers lacking Roman citizenship were crucified in Trastevere (amongst the latter, according to one tradition, St Peter, for having killed a magician, p. 196). Until about 50 or 60 years ago, stabbings were routine in the district, though most often as the result of love dramas or private vendettas. The Trasteverini have always been considered passionate people. Cheap and delicious wine from the Roman countryside further heated their mercurial character, especially in combination with a game called *passatella,* popular at local inns, in which the loser had to 'pass up' his turn at the flask and endure the winner's jeers; or with *morra,* a game of chance played with one's fingers and favoured by the poor, as it did not require possession of a pack of cards (see also p. 250). Today Trastevere has its share of crime, but no more than the rest of the city.

A mid-19th century insurrection against the pope has left more visible traces in Trastevere than elsewhere in Rome. In 1849 rebels on the Janiculum Hill, with the civilian population's support, fought with extraordinary bravery a bloody battle against the papacy's French protectors, in defence of a short-lived 'Roman Republic' set up by the patriots Mazzini and Garibaldi. In 1867, in a house we'll visit, police massacred a local family that had conspired against the papal government. Three years later Rome was reunited with the rest of Italy (p. 67).

That battle, reported by a remarkable American woman journalist, the author and educator Margaret Fuller, and later, by the well-known British historian G. M. Trevelyan, had a considerable impact on English-speaking public opinion, setting it decidedly in favour of the movement for Italian unity and independence. It may also have been responsible for the predilection of Americans for Trastevere. Margaret Fuller, a native of Massachusetts, a poet and philosopher who had been reading the Latin authors in the original since she was eight, was the first editor of the magazine of the Transcendentalist movement, *The Dial* (later edited by her friend Ralph Waldo Emerson) and one of the first American feminists and female liberal writers. In 1846 she was sent to Rome as a foreign correspondent by the *New York Tribune,* and three years later she was personally caught up in the cause of the Italian revolutionists headed by Mazzini and Garibaldi. She married, in secret, one of the rebels, the Marquis Giovanni Angelo Ossoli. During the siege of the Janiculum by the French in 1849 she assisted the wounded rebels as director of the camp hospital set up in Ss. Trinità dei Pellegrini (p. 477), while her husband fought on the hill. The defeat of the Roman Republic persuaded Fuller, now Marchioness Ossoli, to return to America with her husband and child. They arrived in July 1850, but a storm near the shore of Fire Island (Long Island,

542

New York) wrecked their ship and they perished. The manuscript of her day to day chronicle of the Roman revolution that she was bringing back for publication was also lost.

Poverty has had a great impact on the architecture and layout of Trastevere. In the first place, the district is the least 'renovated' in Rome. The very old, humble houses were rarely rebuilt, but simply patched up to their last gasp. Thus many medieval dwellings have survived, giving Trastevere a peculiarly medieval flair. The small, low houses and the need to cram in as many people as possible have made the district the most labyrinthine in Rome. Secondly, poverty encouraged a superabundance of churches, since hardship provided the most fertile ground for mysticism from the time of its earliest settlers. The oriental cults were especially sensitive to the spiritual and emotional needs of the downtrodden. Temples and synagogues proliferated, later to be replaced by Christian churches of all sizes and styles.

Another characteristic of the district is that it has more ancient and modern institutions for social assistance and correction than anywhere else in Rome: hospitals, vocational schools, homes for the poor, for the aged, for orphans, to shield girls from the perils of the world, and for repentant prostitutes. One large building here houses possibly the most comprehensive social help institution ever created, the 18th-century Hospice of St Michael.

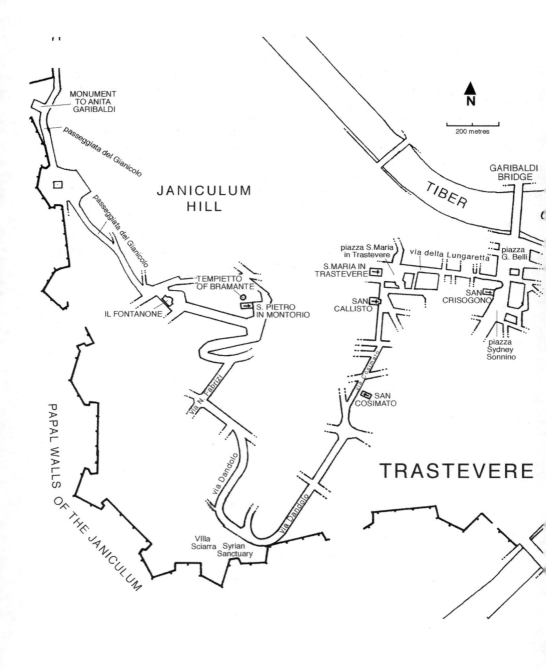

TRASTEVERE
FIRST WALK

1. Piazza Belli, Piazza Sonnino e Viale Trastevere 546
Palazzo Anguillara 547
2. S. Crisogono 548
S. Crisogono 550; S. Agata 551; Ospedale di S. Gallicano 551
3. From S. Crisogono to S. Maria in Trastevere 551
SS. Rufina e Seconda 552; S. Margherita 552
4. S. Maria in Trastevere and St. Calixtus (the man) 553
Palazzo S. Callisto 555; Palazzo Cavalieri 555; S. Maria in Trastevere 555
5. S. Callisto (the church) and S. Cosimato 556
S. Callisto 558; S. Cosimato 558

Midpoint of walk

6. The Janiculum: the Syrian Sanctuary 559
Syrian Sanctuary 560
7. S. Pietro in Montorio and Bramante's Tempietto 560
S. Pietro in Montorio 562; Tempietto 562
8. The Fontanone 563
9. The Janiculum of Garibaldi and Mazzini. (S. Onofrio) 565
Monument to Garibaldi 567; Monument to Anita 567; Villa Lante 567
(S. Onofrio 568)

Starting point: Piazza G. Belli
End point: Piazza Garibaldi
Duration: 4 hours (without the Detours indicated above
between parentheses).

Note: At the time of writing, S. Onofrio is rarely open; you can check by
calling the English-speaking priests at (06) 6864498.

BEFORE GOING

1. Piazza Belli, Piazza Sonnino e Viale Trastevere

Most traffic today flows into Trastevere from Rome over Ponte Garibaldi, a bridge aptly named after the mid-19th-century *condottiere* who led Italians in a fateful battle for freedom atop Trastevere's Janiculum Hill. The bridge leads directly to the heart of the district whose name means 'across the Tiber'. This area covers part of the plain there and up the slope of the Janiculum, and is bordered upstream by another hill, the Vatican, and downstream by a third elevation, Monteverde, semi-deserted until modern times. We too will quite probably be part of that current of traffic when we get to Piazza G.G. Belli just past the bridge, to start the first of these two Trastevere Walks.

We must not forget that Ponte Garibaldi was inaugurated only in 1888; before that, there was no connection between the modern centre of the city and the centre of Trastevere that did not involve a ferry. The only points of dry-shod access were at some distance from this central route, downstream at the Tiber Island with its two ancient Roman bridges (p. 251), and upstream at Ponte Sisto, a connection rebuilt in the renaissance (p. 475). As a result Trastevere is the only part of Rome whose main features have remained almost unaltered since the middle ages.

Created at a time when Rome's entire street network was being overhauled to adapt the city to her new role as capital of Italy, Ponte Garibaldi is the extension across the river of one of the widest new arteries slashing through Rome's centre – Corso Vittorio Emanuele II (p. 470). This was made to continue on the Trastevere side with a similar new avenue, initially called Viale del Re (the King's Road), yet another demonstration of the intense gratitude felt towards the Piedmontese dynasty that had liberated Rome from papal rule. It was re-baptised Viale Trastevere after World War II and the fall of the monarchy. The Viale now cuts Trastevere neatly in two – one part to the west, its back to the Janiculum, the other to the east, running along the river.

Giuseppe Gioacchino Belli

Even though little older than a century, this division has led to a certain difference in character. The western section, which already of old was directly linked to the renaissance district through Ponte Sisto, is more animated and modern-looking; the further-off eastern section, previously served by the more peripheral Isola Tiberina bridges and another, even more distant, bridge (Sublicio, see p. 546), is sleepier.

Entering Trastevere from Ponte Garibaldi allows us to appreciate these distinctions from the start, and highlights some other essential features of the whole district. Our starting point, Piazza G. G. Belli, created together with the bridge, was dedicated, in a belated gesture of recognition, to the bawdy, wise, humane poet of the early 19th century, whose sonnets in the dialect, once destined for destruction by their author himself because of their shocking realism, have survived as among the highest expressions of poetry of the time. Belli is seen today as the truest interpreter of the joys and sorrows of Rome's poorest districts – Trastevere being the poorest, and not the least eminent historically and artistically, as our Walks will amply demonstrate.

In the square is the stern Palazzo Anguillara, a fortified mansion of one of the most important local families, now extinct, typifying a class of Trasteverine citizens who wielded power mainly locally, as if Trastevere were a town in itself, thus stressing its independent and isolated character. These families' names have been given to the different parts of the river drive, the Lungotevere, on the Trastevere side: Lungotevere degli Anguillara is here by Ponte Garibaldi. We'll find reminders in our walk of many of these clans – the Ponziani, the Forteguerri, the Pierleoni, the Stefaneschi, the Alberteschi, the Papareschi or Paparoni – such as their tombs and the stern faces that stare out from their church monuments.

Directly connected with Piazza G. G. Belli in the initial stretch of Viale Trastevere is another square that the city gratefully dedicated to one of its most illustrious citizens, and through him to a whole class that used to be both one of the most vibrant and the most scorned in Rome, the Jews. The square is dedicated to Baron Giorgio Sidney Sonnino, prominent sociologist, finance minister, prime minister and foreign minister of Italy before and after the First World War, one of modern Italy's 'founding fathers' and a Jew. Notably, the square kept its name even under Fascism and its racial laws of 1938. Through Sonnino, the city also meant to honour the Jewish community, which originally was mostly settled in Trastevere and which, even before moving to the opposite bank (p. 541) gave Trastevere and Rome some historic figures, including, as we will see in these Walks (pp. 594, 598), a pope and the head of the first medieval republican government.

ON THE SPOT

1. Piazza Belli, Piazza Sonnino e Viale Trastevere

Take as a reference point a crenelated medieval tower – don't confuse it with a nearby church bell tower – and approach it. In Piazza G. G. Belli, the tower faces the top-hatted statue of Belli (p. 62), a 1913 'homage by the Roman people to their poet,' according to the inscription.

Approach this statue. From here there is a good view of the tower and the adjoining **Palazzo Anguillara**. This fortress-like complex is the sole complete survivor of many such that once dotted the district.

Built in the 11th century – when the Anguillara family, a powerful Trastevere clan, is first mentioned in history – the complex was totally rebuilt in the 15th century. It was fancifully restored in 1902 (for instance, the tower's crenelations were added, as was the rounded double window, from a demolished medieval house in the Ghetto), but by and large it has kept its original appearance.

A misleading tablet on a side of the tower reads 'Casa di Dante' (Dante's House). Dante never lived in Rome, though the building is used for lectures and courses on the greatest Italian poet. This lofty purpose also serves as a pretext to bar the public from the interior, which has a picturesque courtyard.

The Anguillara died out in the 18th century. We'll see their stern tombstones later in this Walk (p. 586).

The square with Belli's monument, the adjacent Piazza Sidney Sonnino on the other side of the tower and then an interminable, wide avenue called Viale Trastevere form a 'modern' thoroughfare, one of the many late 19th century (p. 62) roads that tore their way through the ancient fabric of the city.

Return to the tower. Skirting it, start heading down this graceless, very busy thoroughfare. Turn left at the second crossing into the Via della VII Coorte ('of the Seventh Cohort'), named for an **Ancient Roman police station** at No. 9. Here was based a detail of the police and firefighting force created by Augustus in the 1st century, until at least the 3rd century AD. (We discussed another two of these police stations on p. 427.)

The site, discovered in fairly good condition in 1866, has been allowed to fall back into ruin and is normally locked. The little house at street level was erected around the site soon after the excavation, but the relief with Roman weapons is ancient. On the ancient street level several feet underground is an impressive, large room with a fountain and a wall shrine; partly excavated corridors radiate in different directions. Remains of mosaics and paintings were almost totally obliterated. Of special interest were hundreds of examples of graffiti etched by the ancient Roman policemen, but these, too, have largely disappeared. If you continue past the station building into Via di Montefiore, you will see on the left that it has ventilation openings (with bars) near the present street level. It would be easy to see inside – if only the the interior were lit. But such an economic solution to make an otherwise inaccessible site visible seems beyond the imagination of the city bureaucracy.

BEFORE GOING

2. S. Crisogono

If the creation of Viale Trastevere aimed principally to connect Trastevere directly to the modern centre of Rome, the previous – and only other – urban renewal plan undergone by the district, in the 16th-17th centuries, was prompted mainly by health concerns: the need to decrease its congestion and the spread of disease, climaxing in the periodical plague epidemics that ravaged Rome especially in the middle ages; and to mobilise quickly the evacuation of the ill toward the lazzarettos (the main one was on the nearby Isola Tiberina) and of corpses to mass graves and the sea.

From its origins Trastevere, with its continuous influx of prisoners, slaves and indigent immigrants from other parts of the Roman world, was one of the most unregulated and densely settled parts of the city, more so even than the Suburra, the primeval slums in the ancient core. Throughout history, the ratio here of people to land and of construction to land – at least horizontally, as multi-storeyed houses were rare – was the highest in Rome. In the middle ages Trastevere cannot have been very different from the labyrinthine Muslim suqs of the regions from whence many Trasteverini families hailed. Even today its web of streets and alleys is more intricate than in any other part of Rome, including the congested areas we visited in the renaissance walks. If you need proof, just try finding a one-sheet map of Rome that includes all the streets of Trastevere and their names.

The renaissance and 17th-century renewals consisted in slicing through the urban fabric with a few long, straight and relatively narrow roads, some of which still wear names or nicknames suggesting these characteristics: Lungaretta, Lungarina, Lungara. The first of these we'll first meet at the end of this section, a few steps away from the spot where the worst ever plague epidemic broke out in the 17th century (p. 246).

The section we'll now visit is dominated by one of the most ancient churches in Rome, devoted to one of those mythical saints, Chrysogonos, whose existence today even the Roman Church doubts, and who may, like St. Clement (see above, p. 416) be a conflation of different figures. The

S. Crisogono in the 18th century, before the construction of Viale Trastevere, by Giuseppe Vasi

church was built over an *ecclesia domestica* (see p. 228) and originally, as in many similar cases, may have had the name of the wealthy private benefactor or benefactress who maintained it; quite possibly, in this case, Chrysogonos, an unknown gentleman, perhaps of eastern stock as were many inhabitants here and as his Greek name ('born of gold') suggests. But officially the name is said to belong to a Roman military officer baptised in northern Italy and beheaded under the reign of Diocletian, a major persecutor of Christians. Theological authorities speak of 'a legend' today when mentioning this official titular of the Trastevere church. The two Chrysogoni seem to have been conflated in the early middle ages.

In S. Crisogono we also find, in 10th-century frescoes, the first important reference to another saint, this one real, and one of the most important in Christianity, though mystery shrouds many aspects of his life too. He is St. Benedict, the early 6th-century founder of one of the first and greatest monastic orders, and builder of its first house in the Montecassino abbey (destroyed by Anglo-American bombing in 1944). St. Benedict is remembered in Trastevere because he was said to have been born here, or at least to have lived here with his family in a grand palace. No proof of this exists. Benedict's family, the Anicii, came from Norcia (Nursia), a town that has been Rome's major supplier of pork products in all ages (p. 242). The Anicii could have been involved in that industry, as most Norcia people were; Benedict, though, studied literature in Rome. Since Trastevere was the main distribution and retail centre of pork products from antiquity to at least the 19th century, the Anicii-Trastevere connection could well be real.

ON THE SPOT

2. S. Crisogono

In Via di Montefiore, the houses from No. 22 to No. 10 are picturesque vestiges of medieval Trastevere. In a miserable inn on this street the terrible plague of 1656 began.

Return to Viale Trastevere and cross it. There stands the 17th-century façade of **S. Crisogono**, one of Rome's oldest churches. On the right is its 12th-century bell tower, whose pyramidal top is a 17th-century addition. (Open: 07:00-10:30/Sundays 08:00-12:00; and 16:00-18:00.)

Like many of the most ancient Roman churches, S. Crisogono is actually two churches: an underground one of great antiquity (5th century), and an upper one built many centuries later when crumbling walls and the rising street level – caused in this case by river flooding (p. 140) – made the older church unusable. Not that the 'new' church is very young: it was built in the 12th century, and renovated around 1625.

Ancient Roman columns, with 17th-century stucco capitals, subdivide the stern interior. The floor is Cosmatesque (see glossary); the sumptuous ceiling 17th-century. The triumphal arch is flanked by two ancient Roman columns of porphyry (a rare red marble, now darkened), the largest of their kind in Rome. Over the the 12th-century main altar is a beautiful 17th-century ciborium. In the apse is a framed 13th-century square mosaic of the Virgin and Child between St. Chrysogonos (left) and St. James, perhaps by the great Roman muralist Cavallini. Right of the altar is a 17th-century chapel designed by Bernini, with lively busts of two prelates by his pupils.

The 5th-century church is reached via the sacristy at the end of the left aisle. (Before entering, notice to the right of the door a tablet of 1123 celebrating the consecration of the new church, and on the left a cosmatesque wall shrine of the same period.) This original church incorporated the remains of ancient Roman buildings where an *ecclesia domestica*, or 'home church', called the *Titulus Chrysogoni*, had been for one or more

centuries. Descend a metal staircase about 18 ft (6 m), to a space with a curved back wall. This whole space was originally split horizontally into two floors: note the groove that the intervening floor left in the curved wall. In the ancient church the upper floor was the apse and the lower floor was a semicircular crypt of a type then often used to exhibit relics of martyrs (pp. 367, 431).

The geometrical decoration on the upper part of the wall belongs to the lower part of the apse and is from the 8th century.

The masonry in the middle of the room pertains to the semicircular crypt, except for the high arches, which are modern supports. Near the centre of the masonry is a fresco with three saints (on the left, Chrysogonos), also 8th century.

From this apse-crypt area the 5th-century church (a single nave with no side aisles) extends behind the wall with the metal staircase. Modern supporting masonry now fills it, but the walls are visible. To see one, go to the foot of the staircase and proceed under the (modern) arch to a space with a splendidly preserved 2nd century AD sarcophagus on your right. When it was found here, it was intact and contained the skeleton of a man. The small room opposite the sarcophagus is probably part of the ancient sacristy and has remains of a rich and rare pre-Cosmatesque 10th-century floor. On the right are vestiges of older ancient Roman homes.

Continue, behind the sarcophagus, to the wall of the nave, with remains of 10th-century frescoes illustrating the life of St. Benedict. In the best preserved fresco, he heals a leper with blotchy skin. More rooms of undetermined use have been dug out in this area in 1999.

Backtrack all the way through the apse-crypt area, to the opposite wall of the nave. Here are more frescoes from the 8th century (saints within medallions) and the 10th century. Opposite are two more sarcophagi (the skeletons of a man and child were found in the one with the bust of the deceased and the 'Good Shepherd'). Scattered around are tombstones of different periods, ancient Roman to renaissance.

Returning along this wall, and down four steps, on the left, and through a door there is a baptistry where the rite was still performed by immersion (p. 410). The original circular tub is now split in half by a later wall. There are traces of frescoes.

Go upstairs and leave the church by the side door on the other aisle (if closed, use the main door and go around to the left). Here in the square (Largo S. Giovanni de Matha) you can see the 12th-century flank of the church. The slit windows are original; the others were added later, and the beautiful side doorway dates from the 17th century.

Opposite is the 18th-century façade of **S. Agata** (the church was founded a thousand years earlier), adjacent to that of an Evangelical Baptist Church of 1901. The latter was founded by the British branch of this Protestant denomination, but is presently managed by the American branch.

Take the street that continues the façade of the two churches, Via della Lungaretta ('Little Long Street'). In the late 19th century the new Viale Trastevere bisected this arrow-straight street; both sections are visible from here.

At the first crossing on the left, on the far side (no need to go there – you can see it from the corner) is the very long **Ospedale di S. Gallicano** (St. Gallican's Hospital) for skin diseases, built in the 18th century by Filippo Raguzzini and then the most advanced of its kind in the world. Skin disease, an affliction of the homeless, was once endemic to the district. The hospital, still active, also replaced a leper colony that had been in the area since the middle ages.

BEFORE GOING

3. From S. Crisogono to S. Maria in Trastevere

We will now enter what we described earlier as the more lively section of Trastevere, west of the modern Viale Trastevere, a plain limited on one side by the river, on the other by the Janiculum. This is where most artists of the district lived, including the one who made the best visual record of 19th-century Trastevere, the painter, printmaker and sculptor Bartolomeo Pinelli. Even today this is where we find all the many study centres that have sprung up in Trastevere and most resident foreigners (particularly Americans) live here. During the renaissance, cultural life here had the advantage of direct, stimulating contact with the intellectual ferment of Rome proper, thanks to the bridge rebuilt in the mid-15th century by Sixtus IV, the Ponte Sisto (p. 475), after centuries during which ferry boats had replaced a collapsed ancient bridge. The presence of Ponte Sisto meant that this part of Trastevere was the most visited by 'mainland' Romans, and that it became the place, especially during the renaissance, where many of these Romans built their houses and villas, both on the plain and on the Janiculum slope. So there are quite a few renaissance palaces and pleasure casinos here such as the Farnesina, the Bosco Parrasio with its famous literary academy, Villa Sciarra, Villa Doria-Pamphilj, Giulio Romano's Palazzo Lante and other such highlights that we'll discuss later.

As for the the Trasteverini themselves, the presence of Ponte Sisto did not broaden their horizons much – with due exceptions, naturally – mainly because of their deeply rooted spirit of proud independence, which made some of them boast, up to very recently, that they had never crossed the river, nor did they intend to. The maximum extent of their explorations were the riverside *rioni* ('quarters') of Regola and Ponte, on the opposite bank, and the districts they collectively called 'the hills' (*Monti*) across the river from the Isola Tiberina bridges at the other end of Trastevere. (*Rioni*, an ancient word derived from the Latin *regiones*, is the official term, particular to Rome, for the city districts.) With the populace of those shores Trasteverini entertained a love-hate relationship that produced constant, almost ritual fights, often led by hot-headed *caporioni* ('heads of rioni') who were sometimes awarded the laconic nickname of 'Più', 'the Mostest' (such as in 'Er Più de Trastevere', 'Er Più de Ponte', etc.). Particularly memorable were the fights between Trasteverini and Monticiani, the inhabitants of Monti. In their belligerent activities, the men of Trastevere were conscientiously supported by their women, also considered the fiercest and bravest of Rome, as witnessed by this 19th-century Roman *stornello* ('refrain'):

> Io so' Trasteverina e lo sapete,
> Nun serve, bello mio, che ce rugate;
> So' cortellate quante ne volete!

> I am Trasteverina as you well know,
> There's no point, mate, in bullying me;
> My knife will slash you whenever you ask!

Trasteverina in the 19th century

Fierceness, of course, both in men and women was not always vented just in crime and vendettas. We'll be reminded of this at the start of the 'on the spot' section by a half-forgotten episode of the 19th-century revolutionary struggle against Papal oppression and for Italian unity, freedom and independence, a struggle that was nowhere so alive in Rome as in Trastevere.

ON THE SPOT

3. From S. Crisogono to S. Maria in Trastevere

Continue along Via della Lungaretta. At No. 101, on the right, is a renaissance door. Then at No. 97 is the house where Giuditta Tavani Arquati and a dozen co-conspirators against the papal government were killed in a three-hour battle with papal guards in 1867. Three years later the papal regime fell.

At the end of the block, on the right, is the charming romanesque bell-tower of the small church of **SS. Rufina e Seconda**, built in the 11th century in honour of two martyrs whose legendary existence we discussed elsewhere (p. 400), and often remodelled in recent times. The church, reduced to bare walls and not especially interesting, is entered from No. 92a. It has small catacombs beneath. Continue along Via della Lungaretta. No. 91b on the right houses a home for single women and expectant mothers and a soup kitchen, examples of the myriad welfare institutions that have always dotted Trastevere.

At the end of the block on the right is the 14th-century church of **S. Margherita** (Margaret), entirely rebuilt in the 17th century. Rarely open, it has a painting by Baciccia in a chapel to the left, over the altar. Via della Lungaretta No. 3 is a 17th-century palace; with it the via ends at Piazza S. Maria in Trastevere, hub and pride of the Trastevere district.

BEFORE GOING

4. S. Maria in Trastevere and the story of St. Callixtus

Many fabulous stories surround the foundation and first centuries of S. Maria in Trastevere – one of Rome's great basilicas, and the main church here. Some of these stories are historically certain, other less so. But most appear to reflect two quintessential Trasteverine traits: the close co-existence of people of different ethnic origins and different faiths in its congested quarters, and the quarrelsome character of the inhabitants. They also further confirm a phenomenon that we have pointed out elsewhere, the easy transformation of the practices of one religion into those of another, in this case the Jewish and the Christian.

A club for veterans of the Roman army, or *taberna meritoria*, used to be on or near the present site of the church. One day, some 60 years before Christ, the floor of the taberna began spouting an oily substance, never seen before in Rome. The Jews who at the time populated most of the neighbourhood proclaimed this a miracle and an omen of the coming Messiah. The spot took on a holy connotation. Some decades later, when the Christian Messiah did in fact arrive, those who recognised Him saw the omen confirmed, and in time the venerated site became a small Christian sanctuary. 'In Trastevere's taberna meritoria, oil gushed out and continued flowing for a whole day, meaning that the grace of God would be blessing the peoples', St. Jerome still marvelled four centuries later in his Chronicle. In the early 3rd century the few military pensioners still occupying the taberna moved out and the club was closed. According to the contemporary pagan historian Ælius Lampridius, a furious quarrel erupted between local innkeepers, who considered the former taberna a 'locus publicus' – a commercial site – and wanted to keep it that way, and the Christian faction, at that time led by Callixtus, a Trastevere-born theologian, who squatted in the building and wanted to convert it into a home church (*ecclesia domestica*, p. 228) dedicated to the 'miracle of the oil'. In a surprising denouement, the emperor, Alexander Severus, assigned the place to the Christians, deciding that a site devoted to a god, of whatever nature, would benefit the community more than one devoted to wine. (This story, reported by a contemporary writer, contradicts the idea that pagan authorities were at all times dead set against the Christians. Alexander Severus, of course, ruled a century before the legalization of Christianity by Constantine.)

As for Callixtus, already at that time he was embroiled in another, more intellectual controversy, concerning a slightly different brand of Christianity supported by another theologian, Hippolytus, with a large following in Trastevere. After a long struggle, both Callixtus and his adversary were simultaneously elected pope by their supporters, giving place, for the first time in history, to the conflict of popes and anti-popes, which then went on to plague the church for over twelve centuries (the last anti-pope was elected in 1440), a conflict which can thus be said to have originated in contentious Trastevere. As we'll see when will discuss this shortly in connection with another church dedicated, this time, to Callixtus himself, the dispute between Callixtus and Hippolytus quickly assumed very serious proportions and may even have led to Callixtus' murder.

Two centuries later, the taberna converted into *ecclesia domestica* had been replaced by a large basilica, now called S. Maria in Trastevere; and in the 12th century, the basilica was rebuilt from scratch, either over the first one or nearby, and in greater splendour. All along this time several

S. Maria in Trastevere

clashes between popes and anti-popes took place in this church, and two in particular deserve special mention.

The first, in 366, set the Roman-born, and probably Trasteverine Bishop Ursinus against the Spanish immigrant Bishop Damasus, immediately after the death of pope Liberius (founder of the Basilica Liberiana on the Esquiline, see p. 96). Damasus' partisans elected him pope in the church of S. Lorenzo in Lucina (p. 228). Ursinus' faction proclaimed him pope in S. Maria in Trastevere. Initially, they were both 'popes': 'anti-pope' was an insult mutually bandied about by the contenders, until more permanently assigned to the loser by the winning faction and by history. After minor clashes, Damasus' partisans chose a day when Ursinus' supporters were assembled in S. Maria in Trastevere (or, according to other sources, in the Basilica Liberiana), provided themselves with weapons and caught the opposing faction by surprise; 137 Ursinites were killed, and only a few, Ursinus among them, managed to flee with their lives. Damasus was confirmed pope, and in due course was proclaimed a saint and titular of his own important church (p. 486).

In the 12th century, when the church was rebuilt, the rebuilder was another pope, this time from the Trasteverine Papareschi family. He, too, was a survivor – though not the winner – in another epoch-making pope-antipope struggle. His name was Innocent II, and he could only assume his seat when his opponent, Anaclete II from the Trasteverine Pierleoni family, who had been elected pope the very same day as he, died peacefully after an eight-year reign. The dead Anaclete was then officially demoted to anti-pope and so he remains listed in Church annals to this day. Another peculiarity of Anaclete was that he was of Jewish descent, the only such pope, as far as we know, in history. Of this very interesting man and his influential family, as well as their great importance in the history of Roman Jews, we'll have more to say later (pp. 593-594, 597-598).

S. Maria in Trastevere is the first church in Rome to have been dedicated to the Virgin and was one of the most important centres of early Christianity, along with St. John Lateran, St. Peter's, S. Maria Maggiore and S. Lorenzo in Lucina. As far as the mysterious substance that led to the building of St. Mary in Trastevere is concerned, an explanation emerged in the late 19th century, when natural gas was detected during the construction of the embankment of the nearby stretch of the Tiber. Since such seepage normally indicates the presence of fossil fuel deposits, it was clear that the oily fluid gushing out the floor of the *taberna meritoria* was petroleum, a substance with which Romans were totally unfamilar. The holy 'source of oil' (*fons olei*) is still commemorated by various inscriptions in the church and by the name of a nearby street.

ON THE SPOT

4. S. Maria in Trastevere and the story of St. Callixtus

Entering the square, on the right you will see the Peretti Pharmacy, in business since 1820. If the closing time of the church of S. Maria in Trastevere is near, go there first and visit the square afterwards.

The square centres on a polygonal fountain. A fountain of this shape, perhaps the most ancient of the countless fountains in Rome's piazzas, has been here at least since the early 15th century, though the water was not drinkable until the 16th century, when it was fed by the Pauline aqueduct (p. 563). The fountain has often been rebuilt, though to changing designs. The present, 1873, version closely follows that of 1692. The grand brick building at No. 24 is **Palazzo S. Callisto**, named after the theologian whose *ecclesia domestica* later gave way to the nearby S. Maria in Trastevere, and residence of the cardinal the pope appoints as titular of the basilica. The imposing 17th-century structure is legally part of the Vatican state, with which it shares extraterritorial status (p. 302). The palace has been on the square for at least five centuries in various incarnations, and perhaps for even longer, if it was originally part of a convent built in 828.

To the left is the distinguished 15th- to 16th-century **Palazzo Cavalieri**. Home of a famous 16th-century composer, Emilio de' Cavalieri, it was briefly owned in the early 19th century by the Leopardi family, when its most illustrious member, the great poet Giacomo (p. 61), was a little child. Later it became a half-way house, run by nuns, for women released from the prison that was part of the Hospice of S. Michele (also in Trastevere, pp. 586-587). Later still, civil authorities took it over and turned it into a hostel for runaway girls, which it remains.

The square is dominated by the venerable **S. Maria in Trastevere**, the first church in the world to be dedicated to the Mother of God. It was built in the 4th century over or very near an *ecclesia domestica* (p. 228), enlarged later, entirely rebuilt in the 12th century, then restored several times.

The façade was substantially altered in the 18th and 19th centuries but behind the four early 18th-century statues can still be seen an important medieval mosaic. The Virgin enthroned with Her Child (note at Her feet the two tiny figures of the donors) is flanked by a parade of ten holy women, of disputed symbolic meaning. The eight central figures, large and small, are 12th-century; the three last women on the right were added or redesigned later; the three last on the left, still later (late 14th or early 15th century). Note the different styles. The bell tower is 12th-century; near the top is a small mosaic icon with gold background. In the porch, added in the 18th century, are remains of two 15th-century frescoes (on the left, framed) and many ancient marbles, mostly originating from the church; most notable are the early medieval enclosures running all around the base, the splendid ancient Roman friezes used as a frame around the doors in the middle ages; and the medieval tombstones on the floor and sarcophagi against the left wall.

By and large the interior (open: 07:00-12:00 and 15:00-19:00, and occasionally in between) is that of the 12th century. The columns, unequal in size, originate from ancient Roman buildings, including the temple of an Egyptian cult (some capitals show little heads of Egyptian gods). The Cosmatesque-style floor is mostly modern. The marvellous ceiling was designed in the 17th century by Domenichino, who also painted the *Assumption* at the centre. Approach the main altar. To the right of the central steps, a modern inscription – *fons olei* or 'source of the oil' – replacing an earlier one marks the spot of the 'miracle' that gave the church its origin. Some of the Cosmatesque decoration in this area is 12th century, though partly redone in the 19th century. The original part includes the floor before the altar, elements of the ciborium or canopy (not the roof) and the tall candelabrum. The altar itself harks back to the earliest days of the church.

In the apse are some of Rome's most beautiful

mosaics. They are of different ages, but all are evidence of a return to classical ideals in art, typical of great Roman churches at this stage of the middle ages. On the outer arch, and in the apse proper down to and including the row of sheep, the mosaics are mid-12th century. Expressive and delicate, yet still redolent of the stern Byzantine style, they represent, on the arch, the prophets said to have foretold the advent of Christ, and in the centre Mary and Christ enthroned. Flanking the latter are saints and, far left, the pope who rebuilt the church, Innocent II, holding a model of it. Under the sheep are seven episodes in the Virgin's life by the great late 13th-century Roman muralist Pietro Cavallini; his greater ease of design and psychological insight show growing freedom from the restraints of the Byzantine style. The panel left of the centre window refers to the story of the *taberna meritoria* (p. 553) and the 'source of oil'.

Also in the apse is a 12th-century bishop's chair (only the arm-rests are original). At the far right corner of the church is a harmoniously proportioned chapel designed inside and out (up to the ceiling) by Domenichino. Rich stucco garlands and narrow golden bands of imitation mosaic frame the window above. At this end of the transept is a three-part funerary monument of a cardinal and of his father (to the right), of the early 16th century.

Descend the steps; open a door at the beginning of the aisle to see the other side of the door, framed with Romanesque reliefs of the 10th-12th centuries (a light switch is on the wall). Cross to the far left end of the church. At the end of the transept is a late 16th-century chapel, marvellously decorated. In a room off it is a large and very rare 8th-century icon of the Virgin with Angels. The Virgin is dressed as a Byzantine empress in this Byzantine work, which in ancient days adorned one of the altars.

Also at this end of the transept, on the wall, are two more superb monuments of cardinals, of the early 15th century. Originally in a different position, they were partly dismantled and rebuilt later (a late renaissance painting was included then). The monument on the right is signed, in a long, inscription commemorating the dead cardinal, by an unidentified Magister Paulus. The monument on the left, with an atmosphere-laden relief of the *Dormition of the Virgin*, may also be his work.

Go down the steps on this side. The first door on the right leads to an anteroom where, on the right-hand wall, there are two 1st century AD ancient Roman mosaics. Continue down the aisle to the next chapel, an unusual, lively example of late 16th-century architecture, with ancient Cosmatesque floor. At the end of the aisle is the 18th-century baptistery, originally a chapel where St. Francesca Romana (who lived nearby in the 14th century, p. 595) prayed and had many visions. Cross to the opposite side. At the very beginning of the nave is an exquisite wall shrine by Mino del Reame (probably 15th-century Neapolitan). Over the souvenir shop at the beginning of the aisle is a 15th-century fresco of the Virgin and Child, from a series that once adorned most of the aisle. In the third chapel is a 15th-century wooden crucifix.

BEFORE GOING

5. S. Callisto (the church) and S. Cosimato

Only a short distance from S. Maria in Trastevere, S. Callisto is one of the most enigmatic of Roman churches. If there is any truth to the story that a pit in the church is the very one Callixtus, at the climax of his controversy with the theologian Hippolytus, was thrown in and killed by a mob of furious opponents, perhaps urged on by Hippolytus, then the building must be among Rome's oldest, since the murder took place in the early 3rd century, when Callixtus' dispute with Hippolytus, which is historically documented, was in full swing. Tradition says that the building was, at the time, the house of another prominent cleric by the name of Pontianus, where Callixtus had taken refuge; that some time later it was transformed into an oratory or *ecclesia domestica*, and that later still, in the 8th century, it became a regular church. Yet apart from the pit, and the odd remain of ancient Roman and medieval brickwork that so often emerges wherever you dig in Rome, there is nothing in the building to confirm an extremely ancient origin. The church is first mentioned only in the 12th century, and nothing of the building itself predates the total reconstruction of 1610. Is the site, then, really so ancient? Or is the the connection between the pit and Callixtus' death imaginary, even, perhaps, in the sense that the simple existence of the pit spawned this particular version of Callixtus' death – one of the many cases where a physical feature of a church gives rise to legend, as at S. Prassede (p. 94) and S. Maria in Aracoeli (p. 149)? Another question mark is this church's relationship with the *ecclesia domestica* that Callixtus is known to have established in the area. Was this it, rather than the one which later was replaced by S. Maria in Trastevere nearby? Or there where two? There is no definite answer.

What interests us, in any case, is the history of the titular, who would be among the few, if not the only, Christian martyr whose death was caused not by any official authority but by his fellow citizens, even, perhaps, by other Christians. Only in quarrelsome Trastevere could such a strange instance of martyrology be found. If, in fact, Callixtus was murdered by supporters of the theologian Hippolytus, who was not only a Christian, but such a good one that he was later made a saint, it can be assumed Hippolytus' supporters were also Christian. Another anomaly is the fact that Hippolytus, at the height of his row with Callixtus and after Callixtus had already been elected pope, also had himself proclaimed pope by his own faction. At the time, he was declared a usurper, i.e. an anti-pope, by the higher echelons of the Church. Therefore, following Callixtus' death, far from ascending to the throne as it happened later in the case of Innocent II, he was forced into exile. Callixtus was followed on the throne by Urban, of whom nothing is known except that he was a Roman and that he died five years before Hippolytus, and then by Pontian, who was Callixtus' host at the time of his death and also a Roman. The saga of these people – Callixtus, Hippolytus, Urban and Pontian – all takes place during the reign of Emperor Alexander Severus (AD 222-235), a time of peace for Christians. But when the emperor was murdered and the truculent Maximin of Thrace took his place, persecution of Christians resumed, and the two survivors of these vicissitudes, Pope Pontian and the anti-pope Hippolytus, were exiled to Sardinia, where both died immediately of maltreatment in 235. Then they were both sanctified; the only example, in the case of Hippolytus, of an anti-pope who was proclaimed a saint, in recognition, apparently, of his valour as a theologian and of his martyrdom.

By contrast with the complex and often obscure history of St. Callixtus, that of the eponymous saint of S. Cosimato, the next church on our itinerary, is extremely simple: no saint of this name ever existed. The church of S. Cosimato is named after not one, but two saints – three if you count the fiction. Initially it was dedicated to the Sts. Cosmas and Damian, the eastern doctor-martyrs whose main church we saw near the Forum (p. 193). Over the centuries, their names were fused, creating a third, imaginary figure. But the church and convent of S. Cosimato are of great interest as poignant examples in Rome of ancient monuments converted to everyday use: for over a century now they have been used as a hospital specializing in the afflictions of old age.

ON THE SPOT

5. S. Callisto and S. Cosimato

Leave the church and take the first street on the right out of the square. You are now in Piazza S. Callisto. On the right is **S. Callisto**, with a simple early baroque façade of the early 17th century and the arms of the final rebuilder of St. Peter's, Pope Paul V Borghese. It is occasionally open. The interior was renovated in the 19th and 20th centuries and has simple fixtures and decoration from the last four centuries. The chapel to the left gives a view, through a window to the right of the altar, of the pit in which St. Callixtus is said to have been martyred. (The well-head, an ancient Roman piece, is by the wall outside the chapel. Water from the pit was once deemed a cure for fever.)

Another chapel across the nave has two angels attributed to Bernini. To the right of the main altar is a small sacristy with a late 16th-century wash basin (lavabo). Above it is a small belfry of the same period.

Next to the church is a very large building (1936) by Giuseppe Momo, who also designed the double ramp in the Vatican Museums (p. 355). It contains Vatican offices; connected to Palazzo S. Callisto around the corner (p. 555), it shares the privilege of extra-territorial status (p. 302). Walk past this compound on Via San Cosimato. Where the street ends at Piazza San Cosimato, a heavily eroded tablet of the late 3rd century AD can be seen embedded low in the wall of a house on the left. This inscription, probably found nearby, is a tribute paid by a Trastevere wet nurse, Elpidia, to her dead charge, 'the very sweet and very lovely' Lucia Septimia Patabiniana. She was a young princess, a relative of Syria's famous quasi-independent ruler, Queen Zenobia of Palmyra. It is another echo of the oriental character of ancient Trastevere. At the end of the square, on the left, is **S. Cosimato**.

Enter the hospital grounds at No. 76 (no need for permission) and go straight, through the narrower passage on the left, to the first of two cloisters of the former convent. Built in the early 13th century, it is surrounded by fragments of statuary and inscriptions from ancient Roman, Early Christian and medieval times. Go on around to the left, to the far corridor of the cloister (parallel to the corridor you first entered). Note the ancient ceiling beams here. To the left of the stairs going down is a door leading to the 15th-century convent meeting room. The room, unfortunately closed to visitors, contains age-darkened portraits of the church's benefactors, including a stern-looking Vannozza Catanei, mistress of the notorious Borgia pope (pp. 45, 482).

Climb the steps to the left of the meeting room door to reach the second cloister, also 15th-century. If the windows on the right are open, you will be able to see into the meeting room. A romanesque bell-tower overlooks one side of this cloister.

Leaving the second cloister the way you came in, walk straight ahead and through a large rectangular passage into a triple vestibule (15th-century; two rooms are separated by a 17th-century oak door and the naive ceiling fresco is 19th-century) Go on into a garden with a granite fountain. This garden was once the exterior portico of the church of S. Cosimato on your right.

The church was founded in the 10th century but entirely rebuilt in the 15th. Note the beautiful doorway and delicate cornice. The dark interior is sometimes open. Most of the decoration is early 19th-century, but the refined fresco of the *Virgin and Saints* to the left of the altar is by Antonio da Viterbo, an artist in the circle of Perugino and Pinturicchio. In a chapel to the left of the altar is a beautiful renaissance cenotaph; opposite, the grill behind which the cloistered nuns attended Mass.

Leaving the church, take a look at the original 10th-century entrance at the opposite end of the garden. For a better view, leave the premises where you entered and turn right. In front of the ancient entrance (which on this side consists of a 12th-century romanesque vestibule or porch, *prothyrum*, similar to those of S. Clemente (p.

419) and S. Prassede (p. 106), and includes columns and other ancient Roman spolia) note the difference between the street level and that of the church complex. This is not because of excavation, but because continuous use has maintained the level of the church.

<h2 style="text-align:center">⚜ MIDPOINT OF WALK ⚜</h2>

BEFORE GOING

6. The Janiculum: the Syrian Sanctuary

Our Walk now goes up the Janiculum, Trastevere's hill. The ancient Romans believed it had been colonised by the god Janus, the animistic spirit of doorways and entrances – hence the name. Until recently it did not figure much in the history of the city. It wasn't inside the *pomerium* (p. 471), nor is it counted among the traditional 'seven hills'. Its steepness contributed to its insularity – a regular road to the top was not built until 1867.

In military terms, the hill of Janus, a warlike god, was always of strategic value, as it dominated access to Rome from a point near the natural defence of the river. Indeed, the hill first enters the city annals in the 6th century BC in connection with a successful attack by an Etruscan army. In modern times it witnessed a clamorous military episode: the heroic resistance of anti-papal insurgents in 1849, bent on creating a lay Roman Republic, against vastly superior French forces rushed by Napoleon III to defend the pope. We'll find reminders of that struggle all along this first stretch our walk.

There we'll also find a new, suggestive reminder of the eastern character of ancient Trastevere, the Syrian Sanctuary, one of many oriental temples serving the immigrant population of the district (pp. 540-541). It was built later than other pagan temples in Rome, actually after Christianity had already become the official state religion at the end of the 4th century, possibly in the period when Emperor Julian 'the Apostate' (p. 424) tried to reintroduce paganism. Soon afterwards it was destroyed by fire, perhaps by enraged Christians after Julian's death. Ritual statuettes and a large statue of a Syrian goddess – now in museums – were found during the excavations, either hidden (presumably by Syrian priests) or broken and defaced (by Christians).

The temple abuts one of the aristocratic *vigne* ('vineyards', often luxuriously appointed and including elegant *palazzetti*) that dotted Rome's *disabitato* (p. 28) until the 19th century: Villa Sciarra, named after former owners, the Colonna-Sciarra family (p. 125). In its vast gardens, forces under Garibaldi clashed with the French in one of the longest and most furious battles of 1849, before being forced to the top of the hill, where they had to concede defeat. The villa's elegant 17th-century *palazzetto*, devastated in the battle, was subsequently rebuilt. In 1902 it was bought by the American diplomat George Wurts and his heiress wife Henriette Tower, who embellished it with romantic fountains and copies of ancient statues. After Wurts' death, his widow gave the property to Mussolini as a personal gift, and the Fascist leader made it a public park.

ON THE SPOT

6. The Janiculum: the Syrian Sanctuary

If you are facing the entrance to S. Cosimato, go right to Via Morosini, cross it and continue straight into the long Via Emilio Dandolo. (The names of most streets here are those of the soldiers who fell in the 1849 war.)

Planning this stage: the whole trip uphill can be made with one of the buses that stop on Via Morosini. To visit the Syrian Sanctuary, though, you'll first have to get off at the second stop. Then get back on the bus and go as far as a stop just after the curve into the intersecting Via Nicola Fabrizi. Walk right along Via Fabrizi to its end, and you'll see the bell tower of S. Pietro in Montorio. If you don't take the bus, but would rather shorten this long excursion, you may skip the Syrian Sanctuary and go straight to S. Pietro in Montorio (p. 562). The shortcut consists of walking along Via Morosini to its end, then continuing straight along Viale Mameli to its end in Piazza S. Pietro in Montorio.

The **Syrian Sanctuary** is at Via Dandolo 45 and is usually open till sunset. It is an archæological site, not directly accessible but to be seen from above. Climb the steps to the first landing and move to the fence on the right.

The ruins consist of a rectangular courtyard leading, at one end, to a basilican structure with apse and niches and, at the other (the end nearest the street), a room with remains of a triangular fountain, used perhaps for purification rituals. The temple dates from the 4th century AD but traces of much older temples lie underneath.

Known from early antiquity as 'sacred woods', the area was at one time dedicated to the Furies, avenging deities who tormented criminals. This was where Caius Gracchus (pp. 154, 268), the first great champion of the Roman poor, committed suicide in 121 BC while opponents out to kill him were in hot pursuit. His conservative enemies said the Furies had justly called him to his death near their sanctuary.

In the past the sanctuary grounds were part of Villa Sciarra, but no longer. The villa, now a public park, is entered further uphill (Via Calandrelli). Currently the palazzetto houses the Italian Institute of Germanic (and Scandinavian) Studies, with a large library.

Go back to Via Dandolo and go uphill to a crossing with Via Nicola Frabrizi. Take Via Fabrizi, right, to the end, where you can spot the bell tower of S. Pietro in Montorio, your next destination.

BEFORE GOING

7. S. Pietro in Montorio and Bramante's Tempietto

Silent and poetic though it is today, in ancient Roman times this place was one of the most macabre in the city. Non-Romans and slaves convicted of murder were crucified here. Until Augustus imposed more lenient regulations, relatives were forbidden to recover the bodies. These were left to rot on their crosses, consumed by flocks of crows thought to be divine, as witnessed by a stele found nearby with the inscription *Divas Corniscas Sacrum* ('Sacred to the Holy Crows', though the word *divas* also meant divinatory, as the study of birds was thought to reveal the future, p. 148).

To this site many chroniclers of Early Christianity assign St. Peter's execution (if indeed it took place in Rome). The tradition of Peter's death here is more plausible than the much better known tradition in which he was crucified at the foot of the Vatican obelisk (p. 376). The square would have been appropriate, since he was not a Roman and since, according to the ancients, he had been sentenced not only for preaching Christianity, but also for murder, having caused the fatal fall of the flying magician Simon (p. 196).

This tradition explains the presence here of S. Pietro in Montorio ('on Golden Hill', perhaps a reference to the yellowish soil of the Janiculum). The church harks back to early Christianity, though the exact founding date is unknown and the present architecture dates from 1481. It was restored after being ravaged by the French in 1798 and again in the fighting of 1849.

Near or under the main altar Beatrice Cenci (p. 517) was buried at the end of the 16th century. No inscription has ever marked the location, which remains uncertain; in any case, her body is not there now. Is it elsewhere in the church? Some say marauding troops of revolutionary France, who occupied Rome in 1798 and used this church as a depot, removed it, or even played ball with her skull. Rumour or fact, all this adds another macabre facet to the Cenci saga.

Bramante's Tempietto

In a courtyard of the convent is the exquisite Tempietto ('Little Temple') by Bramante, the great architect's most famous work. The fruit of Bramante's passionate study of ancient Roman monuments, to which he had devoted his first years in Rome (p. 462), the Tempietto caused a sensation when it was unveiled in 1512: here was a perfect synthesis of the canons of classical architecture, reinterpreted through modern values and sensibilities. An inspiration to all high renaissance artists, it is one of history's most influential architectural works. It fuses pagan beauty and Christian spirituality: the first conveyed by proportions so subtly balanced, that the dominant impression is one of noble monumentality despite its tiny size; the second, by an ornate design recalling that of a precious church reliquary.

The temple functioned to preserve a religious legacy, having been built over the alleged site of Peter's crucifixion. Originally it was to be enclosed in a circular, colonnaded cloister, but this was never built.

ON THE SPOT

7. S. Pietro in Montorio and the Tempietto

S. Pietro in Montorio faces a tranquil square half way up the Janiculum which, like a terrace, allows a charming view of Rome. Its linear early renaissance facade recalls that of its contemporaries, S. Maria del Popolo (p. 47) and S. Caterina dei Funari (p. 248). (Open: 08:00-12:00 and 16:00-19:00/18:00 in winter; at other times you can try to gain admission by ringing the bell.)

The church is especially notable for its richly decorated chapels (push the buttons for light). Proceed counter-clockwise. Except where noted, the chapels were decorated in the 16th century. The first on the right contains the wonderful *Scourging of Christ* and other oil paintings by Sebastiano del Piombo, a friend and admirer of Michelangelo, whose style is obvious here. The design may have been supplied by Michelangelo himself, who inspired and/or helped several of his followers in this church.

In the second chapel on the altar is a sweet *Virgin and Child* by Niccolò Pomarancio; it was brought here from the street outside, where it was said to have caused many miracles. The chapel is also frescoed, inside and above, by artists of Pinturicchio's or Peruzzi's circle, who also painted the wall above the next chapel. The last and largest chapel on this side was designed by Vasari, famous both as an artist and as a biographer of the renaissance masters. His fine *Conversion of St. Paul* is over the altar. The dark-bearded man sitting on the far left is a self-portrait. The splendid tombs of cardinals and other statuary on the side walls of this chapel are by Bartolomeo Ammannati, another Michelangel-esque artist and architect, as is the beautiful balustrade with cherubs. Some attribute the design of the cherubs to Michelangelo.

Proceed down the nave. The first, very large chapel on your right was designed by another Michelangelo follower, Daniele da Volterra, to whom the *Baptism of Jesus* over the altar is also attributed. The beautiful second chapel holds the dramatic *Deposition* by Dirk van Baburen, a 17th-century follower of Caravaggio. In the next chapel are the tender *St. Anne with the Virgin and Child*, over the altar, and other frescoes by Antoniazzo Romano (late 15th century) or his school. The next to last chapel, dedicated to St. Francis, was designed by Bernini and decorated by his pupils (17th century). Adorning the last chapel are the *Stigmata of St. Francis* and other frescoes by the late 16th-century Tuscan painter Giovanni De Vecchi. To the right of the exit, on the wall, is a monument to an archbishop by Bregno (late 15th century) or one of his pupils.

The famous **Tempietto** by Bramante is at No. 2 in the square (if closed, ask in the church). Around the first storey, twelve granite columns support a frieze with Christian liturgical symbols. The second storey is surrounded by an airy balustrade and topped by a dome (restored and somewhat modified in the 17th century). Windows and niches running around the two storeys enrich and lighten the structure, which is dramatised by the deep cast shadows. Inside, the division into two storeys is different from that on the outside, since the whole structure above ground forms a single room, while the lower chapel is underground.

The upper room has a beautiful cosmatesque floor. On a 16th-century altar are the coats of arms of King Ferdinand and Queen Isabella of Spain (p. 95), who commissioned the temple when their prayers for the birth of a son were answered. Over the altar, a relief and statue of St. Peter by minor renaissance artists. The statues in the niches are by pupils of Bernini (17th century).

In the lower chapel, reached at the back of the temple via a door and a double staircase created by Bernini, a hole in the ground marks where St. Peter's cross was said to have been placed. The ceiling is stuccoed with episodes from the life of St. Peter, by a minor 17th-century artist. To the left of this courtyard, another wing of the convent houses the Spanish Academy. It includes a renaissance cloister, frescoed in the 16th century with scenes from the life of St. Francis, attributed to Niccolò Pomarancio.

8. The Fontanone

Next we come to another square, dominated by the Fontanone, or 'Big Fountain', as Romans affectionately call this early 17th-century masterpiece. Technically, it is the 'Mostra' or showcase fountain built to adorn the terminus of the Pauline aqueduct serving Trastevere. Another commemorative fountain of the Pauline water is downhill on the bank of the Tiber where we'll see it in the next walk (p. 573). The function of this fountain is therefore like that of the Trevi Fountain (p. 64) and the Fountain of Moses (p. 77) for the aqueducts of the Acqua Vergine and Acqua Felice respectively. The Acqua Paola was the third ancient aqueduct rebuilt in Rome in the late renaissance on the course of one originally built by Emperor Trajan at the end of the 1st century AD.

The special affection that Romans, in particular those of Trastevere, have always felt for the Fontanone is due not only to its beauty, but also to the fact that its water was the first to relieve a thirst for healthy water that the poor Trastevere district had suffered throughout its long history. Inhabitants had always made do with meagre local springs and river water. Some scholars even ask – as one, Cesare D'Onofrio, has recently written – whether 'Trastevere's century-long underdevelopment shouldn't primarily be connected with the age-old scarcity or total absence of running and drinkable water.' Already in ancient times, when imposing aqueducts brought torrents of pure water to Rome (p. 428), the needs of a Trastevere populated by slaves and immigrants were largely neglected. Augustus built a first aqueduct to supply Trastevere with water from Lake Martignano, near Bracciano, about 21 miles (33 km) north of Rome, but it was badly polluted. The real reason Augustus wanted it was to feed the enormous *naumachia* or pool for mock naval battles that his engineers, as we'll see later, built in Trastevere, which he was proud enough to remember in the list of his greatest deeds and testament (p. 224). Frontinus, the head of Rome's water supply in the 1st century AD and author of a famous hydrology treatise, was scandalised: 'it is not clear,' he wrote, 'what could have induced such a provident prince to bring Rome water not only unpleasant but unhealthy, so much so that nobody anywhere wants to drink it.'

Trasteverini waited almost another century before a famously generous emperor, Trajan, brought them decent water, by exploiting other sources in the Bracciano area. But four centuries later, as we know (p. 28), the barbarian Goths cut all the aqueducts to hasten the fall of the besieged city. Rome did not capitulate, at least immediately, but the ploy returned Trastevere to a state of drought. Even when the popes reactivated the first aqueducts, Trastevere was not served by them. The reasons are clearly explained by one of the papal engineers: 'His Holiness does not wish that this water be sold for public fountains in Trastevere because here there are few palaces, little nobility and scant wealth,' he wrote in a report. Even when Pope Paul V Borghese (p. 359) finally rebuilt Trajan's aqueduct to Trastevere, the public use of its water (whose name he felt necessary to change from 'aqua traiana' to 'acqua paola', or 'Pauline water') was limited. Nor did Trastevere ever acquire the same number of splashy fountains that brighten the other districts of Rome.

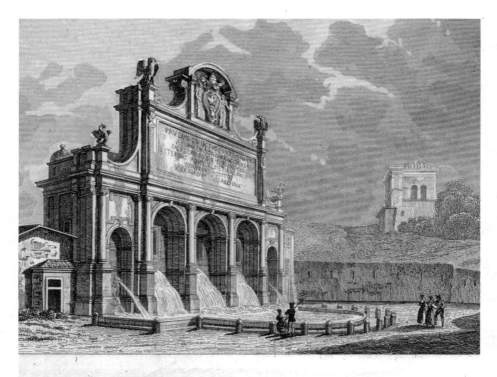

Roma. Fontanone dell' acqua Paola.

The Fontanone in the 1830's

ON THE SPOT

8. The Fontanone

Moving on uphill, we pass on the left a Fascist-style (1941) memorial to the dead of 1849 and to those who fell for Rome's final liberation from papal theocracy in 1870 (p. 67). A porphyry tomb honours Goffredo Mameli, one of the youngest heroes of 1849 and author of a hymn to Italy that became the national anthem (p. 566).

Not far off is the **Fontanone** square. The fountain was commissioned by Pope Paul V from Flaminio Ponzio and Giovanni Fontana, son of Domenico Fontana, who had built the Moses Fountain (p. 77). Paul V was the pope who completed the new St. Peter's Basilica, as we remember when we see four granite columns from the old St. Peter's reused here for the front of the fountain. Two new ones were added on the sides. Other marble pieces came from the Temple of Mars the Avenger in the Forum of Augustus (pp. 178-179).

With its vast, cool basin (added several decades later by a third Fontana architect, Carlo, a distant relative of the other two) and its façade inspired by ancient Roman triumphal arches and enlivened by angels, monsters and dragons, the fountain ranks amongst the most beautiful in Rome.

BEFORE GOING
9. The Janiculum of Garibaldi and Mazzini. (S. Onofrio)

In 1849, the second year of revolutions throughout Europe, Italian patriots led by two leaders, the guerilla general Giuseppe Garibaldi and the political theorist Giuseppe Mazzini, proclaimed Rome a republic. The pope fled. But France's newly elected president Louis Napoleon (nephew of the great Napoleon) was bent on ingratiating himself with conservative circles who were planning a coup to make him emperor, and so he sent 20,000 troops to reclaim Rome for the Pope.

The rebels, mostly students and volunteers, and mostly Italians but also sympathisers from England, Holland, Switzerland, Poland and even France, knew they had no chance against a far better-armed, professional force six times stronger. But they chose to fight, if necessary to the death. 'Rome or death' was their slogan. Mazzini, speaking at the parliament assembled to govern the city, said: 'We must act like men who have the enemy at the gates, and yet also like men who are working for eternity.'

Liberal countries supported Italy's struggle for independence, unity and freedom, which is known as the Risorgimento (Revival). Louis Napoleon himself aided the Risorgimento, after being made emperor (as Napoleon III) two years later. In England, Garibaldi's feats and the enterprises of Mazzini, often a political refugee in London, were followed with no less enthusiasm than the Greek fight for independence from the Turks had been in Byron's time. 'I cannot count the years / That you will drink, like me / The cup of blood and tears, / Ere she to you appears, / Italia, Italia shall be free!' wrote George Meredith.

The rebels fought without pause against overwhelming forces, but after bloody losses and a long siege on the Janiculum they eventually capitulated. (The outcome was not affected by the late arrival of a group of 810 English volunteers – others had been there from the start, see p. 52 – organized by the socialist leader George Holyoake. Her Majesty's Government turned a blind eye to their enterprise on the assumption that their uniforms were 'for the purpose of recognizing each other' and their weapons 'for the purpose of self-defence'.) The popes ruled Rome for 21 more years. The desperate fight of the young Garibaldini moved Europe. The British historian Trevelyan, who has left us a day-to-day account, noted that when motivated, Italians can fight as valiantly as others considered more warlike. 'The Italian character has in it something beyond the reasonable,' he wrote. On the Janiculum, 'when all was lost, the idea of perishing with the murdered Republic seemed to fortify the morale and brace the nerves of the tired men, whose conduct became now more uniformly heroic than it had been during the fortnight past, when it was still possible to indulge a shadowy hope.' The resistance at Villa Sciarra, Villa Corsini, the Casino dei Quattro Venti and the Villa il Vascello (see p. 637) assumed mythical dimensions. Trevelyan later even offered his own translation of a 'Song of Garibaldi' written by Gabriele d'Annunzio:

Villa Corsini, House of the Four Winds,	Villa Corsina, Casa dei Quattro Venti
Smoky prow of the Ship thrust forward	Fumida prua del Vascello protesa
Into the tempest, names for ever	Nella tempesta, alti nomi per sempre
Grand – like Marathon, Platea,	Solenni come Maratona, Platea,

Cremera – once ye were haunts of idleness,	Cremera, luoghi già d'ozii di piaceri
Pleasure and music and frail magnificence,	Di melodie e di magnificenze
Gardens guarded by blind stone statues,	Fuggitive, orti custoditi da cieche
Watered by fountains – all changed suddenly	Statue ed arrisi da fontane serene,
Into a red infernal giddiness.	Trasfigurati subito in rossi inferni
	Vertiginosi.

Here is, in Garibaldi own words, a description of the sacrifice of the 20-year-old poet Goffredo Mameli, as reported in a letter to Mameli's mother:

> It was towards the evening, when Mameli, whom I had kept beside me most of the day as my aide, besought me earnestly to let him go forward into battle, as his position near me seemed to him inglorious. In a few minutes he was brought back past me, gravely wounded, but radiant, his face shining because he had shed his blood for his country. We did not exchange a word, but our eyes met with the love which had long bound us together. I remained behind. He went on, as though in triumph.

Taken to the camp hospital in a nearby church (p. 475-477), the author of the poem that would later become Italy's national hymn died four weeks later, after gangrene had set in.

At least a third of the rebels died or were wounded. Garibaldi survived miraculously, despite having taken part in the heat of battle several times. Followed by his loyal young wife Anita, who had a fever, he eluded pursuing French forces and Austrian police hunting him throughout Italy, and hid in the marshes of the Po valley near Ravenna. There Anita collapsed. 'In putting her down to sleep tonight,' he wrote, 'I thought I saw the death-look in her face.' She passed away in his arms.

Monument to heroes of the post-Garibaldi resistance: the Cairoli Brothers, who led an insurrection in 1867

Today few people, even in Italy, remember all this. The busts on the Janiculum are often defaced by vandals and hastily repaired. People do not connect the names of the streets along the Janiculum slopes with the heroes of the struggle. Recently, a mayor of Rome, ironically the nephew of the sculptor who made the wonderful monument to Anita atop the hill, proposed to change the name of one street from that of one of the bravest defenders of the Roman Republic, fallen at the head of a group of student volunteer cavalry, to that of the American Academy nearby. The project was abandoned with some difficulty. (The authors would like to think that their protests during a press conference given by that mayor and in a letter to the director of the American Academy led to the abandonment of the idea. The splendid work of the American Academy certainly deserves all sorts of recognition, but not this.)

ON THE SPOT

9. The Janiculum of Garibaldi and Mazzini. (S. Onofrio)

This next section is mainly devoted to the events of 1849. If you first wish to see an area where many of the crucial battles were fought, you may take a detour by continuing on Via Garibaldi around the Fontanone, to Porta S. Pancrazio. The description is in 'Fuori le Mura' ('Excursions outside the Walls'), starting on p. 637.

Take, to your right (if you are facing the Fontanone) the Passeggiata del Gianicolo, to a vast square, Piazza Garibaldi. You are now at the summit of the hill. In the middle is the **Monument to Garibaldi**, an excellent work of 1895 by the sculptor Emilio Gallori. From the terrace here one enjoys one of the most beautiful and famous views of Rome, though not as complete a vista as the one we'll see from elsewhere on our way downhill.

An old cannon stored under the parapet here is trotted out daily and fired at noon. Romans have set their watches by it for over two centuries.

There are lavatories near this garage, accessible from the right end of the terrace.

Start walking downhill. In the distance on your left are the pine trees and wonderful formal gardens of Villa Doria-Pamphili (p. 637), created in the mid 17th century by a nephew of Pope Innocent X. The villa was to become one of the main theatres of the 1849 war. From this point on, a crowd of marble busts portray many of the people – both soldiers and politicians – who built and defended the Roman Republic under the leadership of Garibaldi and Mazzini. Mazzini himself has no monument here; his statue is in a large square named after him in a turn-of-the-century neighbourhood (Quartiere Prati).

To your left is the equestrian **Monument to Anita**, Garibaldi's gun-toting Brazilian wife, who died at 28 during the retreat from Rome. She is buried under the monument. The spirited bronze was cast in 1932 by Mario Rutelli, whose Fountain of the Naiads you may have admired earlier (p. 81). Cross the Passeggiata del Gianicolo to see, on

the slope of the hill, the delightful **Villa Lante**, a classically proportioned early 16th-century leisure villa by Raphael's pupil Giulio Romano, who probably took specific suggestions from his master. The villa is now the home of the Finnish Institute of Roman Studies.

Continuing for about 100 yards on this side, you reach a small marble-covered lighthouse, a monument that symbolises Italy's rôle as a beacon to the world. Italian emigrés to Argentina donated it to Rome in 1911. These former Italian citizens had contributed mightily to turning their new country into an extremely prosperous land, as it was then, and felt a special affection for their homeland. At night the lighthouse used to project beams over Rome in the colours of the Italian flag. It stopped doing so at some point, and one wonders if today's Argentinians still feel they should come and fix it, or whether they consider it Rome's responsibility. The terrace by the lighthouse enjoys the most complete view of Rome, ranging – left to right – from Castel Sant'Angelo to Villa Medici and Trinità dei Monti, from the Pantheon's squat dome to the 'Soldiers' Tower' and from the Senator's Palace on the Capitol to the statues silhouetted over S. Giovanni in Laterano, and further into the distance.

If you skip the detour and the church of S. Onofrio you can go back to Piazza Garibaldi and catch a bus for the longish downhill trip. You can take it to the end of the line, which is in a more central part of Rome, past the river, at the beginning of Corso Vittorio. If you follow the detour, partly or in full, you can still avail yourself of the bus and alight at one of its stops, such as S. Onofrio or the Ospedale di Santo Spirito, before it crosses the river.

DETOUR
40 MIN

From the lighthouse, a path through the green leads to a centuries-old oak, dead since 1950. It is a famous tree, not only for having lived at least five hundred years, but because it was here, in its shade that Torquato Tasso came to meditate. Tasso, one of the greatest poets of the renaissance, had taken refuge in the nearby convent of S. Onofrio to try to recover from mental illness.

The steps near the stump take us back to Passeggiata del Gianicolo, which winds down a short distance to the metal gate of **S. Onofrio** (St. Onuphrius). The church is up some stairs. Together with its convent and cloister, it makes an island of serenity after the bustle of the city below. It was founded in 1419 to honour an Early Christian hermit from Persia, so ascetic that he went around clothed only in his own hair. Though restored some decades later, the complex retains most of its original appearance. Here Tasso, sick in body and mind, sought refuge at the end of the 16th century, and here he died the day before he

was to be crowned with laurels at the Capitol as one of the immortals of world literature.

Today the complex is managed by the priests 'of the Atonement', an American branch of the Franciscan Order. Outside, 17th-century frescoes adorn the church wall. The series of three under the porch on your right are by Domenichino, depicting episodes from the *Life of St. Jerome*. (The church is usually open in the morning, except Saturday. At other times you can still try to be admitted by ringing the bell, or you can call the English-speaking priests to make an appointment on (06) 6864998).

Here and there the dark interior shows hints of austere gothic design. Proceed counter-clockwise, using the push-button lights. The first chapel on the right has, on the ceiling, a pure and luminous 15th-century *Annunciation*, a youthful work by

Torquato Tasso's oak tree, before it fell down in 1950

Antoniazzo Romano. The second chapel, decorated with rich 17th-century stuccoes, has a *Madonna* by Annibale Carracci (17th century) or his school over the altar. Past the chapel, on the wall is a monument to an early 16th-century cardinal by Andrea Bregno or his school, and above it a fresco of the same period. The apse has frescoes by Pinturicchio's workshop (early 16th century), with episodes from the life of Mary. Proceeding toward the exit, the first chapel now on your right has a cenotaph to a late 16th-century cardinal with his portrait by Domenichino. In the last chapel, on the right is a 19th-century monument to Torquato Tasso and near the chapel exit is a 17th-century memorial to him. His actual remains are near the church door. Nearby is a 15th-century font. Go into the peaceful cloister of the convent next door, with columns originating from ancient Roman buildings. Under the porches are charming early 17th-century frescoes of episodes from the life of St. Onuphrius, all by minor artists. As you leave the church, at the right end of the porch there is an exquisite chapel of 1620, also frescoed by lesser-known painters.

Cross the street to Salita di S. Onofrio (or you may take a bus downhill directly in front of S. Onofrio to its terminus just across the river). Go down this evocative street (on the left are ancient institutions for the poor) and a short flight of steps. On your left is Piazza della Rovere, were you can take a leisurely look at the powerful Vatican Walls (p. 312) and at the Porta S. Spirito ('of the Holy Spirit'), the only surviving renaissance gate in the Vatican walls. Construction, begun in 1542 by Antonio da Sangallo the Younger, was soon abandoned because, on a suggestion by Michelangelo, it was decided that the

Monument to Torquato Tasso, S. Onofrio

walls should follow a different course. Though unfinished, the classically-inspired gate, adorned by four huge Doric columns, is one of the most solemn and best proportioned in Rome.

END OF DETOUR

From Piazza della Rovere, or from the bus stop at the river entrance of the nearby Ospedale di S. Spirito (Holy Spirit Hospital) several buses go to downtown Rome.

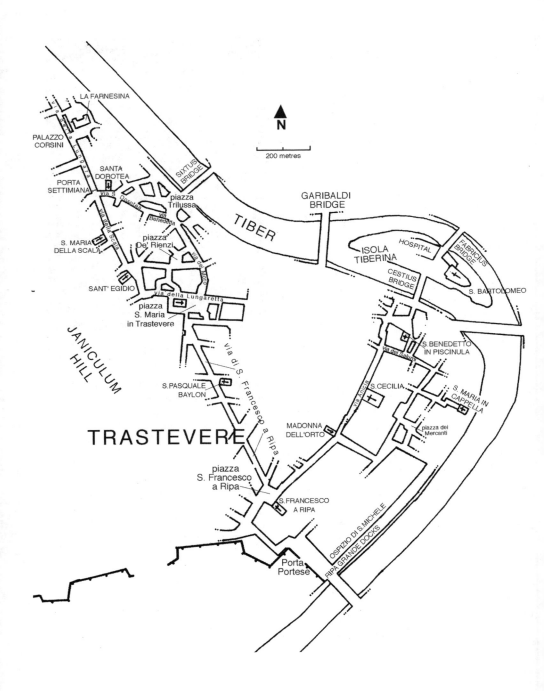

TRASTEVERE
SECOND WALK

1. From Piazza Trilussa to the Farnesina 572
Fontana dell'Acqua Paola 573; Via S. Dorotea 574; House of the Fornarina 574; Porta Settimiana 574; Palazzo Corsini 574
2. La Farnesina 575
(Conservatorio delle Pericolanti 577; S. Maria dei Sette Dolori 577; Bosco Parrasio 577)
3. S. Maria della Scala and S. Egidio 578
4. From Via del Moro to Viale Trastevere 580
Oratorio di Maria Santissima Addolorata e delle Anime del Purgatorio 581; SS. Quaranta Martiri e S. Pasquale di Baylon 582; Fountain of the Prisoner 583

Midpoint of walk

4. From S. Francesco a Ripa to S. Cecilia 584
San Francesco a Ripa 585; (Ospizio di S. Michele 586); Madonna dell'Orto 587
5. S. Cecilia 588
6. From S. Cecilia to S. Benedetto in Piscinula 593
S. Maria in Cappella 594; Palazzo Ponziani 595; S. Andrea dei Vascellari 595; S. Giovanni dei Genovesi 595; Arch of the Tolomei 595; S. Maria della Luce 596; Palazzo Mattei 596; S. Benedetto in Piscinula 596
7. S. Bartolomeo all' Isola 597
S. Giovanni Calibita 598; S. Bartolomeo all' Isola 598; Torre della Pulzella 600

Starting point: Piazza Trilussa
End point: Isola Tiberina and Monte Savello
Duration: 4 hours (without the Detours indicated above between parentheses)

BEFORE GOING

1. From Piazza Trilussa to the Farnesina

Of the three squares – Piazza Trilussa, Piazza Belli and Piazza in Piscinula – that open out from the main bridges to Trastevere and serve as entranceways to different neighbourhoods of the *rione*, (p. 552) Piazza Trilussa is the furthest upstream. It is also the one that had the most direct and all-purpose connection with the other bank until the construction of Ponte Garibaldi in 1888, as the bridges downstream served mainly for the transit of victuals and merchandise to and from Rome's markets. In imperial times, the bridge arriving here from the Campus Martius via the age-old street of the Arenula ('of the little beach', p. 519) was the Agrippa bridge, built by Augustus' son-in-law to link the Campus – the recreational area – to the new attraction created by Augustus at the foot of the Janiculum. This was the 'naumachia', the great pool for mock naval battles fed by the newly built aqueduct of non-potable water (p. 563). Later, the bridge became part of Rome's defences. Chains could be drawn in the water along it to block hostile vessels, while on the Trastevere bank the Aurelian walls (p. 42), aligned with the bridge, continued to the top of the Janiculum and then down, turning south-east, to another point of the river (p. 586).

Agrippa's bridge fell and was rebuilt at least twice, before one particularly violent river flood wrecked it in 590. Thereafter, ferries served this part of Trastevere for over eight centuries, as did the bridge of Castel S. Angelo further north, the final stretch of the pilgrimage route to the Vatican and St Peter's. As we know (p. 442), that bridge, always overcrowded, was the scene of a tragic traffic accident in the Jubilee year 1450. This persuaded Pope Sixtus IV to rebuild Agrippa's bridge for the next Jubilee 25 years later, with advanced techniques that have helped it withstand the current, particularly strong at that point, to this day (p. 475); and he gave it his own name.

Ponte Sisto, named after its rebuilder, was thus a direct link between Trastevere and the Campus Martius, which was becoming the 'Renaissance Quarter'. This fact explains the renaissance look given to this part of Trastevere by several *palazzi* and villas, in contrast to the medieval appearance of most of the district. This is also the neighbourhood that the British historian G. M. Trevelyan called the 'famous Tiber-side slums, crushed in between the river and the Janiculan hill,' where Trastevere's 'most characteristic and primitive inhabitants' lived, i.e. those famous for their short temper and the quick resort to the knife. And indeed it was a place closely connected with two bloody and fateful episodes in Roman history. The first came in 1797, when a gang of papal supporters from Trastevere stabbed to death a General Duphot sent by revolutionary France to propagandise democratic reform. This took place just outside Palazzo Corsini, one of the highlights of this Walk, and led to the deportation of Pope Pius VI to France (p. 67) by Napoleon's troops and to the French occupation of Rome until the end of Napoleon's regime. The second episode came from the opposite end of the political spectrum, the murder of Pius IX's closest assistant at a time when this initially liberal pope had turned conservative for fear of the revolutionary wind blowing through Europe in 1848. The Italian-born but Swiss and French educated minister Pellegrino Rossi was, like Duphot, stabbed to death by a group of Trasteverini who came downtown from the vicinity of Ponte Sisto. Rossi, one of the most moderate and reformist-minded papal cabinet members, but apparently not enough so for the revolutionaries, was felled in front of the Cancelleria palace where he had been speaking to an embryonic form of popular parliament he had persuaded the pope to convene. Later that year, rioting by Trasteverini, led by a Rienzi-like (p. 144) character nicknamed Ciceruacchio, flared into fully fledged insurrection. Early in 1849 the pope fled Rome and the short-lived 'Repubblica Romana' (p. 565) was born. At the time, Rossi's murder was applauded in progressive circles all over the world and especially in England, where it was compared to that of Buckingham in Charles I's day. Margaret Fuller, the Bostonian friend of Emerson and Carlyle then living in Rome, wrote to her mother: 'I never thought to have heard of a violent death with satisfaction; but this act affected me as one of terrible justice.' But many were horrified. The poet Belli, a lifelong staunch supporter of the poor and adversary of the clerical regime, became a conservative and took a job as literary censor for the papal government.

ON THE SPOT

1. From Piazza Trilussa to the Farnesina

To get to this part of Trastevere and Piazza Trilussa, you will probably cross the Ponte Sisto, which we have already seen from the other bank and discussed on p. 475. Piazza Trilussa, named after a dialect poet of Rome – just like the Piazza G.G. Belli, which connects with Ponte Garibaldi immediately downstream and from which we started the previous Walk – is graced by the **Fontana dell'Acqua Paola**, the smaller of the two 'Pauline Water' fountains set one above the other (p. 563), which commemorate the aqueduct rebuilt by Paul V on the ruins of that of Trajan.

This smaller fountain, however, was originally on the opposite river bank, where it was installed as a beautiful backdrop at the end of Via Giulia (p. 474). In 1879 it was dismantled when the Tiber was walled up. Twenty years later, by which time several of the original pieces were damaged or stolen, it was repaired and rebuilt here. The original location is mentioned in the Latin inscription, which speaks of the new water spouting *citratiberim* ('on this side of the Tiber'), whereas the fountain is now clearly *transtiberim* ('across the Tiber').

The fountain was built in 1613, one year after the larger one uphill, by a team of two including Giovanni Fontana, though the official leader here was his prominent Dutch colleague Jan van Zanten (called 'Vasanzio' in Italy). Fontana,

though, had also been in charge of the aqueduct, and the whole enterprise is another example of the great work to make of Rome a 'city of fountains' by two generations of Fontanas – a family of Swiss origins that included Giovanni's brother Domenico and a younger relative, Carlo. By a curious coincidence, the family name Fontana means 'fountain'.

On the other side of the square is a small, eloquent 1950 monument to Trilussa, nom de plume of an early 20th-century Roman dialect poet known for his courageous anti-Fascist stance. It includes one of his ironic sonnets, this one defending freedom of speech; he writes of having to converse with pigs and donkeys to speak his mind.

Left of the fountain take Via Benedetta (from the name of a local family). Passing, on the left at No. 2, a graceful 18th-century terracotta shrine missing its fresco, see on the right at No. 26 a 16th- to 17th-century baroque house with interesting design and ornaments. Opposite it, Nos. 21 and 19 are two contiguous early renaissance buildings, an unusual example for that period of terraced houses in Rome.

Via Benedetta ends into a square dominated by S. Giovanni (John) della Malva (a name of uncertain origin), founded in the middle ages but totally rebuilt in 1845. Opposite, over No. 6, is a pretty 18th-century Madonnella (street shrine). No. 3 may be the stump of a medieval tower; note the sloping base.

At the end of the square, at the beginning of Via

S. Dorotea, take the winding Vicolo Moroni (right) and keep to the right up to No. 15, which is a practically intact medieval single-storey house. Note the typical outdoor staircase, similar to the ones one finds in many medieval villages of central Italy. The roof might have been originally thatched, as were many of the small houses of medieval Trastevere.

The vicolo ends by a ruin, one of the few vestiges of of the Aurelian Walls (p. 42) on this side of the river (another is Porta Settimiana, see below). Leave the vicolo. A few steps further, on **Via S. Dorotea** is the graceful concave façade of the church of the same name, rebuilt in the 18th century over structures seven centuries older. Well known as a centre of charitable activities for the poor of the district, this was where St Joseph Calasanz opened the world's first free primary school (p. 504). The serene interior is occasionally open. Near the main altar is the grave of the church's architect, Giovan Battista Nolli, best known as a famous cartographer of Rome.

At the end of Via S. Dorotea on the right (No. 20) is the **House of the Fornarina**; an unverifiable tradition holds that in the early 16th-century Raphael's beloved 'baker girl' (p. 237) lived here. The 15th-century building, now housing a restaurant, incorporates earlier medieval structures.

We are now at a spacious intersection. On the right is **Porta Settimiana** (Septimian Gate), an archway built at the end of the 2nd century by Emperor Septimius Severus, incorporated in the next century in the Aurelian Walls. At the end of the 15th century it was almost entirely rebuilt by Pope Alexander VI Borgia (p. 45). On the walls are traces of a 17th-century fresco.

Pass the gate. You are now at the beginning of a straight street called Via della Lungara ('Long One'). It was built in the renaissance by Pope Julius II, the patron of both Raphael and Michelangelo, to match his equally long and straight Via Giulia on the other side of the river, along which you strolled (p. 470).

If it is near closing time for the Farnesina Palace (p. 576), go straight there (200 yards on your right) and return here later.

A few yards further down, on the left, is Via Corsini, unchanged enough to look like an old print of Rome. At the beginning of this street is a splendid old magnolia tree from North America. On the right is the garden of the nearby Palazzo Corsini. On the left near No. 5 is a 17th-century street shrine, much faded, over an ancient Roman sarcophagus turned into a fountain. At the end is the entrance to the Botanical Gardens founded in 1883. They contain many rare specimens, including a redwood tree of a species thought to have vanished thousands of years ago but found again in China in 1948.

Return to Via della Lungara and turn left. At No. 10 is the 18th-century **Palazzo Corsini** by Ferdinando Fuga, with its ample façade of sober design. The palace contains an important museum of paintings (see p. 684).

In the 17th century the exiled Queen Christina of Sweden (p. 478), controversial guest of Pope Alexander VII, having left her initial accomodation in Palazzo Farnese, had established her court here. At that time she also started a literary salon which at her death, which took place here, inspired the creation of a famous Italian literary academy nearby (Accademia dell' Arcadia, p. 577). Shortly thereafter, the palace became the seat of an even more famous scientific academy, the oldest surviving in Italy, the Accademia dei Lincei ('of the Lynx-eyed' or sharp-sighted). Galileo was one of its first members. It still operates here and in the Farnesina across the street. (A previous version of the palace had been built here at the end of the 15th century for the Riario family, nephews of Sixtus IV, see p. 314).

Fresco in La Farnesina: Venus and Jupiter, from the Loggia di Psiche

BEFORE GOING

2. La Farnesina

Palazzo, palazzetto or villa? The right definition has not yet been agreed upon, for while the building partakes of all of these architectural models, everyone simply calls it the 'Farnesina' after the name of one of the families who owned it. It is the renaissance jewel of Rome's right bank, built in the early 16th century for one of the richest foreign financiers in the renaissance banking district across the river (p. 439), the Sienese Agostino Chigi. He was famous for lavishly entertaining his clients, including the pope, cardinals and princes; he also invited the most beautiful women and most famous intellectuals. During the Farnesina's Chigi heyday, the most famous parties took place in a pavilion directly on the river, later demolished. There, in a surpassing display of extravagance, servants cleared the table by hurling all the silverware into the river – only to retrieve it later, to be sure, with nets they had placed underwater in advance.

At Chigi's death the villa was sold to the Farnese dukes, who already owned a palace across the river (p. 478).

One of its famous frescoes tell the story of how Venus was jealous of the beauty of Psyche, a mortal, and how Venus' son Cupid, who had fallen in love with Psyche, protected her from his mother's wrath. A reminder of the fervid intellectual life of the times is the fact that the old Greek myth of Cupid and Psyche had just been rediscovered by renaissance scholars when the fresco was painted, and a book on it had been published in Rome a few months earlier.

ON THE SPOT

2. La Farnesina

Across Via della Lungara, in a garden, is the **Farnesina**, designed by Raphael's friend Baldassarre Peruzzi and decorated by Raphael himself, Peruzzi and others. It is now property of the state, used for receptions of the Accademia dei Lincei (p. 574), and houses an important national collection of prints and drawings.

It is open 09:00-13:00 Monday-Saturday. At present, the entrance is at the back. The rear façade was altered in the 19th century, but the Raphaelesque frieze all around under the cornice is original. (Later you can look at the front and at the other original sides from the garden).

Past an entrance hall, decorated recently with mythological subjects, is the Gallery, a vast, harmonious, light-filled room famous for its splendid frescoes of the *Legend of Cupid and Psyche*. Their overall conception was Raphael's, but the actual drawing and painting is mostly by his pupils Giulio Romano, Gianfrancesco Penni and others. The fabulous festoons of flowers and fruits are by another pupil, Giovanni da Udine. In the frescoes, the only figure said to be by Raphael's hand is one of the three Graces in a corner of the ceiling, the one turning her back (first triangle left, on the long side opposite the garden).

Take one of the doors that were on your right when you entered the gallery. You are now in the Hall of the Galatea, one of the most celebrated of Raphael's frescoes, the next to the last panel on the left of the (long) side opposite the windows. An airy, dashing nymph surfs on her clamshell chariot, her exquisite proportions enhanced by the perfect harmony of colours. The resulting balance – the hallmark of Raphael – is such that the figure, despite of its very human, corporeal weight, seems to levitate. The panel left of the Galatea is Sebastiano del Piombo's Polyphemus, the one-eyed giant of the Odyssey. The powerful design is somewhat spoiled by restorations and alterations, including a blue tunic added on the orders of Chigi, it is said, after a prudish lady complained.

Sebastiano also painted the mythological scenes in the lunettes that top all the frescoes. The unexpected dreamy head of a youth in monochrome is attributed to Peruzzi. All the other panels were painted with soft and elegiac landscapes almost a century later by Gaspard Dughet, a specialist of the genre. On the ceiling, Peruzzi painted mythological scenes symbolising the constellations; studies have shown they portray the banker Chigi's horoscope, since they represent the stars over the sky of Siena the night he was born, 1 December 1466.

This room was originally an open gallery facing the garden; only in the 18th century were the arches filled in with windows. Here the banker's famous banquets were usually held.

Return to the large gallery and go straight ahead into the Hall of the Frieze, so-called after the mythological decoration on the upper walls by Peruzzi. The dazzling craftsmanship is a reminder that Peruzzi had started out as a goldsmith.

From the entrance hall go upstairs into another room wonderfully frescoed by Peruzzi, the Hall of Perspectives. All around, framed by grand architectural elements, is a diorama of renaissance Rome; various landmarks can be recognised, such as the Septimian Gate (p. 574; near the first window), the Torre delle Milizie or Soldiers' Tower (p. 151; to the right of the fireplace) and the Octagonal Room at the top of the Holy Spirit Hospital (p. 383; far short side to the right; note a flooding of the Tiber there). The full perspective effect of the views must be appreciated from different points in the room. The rest of the room's decoration – from the Forge of Vulcan over the chimney to the frieze under the ceiling and the many mythological figures – is of varying quality; the hands – not Peruzzi's but surely those of his colleagues or assistants – are not definitely identified. The next room was Chigi's bedroom, its opulent bed removed when the villa was sold.

The room is dominated by an intensely colourful, erotic fresco on the middle wall, The *Wedding Night of Alexander the Great and Roxane*. It is the masterpiece of the fine northern Italian artist,

Giovanni Antonio Bazzi, known as Il Sodoma because of his sexual leanings. Sodoma blossomed under the influence of Leonardo da Vinci – obvious here in the softness of the modelling and in the chiaroscuro – and, after his arrival in Rome, that of Raphael, near whom he had worked in the Vatican. Not as successful is Sodoma's fresco on the chimney wall (*Alexander shows mercy to the family of his vanquished enemy Darius*; below, the *Forge of Vulcan*). Also by Sodoma is the lively battle scene between the windows. The remaining decoration in the room is more run-of-the-mill work by unidentified artists.

Before leaving the Farnesina, don't forget to visit the garden (still charming though much smaller that it was when it extended down to the river) and look back at the main facade of the villa, its porch elegantly laid out between two protruding wings. Most of the walls were once graffito-covered (p. 449).

Return to Porta Settimiana.

DETOUR
25 MIN.

From this side of Porta Settimiana, Via Garibaldi starts uphill toward the Janiculum The street follows the course of the destroyed Aurelian Walls.

At the beginning, on a building on the left is a large Madonnella with a painting restored in 1885. Opposite, over the door of no. 88, a tablet affixed in 1792 announces in Latin that the institution there is a shelter for city girls (*puellas urbanas*) whose poverty endangers their virtue (*egestate periclitantes*). This **Conservatorio** (shelter) **delle Pericolanti** (of the endangered ones), as it was called in Italian, survived until the beginning of the 20th century; its guests paid their way by working at a silk factory in the building.

Toward the end of this straight stretch of the street, at No. 27 on the left, is the 17th-century convent and church of **S. Maria dei Sette Dolori** ('of the Seven Sorrows,') by Borromini. Only the exterior can be seen, with its simple lines and a design both austere and animated, typical of the master's baroque style; the convent's cloistered nuns do not grant admission to occasional visitors. The compound is one of the places used as a field hospital in the Janiculum fighting of 1849. During the German occupation of Rome in 1943-44, it concealed Jews and dissidents.

Across the street, Nos 41-45 is now the national headquarters of the Carabinieri, the military police of papal origins, whose colourful gala uniforms are part of Italian folklore. Originally, though, the large mid-18th century edifice, built by Luigi Vanvitelli, housed Rome's first tobacco factory, and later another shelter for 'pericolanti' girls, this one connected to a linen factory.

This stretch of Via Garibaldi ends at the gate (usually closed) of the **Bosco Parrasio** (Parrhasius Woods), seat of a famous late 17th-century literary club (the Accademia dell' Arcadia, see p. 574) which had some influence on Italian and European literature and manners in the 18th century. It professed to recreate the rural simplicity of a legendary shepherds' society in Arcadia, a central region of ancient Greece; 'extermination of bad taste' was its official aim. Yet rather than resurrecting a supposed artlessness of old, it spawned preciosity and affectedness. Artists and even scientists flocked to the Accademia. Abroad, people like Goethe and Newton were members. In the sloping park, steps created by Antonio Canevari (a Roman architect midway between the baroque and neoclassicim, more famous for his Clocktower in Lisbon) and Niccolò Salvi (of Trevi Fountain fame) were inspired by the famous Scalinata of Piazza di Spagna (p. 57). Circling behind the compound of S. Maria dei Sette Dolori through a maze of typical Trastevere alleys, return to Via Garibaldi and Porta Settimiana.

END OF DETOUR

BEFORE GOING

3. S. Maria della Scala and S. Egidio

Northwest of Viale Trastevere, our Walk moves through the dense fabric of small houses alternating with churches and charitable institutions. Streets and squares are also dotted with countless restaurants that replaced the simple wineries ('osterie') affectionately remembered by older residents, but which serve the same purpose – meeting places for conversation, dining and socialising until late, indoors or, better, outdoors, weather permitting. The old and the new mix everywhere. One of Europe's oldest pharmacies still operates and still sells its ancient nostrums. Shelters and convents that aid their traditional charges – the aged, orphans and young girls – don't turn away tourists seeking bargain accommodation.

At the height of summer, the streets become the scene of one of the district's oldest customs, dating from the middle ages: the 'Festa de Noantri', dialect for 'Our Festival', traditionally a procession but today mainly a feast of song and amusement. It starts on the first Saturday after July 16, when a procession celebrating the Madonna of Trastevere or 'Madonna Fiumarola' ('of the River' in dialect) winds around the neighbourhood, with church and civil authorities at the head of a crowd of locals. The statue of the Madonna that is carried around is kept in the little church of S. Agata on this side of Viale Trastevere, while the vestments, the crowns and jewels donated through the centuries by the populace are kept by the nuns of the church of S. Pasquale, on the other side of the Viale.

You'll also find that this part of Trastevere is not all colourful squares and ancient traditions, but is also a vibrant, modern neighbourhood, rich in cultural and social institutions. One of the most recent, and now world-renowned, is a group of activists originally congregating in the church and convent of S. Egidio. They dedicate themselves to the welfare of immigrants – and beyond that, to helping the underdeveloped countries from which they come, with both material aid and political advice. Founded in 1968 by lay and religious volunteers, the Comunità di S. Egidio has used its popularity among immigrants as leverage to conduct diplomacy and conciliation in their countries' internal and external conflicts. In 1992 it was credited with settling a decades-long civil war in Mozambique. Since then it has promoted negotiations between insurgents and governments in Algeria, Albania, Angola, Guatemala, Lebanon, Somalia and elsewhere. Support groups called the Friends of St Egidio now exist in the United States and elsewhere. To raise money, the Comunità manages its own, popular restaurant in Trastevere, the Trattoria degli Amici ('of the Friends') at Piazza S. Egidio 6 (tel. (06) 5806033, closed Sunday).

ON THE SPOT

3. S. Maria della Scala and S. Egidio

In front of Porta Settimiana take Via della Scala ('of the Stairs'); the name is from the outside staircase of one of the district's medieval houses (pp. 574, 596) – this one no longer standing – under which was found an icon which we'll discuss later. On the right, Nos 28 to 25 are houses of the 15th and 16th centuries, with typical doorways.

We come to a square named after the church there, **S. Maria della Scala**. The church in turn owes its name, and existence, to a painting of the Virgin and Child – the one mentioned above –

said to have miraculous powers. The church was built in the late 16th century to house the image in a worthy place. Its façade is attributed to Ottaviano Mascarino, the interior to Girolamo Rainaldi. If the church is closed, ring at the convent (No. 23) where the Carmelite fathers are usually willing to show people around (leave an offering). The interior is a study in harmony and pathos, undisturbed by the 19th-century restorations. All the art works we shall mention here are 17th century. The most important is the *Beheading of St John the Baptist*, a powerful painting by Caravaggio's follower Gerrit Van Honthorst in the first chapel on the right. All the lovely chapels, with their rich decoration, deserve attention. The main altar, its columned tabernacle and the two beautiful doors at the side are by Carlo Rainaldi, Girolamo's son.

In the choir behind the altar are large paintings of biblical subjects by Luca de la Haye, a Carmelite monk buried in the church. In the sacristy, at the right end of the church, are twelve *papier mâché* Apostles that replaced bronze ones stolen in 1797 by Napoleon's troops. Cross to the other side of the church. At the left end of the transept, over an altar, is the much retouched 16th-century Madonna for whom the church was built. The metal crown is an honour the church used to bestow to images recognised as miraculous. On the sides are busts of the Santacroce family (p. 517), who once sponsored the chapel; the bust to the far right, Prospero, is by Algardi.

As you leave the church, the second to last chapel to your right contains memorabilia of a modern French saint, Theresa of the Infant Jesus. The altar here would boast the famous *Death of the Virgin* by Caravaggio, now at the Louvre, if in 1606 the friars had not rejected it as vulgar (see p. 494 for similar occurrences in Caravaggio's life). Instead there is a painting on the same subject by a Caravaggio imitator, Carlo Saraceni.

If the friar has time, he will also show you the convent's late 17th-century pharmacy (above the present modern one, at No. 23), though most of its original furnishings, precious herbariums, and so on, were put away recently for safety. The convent still produces some popular distillates, once called 'anti-pestilential' and 'anti-hysterical', now called 'perfumed and cleansing waters'.

Opposite the church, at No. 56, is a medieval house with renaissance windows. Pick up on Via della Scala again. On the left, from No. 67 to No. 70, note that the house numbers themselves are late 18th-century antiques; opposite, at No. 9, is a picturesque courtyard of that time. An interesting doorway, two centuries older, is at No. 72. Over it is what remains of a street shrine of the same period. At No. 75 is another late 16th-century doorway. A column on your right, near No. 3, was once part of a medieval porch. In the next alley on the right – the Vicolo del Cedro, 'of the Cedar Tree' – at No. 35 is a narrow, elegant 18th-century house.

Return to Via della Scala; on your right begins the former convent of S. Egidio, which we'll come to in a moment. You are now in Piazza S. Egidio. The convent connects on your right to **S. Egidio**, a 17th-century church, though its foundation dates to the 11th century or earlier. Occasionally open, it is mainly interesting for a grille inside that once separated the cloistered nuns of the nearby convent from others attending Mass. Flanking the church, the building at No. 1b, also 17th-century, is part of the former convent, and presently the seat of the world-renowned S. Egidio Community of social and political activists. The building also houses the Museum of Rome in Trastevere (see p. 687). Opposite, at Nos 7-9, is a late 15th-century palace, with typical doorways and windows and a solemn courtyard. Once owned by the Velli family, another important Trastevere clan (now extinct), its left wing was recently bought by the Orsini family (p. 253) as their residence.

4. From Via del Moro to Viale Trastevere

'Sor delegato mio, nun so' un bojaccia...' ('Mister inspector, sir, I'm not a scoundrel...'): so starts an early 20th-century Trastevere ballad by the Roman vernacular poet Americo Giuliani, 'Er Fattaccio der Vicolo der Moro' ('Bad Mess in Vicolo del Moro') – a poem once famous as a metaphor for the Trasteverine hot but good-hearted temperament, and of the close-knit, passionate family life of the Trastevere slums. The fitting scene of this story, of a young blacksmith arrested for stabbing to death his drunken brother as he defended their mother from his violence, is vicolo, or rather Via del Moro, as proud locals unfailingly correct this constant mis-classification. This commercial and residential street, surely the original of W. W. Story's masterly description of Trastevere (p. 540), ranks as one of the most representative and lively in the district, or at least did so until the modern Viale Trastevere replaced it as the main shopping street. Its countless little shops, windows ablaze with gaslight in the evening; the crowd of the 'minenti' ('eminent' women, meaning any married, non-servant woman) and of the young girls, all promenading 'in capelli' ('in hairs') – that is, without hats, the emblem of the well-to-do ladies who were rare here; the people leaning from windows or peering from behind shutters; the carriage-drawing horses clopping; the bells ringing from the many churches; all composed a memorable urban picture until the mid-20th century. Twice a day, aromas from the pots and pans, and from the stoves themselves, all still fuelled by wood or coal, prevailed over those left in the streets by the horse traffic, and the air was often heavy with smoke. '"Sor'Antonia, ched'è tutto sto fume?" "Gnente, Sor'Anna, coscio le bbrasciole",' begins one of Belli's (p. 62) many courtyard conversations, roughly translatable as: '"Signora Antonia, what's all the smoke?" "Nuttin', Signora Anna, just fixin' the veal chops"'. Today, this mosaic is much less vivid, with vehicular traffic banned, church bells replaced by barely audible tapes, human songs muted or lost in the blare of TV sets and the home-cooking emanations mostly contained.

Walking along Via del Moro and, afterwards, the arrow-straight but less ancient street of S. Francesco a Ripa, by which we'll reach the 'watershed' of Viale Trastevere, we'll also find the first reminders of a vanished aspect of Trastevere: it was above all a Jewish quarter, especially the part nearer the downstream bridge of the Isola Tiberina which we are now approaching. Yes, the original Trasteverini, slaves, prisoners of war, immigrants, could claim all sorts of ethnic origins, though they were mainly from the Middle East. But the Jews flourished and gradually came to dominate the area, assuming key roles in commerce and finance already in ancient times. Then one day in the middle ages, as we know, practically from one month to the next, almost all migrated over the bridge and into the area that became the Ghetto centuries later. The reason for this has never been found, but we'll propose a possible one later.

Here, at a crossing of Via del Moro, we'll be reminded of a curious facet of Jewish life in Trastevere, one totally forgotten. It will be evoked by two streets, one, Via della Pelliccia, leading into the other, Vicolo della Renella, near the riverbank. The Renella (a version of the word 'arenula', meaning 'the little beach', which we earlier encountered as a street name dating to ancient Rome, p. 519) was a sandy landfill on the shore that vanished when the embankment was built. It was a favourite resting and swimming spot for boatmen and dockworkers, and, just before it was swept away, the place for travelling circuses to set up tents. Before that, for centuries, the place had an additional use, attested to by the original name of the present Via della Pelliccia ('of the Fur'; the reason for this more recent name is disputed). It was formerly called Via de' Macelli delle Bufale ('of the Water-buffalo Slaughterhouses'). These were the main establishments in the Renella area, and a traditional monopoly of the Jews. Much of the food for Rome came from the Tyrrhenian sea harbours of Ostia and Fiumicino on flat-bottom barges, towed by men or by water-buffaloes – strong, semi-aquatic bovines imported from India in ancient Roman times and still to be seen on some parts of the Italian coast. (It is their milk that is used for the costliest mozzarella cheese.) At Rome's main river harbour, the Ripa Grande (p. 586), they were let loose into a large enclosure called the 'Bufalara'. Pulling barges was exhausting: the beasts that could not go on were butchered, their meat apparently a mainstay of Jewish cuisine. Gradually, Jewish butchers took over a line of work related mainly to their own tables. They took the animals from the Ripa Grande to the Renella, 1,800 ft (600 m) upstream, and thence to their own slaughterhouses.

At the end of Via S. Francesco a Ripa we'll find the only Jewish institutions left in Trastevere after the Jews' historic move to the right bank. These include a society for the financial, legal and health aid of needy Jews, established in the early 19th century and last of a long series of similar institutions in Trastevere. Others are aid organisations for Jewish children founded after the Second World War.

ON THE SPOT

4. From Via del Moro to Viale Trastevere

From Piazza S. Egidio enter the adjacent Largo Fumasoni Biondi (the wider part of Via della Paglia). On your right is the 12th-century outer wall of the transept of S. Maria in Trastevere (p. 556), with a medieval cornice and other original details. (The apse, of the same date, can be seen by continuing right of the transept wall on Via della Paglia and entering the courtyard at No. 4; return to Largo Fumasoni Biondi afterwards.) At No. 1 of the Largo is the entrance to what was Trastevere's paupers' cemetery for over a millennium. Abandoned at the start of the 20th century, it is now a courtyard with a pine tree connected to an Oratory discussed in the next paragraph. Opposite, at Nos 4-5, is an 18th-century house.

Take Via della Paglia, to the left of No. 1. Here on your right is the early 19th-century **Oratorio di Maria Santissima Addolorata e delle Anime del Purgatorio** ('of Holy Mary of the Sorrows and Souls in Purgatory') with a tiny belfry. The name comes from its being the church of the paupers' cemetery. Both were once well-known for religious plays, which even the pope sometimes attended; renowned artists participated in the staging, foremost among them the water-colourist and sculptor Bartolomeo Pinelli, who lived nearby in a house later demolished (and is commemorated by a modern bust at No. 18 Viale Trastevere, in case you're interested).

Opposite the Oratory, step into the picturesque Vicolo del Piede (with a 16th-century building at the corner) to see, at No. 14, how a 17th-century oratory (prayer hall), now deconsecrated, has become one of many touristy restaurants that have sprung up around here recently. Until the late 19th century, this charming building was the headquarters of the lay Brothers of the Holy Sacrament, who comforted the poor on their deathbeds.

The winding vicolo, which perhaps took its name ('of the foot') from its shape, crosses Via della Pellicia. This in turn ends at Piazza dei Renzi, an isolated place whose former quiet is today spoilt by noisy restaurants. At the corner between this square and Via della Pelliccia is a two-storey medieval house, with a stump of ancient Roman column used as a curbstone. From this square take Vicolo dei Renzi, which ends at the main street of this area, Via del Moro ('of the Moor', from an inn sign). Sticking out at the corner is an upper-class 18th-century house.

On your left Via del Moro ends in Piazza Trilussa – the start of this Walk. Taking Via del Moro in the opposite direction at the next crossing (Via della Pelliccia) we see a busy bar called 'Old Coffee House of the Moor', late 19th-century in appearance, but probably older. It could be the successor of the tavern that gave the street its name, and also of one of the same name where, in 1604, the painter Caravaggio, notorious for his temper (p. 494), threw a dish of artichokes at a waiter's face. Neither identification is certain. The bar now has a turn-of-the-century sign showing 'Bersaglieri' soldiers of Italy's 20th-century colonial wars offering drinks to black girls.

At the crossing here is Via della Pelliccia, once named Via de' Macelli delle Bufale and leading, across Via del Moro, to the 'Renella' and the water-buffalo slaughterhouses, now long gone.

Keep walking on Via del Moro, which ends shortly at Piazza S. Apollonia; then go left into Via della Lungaretta for just a few yards before turning right into Via di S. Callisto. At the end of this irregular street are two delightful tiny medieval houses (Nos. 42 and 44). They say the smaller one is the smallest house in Rome. Proceed to the arch there and pass under. We're again in Piazza S. Callisto, a side of which we visited in the previous Walk. On this side, and just on the corner after the arch, are two old palaces. The one at No. 6, of the late 16th century, was the home of a famous lawyer, Farinacci, who defended Beatrice Cenci (p. 522) – rather weakly, it was said, so as not to displease the pope.

The palace at No. 9, built a few decades earlier, was the first Roman residence of a famous connoisseur and art collector of the first half of the 17th century, the scientist Cassiano del Pozzo, friend of Galileo and supporter of painters both unappreciated, such as Poussin, and famous, such as Luca Giordano. The private museum Pozzo set up in another part of the city played an influential part in the history of baroque art.

Right of these buildings (if you're looking at them) go to the end of the square where Via della Cisterna and Via S. Francesco a Ripa meet. A small but pretty 1927 fountain at the corner is in the form of a wine barrel, a vat and two typical wine measures: a smiling invitation to the traditional Trasteverine consolation. Excavations in Via della Cisterna (no need to go in) in 1886 found the signs of two ancient Roman craft unions, the *eborarii* or merchants of ivory objects, and the *citriarii* or carvers of wood from the famous cedars of Lebanon, workmen of exclusively middle-eastern origin. They are further reminders of Trastevere's oriental character (pp. 540-541). A Vicolo del Cedro (Cedar Lane) is still nearby.

Via S. Francesco a Ripa is named after the church of St Francis, which we'll see in the next section ('Ripa' means 'shore', or more specifically, 'Ripa Grande', the greater river harbour once near the church). The street is another of those long, straight streets created in the 16th-17th century urban renewal here.

Take it to the first crossing. On your left is the church and convent of **SS. Quaranta Martiri e S. Pasquale di Baylon**; the first part of this long name refers to an oratory 'of the Forty Martyrs', here since before the 12th century to commemorate soldiers converted to Christianity and executed in Armenia under Diocletian (4th century), a reminder of the eastern origins of many Trasteverini. (Another, even older oratory dedicated to these saints, stands in the Roman forum, see p. 283). According to the story, possibly true, the soldiers were martyred *en masse* by being left naked on a frozen lake. The second part of the name was added in 1745 when Spain purchased the oratory, rebuilt it as a church and dedicated it to Pascal Baylon, a late 16th-century Spanish saint. Baylon, a mystic and theologian born a simple shepherd, has for centuries been venerated by Trastevere women – especially girls hoping for husbands – as a protector and granter of wishes.

S. Pasquale di Baylon in the 18th century, engraving by Giuseppe Vasi

This belief may have arisen from some old lines of doggerel that calls him a protector of women just to make his name (in dialect) rhyme with 'women': 'Pasquale di Baylonne / protettore delle donne').

The church, still served by Spanish Franciscans, was designed by the central Italian architect Giuseppe Sardi, a follower of Borromini, in a simple but joyous and elegant late baroque. The double-order façade bears the escutcheon of the Spanish Bourbon dynasty and, above it, an oval with the saint's portrait; on the sides is the Franciscan emblem. The interior, rarely open, has harmonious if complex ornamental detailing, and is enlivened by minor Spanish and Italian paintings of the 18th century and later.

The convent behind the church doubled as one of the many charities dotting the street. This one was for orphan girls being prepared to go into the service of well-to-do families.

At the next crossing, on the left is Via Cardinale Merry del Val, where ruins of an ancient Roman palace were dug up accidentally in 1969 and then covered over again. On the right, one can see in the distance, as an end backdrop to Via Luciano Manara, the **Fountain of the Prisoner** (so called from a statue now missing) by Domenico Fontana, the only one saved from the demolition of Sixtus V's Villa Montalto (p. 80), which was rebuilt here.

At the end of Via S. Francesco a Ripa, in the building on the right corner with Viale Trastevere, are the few Jewish institutions remaining in Trastevere, of which the most important is the Jewish Assistance Committee.

On Viale Trastevere, a widening of the avenue on the left, visible from here, is Piazza Mastai, after the controversial mid-19th century Pope Pius IX (p. 572; Mastai was his family name) who built a large tobacco processing compound there. The buildings still serve as offices of the government tobacco monopoly. The popes encouraged tobacco use, dubbing it 'the blessed grass' because they thought it a harmless alternative to wine. It also made them good money, but at least one pope temporarily abolished the monopoly in the 18th century, declaring it 'wrong to impose fiscal penalties on a pleasure that's not sinful'.

❧ MIDPOINT OF WALK ☙

BEFORE GOING

4. From S. Francesco a Ripa to S. Cecilia

The part of Trastevere we now enter was as busy and noisy when it was the immediate hinterland of Rome's main river harbour – the Ripa Grande – as it is now quiet and almost frozen in time. The harbour was destroyed in the late 19th century, and wholesale commerce here came to an end, leaving only some modest retailers, mostly in food and other essentials. The creation of Viale Trastevere divided this neighbourhood from the rest of the Trastevere, increasing its isolation.

In this intimate corner are some of the most poignant memories of the religions – pagan, Jewish, Christian – that once dominated the life of this district which, like all poor areas, found solace in the opium of the people. One of the first streets we see is Via Anicia, named after a prominent pagan dynasty who were said to have a house here, and who are also associated with a pivotal figure of Christianity, St Benedict, and with the greatest family of Jewish Trastevere, the Pierleoni (pp. 593-594).

Here we also find, more than anywhere else in Rome, traces of St Francis, the 'poor fellow from Assisi'. Francis came here often from his native town, to lobby for official recognition of his monastic order (p. 411); historians remind us that he even risked being declared a heretic. We'll enter the very room where this sweetest and yet most powerful figure of medieval Christianity, closest imitator of the life of Christ and future principal patron of Italy, used to stay in the early 13th century between appointments with Vatican officialdom. We will visit the most important Roman church dedicated to him. We'll see his first and most convincing portrait, possibly painted from life. On a street sign, we'll see the name of the noble Roman lady Jacopa de' Settesoli, who helped him obtain papal recognition for his 'order of lesser brethren' at a time when the group destined to revive Christianity and spread the world over consisted of just twelve people. The Ordo Fratrum Minorum was soon after to be followed by a feminine order of the Clarissæ headed by his Assisi friend St Clare.

This is also where we'll first find frequent signs of the intense Jewish presence that survived until the late middle ages: no coincidence, as commerce, lifeline of any activity in the area of the Ripa Grande harbour, and has always gone together with Jewish entrepreneurship Here is the core area where the ancient Jewish colony, established in Trastevere since the time of Pompey (p. 522), first flourished and, where, as Ferdinand Gregorovius, the foremost historian of medieval Rome, noted in the mid-19th century, it 'survived through all the storms of history'. He added in amazement:

> They transmitted their blood unmixed with the blood of Romans or barbarians from generation to generation; they beheld the republic of ancient Rome, Roman Cæsarism, the immense city of marble, a second Frankish empire fall to dust beside them; more indestructible than monuments of bronze, they survived the frightful Nemesis of the centuries; and to this day they continue to pray to Jehovah, the God of Abraham and Moses, in the same streets beside the Tiber.

ON THE SPOT

4. From S. Francesco a Ripa to S. Cecilia

You are now at Piazza **San Francesco a Ripa** ('St Francis by the Docks'), dominated by the church and convent of the same name. Both originate in the 10th century as a Benedictine monastic compound. In 1229, after St Francis' repeated visits, the compound passed to his new monastic order, took the saint's name and underwent the first of several restorations. The church's present façade, by the Roman architect Mattia de' Rossi, dates from 1682, when the church was totally rebuilt. To the right is a Franciscan monastery. (Open: 07:00-12:00 and 16:00-19:00; Sundays and holidays, 07:00-12:30 and 16:00-19:30.)

Start with the first chapel on your left, with the delightful *Nativity of the Virgin* (on the left) by Caravaggio's French follower Simon Vouet (17th century) and over the altar, the *Immaculate Conception* by the Flemish artist Marten de Vos (16th century), also very beautiful. Behind this chapel is the tomb of Giorgio De Chirico, the 20th-century 'metaphysical' painter-sculptor whose house we saw in Piazza di Spagna. In the next chapel is an *Annunciation* by the mannerist Francesco Salviati, one of the first works in Rome by this important Florentine follower of Raphael (16th century). The third chapel contains the body of St Charles of Sezze – who died in the nearby monastery in 1670 – embalmed and coated with wax. On the walls are expressive 17th-century busts of two members of the Mattei family (p. 248).

The last chapel on the left contains the tomb with the famous statue of the *Blessed Ludovica Albertoni* (died 1533), commissioned from Bernini by Ludovica's aristocratic family and erected in 1675. We saw this family's own chapel and house elsewhere (p. 531), but Ludovica was buried here in Trastevere where she had married a nobleman and where she had done most of her philanthropic work, especially after the terrible Sack of 1527 (p. 381).

The display of her divine ecstasy at the moment of death, a peak of mystic – some have said erotic – feeling comparable to that which Bernini had infused into the famous statue of S. Teresa 30 years earlier (p. 74), is amongst the highest expressions of the baroque. Bernini's theatrical flair also shows here in that he had the rear wall of the chapel pushed back to create two partially concealed windows, which throw a dramatic light on the statue. On the sides are two late 16th-century frescoes of the *Blessed Ludovica* (right) and *St Clare*. Over the statue is a painting by Baciccia (17th century) of the *Virgin and Child with St Anne*. Passing before the striking 18th-century main altar, with its 16th-century multi-coloured statue of St Francis carved by a friar, proceed to the chapel to the right of the altar, which contains splendid 18th-century tombs and cenotaphs of the noble Rospigliosi-Pallavicini family (still extant).

Baciccia: Virgin and Child with St. Anne

From a door to the left of the main altar pass into the beautiful late 17th-century sacristy and from it (asking for permission) into a little room with tombstones of the Anguillara, carved with the stern features of 15th- and 16th-century members of that important Trastevere family, whose stronghold we saw earlier (p. 547). Next, steps lead up to St Francis' cell which, despite substantial alterations, is the only space preserved from the church's older, medieval structure. A cabinet there contains a 13th-century portrait of St Francis. Of disputed authorship, and possibly a copy, it is said to be one of the few with the saint's real features, drawn at his death.

Leave the church. The name of a street to its left is another reminder of St Francis. Jacopa de' Settesoli was the influential woman who helped him get papal recognition for his order (her last name – 'of the Seven Suns' – probably comes from her family having a stronghold in the Septizodium, p. 295).

Take Via Jacopa de' Settesoli to the corner with Via Porta Portese. Across this street, and slightly to your right is a run-down red building, a good example of Fascist architecture, which is now enjoying an international comeback as the 'Rationalist' style. It was built in 1936 as the **Casa della GIL** (Gioventù Italiana del Littorio), the headquarters of the Fascist youth group; its present disrepair stems from an ongoing ownership dispute between the city and the government. It was designed by Luigi Moretti, also well known for his work in the Foro Mussolini (p. 606), who would go on in the 1950's to create the Watergate residential complex in Washington. This building bears one of Mussolini's many slogans: 'One must win; even more one must fight'.

If you haven't already crossed the street, do so now at the lights about thirty yards down Via Porta Portese, toward the river; then go under the brick arches there. One of these arches is Porta Portese ('Port Gate'), which can be seen from the other side. Wall and gate were built in the 17th century to replace the collapsing Aurelian Walls that came down near here from the top of the

Janiculum and the Porta Settimiana area where we saw them (p. 574).

Rome's main Jewish cemetery had been near the old and the new walls here since time immemorial. When the anti-Semitic campaign started in the 16th century (p. 524), a wall was built around it. Enlarging the cemetery was forbidden, as were inscriptions on the tombstones, except those of rabbis. The cemetery was closed soon after and the remains moved to the slope of the Aventine overlooking the Circus Maximus (p. 269), then in modern times moved again to Rome's general cemetery (p. 633).

Beyond the gate extends Via Portuense, Port Street, so called because it led to the Ostia seaport, whence most of Rome's supplies had arrived since antiquity. This rather drab area is today the locale of Rome's sprawling, popular flea market. The hangars on the river side of the street were once shipyards, very important since the main river docks, as we'll soon see, were nearby. Pass back through the walls. On your right the street ends in a bridge over the Tiber (on the other bank is the Aventine Hill, pp. 268-274). Cross Via Porta Portese again; the only way to do so safely is to return to the same lights mentioned above.

DETOUR

15 MIN

Go up an elevated walkway along the river, heading left.

The late 19th-century embankment of the river destroyed a major, centuries-old feature of Rome: the main docks here (Porto di Ripa Grande or 'greater river harbour'). Cargo arrived on ships and barges, some drawn by waterbuffalos or men. A customs house was also here. In the middle ages, an iron chain was stretched across the river near here at night to block Arab pirate raids.

Across the street from the walkway is one of the largest social welfare buildings ever built, the 18th-century **Ospizio di S. Michele** (St Michael's Hospice), attributed to Carlo Fontana, Mattia de Rossi and others. By far the biggest of many centres ministering to the district's destitute, it included an orphanage, a home for the elderly, vocational schools, a printshop, a tapestry factory, a metal shop and foundry (still in use; the huge equestrian statue of the Piazza Venezia memorial, p. 535, was cast here, and the statue of Marcus Aurelius on horseback, p. 146, was restored here recently), two churches, a reform school for boys (an exemplary work for which Fontana was helped by Giovan Antonio de' Rossi) and, last but not least, a prison for prostitutes by Ferdinando Fuga. Free music, drawing and sculpture classes were offered until the middle of the last century by top artists, chosen by a committee once headed by the great sculptor Canova. Several famous Roman artists and craftsmen graduated from here. Most of the rooms still look much as they used to. A branch of the Italian national art restoration institute and offices of the Ministry for the Preservation of Cultural Assets have installed themselves here, paradoxically altering for the worse one of the beautiful courtyards. Note the building's ornate doorways, especially the penultimate, with rich stucco cornucopia (horns of plenty).

Just past the cornucopia doorway, go down to street level and continue on the very narrow sidewalk until you face the end of the building. There, carefully cross the river drive to another flight of steps. Take these down to the corner of the St Michael complex; turn around the corner into Via del Porto, walk one block to Piazza dei Mercanti and pick up the main itinerary there (four paragraphs down, starting 'This area...'). You will have missed the Madonna dell'Orto church by going on the detour, but there are directions below if you want to visit it later.

END OF DETOUR

Returning to Piazza S. Francesco a Ripa and passing the church enter Via Anicia. Go down a long, run-down first stretch of this street to the church of the **Madonna dell'Orto** at the first crossing. This is another Trastevere church owing its name, and existence, to a miraculous image of the Virgin, this one found in a vegetable patch ('orto'). It was built in the 16th century by Michelangelo's pupil Guidetto Guidetti, with a façade by Vignola, then restored and redecorated in the 18th century. Open occasionally. Inside, the most striking thing is the rich 18th-century decoration. But most of the paintings are 17th- and late 16th- century; among the latter, some by the Zuccari brothers: the *Annunciation* in the first chapel to the right by Taddeo and, on the sides of the main altar, frescoes by Taddeo and Federico. Over the main altar is the miraculous image, a mid 15th-century work; note the crowns added by church authorities (p. 579).

Parts of the church were once sponsored by countless small tradesmen's guilds such as the grocers, pollaroli (poultry-sellers), millers and vermicellari (spaghetti-makers). In the sacristy is a spunky wooden turkey donated by the pollaroli. The church is connected to an oratory entirely frescoed in the 18th century and, upstairs, to a small museum of the old Roman guilds.

Go down Via Madonna dell'Orto in front of the church, to Via S. Michele, turn left and go to the first crossroad – Via del Porto. From this street turn immediately left into Piazza dei Mercanti.

This area, once predominantly Jewish (an ancient Rua Judæorum – 'Street of the Jews' – was nearby), is one of the most vivid and characteristic corners of the district, though marred by touristy restaurants. There is a series of renaissance houses (Nos 19 to 15 on your right; but No. 14 is a 19th-century imitation). There are also medieval houses (Nos 4-5, across the square – note the little gothic windows hidden by a tree, and a gothic window, formerly a door, around the corner in the alley – and the house beside that one, also facing the next square) and houses of later ages, all in the most colourful jumble.

Go on to the next square, Piazza Santa Cecilia. At No. 19 is the other side of one of the medieval houses we saw in the first square. The early renaissance palazzetto at Nos 16-17 is heavily restored. Also note the unusual 18th-century madonnella above No. 25.

BEFORE GOING

5. S. Cecilia

The transition from paganism to Christianity could be abrupt and traumatic, as the traces of panic and conflict found in the ruins of the Syrian Sanctuary in Trastevere attest (p. 559). Or the beliefs of one faith might mutate slowly into those of another, as we saw in old cult buildings such as S. Lorenzo in Lucina with the healing spring waters (p. 228) and S. Maria in Trastevere with its 'holy oil' (p. 553). In a neighbourhood like the one we now enter, where different religions co-existed for centuries, the transition was even more natural. A striking case – if the conclusions of some recent research are correct – is that of the Bona Dea, the 'Good Goddess', believed to be a healer of eye diseases. This cult, exclusive to women, was so mysterious that the deity's very name was kept secret. It was especially widespread among ancient Rome's poor; one of its main temples was in this part of Trastevere (p. 595). Julius Cæsar's wife was a devotee, and a scandal erupted in 62 BC when a man tried to approach her in the sanctuary. He barely escaped the punishment for males who witnessed the secret rites: blinding.

Scholars think this cult gave way, in Early Christian times, to that of a saint of obscure origins, Cecilia, whose church is one of the foremost in Trastevere and will be our next sight. She is one of Rome's most celebrated martyrs, supposedly harking back to the 2nd or 3rd century. Yet there is no trace of her at that time; her cult appears only some 300 years later. She is unmentioned in early hagiographic compilations and unrepresented in the Early Christian decorated 'gold glasses' that are among our major sources. Church officials consider her legendary, and propose she could have been any pious Christian woman, possibly of the ancient Cæcilian family, and perhaps one who opened a private church or *ecclesia domestica* (p. 228) thought to have been under the present basilica. It is unlikely that hers was the body 'found' in the catacombs centuries later, supposedly thanks to a pope's dream, but probably by grave robbers digging for relics of martyrs.

Yet her particular attributes give us hints about her cult. S. Cecilia is known as the patron of music and musicians, but this tradition is not mentioned before the late 15th century, well after she was supposed to have lived. The reference to music apparently stems from a mistaken transcription of a hymn associated with Cecilia in some medieval books. An original, age-old text said that she sang Christ's praises 'in her heart'. A medieval scribe dropped those three words, making it appear she was a singer.

The age-old version did say, however, that Cecilia was the protector of eyesight – giving her the same miraculous powers attributed, centuries earlier, to the 'Good Goddess'. Inscriptions mentioning the goddess have turned up very near the church of S. Cecilia; her temple was probably also there. All this suggests the one cult may have seamlessly flowed into the other – a theory further supported by the fact the original liturgical words used to invoke Cecilia's protection turn out to be the same as those used to propitiate the Bona Dea.

As first reported, three or four centuries after the purported events, S. Cecilia's legend said an *ecclesia domestica* had opened in the 3rd century AD in a house that belonged to a Christian noblewoman, Cecilia, and her pagan husband, Valerian (the couple's existence is unverifiable). They were both martyred on the emperor's orders when it emerged that Cecilia had vowed to remain a

Paschal discovers the body of St. Cecilia: a 19th-century vision inspired by Maderno's statue

virgin and not consummate her marriage, and that Valerian, persuaded by her guardian angel, had accepted this and himself converted. His execution went smoothly, but hers was difficult (compare to St Agnes' execution, p. 452). It took place in her bathroom, where they first tried to suffocate her with steam from the bath (a not uncommon procedure, see p. 397). This failed when Cecilia's angel appeared and fanned the room with his wings. Then they tried to behead her, but unsuccessfully, so they left her to bleed to death. According to details added later, they inflicted three sword blows to the neck, then desisted because Roman law forbade a fourth. She took three days to die.

In the 9th century Pope Paschal I, one of Rome's great builder popes, said he had found the body of Cecilia, who had directed him herself to her grave in the catacombs (p. 618) in a vision (about discoveries of this kind, see pp. 358, 417). This is the first mention of Cecilia's body; it had not decomposed, but the neck showed cuts, which may have suggested the details of the legend.

Much later, in 1599, there was a sensation when, during a restoration of the church, a body was exhumed from her urn, again intact but with cuts on the neck. Within moments, it crumbled to dust. Several people witnessed this, including the sculptor Stefano Maderno, who later made a statue of the body – a young woman reclining, the face veiled, the neck showing three cuts. This sculpture, his masterpiece, graces the main altar.

In the church, the underground ancient Roman room said to be the place of Cecilia's martyrdom can be visited. It is indeed a bathroom, as its ancient plumbing attests. Of course it could be the room of any house, or even of one of the many public baths of ancient Rome. It could even be, like the pit in S. Prassede or that in St Calixtus or the floor outcrop in S. Maria dell'Ara Coeli, that this structural peculiarity itself inspired one of the main details of the legend.

ON THE SPOT

5. S. Cecilia

On the square is the solemn, columned 18th-century entrance to **S. Cecilia**, a much older convent and church, another of the great basilicas of Trastevere. It was built in the 9th century by Paschal I, one of the great builder popes, over a supposed *ecclesia domestica* (still underneath), to give an appropriate resting place to the corpse he claimed to have found thanks to a vision. Later, convent buildings were added and the church was restored, modified and redecorated several times. Two orders of nuns have owned and managed it for a few centuries: Franciscans, in the convent on the right, and Benedictines on the left.

(Open: 10:00-12:00 and 16:00-18:00, but the nuns often close up earlier.) You can reach one of the convents, with important frescoes, by going through the church, but only on Tuesdays and Thursdays 10:00-11:30, and Sundays and holidays after 11 o'clock Mass. It is worth going straight there if you happen to arrive around those times (the door is at the beginning of the left aisle, the description on p. 592).

The area you first see was mostly created in the 12th century. The original parts consist of a lovely courtyard centred on a large, striking ancient Roman vase (the fountain is modern); the convent on the right with its romanesque windows (the convent on the left is 16th-century); the lower, colonnaded part of the church facade (up to the mosaic frieze with medallion portraits; the upper part is 18th-century); the bell tower; and the porch behind the façade.

In the porch, on the right, is a gorgeous baroque monument to a cardinal who ordered the 1599 restoration of the church during which the putative body of St Cecilia was exhumed. The relief illustrates the event. The architecture is by Girolamo Rainaldi and the statues were designed by Pietro Bernini (Gian Lorenzo's father). Also in the porch are medieval tombstones, some belonging to members of the Ponziani family, who lived nearby, as we'll see. (St Francesca Romana – see pp. 196-197 – was a Ponziani.) When you enter, first pause to absorb the impact of the grand, airy interior, more the great hall of a mansion than a church nave. A 19th-century restoration which, among other things, encased the 9th-century columns of the nave within brick pillars (in order to reinforce the ancient structure) does not spoil the effect; on the contrary, it somehow eases the passage from the original, stark medieval look to the flowery baroque and 18th-century redecoration. To the latter belongs the ceiling fresco by Sebastiano Conca.

The first section of the church forms a vestibule decorated by minor 17th-century painters. To the right and left of the main entrance are two impressive 15th-century tombs of cardinals. The one on the right is of Adam Easton, a Norwich man (by an unidentified, possibly Roman sculptor); the other is of a Cardinal Forteguerri, a relative of the Ponziani, with the main statue and a *Virgin and Child* relief by Mino da Fiesole (the other statuary is by an artist of the Roman school, while the monument itself was reassembled somewhat arbitrarily in the 19th century from fragments found in the church).

Proceed counter-clockwise. At the right end of the vestibule is the Chapel of the Crucifixion built in the 17th century to house a reputedly miraculous image of the Crucifixion (late 14th-century Roman school) now on the chapel altar. Note the splendid 18th-century ceramics on the front of the altar. One of the original 9th-century columns is on one of the walls of the chapel entrance.

The right aisle starts with an (often closed) iron gate, a fine modern work. Beyond this is a corridor frescoed in the 17th century. On the left of the corridor is a 15th-century relief of the *Virgin and Child*, probably once part of the Forteguerri tomb (see above); further on, a round painting by Guido Reni of the *Nuptials of Cecilia and Valerian*. This corridor leads to the upper walls of a room of the Roman house buried below. The room, open only to archæologists, is traditionally said to have been Cecilia's bathroom and the site of her execution. All around are bathroom flues, under metal plates.

S. Cecilia: fresco of saints by Cavallini

There are other parts of the heating system behind the round railing. The room that now incorporates the walls was frescoed in the 17th century. Over an altar is the *Beheading of St Cecilia* by Reni. Note the Cosmatesque floor, rebuilt with patches of the original 12th-century flooring.

Back in the aisle, the next chapel, built in the 15th century, is of the Ponziani family; it has frescoes of the period by Antonio da Viterbo. On the altar is a painting in which St Francesca Romana flanks the Madonna, also 15th-century. The last chapel on the right is a somewhat theatrical creation of 1929. It contains the tomb of a cardinal who in 1901 had restored the crypt, which we'll visit.

At the end of the aisle, a chapel with modern altar has, on the right wall, a severely damaged 12th-century fresco (originally in the church portico) depicting Cecilia's appearance to Pope Paschal in a dream and the rediscovery of her body.

Enter the nave. Under the main altar is *St Cecilia recumbent*, a delicate work of 1599 by Stefano Maderno (no relative of his contemporary Carlo Maderno). Notice the cuts on the neck.

The apse centres on a marble canopy, a ciborium, by Arnolfo di Cambio, signed and dated 1293. Here again the master combines medieval pathos and classical serenity, in the architecture and in the reliefs. These include, on the corners, statuettes of Cecilia and her relatives (one on horseback). Nearby is a Cosmatesque candlestick.

The apse has 9th-century mosaics: Christ is flanked on the left by St Paul, St Cecilia and Pope Paschal I (with the square halo of the living); on the right by St Peter, St Valerian and another saint. Somewhat similar to the great mosaic of St Praxedes (p. 103), which was also commissioned by Pope Paschal I, it too is mainly glass rather than marble, and has the same mystic intensity, typical of the Byzantine style.

Down the other aisle, near the end of the wall is

a monument to a 16th-century bishop recently attributed to Giacomo Della Porta. Just past it are two doors at an angle. The first, only open at certain times (see p. 590; further access restrictions may have been imposed after the publication of this book, as important paintings have been stolen from the convent) leads to the Benedictine convent. You get a view of a 12th-century cloister (one side is embedded in a larger 15th-century porch). Upstairs is the present nuns' choir. There, on a wall which was originally the inside of the church entrance wall, is what remains of the 1293 fresco by Pietro Cavallini of the *Last Judgment*, a monumental work partly destroyed in the 16th-century restoration. Though still imbued with the stiff mysticism of the Byzantine era, the figures display a much wider emotional range, foreshadowing the humanistic spirit that culminated in the Renaissance.

The fresco continued on the side walls with Biblical scenes, probably by Cavallini's assistants. A fragmentary *Annunciation* scene nearby (look for it to the lower right of the door) is 16th-century. Back on the aisle, the other of the two doors leads past a room where two more original 9th-century columns are visible, down to the ancient Roman construction. The ceilings and many of the walls are modern, obscuring the original layout. The ruins seem to belong to two different houses. Assuming that Cecilia and Valerian actually lived here, it is impossible to say which of the rooms were theirs, or just where the 'home church' was located. One theory is that some rooms were at one point converted into a regular church, preceding the present one. Most of the structures are 3rd-4th century AD, but some are much older. The first three rooms (A, B, C; the first possibly a courtyard) belong to the first house, the rest to the other. In this second house, one of the first rooms (D) has several pits or silos. It is thought that at one point this part was converted into a tannery, with pits to soak the skins. Here behind the wall, inaccessible to visitors, is the lower part (E) of Cecilia's reputed bathroom (p. 590). Other flues there confirm the presence of a heating system.

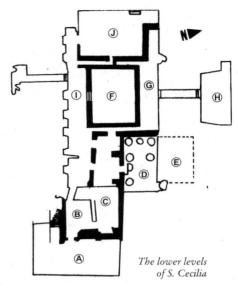

The lower levels of S. Cecilia

Past these rooms is a large space (F) which has been made into a display room. Most interesting is a fragment of a 3rd century sarcophagus with the symbol of Christ as Good Shepherd. On the back is a Cosmatesque cross and a 9th-century inscription exalting Pope Paschal I's recovery of the relics. An adjacent room (G) has very ancient tufa block walls (1st century BC?) and, in the far corner, a niche with a *lararium*, or family shrine, dedicated to Minerva, of the same period. From here a narrow corridor leads to an isolated room (H), perhaps part of the public bath. A bust of Plato found in the putative courtyard (A) is displayed here.

Across the display room, a long corridor (I) leads to the crypt (J), dating from the middle ages but entirely rebuilt and redecorated in 1901. Leave the church and cross the garden to the portico overlooking the square. Inside on the left, a 1st century marble tablet, found nearby, proclaims the enlargement of Rome's official borders (*pomerium*) by Emperors Vespasian and Titus. (For another of these marks see p. 471.) From Piazza S. Cecilia go left into Via S. Cecilia.

BEFORE GOING

6. From S. Cecilia to S. Benedetto in Piscinula

This section takes us to the vicinity of what was said to be – and nothing proves it wasn't – the Rome house of the Anicii of Norcia (p. 584). Here St Benedict, a member of this distinguished family, would have spent his student years. There are also the surviving palaces of some of the late medieval noble families of Trastevere – the Ponziani, ancestors of that beloved Roman figure S. Francesca Romana, and their relatives the Forteguerri. Nearby was (and perhaps still is, embedded in a more modern version) the palace of a wealthy Sienese family, the Tolomei, who moved to Rome in the 14th century after one its members, Pia, was murdered by her husband. Her story is immortalised in Dante's *Divine Comedy*, when the poet visiting the 'ante-Purgatory' meets her ghost, who begs him in wonderfully melodious verses: 'Deh, quando tu sarai tornato al mondo / e riposato della lunga via ... / ricorditi di me che son la Pia' ('Pray, when you have returned to the world / And will be rested after this long journey ... / Remember me, who am Pia' – meaning also 'pious one').

All these families must have been involved in trade, especially of foodstuffs. It is known that the Ponziani were originally butchers. The Anicii, whose ancestral hometown was the traditional supplier of pork products to Rome, were probably in the business too. They would not otherwise have lived in what was both a slum and, thanks to the adjacent Ripa Grande harbour, a hub of foodstuff retail trade. Commerce echoes in the names of many streets and alleys here: 'dei Salumi' – of salt pork; 'dei Vascellari' – of amphors for packing; 'dei Genovesi' – of the Genoese manning the vessels at the harbour – and so on. With the exception of the ancient Anicii, these families had their heyday in the late middle ages – which is why we haven't mentioned the many Jewish families who once dominated in the area: by then, they had already migrated over the river, to what was much later designated the Jewish Ghetto.

But the Jewish imprint is certainly not erased here. We find it in vestiges of a bath for ritual purification and in two of the dozens of synagogues that once existed in Trastevere, one a few ruins, the other almost intact externally. The latter was the most recent of all, having been founded in the 12th century by the well known scholar Rabbi Nathan Ben Yehiel, author of the Aruch, a Talmudic dictionary. He was also a very influential person and the pope's financial manager. Rabbi Benjamin of Tudela, visiting Rome at the time, calls him 'papæ minister, juvenis formosus, prudens ac sapiens' ('a minister of the pope, a handsome young man, wise and erudite'). Also still alive is the memory of the Jewish Pierleoni family, after whom a large tract of the Lungotevere on the opposite riverbank has now been named. The family originated on this side, and lived here many years. It is first recorded in the person of an anonymous Jewish financier, well known consultant and money lender to the papal court. For unclear reasons, quite possibly related to these semi-official functions, he converted to Christianity and is therefore on record with the name Benedictus Christianus. The word spread, with no known basis, that his family was somehow connected with the revered Anicii. His direct descendants were also Christians: his son Leo, named after the then reigning pope, then his grandson Peter of Leo (Petrus Leonis), then another Peter. After Petrus Leonis the whole family assumed the Italian version of his name, Pierleoni.

Within these few generations they accumulated immense riches and honors. Leo was made a baron by the pope, who, the historian Gregorovius writes, owed him money. Starting with his son Petrus Leonis, all the first born were 'Roman consuls', the highest civilian title. Their houses in Trastevere became towers and fortresses. Pierleoni buildings sprang up on the nearby Isola Tiberina, as they became the island's de facto rulers; on the other riverbank, they occupied and fortified the Theatre of Marcellus (p. 253) and built towers near it. The popes even gave them possession of Rome's greatest defensive bulwark, Castel S. Angelo (pp. 385-393).

According to Gregorovius, this extraordinary power flowed from the wealth of these 'medieval Rothschilds', and to the debts that the popes, always needing funds for their struggles against the German emperors, incurred to them. The Pierleoni also become the main supporters of the papacy against the imperial party in a strife involving most of the Roman baronial families and the population itself. It is not surprising that Peter, Benedictus' great-grandson, Papal Legate to France and England, decided to start climbing the ultimate rungs by having the pope make him a cardinal. When the pope died in 1130, Peter was elected pope – under the name Anaclete II – by his many church relations.

We have already related (p. 554) Anaclete's struggle against another pretender to the throne, the imperial candidate, also a Trasteverine and elected the same day by other church notables, as Innocent II. Innocent had not only the emperor's support but, just as importantly, that of the foremost mystic of the day, St Bernard of Clairvaux, founder of the Cistercian monastic order. Bernard persuaded most of the church establishment to declare Anaclete (formerly Peter) an antipope. Yet Anaclete managed to keep the throne until his death eight years later. This cannot be explained except by a new factor: the Roman people's love and respect for the Pierleoni, of which we'll find further evidence later. Only at Anaclete's death could Innocent II peacefully take his place.

ON THE SPOT

6. From S. Cecilia to S. Benedetto in Piscinula

At the first crossing, Via dei Genovesi, on the right above No. 1a is a small walled-up medieval window. Turn right into Via Augusto Jandolo. Past an interesting early 20th-century art nouveau apartment building at the end on your left, walk into No. 6 to see the charming miniature church of **S. Maria in Cappella** ('in the Chapel', a name of uncertain origin).

Built in 1090, it is notable for its simple façade (with a renaissance-style relief) and the bell-tower; the interior, rarely open, has fine ancient columns. The church was connected from the beginning to a hospital which is still on the right. In the 14th century the whole complex was sponsored by a Ponziani nobleman, the father-in-law of St Francesca Romana (pp. 196-197); then in the 17th century it passed to the sponsorship of the Pamphili family. The notorious Donna Olimpia, sister-in-law of the Pamphili pope (p. 457), bought more land adjacent to the hospital garden and transformed the whole thing into a magnificent villa and garden for herself, facing the river. Meanwhile the hospital continued to function.

Originally devoted to the terminally ill (referred to in the words 'morbis chronicis' of a Latin inscription over the door), the hospital is now a home for the aged run by nuns. You may ring and enter to see what is left of Donna Olimpia's garden, a helter-skelter, cheerful mass of greenery. Fountains and other ornaments have vanished, along with elegant buildings, mostly because of the late 19th-century embankment of the river. Some original structures remain embedded in run-down modern buildings.

Backtrack on Via Augusto Jandolo, then go right on Via dei Vascellari ('of the Pottery-makers'; whose products were the containers of choice for foodstuffs). No. 45 on the right is a much restored early renaissance house. Further down on the left, at No. 61, is **Palazzo Ponziani**. In the 14th century a 12-year-old girl, the future saint Francesca Romana, married into the family and moved here. She soon grew famous for her tireless devotion to the sick and poor in a period when famine, civil war and plague racked the district. The medieval palace was remodelled, partially or completely, several times, most recently in the early 19th century, when it became a youth hostel. Still operating, this also takes in foreign students. On the building's far corner (at Via dei Salumi) is an emblem of the Forteguerri family (p. 590), who were related to the Ponziani.

On the other corner, across Via dei Salumi, is a dilapidated little church, **S. Andrea dei Vascellari** ('St Andrew of the Pottery-makers'). Founded in the middle ages but rebuilt in the 17th century, the church is deconsecrated and has been used as a carpenter's workshop since 1942. The workbench is over the main altar.

Take Via dei Salumi ('of the Pork Products') which owes its ancient name to sausage and ham warehouses connected to the river docks. Before the first crossing on the left is a renaissance house (No. 10). Turn left into Vicolo dell'Atleta ('of the Athlete'). On the right at No. 16 are the remains of an ancient house of uncertain date. At No. 14 is a lovely medieval house. It is a former **synagogue**, almost certainly the one known to have been founded in Trastevere in the 12th century by Rabbi Nathan ben Yehiel. Worn Hebrew lettering, which seems to begin with the word 'Nathan', is barely visible at the bottom of the centre column.

When the house was restored in 1849, excavations in front of it turned up the famous statue of a Greek athlete, the *Apoxyomenos*, now in the Vatican Museums (p. 320). This event gave rise to

the street's name. Continue to Via dei Genovesi (a reference to the many Genoese sailors who thronged the area of the river docks) and turn right. In the area on the right occupied by a public school, digs have uncovered remains of another synagogue and of purification baths for Jewish women.

The first crossroads brings you again to Via Anicia again (p. 587). On the left is **S. Giovanni dei Genovesi** ('St John of the Genoese'), a church-hospital complex built in the late 15th century by a Genoese nobleman for sailors from Genoa. The church is occasionally open. In addition, the cloister – perhaps the most attractive of its period in Rome – is open Tuesdays and Thursdays 15:00-18:00 / 14:00-16:00 in winter (closed in August) by ringing the bottom left bell at No. 12.

This is the point at which you can now visit the Madonna dell'Orto church if you missed it earlier by taking the second detour. Simply continue on Via Anicia past No. 12 for one block (description on p. 587). Then return here after your visit.

Leaving S. Giovanni, walk left to an 18th-century building across Via dei Genovesi from S. Giovanni. Two tablets relating to the cult of the Bona Dea (p. 588), found nearby, are embedded in the walls of this building. One is on the corner here, several feet below the street lamp. The other is around the corner on the main façade, to the lower left of a ground floor window. They refer to memorials set up by a certain Bolanus to invoke the protection of the 'Good Goddess' on his home nearby.

Continue on Via Anicia to a covered passage, the medieval **Arch of the Tolomei**. Only the archway interior is authentic; the rest is mostly modern. On the other side of the arch, in front of you is what is left of a renaissance building with a large balcony. This building, which would have replaced a medieval predecessor, is said to have been the palace of Pia dei Tolomei's family, but the identification is uncertain.

Continue downhill through this fascinating corner of Trastevere; at the bottom turn left onto Via della Lungaretta (p. 551). Walk to the first crossing and go left. A few yards further on your right is **S. Maria della Luce** ('St Mary of Light'). Of medieval and possibly even ancient Roman origin, the church was originally called S. Salvatore della Corte ('Holy Saviour of the Court'), perhaps in reference to the ancient cohort, or police precinct, nearby (p. 548). It acquired its present name in the 18th century, in homage to an image of the Virgin, now on the main altar, that was credited with restoring a blind man's sight. It was also almost entirely rebuilt about the same time. The 18th century interior, often open, is of unusual and luminous design.

The original 12th-century apse is visible by turning into the nearby Vicolo del Buco, left of the façade. Embedded in the wall at No. 24 of the Vicolo are the words 'Collegium Ang.', all that remains of an ancient hospital and hospice for English residents, which still existed in the 19th century.

Backtrack to Via della Lungaretta and take it left to Vicolo della Luce. At the corner of the two streets, a carefully restored medieval house. Note the different sets of windows opened in the walls at different periods, the once open-air staircase, and the two columns of the porch, which is now enclosed.

Retrace your steps on Via della Lungaretta, to Piazza in Piscinula (an ancient name referring to baths or to a fish market). The whole left side of the square is formed by **Palazzo Mattei**, a complex of several renaissance buildings.

The construction dates from the early 15th to the mid 16th century, though the foundations are probably centuries older. In it lived the Trastevere branch of the princely Mattei family (whose many palaces we saw on the other side of the river, p. 248). A bloody tragedy took place here in the 16th century, when an internecine feud erupted, killing five family members, including a man at his wedding.

On the opposite side of the square, tucked away in a corner, is a tiny, very old church, S. **Benedetto in Piscinula**. According to tradition, the church was built on the site of the palatial home of St Benedict's family, the Anicii (p. 584), though no definite trace of a house has been found. The church, including the modest façade, was rebuilt in the 19th century, but the oldest original structures go back to the 11th. The delightful bell tower is from the 12th century. In the tower are two medieval bells. The older (11th-century?), on the right, is also the smallest in any Roman belfry. If closed, request admission by ringing the bell at No. 40, but not between 11:00 and 16:30 or after 18:00, when the elderly nuns who run this church are praying or dining. Leave an offering.

The church, with a warm, homely look, has an entrance hall with faded 13th- to 14th-century frescoes. Splendid colours of a 12th-century Cosmatesque floor enliven the dark interior. The columns come from Roman temples of various ages (1st-5th century AD). At the end of the right wall is a damaged 15th-century fresco of *St Anne with the Madonna and Child*. On the altar is a painting of St Benedict, of the same period but much retouched. In a niche over it is a 14th-century Madonna and Child. Past the sacristy is a chapel called 'of the Madonna' because of a venerated painting of the Virgin over the altar (possibly 14th-century, much reworked). Next to this room is a cubicle said to have been St Benedict's praying room in the Anicia house. The tradition cannot be verified, but the cubicle is believed to be older than the church, since it appears to have affected its lay-out.

Leaving the church, cross to the steps on the opposite side of the square. Observe the flank of Palazzo Mattei on your left (including the external closet, a latrine) and glance back to S. Benedetto's bell tower, better visible from here. You are now on the river drive.

BEFORE GOING

7. S. Bartolomeo all' Isola

We told elsewhere the story of the only island in the Tiber's urban stretch in pagan times (p. 246), and of how the Sanctuary of Æsculapius came to be founded there in the 4th century BC, along with Rome's first hospital, which gave the island the character of a health centre that it preserves

Around the year 1000, a church rose over the site of the sanctuary-hospital. River floods, particularly frequent and furious here, swept away this original church and what remained of the sanctuary, but important vestiges of both remain in and near the present church, last of several reconstructions. The history of S. Bartolomeo all' Isola ('on the island') reads like a fairy-tale. It was founded by Otto III, a German emperor descended from Charlemagne (p. 303) and one of the few who briefly managed to extend their empire to its nominal capital, Rome. The young ruler, who had been crowned at the age of two and come to Rome in his teens, lived in a villa on the Aventine Hill (p. 269). There he struck up a friendship with Adalbert, a monk in an Aventine monastery and former bishop of Prague who had retired to Rome for prayer and meditation.

About 997 Adalbert left Rome for missionary work in Germany, where he was murdered by pagan natives in the city of Danzig. Otto had the body returned to Rome, where he built this church to house it. The church was initially dedicated to Adalbert, who was made a saint. As was custom, Otto tried to make his church as famous and attractive as possible by endowing it with relics of many saints and martyrs (p. 400). Besides his friend's body, he imported several more, by purchase or force. His showpiece was the alleged body of St Bartholomew, one of the Twelve Apostles, said to have drifted ashore in Italy from Palestine five centuries earlier after infidels dumped the body in the sea. Another of Otto's finds was the body of St Paulinus, a 4th-century AD senator, poet and bishop. Otto did not enjoy his beloved church for long. He was expelled from Rome by a popular uprising and died at age 22 trying to retake the city, in 1002.

Only a few years later, with St Adalbert's protector gone, the name of the church was changed to S. Bartolomeo, because the relics of one of the Apostles were thought to have greater allure than those of a mere saint. In a further twist, the southern Italian church that had given Otto St Bartholomew's body realised the great treasure it had lost, and claimed to have cheated the emperor by giving him another corpse. It remains unknown whether the relics that purportedly landed in Italy are in this Roman church or in the southern city of Benevento.

Already at the time that the original church was built, life here had begun to change. The island came increasingly within the orbit of the wealthy Jewish families who not only dominated trade in Trastevere and Ripa Grande, but who had already established themselves on the opposite bank too, near the Porticus of Octavia (p. 522). At one point, both bridges serving the island had assumed the collective name of Pons Judæorum, the Jewish bridge. By the 12th century the Pierleoni family had practically colonised the island and set up their fortresses there and beyond.

At the death of the Pierleoni anti-pope Anaclete II, his successor Innocent II had kept up relations with Anaclete's rich and powerful former Jewish clan. Anaclete's brother, Jordan, began serving at the new papal court. But the situation had changed. First, the papacy was no longer in Pierleoni hands. Second, the Pierleoni were increasingly appreciating the popular support they had enjoyed in the struggle for control of the papacy and between themselves and the emperor. So at some point, Jordan turned to the Roman people, who had never forgotten their dream of recovering their liberty and sovereignty, and started a popular party on the heels of the republican, anti-feudal ones that had triumphed in many other Italian cities. Under Jordan's guide this movement led to the successful popular revolution of 1143 (p. 144) and to the approval of the first civic constitution, which revived the Roman Senate. As we know, the autonomous senate did not last long; the popes soon recovered most of their power. But not all. After 1143 there was always at least one officer called a senator representing to some extent the popular will, and this arrangement lasted until the very end of papal rule in Rome. In 1871, the results of the referendum that approved a constitutional and democratic regime and Rome's union to the rest of Italy were announced before the very Capitol building (p. 147) where Jordan had established his Senate.

This may be the last major appearance of the Pierleoni in history, unless we believe a rumour spread in the 15th century that some of them had moved to Austria and originated the imperial Hapsburg dynasty there. The Pierleoni name reappears in the late 19th century, when the ruins of a water-buffalo slaughterhouse, a Jewish monopoly, were uncovered in some very tall houses – thought to be former Pierleoni towers – that were being demolished in the Ghetto opposite Trastevere. Historians theorised that the Pierleoni had put it there, and that perhaps they themselves had gone back to live and work there, returning to their old faith. This is unproven. Yet Rome's great medieval scholar, Gregorovius, seems to have believed it, writing: 'Thus a family of haughty senators and consuls of the Romans reverted by a strange irony to its original conditions.'

Whether they returned to the Ghetto or not, their loss of power in Trastevere, desertion of and then opposition to the papal court, and finally their fight for Roman freedom may well explain one of the unsolved mysteries of Roman history: the abandonment of the Trastevere area by Roman Jews, which happened about this time. They probably felt less secure in two separate groups, and decided to migrate en masse to join the rest of their community on the opposite bank. (p. 522).

ON THE SPOT

7. S. Bartolomeo all' Isola

Go to Isola Tiberina via the bridge. (For the early history of the island, see pp. 246, 251-252.)

The whole left side of the island is occupied by a hospital founded in 1548 and rebuilt in 1930, of friars called the Fatebenefratelli ('The Do-good Brothers'). On its ground floor is the little 17th-century church (restored in the 18th century) of **S. Giovanni Calibita** ('St John the Calibite', or hermit). Open just half an hour daily, from 19:15 to 19:45, it is entered with no problem from inside the hospital. It has a sumptuous, typical 18th-century interior.

Roughly opposite is a small square centering on a 19th-century carved pillar with figures of St Bartholomew and other saints connected with the story of the island. Facing the pillar is **S. Bartolomeo all' Isola**, in its last, baroque incarnation.

The present façade is early 17th-century, but the bell-tower rising on the left is a 12th-century romanesque work that dates back to one of the first renovations. The posted schedule is 07:00-12:00 and 16:00-19:00 / 18:00 in winter, but it is not very reliable.

The wall in the porch belongs, in part, to one of the earliest façades. At the centre an oval mosaic of Christ in the act of blessing dates from the 12th century (a fragment of a much larger work destroyed by floods). Of the same date is the marble door-frame. A Latin inscription at its top recalls the foundation by Otto III (upper line). And in a sentence that confirms the enormous importance relics were accorded as a magnet for pilgrims by the churches that fought over them, it proclaims: 'In this house are … believe it [or not] … such bodies (*corpora*) as those of Paulinus and Bartholomew…' (lower line, in larger letters). The less impressive original martyr, Adalbert, by this early time seems already largely forgotten. The wooden doors are 18th-century.

Two more inscriptions on the sides of the doorway (right, 17th-century; left, 19th-century), describe other merits of the church, such as absolution from sins and liberation from Purgatory, granted to visitors and to anyone who will pay for a Mass for the dead.

The interior is graceful and serene despite jarring modern additions. All the columns are ancient Roman and originate from the 1000 AD church which, in turn, probably got them from the temple of Æsculapius. Stucco capitals were added in the 17th-century renovation, but two columns – the third from the entrance on each side – have kept their splendid and rare bases. Frescoes and paintings are by minor artists from the 17th to the early 19th centuries, some badly damaged by flood waters.

The most interesting artefact in the church, a medieval well-head, is in the middle of the steps to the main altar. It is fascinating for two reasons. First, it covers a pit, 36ft (12m) deep, which may be the very one which served the temple of Æsculapius. Like most ancient 'health sanctuaries' (remember the one at S. Lorenzo in Lucina, p. 228) this one had been built near its own 'sacred spring'. Secondly, the wellhead, dating from the founding of the church in 1000 AD or soon after, is roughly carved all around with figures relating to the beginnings of the church. On the right, the Emperor Otto (but would you say this was a youth of 20?), holding his sceptre and a model of

CHIESA DI S. GIO. COLABITA.

S. Giovanni Calibita, from a pilgrim's guidebook of the 16th-17th centuries; these crude prints continued to be used long after they would have been rejected by grander publications

the church; in the middle, St Adalbert (or St Paulinus); on the left, the Redeemer, and on the back, St Bartholomew. The well-head, made from the stump of a column, has deep indentations on the rim from the long use of ropes or chains to draw a bucket. The pit was used until the early 19th century, when it was closed because the water had become polluted.

The main altar is formed by an ancient Roman tub of porphyry marble, containing the controversial relics of St Bartholomew. In front of the altar are surviving fragments – two square patches – of a splendid Cosmatesque floor which was installed around 1100, but later washed away by flood waters. Go up to the transept via the stairs to the right. On the wall there is a strange, large bronze dish with floral designs, an Arab work of about 1000 AD; the very one, tradition says ignoring the anachronism, on which St Bartholomew's body floated to Italy, and in any case the one Emperor Otto used to bring the remains to Rome.

To the right of the apse is a chapel guarded by two medieval lions, symbolic beasts (p. 230) common in medieval churches. The chapel itself is thought to be extremely old, possibly pre-dating the 1000 AD church. Its present fine ceiling is late 16th-century. Over the altar is a charming medieval fresco (11th-century or later) recently uncovered. A cannon ball embedded near the base of the right-hand wall was shot from the Janiculum Hill during the battle for Rome in 1849 (p. 565).

To the left of the apse is another large chapel, dedicated to St Adalbert and St Paulinus. In the pavement is another square patch of cosmatesque floor. The chapel was sponsored by owners of the water mills on the Tiber, who had adopted St Paulinus as their patron; the mills themselves are depicted in two small 17th-century frescoes near the base of the short wall. (Used to grind wheat from the middle ages to the late 19th century, these mills were so crucial for feeding the city that they were accepted even though they worsened the floods by hindering the water flow.)

From the sacristy, steps lead to a small surviving section of the crypt of the original church (closed at the time of writing), with medieval columns topped by stylised eagles, Otto's imperial emblem. Now leave the church.

Vestiges of the time when the island had been fashioned into a 'ship' in honour of Æsculapius are visible. Cross the church square, the street and the square next to the hospital. Walk left toward the parapet over the river, where you'll find steps down.

Once on the island's modern embankment, go left all the way and around to the other side. Just past the island's tip or 'prow', on a large patch of marble (a fragment of the 'hull') are a bust of Æsculapius, with his symbolic snake twisted around a staff, and a bull's head. The whole is damaged almost beyond recognition.

From here the **Ponte Rotto**, or 'Broken Bridge', (p. 258) and the two bridges to the island (pp. 251, 259) can be viewed close-up.

Leave the island by the bridge opposite the one you came over from Trastevere. As you cross this bridge, turn around to see a massive tower at the left end of the bridge. It dates from at least the 10th century, but in the 12th century the tower, together with an adjacent castle of which little remains, were a Pierleoni family fortress. For centuries this tower has been called, in old-fashioned Italian, **Torre della Pulzella** ('Tower of the Damsel'), and for a curious reason. Peering from a niche in the brickwork – midway between the two slanting iron clamps on the right – is a medieval marble woman's head, of unknown date, meaning and origin. The little sphinx seems an apt symbol for this enigmatic, great, but half-forgotten, Jewish-Christian family of Trastevere, to whom all Rome bears a debt of gratitude.

The bridge leads to Piazza Monte Savello, where several bus lines stop.

Excursions Outside the Walls

1. VILLA BORGHESE AND VILLA GIULIA, VIA FLAMINIA AND PONTE MILVIO, FORO ITALICO

This excursion takes us first to an area of gentle hills and countryside that was partially taken over in the renaissance by the villas of the great Roman families.

The largest (4 miles/6 km around) is Villa Borghese, formerly the property of the princely Borghese family. One of the entrances is opposite Porta Pinciana (p. 86). The park, created in the early 17th century along with the beautiful villa, was totally redesigned in the late 18th century by two Roman architects, Antonio and Mario Asprucci, who commissioned the Tyrolese sculptor Christopher Unterperger to embellish it with casinos, fountains, statues and pseudo-temples in the neoclassical style then turning fashionable. In the early 20th century the king of Italy bought the villa and gardens and donated them to the people, making it Rome's main public park.

Enter the park from the side opposite Porta Pinciana. Before you is a broad avenue. Circling the meadow down on the left is the bridle path, once a most elegant venue for riders but now a bit neglected. Don't go down the avenue; instead take Viale del Museo Borghese on your right. First here is a fine copy of a statue of Lord Byron by Thorvaldsen, given to Rome by the poet's alma mater, Trinity College, Cambridge. It bears the poet's verses to the Eternal City: 'O Rome! My country! City of the soul!' Go on until you get to a piazza with a baroque balustrade and old statues (copies).

Dominating the piazza is the exquisite, ornate early 17th-century **Casino Borghese**, by the northern Italian architect Flaminio Ponzio and his prominent Dutch colleague Jan van Santen, who spent part of his career in Rome as Giovanni Vasanzio. The Casino has always held one of the foremost collections of paintings and sculpture in the world – including many of Bernini's greatest pieces. In the early 19th century it was the favourite residence of Prince Camillo Borghese

and his wife Paolina, Napoleon's sister (p. 99), whose beauty and extravagance were legendary. The Emperor once forced his brother-in-law to sell part of his collection to the Louvre, but the prince quickly replaced it. The collection includes Canova's famous and resplendent statue of the semi-nude Paolina. To visit the museum see p. 683.

To the left of the museum (if you are facing) take Viale dell'Uccelliera, named after the attractive pair of 17th-century structures here, one of which is an *uccelliera* (aviary). Across the street from the aviary take Viale dei Pupazzi. You cnow ross one of the more picturesque, secluded spots of the park and reach the beautiful Fountain of the Seahorses by Unterperger. In the background, note a little neo-classical Temple of Diana. From the fountain take, on the right, Viale dei Cavalli Marini toward an ochre building, the pretty Casino of the Timepiece. It faces Piazza di Siena, an oval in a splendid natural setting amid the umbrella pines of Rome, which is used for spectacles, fashion shows and every April, an international horse show. Do walk over to have a look.

Continue along Viale dei Cavalli Marini away from the fountain. When you get to the little Temple of Faustina (an imitation of the antique), you'll see in front of it Viale Pietro Canonica, named after an illustrious early 20th-century sculptor. The 17th-century house at the entrance here was the home of Canonica, remodelled by him to look like a medieval castle. Now it is home to his collected works (p. 687). Canonica erected two monuments in front of his house: to the Alpine Soldier and to the Mule, honouring these gallant protagonists of the First World War. Take Viale Canonica, and pass Piazza di Siena at your left. The next crossing on the right leads to the Giardino del Lago (Lake Garden).

(If you go straight for about half a mile (800 m) you reach the top of the **Pincio** (p. 51), which was studded with marvelous villas in ancient Roman times. It is not a part of the original Villa Borghese, though it is in the same park. Landscaped in the early 19th century by Giuseppe Valadier in conjunction with the Piazza del

Gardens of the Villa Borghese

Popolo he was rearranging below, the Pincian garden gives a beautiful view of the city. At the turn of the 19th-20th century the Pincian Hill was the elegant place to promenade, by carriage or on foot – as was the case in Paris, during the same *belle époque* period, in the Bois de Boulogne or the Champs Elysées. If you go and take a look, then return here afterwards.)

Restored in the early 20th century, and pleasantly secluded from the rest of the park, one side of the lake garden faces an artificial lake with an island and an imitation Greek temple. Keep to the left, circle the lake and go under the arch. You reach an opening with a large ramp on the right. Take it to go down to Viale delle Belle Arti. On the other side of the viale is a palazzo of 1911, the National Gallery of Modern Art (p. 683).

Take Viale delle Belle Arti to the left. On the right by the ramp is a bronze copy of *Jason* by the

Danish Thorvaldsen, an early 19th-century statue given to Rome by the city of Copenhagen. Topping the steps is a statue of Simon Bolivar by Pietro Canonica (1934); further up is the building of the British School at Rome, an early 20th-century palazzo by Edwin Lutyens, who later built Imperial Delhi. To the left of it are the Romanian Academy and the academies and study centres of other countries.

About 300 yards ahead on Viale delle Belle Arti, on the left, is the entrance to **Villa Giulia** – the residence only, not the related park, which no longer exists. It was named after Pope Julius III, who built it for his family in the mid-16th century. (Don't confuse him with the famous Juli Michelangelo's and Raphael's patron, wh 40 years earlier.) This renaissance jewel of a collaboration of three great art tect Jacopo Vignola, the archit

604

Ceiling decoration in the Villa Giulia

Bartolomeo Ammannati and the architect and painter (and celebrated biographer) Giorgio Vasari. Vignola is responsible for the overall design including the façade, while Ammannati and Vasari developed the scenographic interior. The villa now houses the important **National Museum of Ancient Etruscan and Pre-Roman Art**, and may be visited along with it (p. 682).

The front of the palace has two halls, now the ticket office and library of the museum, with rich frescoes and stuccoes. Especially notable is the library, decorated by Taddeo Zuccaro. Beyond it is a huge courtyard with a portico, frescoed with arbors on the ceiling by the Emilian painter Pietro Venale, to echo the rustic feel of the area, and with grotesques (p. 212) on the walls. The courtyard ends with a beautiful loggia by Ammannati, signed by him at eye level on the last semi-column of the second row (on the right). The loggia gives onto a theatrical, monumental three-tiered nymphæum, a famous creation by Vasari and Ammannati.

There are plans to extend the museum into an early 19th-century palazzina nearby, the Villa Poniatowsky. This was built for a Polish prince of that name to designs by Giuseppe Valadier and will be connected to Villa Giulia by a walkway; the present entrance is at 34, Via di Villa Giulis; enquiries to (06) 8207 7304.

Leaving the villa take the narrower road on the left, Via di Villa Giulia, to Via Flaminia, one of the great roads of the ancient Roman consular grid (p. 43), this one leading to the north. Right of the crossing, if we came from Villa Giulia, is the **Palazzina of Pius IV**, originally an annexe to Villa Giulia. It was confiscated from Pope Julius' family by his successor, Paul IV, who enlarged it and gave it to his nephew Carlo Borromeo (who was later canonised, see p. 225). The Borromeo family owned it until 1929. It was then sold to the Italian government, which has since used it as its embassy to the Vatican.

Amongst past ambassadors was Mussolini's son-in-law, Count Galeazzo Ciano. This young and brilliant diplomat married Mussolini's only daughter, Edda. Ciano had initially served as Foreign Minister, so his appointment as ambassador represented a demotion, caused by his growing, if secret, opposition to the Italian alliance with Germany. Ciano was instrumental in the overthrow and arrest of Mussolini, and in the fall of Fascism. When the dictator was rescued and returned to a semblance of power by Hitler, he had Ciano executed on Hitler's orders, despite Edda's desperate entreaties to save him.

In its enlarged version the palazzina and its elegant loggia are by the Neapolitan architect Pirro Ligorio, but the lower part is the original by Vignola and Ammannati, who also designed the fountain of the Acqua Vergine below (it has undergone several remodellings).

Go 300 yards further along Via Flaminia, past the crossing with Via delle Belle Arti. On the right, at the corner with Via E. Chiaradia, is another work designed by Vignola for Pope Julius III: the so-called **Tempietto di S. Andrea** ('Little Temple to St. Andrew'). Julius built the church to fulfil a vow he had made, when still a priest, on the saint's feast day during the Sack of Rome (p. 381), after he managed to escape the marauding troops who had captured him.

Admire this 1553 church for its façade of sober salt-and-pepper marble (*peperino*) and for the way the light plays on the pilasters, the triangular gable and the great side niches, contrasting with the chunkiness of the structure. Notice the tension between the plain cubic shape and the curve of the dome, a motif soon to be picked up by the baroque. The frescoed interior is usually closed.

Proceeding for about two thirds of a mile (1 km), in Piazza Apollodoro on the right is the **Palazzetto dello Sport** stadium, seating 5,000, completed in 1958 by Pierluigi Nervi and Annibale Vitellozzi. It is based on the circular plan of the larger Palazzo dello Sport in the EUR district (p. 629), but employs different materials and techniques. A few yards away, on Via de Coubertin, is the brand-new **Auditorium of Rome** (1997-2002), seating 8,000, built for the Roman classical-music orchestra of the Accademia di S. Cecilia by

another world-renowned Italian architect, Renzo Piano. It consists of three auditoria of different sizes around a central open-air theatre. Its design is one of the most advanced anywhere, not least in terms of acoustics. During construction an ancient Roman farmhouse was unearthed that dated back to the Republic; its ruins have been turned into a museum.

On the other side of Via Flamminia, two more constructions are currently being completed. One is a sprawling national museum of contemporary art bearing, in imitation of fashionable foreign acronyms such as MoMA, the unpronounceable name MAXXI, meaning, according to its inventors, 'Museum of Art in the XXIst Century'. It is by an Anglo-Iraqi architect known for her daring projects, Zaha Hadid. Nearby another large futuristic building is taking shape, by the Roman architect Massimiliano Fuksas; this is meant to house an Italian Space Agency.

Hadid's model for the new museum has been described by the New York Times as 'an achingly modern mesh of overlapping steel and glass corridors,' and 'a twisted and tangled railway yard.' The frenzied arrival of gigantic, new-age buildings such as those that are sprouting up in Rome (see also pp. 223, 636) devouring large slices of the city budget, does not lack critics. They stress that though perhaps appropriate to less 'eternal' cities in America or Australia, these new-fangled structures are out of place here and could even cost Rome its millennial identity. As one prominent Roman architect put it: 'these buildings have nothing to do with this city. They are like alien spaceships.'

Another mile along Via Flaminia brings you up to the Tiber (you can use the tram part of the way) and the extremely ancient **Milvian** (or **Mulvian**) **Bridge**, built in 109 BC in stone to replace an age-old wooden bridge. Tacitus reports that in the time of Nero (1st century AD) the bridge was 'famous for its nocturnal attractions' and that the young emperor went there 'for his debaucheries'. Throughout the centuries, the bridge played a key role in the history of Rome, as all roads from the north led over it. It was, for instance, the site of the epochal battle between co-emperors Constantine and Maxentius, where the latter was killed and Christianity triumphed (p. 198).

Little remains of the original structure of the four-arched bridge. The two nearest arches are original; the rest, including ends and parapets, results from countless restructurings and expansions that began with Belisarius (p. 86) in the 6th century and ended after the bridge was blown up in the 1849 war (p. 565). The present appearance is mostly due to the restoration by Giuseppe Valadier, done to celebrate the return to Rome of Pope Pius VII from a Napoleonic prison (p. 67). The two statues are (left) early 18th and (right) 19th century.

Downstream from the Milvian Bridge and in front of the next bridge (within walking distance along Lungotevere Maresciallo Diaz) is a complex built by the Fascist régime between 1928 and 1937 as a showpiece for athletic and paramilitary activities, the **Foro Italico** (originally Foro Mussolini). At its front is a striking 119 ft (36 m) obelisk made in 1932 of a single piece of white Carrara marble and dedicated to Mussolini. The compound shows how Fascist architecture evolved from a decorative, detailed style to the abstract, austere lines of the so-called 'rationalist' style that would find its most complete and well-known expression in the EUR district (p. 628). The obelisk, by Costantino Costantini, combines the new trends with cubist and art deco motifs. Most of the buildings in the earlier style are by the original planner of the compound, Enrico del Debbio; the later planning and construction was mostly by Luigi Moretti (whose work we first met in Trastevere; he later built the Watergate complex in Washington). Typical of Del Debbio's manner is the first large building one reaches (1928), presently housing the Italian centre for Olympic sports (CONI), and, behind it, the spectacular 1933 **Stadio dei Marmi** ('Stadium of the Marble Statues'). You can normally cross the building from the main entrance to reach the stadium. The 60 statues of athletes surrounding the stadium, providing a sort of anthology of Fascist sculpture, were each donated by a separate Italian city. Apart from its strident rhetoric, the ensemble had originality and a certain majesty, especially when it benefited from the serene natural backdrop of a verdant slope (the Monte Mario hill). Unfortunately, the beautiful natural setting has been blocked and defaced since 1990, when another stadium, huge and downright ugly, was built alongside the Stadio dei Marmi for the World Cup.

Right behind the obelisk is an Avenue of the (Fascist) Empire created in 1937 by Luigi Moretti, with beautiful ancient Roman-style floor mosaics and large marble blocks inscribed with momentous dates of the Fascist régime; the last ones, however, were added after its demise. The whole is in a state of pathetic neglect. The future fate of the Stadio dei Marmi and other parts of the Forum is unclear. The government would like to privatise them, but proposals for a sale to American investors were rejected in 2000.

Two other architecturally interesting buildings of the same era are on the fringes of the compound, about 300 yards further along another segment of the Lungotevere (Lungotevere Maresciallo Cadorna) and just before the crossing with Via Morra di Lavriano. The one nearest to the river, built in 1933 by Del Debbio in the rationalist style as a guest-house for the Forum, is now a youth hostel. In front of it is the profoundly innovative Fencing House by Moretti (1936), sadly damaged and neglected since its conversion into a Carabinieri police station. On a side wall of the building is an impressive mosaic by Angelo Canevari.

Looking from these buildings up the slope of the Monte Mario hill one sees, on the right among trees, the outline of Villa Madama, begun by Raphael in 1518, two years before his death. His followers then only partially completed it, based on his plans. It beautifully exemplifies a suburban patrician renaissance villa, with paintings and stuccos by Raphael's pupils, Giulio Romano and Giovanni da Udine. Unfortunately. it is closed to the public and only used for official functions.

2. PORTA PIA, S. AGNESE AND S. COSTANZA, THE CATACOMBS OF S AGNESE AND S. PRISCILLA, PONTE NOMENTANO, VILLA ADA

Porta Pia is the name given in 1564 to an ancient gate of the Aurelian Walls (for this name change see p. 70), when Michelangelo rebuilt it a few months before his death.

The master designed the side facing Via XX Settembre (the other is 19th-century) in his usual grand and imposing style; but the elaborate ornamentation of this, his last work, points for the first time to the coming baroque. Note high up the curious bowl-and-stole motifs. They may refer to the plate on which the priests rest the Host during Mass, but they could also allude to the combined art of barber and surgeon, the original vocation of the family of the reigning Pope Pius IV Medici (p. 70). The shield with angels is by followers of Michelangelo.

Inside the gate is a **Museum of the Bersaglieri**, open Tuesdays and Thursdays, 09:00-13:00. The Bersaglieri were an elite unit of sharpshooters, who are also commemorated by a monument (1932) in the centre of the square. In 1870 they made a famous breach in the city walls to enter the city; if you are looking at the gate from its 19th-century side, it was about 200 ft (60 m) to the right and the site is now marked by a column.

At the gate begins Via Nomentana, an arm of the ancient consular road grid that passed through the ancient town of Mentana (it also gave its original name to the gate).

Note: bus lines descend Via Nomentana with stops near Villa Torlonia, St Agnes and the junction leading to the Nomentano Bridge.

Outside the gate, a third of a mile on the right, is **Villa Torlonia**. This vast neo-classical complex, built in the early 19th century for a rich banking family ennobled by the pope a century earlier) was the home of Mussolini in the 1930's, when he rented a wing from the old prince (both families lived on the property). After the war the villa became the English Overseas School in Rome. It was then given to the city of Rome to be turned into offices and a public park.

Though first conceived by Giuseppe Valadier, this complex was mostly realised in the early 19th century by the Piedmontese architect Giovan Battista Caretti, who also designed the main residence. Part of the compound is now open to the public. In the middle of the park is the residence, decorated and frescoed by the Purists, Italian artists who took their inspiration from the German Nazarene School (see glossary). The ballroom has friezes and stuccoes by Thorvaldsen and Canova. The separate bedrooms of Mussolini and his wife – the patient Donna Rachele, though not so patient that the dictator ever dared to bring his lover Claretta Petacci here (p. 633) – are on the upper floor, though the original furniture is gone.

There are other interesting buildings here, by minor Italian architects, dating from the mid 19th century to the 1920's. One is the Villino dei Principi ('Little Villa of the Princes'), another is the Casa delle Civette ('House of the Owls'), which houses a decorative arts museum (see p. 685) interesting mainly for its modern stained glass windows and for the collection of 1920's-1940's stained glass and other art of the time (including work by Cesare Picchiarini and the group of designers around him, in particular Duilio Cambellotti). The neo-classical theatre, preceded by a striking semi-circular colonnade, has frescoes by Costantino Brumidi, who went on to fresco the dome of the Capitol in Washington DC. The staff are enthusiastic and helpful. The park is in the Romantic style, with artificial ruins and exotic plants. Extensive 2nd and 3rd century Jewish catacombs were discovered under the grounds here in the early 20th century, but are usually closed (see p. 657). A 'Museum of the Holocaust' commemorating the war-time tragedy of Roman Jews (p. 525) is being planned for this area.

About two thirds of a mile further along on the left (at Via Nomentana Nos 349-353) are **S. Agnese fuori le Mura** ('outside the Walls') and **S. Costanza** ('St Constance'). This confusing complex can only be understood if one keeps the

607

Santa Agnese Santa Costanza monumental complex in the 16th century

historical relation between the parts in mind. It was created between 337 and 350 thanks to the interest and financial support of Princess Constantina, the daughter of Emperor Constantine (who legalised Christianity, see p. 198), near the spot where the supposed remains of St Agnes lay in the local catacombs. Agnes was a 13-year-old virgin said to have been martyred about 50 years earlier near the Stadium of Domitian (see p. 452). This burial-ground origin, as we have seen, is common to most churches founded in the time of Constantine; the greatest similarity here is with S. Lorenzo fuori le Mura (p. 633).

The complex comprises: 1) the catacombs; 2) next to them, the almost vanished 4th-century Constantinian basilica devoted to St Agnes, 3) the imperial mausoleum, built for Constantina along with and next to the early basilica (it was later turned into a church and called S. Costanza after a real or imaginary Christian martyr, probably a case of association with the name of Constantina); 4) a much smaller basilica dedicated to St Agnes, built near the catacombs 300 years later, in the 7th century, when the earlier basilica had to be abandoned; this 'new' basilica still operates and is today the fulcrum of the complex: like many such ancient churches, it has been below street level for centuries; 5) a large entrance building, built between the renaissance and the 19th century.

The fact that it is not possible to visit these various elements one at a time, or even in chronological order, increases the confusion.

From the corner near No. 353, first look at the lovely, small apse of the 7th-century basilica, next to a 15th-century bell tower with two levels of renaissance double windows. Notice how far underground the church stands. On the right is the entrance to the *matroneum*, a gallery to which women were restricted in the primitive church.

The complex is open: 09:00-12:00 and 16:00-18:00, except on the mornings of holy days and Monday afternoons. The main entrance is at No. 349, through the courtyard, which is surrounded by the church offices of the newest building.

One of the upper storey rooms on the right witnessed a frightening accident in the mid-19th century: the floor collapsed during a ceremonial visit by Pope Pius IX and his entourage. Everyone ended up on the ground floor, more or less unharmed. The pope declared this to be a miracle and confirmation that he was under the special protection of the Virgin Mary; and the incident led to his increased emphasis on the cult of Mary, culminating in his controversial proclamation of the Dogma of the Immaculate Conception (p. 60). A fresco representing the incident is behind the glass on the right (difficult, but not impossible to see through crevices at eye level). Other rooms off the courtyard, generally not open, have remains of renaissance frescoes.

Continue out from the courtyard. The 16th-century portal on the right bears the arms of Pope Julius II, patron of both Raphael and Michelangelo. A solemn late 16th-century marble staircase decorated with plaques, catacomb finds and medieval fragments leads, through a wide door, to the 7th-century basilica below, built by Pope Honorius I. It is a shining example of a Christian church influenced by the Byzantine style. This is evident in the narthex (the atrium separate from the rest of the church, where the unbaptised, called 'catecumens', and penitents had to stay), in the *matronea* (at the end of the upper left *matroneum* is the entrance you had seen from above and outside) and in the mosaic of the apse.

Dividing the interior are columns with beautiful Corinthian capitals, possibly from the earlier basilica. The columns of the *matronea* were made for this church. The ceiling is 17th-century with 19th-century restorations. The luminous 7th-century apsidial mosaic depicts St Agnes with flames and a sword at her feet, and in a gold medallion in her dress the phoenix or 'bird of resurrection'; all are symbols of her arduous martyrdom (p. 452). At her sides are two popes, one, Honorius I, bearing the model of his church. A 17th-century canopy or ciborium with porphyry columns stands over the main altar, which in turn rests over the presumed relics of St Agnes and St Emerentiana (her foster-sister, according to tradition). An exquisite statue of St Agnes on the altar is by the French sculptor Nicolas Cordier, nicknamed Il Francesino. He added head, hands and gilded dress to an ancient alabaster torso.

To visit the catacombs, wait by a door to the left of the narthex door for a custodian in charge to help you. The underground area extends for several miles on three levels that were dug mostly in the 3rd and 4th centuries (see the Glossary for catacombs in general).

On emerging, note the plain, mainly brick façade of St Agnes (heavily restored). Through a gate opposite the façade, and then left, the same custodian can show you the Mausoleum of Constantina (or you can go alone). From the courtyard before the mausoleum on the right the ruins of the original 4th-century basilica are visible: a gigantic structure similar to the basilica of S. Lorenzo, and four times larger than the later basilica of St Agnes you have just visited.

The **Mausoleum of Constantina** (S. Costanza) is an exceptional and well-preserved example of a circular Early Christian structure built on a central plan, deriving directly from ancient Roman models (the circular temple, nymphæum and mausoleum).

The building, in front of which is an outer narthex, is striking for its perfect structural rhythm. The interior is beautifully light-filled thanks to the dozen big windows under a huge dome (made of a mixture of a lightweight tufa stone and pumice). The domed centre rests on twelve pairs of splendid columns and capitals, all spolia from older buildings. The circular aisle is barrel-vaulted and the vaults bear stupendous 4th-century mosaics, the oldest of this type extant and a remarkable example of Roman art. Divided in compartments, they become increasingly complex as one advances from the entrance by going either way toward the niche in the rear, where the sarcophagus of the princess was. The design is based on traditional ancient Roman imagery, here reinterpreted according to Christian symbolism. Geometrical patterns are followed by grape harvest themes (vines with cupids crushing grapes, oxcarts, fruits, flowers and birds) and then by food for a banquet. The two symmetrical medallions in the middle of the harvest scenes probably portray Constantina (to the left facing away from the entrance) and her husband Hannibalian. The two little side-apses contain later mosaics, tentatively dated to the 5th or 6th centuries, beautifully framed by leaves and fruit. On the left the young Christ on a landscaped background, delivers the symbols of divine law to Peter and Paul (the *traditio legis*). The right-hand mosaic, heavily damaged, showed St Peter receiving the keys (the *traditio clavium*); the keys were replaced by a scroll in an early 19th-century restoration. The arms of the aisle converge on the niche on the back, which originally held the marvellous porphyry sarcophagus. This is a cast: the original was moved in the 16th century to the Vatican Museums (p. 326).

Back on Via Nomentana, you have three options.

A minor sight, the ruin of the brick mausoleum of an Imperial officer – a freedman of Emperor Hadrian, mid-2nd century – is not far. To see it, go back to Via Nomentana and proceed another 750 yards away from the centre. Take Via Cheren on the left and then Via Chisimaio. In Piazza Elio Callisto is the ruin of the brick tomb of Elius Callistus, which since the middle ages has been called the **Sedia del Diavolo** ('Devil's Chair').

The second option is to continue, after the St Agnes-St Constance visit, for about a mile on Via Nomentana away from the centre (or only half that if you have been to the 'Devil's Chair'). When you get near Via Trompia, Via Nomentana forks. The left part is 'new' Via Nomentana. Continue on the right part, which retraces the old Via

Tourists exploring the catacombs, c. 1830

Nomentana. Three hundred yards further on is the 1st or 2nd century AD **Nomentano Bridge** over the Aniene river, an affluent of the Tiber.

The beautiful interior of the central arch, in a dark stone edged with white travertine marble, is the oldest part. The upper part was redone and raised by the Byzantine general Narses in 552 as part of a plan to fortify Rome against invading Goths. On the keystone of the arch away from the city note, over a badly worn bull's head, the relief of a club, symbol of Hercules the protector of herds (pp. 259-260); reminders of a time when the bridge was mostly used by migrating herdsmen and their cattle. Further on, on the right, is a latrine, better visible from the outside, added when a permanent guard was installed here by order of Pope Nicholas V in the mid-15th century. Nicholas, who also restored and further fortified the bridge, had his initials 'N.P.V.' affixed over the arch facing the city; the populace maliciously interpreted these letters as meaning 'Nessun Papa Volemo' ('No Pope Wanted'). Here Pope Leo III had welcomed Charlemagne when he arrived in 800 AD to be crowned emperor (p. 303). With its picturesque towers and crenelations (added in the 19th century), this bridge has been the subject of countless paintings from the 17th century on.

The third option as you leave the St Agnes-St Constance complex is to walk toward the centre to go right on Via Nomentana to the first street on the right, Via S. Costanza. Take it and its continuations more or less straight for about 900 yards (1 km) to another ancient consular way, the Via Salaria. On Via Salaria are Villa Ada, the former residence of the Savoys (former kings of Italy), and the Catacombs of Priscilla.

With the usual reservations regarding the actual existence and names of public transport, from the area of St Agnes we suggest you take bus 168 at the beginning of Via S. Costanza, for just a few stops to Piazza Verbano. It is then a short walk on Via di Villa Ada to Via Salaria: turn right when you reach it. The entrance to the villa grounds, of moderate interest, is not far. **Villa Ada** was the private home of Victor Emmanuel III. It was here that, on 25

Veiled worshipper, from the Catacombs of Priscilla

July 1943, he ordered the arrest of Mussolini, whom the Grand Fascist Council had just deposed (p. 530). Now it is the residence of the Egyptian ambassador.

Continue along Via Salaria, keeping the grounds of Villa Ada to your left. Just past Piazza Priscilla, at No. 430 Via Salaria, are the **Catacombs of Priscilla**, among the oldest (mid-2nd century) and most important of all the catacombs (for catacombs in general, see Glossary). Of special interest are the primitive frescoes with biblical scenes, as well as the oldest representation of the Virgin in the catacombs. A nun will guide you expertly.

To return to the city centre you can catch a bus nearby. Get off the bus for a few minutes at the Via Tagliamento stop, just before Piazza Buenos Aires, to see the **Coppedè Quarter** between Via Tagliamento and Piazza Mincio. This small residential complex) was built between 1919 and 1923 by the Florentine architect Gino Coppedè in a fanciful, amusing variant of the *art nouveau* style, inspired by medieval motifs.

3. PORTA LATINA, PORTA
S. SEBASTIANO AND VIA APPIA,
VIA TUSCOLANA

Planning: this is a long excursion where you cannot rely entirely on public transport; and owing to traffic restrictions we don't recommend private cars. But one can divide the walk into segments; and buses do cover some stretches. Another possible solution is a newly established, special-fare bus line covering most of the route, called the 'Archeobus' (assuming it still exists; some of these city initiatives don't last). It leaves downtown Rome (Piazza San Marco, near Piazza Venezia) every hour on the hour from 09:00 to 17:00 and lets you get off at any stop along the way, visit nearby sites and then hop back on one of the following buses one hour later, with the same ticket.

One drawback of the Archeobus is that it skips a long segment of the Via Appia, from the tomb of Cecilia Metella to the Via Erode Attico crossing (pp. 619-620). On the other hand it does take you to Villa dei Quintili on Via Appia Nuova and, next to Via Appia Nuova, to spectacular ancient aqueducts which are otherwise hard to get to.

Other, ordinary buses go to different points of the route. No. 218 from Piazza San Giovanni in Laterano covers the first stretch. It can take you to Porta San Sebastiano (where the Via Appia begins); this area includes the nearby Porta Latina. Taking the same bus – either from its Piazza San Giovanni terminus in a separate excursion, or picking it up again at its first stop on the Via Appia – you can reach the area behind the Catacombs of St Calixtus, where the other terminus lies. You can then walk to the Catacombs of St Sebastian, the Circus of Maxentius and Cecilia Metella's Mausoleum, all relatively close by. From the Mausoleum you can return to the city with a bus No. 660 that stops at a nearby Via Appia crossing; this bus will take you to the Arco di Travertino metro station. The city centre is in the Anagnina direction.

More remote areas of the Via Appia can be reached by buses 765 and 664, both of which connect with the Arco di Travertino metro station.

The solitary, picturesque Via di Porta S. Sebastiano starts from Piazzale Numa Pompilio, which centres on a small mound of bricks – a nondescript 11th- or 12th-century ruin. This via is more or less a continuation of the avenue in front of the Baths of Caracalla; therefore, as we saw on p. 274, it is already part of the Via Appia as originally laid out in very ancient times. Just before the beginning of the road, on the left, rose two *mutationes*, 'service stations' for the cars and horses starting trips along the Via Appia. One (*Mutatio Cæsaris*) was for the imperial mail and other official vehicles; the other was for private vehicles. But none of that survives.

About 100 yards along Via di Porta San Sebastiano, on the right, is the little church of **S. Cesareo de Palatio**, whose unassuming early 17th-century façade masks structural elements dating back to the 8th century. These in turn stand over a 2nd century building, a fact that gave the church its name in the middle ages. Unfortunately the church is normally closed to the public.

The 17th-century interior has attractive marble furnishings made by recycling cosmatesque elements, probably of the 12th century. Under the altar, two angels in a 15th-century relief hold back a marble curtain giving light to a crypt. All around there are 17th-century frescoes, for the most part representing episodes from the *Life of St Cæsareus*. The most important are in the apse, by Cavaliere d'Arpino, an eclectic follower of Michelangelo whose rivalry with Caravaggio is famous. Steps left of the entrance lead down to the Roman 2nd century building, of which a great black-and-white mosaic floor with marine themes survives. It belonged almost certainly to a bath building, perhaps the Baths of Emperor Commodus, known to have been in the neighbourhood. The mosaic covers two large rooms, corresponding to the entire area of the church.

Next to the church, at No. 8, is the 15th-century **House of Cardinal Bessarion**, a pretty but much restored house where this prelate, a noted humanist, entertained the Roman intelligentsia of the early renaissance. It is not often open, but a frescoed loggia is visible from the gate. Ahead on the right, at No. 12, is the 16th-century **Villa Appia of the Sirens**, which is always closed but worth a look, even if only from the outside.

Across the street, at No. 9 is the fascinating **Sepulchre of the Scipios**. Alas, it is nearly always closed to the public because it is falling apart and no state or city authority seems interested in saving it. Arguably the most important of the monuments in the area, it is the burial place of a most ancient and celebrated family that gave Rome Scipio the African, who vanquished Hannibal, and Scipio the Emilian, who destroyed Carthage. Their particular graves have not been identified but those of various other family members have. This small necropolis, whose existence had always been known from ancient texts, came to light by chance in the 18th century, causing enormous excitement.

Most of the graves date from the 4th to 2nd centuries BC, which shows how exceptional they are; by comparison the Christian catacombs came four and five centuries later. A few of the tombs and plaques are copies, since the originals were removed to the Vatican Museums.

The plentiful inscriptions have great historical interest. Some, dedicated to adolescents, are touching: 'Beneath this stone lie the great knowledge and high virtue of one who had a short life. Do not ask what high offices he held, for he held none … He did not have time…'; 'You were a flamine priest and wore the cap [see p. 223, 281] but Death intervened and your glories were all too short'. According to ancient texts, the Scipios had welcomed in their sepulchre the body of Ennius, a great 3rd-2nd century BC poet, which hasn't been found. But a portrait carving discovered here and now in the Vatican Museums could be his.

From the sepulchre, or from an entrance next to No. 9, go into a public garden with another very interesting archæological find (also closed!), the **Columbarium** (a room with recesses for funerary urns) of Pomponius Hylas, a well-to-do 1st century Roman citizen.

S. Giovanni in Oleo, with the Porta Latina behind

The underground room, discovered in 1831, held the ashes of Pomponius and those of his family, servants and freedmen. It is reached via the original stairs; it contains elaborate architectural details and is decorated with stuccoes, mosaics and paintings.

Leave the public garden from the exit by the Columbarium into Via di Porta Latina. Immediately on the right is the tiny **Oratorio di S. Giovanni in Oleo** ('of St John in the Oil'), an octagonal temple built in the early 16th century by a French prelate to replace a very ancient chapel which in turn had been built on the spot where, according to one legend, St John the Evangelist – an uncertain figure historically, and not otherwise known to have been in Rome – emerged unharmed from being dipped in boiling oil. The architect is unknown, but the upper section with the beautiful frieze was added by Borromini a century and a half later.

Over the door is the coat of arms of the donor-prelate, Benedetto Adamo, with his motto (in French): 'At God's pleasure'. On the door-frame

613

itself there are the roughly scratched names of 18th-century tourists ('Antonio Tasso of Lucca, sol[dier], 1761', etc.) Inside, 17th-century frescoes illustrate the torture of St John.

An old wall shrine across the street with recently added statuette, belonging to a convent, is probably 17th century and was placed there by a certain Arcangelo Carpino with the inscription: 'O ye faithful passers-by, say an Our Father and a Hail Mary, for the souls who have left this world.'

Behind the Oratory is the **Porta Latina**, a gate in the 3rd century Aurelian Walls and one of the best preserved. Via Latina, directed to central and southern Italy, started from it. Pass through the gate to look at the outer façade, lined with travertine marble and framed by two cylindrical towers (the right one is medieval, built over an ancient tomb). From here, be sure to also admire the picturesque walls, left and right.

The five windows up at the walkway level were added around 400 AD. The keystone bears a monogram of Christ, with the Alfa and Omega letters. Under the arch are signs that the arch had wooden doors, and runners for a portcullis or sliding shutter, a usual feature of such gates. The keystone of the interior side has a Byzantine cross (compare it with the analogous keystones of Porta Pinciana, p. 86, and Porta San Sebastiano, p. 615).

Go back on Via di Porta Latina about 50 yards and take the street going right. At the end, on the right, is the delightful little medieval church of **S. Giovanni a Porta Latina**, a favourite wedding venue for Romans. (This St John is the one mentioned above, supposedly emerged unscathed from the boiling oil.) It was founded in the 5th century but the present church is 8th-century. The pretty romanesque bell-tower is 12th-century. The court before the church is shaded by a tall cedar of Lebanon. On the left is a very old (9th-century) well inscribed in Latin: 'Anyone thirsty, come drink. I, Stephen...' Stephen could be one of the medieval Fathers we know lived here, vowing total poverty and supporting the church with their own poor means. Centuries later, when this whole area was completely abandoned, the church

remained a refuge for hermits who kept it in repair with the donations of passers-by. (Open 07:00-12:00 and sometimes in the afternoon.)

The portico has ancient Roman marble fragments and bits of frescoes. The vari-coloured columns in both the portico and church are spolia from ancient temples. The frescoes of both nave and apse are 12th-century, with scenes from the Old and New Testaments and symbols of the evangelists. These frescoes are important in that they signal the abandonment of the prevailing Byzantine influence and, in reverting to more classical forms, prefigure the style about to mature in Rome, represented by the great Cavallini. The apse is partially paved with pre-cosmatesque coloured marbles, and the riser of the step separating it from the nave is decorated with elegant spirals.

Go back to the public garden and across it back to Via di Porta San Sebastiano, then go left. The Via ends with the so-called **Arch of Drusus**, actually an arch of the 3rd century 'Antonine'

Arch of Drusus

aqueduct built to supply the Baths of Caracalla (p. 276), subsequently embellished. The name derives from it having been confused in the middle ages with a triumphal arch to a Roman military hero, thought to have existed in this area. Other ruins of the aqueduct are nearby.

This is one of the most picturesque and famous ruins in Rome. In antiquity the arch was sheathed in marble and decorated with columns to match the Appian Gate (also called Porta San Sebastiano), which is behind it: together they formed a fortified courtyard, and for centuries an armed garrison stood guard here, the only inhabited spot in a deserted zone.

Behind the arch, at No. 18, is the Museum of the Walls (09:00-19:00, Sundays to 17:00.) Besides having interesting wall-related exhibits, the museum allows a visit to the interior spaces of the Gate. (The secretary of the Fascist Party, Ettore Muti, lived here in the 1940's, and some black and white mosaics inside date from then.) In addition, one can take a stroll on the walkway of the wall.

Porta San Sebastiano, to the right behind the arch, used to be called Porta Appia because the consular Via Appia passed through it (now the Via Appia starts just beyond the gate). Its present, medieval name came from the nearby catacombs dedicated to the famous martyr (pp. 295, 618). This is one of the Aurelian Walls' most imposing and best preserved gates, even though the late 3rd century structure was repeatedly remodelled during the next three centuries, when it was changed from two-arched to one-arched and the two towers were enlarged and raised.

A Byzantine cross was added on the internal keystone of the arch; with its Greek inscription invoking God, St Cono and St George, protectors of imperial Byzantine troops (p. 262), it gives thanks for the gate having withstood an invasion of barbarian Goths. The track for the portcullis is visible. Also note a rough incision in the stone of the Archangel Gabriel. This commemorates the victory of the local militia under Giacomo Ponziani of Trastevere (a member of St Francesca Romana's family, p. 595) in the 14th century over

the King of Naples, who wanted to impose a protectorate on other Italian regions.

The gate is best appreciated from the outside, with its powerful towers and the two covered galleries and crenelated walkway topping the arch.

(If you've just come through the gate (Viale di Porta Ardeatina) you may wish to walk the atmospheric length of walls to your right – a longish detour, but you can do just part of it. To do this, first cross the modern Via Cristoforo Colombo, before reaching the massive **Bastion of Sangallo** added to the walls in 1537 by Antonio Sangallo the Younger. From here the walls go on, up and then down for a beautiful stretch dotted with towers mostly restored in the renaissance, until they reach Porta S. Paolo, p. 623.)

The ancient **Via Appia** now starts past Porta S. Sebastiano, retracing the old road exactly. As already noted, it originally began further in (p. 274), at a gate in the Republican walls called Porta Capena. This was in 312 BC. The road was named after its builder, Appius Claudius, a celebrated figure of the patrician class, a developer responsible for other major public works including the first aqueduct, and also a well-known politician, jurist, grammarian and poet. Because this was the first of a great network of strategic roads radiating from Rome – originally with a military purpose – and because of the splendour of the funerary monuments that came to line it, from the outset it was dubbed *Regina Viarum*, Queen of Roads. (Burials were not allowed within the city limits. The tombs of the Scipios, which we have just seen within the Aurelian walls, go back to the time when that part of the road was outside the city walls.) The Via Appia never outwore the nickname: even as it fell into ruin, its beauty, solemnity, picturesqueness and significance endured.

Initially the road went only as far as Capua near Naples, an allied city in the first phase of the expansion of the Republic (p. 20). A century later it was extended to Brindisi, a major harbour town on the east coast of Italy. It thus became Rome's main link not only to the south, but to the entire Orient. Later (p. 620) we'll say more about the

Via Appia in the 1st century: a 19th-century reconstruction

technical aspects of this road, as of the others that came to be part of the empire-wide network of 'consular' roads.

The Via begins between two renaissance doorways. About 100 yards further, on the right, stands a copy of the first milestone (the original was taken during the renaissance to decorate the Capitol, p. 145). A few hundred feet ahead, under the railroad viaduct, on the right, recent digs have revealed what are probably remains of the **Temple of Mars** (p. 255), one of Rome's oldest. This is why this stretch was also called Clivus Martis. A traditional summer parade of the Roman cavalry started there. A bit further, the Via crosses a ditch, the Almone ditch, of great mythical importance – obscure today – for ancient Romans, whose priests of Cybele (p. 290) found it necessary to wash the statue of their goddess in it yearly.

On the right, at No. 42, is an official station for Via Appia visitors, with restrooms, a souvenir shop and, at least at present, moderately priced bicycle rentals. The bikes are very good and can be quite helpful, especially if you extend your visit to side trips such as the one starting on Via della Caffarella described on p. 617.

Past that, on the left at No. 41, but hard to see, is the ruin of a tomb which tradition assigns to Geta, Emperor Caracalla's brother and victim (p. 165). A small house was built over it in the 16th century. Further on, in No. 64 on the right is a round tomb over a square base.

A little further, at the fork in the road with Via Ardeatina, is a little church called **Domine Quo Vadis** ('Lord, where goest thou?'), medieval but rebuilt in the 17th century. The name comes from a question which, according to legend, a stunned St Peter, fleeing from Rome (p. 274) to escape martyrdom, put to an apparition of Jesus who faced him at this spot. The vision replied: 'Venio iterum crucifigi' ('I came to be crucified again'). The Apostle realised this was a reproach for his own cowardice, and went back to Rome and to his doom (p. 48). Open unpredictably.

Inside the church is a replica (the original is in the basilica of St Sebastian) of a stone with what are supposed to be Christ's footprints (a 17th-century inscription mentions 'His holy feet'). The original stone is indeed ancient Roman, but it is thought to be a very common form of *ex voto*, or pledge to the gods, that travellers used to make at the start of a journey. These footprints give the church its official name, S. Maria in Palmis ('St Mary of the Footprints').

Across the road, almost in front of the church but obscured by other buildings, is the ruin of a tomb identified as the **Mausoleum of Priscilla,** wife of a powerful former slave of Emperor Domitian (1st century AD). A contemporary writer, Statius, says the freedman Abscantus loved his wife passionately and had her body embalmed and put in a sumptuous marble coffin (never found). Statues representing Priscilla as several goddesses adorned the tomb. These were possibly set in the niches visible on the upper of two brick cylinders at the top of the mausoleum.

At the junction here is a first entrance to the catacombs of St Callixtus. But there is another further down the road, which will allow you to see additional sights on the way.

Some 150 yards ahead, on the left (Via della Caffarella) is a chapel shaped like a round little temple. It was built in 1539 by the English cardinal Reginald Pole, an opponent of England's break with the Roman Catholic Church, in gratitude for having survived an assassination attempt by agents of King Henry VIII. The king took revenge by executing Pole's mother and other relatives in England. Later, Pole was almost elected pope. When the Roman Catholic Mary Tudor became Queen of England, Pole became one of her closest advisers and was appointed Archbishop of Canterbury. He died only a few hours after his queen, and was buried in Canterbury Cathedral

near the shrine of St Thomas à Becket.

(A possible detour starts here. Less than a mile down Via della Caffarella, at the curve near No. 15, is the entrance to a park-like area, the valley of the Almone ditch, with interesting sights. (This entrance sometimes looks closed, but it isn't; also it has an accessway for bikes.) About a mile from the entrance, left of the main path, encased in a farmhouse, is a well-preserved temple-like building of the 2nd century AD, adorned with semi-columns and capitals. The building is in brick of two colours, yellow for structural elements and red for details; drawings by renaissance artists show it originally had a portico in front. It has been identified as the tomb of Annia Regilla, wife of a famous 2nd century orator and consul, or as a temple to the 'God of Return' (Deus Rediculus), who was worshipped before the start of a journey (this god 'of return' supposedly also persuaded the Carthaginian general Hannibal to stop ravaging Italy and go home to Africa, p. 256). Both identifications are unlikely. Another mile further, on the main path is the Grotto of the Nymph Egeria, a 2nd century AD fountain-like structure, or nymphæum, near a mineral water spring. This is the spot where, according to legend, the wise nymph Egeria used to meet the king Numa Pompilius (successor to Romulus) to give him advice. Where the valley meets the modern highway (Via Appia Nuova) is another temple-like building, an unidentified 2nd-century AD tomb misnamed 'Constantine's Columbarium'.)

Continuing along the Via Appia, about 300 yards after the Cardinal Pole chapel is the ruin of a large tomb topped with trees. Shortly after that, in a restaurant at No. 87, are the ruins of a large columbarium (originally three large rooms with hundreds of recesses for funerary urns) that Augustus built for the ashes of his freedmen.

Near No. 103 was the second milestone. No. 103-105 is Villa Casale, with a 4th-century AD underground tomb (Vibia's Hypogeum) with frescoes and small catacombs. The villa is privately owned and is not opened.

About 200 yards further on, at Nos. 102 and

110 are the pedestrian and vehicular entrances to the **Catacombs of St Calixtus**, the largest in Rome. They extend on four labyrinthine levels and are partly unexplored. (Guided visits 08:30-12:00 and 14:30-17:00, closed Wednesdays. For catacombs in general, see Glossary.)

These catacombs date from the 3rd and 4th centuries AD and are the most important from the standpoint of Church history. For at least two centuries this was the 'official' cemetery of the popes, then simply called bishops of Rome, many of whom were martyrs. The tomb from which the putative body of St Cecilia was taken in the 800's (p. 589) is here, plus important frescoes and an inscription dated 298 AD that for the first time, as far as we know, calls the Rome's bishop the 'pope.' The guided tour gives a good description.

Near the catacombs' entrance are two small basilica churches of 220 AD, called Cellæ Trichoræ because they each have three small apses. One has been turned into a display room, with relics from the catacombs.

Back on Via Appia, 300 yards further on, and left at the intersection of Via Appia Pignatelli (No. 119), there are extensive Jewish catacombs discovered in 1859. They are presently accessible only by special permit.

Jewish catacombs, the oldest in Rome, were the models for Christian ones. They are structurally and decoratively similar, except for the different religious symbols and the lack of human figures in the Jewish ones, as mandated by Jewish tradition.

Continue 300 yards further to the church and **catacombs of St Sebastian** on the right. Best to start your visit with the latter, as the church comes at the end of the tour. (Guided visits 09:00-12:00 and 14:30-17:00, closed Thursdays.) These catacombs have been accessible through the centuries and are therefore severely defaced; also they have suffered misguided restorations and additions in modern times. Still, they remain fascinating for their paintings, stuccos and inscriptions.

There are four levels but only the second, developed between the 1st and 5th century AD, is usually visited. Three large burial sites are of key importance. Individual guides may take different routes but generally everyone ends up in a place that in ancient times was supposedly used for funerary banquets. This room was shortened when the church was created. From there one goes to the basilica sacristy.

The **Basilica di S. Sebastiano** was built in the 4th century under Emperor Constantine to celebrate a tradition according to which St Peter and St Paul were temporarily buried in the catacombs below. (The original name of the church was the Basilica of the Apostles.) By the middle ages a new tradition emerged, that the catacombs also held the body of St Sebastian, a Christian Imperial guard officer born in Gaul of a northern Italian family, and martyred by Emperor Diocletian (end of the 3rd century) to quell Christianity in the military (see p. 285). Thus the church got its present name. It was rebuilt in the 13th century, when the arches of the aisles were walled up, and in the 17th century, when a new porticoed façade, with granite columns from the old basilica, was designed by Flaminio Ponzio and Giovanni Vasanzio.

The stern interior has a beautiful Vasanzio ceiling with a colourful figure of St Sebastian. The chapel of relics – first on the right – contains an arrow said to be from the saint's martyrdom, and a marble slab with footprints Christ left in the 'Quo Vadis' episode (p. 617). The next chapel, large and apsed, was made in 1706 for a noble family by Carlo Maratta, Alessandro Specchi and Carlo Fontana. On the other side, the last chapel before you leave is over the crypt where St Sebastian's body was supposedly found. The beautiful recumbent *St Sebastian* is the masterpiece of the 17th-century Roman sculptor Antonio Giorgetti.

On the Via Appia again, walk up another few hundred yards to a crossing with Via San Sebastiano. On the left are imposing remains of a suburban residence of Emperor Maxentius (early 4th century AD), mortal enemy of his co-emperor and future nemesis Constantine (p. 198). It included a villa, now almost gone, a sports complex and the temple-like **Tomb of Romulus**, which Maxentius built for his son Romulus, who drowned in his teens in the Tiber. The site is sporadically open (mostly on Sundays), but the tomb is visible from the road in front of the intersection.

Partly embedded in a farmhouse, this sepulchral temple – the young prince had been pronounced a divinity at his death – was in a great porticoed square, of which three tall walls remain. The interior, inspired by the Pantheon, comprised a high podium and an upper floor, and was lit from a great oculus in the dome. The tomb proper was in the podium, in a round space still visible from the outside through the little windows. An image of this structure on a coin was long thought to depict a temple in the Roman Forum, with confusing consequences (p. 286).

From a bit further on, at No. 149, you can see what remains of the **Circus of Maxentius**, built for chariot racing and also dedicated by the emperor to his dead boy.

Almost as big as the Circus Maximus (513 x 90 metres) and better preserved, it followed the same plan: a central 'spine' and conical columns (*metæ*) at both ends of the circuit along which chariots raced. These emerged from boxes, *carceres*, located between two tall towers (the right one survives almost complete). The short rounded end still has the archway for the chariots' exit.

One of the decorations of the spine was an obelisk which Maxentius took from Domitian's Stadium or the nearby sanctuary of Isis (p. 114). Bernini subsequently took it to adorn his Piazza Navona fountain (p. 458), thus returning it to its original area.

At the Via Appia's second mile (or third kilometre) is the **Tomb of Cecilia Metella** (mid 1st century BC), one of the most famous monuments in Rome, featured in countless paintings, old prints and photographs for the evocative picture it composes with the ancient road. This great marble-covered cylindrical mausoleum (with a diameter of about 100 ft/30 m) contained, as stated on the tablet, the remains of Cecilia, a woman of a very old and famous plebeian family, the Cecilii. She was daughter of a consul and general of the late Republic who had conquered Crete, and wife of Crassus, son of the Triumvir of the same name and a general in Caesar's conquest of Gaul (France). In the middle ages the monument was raised and crenellated, to add it as a bastion to the fortified complex that continues across the street.

The beautiful frieze high up is adorned with Gallic shields, a reminder of the deeds of Crassus, and ox heads (which is why this neighbourhood has been named Capodibove – 'oxhead' – throughout the centuries). The monument is usually open until sunset and the sepulchral cell may be visited.

Tomb of Cecilia Metella, in a typically picturesque 19th-century print

Rooms adjacent to the mausoleum, which were part of the nearby fortifications, contain marble fragments and inscriptions from other tombs.

The castle near the mausoleum is 11th-century. It was restored and reinforced in the 14th century by the Caetani family (p. 248), then joined to the mausoleum to create a single fortified complex. Only a few ruins remain of the walls of the castle, with mullioned windows and towers. A gothic church – a style unusual in Rome – across the street, now abandoned and roofless, belonged to the same complex.

The tomb of Cecilia Metella marks the end of the better known part of the Via Appia. But an alluring stretch lies ahead, the road continuing in solitary splendour for another eight miles (13 km) or so, shaded by pine and cypress trees and punctuated by a series of tombs. Short sections of the original pavement appear.

This final stretch is also the one that best suggests the appearance and characteristics of these Roman consular roads, which at the height of the Empire covered most of Europe and more. They were wide enough for two large carts side by side, and were flanked on both sides by wide unpaved footpaths. The roadbed had four layers of different materials, each 1-2 ft (30-60 cm) deep. The top layer consisted of large silica or basaltic polygonal stones (*basoli*) so close-fitting, that the surface stayed flat and without potholes even in heavy traffic and in sections which are now disconnected and bumpy. The roads were marked by milestones and at regular intervals of ten or twenty miles there were service stations (*mutationes*) for resting or changing the horses. At intervals of one day's travel there were motel-like structures, mostly with baths, for resting or overnight stays.

The first major monument in this stretch is about two-thirds of a mile (about 1 km) away on the left (on the right is the end of the fence of a modern military complex). It is the tomb of one Marcus Servilius, adorned with marble fragments, discovered in 1808 by Antonio Canova. As the tablet says, the great sculptor left the fragments on site, feeling they should remain in place, and not sold or dispersed as was the custom at the time. The result is that many have been stolen, according to the custom of our time.

On the same side, 400 yards further on, is a 2nd century AD brick structure, perhaps a fountain or nymphæum, traditionally called the '**Temple of Jove**' (some scholars do not rule out the possibility that it may have been just that). Another 2000 ft (about 600 m) further on, opposite No. 223, is a 2nd century AD brick mausoleum in the shape of a small square temple on a high base, in good condition, with little windows and an elaborate rear facade. Just past this is the **Tomb of the Rabirii**, a 1st century AD family. (The three portraits – the freedman of a well-known banker, his wife and a priestess of Isis among the symbols of her cult – are copies.)

Next comes the intersection with Via Tor Carbone (right) and Via Erode Attico (left).

(Planning: A striking archæological site of the Via Appia in its next stretch is the Villa of the Quintilii , about ²/₃ of a mile – 1 km – from here. The problem is that the entrance to the site is not on the Via Appia but on the fairly distant Via Appia Nuova, which runs parallel'to it. An entrance to the Via Appia is being considered, but check with the Soprintendenza Archeologica, p. 657. If your main purpose is an extensive visit to this site, rather than just the glimpse you can get from the Via Appia – see below – you should detour here at the crossing with Via Erode Attico, down which the No. 765 bus can be caught as it goes left. At the terminus near the Metro station catch No. 664, which after a few stops will drop you right to the front of the entrance, Via Appia Nuova 1092. All this could take anywhere from 20 minutes to an hour.

The 'Archeobus' mentioned in the note on p. 612 has a stop at the Villa Quintilii entrance. It is also the only public transport to the aqueducts mentioned below.

Via Erode Attico and its continuations connect the ancient Via Appia with the 'modern' Via Appia Nuova, which since the 16th century, when the Via Appia was definitively abandoned, replaced it for most of its southern course. Beyond the Via Appia Nuova one can see in the distance the spectacular run of some of the old Roman aqueducts.)

A few hundred feet past the crossing with Via Erode Attico, the Via Appia, which was perfectly straight up to here, bends slightly to the left. This was most probably done to avoid a zone considered sacred: this was where the Romans thought that, at the birth of their city, the border with Alba Longa ran. Alba Longa (near the modern Castelgandolfo), was, they thought, the city of Rea Silvia and of their other ancestors (p. 153). Right of the road are mounds related to this aura of sacredness. The first is traditionally called the **Tomb of the Curiatii**. It was said to hold the remains of three brothers from Alba Longa, the Curiatii, killed in a famous duel with three Roman brothers, the Horatii, ending a decisive war between the two cities. (The ruins on top belong to a sanctuary built much later, possibly under Emperor Augustus, who attached political importance to highlighting the heroic past of Rome.)

The Roman historian Livy, another idealizer of the Roman past, in describing the episode, speaks of Roman triplets picked to duel with triplets from Alba Longa, both sides having agreed to abide by the result to end the war. The Curiatii killed two of the Horatii, but the third, with a trick, killed all the Curiatii.

Another 200 yards further on, a giant pyramid-shaped tomb on the left stands solid, though most of the base is gone. Just 50 yards further on and to the right are two more mounds, said to be the Tombs of the Horatii – an identification based, again, more on legend than on history.

Slightly further along, on hilly ground to the left, are the scattered ruins of the **Villa of the Quintilii**. This compound – the largest villa of the ancient Roman suburbia – was the ancestral residence of a very rich patrician clan, the Quintilii, whose roots dated back several centuries to the city of Alba Longa. In the 2nd century AD, the tyrant Emperor Commodus executed the only survivors of the family, two brothers, under the accusation of conspiracy – in fact, just to confiscate this property. The somewhat ghostly ruins emanate a sense of grandiosity and of a mysterious past, which over the centuries contributed to giving these meadows the odd local name of 'Roma Vecchia' ('Old Rome').

From the Via Appia enclosure one sees a large curved annexe, possibly a nymphæum, near the road and other monumental ruins at various distances. Entering from the Via Appia Nuova (see note above) one can also visit these other large ruins: the villa proper (on the left), a theatre-like building, baths and a cistern. A small museum exhibits a few of the countless statues and other artworks found in the villa during excavations that were begun in the 18th century. Most of these finds, though, are in larger museums in Rome (Museo Nazionale Romano), in the Vatican and abroad (the Louvre in Paris, the Hermitage in St Petersburg.)

Near the sixth Roman mile, at No. 291 and just before an intersection is, on the left, the biggest ruin of a tomb on the whole Via Appia, the **Casal Rotondo** ('Round Farmhouse').

The tomb dates from the Augustan era (1st century) and has been restored many times. The massive cylinder on a square base (measuring 115 ft/35 m per side) contained the remains of important people, but exactly who is unknown. For many centuries it has been used as the base for a farmhouse, with garden and truck patch, presenting a picturesque, fairy-tale scene that has inspired artists down the ages. Before it is a wall built by a 19th-century archæologist to display the marble fragments of the decoration of the tomb. Notice the theatrical masks.

Past the crossing with Via di Casal Rotondo and Via Torricola, on the left over the remains of another big Roman tomb, is a 12th-century tower called the **Tor in Selce** ('Flint Tower'). With its alternating black and white bands, it resembles other fortified structures of the period, such as the Tor de' Conti (p. 192), only here many of the white fragments come from the decorative marble scattered in the area.

Anonymous, ill-preserved tombs succeed one another on boths sides of the road, which then crosses the modern ring road around Rome (Grande Raccordo Anulare). About $1^1/_4$ miles (2 km) past this on the left, is a large cylindrical, domed mausoleum dating from late imperial times, called the **Berretta del Prete** ('Priest's Cap') owing to its shape. Its plan recalls closely that of the Mausoleum of Constantina (p. 609), of the same era. In the middle ages a little church dedicated to **Maria Madre di Dio** ('Mary Mother of God') was installed within. Another two thirds of a mile (1 km) further ahead on the right, is the ruin of a two-level cylindrical structure of the 3rd century AD, which most scholars believe to be the Mausoleum of Emperor Gallienus (p. 102), one of whose villas was near here (traces have been found). At this point we are not far from Ciampino, Rome's secondary airport, and the ancient Via Appia shortly connects with the Via Appia Nuova.

From the crossing at Casal Rotondo (see above) you can reach one of the most interesting parts of the nearby Via Tuscolana, a very ancient road that started at the Asinaria Gate (p. 402).

Walk downhill along Via Casal Rotondo to Via Appia Nuova, where you can take bus No. 654. The bus reaches Via Tuscolana near the Cinecittà metro stop. (The A line serves the whole urban stretch of this road, so you can also come here directly from the centre of town.)

Cinecittà has been the the hub of the Italian movie industry since 1937, when a film studio complex next to the metro stop was built. Designed by Enrico Peressutti, the complex used to be the largest in Europe. Its history is closely linked to that of the great Italian director Federico Fellini, who celebrated it in his film *Intervista* of 1987. The complex, whose simple lines rise amid greenery, can be visited only with credentials, but it is visible from the entrance.

As well as the studios, the complex contains two other historic buildings. One is the Centre for Experimental Theatre, a little further on (towards central Rome) and across the street; this is a school that has produced many famous Italian filmmakers. The other, a hundred yards past the school and on the same side of Cinecittà, is the LUCE National Institute, a vast, yellow semicircular mass looming amid trees, where propaganda newsreels were produced during the Fascist period.

In front of the Experimental Theatre centre is the monumental commercial complex of **Cinecittà 2**, completed in 1992. It has two parts. The front is a shopping mall, made of pre-fabricated, painted aluminium and glass modules, and designed by Nicola Di Cagno and others. The other part is a group of marble and glass office buildings by the architect Carlo Costantini. The whole complex rises on the field where the chariots raced in the 1950's remake of *Ben Hur*. Usually there are huge papier-mâché props used by nearby studios peeping out at its sides.

Next you can visit an interesting archæological site, the **Parco degli Acquedotti** ('Park of Aqueducts'). Go towards downtown Rome for about two thirds of a mile (1 km) – you can take the metro to the Lucio Sesto station – then take Via Valerio Publicola on your left for about a third of a mile (500 m). Amidst the greenery rise the Aqueduct of the Acqua Felice ('Happy Water') – a Roman structure restored in the late 16th century (see pp. 70, 77) – and the Claudian Aqueduct (p. 632). The ruins of a 2nd-century BC Roman house, the so-called Villa delle Vignacce ('of Old Vines'), are also visible.

Also worth seeing is the beautiful Porta Furba ('Furba Gate') which Pope Sixtus V had built into an archway of his Acqua Felice aqueduct ('furba' is a corruption of the word 'forma', the arch of an aqueduct). To reach the gate from the Park of Aqueducts, take the metro for two stops from the Lucio Sestio station toward the centre, then go a third of a mile (500 m) uphill along Via Tuscolana. Next to the gate also note the elegant, 18th-century Fountain of Furba Gate. (To return to central Rome from here, walk back downhill and take the metro from the Porta Furba station.)

4. FROM PORTA S. PAOLO TO EUR

The starting point of this excursion, Porta S. Paolo, is easily reached by public transport, including the subway (S. Paolo station on the B Line).

Porta S. Paolo ('St Paul's Gate') is the ancient Porta Ostiensis, so called because the road passing under it led to the port town of Ostia. It is one of the most beautiful and best preserved gates in the wall.

The side facing the city has its original 3rd century façade, built together with the Aurelian Walls. (In the middle ages a wall shrine honouring St Peter was added.) The powerful outer side was rebuilt and raised in the 5th century, when the two round towers were also added (as with Porta S. Sebastiano, p. 615). Seen from a distance from outside, along with the nearby pyramid (see below) and the turreted old walls on the right, this is a classic picture-postcard view of Rome. The barbarian Goths entered Rome from here in the late 6th century.

Inside the gate is the small **Museum of the Via Ostiensis**, entered from Via Persichetti. (Open: Tuesday to Sunday 09:00-13:30, also Tuesday and Thursday 14:30-16:30; closed Monday.)

To the left of the gate (if you are outside the walls) is a monument dating from the early days of the Empire, the **Pyramid of Caius Cestius Epulo**. It is a tomb built to mimic an Egyptian one, for a high official (prætor and tribune) in the reign of Augustus.

It dates from before 12 BC, though exactly when is unknown. It is the only remaining one, and the grandest (120ft / 36m high) of a few like it in ancient Rome. The word 'Epulo' is not part of the name of the deceased, but means that besides his important duties, he was one of the seven men in charge of organising the grand state banquets (*epulæ*). An inscription, down where a 1663 restoration is also mentioned, says the heirs to Cestius built the pyramid in 330 days. The tomb looked more imposing when it was built, as the raised street level makes it seem smaller. But if you turn into Via Persichetti right of the pyramid, you can see the original level and also the two small columns framing the entrance to the sepulchre.

Near the walls, a plaque commemorates the heroic but vain resistance of a few hundred Italian soldiers and civilians who died opposing the entry of German troops in Rome on 10 September 1943.

Turning behind the pyramid into Via Caio Cestio, No. 6 is the entrance to the **Protestant Cemetery** (this or English Cemetery have been the everyday names of the cemetery since it was established in the early 18th century, though its official name is Non-Catholic Cemetery). It is renowned for its serene beauty, pine and cypress trees, and its view of the pyramid. Keats' grave is visible from the outside, through the last slit in the encircling wall in Via C. Cestio, to the left of the entrance. (Closed Wednesday. Open: 08:20-11:30 and 15:20-17:30 March-September, 14:20-16:30 October-February.)

People of all faiths or none, and Catholics who opted to be buried with their non-Catholic relatives are buried here. Where non-Catholics were interred before this cemetery was created is unknown; at least some were probably buried in unconsecrated soil by the Muro Malo ('Evil Wall') at the foot of the Pincio (p. 43), along with prostitutes and suicides. Until the mid-19th century, daytime funeral processions were banned for Protestants in Rome, though this was in part to protect the cortege from assault by religious fanatics. (For other restrictions on Protestantism in Rome see St Paul's within the Walls, p. 81.)

'The most beautiful thing in Italy, almost,' wrote the novelist Henry James around 1900 about this place, 'seemed to me … the exquisite summer luxuriance of that spot... below the great grey wall, the cypresses and the time-silvered Pyramid. It is tremendously, inexhaustibly touching – its effect never fails to overwhelm.'

The entrance is at a section called the 'New Cemetery' laid out against the Aurelian Walls. Skirting the walls to the left on the higher path, near the next-to-the-last tower, is the grave of August von Goethe, the German poet's illegitimate son, who died before his father in 1830. (Goethe himself visited the cemetery in 1786 and thought of being buried here, as he wrote in these lines: 'Oh, if only the god Hermes could lead me one day here, near the Cestius pyramid, gently down to Hades…') Nearby is the grave of the German writer Malvida von Meysenburg, a friend of Wagner, Herzen, Nietzsche and Mazzini, who died in 1903.

Next to the last tower a stone covers the ashes of the English Romantic poet Percy Bysshe Shelley (p. 56), who drowned at the age of 30, while sailing off the coast north-west of Rome in 1822. His friend Lord Byron had the body cremated in his presence on the beach. The simple tombstone here is engraved with the Latin words *cor cordium* ('heart of all hearts') and three lines from Ariel's song in Shakespeare's *The Tempest*: 'Nothing of him that doth fade/But doth suffer a sea-change/Into something rich and strange'. Shelley had visited the cemetery shortly before his death, and written: 'It might make one in love with death, to be buried in so sweet a place.' This, incidentally, reinforces the suspicion, never seriously entertained in England but for which there is some evidence, that his drowning was suicide.

A few steps further on, to the left, is the grave of the American sculptor, poet and jurist William Wetmore Story (pp. 83, 540), buried under his own sculpture (and his only famous one), the *Angel of Grief*.

At the end of this section one passes into the 'old cemetery', the first patch of land the papal government donated for this purpose. Here, near the farthest left-hand corner, shaded by pine trees, lies that other supreme exponent of English Romanticism, John Keats, who died of tuberculosis in Rome at the age of 25 in 1821 (see pp. 55-57). In accordance with his wishes, a simple, unnamed tombstone bears the words: 'Here lies one whose name was writ in water'. Nearby lies the friend who assisted Keats during his agony, the English painter Joseph Severn, who himself died in Rome 54 years later.

Near the centre of the 'old cemetery' is the grave of the American architect William Rutherford Mead, part of the famous McKim Mead White partnership. Their work was heavily influenced by the renaissance and by classical Rome (New York's Penn Station, based on the Baths of Caracalla and crazily demolished in the 1960's, was one example). Mead in retirement became director of the American Academy in Rome, where he died in 1928.

Between the cemetery and the nearby Tiber is a coastal plain. Its flatness, and the presence of the river made this an important commercial area in ancient Rome. You may recall that the first river harbour and related storage buildings in Rome were behind the Fora, that is, right behind the markets they served (pp. 256-257). Even by Republican times, however, these facilities proved insufficient, nor could they be enlarged, as there were hills in the way on both sides. Thus, at the end of the 2nd century BC, the plain before us started turning into a shipping complex with increasingly large docks and buildings, called the Emporium. By imperial times so many goods were entering from around the world that the terracotta jugs (*amphorae*) carrying many of the foodstuffs became a problem. They were crushed on arrival, but the shards eventually piled up to form a real hill, the **Mons Testaceus** ('Mount of Shards'), which still exists and gives the entire neighbourhood its age-old name: Monte Testaccio. To see this famous artificial hill, walk along Via Caio Cestio away from the pyramid to Via Zabaglia. The 120ft /36m high hill is before you.

Via di Monte Testaccio circles it. Follow it round to the left, to see the hill from all sides. In various spots the shards peep out from between the soil and the grass. A road runs over it, probably the original one taken by carts going to the top with their loads of shards. It is closed now to prevent 'Sunday archaeologists' from doing more damage than they already have. The top-layer amphorae are mainly 2nd-3rd century AD and come from Spain and Africa. They bear the names of the factories of provenance on the handles, while painted on the jugs are the names of the

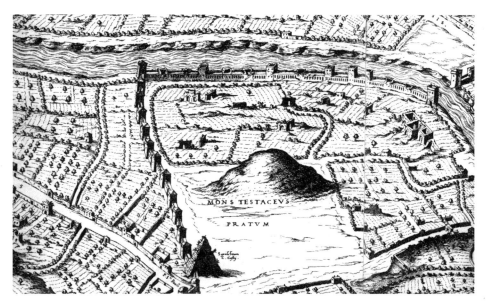

Monte Testaccio and surrounding area in the 16th century

ruling consuls (a sort of 'consular date'), the name of the exporter and marks of control at point of departure and arrival. The mound, practically unexplored, may contain much precious information on ancient Roman economic history.

In the middle ages the commercial buildings of the Emporium fell into disrepair. The area became a venue for religious processions (the cross was put on the hill then). Later, it became a place for sports and races. The popes nicknamed it 'the fields of the Roman people'; it was an extremely popular spot until recently for hiking, saltarello and tarantella dancing, flirting and picnicking with wine cooled in the many grottoes hereabouts. These idyllic scenes were the subject of many a painting and print until the late 19th century.

To reach our next destination, S. Paolo fuori le Mura, you must go back to Porta S. Paolo and take the metro at the Piramide station on Piazzale Ostiense. Go two stops (to the S. Paolo station) in the Laurentina direction.

Approach the church of **S. Paolo fuori le Mura**

('St Paul's outside the Walls'), dedicated in 324 to the converted Jew from the East who brought Christianity to Rome, and hence the world, earning the title 'Apostle to the Nations'. This is the second largest Christian basilica in Rome after St Peter's. Like St Peter's, it was built by the emperor Constantine, and like St Peter's and other Constantinian churches, it was built over an ancient chapel above the tomb of the saint. At the turn of the same century, the church was enlarged and splendid decorations added under emperors Theodosius and Honorius. Sadly, an 1823 fire partly destroyed this very rich basilica; what we see now is a sterile 19th-century reconstruction. For a long period during the middle ages, the church had been converted, along with neighbouring buildings, into a fortress called Johannipolis ('John's Citadel') for its creator, Pope John I. In those years St Paul's, like other *disabitato* churches (pp. 402, 635–636), served to defend the city against barbarian and Muslim raids. No trace remains of these activities, however.

The church has several entrances. Our description starts from the main entrance, so go around to the front if you arrived by public transport.

The façade, which retraces the original design of the church, has 19th-century mosaics replacing those by the great Pietro Cavallini destroyed in the fire; a few over-restored fragments are inside. (Open: 07:00-19:00.)

In front of the church is a square 19th-century portico. In the middle is a statue of St Paul by Pietro Canonica. Of all this modern stuff the most notable piece is the bronze door in the middle, by Antonio Maraini, with vigorous reliefs of episodes from the lives of Sts Paul and Peter, with an art deco cross with silver inlays as its centrepiece.

The interior was rebuilt on the original plan. The five naves evoke the majesty – if not the mystical aura – of the great early Christian churches. Over the shining columns of the central nave runs a series of 19th-century frescoes; these only make one weep for the 14th-century ones by Pietro Cavallini, which could at least have been partly saved, the entire right wall having survived the fire. In an age when people knew better, however, they

S. Paolo fuori le mura

were destroyed by the very restorers. Even the great mosaic on this side of the triumphal arch, an almost total 19th-century reconstruction of the 4th-century work (as modified and redrawn in the 9th century) leaves one cold. (On the arch are the inscriptions extolling emperors Theodosius and Honorius; the sister of the latter, Galla Placidia, who ordered and financed the original decorations; and the pope who some decades later effected the first of many restorations, St Leo the Great.)

The most impressive things in this section are the original bronze doors. Removed from their original position at the main entrance, they are now inside the side door, or holy door (if you are in the church, on the left). They were commissioned by the church's abbot, bishop Hildebrand, later Pope Gregory VII (p. 303), financed by a consul Panthaleon from Amalfi (near Naples) and cast in 1070 in Constantinople by the Byzantine master Staurachios of Scio. The three names are in the lower part on the right side. The doors represent, in lively but now hard-to-discern vignettes, episodes from the lives and martyrdoms of Christian prophets, evangelists and apostles.

On reaching the transept, which mostly survived the fire, one gets a sense of the original appearance. Dominating the apse is a huge mosaic made around 1220 by Venetian artists called to Rome by the reigning pope Honorius III as a copy of the original mosaic, which was disintegrating after 700 years. Despite 19th-century restoration – in the upper area and the larger figures – this is an impressive work, thanks to the celebrated colouristic skills of the Venetians and also to the minute detail. Note the tiny figure of Pope Honorius III (of the powerful Savelli family, p. 270) who commissioned the mosaic: he crouches by the knotty right foot of Christ, who is blessing 'Greek-style'. In the band below, apostles and saints flank a jewelled cross. Note the microscopic Redeemer in its centre, and the symbols of His Passion at His sides. Unfortunately now invisible, because covered by marble furnishings, is the area below the cross, with a group of 'holy innocents' flanked by monk Adinulph and the basilica's abbot Giovanni, of the Orsini family (p. 253; later Pope Nicholas III). Outside the arch of the apse are the heavily restored fragments of the Pietro Cavallini mosaics originally on the façade. There are some more fragments on the inside of the triumphal arch, across from the apsidal mosaic.

In the middle of the transept the canopy, or ciborium, in the svelte Tuscan Gothic style, is the oldest work in Rome by the Sienese sculptor Arnolfo di Cambio (1285), possibly in collaboration with Cavallini ('Hoc opus ...' – 'this work is by Arnolfo with his partner Petro', it says under the base of the spires, but Petro could also have been a great Cosmatesque marble-worker known to be active at this time). The work is remarkable for its monumentality, imaginativeness of decoration and beauty of sculptural detail. Don't miss, in the corner niches, the powerful St Paul with his Sword, and the fresh realism of the figure of the abbot of the time, Bartholomew, book in hand.

Under the ciborium is the altar. Beneath this is the 4th-century tomb of the Apostle, which is preceded by a crypt. The original inscription on the sarcophagus reads *Paul, Apostle Martyr*.

To the left of the altar (if you are looking at the front of the church) near the transept wall is another precious object, the Easter Candelabrum, a tiered marble shaft signed in 1170 by Nicola d'Angelo and Pietro Vassalletto. At its base are figures of women strangling human-faced monsters, a motif taken from Early Christian reliefs. In the centre of the shaft is Christ rising to Heaven; elsewhere crude yet effectively rendered episodes from the Passion.

Just left of the apse is the Chapel of the Sacrament by Carlo Maderno (1623). It survived the fire and Cavallini is buried here. Tradition says that when the great artist was old and almost blind, he concentrated on wood carving, and made the beautiful crucifix in this chapel. Even if that is uncertain, the work is highly expressive and first rate; it influenced the design of similar objects throughout the 14th century. To the left is the 13th-century mosaic of the *Madonna* before which S. Ignazio da Loyola (p. 112) took his priestly vows.

S. Paolo fuori le mura, detail of crucifix attributed to Cavallini

Tradition also holds that St Bridget of Sweden (p. 480) used to pray before this crucifix; her statue at prayer by Stefano Maderno (the early 17th-century sculptor famous for his statue of St Cecilia, p. 589) is in a niche. To the right of the Crucifix is a damaged, much venerated 14th-15th century wooden statue of St Paul that survived the fire.

From this end of the transept you may exit through a side door briefly to see a portico restored with the columns of the old basilica. Words on the first column on the right of the inside row mention 'Siricius episcopus', the Pope Siricius who in 390 consecrated the basilica after its first reconstruction.

Go back in. At both ends of the transept note the altars veneered with precious malachite and lapis lazuli, a post-fire donation from the Tsar. From one arm of the transept enter the souvenir shop where there are 13th-century frescoes, unfortunately very worn and repainted. Access to the beautiful early 13th-century cloister is through here. Built by cosmatesque marble-workers, it holds its own with the cloister of St John Lateran (p. 408) for the gracefulness of its double colonnettes and the splendour of the multi-coloured, inlaid architectural elements. It may even be by the

627

same hands. There are marble fragments and inscriptions from the primitive basilica and nearby burial grounds (p. 625). The most important objects include a 4th-century sarcophagus front representing the delivery of the Laws of Moses (*traditio legis*), and a grandiose sarcophagus, also 4th-century, with a marine scene on one side and on the other the contest of Apollo and the satyr Marsyas (who claimed to be the better musician and was flayed by the victorious god).

On the side of the cloister, left of its entrance, is an exhibition room with a tryptich, *Madonna and Child with Saints*, by Antoniazzo Romano or his circle, and other paintings. A precious Bible from the era of Charlemagne, from the nearby monastery, is often displayed here. Past this room is a hall with a great statue of pope Gregory XVI, and on the walls there are 15th-century frescoes and 13th-century mosaics from the decoration of the apse. From here exit onto Via Ostiense. (Ask in the sacristy or call beforehand 06/5410341 to visit the monastery next door. A museum there has a major collection of inscriptions from the old basilica, many of the frescoed medallions painted in the high middle ages with portraits of the earliest popes and interesting paintings.)

In the foreground on this side stands a graceless, lighthouse-shaped 19th-century bell tower. About 300 yards away on the Via Ostiense, under a protective structure, is a burial site (1st century BC to 4th century AD), pagan but with a few Christian tombs. The ruin consists mainly of columbaria and modest burial rooms. Other parts of this necropolis are on the edge of the road, under a tufa stone mound. (Via delle Sette Chiese intersects Viale Ostiense on this side, and about 300 yards away – to the right, at No. 42 – is the entrance to the highly interesting Catacombs of Commodilla, unfortunately accessible only with permission from the Vatican, see p. 659).

Take the metro again in the Laurentine direction to the 'Eur Palasport' stop. This is the EUR quarter, Rome's only true 'satellite-city'. It is interesting for its Fascist (now called 'Rationalist') architecture, and the way in which its architecture and layout were used in subsequent urban developments. The neighbourhood began life around 1938 as a dormitory community, based on Mussolini's plan to extend the city toward the sea. The plan changed two years later: the regime decided to hold a great fair here in 1942 to honour the 20th year of Fascism. This was a strange idea, as Italy was now immersed in world war. The project was soon dropped, and the half-built monumental structures were devastated first by German occupiers and then by wartime refugees. Yet the acronym EUR ('Universal Exposition of Rome') stuck. In 1951 the buildings were repaired and construction restarted; more buildings were added in the 1950's and 1960's. Many larger buildings became offices. Today the district is a major government centre; private residences have also multiplied.

Two concepts inspired the layout and style of EUR, which transcends the Fascist 'Rationalist' architecture of the time. One was a long-dreamed-of utopia, the 'ideal city'. As long ago as the 15th century a famous painting attributed to the Sienese Francesco di Giorgio Martini had depicted such a city, to be governed by reason and harmony. A copy of the painting was deliberately included in the original EUR project. The other concept was 'metaphysical': a trend in Italian art that had influenced painting and sculpture, called the Metaphysical School (De Chirico, Carrà, Boccioni and others), now left its mark on these buildings, especially those of the original nucleus. They are monumental and daring, yet stark, understated and somewhat mysterious. This highly original style, developed by talented architects under the supervision of Marcello Piacentini, is today being reassessed by architects worldwide.

The grid-like street plan, echoing ancient Roman cities, developed around a core of long perpendicular axes. North-south is the wide Via Cristoforo Colombo; other great avenues run east-west. Where all these intersect they form sweeping squares; monotony is avoided by plenty of landscaping (44% of the area is green, and to the south is a sparkling artificial lake).

The heart of EUR is Piazza Marconi (from the EUR Palasport metro station find Via Cristoforo Colombo nearby and take it three blocks uphill, going north). It is dominated by a commemorative **Stele to Guglielmo Marconi**, the inventor of the radio, made of colossal marble blocks sculpted in high relief by Arturo Dazzi (1959).

One block up, Via Cristoforo Colombo intersects the first of the east-west avenues, the Viale della Civiltà del Lavoro ('of the Civilization of Labour'). At its end are the two most famous EUR buildings (both clearly visible from here). To the west (that is, to the left, if the Marconi stele is behind you) is the **Palazzo della Civiltà del Lavoro** by Giovanni Guerrini, Ernesto Bruno La Padula and Mario Romano (1939). After the war populist political correctness added the words 'del lavoro' to both palace and avenue, which were originally devoted to 'civilization' *tout court.*

The palace is perhaps the most heartfelt expression of the artistic spirit of EUR: 223 ft (68 m) tall, the linear design contrasts with the almost hypnotic rhythm of the arches. Decoration is absent save the statues at the base and a famous Mussolini phrase at the top celebrating the Italian genius: 'A people of artists and heroes, of saints and thinkers, of scientists, of navigators and of transmigrators'.

To the east is the grandiose **Palazzo dei Congressi** by Adalberto Libera (1939).

Another block up, a square recently rededicated to the United Nations consists of two symmetrical buildings with a large semi-circular portico inspired by the Markets of Trajan (p. 182), (1937, by Giovanni Muzio, Mario Paniconi and Giulio Pediconi).

Return to Piazza Marconi. On its east side are two symmetrical buildings linked by an open portico, adorned in the rear by mosaics by the Futurists Enrico Prampolini and Fortunato Depero. The building to the north houses the Museum of Traditional and Folk Art and the south one the Pigorini Museum of Prehistoric and Ethnographic Art, among the most important of their kind (pp. 686-687). There are other major museums nearby: behind the Prehistoric Museum is the Museum of the Early Middle Ages, with exhibits from the 4th to the 10th centuries. At the very end of Via della Civiltà Romana (off the east side of the square and beyond the Via dell'Arte crossing) is the **Museum of Roman Civilization** (p. 686), an imposing building by Pietro Aschieri, Domenico Bernardini, Cesare Pascoletti and Gino Peressutti (1939-41).

This extremely informative museum contains casts of statues, models of Roman buildings and fortressess, and a huge, accurate model of imperial Rome (it was used as a prop and reference in the 2000 Hollywood movie *Gladiator*). There are also, casts of every panel of Trajan's Column (p. 186).

Return to Via dell'Arte and descend it going left. The spirited elliptical building on the left, in a widening called Piazzale Giulio Pastore, the **Palazzo INAIL**, was designed by Fabio Dinelli in 1960 and modified by Gino Valle and Carlo Costantini in 1995. Continue and turn right at the crossing with Viale Europa, another of the large east-west avenues. In the distance is the church of **SS. Pietro e Paolo** (1938-59) by Arnaldo Foschini.

As is always true of well-proportioned buildings, simplicity of form makes this church look smaller. One wouldn't think it is 225 ft tall (69 m) and that the dome is 87 ft (27 m) wide.

From Viale Europa pick up Viale Cristoforo Colombo again, taking it left. It crosses Viale America (south and parallel to Viale Europa) and splits to go around the EUR lake: three ponds totalling 420 ft (128 m) across, running for about two thirds of a mile (1 km) parallel to the avenues. This scenic park, created in the 1960's, is sadly marred by heavy traffic and smog today. The landscaping between the two lanes of traffic, with its fountains and little waterfalls, is by Raffaele De Vico. The great building with a glass and metal façade on the left if you are crossing the lake is by Ugo Ratti and Marco Bacigalupo (1962). On the other side is the **Palazzo dello Sport** by the great Pierluigi Nervi and Marcello Piacentini: a vast circular glass structure with a dome 309 ft (94 m) wide. Before it stands a statue, *The Olympic Flame*, by the Sicilian sculptor Emilio Greco.

5. FROM S. CROCE IN GERUSALEMME TO PORTA MAGGIORE AND S. LORENZO FUORI LE MURA

Planning: at the time of writing, this whole excursion can be done by tram. We'll tell you where to get on and off.

If you'd rather walk, from Porta S. Giovanni(p. 402) follow the outside of the Aurelian Walls on Viale Castrense along a long, straight stretch of the walls, which are majestic and quite well preserved here; continue to the crossing with Via Nola.

If you take the tram, the station is at the beginning of Viale Carlo Felice, inside the Walls and off Piazza di Porta S. Giovanni (board any tram in the direction that stays on Viale Carlo Felice). Get off at the first stop and go through the walls by the opening on the right, to see, again on the right, the walls from the outside.

The first opening through the walls here, at the Via Nola crossing, is modern. Next to it, at the top of some steps is the picturesque, late 15th-century **Oratorio di S. Maria del Buon Aiuto** ('of the Good Help') restored in the 19th century.

Usually closed, it contains a heavily restored fresco, perhaps by Antoniazzo Romano.

From the outside, the walls form a wide arc; this in fact is all that is left of the **Castrense Amphitheatre**, the only true amphitheatre (p. 205) of ancient Rome, apart from the Colosseum, of which anything survives. It was built in the early 3rd century AD and incorporated into the Aurelian Walls later in the century, when those were built. This great theatre, almost half the size of Colosseum, was all brick with the usual tiers of superimposed columns. Only the first tier remains, plus a bit of the second (next to the Oratorio di S. Maria). The interior may be seen from inside the walls; go to No. 54 at the adjacent Piazza Santa Croce to request access through a convent there, or ask in the sacristy of the nearby church.

The theatre was called Castrense, Latin for 'of the fort', because it was reserved for military and court-related spectacles. It belonged to a complex of buildings of a public character, the Sessorium ('Residence'), which included a residence for the emperors.

Crossing the walls into Piazza Santa Croce, let's see what remains of those buildings. The most important is a large hall of the imperial residence, which the emperor Constantine's family converted into the church of **Santa Croce in Gerusalemme** ('The Holy Cross in Jerusalem'). This 4th century conversion was done to provide a solemn shelter for the relics of the True Cross of Christ, which Constantine's mother, St Helena, claimed to have found in Palestine and brought to Rome (see p. 368). The structure was remodelled at least six times, most recently in the mid 18th century by the Roman architect Domenico Gregorini and his Sicilian colleague Pietro Passalacqua. It was they who created the theatrical façade, in the Borrominesque style of concave and convex surfaces, and crowned with statues of the Evangelists, Constantine and St Helena. Foundations and walls remain part of the original structure.

The church is one of the seven on the traditional tour of pilgrims seeking indulgences (see p. 92). It has on both sides a late 10th-century convent; the eight-storey Romanesque bell-tower in the background was built 150 years later. The church entrance is an elegant elliptic atrium, with a small dome and columns from the original church portico leaning against pilasters. (Open: 07:00-13:00 and 15:30-19:00.)

Gigantic ancient granite columns divide the interior. The wooden ceiling has an early 18th-century fresco of the *Virgin Introducing St Helena and Constantine to the Trinity* by the distinguished exponent of the Neapolitan school, Corrado Giaquinto. The fine cosmatesque floor (restored) is 12th-century. At the front of the nave are two late 15th-century holy water fonts with carvings of fish on the inside.

There is a notable painting by Carlo Maratta (17th-18th century) over the second altar of the right aisle: *The Antipope Victor IV Led by St Bernard to Submit to Pope Innocent II* (an episode in the incessant struggle between popes, anti-popes

S. Croce in Gerusalemme in the 18th century; engraving by Giuseppe Vasi

and their secular backers for domination of Rome in the middle ages). In the presbytery is an 18th-century ciborium (marble canopy) resting on the columns of an older, 12th-century one. In the apse is the tomb of a 16th-century cardinal by Jacopo Sansovino, with statues of Solomon and David. Above it is a tabernacle with angels designed by Carlo Maderno. In the vault of the apse is a grandiose late 15th-century fresco, episodes from the *Invention ('Finding') of the True Cross* and *Christ Blessing*, possibly by Antoniazzo Romano.

From the end of the right aisle one descends to the sumptuous Chapel of St Helena, supposedly created by the empress herself. On its ground she strewed soil she had collected from the Via Dolorosa in Jerusalem; this soil – presumably still under the flooring – gave the church its name of 'in Jerusalem'. The vault has a splendid 15th to 16th-century mosaic, perhaps by Melozzo da Forlì, replacing an earlier one – famous in the middle ages – provided by a descendant of Helena in the 5th century. On the walls are late 16th-century

frescoes by Niccolò Pomarancio. Passing an adjacent chapel, go back up to the presbytery and hence to the nearby Chapel of the Relics. Inside a reliquary by Valadier are the fragments of the Cross found by St Helena.

Leaving the basilica by the aisle on this side, take a look at the delicate 16th-century funerary monument to a Belgian sculptor, a gift of his friends, at the end of the aisle, left of the entrance.

Excavations in 1968 uncovered the baptistery of the primitive church (currently not open).

A vast convent stands next to the church, built in the 10th century, partly over the Castrense Amphitheatre. It includes a beautiful 18th-century library frescoed by Giovanni Paolo Pannini.

To the left of the church all the space included in the curve of the Aurelian Walls was originally part of the Sessorium compound; ruins of an apsed rectangular hall can still be seen. The modern buildings there now are museums, including the important **Museum of Musical Instruments** (for all of these, see p. 687).

631

The street facing the church on the other side of the square is the final stretch of the long 'Via Felice' laid out by Sixtus V and his successors to connect their new 'downtown' with the *disabitato* and to include historic churches such as St John Lateran and Santa Croce in the new network of streets (see p. 92).

Leave the square going right (if you are exiting the church) into Via Eleniana, an ancient Roman street originally leading to the Sessorium. Ruins of the Sessorium baths are visible through a gate. You now approach an ancient Roman wall, whose left and right sides have different origins. The left part is the first urban segment of the Aqueduct of Nero, parts of which you've probably already seen in Piazza S. Giovanni (pp. 404, 410) and on the slope of the Palatine (p. 431) where it proceeded to service the imperial palaces.

The aqueduct was actually built by Emperor Claudius, predecessor to Nero, in 50 AD; Nero merely reinforced and extended it.

The part of the wall extending right of the grassy knoll is a continuation of the Aurelian Walls. Cross to the other side to see how the wall continues (at your left) at a right angle and then incorporates a great gate, the **Porta Maggiore**, one of ancient Rome's most majestic architectural works. This titanic 1st century structure was originally not a gate, but was built to collect in its attic the waters of most aqueducts leading to the city. Only two centuries later was it incorporated into the city walls and made into a gate.

The power and beauty of the Porta Maggiore derive in part from the deliberate contrast between the big, coarse travertine marble blocks lining it and the polished surface of the attic, which lists the emperors who built and restored the structure. The name of the gate is medieval and refers neither to its size nor its importance but to the fact that it leads to the church of S. Maria Maggiore. The original name was Prænestina, because it was crossed by the road to Præneste (now Palestrina). The flagstones under the gate are original; the rest of the Prænestine Way still exists as a modern road.

Before the gate is the extremely interesting and in part at least very well preserved **Tomb of Marcus Vergilius Eurisaces**, a wealthy 1st century BC baker. It is thus about one century older than the gate. Recall that tombs were forbidden inside Rome but are a common sight at the beginning of the various consular roads.

Eurisaces, a freedman who, as the inscription says, had become an official contractor providing bakery goods (*pistor redemptor*), had grown rich by serving both sides in the civil wars preceding the end of the Republic. The monument's reliefs show elements of a bakery; the frieze illustrates the baking and selling of bread.

The pen for animals destined to the ancient circus games used to be just inside the gate at Piazza di Porta Maggiore.

Outside the gate (Piazzale Labicano), on the left, inside a railway embankment, is a unique early 1st-century AD underground sanctuary, the so-called **Neo-Pythagorean Basilica**. It was found by accident in 1917, when a train track collapsed, but after the Second World War it was closed to the public. During the 2000 Jubilee year, the 'political archæological complex' announced with a straight face that it had just 'discovered' the site, which after a hasty restoration was reopened to the acclamation of an obedient press. The festivities over, the site was closed again (special permits are sometimes available, see p. 657).

It is a large basilical space, created by digging from above into the ground of tufa stone. It has a nave, two aisles and abundant stucco decoration, but the original use is unknown. Though it could have been a tomb, the vestiges of pedestals and niches that could have held cult paraphernalia recall a pagan place of worship. The stuccoes have Greek-mythological or naturalistic subjects. One French historian hypothesized, on the basis of a scene in the apse thought to depict the Greek poetess Sappho jumping off a cliff into the sea, that this was a 'neo-pythagorean' sanctuary, because a cult based on the teachings of the ancient Greek philosopher Pythagoras saw in the suicide of Sappho a symbol of reincarnation. It appears the underground basilica was sacked and abandoned shortly after it was built, possibly when the Emperor Claudius instigated a persecution of neo-pythagorean cults.

From Porta Maggiore a long avenue, Scalo S. Lorenzo, leads to Piazzale del Verano in front of Rome's main cemetery. Trams passing Porta Maggiore will take you there in a few stops.

The cemetery is called **Campo Verano**, the Veranian Field, because the land once belonged to Lucius Verus, brother and co-emperor of Marcus Aurelius. It became a cemetery in 1831 during a cholera epidemic when the French authorities then occupying Rome decided that burial in churches and a hodgepodge of small yards wasn't right for a modern city.

The oldest part, near the entrance, was designed by Giuseppe Valadier and is followed, on the left, by a more recent addition and by the Jewish section, where the remains of older Jewish cemeteries were transferred (see p. 269, 586). Few of the funerary monuments are of major historical or artistic interest. In a section to the left of the entrance, however, is the tomb of Gioacchino Belli, Rome's great vernacular poet of the 19th century, whose immortal sonnets we often quote in this guide, and that of Trilussa, his 20th-century follower. To the right of the Viale Principale (the central avenue), starting at the entrance, are the graves of the famous actor and film director Vittorio De Sica, the Nobel prize-winning poet Giuseppe Ungaretti, and, further on, the novelist Alberto Moravia.

A reminder of a tragic episode of recent history is the large glass-fronted chapel containing the remains of Claretta Petacci, Mussolini's mistress (midway down the modern addition near a section called 'Evangelical'). Petacci refused to abandon the former dictator at the end of the war and was executed together with him by partisans in 1945, her body later being hung upside down next to that of her lover in a Milan square.

To the left of the cemetery entrance on the piazzale is the church of **S. Lorenzo fuori le Mura** ('St Lawrence outside the Walls'), all that remains of the large compound that sprang up around the grave of Lawrence, a much venerated Spanish deacon, or social worker, martyred in the 3rd century. (The area has been a burial site since antiquity.)

A first, enormous basilica had been built here in the 4th century, perhaps by Constantine himself, but of that only a little survives, discovered recently along the cemetery wall on the right. (It is conceivable that the columns and some of the marble furnishings of the present church come from the earlier basilica.)

What exists now is an unusual mix of two smaller later buildings: one from the 6th century, built by Pope Pelagius over the presumed grave of the saint, at a short distance from the original basilica and parallel to it; and another, somewhat larger, from the 12th-13th centuries, that Pope Honorius III joined to the first lengthways to form a single long building (although the two axes diverge slightly). The two buildings, which were orientated in opposite directions, were joined back to front; the rear (older) building was turned into the presbytery of the composite church, which involved burying some sections under raised floors.

S. Lorenzo fuori le mura

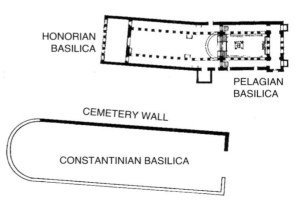

S. Lorenzo fuori le mura in the early 20th century

Although this composite basilica was partly destroyed in the Second World War during an allied air raid on a nearby railway depot – the only serious bombing in Rome – it was rebuilt using the original materials.

One enters the newer ('Honorian') part of the church through a harmonious 13th-century portico by Vassalletto, one of the foremost members of the famous Cosmati clan (see Glossary). Note the refined architrave and cornice over ancient columns with elaborate Ionic capitals. The little scene over the 4th column shows Honorius introducing the commander of the Fifth Crusade (the disastrous enterprise for which this pope is remembered) to St Lawrence (missing). Inside the portico are: right, an 11th-century funerary monument under a small canopy supported on colonnettes, and a 4th-century sarcophagus with biblical episodes; on the façade wall, an exceptional 5th-6th century sarcophagus with a primitive and lively bas-relief of wine-making children, and the usual

romanesque lions (p. 230); left, the modern tomb of the post-war statesman Alcide De Gasperi by Giacomo Manzù. All around there are remains of 12th-13th century frescoes with episodes from the life of St Lawrence (the ones on the left were repainted in the 19th century).

Open: 07:00-12:00 and 15:30-18:00 in winter, 20:00 in summer.

Rows of great granite columns with Ionic capitals, all antique spolia, articulate the Honorian church. The marvellous floor, beautiful pulpits in the nave and Easter candelabrum are 12-13th century and Cosmatesque. Note the eagle grasping its prey in the right pulpit. There is more Cosmati work right of the entrance, in the canopy over the tomb of a 13th-century cardinal, itself a recycled 2nd-3rd century AD Roman sarcophagus.

Reaching the main altar, we find ourselves at the point of junction between the two parts of the basilica; the curves of the apse of the older ('Pelagian') church is in fact marked exactly by the platform of the altar.

Under the altar, steps lead to the original crypt under the Pelagian church that contained the grave of St Lawrence, to which the supposed relics of other saints were added later. The crypt, remodelled in the 19th century, was originally of the 'confessio' type, designed for the exhibition of relics to pilgrims, as we saw in St Peter's and other early basilicas (see p. 361).

We now enter the Pelagian part of the church. When this became, as explained above, the presbytery of the composite building, its nave was raised, and all the space underneath filled with soil; the lower parts of the two lateral aisles were also filled, bringing them to the same level as the new nave.

In modern times all the soil was dug out. We'll get to the space that was recovered under the nave later. As to the aisles, when the Ionic bases and lower sections of the ten splendid 4th-century columns (with Corinthian capitals, in two rows of five) re-emerged, the Pelagian church regained its original magnificence.

Victory and trophy motifs adorn the first two

capitals on both rows. The splendid entablature over the columns consists of elaborate ancient friezes, all spolia; over those in turn smaller, 6th-century columns with capitals support a corridor, once the *matroneum* or women's gallery.

The back wall of the present basilica used to be the internal façade of the Pelagian church, which, as you will recall, originally faced the opposite way from the Honorian building (though the entrance was on the side, due to the presence of a landfill). The triumphal arch which now separates the two halves originally belonged to the Pelagian church and of course faced the faithful who had their backs to the internal façade. That is why its beautiful Byzantine-style mosaic (comparable and somewhat similar to the best in Italy, those of Ravenna) faces the 'wrong' way. The mosaic, by three different late 6th-century artists, represents Jesus with (right) Sts Peter and Lawrence and Pope Pelagius with a model of this church, and (left) Sts Paul, Stephen and Hippolytus. On the sides are Jerusalem and Bethlehem; on the underside, garlands of fruits and flowers.

Standing nearby is a very ornate 13th-century Cosmatesque episcopal chair, while the presbytery has an exceptional marble canopy (ciborium) with a pyramidal roof. This is the oldest signed and dated (1148) work of Rome's cosmatesque marble workers, four 'sons of Paolo' whose names, Giovanni, Pietro, Angelo and Sasso, are in the architrave. On the sides are two plain, elegant marble benches terminating with marble lions, probably by Vassalletto.

From the end of both aisles we can now descend to the original level of the Pelagian church, that is to the space that, filled with soil when the two buildings were joined, was later dug out (see above). In the late 19th century, when this space was re-discovered, it was devoted to a new, larger crypt, including at one end a rich burial chapel for Pope Pius IX, the controversial pope of the Risorgimento era. The chapel is contained in what was originally a small interior portico (*endonarthex*) at the front of the Pelagian church (remember that the entrance to the church was on

this side). Let's go back upstairs.

The walls of the Pelagian church include early medieval fresco fragments. Some were removed and are now in the right-hand aisle of the Honorian church. If we go to the end of this aisle we come to the Chapel of St Tarcisius, with (left) *The Beheading of John the Baptist* by Giovanni Serodine, a 17th-century painter whose vigorous style has recently been favourably reassessed by scholars. Both this and the opposite aisle have interesting tombs of 17th-century gentlemen. Especially notable in the left aisle is a grand funerary monument designed by Pietro da Cortona, which doubles as the entrance (now unused) to the Catacombs of Ciriaca below. The attractive monument includes busts of two dignitaries of the papal administration, by the Fleming François Duquesnoy.

The end of the right aisle leads to the 19th-century sacristy and on to the beatiful romanesque cloister (12th-13th century), unique in Rome for its second floor with mullioned windows. Inscribed tablets and other marble pieces, both ancient Roman and medieval, are all around; also, a large bomb fragment from the 1943 air raid.

Access to the **Catacombs of Ciriaca** is through the cloister. (Ask in the sacristy to be accompanied.) This is a cemetery developed inside the property of a certain Ciriaca, one of the many ancient Roman ladies who supported the Christian church before it became legitimate (p. 228). St Lawrence was said to have been buried here by her. The catacomb has three levels – the upper two are Christian, the lower one pagan – with interesting fragments and pictures. Most of the underground passages are unexplored; they extend for miles, and some are said to connect to the distant Catacombs of St Agnes (p. 609).

Leave the church. Notice the romanesque 12th-century bell tower and, on the right, the 12th-century monastery with a four-arched portico resting on ancient columns and pretty mullioned windows on an upper floor. A medieval tower rises further back.

This is all that remains of a fortified compound,

Chiesa del Giubileo
model by Richard Meier

nicknamed Laurentiopolis or 'the city of Lawrence', that gradually grew around this ecclesiastical complex when its neighbourhood became increasingly desolate as people moved to the new 'abitato' (p. 28) or downtown. The same thing happened when a citadel rose near St John Lateran (p. 404) and when 'Johannipolis' was created near S. Paolo fuori le Mura (p. 625).

(Here you have a choice: 1) From here, with a change at Porta Maggiore, you can return to St John Lateran by taking the tram. 2) If you wish, and if you haven't been there yet, you can also reach from here the picturesque Tiburtina Gate by walking along Via Tiburtina for half a mile to Porta S. Lorenzo and then following the directions on p. 102.)

Outside Porta Maggiore, $4^1/_2$ miles (7 km) directly east on Via di Tre Teste, is the **Chiesa del Giubileo** ('Church of the Jubilee Year') – also called 'S. Cuore del Suffragio' or 'Dives in Misericordia' – by the renowned American architect Richard Meier.

To get there you can take trams Nos 5, 14 or 19 at or near Porta Maggiore to their terminus. From there, bus No. 556 reaches (at its terminus) the vicinity of the church. Come back the same way to Porta Maggiore or (trams Nos 5 and 14 only) to the more central Termini station.

This is the first important church built in Rome by a non-Italian in over a century, and a rare example in Italy of the fractured, centrifugal style, rich in a diversity of gradients and slants on the external surfaces, adopted by some of today's most adventurous architects. In Meier, unlike his American colleague, Frank Gehry and others who aim to make æsthetic capital from spectacular disorder, the style produces a sense of peace and symmetry. The sophisticated construction technique is, however, wholly Italian. The Vatican commissioned this as the parish church of this low-income neighbourhood, and it will be a key part of a new housing development project.

The complex is divided into sacred (church proper, meditation court) and secular areas (community centre, open square for assemblies). The structure is based on a series of squares and four circles. Three huge, pre-fabricated concrete shells symbolising the Holy Trinity make up the body of the church; the builders had to invent a special machine to hoist them into place. 'Zenithal' side lights hanging between the shells enliven the nave with shifting patterns of light and shade.

6. PORTA S. PANCRAZIO, VILLA DORIA PAMPHILI AND THE BASILICA OF S. PANCRAZIO

Planning: At the time of writing Porta S. Pancrazio and the church of St Pancras can be reached by bus from central Rome (No. 870, leaving from Via Paola near the river end of Corso Vittorio).

During restoration of St Pancrazio in 2001 part of a roof caved in and the church is now closed indefinitely. You may check out the situation at www.sanpancrazio.org or call (06) 58104580.

Porta S. Pancrazio ('St Pancras' Gate') is part of the 17th-century Vatican Walls (p. 303) but is only a few yards from the spot where the corresponding gate in the Aurelian Walls once stood. (Except for a few ruins, the Aurelian Walls no longer exist on this bank of the Tiber. The ancient Roman gate was called Aurelia, not because of the walls, but because the much older Via Aurelia started here.) The present gate is a 19th-century 'neo-classical' reconstruction. French cannonades against the defenders of the short-lived Roman Republic in 1849 (p. 565) destroyed the original. There are mementos of this conflict sprinkled throughout the neighbourhood, and a small museum devoted to it at the top of the gate. (Open: Tuesday, Wednesday and Thursday 09:00-12:00.)

To the right of Porta S. Pancrazio, go through iron gates into the Janiculum gardens. Just to the left is the renaissance façade of a house where Michelangelo is said to have lived – not here, however, but near Piazza Venezia: the house was demolished in 1941 and the façade moved here, where it serves as a false front for a water cistern.

Outside the iron gates once more, take Via S. Pancrazio to the right. About 100 yards further on, at No. 6-8, is the Vascello ('Vessel'), a baroque villa with the house shaped like a boat designed in 1633 by the only female architect in 17th-century Italy, Plautilla Bricci. Here the heroes of the 1849 Republic barricaded themselves in for a last-ditch defence (pp. 565-566). A plaque commemorates this. Traces of the French cannonball attacks still mark the wall.

[The following paragraphs describe Villa Doria Pamphili first, S. Pancrazio second. It is hard to combine these two sites into one walk, because, though the church is in the grounds of the Villa, there is no connection between them. Providing of course that the church is now open again, one solution is to first see the church and then enter the villa from a secondary entrance (for those leaving the church compound, this is immediately to the left and up a ramp). Then pick up the walk where the commemorative arch is mentioned below.]

Here, where the road forks and the ancient Aurelian Way veers right, is the entrance to **Villa Doria Pamphili**, a superb example of a suburban residence of a grand Roman family (a member was Pope Innocent X, patron of Bernini, p. 456). Partly designed by the prominent 17th-century architect and sculptor Alessandro Algardi, it became run down after the government acquired it in the 1960's and opened most of its grounds to the public. The main building and adjacent gardens were reserved for official functions. (Open: 07:00-18:00 October-March; 07:00-20:00 April-September; 07:00-21:00 May-August.)

Beware: the gates shut with no forewarning at the marked time, and crossing the park takes about 40 minutes. Since park personnel are few, there have been cases of visitors being trapped in the park for hours after the closing time.

At the end of the entrance avenue is a great commemorative arch, built in the 1800's on the spot where French artillery destroyed an annexe occupied by Republican fighters. Take the trail (Viale del Casino Corsini) right of the arch to a small 18th-century palace formerly called Corsini. From here take Viale Angelo Pancalli and then Viale Bartolomeo Rozat to the right (heroes of the 1849 battle – one a Roman man of the people, the other a Swiss intellectual volunteer). You reach the arches of the Pauline aqueduct, built by Pope Paul V Borghese (who also completed St Peter's) to bring water to Trastevere (p. 563). It partly reuses an aqueduct originally built by the emperor Trajan in the 2nd century AD. Observe the beautiful arch spanning the Aurelian Way, which here

Villa Doria Pamphili in the 19th century

borders the park. Go on to the right, skirting the area set aside for official functions. Take Viale del Maglio, then Viale della Fontana di Venere (named for a lovely but badly damaged Fountain of Venus Rising from the Waters set in a sustaining wall). When you are near a flight of steps, instead of going up, take Viale del Giardino del Teatro to a 17th-century complex called 'the Theatre'. This consists of an artificial grotto with marine divinities and a beautiful exedra on the right and a 19th-century Fountain of Cupid – missing its Cupid – on the left.

Go back and up the flight of steps. From the top there is a view of the elegant **Casino delle Allegrezze** ('of Joys') – also called del Bel Respiro ('of Fresh Air') – designed by Algardi for the princely family and now reserved for state functions. A formal garden surrounds it.

From here go right (assuming your back is to

the steps). First you come to (on the right) a late 19th-century annexe to the Casino adorned with ancient columns and sculptural fragments in the walls. These come from a nearby ancient Roman cemetery of which there are ample remains (closed to the public). At the end of the path take, on the left, an avenue to the touching Monument to the Fallen French of 1849. Sadly, its neo-classical statue has recently lost its head. One of the princes, moved by Christian piety, as the inscription says, decided to honour the fallen enemy by burying their remains on the grounds of the villa and raising this memorial. Further on, to the right, is the plain 17th-century Villa Vecchia ('Old Villa'), rebuilt in the 18th century.

In the valley below are two works by Algardi, the Fountain of the Snail, in which the artist used a snail originally made by his friend Bernini for a fountain in Piazza Navona (replaced by a statue of a Moor, pp. 460-461), and the Fountain of the Lily. A canal with three cascades begins at the Lily Fountain and drops into a pond. Walk around the pond to Viale 8 Marzo. This leads to a secondary exit to Via Vitellia, where there is a bus stop.

Take Via Vitellia left skirting the Villa for less than half a mile (about 700 m), to a widening called Piazza S. Pancrazio. On the left here is a courtyard with a garden and the austere **Basilica of S. Pancrazio** (St Pancras) founded in the early 6th century over the spot where Pancras, a 14-year-old Christian, was said to have been beheaded three centuries earlier, his body being buried in the catacombs below. (The church may still be closed for repairs; see p. 637.)

The plain façade is 15th-century. Two columns from the primitive church flank the main portal. Countless rebuildings have almost obliterated the original structure; only the exterior of the apse and a few parts of the old walls remain. The spacious interior is the result of 17th- and 19th-century restorations (the latter after the devastation of the 1849 conflict). The church still projects an aura of solitude and remoteness, as if lost in time. Ask in the sacristy about access to the catacombs.

The 17th-century ceiling centres on a wooden image of the martyr. Along the walls there are remains of a medieval marble pulpit, of an altar and of other furnishings, also medieval and all in the cosmatesque manner. Over another altar at the end of the left aisle is *S. Teresa* by Palma the Younger, one of the finer painters of 16th century Venice. The modern ciborium rests on medieval porphyry columns. From the sides one can descend to a semicircular crypt, designed to allow an easy-in easy-out traffic of pilgrims viewing the relics, and the oldest example of this arrangement after St Peter's. It contains relics and a cosmatesque altar.

Between the 3rd and the 4th pilaster, on the right, is the entrance to the **Catacombs of Ottavilla**, named after the Roman lady who was said to have saved and buried the body of St Pancras here. It is a great underground cemetery whose several levels, mostly unexplored, contain traces of pictures and reliefs. Some archæological finds – amphoræ, plaques and fragments – are exhibited separately (ask in the sacristy).

Further Reading

Ackerman, J. S. *The Architecture of Michelangelo*, London 1961

Bailey, J. B. *Letarouilly on Renaissance Rome*, New York 1984

Balsdon, J. P. V. D. *Life and Leisure in Ancient Rome*, London 1969

Barkan, L. *Unearthing the Past: Archæology and Æsthetics in the Making of Renaissance Culture*, New Haven 1999

Bellori, G. P. *Le vite de' pittori, scultori et architetti moderni (Documents of Art and Architectural History, Series 1: Vol. 4)* Williamstown Mass. 1980

Beny, R. and Gunn, P. *The Churches of Rome*, New York 1981

Birindelli, M. *Roma italiana, come fare e disfare una città*, Rome 1978

Blunt, A. *A Guide to Baroque Rome: the Churches*, London 2006

—— *Roman Baroque*, London 2001

—— *Borromini*, Cambridge, Mass. 1979

Boethius, A. *The Golden House of Nero*, Ann Arbor 1960

—— and Ward-Perkins, J. B. *Etruscan and Roman Architecture*, Harmondsworth 1970

Boorsch, S. 'The Building of the Vatican', *Metropolitan Museum of Art Bulletin*, 3, 1982

Bowersock, G. W. *Julian the Apostate*, Cambridge Mass. 1981

Bowersock, G. W., Brown, P., Grabar, O. (Editors) *Late Antiquity: A Guide to the Postclassical World*, Cambridge, Mass. 1999

Burchard (Burckard), J. *Liber Notarum 1473-1506* (edited E. Celani, Città di Castello 1903; partial French translation by J. Turmel, Paris 1932; partial Italian translation by L. Bianchi, Milan 1988).

Caracciolo, A. *Roma Capitale. Dal Risorgimento alla crisi dello Stato liberale*, Roma 1984

Carcopino, J. *La vie quotidienne à Rome à l'apogée de l'Empire*, Paris 1939

Coarelli, F. *Guida archeologica di Roma*, Milano 1974

Condivi, A., intro. Charles Robertson, *Life of Michelangelo,* London 2006

Connors, J. *Borromini and the Roman Oratory*, Cambridge, Mass. 1980

de Guttry, I. *Guida di Roma Moderna*, Roma 1989

Delaine, J. 'Recent Research on Roman Baths', *Journal of Roman Archæology*, 1, 1988

Delehaye, H. *The Legends of the Saints, an Introduction to Hagiography*, 1907, Engl. translation Notre Dame, Indiana 1961

D'Onofrio, C. *Castel S. Angelo*, Roma 1972

—— *Renovatio Romæ*, Roma 1973

—— *Il Tevere*, Roma 1980

—— *Le fontane di Roma*, Roma 1986

—— *Un popolo di statue racconta*, Roma 1990

—— *Gli obelischi di Roma*, Roma 1992

Dudley, D. R. *Urbs Roma, a Source Book of Classical Texts on the City*, Aberdeen 1967

Duffy, Eamon *Saints and Sinners – a History of the Popes,* London and New Haven 1997

Earl, D. *The Age of Augustus,* New York 1980

Enggass, R. *Early 18th-Century Sculpture in Rome*, London 1976

Ferrari, G. *Early Roman Monasteries*, Vatican City 1957

Finelli, L., Insolera, I., Marcianò, A. D. *Il Ghetto*, Rome 1986

Fisher Pace, U. V. *Kunstdenkmäler in Rom*, Darmstadt 1989

Geller, R. L. *Jewish Rome*, Rome 1983

Gnoli, U. *Cortigiane romane*, Arezzo 1941

Gregorovius, F. *History of the City of Rome in the Middle Ages*, London 1894 repr. New York 1967

Grimal, P. *La Vie à Rome dans l'Antiquité*, Paris 1953

—— *Les jardins romains* (2nd. ed.) Paris 1969

—— *The Civilization of Rome* London 1963

Hall, James, *Michelangelo and the reinvention of the human body*, London 2005

Hare, A. *Walks in Rome*, London 1878

Haskell, Francis *Patrons and Painters: Art and Society in Baroque Italy*, New Haven 1980

Hatfield, R. *The Wealth of Michelangelo*, Rome 2002

Heer, F. *Mittelalter*, Munich 1961, transl. as *The Medieval World*, New York 1963

Hempel, E. *Francesco Borromini*, Vienna 1924

Heydenreich, L. and Lotz W. *Architecture in Italy 1400 to 1600*, Harmondsworth 1974

Hibbard, Howard, *Bernini*, Harmondsworth 1975 and later

Hibbard, Howard, *Michelangelo*, Harmondsworth 1975 and later

Holanda, Francisco de, intro. David Hemsoll, *Dialogues with Michelangelo*, London 2006

Hopkins, K. and Beard, M. *The Colosseum*, London 2005

Kostof, S. *The Third Rome 1870-1950*, Berkeley 1973

Krautheimer, R. *Rome, Profile of a City, 312-1308*, Princeton 1980

—— *The Rome of Alexander VII, 1655-1667*, Princeton 1985

—— *Early Christian and Byzantine Architecture*, (4th ed.) Harmondsworth 1986

—— *Corpus Basilicarum christianarum Romæ*, Vatican City 1937

Iversen, E. *Obelisks in Exile, I: The Obelisks of Rome*, Copenhagen 1968

Lanciani, R. *The Ruins and Excavations of Ancient Rome*, London 1897

—— *The Destruction of Ancient Rome*, New York 1899

—— *The Golden Days of the Renaissance in Rome*, New York 1906

Langdon, Helen, *Caravaggio, a Life*, London 1999

Langdon, Helen, intro. *Lives of Caravaggio (Mancini, Baglione, Bellori)*, London 2005

Lees-Milne, James, *Roman Mornings*, London 1956

Llewellyn, P. *Rome in the Dark Ages*, New York 1971

MacDonald, W. *The Architecture of the Roman Empire*, New Haven-London 1965

MacDonald, W. *The Pantheon*, Harvard 1976

Mâle, E. and Buxton, D. *The Early Churches of Rome*, London 1960

Majanlahti, Anthony, *The Families who made Rome: A History and a Guide*, London 2005

Mallet, M. E. *The Borgias*, Chicago 1987

Markus, R. A. *Gregory the Great and His World*, Cambridge 1998

Millon, G. R. *St. Paul's within the Walls*, Dublin 1982

Montagu, J. *Roman Baroque Sculpture*, London 1989

Müller Karpe, H. *Vom Anfangs Rom*, Heidelberg 1959

Muñoz, A. *Roma barocca*, Milan-Rome 1928

Nash, E. *Pictorial Dictionary of Ancient Rome* (2nd ed.) London 1968

Norberg-Schulz, C. *Baroque Architecture*, London, 1979

Partner, P. *The Lands of St. Peter*, London 1972

Pietrangeli, C. *I Musei Vaticani. Cinque secoli di storia*, Rome 1985

Pope-Hennessy, J. *Italian Gothic Sculpture,* London 1996

—— *Italian Renaissance Sculpture*, London 1996

—— *Italian High Renaissance & Baroque Sculpture*, London 1996

Portoghesi, P. *Roma barocca*, Rome 1982

—— *The Rome of Borromini; Architecture and Language,* New York 1968

Proia, A. and Romano, P. *Vecchio Trastevere*, Rome 1935

Redig de Campos, D. *The 'Stanze' of Raphael*, Rome 1963

Simoncini, G. *'Roma Restaurata' rinnovamento urbano al tempo di Sisto V*, Firenze 1990

Steinberg, L. *Borromini's San Carlo alle Quattro Fontane*, New York 1977

Stinger, C. L. *The Renaissance in Rome*, Bloomington, Ind. 1998

Tierney, B. *The Crisis of Church and State, 1050-1300*, Englewood Cliffs, N. J. 1964

Tucci, P. L., *Laurentius Manlius, la riscoperta dell'antica Roma*, Rome 2001

Varriano, J. L. *Italian Baroque and Rococo Architecture*, New York 1986

Vasari, G. *Lives of the Artists: Biographies of the Most Eminent Architects, Painters, and Sculptors of Italy*, New York 1986 and many other editions

Vasari, G., intro. David Hemsoll, *Life of Michelangelo,* London 2006

Vasari, G., intro. Jill Burke, *Life of Raphael,* London 2004

Wey, Francis, introduced by W. W. Story, *Rome,* London 1872 and later

Wittkower, R. *Gian Lorenzo Bernini*, London 1955

—— *Art and Architecture in Italy 1600-1750*, Harmondsworth 1958

Wurm, H. *Der Palazzo Massimo alle Colonnne*, Berlin 1965

Yegül, F. *Baths and Bathing in Classical Antiquity*, Cambridge, Mass. 1992

Popes

Antipopes are in [square brackets].
The origin of non-Italian popes is given, and some family names.
The conventional numbers are given; St. Peter is not traditionally counted as a pope

St. Peter (32-67)
1. St. Linus (67-76)
2. St. Anacletus (Cletus) (76-88)
3. St. Clement I (88-97)
4. St. Evaristus (97-105) (Greek)
5. St. Alexander I (105-115)
6. St. Sixtus I (115-125) - also called Xystus I
7. St. Telesphorus (125-136) (Greek)
8. St. Hyginus (136-140) (Greek)
9. St. Pius I (140-155)
10. St. Anicetus (155-166) (Syrian)
11. St. Soter (166-175)
12. St. Eleutherius (175-189) (Greek)
13. St. Victor I (189-199) (African)
14. St. Zephyrinus (199-217)
15. St. Callistus I (217-22)
    [St. Hippolytus (217-235)]
16. St. Urban I (222-30)
17. St. Pontian (230-35)
18. St. Anterus (235-36) (Greek)
19. St. Fabian (236-50)
20. St. Cornelius (251-53)
    [Novatian (251)]
21. St. Lucius I (253-54)
22. St. Stephen I (254-257)
23. St. Sixtus II (257-258)
24. St. Dionysius (260-268)
25. St. Felix I (269-274)
26. St. Eutychian (275-283)
27. St. Gaius (or Caius) (283-296)
28. St. Marcellinus (296-304)
29. St. Marcellus I (c. 308-309)
30. St. Eusebius (310) (Greek)
31. St. Miltiades (or Melchiades) (311-14) (African)
32. St. Sylvester I (314-35)
33. St. Marcus (336)

34. St. Julius I (337-52)
35. Liberius (352-66)
    [St. Felix II (355-365)]
36. St. Damasus I (366-83) (Spanish)
    [Ursinus (366-67)]
37. St. Siricius (384-99)
38. St. Anastasius I (399-401)
39. St. Innocent I (401-17)
40. St. Zosimus (417-18) (Greek)
41. St. Boniface I (418-22)
    [Eulalius (418-419)]
42. St. Celestine I (422-32)
43. St. Sixtus III (432-40)
44. St. Leo I (the Great) (440-61)
45. St. Hilarus (461-68)
46. St. Simplicius (468-83)
47. St. Felix III (II) (483-92)
48. St. Gelasius I (492-96) (African)
49. Anastasius II (496-98)
50. St. Symmachus (498-514)
    [Laurence (498-499; 501-506)]
51. St. Hormisdas (514-23)
52. St. John I (523-26)
53. St. Felix IV (III) (526-30)
    [Dioscorus (530) (Egyptian)]
54. Boniface II (530-32)
55. John II (533-35) (*Mercury*; the first to change his name)
56. St. Agapitus I (535-36)
57. St. Silverius (536-37)
58. Vigilius (537-55)
59. Pelagius I (556-61)
60. John III (561-74)
61. Benedict I (575-79)
62. Pelagius II (579-90)
63. St. Gregory I (the Great) (590-604)
64. Sabinian (604-606)

65. Boniface III (607)
66. St. Boniface IV (608-15)
67. St. Deusdedit (Adeodatus I) (615-18)
68. Boniface V (619-25)
69. Honorius I (625-38)
70. Severinus (640)
71. John IV (640-42) (Dalmatian)
72. Theodore I (642-49) (Greek)
73. St. Martin I (649; deposed 653; died 655)
74. St. Eugenius I (654-57)
75. St. Vitalian (657-72)
76. Adeodatus (II) (672-76)
77. Donus (676-78)
78. St. Agatho (678-81)
79. St. Leo II (682-83)
80. St. Benedict II (684-85)
81. John V (685-86) (Syrian)
82. Conon (686-87)
    [Theodore (687)]
    [Paschal (687)]
83. St. Sergius I (687-701) (Syrian)
84. John VI (701-05) (Greek)
85. John VII (705-07) (Greek)
86. Sisinnius (708) (Syrian)
87. Constantine I (708-15) (Syrian)
88. St. Gregory II (715-31)
89. St. Gregory III (731-41) (Syrian)
90. St. Zacharias (741-52) (Greek)
    Stephen II (four days in 752)
91. Stephen II (III) (752-57)
92. St. Paul I (757-67)
    [Constantine (767-768)]
    [Philip (768)]
93. Stephen III (IV) (767-72)
94. Adrian I (772-95)
95. St. Leo III (795-816)
96. Stephen IV (V) (816-17)
97. St. Paschal I (817-24)
98. Eugene II (824-27)
99. Valentine (827)
100. Gregory IV (827-44)
    [John (844)]
101. Sergius II (844-47)
102. St. Leo IV (847-55)
103. Benedict III (855-58)
    [Anastasius Bibliothecarius (855)]
104. St. Nicholas I (the Great) (858-67)
105. Adrian II (867-72)

106. John VIII (872-82)
107. Marinus I (882-84)
108. St. Adrian III (884-85)
109. Stephen V (VI) (885-91)
110. Formosus (891-96)
111. Boniface VI (896)
112. Stephen VI (VII) (896-97)
113. Romanus (897)
114. Theodore II (897)
115. John IX (898-900)
116. Benedict IV (900-03)
117. Leo V (903; murdered 904)
    [Christopher (903-904)]
118. Sergius III (904-11)
119. Anastasius III (911-13)
120. Lando (913-14)
121. John X (914; deposed 928; murdered 929)
122. Leo VI (928)
123. Stephen VII (VIII) (929-31)
124. John XI (931-35)
125. Leo VII (936-39)
126. Stephen VIII (IX) (939-42)
127. Marinus II (Martin III) (942-46)
128. Agapitus II (946-55)
129. John XII (955-63)
130. Leo VIII (963; deposed 964; died 966)
131. Benedict V (964)
132. John XIII (965-72)
133. Benedict VI (973-74)
    [Boniface VII (974)]
134. Benedict VII (974-83)
135. John XIV (983-84)
    [Boniface VII (again; 984-985)]
136. John XV (985-96)
137. Gregory V (996-99) (Carinthian)
    [John XVI (997-998)]
138. Sylvester II (999-1003) (French)
139. John XVII (1003)
140. John XVIII (1003-09)
141. Sergius IV (1009-12)
    [Gregory VI (1012)]
142. Benedict VIII (1012-24) *(Theophylact II of the Counts of Tusculum)*
145. John XIX (1024-32) *(Romanus of the Counts of Tusculum)*
144. Benedict IX (1032-44; 1045; 1047-deposed 1048) *(Theophylact III of the Counts of Tusculum)*

145. Sylvester III (1045; deposed)
146. Gregory VI (1045-deposed 1046)
147. Clement II (1046-47) (Saxon)
148. Damasus II (1048) (Bavarian)
149. St. Leo IX (1049-54) (Alsatian)
150. Victor II (1055-57) (Lorrainer)
151. Stephen IX (X) (1057-58)
    [Benedict X (1058-59)]
152. Nicholas II (1058-61) (Lorrainer)
153. Alexander II (1061-73)
    [Honorius II (1061-64)]
154. St. Gregory VII (1073-85)
    [Clement III (1080; 1084-1100)]
155. Blessed Victor III (1086-87)
156. Blessed Urban II (1088-99) (French)
157. Paschal II (1099-1118)
    [Theodoric (1100-1101)]
    [Albert (1101-02)]
    [Sylvester IV (1105-11)]
158. Gelasius II (1118-19)
    [Gregory VIII (1118-21)]
159. Callistus II (1119-24) (Burgundian)
160. Honorius II (1124-30)
    [Celestine II (1124)]
161. Innocent II (1130-43)
    [Anacletus II (1130-1138)]
    [Victor IV (1138)]
162. Celestine II (1143-44)
163. Lucius II (1144-45)
164. Blessed Eugene III (1145-53)
165. Anastasius IV (1153-54)
166. Hadrian IV (1154-59) (English)
167. Alexander III (1159-81)
    [Victor IV (not identical) (1159-64)]
    [Paschal III (1164-68)]
    [Callistus III (1168-79)]
    [Innocent III (1179-80)]
168. Lucius III (1181-85)
169. Urban III (1185-87)
170. Gregory VIII (1187)
171. Clement III (1187-91)
172. Celestine III (1191-98)
173. Innocent III (1198-1216)
174. Honorius III (1216-27)
175. Gregory IX (1227-41) *(Ugolino of the Counts of Segni)*
176. Celestine IV (1241)
177. Innocent IV (1243-54)

178. Alexander IV (1254-61)
179. Urban IV (1261-64) (French)
180. Clement IV (1265-68) (French)
181. Blessed Gregory X (1271-76) *(Tedaldo Visconti)*
182. Blessed Innocent V (1276)
183. Hadrian V (1276) *(Ottobono Fieschi)*
184. John XXI (1276-77) (thanks to a medieval mistake, there is no John XX) (Portuguese)
185. Nicholas III (1277-80) *(Giovanni Gaetano Orsini)*
186. Martin IV (1281-85) (French)
187. Honorius IV (1285-87) *(Giacomo Savelli)*
188. Nicholas IV (1288-92)
189. St. Celestine V (1294; resigned)
190. Boniface VIII (1294-1303)

AVIGNONESE POPES
191. Blessed Benedict XI (1303-04)
192. Clement V (1305-14) (French)
193. John XXII (1316-34) (French)
    [Nicholas V (1328-30)]
194. Benedict XII (1334-42) (French)
195. Clement VI (1342-52) (French)
196. Innocent VI (1352-62) (French)
197. Blessed Urban V (1362-70) (French)
198. Gregory XI (1370-78) (French)
199. Urban VI (1378-89)

STAYED IN AVIGNON AS ANTI-POPES
    [Clement VII (1378-94) (French)]
    [Benedict XIII (1394-1417; died 1423) (Aragonese)]
    [Clement VIII (1423-29) (Spanish)]
    [Benedict XIV (1425-?) (French)]

200. Boniface IX (1389-1404) *(Pietro Tomacelli)*
201. Innocent VII (1404-06)
202. Gregory XII (1406- abdicated 1415; died 1417) *(Angelo Correr)* (returns to Rome)

ELECTED BY THE RIVAL COUNCIL OF PISA (NON-ECUMENICAL)
    [Alexander V (1409-10) (Cretan)]
    [John XXIII (1410-15; died 1419)]

203. Martin V (1417-31) *(Odo Colonna)*
204. Eugenius IV (1431-47)

[Felix V (1439-49) *(Amadeus of Savoy)*]
205. Nicholas V (1447-55)
206. Callistus III (1455-58) *(Alfonso Borgia)* (Spanish)
207. Pius II (1458-64) *(Æneas Silvio Piccolomini)*
208. Paul II (1464-71) *(Pietro Barbo)*
209. Sixtus IV (1471-84) *(Francesco della Rovere)*
210. Innocent VIII (1484-92) *(Giambattista Cybo)*
211. Alexander VI (1492-1503) *(Roderigo de Borgia)* (Spanish)
212. Pius III (1503) *(Francesco Todeschini)*
213. Julius II (1503-13) *(Giuliano della Rovere)*
214. Leo X (1513-21) *(Giovanni de' Medici)*
215. Adrian VI (1522-23) *(Adrian Florensz. Dedel)*
216. Clement VII (1523-34) *(Giulio de' Medici)*
217. Paul III (1534-49) *(Alessandro Farnese)*
218. Julius III (1550-55) *(Giovanni del Monte)*
219. Marcellus II (1555) *(Marcello Cervini)*
220. Paul IV (1555-59) *(Giovanni Pietro Carafa)*
221. Pius IV (1559-65) *(Giovanni Angelo Medici)*
222. St. Pius V (1566-72) *(Michele Ghislieri)*
223. Gregory XIII (1572-85) *(Ugo Buoncompagni)*
224. Sixtus V (1585-90) *(Felice Peretti)*
225. Urban VII (1590) *(Giambattista Castagna)*
226. Gregory XIV (1590-91) *(Nicolò Sfondrati)*
227. Innocent IX (1591) *(Giovanni Antonio Facchinetti)*
228. Clement VIII (1592-1605) *(Ippolito Aldobrandini)*
229. Leo XI (1605) *(Alessandro de' Medici)*
230. Paul V (1605-21) *(Camillo Borghese)*
231. Gregory XV (1621-23) *(Alessandro Ludovisi)*
232. Urban VIII (1623-44) *(Maffeo Barberini)*
233. Innocent X (1644-55) *(Giambattista Pamfili)*
234. Alexander VII (1655-67) *(Fabio Chigi)*
235. Clement IX (1667-69) *(Giulio Rospigliosi)*
236. Clement X (1670-76) *(Emilio Altieri)*

237. Blessed Innocent XI (1676-89) *(Benedetto Odescalchi)*
238. Alexander VIII (1689-91) *(Pietro Ottoboni)*
239. Innocent XII (1691-1700) *(Antonio Pignatelli)*
240. Clement XI (1700-21) *(Gianfrancesco Albani)*
241. Innocent XIII (1721-24) *(Michelangelo de' Conti)*
242. Benedict XIII (1724-30) *(Pietro Francesco Orsini-Gravina)*
243. Clement XII (1730-40) *(Lorenzo Corsini)*
244. Benedict XIV (1740-58) *(Prospero Lorenzo Lambertini)*
245. Clement XIII (1758-69) *(Carlo della Torre Rezzonico)*
246. Clement XIV (1769-74) *(Lorenzo Ganganelli)*
247. Pius VI (1775-99) *(Giovanni Angelo Braschi)*
248. Pius VII (1800-23) *(Barnaba Chiaramonti)*
249. Leo XII (1823-29) *(Annibale della Genga)*
250. Pius VIII (1829-30) *(Francesco Saverio Castiglione)*
251. Gregory XVI (1831-46) *(Bartolomeo Cappellari)*
252. Blessed Pius IX (1846-78) *(Giovanni Maria Mastai-Ferretti)*
253. Leo XIII (1878-1903) *(Gioacchino Vincenzo Pecci)*
254. St. Pius X (1903-14) *(Giuseppe Sarto)*
255. Benedict XV (1914-22) *(Giacomo della Chiesa)*
256. Pius XI (1922-39) *(Achille Ratti)*
257. Pius XII (1939-58) *(Eugenio Pacelli)*
258. Blessed John XXIII (1958-63) *(Angelo Giuseppe Roncalli)*
259. Paul VI (1963-78) *(Giovanni Battista Montini)*
260. John Paul I (1978) *(Albino Luciani)*
261. John Paul II (1978-2005) *(Karol Josef Wojtyla)* (Polish)
262. Benedict XVI (2005–) *(Josef Ratzinger)* (German)

Emperors

Julian and Claudian dynasty
31BC-14AD Augustus
14-37 Tiberius
37-41 Caligula
41-54 Claudius
54-68 Nero

Year of the Four Cæsars
68-69 Galba
69 Otho
69 Vitellius

Flavian Dynasty
69-79 Vespasian
79-81 Titus
81-96 Domitian

Emperors by adoption
96-98 Nerva
98-117 Trajan
117-138 Hadrian

Antonine dynasty
138-161 Antoninus Pius
161-180 Marcus Aurelius
161-166 Lucius Verus
180-192 Commodus

Year of the Five Cæsars
193 Pertinax
193 Julian
193-194 Pescennius Niger
193-197 Clodius Albinus

Severan dynasty
193-211 Septimius Severus
211-217 Caracalla
211-212 Geta

218 Macrinus and
Diadumenianus
218-22 Heliogabalus
222-235 Alexander Severus

Soldier Cæsars
238 Gordian I
238 Gordian II
238 Pupienus (Maximus)
238 Balbinus
238-244 Gordian III
244-249 Philip the Arab
249-251 Decius
251-253 Trebonianus Gallus
and Volusianus
253 Æmilianus
253-260 Valerian
260-268 Gallienus
268-270 Claudius II
270 Quintillus
270-275 Aurelian
275-276 Tacitus
276 Florianus
276-282 Probus
282-283 Carus
283-285 Carinus
283-284 Numerianus

Tetrarchy
284-305 Diocletian
286-305 Maximianus
305-311 Galerius
305-306 Constantius I
306-307 Flavius Severus
306-312 Maxentius
308-324 Licinius
310-313 Maximinus Daia

**From Constantine to
Theodosius**
306-337 Constantine I
337-340 Constantine II
337-361 Constantius II
337-350 Constans I
361-363 Julian the Apostate
363-364 Jovian
364-375 Valentinian I
364-378 Valens
367-383 Gratian
375-392 Valentinian II
378-395 Theodosius I the
Great

Western Empire
395-423 Honorius
421 Constantine III
425-455 Valentinian III
455 Petronius Maximus
455-456 Avitus
457-461 Majorian
461-465 Libius Severus
467-472 Anthemius
472 Olybrius
473-474 Glycerius
474-480 Julius Nepos
475-476 Romulus Augustulus

Glossary

'Abitato' and **'disabitato'** The barbarians who besieged Rome after the fall of the Empire severed the aqueducts, forcing the citizenry to abandon the hills for lack of water. These densely-populated areas, the first to be settled a thousand years earlier, now became largely deserted, with the result that large areas within the city walls would remain empty for centuries. These areas soon became collectively known as the 'disabitato' ('depopulated'), to distinguish them from those that had always remained inhabited – the 'abitato'. In the 19th century the disabitato was still just that – rustic patches, vineyards and gardens punctuated by the occasional ruin. Eventually these areas were rebuilt, but even to this day some of them convey a feeling of solitude. See also p. 28.

Aisle The side corridors of a nave, separated from it by columns or piers.

Amphitheatre The word – meaning 'a double theatre' or 'a theatre on both sides' – is Greek, but the invention is Roman, and the prototypes were built in Italy in the 1st century. BC. Since theatres were semicircular, a 'double theatre' formed a whole circle (or, more often, an oval). Such shape was an answer to a specific form of entertainment favored by the Romans: gladiatorial games and wild beast hunts. The prototypes were in wood, and some consisted literally of two theatres which could be used singly or together by rotating them on a pivot. Rome's first permanent stone amphitheatre, built under Augustus by his general Statilius Taurus, was destroyed in the great fire under Nero in 64 AD. The huge Amphiteatrum Flavium (only much later called the Colosseum) was built by Jewish war prisoners under the emperors Vespasian and Titus (AD 69-81) on the site of Nero's demolished Domus Aurea. A smaller amphitheatre, called Castrense, was built about two centuries later. Its ruins still exist.

Apse Curved or semicircular part of a wall, often specially decorated, housing an artwork or dedicated to a particular function. In a church, it is the backdrop to the nave and usually contains the choir and the bishop's chair. The aisles (qv) may also end in apses.

Architrave Beam or lowest division of the entablature which extends from column to column. The term also applies to to the moulded frame round a door or window.

Art Deco Highly geometric style of building and decoration popular in the 1930's; overlaps with other movements such as the Bauhaus and Razionalismo (qv).

Art Nouveau Stylistic movement of the turn of the 20th century, characterized by a delicate sensuality of forms, and sinuous lines, particularly the famous 'whiplash' line. Had limited impact in Italy.

Atrium Entrance hall of a Roman house, with the roof open to the sky in the middle. Sometimes the rim of the roof aperture was supported by four or more columns. In later architecture and in churches the term denotes a forecourt.

Baldaquin or **Baldacchino** A specially imposing, roofed ciborium (qv) on an altar. Can be of cloth, bronze or marble, or a combination of them. Also, a cloth canopy carried over an eminent person.

Barocco, baroque The word 'baroque', originally used in a negative sense to mean 'capricious' or 'irregular', came later to indicate an ornate, emotional style – particularly of architecture, but also of sculpture and painting – which originated in Rome at the end of the 16th century in reaction to the simplicity and 'classical' straightforwardness of renaissance art. It was soon harnessed to the educational and inspirational purposes of the Counter-Reformation. Baroque spread to the rest of Italy and then Europe, assuming ever freer, more exuberant features, until the middle of the 18th century, when opposite trends in the direction of austerity and linearity started to take hold.

Basilica Greek word meaning 'royal building'. The basilica, though, is not a Greek but a Roman invention. It is a large, rectangular roofed building, of one or (less commonly) two storeys, the central area divided by rows of columns and lit by a clearstorey (the windows in the upper section of a higher central nave). This very successful model was later adopted by the Christians for their churches. Among the few differences: pagan basilicas were surrounded not only by walls but by giant porticoes, usually two-storied; also, the main entrance was on the long side instead of the short. Pagans did not use basilicas for religious purposes; for that they had temples. Temples were usually reserved for priests, while worshippers assembled outside. Christians, in contrast, wanted everybody inside. That's why they adopted an architectural model, the basilica, eminently suitable for large gatherings. All the great early churches, starting with those built by the emperor Constantine, who legalized Christianity, were basilicas. More recently, the name 'basilica' has been applied as a badge of distinction to very important churches, whatever their shape.

Basolato Common type of ancient Roman road pavement, made of large, approximately square or rectangular stone slabs called 'basoli' or 'basole.' Predecessor of selciato (qv).

Baths As an aid to hygiene and a form of entertainment, baths go back to ancient Egyptian and Ægean civilizations, yet it was the Romans who, beginning in the age of Augustus, elevated them to a peak of popularity and architectural creativity. All Roman baths followed the same essential layout, differing only in size. Bathers could choose between hot, warm and cold pools. Dressing areas, oiling rooms and saunas were standard services. To one side was an outdoor swimming pool for summer use. The baths proper were situated within a vast courtyard for callisthenics, appointed with gardens, gyms, shops, a stadium and even a library. See also pp. 275-276.

Bishop's Chair or **Throne** Feature of many, especially medieval, churches, where it was used on the occasion of a visit by a high prelate, such as the cardinal titular, or the pope.

Byzantine style The Eastern Empire developed its own style of art and architecture from the 6th century AD, called Byzantine after the Empire's capital Byzantium (Constantinople, later Istanbul). Its influence spread beyond the frontiers of the East-Roman (Byzantine) Empire throughout Western and Eastern Europe up to the end of the middle ages (later in the east). In Italy, Byzantine art had great impact owing to the reconquest of parts of the peninsula by the Eastern Emperor Justinian in the 6th century and intermittent Byzantine rule for over 200 years in Rome and longer in the southern regions. In Rome its influence was mainly seen in mosaic, a medium felt to be specially apt to express the emphatic, transcendent mysticism typical of Byzantine religious representations. Stylistically this spiritual intensity translated into austerity of design and two-dimensionality; characteristics so marked, at times, as to confer an hypnotic, other-worldly quality.

Catacombs Underground cemeteries used since the remotest antiquity in the Mediterranean world, particularly in places, such as Rome, where the volcanic ground made digging easy and burial inexpensive. Several religions also came to prefer burial to cremation, which the pagans favoured. The earliest catacombs were · Jewish, and served as models for the Christian catacombs. The use of cremation among the pagans went into decline in the 2nd century, around the time of Hadrian, and in the succeeding centuries catacombs spread rapidly as Christianity took widespread root. Their use peaked around the mid-4th century; then, with the fall of the Empire and the depopulation of Rome, they went into disuse. By the middle ages their very existence was forgotten, until they were rediscovered accidentally in 1578. The Roman catacombs have as many as five levels, and are frequently 66 ft (20 m) or more deep. They can extend across vast distances, through narrow, labyrinthine corridors. The families of the deceased used to celebrate rites and keep funerary shrines there. In some cases the catacombs also served as hiding places during religious or even secular persecutions, though how often is unclear. However, a widespread notion that early Christians used the catacombs as secret places of worship appears unfounded. It is thought that the name 'catacombs,' dating back only to the rule of the Greek-speaking Byzantines in Rome (6th-8th century), is Greek, and that it originates from the Catacombs of St Sebastian which were 'near a quarry' ('kata kumbas').

Cenotaph Monument to a person or persons buried elsewhere.

Ciborium Marble or bronze canopy, often propped on four columns, over or near the altar. It generally serves as the keeping place of the Eucharist or, less often, of relics. It is often also called the tabernacle (qv).

Circus In Roman architecture a long rounded building with oblong ends and with tiered seating on both sides. See also pp. 265-267.

Columbarium An ancient Roman burial place, so called because it was constructed with niches or shelves on every wall like dovecotes or *columbaria*.

Cornice The top, projecting section of an entab-lature. Any projecting ornamental moulding along the top of a building, wall, arch, etc.

Cosmati work Vivid, multicoloured marble work which decorates pavements, columns, pulpits, tombs etc. in many late 12th- to late 13th-century Roman churches. It was created by generations of masons, sculptors and architects mostly belonging to a family called Cosma. See also Artists' Index.

Disabitato see 'Abitato'

Diaconiæ Churches that originally doubled as welfare centers and food distribution centers to help a populace ravaged by famine and disease. The first ones were part of a chain conceived by the remarkable 6th-century pope St Gregory the Great to distribute the produce from church-owned farms in the countryside around Rome, a critical programme amid the desperate poverty that followed the fall of the Empire.

Drum or **Tambour** Vertical, round band, often with columns, at the base of a dome.

Easter candelabrum Large, freestanding candelabrum found in many churches. It is the only relic of a medieval Easter liturgy called 'Tenebræ' (Latin for 'darkness'), in which the death and resurrection of of the Lord were celebrated at night, with the darkness in the church broken only by light from this candelabrum.

Ecclesia domestica or **Titulus** Many of the earliest Christian churches were not churches: they were the homes of well-to-do believers, placed at the disposal of the other faithful so they could perform their rites sheltered from official persecution. They were also important meeting places for the early church hierarchy, and at one point there was one such home church ('ecclesia domestica') for each region of the city of Rome. After the legalization of Christianity, many of these homes became regular churches, and the ancient network of home churches was converted into the still existing system of parish churches. Ecclesiæ domesticæ were also called *Tituli* or 'titles' because, in their function as proto-parishes, they were usually entrusted to particular clerics and recognized as their 'titles.' In a somewhat similar way the term 'cardinal's title' ('titolo cardinalizio') is used today for major churches, each of which is assigned to the sponsorship of a particular cardinal.

Entablature A horizontal architectural member supported by columns or pilasters and usually consisting of architrave, frieze, and cornice.

Floreal In decorative arts, an Italian variant of Art Nouveau (qv) and of the Liberty style (qv) emphasizing the naturalistic motifs of both, such as leaves and flowers (hence the name).

Foricæ Public lavatories of ancient Rome. Since the apartments in the ancient Roman 'insula' (qv), as opposed to houses, had no lavatories, most people used the foricæ. They consisted of rows of marble seats, could be quite luxurious and, like the public baths, were popular socializing spots. The ruins of several survive in Rome.

Frieze The middle division of an entablature, usually decorated but sometimes plain; the decorated band along the upper part of an internal wall, immediately below the cornice

Futurism Italian *avant-garde* movement launched in 1908 by Marinetti and inspired by the dynamism of the modern city. Futurism faltered during the First World War and attempts to revive it foundered in its association with Fascism.

Gothic style Style of architecture and decoration originating in northern France in the late 12th century. It is characterized by verticality and lightness – in contrast to the horizontality and massiveness of the Romanesque. Technically, these qualities are made possible by a widespread use of buttresses, ogival cross-vaults and by the pointed arch (as opposed to the round arch of the Romanesque). It had very limited influence in Rome, where its characteristic elements (the pointed arch, the ogival cross-vault) are just

hinted at, and only in a very few churches. In sculpture and painting, the terms 'Gothic', 'Late Gothic' and 'International Gothic' are sometimes used to describe schools of the 13th and 14th centuries. See also pp. 313-314.

Graffito or **Sgraffito** ('scratched') A drawing scratched onto a wall or more specifically by scratching through a layer of paint or other material to reveal a ground of a different colour. See also p. 449.

Grotesques Fanciful decoration composed of small, loosely connected motifs including human figures, monkeys, sphinxes etc.. The term derives from ancient Roman decorations which came to light in the renaissance after being buried in subterranean ruins known as *grotte*.

Hellenistic A term applied to Greek culture between Alexander and Augustus, (approximately from 323 to 27 BC). Imperial Roman architecture may be regarded as its logical develoment. See also p. 311.

Home church see Ecclesia domestica.

Icon A holy image painted on wood or metal, typical of Byzantine art and of the Orthodox religion.

Iconostasis In eastern (Greek or Byzantine) churches, a screen or partition with doors and tiers of icons, separating the section that contains the altar from the nave.

Insula In ancient Rome, a block with one or more apartment buildings, which were usually rented (as opposed to the self-contained, one-family houses of the upper class, which were owned and had an entirely different layout). Insula apartments, unlike houses, lacked running water and had no kitchens or bathrooms. So tenants resorted to take-away food from the ground floor *tabernæ* (qv), to public baths and public lavatories, *foricæ* (qv).

Iseum Temple devoted to the Egyptian goddess Isis. One large such temple existed in Rome's Campus Martius; a smaller, older one was on the Capitol.

Lantern Small, generally round, structure atop a

dome, often letting in light.

Liberty style Although originating in London, where it was applied to the drawings of Arthur Lesenby Liberty and to the products sold at the Liberty store, this term is, strangely enough, more widespread in Italy than in England. In Rome it connotes a variant of Art Nouveau found in decorative arts and in some buildings, overlapping with Floreal style (qv).

Loggia In Rome, a roofed balcony, often arcaded and whose arches are supported by small columns or pilasters. In Florence and other Italian cities, the same word is used for medieval and Renaissance buildings open on one side, arcaded, used as meeting points for merchants and others.

Madonnella see Tabernacle.

Mannerism Painting style that flourished in the second half of the 16th century, characterised by mannered elegance, formal virtuosity and a dose of extravagance that betrays the restlessness at its source. As a reaction to the values of balance, measuredness and proportion that had triumphed in the High Renaissance, it is reminiscent of the baroque. Mannerism originated in Italy, but its most characteristic exponents also worked elsewhere in Europe, notably in France (the 'Fontainebleau school').

Matronea Side galleries, usually on an upper level, where in the oldest Christian churches women were confined.

Metaphysical art Term applied to the work of De Chirico, Carrà and other modern Italian painters and sculptors. Although the actual metaphysics are obscure, the works undoubtedly create an atmosphere of mystery. The style also had an impact on architecture. See also p. 628.

Mithræum or **Mithraic temple** Building devoted to the Persian cult of Mithras, one of many oriental religions in Rome and the last pagan religion to survive there. Mithraism had some affinities with Christianity, though it admitted only men and stressed loyalty and courage, rather than love (for this reason it was especially popular with the military). For the symbolism of Mithraic images see p. 322

Mullioned window A window divided in two or more lights by vertical dividers called mullions.

Narthex In early Christian churches, a portico against the façade or on the inside, reserved to those not yet baptized and to penitents, who were not yet allowed into the church proper.

Nave Central and largest space of a church, usually (but not always) flanked by aisles (qv) and crossed (but not always) by a transept (qv).

Nazarenes Group of German painters in Rome in the early 19th C, including Overbeck, Koch, Veit, Reinhart and Hoffmann. Working toward a renewal of art on religious and nationalistic foundations, they drew inspiration from the simplicity of composition and colour of the early renaissance Italian paintings. The movement strongly influenced painting in Germany and elsewhere in Europe, well into and past the 19th century.

Neoclassicism A revival of the canons of Greek and Roman classical art, begun in the mid-18th century in reaction to the baroque, and lasting until the early 19th century and sometimes beyond. It was stimulated by the first serious efforts in archæology and æsthetic studies, especially those of the German J. J. Winckelmann. It also had its underpinnings in the political-philosophical movement of the Enlightenment, based on reason and the ancient virtues, values widely praised during the French Revolution and the subsequent upheavals. Its greatest adherents worked in the visual arts: sculpture (Canova, Thorvaldsen), painting (especially in France), architecture (in Rome, Valadier) and the decorative arts; but its impact can also be seen in music and literature.

Nymphæum Architectural element that suggests the abode of water deities, the nymphs. In classical times, a fountain, pool or other ornamental feature of a building or garden; in the baroque, more often an artificial grotto.

Odeon or **odeum** Greek or Roman concert hall, shaped like a small theatre.

Orans or **orant** (from the Latin *orare*, to pray.) An early Christian representation, in art, of a praying figure, arms outstretched. This ancient ritual gesture is both Jewish and Christian.

Oratory or **oratorium** Chapel or other place devoted to prayer. An oratorio is a religious music-drama, a form pioneered at the Oratory of the Filippini in Rome.

Palladian Architectural style derived from the buildings and publications of Palladio which crystallised various renaissance notions, notably that of Roman symmetrical planning and harmonic proportions, and aimed to recapture the splendour of antiquity. Despite being thought to be 'impure' by later neo-classical architects, Palladio's ideas came to be accepted almost blindly as the classical canon all over the world.

Pendentive A curved section connecting the angle of two walls to the base of a dome, it is one of the means by which a circular dome is supported over a square or polygonal chamber. In baroque architecture it forms an important part of the decorative scheme.

Peristyle or **Peristilium** A courtyard with columns.

Pomerium The official city limits of ancient Rome.

Portico or **porticus** Roofed space forming the entrance and centrepiece of the facade of a temple, house or church. In ancient Rome, a large colonnaded area. See also pp. 245-246

Pre-Raphaelite school Mid-19th century English artistic movement somewhat similar to the Nazarene school of Germany (qv), aiming at a return to the spontaneity and simplicity of the early renaissance.

Presbytery The part of a church with the High Altar, from which the priests conduct services, usually raised a step or two. A 'triumphal arch' and, in Greek or Byzantine churches, an iconostasis (qv) often separate the area of the presbytery from the nave.

Prothyrum Stone vestibule with small columns and a friezed architrave, often followed by a courtyard, at the entrance of some medieval churches.

Razionalismo, Rationalism Stylistic current in Italian architecture, begun in the pre-war Fascist years, that shared with the German Bauhaus style the 'rational' principle that every form must be justified by its function.

Renaissance Generally applied to the intellectual movement beginning in the 14th century and culminating in the 16th (the 'High Renaissance'). An exact definition is much debated but essentially the term denotes the 'rebirth' of interest in classical learning, art and architecture during the period.

Rococo Architectural and decorative style of the 18th century, derived from the baroque and based on gracefulness, elegance and fanciful curved forms. It emerged in France (the name is based on the French 'rocaille', meaning shell-like forms) and spread to the rest of Europe, but is rare in Rome.

Romanesque Architectural style that prevailed in Western Europe from the late 11th to the early 13th centuries. It derives from provincial, folk-like currents in the late Roman Empire as opposed to the 'aristocratic' classical style (a social trend which coincided with the separation of national, or 'romance', languages from Latin – hence the name). Of endearing simplicity, the Romanesque is characterized by squatness (as opposed to the vertical thrust of the Gothic), the round arch and, often, ornamental elements accenting the structural lines. The term is often extended to the sculpture and painting of the same period; the latter typified in Rome by the 11th century frescoes of S. Clemente (one containing the earliest extant record of the Italian language).

Romanticism Multifaceted cultural movement that began in the very late 18th century. Its tone contrasts with the rational, 'enlightened' approach of the rival style of neoclassicism. Unlike the latter, it affirmed individualism against the abstract beauty of the Greco-Roman tradition, and rejected strict formalism and rigorous design in favour of spontaneity, emotion and impulse, drawing on Christian values of humanity and passion. As an æsthetic current, it manifested itself in literature, in the visual arts and especially music.

'Roma quadrata' ('Square Rome') The original city of Rome, as it was founded and walled on top of the Palatine.

Selciato The typical paving stones of Roman streets between the middle ages and modern times, until the advent of asphalt. Selci (from the Latin *silex*, flint) were small truncated pyramids; they replaced the much larger, flatter slabs of flint (see 'basolato') of ancient Rome. See also p. 106.

Spolia Marble slabs, or other architectural elements, plundered from earlier buildings for re-use. This practice, sporadic in the late Roman Empire, became widespread after its fall. Whole columns were favorite spolia objects, as after the empire both materials and skills to produce them were lacking. A large proportion of the columns in Rome's churches and other classical buildings are spolia from pagan temples, basilicas or other monuments.

Tabernæ Ancient Roman shops, on the ground floor of the *insulæ*, or apartment houses (qv). They typically included a large room at mezzanine level, with a window over the shop door, for the shop-keeper and his family. Tabernæ, like the apartments, were rented out by landlords. Ancient authors say that when shopkeepers were late with the rent, landlords would threaten to trap them upstairs by removing the portable ladder to the store below. Many of the stores sold take-away food, because the apartments lacked kitchens. They also lacked bathrooms, and so most people used public lavatories (*foricæ*, qv).

Tabernacle In churches, a receptacle for the consecrated Host (on the altar) and of the Holy Oil (generally on a wall); also, a shrine-like, canopied free-standing structure, alternatively called a *baldaquin* or a *ciborium* (qqv). The word also denotes wall shrines, including those in the streets commonly called *madonnelle* (from a painted sacred image that often, though not always, represents the Madonna – see also p. 66).

Tablinum The living room of an ancient Roman house. It opened on an atrium, and in the earliest times it could include the master bedroom. Family archives (*tabulæ*) were kept there, hence the room's name.

Tesseræ Small pieces of marble or glass used in mosaics. The former were preferred for floor moisaics, the latter for wall mosaics, but there are exceptions.

Titulus see Ecclesia domestica.

Transept Major space before the altar area that runs perpendicular to the nave and gives the church the shape of a cross.

Travertine A calcareous rock quarried at Tivoli near Rome, of a dirty-white color which Rome's brilliant sunlight endows with yellow or pinkish hues. Many of Rome's finest edifices, including St. Peter's, both ancient and modern, are built of travertine or faced with it.

Triclinium The dining room of an ancient-Roman house.

Triumphal Arch An arch erected in honour of an important person, usually an emperor or general, and often used as a passageway for triumphal parades. In churches it is the arch separating the presbytery (qv) from the nave (qv).

Tufa A brown-red, soft volcanic rock common in Southern Italy, suitable for construction work. Used in early columns, temples and basilicas, it was later generally replaced by marble.

Ustrinum, plural **ustrina** A crematory oven and its building, often monumental.

Practical information

A city in flux: Official schedules and phone numbers, monument and church opening hours, as well as bus numbers and routes are constantly changing in Rome. Some museum opening hours have changed 35 times in the past 20 years; other site schedules are hardly more stable. It's rarely clear whether something is accessible, and when. The telephone system, with most of the numbers, has changed three times in a decade and is being overhauled again. Repeated bus and train route changes have triggered public resentment; currently, not only are most bus lines changing, but there is a plan to replace all the bus numbers. Recently the city announced it will hire a German firm to draw a new, and, let us hope, final public transportation plan, but nothing has come of this yet.

Given the situation, we debated whether to include schedules, phone numbers and bus routes at all. We have done so, partly because some of it will remain valid, and partly because, even when outdated, it could maintain some value in helping you find your way around.

So we strongly stress the need to confirm the information in the book before relying on it, by either calling the sites (numbers are available through the telephone information service) or using the daily press. Newsstands should have current public transportation maps, or you can try calling the ATAC transit agency at (06) 800431784, or consulting ATAC's English-language information site on the Web at: www.atac.roma.it/ trasroma/indexuk.htm.

When telephoning anywhere in Rome, even from within the city, the city code (06) must currently be added before any number dialled.

The city maintains a 24-hour general information number, 06 06 06, where they try to help with any problem relating to city services or other counselling. Between 4 pm and 7 pm the operators include staff fluent in all major languages. Lastly, the city has promised to provide updated information on the accessibility of monuments at the numbers (06) 82059127, (06) 4815576, (06) 39967700, (06) 36004399 or (06) 39749907; some of the operators speak English.

Some archæological sites normally closed to the public may be visited by special permission. The telephone numbers to try are: (06) 6790110 (sites under Italian government control, Soprintendenza Archeologica di Roma); (06) 67103819 (sites under city government control, Sovraintendenza Comunale); (06) 4465610 (sites under Vatican control, Pontificia Commissione di Archeologia Sacra).

Some Practical Hints

The importance of small change Besides being used for all the usual purposes, including public phones and vending machines, small change is precious to the tourist in Rome for a special reason: artworks in churches are usually lit by coin-operated devices. These gadgets are not standardized, so you will need coins of all denominations, and a single church can gobble up your entire monetary reserve.

So take along plenty of change. Remember that this reserve won't be very easy to replenish, because for some reason stores in Rome are perennially short of change.

Public telephones, by the way, are at this writing being converted for use with magnetic cards which will be sold by tobacconists.

Crossing a Roman street Roman traffic? Madness. That's the unanimous opinion of arriving foreigners.

Yet there is some method in the madness, which explains why accidents, at least involving pedestrians, are not especially frequent in Rome.

Many city dwellers lavish attention on rules, and neglect actual situations. The opposite is true in Rome. Traffic lights, stop signs and crosswalks are rare and not much relied on. Instead, drivers and pedestrians pay close attention to each other. The relative lack of regulation is the result of the old city's topography; trying to regulate so many winding streets and crooked intersections would virtually halt traffic.

Some pedestrians seem almost absentmindedly to brave the speeding vehicles, but rest assured, they are quite aware of the surroundings activity. Their nonchalance is a ploy, a display of unpredictability, meant to keep the drivers on guard. Drivers, for their part, are acutely conscious of the pedestrians, but try to look as if they are not and keep forging ahead until they are forced to stop.

Church sightseeing: precautions With the exception of major basilicas such as St. Peter's and others a strict dress code is not enforced in churches. But somewhat conservative attire is recommended; short shorts and miniskirts are not always found acceptable.

Sightseeing is frowned upon during religious services. If you want to move around while these take place, do so with extreme discretion.

At other times please behave respectfully and refrain from loud talking. In some cases, you can venture into the side chapels and even go behind the main altar, in the presbytery area - but the access must be clearly open. If in doubt, ask at the sacristy.

If the sacristan does something special for you, such as accompanying you and showing you things, you should tip him. Offerings are sorely needed and you may leave them in the designated boxes. Some churches sell publications and postcards about themselves - the postcards are nicer and cheaper here than in shops.

Church names Regarding church names: *San, Sant', Santo, Santa* , often abbreviated as 'S.', are variants of the Italian word for 'Saint'; the abbreviation 'SS.' means 'Saints'; 'Ss.' means 'most holy' (*Santissimo*).

The term 'basilica' indicates churches laid out as were ancient Roman basilicas (see glossary) but it is also used for some churches of key importance regardless of their architecture. But one can very well avoid these distinctions and stick to the word 'church'. Each city has a 'cathedral', the church of the city's highest bishop; in Rome, this is St Peter's, the pope's church.

Street names made simpler *Piazza* is a square and *via* is a street; that much almost everybody knows; but it may be useful to know that a *viale* is a wide street, or avenue, while a *vicolo* is a narrow street, or alley.

There is only one authentic *Corso* – Rome's Main Street – and in origin the word meant 'the racetrack'. But by extension, *corso* has come to be applied to other important streets in Rome (and in a thousand other Italian towns). Among these streets is Corso Vittorio Emanuele II, named after the king who united Italy in the 19th century; in every day use, this unwieldy name is abbreviated to Corso Vittorio.

Other street terminology: *Borgo*: a street in the Borgo district; *Clivo*: a more ancient name for *salita* (see below) *Largo*: the square-like widening of a street; *Lungotevere*: the riverside drive; *Piazzale*: an esplanade; *Ponte*: a bridge; *Passeggiata*: an avenue originally meant for strolling; *Salita*: an uphill road.

Names of most streets, piazzas, etc. usually include the words *di*, *del*, *della* and such like, the articles and prepositions preceding the actual name. But these words can be omitted in everyday use. Thus, 'Via del Babuino' can simply be called 'Via Babuino'. In our index of places we prefer these commonly accepted Roman names for streets and piazzas to the punctilious forms adopted by the city bureaucracy.

Some visual aids Certain publications on sale in Rome at newsstands and elsewhere can be helpful in visualizing the ancient city landmarks. We recommend the large and inexpensive photographs of a unique and exceptionally detailed model of the city, the original of which is in the far-off Museum of Roman Civilization. There are two of these reproductions, photographed from different angles. They are both entitled *Roma Imperatoris Constantini Ætate* (Latin for 'Rome at the time of Emperor Constantine').

Also useful is a red booklet called *Rome - Past and Present*, in which reconstructions of monuments drawn on clear plastic are superimposed on photos of their present ruins.

To take full advantage of public transport, really essential in Rome for an exhaustive sightseeing programme, we suggest that you integrate the necessarily schematic information provided by this book with one of the detailed, large bus-maps on sale at newsstands.

Finding a lavatory Public lavatories are rare in Rome, but you can find a haven in any of the ubiquitous 'bars,' which in Italy are coffee and snack shops. Order anything – the famous espresso coffee or a glass of spring water (*acqua minerale*, pronounced AK-wah mee-neh- RAH-leh) – or just give a tip, and ask for the *gabinetti* (gah-bee-NET-tee).

Be ready for a less than ideal hygiene situation. It's a good idea to bring your own toilet paper.

A warning about 'bar' prices Most Italian coffeeshops charge significantly more for customers who sit at a table. (This is legal, as most 'bar' prices, both standing and seating, are set by city regulation.) Eat standing if you want to pay less. Do not try to sit after having paid the standing price, if you don't want to be asked to pay the difference.

Opening hours Most stores in Rome are open in the morning and the afternoon, with a long intermission for lunch and siesta. As a rule of thumb, closing time is at 1 pm, reopening at 4 pm (half an hour earlier in summer) then closing again at 7.30 pm (half an hour later in summer). Foodstores and supermarkets tend to close somewhat later, and many stay open through lunch. All non-food stores are closed on Sundays, many on Saturdays too; foodstores and supermarkets are usually closed on Sunday afternoon only (there is only one, at the forefront of a movement for the liberalization of opening hours, which is open seven days a week despite the frequent fines it gets from the city authorities, has no midday closure and stays open late in the evening: the little 'Forno' supermarket opposite the Trevi Fountain.)

Banks are open twice a day but in the afternoon have very short hours. Some are open on Saturday morning, all are closed on Sunday.

Shopping Famous for shopping is the Piazza di Spagna-Via Condotti area, with all the intersecting streets such as Via Frattina, Via Mario dei Fiori, Via Bocca di Leone, Via della Croce and Via delle Carrozze. The shop windows there give a fairly complete idea of what the Italian fashion industry has been up to in all fields of women's and men's apparel and accessories. For antiques there are two main streets: Via del Babuino with some very old establishments, Via dei Coronari with younger firms and possibly less expensive merchandise. Only one store, in Piazza Fontanella di Borghese, specializes in marble antiquities. Rome's big flea market is at Porta Portese (see p. 586), fully open only on Sundays.

Language As you probably know, many centuries of political division and of foreign domination have made it so that every region, every city and even every nook and cranny of Italy has its own dialect, often very different from the one nearby, even over a short distance. Most people, though, also speak a common Italian idiom recognized in all the rest of Italy and taught in schools. Our guidebook is sprinkled with the immortal verses of the poet of Rome, the 19th century poet Gioacchino Belli, the purest expression of the Roman dialect. Yet you will not hear this deepest dialect spoken very often. What you will hear most will be the official idiom, almost always tinted, however, in more or less marked way, by its dialectal background. If one of your purposes in Rome is to learn Italian, or perfect your Italian, be of good heart: the accent that you will draw from listening to the everyday language will be good, even from the 'academic' point of view. A common saying in Italy is that perfect Italian is 'Tuscan language in a Roman's mouth' ('lingua toscana in bocca romana'). This is undoubtedly due to the closeness of the language, in Rome, to its Latin origins. Some dialect words, indeed, are pure Latin, not spoken in other parts of Italy: for instance the very frequently used dialectal word 'mo', meaning 'now', is the abbreviation of the Latin 'modo'. You only hear it in the Rome area. Also, the only place where you hear the vowels 'e' and 'o' pronounced correctly according to the words they belong to, i.e. sometimes 'open' and sometimes 'closed', is Rome.

The Tuscan, or Florentine, written version of Italian was chosen four centuries ago as representative of all Italian language by the most important literary academy of the time, the Accademia della Crusca, for the simple reason that Florentine 'vulgar' had been used by the three giants of Italian literature, Dante, Petrarca and Boccaccio, for their masterworks in the 14th century. This was the period when Latin – a dead language since many centuries in its spoken form, started being abandoned in its written form too, and replaced by the so-called 'vulgar', the everyday language of the people. In Rome, Tuscan, imported to the city by the many artists and writers that served the papacy in the Renaissance, assumed the particular accents of the place. Later, and especially after the unification of Italy and the establishment of the Italian government in Rome, Italian language with a Roman flavour acquired a certain connotation of superiority not only from the political and historic importance of Rome, but from Rome being the capital. Today another reason why Italian with a Roman accent has a particular authority in the country is that it is commonly heard on television and radio, the programmes of which originate almost totally from Rome.

Finally: in an emergency
The emergency services can be reached on:
112 – '*Carabinieri*' – national police
113 – City police
114 – Emergencies involving children
115 – Fire (city services)
1515 – Fire (countryside, forest)
118 – Medical emergency
(06) 58201030 – Medical advice
(06) 3054343, (06) 490663 – Poison emergency
803116 – Road (car) help

170 – International calls through an operator
  Consular services are available from
UK: Via XX Settembre 80a; open weekdays 9.15 am and 1.30 pm. Tel (06) 482 5441 or (06) 482 5551; outside normal working hours, in the event of an emergency, tel (06) 482 5400/8893.
Eire Piazza di Campitelli 3, 00186 Roma; tel: (06) 697 9121
US Via Vittorio Veneto 119/A, 00187 Roma; tel (06) 467 41
Canada: Via Zara 30, 00198 Roma; tel (06) 445 981
Australia: 25c Corso Trieste, 00198 Roma; tel (06) 852 721
New Zealand Via Zara 28, 00198 Roma; tel (06)441 7171
South Africa: Via Tanaro 14, 00198 Roma; tel (06) 8419794 or (06) 852 541

Getting to Rome

By air
Most longhaul flights to Rome land to the Leonardo da Vinci airport located at Fiumicino, a seaside town about 20 miles from the capital. Budget airlines from European cities tend to use the smaller Ciampino airport about 10 miles from Rome on the new Appian Way. The latter is in fact preferable, since as well as being nearer it has a good bus/train connection with the city. You will not always find taxis stationed here, but they pop in frequently.

Leonardo da Vinci (also called Fiumicino) airport is more complicated. If you travel in great style and are bound for one of the high-rated hotel, they will send a car to pick you up at the airport if you request it when reserving your room, but they will add an outlandish fee to the final bill (the Excelsior Hotel, for instance, charges 108 euros.) If door-to-door transport is a must for you, which will be if you have a lot of baggage, the alternative is, of course, an ordinary cab, which would cost about 40 euros. Unfortunately many taxis try to overcharge or even downright cheat on tourists. So, unless you speak the language and can strike a definite bargain, you are liable to have an unpleasant experience. If you can come to a clear understanding, insist for a reasonable flat rate, or, if they tell you that they will apply the meter fare, make sure they do not spring upon you any extra charge on arrival; or ask that they specify any extra charges (for instance, referring to the baggage) beforehand. In any case, stick to the authorized taxis stationed outside the building, and avoid the fly-by-night, unmarked car driver that accosts you inside offering his services. Tipping is absolutely optional, and in any case can be very modest.

If you cannot come to a clear understanding with a cab driver, we suggest the limousine service that has an office on the ground floor of the airport. Their basic fare is higher (about 50 Euros), but there are no surprises and the personnel are courteous and helpful.

If you travel light, there is an inexpensive train service from the airport to the city. Once there, though, you will again be faced with the need to take a cab or a bus to your destination. The situation concerning this train is somewhat complex. When you get to the train station of the airport, you see two platforms in front of you. The one to the right is marked 'Rome': the trains there will take you to the main train station (Termini) in Rome. The one to the left is not marked at all, or there will be signs and/or voice announcements mentioning minor, obscure destinations. You will be naturally led to take the train on the right platform, yet the one on the left may be more convenient. Even if the signs do not say so, all these trains will also go to Rome – before proceeding to further, regional destinations – and the only difference with the 'official' Rome train will be that instead of ending their trip at the main Termini station, they will stop at two peripheral Rome stations (Trastevere, Ostiense), before proceeding to farther, provincial destinations. Yet those peripheral Rome stations may be closer to your final destination than the main Termini station; or the public transportation that you will find there may be more convenient in your case. Further advantages of the 'left wing' trains are that they depart more frequently than the 'right wing'; also, they cost less.

If you do not feel sure, though, by all means take the 'official' Rome train to Termini.

All tickets must be bought beforehand at a tobacconist shop near the trains. An important warning: tickets need to be obliterated, before boarding, at the little yellow machines that you will see. If you forget to do it, you are liable to a stiff fine after the train leaves.

By train

Most inter-city trains stop at the central Termini station (see p. 80), and a few at the suburban Tiburtina station. Both these stations are served by taxis, which are easier to deal with than airport taxis (the distances being much shorter, the fare is always metered; but beware the 'extras'); and by buses to the more central Rome areas. An underground metro station is accessible directly from the Termini station, and both the existing metro lines intersect there.

A large bus-terminal area in the Piazza dei Cinquecento opposite the Termini station serves several buses directed to the center, such as the 175 and 90 for the areas of Piazza Barberini, Via del Tritone and Via del Corso and the 64 and 170 for the areas of Via Nazionale and Piazza Venezia. Tiburtina station is connected to the centre by bus 492.

By car

If you arrive by car, the best advice you can get is to park it as soon as possible in your hotel's garage (if it has one) or in one of the few public garages (such as the one under Villa Borghese) and forget about it for the rest of your stay. Driving in downtown Rome requires special permits, except for a few hours each day, is very difficult thanks to the labyrinthine, mostly one-way streets, and rules change according to the day of the week and the hours of the day. Recently, cameras on the alert for trespassers have been installed at some crossings, and you or your car rental agency are exposed to fines for violations you'll not even know you committed.

Getting around Rome

Public transport in Rome is fast, passably frequent, cheap and widespread. There are two draw-backs: the system is awfully crowded and you will probably have to stand; it is difficult to identify the routes and find your stops. On this, more later. First some general information.

BUSES AND TRAMS. You cannot pay your fare aboard; you must arrive with your ticket. Once aboard you have to validate the ticket by sliding it into stamping machines near the vehicle's entrances. If the machines do not work, tell the driver.

The rule that the fare is not payable aboard, which is justified by a number of practical considerations, should have as a corollary that tickets are easy to find and purchase. But they are not. The undercurrent of chaos that winds its way through Rome's best organizational efforts sees to it that tickets are an elusive commodity.

Tickets are supposed to be sold 1) at tobacconists; 2) at news-stands; 3) at special transit authority kiosks. But tobacconists and news-stands are often out of them. The special kiosks have the tickets, but they are few and far between (see list of these kiosks below).

To minimize the difficulty, it is advisable to get long-term passes, which are valid on all lines, including metro lines (see below). These passes are no easier to find than tickets, but at least, once you have them, you have solved your problem for a number of days. Moreover, passes have other advantages over tickets: they are proportionately cheaper, and you do not need to validate them in the stamping machine. On a crowded bus you will appreciate that very much.

At the time of writing, there are two main categories of passes:

– Weekly passes. They start on any day you choose. They are difficult to find, but the special kiosks of the transit authority usually have them.

– Monthly passes. In proportion to their duration, they are the cheapest, but they start on the first of the month and not on the day of your choice. Also, by the tenth of the month or so they are all gone.

According to present rules, a ticket is valid for unlimited bus or tram trips during an $1^1/_4$ hour period; it can also be used on the metro, but for one trip only.

Although the tickets or passes are not checked aboard by the driver, it is not a good idea to attempt riding without them. Controllers board the buses occasionally, and to be found ticketless is both embarrassing and expensive.

A peculiarity of the Roman bus system is the impatience of the drivers. They seem in a perpetual hurry and won't stop at stops unless you wave at them energetically. So beware: if you just stand at the stop in solitary absent-mindedness, and don't wave as the bus approaches, you risk being left behind. Once aboard, request your stop by ringing, and prepare to get off (from the middle door) well in time, since drivers don't wait for slow-pokes. If the bus is crowded, make your way out with the liberal use of the words 'Scusi' ('excuse me', pron. SKOO-zee) and 'Scende?' ('are you getting off?', pron. SHEHN-deh).

The fact that buses do not stop at all stops complicates counting stops as you ride, which is necessary if you want to follow the suggestions of this book about using buses. To count stops, you will have to look out the windows and take into account stops that have been skipped. This is not too difficult, however, because most bus stop signs are conspicuous.

At present, buses are boarded from the rear, but you may use the front door if you have a pass; buses are exited from the middle. These regulations (which may change) are routinely violated by agile locals, but we don't recommend that, at least until you have developed some feel for the situation.

A note of caution: pickpockets, especially street urchins, use buses as their primary field of action. Always mind your wallet, and check the clasp of your handbag. We take this opportunity to warn you against gangs of children and/or teenagers, often led by women who accost you in the streets waving pieces of cardboard or paper. The intention is to confuse you while the small fry, under the paper cover, pick your pockets with Dickensian dexterity. Just shoo them all away very energetically.

LIST OF KIOSKS of the transit authority (subject to frequent change):

- Piazza dei Cinquecento (main railroad station). There is a double booth in the piazza in front of Termini railway station. One booth sells tickets; the other, marked 'Informazioni', sells weekly passes and gives information.

- Piazza Venezia. There is sometimes a mobile kiosk (actually, a parked bus) in front of Palazzo Venezia during the main tourist seasons.

- Piazza della Città Leonina (behind St. Peter's square)

- Piazza San Silvestro

- Largo Argentina

- Piazzale Flaminio

AT NIGHT: Ordinary buses, trams and the metro do not run at night. A few night-only buses called 'Notturni' are listed on bus stop signs.

COMPLICATIONS: Some aspects of Rome's bus and tram system are not only complicated, but maddening. This is mainly because the system does not consist of one network, but three. On the stretches where these networks overlap, the stops sometimes coincide, sometimes don't. You may see people running from one stop to the other on the same street trying to catch the first of more than one bus going to the same destination.

The three networks are:

- Ordinary buses and trams

- Express buses ('Linea espressa'). These buses (most are extra-long) sometimes cover the same routes as the ordinary ones, sometimes not.

- Minibuses. These are small electric vehicles used in the core of Rome to reduce pollution. They are hard to catch and it's not easy to understand where they're going.

We do give a list, below, of tram and bus routes with many provisos: these routes keep changing; the return route often differs from the outgoing one; routes can change on Sundays, holidays, during constructions, strikes and political demonstrations. The changes are only sometimes noted on some bus signs. It happened to us, once, that the driver had forgotten what his way should be for that day.

A CENTRAL TRAM LINE? To connect the main railways station (Termini) with the downtown, the city is considering creating a special tram line through parts of the centre, along the wide Via Nazionale and on to Piazza Venezia and Largo Argentina. There it would connect with the No. 8 tram, which links central Rome with the Trastevere district and the outskirts.

This project would revolutionize the transport system. It would eliminate all bus route segments along the very busy, central and long Via Nazionale, easing traffic and cutting pollution. But nobody knows if and when it will be actually implemented. The last time we asked, we were told: 'Perhaps tomorrow, perhaps never. It depends on the political atmosphere.'

THE METRO There are only two underground train lines, A and B, running a total distance of 36 km. There is a C line in the works, but when it will be completed is unknown. Trains run from 5.30 am to 11.30 pm .Prices are the same for any distance. Bus tickets are usable on the metro during their 75 minutes of validity, but only once. For other metro trips a fresh bus ticket, or a metro ticket obtainable at stations, is required.

RIVER BUSES These ply the Tiber between Ponte Milvio and the Tiber Island, with stops in between. Currently the boats run at half-hour intervals between 7.30 am and 8 pm, but the city plans to extend the service.

Map of metro, suburban and regional train lines

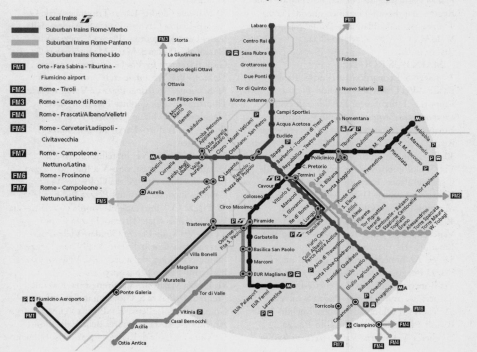

665

MAIN TRAM ROUTES

2 Piazzale Flaminio – Piazza Marina–Via Flaminia–Viale Tiziano–Piazzale Cardinal Consalvi–Viale Pinturicchio–Piazza Mancini *(returns by Piazza Mancini–Piazza Carracci–Via Flaminia–Piazza Marina–Piazzale Flaminio)*.
3 Stazione Trastevere (Piazzale F. Biondo)–Viale Trastevere–Ponte Sublicio–Viale Aventino– Piazza Colosseo–Piazza Porta S. Giovanni– Piazza Porta Maggiore–Piazzale Verano– Viale Regina Margherita–Piazza Ungheria–Piazza Thorvaldsen
8 Casaletto–Circonvallazione Gianicolense –Stazione Trastevere–Viale Trastevere–Piazza S. Sonnino–Via Arenula–Via Torre Argentina
14 Viale. P. Togliatti–Via Prenestina–Largo Preneste–Via Prenestina– Piazza Porta Maggiore– Piazza Vittorio Emanuele II–Via Napoleone III–Via Amendola (Stazione Termini)
19 Piazza Gerani–Via Bresadola–Via Prenestina–Largo Preneste–Via Prenestina–Piazza Porta Maggiore–Piazzale Verano–Viale Regina Margherita–Piazza Ungheria–Piazza Thorvaldsen–Via Flaminia–Ponte Matteotti–Viale Milizie–Via Ottaviano–Piazza Risorgimento

MAIN BUS ROUTES

23 Largo S. Leonardo Murialdo–S. Paolo Basilica–Via Ostiense–Piramide–Piazza Emporio– Lungotevere Tebaldi *(returns by Lungotevere Farnesina)*–Ponte Vittorio Emanuele II *(returns by Piazza Rovere)*–Piazza Risorgimento–Largo Trionfale–Piazzale Clodio
30 Stazione Laurentina–Viale Aeronautica–Via C. Colombo–Viale Marco Polo–Piazzale Ostiense–Piazza Emporio–Piazza Venezia–Corso Vittorio Emanuele II–Piazza Cavour–Piazza Mazzini–Piazzale Clodio *Linea Espressa*
40 Stazione Termini–Via Nazionale–Piazza Venezia–Largo Torre Argentina–Corso Vittorio Emanuele II- Piazza Pia *Linea Espressa*
52 Via Archimede–Piazzale Don Minzoni–Piazza Pitagora–Via Po *(returns by Via Pinciana)*–Via Boncompagni–Via V. Veneto–Piazza Barberini–Largo Tritone–Piazza S. Silvestro
53 Via XVII Olimpiade–Piazza Euclide–Viale Parioli–Piazza Santiago del Cile–Piazza Ungheria–Via Salaria–Via Po *(returns by Via Pinciana)*–Via V. Veneto–Piazza Barberini–Piazza S. Silvestro *Weekdays only*
60 Piazzale Partigiani–Viale Aventino– Colosseo–Piazza Venezia–Via Nazionale– Piazza Repubblica–Via XX Settembre– Piazzale Porta Pia–Via Nomentana– Corso Sempione– Via Nomentana–Via E. Romagnoli–Largo S. Pugliese *Linea Espressa*
61 Piazza R. B. Crivelli–Via F. Fiorentini–Via Monti Tiburtini–Largo R. Lanciani–Piazza Massa Carrara–Piazza Bologna–Via G. B. Morgagni–Piazzale Porta Pia–Via Cernaia–Piazza Barberini–Largo Tritone–Piazza S. Silvestro
62 Piazza Bologna–Via Nomentana–Piazzale Porta Pia–Piazza Barberini–Piazza S. Silvestro–Piazza Venezia–Largo Argentina–Corso Vittorio Emanuele II–Piazza Pia
64 Stazione Termini–Piazza Repubblica–Via Nazionale–Piazza Venezia–Largo Argentina–Piazza S. Andrea della Valle–Corso Vittorio Emanuele II–Largo Porta Cavalleggeri–Stazione San Pietro
70 Piazzale Clodio–Largo Trionfale–Viale G. Cesare–Piazza Cavour–Piazza S. Andrea della Valle–Largo Argentina–Piazza Venezia–Via Nazionale–Piazza S. Maria Maggiore–Via G. Giolitti *(returns by Via G. Giolitti–Stazione Termini–Via Nazionale etc)*
71 Stazione Tiburtina–Piazzale Verano–Piazzale Tiburtino–Via G. Giolitti–Piazza S. Maria Maggiore–Via Milano *(returns by Via A. De Pretis)*–Via Traforo–Largo Tritone–Piazza Indipendenza
75 Via A. Poerio–Via Fratelli Bonnet–Via Dandolo–Viale Trastevere–Via Induno–Piazza Emporio–Piramide–Piazza Colosseo–Via Cavour–Stazione Termini–Piazza Indipendenza
80 Piazza O. Vimercati–Via Monte Cervialto–Via Valle Melaina–Viale Tirreno–Piazza Conca d'Oro–Via Valli–Piazza Gondar–Viale Libia–Piazza Istria–Corso Trieste–Via Nizza–Piazza Fiume–Via Boncompagni–Via V. Veneto–Piazza Barberini–Piazza S. Silvestro
81 Piazza Malatesta–Via Prenestina–Piazzale Prenestino–Piazza S. Giovanni in Laterano–Colosseo–Via L. Petroselli–Piazza Venezia–Largo Argentina–Piazza S. Andrea della Valle–Ponte Cavour–Via Cola di Rienzo–Piazza Risorgimento

(returns by Piazza Risorgimento –Via Cola di Rienzo–Ponte Margherita–Piazza Augusto Imperatore–Via del Corso–Piazza Venezia etc)
85 Via Arco di Travertino–Largo Colli Albani *(this direction only)*–Via Tuscolana–Piazza Ragusa–Piazza S. Giovanni in Laterano–Via Labicana–Piazza Colosseo–S. Andrea della Valle– Corso Rinascimento–Piazza Cavour
87 Largo Colli Albani–Via C. Baronio–Piazza Tuscolo–Piazza S. Giovanni in Laterano–Piazza Colosseo–Piazza Venezia–Largo Argentina–Piazza S. Andrea della Valle–Corso Rinascimento– Piazza Cavour
95 Piazzale Partigiani–Piramide–Via Zabaglia–Piazza Bocca della Verità–Via Teatro di Marcello–Piazza Venezia–Largo Chigi–Largo Tritone–Piazza Barberini–Via V. Veneto–Viale G. Washington *(returns by Viale. G. Washington– Piazzale Flaminio–Via V. Veneto etc.)*
116 (Minibus) Via V. Veneto – Piazza Barberini–Via Tritone–Piazza Spagna–Piazza S. Silvestro–Piazza Ponte Umberto I–Corso Rinascimento–Piazza Campo de' Fiori–Piazza Farnese–Lungotevere Sangallo *(returns by Lungotevere Sangallo–Piazza Farnese–Piazza Campo de' Fiori–Corso Rinascimento–Piazza Rotondo–Piazza Colonna– Via Tritone–Piazza Barberini–Via V. Veneto– Viale S. Paolo del Brasile–Piazzale Canestre–Viale Cavalli Marini–Via V. Veneto)*
117 (Minibus) Piazza S. Giovanni in Laterano–Via Claudia–Piazza Colosseo–Via dei Serpenti–Via Milano– Largo Tritone–Piazza Spagna–Via del Corso *(returns by Via del Corso–Piazza Venezia–Via Nazionale–Via dei Serpenti–Piazza Colosseo–Via Labicana–Piazza S. Giovanni in Laterano)*
118 (Minibus) Piazzale Ostiense–Viale Piramide Cestia– Viale Aventino–Viale Terme di Caracalla–Via Appia Antica–Via Appia Pignatelli–Via Annia Regilla–Largo Claudiani
119 (Minibus) Via del Corso–Piazza Venezia–Via del Corso–Via Tritone–Piazza Barberini–Via V. Veneto–Porta Pinciana–Via V. Veneto–Piazza Barberini–Piazza Spagna–Via Babuino–Piazza Popolo–Via del Corso
160 Piazza E. Rufino–Via C. Colombo–Viale G.

Baccelli–Via Cerchi–Via L. Petroselli–Piazza Venezia–Via del Corso–Largo Chigi–Piazza S. Silvestro *(returns by Piazza S. Silvestro–Via del Corso–Piazza Venezia–Via L. Petroselli–Via Circo Massimo–Viale G. Baccelli–Viale Porta Ardeatina–Via C. Colombo–Viale Tor Marancia–Piazza F. M. Lante–Piazza E. Rufino)*
170 Stazione Termini–Piazza Repubblica–Via Nazionale–Piazza Venezia–Piazza Bocca della Verità–Lungotevere Aventino–Lungotevere Testaccio–Via C. Pascarella *(returns by Via C. Porta)*–Viale Trastevere–Stazione Trastevere–Viale G. Marconi–Via C. Colombo–Viale Civiltà del Lavoro–Piazzale Agricoltura
175 Piazzale Partigiani–Piramide–Via S. Saba–Piazzale U. La Malfa–Piazza Colosseo *(except holidays)*–Piazza Venezia–Via del Corso–Largo Chigi–Largo Tritone–Piazza Barberini–Piazza Repubblica–Stazione Termini
280 Piazza Mancini–Lungotevere Maresciallo Cadorna–Piazza Mazzini–Via Lepanto–Piazza Cavour–Lungotevere Sassia *(returns by Lungotevere Fiorentini)*–Lungotevere Anguillara *(returns by Lungotevere Cenci)* Piazza Emporio–Piramide–Piazzale Partigiani
492 Stazione Tiburtina–Piazzale Verano–Via Volturno–Via Cernaia–Via del Tritone–Piazza Venezia–Largo Argentina–Piazza S. Andrea della Valle–Piazza Cavour–Piazza Risorgimento–Stazione Cipro–Musei Vaticani
628 Piazza C. Baronio–Piazza Zama–Viale Terme di Caracalla–Piazza Bocca della Verità–Via Teatro di Marcello–Piazza Venezia–Largo Argentina– Lungotevere Augusta–Piazza G. Mazzini –Piazzale Maresciallo Giardino *(returns by Piazzale Maresciallo Giardino–Piazza G. Mazzini– Piazza Augusto Imperatore–Via del Corso–Piazza Venezia etc)*
850 Piazza Porta S. Giovanni–Via Labicana–Piazza Colosseo–Piazza Venezia–Piazza S. Silvestro
870 Via Paola–Piazza Rovere–Passeggiata del Gianicolo–Via G. Carini–Piazza S. Pancrazio–Via Vitellia– Circonvallazione Gianicolense–Via Casaletto *(and on return only Viale. I. Newton)*–Via Portuense–Via Trullo

Staying in Rome

It's best to lodge dowtown, the area the locals (not very accurately) call the historic centre. Commuting from the outskirts could halve your time in Rome, owing to the traffic.

The following hotels have the best combination of central location, pleasant ambience, good service, and prices that are reasonable for the level of accommodation. Notice the 'Convent lodging' category: this is Rome's best kept secret for good, affordable lodgings. These convents are centrally located, clean and quiet. The drawbacks: they have no restaurants (although they usually offer breakfast), and they have curfews, usually midnight.

Several hotels have recently been bought by international hotel chains, some of which have added their names to the historic Roman names. In these cases, we've put the "new" part of the names in parentheses.

✻✻✻
✻✻

PIAZZA DEL POPOLO AREA

De Russie, Via del Babuino 9, 00187 Roma, tel. (06) 3288881, fax (06) 32888888, (Reservations @hotelderussie.it) One of the most famous hotels of 'Romantic Rome' (see p. 51), recently bought and renovated by the Forte chain. Once called the 'hotel of kings' for its royal clientèle, it has the most splendid interior garden of any Rome hotel on the slope of the Pincian Hill, dating back to the 18th C.

PIAZZA DI SPAGNA/ PIAZZA BARBERINI AREA

Hassler Villa Medici, Piazza Trinità dei Monti 6, 00186 Roma, tel. (06) 699340, fax (06) 6789991, (booking@hotelhassler.it) Atop the Spanish Steps, looking out on a breathtaking panorama. Well known for its discreet elegance and old-world charm. Wonderful roof garden restaurant in summer. (See p. 88.)

PANTHEON AREA

Grand Hotel de la Minerve, Piazza della Minerva 69, 00186 Roma, tel. (06) 695201, fax (06) 6794165, (minerva@hotel-invest.com) Recently renovated, in a 17th-C. palace building in the heart of Rome. It is next door to the Pantheon and a few steps from Piazza Navona.

VIA VENETO

(Westin) Excelsior, Via Veneto 125, 00187 Roma, tel. 0647081, fax 064826205, (www.westin.com/excelsiorrome). The epitome of the legendary 'dolce vita' (see p. 85). The slightly out-of-centre location isn't totally ideal for a walking tourist, but for posh accommodation and excellent cuisine, you can't do much better. Prices for a double start at 500 euros daily, ranging up to 9,000 euros daily for the majestic penthouse suite, Villa La Cupola.

(Meridien) Eden Via Ludovisi 49, 00187 Roma, tel. (06) 478121, fax 064821, (www.hotel-eden.it) Very near the Excelsior – again, the location isn't ideal for walking tours – but it boasts wonderful views and a restaurant that some consider the best in Rome.

PIAZZA DELLA REPUBLICA

Exedra, Piazza della Republica 47, 00185 Roma, tel. (06) 469381, fax (06) 48938000, (www.boscolohotels.com) A new hotel on a grand scale, with plush lobby, unusually spacious rooms and a small rooftop pool.

✤✤
✤✤

PIAZZA DI SPAGNA/PIAZZA BARBERINI

(Continental) De la Ville, Via Sistina, 00187 Roma, tel. 800 3270200, (www. intercontinental.com) At the top of the Spanish Steps. The panoramic view from the upper floors takes in Rome's rooftops and some of the great monuments. (see p. 88).

PIAZZA DI SPAGNA/IL CORSO

Hotel d'Inghilterra,Via Bocca di Leone 14, tel. (06) 6799811, fax (06) 6798601, (www.charminghotels.it/inghilterra) Between Via Condotti and Piazza di Spagna, once a favorite of British visitors, located since 1850 in a former annexe of the princely Palazzo Torlonia.

FORA

Forum, Via Tor de' Conti 24, 00184 Roma, tel.(06) 6792446, fax (06) 6786479, (forum@venere.it) Most windows give a view over both the Roman Forum and the Imperial Fora.

PIAZZA NAVONA

Raphael, Largo Febo 2, 00186 Roma, tel. (06) 650881. A dazzling façade covered with climbing vines, shimmering with sun behind the joyous Piazza Navona. A watering place for out-of-town politicians. The famous premier Bettino Craxi lived here in the 1980s before fleeing Italy under corruption charges.

✤✤✤

IL CORSO/VIA DEL TRITONE

Nazionale, Piazza Montecitorio 131, 00186 Roma, tel. (06) 6789251. Comfortable rooms at reasonable prices, next door to the Italian parliament. A mostly political clientele.
Lugano, Via del Tritone 132, 00187 Roma, tel. (06) 42014952, fax (06) 4745502, (h.lugano @mcclink.it) In the upper floors of a stately 'Belle époque' building. Old style, large, comfortable rooms.

IL CORSO/TREVI FOUNTAIN

Accademia, Piazza dell'Accademia di San Luca, 00187 Roma, tel. (06) 69922607, fax (06) 6785897. (www.accademiahotel.com) A short distance from the Trevi Fountain and on the edge of hyper-central Via del Tritone, you couldn't be better situated to catch any of the many buses that stop there or to walk anywhere in the centre.

PANTHEON AREA

Santa Chiara, Via di S. Chiara 21, 00186 Roma, tel. (06) 6872979, fax (06) 6873144, (www. albergosantachiara.com) Until very recently directly managed by a nun order near the house where St Francis' companion, St Claire, once lived, it preserves a very quiet atmosphere and includes the well-known Restaurant Eau Vive (see p. 670).

FORA

Fori Imperiali-Cavalieri, Via Frangipani 34, 00184 Roma, tel.(06) 6796246, fax (06) 6797203, (www.cavalieri.it). In a quiet area just behind the Imperial Fora.

✽✽✽ / ✽✽

PANTHEON AREA

Cesàri, Via di Pietra 89a, tel. (06) 6792386, fax (06) 6790362. A few steps from the Temple of Hadrian and the Pantheon, and among the oldest and most historic hotels in the centre of Rome.

TREVI FOUNTAIN

Fontana, Piazza di Trevi 96, 00187 Roma tel. (06) 6786113, fax (06) 6790024. Surprisingly quiet for being across the piazza from the Trevi fountain. Roof garden.
Trevi, Vicolo del Babuccio 20, 00187 Roma, tel. (06) 6789563, fax (06) 69941407, (info@gruppo trevi.it). Roof garden.

CAMPO DE' FIORI/CORSO VITTORIO

Smeraldo, Via dei Chiodaroli 9, 00186 Roma, tel. 066875929, fax (06) 68805495. Near Piazza Navona and Campo de' Fiori, and behind Largo Argentina, hub of many bus lines.
Rinascimento, Via del Pellegrino 122, 00186 Roma, tel. (06) 6568011. Handy for the Vatican-Castel S. Angelo.

✽✽ / ✽

PIAZZA NAVONA AREA

Due Torri, Vicolo del Leonetto 23, 00186 Roma, tel. (06) 6565442, (06) 6540956. Charming, in a quiet back street.

FORA, VIA NAZIONALE

Nerva, Via Tor de' Conti 3, 00184 Roma, tel. (06) 6793764, (06) 6781835.

Grifo, Via del Boschetto 144, 00184 Roma, tel. (06) 4742323, (06) 4871395. On the corner of the Via Nazionale.

S. MARIA MAGGIORE, TERMINI

Liberiano, Via di S. Prassede 25, 00184 Roma, tel. (06) 4883804. Quiet, clean, family managed.

CAMPO DE' FIORI

POMEZIA, Via dei Chiavari 12, 00186 Roma, tel. and fax (06) 6861371.

CONVENT LODGING

FORA, VIA NAZIONALE

Dominican sisters, **Il Rosario**, Via S. Agata dei Goti 10, 00184 Roma, tel. (06) 6792346.

TRASTEVERE

Vicariate house, **Santa Francesca Romana**, Via dei Vascellari 61, 00153 Roma, tel. & fax (06) 5812125.

AVENTINO

English sisters, **Villa Rosa**, Via delle Terme Deciane 5, 00153 Roma, tel.(06) 5717091, fax (06) 5745275.
Cistercian fathers, Piazza del Tempio di Diana 14, 00153 Roma, tel. 5717021, fax (06) 57170267.
Armenian fathers, Via S. Anselmo, 00153 Roma, tel. (06) 5743550.
S. Anselmo convent, Via S. Anselmo, 00153 Roma, tel. (06) 5791264.

Eating and drinking in Rome

Roman places to eat come in roughly four categories. **Ristoranti**, or restaurants, are at the more expensive end and sometimes are more elegant looking, but the borderline between a ristorante and the next category, trattorie, is very fuzzy. It is mainly a question of service, of decor - for which Italians don't care much anyway - and of course of price. The chef of a restaurant may be a higher paid professional (but not always!) whereas trattorie can be more of the mom and pop variety (but again, not always: and in any case, the end result is not necessarily worse). The table appointments range from luxurious to adequate to tacky, but hygiene-wise you are generally safe in Rome, as control is strict.

Trattorie, like restaurants, offer a full range menu. They are simple in appearance, the decor, if one can call it that, leans to wine bottles on a shelf, a fresco painting of the Roman campagna on a wall, a medley of possibly kitschy pictures along with photos of the favorite soccer team, family pictures and postcards from friends and customers near the cash register. A step down from the trattoria, both gastronomically and price-wise, is the **pizzeria** with a simpler menu, few or no meat dishes and an even plainer version of the typical trattoria decor. But you can get delicious pizza at some (actually, very few) trattorias or restaurants.

And finally there are the **caffés**, or bars (they are the same thing). In addition to coffee, tea, ice cream, wine and spirits they offer a varying range of food, from unassuming but generally good sandwiches in most of them, to some bars offering pasta and other hot prepared dishes. The service is faster than in a trattoria, the price not necessarily lower. As a rule, prices in a bar are substantially higher if you are served at a table rather than if you stand at the counter. And forget about picking up your order yourself at the counter and then taking it to a table. That is not done.

One thing that needs stressing again is that Romans, and Italians in general, are not particular about decor and 'atmosphere' in an eating place, they care primarily about the food. As a consequence, exaggerated and artificially created 'atmosphere' can be indicative of an effort to lure foreigners to places of dubious quality the natives would not be caught dead in. Thus if you detect too much of a decor-related effort (even things that in another country would be taken for granted, such as coloured table cloths or candles), or an excessive accent on folk motifs (such as the place's name or the menu being in the Roman dialect, or – Heaven forbid — waiters wearing funny costumes), you enter at your gastronomic and financial peril.

The 'no atmosphere' principle does not extend to location, which of course can be more or less panoramic and more or less attractive. Also, in summer months – and in the spring and fall, weather permitting – an important consideration in your dining enjoyment will be whether there is outdoor seating or not. Most locals prefer outside seating which most, but not all, eating establishments have.

Now about the food. Pricier restaurants and luxury hotels offer international cuisine; all the others stick to Italian, and possibly Roman, dishes. The differences here are subtle. Rome does have its own native dishes. But this being the capital, and the focal point of Italy geographically, a wide range of other gastronomic possibilities are also available. The greatest influence cames from the regions around Rome: Neapolitan, Abruzzese and Tuscan dishes – and from the famous gastronomic region in the north, Emilia (includes Bologna). Many restaurants and trattorias have a full range of all of these dishes. Others specialize in one or the other regional specialties (for instance, Abruzzese restaurants will emphasize roasts; Tuscan restaurants are bound to have the Florentine steak, which is the only really outstanding beefsteak in Italy). But 'regional' restaurants will not necessarily be better in terms of quality, not even in their own regional range, that non-regional ones. Most restaurants and trattorias will include specifically Roman dishes in their menu, but some will stress this local cuisine more than others, or be mostly confined to it. We suggest you go to the latter if you are curious about Roman cuisine.

What dishes and foods are specifically Roman? Here are a few you are likely to happen upon in menus: 'bollito misto' (a very simple, but very tasty, selection of boiled meats with green sauce); 'fritto misto alla Romana' (fried vegetables, including the airy and delicious zucchini heads, and/or fried offal including brains, kidneys, liver et alia); 'coda alla vaccinara' ('cattleman style': oxtail in a stew); 'carciofi alla Romana' (stewed artichokes, the tender kind where one eats everything, not the heart only); 'carciofi alla giudìa' ('Jewish style' artichokes: deep fried, and one eats everything; the leaves seem spiny, but in fact are only crunchy, and altogether this is perhaps the most delicious dish that Roman cuisine can offer). 'Saltimbocca [Jump-in-your-mouth] alla romana' and 'Piccatina al limone' are thin veal slices, the former rolled with prosciutto (Italian raw ham), the latter served with a lemon and parsley sauce. Rome, and generally Italy, is not great beef country, and you will generally get veal – a delicate, but essentially duller meat. In Rome, though, an exquisite meat specialty, best eaten in spring, is 'abbacchio', roast baby lamb (occasionally, baby goat). If neither too fat nor too lean, 'abbacchio', which usually comes 'con patate' (with roast potatoes) can be a real treat. An old, inexpensive and popular Roman dish is 'trippa', a stew in a tomato or white sauce. Trippa means tripes (the veal's spongy stomach), and the name says it all. It can be a delicate dish, but only the more adventurous will try it. An even older, cheaper, even more popular with some but certainly even more controversial Roman dish is 'pagliata', the stewed intestines of the animal. But today it is very hard to find: since with the 'mad cow' woe that has hit Italy and Europe, the sale of some bovine parts has been banned, and 'pagliata' is one.

Of the tens of thousands of recipes for spaghetti and *pasta asciutta* ('dry pasta', as against pasta in a soup), only a couple are specifically Roman. One is 'pasta al pecorino', i.e. with the piquant 'pecorino' or sheep cheese, plus pepper, rather than with the mellow, ubiquitous grated 'parmesan'. Another is 'gnocchi alla romana' (potato dumplings). 'Spaghetti alla puttanesca' ('the whore's way') with capers, olives and tomato sauce is Roman only in its gimmicky name, a recent and yet untested recipe. Besides that, Romans share their pasta recipes with the rest of Italy. Pasta comes in many different shapes and two basic forms: the dry, machine made, store-bought one; or the 'fresh' one with egg mixed into the flour, frequently home-made, different but not necessarily better. The dominant recipes are Neapolitan (tomato) or Bolognese (meat sauce) or, distant third, Genoese ('pesto', basil with garlic). Pasta 'in bianco' ('the white way': butter and parmesan only) is good for sensitive stomachs and is a nice alternative; it is especially good with 'fresh' pasta. Elaborate regional preparations most common in Rome are: 'spaghetti alla matriciana' (from the Abuzzi town of Amatrice: tomato and grated 'pecorino' cheese, with bacon bits) e 'alla carbonara' ('the coalman's way': eggs and bacon bits); 'maccheroni ai quattro formaggi' ('with four cheeses': mozzarella; edam; gruyère; grated parmesan), 'vermicelli alle vongole' (Neapolitan, with tiny clams, garlic, parsley). (Vermicelli and maccheroni are forms of long pasta not dissimilar to spaghetti.)

When it comes to spaghetti, a few tips on graceful dining. With the tip of your fork, disentangle a few – five or six – strands, and pull them to a side of your plate. Start turning the fork so the strands will wrap around it. When they are more or less gathered up, raise the fork and eat. Any spaghetti ends dangling out your mouth, lift with the fork and push them in too, that is all that there is to it. Helping oneself with a spoon is a no-no.

All Mediterranean fish, and some imported ocean fish, is found in Rome. But only in pricier restaurants and those – of any price – specializing in fish will you find a good selection and the fish will not be frozen. (By law, restaurants serving frozen fish must say so on the menu.) Also, before you order specific fish, as opposed to miscellaneous 'seafood', it is customary to see it first ; if really fresh, the eye must still look lively and the body should glisten. So do not hesitate to ask the waiter to bring it out, and turn it down if you are not happy with what you see.

One Roman fish speciality – once, the food of the poor – is 'filetti di baccalà', fillets of dried codfish. For that you do not need to go to fish places, since baccalà, being preserved, does not need to be freshly supplied. It can be stewed ('baccalà in umido') or, more often, deep-fried ('baccalà fritto'). Romans swear by it, but it is an acquired taste. In winter, places that offer 'baccalà' may also have 'puntarelle' ('pointy leaves'). This is a Roman specialty, long, thin, crunchy greens of the fennel family, served with an anchovy and garlic sauce.

Vegetables are fresh and good everywhere and at all times, though spring is the best season. Wonderful large heads of fresh 'porcini' mushrooms are best in fall and winter. They can be considered either as a main dish or as an hors-d'oeuvre or side dish ('contorno'). Of the cheeses, pecorino and mozzarella are regional specialties. Mozzarella comes in two versions, one, more expensive but creamier and tastier, from the milk of water buffaloes – which still roam the region between Rome and Naples; the other from cow milk. Both are delicious, and, besides being the the staple of Neapolitan pizza, are also found in a simple and healthy dish from the south of Rome: 'insalata (salad) caprese' from the island of Capri.

Neither Italians nor their eating places are strong on desserts, which tend to repeat themselves and are unexciting. In Rome, the more elaborate exist mainly for the benefit of foreigners and children. Locals confine themselves to fruits and fruit salads ('macedonia'), or to simple creations such as ice cream, crème caramel (a flan) and tiramisù ('pick me up', a coffee-based concoction). Espresso coffee is not at its best in restaurants, since, by regulation, only bars can make it; restaurants will send a waiter to buy it and bring it to you, but by then it will be getting cold. All in all, many people in restaurants skip dessert entirely, or, adding a pleasant stroll, go to the corner bar to round off dinner with ice cream and coffee or possibly a liqueur. If you want an Italian favorite digestive herb liqueur, and want to wonder at its almost unbearable bitterness, try Fernet Branca.

Speaking of coffee bars, we take the opportunity to recommend their delicious fresh squeezed orange juice ('spremuta d'arancio'), available in winter. Absolutely best for ice-creams and sherbets is Pasticceria Giolitti (see p.), although its 'pasticceria' proper ('paste') is nothing to boast about – as hinted above, sweets are not the thing in Rome. Ice cream lovers should also try a specialty that is served mainly around Piazza Navona, the 'tartufo', a luscious 'truffle' of bittersweet chocolate and whipped cream. Get it where it was invented, the bar 'Tre Scalini.' It is cheaper as take-out and you can sit on a bench in the piazza (p. 000).

Wine. You will find adequate selections of Italian and foreign wines in Roman eateries, proportionate, of course, to their rank and price. Except for the higher-end places, all the others will also offer their own 'open', or carafe, wine, usually local and in any case Italian. Rome's countryside does not boast any really high-class vintages, although there is wine produced in the nearby hills of the Roman Campagna that has its devotees and is in fact excellent and very characteristic. It is called 'Vino dei Castelli' (wine of the castles), and its only problem is that it does not travel well and does not keep very long. Once it was ubiquitous, and the annals of alcoholic bliss in Rome since at least the middle ages, which include Belli's immortal sonnets, have 'Vino dei Castelli' as understood prop. Today, when the supply is no longer direct from vintner to restaurant, it has become hard to find this wine ripe and at the same time fresh from the cask. One restaurant that makes a point of having good Vino dei Castelli is La Carbonara on Campo dei Fiori. The white is the best, and it has to be drunk cool; in summer, don't ask for the large carafe, or it will get warm before you finish it; order the smallest amount ('un quarto', a quarter of a litre), and refill as needed. To add ice is to spoil it.

The above concerns Italian restaurants. Rome also has a few 'ethnic' restaurants such as Chinese, none known to be outstanding. Recently, perhaps as a consequence of a closer European union, several British-pub-like and Irish-pub-like places have sprung up, with a good choice of draught and bottle beers. These places are still finding their way and we can't vouch for the quality of their food and drink. But the latter are presumably adequate, as it is well known that an ambassador from an English-speaking country needed to be recalled recently because of his too frequent visits to these establishments. Last but not least are 'enotecas', i.e. 'wine libraries', places that offer wine and cheese, and perhaps some cold buffet; the wine selection is supposed to be broad, good bottled wine can be tasted by the glass and the price is usually moderate.

All eating places are closed one day a week, and two weeks or longer in the summer in rotation (which may change from year to year). Reservations are recommended, but not essential. The less expensive places won't take reservations and it is better to go well in time.

Tipping: usually service is included in the bill so you should leave little – just round off the figure – or even no tip.

Selected Restaurants

Of the hundreds of Roman eateries these are our pick. Most are in the *centro* or in Trastevere, a few are near Via Veneto and in Parioli and one in Testaccio. All restaurants have outside seating in summer, except where noted.

In the better restaurants a reservation is often necessary. In summer, most restaurants go on vacation at different periods for weeks; call before you go.

An all-in-one food experience is offered by **La Città del Gusto**, or 'the city of taste', a new enterprise just started up by a group of Roman gourmets in an old building at Via Enrico Fermi 161, near Piazza Marconi. Its five floors are host to cooking schools, a shop of kitchen gadgets and several traditional and avant garde restaurants. In a 'kitchen theatre' well known chefs demonstrate how to prepare dishes that are then served. A 'theatre of wine' is also open for dinner. For information or resevations call (06) 55112277 (also 55112264 or 55112211).

Luxury

Passetto, Via Zanardelli 14 near Piazza Navona, (06) 688(06)569. Classic international cuisine.

La Rosetta, Via della Rosetta 9 near the Pantheon, (06) 6861002. Specializes in fish.

El Toulà, Via della Lupa 29b, (06) 6873498, Venetian cuisine. Closed Sun. and Sat. for lunch. No outside seating.

The following, all hotel restaurants, are particularly expensive.

La Terrazza, Hotel Eden, Via Ludovisi 49 near Via Veneto, (06) 47812752. Rooftop restaurant, great views.

Hassler Villa Medici. Piazza Trinità dei Monti 6, ((06)) 699340. Wonderful roof garden dining in summer.

St. Regis Grand. Via Vittorio Emanuele Orlando 3, tel ((06)) 47091. One of Rome's best restaurants in the historic Grand Hotel (p. 77), recently renovated and renamed.

Excelsior, Via Veneto 125, tel. (06)47081. Famous for its 'dolce vita' ambience; top international cuisine.

Expensive and elegant

Nino, Via Borgognona 11 near Piazza di Spagna, (06) 6795676. Closed Sun. No outside seating.

Fontanella, Largo Fontanella di Borghese 86, (06) 6871092. Closed Mon. Bistecca alla Fio-rentina and other staples of Tuscan cuisine.

Piperno, Via Monte Cenci 9 near Ghetto, The menu includes Carciofi alla Giudia and other Roman dishes. (06) 654(06)29. Closed Mon.

Bolognese, Piazza del Popolo 1, (06) 3611426. Bologna cuisine with its glorious pasta, ragù, lasagne and other specialities.

Café de Paris, Via Veneto, (06) 26885284. Closed Mon. One of the 'historic' café-restaurans of Via Veneto.

Doney, Via Veneto 145, (06) 4827107. Closed Mon. Immortalised, like the Café de Paris, in Fellini's film *La Dolce Vita.*. Both restaurants serve excellent international fare.

Hosteria del Pesce, Via Manserrato 32, ((06)) 6865617. Closed Sun. The finest seafood laid out for customers to inspect.

RESTAURANTS

Expensive-moderate

Giggetto, Via Portico d'Ottavia 22 in the Ghetto, (06) 6861105. Closed Monday. The menu includes Carciofi alla Giudia, Coda alla Vaccinara and Filetti di Baccalà

Fortunato al Pantheon, (06) 6792788. Closed Sun. Tuscan cuisine in a lively setting.

La Carbonara, Campo de' Fiori 23, (06) 6864783, Rome and Amatriciana specialties, closed Tue. in winter and Sat. in summer.

Taverna Angelica, Borgo Vittorio 14 near St. Peter's, (06) 6874514, creative cuisine.

Pancrazio, Piazza del Biscione 92 near Campo de' Fiori, (06) 6861246. Dining within the substructures of the Theatre of Pompey. No outside seating.

Sabatini, Piazza S. Maria in Trastevere 13, (06) 5812026. Closed Wed.

Canova, Piazza del Popolo 16, (06) 3612231, interior garden. Closed Mon.

Vecchia Roma, Piazza Campitelli, (06) 6864604. Closed Wed.

Otello, Via della Croce 81 near Piazza di Spagna. (06) 671188. Closed Sun. Popular with expatriates. In summer, dining in colourful old courtyard.

Taverna Flavia, Via Flavia 9 near Via XX Settembre, ((06)) 474214. An excellent steak, good international cuisine. Closed Sun.

Checchino v. Monte Testaccio 30, Roman cuisine including 'Rigatoni with Pagliata', 'Trippa alla Romana', 'Coda alla Vaccinara.'

Giuseppe, Via Angelo Brunetti 59 near Piazza del Popolo, (06) 3219019. Closed Sun.

I Due Ladroni, Piazza Nicosia 24 (Via della Scrofa) (06) 6861013. Closed Sun.

Eau Vive, Via Monterone 85 (off Piazza S. Eustachio), (06) 68802571. Roman catholic lay missionaries, mostly French ladies. Excellent French and exotic cuisine. You might see some cardinals dining here. No outside seating.

Enoteca Capranica, Piazza Capranica 100, tel. ((06)) 69940922. One of the best of its type.

Moderate

Fiammetta on Piazza Fiammetta 8, near Piazza Navona, (06) 6875777. Tuscan cuisine, they serve pizza too.

Al Pompiere, Via S. Maria dei Calderari 38, (06) 6868377. No outside seating.

Tullio, Via S. Nicolò da Tolentino 26, tel. (06) 4818564. Tuscan cuisine.

Ristorante Abruzzi, Via del Vaccaro 1 near Piazza SS. Apostoli, (06) 6793897, Abruzzese cuisine

Alla Rampa, Piazza Mignanelli 18 (adjoining Piazza di Spagna).

Da Benito e Gilberto, Via del Falco 10, St. Peter's area, (06) 6867769

Al Piccolo Arancio, Vicolo Scanderbeg 12 near Trevi fountain, (06) 6786139. Closed Sun.

Trattoria Scavolino, also called Bella Roma, Vicolo Scavolino 74, near Trevi fountain, (06) 679 0974. Menu includes very good fish. Closed Sat.

La Sagrestia, Via del Seminario 89 near Pantheon, (06) 6797581. Closed Wed. Extensive menu and one of the best pizzas in Rome.

La Berninetta Via Pietro Cavallini 14 near Piazza Cavour, (06) 3204405, menu includes Carciofi alla Giudia. No outside seating.

Taverna Romana, Via Madonna dei Monti 79, a parallel of Via Cavour near the Fora. Typical Roman cuisine, popular with a nearby seminary. No outside seating. . Closed Sun and during August.

Ai Piani, Via Francesco Denza 35 and Via del S. Cuore di Maria 22, tel. ((06)) 8075412 and ((06)) 8079704 both in the Parioli district (near Piazza Euclide). Closed Mon.

La Matriciana, Via del Viminale 44, (06) 48986848. Across the street from the Teatro dell'Opera.

Fiaschetteria Beltrame, Via della Croce 39, near Piazza di Spagna. Very good 'mom and pop' cuisine. No outside seating.

Pierluigi, Piazza dei Ricci near Via Giulia, (06) 6868717. Very Roman, no tourists. Closed Mon.

La Bottega del Vino, Via S. Maria del Pianto 9a, (06) 6865970, a wine and cold buffet place.

Enoteca Ferrara, Piazza Trilussa 41 (Trastevere), (06) 58333920, wine and cheese.

Inexpensive

Al Picchio, Via del Lavatore 40 near Trevi fountain, ((06)) 6781602, never closed.

Brek, Largo Argentina 1, (06) 68210353, never closed. Self-service, but well prepared food.

Birreria Peroni, Via S. Marcello 19 near Piazza SS. Apostoli (06) 6795310, an authentic early 20th-century. 'beer hall' with a long list of simple dishes; no outside seating. Closed Sun.

Pizzeria Baffetto, Via del Governo Vecchio. Very popular in the evening with the young set, both Roman and foreign. No reservations. Go early or queue.

Pizzeria La Montecarlo, Vicolo Savelli near Corso Vittorio. This pizza place and the one above are near to each other and managed by the same people; when one is closed or full, the other is open or may have a shorter queue.

Outside the Walls (medium priced)

Sora Rosa - Villa Tor Carbone, Via Tor Carbone 74, ((06)) 990453. Closed Mon. Devilled roast chicken, fish, beef fillet.

Scarpone, Via S. Pancrazio 15, ((06)) 5890094. Closed Mon.

Gelaterie (ice cream bars)

Giolitti, Via degli Uffici del Vicario (see p. 232) closed Mon.

'Tre Scalini', Piazza Navona. Closed Mon. Speciality is 'tartufo' (see p. 456).

Il Gelato di San Crispino, 42 Via della Panetteria, near the Trevi Fountain. Closed Tues. Describes itself as a 'laboratory', researching new flavours and textures.

Il Palazzo del Freddo di Giovanni Fassi, 65 Via Principe Eugenio, near Piazza Vittorio. Closed Mon. Excellent, old-style Sicilian ice-cream.

Tourists arriving in a Roman tavern, 19th century engraving by Achille Pirelli

Accessibility and conservation of Rome's monuments

The public has less access to Rome's key monuments today than ever before in recent decades. The reason boils down to politics and the pork barrel. Visitors today are delighted to find the city spruced up, thanks to a much-publicized campaign of renovations during the 'Jubilee Year 2000', and eager to visit newly advertised archæological sites and just-reopened museums. What the publicity doesn't say is that for each landmark newly opened, two have been closed. Moreover, some key sights that have been closed for thirty or more years, and whose reopening had been pledged for the new millennium, are still closed. Meanwhile, hasty renovations and ill advised archæological work have done serious damage, while old, persistent problems have been ignored.

Corruption and political patronage have plagued all Italy in the post-war period. But Rome has always added a special twist: a symbiotic relationship between the political powers and a vast army of antiquarians, archæologists and art restorers, its ranks teeming with the beneficiaries of cronyism and nepotism. Rome's fragile cultural treasures are pawns in the internal squabbles of this 'political-antiquarian complex,' and sources of revenue for private interests. In the early years of the new millennium, three factors have brought this situation to a climax: the polarization, for the first time since World War II, of Italy's life into two factions, right and left; the inclusion, by both these factions, of programmes for the preservation and expansion of Italy's 'cultural assets' in their electoral propaganda; and the Jubilee in 2000, which allowed the authorities to flood Rome with taxpayer's money from all over Italy for renovation projects. Politics, demagoguery and the prospect of easy profits converged on Rome's artistic and archæological assets.

Many buildings have been repainted and renovated. But repainting a building is no big deal, and damaging it is easy. On one palace downtown, there was once historic graffiti, probably left by troops accompanying emperor Charles V in a famous visit to Rome in the 1500's. A hasty repainting of the building erased these historic records. The famous Galleria Borghese was refurbished and repainted, but the job, at least on the outside, was so shoddy that chunks of the back façade were dropping off within months of the inauguration. The roof of S. Pancrazio basilica caved in, not actually during renovation, but immediately afterwards. Worst of all was a needless attempt to replace a perfectly serviceable pavilion over the precious Ara Pacis. This project, contracted out without any competitive process, spawned an explosive controversy due to the total inappropriateness of the new structure, called 'a horror' even by a government official. The project was frozen, the pavilion partly dismantled and the Ara Pacis, a fundamental document of Augustan and Imperial Rome, has been out of sight for years.

Beyond the foregoing is the internationally debated question of whether over-cleaning and over-restoring accelerate deterioration. If this risk exists, Rome will witness a sad fate for the thousands of artifacts in all media on which its army of government-financed restorers has laid hands. Unfortunately there is already abundant cause for alarm.

As for the new archæological campaigns, a few led to some, generally minor, finds and some to overdue renovations, such as those of the Domus Aurea and the Crypta Balbi. But most had meager, mediocre or even disastrous results. The worst was an enormously costly effort to unearth the Imperial Fora in central Rome and turn them into an 'archæological park,' which revealed nothing new and made it harder to see what was there before. Thus, one of Rome's formerly most solemn, impressive features has become a jumbled, almost squalid zone.

The importance of the landmarks and sites now relegated to a growing 'Roma invisibile' cannot be overstated. Some truly essential features of the Roman Forum, such as the House of the Vestals, have been put off-limits. Most of the Palatine Hill, including the old Imperial palace, the ancestral temples and the prehistoric settlements that were Rome's cradle, are now blocked off – perhaps temporarily, but temporary in Rome can mean decades. The Colosseum, which until recently had several freely accessible entrances, now for the first time has endless queues at a single box office. Closed off, allegedly for safety reasons, are the Tomb of the Scipios – perhaps the Appian Way's most fascinating monument – and most other sites along the Way, plus the underground areas of many churches. Other renowned landmarks that were inaccessible for decades, and whose re-openings were promised for the new millennium, are still closed at the time of writing; while the Museum of Rome, repository of tens of thousands of fascinating documents, closed since 1966, has been re-opened; only a small fraction of its collections are visible. The 'antiquarium' of the Forum, open until recently, is now closed for undisclosed reasons.

Public access can, obviously, come into conflict with conservation efforts. But this conflict exists only when the former disrupts the latter. Not in the other cases – and not when the money to protect monuments and public safety is there, but is wasted on more eye-catching and vote-grabbing ventures.

Museums

This section lists all the museums of Rome, organized in order of importance within the following categories:

In the Vatican
   1) Main Vatican Museums and Palaces, p. 680
   2) Other collections in the Vatican, p. 680
In the city
   3) Major art museums, p. 682
   4) Other important art collections, p. 684
   5) Art collections of a lesser scope, p. 685
   6) Historical museums, p. 686
   7) Other museums, p. 687

NOTE: Opening hours are subject to constant change and it is always advisable to confirm by telephone.

Museums in the Vatican

1) Main Vatican museums and palaces

VATICAN MUSEUMS ('Musei Vaticani') Viale Vaticano. These are the only museums that are part of one of our Walks, where they are described in detail (see pp. 307-355.). Open. July 1 to September 30 and at Easter, Monday-Friday 08.45-16.45, Saturday 08.45-13.45. Other times, 08.45-13.45; no admittance in the last hour. Closed on Sunday, except the last Sunday of every month, when admission is free. Also closed on holidays. January 1 and 6, February 11, March 19, Easter and Easter Monday, May 1, Ascension Day, Corpus Christi Day, June 29, August 14-15, November 1 and December 8, 25 and 26.

In summer the Pinacoteca inside the complex closes at 13:30; the Belvedere courtyard area closes between 13.45 and 14.45. For more information and/or confirmation, call (06) 6982. Other Vatican museums are described below.

2) Other collections in the Vatican

ARCHÆOLOGICAL MUSEUM ('Museo Gregoriano Profano') See p. 355.
Greek and Roman statuary were moved here recently from the complex of St.John Lateran. The museum consists of three sections: Roman sculpture of the Imperial Age; Roman replicas of Greek originals of the

'classical' period, plus some Greek originals; various Roman sculptures in chronological order.

CHRISTIAN MUSEUM ('Museo Pio Cristiano') See p. 355.

This collection and that of the Museum that follows are exhibited in the same section of the Vatican Museums. Hours are usually shorter than those of the rest of the Museums.

Items from the catacombs and the early Christian churches. Of special interest, the statuette of *The Good Shepherd*, possibly (but not probably) a symbolic representation of Christ, of the 3rd-4th centuries AD (greatly restored). A series of sarcophagi narrate Biblical stories through their reliefs. One section is reserved to Judaica, including very ancient Jewish inscriptions. In the last room there is a fascinating floor mosaic depicting Roman athletes and referees, which came from one of the great Roman baths.

EGYPTIAN MUSEUM ('Museo Gregoriano Egizio') See p. 317.

Contains many rare pieces, such as a fragment of a statue of Pharaoh Ramses II, the enemy of Moses, a statue of his mother Queen Tuya, finely painted coffins with mummies, ancient Roman works in the Egyptian style and works from Assyria and Mesopotamia.

ETRUSCAN MUSEUM ('Museo Gregoriano Etrusco') See p. 326.

(Closed for restoration at time of writing). Second in importance only to the National Etruscan Museum (p. 682).

Among the most famous exhibits here are the contents of the tomb of an Etruscan family of the 7th century BC, found intact in the early 19th century.

MISSIONARY-ETHNOLOGICAL MUSEUM ('Museo Missionario Etnologico') see p. 355).

(Closed for restoration at time of writing).

Artefacts from all continents except Europe, mostly collected by Roman Catholic missions, and mostly illustrating present and past religions. The vast collection contains ceremonial objects and ethnographic documents from all corners of the globe. The North American section includes works of the German sculptor Ferdinand Pettrich, who depicted the customs of the Native Americans in the early 19th century from life.

TREASURY OF ST. PETER (in St Peter's, see p. 370).

A wonderful collection of objects connected to the history of the basilica, many from the old basilica (including the 9th-century gilt weathercock that topped the bell tower). Ivory, cloth, wooden and silver artifacts – among them chandeliers attributed to Cellini – compose a fascinating sampler of the 'minor arts', from the late Roman Empire to the renaissance. Of great interest is the *Sarcophagus of Junius Bassus*, a governor of Rome who converted to Christianity in 359. The star attraction of the Treasure is the majestic bronze *Tomb of Pope Sixtus IV* (1493) the masterpiece of Antonio Pollaiuolo.

Museums in the city:

3) Major art museums

CAPITOLINE MUSEUMS ('Musei Capitolini') Piazza del Campidoglio, tel. (06) 39746221, (06) 67102071. Open 09:00-19:00, Sun 09:00-13:30; closed Mon.

Second only to those of the Vatican for diversity and importance, these collections were started around the same time (late 15th century), and are the oldest museums in the world specifically intended for the public. The works of art, which are owned by the city, are housed in the two palaces on the sides of Piazza del Campidoglio (see p. 147). The palace on the right (as you arrive on the piazza from the ramp) has magnificent frescoed halls currently used for official functions of the city government. They also house two world-famous bronzes, the *Capitoline Wolf* (pp. 164, 165) and the *Boy with the Thorn*. Other Greek and Roman statuary of importance is in nearby rooms. A gallery of paintings includes first-class works by Caravaggio, Guercino, Domenichino, Reni and Rubens. The original of the world-famous equestrian statue of *Marcus Aurelius* stands in a courtyard, together with the colossal *Head of Constantine* from the Basilica of Maxentius (pp. 286-287).

The palace on the left (admission with the same ticket) houses a large collection of Greek and Roman sculpture, including masterpieces such as the *Capitoline Venus*, the *Dying Galatian*, the *Laughing Satyr* (which inspired Nathaniel Hawthorne's novel *The Marble Faun*, p. 492); and 65 busts of Roman Emperors, of great artistic and historic importance.

From these buildings an underground gallery leads to ruins of a temple and to the ancient Roman Tabularium, facing the Roman Forum.

ARCHÆOLOGICAL MUSEUM ('Museo Nazionale Romano') Main branch at Palazzo Massimo in Piazza dei Cinquecento 67, tel. (06) 4815576. Other branches: in the nearby Baths of Diocletian (entrance on Piazza dei Cinquecento 78, tel (06) 4815576); also nearby, at Via V. E. Orlando in the so-called Planetarium; and in Palazzo Altemps, piazza S. Apollinare 46 (tel. (06) 6833759). Daily 09:00-19:00, closed Mon. General information also obtainable at (06) 39967700.

Another highly important collection of Roman and Greek art (sculpture, frescoes, mosaics), this one owned by the Italian government. It consists mainly of items found in Rome and surroundings after the annexation of Rome to the Italian state in 1870. Among the world-famous pieces. the *Daughters of Niobe* from Sallust's Villa, the *Girl from Antium*, the *Ludovisi Throne* (the authenticity of which, however, is not universally recognised). The museum also possesses an immense collection of ancient coins.

The branch within the Baths of Diocletian allows a visit to some parts of the Baths, including a courtyard remodelled by Michelangelo and contains, besides several important pieces, an interesting section on ancient inscriptions.

NATIONAL ETRUSCAN MUSEUM ('Museo Nazionale di Villa Giulia') Piazzale di Villa Giulia 9 [Via delle Belle Arti], tel. (06) 320 1951. Tues, Thurs, Fri, Sat 09:00-2, Wed. 09:00-19:30, Sun. 09:00- 13:00. See p. 604.

The most important collection in the world of Etruscan artefacts. The Etruscans, a people of unknown origins, dominated central and northern Italy before the foundation of Rome. Subjugated by the Romans, they continued for some centuries to exert a significant influence on the religious, political and artistic life of Italy and of Rome itself, but then disappeared as a distinct national and ethnic group. Their script has never been completely deciphered.

The remains of other pre-Roman civilizations of Italy, harking back to the Bronze Age, are also exhibited in the museum. Among the most famous items of Etruscan art are the *Sarcophagus of the Bride and Bridegroom* and *Heracles fighting Apollo*, both from the 6th century BC. The museum is housed in the splendid villa of a renaissance Pope, Julius III, built in the mid 16th century by two great architects, Vignola and Ammannati, in collaboration with the painter, architect and art historian Vasari.

PALAZZO BARBERINI ('Galleria Nazionale d'Arte Antica') Via Quattro Fontane 13. Tel. (06) 4814591. Daily 09:00-19:00, closed Mon.

This great state collection, housed in one of Rome's grand palaces (p. 83), consists mainly of 13th- to 16th-century paintings from various Italian schools, plus some by northern European artists. Works by Fra Angelico, Lippi, Raphael, Titian, Tintoretto, Holbein and many others are exhibited. Among the most famous are Raphael's portrait of a woman traditionally said to be his lover, *La Fornarina* (pp. 237, 254) and Holbein's portrait of *Henry VIII*, painted on the occasion of his fourth marriage. From the gallery of paintings one passes to a wing of original 18th-century rooms, which are finely decorated and exhibit furniture, clothes and art objects of the same period (this wing is sometimes closed). The splendid main hall of the palace has an enormous ceiling fresco, the masterpiece of Pietro da Cortona.

BORGHESE GALLERY at Villa Borghese, the main city park. Tel. (06) 328101. Daily 09:00-17:00, Sun 09:00-13:00, closed Mon. Reservation sometimes required.

Once the property of the princely Borghese family and now owned by the state, this is one of the richest single-owner art collections in the world. It is housed in an elaborately frescoed 17th-century villa (p. 602), formerly one of the Borghese residences (the family survives, but lives elsewhere). The ground floor is devoted to ancient and modern sculpture, including masterpieces by Bernini (including the *Rape of Proserpine* and *Apollo and Daphne*) and Canova (the famous semi-nude, life-size portrait of Napoleon's scandalous sister Paolina, who had married into the Borghese family, p. 99). Paintings on the upper floor include famous works by Italian artists of the renaissance (Raphael, Correggio, Titian, Antonello da Messina) and of the 17th century (Caravaggio, Guercino, Domenichino).

MODERN ART GALLERY ('Galleria Nazionale d'Arte Moderna e Contemporanea') Viale delle Belle Arti 131, tel. (06) 322981 or (06) 3224151. Daily 09:00-19:00, Sun 09:00-13:30, closed Mon. See p. 603.

The most important collection of Italian modern painting and sculpture, from the late 19th century to the present. All the best known Italian art movements, such as the Macchiaioli and the Futurists, and most contemporary Italian artists are represented. There is also a selection of foreign works.

4) Other important art collections

PALAZZO CORSINI ('Galleria Nazionale di Palazzo Corsini') Via della Lungara 10, tel. (06) 68802323. Daily 09:00-14:00, Sun. 09:00-13:00, closed Mon.) See p. 574.
PALAZZO SPADA ('Galleria Spada') Piazza Capodiferro 9, tel. (06) 32810, (06) 6861158. Daily 09:00-2, Sun. 09:00-13:00 See p. 474.
PALAZZO DORIA ('Galleria Doria Pamphili') Piazza Collegio Romano 2, tel. (06) 6797323. Daily 10:00-17:00 (12:30 for the apartments), closed Thurs. See p. 535.
PALAZZO COLONNA ('Galleria Colonna') Via della Pilotta 17 [near Piazza Venezia], tel. (06) 679 4362. Sat. only, 09:00-13:00 Closed in Aug. See p. 129.

These four great collections are all housed in the splendid palaces of the princely Roman families who owned them originally. This affords the special pleasure of admiring art in a historic, private interior, rather than in the impersonal setting of a museum. Two of these families, the Corsini and the Spada, have died out, and their collections now belong now to the state, but the Doria and the Colonna still own both palaces and their collections. Moreover the Doria, who live in a small section of their immense palace, allow visitors into the 'official' rooms of their residence (by guided tour that takes place earlier in the morning and requires a separate ticket). The bulk of all four collections is 17th-century work. For this period, so important in the art history of Rome, the collections offer an unparalleled selection of works. All the great Italian artists of that century are represented, as well as many foreign painters, especially those who had settled in Rome (see p. 50).

In the Corsini collection, one of the portraits by Reni is traditionally said to be of Beatrice Cenci (p. 517), although that identification is doubtful. Another highlight is a wonderful Murillo *Madonna and Child*. The Colonna col-

lection includes the famous *Bean Eater* by Annibale Carracci; the Doria collection, the greatest picture painted in Italy by Velázquez, the portrait of *Pope Innocent X Doria Pamphili*. The Colonna and Doria collections also include important Renaissance works. Among those in the Colonna collection are works by Bronzino, Botticelli and Veronese; in the Doria collection are several pictures of the Venetian school (by Bellini, Titian, Tintoretto, the Bassanos, etc.).

GALLERY OF THE ACADEMY OF ST. LUKE ('Accademia di San Luca') Piazza Accademia di San Luca, tel. (06) 678 9243. Open Mon., Wed. and Fri. 10:00-13:00. See p. 63.

Although it does not include world-famous works, this is a fine selection of paintings, plus some sculptures, collected by the five-century old Academy, named after the patron saint of artists, which is housed in the building. The majority of the works are renaissance and baroque, and by artists born or operating in Rome, including Raphael. But other periods and other schools such as the Venetian (Titian and others) and the Dutch are also represented.

PALAZZO VENEZIA ('Museo di Palazzo Venezia') Via del Plebiscito 118, tel. (06) 679 8865. Daily 09:00-13:30, Sun. 09:00-12:30, closed Mon.; in summer, the museum is additionally open Tues. & Thurs. 15:00-18:00. See p. 535.

Mostly devoted to the so-called 'minor arts' – silver, ivories, tapestry, ceramics etc. – but also exhibits a selection of Italian paintings from the 15th to the 18th centuries and interesting sculpture. The latter includes a fine bust of *Pope Paul II*, the founder of the palace. Non-museum rooms of the palace, including the 'Sala del Mappamondo' ('Room of the Globe') which was Mussolini's private office, are open to the public on the occasion of special shows.

ANTIQUARIUM OF THE PALATINE in the Forum-Palatine site (p. 294), and with the same opening hours.

A fascinating collection of objects found on the site, among them the famous graffito *Alexamenos Worships His God*.

BARRACCO MUSEUM ('Museo Barracco di scultura antica') Corso Vittorio Emanuele II 168, tel. (06) 68806848. Daily 09:00-19:00, Sun. 09:00-13:30, closed Mon. See p. 487.

Small but refined collection of ancient sculpture, including rare Greek originals and Egyptian, Assyrian and Phoenician works. Visitors to the museum can request to see the vestigial ruins of a 4th-5th century AD ancient Roman house in the basement.

MUSEUM OF ORIENTAL ART ('Museo Nazionale d'Arte Orientale') Via Merulana 248, tel. (06) 735 9946. Daily 09:00-19:00, closed Mon. See p. 100.

An extensive and important collection of Eastern artefacts of artistic or historical value, from the Middle East to Japan, many of them the fruits of Italian archæological exploration.

5) Art collections of a lesser scope

AURORA PAVILION ('Casino dell'Aurora') Via Lombardia 44. Admission by appointment only, to be requested from the Boncompagni Administration at this address.

Situated in a surviving corner of the old Villa Ludovisi (see p. 83) this contains the famous ceiling fresco, *Aurora* by Guercino, and other works by Guercino and his contemporaries.

PALLAVICINI PAVILION ('Casino Pallavicini') Via XXIV Maggio 43. Open only the first day of every month, 10:00-12:00 & 15:00-17:00.

The only exhibit is a fabulous ceiling fresco by Guido Reni, also called *Aurora*. The pavilion is an annexe of the villa of the aristocratic Pallavicini-Rospigliosi family, who live here.

MASSIMO-LANCELLOTTI PAVILION ('Casino Massimo Lancellotti') Via Boiardo 16, tel. (06) 70495651. Tue. & Thurs. 10:00-12:00 & 16:00-19:00 ., Sun. 09:00-12:00.

Important 19th century frescoes of the German Nazarene School, including works by Friedrich Overbeck, Anton Koch et al.

CENTRALE MONTEMARTINI Via Ostiense 106, tel. (06) 5754207. Daily 10:00-18:00, closed Mon.

Relatively minor ancient Roman works from the store-rooms of the Capitoline Museums, exhibited in a decommissioned power station.

CITY GALLERY OF MODERN ART ('Galleria Comunale d'Arte Moderna e Contemporanea') Via Francesco Crispi 24, tel. (06) 4742848 and Via Cagliari 29, tel. (06) 8844930. Daily 09:00-19:00, Sun. 09:00-14:00.

City-owned paintings by Italian, and especially Roman, artists from the late 19th century onwards.

GALLERY OF CONTEMPORARY ART **Termini Station, 2nd floor.**

Due to open shortly; advance publicity claims it will be 'worth getting to the station early for.'

MUSEUM OF VILLA TORLONIA ('Museo della Casina delle Civette') Via Nomentana 70, tel. (06) 44250072. Daily 09:00-17:00, closed Mon. See p. 607.

Modern decorative arts, especially stained glass windows and furniture.

6) Historical museums

ROME HISTORICAL MUSEUM ('Museo di Roma') Piazza San Pantaleo 10, tel. (06) 687 5880. See p. 506.

A vast collection of art and objects documenting the life of Rome (especially in the last few centuries), in a grand 18th-century palace. Because of perennial and apparently insoluble organizational problems, the collection, once fully accessible, is now only shown piecemeal.

MUSEUM OF ROMAN CIVILIZATION ('Museo della Civiltà Romana') Piazza Giovanni Agnelli (in the EUR district, see p. 629), tel. (06) 5926041. Open Tues. to Sat. 09:00-13:30; Tues. and Thurs. also 15:00-18:00; Sun. 09:00-13:00; closed Mon. See p. 629. Close to that of the Early Middle Ages, listed next, so the two can conveniently be visited together. See below.

The collection is entirely composed of reproductions and scale models of ancient Roman monuments, buildings and artifacts, and is meant to illustrate the whole spectrum of Roman civilization, from bridge-building to music. Includes two outstanding items: a plaster cast of all the panels of Trajan's Column (p. 184), made in the late 19th century at the expense of Napoleon III; and a fabulous reconstruction (on a scale of 1:250) of the entire city of Rome as it was at the time of Emperor Constantine (4th century AD).

MUSEUM OF THE EARLY MIDDLE AGES ('Museo dell'Alto Medioevo') Viale Lincoln 3 (in the EUR district, see p. 629), tel. (06) 592 5806. Daily 09:00-14:00, Sun. 09:00-13:00. See p. 629.

This museum, which is within walking distance of the Museum of Roman Civilization the 10th centuries AD. They are art objects, weapons, clothes, furnishings, etc. from the Roman, barbarian and Byzantine civilizations.

MUSEUM OF PREHISTORY ('Museo Preistorico ed Etnografico L. Pigorini') Piazza G. Marconi 14, in the EUR district. Daily 09:00-14:00, Sun. 09:00-13:00. See p. 629.

Founded in 1875, offers major prehistoric and ethnographic exhibits, from those collected in the 17th century by the famous Jesuit scholar Athanasius Kirchner to those derived from recent Italian scientific expeditions.

RISORGIMENTO MUSEUM ('Museo Centrale del Risorgimento') Piazza Venezia, entrance on the left flank of the Vittoriano monument. Tel. (06) 6793598. Daily 10:00-18:00; closed in August. See p. 535.

Documents the Risorgimento movement for Italy's reunification and liberation from foreign rule. This movement lasted from the early 19th century until the First World War, when Italy recovered the last of its ethnic Italian territories.

NAPOLEONIC MUSEUM ('Museo Napoleonico') Piazza di Ponte Umberto I, tel (06) 68806286. Tues. to Sat. 09:00-19:00, Sun. 09:00-13:00; closed Mon. See p. 492.

Memorabilia of Napoleon I and of his relations, some of whom spent part of their lives in Rome. From the sword of the great Napoleon to the game board he used on St. Helena, and from the jewels of his seductive sister Paolina to the death mask of his nephew Napoleon III, the tragic history of the clan is illustrated with fascinating immediacy and authenticity.

MUSEUM OF THE RESISTANCE ('Museo Storico della Liberazione di Roma') Via Tasso 145, tel. (06) 7003866. Tue. Thur. & Fri. 16:00-19:00 , Sat. & Sun. 09:00:30-12:30.

Housed in the notorious building used by the torturers of the German SS to hold their Italian prisoners. Now rarely open and in deplorable condition.

7) Other museums

MUSEUM OF ROME IN TRASTEVERE (Museo di Roma in Trastevere') Piazza S. Egidio 1B, tel (06) 5816563. Open 10:00-21:00, closed Mon. See p. 579.

Mostly prints and drawings, the interesting exhibits include many originals from the famous collection of watercolours, 'Vanishing Rome', by the late-19th century Roman-Swiss artist Ettore Roesler Franz.

MUSEUM OF MEDICINE AND SURGERY ('Museo Storico Nazionale dell'Arte Sanitaria') inside Hospital of S. Spirito, Lungotevere in Sassia 1, tel. (06) 68351. Mon., Wed. & Fri. 10:00-12:00. See p. 383.

Surgical and medical tools and amulets from different eras and civilizations.

MUSEUM OF CRIMINOLOGY ('Museo Criminologico di Roma') Via del Gonfalone 29, corner of Via Giulia, tel. (06) 68300234. Call for admission times.

Housed in the former prison building of the 17th century 'Carceri Nuove' (p. 472), the museums traces the history of Italy's prison system and displays the sometimes gory punishments inflicted over the centuries.

MUSEUM OF ITALIAN FOLKLORE ('Museo delle Arti e Tradizioni Popolari') Piazza G. Marconi 8, in the EUR district. Tel. (06) 5926148. Daily 09:00-14:00, Sun. 09:00-13:00, closed Mon. See p. 629.

Rare artefacts of Italian popular life, as it was before two world wars and the economic development of Italy in the late 20th century.

MUSEUM OF MUSICAL INSTRUMENTS ('Museo degli Strumenti Musicali') Piazza S. Croce in Gerusalemme 9A, tel. (06) 701 4796. Daily 09:00-13:30, closed Sun. See p. 631.

Over 3,000 items, from antiquity until the 19th century

JEWISH MUSEUM ('Museo di Arte Ebraica') Lungotevere Cenci, tel. 066875051. Daily 09:30 -14:00 and 15:00-17:00; Sun. 09:00:30-14:00; closed Sat. See p. 521.

Religious objects and objects related to the life of Rome's Jewish community.

KEATS AND SHELLEY MEMORIAL HOUSE, Piazza di Spagna 26, tel. (06) 6784235. Weekdays only 09:00-13:00 & 15:00-17:30. See p. 57.

In the apartment where the English romantic poet John Keats died, documents of his times and of his circle of friends in Rome.

GOETHE MUSEUM ('Museo Goethe') Via del Corso 18, tel. (06) 32650412. Daily 10:00-18:00. See p. 51.

Goethe memorabilia, especially relating to his Italian travels.

CANONICA MUSEUM Viale P. Canonica 2 at Villa Borghese, tel. (06) 8842279, Daily 09:00-19:00, Sun 09:00-13:30, closed Mon. See p. 602.

The works of sculptor Canonica (1869 - 1959) exhibited in the house where he lived.

MARIO PRAZ MUSEUM Via Zanardelli 2, tel. (06) 6861089. Daily 09:00-13:00 & 14:30-18:30, closed Mon.

A large collection of Empire-style furniture in the home of a noted Italian scholar.

MUSEUM OF PASTA ('Museo delle Paste Alimentari') Piazza Scanderbeg 117, tel. (06) 6991120. Daily 09:00-17:00.

The history of spaghetti. Near Fontana di

Trevi. Moderate fun at a rather stiff price.

'MUSEUM OF PURGATORY' Lungo-
tevere Prati 12, tel. (06) 68806517. Daily 07:30
-12:30 & 17:00-18:30.

Affectionately called a 'museum' by sympa-
thizers, this is in fact a tiny collection of papers
posted on the wall of a church sacristy. But
they are startling papers indeed: messages from
the netherworld by Christian souls suffering in
Purgatory, who ask the living for help to get
into Paradise! The collection was started in
1893 (an epoch of widespread belief in spiritu-
alism) by a French priest who founded a
religious brotherhood exclusively devoted to
praying for the dead. It includes paranormal
and otherwise miraculous documents dating
from 1696 to 1919. A visit to this uniquely
Roman exhibition has the added advantage of
letting you see the sleepy, strangely affecting,
neo-Gothic church (1917).

CHILDREN'S MUSEUM ('Explora, il
Museo di Bambini') Via Flaminia 82, tel (06)
3613776, www.mdbr.it.

Call for admission times. Educational and
amusing things to look at and handle.

ROMANUM MUSEUM

*Opening page of an early compendium of Roman antiquities:
allegory of Rome by Carlo Maratta*

Index of Artists

To help the reader visualize the artists' œuvre, entries include a list of their works encountered in the Walks. As the purpose is comparison, however, if just one work is encountered it may not be pointed out in the entry. Question marks beside an entry denote doubts about an attribution. To make this section as useful as possible some information may be found repeated from the body of the book.

Alberti, Leon Battista – architect (1406-1472) 307, 533. Genoese of Florentine family, among the first to readopt ancient classical art's technical and æsthetic principles. His theories and his works in different Italian regions deeply influenced renaissance architecture. Artistic adviser to the popes, he told them : 'If the authority of the Church is visibly displayed in majestic buildings, the whole world will accept it.'

Algardi, Alessandro – sculptor and architect (c. 1600-1654) 127, 169, 369, 460, 469, 579, 637-9. Though influenced by his great and exuberant contemporary, Bernini, Algardi retained a sedate, meditative approach that gives his works smooth balance and (the portraits) psychological truth.
- Busts of the Frangipane, S. Marcello 127
- Reliefs, SS. Luca e Martina 169
- Relief of *Attila the Hun*, St. Peter's 369
- Relief of *Leo XI* St. Peter's 369
- *Miracle of St. Agnes' Hair*, S. Agnese in Agone 460
- *St. Philip and the Angel*, Chiesa Nuova 469
- Bust of *Prospero Santacroce* , S. Maria della Scala 579

- Villa Doria Pamphili and Casino delle Allegrezze 637-9
- Fountain of the Lily and Fountain of the Snail 638-9

Ammannati, Bartolomeo – architect and sculptor (1511-1592) 89, 227, 562, 603, 604-5, 683. Refinement and intellectualism characterize this Tuscan follower of Michelangelo.
- Villa Medici (with A. Lippi) 89, 603-4
- Palazzo Ruspoli 227
- Chapel and statuary in S. Pietro in Montorio 562
- Villa Giulia (with Vasari and Vignola) 603-4
- Palazzina of Pio IV and its fountain (with Vignola) 604-5

Andrea del Castagno – painter (early 15th C.) 329, 331. One of the first Florentine painters to be called to the Vatican. Famous for the power of his works and a realism still uncommon in the period.

Angelico (Fra' Giovanni da Fiesole) – painter (c. 1390-1455) 118, 313, 329, 335, 338, 372, 683. Major exponent of the late gothic style, famous for gem-like colours and deep spirituality. A friar who 'never painted a crucifix without tears in his eyes' (Vasari).
- *Madonna and Child with Saints*, Vatican Pinacoteca 313

- Chapel frescoed in one of the Vatican Palaces 335

Antoniazzo Romano – painter (15th-early 16th C) 100, 116, 238, 256, 263, 383, 407, 472, 493, 504, 562, 568-9, 628, 630, 631. A simple, solemn artist, a bit old-fashioned for his time.
- Frescoes, SS. Vito e Modesto (?) 100
- *Cardinal Torquemada giving dowries*, S. Maria sopra Minerva 116
- *Annunciation* (?), Pantheon 238
- Fresco, S. Nicola in Carcere 256
- *Madonna of Consolation* and frescoes, S. Maria della Consolazione 263
- *Madonna and Child*, fresco, Annunziatina 383
- Ciborium panels, S. Giovanni in Laterano 407
- Frescoes, S. Spirito dei Napoletani (?) 472
- *Madonna and Child with Saints*, S. Antonio dei Portoghesi 493
- *Madonna and Child with Saints*, S. Paolo fuori le Mura 628
- Frescoes, S. Pietro in Montorio 562
- *Annunciation* , S. Onofrio, 568-9
- *Madonna and Child with Saints*, S. Paolo fuori le Mura (?) 628
- Fresco, S. Maria del Buon Aiuto (?) 630
- Fresco, S. Croce in Gerusalemme (?) 631

- Mosaics, S. Paolo dentro le Mura 81

Cadorin, Guido – painter (active 1892-1976) 85. Friend and protegé of the poet D'Annunzio in the late 1920's, his frescoes of high society in the former Albergo Ambasciatori, rightly described as 'seductive' in the hotel's publicity, are his most enduring work.

Calini, Leo (1903-1985), and **Montuori, Eugenio** (1907-1982), architects, 80. The completion and renovation (with others) of the Termini station is the major work of this team, who were also responsible for a large number of public, office and residential buildings in the outlying districts of post-war Rome.

Cambellotti, Duilio – painter, sculptor, designer and illustrator (1876-1960) 393, 521, 607. Trained as an illustrator and designer in an Art Nouveau vein, he later developed, both as a painter and sculptor, a forceful narrative and vaguely symbolist style. Very influential in the development of Italian arts and crafts, advertising art and scene design between the wars.

FRESCOES:
- Castel S. Angelo 393

STAINED GLASS:
- (with C. Picchiarini, *qv*), Synagogue 521

DRAWINGS :
- Casa delle Civette 607

Campigli, Massimo – painter (1875-1971) 355. Started working in Paris in a milieu dominated by cubism and the rediscovery of primitive and archaic art. Influenced by the latter, he created toy-like, modular images with an atemporal and mythological aura, a style reinforced and personalized after his return to Italy in the 1920's by his encounter with Etruscan art.

Canevari, Angelo – painter (1901-1955) 606. One of the most successful designers associated with a mosaics school founded near Venice in the 1920's and still active, the 'Scuola Mosaicisti del Friuli.'

Canevari, Antonio – architect (1681-*c.* 1750) 577. Roman architect midway between the baroque and neoclassicism, more famous for his clocktower in Lisbon.

Canonica, Pietro – sculptor (1869-1959) 602, 603, 626, 687. From Turin in northern Italy, best known for his poised, psychologically penetrating but rigidly academic portraiture.
- Monument to the Alpine Soldier 602
- Monument to the Mule 602
- *Simon Bolívar* 603
- *St. Paul*, 626

Canova, Antonio – sculptor (1757-1822) 129, 322, 369, 371, 373, 493, 534, 587, 602, 620, 683. One of the most famous artists of his time, he almost personifies neoclassical sculpture (*see* Glossary). No artist knew better how to revive the ideals of classical art, under those principles of 'noble simplicity, calm grandeur' that Winckelmann had declared as central to the classical vision. To them Canova added a touch of late-18th-C grace.
- Statue of Paolina Borghese 602
- Funerary stele, the porch of SS. Apostoli 129
- Monument to Clement XIV, SS. Apostoli 129
- *Perseus, Kreugas and Damoxenos,* the Belvedere Court 322
- Tomb of Pope Clement XIII, St. Peter's 368
- Cenotaph of the last Stuarts, St. Peter's 370
- Monument to Pope Pius VI, the Sacred Grottoes (with A. Tadolini) 372
- Relief in S. Antonio dei

Portoghesi 493
- Tomb in S. Marco 534

Capponi, Luigi – sculptor (15th-16th C) 263, 372, 433. Member of the Bregno group.
- Crucifixion, relief, S. Maria della Consolazione 263
- Monument to the Bonsi brothers and reliefs of episodes in St. Gregory's life, S. Gregorio Magno 433
- Relief of Madonna and Child, the Sacred Grottoes (?) 372

Caravaggio (Michelangelo Merisi da) – painter (1572-1610) 45, 48, 53, 85, 316, 494, 498, 499, 512, 516, 579, 582, 612, 682, 683. One of the pivotal figures in the history of painting. Came to Rome at the age of 20 from Northern Italy, and in a brief period created a style where violent contrasts between light and shade and a concentration on the humblest aspects of daily life combined to make a revolutionary naturalism. This style overwhelmed contemporaries and spread throughout Europe See further pp. 494.
- *Conversion of St. Paul* and *Crucifixion of St. Peter*, S. Maria del Popolo 48
- *St. Francis with a Skull*, Church of the Capuchins 85
- *Deposition*, Vatican Pinacoteca 316
- *Madonna of the Pilgrims*, S. Agostino 498
- *Calling of St. Matthew, Martyrdom of St. Matthew* and *St. Matthew and the Angel*, S. Luigi de' Francesi 499

Caretti, Giovan Battista – architect, painter and interior decorator (1803-after 1850) 607. His rather pompous late-renaissance style, with classic accents, was found suitable for new palaces that, like that of the Torlonia, strived to compete in grandeur with those of the longer-established Roman nobility.

693

others such as the Vassallettos, operating in Rome, late 12th-late 13th C. They are especially famous for vivid, multicoloured patterns executed in marble, which decorate pavements, columns, pulpits, tombs etc. in many Roman churches (the Cosmatesque style)

SCULPTURE/ARCHITECTURE

- Tomb of a cardinal, S. Maria Maggiore (Giovanni Cosma) 98-9
- Tomb of a bishop, S. Maria sopra Minerva (Giovanni Cosma) 118
- Tomb of a cardinal, S. Balbina (Giovanni Cosma) 274
- Entrance, S. Antonio Abate (Vassalletto) 100
- Relief under the porch of SS. Apostoli (Vassalletto) 129
- Baldaquin, S. Maria in Cosmedin (Deodatus Cosma) 260
- Cloister, S. Giovanni in Laterano (Vassalletto) 409
- Pulpits, S. Maria in Ara Coeli (Lorenzo Cosma and son) 149-50
- Cloister, S. Paolo fuori le Mura (Vassalletto) (?) 627-8
- Easter candelabrum, S. Paolo fuori le Mura (Vassalletto and Nicolò D'Angelo) 627
- Wall shrine, S. Tommaso in Formis 429
- Spiral columns, S. Saba (Vassalletto) 273
- Columns, S. Alessio (Lorenzo and Jacopo Cosma) 271
- Doorway, S. Saba (Jacopo Cosma) 273
- Portico and benches, S. Lorenzo fuori le Mura (Vassalletto) 634
- Ciborium, S. Lorenzo fuori le Mura (Giovanni, Pietro, Angelo and Sasso) 635

Costa, Luigi see **Armanni, Osvaldo**

Costantini, Carlo – architect (b. 1940) 622, 629. Member of a younger generation of Roman architects exploring new construction techniques to create a light, dynamic architecture that is also energy efficient.
- Office buildings, Cinecittà 2, 622
- Renovation of the Palazzo INAIL at EUR (with Fabio Dinelli) 629

Costantini, Costantino – architect (active 1920s-1930s) 606. Combined Art Deco and the 'rationalist' style in a fluid personal style that was highly influential. Designed some official Fascist-era buildings outside Rome.

Courtois brothers: Guillaume (painter, 1628-1679) **and Jacques**, also called **Il Borgognone** (painter, 1621-1676) 56, 225, 316, 409. Best known for their battle scenes; those of Jacques are dramatic and intensely colourful.
- Crucifixion (by Jacques), S. Carlo al Corso 225
- Battle (by Jacques), Vatican Pinacoteca 316
- Fresco (by Guillaume), S. Giovanni in Laterano 409

Crespi, Giuseppe Maria – painter (1665-1747) 316. Subtle naturalist painter in the tradition of Caravaggio and the Carracci, he operated mainly in the Po Valley in northern Italy.

Crivelli, Carlo – painter (c. 1432- c. 1496) 306. This important master from the Veneto region combined Renaissance advances in perspective and modelling with bold experiments with the human figure, including distorting it for expressive purposes.

Croce, Baldassarre – painter (1558-1628) 76

d'Angelo, Nicolò see 'Cosma family',

SCULPTURE Easter candelabrum

da Cortona, da Fiesole, da Pisa, da Vinci, da Volterra etc. see **Pietro da Cortona, Mino da Fiesole, Isaia da Pisa, Leonardo da Vinci, Daniele da Volterra** and **Francesco da Volterra etc.**

da Sangallo see **Sangallo**

Daddi, Bernardo – painter (1290-c. 1348) 313. One of the so-called 'Primitives,' tied to the stiff, intensely mystical early medieval style, which in turn draws on the Byzantine tradition.

Dalmata see **Giovanni Dalmata**

Daniele da Volterra (D. Ricciarelli) – painter and sculptor (1509-1566) 88, 349, 485, 505, 562. Through his teachers Sodoma and Peruzzi, a brilliant inheritor of the vision of Raphael and, even more, of Michelangelo, which he imbued with his own sense of colour and drama.
- *Descent from the Cross* and *Assumption*, Trinità de' Monti, 88
- *Baptism of Jesus* and chapel, S. Pietro in Montorio 562
- Façade frescoes, Palazzo Massimo Istoriato 505

David, Jacques-Louis – painter (1748-1825) 89. Dramatic interpreter of historical subjects and foremost exponent of neoclassicism in France. With a clear, cogent brushwork he gave his paintings a moral and political content, which he put at the service first of the French Revolution, then of Napoleon.

Dazzi, Arturo – painter and sculptor (1881-1966) 629. A simple stonemason, he acquired technical abilities and a convincing monumental style which won him commissions first for work on the Altar of the Fatherland, then during the Fascist regime and after.

de Boulogne see **Valentin de Boulogne**

de Bruyn see **Bruyn**

De Chirico, Giorgio – painter and sculptor (1888-1978) 58, 585, 629. The main founder of the 'metaphysical' school of painting, a blend of classicism and surrealism that De Chiric developed after years of study of

German art and philosophy in Munich, and later under various influences in the intense milieu of Paris. Already then, and after his return to Italy in the war years, his enigmatic images of dreamy cityscapes and lively mannequins won him international fame. Their repeated classical and geometrical allusions had a deep impact on Italian visual culture between the two wars, especially architecture, as can be seen at EUR, for example.

de la Haye see **Haye**

del Castagno, del Piombo, della Francesca etc. see **Andrea del Castagno, Sebastiano del Piombo, Piero della Francesca**

Del Debbio, Enrico – architect (1881-1973). Planner of the earlier part of the Foro Mussolini complex and one of its builders. Major exponent of the Fascist ('Rationalist') style. 606
- Foro Mussolini and Stadio dei Marmi 606
- Guest House of the Foro Mussolini 606

Della Porta, Giacomo – architect and sculptor (1533-1602) 52-3, 88, 99, 112, 130, 131, 241, 256, 358, 359, 362, 366, 369, 407, 444, 450, 458, 460, 472, 474, 499, 502, 520, 520, 526, 527, 531, 532, 591-2. Pupil of Vignola, with whom he moves in the wide wake of Michelangelo's influence. Della Porta and Vignola are among the last exponents of the mature renaissance before the advent of the baroque. Della Porta is one of the architects to whom Rome owes most of its appearance today; his presence is ubiquitous in churches, palaces and countless fountains.
CHURCHES:
- S. Attanasio dei Greci 52-53
- Ss. Trinità dei Monti 77, 88
- Il Gesù (façade; with Vignola) 112
- Oratory of the Crucifix (façade) 130
- S. Maria in Via (with C. Rainaldi) 121
- S. Nicola in Carcere 256
- S. Giovanni dei Fiorentini (dome, with C. Maderno) 444
- S. Luigi dei Francesi (façade) 499
PALAZZI:
- Farnese (rear façade, with Vignola) 474
- della Sapienza ('of Wisdom') 502
- in Via Tor de' Specchi 532
CHAPELS:
- St. Peter's 366, 369
- S. Maria Maggiore 99
FOUNTAINS:
- Pantheon 241, Piazza S. Simeone 450, Piazza Navona 458, 460, of the Tureen 472, Piazza Giudĩa 520, 526, of the Tortoises (with Landini) 527, Piazza Campitelli 531, Piazza Aracoeli 532
SCULPTURE:
- Monument to a bishop,S. Cecilia (?) 591-592

Della Porta, Giovan Battista – sculptor (1542-1597) 77, 94

Della Porta, Guglielmo – sculptor and architect (1500-1577) 149, 361, 369. Genoese, he worked in Rome mainly for the Farnese family. Michelangelo's influence is evident especially in his masterpiece, the Tomb of Paul III in St. Peter's.
- Tomb of Paul III in St. Peter's 361, 369
- Statue of Paul III in S. Maria in Ara Coeli (?) 149

De Marcillat see **Marcillat**

Depero, Fortunato – painter (1892-1960) 629. In his work, Futurism and Expressionism fuse through an ironic use of lines and vivid colour.

de' Rossi, Giovan Antonio (1619-1695) and **de' Rossi, Mattia** (1637-1695) 62-3, 114, 585, 587. Another Roman family team in the second rank of the innovative circle of architects that created the Roman baroque.
- Palazzo Altieri 114
- S. Andrea delle Fratte, completion of Borromini's work after his death (Giovan Antonio only) 62-3
- Façade, S. Francesco a Ripa (Mattia only) 585
- Boys reformatory, Ospizio di S. Michele, (Giovan Antonio with Carlo Fontana) 587

De Sanctis, Francesco – architect (1693-1740) 55, 57. Best known for the Spanish Steps of Piazza di Spagna, for which he drew inspiration from Alessandro Specchi's Porto di Ripetta, later destroyed.

De Vecchi, Giovanni – painter (1536-1614) 562. Central Italian mannerist.

De Vico, Raffaele – architect (1881-1969) 629. Landscape specialist.

De Vos see **Vos**

Dinelli, Fabio – architect and engineer (1982-1985) 629. Best known for his work at EUR.

Domenichino (Domenico Zampieri) – painter (1581-1641) 76, 77, 79-80, 85, 94, 106, 108, 193, 316, 366, 432, 450, 480, 499-500, 508-510, 512-3, 513, 527, 555, 556, 568, 682, 683. The favourite student of Annibale Carracci (qv). His serene, incisive and at times monumental style follows the renaissance tradition of balance and ideal proportion, but a delicate matching of hues and a studied symmetry of shapes add an abstract, at times almost surreal atmosphere. These qualities made of him one of the seminal artists of the early baroque, influential down to our days.
OIL PAINTINGS:
- *Madonna and Child with St. Francis*, S. Maria della Vittoria 76
- *Madonna and Child with Saints*, S. Lorenzo in Miranda 193
- *Martyrdom of St. Sebastian*, S. Maria degli Angeli 79-80
- *Ecstasy of St. Francis* and *Death of St. Francis*, Church of the Capuchins 85

- Portrait of a cardinal and *The Liberation of St. Peter*, in S. Pietro in Vincoli 108
- *Scourging of St. Andrew*, Chapel of St. Andrew, S. Gregorio Magno 432
- *The Last Communion of St. Jerome*, Vatican Pinacoteca 316
- Portrait of a cardinal, S. Onofrio 568

FRESCOES IN:
- S. Maria degli Angeli 79-80
- S. Pudenziana (?) 94
- Palazzo Farnese 480
- S. Luigi dei Francesi 499-500
- S. Andrea della Valle 508-10
- S. Carlo ai Catinari 512-3, 516
- S. Onofrio 568
- S. Maria in Trastevere 555

OTHER:
- Doorway, Palazzo Lancellotti 450
- Ceiling with *Assumption*, S. Maria in Trastevere 555

Donatello (D. de' Bardi) – sculptor (1386-1466) 151. No major works by this revolutionary Florentine sculptor survive in Rome, where he is represented only by the Ciborium in the Treasury of St. Peter's and by a half-destroyed relief in St. Mary in Ara Coeli.

Dughet, Gaspard – painter (1615-1675) 106, 576. Strongly influenced by his teacher and brother-in-law, Poussin; produced some of the finest landscape paintings of his century in Rome.

FRESCOES IN:
- S. Martino ai Monti 106
- Farnesina 576

Duquesnoy, François also called **Francesco Fiammingo** – sculptor (*c.* 1597-1643) 368, 635. Flemish, active after 1618 in Rome, where he became part of the circle around Bernini, and distinguished himself by sedate works with a classical accent.
- *St. Andrew* in St. Peter's 368
- *Two Papal Dignitaries*, S. Lorenzo fuori le mura 635

Fabullus – painter (1st C. AD) 210, 212-3. Nero's favourite painter and the greatest of his era. None of his frescoes is still legible, but their rediscovery in the early renaissance was influential on Raphael and others of his day.

Ferrari, Ettore – sculptor and painter (1845-1929) 484. Strongly motivated in his work by social and political themes, and a follower of the strictly secular, anti-monarchical ideology of Mazzini, he became the head of Rome's Masons until the arrival of Fascism.

Fiammeri, Giambattista – painter (1530-1606) 72. Jesuit priest who gave expression to the ideology of the Order in zealous martyrdom scenes.

Filarete, Il (Antonio Averulino) – sculptor and architect (*c.* 1400-*c.* 1469) 361, 365. Probably the pupil of one of the greatest Florentine sculptors, Lorenzo Ghiberti, but mostly active as an architect (in northern Italy)

Fontana, Carlo – architect (*c.* 1643-1714) 125, 376, 564, 573, 618. Distantly related to Domenico Fontana, he was trained in the school of Pietro da Cortona and long worked for Bernini. His talents, in a markedly theatrical vein, found high expression in the church of S. Marcello, while the Ospizio di S. Michele attests to his advanced technique.
- Church of S. Marcello 125
- Fountain in Piazza S. Pietro 376
- Hospice of S. Michele 564
- Basin of Fontanone on Janiculum 573
- Chapel, S. Sebastiano (with G. Vasanzio and C. Maratta) 618

Fontana, Domenico – architect (1543-1607) 68, 70, 77, 98, 129, 376-377, 409, 573, 583. First of a family of northern Italian architects to emigrate to Rome, where they operated for two centuries (mid-16th to mid-

18th). The family included, besides many Fontanas, Carlo Maderno and Francesco Borromini. As chief architect to Sixtus V, Domenico carried out the works of urban renewal and daring engineering that made this builder pope famous.
- Transportation and erection of the obelisk in St. Peter's Square 376-7
- Sistine Chapel of S. Maria Maggiore 98

PALACES:
- Lateran 409
- Quirinal (with others) 68

FOUNTAINS:
- of Moses 77
- in the cloister of SS. Apostoli 129
- of the Prisoner 583

Fontana, Giovanni – architect (1540-1614) 564, 573. Brother of Domenico and working in a similar vein.
- Fontanone (The Big Fountain) on the Janiculum (with F. Ponzio) 564
- Fountain of the Pauline Water (with G. Vasanzio) 573

Fontebuoni, Anastasio – painter (1571-1626) 107, 273, 274. Florentine pupil of Passignano.
- *Annunciation*, S. Lucia in Selci 107
- Frescoes, S. Prisca 273
- Frescoes, S. Balbina 274

Fortuny y Carbò, Mariano – painter and designer (1838-1874) 39. Catalan artist, influential to this day in decoration and fashions, especially textile design.

Foschini, Arnaldo – architect (1884-1968) 629. Working in an updated, personal Art Deco manner throughout the 1930's, and later famous for his church at EUR, he designed many residential, church and public buildings in Rome.

Fra Angelico *see* **Angelico.**

Fragonard, Jean Honoré – painter (1732-1806) 56. One of the best known and most characteristic

Maratta, Carlo – painter (1625-1713) 79, 80, 225, 316, 534, 618, 630. His early academic style gradually gave way to a more baroque freedom, achieving genuine grandeur and acuity in his portraiture.
- *Baptism of Jesus*, S. Maria degli Angeli 80
- *St. Ambrose and St. Charles Borromeo in Glory*, S. Carlo al Corso 225
- Portrait of *Clement IX* Vatican Pinacoteca 316
- *Adoration of the Magi*, S. Marco 534
- *The Antipope Victor II*, S. Croce in Gerusalemme 630
- Design of his own tomb, S. Maria degli Angeli 79
- Design of a chapel in S. Sebastiano (with A. Specchi and C. Fontana) 618

Marcillat, Guillaume de – painter and stained glass artist (?-1529) 48. French. Although he tried his hand at frescoing in the Vatican, where he assisted in the Stanze decoration, his fame is due to his beautiful stained glass windows.

Martini, Francesco di Giorgio see **Francesco di Giorgio Martini**

Martini, Simone – painter (*c.* 1284-1344) 313. No works in Rome except in museums. A follower of Giotto, he stressed the decorative, fable-like aspects of his narrative, in a style sometimes called 'late gothic'.

Marucelli, Paolo – architect and sculptor (1594-1649) 501. Roman. Distinguished exponent of the baroque, especially active in his home town. The façade of Palazzo Madama is his most famous work.

Marzi, Renzo – painter, sculptor and decorator (1912-1992) 369. One of the very few pupils of the master glass-maker Cesare Picchiarini (*qv*), whose school he still attended when he made the Holy Spirit window in St.

Peter's. Later, he expanded his expertise to other media, acquiring renown as a decorator.

Masaccio – painter (1401-1428) 420. A Tuscan initially associated with the older painter Masolino da Panicale in Florence, and a licensed physician, he departed from the sweet, fable-like late gothic painting of his circle to adopt a darker palette and an unprecedentedly stark, tragic vision of the human condition. In this he was perhaps helped by his direct medical experience. He also innovated with the use of light from definite directions and the use of shadows. It was a revolution, which made of him the recognised prime mover of realism in the renaissance. His masterpiece is the Brancacci Chapel in S. Maria del Carmine, Florence. He died in Rome at only 27 years of age.

Mascarino or **Mascherino, Ottaviano** – architect and painter (1524-1606) 68, 516, 569. Pupil of Vignola, adding manner and grace to his master's style.
- Quirinal Palace (with others) 68
- Palace of Monte di Pietà 516
- Church of S. Maria della Scala (façade) (?) 579

Maso del Bosco or **Boscoli** – sculptor (1507-1574) 108. One of a group of minor sculptors active in the town of Fiesole near Florence, where he first met Michelangelo.

Masolino da Panicale – painter (*c.* 1383-*c.* 1444) 313, 420-1. One of a number of Florentines painting in the hyper-decorative late gothic style, which he toned down after his encounter with the much younger Masaccio, whom he followed toward a greater naturalism without ever achieving the same depth.
- *Crucifixion*, Vatican Pinacoteca 313
- Frescoes, S. Clemente 420-1

Matisse, Henri – painter, sculptor and decorator (1869-1954) 340. Twentieth-century master of colour, famous for his cutouts.

Maturino da Firenze – painter (d. 1528) 449. With Raphael and Polidoro da Caravaggio, one of the first to use 'graffito' work on Rome buildings.

Mazzoni, Giulio – sculptor, stucco-maker and painter (*c.* 1525-after 1589) 479. Pupil of Vasari and the most accomplished specialist stucco-worker of the late renaissance, as witness his work in Palazzo Spada.

Mazzoni del Grande, Angiolo – architect (1894-1979) 80. All his best known works are public buildings realised within the accepted formulas of the Fascist period. The Termini station is his masterpiece.

Mead, William R. – architect (1846-1928) 624. American, part of the famous McKim Mead White partnership. Their work was heavily influenced by the renaissance and by classical Rome (Pennsylvania Sation, Bellevue Hospital in New York). Director of the American Academy in Rome from 1908 until his death 20 years later.

Meier, Richard – architect (b. 1934) 223, 636. American. Works in a fractured, centrifugal style, breaking up the external surfaces with a diversity of gradients and slants; but unlike colleagues who aim to make æsthetic capital from the spectacular disorder of such a style, Meier creates a sense of peace and symmetry.
- Pavilion of the Ara Pacis 223
- Church of Dives in Misericordia 636

Melozzo da Forlì – painter (1438-1494) 68, 117, 129, 238, 314, 336, 352, 371, 407, 483, 534, 631. From central-north Italy, follower and perhaps pupil of Piero della Francesca.

school of stained glass making, he worked at the centre of a group of artists that included Duilio Cambellotti and Renzo Marzi.
- Synagogue windows 521
- Casa delle Civette 607

Pictor, Petrus see **Petrus Pictor**

Piero della Francesca – painter (c. 1417-1492) 98, 329, 331, 335. This great artist from Umbria, one of the giants of Renaissance painting – a master of perspective, lighting and atmosphere – worked for years in Rome. Yet he has left almost no traces there, partly due to the destruction of his Vatican frescoes when they were replaced by Raphael's.

Pietro da Cortona (P. Berrettini) – painter and architect (1596-1669) 68, 84, 102, 112, 127, 167-9, 193, 224, 225, 340, 366, 445, 450, 466, 467, 469, 516, 534, 635, 683. Major exponent of the Roman baroque. His paintings, genial and vivid, make full and sometimes spectacular use of perspective. As an architect, he inherited some of Michelangelo's combination of movement and monumentality, while marking a return of the baroque toward simpler, classical patterns.

PAINTING:
- Fresco, Palazzo Barberini hall 84
- Frescoes, Quirinal Palace 68
- Frescoes, S. Bibiana 102
- Frescoes and stuccos, S. Carlo al Corso 225
- Frescoes and decoration of chapel, the Apostolic Palace 340
- Frescoes and canvases, Chiesa Nuova and Rooms of St. Philip Neri 469
- *S. Dafrosa*, S. Bibiana 102
- *Martyrdom of St. Lawrence*, S. Lorenzo in Miranda 193
- *The Trinity*, St. Peter's 366
- *The Nativity*, S. Salvatore in Lauro 450
- *St. Charles Leading a Procession*

during the Plague, S. Carlo ai Catinari 516

ARCHITECTURE:
- SS. Luca e Martina 167-9
- S. Maria della Pace (façade) and design of the piazza 464-6
- S. Maria in Via Lata (façade) 127
- S. Carlo al Corso (dome) 224
- S. Giovanni dei Fiorentini (presbytery) 445
- Chapel of St. Francis Xavier, Il Gesù 112
- Chapel, S. Marco 534
- Cenotaph, S. Lorenzo fuori le Mura 635

Pinelli, Bartolomeo – painter, sculptor, printmaker and illustrator (1781-1835) 581. Roman, in love with the city's ancient past and with the popular spirit of his own time, he translated both in an impeccable neoclassical style and a vast repertory of Roman lore and costumes.

Pinturicchio (Bernardino di Betto) – painter (c. 1454-1513) 45, 48, 150, 314, 329, 331, 340-1, 350-1, 562, 568. Pupil of Perugino. Emphasizing with vivid accents the combination of line and colour he learned from his master, he used it in the service of a great narrative talent. Raphael was his fellow student.

FRESCOES IN:
- S. Maria del Popolo, (with pupils) 48
- Borgia Apartment, Vatican 330, 340-1
- Sistine Chapel (with Perugino), the Vatican 350-2
- S. Maria in Ara Coeli 150
- S. Onofrio (school) 568
- S. Pietro in Montorio (school) 562

ALTARPIECE:
Coronation of the Virgin, Vatican Pinacoteca 306

Piranesi, Giovanni Battista – printmaker, decorator and architect (1720-1788) 64, 88, 262. Venetian-born, but possibly did more than any other artist to create an enduring

vision of ancient Rome. Classical architecture and design, which he studied in very considerable depth, were reinterpreted in some of the most dramatic and beautiful prints ever made.

Poelenburg, Cornelis – painter (c. 1586-1667) 50. Dutch painter of delicate landscapes.

Polidoro da Caravaggio – painter (c. 1500-1546) 449, 472. With Raphael and Maturino da Firenze, one of the first to use 'graffito' work on Rome buildings.

Pollaiuolo, Antonio e Piero (A. and P. Benci) – painters, sculptors, goldsmiths and print-makers (15th C.) 108, 164, 370, 681. Antonio – the better known of the Florentine brothers who often worked together – was one of the most brilliant sculptors and painters of the early Renaissance. His virtuosity as a goldsmith is evident in works of incisive detail and in sculptured portraits of subtle psychological impact.

SCULPTURE:
- Twins suckling the Capitol's she-wolf (reproduction) 164
- Tomb of Pope Innocent VIII in St. Peter's 370
- Tomb of Pope Sixtus IV, Treasury of St. Peter's 681

Polyclitus – sculptor (5th C. BC) 319, 326. The first to study the human body's proportions and the dynamics of its balance, producing masterful and immensely influential works. See further p. 319.

Pomarancio, Cristoforo (C. Roncalli) – painter (1552-1626) 108, 130, 131, 263. Pupil of Niccolò Pomarancio, whose nickname he inherited. Mannerist. A lyricism, albeit rather academic, underlies his works, accompanied by vivid colours and occasional naturalistic accents.

Antonio the Elder, whose style and technical approach he shared.
- Ceiling of S. Maria Maggiore 97
- Cloister of S. Pietro in Vincoli 108
- Palazzo Sant'Apostoli (?) 129

Sansovino, Andrea (A. Contucci) – sculptor and architect (1460-1529) 48, 126, 150, 427, 428, 466, 498. Probably a pupil of A. Pollaiuolo in Florence, in Rome he tempered his Tuscan warmth with the classical austerity of the Bramante circle.

SCULPTURE:
- *St. Anne with the Virgin and the Child*, S. Agostino 498
- Two tombs in the presbytery of S. Maria del Popolo 48
- *Tomb of Cardinal Michiel*, S. Marcello (with J. Sansovino) 126
- Tomb, S. Maria in Ara Coeli 150
- Fountain of the Navicella (?) 427
- Relief of the *Virgin* on the façade of S. Maria dell'Anima 466

ARCHITECTURE:
- S. Maria in Domnica (façade) 428

Sansovino, Jacopo (J. Tatti) – sculptor and architect (1486-1570) 126, 340-41, 444, 461, 473, 497, 498, 500, 631. Pupil of Andrea Sansovino. As an architect worked mainly in Venice (Piazza S. Marco) His eloquent sculptures show the influence of both his master and Michelangelo.

SCULPTURE:
- *St. James*, S. Maria di Monserrato 473
- *Madonna del Parto*, S. Agostino 497
- *Tomb of Cardinal Michiel*, S. Marcello (with A. Sansovino) 126
- Cardinal's tomb, S. Croce in Gerusalemme (with C. Maderno) 631

ARCHITECTURE:
- Fireplace in the Borgia Apartment of the Apostolic Palace 340-1

- S. Giovanni dei Fiorentini (general plan) 444
- Palazzo Lante 500

Saraceni, Carlo – painter (1579-1620) 579. Influenced by Caravaggio, but with a Venetian feeling for colour.

Sardi, Giuseppe – architect (1680-1753) 583. From central Italy. A late follower of Borromini.

Sassetta, Stefano – painter (c. 1400-1450) 313. The greatest Sienese painter of the early 15th C.

Sassoferrato, Il (G. B. Salvi) – painter (1605-1685) 108, 271. Purity of design and sweet colouring characterise his renewal of the tradition of Raphael and Domenichino.
- Fresco, S. Francesco di Paola 108
- *The Virgin between St. Dominic and St. Catherine*, S. Sabina 271

Sebastiano del Piombo (S. Luciani) – painter (c. 1485-1547) 48, 446, 448, 562, 576. Trained in Venice, where he added a perfect command of colour to a personal taste for monumental composition. In Rome came under the influence of his friend Michelangelo and of Raphael, as can be seen in the powerful works of his maturity.
- *Birth of the Virgin*, S. Maria del Popolo 48
- *Scourging of Christ*, S. Pietro in Montorio 562
- Frescoes, Farnesina Palace 576

Serlio, Sebastiano – architect (1475-1555) 109. From Bologna, best known as the author of a treatise that contributed new ideas and patterns to architecture for the next two centuries and longer.

Sermoneta, Il (Girolamo Siciolante) – painter (1521-c.1580) 264. Pupil and assistant of Perino del Vaga, active in the mannerist circle of painters in Rome.

Serodine, Giovanni – painter (1594-1630) 635. Artist from

northern Italy who spent most of his career in Rome and whose vigorous style has recently been favourably reassessed by critics.

Severn, Joseph – painter (1793-1872) 55-6, 61, 624. British painter and miniaturist; friend of Keats in Rome.

Siciolante, Girolamo *see* Sermoneta, Il

Signorelli, Luca – painter (c. 1455-1523) 329, 343, 351. This early renaissance artist is considered Michelangelo's only real precursor in his celebration of the dynamism and flexibility of the human body. Except for the Sistine frescoes and in museums, there are no works by him in Rome. But his absolute masterpiece, his *Last Judgement* frescoes in the not-too-distant cathedral of Orvieto, are important precursors of Michelangelo's work on the same subject 34 years later.

Simonetti, Michelangelo – architect (1724-1787) 325. Roman, mainly known for his contruction of the main body of the Vatican museums. Considered responsible for the demolition there of a chapel with priceless frescoes by Mantegna.

Skopas – sculptor (4th C. BC) 322. One of the most dynamic and dramatic classical sculptors of Greece, famous throughout antiquity for his ability to translate into stone the sentiments of passion and violence.

Sodoma, Il (Giovan Antonio Bazzi) – painter (1477-1549) 339, 576-7. His nickname may well refer to his sexual leanings. Sodoma had success in northern Italy, where he was heavily influenced by Leonardo. That influence, to which he added after his arrival in Rome that of Raphael, near whom he worked in the Vatican, is obvious in the Farnesina frescoes with their soft modelling and *chiaroscuro* .

Soria, Giovan Battista – architect (1581-1651) 76, 432-433, 516. Created an austere baroque style under the influence of Maderno and Pietro da Cortona; S. Gregorio Magno is considered to be his masterpiece.
- S. Maria della Vittoria (façade) 76
- S. Gregorio Magno 432-3
- S. Carlo ai Catinari (with R. Rosati) 516

Specchi, Alessandro – architect (1668-1729) 125, 480, 618. Pupil of Carlo Fontana but came under the influence of Borromini. His masterpiece, sadly destroyed, was the Porto di Ripetta (a minor harbour on Via Ripetta), which inspired De Sanctis' Spanish Steps.
- Palazzo on the Corso 125
- Palazzo Roccagiovine 480
- Chapel in S. Sebastiano (with C. Maratta and C. Fontana) 618

Staurachios of Scio – goldsmith and ironsmith (late 11th C.) 626. Known only for the bronze doors of St. Paul's basilica, imported to Rome, though whether he designed as well as executed these is unclear.

Story, William Wetmore – sculptor (1819-1895) 83, 540, 580, 624. Brilliant American jurist turned sculptor, who spent his artistic life in Rome. Virtually forgotten except for the widely-copied *Weeping Angel* in Rome's Protestant Cemetery.

Street, George Edmund – architect (1824-1881) 52, 81. Inspired by the socio-political writings of Ruskin to emphasize refined craftsmanship and simple but colourful materials.
- Church of All Saints 52
- S. Paolo dentro le Mura 81

Swanevelt see **Van Swanevelt**

Sweerts, Michiel – painter (1624-1664) 50. Flemish artist influenced by Caravaggio and the Bamboccianti, though with a delicate grey tonality of his own. Joined a missionary society and probably died in Goa.

Taccone, Paolo see **Paolo Romano**

Tadolini family – Dynasty of Roman sculptors whose first and most famous member was **Adamo** (1788-1868) 53, 61, 362, 373
- *St. Paul* in front of St. Peter's 362
- *Pius VI* (with Canova), the Sacred Grottoes 373

Thorvaldsen, Bertel – sculptor (1770-1844) 82, 88, 238, 370, 602, 603. Danish follower of Canova and one of the most successful neo-classicists. He spent most of his career in Rome, where he was prominent in intellectual circles and the foreign community.
- *Tomb of Cardinal Consalvi*, Pantheon 238
- *Tomb of Pope Pius VII*, St. Peter's 370
- *Byron* 602
- *Jason* 603

Tibaldi, Pellegrino – painter, architect and sculptor (1527-1596) 393, 499. Part of the circle of Raphael's assistants, but was more influenced by Michelangelo. His many architectural works are all in Milan.
- Decoration of the Pauline Room, Castel S. Angelo (with Perino del Vaga) 393
- Frescoes in S. Luigi de' Francesi 499

Tischbein, Johann – painter (1751-1829) 51, 124. A sensitive pre-romantic painter, he was Goethe's travel companion and they briefly shared an apartment in Rome. His portrait of the poet in the Roman countryside is among his best-known works.

Titian (Tiziano Vecellio) – painter (c. 1490-1576) 315, 683, 684. No works of this giant of the Venetian school are in Rome except in museums.

Torriti, Jacopo – painter (13th-14th C.) 97, 408. His mosaics react against Byzantine art by returning to the naturalism and solidity of ancient Roman design and composition.
MOSAICS IN:
- S. Maria Maggiore 97
- S. John Lateran (with J. da Camerino) (copy) 408

Turner, J. M. W. – painter (1775-1851) 56. British. Great colourist of extraordinary intensity and modernity.

Unterberger, Cristoforo – painter (1732-1798) 602-3. From an old family of painters from the northern Veneto region, he is best known in Rome for the collaboration he gave the Asprucci brothers as a designer and planner in the Villa Borghese, including the creation of the beautiful Fontana dei Cavalli Marini ('of the Seahorses').

Vacca, Flaminio – sculptor and architect (1538-1605) 77, 231, 239. Born, probably in Rome, into the aristocratic Spanish family De Vaca, which had joined the court of the Spanish pope Alexander VI. Designed several minor works around the city. Also well known as an amateur archæologist and author of archæological memoirs.

Vaccaro, Giuseppe – architect (1896-1970), 85. A frequent collaborator of Marcello Piacentini and, with him, the designer of some impressive buildings on the Via Veneto.

Valadier, Giuseppe – architect and archæologist (1762-1839) 45, 47, 53, 64, 129, 224, 287, 362, 506, 602, 604, 606, 607, 631, 633. Neo-classicist renowned both for his buildings and for his studies of urban planning.
- Layout of Piazza del Popolo and landscaping of Pincian Hill 45, 47, 602
- Calcografia Nazionale 64
- Redesign of the façade of SS. Apostoli 129

Index of people and gods

Index of Places

Front cover: Bernini's Fountain of the Rivers, Piazza Navona (Cesare D'Onofrio)
Front cover flap: View from the Spanish Steps (Cesare D'Onofrio)
Back cover: Galatea, by Raphael, Farnesina
Back cover flap: Sculpture at EUR (Cesare D'Onofrio)

All colour photographs by Cesare D'Onofrio, except pp. 34-35, courtesy Scala
Black and white illustrations from the archives of Newton Compton and Pallas Athene

Inside cover maps: courtesy ATAC Rome
Maps pp. 2-3 and 4-5: drawn by Touring Club Italiano
All internal diagrams and maps © Mauro Lucentini
Illustrations from the archives of Newton Compton and Pallas Athene

Translations of sonnets by G. G. Belli © Mauro Lucentini

This book is part of the Pallas Guides series, published by Pallas Athene.
If you would like further information about the series, please write to:
Pallas Athene, 42 Spencer Rise, London NW5 1AP
or visit our website **www.pallasathene.co.uk**

Series editor: Alexander Fyjis-Walker
Editorial assistants: Lisa Adams, Jessica Fisher, Jim McCue and Piers Blofeld;
   mapwork by Kicca Tommasi
Series designer: James Sutton

This edition first published by Pallas Athene London, 2006

ISBN 1 873429 91 6

Printed through World Print, China